Readings in Cognitive Science

A Perspective from Psychology and Artificial Intelligence

Readings in Cognitive Science

A Perspective from Psychology and Artificial Intelligence

Allan Collins
BBN Laboratories

and

Edward E. Smith
University of Michigan

MORGAN KAUFMANN PUBLISHERS, INC.
SAN MATEO, CALIFORNIA

President and Editor *Michael B. Morgan*
Production Manager *Shirley Jowell*
Permissions Assistant *Elizabeth Myhr*
Copy Editor *Lynn Dupre*
Cover Designer *Rick Van Genderen*
Typesetter *Technically Speaking Publications*
Indexers *Kevin Biolsi* and *Kenneth Gray*
Research Assistant *Pamela Ellis*

Library of Congress Cataloging-in-Publication Data is Available
88-23094
ISBN 1-55860-013-2

Morgan Kaufmann Publishers, Inc.
Editorial Office: 2929 Campus Drive, San Mateo, California 94403
Order from: P.O. Box 50490, Palo Alto, California 94305
© 1988 by Morgan Kaufmann Publishers, Inc.
All rights reserved.
Printed in the United States of America

92 91 90 89 88   5 4 3 2 1

Contents

Contents

Chapter 3   *Categorization*

Chapter 4   *Learning*

Chapter 5 Thinking

Chapter 6 Perception

Acknowledgments

We thank Dan Bobrow, John Seely Brown, Chip Bruce, Mark Burstein, Ken Forbus, Dedre Gentner, Zenon Pylyshyn, Lance Rips, Kurt Van-Lehn, Barbara White, and one anonymous reviewer for their advice and suggestions on the book.

Anderson, J. R., "A Speading Activation Theory of Memory", *Journal of Verbal Learning and Verbal Behavior*, 22:261-295, 1983. ©1983, Academic Press, Inc. Reprinted with the permission of the publisher and the author.

Anderson, J. R., "Aquisition of Cognitive Skill", *Psychological Review*, 89:369-406, 1982. ©1982 by the American Psychological Association. Reprinted with the permission of the publisher and the author.

Brown, J. S. & K. VanLehn, "Repair Theory: A Generative Theory of Bugs in Procedural Skills", *Cognitive Science* 4:379-426, 1980. ©1980 by Ablex Publishing Corporation. Reprinted with the permission of the publisher and the author.

Chase, W. G. H. & H. A. Simon, "The Mind's Eye in Chess", *Visual Information Processing*, 215-281, 1973. ©1973 by Academic Press Inc. Reprinted with the permission of the publisher and the author.

Collins, A. M. & E. F. Loftus, "A Spreding Activation Theory of Semantic Processing", *Psychological Review*, 82:407-428, 1975. ©1975 by the American Psychological Association. Reprinted with the permission of the publisher and the author.

deKleer, J. & J. S. Brown, "Assumptions and Ambiguities in Mechanistic Mental Models", in D. Gentner & A. L. Stevens (eds.), *Mental Modes*, 155-190, Hillsdale, NJ: Erlbaum, 1983. ©1983 by Lawrence Erlbaum Publishers. Reprinted with the permission of the publisher and the author.

Fodor, J. A., "Precis of the Modularity of Mind", *Behavioral and Brain Sciences*, 8:1-5, 1984. ©1984 by Cambridge University Press. Reprinted with the permission of the publisher and the author.

Gentner, D., "Structure-Mapping: A Theoretical Framework for Analogy", *Cognitive Science*, 7:155-170, 1983. ©1983 by Ablex Publishing Corporation. Reprinted with the permission of the publisher and the author.

Hayes, P. J., "Naive Physics 1: Ontology for Liquids", in J. R. Hobbs & R. C. Moore (eds.), *Formal Theories of the Common Sense World*, 71-107, Norwood, N.J.: Ablex, 1985. ©1985 by Ablex Publishing Corporation. Reprinted with the permission of the publisher and the author.

Hayes-Roth, B. & Hayes-Roth, F., "A Cognitive Model of Planning", *Cognitive Science*, 3:275-310, 1979. ©1979 by Ablex Publishing Corporation. Reprinted with the permission of the publisher and the author.

Johnson-Laird, P. N., *Mental Models* Chapter 5:94-125, 1983. ©1983 by Harvard University

Press. Reprinted with the permission of the publisher and the author.

Kosslyn, S. M., "Seeing and Imagining in the Cerebral Hemispheres: A Computational Approach", *Psychological Review*, 94:148-175, 1987. ©1987 by the American Psychological Association. Reprinted with the permission of the publisher and the author.

Marr, D. & T. Poggio, "A Computational Theory of Human Stereo Vision", *Proceedings of the Royal Society of London, Series B*, 204:301-328, 1979. ©1979 by the Royal Society of London. Reprinted with the permission of the publisher and the author.

McClelland, J. L., D. E. Rumelhart, & G. E. Hinton, "The Appeal of Parallel Distributed Processing", in D. E. Rumelhart, J. L. McClelland and the PDP Research Group (eds.), *Parallel Distributed Processing*, vol. 1:3-40, 1986. ©1986 by the MIT Press. Reprinted with the permission of the publisher and the author.

McClelland, J. L. & D. E. Rumelhart, "An Interactive Activation Model of Context Affects in Letter Perception: Part 1. An Account of Basic Findings", *Psychological Review*, 88:375-407, 1981. ©1981 by the American Psychological Association. Reprinted with the permission of the publisher and the author.

Minsky, M., "A Framework for Representing Knowledge", in P. H. Winston (ed.), *The Psychology of Computer Vision*, 211-277, New York: McGraw Hill, 1975. © 1975 by McGraw Hill Book Co. Reprinted with the permission of the publisher and the author.

Mitchell, Tom M., Richard M. Keller, and T. Kedar-Cabelli, "Explanation-Based Generalization: A Unifying View", *Machine Learning 1*:47-80, 1986. ©1986 Kluwer Academic Publishers.

Newell, A., & H. A. Simon, "GPS: A Program that Simulates Human Thought", in E. A. Feigenbaum & J. Feldman (eds.), *Computers and Thought*, 279-293, R. Oldenbourg KG., 1963. ©1963 by R. Oldenbourg KG. and the author.

Pylynshyn, Z., "The Imagery Debate: Analogue Media Versus Tacit Knowledge", *Psychological Review*, 88:16-45, 1981. ©1981 by the American Psychological Association. Reprinted with the permission of the publisher and the author.

Quillian, M. R., "Semantic Memory", in M. Minsky (ed.), *Semantic information processing*, 216-260, Cambridge, MA: MIT Press, 1968. ©1968 by MIT Press. Reprinted with the permission of the publisher and the author.

Rosch, E., "Principles of Categorization", in E. Rosch & B. B. Lloyd (eds.), *Cognition and Categorization*, 27-48, Hillsdale, NJ: Erlbaum, 1978. ©1978 by Lawrence Erlbaum Publishers. Reprinted with the permission of the publisher and the author.

Rumelhart, D. E., G. E. Hinton & R. J. Williams, "Learning Internal Representations by Error Propagation", in D. E. Rumelhart, J. L. McClelland, and the PDP Research Group (eds.), *Parallel Distributed Processing*, vol. 1:318-362, Cambridge, MA: MIT Press, 1986. ©1986 by MIT Press. Reprinted with the permission of the publisher and the author.

Rumelhart, D. E., P. Smolensky, J. L. McClelland, & G. E. Hinton, *Schemata and Sequential Thought* "Processes in PDP Models", in J. L. McClelland, D. E. Rumelhart and the PDP Research Group (eds.), *Parallel Distributed Processing*, vol. 2:7-57, Cambridge, MA: MIT Press, 1986. ©1986 by MIT Press. Reprinted with the permission of the publisher and the author.

Searle, J. R., "Minds, Brains and Programs", *Behavioral and Brain Sciences*, 3:417-424, with commentaries by Block and Fodor, 1980. ©1980 by Cambridge University Press. Reprinted with the permission of the publisher and the author.

Schank, R. C. & R. P. Abelson, *Scripts, Plans, Goals and Understanding*, Chapters 1-3:1-68, Hillsdale, NJ: Erlbau, 1977. ©1977 by Lawrence Erlbaum. Reprinted with the permission of the publisher and the author.

Shepard, R. N. & J. Metzler, "Mental rotation of three-dimensional objects", *Science*, 171:791-703, 1971. ©1971 by the American Association for the Advancement of Science. Reprinted with the permission of the publisher and the author.

Turing, A. M., "Computing Machinery and Intelligence", *Mind*, 59:433-460, 1950. ©1950 by xford University Press, Oxford, England. Reprinted with the permission of the publisher and the author.

Tversky, A., "Features of similarity", *Psychological Review*, 84:327-352, 1977. ©1977 by the American Psychological Association. Reprinted with the permission of the publisher and the author.

Tversky, A. & D. Kahneman, "Extensional versus intuitive reasoning: The conjunction fallacy in probability judgments", *Psychological Review*, 90:293-315, 1983. ©1983 by the American Psychological Association. Reprinted with the permission of the publisher and the author.

Ullman, S., "Visual Routines", *Cognition*, *18*:97-160, 1984. ©1984 by Elsevier Publishers, Amsterdam. Reprinted with the permission of the publisher and the author.

Wilensky, R., "Meta planning: Representing and using knowledge about planning in problem solving and natural language understanding", *Cognitive Science*, *5*:197-234, 1984. ©1984 by Ablex Publishing Corporation. Reprinted with the permission of the publisher and the author.

Woods, W. A., "What's in a link: Foundations for semantic networks", in D. G. Bobrow and A. Collins (eds.), *Representations and Understanding: Studies in Cognitive Science*, 35-84, New York: Academic Press, 1975. ©1975 by Academic Press. Reprinted with the permission of the publisher and the author.

A Perspective on Cognitive Science

As the term is most generally used, *cognitive science* refers to the interdisciplinary study of the acquisition and use of knowledge. The field includes as contributing disciplines: artificial intelligence, cognitive psychology, linguistics, philosophy of mind and language, anthropology, neuroscience, and education. As we might surmise from this list, the cognitive-science movement is far-reaching and diverse, containing within it several viewpoints. The present collection of readings focuses on one of these perspectives—that provided by the interface between artificial intelligence and cognitive psychology. Hereafter, we use the term *cognitive science* to refer to only this perspective.

The perspective of interest grew out of two developments: (1) the invention of computers and the attempts soon thereafter to design programs that could do the kinds of tasks that humans do, and (2) the development of information-processing psychology, later called cognitive psychology, which attempted to specify the internal processing involved in perception, memory, and thought. Cognitive science was a synthesis of the two, concerned both with the details of human cognitive processing and with the computational modeling of those processes.

Cognitive science and artificial intelligence arose at about the same time, in the late 1950s. Cognitive science (called *cognitive simulation* at the outset) developed primarily at the Carnegie Institute of Technology (now Carnegie-Mellon University), whereas artificial intelligence developed primarily at the Massachusetts Institute of Technology (MIT). (Of course, other institutions were involved to a lesser degree; we are painting in broad strokes here.) MIT has always specialized in languages or tools for building intelligent programs, starting with LISP. Carnegie, on the other hand, focused on developing formalisms, such as means–ends analysis, which are standard methods for representing and implementing cognitive processes. When, a little later, Stanford University entered the field of artificial intelligence, it focused most of its efforts on building expert systems, such as Dendral or Mycin. These three universities remain major centers of artificial intelligence today.

1. Formalisms in Cognitive Science

The above three foci—(1) formalisms, (2) tools, and (3) programs—have turned out to be the three major bases for progress in artificial intelligence. Artificial intelligence develops better formalisms for solving problems, accumulates more powerful tools for building programs by turning these formalisms into programming languages, and develops more and more programs using these formalisms and tools. By contrast, psychology historically has made progress mainly by accumulating empirical phenomena and data, with far less emphasis on theorizing of the sort found in artificial intelligence. In particular, psychological theories have tended to be constructed just to account for the data in some experimental paradigm, and have tended to have an impoverished sense of mechanism, no doubt a remnant of the behavioristic or stimulus–response approach that dominated psychology from the 1920s through the 1950s.

What was needed for a science of cognition was a much richer notion of knowledge representation and process mechanisms. That is what artificial intelligence has provided. Cognitive psychologists now have a rich set of formalisms to use in characterizing human cognition. New formalisms have been developed every 2 or 3 years. The following is a sampling of some of the most important formalisms:

Means–ends analysis (Newell & Simon, 1963) is a method for solving problems that involves setting up subgoals and applying operators that reduce the difference between the current state and goal. This is a process formalism that has been applied in a wide variety of problem-solving tasks.

Discrimination nets (Feigenbaum, 1963) are a means of representing knowledge in a tree structure such that each branch point discriminates one set of objects from another on the basis of some feature. By determining the value of each feature at consecutive branch points (as in the game Twenty Questions), one can identify any object at a terminal node in the discrimination net.

Semantic networks (Quillian, 1968) are a means of representing knowledge in which any concept is represented by a set of properties, which in turn consist of pointers to other concepts. The properties are made up of attribute–value pairs, so that an oriole might be represented by the pairs: superset = bird, color = orange, location = Eastern United States. Any amount of information can be represented in this format.

Intersection search or marker passing (Quillian, 1968) is a process formalism for finding a connection between concepts in a semantic network. The scheme is to start out in parallel from the given concepts following pointers, and to leave a marker at each concept along the way. When a marker is encountered that originated at a different concept, an intersection is found and the path between the concepts can be identified.

Production systems (Newell & Simon, 1972) are both a representational and a process formalism. Knowledge is represented as condition–action pairs called production rules (e.g., "If it has a long neck and brown blotches, infer that it is a giraffe"). A production system operates roughly as follows: If the current state satisfies one of the rules, it fires, which changes the current state, so then either a new rule fires or the system stops.

Semantic primitives (Schank, 1972; Norman & Rumelhart, 1975) involve the notion of representing different actions or verbs in terms of a small number of primitive acts (e.g., object transfer, idea transfer). The goal was to be able to represent all the paraphrases of a single idea with the same representation (e.g., Mary gave the ball to John; John got the ball from Mary).

Constraint satisfaction (Fikes, 1970; Waltz, 1975) is a technique used in problem solving and scene recognition where an interpretation of one element in a problem or scene constrains the interpretation of related elements. The process continues (sometimes backtracking) until an overall interpretation is found that satisfies the constraints among all the elements.

Frames and scripts (Minsky, 1975; Schank & Abelson, 1977) are extensions of semantic networks. Frames and scripts represent complex concepts (e.g., going to a restaurant) in terms of structured units with specific slots (e.g., being seated, ordering), with possible default values (e.g., ordering from a menu), and with a range of possible values associated with any slot.

Incremental qualitative analysis (deKleer, 1979) is a means for describing what happens in a system when a change is introduced. Each element or device in the system has a set of rules associated with it that describes the set of qualitative changes in its outputs, given any possible qualitative change in its inputs.

These examples show the wide range of formalisms that has accumulated over the years. We stop in 1979, not because no formalisms were developed after that, but because it is not clear which of the new formalisms will have staying power. It should be clear, however, that any cognitive scientist is now armed with a powerful set of formalisms for analyzing human cognition. These formalisms are part of the critical substance of cognitive science that students need to learn.

2. Artificial Intelligence as Theoretical Psychology

Many sciences have developed two branches, with theoreticians on one side and experimentalists on the other. This is a natural division, because theory and experiment call for different talents. There may not always be a tight coupling between the two branches, but in most fields theory and experiment clearly constrain each other.

From the behaviorist revolution of the early 1900s until recently, psychology deemphasized theory. With few exceptions, you had to prove yourself as an experimenter in order to be allowed to theorize at all. One leading psychologist characterized a book that he admired, *Language and Perception* by George Miller and Philip Johnson–Laird, as "philosophic and linguistic speculation," rather than as theoretical psychology, even though it was written by two psychologists. Without a theoretical emphasis, psychology was severely limited as a science. Unless there is a healthy interplay between experiment and theory, a field can end up producing 50 years of research to which hardly anyone pays attention.

An effect that has emerged from the cognitive–science movement is that artificial intelligence has become a kind of theoretical psychology. Researchers who want to develop psychological theory can become artificial–intelligence researchers without making their marks as experimentalists. So now, as in physics, there are both experimental and theoretical branches of psychology, and cognitive science is the interface where theorists and experimentalists sort things out.

3. Computation as a Language for Psychological Theories

It is often argued that the computer is only a metaphor for how people think. Although computers can be regarded as a metaphor for the mind, this should not disguise the more important role that computation is playing in relation to psychology. Like mathematics, computation has become a language for constructing theories of the mind. Like mathematics (and unlike natural language), computation is a formal language that imposes a set of constraints on the kind of theories that can be constructed.

In the social sciences, computation is becoming the language of choice. It has several advantages over mathematics for constructing psychological theories:

- *Computational models are process–oriented*. Mathematical models are often static, whereas computational models are inherently process models. Because what is being described are processes (e.g., thinking, learning, perceiving), computation is better suited for modeling.

- *Computational models can be content–dependent*. A central concern of artificial intelligence has been the representation of knowledge. Hence, most computational models of human cognition have been models both of knowledge representation and of processing (although connectionist models—e.g., McClelland, Rumelhart & Hinton, 1986, reprinted in this volume—make minimal assumptions about knowledge representation). Mathematical models, particularly in psychology, have been content–independent.

- *Computational models are goal–oriented*. Programs, like people and animals, are inherently goal–oriented, whereas mathematics is not. Before computation, talk of goals and desires was disparaged as vitalism. Today, we understand what it means for a formal model to be goal–oriented.

But computation, until recent years, has had one big disadvantage as a language for modeling cognition. Most of the computer models and formalisms (except intersection search and production systems) have been serial, whereas many aspects of the human mind involve parallel processing. Perhaps the highest–fidelity model of the human mind will consist of a serial executive acting on a parallel–processing system. Now that the cost of computation has decreased enough that it is feasible to start building parallel machines, we will begin to develop computational formalisms and models that better reflect the actual architecture of the mind.

4. The Goal of this Book

The goal of this book is to bring together important articles that fall in the intersection between artificial intelligence and cognitive psychology. We assume that the readers are mainly graduate students in cognitive science, cognitive psychology, and artificial intelligence. We have selected papers that are near the center of research in the particular perspective of cognitive science on which we are focusing, omitting large areas such as linguistics, anthropology, neuroscience, and education. Our bias is toward topics that have been studied in both artificial intelligence and cognitive psychology. Topics that are dear to the heart of one field but not the other have been left out: For artificial intelligence, such topics include theorem proving, nonmonotonicity, dependency-directed backtracking, and higher-order languages; for cognitive psychology, the omissions include attention, short-term memory, motor behavior, and decision making. In addition, we generally have not included studies of language understanding and production; many of these studies fit in the intersection of artificial intelligence and cognitive psychology—so many, in fact, that adequate coverage of this area requires a separate book of readings (e.g., Grosz, Sparck–Jones & Webber, 1986).

As much as possible, we have tried to select classic papers that are highly referenced and that are of value as a collection. We also considered the readability of our selections, however, so we omitted many papers that might be considered classics. Our ideal paper related theoretical ideas to empirical results. We also tried to select readings representative of the major research areas in cognitive science and, to some extent, of the major researchers.

The book proceeds from the most general issues to the more specific research areas. Part 1, *Foundations*, introduces the general assumptions of the enterprise of computational modeling and the issue of what kind of cognitive architecture the mind has. Part 2, *Representation*, deals with three approaches to representation: semantic networks, schemas or frames, and mental models. A fourth approach, production systems, which might have been treated separately, is reflected in the Newell and Simon paper in Cognitive Architecture and the Anderson paper on Learning. Parts 3 through 6— on *Categorization*, *Learning*, *Thinking*, and *Perception*—address the major research areas in cognitive science.

5. References

deKleer, J. (1979). The origin and resolution of ambiguities in causal arguments. In *Proceedings of the Sixth International Joint Conference on Artificial Intelligence* (pp. 197–203). San Mateo, CA: Morgan Kaufmann.

Feigenbaum, E.A. (1963). The simulation of verbal learning behavior. In E.A. Feigenbaum & J. Feddman (Eds.), *Computers and Thought* (pp. 297–309). New York: McGraw-Hill.

Fikes, R.E. (1970). REF-ARF: A system for solving problems stated as procedures. *Artificial Intelligence*, *1*, 27–120.

Grosz, B.J., Sparck-Jones, K. & Webber, B.L. (1986). *Readings in Natural Language Processing*. San Mateo, CA: Morgan Kaufmann.

McClelland, J.L., Rumelhart, D.E. & Hinton, G.E. (1986). The appeal of parallel distributed processing. In D.E. Rumelhart, J.L. McClelland & the PDP Research Group (Eds.), *Parallel Distributed Processing* (pp. 3–44). Cambridge, MA: MIT Press.

Minsky, M. (1975). A framework for representing knowledge. In P.H. Winston (Ed.), *The Psychology of Computer Vision* (pp. 211–277). New York: McGraw-Hill.

Newell, A. & Simon, H.A. (1963). GPS: A program that simulates human thought. In E.A. Feigenbaum & J. Feldman (Eds.), *Computers and Thought* (pp. 279–296). New York: McGraw-Hill.

Newell, A. & Simon, H.A. (1972). *Human Problem Solving*. Englewood Cliffs, NJ: Prentice-Hall.

Norman, D.A., Rumelhart, D.E. & the LNR Research Group (1975). *Explorations in Cognition*. San Francisco: W.H. Freeman.

Quillian, M.R. (1968). Semantic memory. In M. Minsky (Ed.), *Semantic Information Processing* (pp. 216–270). Cambridge, MA: MIT Press.

Schank, R.C. (1972). Conceptual dependency: A theory of natural language understanding. *Cognitive Psychology*, *3*, 552–631.

Schank, R.C. & Abelson, R.P. (1977). *Scripts, Plans, Goals, and Understanding*. Hillsdale, NJ: Lawrence Erlbaum Associates.

Waltz, D. (1975). Understanding line drawings of scenes with shadows. In P.H. Winston (Ed.), *The Psychology of Computer Vision* (pp. 19–91). New York: McGraw-Hill.

Chapter 1

Foundations

Mind and Machines

Turing's classic paper raised an issue that lies at the heart of cognitive science: Can a machine display the same kind of intelligence as does a human being? To the extent that the answer is "yes," it should be possible to develop a science that studies intelligence, regardless of how it is implemented. To gain leverage on this question, Turing proposed that we see how well we can discriminate humans from programs by the answers the two give to questions; this proposal is the birth of the *Turing test*.

Searle's paper, published thirty years after Turing's paper, challenges the validity of the Turing test in particular, and of the computational-modeling perspective of cognitive science in general. Searle attempts to show that, if a theory of language were modeled in a computer program, the program would not really understand language. The Searle paper is accompanied by two of the rebuttals that appeared with it when it was originally published.

MIND

A QUARTERLY REVIEW

OF

PSYCHOLOGY AND PHILOSOPHY

COMPUTING MACHINERY AND INTELLIGENCE

By A. M. Turing

1. The Imitation Game.

I PROPOSE to consider the question, 'Can machines think?' This should begin with definitions of the meaning of the terms 'machine' and 'think'. The definitions might be framed so as to reflect so far as possible the normal use of the words, but this attitude is dangerous. If the meaning of the words 'machine' and 'think' are to be found by examining how they are commonly used it is difficult to escape the conclusion that the meaning and the answer to the question, 'Can machines think?' is to be sought in a statistical survey such as a Gallup poll. But this is absurd. Instead of attempting such a definition I shall replace the question by another, which is closely related to it and is expressed in relatively unambiguous words.

The new form of the problem can be described in terms of a game which we call the 'imitation game'. It is played with three people, a man (A), a woman (B), and an interrogator (C) who may be of either sex. The interrogator stays in a room apart from the other two. The object of the game for the interrogator is to determine which of the other two is the man and which is the woman. He knows them by labels X and Y, and at the end of the game he says either 'X is A and Y is B' or 'X is B and Y is A'. The interrogator is allowed to put questions to A and B thus:

C: Will X please tell me the length of his or her hair?

Now suppose X is actually A, then A must answer. It is A's object in the game to try and cause C to make the wrong identification. His answer might therefore be

'My hair is shingled, and the longest strands are about nine inches long.'

In order that tones of voice may not help the interrogator the answers should be written, or better still, typewritten. The ideal arrangement is to have a teleprinter communicating between the two rooms. Alternatively the question and answers can be repeated by an intermediary. The object of the game for the third player (B) is to help the interrogator. The best strategy for her is probably to give truthful answers. She can add such things as 'I am the woman, don't listen to him!' to her answers, but it will avail nothing as the man can make similar remarks.

We now ask the question, 'What will happen when a machine takes the part of A in this game?' Will the interrogator decide wrongly as often when the game is played like this as he does when the game is played between a man and a woman? These questions replace our original, 'Can machines think?'

2. Critique of the New Problem.

As well as asking, 'What is the answer to this new form of the question', one may ask, 'Is this new question a worthy one to investigate?' This latter question we investigate without further ado, thereby cutting short an infinite regress.

The new problem has the advantage of drawing a fairly sharp line between the physical and the intellectual capacities of a man. No engineer or chemist claims to be able to produce a material which is indistinguishable from the human skin. It is possible that at some time this might be done, but even supposing this invention available we should feel there was little point in trying to make a 'thinking machine' more human by dressing it up in such artificial flesh. The form in which we have set the problem reflects this fact in the condition which prevents the interrogator from seeing or touching the other competitors, or hearing their voices. Some other advantages of the proposed criterion may be shown up by specimen questions and answers. Thus:

Q: Please write me a sonnet on the subject of the Forth Bridge.

A: Count me out on this one. I never could write poetry.

Q: Add 34957 to 70764

A: (Pause about 30 seconds and then give as answer) 105621.

Q: Do you play chess?

A: Yes.

Q : I have K at my K1, and no other pieces. You have only K at K6 and R at R1. It is your move. What do you play?

A : (After a pause of 15 seconds) R-R8 mate.

The question and answer method seems to be suitable for introducing almost any one of the fields of human endeavour that we wish to include. We do not wish to penalise the machine for its inability to shine in beauty competitions, nor to penalise a man for losing in a race against an aeroplane. The conditions of our game make these disabilities irrelevant. The 'witnesses' can brag, if they consider it advisable, as much as they please about their charms, strength or heroism, but the interrogator cannot demand practical demonstrations.

The game may perhaps be criticised on the ground that the odds are weighted too heavily against the machine. If the man were to try and pretend to be the machine he would clearly make a very poor showing. He would be given away at once by slowness and inaccuracy in arithmetic. May not machines carry out something which ought to be described as thinking but which is very different from what a man does? This objection is a very strong one, but at least we can say that if, nevertheless, a machine can be constructed to play the imitation game satisfactorily, we need not be troubled by this objection.

It might be urged that when playing the 'imitation game' the best strategy for the machine may possibly be something other than imitation of the behaviour of a man. This may be, but I think it is unlikely that there is any great effect of this kind. In any case there is no intention to investigate here the theory of the game, and it will be assumed that the best strategy is to try to provide answers that would naturally be given by a man.

3. The Machines concerned in the Game.

The question which we put in § 1 will not be quite definite until we have specified what we mean by the word 'machine'. It is natural that we should wish to permit every kind of engineering technique to be used in our machines. We also wish to allow the possibility than an engineer or team of engineers may construct a machine which works, but whose manner of operation cannot be satisfactorily described by its constructors because they have applied a method which is largely experimental. Finally, we wish to exclude from the machines men born in the usual manner. It is difficult to frame the definitions so as to satisfy these three conditions. One might for instance insist that the team of

engineers should be all of one sex, but this would not really be satisfactory, for it is probably possible to rear a complete individual from a single cell of the skin (say) of a man. To do so would be a feat of biological technique deserving of the very highest praise, but we would not be inclined to regard it as a case of 'constructing a thinking machine'. This prompts us to abandon the requirement that every kind of technique should be permitted. We are the more ready to do so in view of the fact that the present interest in 'thinking machines' has been aroused by a particular kind of machine, usually called an 'electronic computer' or 'digital computer'. Following this suggestion we only permit digital computers to take part in our game.

This restriction appears at first sight to be a very drastic one. I shall attempt to show that it is not so in reality. To do this necessitates a short account of the nature and properties of these computers.

It may also be said that this identification of machines with digital computers, like our criterion for 'thinking', will only be unsatisfactory if (contrary to my belief), it turns out that digital computers are unable to give a good showing in the game.

There are already a number of digital computers in working order, and it may be asked, 'Why not try the experiment straight away? It would be easy to satisfy the conditions of the game. A number of interrogators could be used, and statistics compiled to show how often the right identification was given.' The short answer is that we are not asking whether all digital computers would do well in the game nor whether the computers at present available would do well, but whether there are imaginable computers which would do well. But this is only the short answer. We shall see this question in a different light later.

4. Digital Computers.

The idea behind digital computers may be explained by saying that these machines are intended to carry out any operations which could be done by a human computer. The human computer is supposed to be following fixed rules; he has no authority to deviate from them in any detail. We may suppose that these rules are supplied in a book, which is altered whenever he is put on to a new job. He has also an unlimited supply of paper on which he does his calculations. He may also do his multiplications and additions on a 'desk machine', but this is not important.

If we use the above explanation as a definition we shall be in danger of circularity of argument. We avoid this by giving an outline of the means by which the desired effect is achieved. A digital computer can usually be regarded as consisting of three parts:

    (i) Store.
    (ii) Executive unit.
    (iii) Control.

The store is a store of information, and corresponds to the human computer's paper, whether this is the paper on which he does his calculations or that on which his book of rules is printed. In so far as the human computer does calculations in his head a part of the store will correspond to his memory.

The executive unit is the part which carries out the various individual operations involved in a calculation. What these individual operations are will vary from machine to machine. Usually fairly lengthy operations can be done such as 'Multiply 3540675445 by 7076345687' but in some machines only very simple ones such as 'Write down 0' are possible.

We have mentioned that the 'book of rules' supplied to the computer is replaced in the machine by a part of the store. It is then called the 'table of instructions'. It is the duty of the control to see that these instructions are obeyed correctly and in the right order. The control is so constructed that this necessarily happens.

The information in the store is usually broken up into packets of moderately small size. In one machine, for instance, a packet might consist of ten decimal digits. Numbers are assigned to the parts of the store in which the various packets of information are stored, in some systematic manner. A typical instruction might say—

'Add the number stored in position 6809 to that in 4302 and put the result back into the latter storage position'.

Needless to say it would not occur in the machine expressed in English. It would more likely be coded in a form such as 6809430217. Here 17 says which of various possible operations is to be performed on the two numbers. In this case the operation is that described above, viz. 'Add the number...'. It will be noticed that the instruction takes up 10 digits and so forms one packet of information, very conveniently. The control will normally take the instructions to be obeyed in the order of the positions in which they are stored, but occasionally an instruction such as:

'Now obey the instruction stored in position 5606, and continue from there'

may be encountered, or again

'If position 4505 contains 0 obey next the instruction stored in 6707, otherwise continue straight on.'

Instructions of these latter types are very important because they make it possible for a sequence of operations to be repeated over and over again until some condition is fulfilled, but in doing so to obey, not fresh instructions on each repetition, but the same ones over and over again. To take a domestic analogy. Suppose Mother wants Tommy to call at the cobbler's every morning on his way to school to see if her shoes are done, she can ask him afresh every morning. Alternatively she can stick up a notice once and for all in the hall which he will see when he leaves for school and which tells him to call for the shoes, and also to destroy the notice when he comes back if he has the shoes with him.

The reader must accept it as a fact that digital computers can be constructed, and indeed have been constructed, according to the principles we have described, and that they can in fact mimic the actions of a human computer very closely.

The book of rules which we have described our human computer as using is of course a convenient fiction. Actual human computers really remember what they have got to do. If one wants to make a machine mimic the behaviour of the human computer in some complex operation one has to ask him how it is done, and then translate the answer into the form of an instruction table. Constructing instruction tables is usually described as 'programming'. To 'programme a machine to carry out the operation A' means to put the appropriate instruction table into the machine so that it will do A.

An interesting variant on the idea of a digital computer is a 'digital computer with a random element'. These have instructions involving the throwing of a die or some equivalent electronic process; one such instruction might for instance be, 'Throw the die and put the resulting number into store 1000'. Sometimes such a machine is described as having free will (though I would not use this phrase myself). It is not normally possible to determine from observing a machine whether it has a random element, for a similar effect can be produced by such devices as making the choices depend on the digits of the decimal for π.

Most actual digital computers have only a finite store. There is no theoretical difficulty in the idea of a computer with an unlimited store. Of course only a finite part can have been used at any one time. Likewise only a finite amount can have been constructed, but we can imagine more and more being added as required. Such computers have special theoretical interest and will be called infinitive capacity computers.

The idea of a digital computer is an old one. Charles Babbage, Lucasian Professor of Mathematics at Cambridge from 1828 to 1839, planned such a machine, called the Analytical Engine, but it was never completed. Although Babbage had all the essential ideas, his machine was not at that time such a very attractive prospect. The speed which would have been available would be definitely faster than a human computer but something like 100 times slower than the Manchester machine, itself one of the slower of the modern machines. The storage was to be purely mechanical, using wheels and cards.

The fact that Babbage's Analytical Engine was to be entirely mechanical will help us to rid ourselves of a superstition. Importance is often attached to the fact that modern digital computers are electrical, and that the nervous system also is electrical. Since Babbage's machine was not electrical, and since all digital computers are in a sense equivalent, we see that this use of electricity cannot be of theoretical importance. Of course electricity usually comes in where fast signalling is concerned, so that it is not surprising that we find it in both these connections. In the nervous system chemical phenomena are at least as important as electrical. In certain computers the storage system is mainly acoustic. The feature of using electricity is thus seen to be only a very superficial similarity. If we wish to find such similarities we should look rather for mathematical analogies of function.

5. *Universality of Digital Computers.*

The digital computers considered in the last section may be classified amongst the 'discrete state machines'. These are the machines which move by sudden jumps or clicks from one quite definite state to another. These states are sufficiently different for the possibility of confusion between them to be ignored. Strictly speaking there are no such machines. Everything really moves continuously. But there are many kinds of machine which can profitably be *thought of* as being discrete state machines. For instance in considering the switches for a lighting system it is a convenient fiction that each switch must be definitely on or definitely off. There must be intermediate positions, but for most purposes we can forget about them. As an example of a discrete state machine we might consider a wheel which clicks round through 120° once a second, but may be stopped by a lever which can be operated from outside; in addition a lamp is to light in one of the positions of the wheel. This machine could be described abstractly as follows. The internal state of the machine (which is described by the position of the wheel) may be q_1, q_2 or q_3. There is an input signal i_0 or i_1 (position of lever). The internal state at any moment is determined by the last state and input signal according to the table

		Last State		
		q_1	q_2	q_3
Input	i_0	q_2	q_3	q_1
	i_1	q_1	q_2	q_3

The output signals, the only externally visible indication of the internal state (the light) are described by the table

State	q_1	q_2	q_3
Output	o_0	o_0	o_1

This example is typical of discrete state machines. They can be described by such tables provided they have only a finite number of possible states.

It will seem that given the initial state of the machine and the input signals it is always possible to predict all future states. This is reminiscent of Laplace's view that from the complete state of the universe at one moment of time, as described by the positions and velocities of all particles, it should be possible to predict all future states. The prediction which we are considering is, however, rather nearer to practicability than that considered by Laplace. The system of the 'universe as a whole' is such that quite small errors in the initial conditions can have an overwhelming effect at a later time. The displacement of a single electron by a billionth of a centimetre at one moment might make the difference between a man being killed by an avalanche a year later, or escaping. It is an essential property of the mechanical systems which we have called 'discrete state machines' that this phenomenon does not occur. Even when we consider the actual physical machines instead of the idealised machines, reasonably accurate knowledge of the state at one moment yields reasonably accurate knowledge any number of steps later.

As we have mentioned, digital computers fall within the class of discrete state machines. But the number of states of which such a machine is capable is usually enormously large. For instance, the number for the machine now working at Manchester it about $2^{165,000}$, i.e. about $10^{50,000}$. Compare this with our example of the clicking wheel described above, which had three states. It is not difficult to see why the number of states should be so immense. The computer includes a store corresponding to the paper used by a human computer. It must be possible to write into the store any one of the combinations of symbols which might have been written on the paper. For simplicity suppose that only digits from 0 to 9 are used as symbols. Variations in handwriting are ignored. Suppose the computer is allowed 100 sheets of paper each containing 50 lines each with room for 30 digits. Then the number of states is $10^{100 \times 50 \times 30}$, i.e. $10^{150,000}$. This is about the number of states of three Manchester machines put together. The logarithm to the base two of the number of states is usually called the 'storage capacity' of the machine. Thus the Manchester machine has a storage capacity of about 165,000 and the wheel machine of our example about 1·6. If two machines are put together their capacities must be added to obtain the capacity of the resultant machine. This leads to the possibility of statements such as 'The Manchester machine contains 64 magnetic tracks each with a capacity of 2560, eight electronic tubes with a capacity of 1280. Miscellaneous storage amounts to about 300 making a total of 174,380.'

Given the table corresponding to a discrete state machine it is possible to predict what it will do. There is no reason why this calculation should not be carried out by means of a digital computer. Provided it could be carried out sufficiently quickly the digital computer could mimic the behaviour of any discrete state machine. The imitation game could then be played with the machine in question (as B) and the mimicking digital computer (as A) and the interrogator would be unable to distinguish them. Of course the digital computer must have an adequate storage capacity as well as working sufficiently fast. Moreover, it must be programmed afresh for each new machine which it is desired to mimic.

This special property of digital computers, that they can mimic any discrete state machine, is described by saying that they are *universal* machines. The existence of machines with this property has the important consequence that, considerations of speed apart, it is unnecessary to design various new machines to do various computing processes. They can all be done with one digital computer, suitably programmed for each case. It will be seen that as a consequence of this all digital computers are in a sense equivalent.

We may now consider again the point raised at the end of §3. It was suggested tentatively that the question, 'Can machines think?' should be replaced by 'Are there imaginable digital computers which would do well in the imitation game?' If we wish we can make this superficially more general and ask 'Are there discrete state machines which would do well?' But in view of the universality property we see that either of these questions is equivalent to this, 'Let us fix our attention on one particular digital computer C. Is it true that by modifying this computer to have an adequate storage, suitably increasing its speed of action, and providing it with an appropriate programme, C can be made to play satisfactorily the part of A in the imitation game, the part of B being taken by a man?'

6. Contrary Views on the Main Question.

We may now consider the ground to have been cleared and we are ready to proceed to the debate on our question, 'Can machines think?' and the variant of it quoted at the end of the last section. We cannot altogether abandon the original form of the problem, for opinions will differ as to the appropriateness of the substitution and we must at least listen to what has to be said in this connexion.

It will simplify matters for the reader if I explain first my own beliefs in the matter. Consider first the more accurate form of the question. I believe that in about fifty years' time it will be possible to programme computers, with a storage capacity of about 10^9, to make them play the imitation game so well that an average interrogator will not have more than 70 per cent. chance of making the right identification after five minutes of questioning. The original question, 'Can machines think?' I believe to be too meaningless to deserve discussion. Nevertheless I believe that at the end of the century the use of words and general educated opinion will have altered so much that one will be able to speak of machines thinking without expecting to be contradicted. I believe further that no useful purpose is served by concealing these beliefs. The popular view that scientists proceed inexorably from well-established fact to well-established fact, never being influenced by any unproved conjecture, is quite mistaken. Provided it is made clear which are proved facts and which are conjectures, no harm can result. Conjectures are of great importance since they suggest useful lines of research.

I now proceed to consider opinions opposed to my own.

(1) *The Theological Objection.* Thinking is a function of man's immortal soul. God has given an immortal soul to every man and woman, but not to any other animal or to machines. Hence no animal or machine can think.

I am unable to accept any part of this, but will attempt to reply in theological terms. I should find the argument more convincing if animals were classed with men, for there is a greater difference, to my mind, between the typical animate and the inanimate than there is between man and the other animals. The arbitrary character of the orthodox view becomes clearer if we consider how it might appear to a member of some other religious community. How do Christians regard the Moslem view that women have no souls? But let us leave this point aside and return to the main argument. It is admitted that there are certain things that He cannot do such as making one equal to two, but should we not believe that He has freedom to confer a soul on an elephant if He sees fit? We might expect that He would only exercise this power in conjunction with a mutation which provided the elephant with an appropriately improved brain to minister to the needs of this soul. An argument of exactly similar form may be made for the case of machines. It may seem different because it is more difficult to "swallow". But this really only means that we think it would be less likely that He would consider the circumstances suitable for conferring a soul. The circumstances in question are discussed in the rest of this paper. In attempting to construct such machines we should not be irreverently usurping His power of creating souls, any more than we are in the procreation of children: rather we are, in either case, instruments of His will providing mansions for the souls that He creates.

However, this is mere speculation. I am not very impressed with theological arguments whatever they may be used to support. Such arguments have often been found unsatisfactory in the past. In the time of Galileo it was argued that the texts, "And the sun stood still . . . and hasted not to go down about a whole day" (Joshua x. 13) and "He laid the foundations of the earth,

¹ Possibly this view is heretical. St. Thomas Aquinas (*Summa Theologica*, quoted by Bertrand Russell, p. 480) states that God cannot make a man to have no soul. But this may not be a real restriction on His powers, but only a result of the fact that men's souls are immortal, and therefore indestructible.

that it should not move at any time" (Psalm cv. 5) were an adequate refutation of the Copernican theory. With our present knowledge such an argument appears futile. When that knowledge was not available it made a quite different impression.

(2) *The 'Heads in the Sand' Objection.* "The consequences of machines thinking would be too dreadful. Let us hope and believe that they cannot do so."

This argument is seldom expressed quite so openly as in the form above. But it affects most of us who think about it at all. We like to believe that Man is in some subtle way superior to the rest of creation. It is best if he can be shown to be *necessarily* superior, for then there is no danger of him losing his commanding position. The popularity of the theological argument is clearly connected with this feeling. It is likely to be quite strong in intellectual people, since they value the power of thinking more highly than others, and are more inclined to base their belief in the superiority of Man on this power.

I do not think that this argument is sufficiently substantial to require refutation. Consolation would be more appropriate: perhaps this should be sought in the transmigration of souls.

(3) *The Mathematical Objection.* There are a number of results of mathematical logic which can be used to show that there are limitations to the powers of discrete-state machines. The best known of these results is known as Gödel's theorem,¹ and shows that in any sufficiently powerful logical system statements can be formulated which can neither be proved nor disproved within the system, unless possibly the system itself is inconsistent. There are other, in some respects similar, results due to *Church, Kleene, Rosser,* and *Turing.* The latter result is the most convenient to consider, since it refers directly to machines, whereas the others can only be used in a comparatively indirect argument: for instance if Gödel's theorem is to be used we need in addition to have some means of describing logical systems in terms of machines, and machines in terms of logical systems. The result in question refers to a type of machine which is essentially a digital computer with an infinite capacity. It states that there are certain things that such a machine cannot do. If it is rigged up to give answers to questions as in the imitation game, there will be some questions to which it will either give a wrong answer, or fail to give an answer at all however much time is allowed for a reply. There may, of course, be many such questions, and questions which cannot be answered by one machine may be satisfactorily

¹ Author's names in italics refer to the Bibliography.

answered by another. We are of course supposing for the present that the questions are of the kind to which an answer 'Yes' or 'No' is appropriate, rather than questions such as 'What do you think of Picasso?' The questions that we know the machines must fail on are of this type, "Consider the machine specified as follows. . . . Will this machine ever answer 'Yes' to any question?" The dots are to be replaced by a description of some machine in a standard form, which could be something like that used in §5. When the machine described bears a certain comparatively simple relation to the machine which is under interrogation, it can be shown that the answer is either wrong or not forthcoming. This is the mathematical result: it is argued that it proves a disability of machines to which the human intellect is not subject.

The short answer to this argument is that although it is established that there are limitations to the powers of any particular machine, it has only been stated, without any sort of proof, that no such limitations apply to the human intellect. But I do not think this view can be dismissed quite so lightly. Whenever one of these machines is asked the appropriate critical question, and gives a definite answer, we know that this answer must be wrong, and this gives us a certain feeling of superiority. Is this feeling illusory? It is no doubt quite genuine, but I do not think too much importance should be attached to it. We too often give wrong answers to questions ourselves to be justified in being very pleased at such evidence of fallibility on the part of the machines. Further, our superiority can only be felt on such an occasion in relation to the one machine over which we have scored our petty triumph. There would be no question of triumphing simultaneously over all machines. In short, then, there might be men cleverer than any given machine, but then again there might be other machines cleverer again, and so on.

Those who hold to the mathematical argument would, I think, mostly be willing to accept the imitation game as a basis for discussion. Those who believe in the two previous objections would probably not be interested in any criteria.

(4) *The Argument from Consciousness.* This argument is very well expressed in *Professor Jefferson's* Lister Oration for 1949, from which I quote. "Not until a machine can write a sonnet or compose a concerto because of thoughts and emotions felt, and not by the chance fall of symbols, could we agree that machine equals brain—that is, not only write it but know that it had written it. No mechanism could feel (and not merely

artificially signal, an easy contrivance) pleasure at its successes, grief when its valves fuse, be warmed by flattery, be made miserable by its mistakes, be charmed by sex, be angry or depressed when it cannot get what it wants."

This argument appears to be a denial of the validity of our test. According to the most extreme form of this view the only way by which one could be sure that a machine thinks is to be the machine and to feel oneself thinking. One could then describe these feelings to the world, but of course no one would be justified in taking any notice. Likewise according to this view the only way to know that a *man* thinks is to be that particular man. It is in fact the solipsist point of view. It may be the most logical view to hold but it makes communication of ideas difficult. A is liable to believe 'A thinks but B does not' whilst B believes 'B thinks but A does not'. Instead of arguing continually over this point it is usual to have the polite convention that everyone thinks.

I am sure that Professor Jefferson does not wish to adopt the extreme and solipsist point of view. Probably he would be quite willing to accept the imitation game as a test. The game (with the player B omitted) is frequently used in practice under the name of *viva voce* to discover whether some one really understands something or has 'learnt it parrot fashion'. Let us listen in to a part of such a *viva voce*:

Interrogator: In the first line of your sonnet which reads 'Shall I compare thee to a summer's day', would not 'a spring day' do as well or better?

Witness: It wouldn't scan.

Interrogator: How about 'a winter's day'. That would scan all right.

Witness: Yes, but nobody wants to be compared to a winter's day.

Interrogator: Would you say Mr. Pickwick reminded you of Christmas?

Witness: In a way.

Interrogator: Yet Christmas is a winter's day, and I do not think Mr. Pickwick would mind the comparison.

Witness: I don't think you're serious. By a winter's day one means a typical winter's day, rather than a special one like Christmas.

And so on. What would Professor Jefferson say if the sonnet-writing machine was able to answer like this in the *viva voce*? I do not know whether he would regard the machine as 'merely artificially signalling' these answers, but if the answers were as satisfactory and sustained as in the above passage I do not think he would describe it as 'an easy contrivance'. This phrase is, I think, intended to cover such devices as the inclusion in the machine of a record of someone reading a sonnet, with appropriate switching to turn it on from time to time.

In short then, I think that most of those who support the argument from consciousness could be persuaded to abandon it rather than be forced into the solipsist position. They will then probably be willing to accept our test.

I do not wish to give the impression that I think there is no mystery about consciousness. There is, for instance, something of a paradox connected with any attempt to localise it. But I do not think these mysteries necessarily need to be solved before we can answer the question with which we are concerned in this paper.

(5) *Arguments from Various Disabilities.* These arguments take the form, "I grant you that you can make machines do all the things you have mentioned but you will never be able to make one to do X". Numerous features X are suggested in this connexion. I offer a selection :

Be kind, resourceful, beautiful, friendly (p. 448), have initiative, have a sense of humour, tell right from wrong, make mistakes (p. 448), fall in love, enjoy strawberries and cream (p. 448), make some one fall in love with it, learn from experience (pp. 456 f.), use words properly, be the subject of its own thought (p. 449), have as much diversity of behaviour as a man, do something really new (p. 450). (Some of these disabilities are given special consideration as indicated by the page numbers.)

No support is usually offered for these statements. I believe they are mostly founded on the principle of scientific induction. A man has seen thousands of machines in his lifetime. From what he sees of them he draws a number of general conclusions. They are ugly, each is designed for a very limited purpose, when required for a minutely different purpose they are useless, the variety of behaviour of any one of them is very small, etc., etc. Naturally he concludes that these are necessary properties of machines in general. Many of these limitations are associated with the very small storage capacity of most machines. (I am assuming that the idea of storage capacity is extended in some way to cover machines other than discrete-state machines.

The exact definition does not matter as no mathematical accuracy is claimed in the present discussion.) A few years ago, when very little had been heard of digital computers, it was possible to elicit much incredulity concerning them, if one mentioned their properties without describing their construction. That was presumably due to a similar application of the principle of scientific induction. These applications of the principle are of course largely unconscious. When a burnt child fears the fire and shows that he fears it by avoiding it, I should say that he was applying scientific induction. (I could of course also describe his behaviour in many other ways.) The works and customs of mankind do not seem to be very suitable material to which to apply scientific induction. A very large part of space-time must be investigated, if reliable results are to be obtained. Otherwise we may (as most English children do) decide that everybody speaks English, and that it is silly to learn French.

There are, however, special remarks to be made about many of the disabilities that have been mentioned. The inability to enjoy strawberries and cream may have struck the reader as frivolous. Possibly a machine might be made to enjoy this delicious dish, but any attempt to make one do so would be idiotic. What is important about this disability is that it contributes to some of the other disabilities, *e.g.* to the difficulty of the same kind of friendliness occurring between man and machine as between white man and white man, or between black man and black man.

The claim that " machines cannot make mistakes " seems a curious one. One is tempted to retort, " Are they any the worse for that ? " But let us adopt a more sympathetic attitude, and try to see what is really meant. I think this criticism can be explained in terms of the imitation game. It is claimed that the interrogator could distinguish the machine from the man simply by setting them a number of problems in arithmetic. The machine would be unmasked because of its deadly accuracy. The reply to this is simple. The machine (programmed for playing the game) would not attempt to give the *right* answers to the arithmetic problems. It would deliberately introduce mistakes in a manner calculated to confuse the interrogator. A mechanical fault would probably show itself through an unsuitable decision as to what sort of a mistake to make in the arithmetic. Even this interpretation of the criticism is not sufficiently sympathetic. But we cannot afford the space to go into it much further. It seems to me that this criticism depends on a confusion between two kinds of mistake. We may call them 'errors of functioning' and 'errors of conclusion'. Errors of functioning are due to some mechanical or electrical fault which causes the machine to behave otherwise than it was designed to do. In philosophical discussions one likes to ignore the possibility of such errors; one is therefore discussing 'abstract machines'. These abstract machines are mathematical fictions rather than physical objects. By definition they are incapable of errors of functioning. In this sense we can truly say that 'machines can never make mistakes'. Errors of conclusion can only arise when some meaning is attached to the output signals from the machine. The machine might, for instance, type out mathematical equations, or sentences in English. When a false proposition is typed we say that the machine has committed an error of conclusion. There is clearly no reason at all for saying that a machine cannot make this kind of mistake. It might do nothing but type out repeatedly '0 = 1'. To take a less perverse example, it might have some method for drawing conclusions by scientific induction. We must expect such a method to lead occasionally to erroneous results.

The claim that a machine cannot be the subject of its own thought can of course only be answered if it can be shown that the machine has *some* thought with *some* subject matter. Nevertheless, 'the subject matter of a machine's operations' does seem to mean something, at least to the people who deal with it. If, for instance, the machine was trying to find a solution of the equation $x^2 - 40x - 11 = 0$ one would be tempted to describe this equation as part of the machine's subject matter at that moment. In this sort of sense a machine undoubtedly can be its own subject matter. It may be used to help in making up its own programmes, or to predict the effect of alterations in its own structure. By observing the results of its own behaviour it can modify its own programmes so as to achieve some purpose more effectively. These are possibilities of the near future, rather than Utopian dreams.

The criticism that a machine cannot have much diversity of behaviour is just a way of saying that it cannot have much storage capacity. Until fairly recently a storage capacity of even a thousand digits was very rare.

The criticisms that we are considering here are often disguised forms of the argument from consciousness. Usually if one maintains that a machine *can* do one of these things, and describes the kind of method that the machine could use, one will not make much of an impression. It is thought that the method (whatever it may be, for it must be mechanical) is really rather base. Compare the parenthesis in Jefferson's statement quoted on p. 21.

(6) *Lady Lovelace's Objection.* Our most detailed information of Babbage's Analytical Engine comes from a memoir by *Lady Lovelace.* In it she states, "The Analytical Engine has no pretensions to *originate* anything. It can do *whatever we know how to order it* to perform" (her italics). This statement is quoted by Hartree (p. 70) who adds: "This does not imply that it may not be possible to construct electronic equipment which will 'think for itself', or in which, in biological terms, one could set up a conditioned reflex, which would serve as a basis for 'learning'. Whether this is possible in principle or not is a stimulating and exciting question, suggested by some of these recent developments. But it did not seem that the machines constructed or projected at the time had this property".

I am in thorough agreement with Hartree over this. It will be noticed that he does not assert that the machines in question had not got the property, but rather that the evidence available to Lady Lovelace did not encourage her to believe that they had it. It is quite possible that the machines in question had in a sense got this property. For suppose that some discrete-state machine has the property. The Analytical Engine was a universal digital computer, so that, if its storage capacity and speed were adequate, it could by suitable programming be made to mimic the machine in question. Probably this argument did not occur to the Countess or to Babbage. In any case there was no obligation on them to claim all that could be claimed.

This whole question will be considered again under the heading of learning machines.

A variant of Lady Lovelace's objection states that a machine can 'never do anything really new'. This may be parried for a moment with the saw, 'There is nothing new under the sun'. Who can be certain that 'original work' that he has done was not simply the growth of the seed planted in him by teaching, or the effect of following well-known general principles. A better variant of the objection says that a machine can never 'take us by surprise'. This statement is a more direct challenge and can be met directly. Machines take me by surprise with great frequency. This is largely because I do not do sufficient calculation to decide what to expect them to do, or rather because, although I do a calculation, I do it in a hurried, slipshod fashion, taking risks. Perhaps I say to myself, 'I suppose the voltage here ought to be the same as there: anyway let's assume it is'.

Naturally I am often wrong, and the result is a surprise for me for by the time the experiment is done these assumptions have been forgotten. These admissions lay me open to lectures on the subject of my vicious ways, but do not throw any doubt on my credibility when I testify to the surprises I experience.

I do not expect this reply to silence my critic. He will probably say that such surprises are due to some creative mental act on my part, and reflect no credit on the machine. This leads us back to the argument from consciousness, and far from the idea of surprise. It is a line of argument we must consider closed, but it is perhaps worth remarking that the appreciation of something as surprising requires as much of a 'creative mental act' whether the surprising event originates from a man, a book, a machine or anything else.

The view that machines cannot give rise to surprises is due, I believe, to a fallacy to which philosophers and mathematicians are particularly subject. This is the assumption that as soon as a fact is presented to a mind all consequences of that fact spring into the mind simultaneously with it. It is a very useful assumption under many circumstances, but one too easily forgets that it is false. A natural consequence of doing so is that one then assumes that there is no virtue in the mere working out of consequences from data and general principles.

(7) *Argument from Continuity in the Nervous System.* The nervous system is certainly not a discrete-state machine. A small error in the information about the size of a nervous impulse impinging on a neuron, may make a large difference to the size of the outgoing impulse. It may be argued that, this being so, one cannot expect to be able to mimic the behaviour of the nervous system with a discrete-state system.

It is true that a discrete-state machine must be different from a continuous machine. But if we adhere to the conditions of the imitation game, the interrogator will not be able to take any advantage of this difference. The situation can be made clearer if we consider some other simpler continuous machine. A differential analyser will do very well. (A differential analyser is a certain kind of machine not of the discrete-state type used for some kinds of calculation.) Some of these provide their answers in a typed form, and so are suitable for taking part in the game. It would not be possible for a digital computer to predict exactly what answers the differential analyser would give to a problem, but it would be quite capable of giving the right sort of answer. For instance, if asked to give the value of π (actually about 3·1416) it would be reasonable to choose at random between the values 3·12, 3·13, 3·14, 3·15, 3·16 with the probabilities of 0·05, 0·15, 0·55, 0·19, 0·06 (say). Under these circumstances it would be very difficult for the interrogator to distinguish the differential analyser from the digital computer.

(8) *The Argument from Informality of Behaviour.* It is not possible to produce a set of rules purporting to describe what a man should do in every conceivable set of circumstances. One might for instance have a rule that one is to stop when one sees a red traffic light, and to go if one sees a green one, but what if by some fault both appear together? One may perhaps decide that it is safest to stop. But some further difficulty may well arise from this decision later. To attempt to provide rules of conduct to cover every eventuality, even those arising from traffic lights, appears to be impossible. With all this I agree.

From this it is argued that we cannot be machines. I shall try to reproduce the argument, but I fear I shall hardly do it justice. It seems to run something like this. 'If each man had a definite set of rules of conduct by which he regulated his life he would be no better than a machine. But there are no such rules, so men cannot be machines.' The undistributed middle is glaring. I do not think the argument is ever put quite like this, but I believe this is the argument used nevertheless. There may however be a certain confusion between 'rules of conduct' and 'laws of behaviour' to cloud the issue. By 'rules of conduct' I mean precepts such as 'Stop if you see red lights', on which one can act, and of which one can be conscious. By 'laws of behaviour' I mean laws of nature as applied to a man's body such as 'if you pinch him he will squeak'. If we substitute 'laws of behaviour which regulate his life' for 'laws of conduct by which he regulates his life' in the argument quoted the undistributed middle is no longer insuperable. For we believe that it is not only true that being regulated by laws of behaviour implies being some sort of machine (though not necessarily a discrete-state machine), but that conversely being such a machine implies being regulated by such laws. However, we cannot so easily convince ourselves of the absence of complete laws of behaviour as of complete rules of conduct. The only way we know of for finding such laws is scientific observation, and we certainly know of no circumstances under which we could say, 'We have searched enough. There are no such laws.'

We can demonstrate more forcibly that any such statement would be unjustified. For suppose we could be sure of finding such laws if they existed. Then given a discrete-state machine it should certainly be possible to discover by observation sufficient about it to predict its future behaviour, and this within a reasonable time, say a thousand years. But this does not seem to be the case. I have set up on the Manchester computer a small programme using only 1000 units of storage, whereby the machine supplied with one sixteen figure number replies with another within two seconds. I would defy anyone to learn from these replies sufficient about the programme to be able to predict any replies to untried values.

(9) *The Argument from Extra-Sensory Perception.* I assume that the reader is familiar with the idea of extra-sensory perception, and the meaning of the four items of it, *viz.* telepathy, clairvoyance, precognition and psycho-kinesis. These disturbing phenomena seem to deny all our usual scientific ideas. How we should like to discredit them! Unfortunately the statistical evidence, at least for telepathy, is overwhelming. It is very difficult to rearrange one's ideas so as to fit these new facts in. Once one has accepted them it does not seem a very big step to believe in ghosts and bogies. The idea that our bodies move simply according to the known laws of physics, together with some others not yet discovered but somewhat similar, would be one of the first to go.

This argument is to my mind quite a strong one. One can say in reply that many scientific theories seem to remain workable in practice, in spite of clashing with E.S.P.; that in fact one can get along very nicely if one forgets about it. This is rather cold comfort, and one fears that thinking is just the kind of phenomenon where E.S.P. may be especially relevant.

A more specific argument based on E.S.P. might run as follows: " Let us play the imitation game, using as witnesses a man who is good as a telepathic receiver, and a digital computer. The interrogator can ask such questions as ' What suit does the card in my right hand belong to ? ' The man by telepathy or clairvoyance gives the right answer 130 times out of 400 cards. The machine can only guess at random, and perhaps gets 104 right, so the interrogator makes the right identification." There is an interesting possibility which opens here. Suppose the digital computer contains a random number generator. Then it will be natural to use this to decide what answer to give. But then the random number generator will be subject to the psycho-kinetic powers of the interrogator. Perhaps this psycho-kinesis might cause the machine to guess right more often than would be expected on a probability calculation, so that the interrogator

might still be unable to make the right identification. On the other hand, he might be able to guess right without any questioning, by clairvoyance. With E.S.P. anything may happen.

If telepathy is admitted it will be necessary to tighten our test up. The situation could be regarded as analogous to that which would occur if the interrogator were talking to himself and one of the competitors was listening with his ear to the wall. To put the competitors into a ' telepathy-proof room ' would satisfy all requirements.

7. *Learning Machines.*

The reader will have anticipated that I have no very convincing arguments of a positive nature to support my views. If I had I should not have taken such pains to point out the fallacies in contrary views. Such evidence as I have I shall now give.

Let us return for a moment to Lady Lovelace's objection, which stated that the machine can only do what we tell it to do. One could say that a man can ' inject ' an idea into the machine, and that it will respond to a certain extent and then drop into quiescence, like a piano string struck by a hammer. Another simile would be an atomic pile of less than critical size : an injected idea is to correspond to a neutron entering the pile from without. Each such neutron will cause a certain disturbance which eventually dies away. If, however, the size of the pile is sufficiently increased, the disturbance caused by such an incoming neutron will very likely go on and on increasing until the whole pile is destroyed. Is there a corresponding phenomenon for minds, and is there one for machines ? There does seem to be one for the human mind. The majority of them seem to be ' sub-critical ', *i.e.* to correspond in this analogy to piles of sub-critical size. An idea presented to such a mind will on average give rise to less than one idea in reply. A smallish proportion are super-critical. An idea presented to such a mind may give rise to a whole ' theory ' consisting of secondary, tertiary and more remote ideas. Animals minds seem to be very definitely sub-critical. Adhering to this analogy we ask, ' Can a machine be made to be super-critical ? '

The ' skin of an onion ' analogy is also helpful. In considering the functions of the mind or the brain we find certain operations which we can explain in purely mechanical terms. This we say does not correspond to the real mind : it is a sort of skin which we must strip off if we are to find the real mind. But then in what remains we find a further skin to be stripped off, and so on.

Proceeding in this way do we ever come to the 'real' mind, or do we eventually come to the skin which has nothing in it? In the latter case the whole mind is mechanical. (It would not be a discrete-state machine however. We have discussed this.)

These last two paragraphs do not claim to be convincing arguments. They should rather be described as 'recitations tending to produce belief'.

The only really satisfactory support that can be given for the view expressed at the beginning of §6, will be that provided by waiting for the end of the century and then doing the experiment described. But what can we say in the meantime? What steps should be taken now if the experiment is to be successful?

As I have explained, the problem is mainly one of programming. Advances in engineering will have to be made too, but it seems unlikely that these will not be adequate for the requirements. Estimates of the storage capacity of the brain vary from 10^{10} to 10^{15} binary digits. I incline to the lower values and believe that only a very small fraction is used for the higher types of thinking. Most of it is probably used for the retention of visual impressions. I should be surprised if more than 10^9 was required for satisfactory playing of the imitation game, at any rate against a blind man. (Note—The capacity of the *Encyclopaedia Britannica*, 11th edition, is 2×10^9.) A storage capacity of 10^7 would be a very practicable possibility even by present techniques. It is probably not necessary to increase the speed of operations of the machines at all. Parts of modern machines which can be regarded as analogues of nerve cells work about a thousand times faster than the latter. This should provide a 'margin of safety' which could cover losses of speed arising in many ways. Our problem then is to find out how to programme these machines to play the game. At my present rate of working I produce about a thousand digits of programme a day, so that about sixty workers, working steadily through the fifty years might accomplish the job, if nothing went into the waste-paper basket. Some more expeditious method seems desirable.

In the process of trying to imitate an adult human mind we are bound to think a good deal about the process which has brought it to the state that it is in. We may notice three components,

(a) The initial state of the mind, say at birth,

(b) The education to which it has been subjected,

(c) Other experience, not to be described as education, to which it has been subjected.

Instead of trying to produce a programme to simulate the adult mind, why not rather try to produce one which simulates the child's? If this were then subjected to an appropriate course of education one would obtain the adult brain. Presumably the child-brain is something like a note-book as one buys it from the stationers. Rather little mechanism, and lots of blank sheets. (Mechanism and writing are from our point of view almost synonymous.) Our hope is that there is so little mechanism in the child-brain that something like it can be easily programmed. The amount of work in the education we can assume, as a first approximation, to be much the same as for the human child.

We have thus divided our problem into two parts. The child-programme and the education process. These two remain very closely connected. We cannot expect to find a good child-machine at the first attempt. One must experiment with teaching one such machine and see how well it learns. One can then try another and see if it is better or worse. There is an obvious connection between this process and evolution, by the identifications

Structure of the child machine = Hereditary material
Changes   "   = Mutations
Natural selection   = Judgment of the experimenter

One may hope, however, that this process will be more expeditious than evolution. The survival of the fittest is a slow method for measuring advantages. The experimenter, by the exercise of intelligence, should be able to speed it up. Equally important is the fact that he is not restricted to random mutations. If he can trace a cause for some weakness he can probably think of the kind of mutation which will improve it.

It will not be possible to apply exactly the same teaching process to the machine as to a normal child. It will not, for instance, be provided with legs, so that it could not be asked to go out and fill the coal scuttle. Possibly it might not have eyes. But however well these deficiencies might be overcome by clever engineering, one could not send the creature to school without the other children making excessive fun of it. It must be given some tuition. We need not be too concerned about the legs, eyes, etc. The example of Miss *Helen Keller* shows that education can take place provided that communication in both directions between teacher and pupil can take place by some means or other.

We normally associate punishments and rewards with the teaching process. Some simple child-machines can be constructed or programmed on this sort of principle. The machine has to be so constructed that events which shortly preceded the occurrence of a punishment-signal are unlikely to be repeated, whereas a reward-signal increased the probability of repetition of the events which led up to it. These definitions do not presuppose any feelings on the part of the machine. I have done some experiments with one such child-machine, and succeeded in teaching it a few things, but the teaching method was too unorthodox for the experiment to be considered really successful.

The use of punishments and rewards can at best be a part of the teaching process. Roughly speaking, if the teacher has no other means of communicating to the pupil, the amount of information which can reach him does not exceed the total number of rewards and punishments applied. By the time a child has learnt to repeat 'Casabianca' he would probably feel very sore indeed, if the text could only be discovered by a 'Twenty Questions' technique, every 'NO' taking the form of a blow. It is necessary therefore to have some other 'unemotional' channels of communication. If these are available it is possible to teach a machine by punishments and rewards to obey orders given in some language, e.g. a symbolic language. These orders are to be transmitted through the 'unemotional' channels. The use of this language will diminish greatly the number of punishments and rewards required.

Opinions may vary as to the complexity which is suitable in the child machine. One might try to make it as simple as possible consistently with the general principles. Alternatively one might have a complete system of logical inference 'built in'.[1] In the latter case the store would be largely occupied with definitions and propositions. The propositions would have various kinds of status, e.g. well-established facts, conjectures, mathematically proved theorems, statements given by an authority, expressions having the logical form of proposition but not belief value. Certain propositions may be described as 'imperatives'. The machine should be so constructed that as soon as an imperative is classed as 'well-established' the appropriate action automatically takes place. To illustrate this, suppose the teacher says "Teacher says 'Do your homework now'" to be included amongst the well-established facts. Another such fact might be,

[1] Or rather 'programmed in' for our child-machine will be programmed in a digital computer. But the logical system will not have to be learnt.

"Everything that teacher says is true". Combining these may eventually lead to the imperative, 'Do your homework now', being included amongst the well-established facts, and this, by the construction of the machine, will mean that the homework actually gets started, but the effect is very satisfactory. The processes of inference used by the machine need not be such as would satisfy the most exacting logicians. There might for instance be no hierarchy of types. But this need not mean that type fallacies will occur, any more than we are bound to fall over unfenced cliffs. Suitable imperatives (expressed *within* the systems, not forming part of the rules of the system) such as 'Do not use a class unless it is a subclass of one which has been mentioned by teacher' can have a similar effect to 'Do not go too near the edge'.

The imperatives that can be obeyed by a machine that has no limbs are bound to be of a rather intellectual character, as in the example (doing homework) given above. Important amongst such imperatives will be ones which regulate the order in which the rules of the logical system concerned are to be applied. For at each stage when one is using a logical system, there is a very large number of alternative steps, any of which one is permitted to apply, so far as obedience to the rules of the logical system is concerned. These choices make the difference between a brilliant and a footling reasoner, not the difference between a sound and a fallacious one. Propositions leading to imperatives of this kind might be "When Socrates is mentioned, use the syllogism in Barbara," or "If one method has been proved to be quicker than another, do not use the slower method". Some of these may be 'given by authority', but others may be produced by the machine itself, e.g. by scientific induction.

The idea of a learning machine may appear paradoxical to some readers. How can the rules of operation of the machine change? They should describe completely how the machine will react whatever its history might be, whatever changes it might undergo. The rules are thus quite time-invariant. This is quite true. The explanation of the paradox is that the rules which get changed in the learning process are of a rather less pretentious kind, claiming only an ephemeral validity. The reader may draw a parallel with the Constitution of the United States.

An important feature of a learning machine is that its teacher will often be very largely ignorant of quite what is going on inside, although he may still be able to some extent to predict his pupil's behaviour. This should apply most strongly to the later education of a machine arising from a child-machine of well-tried design (or programme). This is in clear contrast with normal procedure when using a machine to do computations: one's object is then to have a clear mental picture of the state of the machine at each moment in the computation. This object can only be achieved with a struggle. The view that 'the machine can only do what we know how to order it to do',[1] appears strange in face of this. Most of the programmes which we can put into the machine will result in its doing something that we cannot make sense of at all, or which we regard as completely random behaviour. Intelligent behaviour presumably consists in a departure from the completely disciplined behaviour involved in computation, but a rather slight one, which does not give rise to random behaviour, or to pointless repetitive loops. Another important result of preparing our machine for its part in the imitation game by a process of teaching and learning is that 'human fallibility' is likely to be omitted in a rather natural way, i.e. without special 'coaching'. (The reader should reconcile this with the point of view on pp. 24, 25.) Processes that are learnt do not produce a hundred per cent. certainty of result; if they did they could not be unlearnt.

It is probably wise to include a random element in a learning machine (see p. 438). A random element is rather useful when we are searching for a solution of some problem. Suppose for instance we wanted to find a number between 50 and 200 which was equal to the square of the sum of its digits, we might start at 51 then try 52 and go on until we got a number that worked. Alternatively we might choose numbers at random until we got a good one. This method has the advantage that it is unnecessary to keep track of the values that have been tried, but the disadvantage that one may try the same one twice, but this is not very important if there are several solutions. The systematic method has the disadvantage that there may be an enormous block without any solutions in the region which has to be investigated first. Now the learning process may be regarded as a search for a form of behaviour which will satisfy the teacher (or some other criterion). Since there is probably a very large number of satisfactory solutions the random method seems to be better than the systematic. It should be noticed that it is used in the analogous process of evolution. But there the systematic method is not possible. How could one keep track

[1] Compare Lady Lovelace's statement (p. 450), which does not contain the word 'only'.

of the different genetical combinations that had been tried, so as to avoid trying them again?

We may hope that machines will eventually compete with men in all purely intellectual fields. But which are the best ones to start with? Even this is a difficult decision. Many people think that a very abstract activity, like the playing of chess, would be best. It can also be maintained that it is best to provide the machine with the best sense organs that money can buy, and then teach it to understand and speak English. This process could follow the normal teaching of a child. Things would be pointed out and named, etc. Again I do not know what the right answer is, but I think both approaches should be tried.

We can only see a short distance ahead, but we can see plenty there that needs to be done.

BIBLIOGRAPHY

Samuel Butler, Erewhon, London, 1865. Chapters 23, 24, 25, *The Book of the Machines.*
Alonzo Church, " An Unsolvable Problem of Elementary Number Theory ", *American J. of Math.*, 58 (1936), 345-363.
K. Gödel, " Über formal unentscheidbare Sätze der Principia Mathematica und verwandter Systeme, I ", *Monatshefte für Math. und Phys.*, (1931), 173-189.
D. R. Hartree, *Calculating Instruments and Machines*, New York, 1949.
S. C. Kleene, " General Recursive Functions of Natural Numbers ", *American J. of Math.*, 57 (1935), 153-173 and 219-244.
G. Jefferson, " The Mind of Mechanical Man ". Lister Oration for 1949. *British Medical Journal*, vol. i (1949), 1105-1121.
Countess of Lovelace, 'Translator's notes to an article on Babbage's Analytical Engine', *Scientific Memoirs* (ed. by R. Taylor), vol. 3 (1842), 691-731.
Bertrand Russell, *History of Western Philosophy*, London, 1940.
A. M. Turing, " On Computable Numbers, with an Application to the Entscheidungsproblem ", *Proc. London Math. Soc.* (2), 42 (1937), 230-265.

Victoria University of Manchester.

Minds, brains, and programs

John R. Searle

*Department of Philosophy, University of California, Berkeley, Calif.
94720*

Abstract: This article can be viewed as an attempt to explore the consequences of two propositions. (1) Intentionality in human beings (and animals) is a product of causal features of the brain. I assume this is an empirical fact about the actual causal relations between mental processes and brains. It says simply that certain brain processes are sufficient for intentionality. (2) Instantiating a computer program is never by itself a sufficient condition of intentionality. The main argument of this paper is directed at establishing this claim. The form of the argument is to show how a human agent could instantiate the program and still not have the relevant intentionality. These two propositions have the following consequences: (3) The explanation of how the brain produces intentionality cannot be that it does it by instantiating a computer program. This is a strict logical consequence of 1 and 2. (4) Any mechanism capable of producing intentionality must have causal powers equal to those of the brain. This is meant to be a trivial consequence of 1. (5) Any attempt literally to create intentionality artificially (strong AI) could not succeed just by designing programs but would have to duplicate the causal powers of the human brain. This follows from 2 and 4.

"Could a machine think?" On the argument advanced here *only* a machine could think, and only very special kinds of machines, namely brains and machines with internal causal powers equivalent to those of brains. And that is why strong AI has little to tell us about thinking, since it is not about machines but about programs, and no program by itself is sufficient for thinking.

Keywords: artificial intelligence; brain; intentionality; mind

What psychological and philosophical significance should we attach to recent efforts at computer simulations of human cognitive capacities? In answering this question, I find it useful to distinguish what I will call "strong" AI from "weak" or "cautious" AI (Artificial Intelligence). According to weak AI, the principal value of the computer in the study of the mind is that it gives us a very powerful tool. For example, it enables us to formulate and test hypotheses in a more rigorous and precise fashion. But according to strong AI, the computer is not merely a tool in the study of the mind; rather, the appropriately programmed computer really *is* a mind, in the sense that computers given the right programs can be literally said to *understand* and have other cognitive states. In strong AI, because the programmed computer has cognitive states, the programs are not mere tools that enable us to test psychological explanations; rather, the programs are themselves the explanations.

I have no objection to the claims of weak AI, at least as far as this article is concerned. My discussion here will be directed at the claims I have defined as those of strong AI, specifically the claim that the appropriately programmed computer literally has cognitive states and that the programs thereby explain human cognition. When I hereafter refer to AI, I have in mind the strong version, as expressed by these two claims.

I will consider the work of Roger Schank and his colleagues at Yale (Schank & Abelson 1977), because I am more familiar with it than I am with any other similar claims, and because it provides a very clear example of the sort of work I wish to examine. But nothing that follows depends upon the details of Schank's programs. The same arguments would apply to Winograd's SHRDLU (Winograd 1973), Weizenbaum's ELIZA (Weizenbaum 1965), and indeed any Turing machine simulation of human mental phenomena.

Very briefly, and leaving out the various details, one can describe Schank's program as follows: the aim of the program is to simulate the human ability to understand stories. It is characteristic of human beings' story-understanding capacity that they can answer questions about the story even though the information that they give was never explicitly stated in the story. Thus, for example, suppose you are given the following story: "A man went into a restaurant and ordered a hamburger. When the hamburger arrived it was burned to a crisp, and the man stormed out of the restaurant angrily, without paying for the hamburger or leaving a tip." Now, if you are asked "Did the man eat the hamburger?" you will presumably answer, "No, he did not." Similarly, if you are given the following story: "A man went into a restaurant and ordered a hamburger; when the hamburger came he was very pleased with it; and as he left the restaurant he gave the waitress a large tip before paying his bill," and you are asked the question, "Did the man eat the hamburger?," you will presumably answer, "Yes, he ate the hamburger." Now Schank's machines can similarly answer questions about restaurants in this fashion. To do this, they have a "representation" of the sort of information that human beings have about restaurants, which enables them to answer such questions as those above, given these sorts of stories. When the machine is given the story and then asked the question, the machine will print out answers of the sort that we would expect human beings to give if told similar stories. Partisans of strong AI claim that in this question and answer sequence the machine is not only simulating a human ability but also

1. that the machine can literally be said to *understand* the story and provide the answers to questions, and

2. that what the machine and its program do *explains* the human ability to understand the story and answer questions about it.

Both claims seem to me to be totally unsupported by Schank's work, as I will attempt to show in what follows.

One way to test any theory of the mind is to ask oneself what it would be like if my mind actually worked on the principles that the theory says all minds work on. Let us apply this test to the Schank program with the following *Gedankenexperiment*. Suppose that I'm locked in a room and given a large batch of Chinese writing. Suppose furthermore (as is indeed the case) that I know no Chinese, either written or spoken, and that I'm not even confident that I could recognize Chinese writing as Chinese writing distinct from, say, Japanese writing or meaningless squiggles. To me, Chinese writing is just so many meaningless squiggles. Now suppose further that after this first batch of Chinese writing I am given a second batch of Chinese script together with a set of rules for correlating the second batch with the first batch. The rules are in English, and I understand these rules as well as any other native speaker of English. They enable me to correlate one set of formal symbols with another set of formal symbols, and all that "formal" means here is that I can identify the symbols entirely by their shapes. Now suppose also that I am given a third batch of Chinese symbols together with some instructions, again in English, that enable me to correlate elements of this third batch with the first two batches, and these rules instruct me how to give back certain Chinese symbols with certain sorts of shapes in response to certain sorts of shapes given me in the third batch. Unknown to me, the people who are giving me all of these symbols call the first batch "a script," they call the second batch a "story," and they call the third batch "questions." Furthermore, they call the symbols I give them back in response to the third batch "answers to the questions," and the set of rules in English that they gave me, they call "the program." Now just to complicate the story a little, imagine that these people also give me stories in English, which I understand, and they then ask me questions in English about these stories, and I give them back answers in English. Suppose also that after a while I get so good at following the instructions for manipulating the Chinese symbols and the programmers get so good at writing the programs that from the external point of view – that is, from the point of view of somebody outside the room in which I am locked – my answers to the questions are absolutely indistinguishable from those of native Chinese speakers. Nobody just looking at my answers can tell that I don't speak a word of Chinese. Let us also suppose that my answers to the English questions are, as they no doubt would be, indistinguishable from those of other native English speakers, for the simple reason that I am a native English speaker. From the external point of view – from the point of view of someone reading my "answers" – the answers to the Chinese questions and the English questions are equally good. But in the Chinese case, unlike the English case, I produce the answers by manipulating uninterpreted formal symbols. As far as the Chinese is concerned, I simply behave like a computer; I perform computational operations on formally specified elements. For the purposes of the Chinese, I am simply an instantiation of the computer program.

Now the claims made by strong AI are that the programmed computer understands the stories and that the program in some sense explains human understanding. But we are now in a position to examine these claims in light of our thought experiment.

1. As regards the first claim, it seems to me quite obvious in the example that I do not understand a word of the Chinese stories. I have inputs and outputs that are indistinguishable from those of the native Chinese speaker, and I can have any formal program you like, but I still understand nothing. For the same reasons, Schank's computer understands nothing of any stories, whether in Chinese, English, or whatever, since in the Chinese case the computer is me, and in cases where the computer is not me, the computer has nothing more than I have in the case where I understand nothing.

2. As regards the second claim, that the program explains human understanding, we can see that the computer and its program do not provide sufficient conditions of understanding since the computer and the program are functioning, and there is no understanding. But does it even provide a necessary condition or a significant contribution to under-

standing? One of the claims made by the supporters of strong AI is that when I understand a story in English, what I am doing is exactly the same – or perhaps more of the same – as what I was doing in manipulating the Chinese symbols. It is simply more formal symbol manipulation that distinguishes the case in English, where I do understand, from the case in Chinese, where I don't. I have not demonstrated that this claim is false, but it would certainly appear an incredible claim in the example. Such plausibility as the claim has derives from the supposition that we can construct a program that will have the same inputs and outputs as native speakers, and in addition we assume that speakers have some level of description where they are also instantiations of a program. On the basis of these two assumptions we assume that even if Schank's program isn't the whole story about understanding, it may be part of the story. Well, I suppose that is an empirical possibility, but not the slightest reason has so far been given to believe that it is true, since what is suggested – though certainly not demonstrated – by the example is that the computer program is simply irrelevant to my understanding of the story. In the Chinese case I have everything that artificial intelligence can put into me by way of a program, and I understand nothing; in the English case I understand everything, and there is so far no reason at all to suppose that my understanding has anything to do with computer programs, that is, with computational operations on purely formally specified elements. As long as the program is defined in terms of computational operations on purely formally defined elements, what the example suggests is that these by themselves have no interesting connection with understanding. They are certainly not sufficient conditions, and not the slightest reason has been given to suppose that they are necessary conditions or even that they make a significant contribution to understanding. Notice that the force of the argument is not simply that different machines can have the same input and output while operating on different formal principles – that is not the point at all. Rather, whatever purely formal principles you put into the computer, they will not be sufficient for understanding, since a human will be able to follow the formal principles without understanding anything. No reason whatever has been offered to suppose that such principles are necessary or even contributory, since no reason has been given to suppose that when I understand English I am operating with any formal program at all.

Well, then, what is it that I have in the case of the English sentences that I do not have in the case of the Chinese sentences? The obvious answer is that I know what the former mean, while I haven't the faintest idea what the latter mean. But in what does this consist and why couldn't we give it to a machine, whatever it is? I will return to this question later, but first I want to continue with the example.

I have had the occasions to present this example to several workers in artifical intelligence, and, interestingly, they do not seem to agree on what the proper reply to it is. I get a surprising variety of replies, and in what follows I will consider the most common of these (specified along with their geographic origins).

But first I want to block some common misunderstandings about "understanding": in many of these discussions one finds a lot of fancy footwork about the word "understanding." My critics point out that there are many different degrees of understanding; that "understanding" is not a simple two-place predicate; that there are even different kinds and levels of understanding, and often the law of excluded middle doesn't even apply in a straightforward way to statements of the form "x understands y"; that in many cases it is a matter for decision and not a simple matter of fact whether x understands y; and so on. To all of these points I want to say: of course, of course. But they have nothing to do with the points at issue. There are clear cases in which "understanding" literally applies and clear cases in which it does not apply; and these two sorts of cases are all I need for this argument.[2] I understand stories in English; to a lesser degree I can understand stories in French; to a still lesser degree, stories in German; and in Chinese, not at all. My car and my adding machine, on the other hand, understand nothing: they are not in that line of business. We often attribute "understanding" and other cognitive predicates by metaphor and analogy to cars, adding machines, and other artifacts, but nothing is proved by such attributions. We say, "The door knows when to open because of its photoelectric cell," "The adding machine knows how (understands how, is able) to do addition and subtraction but not division," and "The thermostat perceives changes in the temperature." The reason we make these attributions is quite interesting, and it has to do with the fact that in artifacts we extend our own intentionality;[3] our tools are extensions of our purposes, and so we find it natural to make metaphorical attributions of intentionality to them; but I take it no philosophical ice is cut by such examples. The sense in which an automatic door "understands instructions" from its photoelectric cell is not at all the sense in which I understand English. If the sense in which Schank's programmed computers understand stories is supposed to be the metaphorical sense in which the door understands, and not the sense in which I understand English, the issue would not be worth discussing. But Newell and Simon (1963) write that the kind of cognition they claim for computers is exactly the same as for human beings. I like the straightforwardness of this claim, and it is the sort of claim I will be considering. I will argue that in the literal sense the programmed computer understands what the car and the adding machine understand, namely, exactly nothing. The computer understanding is not just (like my understanding of German) partial or incomplete; it is zero.

Now to the replies:

I. The systems reply (Berkeley). "While it is true that the individual person who is locked in the room does not understand the story, the fact is that he is merely part of a whole system, and the system does understand the story. The person has a large ledger in front of him in which are written the rules, he has a lot of scratch paper and pencils for doing calculations, he has 'data banks' of sets of Chinese symbols. Now, understanding is not being ascribed to the mere individual; rather it is being ascribed to this whole system of which he is a part."

My response to the systems theory is quite simple: let the individual internalize all of these elements of the system. He memorizes the rules in the ledger and the data banks of Chinese symbols, and he does all the calculations in his head. The individual then incorporates the entire system. There isn't anything at all to the system that he does not encompass. We can even get rid of the room and suppose he works outdoors. All the same, he understands nothing of the Chinese, and a fortiori neither does the system, because there isn't anything in the system that isn't in him. If he doesn't understand, then there is no way the system could understand because the system is just a part of him.

Actually I feel somewhat embarrassed to give even this answer to the systems theory because the theory seems to me so unplausible to start with. The idea is that while a person doesn't understand Chinese, somehow the conjunction of that person and bits of paper might understand Chinese. It is not easy for me to imagine how someone who was not in the grip of an ideology would find the idea at all plausible. Still, I think many people who are committed to the ideology of strong AI will in the end be inclined to say something very much like this; so let us pursue it a bit further. According to one version of this view, while the man in the internalized

systems example doesn't understand Chinese in the sense that a native Chinese speaker does (because, for example, he doesn't know that the story refers to restaurants and hamburgers, etc.); still "the man as a formal symbol manipulation system" really does understand Chinese. The subsystem of the man that is the formal symbol manipulation system for Chinese should not be confused with the subsystem for English.

So there are really two subsystems in the man; one understands English, the other Chinese, and "it's just that the two systems have little to do with each other." But, I want to reply, not only do they have little to do with each other, they are not even remotely alike. The subsystem that understands English (assuming we allow ourselves to talk in this jargon of "subsystems" for a moment) knows that the stories are about restaurants and eating hamburgers, he knows that he is being asked questions about restaurants and that he is answering questions as best he can by making various inferences from the content of the story, and so on. But the Chinese system knows none of this. Whereas the English subsystem knows that "hamburgers" refers to hamburgers, the Chinese subsystem knows only that "squiggle squiggle" is followed by "squoggle squoggle." All he knows is that various formal symbols are being introduced at one end and manipulated according to rules written in English, and other symbols are going out at the other end. The whole point of the original example was to argue that such symbol manipulation by itself couldn't be sufficient for understanding Chinese in any literal sense because the man could write "squoggle squoggle" after "squiggle squiggle" without understanding anything in Chinese. And it doesn't meet that argument to postulate subsystems within the man, because the subsystems are no better off than the man was in the first place; they still don't have anything even remotely like what the English-speaking man (or subsystem) has. Indeed, in the case as described, the Chinese subsystem is simply a part of the English subsystem, a part that engages in meaningless symbol manipulation according to rules in English.

Let us ask ourselves what is supposed to motivate the systems reply in the first place; that is, what independent grounds are there supposed to be for saying that the agent must have a subsystem within him that literally understands stories in Chinese? As far as I can tell the only grounds are that in the example I have the same input and output as native Chinese speakers and a program that goes from one to the other. But the whole point of the examples has been to try to show that that couldn't be sufficient for understanding, in the sense in which I understand stories in English, because a person, and hence the set of systems that go to make up a person, could have the right combination of input, output, and program and still not understand anything in the relevant literal sense in which I understand English. The only motivation for saying there must be a subsystem in me that understands Chinese is that I have a program and I can pass the Turing test; I can fool native Chinese speakers. But precisely one of the points at issue is the adequacy of the Turing test. The example shows that there could be two "systems," both of which pass the Turing test, but only one of which understands; and it is no argument against this point to say that since they both pass the Turing test they must both understand, since this claim fails to meet the argument that the system in me that understands English has a great deal more than the system that merely processes Chinese. In short, the systems reply simply begs the question by insisting without argument that the system must understand Chinese.

Furthermore, the systems reply would appear to lead to consequences that are independently absurd. If we are to conclude that there must be cognition in me on the grounds that I have a certain sort of input and output and a program in between, then it looks like all sorts of noncognitive subsystems are going to turn out to be cognitive. For example, there is a level of description at which my stomach does information processing, and it instantiates any number of computer programs, but I take it we do not want to say that it has any understanding [cf. Pylyshyn: "Computation and Cognitition" BBS 3(1) 1980]. But if we accept the systems reply, then it is hard to see how we avoid saying that stomach, heart, liver, and so on, are all understanding subsystems, since there is no principled way to distinguish the motivation for saying the Chinese subsystem understands from saying that the stomach understands. It is, by the way, not an answer to this point to say that the Chinese system has information as input and output and the stomach has food and food products as input and output, since from the point of view of the agent, from my point of view, there is no information in either the food or the Chinese – the Chinese is just so many meaningless squiggles. The information in the Chinese case is solely in the eyes of the programmers and the interpreters, and there is nothing to prevent them from treating the input and output of my digestive organs as information if they so desire.

This last point bears on some independent problems in strong AI, and it is worth digressing for a moment to explain it. If strong AI is to be a branch of psychology, then it must be able to distinguish those systems that are genuinely mental from those that are not. It must be able to distinguish the principles on which the mind works from those on which nonmental systems work; otherwise it will offer us no explanations of what is specifically mental about the mental. And the mental-nonmental distinction cannot be just in the eye of the beholder but it must be intrinsic to the systems; otherwise it would be up to any beholder to treat people as nonmental and, for example, hurricanes as mental if he likes. But quite often in the AI literature the distinction is blurred in ways that would in the long run prove disastrous to the claim that AI is a cognitive inquiry. McCarthy, for example, writes, "Machines as simple as thermostats can be said to have beliefs, and having beliefs seems to be a characteristic of most machines capable of problem solving performance" (McCarthy 1979). Anyone who thinks strong AI has a chance as a theory of the mind ought to ponder the implications of that remark. We are asked to accept it as a discovery of strong AI that the hunk of metal on the wall that we use to regulate the temperature has beliefs in exactly the same sense that we, our spouses, and our children have beliefs, and furthermore that "most" of the other machines in the room – telephone, tape recorder, adding machine, electric light switch, – also have beliefs in this literal sense. It is not the aim of this article to argue against McCarthy's point, so I will simply assert the following without argument. The study of the mind starts with such facts as that humans have beliefs, while thermostats, telephones, and adding machines don't. If you get a theory that denies this point you have produced a counterexample to the theory and the theory is false. One gets the impression that people in AI who write this sort of thing think they can get away with it because they don't really take it seriously, and they don't think anyone else will either. I propose for a moment at least, to take it seriously. Think hard for one minute about what would be necessary to establish that that hunk of metal on the wall over there had real beliefs, beliefs with direction of fit, propositional content, and conditions of satisfaction; beliefs that had the possibility of being strong beliefs or weak beliefs; nervous, anxious, or secure beliefs; dogmatic, rational, or superstitious beliefs; blind faiths or hesitant cogitations; any kind of beliefs. The thermostat is not a candidate. Neither is stomach, liver, adding machine, or telephone. However, since we are taking the idea seriously, notice that its truth would be fatal to strong AI's claim to be a science of the mind. For now the mind is everywhere. What we wanted to know is what distinguishes

the mind from thermostats and livers. And if McCarthy were right, strong AI wouldn't have a hope of telling us that.

II. The Robot Reply (Yale). "Suppose we wrote a different kind of program from Schank's program. Suppose we put a computer inside a robot, and this computer would not just take in formal symbols as input and give out formal symbols as output, but rather would actually operate the robot in such a way that the robot does something very much like perceiving, walking, moving about, hammering nails, eating, drinking – anything you like. The robot would, for example, have a television camera attached to it that enabled it to 'see,' it would have arms and legs that enabled it to 'act,' and all of this would be controlled by its computer 'brain.' Such a robot would, unlike Schank's computer, have genuine understanding and other mental states."

The first thing to notice about the robot reply is that it tacitly concedes that cognition is not soley a matter of formal symbol manipulation, since this reply adds a set of causal relation with the outside world [cf. Fodor: "Methodological Solipsism" BBS 3(1) 1980]. But the answer to the robot reply is that the addition of such "perceptual" and "motor" capacities adds nothing by way of understanding, in particular, or intentionality, in general, to Schank's original program. To see this, notice that the same thought experiment applies to the robot case. Suppose that instead of the computer inside the robot, you put me inside the room and, as in the original Chinese case, you give me more Chinese symbols with more instructions in English for matching Chinese symbols to Chinese symbols and feeding back Chinese symbols to the outside. Suppose, unknown to me, some of the Chinese symbols that come to me come from a television camera attached to the robot and other Chinese symbols that I am giving out serve to make the motors inside the robot move the robot's legs or arms. It is important to emphasize that all I am doing is manipulating formal symbols: I know none of these other facts. I am receiving "information" from the robot's "perceptual" apparatus, and I am giving out "instructions" to its motor apparatus without knowing either of these facts. I am the robot's homunculus, but unlike the traditional homunculus, I don't know what's going on. I don't understand anything except the rules for symbol manipulation. Now in this case I want to say that the robot has no intentional states at all; it is simply moving about as a result of its electrical wiring and its program. And furthermore, by instantiating the program I have no intentional states of the relevant type. All I do is follow formal instructions about manipulating formal symbols.

III. The brain simulator reply (Berkeley and M.I.T.). "Suppose we design a program that doesn't represent information that we have about the world, such as the information in Schank's scripts, but simulates the actual sequence of neuron firings at the synapses of the brain of a native Chinese speaker when he understands stories in Chinese and gives answers to them. The machine takes in Chinese stories and questions about them as input, it simulates the formal structure of actual Chinese brains in processing these stories, and it gives out Chinese answers as outputs. We can even imagine that the machine operates, not with a single serial program, but with a whole set of programs operating in parallel, in the manner that actual human brains presumably operate when they process natural language. Now surely in such a case we would have to say that the machine understood the stories; and if we refuse to say that, wouldn't we also have to deny that native Chinese speakers understood the stories? At the level of the synapses, what would or could be different about the program of the computer and the program of the Chinese brain?"

Before countering this reply I want to digress to note that it is an odd reply for any partisan of artificial intelligence (or functionalism, etc.) to make: I thought the whole idea of strong AI is that we don't need to know how the brain works to know how the mind works. The basic hypothesis, or so I had supposed, was that there is a level of mental operations consisting of computational processes over formal elements that constitute the essence of the mental and can be realized in all sorts of different brain processes, in the same way that any computer program can be realized in different computer hardwares: on the assumptions of strong AI, the mind is to the brain as the program is to the hardware, and thus we can understand the mind without doing neurophysiology. If we had to know how the brain worked to do AI, we wouldn't bother with AI. However, even getting this close to the operation of the brain is still not sufficient to produce understanding. To see this, imagine that instead of a mono-lingual man in a room shuffling symbols we have the man operate an elaborate set of water pipes with valves connecting them. When the man receives the Chinese symbols, he looks up in the program, written in English, which valves he has to turn on and off. Each water connection corresponds to a synapse in the Chinese brain, and the whole system is rigged up so that after doing all the right firings, that is after turning on all the right faucets, the Chinese answers pop out at the output end of the series of pipes.

Now where is the understanding in this system? It takes Chinese as input, it simulates the formal structure of the synapses of the Chinese brain, and it gives Chinese as output. But the man certainly doesn't understand Chinese, and neither do the water pipes, and if we are tempted to adopt what I think is the absurd view that somehow the *conjunction* of man *and* water pipes understands, remember that in principle the man can internalize the formal structure of the water pipes and do all the "neuron firings" in his imagination. The problem with the brain simulator is that it is simulating the wrong things about the brain. As long as it simulates only the formal structure of the sequence of neuron firings at the synapses, it won't have simulated what matters about the brain, namely its causal properties, its ability to produce intentional states. And that the formal properties are not sufficient for the causal properties is shown by the water pipe example: we can have all the formal properties carved off from the relevant neurobiological causal properties.

IV. The combination reply (Berkeley and Stanford). "While each of the previous three replies might not be completely convincing by itself as a refutation of the Chinese room counterexample, if you take all three together they are collectively much more convincing and even decisive. Imagine a robot with a brain-shaped computer lodged in its cranial cavity, imagine the computer programmed with all the synapses of a human brain, imagine the whole behavior of the robot is indistinguishable from human behavior, and now think of the whole thing as a unified system and not just as a computer with inputs and outputs. Surely in such a case we would have to ascribe intentionality to the system."

I entirely agree that in such a case we would find it rational and indeed irresistible to accept the hypothesis that the robot had intentionality, as long as we knew nothing more about it. Indeed, besides appearance and behavior, the other elements of the combination are really irrelevant. If we could build a robot whose behavior was indistinguishable over a large range from human behavior, we would attribute intentionality to it, pending some reason not to. We wouldn't need to know in advance that its computer brain was a formal analogue of the human brain.

But I really don't see that this is any help to the claims of strong AI; and here's why: According to strong AI, instantiating a formal program with the right input and output is a sufficient condition of, indeed is constitutive of, intentionality. As Newell (1979) puts it, the essence of the mental is the operation of a physical symbol system. But the attributions of intentionality that we make to the robot in this example have nothing to do with formal programs. They are simply based on the assumption that if the robot looks and behaves sufficiently like us, then we would suppose, until proven otherwise, that it must have mental states like ours that cause and are expressed by its behavior and it must have an inner mechanism capable of producing such mental states. If we knew independently how to account for its behavior without such assumptions we would not attribute intentionality to it, especially if we knew it had a formal program. And this is precisely the point of my earlier reply to objection II.

Suppose we knew that the robot's behavior was entirely accounted for by the fact that a man inside it was receiving uninterpreted formal symbols from the robot's sensory receptors and sending out uninterpreted formal symbols to its motor mechanisms, and the man was doing this symbol manipulation in accordance with a bunch of rules. Furthermore, suppose the man knows none of these facts about the robot, all he knows is which operations to perform on which meaningless symbols. In such a case we would regard the robot as an ingenious mechanical dummy. The hypothesis that the dummy has a mind would now be unwarranted and unnecessary, for there is now no longer any reason to ascribe intentionality to the robot or to the system of which it is a part (except of course for the man's intentionality in manipulating the symbols). The formal symbol manipulations go on, the input and output are correctly matched, but the only real locus of intentionality is the man, and he doesn't know any of the relevant intentional states; he doesn't, for example, *see* what comes into the robot's eyes, he doesn't *intend* to move the robot's arm, and he doesn't *understand* any of the remarks made to or by the robot. Nor, for the reasons stated earlier, does the system of which man and robot are a part.

To see this point, contrast this case with cases in which we find it completely natural to ascribe intentionality to members of certain other primate species such as apes and monkeys and to domestic animals such as dogs. The reasons we find it natural are, roughly, two: we can't make sense of the animal's behavior without the ascription of intentionality, and we can see that the beasts are made of similar stuff to ourselves – that is an eye, that a nose, this is its skin, and so on. Given the coherence of the animal's behavior and the assumption of the same causal stuff underlying it, we assume both that the animal must have mental states underlying its behavior, and that the mental states must be produced by mechanisms made out of the stuff that is like our stuff. We would certainly make similar assumptions about the robot unless we had some reason not to, but as soon as we knew that the behavior was the result of a formal program, and that the actual causal properties of the physical substance were irrelevant we would abandon the assumption of intentionality. [See "Cognition and Consciousness in Nonhuman Species" *BBS* 1(4) 1978.]

There are two other responses to my example that come up frequently (and so are worth discussing) but really miss the point.

V. The other minds reply (Yale). "How do you know that other people understand Chinese or anything else? Only by their behavior. Now the computer can pass the behavioral tests as well as they can (in principle), so if you are going to attribute cognition to other people you must in principle also attribute it to computers."

This objection really is only worth a short reply. The problem in this discussion is not about how I know that other people have cognitive states, but rather what it is that I am attributing to them when I attribute cognitive states to them. The thrust of the argument is that it couldn't be just computational processes and their output because the computational processes and their output can exist without the cognitive state. It is no answer to this argument to feign anesthesia. In "cognitive sciences" one presupposes the reality and knowability of the mental in the same way that in physical sciences one has to presuppose the reality and knowability of physical objects.

VI. The many mansions reply (Berkeley). "Your whole argument presupposes that AI is only about analogue and digital computers. But that just happens to be the present state of technology. Whatever these causal processes are that you say are essential for intentionality (assuming you are right), eventually we will be able to build devices that have these causal processes, and that will be artificial intelligence. So your arguments are in no way directed at the ability of artificial intelligence to produce and explain cognition."

I really have no objection to this reply save to say that it in effect trivializes the project of strong AI by redefining it as whatever artificially produces and explains cognition. The interest of the original claim made on behalf of artificial intelligence is that it was a precise, well defined thesis: mental processes are computational processes over formally defined elements. I have been concerned to challenge that thesis. If the claim is redefined so that it is no longer that thesis, my objections no longer apply because there is no longer a testable hypothesis for them to apply to.

Let us now return to the question I promised I would try to answer: granted that in my original example I understand the English and I do not understand the Chinese, and granted therefore that the machine doesn't understand either English or Chinese, still there must be something about me that makes it the case that I understand English and a corresponding something lacking in me that makes it the case that I fail to understand Chinese. Now why couldn't we give those somethings, whatever they are, to a machine?

I see no reason in principle why we couldn't give a machine the capacity to understand English or Chinese, since in an important sense our bodies with our brains are precisely such machines. But I do see very strong arguments for saying that we could not give such a thing to a machine where the operation of the machine is defined solely in terms of computational processes over formally defined elements; that is, where the operation of the machine is defined as an instantiation of a computer program. It is not because I am the instantiation of a computer program that I am able to understand English and have other forms of intentionality (I am, I suppose, the instantiation of any number of computer programs), but as far as we know it is because I am a certain sort of organism with a certain biological (i.e. chemical and physical) structure, and this structure, under certain conditions, is causally capable of producing perception, action, understanding, learning, and other intentional phenomena. And part of the point of the present argument is that only something that had those causal powers could have that intentionality. Perhaps other physical and chemical processes could produce exactly these effects; perhaps, for example, Martians also have intentionality but their brains are made of different stuff. That is an empirical question, rather like the question whether photosynthesis can be done by something with a chemistry different from that of chlorophyll.

But the main point of the present argument is that no purely formal model will ever be sufficient by itself for intentionality because the formal properties are not by themselves constitutive of intentionality, and they have by themselves no causal powers except the power, when instantiated, to produce the next stage of the formalism when the machine is running. And any other causal properties that particular realizations of the formal model have, are irrelevant to the formal model because we can always put the same formal model in a different realization where those causal properties are obviously absent. Even if, by some miracle, Chinese speakers exactly realize Schank's program, we can put the same program in English speakers, water pipes, or computers, none of which understand Chinese, the program notwithstanding.

What matters about brain operations is not the formal shadow cast by the sequence of synapses but rather the actual properties of the sequences. All the arguments for the strong version of artificial intelligence that I have seen insist on drawing an outline around the shadows cast by cognition and then claiming that the shadows are the real thing.

By way of concluding I want to try to state some of the general philosophical points implicit in the argument. For clarity I will try to do it in a question and answer fashion, and I begin with that old chestnut of a question:

"Could a machine think?"

The answer is, obviously, yes. We are precisely such machines.

"Yes, but could an artifact, a man-made machine, think?"

Assuming it is possible to produce artificially a machine with a nervous system, neurons with axons and dendrites, and all the rest of it, sufficiently like ours, again the answer to the question seems to be obviously, yes. If you can exactly duplicate the causes, you could duplicate the effects. And indeed it might be possible to produce consciousness, intentionality, and all the rest of it using some other sorts of chemical principles than those that human beings use. It is, as I said, an empirical question.

"OK, but could a digital computer think?"

If by "digital computer" we mean anything at all that has a level of description where it can correctly be described as the instantiation of a computer program, then again the answer is, of course, yes, since we are the instantiations of any number of computer programs, and we can think.

"But could something think, understand, and so on *solely* in virtue of being a computer with the right sort of program? Could instantiating a program, the right program of course, by itself be a sufficient condition of understanding?"

This I think is the right question to ask, though it is usually confused with one or more of the earlier questions, and the answer to it is no.

"Why not?"

Because the formal symbol manipulations by themselves don't have any intentionality; they are quite meaningless; they aren't even *symbol* manipulations, since the symbols don't symbolize anything. In the linguistic jargon, they have only a syntax but no semantics. Such intentionality as computers appear to have is solely in the minds of those who program them and those who use them, those who send in the input and those who interpret the output.

The aim of the Chinese room example was to try to show this by showing that as soon as we put something into the system that really does have intentionality (a man), and we program him with the formal program, you can see that the formal program carries no additional intentionality. It adds nothing, for example, to a man's ability to understand Chinese.

Precisely that feature of AI that seemed so appealing – the distinction between the program and the realization – proves fatal to the claim that simulation could be duplication. The distinction between the program and its realization in the hardware seems to be parallel to the distinction between the level of mental operations and the level of brain operations. And if we could describe the level of mental operations as a formal program, then it seems we could describe what was essential about the mind without doing either introspective psychology or neurophysiology of the brain. But the equation, "mind is to brain as program is to hardware" breaks down at several points, among them the following three:

First, the distinction between program and realization has the consequence that the same program could have all sorts of crazy realizations that had no form of intentionality. Weizenbaum (1976, Ch. 2), for example, shows in detail how to construct a computer using a roll of toilet paper and a pile of small stones. Similarly, the Chinese story understanding program can be programmed into a sequence of water pipes, a set of wind machines, or a monolingual English speaker, none of which thereby acquires an understanding of Chinese. Stones, toilet paper, wind, and water pipes are the wrong kind of stuff to have intentionality in the first place – only something that has the same causal powers as brains can have intentionality – and though the English speaker has the right kind of stuff for intentionality you can easily see that he doesn't get any extra intentionality by memorizing the program, since memorizing it won't teach him Chinese.

Second, the program is purely formal, but the intentional states are not in that way formal. They are defined in terms of their content, not their form. The belief that it is raining, for example, is not defined as a certain formal shape, but as a certain mental content with conditions of satisfaction, a direction of fit (see Searle 1979), and the like. Indeed the belief as such hasn't even got a formal shape in this syntactic sense, since one and the same belief can be given an indefinite number of different syntactic expressions in different linguistic systems.

Third, as I mentioned before, mental states and events are literally a product of the operation of the brain, but the program is not in that way a product of the computer.

"Well if programs are in no way constitutive of mental processes, why have so many people believed the converse? That at least needs some explanation."

I don't really know the answer to that one. The idea that computer simulations could be the real thing ought to have seemed suspicious in the first place because the computer isn't confined to simulating mental operations, by any means. No one supposes that computer simulations of a five-alarm fire will burn the neighborhood down or that a computer simulation of a rainstorm will leave us all drenched. Why on earth would anyone suppose that a computer simulation of understanding actually understood anything? It is sometimes said that it would be frightfully hard to get computers to feel pain or fall in love, but love and pain are neither harder nor easier than cognition or anything else. For simulation, all you need is the right input and output and a program in the middle that transforms the former into the latter. That is all the computer has for anything it does. To confuse simulation with duplication is the same mistake, whether it is pain, love, cognition, fires, or rainstorms.

Still, there are several reasons why AI must have seemed – and to many people perhaps still does seem – in some way to reproduce and thereby explain mental phenomena, and I believe we will not succeed in removing these illusions until we have fully exposed the reasons that give rise to them.

First, and perhaps most important, is a confusion about the notion of "information processing": many people in cognitive science believe that the human brain, with its mind, does something called "information processing," and analogously the computer with its program does information processing; but fires and rainstorms, on the other hand, don't do information processing at all. Thus, though the computer can simulate the formal features of any process whatever, it stands in a special relation to the mind and brain because when the computer is properly programmed, ideally with the same program as the brain, the information processing is identical in the two cases, and this information processing is really the essence of the mental. But the trouble with this argument is that it rests on an ambiguity in the notion of "information." In the sense in which people "process information" when they reflect, say, on problems in arithmetic or when they read and answer questions about stories, the programmed computer does not do "information processing." Rather, what it does is manipulate formal symbols. The fact that the programmer and the interpreter of the computer output use the symbols to stand for objects in the world is totally beyond the scope of the computer. The computer, to repeat, has a syntax but no semantics. Thus, if you type into the computer "2 plus 2 equals?" it will type out "4." But it has no idea that "4" means 4 or that it means anything at all. And the point is not that it lacks some second-order information about the interpretation of its first-order symbols, but rather that its first-order symbols don't have any interpretations as far as the computer is concerned. All the computer has is more symbols. The introduction of the notion of "information processing" therefore produces a dilemma: either we construe the notion of "information processing" in such a way that it implies intentionality as part of the process or we don't. If the former, then the programmed computer does not do information processing, it only manipulates formal symbols. If the latter, then, though the computer does information processing, it is only doing so in the sense in which adding machines, typewriters, stomachs, thermostats, rainstorms, and hurricanes do information processing; namely, they have a level of description at which we can describe them as taking information in at one end, transforming it, and producing information as output. But in this case it is up to outside observers to interpret the input and output as information in the ordinary sense. And no similarity is established between the computer and the brain in terms of any similarity of information processing.

Second, in much of AI there is a residual behaviorism or operationalism. Since appropriately programmed computers can have input-output patterns similar to those of human beings, we are tempted to postulate mental states in the computer similar to human mental states. But once we see that it is both conceptually and empirically possible for a system to have human capacities in some realm without having any intentionality at all, we should be able to overcome this impulse. My desk adding machine has calculating capacities, but no intentionality, and in this paper I have tried to show that a system could have input and output capabilities that duplicated those of a native Chinese speaker and still not understand Chinese, regardless of how it was programmed. The Turing test is typical of the tradition in being unashamedly behavioristic and operationalistic, and I believe that if AI workers totally repudiated behaviorism and operationalism much of the confusion between simulation and duplication would be eliminated.

Third, this residual operationalism is joined to a residual form of dualism; indeed strong AI only makes sense given the dualistic assumption that, where the mind is concerned, the brain doesn't matter. In strong AI (and in functionalism, as well) what matters are programs, and programs are independent of their realization in machines; indeed, as far as AI is concerned, the same program could be realized by an electronic machine, a Cartesian mental substance, or a Hegelian world spirit. The single most surprising discovery that I have made in discussing these issues is that many AI workers are quite shocked by my idea that actual human mental phenomena might be dependent on actual physical-chemical properties of actual human brains. But if you think about it a minute you can see that I should not have been surprised; for unless you accept some form of dualism, the strong AI project hasn't got a chance. The project is to reproduce and explain the mental by designing programs, but unless the mind is not only conceptually but empirically independent of the brain you couldn't carry out the project, for the program is completely independent of any realization. Unless you believe that the mind is separable from the brain both conceptually and empirically – dualism in a strong form – you cannot hope to reproduce the mental by writing and running programs since programs must be independent of brains or any other particular forms of instantiation. If mental operations consist in computational operations on formal symbols, then it follows that they have no interesting connection with the brain; the only connection would be that the brain just happens to be one of the indefinitely many types of machines capable of instantiating the program. This form of dualism is not the traditional Cartesian variety that claims there are two sorts of *substances*, but it is Cartesian in the sense that it insists that what is specifically mental about the mind has no intrinsic connection with the actual properties of the brain. This underlying dualism is masked from us by the fact that AI literature contains frequent fulminations against "dualism"; what the authors seem to be unaware of is that their position presupposes a strong version of dualism.

"Could a machine think?" My own view is that *only* a machine could think, and indeed only very special kinds of machines, namely brains and machines that had the same causal powers as brains. And that is the main reason strong AI has had little to tell us about thinking, since it has nothing to tell us about machines. By its own definition, it is about programs, and programs are not machines. Whatever else intentionality is, it is a biological phenomenon, and it is as likely to be as causally dependent on the specific biochemistry of its origins as lactation, photosynthesis, or any other biological phenomena. No one would suppose that we could produce milk and sugar by running a computer simulation of the formal sequences in lactation and photosynthesis, but where the mind is concerned many people are willing to believe in such a miracle because of a deep and abiding dualism: the mind they suppose is a matter of formal processes and is independent of quite specific material causes in the way that milk and sugar are not.

In defense of this dualism the hope is often expressed that the brain is a digital computer (early computers, by the way, were often called "electronic brains"). But that is no help. Of course the brain is a digital computer. Since everything is a digital computer, brains are too. The point is that the brain's causal capacity to produce intentionality cannot consist in its instantiating a computer program, since for any program you like it is possible for something to instantiate that program and still not have any mental states. Whatever it is that the brain does to produce intentionality, it cannot consist in instantiating a program since no program, by itself, is sufficient for intentionality.

ACKNOWLEDGMENTS
I am indebted to a rather large number of people for discussion of these matters and for their patient attempts to overcome my ignorance of artificial intelligence. I would especially like to thank Ned Block, Hubert Dreyfus, John Haugeland, Roger Schank, Robert Wilensky, and Terry Winograd.

NOTES
1. I am not, of course, saying that Schank himself is committed to these claims.

2. Also, "understanding" implies both the possession of mental (intentional) states and the truth (validity, success) of these states. For the purposes of this discussion we are concerned only with the possession of the states.

3. Intentionality is by definition that feature of certain mental states by which they are directed at or about objects and states of affairs in the world. Thus, beliefs, desires, and intentions are intentional states; undirected forms of anxiety and depression are not. For further discussion see Searle (1979c).

Open Peer Commentary

by **Ned Block**
Department of Linguistics and Philosophy, Massachusetts Institute of Technology, Cambridge, Mass. 02139

What intuitions about homunculi don't show

Searle's argument depends for its force on intuitions that certain entities do not think. There are two simple objections to his argument that are based on general considerations about what can be *shown* by intuitions that something can't think.

First, we are willing, and rightly so, to accept counterintuitive consequences of claims for which we have substantial evidence. It once seemed intuitively absurd to assert that the earth was whirling through space at breakneck speed, but in the face of the evidence for the Copernican view, such an intuition should be (and eventually was) rejected as irrelevant to the truth of the matter. More relevantly, a grapefruit-sized head-enclosed blob of gray protoplasm seems, at least at first blush, a most implausible seat of mentality. But if your intuitions still balk at brains as seats of mentality, you should ignore your intuitions as irrelevant to the truth of the matter, given the remarkable evidence for the role of the brain in our mental life. Searle presents some alleged counterintuitive consequences of the view of cognition as formal symbol manipulation. But his argument does not even have the right *form*, for in order to know whether we should reject the doctrine because of its alleged counterintuitive consequences, we must know what sort of evidence there is *in favor* of the doctrine. If the evidence for the doctrine is overwhelming, then incompatible intuitions should be ignored, just as should intuitions that the brain couldn't be the seat of mentality. So Searle's argument has a missing premise to the effect that the evidence *isn't* sufficient to overrule the intuitions.

Well, is such a missing premise *true?* I think that anyone who takes a good undergraduate cognitive psychology course would see enough evidence to justify *tentatively* disregarding intuitions of the sort that Searle appeals to. Many theories in the tradition of thinking as formal symbol manipulation have a moderate (though admittedly not overwhelming) degree of empirical support.

A second point against Searle has to do with another aspect of the logic of appeals to intuition. At best, intuition reveals facts about our *concepts* (at worst, facts about a motley of factors such as our prejudices, ignorance, and, still worse, our lack of imagination – as when people accepted the deliverance of intuition that two straight lines cannot cross twice). So even if we were to accept Searle's appeal to intuitions as showing that homunculus heads that formally manipulate symbols do not think, what this would show is that our formal symbol-manipulation theories do not provide a sufficient condition for the application of our ordinary intentional concepts. The more interesting issue, however, is whether the homunculus head's formal symbol manipulation falls in the same scientific natural kind (see Putnam 1975a) as our intentional processes. If so, then the homunculus head does think in a reasonable scientific sense of the term – and so much the worse for the ordinary concept. Moreover, if we are very concerned with ordinary intentional concepts, we can give sufficient conditions for their application by building in ad hoc conditions designed to rule out the putative counterexamples. A first stab (inadequate, but improvable – see Putnam 1975b, p. 435; Block 1978, p. 292) would be to add the condition that in order to think, realizations of the symbol-manipulating system must not have operations mediated by entities that themselves have symbol manipulation typical of intentional systems. The ad hocness of such a condition is not an objection to it, given that what we are trying to do is "reconstruct" an everyday concept out of a scientific one; we can expect the everyday concept to be scientifically characterizable only in an unnatural way. (See Fodor's commentary on Searle, this issue.) Finally, there is good reason for thinking that the Putnam-Kripke account of the semantics of "thought" and other intentional terms is correct. If so, and if the formal symbol manipulation of the homunculus head falls in the same natural kind as our cognitive processes, then the homunculus head *does* think, in the ordinary sense as well as in the scientific sense of the term.

The upshot of both these points is that the real crux of the debate rests on a matter that Searle does not so much as mention: what the *evidence* is for the formal symbol-manipulation point of view.

Recall that Searle's target is the doctrine that cognition is formal symbol manipulation, that is, manipulation of representations by mechanisms that take account only of the forms (shapes) of the representations. Formal symbol-manipulation theories of cognition postulate a variety of mechanisms that generate, transform, and compare representations. Once one sees this doctrine as Searle's real target, one can simply ignore his objections to Schank. The idea that a machine programmed à la Schank has anything akin to mentality is not worth taking seriously, and casts as much doubt on the symbol-manipulation theory of thought as Hitler casts on doctrine favoring a strong executive branch of government. Any plausibility attaching to the idea that a Schank machine thinks would seem to derive from a crude Turing test version of behaviorism that is anathema to most who view cognition as formal symbol manipulation.[1]

Consider a robot akin to the one sketched in Searle's reply II (omitting features that have to do with his criticism of Schank). It simulates your input-output behavior by using a formal symbol-manipulation theory of the sort just sketched of your cognitive processes (together with a theory of your noncognitive mental processes, a qualification omitted from now on). Its body is like yours except that instead of a brain it has a computer equipped with a cognitive theory true of you. You receive an input: "Who is your favorite philosopher?" You cogitate a bit and reply "Heraclitus." If your robot doppelgänger receives the same input, a mechansim converts the input into a description of the input. The computer uses its description of your cognitive mechanisms to deduce a description of the product of your cogitation. This description is then transmitted to a device that transforms the description into the noise "Heraclitus."

While the robot just described behaves just as you would given any input, it is not obvious that it has any mental states. You cogitate in response to the question, but what goes on in the robot is manipulation of *descriptions of your cogitation* so as to produce the same response. It isn't obvious that the manipulation of *descriptions* of cogitation in this way is *itself* cogitation.

My intuitions agree with Searle about this kind of case (see Block, forthcoming), but I have encountered little agreement on the matter. In the absence of widely shared intuition, I ask the reader to pretend to have Searle's and my intuition on this question. Now I ask another favor, one that should be firmly distinguished from the first: take the leap from intuition to fact (a leap that, as I argued in the first four paragraphs of this commentary, Searle gives us no reason to take). Suppose, for the sake of argument, that the robot described above does not in fact have intentional states.

What I want to point out is that even if we grant Searle all this, the doctrine that cognition is formal symbol manipulation remains utterly unscathed. For it is no part of the symbol-manipulation view of cognition that the kind of manipulation attributed to *descriptions* of our symbol-manipulating cognitive processes is itself a cognitive process. Those who believe formal symbol-manipulation theories of intentionality must assign intentionality to *anything of which the theories are true*, but the theories cannot be expected to be true of devices that use them to mimic beings of which they are true.

Thus far, I have pointed out that intuitions that Searle's sort of homunculus head does not think do not challenge the doctrine that thinking is formal symbol manipulation. But a variant of Searle's example, similar to his in its intuitive force, but that avoids the criticism I just sketched, can be described.

Recall that it is the aim of cognitive psychology to decompose mental processes into combinations of processes in which mechanisms generate representations, other mechanisms transform representations, and still other mechanisms compare representations, issuing reports to still other mechanisms, the whole network being appropriately connected to sensory input transducers and motor output devices. The goal of such theorizing is to decompose these processes to the point at which the mechanisms that carry out the operations have no internal goings on that are themselves decomposable into

symbol manipulation by still further mechanisms. Such ultimate mechanisms are described as "primitive," and are often pictured in flow diagrams as "black boxes" whose realization is a matter of "hardware" and whose operation is to be explained by the physical sciences, not psychology. (See Fodor 1968; 1980; Dennet 1975)

Now consider an ideally completed theory along these lines, a theory of *your* cognitive mechanisms. Imagine a robot whose body is like yours, but whose head contains an army of homunculi, one for each black box. Each homunculus does the symbol-manipulating job of the black box he replaces, transmitting his "output" to other homunculi by telephone in accordance with the cognitive theory. This homunculi head is just a variant of one that Searle uses, and it completely avoids the criticism I sketched above, because the cognitive theory it implements is actually *true* of it. Call this robot the cognitive homunculi head. (The cognitive homunculi head is discussed in more detail in Block 1978, pp. 305–10.) I shall argue that even if you have the intuition that the cognitive homunculi head has no intentionality, you should not regard this intuition as casting doubt on the truth of symbol-manipulation theories of thought.

One line of argument against the cognitive homunculi head is that its persuasive power may be due to a "not seeing the forest for the trees" illusion (see Lycan's commentary, this issue, and Lycan, forthcoming). Another point is that brute untutored intuition tends to balk at assigning intentionality to *any* physical system, including Searle's beloved brains. Does Searle really think that it is an initially congenial idea that a hunk of gray jelly is the seat of his intentionality? (Could one imagine a less likely candidate?) What makes gray jelly so intuitively satisfying to Searle is obviously his knowledge that brains are the seat of *our* intentionality. But here we see the difficulty in relying on considered intuitions, namely that they depend on our beliefs, and among the beliefs most likely to play a role in the case at hand are precisely our doctrines about whether the formal symbol-manipulation theory of thinking is true or false.

Let me illustrate this and another point via another example (Block 1978, p. 291). Suppose there is a part of the universe that contains matter that is infinitely divisible. In that part of the universe, there are intelligent creatures much smaller than our elementary particles who decide to devote the next few hundred years to creating out of their matter substances with the chemical and physical characteristics (except at the subelementary particle level) of our elements. The build hordes of space ships of different varieties about the sizes of our electrons, protons, and other elementary particles, and fly the ships in such a way as to mimic the behavior of these elementary particles. The ships contain apparatus to produce and detect the type of radiation elementary particles give off. They do this to produce huge (by our standards) masses of substances with the chemical and physical characteristics of oxygen, carbon, and other elements. You go off on an expedition to that part of the universe, and discover the "oxygen" and "carbon." Unaware of its real nature, you set up a colony, using these "elements" to grow plants for food, provide "air" to breathe, and so on. Since one's molecules are constantly being exchanged with the environment, you and other colonizers come to be composed mainly of the "matter" made of the tiny people in space ships.

If *any* intuitions about homunculi heads are clear, it is clear that coming to be made of the homunculi-infested matter would not affect your mentality. Thus we see that intuition need not balk at assigning intentionality to a being whose intentionality owes crucially to the actions of internal homunculi. *Why* is it so obvious that coming to be made of homunculi-infested matter would not affect our sapience or sentience? I submit that it is because we have all absorbed enough neurophysiology to *know* that changes in particles in the brain that do not affect the brain's basic (electrochemical) mechanisms do not affect mentality.

Our intuitions about the mentality of homunculi heads are obviously influenced (if not determined) by what we believe. If so, then the burden of proof lies with Searle to show that the intuition that the cognitive homunculi head has no intentionality (an intuition that I and many others do not share) is not due to doctrine hostile to the symbol-manipulation account of intentionality.

In sum, an argument such as Searle's requires a careful examination of the source of the intuition that the argument depends on, an examination Searle does not begin.

Acknowledgment
I am grateful to Jerry Fodor and Georges Rey for comments on an earlier draft.

Note
1. While the crude version of behaviorism is refuted by well-known arguments, there is a more sophisticated version that avoids them; however, it can be refuted using an example akin to the one Searle uses against Schank. Such an example is sketched in Block 1978, p. 294, and elaborated in Block, forthcoming.

by J. A. Fodor

Department of Psychology, Massachusetts Institute of Technology, Cambridge, Mass. 02139

Searle on what only brains can do

1. Searle is certainly right that instantiating the same program that the brain does is not, in and of itself, a sufficent condition for having those propositional attitudes characteristic of the organism that has the brain. If some people in AI think that it is, they're wrong. As for the Turing test, it has all the usual difficulties with predictions of "no difference"; you can't distinguish the truth of the prediction from the insensitivity of the test instrument.[1]

2 However, Searle's treatment of the "robot reply" is quite unconvincing. Given that there are the right kinds of causal linkages between the symbols that the device manipulates and things in the world – including the afferent and efferent transducers of the device – it is quite unclear that intuition rejects ascribing propositional attitudes to it. All that Searle's example shows is that the kind of causal linkage he imagines – one that is, in effect, mediated by a man sitting in the head of a robot – is, unsurprisingly, not the right kind.

3 We don't know how to say what the right kinds of causal linkage are. This, also, is unsurprising since we don't know how to answer the closely related question as to what kinds of connection between a formula and the world determine the interpretation under which the formula is employed. We don't have an answer to this question for *any* symbolic system; a fortiori, not for mental representations. These questions are closely related because, given the mental representation view, it is natural to assume that what makes mental states intentional is primarily that they involve relations to semantically interpreted mental objects; again, relations of the right kind.

4 It seems to me that Searle has misunderstood the main point about the treatment of intentionality in representational theories of the mind; this is not surprising since proponents of the theory – especially in AI – have been notably unlucid in expounding it. For the record, then, the main point is this: intentional properties of propositional attitudes are viewed as inherited from semantic properties of mental representations (and not from the functional role of mental representations, unless "functional role" is construed broadly enough to include symbol-world relations). In effect, what is proposed is a reduction of the problem *what makes mental states intentional* to the problem *what bestows semantic properties on (fixes the interpretation of) a symbol.* This reduction looks promising because we're going to have to answer the latter question anyhow (for example, in constructing theories of natural languages); and we need the notion of mental representation anyhow (for example, to provide appropriate domains for mental processes).

It may be worth adding that there is nothing new about this strategy. Locke, for example, thought (a) that the intentional properties of mental states are inherited from the semantic (referential) properties of mental representations; (b) that mental processes are formal (associative); and (c) that the objects from which mental states inherit their intentionality are the same ones over which mental processes are defined: namely ideas. It's my view that no serious alternative to this treatment of propositional attitudes has ever been proposed.

5 To say that a computer (or a brain) performs formal operations on symbols is not the same thing as saying that it performs operations on formal (in the sense of "uninterpreted") symbols This equivocation occurs repeatedly in Searle's paper, and causes considerable confusion. If there are mental representations they must, of course, be interpreted objects; it is because they are interpreted objects that mental states are intentional. But the brain might be a computer for all that.

6. This situation – needing a notion of causal connection, but not knowing which notion of causal connection is the right one – is entirely familiar in philosophy. It is, for example, extremely plausible that "a perceives b" can be true only where there is the right kind of causal connection between a and b. And we don't know what the right kind of causal connection is here either.

Demonstrating that some kinds of causal connection are the *wrong* kinds would not, of course, prejudice the claim. For example, suppose we interpolated a little man between a and b, whose function it is to report to a on the presence of b. We would then have (inter alia) a sort of causal link from a to b, but we wouldn't have the sort of causal link that is required for a to perceive b. It would, of course, be a fallacy to argue from the fact that this causal linkage fails to reconstruct perception to the conclusion that *no* causal linkage would succeed. Searle's argument against the "robot reply" is a fallacy of precisely that sort.

7. It is entirely reasonable (indeed it must be true) that the right kind of causal relation is the kind that holds between our brains and our transducer mechanisms (on the one hand) and between our brains and distal objects (on the other). It would not begin to follow that *only* our brains can bear such relations to transducers and distal objects; and it would also not follow that being the same sort of thing our brain is (in any biochemical sense of "same sort") is a necessary condition for being in that relation; and it would also not follow that formal manipulations of symbols are not among the links in such causal chains. And, even if our brains *are* the only sorts of things that can be in that relation, the fact that they are might quite possibly be of no particular interest; that would depend on *why* it's true.[2]

Searle gives no clue as to why he thinks the biochemistry is important for intentionality and, prima facie, the idea that what counts is how the organism is connected to the world seems far more plausible. After all, it's easy enough to imagine, in a rough and ready sort of way, how the fact that my thought is causally connected to a tree might bear on its being a thought about a tree. But it's hard to imagine how the fact that (to put it crudely) my thought is made out of hydrocarbons could matter, except on the unlikely hypothesis that only hydrocarbons can be causally connected to trees in the way that brains are.

8. The empirical evidence for believing that "manipulation of symbols" is involved in mental processes derives largely from the considerable success of work in linguistics, psychology, and AI that has been grounded in that assumption. Little of the relevant data concerns the simulation of behavior or the passing of Turing tests, though Searle writes as though all of it does. Searle gives no indication *at all* of how the facts that this work accounts for are to be explained if not on the mental-processes-are-formal-processes view. To claim that there is no argument that symbol manipulation is necessary for mental processing while systematically ignoring all the evidence that has been alleged in favor of the claim strikes me as an extremely curious strategy on Searle's part.

9. Some necessary conditions are more interesting than others. While connections to the world and symbol manipulations are both presumably necessary for intentional processes, there is no reason (so far) to believe that the former provide a theoretical domain for a science; wheras, there is considerable a posteriori reason to suppose that the latter do. If this is right, it provides some justification for AI practice, if not for AI rhetoric.

10. *Talking* involves performing certain formal operations on symbols: stringing words together. Yet, not everything that can string words together can talk. It does not follow from these banal observations that what we utter are uninterpreted sounds, or that we don't understand what we say, or that whoever talks talks nonsense, or that only hydrocarbons can assert – similaly, mutatis mutandis, if you substitue "thinking" for "talking."

Notes

1. I assume, for simplicity, that there is only one program that the brain instantiates (which, of course, there isn't). Notice, by the way, that even passing the Turing test requires doing more than *just* manipulating symbols. A device that can't run a typewriter can't play the game.

2. For example, it might be that, in point of physical fact, only things that have the same simultaneous values of weight, density, and shade of gray that brains can have can do the things that brains can. This would be surprising, but it's hard to see why a psychologist should care much. Not even if it turned out – still in point of physical fact – that brains are the only things that *can* have that weight, density, and color. If *that's* dualism, I imagine we can live with it.

ACKNOWLEDGMENT

I am indebted to Paul Kube for discussion of these issues.

References

Anderson, J. (1980) Cognitive units. Paper presented at the Society for Philosophy and Psychology, Ann Arbor, Mich.   [RCS]

Block, N. J. (1978) Troubles with functionalism. In: *Minnesota studies in the philosophy of science, vol. 9*, ed. C. W. Savage, Minneapolis: University of Minnesota Press.   [NB, WGL]
   (forthcoming) Psychologism and behaviorism. *Philosophical Review.*   [NB, WGL]

Bower, G. H.; Black, J. B., & Turner, T. J. (1979) Scripts in text comprehension and memory. *Cognitive Psychology* 11: 177–220.   [RCS]

Carroll, C. W. (1975) *The great chess automaton.* New York: Dover.   [RP]

Cummins, R. (1977) Programs in the explanation of behavior. *Philosophy of Science* 44: 269–87.   [JCM]

Dennett, D. C. (1969) *Content and consciousness.* London: Routledge & Kegan Paul.   [DD,TN]
   (1971) Intentional systems. *Journal of Philosophy* 68: 87–106.   [TN]
   (1972) Reply to Arbib and Gunderson. Paper presented at the Eastern Division meeting of the American Philosophical Association. Boston, Mass.   [TN]
   (1975) Why the law of effect won't go away. *Journal for the Theory of Social Behavior* 5: 169–87.   [NB]
   (1978) *Brainstorms.* Montgomery, Vt.: Bradford Books.   [DD, AS]

Eccles, J. C. (1978) A critical appraisal of brain-mind theories. In: *Cerebral correlates of conscious experiences*, ed. P. A. Buser and A. Rougeul-Buser, pp. 347–55. Amsterdam: North Holland.   [JCE]
   (1979) *The human mystery.* Heidelberg: Springer Verlag.   [JCE]

Fodor, J. A. (1968) The appeal to tacit knowledge in psychological explanation. *Journal of Philosophy* 65: 627–40.   [NB]
   (1980) Methodological solopsism considered as a research strategy in cognitive psychology. *The Behavioral and Brain Sciences* 3:1.   [NB, WGL, WES]

Freud, S. (1895) Project for a scientific psychology. In: *The standard edition of the complete psychological works of Sigmund Freud*, vol. 1, ed. J. Strachey. London: Hogarth Press, 1966.   [JCM]

Frey, P. W. (1977) An introduction to computer chess. In: *Chess skill in man and machine*, ed. P. W. Frey. New York, Heidelberg, Berlin: Springer-Verlag.   [RP]

Fryer, D. M. & Marshall, J. C. (1979) The motives of Jacques de Vaucanson. *Technology and Culture* 20: 257–69.   [JCM]

Gibson, J. J. (1966) *The senses considered as perceptual systems.* Boston: Houghton Mifflin.   [TN]
   (1967) New reasons for realism. *Synthese* 17: 162–72.   [TN]
   (1972) A theory of direct visual perception. In: *The psychology of knowing* ed. S. R. Royce & W. W. Rozeboom. New York: Gordon & Breach.   [TN]

Graesser, A. C.; Gordon, S. E.; & Sawyer, J. D. (1979) Recognition memory for typical and atypical actions in scripted activities: tests for a script pointer and tag hypotheses. *Journal of Verbal Learning and Verbal Behavior* 1: 319–32.   [RCS]

Gruendel, J. (1980). Scripts and stories: a study of children's event narratives. Ph.D. dissertation, Yale University.   [RCS]

Hanson, N. R. (1969) *Perception and discovery.* San Francisco: Freeman, Cooper.   [DOW]

Hayes, P. J. (1977) In defence of logic. In: *Proceedings of the 5th international joint conference on artificial intelligence*, ed. R. Reddy. Cambridge, Mass.: M.I.T. Press.   [WES]

Hobbes, T. (1651) *Leviathan.* London: Willis.   [JCM]

Hofstadter, D. R. (1979) *Gödel, Escher, Bach.* New York: Basic Books.   [DOW]

Householder, F. W. (1962) On the uniqueness of semantic mapping. *Word* 18: 173–85.   [JCM]

Huxley, T. H. (1874) On the hypothesis that animals are automata and its history. In: *Collected Essays*, vol. 1. London: Macmillan, 1893.   [JCM]

Kolers, P. A. & Smythe, W. E. (1979) Images, symbols, and skills. *Canadian Journal of Psychology* 33: 158–84.   [WES]

Kosslyn, S. M. & Shwartz, S. P. (1977) A simulation of visual imagery. *Cognitive Science* 1: 265–95.   [WES]

Lenneberg, E. H. (1975) A neuropsychological comparison between man, chimpanzee and monkey. *Neuropsychologia* 13: 125.   [JCE]

Libet, B. (1973) Electrical stimulation of cortex in human subjects and conscious sensory aspects. In: *Handbook of sensory physiology*, vol. II, ed. A. Iggo, pp. 743–90. New York: Springer-Verlag.   [BL]

Libet, B., Wright, E. W., Jr., Feinstein, B., and Pearl, D. K. (1979) Subjective referral of the timing for a conscious sensory experience: a functional role for the somatosensory specific projection system in man. *Brain* 102:191–222.   [BL]

Longuet-Higgins, H. C. (1979) The perception of music. *Proceedings of the Royal Society of London* B 205:307–22.   [JCM]

Lucas, J. R. (1961) Minds, machines, and Gödel. *Philosophy* 36:112–127.   [DRH]

Lycan, W. G. (forthcoming) Form, function, and feel. *Journal of Philosophy.*   [NB, WGL]

McCarthy, J. (1979) Ascribing mental qualities to machines. In: *Philosophical perspectives in artificial intelligence*, ed. M. Ringle. Atlantic Highlands, N.J.: Humanities Press.   [JM, JRS]

Marr, D. & Poggio, T. (1979) A computational theory of human stereo vision. *Proceedings of the Royal Society of London* B 204:301–28.   [JCM]

Marshall, J. C. (1971) Can humans talk? In: *Biological and social factors in psycholinguistics*, ed. J. Morton. London: Logos Press.   [JCM]
   (1977) Minds, machines and metaphors. *Social Studies of Science* 7:475–88.   [JCM]

Maxwell, G. (1976) Scientific results and the mind-brain issue. In: *Consciousness and the brain*, ed. G. G. Globus, G. Maxwell, & I. Savodnik. New York: Plenum Press.   [GM]
   (1978) Rigid designators and mind-brain identity. In: *Perception and cognition: Issues in the foundaions of psychology*, Minnesota Studies in the Philosophy of Science, vol. 9, ed. C. W. Savage. Minneapolis: University of Minnesota Press.   [GM]

Mersenne, M. (1636) *Harmonie universelle.* Paris: Le Gras.   [JCM]

Moor, J. H. (1978) Three myths of computer science. *British Journal of the Philosophy of Science* 29:213–22.   [JCM]

Nagel, T. (1974) What is it like to be a bat? *Philosophical Review* 83:435–50.   [GM]

Natsoulas, T. (1974) The subjective, experiential element in perception. *Psychological Bulletin* 81:611–31.   [TN]
   (1977) On perceptual aboutness. *Behaviorism* 5:75–97.   [TN]
   (1978a) Haugeland's first hurdle. *Behavioral and Brain Sciences* 1:243.   [TN]
   (1979b) Residual subjectivity. *American Psychologist* 33:269–83.   [TN]
   (1980) Dimensions of perceptual awareness. Psychology Department, University of California, Davis. Unpublished manuscript.   [TN]

Nelson, K. & Gruendel, J. (1978) From person episode to social script: two dimensions in the development of event knowledge. Paper presented at the biennial meeting of the Society for Research in Child Development, San Francisco.   [RCS]

Newell, A. (1973) Production systems: models of control structures. In: *Visual information processing*, ed. W. C. Chase. New York: Academic Press.   [WES]
   (1979) Physical symbol systems. Lecture at the La Jolla Conference on Cognitive Science.   [JRS]
   (1980) Harpy, production systems, and human cognition. In: *Perception and production of fluent speech*, ed. R. Cole. Hillsdale, N.J.: Erlbaum Press.   [WES]

Newell, A. & Simon, H. A. (1963) GPS, a program that simulates human thought. In: *Computers and thought*, ed. A. Feigenbaum & V. Feldman, pp. 279–93. New York: McGraw Hill.   [JRS]

Panofsky, E. (1954) *Galileo as a critic of the arts.* The Hague: Martinus Nijhoff.   [JCM]

Popper, K. R. & Eccles, J. C. (1977) *The self and its brain.* Heidelberg: Springer-Verlag.   [JCE, GM]

Putnam, H. (1960) Minds and machines. In: *Dimensions of mind*, ed. S. Hook, pp. 138–64. New York: Collier.   [MR, RR]
   (1975a) The meaning of "meaning." In: *Mind, language and reality*. Cambridge University Press.   [NB, WGL]
   (1975b) The nature of mental states. In: *Mind, language and reality*. Cambridge: Cambridge University Press.   [NB]
   (1975c) Philosophy and our mental life. In: *Mind, language and reality*. Cambridge: Cambridge University Press.   [MM]
Pylyshyn, Z. W. (1980a) Computation and cognition: issues in the foundations of cognitive science. *Behavioral and Brain Sciences* 3.   [JRS, WES]
   (1980b) Cognitive representation and the process-architecture distinction. *Behavioral and Brain Sciences*.   [ZWP]
Russell, B. (1948) *Human knowledge: its scope and limits*. New York: Simon and Schuster.   [GM]
Schank, R. C. & Abelson, R. P. (1977) *Scripts, plans, goals, and understanding*. Hillsdale, N.J.: Lawrence Erlbaum Press.   [RCS, JRS]
Searle, J. R. (1979a) Intentionality and the use of language. In: *Meaning and use*, ed. A. Margalit. Dordrecht: Reidel.   [TN, JRS]
   (1979b) The intentionality of intention and action. *Inquiry* 22:253–80.   [TN, JRS]
   (1979c) What is an intentional state? *Mind* 88:74–92.   [JH, GM, TN, JRS]
Sherrington, C. S. (1950) Introductory. In: *The physical basis of mind*, ed. P. Laslett, Oxford: Basil Blackwell.   [JCE]
Slate, J. S. & Atkin, L. R. (1977) CHESS 4.5 – the Northwestern University chess program. In: *Chess skill in man and machine*, ed. P. W. Frey. New York, Heidelberg, Berlin: Springer Verlag.
Sloman, A. (1978) *The computer revolution in philosophy*. Harvester Press and Humanities Press.   [AS]
   (1979) The primacy of non-communicative language. In: *The analysis of meaning (informatics 5)*, ed. M. McCafferty & K. Gray. London: ASLIB and British Computer Society.   [AS]

Smith, E. E.; Adams, N.; & Schorr, D. (1978) Fact retrieval and the paradox of interference. *Cognitive Psychology* 10:438–64.   [RCS]
Smythe, W. E. (1979) *The analogical/propositional debate about mental representation: a Goodmanian analysis*. Paper presented at the 5th annual meeting of the Society for Philosophy and Psychology, New York City.   [WES]
Sperry, R. W. (1969) A modified concept of consciousness. *Psychological Review* 76:532–36.   [TN]
   (1970) An objective approach to subjective experience: further explanation of a hypothesis. *Psychological Review* 77:585–90.   [TN]
   (1976) Mental phenomena as causal determinants in brain function. In: *Consciousness and the brain*, ed. G. G. Globus, G. Maxwell, & I. Savodnik. New York: Plenum Press.   [TN]
Stich, S. P. (in preparation) On the ascription of content. In: *Entertaining thoughts*, ed. A. Woodfield.   [WGL]
Thorne, J. P. (1968) A computer model for the perception of syntactic structure. *Proceedings of the Royal Society of London* B 171:377–86.   [JCM]
Turing, A. M. (1964) Computing machinery and intelligence. In: *Minds and machines*, ed. A. R. Anderson, pp.4–30. Englewood Cliffs, N.J.: Prentice-Hall.   [MR]
Weizenbaum, J. (1965) Eliza – a computer program for the study of natural language communication between man and machine. *Communication of the Association for Computing Machinery* 9:36–45.   [JRS]
   (1976) *Computer power and human reason*. San Francisco: W. H. Freeman.   [JRS]
Winograd, T. (1973) A procedural model of language understanding. In: *Computer models of thought and language*, ed. R. Schank & K. Colby. San Francisco: W. H. Freeman.   [JRS]
Winston, P. H. (1977) *Artificial intelligence*. Reading, Mass. Addison-Wesley;   [JRS]
Woodruff, G. & Premack, D. (1979) Intentional communication in the chimpanzee: the development of deception. *Cognition* 7:333–62.   [JCM]

Cognitive Architecture

With regard to the overall architecture of the mind and of other adaptive systems, the traditional view has been inherited from von Neumann. Roughly, sets of symbols are moved about from one memory store to another, and are processed by explicit rules applied in sequence. In recent times, this view has been best articulated by Newell, Simon, and their coworkers. The reading from Newell and Simon is taken from these authors' well-known book on problem solving. In this selection, the emphasis is on what the components are of the human information-processing system (IPS), in particular working memory and long-term memory, and on how information is stored in and transferred into these memories. Other important notions developed in this book are only alluded to in the selection, but are represented in other readings in this collection. These notions included *production systems*, or structured sets of pattern–action rules, and *protocol analysis*, a methodology for studying the details and time course of problem solving. One of the tasks they studied, which is alluded to in their chapter, is solving cryptarithmetic problems (e.g., SEND + MORE = MONEY), where the task is to figure out the assignment of digits to letters such that the equation holds.

The major challenge to the rule-based, *symbolic architecture* championed by Newell and Simon is a *connectionist architecture*, represented here by the McClelland, Rumelhart, and Hinton chapter. McClelland and colleagues reject the notion that intelligent processes consist of the sequential application of explicit rules. Instead, they posit a large number of simple processing units, operating in parallel, where each unit sends excitatory and/or inhibitory signals to other units. In some cases, the units stand for possible hypotheses about the state of the world; in other cases, the units stand for goals and actions. In all cases, information processing takes place through the interactions of a large number of units. The McClelland, Rumelhart, and Hinton chapter offers a glimpse of the varieties of intelligent behavior that connectionist models have thus far produced.

One major point of agreement between the traditional view of Newell and Simon and the new connectionist view is that, where possible, all relevant knowledge is brought to bear on any problem posed to the system. Fodor's article takes issue with this point. Fodor thinks that some of the mind is organized into separate modules, each module dealing with only a very limited set of information. Few people doubt that human sensory systems have a modular organization, but Fodor also argues that some higher cognitive processes are organized in this way as well.

THE THEORY
OF
HUMAN PROBLEM SOLVING

by Allen Newell & H. A. Simon
(Chapter 14)

In Chapters 5 through 13 we reviewed a considerable body of data that describes the task environments for three problem solving tasks and that provides detailed pictures of the behavior of human subjects when confronted with these tasks. In all this analysis we have remained within an information processing framework. But in other respects we have proceeded quite inductively, developing each theory of behavior largely from close observation of the behavior itself and adapting the theory to differences in task environment and response. It is now time to bring together what we have learned into a general theoretical statement about the processes of human problem solving, the characteristics of the information system that carries out the processes, and the nature of the task environments in which the processes operate.

THE FORM OF THE THEORY

Let us start with five very general propositions, which are supported by the entire body of analysis in the book and which pose the basic questions that this chapter must answer:

1. Humans, when engaged in problem solving in the kinds of tasks we have considered, are representable as information processing systems.

2. This representation can be carried to great detail with fidelity in any specific instance of person and task.

3. Substantial subject differences exist among programs, which are not simply parametric variations but involve differences of program structure, method, and content.

3. Substantial task differences exist among programs, which also are not simply parametric variations but involve differences of structure and content.

5. The task environment (plus the intelligence of the problem solver) determines to a large extent the behavior of the problem solver, independently of the detailed internal structure of his information processing system.

What theory of human problem solving fits these generalizations? Given the substantial differences among individuals and among tasks, does a single theory of problem solving exist, or only a congeries of separate theories? What is invariant over task and over problem solver that could constitute the basic theory? Further, what determines the aspects that are not invariant? For if we wish to understand the problem solving of many subjects over many tasks, the changed aspects are as important as the invariants. And overshadowing all: what can the theory of human problem solving be, when the shaping influence of the task environment seems to make the specifics of the problem solver's internal structure almost irrelevant?

These questions are not unique to our particular enterprise. In one guise or another they confront all attempts to develop human psychology. Both the specific variation in behavior by individual and by task, and the general predictability of intelligent behavior from the requirements of the task, are pervasive features of human behavior. Many answers to the questions have been proposed: postulating a representative subject, asserting that scientific psychology is only statistical (nomothetic), asserting that only what is common to all humans is scientific, abandoning all contents as too contingent to be of interest, or retreating to learning as the only fundamental topic of a scientific psychology. We propose below a different answer that seems to us both indicated by the studies of this book and supported by much additional evidence as well.

The shape of the theory we propose can be captured by four propositions:

1. A few, and only a few, gross characteristics of the human IPS are invariant over task and problem solver.

2. These characteristics are sufficient to determine that a task environment is represented (in the IPS) as a problem space, and that problem solving takes place in a problem space.

3. The structure of the task environment determines the possible structures of the problem space.

4. The structure of the problem space determines the possible programs that can be used for problem solving.

The main sections of this chapter develop these four propositions: the fundamental characteristics of the IPS; the problem space; the structure of the task environment; and the nature of the programs. Points 3 and 4 above speak only of *possibilities*, so that a fifth section must deal with the determination both of the actual problem space and of the actual program from their respective possibilities.

The evidence and analysis of this book provide various degrees of explication and support for the different parts of the theory. But each part requires description so that the total shape of the proposed theory can be seen. Before we enter on these sections, we sketch the general nature of the argument implied in the four propositions above, and comment on the scope of the theory.

The General Argument

The argument starts from the observation that adaptive devices shape themselves to the environment in which they are embedded. As we discussed thoroughly in Chapter 2, and have illustrated throughout the book, a system that is not flexible enough to meet the demands of its environment is not adaptive. Thus, only some rather general features of the structure of an adaptive IPS can show through to task behavior. In extreme environments, of course, this is not true, for (tautologically) these are environments where adaptation breaks down—and the structure of the IPS does consequently show through. But the environments studied in this book have no such extreme characteristics, at least for humans as intelligent and well educated as our subjects.

What features of an adaptive IPS will show through is not yet derivable a priori. These features have to do chiefly with the kinds of memories available to the IPS as characterized by memory sizes, rates of reading and writing, and accessing modes. It is noteworthy that with general-purpose computers, also, a few gross features of the devices largely determine performance, and these features are again memory sizes, and rates and ways of accessing. This characteristic of computers also arises because the flexibility of the program mediates between the detailed structure of the computer (its detailed order code and timing) and the structure of problems of practical concern (the situations to which it is to be adapted).

The particular memories and processing rates that characterize human beings determine that the problem space is a major invariant of problem solving—that all problem solving occurs in some problem space. The argument, as detailed later in the chapter, though not logically conclusive, has considerable force. IPS's with different characteristics from the human ones might not solve problems in the same way, and might not employ problem spaces to organize their efforts.

Although the IPS dictates that problem solving shall take place in some problem space, the task environment determines the structure of that space. For problem solving can be effective only if significant information about the objective environment is encoded in the problem space, where it can be used by the problem solver. There can be no guarantee, of course, that all the relevant information in the task environment is reflected in the problem space. Thus, the question remains of how the particular problem space used by a problem solver is determined. The studies in this book do not shed much light on the determining mechanisms. They do make it clear, however, that information about the general intelligence of the problem solver plus his knowledge in relevant domains is often sufficient to predict what problem space he will use. Thus, the task environment remains the overwhelming determinant of the problem space.

The question now turns to determining the actual program used by a problem solver. Since the function of the program is to search in the problem space, it must make the decisions necessary to operate in such a space: basically, select operators and evaluate knowledge states. Only that information is available for making these decisions which has been embedded in the problem space after its extraction from the task environment. Thus, the possible programs can be sharply categorized by the kinds of information available.

Again the problem solver selects a particular program out of the possible ones. And, again, the studies of this book do not much illuminate the mechanisms of selection or construction that determine which program will be used. But, as with the problem space, the selection is rather narrow and well structured.

The theory just outlined fits our five initial propositions. It provides much more, of course, in its concrete detail. But it also leaves a number of unfinished issues and poses a number of questions, some new and some simply refurbished. The question of scope is important enough to be taken up now; others will emerge in the ensuing discussion.

The Scope of the Theory

The very first figure we presented in Chapter 1 attempted to summarize the dimensions along which the human system could vary. The present study focused on a small slice from this total space. To quote that chapter (pp. 3–4):

The present study is concerned with the performance of intelligent adults in our own culture. The tasks discussed are short (half hour), moderately difficult problems of a symbolic nature. The three main tasks we use—chess, symbolic logic, and algebra-like puzzles (called cryptarithmetic puzzles)—typify this class of problems. The study is concerned with the integrated. It is not centrally concerned with perception, motor skill, or what are called personality variables. The study is concerned primarily with performance, only a little with learning, not at all with development, or differences related to age. Finally, it is concerned with integrated activities, hence deemphasizes the details of processing on the time scale of elementary reactions (that is, half a second or less). Similarly, long-term integrated activities extending over periods of days or years receive no attention.

Because our empirical study has kept close to the focus so delineated (though, as we noted, it is a focus, not a set of boundaries), the data upon which our theory is based are quite narrow. The arguments from the data are more general, however —especially those based on the relation of task environment to adaptive organism. Hence we believe that the theory we are putting forth is much broader than the specific data on which we are erecting it. Indeed, we have elsewhere used the same general approach to explore broader domains than those of this book,[1] but we have chosen here to hold to the rather specific focus enunciated above, rather than to assemble evidence from widely scattered realms of psychology.

In spite of the restricted scope of the explicit evidential base of the theory, we will put it forth as a general theory of problem solving, without attempting to assess the boundaries of its applicability. It is clearly broader than the three tasks. On the other hand, the evidence at hand is ill-suited to define the limits of its scope. From the nature of the arguments, of course, one can see some of the conditions that must be present for the theory to be valid (e.g., conditions that characterize the basic memory structures of the adult human IPS).

FUNDAMENTAL CHARACTERISTICS OF THE IPS

We devoted Chapter 2 to providing an explicit set of assumptions for an information processing system, defining such components as symbol, symbol structure, designation, memory, processor, information process, program, and primitive process. All the models of human behavior developed in the book have been instances of such a system, and these features of the IPS are present in all subjects performing all tasks.

But these assumptions leave much unspecified. They admit arbitrary programs, which in turn can generate arbitrarily varied behavior. In discussing specific situations, we even emphasized the remaining freedom of specification by using various programming organizations as the situation and data seemed to demand. Now we wish to see what else we can say about the basic characteristics of the IPS. We will review part of the material of Chapter 2, but only to the extent required to discuss the new assumptions.

Only a few additional characteristics of the IPS seem to be invariant over problem solver and task. (1) One such set of invariants are the size, access characteristics, and read and write times for the various memories in the human IPS.

(2) Related to these invariants are the serial character of the information processing and the rate at which the elementary information processes can be performed. (3) Somewhat different in kind are two invariant aspects of the global program organization: its production-like and its goal-like character.

We will take up each of these characteristics below. We will be concerned not only with those that seem to affect problem solving performance, but also with other characteristics that are invariant in the human, but do not seem important for our theory.

The invariants to be discussed gain their relevance because of the way they determine and affect the information processing in problem solving situations. But the existence of many of them is independently validated by a variety of experimental psychological studies. We will not attempt an extensive review and evaluation of this external literature, partly because the demands of a serious review would exceed the limits in an already long and detailed book, and partly because, as we have stressed several times, only gross characterizations are relevant to problem solving. Much of the detail in the literature is too fine for application here.

Long-Term Memory (LTM)

The smallest units of information held in the memories of the IPS are symbols. There is no evidence that the human LTM is fillable in a lifetime, or that there is a limit on the number of distinguishable symbols it can store. Hence, we assume that the IPS has a potentially infinite vocabulary of symbols, and an essentially infinite capacity for symbol structures.

The human memory is usually described as associative. Associativity is achieved in the hypothesized IPS by storing information in long-term memory in symbol structures, each consisting of a set of symbols connected by relations. As new symbol structures are stored in LTM, they are designated by symbols drawn from the potential vocabulary. These new names can, in turn, be embedded as symbols in other symbol structures.

Unfortunately, we do not have operational specifications for the precise behavioral properties of the human associative memory. Thus, we do not know whether forms of associativity other than the one sketched above are needed. An example of such additional capability would be content addressing, whereby newly constructed symbol structures could designate stored symbol structures without previous assignment of addresses to the latter. The kind of associativity described above seems to be appropriate for the tasks we have examined in this book—even for the chess perception data in Chapter 13. But our tasks do not involve extensive processing in long-term memory, which might call for other forms of association.

Through learning, certain stimuli, or patterns of stimuli, from the input channels come to be designated by particular symbols—become recognizable. We call these recognizable stimulus patterns *chunks*. The stored symbols, then, serve as the internal representations for the corresponding stimulus patterns or chunks; and the chunks, on recognition, evoke their stored designators. The chunks are not innate, but develop through learning. For our subjects the letter D, the number 4, and a chess Bishop were all recognizable patterns. But for an experienced chess

[1] To be specific: concept formation (Gregg and Simon, 1967a; Newell and Simon, 1967; Simon and Kotovsky, 1963), algebra word problems (Paige and Simon, 1967), music (Simon and Sumner, 1968), verbal learning (Gregg and Simon, 1967b; Simon and Feigenbaum, 1964), creativity (Newell, Shaw, and Simon, 1962), administrative and organizational behavior (March and Simon, 1958; Simon, 1947), scientific discovery (Simon, 1966b), emotion (Simon, 1967a), and perception (Simon, 1967b; Simon and Barenfeld, 1969).

player, the configuration known as a fianchettoed short-castled position is also a single recognizable chunk, representable internally by a single symbol, although it is an arrangement of six chessmen.

Numerous experiments, especially reaction-time and recognition experiments, show that the time required to read a symbol structure from long-term memory is of the order of a few hundred milliseconds. So-called associative reaction times are obtained by requiring a subject to recognize a stimulus and then produce some sort of response associated with it (e.g., name a color or give the superordinate of a stimulus word). Such tasks, which involve both stimulus recognition processes and retrieval processes in LTM, typically give reactions times of one-half second to a second or a little more (Woodworth and Schlosberg, 1954, pp. 56–58). Although the times increase somewhat with all sorts of difficulties and uncertainties in the tasks, and with the size of the retrieval ensemble, in no case do they become much longer than this—the reactions never take many seconds. Moreover, reading LTM does not seem to call for scanning, which would produce read times proportional to size of memory.[2]

To write in LTM is another story altogether. Data from rote learning experiments indicate that to store (fixate) a symbolized internal representation of a stimulus containing K familiar subpatterns (including the capacity to recognize the newly formed chunk) requires about 5K to 10K seconds of processing time.

Much less systematic attention has been given in psychology to establishing this LTM fixation parameter than to determining reaction times. A number of experiments, however, yield data that support a time parameter of about five to ten seconds per chunk. Calculating time per chunk from learning time per syllable requires an estimate of the number of chunks that have to be fixated in learning each syllable, and an allowance for the fraction of the subject's total learning time that is spent in processes other than fixation (e.g., reading the stimulus, responding). On the basis of the EPAM model (Feigenbaum, 1961), it can be postulated that fixation of a low-meaningful CVC nonsense syllable pair in the paired-associate paradigm involves storing about seven new chunks (two for the stimulus, which need only be recognized, three for the three letters of the response syllable, and two for the pair). Similarly, fixation of each member of a list in the serial anticipation paradigm involves storing about four new chunks (one for each letter in the syllable, and one to add it to the series).

With these assumptions about numbers of chunks to be fixated, and without allowance for processes other than fixation, experiments reported by Underwood and Schultz (1960, in experiments 1, 4, and 7) give times of 13.0, 11.8, and 8 seconds per chunk with lists of eight paired-associate syllables, and (their experiment 3) 11.2 seconds per chunk for syllables in a serial list. The classical experiments of Hovland (1938a, b, and c) give 10 seconds per chunk for serial lists and (Hovland, 1949) 8 seconds per chunk for paired-associate learning. All of these experiments used college sophomores as subjects, and standard CVC syllables of relatively low association value. The slightly lower times reported by Hovland may reflect the

fact that he used the pronunciation method in his experiments, while Underwood and Schultz used the spelling method. If we estimate the number of chunks under the pronunciation method as only 6 and 3, instead of 7 and 4, for the two paradigms, respectively (assuming that a CVC syllable contains only two aural chunks), then Hovland's data would give 13.3 seconds per chunk with the serial anticipation method and 9.3 seconds per chunk with the paired-associate method. Bugelski's (1962) experiments showing the constancy of paired-associate learning time with different memory drum speeds also yield fixation times per chunk of about nine seconds for a wide range of drum speeds.

Not all experiments, however, are fully consonant with these, and much work still needs to be done to establish the fixation parameter firmly, and to determine the conditions that alter it. Ebbinghaus (1964) reported learning times of ten or twelve seconds per *syllable*—that is, two or three seconds per chunk—using himself as subject in serial anticipation experiments. The times reported by Lyon (1914) in his pioneering experiments with himself as subject were also in the neighborhood of three seconds per chunk. The fast fixation rates in these two series of experiments might be attributed to the experience of the subjects or their intelligence, but we simply do not know whether these factors can explain the difference. Experiments with mnemonic schemes appear to show also that responses that are familiar meaningful words can be learned in two or three seconds if associated "meaningfully" with previously overlearned stimuli. There is at least a hint—but little more—in these data that actually storing the new chunks requires much less time than indexing them for retrieval on presentation of the appropriate stimulus.

Until the fine structure of the fixation process is more thoroughly studied and better understood, however, and the factors accounting for differences in the speed of fixation determined, it is probably reasonable to take five to ten seconds per chunk as a typical fixation time, with some confidence that the parameter is correct within a half order of magnitude.

Little is known about the exact nature of the accessing potentialities that are created by fixation in LTM, except that the learner can exercise relatively little direct control over the process. The important fact, for our purposes, is that it takes at least a half order or full order of magnitude longer (i.e., five or ten times longer) to write in LTM than to read LTM. Thus, although an IPS can fixate some new symbols in LTM during the course of a ten-minute problem solving experience, the total number fixated will be modest (almost certainly less than fifty, since most of the IPS's activity will be devoted to processes other than fixation). This large difference between reading and writing times in LTM has much to do with the problem solving strategies that are available to a human IPS.

We have postulated that symbols in the memory of the IPS can designate not only familiar sensory patterns, but also processes of the IPS and output motor patterns (output messages). Learning very probably produces unitary designation of structures of primitive processes—of subroutines—as well. The available data certainly are not clear on these points, mostly because the matter has not hitherto been looked at in this way by experimentalists. Nor is the transition from discrete symbolic structures to continuous motor behavior well understood (but see Bernstein, 1967). But in the absence of contrary data we assume that these other designations, of processes and output motor patterns, are similar to designations of

[2] There is, of course, behavior involving repeated accesses to LTM in attempts to remember something not retrieved "immediately," but such behavior does not fit the notion of a longer access time in the usual sense.

sensory patterns, and that symbolized processes and symbolized motor patterns require reading and writing times of the same order of magnitude as those for sensory patterns.

Short-Term Memory (STM)

The IPS has a short-term memory of very small capacity. It appears that the contents of STM at any given moment consist of a small set of symbols, each of which can designate an entire structure of arbitrary size and complexity in LTM. It is customary to measure the capacity of STM in symbols (or equivalently in chunks). Simple digit-span experiments show this capacity to be about five to seven symbols ["seven, plus or minus two," as George Miller (1956) put it in his well-known paper], and the capacity seems not to vary much over a wide range of tasks.

The STM seems to be immediately and completely available to the IPS processes. There are no studies that show convincingly how the accessing takes place. The memory is small enough so that it would be difficult to distinguish rapid serial scanning from direct addressing (i.e., a fixed set of cells holding the symbols) or from various content-addressing schemes. At the problem solving level such details make no difference at all. The STM can be defined functionally as comprising the set of symbols that are available to an IPS process at a given instant of time.

The details of how the IPS assembles and holds the inputs and outputs of its information processes are not known. It is most plausible to assume that these inputs and outputs must reside in STM at execution time. The evidence for this assumption is all circumstantial: again, the problem has not been posed experimentally in exactly these terms. But only a very few symbols can be retained in STM—perhaps not more than two—when even a simple processing task (e.g., counting backwards by threes) is interposed between presentation and recall. And almost all tasks that require attention, in some intuitive sense, subtract from the effective capacity of STM as measured by standard tests. It is plausible to suppose that the remaining "missing" capacity is being occupied by the inputs and outputs of the processes (and possibly by information for a stack of subprocesses).

There is good evidence that information in STM decays. (There is controversy—irrelevant here—over whether that decay is caused by interference among symbols in the memory or is a strictly time-dependent process.) For example, there is substantial evidence for rehearsal processes when a person has to maintain information in STM. The decay is another detail of memory that is unimportant for the explanation of problem solving. The reason is not far to seek. Since the problem solving activity is self-paced, the problem solver can adjust his rate and style of processing information so that he does not appear either to have a rapidly decaying STM or to rehearse. Decay and rehearsal might indeed have effects on problem solving—for example, a more reliable STM might permit problem solvers to work at somewhat faster rates. But the effect could be absorbed by the parameters measuring processing speed, hence an additional parameter would not be required to represent the time constant of STM decay.

The analysis above is only a first approximation, of course. STM errors may be caused primarily by decay in conjunction with rehearsal strategies. Such errors, according to the paragraph above, will occur infrequently, but when they do, they may have large effects: for example, S3 spent a long time on his cryptarithmetic problem because he did not recall that T = 0 so that E could not be 0. In fact, the argument from adaptivity breaks down here, precisely because the general processing program limits errors to low frequencies. To predict these errors, rather than taking them as exogenous events as we did in Chapter 6, could well require an explicit model of the decay of STM.

Elementary Processes

As postulated in Chapter 2 and repeated above, all processes take their inputs from STM and leave their outputs in STM (excepting only processes for reading or storing in other memories). How much processing an IPS can accomplish per unit of time depends on three parameters: (1) the number of processes it can do simultaneously, (2) the time it takes to do each process, and (3) the amount of work done by each individual process.

Serial Processing. As far as simultaneity is concerned, the answer is unequivocal: the human IPS is basically a serial system: it can execute one elementary information process at a time. This assertion is often misunderstood and equally often rejected, especially since the underlying physiological system is highly parallel. Let us be clear about it. Assuming that the IPS is serial does not imply that it accesses the various memories by means of a serial scan (i.e., a scanning process with read time proportional to memory size). The human LTM clearly does not operate this way and the STM *acts* as if it didn't, whether it does or not. Again, assuming an IPS to be serial does not imply that it cannot be aware of many things at once in the environment (or some other dynamic memory), in the sense of detecting and recognizing when a single one of them occurs. On the other hand, the statement that an IPS is a serial system asserts more than the bare logical necessity that behavior be serial if the information produced by a first process is required as input to a second. A serial IPS is one that can execute a single elementary information process at one time.

A paradigmatic experiment for seriality is the following: let there be some operation, Q, which the problem solver has learned well and which yields a final output of *yes* or *no*. Let this operation be performed on symbols of a given class. Then, present the IPS simultaneously with K symbols, S_1, S_2, . . . , S_K, and ask it to give the K answers as quickly as possible. The IPS is a *serial machine* (with respect to operation Q) if the time required to give the K answers is proportional to K, and a *parallel machine* (with respect to Q) if the time is independent of K.

For example, suppose the task, Q, is to divide various numbers by a given integer, say 7. The output is *yes* if a number is exactly divisible by 7 and *no* if it isn't. A test with K = 1 is the number:

35642

A test with K = 2 is the pair of numbers:

$$35642$$
$$69416$$

If the human IPS were a parallel processor, then it should do the second problem as fast as the first (due account being taken of the time required to state two results—*no, no*—versus one result, *no*). It is possible for an IPS to be parallel for two activities, but not parallel for three or four, since the processor may be capable of carrying along only two independent control sequences.[3]

In terms of this test, the human is a completely serial IPS for almost all information processing operations. There is some uncertainty whether this is true with respect to highly automated activities, since some parallelism then does appear, but with concomitant changes in the actual task being performed. With respect to motor activities, if the performing motor systems are physically independent then parallelism can exist. But whenever central control is involved, seriality reestablishes itself. The old trick of patting one's head with one hand while rubbing one's stomach in a clockwise direction with the other hand illustrates the extent—and limits—of parallelism in motor activity.

Processing Rate. The second factor determining how much processing the IPS can do is the unit time it takes to execute each information process. For elementary processes, memory access time provides an ultimate lower bound on processing time, for either a process takes as its inputs symbols already in STM or it gets the inputs from another memory (either LTM or the external environment). It can only avoid taking time to input from the latter memories, with their 100-millisecond access times, if it can get along with what is already in STM. But since this memory is very small, a process using no other inputs would soon have only itself to feed upon.

It would, of course, be possible for elementary processes to be much *slower* than the memory access time. Actually they appear not to be slower, for rather careful experiments show that the elementary processes in STM take times of the order of 40 milliseconds (e.g., Sternberg, 1966). This duration might as well be identified with the unit access time from LTM. Such an agreement, with processing times slightly shorter than access time, yields a satisfactory picture of a balanced system.[4]

Nature of Elementary Processes. The final factor that determines the speed of processing is how much work each process accomplishes. The elementary processes (those that take only 40 milliseconds) seem to be the simplest imaginable sorts of compare and replace operations. In Chapter 2 we listed the basic types of elementary processes, observing that we were not in any position to select a specific unique set for our IPS, and that many alternative bases were sufficient to build up arbitrary programs. We are in no better position now to specify the set of basic processes, although later we will say a little more about it in discussing the production-like character of programs. The small size of STM does imply that most elementary processes involve only one or two input and output symbols. Otherwise they could not operate incrementally in a seven-symbol memory whose function is not only to hold the symbols for the immediate processes, but also to keep sufficient dynamic context (e.g., temporary symbols, place-keepers in processes and lists, local goals, and so on) to maintain coherence among the larger processes.

All more complex processes seem to involve either access to LTM or subdivision of the processes into sequences of subprocesses (i.e., into programs). For instance, if a man knows all two-digit by two-digit products, he can multiply 37×43 "instantly"—that is, almost as fast as 7×3—by reading the product out of LTM. If (more commonly) he knows only the 12×12 multiplication table, he may multiply 37×43 by carrying out a sequence of operations, involving, say, digit-by-digit multiplication and addition. One finds no experimental evidence for yet another process—quite different from either of the above—that computes 37×43 entirely within the STM.[5]

The analysis above implies that the time for a composite algorithm can be viewed as a sum of times for the elementary component processes (given the actual sequence executed). From an empirical standpoint, the matter is cloudy. While experiments have obtained simple linear times for linear searches (e.g., running down the alphabet) (Landauer, 1962), composite models of more complex processes run into difficulties (Olshavsky, 1965). One recent study on mental multiplication has had some success in predicting total times by adding up the component times (mostly memory transfer times) (Dansereau, 1969), but the evidence is still incomplete, and we will not attempt any detailed time accounting here.

Perception and Sensory Modality

One of the best-documented characteristics of human processing is that it has separate sensory systems for acquiring different kinds of information about the external environment. We even know a good deal about the physiology of the sensory systems and can trace their structure and function a good way toward the central nervous system. There is also by now good psychological evidence for the existence of very short-term sensory stores (with retention times of the order of a second at most) involving rather intricate mechanisms of masking, decay, and trans-

---

[3] Indeed, some computers have existed (e.g., the SAGE air defense computer) that carried two numbers in each word (the *x* and *y* coordinates of a point) and operated simultaneously and independently on both.

[4] Evolutionary arguments might be used against the possibility of a processing time of, say, a microsecond. This would leave the system idle most of the time while waiting for the next symbol structure from LTM or the visual display. How would such a processing mechanism ever evolve?

[5] It is doubtful whether any such process could be realized in the human. The computer algorithms that avoid dependence on long-term memory employ representations, such as binary, that simplify addition and multiplication. Such algorithms require processes for converting numbers from one base to another (e.g., $37 \times 43 \Rightarrow 100101 \times 101011$) and they also require substantial short-term memory to hold the intermediate results.

fer between these and the central STM. A general picture of the sensory system can be found in Geldard (1953) and in Gibson (1966), of the sensory stores in Neisser (1967) and in Haber (1969).

None of the data on problem solving appear to depend critically on the detail of any of these phenomena. Such detail might well be important for tasks different from those we have studied, but not for the particular phenomena we seek to explain. Moreover, such detail may be important in explaining the processes of reading information from the external environment, or writing it externally. For the purpose of understanding problem solving, however, we need only postulate the processes can be summarized in simple ways—we need only postulate that externally written letters are recognized directly and produce corresponding internal symbols in short-term memory.

For example, the characteristics of the so-called visual buffer store have been determined (originally by Sperling, 1960) from tasks in which a subject is asked to recall a subset of information from a visual display a short time after he has seen it, but without forewarning (while he was actually looking at it) as to which part of the information he would be expected to retain. In our problem solving tasks, the external displays remain visible to the subject, hence the theory need not distinguish between information he retrieves from external displays and information he retrieves from the visual buffer store. The buffer store may be present and active in the system—it simply does not affect problem solving behavior significantly at the level of detail that we are considering, or cause inexplicable discontinuities of behavior.

Other details of the visual sensory system, including the system for visual pattern recognition, become irrelevant by reason of the nature of the problem materials. In all three classes of problems we have examined, the visual displays are rather simple arrangements of discrete elements that the subject can recognize immediately. In the cryptarithmetic task the elements are familiar roman letters and arabic numerals. In the logic task they are letters, punctuation marks, and a small set of symbols that the subjects are encouraged to recognize as *horseshoe*, *wedge*, *dot*, and *tilde*. In chess the elements are squares and chessmen, the latter belonging to six familiar types. Recognition of any of these elements, under the conditions of illumination and distance in which the experiments were run, is a nonproblematic process, requiring perhaps forty or fifty milliseconds, which we can take as an unanalyzed primitive process.

The geometric configurations of the elementary symbols are also rather simple in these tasks. In cryptarithmetic the symbols are arranged in a rectangle, in rows and columns. The subjects' previous experiences with the conventions of arithmetic encourage them to encode them that way, and there is no evidence that any subject treated the geometric pattern in any other way. In logic the expressions appear visually as horizontal strings of the elementary symbols. By interpretation of the parenthesis notation, they can also readily be encoded as phrase-structure trees, as we have already seen. These expressions are arranged, in turn, in a vertical column. In chess the board is an 8 × 8 square. The rules of the game encourage encoding the more complex geometric patterns according to the sixteen possible directions for legal chess moves.

These geometric characteristics of the visual displays, combined with the cultural expectations of the subjects, give some assurance that unknown properties of the visual pattern-recognition system were unlikely to exercise a major influence on behavior.

As another example, consider the effect of obtaining information in one or another sensory modality. For our theory the basic structural characteristics of LTM and STM are independent of the original sensory modalities of the information stored. What we mean by this postulate should be clear from the discussion of chess perception in Chapter 13. It does not mean that the IPS cannot distinguish between stored information that represents visual images, say, and information that represents aural images. As the analysis of chess perception shows, stored information acquires its modality, not by "hardware" differentiation between modes in the central structures, but by the specific ways in which these central capabilities are used to organize the information.

An internal encoding of information preserves the sensory modality to the extent that (1) stimuli that are similar (externally) in that modality have similar encodings, and (2) portions of stimuli that are directly related (externally) correspond to internal symbols with directly-coded relations—that is, to the extent that external and internal structures are isomorphic. As an example of the first aspect—similarity—we would regard an encoding of words as aural if both "taut" and "taught" had identical encodings. On the other hand, we might regard the encoding as visual if the representations of "tout" and "taut" were more nearly alike than those of "taut" and "taught."

The second aspect—relational isomorphism—is more subtle. It is illustrated by our earlier discussion of tic-tac-toe, Number Scrabble, and the magic square (Chapter 3). If Number Scrabble were being played without an external display, a subject's attempt to build a winning triplet from 3 and 9 would demonstrate that his internal representation was not visual, since these two numbers do not lie in a line in the magic square.

There is only modest evidence in the problem solving protocols for the role, if any, played by the sensory modalities in the internal encodings of information. In all three tasks, of course, the external visual stimulus, which was continually available to the subjects, played a major role. Hence, complete programs to represent performances on these tasks would have to include processes for scanning and recognizing components of these external displays.

External Memory (EM)

An IPS with only a STM and LTM possessing the characteristics we have described will behave very differently in a problem solving situation from an IPS, otherwise identical, that is also provided with external memories—paper, say, or a chessboard. The simplest evidence for this, if evidence is needed, is to compare the times required for a person to multiply two four-digit numbers with and without paper and pencil. The ratio of times is about 1 to 100.

Much of the difficulty in doing arithmetic mentally comes from the slow write times of internal LTM and the small size of STM. But the matter is deeper than that. Compare analyzing a chess situation with the board in view and not in view (i.e., blindfold analysis), or doing DONALD+GERALD given the display or entirely "in the head." Even when writing into the EM is not permitted, and only scanning it is allowed, dispensing with the external display makes the task much harder.

For our theory, specification of the EM's available to the problem solver is absolutely essential. These memories must be specified in the same terms as those we have used for the internal memories: symbol capacities, accessing characteristics, and read and write times (with decay times, if relevant). The problem solving program adopted by the IPS will depend on the nature of the available EM every bit as intimately as it depends on the nature of its "built-in" internal STM and LTM.

From a functional viewpoint, the STM should be defined, not as an internal memory, but as the combination of (1) the internal STM (as measured by the usual psychological tests) and (2) the part of the visual display that is in the subject's foveal view. The latter augmentation of the short-term store is, of course, a read-only memory. But it increases the short-term capacity and enhances the stability of the memory considerably.[6]

How, empirically, the two memories are merged is not clear, for again the appropriate experimental questions have not been asked. The merging issue is whether, in order to use any information in the EM to affect behavior, it must be read into the internal STM and symbolized there, or whether the foveal symbols in the EM, once recognized and remaining in foveal view, are part of the STM without further acts of reading and re-recognition. Reaction-time experiments do not address the question, since they almost always involve a change in external stimulus, after which, obviously, an act of recognition is required.

Similarly, it is not clear whether only the instantaneous foveal region can be merged with STM or whether a somewhat larger region, connected by adequately indexed saccades, might be available. To initiate saccadic processes takes times of the order of a hundred milliseconds, but so do rehearsals. Thus, the larger memory region could strongly affect the reliability and availability of dynamic information by permitting modified rehearsal strategies. The external augmentation is read-only memory, to be sure, but it can relieve the internal STM of maintaining fixed information that it must have. For all fixed information cannot be kept in LTM; accessing information is also required, to permit long-term information to be retrieved. The external augmentation could hold such information.

In short, although we have few independent data suited to defining precisely how EM can augment STM, the two components do appear to form a single functional unit as far as the detailed specification of a problem solving IPS is concerned.

Except for the phenomena just discussed, EM, like LTM, must be deliberately

[6] An auditory analog of this *attentional memory* would seem possible, except that most auditory information is highly time-varying, so cannot be used as an extension of memory. If continuous tones of varying pitch and intensity carry the information, then the analog probably does exist. It is not clear whether tactile and olfactory analogs exist, or whether they have to be sampled and input into internal STM as discrete symbols.

accessed both for reading and for writing. EM, like LTM, is essentially infinite in capacity. However, it is not associative, but rather must be accessed by means ranging from linear scanning to random accessing from addresses held in STM.[7] It takes a few hundred milliseconds either to read from a fixated domain to STM or to perform a saccade to another arbitrary point in the visual field. Thus, reading either from located domains of EM or from LTM requires times of the same order of magnitude.

There are, of course, more remote EM's, such as the work sheet on the side of the table, the sheet under the sheet now being worked on, nearby books, books in the library, and so on. Accessing times become increasingly large as more extensive motor behavior and physical distance are involved in retrieval.

The time to record a new structure in an appropriate EM tends to be much shorter than the time (five or ten seconds per symbol) required to record new structures in LTM. External writing time is, however, somewhat longer than the time required to write in STM. Furthermore, it depends critically on there being easily recorded external symbols to represent each of the internal symbols. If certain internal symbols do not have simple recordable external names, then storing in the EM may become very slow—even problematic. A beginning learner trying to write down the Chinese ideograms for words already fixated in his oral vocabulary would illustrate this well. Something like a second per symbol may be taken as the writing rate for overlearned symbols. The alphabet can be written in less than half a second per symbol (letter), and typists can type perhaps one symbol (word) per second, but the symbols in these instances are very simple and highly overlearned.

If we look at the EM's in our tasks, we see that all three had displays larger than could be held in immediate attention. Consequently, all three tasks involved scanning behavior as integral parts of the problem solving programs. The chess task had the peculiarity that no writing at all was permitted—the touch-move rule being enforced in the experiments. In the cryptarithmetic task the EM was a blackboard display. Most experiments with this task allowed digits to be written in physical association with the letter occurrences to which they were assigned. Information other than letter assignments was not permitted to be recorded [e.g., (R odd) or values of the carries]. In one experiment (S3) the subject was permitted to avoid part of his loss of information by maintaining two displays for two alternative hypothetical assignments of the digits. In another, where we had eye movements, no writing whatsoever was permitted on the display, but the subject was given a verbal-auditory EM for letter-digit assignments. In the logic task the EM was altered simply by annexing new logic expressions to the display without modifying or erasing those already there.

Each of these different arrangements of EM affected profoundly the problem solving programs that subjects used for the task. For instance, the progressive-deepening-search strategy, with its striking characteristic of returning to the initial position and retracing the search, stands out in chess where no external writing was allowed. In every example, the IPS's inferred to describe our subjects incorporated

[7] Actually, it is not known empirically whether or not eye movements to a previously known location in EM to pick up information require the use of STM.

the searches of the EM in their program structures. A problem solving program cannot be specified independently of its EM any more than it can be specified independently of its internal STM and LTM. Hence, one can predict the problem solving program of an IPS only after characterizing the EMs available to it.

extensively in cryptarithmetic and partially in chess. We cannot yet prove the correctness of this judgment, and we suspect that the ultimate verification may depend on this organization's proving relatively satisfactory in many different small ways, no one of them decisive. Let us list, without explicit support, some features of productions and production systems that point to their being an appropriate theoretical construct:

1. A production system is capable of expressing arbitrary calculations. Thus, it allows the human IPS the information processing capabilities we know he has.

2. A production system encodes homogeneously the information that instructs the IPS how to behave. In contrast, the standard control-flow system divides program information into the content of the boxes, on the one hand, and the structure of the flow diagram, on the other. In a production system this division does not exist, except to the extent that the ordering of productions carries additional information. Production systems are the most homogeneous form of programming organization known.

3. In a production system, each production is independent of the others—a fragment of potential behavior. Thus the law of composition of productions systems is very simple: manufacture a new production and add it to the set. This arrangement provides simple ways for a production system to grow naturally from incremental experience.

4. The production itself has a strong stimulus-response flavor. It is overly simple to identify the two constructs, since productions also have additional properties of matching, operand identification, and subroutine calling that are not apparent in any of the usual formulations of S-R theory [or even S-R theory extended to meet the demands of internal processing (Berlyne, 1965; Millenson, 1967)]. Nevertheless, productions might well express the kernel of truth that exists in the S-R position.

5. The productions themselves seem to represent meaningful components of the total problem solving process and not just odd program fragments. This is true in part because we, the scientists, sought to define them that way. Nonetheless it remains true that such an organization of meaningful pieces describes the data. (Later in the chapter we will provide some additional support for this assertion.)

6. The dynamic working memory for a production system is the STM (i.e., the memory on which its productions are contingent, and which they modify). This conception fits well the functional definition of the STM as the collection of information of which the subject is aware at any moment of time.[9] This is not the case with most other program organi-

[9] *Awareness* here means that the subject's immediately subsequent behavior can be a function of the given information. It does not mean that the subject can report that he has the information. For example, he may be too absorbed in the task to be "aware" in this monitoring sense; and interrupting to evoke a reporting program may result in the loss of the information from STM.

Production-like Character of the Program

What can be said of the overall program organization of the problem solver? The most important aspect—the problem space—will be discussed in the next section. But even after the problem space has been specified, the program must still be organized in some way out of elementary processes. If we were talking of computers, we would ask what programming language is to be used. Here, since it is not clear to what extent behavior is governed by interpreted symbol structures and to what extent it is produced in some more direct way, we simply ask what the program organization is.

Throughout the book we have made use of a wide range of organizational techniques known to the programming world: explicit flow control, subroutines, recursion, iteration statements, local naming, production systems, interpreters, and so on. Does the empirical evidence permit any narrowing of this range? There are few experimental data beyond those provided in this book that are helpful for answering these questions. Not much is to be expected, of course, since such questions have not yet been posed experimentally.

From one viewpoint the question of program organization is as irrelevant to problem solving as the question of perceptual organization. For all programming languages have about the same power of expression—anything that can be stated in one programming language can be stated in the others.[8] If any reasonable organization were chosen, programs could be constructed to produce any of the behaviors that we have studied.

The reason for nevertheless concerning ourselves with program organization is twofold. First, to discuss problem solving systems in detail one must adopt *some* programming language. Failing to adopt any language precludes speaking on such topics as the structure of problem solving methods. One cannot, as with perception, simply ignore the detail. Second, the program representation may have second-order effects. For instance, adopting a particular representation may make it easier to determine in detail what program is being used, or easier to understand how learning and assembly of programs take place.

We confess to a strong premonition that the actual organization of human programs closely resembles the production system organization, which we used

[8] This may seem an exaggerated claim for computer programming languages. But many of the important differences among such languages as machine language, assembly language, FORTRAN, ALGOL, IPL, LISP, COMIT, SNOBOL, and so on, lie in naming ability, in data structures available, or in basic system features such as memory allocation. Given the associative character of long-term memory and the complete-accessing character of short-term memory, none of the above differences is relevant to the question of program organization as posed here.

organization, but depends on the particular productions that the system contains.

The explicit assumption that the IPS is organized as a production system makes its elementary processes more definite. Discriminating becomes simply the act of selecting the next production—that is, matching the conditions of productions to the contents of STM. This discriminative act may permit an indefinitely broad selectivity—the breadth depending on the number of productions available. At the most basic level, symbol structures are created by the action of a production's placing a new expression in STM. These new expressions may be assembled from parts of existing expressions, detected and designated by matching the production's condition to particular contents of STM. The elementary read operation is simply the operation of extracting these parts of the contents of STM.

It would be difficult—perhaps impossible—to determine for a production system whether new expressions were freshly created in STM or generated by modification of the previous contents. Suppose, in solving a cryptarithmetic problem, STM at one moment contains (A = 4 new), and a moment later simply (A = 4). The tag, *new*, might have been deleted, or another expression without the tag created. Our models of the immediate processor have not been detailed enough to distinguish between these two schemes.

The only other elementary processes a production system requires are processes to write in LTM and processes to interface with the external world. Explicit processes for shuffling information within STM are not needed, for the match process treats STM as a content-addressed memory. Retrieval from LTM, as we have noted, *is* just the process of selecting one production from memory (or, at least, this would be the most obvious way to arrange the memory). Exact specification of the remaining processes—writing in LTM and reading and writing in EM—lies outside the information that can be gleaned from the data we present in this book.

In summary, we do not think a conclusive case can be made yet for production systems as *the* appropriate form of program organization. Many of the arguments listed above raise difficulties. Nevertheless, our judgment stands that we should choose production systems as the preferred language for expressing programs and program organization. We will do so in the remainder of this chapter.

Goal-like Character of the Program

The final aspect of consistency in the human IPS, invariant over people and over tasks, is the existence of goals. Human behavior, viewed externally, clearly is goal-directed, and we have assumed as much throughout the whole book. This is not the question. The question is whether this goal-directedness has structural significance in the IPS. For teleological behavior can be obtained in many ways, as has often been remarked in the cybernetic literature. Thus, one can interpret water as "seeking its own level" or a stone as having the goal of falling.

We postulate for the IPS of the theory that it does have goals, where a goal is a symbol structure with certain characteristics:

---

zation schemes (e.g., the GPS flow diagram in Figure 8.7 or the programs in sequential algebraic languages, such as that for LT in Figure 4.8) in which the relation to directly defined psychological constructs, such as STM, is not clear. All these other organizations contain implicitly an unknown amount of machinery that still requires psychological explanation.

7. For a production system it remains to specify the matching, the operand definition, the subroutining, and the sequential flow of control on the action side. All these seem amenable to explanation. For instance, each production may possess only a single action operator. In such a scheme the hypothesized action sequences—such as FC followed by PC in the productions for cryptarithmetic—would simply be our shorthand for an iteration through STM in which the output of the first production includes a unique symbol (a linking symbol) to identify the next stage of the action sequence. In this view, the subroutine pointer stack consists of the linking symbols in STM. In such a system almost all the program control apparatus is assimilated to the structure of STM.

In all events, the gap between program organization and the experimental psychology of immediate memory and processing seems smaller for production systems than for other program organizations.

8. There is an intriguing possibility that a production system offers a viable model of LTM. Possibly there is no LTM for facts distinct from the production system—that is, no basic distinction between data and program; rather the LTM *is* just a very large production system. If this were the case, the act of taking a new item into LTM would be equivalent to creating a new production (or productions). We will explore this suggestion a bit further in the section on the determination of programs.

A production system, unlike some other programming organizations, offers a nice balance between stimulus-bound activity and stimulus-independent activity. The production system itself is totally stimulus bound, if by *stimulus* one means the contents of the dynamic working memory (i.e., STM). All connection between two adjacent actions is mediated by the stimulus so defined. (As we commented above, this is not absolutely true for productions that have sequential action parts, but these may be eliminated in the way we have suggested.) But this stimulus is per se neither internal nor external, if we take the view that STM is a combination of the internal short-term store and the foveal parts of the visual field (plus of course the symbols that have just been stored in STM upon recognition of other external stimuli). If the vast majority of the productions executed are reactions to internally produced symbols, then the system will appear not to be stimulus bound. On the other hand, if almost all productions take as part of their condition an external symbol, then the system will appear to be very stimulus bound. Thus, the overly focused nondistractable character of programming models—which has seemed to some to be characteristic of them (Reitman, 1965; Neisser, 1963)—is not a structural feature of a production

1. A goal carries a test to determine when some state of affairs has been attained, in which case the goal is satisfied. This test, of course, may simply be a symbol structure to be fed to a testing process elsewhere defined.

2. A goal is capable of controlling behavior under appropriate conditions. We then say that the IPS is attempting to attain the goal. The control takes the form of evoking patterns of behavior that have a rational relation to the goal—i.e., methods for attaining the goal.

We have had to state these specifications very generally, since we have no good empirical information about the actual variety of goals. Goals seem to be highly diverse, but this diversity may have to do mostly with the many ways for specifying desired situations. The important question is whether goals are incorporated in symbolic structures like those defined above, or whether, alternatively, the equivalent behavior occurs because it is encoded into the program in other ways. In the former case, but not in the latter, we would say that the system has goals.

This book has offered examples of both kinds of behavior.

In cryptarithmetic, production P1 states: given a new piece of information about a letter, find an occurrence of that letter and attempt to use the new information. From observation of the subject's behavior, it can appear that he has the goal of using new information. Internally, in the program, there exists no data structure that *is* the goal; instead, a single production produces the behavior.

By way of contrast, production P2 states: to get the value of a letter, go to a location of an occurrence of that letter and process the column containing it. The "to get" condition of P2 is satisfied only if there exists an explicit symbolic structure that can be interpreted as the goal of obtaining the value of a letter. A system containing P2 uses goals.

Using goals has real consequences for the structure of the IPS. If there are goals, then the program must contain processes for creating goals, testing them, updating them, selecting methods for attempting them, evoking them, discarding them, and so on. Thus, a number of detailed specifications must be met by any IPS that represents human activity directed toward goals.[10]

Since directed activity does take place in a problem solving system, the important issue is to distinguish goal behavior from other forms of directed behavior. We can list a number of criteria for making the distinction, which all depend on the fact that the symbolized goal structure gives the system a way of remembering both that it has a goal and where it is along the way toward attaining that goal. Other systems for directed behavior are more stimulus bound, since they do not retain explicit data about progress toward goals in order to organize behavior. Thus, a key behavioral feature of goals is that they produce correlations of behavior over long time intervals.

10 This argument is an instance of a more general principle: that the data types of an information processing system imply that the operations proper to those data types must be included in the repertoire of the system. Thus, knowing of a computer that its data types are addresses, boolean vectors, integers, and single-precision floating-point numbers goes a long way toward predicting its order code.

Some specific criteria for recognizing a goal-directed IPS are:

1. *Interruptibility.* If the IPS is removed or distracted from a situation, it later returns to directed activity at the same point.

2. *Subgoaling.* The IPS itself interrupts its activity toward a goal to engage in an activity that is a means to that goal, and then returns (often after considerable time lapse) to the activity directed toward the original goal, making use of the means produced by the subgoal.

3. *Depth-first subgoaling.* When the subgoaling behavior indicated above occurs to a depth of several goals, the evidence is particularly conclusive.

4. *Equifinality.* If one method for attaining a goal is attempted and fails, another method toward the same goal, often involving quite different overt behavior, is then attempted.

5. *Avoidance of repetition.* More generally, the system operates with memory of its history of attempts on goals, so as to avoid repetition of behavior.

6. *Consummation.* If the goal situation is attained, effort is terminated with respect to that goal.

The evidence for goal activity is abundant in the protocols we have studied. Thus, we conclude that the human IPS invariably has goal structures. However, it must not be assumed that all or most directed activity is achieved by means of goal structures.

Summary

In sum, the important characteristics of the human IPS that influence its programs for handling problem solving tasks are:

1. It is a serial system consisting of an active processor, input (sensory) and output (motor) systems, an internal LTM and STM and an EM.

2. Its LTM has unlimited capacity and is organized associatively, its contents being symbols and structures of symbols. Any stimulus configuration that becomes a recognizable configuration (chunk) is designated in LTM by a symbol. Writing a new symbol structure that contains K familiar symbols takes about 5K to 10K seconds of processing time. Accessing and reading a symbol out of LTM takes a few hundred milliseconds.

3. Its STM holds about five to seven symbols, but only about two can be retained for one task while another unrelated task is performed. All the symbols in STM are available to the processes (i.e., there is no accessing or search of STM).

4. Its STM and LTM are homogeneous, in that sensory patterns in all sensory modalities, processes, and motor patterns are symbolized and handled identically in STM and LTM.

5. Its elementary processes take times of the order of fifty milliseconds,

but the overall rate of processing is fundamentally limited by read rates from LTM and EM.

6. EM (the immediately available visual field) has access times of the order of a hundred milliseconds (the saccade) and read times to STM of the order of fifty milliseconds. Write times are of the order of a second per symbol for overlearned external symbols.

7. Its program is structured as a production system, the conditions for evocation of a production being the presence of appropriate symbols in the STM augmented by the foveal EM.

8. It possesses a class of symbol structures, the goal structures, that are used to organize problem solving.

THE PROBLEM SPACE

We postulate that problem solving takes place by search in a problem space. This principle is a major invariant of problem solving behavior that holds across tasks and across subjects.

In making this claim we should perhaps recall the scope of the theory being put forth. We do not know what part of all human problem solving activity employs a problem space, but over the range of tasks and individuals we have studied—a broad enough spectrum to make the commonalities nontrivial—a problem space is always used.

This statement does not mean that all behavior *relevant* to problem solving is search in a problem space. Initially, when a problem is first presented, it must be recognized and understood. Then, a problem space must be constructed or, if one already exists in LTM, it must be evoked. Problem spaces can be changed and modified during the course of solving. These activities, crucial to problem solving, need not themselves be searches in a problem space.

The statement that problem solving takes place by search in a problem space does not mean that the human has a preferred problem formulation. In Chapter 3 we adopted a carefully neutral stance as to how problems were formulated. We defined two alternatives—the set-predicate formulation and the search formulation—and left open the possibility that there might be others. Any collection of symbol structures giving information about a task environment, together with interpreters to control the behavior of the IPS toward the achievement of some state of affairs, could constitute another problem formulation. However, the evidence we have gathered from the three tasks available to us indicates that a human will preferentially employ the search formulation.

The purpose of this section is twofold. First we need to review and summarize the concept of a problem space—introduced in Chapter 3 simply as the space (1) where problem solving takes place and (2) that contains not only the actual solution but possible solutions that the problem solver might consider. In subsequent chapters the problem space was given several concrete forms, each adapted to the task situation at hand.

Second, we wish to show that a number of the features of the problem spaces we have observed are consistent with the basic invariant characteristics of the IPS discussed in the previous section. The arguments are not so strong that we can claim to derive the existence and nature of the problem space from the IPS characteristics, but we hope to make the interdependence of the two structures plausible.

The Definition of Problem Space

A problem space consists of:

1. A *set of elements*, U, which are symbol structures, each representing a state of knowledge about the task.

2. A *set of operators*, Q, which are information processes, each producing new states of knowledge from existing states of knowledge.

3. An *initial state of knowledge*, u_0, which is the knowledge about the task that the problem solver has at the start of problem solving.

4. A *problem*, which is posed by specifying a set of final, desired states G, to be reached by applying operators from Q.

5. The *total knowledge available* to a problem solver when he is in a given knowledge state, which includes (ordered from most transient to most stable):

    (a) *Temporary dynamic information* created and used exclusively within a single knowledge state.

    (b) The *knowledge state* itself—the dynamic information about the task.

    (c) *Access information* to the additional symbol structures held in LTM or EM (the *extended knowledge state*).

    (d) *Path information* about how a given knowledge state was arrived at and what other actions were taken in this state if it has already been visited on prior occasions.

    (e) *Access information to other knowledge states* that have been reached previously and are now held in LTM or EM.

    (f) *Reference information* that is constant over the course of problem solving, available in LTM or EM.

To recall an example, in chess the elements of the problem space are chess positions; the operators are moves; the initial state is the given position; the final state depends on evaluations, but is related to checkmate; the extended knowledge state is the set of static relations among pieces that the problem solver has not yet extracted, but which are available through the display of the position in EM; the only other accessible knowledge state is the original position available in the display; path information includes (say) that the player has already looked at Bishop moves in the current position; temporary information is (say) the system's current position in a generator of all moves that defend a given man; and constant information includes the conventional values of the pieces, which are available in LTM for use in evaluating exchanges.

and their typical durations, or residence times, during problem solving. We believe that there are deep structural relations between the organization and parameters of the IPS and the problem space, respectively—that many characteristics of the latter are adaptations to constraints imposed by the former. In this section we will undertake to exhibit some of these structural relations.

Residence Times and the Size of the Knowledge State

We have defined the problem solver's knowledge state as that portion of his total knowledge which represents his dynamic information about the task. From the protocol data in all three tasks, the residence times in a knowledge state (i.e., the times between the moves that change current knowledge of the task) appear typically to be of the order of seconds. Table 14.1 gives the average durations for a subject in each of the tasks.[11] The durations range from two to eight seconds. The lowest average, from the PBG of S2 on CROSS+ROADS, was based on both protocol and eye-movement data, hence permitted a more fine-grained analysis (e.g., one that included recall operators) than the others. A move from one knowledge state to another generally means storage of some new information. Hence, we can infer something about the probable size of a knowledge state and the memories in which it might be stored from our knowledge of the speeds of the IPS's storage processes.

TABLE 14.1
average residence time in a knowledge state

SUBJECT AND TASKS	SECONDS
S2 on CROSS+ROADS	1.9
S5 on DONALD+GERALD	5.6
S2 on chess position A	6.2
S8 on logic problem D1	7.7

During very short time intervals—less than 100 milliseconds, say—symbols can be stored only in STM, where we would expect most of the within-state temporary symbols also to be held. Over residence times of several seconds, however, symbols can also be stored in LTM or EM. Hence the knowledge state can contain more information than is held in STM.

The increments of information from one knowledge state to the next are

[11] The average duration is total time divided by total number of nodes in the PBG. These averages have been calculated for only a few subjects, but we are concerned here with an order-of-magnitude estimate of average duration, and these illustrative data suffice for that.

The concept of *available* in point 5 means that the information may be used in decision processes or in applying operators and will be forthcoming if it is called for. We distinguish in point 5 between the knowledge state itself, which is *directly* available, and the extended knowledge state, for which only access information is available. Similarly, the problem solver does not have available the information in the other knowledge states to which he might go if he were to abandon the current one, but he does have access information enabling him to recall them (if he did not, he could never get to them).

Invariant Features of Problem Spaces

A series of generalizations about the problem space hold for the tasks and subjects we have studied. We postulate these generalizations as invariant features of problem spaces used by humans:

1. The set of knowledge states is generated from a finite set of objects, relations, properties, and so on, and can be represented as a closed space of knowledge.
2. The set of operators is small and finite (or at least finitely generated).
3. The available set of alternative nodes in the space to which the problem solver might return is very small; in fact, it usually contains only one or two nodes.
4. The residence time in each particular knowledge state before generation of the next state is of the order of seconds.
5. The problem solver remains within a given problem space for times of the order of at least tens of minutes.
6. Problem solving takes place by search in the problem space—i.e., by considering one knowledge state after another until (if the search is successful) a desired knowledge state is reached. The moves from one state to the next are mostly incremental.
7. The search involves backup—that is, return from time to time to old knowledge states and hence the abandonment of knowledge-state information (although not necessarily of path information).
8. The knowledge state is typically only moderate in size—containing at most a few hundred symbols, more typically a few dozen.

We wish to relate the problem space, and these regularities describing it, to the basic characteristics of the IPS.

Residence Time

Earlier, we characterized the human IPS in terms of its seriality, the sizes and access times of its memories, and the speeds of its processes. In the last section we characterized the problem space and the knowledge state in terms of their sizes limited by the amounts that can be stored during the residence interval. If a subject moves through the problem space at an average rate of five seconds per node, he cannot record very much information about the task in his LTM, which requires times of the order of 5K seconds to fixate a new symbol structure containing K symbols. But he can record *something*, especially if the knowledge is incremental.

The possibilities for storage of new information in EM are slightly more generous. Our tasks show that the subjects add to EM only sporadically, but then with a marked effect on their styles of problem solving. Slight differences in task structure (beyond the range we have studied) might make a real difference in strategies for external storage. For example, a man trying to solve complex equations, or a man writing a computer program, generally writes almost continually on scratch paper, thus putting a significant amount of his current knowledge into EM.

In summary, from a comparison of the memory write times of the IPS with the typical residence time in a single knowledge state, we can localize the current knowledge state as the content of STM together with a small quantity of information in LTM, plus a variable amount (a modest amount in our tasks) in EM.

Residence Times and Availability. By our definition of the current knowledge state, we require that the information in it actually be available to the problem solver in making his move to the next knowledge state. The information that is held in STM is immediately available. The same may be true for the part of the knowledge state that is in LTM, since it is retrievable within a few hundred milliseconds and without the execution of deliberate retrieval programs (e.g., it can be retrieved upon simple recognition of a familiar symbol in STM). There is a question as to whether this information will be retrieved when appropriate, but the situation is maximally favorable to its being called, for the information is both recent and in context. However, there is no absolute assurance that it will always be retrieved; in fact, some of the errors that plague problem solvers can be localized at this interface (e.g., in cryptarithmetic, S3's failure to recall that T = 0).

The situation with respect to EM is different. As long as information is within foveal view, it is effectively part of STM. But if it is outside the fovea, difficulties arise in guaranteeing its availability during the residence time of a knowledge state. Within an interval of several seconds, much external information can be accessed and read, but doing so requires explicit programs, especially for scanning it to bring the relevant parts within foveal view.

Hence, if all the information in EM is invariably to be available, the programs must be rather systematic and compulsive in their accessing behavior. Our observations of human behavior, especially in logic and chess, suggest that access to the EM depends on specific searches triggered by specific conditions (except for the initial orientation to a new external stimulus). Under these circumstances, it is necessary to define an *extended knowledge state* that is larger than the immediate knowledge state, but that can be accessed selectively within the course of processing during residence at a single node.

It follows also from these considerations that the immediate knowledge state is always kept small by the requirement of availability, but that the extended

knowledge state may grow continually, provided the problem solver has appropriate selective accessing programs.[12]

Other factors are important in determining the sizes of the immediate and extended knowledge states held in EM. One of these is the actual physical limit on available EM—when the blackboard is filled, nothing more can be written unless something is first erased.

A second factor is more interesting, for it involves the cooperative action of internal LTM with EM. The most severe limit on LTM is the five-second-per-symbol write time; the most severe limit on EM is the search time to locate a relevant item for reading. It is sometimes efficient to store information in EM because it can be recorded rapidly, but to store *index entries* (i.e., accessing information) in LTM so that the EM can be read quickly. In fact, an EM of more than very modest size is almost useless for problem solving without such a complementary internalized index.

Processing Speeds and Residence Times. The information we possess about the processing rates of the human IPS provides another heuristic argument for expecting the typical residence time in a knowledge state to be a matter of seconds rather than minutes. What is the IPS doing during this time? It is exploring the extended knowledge state and then, on the basis of that exploration, selecting and executing an operator to obtain new knowledge—and thus move to a new knowledge state.

Our empirical knowledge of the operators actually employed shows that they are characteristically algorithmic subroutines (e.g., applying a rule in logic, processing a column in cryptarithmetic) that require a few seconds for execution by the human IPS.

But why could not the search for and the selection of the appropriate operator take several minutes? An extended search of this kind through a large knowledge state implies a commitment to spending much time deciding what to do, rather than making many small, incremental decisions, each on a new base of information. The problematic character of the task situations argues against the efficacy of the former procedure. The problem solver's information is not shaped precisely enough to permit him to engage profitably in such extended preparatory activity. A better balance between decision times and operator execution times provides a better use of the serial processing capacity—and implies residence times of the order of seconds, rather than minutes.

Cumulation of Knowledge

It is natural to think of problem solving as achieved by the accumulation of knowledge. It could hardly work in any other way. But from just this we would

[12] If we observe that the recognition process is a powerful selective accessing mechanism to the internal memory, then we see why the limits on content of the knowledge state in internal memory are so much broader than the limits for EM, which has no correspondingly powerful mechanism.

expect a different organization of knowledge from the one we have observed and described—instead of information organized in discrete current knowledge states, with some limited backup capability, we would have expected to return to a previous state. The IPS would never need to return to the extended state. Indeed, LTM appears to work this way. With each week or year of life, we are informationally richer than we were before, and we never return to earlier states of ignorance or innocence until senility or pathologies overtake us.

Yet from our descriptions of behavior in problem spaces, it appears rather evident that search often does return to earlier knowledge states. The underlying reason for this phenomenon lies in the same properties of the IPS we have referred to previously. STM is too small to hold a continually growing knowledge state. If the cumulation were assigned to EM, the accessing cost would grow to unacceptable levels with the increase in information. Cumulation in LTM would avoid this disadvantage, but only by incurring large time costs for storing the information.

Memory Requirements for Backup. From time to time subjects abandon the current information state they have reached and return to a prior state. They do not, however, retain the information that would permit them to return to *any* node they have visited previously. On the contrary, at any given point in the search only one or two nodes are commonly available as backup to the current one. The reason for this is again to be found in the limits upon memory and, in particular, limits on the rate at which information can be stored.

Alternative knowledge states must be held in some memory. In view of the preemption of the STM by the current state and transient information, other states must be held primarily in LTM or EM. With either alternative, or both, the limiting factor is the number of such states that can be recorded in the times available. Of course the IPS could devote much, or most, of its time to storing such information, but only at the expense of slowing down its exploration and discovery of new information. In general, the programs we have studied avoid this expense, and they have, as a consequence, only rather rudimentary backup capabilities.

Reasons for Backup. The memory limitation argument implies only that the current knowledge state will not become arbitrarily large. It does not prove that information will be retained for returning to previous states. Indeed, some organizations of knowledge states do not make any provision for backup. For example, in cryptarithmetic (working in the basic problem space), when a contradiction arises from the assignments made up to a particular point, the contradiction could be resolved by changing one or more of the assignments independently of the order in which they were originally made—the order information would not need to be retained. In this case (as with S6 to some extent) the system would rarely return to a previous state of knowledge and then only by chance.

There are several reasons why a system will usually be more efficient that retains some capability for returning to previous knowledge states. A knowledge state may contain false information—as a result of errors in processing or recall. A knowledge state may also contain conditional information, where assumptions are made deliberately in order to work out their consequences (the conditional assignments of cryptarithmetic and the alternative moves of chess are both examples of conditional information).

In the cases either of error or of a rejected hypothesis it is desirable to abandon information if it proves inappropriate. If an error is discovered, then all the information in which the error is implicated through subsequent processing may need to be eliminated from the knowledge state. If a hypothesized alternative proves infeasible (e.g., a conditional assignment in cryptarithmetic leads to a contradiction) or undesirable (e.g., a sequence of chess moves is evaluated as unsatisfactory), all the inferred knowledge that depends on the hypothesis needs to be removed.

Insofar as increased search costs are incurred with increase in the size of the knowledge state, it may even be worthwhile to purge the current knowledge state of information that has been determined to be irrelevant. (Odd pages from the previous draft of a manuscript are best placed in the wastebasket, not left on the writing desk.)

Backup Mechanisms. Backup to a previous state may be more or less difficult. If the total knowledge state is a collection of symbol structures, each expressing a portion of the whole, abandonment of some symbol structures simply drops them out. Then the IPS automatically returns to a prior state—that state does not have to be stored as a separate, identifiable entity.

How the "dropping out" is accomplished is another matter. If the symbols were in EM, then dropping out may mean erasing them or discarding the workspace on which they were registered. It is much less clear from the evidence what capabilities the human IPS possesses for dropping out information from its internal memories. Symbols in STM can apparently simply be "written over," but it is possible that the only forgetting in LTM is that which results from modification or obliteration of the recognition capabilities that index it. In any event, elimination from LTM appears subject to very little, if any, systematic program control.

A quite different kind of backup capability is provided by the external displays, such as the chessboard. Here the initial problem state is recorded in an EM, from which it can be recovered with confidence. The presence or absence of a permanent external display of the initial problem state may largely determine the backup procedure actually adopted by the problem solver.

Noncumulative Memories. In problem solving, the knowledge state is by no means always stored in a way that facilitates returning to earlier states. When cryptarithmetic problems are solved in the basic problem space, moves from one knowledge state to another replace one piece of information with another, so that the earlier state is not recoverable from the external display and is not recoverable at all unless appropriate path information is kept elsewhere in memory.

A pure example of a noncumulative memory is the familiar 15-puzzle, shown in Figure 14.1. The state is changed in this puzzle by moving any one of the blocks adjacent to the empty space into that space. The aim of the game is to get from some initial arrangement of the blocks to one in which all the blocks are arranged in the order of their numbers.

It is extremely difficult to do this task in one's head because the number of blocks is too large for STM. Most people try to solve the puzzle by manipulating the display—moving the blocks. But then their knowledge state consists almost entirely of the current state of the display. Their only ability to return to prior states depends on storing a few of the most recent moves in STM and restoring the display to a just prior one by performing the inverse operations.

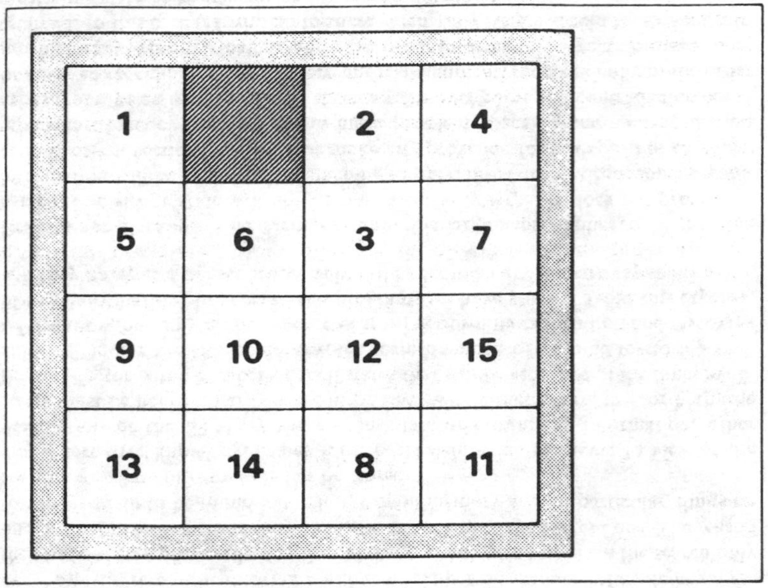

Models and Descriptions. We can distinguish, roughly, two poles in the representation of the knowledge space. One of these, the *model*, is typified by the 15-puzzle, the chessboard, and by the cryptarithmetic display in the case where the problem solver enters on it the current set of assignments. In the case of a model, the current knowledge state can be viewed as a vector of fixed dimensionality. A move from one node to another consists in changing the values of one or more components of this vector. Previous knowledge states can be recovered only if previous values of vector components are retained, together with path information, or if the change operators that have been applied (or their inverses) are retained. In the chess mating combinations program described in Chapter 13, the latter mechanism was employed to permit arbitrary backup to previously visited nodes.

The use of the model format generally discourages return to prior states, since the representation of the current situation itself is independent of the route by which it was reached. As we have just indicated, auxiliary information must therefore be retained in order to permit backup.

At the other pole from the model is the *description*, typified by the display of initial and derived expressions in the logic problems. In general, a description is a set of statements in some language (1) whose conjunction describes the current (extended) knowledge state and (2) whose validity is unconditional and does not depend on the node at which they are known.

In a description, statements that are known at one node may be *unknown* at another node (hence not part of that knowledge state), but they are not *false* at that node. The elements of a model can also be interpreted as statements, but only if they are made conditional—say, by subscripting them with the name of the node—so that they are only asserted to hold at a particular node.

Descriptions, unlike models, cumulate, hence do not require erasing in order to move to a new knowledge state. If the memory in which the description is held has ordering properties (e.g., a list on a sheet of paper), then the elements of a description will generally be entered in the order in which they are added to the state of knowledge. To this extent, some earlier states of knowledge can be recovered automatically by ignoring the subsequent items in the description.

An actual knowledge state can combine both model and descriptive aspects, of course. The part of the knowledge state held in LTM is apt to be descriptive, partly because some order information is almost always recorded with it, partly because there are no systematic erasing mechanisms, as required for a model. On the other hand, the part of the knowledge state held in EM—particularly if a formatted display is used—is likely to constitute a model. However, these generalizations have exceptions. When a problem is small enough to be solved in the head with STM alone, it is most apt to be represented by a model. On the other hand, we have already noted that the external display in the logic problems is description-like in character.

Long-term Cumulation. Because the external memory can accumulate information continuously and indefinitely (as with the logic display), we had to distinguish the immediate knowledge state from the extended knowledge state. If we take periods of time much longer than those needed to solve single problems—days, weeks, or years—then an indefinite amount of information can also accumulate in LTM. After such accumulation, the human IPS does not return to earlier states. Many terms are used to designate this longer-run cumulation: learning, education, training, experience, and so on. It is not necessary to distinguish among these here.

Thus, no sharp line can be drawn between the short-run cumulative changes in information during a problem solving session, which we have called moves in the problem space, and the long-run changes called learning. We must think of search as having a short-run component involving exploring and returning, riding atop a slower, gradual cumulation. Because of the time scales of the experiments, the tasks we have explored have not provided much evidence of this two-level movement. We did, however, see some effects of learning in logic, and we can assert with reasonable assurance that it occurs generally.

FIGURE 14.1
the 15-puzzle (the problem is to slide the small tiles about, making use of the single empty space, until they are arranged in ascending numerical order; in the position shown, this can be accomplished by moving the following pieces in sequence: 2-3-12-8-11-15-8-12-7-8-15-12-11-16.)

Closure of the Problem Space

We can now treat explicitly a property of the problem space that has been implicit throughout our discussion: that the space is in some sense closed under the operations that transform one current knowledge state into another. The closure property we refer to is empirical and approximate, not formal. As with the other properties of the problem space, we wish to show that its (empirically) closed character is intimately related to the properties of the IPS.

Given other things we know about the problem solving human IPS, the closure property is not trivial. The human problem solver has an internal LTM in which is stored an enormous—essentially infinite—baggage. If we allow him to locomote, to reach a shelf of books, or even to glance freely around the laboratory, the totality of external information stored about him, to which he has access, is also essentially infinite. (*Infinite*, in this context, need mean only: far more than he could possibly scan during a problem solving session.) It is a striking fact that the problem solver usually evokes an extremely limited part of his internal store, and attends to an extremely limited part of his external environment. What is grossly irrelevant to the task in either of these memories could just as well not be there. We never detect either its presence or absence. [Exercise for the reader: from any one of the problem solving protocols reconstruct: (1) the extent of the subject's knowledge of Latin, ceramics, or modern history, or (2) a description of the room in which the experiment was performed.]

At any given point in its history, the IPS has available in its LTM a set of discriminations it can make, a set of relations and features it can notice, and a set of processing operations it can perform (nonproblematically). On exposure to a task a certain collection of such symbol structures and processes is evoked—in a later section we will discuss how this might come about. These structures and processes define the problem space: certain predicates can and will be noticed, certain operations can and will be performed. If the IPS is a production system, these two aspects of its performance will be determined by the condition and action parts, respectively, of its productions. Since the set of structures and processes—the productions, if you will—is finite, so also will be the problem space, at least initially.

The question is why it remains finite—why the IPS does not continually wander into new regions of LTM and EM. Our hypothesis is that the kinds of information produced by the problem solving processes—namely, the knowledge states—are all of a piece with the information initially evoked, and do not have associations, via the productions, with other materials in memory to evoke new information that would continually enlarge the problem space. If only algebraic operations are performed on algebraic expressions, then only new algebraic expressions are produced, and these evoke, in turn, only algebraic operations. Substitute for "algebraic" the name of any other task domain and the propositions remain true.

The closed character of a problem space is closely akin to functional fixity. The subject immerses himself in an informational environment that evokes only elements belonging to that environment. No *absolute* bar—independent of his production system—prevents him from generating ideas that go outside the stand-ard problem space. Recall that S8, in cryptarithmetic, spent 40 minutes exploring alternative methods before settling in to the standard augmented problem space. In the tasks we examined, closure was the rule, but we can conceive of other tasks where a program might be evoked that would cause extensive search through LTM (e.g., free association) or actual physical search of the external environment (e.g., a manned landing on the Moon) or of a library (e.g., browsing).

Only in the case of at least approximate closure is it useful, or even operationally meaningful, to speak of problem solving as taking place in a problem space. The concept of problem space permits us to mark off a small portion of the internal and external memory and information sources, and to postulate the irrelevance of anything that lies outside the lines of demarcation. To assert that the problem solving takes place in this problem space is to say that the problem solving processes will never (or seldom) carry thought beyond these boundaries.

The closure of the problem space permits a relatively small production system to guide the behavior of the problem solver (or to describe it, from the viewpoint of the psychologist). The exact size of the production system does not seem to be an important descriptive parameter. It is certainly important that it be small enough to allow it to be discovered and analyzed. But additional productions come into use and into view with every new aspect of significant variety in the task environment. The point at which analysis stops is dictated by the frequency with which particular productions are evoked (recall Figures 6.10 and 7.29, which show the diminishing marginal explanatory utility of the successive productions for cryptarithmetic). The subject undoubtedly has other productions in LTM, especially to deal with error conditions, that we simply did not detect. In chess this was especially evident, for our catalog of productions for move generation (Table 12.2) was quite insufficient to cover the entire play of a chess game.

Possibly, in working on a task a *context* is somehow selected, so that a subset of the productions in LTM becomes the operative system; and there is then a boundary in LTM around it. While there is ample evidence for the presence of such context effects, nothing in our study identifies the context-establishing or context-maintaining mechanisms. It is quite possible that each production is selected, when it is to be used, from a very large set, which we simply never observe because the selection is limited, by the limited contents of STM, to a very small subset.

When Does the Problem Space Exist?

The concept of problem space is useful for describing behavior, therefore, only if the information accumulated during the course of the behavior remains pretty well confined within closed boundaries. Is the converse true: that whenever the sequence of knowledge states in observed behavior stays within a closed space, it is useful to regard that space as a *problem space*? Without trying to provide a definitive answer to what is essentially a question of word usage, we can illuminate the issues with some examples.

Provide a subject with paper and pencil and ask him to multiply 1492×1762. When he is done, his paper will look something like this:

1. At the outset the algorithm is followed by reference, step by step, to a recipe stored in EM.

2. The recipe is memorized (stored internally) but still has to be executed by step-by-step interpretation.

3. The memorized recipe is "mechanized"—that is to say, compiled in the internal language of programs, so that it can now be executed directly and without interpretation.

4. More or less independently of the previous sequence, an understanding may be acquired of the logical justification for the algorithm—of why it works. Observe that a high level of mechanization can be achieved in executing the algorithm, without any evidences of understanding; and a high level of understanding can be achieved at a stage where the algorithm still has to be followed from an externally stored recipe. (The latter is likely to be true only of relatively elaborate algorithms—e.g., the simplex algorithm for linear programming.)

Essentially the same problem space can be used to describe the behavior, regardless of where it stands along these developmental sequences. The level of understanding is likely to affect performance primarily in recovery from error or interruption. Over longer periods of time it also affects the ease with which the subject acquires or retains the algorithm in memory, but that is an issue that goes beyond the scope of the present study. Finally, it may be exhibited in the subject's flexibility in adopting shortcuts and adapting the algorithm to special cases. A high degree of mechanization, on the other hand, may actually inhibit the use of special procedures for special cases.

Algorithms. When a subject is using a highly specific algorithm (e.g., the simplex algorithm for linear programming) to solve a problem in a highly mechanical way and with a low error rate (hence with little occasion to use procedures that stand outside the formal algorithm), it adds little to our knowledge about him to say that "he is engaged in problem solving activity." We might as well say that "he is carrying out the XYZ algorithm." None of the phenomena that make problem solving interesting are likely to appear in his behavior, precisely because the algorithm has been tailored (1) to guarantee solution of problems of the class in question, (2) to operate smoothly within the limits of the IPS with whatever specific EM aids are provided, and (3) to avoid searches as much as possible.

If we wish to have a term to refer to these arbitrarily varied sequences of behavior that are carried out under control of specific algorithms, we can call them *programmed activity*. They take place in problem spaces, but are to be distinguished (at least as a matter of degree) from the *unprogrammed activity*—i.e., less stereotyped and mechanized activity, involving search and backup—that we have treated in this book as problem solving behavior (March and Simon, 1958).

Planning. Problem solving within the context of a plan has somewhat the same flavor as executing a specialized algorithm, for plans are structurally identical to programs. They are symbolic structures, available in LTM (or in EM), that are used to guide action in exploring the problem space.

```
   1492
   1762
   2984
   8952
  10444
   1492
2628904
```

There is no difficulty in describing his problem space, if he has one at all, just as we have done for the other tasks. Essentially, it is the space of all complete and incomplete arrays of the sort illustrated above (supplemented by information about the carries, which our subject presumably held temporarily in STM). It is clear enough from the display that the subject solved the problem by factoring it, more or less as follows:

$$(1492 \times 1762) = (1492 \times 2) + (1492 \times 6 \times 10)$$
$$+ (1492 \times 7 \times 100) + (1492 \times 1 \times 1000).$$

One could speak of the subgoals of carrying out the one-digit multiplications, shifting left, and performing the final addition.

If the subject were reasonably skilled in arithmetic, the description above, referring to goals, would not provide a veridical analysis of his behavior. If he provided a protocol, we would not expect to find goal statements in it, or evidences of explicit goal structures. In common-sense terms, we might not refer to him as solving a problem at all, but simply as following "mechanically" a well-learned algorithm for multiplication.

On the other hand, if the subject were interrupted in midstream—after the second multiplication, say—he would probably not start off from the beginning again, but would take up where he left off. If he were interrupted in the *middle* of a multiplication, however, he probably would redo that whole multiplication, not trusting his STM to retain the proper value of the carry. (That is, the acceptable interruption points would be points where no essential information was being held in STM.)

The "mechanization" of the algorithm appears to be a matter of degree along another dimension also. If our subject were an elementary school child, his protocol might reveal more or less definite traces of a verbal recipe he was following: "First, I must multiply by the digit on the right of the multiplier...." At a very early stage, we might discover him actually listening to a teacher, and following her instructions step by step.

Finally, if we asked someone, fully able to execute the standard multiplication algorithm, to *explain* why it gave him the right answer, we might receive from him a more or less coherent reply, or none at all.

If the reader finds it difficult to reconstruct these various performances in his imagination, because he is too familiar with the multiplication algorithm, let him introspect about algorithms he knows less well—the algorithm for extracting square roots, say, or for checking multiplications by "casting out nines." He will be aware of a typical developmental sequence:

Plans involve exactly the same kind of commitment that we find in following algorithms like the simplex algorithm. Some prior activity—the development of the plan—results in a conviction that the plan is worth pursuing. Thereupon, there occurs implementation activity to carry out the plan. Plans, like those in the logic task, range from two-step affairs to rather lengthy sequences. There is no rigid boundary between behavior in which the subject is searching in the problem space (unprogrammed activity) and his behavior when he is following a predetermined plan (programmed activity). The programmed and unprogrammed aspects of his behavior are so interwoven that we have found it convenient to treat them both as interrelated components of his total problem solving activity.

Conclusion: Problem Space and IPS

In summary, we have discussed most of the regularities that problem spaces seem to possess, as listed in the beginning of this section. (The only listed item not mentioned is the nature of path information, where we have been silent because we have little to say.) We have tried to show the consistency between these regularities and the basic characteristics of the human IPS and to show, thereby, the plausibility of the idea that problem solving behavior takes the form of a search through a problem space.

We have not derived the problem space concept from the IPS characteristics, in the sense of showing that, given this kind of IPS, it is *necessary* that it search a problem space in order to solve problems. A proof, even if it exists, is well beyond the current state of understanding. To carry out such a demonstration, for instance, some way is needed to represent the set of all possible programs that accomplishes a given set of functions under specified structural limits. We know of no such representation.

The Appeal of
Parallel Distributed Processing

J. L. McCLELLAND, D. E. RUMELHART, and G. E. HINTON

What makes people smarter than machines? They certainly are not quicker or more precise. Yet people are far better at perceiving objects in natural scenes and noting their relations, at understanding language and retrieving contextually appropriate information from memory, at making plans and carrying out contextually appropriate actions, and at a wide range of other natural cognitive tasks. People are also far better at learning to do these things more accurately and fluently through processing experience.

What is the basis for these differences? One answer, perhaps the classic one we might expect from artificial intelligence, is "software." If we only had the right computer program, the argument goes, we might be able to capture the fluidity and adaptability of human information processing.

Certainly this answer is partially correct. There have been great breakthroughs in our understanding of cognition as a result of the development of expressive high-level computer languages and powerful algorithms. No doubt there will be more such breakthroughs in the future. However, we do not think that software is the whole story.

In our view, people are smarter than today's computers because the brain employs a basic computational architecture that is more suited to deal with a central aspect of the natural information processing tasks that people are so good at. In this chapter, we will show through examples that these tasks generally require the simultaneous consideration of many pieces of information or constraints. Each constraint may be imperfectly specified and ambiguous, yet each can play a potentially decisive role in determining the outcome of processing. After examining these points, we will introduce a computational framework for modeling cognitive processes that seems well suited to exploiting these constraints and that seems closer than other frameworks to the style of computation as it might be done by the brain. We will review several early examples of models developed in this framework, and we will show that the mechanisms these models employ can give rise to powerful emergent properties that begin to suggest attractive alternatives to traditional accounts of various aspects of cognition. We will also show that models of this class provide a basis for understanding how learning can occur spontaneously, as a by-product of processing activity.

Multiple Simultaneous Constraints

Reaching and grasping. Hundreds of times each day we reach for things. We nearly never think about these acts of reaching. And yet, each time, a large number of different considerations appear to jointly determine exactly how we will reach for the object. The position of the object, our posture at the time, what else we may also be holding, the size, shape, and anticipated weight of the object, any obstacles that may be in the way—all of these factors jointly determine the exact method we will use for reaching and grasping.

Consider the situation shown in Figure 1. Figure 1A shows Jay McClelland's hand, in typing position at his terminal. Figure 1B indicates the position his hand assumed in reaching for a small knob on the desk beside the terminal. We will let him describe what happened in the first person:

On the desk next to my terminal are several objects—a chipped coffee mug, the end of a computer cable, a knob from a clock radio. I decide to pick the knob up. At first I hesitate, because it doesn't seem possible. Then I just reach for it, and find myself grasping the knob in what would normally be considered a very awkward position—but it solves all of the constraints. I'm not sure what all the details of the movement were, so I let myself try it a few times more. I observe that my right hand is carried up off the keyboard, bent at the elbow, until my forearm is at about a 30° angle to the desk top and parallel to the side of the terminal. The palm is facing downward through most of this. Then, my arm extends and lowers down more or less parallel to the edge of the desk and parallel to the side of the terminal and, as it drops, it turns about 90° so that the palm is facing the cup and the thumb and index finger are below. The turning motion occurs just in time, as my hand drops, to avoid hitting the coffee cup. My index finger and thumb close in on the knob and grasp it, with my hand completely upside down.

Though the details of what happened here might be quibbled with, the broad outlines are apparent. The shape of the knob and its position on the table; the starting position of the hand on the keyboard; the positions of the terminal, the cup, and the knob; and the constraints imposed by the structure of the arm and the musculature used to control it—all these things conspired to lead to a solution which exactly suits the problem. If any of these constraints had not been included, the movement would have failed. The hand would have hit the cup or the terminal—or it would have missed the knob.

The mutual influence of syntax and semantics. Multiple constraints operate just as strongly in language processing as they do in reaching and grasping. Rumelhart (1977) has documented many of these multiple constraints. Rather than catalog them here, we will use a few examples from language to illustrate the fact that the constraints tend to be reciprocal: The example shows that they do not run only from syntax to semantics—they also run the other way.

It is clear, of course, that syntax constrains the assignment of meaning. Without the syntactic rules of English to guide us, we cannot correctly understand who has done what to whom in the following sentence:

The boy the man chased kissed the girl.

But consider these examples (Rumelhart, 1977; Schank, 1973):

I saw the grand canyon flying to New York.
I saw the sheep grazing in the field.

Our knowledge of syntactic rules alone does not tell us what grammatical role is played by the prepositional phrases in these two cases. In the first, "flying to New York" is taken as describing the context in which the speaker saw the Grand Canyon—while he was flying to New York. In the second, "grazing in the field" could syntactically describe an analogous situation, in which the speaker is grazing in the field, but this possibility does not typically become available on first reading. Instead we assign "grazing in the field" as a modifier of the sheep (roughly, "who were grazing in the field"). The syntactic structure of each of

FIGURE 1. *A:* An everyday situation in which it is necessary to take into account a large number of constraints to grasp a desired object. In this case the target object is the small knob to the left of the cup. *B:* The posture the arm arrives at in meeting these constraints.

A

B

these sentences, then, is determined in part by the semantic relations that the constituents of the sentence might plausibly bear to one another. Thus, the influences appear to run both ways, from the syntax to the semantics and from the semantics to the syntax.

In these examples, we see how syntactic considerations influence semantic ones and how semantic ones influence syntactic ones. We cannot say that one kind of constraint is primary.

Mutual constraints operate, not only between syntactic and semantic processing, but also within each of these domains as well. Here we consider an example from syntactic processing, namely, the assignment of words to syntactic categories. Consider the sentences:

> I like the joke.
> I like the drive.
> I like to joke.
> I like to drive.

In this case it looks as though the words *the* and *to* serve to determine whether the following word will be read as a noun or a verb. This, of course, is a very strong constraint in English and can serve to force a verb interpretation of a word that is not ordinarily used this way:

> I like to mud.

On the other hand, if the information specifying whether the function word preceding the final word is *to* or *the* is ambiguous, then the typical reading of the word that follows it will determine which way the function word is heard. This was shown in an experiment by Isenberg, Walker, Ryder, and Schweikert (1980). They presented sounds halfway between *to* (actually /tˊ/) and *the* (actually /dˊ/) and found that words like *joke*, which we tend to think of first as nouns, made subjects hear the marginal stimuli as *the*, while words like *drive*, which we tend to think of first as verbs, made subjects hear the marginal stimuli as *to*. Generally, then, it would appear that each word can help constrain the syntactic role, and even the identity, of every other word.

Simultaneous mutual constraints in word recognition. Just as the syntactic role of one word can influence the role assigned to another in analyzing sentences, so the identity of one letter can influence the identity assigned to another in reading. A famous example of this, from Selfridge, is shown in Figure 2. Along with this is a second example in which none of the letters, considered separately, can be identified unambiguously, but in which the possibilities that the visual

FIGURE 2. Some ambiguous displays. The first one is from Selfridge, 1955. The second line shows that three ambiguous characters can each constrain the identity of the others. The third, fourth, and fifth lines show that these characters are indeed ambiguous in that they assume other identities in other contexts. (The ink-blot technique of making letters ambiguous is due to Lindsay and Norman, 1972).

information leaves open for each so constrain the possible identities of the others that we are capable of identifying all of them.

At first glance, the situation here must seem paradoxical: The identity of each letter is constrained by the identities of each of the others. But since in general we cannot know the identities of any of the letters until we have established the identities of the others, how can we get the process started?

The resolution of the paradox, of course, is simple. One of the different possible letters in each position fits together with the others. It appears then that our perceptual system is capable of exploring all these possibilities without committing itself to one until all of the constraints are taken into account.

Understanding through the interplay of multiple sources of knowledge. It is clear that we know a good deal about a large number of different standard situations. Several theorists have suggested that we store this knowledge in terms of structures called variously: *scripts* (Schank, 1976), *frames* (Minsky, 1975), or *schemata* (Norman & Bobrow, 1976; Rumelhart, 1975). Such knowledge structures are assumed to be the basis of comprehension. A great deal of progress has been made within the context of this view.

However, it is important to bear in mind that most everyday situations cannot be rigidly assigned to just a single script. They generally involve an interplay between a number of different sources of information. Consider, for example, a child's birthday party at a restaurant. We know things about birthday parties, and we know things about restaurants, but we would not want to assume that we have explicit knowledge (at least, not in advance of our first restaurant birthday party) about the conjunction of the two. Yet we can imagine what such a party might be like. The fact that the party was being held in a restaurant would modify certain aspects of our expectations for birthday parties (we would not expect a game of Pin-the-Tail-on-the-Donkey, for example), while the fact that the event was a birthday party would inform our expectations for what would be ordered and who would pay the bill.

Representations like scripts, frames, and schemata are useful structures for encoding knowledge, although we believe they only approximate the underlying structure of knowledge representation that emerges from the class of models we consider in this book, as explained in Chapter 14. Our main point here is that any theory that tries to account for human knowledge using script-like knowledge structures will have to allow them to interact with each other to capture the generative capacity of human understanding in novel situations. Achieving such interactions has been one of the greatest difficulties associated with implementing models that really think generatively using script- or frame-like representations.

PARALLEL DISTRIBUTED PROCESSING

In the examples we have considered, a number of different pieces of information must be kept in mind at once. Each plays a part, constraining others and being constrained by them. What kinds of mechanisms seem well suited to these task demands? Intuitively, these tasks seem to require mechanisms in which each aspect of the information in the situation can act on other aspects, simultaneously influencing other aspects and being influenced by them. To articulate these intuitions, we and others have turned to a class of models we call *Parallel Distributed Processing* (PDP) models. These models assume that information processing takes place through the interactions of a large number of simple processing elements called units, each sending excitatory and inhibitory signals to other units. In some cases, the units stand for possible hypotheses about such things as the letters in a particular sentence. In these cases, the activations stand roughly for the strengths associated with the different possible hypotheses, and the interconnections among the units stand for the constraints the system knows to exist between the hypotheses. In other cases, the units stand for possible goals and actions, such as the goal of typing a particular letter, or the action of moving the left index finger, and the connections relate goals to subgoals, subgoals to actions, and actions to muscle movements. In still other cases, units stand not for particular hypotheses or goals, but for aspects of these things. Thus a hypothesis about the identity of a word, for example, is itself distributed in the activations of a large number of units.

PDP Models: Cognitive Science or Neuroscience?

One reason for the appeal of PDP models is their obvious "physiological" flavor: They seem so much more closely tied to the physiology of the brain than are other kinds of information-processing models. The brain consists of a large number of highly interconnected elements (Figure 3) which apparently send very simple excitatory and inhibitory messages to each other and update their excitations on the basis of these simple messages. The properties of the units in many of the PDP models we will be exploring were inspired by basic properties of the neural hardware. In a later section of this book, we will examine in some detail the relation between PDP models and the brain.

The Microstructure of Cognition

The process of human cognition, examined on a time scale of seconds and minutes, has a distinctly sequential character to it. Ideas come, seem promising, and then are rejected; leads in the solution to a problem are taken up, then abandoned and replaced with new ideas. Though the process may not be discrete, it has a decidedly sequential character, with transitions from state-to-state occurring, say, two or three times a second. Clearly, any useful description of the overall organization of this sequential flow of thought will necessarily describe a sequence of states.

But what is the internal structure of each of the states in the sequence, and how do they come about? Serious attempts to model even the simplest macrosteps of cognition—say, recognition of single words—require vast numbers of microsteps if they are implemented sequentially. As Feldman and Ballard (1982) have pointed out, the biological hardware is just too sluggish for sequential models of the microstructure to provide a plausible account, at least of the microstructure of *human* thought. And the time limitation only gets worse, not better, when sequential mechanisms try to take large numbers of constraints into account. Each additional constraint requires more time in a sequential machine, and, if the constraints are imprecise, the constraints can lead to a computational explosion. Yet people get faster, not slower, when they are able to exploit additional constraints.

Parallel distributed processing models offer alternatives to serial models of the microstructure of cognition. They do not deny that there is a macrostructure, just as the study of subatomic particles does not deny the existence of interactions between atoms. What PDP models do is describe the internal structure of the larger units, just as subatomic physics describes the internal structure of the atoms that form the constituents of larger units of chemical structure.

We shall show as we proceed through this book that the analysis of the microstructure of cognition has important implications for most of the central issues in cognitive science. In general, from the PDP point of view, the objects referred to in macrostructural models of cognitive processing are seen as approximate descriptions of emergent properties of the microstructure. Sometimes these approximate descriptions may be sufficiently accurate to capture a process or mechanism well enough; but many times, we will argue, they fail to provide sufficiently elegant or tractable accounts that capture the very flexibility and open-endedness of cognition that their inventors had originally intended to capture. We hope that our analysis of PDP models will show how an

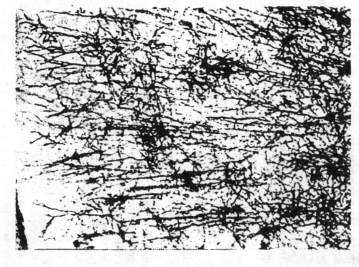

FIGURE 3. The arborizations of about 1 percent of the neurons near a vertical slice through the cerebral cortex. The full height of the figure corresponds to the thickness of the cortex, which is in this instance about 2 mm. (From *Mechanics of the Mind,* p. 84, by C. Blakemore, 1977, Cambridge, England: Cambridge University Press. Copyright 1977 by Cambridge University Press. Reprinted by permission.)

Though the appeal of PDP models is definitely enhanced by their physiological plausibility and neural inspiration, these are not the primary bases for their appeal to us. We are, after all, cognitive scientists, and PDP models appeal to us for psychological and computational reasons. They hold out the hope of offering computationally sufficient and psychologically accurate mechanistic accounts of the phenomena of human cognition which have eluded successful explication in conventional computational formalisms; and they have radically altered the way we think about the time-course of processing, the nature of representation, and the mechanisms of learning.

models in this domain. These models have not developed far enough to capture the full details of obstacle avoidance and multiple constraints on reaching and grasping, but there have been applications to two problems with some of these characteristics.

Finger movements in skilled typing. One might imagine, at first glance, that typists carry out keystrokes successively, first programming one stroke and then, when it is completed, programming the next. However, this is not the case. For skilled typists, the fingers are continually anticipating upcoming keystrokes. Consider the word *vacuum.* In this word, the *v*, *a*, and *c* are all typed with the left hand, leaving the right hand nothing to do until it is time to type the first *u*. However, a high speed film of a good typist shows that the right hand moves up to anticipate the typing of the *u*, even as the left hand is just beginning to type the *v*. By the time the *c* is typed the right index finger is in position over the *u* and ready to strike it.

When two successive key strokes are to be typed with the fingers of the same hand, concurrent preparation to type both can result in similar or conflicting instructions to the fingers and/or the hand. Consider, in this light, the difference between the sequence *ev* and the sequence *er*. The first sequence requires the typist to move up from home row to type the *e* and to move down from the home row to type the *v*, while in the second sequence, both the *e* and the *r* are above the home row.

The hands take very different positions in these two cases. In the first case, the hand as a whole stays fairly stationary over the home row. The middle finger moves up to type the *e*, and the index finger moves down to type the *v*. In the second case, the hand as a whole moves up, bringing the middle finger over the *e* and the index finger over the *r*. Thus, we can see that several letters can simultaneously influence the positioning of the fingers and the hands.

From the point of view of optimizing the efficiency of the typing motion, these different patterns seem very sensible. In the first case, the hand as a whole is maintained in a good compromise position to allow the typist to strike both letters reasonably efficiently by extending the fingers up or down. In the second case, the need to extend the fingers is reduced by moving the whole hand up, putting it in a near-optimal position to strike either key.

Rumelhart and Norman (1982) have simulated these effects using PDP mechanisms. Figure 4 illustrates aspects of the model as they are illustrated in typing the word *very*. In brief, Rumelhart and Norman assumed that the decision to type a word caused activation of a unit for that word. That unit, in turn, activated units corresponding to each of the letters in the word. The unit for the first letter to be typed was made to inhibit the units for the second and following letters, the unit

examination of the microstructure of cognition can lead us closer to an adequate description of the real extent of human processing and learning capacities.

The development of PDP models is still in its infancy. Thus far the models which have been proposed capture simplified versions of the kinds of phenomena we have been describing rather than the full elaboration that these phenomena display in real settings. But we think there have been enough steps forward in recent years to warrant a concerted effort at describing where the approach has gotten and where it is going now, and to point out some directions for the future.

The first section of the book represents an introductory course in parallel distributed processing. The rest of this chapter attempts to describe in informal terms a number of the models which have been proposed in previous work and to show that the approach is indeed a fruitful one. It also contains a brief description of the major sources of the inspiration we have obtained from the work of other researchers. This chapter is followed, in Chapter 2, by a description of the quantitative framework within which these models can be described and examined. Chapter 3 explicates one of the central concepts of the book: *distributed representation*. The final chapter in this section, Chapter 4, returns to the question of demonstrating the appeal of parallel distributed processing models and gives an overview of our explorations in the microstructure of cognition as they are laid out in the remainder of this book.

EXAMPLES OF PDP MODELS

In what follows, we review a number of recent applications of PDP models to problems in motor control, perception, memory, and language. In many cases, as we shall see, parallel distributed processing mechanisms are used to provide natural accounts of the exploitation of multiple, simultaneous, and often mutual constraints. We will also see that these same mechanisms exhibit emergent properties which lead to novel interpretations of phenomena which have traditionally been interpreted in other ways.

Motor Control

Having started with an example of how multiple constraints appear to operate in motor programming, it seems appropriate to mention two for the second to inhibit the third and following letters, and so on. As a result of the interplay of activation and inhibition among these units, the unit for the first letter was at first the most strongly active, and the units for the other letters were partially activated.

Each letter unit exerts influences on the hand and finger involved in typing the letter. The v unit, for example, tends to cause the index finger to move down and to cause the whole hand to move down with it. The e unit, on the other hand, tends to cause the middle finger on the left hand to move up and to cause the whole hand to move up also. The r unit also causes the left index finger to move up and the left hand to move up with it.

The extent of the influences of each letter on the hand and finger it directs depends on the extent of the activation of the letter. Therefore, at first, in typing the word very, the v exerts the greatest control.

Because the e and r are simultaneously pulling the hand up, though, the v is typed primarily by moving the index finger, and there is little movement on the whole hand.

Once a finger is within a certain striking distance of the key to be typed, the actual pressing movement is triggered, and the keypress occurs. The keypress itself causes a strong inhibitory signal to be sent to the unit for the letter just typed, thereby removing this unit from the picture and allowing the unit for the next letter in the word to become the most strongly activated.

This mechanism provides a simple way for all of the letters to jointly determine the successive configurations the hand will enter into in the process of typing a word. This model has shown considerable success predicting the time between successive keystrokes as a function of the different keys involved. Given a little noise in the activation process, it can also account for some of the different kinds of errors that have been observed in transcription typing.

The typing model represents an illustration of the fact that serial behavior—a succession of key strokes—is not necessarily the result of an inherently serial processing mechanism. In this model, the sequential structure of typing emerges from the interaction of the excitatory and inhibitory influences among the processing units.

Reaching for an object without falling over. Similar mechanisms can be used to model the process of reaching for an object without losing one's balance while standing, as Hinton (1984) has shown. He considered a simple version of this task using a two-dimensional "person" with a foot, a lower leg, an upper leg, a trunk, an upper arm, and a lower arm. Each of these limbs is joined to the next at a joint which has a single degree of rotational freedom. The task posed to this person is to reach a target placed somewhere in front of it, without taking any steps and without falling down. This is a simplified version of the situation in which a real person has to reach out in front for an object placed somewhere in the plane that vertically bisects the body. The task is not as simple as it looks, since if we just swing an arm out in front of ourselves, it may shift our center of gravity so far forward that we will lose our balance. The problem, then, is to find a set of joint angles that simultaneously solves the two constraints on the task. First, the tip of the forearm must touch the object. Second, to keep from falling down, the person must keep its center of gravity over the foot.

To do this, Hinton assigned a single processor to each joint. On each computational cycle, each processor received information about how far the tip of the hand was from the target and where the center of gravity was with respect to the foot. Using these two pieces of information, each joint adjusted its angle so as to approach the goals of maintaining

Response System

Keypress Schemata

Word Schema

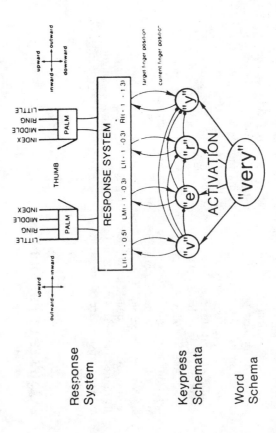

FIGURE 4. The interaction of activations in typing the word *very*. The *very* unit is activated from outside the model. It in turn activates the units for each of the component letters. Each letter unit specifies the target finger positions, specified in a keyboard coordinate system. L and R stand for the left and right hands, and I and M for the index and middle fingers. The letter units receive information about the current finger position from the response system. Each letter unit inhibits the activation of all letter units that follow it in the word; inhibitory connections are indicated by the lines; with solid dots at their terminations. (From "Simulating a Skilled Typist: A Study of Skilled Motor Performance" by D. E. Rumelhart and D. A. Norman, 1982. *Cognitive Science*, 6, p. 12. Copyright 1982 by Ablex Publishing. Reprinted by permission.)

Perception

Stereoscopic vision. One early model using parallel distributed processing was the model of stereoscopic depth perception proposed by Marr and Poggio (1976). Their theory proposed to explain the perception of depth in random-dot stereograms (Figure 6) in terms of a simple distributed processing mechanism.

Random-dot stereograms present interesting challenges to mechanisms of depth perception. A stereogram consists of two random-dot patterns. In a simple stereogram such as the one shown here, one pattern is an exact copy of the other except that the pattern of dots in a region of one of the patterns is shifted horizontally with respect to the rest of the pattern. Each of the two patterns—corresponding to two retinal images—consists entirely of a pattern of random dots, so there is no information in either of the two views considered alone that can indicate the presence of different surfaces, let alone depth relations among those surfaces. Yet, when one of these dot patterns is projected to the left eye and the other to the right eye, an observer sees each region as a surface, with the shifted region hovering in front of or behind the other, depending on the direction of the shift.

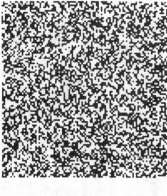

FIGURE 6. Random-dot stereograms. The two patterns are identical except that the pattern of dots in the central region of the left pattern are shifted over with respect to those in the right. When viewed stereoscopically such that the left pattern projects to the left eye and the right pattern to the right eye, the shifted area appears to hover above the page. Some readers may be able to achieve this by converging to a distant point (e.g., a far wall) and then interposing the figure into the line of sight. (From *Vision*, p. 9, by D. Marr, 1982, San Francisco: Freeman. Copyright 1982 by W. H. Freeman & Co. Reprinted by permission.)

balance and bringing the tip closer to the target. After a number of iterations, the stick-person settled on postures that satisfied the goal of reaching the target and the goal of maintaining the center of gravity over the "feet."

Though the simulation was able to perform the task, eventually satisfying both goals at once, it had a number of inadequacies stemming from the fact that each joint processor attempted to achieve a solution in ignorance of what the other joints were attempting to do. This problem was overcome by using additional processors responsible for setting combinations of joint angles. Thus, a processor for flexion and extension of the leg would adjust the knee, hip, and ankle joints synergistically, while a processor for flexion and extension of the arm would adjust the shoulder and elbow together. With the addition of processors of this form, the number of iterations required to reach a solution was greatly reduced, and the form of the approach to the solution looked very natural. The sequence of configurations attained in one processing run is shown in Figure 5.

Explicit attempts to program a robot to cope with the problem of maintaining balance as it reaches for a desired target have revealed the difficulty of deriving explicitly the right combinations of actions for each possible starting state and goal state. This simple model illustrates that we may be wrong to seek such an explicit solution. We see here that a solution to the problem can emerge from the action of a number of simple processors each attempting to honor the constraints independently.

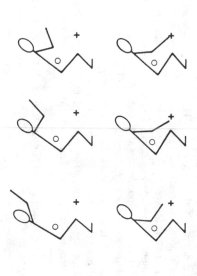

FIGURE 5. A sequence of configurations assumed by the stick "person" performing the reaching task described in the text, from Hinton (1984). The small circle represents the center of gravity of the whole stick-figure, and the cross represents the goal to be reached. The configuration is shown on every second iteration.

What kind of a mechanism might we propose to account for these facts? Marr and Poggio (1976) began by explicitly representing the two views in two arrays, as human observers might in two different retinal images. They noted that corresponding black dots at different per-ceived distances from the observer will be offset from each other by different amounts in the two views. The job of the model is to deter-mine which points correspond. This task is, of course, made difficult by the fact that there will be a very large number of spurious correspondences of individual dots. The goal of the mechanism, then, is to find those correspondences that represent real correspondences in depth and suppress those that represent spurious correspondences.

To carry out this task, Marr and Poggio assigned a processing unit to each possible conjunction of a point in one image and a point in the other. Since the eyes are offset horizontally, the possible conjunctions occur at various offsets or disparities along the horizontal dimension. Thus, for each point in one eye, there was a set of processing units with one unit assigned to the conjunction of that point and the point at each horizontal offset from it in the other eye.

Each processing unit received activation whenever both of the points the unit stood for contained dots. So far, then, units for both real and spurious correspondences would be equally activated. To allow the mechanism to find the right correspondences, they pointed out two general principles about the visual world: (a) Each point in each view generally corresponds to one and only one point in the other view, and (b) neighboring points in space tend to be at nearly the same depth and therefore at about the same disparity in the two images. While there are discontinuities at the edges of things, over most of a two-dimensional view of the world there will be continuity. These princi-ples are called the *uniqueness* and *continuity* constraints, respectively.

Marr and Poggio incorporated these principles into the interconnec-tions between the processing units. The uniqueness constraint was cap-tured by inhibitory connections among the units that stand for alterna-tive correspondences of the same dot. The continuity principle was captured by excitatory connections among the units that stand for simi-lar offsets of adjacent dots.

These additional connections allow the Marr and Poggio model to "solve" stereograms like the one shown in the figure. At first, when a pair of patterns is presented, the units for all possible correspondences of a dot in one eye with a dot in the other will be equally excited. However, the excitatory connections cause the units for the correct conjunctions to receive more excitation than units for spurious conjunc-tions, and the inhibitory connections allow the units for the correct conjunctions to turn off the units for the spurious connections. Thus, the model tends to settle down into a stable state in which only the correct correspondence of each dot remains active.

There are a number of reasons why Marr and Poggio (1979) modi-fied this model (see Marr, 1982, for a discussion), but the basic mechanisms of mutual excitation between units that are mutually con-sistent and mutual inhibition between units that are mutually incompa-tible provide a natural mechanism for settling on the right conjunctions of points and rejecting spurious ones. The model also illustrates how general principles or rules such as the uniqueness and continuity princi-ples may be embodied in the connections between processing units, and how behavior in accordance with these principles can emerge from the interactions determined by the pattern of these interconnections.

Perceptual completion of familiar patterns. Perception, of course, is influenced by familiarity. It is a well-known fact that we often misper-ceive unfamiliar objects as more familiar ones and that we can get by with less time or with lower-quality information in perceiving familiar items than we need for perceiving unfamiliar items. Not only does familiarity help us determine what the higher-level structures are when the lower-level information is ambiguous; it also allows us to fill in missing lower-level information within familiar higher-order patterns. The well-known *phonemic restoration effect* is a case in point. In this phenomenon, perceivers hear sounds that have been cut out of words as if they had actually been present. For example, Warren (1970) presented *legi#lature* to subjects, with a click in the location marked by the #. Not only did subjects correctly identify the word *legislature*; they also heard the missing /s/ just as though it had been presented. They had great difficulty localizing the click, which they tended to hear as a disembodied sound. Similar phenomena have been observed in visual perception of words since the work of Pillsbury (1897).

Two of us have proposed a model describing the role of familiarity in perception based on excitatory and inhibitory interactions among units standing for various hypotheses about the input at different levels of abstraction (McClelland & Rumelhart, 1981; Rumelhart & McClelland, 1982). The model has been applied in detail to the role of familiarity in the perception of letters in visually presented words, and has proved to provide a very close account of the results of a large number of experiments.

The model assumes that there are units that act as detectors for the visual features which distinguish letters, with one set of units assigned to detect the features in each of the different letter-positions in the word. For four-letter words, then, there are four such sets of detectors. There are also four sets of detectors for the letters themselves and a set of detectors for the words.

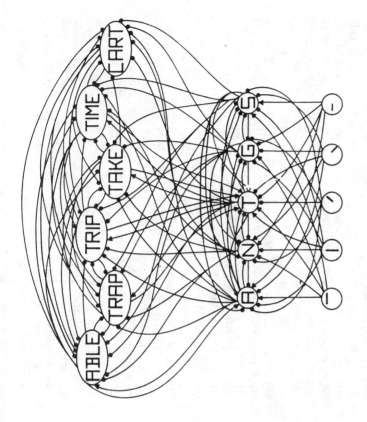

FIGURE 7. The unit for the letter *T* in the first position of a four-letter array and some of its neighbors. Note that the feature and letter units stand only for the first position; in a complete picture of the units needed from processing four-letter displays, there would be four full sets of feature detectors and four full sets of letter detectors. (From "An Interactive Activation Model of Context Effects in Letter Perception: Part 1. An Account of Basic Findings" by J. L. McClelland and D. E. Rumelhart. 1981, *Psychological Review*, 88, p. 380. Copyright 1981 by the American Psychological Association. Reprinted by permission.)

In the model, each unit has an activation value, corresponding roughly to the strength of the hypothesis that what that unit stands for is present in the perceptual input. The model honors the following important relations which hold between these "hypotheses" or activations: First, to the extent that two hypotheses are mutually consistent, they should support each other. Thus, units that are mutually consistent, in the way that the letter *T* in the first position is consistent with the word *TAKE*, tend to excite each other. Second, to the extent that two hypotheses are mutually inconsistent, they should weaken each other. Actually, we can distinguish two kinds of inconsistency: The first kind might be called between-level inconsistency. For example, the hypothesis that a word begins with a *T* is inconsistent with the hypothesis that the word is *MOVE*. The second might be called mutual exclusion. For example, the hypothesis that a word begins with *T* excludes the hypothesis that it begins with *R* since a word can only begin with one letter. Both kinds of inconsistencies operate in the word perception model to reduce the activations of units. Thus, the letter units in each position compete with all other letter units in the same position, and the word units compete with each other. This type of inhibitory interaction is often called *competitive inhibition*. In addition, there are inhibitory interactions between incompatible units on different levels. This type of inhibitory interaction is simply called *between-level inhibition*.

The set of excitatory and inhibitory interactions between units can be diagrammed by drawing excitatory and inhibitory links between them. The whole picture is too complex to draw, so we illustrate only with a fragment: Some of the interactions between some of the units in this model are illustrated in Figure 7.

Let us consider what happens in a system like this when a familiar stimulus is presented under degraded conditions. For example, consider the display shown in Figure 8. This display consists of the letters *W, O,* and *R*, completely visible, and enough of a fourth letter to rule out all letters other than *R* and *K*. Before onset of the display, the activations of the units are set at or below 0. When the display is presented, detectors for the features present in each position become active (i.e., their activations grow above 0). At this point, they begin to excite and inhibit the corresponding detectors for letters. In the first three positions, *W, O,* and *R* are unambiguously activated, so we will focus our attention on the fourth position where *R* and *K* are both equally consistent with the active features. Here, the activations of the detectors for *R* and *K* start out growing together, as the feature detectors below them become activated. As these detectors become active, they and the active letter detectors for *W, O,* and *R* in the other positions start to activate detectors for words which have these letters in

them and to inhibit detectors for words which do not have these letters. A number of words are partially consistent with the active letters, and receive some net excitation from the letter level, but only the word *WORK* matches one of the active letters in all four positions. As a result, *WORK* becomes more active than any other word and inhibits the other words, thereby successfully dominating the pattern of activation among the word units. As it grows in strength, it sends feedback to the letter level, reinforcing the activations of the *W, O, R,* and *K* in the corresponding positions. In the fourth position, this feedback gives *K* the upper hand over *R*, and eventually the stronger activation of the perception of letters in unfamiliar letter strings which are word-like but not themselves actually familiar.

One way of accounting for such performances is to imagine that the perceiver possesses, in addition to detectors for familiar words, sets of detectors for regular subword units such as familiar letter clusters, or that they use abstract rules, specifying which classes of letters can go with which others in different contexts. It turns out, however, that the model we have already described needs no such additional structure to produce perceptual facilitation for word-like letter strings; to this extent it acts as if it "knows" the orthographic structure of English. We illustrate this feature of the model with the example shown in Figure 9, where the nonword *YEAD* is shown in degraded form so that the second letter is incompletely visible. Given the information about this letter, considered alone, either *E* or *F* would be possible in the second position. Yet our model will tend to complete this letter as an *E*.

The reason for this behavior is that, when *YEAD* is shown, a number of words are partially activated. There is no word consistent with *Y, E* or *F, A,* and *D,* but there are words which match *YEA_ (YEAR,* for example) and others which match _*EAD (BEAD, DEAD, HEAD,* and *READ,* for example). These *and* other near misses are partially activated as a result of the pattern of activation at the letter level. While they compete with each other, none of these words gets strongly enough activated to completely suppress all the others. Instead, these units act as a group to reinforce particularly the letters *E* and *A.* There are no close partial matches which include the letter *F* in the second position, so this letter receives no feedback support. As a result, *E* comes to dominate, and eventually suppress, the *F* in the second position.

The fact that the word perception model exhibits perceptual facilitation to pronounceable nonwords as well as words illustrates once again how behavior in accordance with general principles or rules can emerge from the interactions of simple processing elements. Of course, the behavior of the word perception model does not implement exactly any of the systems of orthographic rules that have been proposed by linguists (Chomsky & Halle, 1968; Venesky, 1970) or psychologists (Spoehr & Smith, 1975). In this regard, it only approximates such rule-based descriptions of perceptual processing. However, rule systems such as Chomsky and Halle's or Venesky's appear to be only approximately honored in human performance as well (Smith & Baker, 1976). Indeed, some of the discrepancies between human performance data and rule systems occur in exactly the ways that we would predict from the word perception model (Rumelhart & McClelland, 1982). This illustrates the possibility that PDP models may provide more accurate accounts of the details of human performance than models

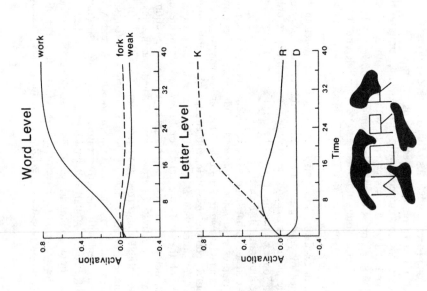

FIGURE 8. A possible display which might be presented to the interactive activation model of word recognition, and the resulting activations of selected letter and word units. The letter units are for the letters indicated in the fourth position of a four-letter display.

K detector allows it to dominate the pattern of activation, suppressing the *R* detector completely.

This example illustrates how PDP models can allow knowledge about what letters go together to form words to work together with natural constraints on the task (i.e., that there should only be one letter in one place at one time), to produce perceptual completion in a simple and direct way.

Completion of novel patterns. However, the perceptual intelligence of human perceivers far exceeds the ability to recognize familiar patterns and fill in missing portions. We also show facilitation in the can access information in memory based on nearly any attribute of the representation we are trying to retrieve.

Of course, some cues are much better than others. An attribute which is shared by a very large number of things we know about is not a very effective retrieval cue, since it does not accurately pick out a particular memory representation. But, several such cues, in conjunction, can do the job. Thus, if we ask a friend who goes out with several women, "Who was that woman I saw you with?", he may not know which one we mean—but if we specify something else about her—say the color of her hair, what she was wearing (in so far as he remembers this at all), where we saw him with her—he will likely be able to hit upon the right one.

It is, of course, possible to implement some kind of content addressability of memory on a standard computer in a variety of different ways. One way is to search sequentially, examining each memory in the system to find the memory or the set of memories which has the particular content specified in the cue. An alternative, somewhat more efficient, scheme involves some form of indexing—keeping a list, for every content a memory might have, of which memories have that content.

Such an indexing scheme can be made to work with error-free probes, but it will break down if there is an error in the specification; of the retrieval cue. There are possible ways of recovering from such errors, but they lead to the kind of combinatorial explosions which plague this kind of computer implementation.

But suppose that we imagine that each memory is represented by a unit which has mutually excitatory interactions with units standing for each of its properties. Then, whenever any property of the memory became active, the memory would tend to be activated, and whenever the memory was activated, all of its contents would tend to become activated. Such a scheme would automatically produce content addressability for us. Though it would not be immune to errors, it would not be devastated by an error in the probe if the remaining properties specified the correct memory.

As described thus far, whenever a property that is a part of a number of different memories is activated, it will tend to activate all of the memories it is in. To keep these other activities from swamping the "correct" memory unit, we simply need to add initial inhibitory connections among the memory units. An additional desirable feature would be mutually inhibitory interactions among mutually incompatible property units. For example, a person cannot both be single and married at the same time, so the units for different marital states would be mutually inhibitory.

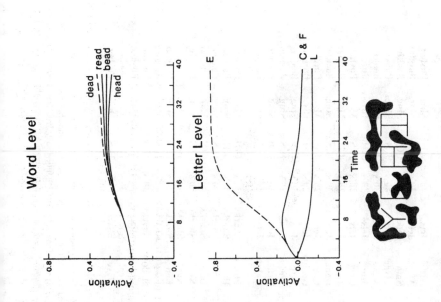

FIGURE 9. An example of a nonword display that might be presented to the interactive activation model of word recognition and the response of selected units at the letter and word levels. The letter units illustrated are detectors for letters in the second input position.

based on a set of rules representing human competence—at least in some domains.

Retrieving Information From Memory

Content addressability. One very prominent feature of human memory is that it is content addressable. It seems fairly clear that we

McClelland (1981) developed a simulation model that illustrates how a system with these properties would act as a content addressable memory. The model is obviously oversimplified, but it illustrates many of the characteristics of the more complex models that will be considered in later chapters.

Consider the information represented in Figure 10, which lists a number of people we might meet if we went to live in an unsavory neighborhood, and some of their hypothetical characteristics. A subset

of the units needed to represent this information is shown in Figure 11. In this network, there is an "instance unit" for each of the characters described in Figure 10, and that unit is linked by mutually excitatory connections to all of the units for the fellow's properties. Note that we have included property units for the names of the characters, as well as units for their other properties.

Now, suppose we wish to retrieve the properties of a particular individual, say Lance. And suppose that we know Lance's name. Then we can probe the network by activating Lance's name unit, and we can see what pattern of activation arises as a result. Assuming that we know of no one else named Lance, we can expect the Lance name unit to be hooked up only to the instance unit for Lance. This will in turn activate the property units for Lance, thereby creating the pattern of

The Jets and The Sharks

Name	Gang	Age	Edu	Mar	Occupation
Art	Jets	40's	J.H.	Sing.	Pusher
Al	Jets	30's	J.H.	Mar.	Burglar
Sam	Jets	20's	COL.	Sing.	Bookie
Clyde	Jets	40's	J.H.	Sing.	Bookie
Mike	Jets	30's	J.H.	Sing.	Bookie
Jim	Jets	20's	J.H.	Div.	Burglar
Greg	Jets	20's	H.S.	Mar.	Pusher
John	Jets	20's	J.H.	Mar.	Burglar
Doug	Jets	30's	H.S.	Sing.	Bookie
Lance	Jets	20's	J.H.	Mar.	Burglar
George	Jets	20's	J.H.	Div.	Burglar
Pete	Jets	20's	H.S.	Sing.	Bookie
Fred	Jets	20's	H.S.	Sing.	Pusher
Gene	Jets	20's	COL.	Sing.	Pusher
Ralph	Jets	30's	J.H.	Sing.	Pusher
Phil	Sharks	30's	COL.	Mar.	Pusher
Ike	Sharks	30's	J.H.	Sing.	Bookie
Nick	Sharks	30's	H.S.	Sing.	Pusher
Don	Sharks	30's	COL.	Mar.	Burglar
Ned	Sharks	30's	COL.	Mar.	Bookie
Karl	Sharks	40's	H.S.	Mar.	Bookie
Ken	Sharks	20's	H.S.	Sing.	Burglar
Earl	Sharks	40's	H.S.	Mar.	Burglar
Rick	Sharks	30's	H.S.	Div.	Burglar
Ol	Sharks	30's	COL.	Mar.	Pusher
Neal	Sharks	30's	H.S.	Sing.	Bookie
Dave	Sharks	30's	H.S.	Div.	Pusher

FIGURE 10. Characteristics of a number of individuals belonging to two gangs, the Jets and the Sharks. (From "Retrieving General and Specific Knowledge From Stored Knowledge of Specifics" by J. L. McClelland. 1981. *Proceedings of the Third Annual Conference of the Cognitive Science Society,* Berkeley, CA. Copyright 1981 by J. L. McClelland. Reprinted by permission.)

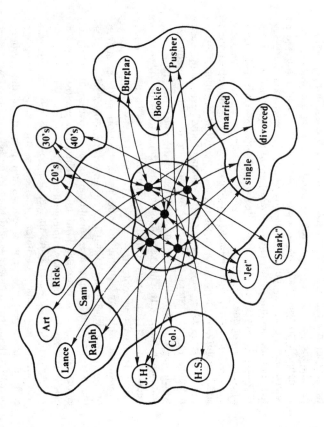

FIGURE 11. Some of the units and interconnections needed to represent the individuals shown in Figure 10. The units connected with double-headed arrows are mutually excitatory. All the units within the same cloud are mutually inhibitory. (From "Retrieving General and Specific Knowledge From Stored Knowledge of Specifics" by J. L. McClelland, 1981, *Proceedings of the Third Annual Conference of the Cognitive Science Society,* Berkeley, CA. Copyright 1981 by J. L. McClelland. Reprinted by permission.)

activation corresponding to Lance. In effect, we have retrieved a representation of Lance. More will happen than just what we have described so far, but for the moment let us stop here.

Of course, sometimes we may wish to retrieve a name, given other information. In this case, we might start with some of Lance's properties, effectively asking the system, say "Who do you know who is a Shark and in his 20s?" by activating the Shark and 20s units. In this case it turns out that there is a single individual, Ken, who fits the description. So, when we activate these two properties, we will activate the instance unit for Ken, and this in turn will activate his name unit, and fill in his other properties as well.

Graceful degradation. A few of the desirable properties of this kind of model are visible from considering what happens as we vary the set of features we use to probe the memory in an attempt to retrieve a particular individual's name. Any set of features which is sufficient to uniquely characterize a particular item will activate the instance node for that item more strongly than any other instance node. A probe which contains misleading features will most strongly activate the node that it matches best. This will clearly be a poorer cue than one which contains no misleading information—but it will still be sufficient to activate the "right answer" more strongly than any other, as long as the introduction of misleading information does not make the probe closer to some other item. In general, though the degree of activation of a particular instance node and of the corresponding name nodes varies in this model as a function of the exact content of the probe, errors in the probe will not be fatal unless they make the probe point to the wrong memory. This kind of model's handling of incomplete or partial probes also requires no special error-recovery scheme to work—it is a natural by-product of the nature of the retrieval mechanism that it is capable of graceful degradation.

These aspects of the behavior of the Jets and Sharks model deserve more detailed consideration than the present space allows. One reason we do not go into them is that we view this model as a stepping stone in the development of other models, such as the models using more distributed representations, that occur in other parts of this book. We do, however, have more to say about this simple model, for like some of the other models we have already examined, this model exhibits some useful properties which emerge from the interactions of the processing units.

Default assignment. It probably will have occurred to the reader that in many of the situations we have been examining, there will be other

activations occurring which may influence the pattern of activation which is retrieved. So, in the case where we retrieved the properties of Lance, those properties, once they become active, can begin to activate the units for other individuals with those same properties. The memory unit for Lance will be in competition with these units and will tend to keep their activation down, but to the extent that they do become active, they will tend to activate their own properties and therefore fill them in. In this way, the model can fill in properties of individuals based on what it knows about other, similar instances.

To illustrate how this might work we have simulated the case in which we do not know that Lance is a Burglar as opposed to a Bookie or a Pusher. It turns out that there are a group of individuals in the set who are very similar to Lance in many respects. When Lance's properties become activated, these other units become partially activated, and they start activating their properties. Since they all share the same "occupation," they work together to fill in that property for Lance. Of course, there is no reason why this should necessarily be the right answer, but generally speaking, the more similar two things are in respects that we know about, the more likely they are to be similar in respects that we do not, and the model implements this heuristic.

Spontaneous generalization. The model we have been describing has another valuable property as well—it tends to retrieve what is common to those memories which match a retrieval cue which is too general to capture any one memory. Thus, for example, we could probe the system by activating the unit corresponding to membership in the Jets. This unit will partially activate all the instances of the Jets, thereby causing each to send activations to its properties. In this way the model can retrieve the typical values that the members of the Jets have on each dimension—even though there is no one Jet that has these typical values. In the example, 9 of 15 Jets are single, 9 of 15 are in their 20s, and 9 of 15 have only a Junior High School education; when we probe by activating the Jet unit, all three of these properties dominate. The Jets are evenly divided between the three occupations, so each of these units becomes partially activated. Each has a different name, so that each name unit is very weakly activated, nearly cancelling each other out.

In the example just given of spontaneous generalization, it would not be unreasonable to suppose that someone might have explicitly stored a generalization about the members of a gang. The account just given would be an alternative to "explicit storage" of the generalization. It has two advantages, though, over such an account. First, it does not require any special generalization formation mechanism. Second, it can provide us with generalizations on unanticipated lines, on demand.

Thus, if we want to know, for example, what people in their 20s with a junior high school education are like, we can probe the model by activating these two units. Since all such people are Jets and Burglars, these two units are strongly activated by the model in this case; two of them are divorced and two are married, so both of these units are partially activated.[1]

The sort of model we are considering, then, is considerably more than a content addressable memory. In addition, it performs default assignment, and it can spontaneously retrieve a general concept of the individuals that match any specifiable probe. These properties must be explicitly implemented as complicated computational extensions of other models of knowledge retrieval, but in PDP models they are natural by-products of the retrieval process itself.

REPRESENTATION AND LEARNING IN PDP MODELS

In the Jets and Sharks model, we can speak of the model's *active representation* at a particular time, and associate this with the pattern of activation over the units in the system. We can also ask: What is the stored knowledge that gives rise to that pattern of activation? In considering this question, we see immediately an important difference between PDP models and other models of cognitive processes. In most models, knowledge is stored as a static copy of a pattern. Retrieval amounts to finding the pattern in long-term memory and copying it into a buffer or working memory. There is no real difference between the stored representation in long-term memory and the active representation in working memory. In PDP models, though, this is not the case. In these models, the patterns themselves are not stored. Rather, what is stored is the *connection strengths* between units that allow these patterns to be re-created. In the Jets and Sharks model, there is an instance unit assigned to each individual, but that unit does not contain a copy of the representation of that individual. Instead, it is simply the case that the connections between it and the other units in the system are such that activation of the unit will cause the pattern for the individual to be reinstated on the property units.

[1] In this and all other cases, there is a tendency for the pattern of activation to be influenced by partially activated, near neighbors, which do not quite match the probe. Thus, in this case, there is a Jet Al, who is a Married Burglar. The unit for Al gets slightly activated, giving Married a slight edge over Divorced in the simulation.

This difference between PDP models and conventional models has enormous implications, both for processing and for learning. We have already seen some of the implications for processing. The representation of the knowledge is set up in such a way that the knowledge necessarily influences the course of processing. Using knowledge in processing is no longer a matter of finding the relevant information in memory and bringing it to bear; it is part and parcel of the processing itself.

For learning, the implications are equally profound. For if the knowledge is the strengths of the connections, learning must be a matter of finding the right connection strengths so that the right patterns of activation will be produced under the right circumstances. This is an extremely important property of this class of models, for it opens up the possibility that an information processing mechanism could learn, as a result of tuning its connections, to capture the interdependencies between activations that it is exposed to in the course of processing.

In recent years, there has been quite a lot of interest in learning in cognitive science. Computational approaches to learning fall predominantly into what might be called the "explicit rule formulation" tradition, as represented by the work of Winston (1975), the suggestions of Chomsky, and the ACT* model of J. R. Anderson (1983). All of this work shares the assumption that the goal of learning is to formulate explicit rules (propositions, productions, etc.) which capture powerful generalizations in a succinct way. Fairly powerful mechanisms, usually with considerable innate knowledge about a domain, and/or some starting set of primitive propositional representations, then formulate hypothetical general rules, e.g., by comparing particular cases and formulating explicit generalizations.

The approach that we take in developing PDP models is completely different. First, we do not assume that the goal of learning is the formulation of explicit rules. Rather, we assume it is the acquisition of connection strengths which allow a network of simple units to act *as though* it knew the rules. Second, we do not attribute powerful computational capabilities to the learning mechanism. Rather, we assume very simple connection strength modulation mechanisms which adjust the strength of connections between units based on information locally available at the connection.

These issues will be addressed at length in later sections of this book. For now, our purpose is to give a simple, illustrative example of the connection strength modulation process, and how it can produce networks which exhibit some interesting behavior.

Local vs. distributed representation. Before we turn to an explicit consideration of this issue, we raise a basic question about

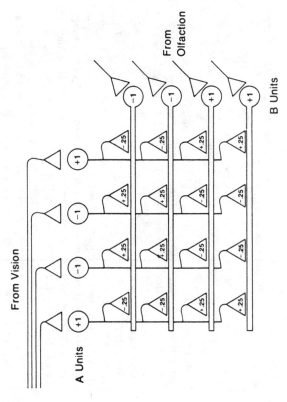

A Units

From Vision

From Olfaction

B Units

representation. Once we have achieved the insight that the knowledge is stored in the strengths of the interconnections between units, a question arises. Is there any reason to assign one unit to each pattern that we wish to learn? Another possibility—one that we explore extensively in this book—is the possibility that the knowledge about any individual pattern is not stored in the connections of a special unit reserved for that pattern, but is distributed over the connections among a large number of processing units. On this view, the Jets and Sharks model represents a special case in which separate units are reserved for each instance.

Models in which connection information is explicitly thought of as distributed have been proposed by a number of investigators. The units in these collections may themselves correspond to conceptual primitives, or they may have no particular meaning as individuals. In either case, the focus shifts to patterns of activation over these units and to mechanisms whose explicit purpose is to learn the right connection strengths to allow the right patterns of activation to become activated under the right circumstances.

In the rest of this section, we will give a simple example of a PDP model in which the knowledge is distributed. We will first explain how the model would work, given pre-existing connections, and we will then describe how it could come to acquire the right connection strengths through a very simple learning mechanism. A number of models which have taken this distributed approach have been discussed in this book's predecessor, Hinton and J. A. Anderson's (1981) *Parallel Models of Associative Memory*. We will consider a simple version of a common type of distributed model, a *pattern associator*.

Pattern associators are models in which a pattern of activation over one set of units can cause a pattern of activation over another set of units without any intervening units to stand for either pattern as a whole. Pattern associators would, for example, be capable of associating a pattern of activation on one set of units corresponding to the appearance of an object with a pattern on another set corresponding to the aroma of the object, so that, when an object is presented visually, causing its visual pattern to become active, the model produces the pattern corresponding to its aroma.

How a pattern associator works. For purposes of illustration, we present a very simple pattern associator in Figure 12. In this model, there are four units in each of two pools. The first pool, the A units, will be the pool in which patterns corresponding to the sight of various objects might be represented. The second pool, the B units, will be the pool in which the pattern corresponding to the aroma will be represented. We can pretend that alternative patterns of activation on

the A units are produced upon viewing a rose or a grilled steak, and alternative patterns on the B units are produced upon sniffing the same objects. Figure 13 shows two pairs of patterns, as well as sets of interconnections necessary to allow the A member of each pair to reproduce the B member.

The details of the behavior of the individual units vary among different versions of pattern associators. For present purposes, we'll assume that the units can take on positive or negative activation values, with 0 representing a kind of neutral intermediate value. The strengths of the interconnections between the units can be positive or negative real numbers.

The effect of an A unit on a B unit is determined by multiplying the activation of the A unit times the strength of its synaptic connection with the B unit. For example, if the connection from a particular A unit to a particular B unit has a positive sign, when the A unit is effects are produced if an element of the pattern is distorted—or if the model is damaged, either by removing whole units, or random sets of connections, etc. Thus, their pattern retrieval performance of the model degrades gracefully both under degraded input and under damage.

How a pattern associator learns. So far, we have seen how we as model builders can construct the right set of weights to allow one pattern to cause another. The interesting thing, though, is that we do not need to build these interconnection strengths in by hand. Instead, the pattern associator can teach itself the right set of interconnections through experience processing the patterns in conjunction with each other.

A number of different rules for adjusting connection strengths have been proposed. One of the first—and definitely the best known—is due to D. O. Hebb (1949). Hebb's actual proposal was not sufficiently quantitative to build into an explicit model. However, a number of different variants can trace their ancestry back to Hebb. Perhaps the simplest version is:

> When unit A and unit B are simultaneously excited, increase the strength of the connection between them.

A natural extension of this rule to cover the positive and negative activation values allowed in our example is:

> Adjust the strength of the connection between units A and B in proportion to the product of their simultaneous activation.

In this formulation, if the product is positive, the change makes the connection more excitatory, and if the product is negative, the change makes the connection more inhibitory. For simplicity of reference, we will call this the *Hebb rule*, although it is not exactly Hebb's original formulation.

With this simple learning rule, we could train a "blank copy" of the pattern associator shown in Figure 12 to produce the B pattern for rose when the A pattern is shown, simply by presenting the A and B patterns together and modulating the connection strengths according to the Hebb rule. The size of the change made on every trial would, of course, be a parameter. We generally assume that the changes made on each instance are rather small, and that connection strengths build up gradually. The values shown in Figure 13A, then, would be acquired as a result of a number of experiences with the A and B pattern pair.

excited (activation greater than 0), it will excite the B unit. For this example, we'll simply assume that the activation of each unit is set to the sum of the excitatory and inhibitory effects operating on it. This is one of the simplest possible cases.

Suppose, now, that we have created on the A units the pattern corresponding to the first visual pattern shown in Figure 13, the rose. How should we arrange the strengths of the interconnections between the A units and the B units to reproduce the pattern corresponding to the aroma of a rose? We simply need to arrange for each A unit to tend to excite each B unit which has a positive activation in the aroma pattern and to inhibit each B unit which has a negative activation in the pattern. It turns out that this goal is achieved by setting the strength of the connection between a given A unit and a given B unit to a value proportional to the product of the activation of the two units. In Figure 12, the weights on the connections were chosen to allow the A pattern illustrated there to produce the illustrated B pattern according to this principle. The actual strengths of the connections were set to ±.25, rather than ±1, so that the A pattern will produce the right magnitude, as well as the right sign, for the activations of the units in the B pattern. The same connections are reproduced in matrix form in Figure 13A.

Pattern associators like the one in Figure 12 have a number of nice properties. One is that they do not require a perfect copy of the input to produce the correct output, though its strength will be weaker in this case. For example, suppose that the associator shown in Figure 12 were presented with an A pattern of (1,−1,0,1). This is the A pattern shown in the figure, with the activation of one of its elements set to 0. The B pattern produced in response will have the activations of all of the B units in the right direction; however, they will be somewhat weaker than they would be. had the complete A pattern been shown. Similar

	+1	−1	−1	+1	
	−.25	+.25	+.25	−.25	−1
	−.25	+.25	+.25	−.25	−1
	+.25	−.25	−.25	+.25	+1
	+.25	−.25	−.25	+.25	+1

	−1	+1	−1	+1	
	+.25	−.25	+.25	−.25	−1
	−.25	+.25	−.25	+.25	+1
	−.25	+.25	−.25	+.25	+1
	+.25	−.25	+.25	−.25	−1

FIGURE 13. Two simple associators represented as matrices. The weights in the first two matrices allow the A pattern shown above the matrix to produce the B pattern shown to the right of it. Note that the weights in the first matrix are the same as those shown in the diagram in Figure 12

```
[ - + + - ]   [ - + - + ]   [       ++  -- ]
[ + + + - ] + [ + - + + ] = [ --        ++ ]
[ - + - - ]   [ - + - + ]   [       --  ++ ]
[ + - - + ]   [ + - + - ]   [ ++        -- ]
```

FIGURE 14. The weights in the third matrix allow either A pattern shown in Figure 13 to recreate the corresponding B pattern. Each weight in this case is equal to the sum of the weight for the A pattern and the weight for the B pattern, as illustrated.

It is very important to note that the information needed to use the Hebb rule to determine the value each connection should have is *locally available* at the connection. All a given connection needs to consider is the activation of the units on both sides of it. Thus, it would be possible to actually implement such a connection modulation scheme locally, in each connection, without requiring any programmer to reach into each connection and set it to just the right value.

It turns out that the Hebb rule as stated here has some serious limitations, and, to our knowledge, no theorists continue to use it in this simple form. More sophisticated connection modulation schemes have been proposed by other workers; most important among these are the delta rule, discussed extensively in Chapters 8 and 11; the competitive learning rule, discussed in Chapter 5; and the rules for learning in stochastic parallel models, described in Chapters 6 and 7. All of these learning rules have the property that they adjust the strengths of connections between units on the basis of information that can be assumed to be locally available to the unit. Learning, then, in all of these cases, amounts to a very simple process that can be implemented locally at each connection without the need for any overall supervision. Thus, these models which incorporate these learning rules train themselves to have the right interconnections in the course of processing the members of an ensemble of patterns.

Learning multiple patterns in the same set of interconnections. Up to now, we have considered how we might teach our pattern associator to associate the visual pattern for one object with a pattern for the aroma of the same object. Obviously, different patterns of interconnections between the A and B units are appropriate for causing the visual pattern for a different object to give rise to the pattern for its aroma. The same principles apply, however, and if we presented our pattern associator with the A and B patterns for steak, it would learn the right set of interconnections for that case instead (these are shown in Figure 13B). In fact, it turns out that we can actually teach the same pattern associator a number of different associations. The matrix representing the set of interconnections that would be learned if we taught the same pattern associator both the rose association and the steak association is shown in Figure 14. The reader can verify this by adding the two matrices for the individual patterns together. The reader can also verify that this set of connections will allow the rose A pattern to produce the rose B pattern, and the steak A pattern to produce the steak B pattern: when either input pattern is presented, the correct corresponding output is produced.

The examples used here have the property that the two different visual patterns are completely uncorrelated with each other. This being the case, the rose pattern produces no effect when the interconnections for the steak have been established, and the steak pattern produces no effect when the interconnections for the rose association are in effect. For this reason, it is possible to add together the pattern of interconnections for the rose association and the pattern for the steak association, and still be able to associate the sight of the steak with the smell of a steak and the sight of a rose with the smell of a rose. The two sets of interconnections do not interact at all.

One of the limitations of the Hebbian learning rule is that it can learn the connection strengths appropriate to an entire ensemble of patterns only when all the patterns are completely uncorrelated. This restriction does not, however, apply to pattern associators which use more sophisticated learning schemes.

Attractive properties of pattern associator models. Pattern associator models have the property that uncorrelated patterns do not interact with each other, but more similar ones do. Thus, to the extent that a new pattern of activation on the A units is similar to one of the old ones, it will tend to have similar effects. Furthermore, if we assume that learning the interconnections occurs in small increments, similar patterns will essentially reinforce the strengths of the links they share in common with other patterns. Thus, if we present the same pair of patterns over and over, but each time we add a little random noise to each element of each member of the pair, the system will automatically learn to associate the central tendency of the two patterns and will learn to ignore the noise. What will be stored will be an average of the similar patterns with the slight variations removed. On the other hand, when we present the system with completely uncorrelated patterns, they will not interact with each other in this way. Thus, the same pool of units can extract the central tendency of each of a number of pairs of unrelated patterns. This aspect of distributed models is exploited extensively in Chapters 17 and 25 on distributed memory and amnesia.

COME. These phenomena mirror those observed in the early phases of acquisition of control over past tenses in young children.

The generativity of the child's responses—the creation of regular past tenses of new verbs and the overregularization of the irregular verbs—has been taken as strong evidence that the child has induced the rule which states that the regular correspondence for the past tense in English is to add a final *ed* (Berko, 1958). On the evidence of its performance, then, the model can be said to have acquired the rule. However, no special rule-induction mechanism is used, and no special language-acquisition device is required. The model learns to behave in accordance with the rule, not by explicitly noting that most words take *ed* in the past tense in English and storing this rule away explicitly, but simply by building up a set of connections in a pattern associator through a long series of simple learning experiences. The same mechanisms of parallel distributed processing and connection modification which are used in a number of domains serve, in this case, to produce implicit knowledge tantamount to a linguistic rule. The model also provides a fairly detailed account of a number of the specific aspects of the error patterns children make in learning the rule. In this sense, it provides a richer and more detailed description of the acquisition process than any that falls out naturally from the assumption that the child is building up a repertoire of explicit but inaccessible rules.

There is a lot more to be said about distributed models of learning, about their strengths and their weaknesses, than we have space for in this preliminary consideration. For now we hope mainly to have suggested that they provide dramatically different accounts of learning and acquisition than are offered by traditional models of these processes. We saw in earlier sections of this chapter that performance in accordance with rules can emerge from the interactions of simple, interconnected units. Now we can see how the acquisition of performance that conforms to linguistic rules can emerge from a simple, local, connection strength modulation process.

We have seen what the properties of PDP models are in informal terms, and we have seen how these properties operate to make the models do many of the kinds of things that they do. The business of the next chapter is to lay out these properties more formally, and to introduce some formal tools for their description and analysis. Before we turn to this, however, we wish to describe some of the major sources of inspiration for the PDP approach.

Extracting the structure of an ensemble of patterns. The fact that similar patterns tend to produce similar effects allows distributed models to exhibit a kind of spontaneous generalization, extending behavior appropriate for one pattern to other similar patterns. This property is shared by other PDP models, such as the word perception model and the Jets and Sharks model described above; the main difference here is in the existence of simple, local, learning mechanisms that can allow the acquisition of the connection strengths needed to produce these generalizations through experience with members of the ensemble of patterns. Distributed models have another interesting property as well. If there are regularities in the correspondences between pairs of patterns, the model will naturally extract these regularities. This property allows distributed models to acquire patterns of interconnections that lead them to behave in ways we would ordinarily take as evidence for the use of linguistic rules.

A detailed example of such a model is described in Chapter 18. Here, we describe the model very briefly. The model is a mechanism that learns how to construct the past tenses of words from their root forms through repeated presentations of examples of root forms paired with the corresponding past-tense form. The model consists of two pools of units. In one pool, patterns of activation representing the phonological structure of the root form of the verb can be represented, and, in the other, patterns representing the phonological structure of the past tense can be represented. The goal of the model is simply to learn the right connection strengths between the root units and the past-tense units, so that whenever the root form of a verb is presented the model will construct the corresponding past-tense form. The model is trained by presenting the root form of the verb as a pattern of activation over the root units, and then using a simple, local, learning rule to produce the correct pattern of activation over the past-tense units. The model is tested by simply presenting the root form as a pattern of activation over the root units and examining the pattern of activation produced over the past-tense units.

The model is trained initially with a small number of verbs children learn early in the acquisition process. At this point in learning, it can only produce appropriate outputs for inputs that it has explicitly been shown. But as it learns more and more verbs, it exhibits two interesting behaviors. First, it produces the standard *ed* past tense when tested with pseudo-verbs or verbs it has never seen. Second, it "overregularizes" the past tense of irregular words it previously completed correctly. Often, the model will blend the irregular past tense of the word with the regular *ed* ending, and produce errors like *CAMED* as the past of

ORIGINS OF PARALLEL DISTRIBUTED PROCESSING

The ideas behind the PDP approach have a history that stretches back indefinitely. In this section, we mention briefly some of the people who have thought in these terms, particularly those whose work has had an impact on our own thinking. This section should not be seen as an authoritative review of the history, but only as a description of our own sources of inspiration.

Some of the earliest roots of the PDP approach can be found in the work of the unique neurologists, Jackson (1869/1958) and Luria (1966). Jackson was a forceful and persuasive critic of the simplistic localizationist doctrines of late nineteenth century neurology, and he argued convincingly for distributed, multilevel conceptions of processing systems. Luria, the Russian psychologist and neurologist, put forward the notion of the *dynamic functional system*. On this view, every behavioral or cognitive process resulted from the coordination of a large number of different components, each roughly localized in different regions of the brain, but all working together in dynamic interaction. Neither Hughlings-Jackson nor Luria is noted for the clarity of his views, but we have seen in their ideas a rough characterization of the kind of parallel distributed processing system we envision.

Two other contributors to the deep background of PDP were Hebb (1949) and Lashley (1950). We already have noted Hebb's contribution of the Hebb rule of synaptic modification; he also introduced the concept of cell assemblies—a concrete example of a limited form of distributed processing—and discussed the idea of reverberation of activation within neural networks. Hebb's ideas were cast more in the form of speculations about neural functioning than in the form of concrete processing models, but his thinking captures some of the flavor of parallel distributed processing mechanisms. Lashley's contribution was to insist upon the idea of distributed representation. Lashley may have been too radical and too vague, and his doctrine of equipotentiality of broad regions of cortex clearly overstated the case. Yet many of his insights into the difficulties of storing the "engram" locally in the brain are telling, and he seemed to capture quite precisely the essence of distributed representation in insisting that "there are no special cells reserved for special memories" (Lashley, 1950, p. 500).

In the 1950s, there were two major figures whose ideas have contributed to the development of our approach. One was Rosenblatt (1959, 1962) and the other was Selfridge (1955). In his *Principles of Neurodynamics* (1962), Rosenblatt articulated clearly the promise of a neurally inspired approach to computation, and he developed the *perceptron convergence procedure*, an important advance over the Hebb rule for changing synaptic connections. Rosenblatt's work was very controversial at the time, and the specific models he proposed were not up to all the hopes he had for them. But his vision of the human information processing system as a dynamic, interactive, self-organizing system lies at the core of the PDP approach. Selfridge's contribution was his insistence on the importance of interactive processing, and the development of *Pandemonium*, an explicitly computational example of a dynamic, interactive mechanism applied to computational problems in perception.

In the late 60s and early 70s, serial processing and the von Neumann computer dominated both psychology and artificial intelligence, but there were a number of researchers who proposed neural mechanisms which capture much of the flavor of PDP models. Among these figures, the most influential in our work have been J. A. Anderson, Grossberg, and Longuet-Higgins. Grossberg's mathematical analysis of the properties of neural networks led him to many insights we have only come to appreciate through extensive experience with computer simulation, and he deserves credit for seeing the relevance of neurally inspired mechanisms in many areas of perception and memory well before the field was ready for these kinds of ideas (Grossberg, 1978). Grossberg (1976) was also one of the first to analyze some of the properties of the competitive learning mechanism explored in Chapter 5. Anderson's work differs from Grossberg's in insisting upon distributed representation, and in showing the relevance of neurally inspired models for theories of concept learning (Anderson, 1973, 1977); the work in Chapters 17 and 25 on distributed memory and amnesia owes a great deal to Anderson's inspiration. Anderson's work also played a crucial role in the formulation of the *cascade* model (McClelland, 1979), a step away from serial processing down the road to PDP. Longuet-Higgins and his group at Edinburgh were also pursuing distributed memory models during the same period, and David Willshaw, a member of the Edinburgh group, provided some very elegant mathematical analyses of the properties of various distributed representation schemes (Willshaw, 1981). His insights provide one of the sources of the idea of coarse coding described at length in Chapter 3. Many of the contributions of Anderson, Willshaw, and others distributed modelers may be found in Hinton and Anderson (1981). Others who have made important contributions to learning in PDP models include Amari (1977a), Bienenstock, Cooper, and Munro (1982), Fukushima (1975), Kohonen (1977, 1984), and von der Malsburg (1973).

Toward the middle of the 1970s, the idea of parallel processing began to have something of a renaissance in computational circles. We have already mentioned the Marr and Poggio (1976) model of stereoscopic the nature of the enterprise we are all involved in, and that it does justice to the potential of the PDP approach.

ACKNOWLEDGMENTS

This research was supported by Contract N00014-79-C-0323, NR 667-437 with the Personnel and Training Research Programs of the Office of Naval Research, by grants from the System Development Foundation, and By a NIMH Career Development Award (MH00385) to the first author.

depth perception. Another model from this period, the *HEARSAY* model of speech understanding, played a prominent role in the development of our thinking. Unfortunately, HEARSAY's computational architecture was too demanding for the available computational resources, and so the model was not a computational success. But its basically parallel, interactive character inspired the interactive model of reading (Rumelhart, 1977), and the interactive activation model of word recognition (McClelland & Rumelhart, 1981; Rumelhart & McClelland, 1982).

The ideas represented in the interactive activation model had other precursors as well. Morton's *logogen* model (Morton, 1969) was one of the first models to capture concretely the principle of interaction of different sources of information, and Marslen-Wilson (e.g., Marslen-Wilson & Welsh, 1978) provided important empirical demonstrations of interaction between different levels of language processing. Levin's (1976) *Proteus* model demonstrated the virtues of activation-competition mechanisms, and Glushko (1979) helped us see how conspiracies of partial activations could account for certain aspects of apparently rule-guided behavior.

Our work also owes a great deal to a number of colleagues who have been working on related ideas in recent years. Many of these colleagues appear as authors or coauthors of chapters in this book. But there are others as well. Several of these people have been very influential in the development of the ideas in this book. Feldman and Ballard (1982) laid out many of the computational principles of the PDP approach (under the name of *connectionism*), and stressed the biological implausibility of most of the prevailing computational models in artificial intelligence. Hofstadter (1979, 1985) deserves credit for stressing the existence of a subcognitive—what we call microstructural—level, and pointing out how important it can be to delve into the microstructure to gain insight. A sand dune, he has said, is not a grain of sand. Others have contributed crucial technical insights. Sutton and Barto (1981) provided an insightful analysis of the connection modification scheme we call the *delta rule* and illustrated the power of the rule to account for some of the subtler properties of classical conditioning. And Hopfield's (1982) contribution of the idea that network models can be seen as seeking minima in energy landscapes played a prominent role in the development of the Boltzmann machine (Chapter 7), and in the crystallization of the ideas presented in Chapters 7 and 14 on harmony theory and schemata.

The power of parallel distributed processing is becoming more and more apparent, and many others have recently joined in the exploration of the capabilities of these mechanisms. We hope this book represents

Précis of *The Modularity of Mind*

Jerry A. Fodor
*Department of Psychology, Massachusetts Institute of Technology,
Cambridge, Mass. 02139*

Abstract: *The Modularity of Mind* proposes an alternative to the "New Look" or "interactionist" view of cognitive architecture that has dominated several decades of cognitive science. Whereas interactionism stresses the continuity of perceptual and cognitive processes, modularity theory argues for their distinctness. It is argued, in particular, that the apparent plausibility of New Look theorizing derives from the failure to distinguish between the (correct) claim that perceptual processes are *inferential* and the (dubious) claim that they are *unencapsulated*, that is, that they are arbitrarily sensitive to the organism's beliefs and desires. In fact, according to modularity theory, perceptual processes are computationally isolated from much of the background knowledge to which cognitive processes have access. The postulation of autonomous, domain-specific psychological mechanisms underlying perceptual integration connects modularity theory with the tradition of faculty psychology, in particular, with the work of Franz Joseph Gall. Some of these historical affinities, and some of the relations between faculty psychology and Cartesianism, are discussed in the book.

Keywords: Cartesianism; cognition; faculty psychology; interactionism; language; modularity; neuropsychology; perception; phrenology

Everybody knows that something is wrong. But it is uniquely the achievement of contemporary philosophy – indeed, it is uniquely the achievement of contemporary *analytical* philosophy – to have figured out just what it is. What is wrong is that not enough distinctions are being made. If only we made all the distinctions that there are, then we should all be as happy as kings. (Kings are notoriously *very* happy.)

The Modularity of Mind (henceforth *Modularity*) is a monograph much in the spirit of that diagnosis. I wanted to argue there (and will likewise argue here) that modern Cognitivism failed, early on, to notice a certain important distinction: roughly, a distinction between two ways in which computational processes can be "smart." Because it missed this distinction, Cognitivism failed to consider some models of mental architecture for which a degree of empirical support can be marshaled, models that may, indeed, turn out to be true. If these models *are* true, then standard accounts of the nature of cognition and perception – and of the relations between them – are seriously misled, with consequences that can be felt all the way from artificial intelligence to epistemology. That was my story, and I am going to stick to it.

"What," you will ask, "was this missed distinction; who missed it; and how did missing it lead to these horrendous consequences?" I offer a historical reconstruction in the form of a fairy tale. None of what follows actually happened, but it makes a good story and has an edifying moral.

So then: Once upon a time, there was a Wicked Behaviorist. He was, alas, a mingy and dogmatic creature of little humor and less poetry; but he did keep a clean attic. Each day, he would climb up to his attic and throw things out, for it was his ambition eventually to have *almost nothing in his attic at all.* (Some people whispered that this was his *only* ambition, that the Wicked Behav-

iorist was actually just a closet Ontological Purist. For all I know, they were right to whisper this.)

Anyhow, one day when the Wicked Behaviorist was upstairs cleaning out his attic, the following Very Interesting Thought occurred to him. "Look," he said to himself, "*I can do without perceptual processes.*" (Because he had been educated in Vienna, the Wicked Behaviorist usually thought in the formal mode. So what actually occurred to him was that he could do without a *theory* of perceptual processes. It comes to much the same thing.) "For," it continued to occur to him, "perceptual identification reduces without residue to discriminative responding. And discriminative responding reduces without residue to the manifestation of conditioned (as it might be, operant) reflexes. And the theory of conditioned reflexes reduces without residue to Learning Theory. So, though learning is one of the things that there are, perceptual processes are one of the things there aren't. There also aren't: The True, or The Beautiful, or Santa Claus, or Tinkerbell; and unicorns are metaphysically impossible and George Washington wore false teeth. So there. Grrr!" He really was a *very* Wicked Behaviorist.

Fortunately, however, in the very same possible world in which the WB eked out a meager existence as a value of a bound variable (for who would call that living?), there was also a Handsome Cognitivist. And whereas the WB had this preference for clean attics and desert landscapes, the HC's motto was: "The more the merrier, more or less!" It was the HC's view that almost nothing reduces to almost anything else. To say that the world is so full of a number of things was, he thought, putting it mildly; for the HC, every day was like Christmas in Dickens, ontologically speaking. In fact, far from wishing to throw old things out, he was mainly interested in turning new things up. "Only collect," the HC was often heard to say.

Above all – and this is why I'm telling you this story – the HC wanted mental processes in general, and perceptual processes in particular, to be part of his collection.

Moreover, the HC had an argument. "Perceptual processes," he said, *"can't* be reflexes because, whereas reflexes are paradigmatically dumb, perceptual processes are demonstrably smart. Perception is really a part of cognition; it involves a kind of *thinking.*"[1]

"And what demonstrates that perceptual processes are smart?" grumbled the Wicked Behaviorist.

"I will tell you," answered the Handsome Cognitivist. "What demonstrates that perceptual processes are smart is *Poverty of The Stimulus Arguments.*" [A Poverty of The Stimulus Argument alleges that there is typically *more information* in a perceptual response than there is in the proximal stimulus that prompts the response; hence perceptual integration must somehow involve the *contribution* of information by the perceiving organism. [See Chomsky: "Rules and Representations" *BBS* 3(1) 1980.] No one knows how to quantify the relevant notion of information, so it is hard to show conclusively that this sort of argument is sound. On the other hand, such phenomena as the perceptual constancies have persuaded almost everybody – except Gibsonians and Wicked Behaviorists [see Ullman: "Against Direct Perception" *BBS* 3(3) 1980, and Rachlin: "Pain and Behavior," this issue) – that Poverty of The Stimulus Arguments have to be taken very seriously. I shall assume, in what follows, that that is so.] "Poverty of The Stimulus Arguments," continued the HC, "show that perceptual identifications can't be reflexive responses to proximal stimulus invariants. In fact, Poverty of The Stimulus Arguments strongly suggest that perceptual identifications depend on some sort of *computations*, perhaps on computations of quite considerable complexity. So, once we have understood the force of Poverty of The Stimulus Arguments, we see that there probably are perceptual processes after all." "And," the HC added in a rush, "I believe that there are Truth and Beauty and Santa Claus and Tinkerbell too (only you have to read the existential quantifier leniently). And I believe that for each drop of rain that falls / A flower is born. So *there.*" (Some people whispered that the Handsome Cognitivist, though he was *very* handsome, was perhaps just a little wet. For all I know, they were right to whisper that, too.) End of fairy tale.

My point is this: Modern Cognitivism starts with the use of Poverty of The Stimulus Arguments to show that perception is smart, hence that perceptual identification can't be reduced to reflexive responding. However – and I think this is good history and not a fairy tale at all – in their enthusiasm for this line of argument, early Cognitivists failed to distinguish between two quite different respects in which perceptual processes might be smarter than reflexes. Or, to put it the other way around, they failed to distinguish between two respects in which perception might be similar to cognition. It's at precisely this point that *Modularity* seeks to insert its wedge.

Reflexes, it is traditionally supposed, are dumb in two sorts of ways: They are *noninferential* and they are *encapsulated.*[2] To say that they are noninferential is just to say that they are supposed to depend on "straight-through" connections. On the simplest account, stimuli elicit reflexive responses directly, without mediating mental processing. It is my view that the HC was right about

perceptual processes and reflexive ones being different in *this* respect; Poverty of The Stimulus Arguments do make it seem plausible that a lot of inference typically intervenes between a proximal stimulus and a perceptual identification.

By contrast, to describe reflexes as encapsulated is to say that they go off largely without regard to the beliefs and utilities of the behaving organism; to a first approximation, all that you need do to evoke a reflex is to present the appropriate eliciting stimulus. Here's how *Modularity* put this point:

> Suppose that you and I have known each other for many a long year . . . and you have come fully to appreciate the excellence of my character. In particular, you have come to know perfectly well that under no conceivable circumstances would I stick my finger in your eye. Suppose that this belief of yours is both explicit and deeply felt. You would, in fact, go to the wall for it. Still, if I jab my finger near enough to your eyes, and fast enough, you'll blink. . . . [The blink reflex] has no access to what you know about my character or, for that matter, to any other of your beliefs, utilities [or] expectations. For this reason the blink reflex is often produced when sober reflection would show it to be uncalled for. . . . (p. 71)

In this respect reflexes are quite unlike a lot of "higher cognitive" behavior, or so it would certainly seem. Chess moves, for example, aren't elicited willy-nilly by presentations of chess problems. Rather, the player's moves are determined by the state of his utilities (is he trying to win? or to lose? or is he, perhaps, just fooling around?) and by his beliefs, including his beliefs about the current state of the game, his beliefs about the structure of chess and the likely consequences of various patterns of play, his beliefs about the beliefs and utilities of his opponent, his beliefs about the beliefs of his opponent about *his* beliefs and utilities, and so on up through ever so many orders of intentionality.

So, then, cognition is smart in two ways in which reflexes are dumb. Now the question arises: What is *perception* like in these respects? *Modularity* offers several kinds of arguments for what is, really, a main thesis of the book: Although perception is smart like cognition in that it is typically inferential, it is nevertheless dumb like reflexes in that it is typically encapsulated. Perhaps the most persuasive of these arguments – certainly the shortest – is one that adverts to the persistence of perceptual illusions. The apparent difference in length of the Mueller–Lyer figures, for example, doesn't disappear when one learns that the arrows are in fact the same size. It seems to follow that at least *some* perceptual processes are insensitive to at least some of one's beliefs. Very much wanting the Mueller–Lyer illusion to go away doesn't make it disappear either; it seems to follow that at least some perceptual processes are insensitive to at least some of one's utilities. The ecological good sense of this arrangement is surely self-evident. Prejudiced and wishful seeing makes for dead animals.

This sort of point seems pretty obvious; one might wonder how Cognitivist enthusiasm for "top down," "cognitively penetrated" perceptual models managed to survive in face of it. I think we have already seen part of the answer: Cognitivists pervasively confused the question about the encapsulation of perception with the question about its computational complexity. Because they believed – rightly – that Poverty of The Stimulus Arguments settled the second question, they never seriously considered the issues implicit in the first one. You can actually *see* this confusion being perpetrated in some of the early Cognitivist texts. The following passage is from Bruner's "On Perceptual Readiness":

Let it be plain that no claim is being made for the utter indistinguishability of perceptual and more conceptual inferences. . . . I may know that the Ames distorted room that looks so rectangular is indeed distorted, but unless conflicting cues are put into the situation . . . the room still looks rectangular. So too with such compelling illusions as the Mueller–Lyer: In spite of knowledge to the contrary, the line with the extended arrowheads looks longer than the equal-length line with arrowheads inclined inward. *But these differences, interesting in themselves, must not lead us to overlook the common feature of inference underlying so much of cognitive activity.* (Bruner 1973, p. 8; emphasis added)

The issue raised by the persistence of illusion is not, however, whether some inferences are "more conceptual" than others – whatever, precisely, that might mean. Still less is it whether perception is in some important sense inferential. Rather, what's at issue is: How rigid is the boundary between the information available to cognitive processes and the information available to perceptual ones? How much of what you know/believe/desire actually does affect the way you see? The persistence of illusion suggests that the answer must be: "at most, less than all of it."

So far, my charge has been that early Cognitivism missed the distinction between the inferential complexity of perception and its cognitive penetrability. But, of course, it's no accident that it was just that distinction that Cognitivists confused. Though they are independent properties of computational systems, inferential complexity and cognitive penetrability are intimately related – so intimately that, unless one is *very* careful, it's easy to convince oneself that the former actually entails the latter. [For discussion see Pylyshyn: "Computation and Cognition"*BBS* 3(1) 1980.]

What connects inferential complexity and cognitive penetrability is the truism that inferences need premises. Here's how the argument might seem to go: Poverty of The Stimulus Arguments show that the organism must contribute information to perceptual integrations; "perceptual inferences" just *are* the computations that effect such contributions. Now, this information that the organism contributes – the premises, as it were, of its perceptual inferences – must include not just sensory specifications of current proximal inputs but also "background knowledge" drawn from prior experience or innate endowment; for what Poverty of The Stimulus Arguments show is precisely that sensory information alone underdetermines perceptual integrations. But, surely, the availability of background knowledge to processes of perceptual integration *is* the cognitive penetration of perception. So if perception is inferentially elaborated, it *must* be cognitively penetrated. Q.E.D.

What's wrong with this argument is that it depends on what one means by cognitive penetration. One might mean the availability to perceptual integration of some

information not given in the proximal array. Because Poverty of The Stimulus Arguments show that some such information must be available to perceptual integration, it follows that to accept Poverty of The Stimulus Arguments is to accept the cognitive penetrability of perception *in this sense*. But one might also mean by the cognitive penetrability of perception that *anything that the organism knows, any information that is accessible to any of its cognitive processes*, is ipso facto available as a premise in perceptual inference. This is a much more dramatic claim; it implies the *continuity* of perception with cognition. And, if it is true, it has all sorts of interesting epistemic payoff (see Fodor 1984). Notice, however, that this stronger claim does not follow from the inferential complexity of perception.

Why not? Well, for the following boring reason. We can, in principle, imagine three sorts of architectural arrangements in respect of the relations between cognition and perception: *no* background information is available to perceptual integration; *some but not all* background information is available to perceptual integration; *everything one knows* is available to perceptual integration. Because Poverty of The Stimulus Arguments imply the inferential elaboration of perception, and because inferences need premises, the first of these architectures is closed to the Cognitivist. But the second and third are still open, and the persistence of illusions is prima facie evidence that the second is the better bet.

We arrive, at last, at the notion of a psychological module. A module is (inter alia) an informationally encapsulated computational system – an inference-making mechanism whose access to background information is constrained by general features of cognitive architecture, hence relatively rigidly and relatively permanently constrained. One can conceptualize a module as a special-purpose computer with a proprietary database, under the conditions that: (a) the operations that it performs have access *only* to the information in its database (together, of course, with specifications of currently impinging proximal stimulations); and (b) at least some information that is available to at least some cognitive process is *not* available to the module. It is a main thesis of *Modularity* that perceptual integrations are typically performed by computational systems that are informationally encapsulated in this sense.

Modularity has two other main theses, which I might as well tell you about now. The first is that, although informational encapsulation is an essential property of modular systems, they also tend to exhibit other psychologically interesting properties. The notion of a module thus emerges as a sort of "cluster concept," and the claim that perceptual processes are modularized implies that wherever we look at the mechanisms that effect perceptual integration we see that this cluster of properties tends to recur. The third main thesis is that, whereas perceptual processes are typically modularized – hence encapsulated, hence stupid in one of the ways that reflexes are – the really "smart," really "higher" cognitive processes (thinking, for example) are not modular and, in particular, not encapsulated. So *Modularity* advocates a *principled distinction* between perception and cognition in contrast to the usual Cognitivist claims for their continuity.

Since *Modularity* goes into all of this in some detail, I

don't propose to do so here; otherwise, why would you buy the book? But I do want to stress the plausibility of the picture that emerges. On the one hand, there are the perceptual processes; these tend to be input driven, very fast, mandatory, superficial, encapsulated from much of the organism's background knowledge, largely organized around bottom-to-top information flow, largely innately specified (hence ontogenetically eccentric), and characteristically associated with specific neuroanatomical mechanisms (sometimes even with specific neuroanatomical loci). They tend also to be domain specific, so that – to cite the classic case – the computational systems that deal with the perception/production of language appear to have not much in common with those that deal with, for example, the analysis of color or of visual form (or, for that matter, the analysis of nonspeech auditory signals). So strikingly are these systems autonomous that they often rejoice in their proprietary, domain-specific pathologies: compare the aphasias and agnosias. *Modularity* takes the view that it is high time to praise Franz Joseph Gall for having predicted the existence of psychological mechanisms that exhibit this bundle of properties. (Gall was approximately a contemporary of Jane Austen's, so you see how far we have come in cognitive psychology – and in the novel, for that matter.) It is precisely in the investigation of these "vertical faculties" that modern Cognitivism has contributed its most important insights, and *Modularity* suggests that this is no accident. Precisely because the perceptual mechanisms are encapsulated, we can make progress in studying them without having to commit ourselves about the general nature of the cognitive mind.

On the other hand, there are the true higher cognitive faculties. So little is known about them that one is hardput even to say *which* true higher cognitive faculties there are. But "thought" and "problem solving" are surely among the names in the game, and here *Modularity*'s line is that these are everything that perception is not: slow, deep, global rather than local, largely under voluntary (or, as one says, "executive") control, typically associated with diffuse neurological structures, neither bottom-to-top nor top-to-bottom in their modes of processing, but characterized by computations in which information flows every which way. Above all, they are paradigmatically *un*encapsulated; the higher the cognitive process, the more it turns on the integration of information across superficially dissimilar domains. *Modularity* assumes that in this respect the higher cognitive processes are notably similar to processes of scientific discovery – indeed, that the latter are the former writ large. Both, of course, are deeply mysterious; we don't understand nondemonstrative inference in either its macrocosmic or its microcosmic incarnation.

If much of the foregoing is right, then mainstream Cognitive science has managed to get the architecture of the mind *almost exactly backwards*. By emphasizing the continuity of cognition with perception, it missed the computational encapsulation of the latter. By attempting to understand thinking in terms of a baroque proliferation of scripts, plans, frames, schemata, special-purpose heuristics, expert systems, and other species of domain-specific intellectual automatisms – jumped-up habits, to put it in a nutshell – it missed what is most characteristic, and most puzzling, about the higher cognitive mind: its

nonencapsulation, its creativity, its holism, and its passion for the analogical. One laughs or weeps according to one's temperament. It was, perhaps, Eeyore who found precisely the right words: "'Pathetic,' he said, 'That's what it is, pathetic.'"

Well, yes, but *is* much of this right? I want at least to emphasize its plausibility from several different points of view. Perception is above all concerned with keeping track of the state of the organism's local spatiotemporal environment. Not the distant past, not the distant future, and not – except for ecological accidents like stars – what is very far away. Perception is built to detect what is right here, right now – what is available, for example, for eating or being eaten by. If this is indeed its teleology, then it is understandable that perception should be performed by fast, mandatory, encapsulated, . . . etc. systems that – considered, as it were, detection-theoretically – are prepared to trade false positives for high gain. It is, no doubt, important to attend to the enternally beautiful and to believe the eternally true. But it is more important not to be eaten.

Why, then, isn't perception even stupider, even less inferential than it appears to be? Why doesn't it consist of literally reflexive responses to proximal stimulations? Presumably because there is so much more variability in the proximal projections that an organism's environment offers to its sensory mechanisms than there is in the distal environment itself. This kind of variability is by definition irrelevant if it is the distal environment that you care about – which, of course, it almost always is. So the function of perception, from this vantage point, is to propose to thought a representation of the world from which such irrelevant variability has been effectively filtered. What perceptual systems typically "know about" is how to infer current distal layouts from current proximal stimulations: the visual system, for example, knows how to derive distal form from proximal displacement, and the language system knows how to infer the speaker's communicative intentions from his phonetic productions. Neither mechanism, on the present account, knows a great deal else, and that is entirely typical of perceptual organization. Perceptual systems have access to (implicit or explicit) theories of the mapping between distal causes and proximal effects. But that's all they have.

If the perceptual mechanisms are indeed local, stupid, and extremely nervous, it is teleologically sensible to have the picture of the world that they present tempered, reanalyzed, and – as Kant saw – above all *integrated* by slower, better informed, more conservative, and more holistic cognitive systems. The purposes of survival are, after all, *sometimes* subserved by knowing the truth. The world's deep regularities don't show in a snapshot, so being bullheaded, ignoring the facts that aren't visible on the surface – encapsulation in short – is not the cognitive policy that one wants to pursue *in the long run*. The surface plausibility of the *Modularity* picture thus lies in the idea that Nature has contrived to have it both ways, to get the best out of fast dumb systems *and* slow contemplative ones, by simply refusing to choose between them. That is, I suppose, the way that Nature likes to operate: "I'll have some of each" – one damned thing piled on top of another, and nothing in moderation, ever.

It will have occurred to you, no doubt, that Cognitivism could quite possibly have hit on the right doctrine, even if it did so for the wrong reasons. Whatever confusions may have spawned the idea that perception and cognition are continuous, and however plausible the encapsulation story may appear to be a priori, there is a lot of experimental evidence around that argues for the effects of background knowledge in perception. If the mind really is modular, those data are going to have to be explained away. I want to say just a word about this.

There are, pretty clearly, three conditions that an experiment has to meet if it is to provide a bona fide counter-instance to the modularity of a perceptual system.

1. It must, of course, demonstrate the influence of background information in some computation that the system performs. But, more particularly, the background information whose influence it demonstrates must be *exogenous* from the point of view of the module concerned. Remember, each module has its proprietary database; whatever information is in its database is ipso facto available to its computations. So, for example, it would be no use for purposes of embarrassing modularity theory to show that words are superior to nonwords in a speech perception task. Presumably, the language processing system has access to a grammar of the language that it processes, and a grammar must surely contain a lexicon. What words are in the language is thus one of the things that the language module can plausibly be assumed to know consonant with its modularity.

2. The effect of the background must be distinctively perceptual, not postperceptual and not a criterion shift. For example, it is of no use to demonstrate that utterances of "implausible" sentences are harder to process than utterances of "plausible" ones if it turns out that the mechanism of this effect is the hearer's inability to believe that the speaker could have said what it sounded like he said. No one in his right mind doubts that perception interacts with cognition *somewhere*. What's at issue in the disagreement between modularity theory and "New Look" Cognitivism (e.g., Bruner 1973) is the *locus* of this interaction. In practice, it usually turns out that the issue is whether the recruitment of background information in perception is *predictive*. Modularity theory says almost never; New Look Cognitivism says quite a lot of the time.

3. The cognitively penetrated system must be the one that shoulders the burden of perceptual analysis in normal circumstances, and not, for example, some backup, problem-solving type of mechanism that functions only when the stimulus is too degraded for a module to cope with. Therefore, it is of no use to show that highly redundant lexical items are easier to understand than less redundant ones when the speech signal is very noisy – unless, of course, you can also show that the perception of very noisy speech really is bona fide speech perception.

So far as I know, there is very little in the experimental literature that is alleged to demonstrate the cognitive penetration of perception that meets all three of these conditions (to say nothing of replicability). This isn't to claim that such experiments cannot be devised or that, if devised, they might not prove that New Look Cognitivism is right after all. I claim only that, contrary to the textbook story, the empirical evidence for the continuity of perception with cognition is not overwhelming when contemplated with a jaundiced eye. There is, in any event, something for laboratory psychology to do for the

next twenty years or so: namely, try to develop some designs subtle enough to determine who's right about all this.

"But look," you might ask, "why do you care about modules so much? You've got tenure; why don't you take off and go sailing?" This is a perfectly reasonable question and one that I often ask myself. Answering it would require exploring territory that I can't get into here and raising issues that *Modularity* doesn't even broach. But roughly, and by way of striking a closing note: The idea that cognition saturates perception belongs with (and is, indeed, historically connected with) the idea in the philosophy of science that one's observations are comprehensively determined by one's theories; with the idea in anthropology that one's values are comprehensively determined by one's culture; with the idea in sociology that one's epistemic commitments, including especially one's science, are comprehensively determined by one's class affiliations; and with the idea in linguistics that one's metaphysics is comprehensively determined by one's syntax. All these ideas imply a sort of relativistic holism: because perception is saturated by cognition, observation by theory, values by culture, science by class, and metaphysics by language, rational criticism of scientific theories, ethical values, metaphysical world-views, or whatever can take place only *within* the framework of assumptions that – as a matter of geographical, historical, or sociological accident – the interlocutors happen to share. What you can't do is rationally criticize the framework.

The thing is: I *hate* relativism. I hate relativism more than I hate anything else, excepting, maybe, fiberglass powerboats. More to the point, I think that relativism is very probably false. What it overlooks, to put it briefly and crudely, is the fixed structure of human nature. (This is not, of course, a novel insight; on the contrary, the *malleability* of human nature is a doctrine that relativists are invariably much inclined to stress. See, for example, John Dewey in *Human Nature and Conduct* [1922].) Well, in cognitive psychology the claim that there is a fixed structure of human nature traditionally takes the form of an insistence on the the heterogeneity of cognitive mechanisms and on the rigidity of the cognitive architecture that effects their encapsulation. If there are faculties and modules, then not everything affects everything else; not everything is plastic. Whatever the All is, at least there is more than One of it.

These are, as you will have gathered, not issues to be decisively argued – or even perspicuously formulated – in the course of a paragraph or two. Suffice it that they seem to be the sorts of issues that our cognitive science ought to bear on. And they are intimately intertwined: surely, *surely*, no one but a relativist would drive a fiberglass powerboat.

Coming in our next installment: "Restoring Basic Values: Phrenology in an Age of License." Try not to miss it!

NOTES

1. See, for example, Gregory (1970, p. 30): "perception involves a kind of problem-solving; a kind of intelligence." For a more recent and comprehensive treatment that runs along the same lines, see Rock (1983).

2. I don't at all care whether these "traditional assumptions" about reflexes are in fact correct, or even whether they were traditionally assumed. What I want is an ideal type with which to compare perception and cognition.

Chapter 2
Representation

Semantic Memory and Spreading Activation

The Quillian paper introduced the notion of a *semantic network* as a formalism for representing concepts. Along with this representation, Quillian proposed *spreading activation* (or *marker passing*) as a means for searching a semantic network. A semantic network went beyond a simple associative network (familiar to many psychologists) in that it permitted different kinds of relations, or links, which were labeled differentially. Labeled links are critical in using the network to answer questions. These ideas proved seminal in both artificial intelligence and cognitive psychology, and inspired a host of models in both fields.

The use of labeled links was not without its problems, and Woods directly attacked some of these in his paper. Woods' goal was to systematize the way links are used in semantic networks. This effort led to substantial work on knowledge representation in artificial intelligence, such as KL-ONE where the goal was to develop a small set of link types that were used in systematic ways (see Brachman, R. J. & Smolze, J. G. (1985). An overview of the KL-ONE knowledge representation system. *Cognitive Science*, *9*, 171–216).

Semantic networks were soon introduced into psychology (see Collins, A. & Quillian, M. R. (1969) Retrieval time from semantic memory, *Journal of Verbal Learning and Verbal Behavior, 8*, 240–248). These theoretical ideas stimulated a host of studies on *semantic memory*—roughly, people's knowledge about word meanings and about the basic facts of the world. A typical experiment required that subjects determine as quickly as possible the truth value of propositions like *A canary has wings*, and then related the decision times to an underlying semantic-network model. Much of this work is reviewed in the Collins and Loftus paper, which argues that empirical findings can be accounted for in terms of the formalisms originally proposed by Quillian.

Of course, much of the knowledge we have in memory is not about general information, but rather consists of personal episodes and is accordingly referred to as *episodic memory* by psychologists. It turns out, however, that the propositions constituting episodic knowledge can also be represented by a "semantic" network. This possibility is amply demonstrated in the Anderson selection, where Anderson develops a quantitative version of a spreading-activation model, and shows that this model can account for a variety of experimental findings. The semantic network and spreading-activation process described in this selection form a major part of Anderson's ACT model; another component of this model, the production system, is described in the Anderson paper in Part 4, *Learning*.

4. Semantic Memory

M. Ross Quillian

4.1 The Role of Semantic Memory

The central question asked in this research has been: What constitutes a reasonable view of how semantic information is organized within a person's memory? In other words: What sort of representational format can permit the "meanings" of words to be stored, so that humanlike use of these meanings is possible? In the next section an answer to this question is proposed in the form of a complicated but precisely specified model of such a memory structure. The test of this model is its ability to shed light on the various types of behavior dependent on semantic memory, preferably both by accounting for known phenomena and by generating new research data. The model's use in explicating various memory-dependent behaviors will be considered.

The first of these memory-dependent tasks is relatively straightforward: to compare and contrast the meanings of two familiar English words. The first half of this chapter will show that a computer memory, containing information organized as the model dictates, can provide a reasonable simulation of some aspects of human capability at this task. One program, given pairs of English words, locates relevant semantic information within the model memory, draws inferences on the basis of this, and thereby discovers various relationships between the meanings of the two words. Finally, it creates English text to express its conclusions. The design principles embodied in the mem-

*Recent follow-up work to the research reported in this chapter is described in Quillian, R., "The Teachable Language Comprehender: A Program to Understand English," to be published in a forthcoming issue of *Communications of the Association for Computing Machinery*.

ory model, together with some of the methods used by the program, constitute one theoretical view of how human memory for semantic and perhaps other conceptual material may be represented, organized, and used.

The second behavior investigated in the light of the same theoretical framework is very much more complex: the processing of English text done by a person during careful reading, and which will lead that person to report that he has to some extent "understood" the text. The second part of this chapter is devoted to showing how the representational format and memory model developed and used in the computer program can also serve, first as a methodological innovation to enable collection of new data about the process by which text is understood, and second as part of a theoretical explanation of how that process occurs. This section consists primarily of an analysis of one subject's "thinking aloud" protocol, collected as she performed a complex linguistic task.

4.1.1 Prior Literature: What is to be Stored in Semantic Memory

Literature relevant to the question of what semantic information is and how it may be stored and used in a person's brain includes a sizable portion of philosophy, a good part of psychology, some of linguistics, and much of that computer programming literature which deals with natural-language processing, list processing, or heuristic programs. In this chapter, therefore, prior works will be mentioned only as they help to clarify what our memory model is, or is not, intended to accomplish.

One issue facing the investigator of semantic memory is: exactly what is it about word meanings that is to be considered? First, the memory model here is designed to deal with exactly complementary kinds of meaning to that involved in Osgood's "semantic differential" (57). While the semantic differential is concerned with people's feelings in regard to words, or the words' possible emotive impact on others, this model is explicitly designed to represent the nonemotive, relatively "objective" part of meaning.

The next relevant distinction is between learning and performance. As a theory, this model does not deal directly with the acquisition of semantic information but only with what eventually results after a long period of such acquisition. The problem of how humans acquire long-term semantic concepts is simply finessed by having a trained adult (a "coder") build the memory model primarily by hand.

The model is designed to enable representation and storage of any and all of the nonemotive parts of word meanings, of the sort presumably responsible for the fact that a conditioned response to a word generalizes more readily to words close to it in meaning than to words close in sound (for example, from "style" to "fashion" more readily than from "style" to "stile," 15, 68). More important, the model seeks to represent the memory that a person continuously calls upon in his everyday language behavior.

The memory most generally involved in language is what one might call "recognition memory" as distinguished from "recall memory." For example, if a reader is told that the word "the" can mean "her," he may not immediately *recall* how this can be so. However, if he encounters text that says, "I took my wife by the hand," he will have no hesitation in recognizing what "the" means. It is this sort of recognition capability, not, in general, recall, that a store of semantic information must support, and that is the exclusive concern of this paper. Since one ready source of such semantic information is an ordinary dictionary, a coder building this memory model takes much of his information from the dictionary. No less important, however, the coder will at the same time use common knowledge which he himself possesses and must use to read the dictionary material intelligently: the fund of knowledge that constitutes his own semantic memory.

4.1.2 Semantic Memory in Psychology and Simulation Programs

Another historically important issue for memory is the use it makes of associative links. Early philosophical work on "verbal learning," and behavioristic accounts of performance such as Skinner's (77), all make the assumption, to one degree or another, that cognitive and memory structure consists of nothing more than an aggregate of associated elements. At the same time another tradition and body of work is based on the assumption that attributes and (often) "plans," make up the representational medium in which cognitive processes occur. The notion that attributes (*labeled associations*) are a key part of the thought medium was apparently first recognized and incorporated into a comprehensive theory by Otto Selz (see reference 18). This notion can be found well stated for clinical psychologists by Kelly (33), for psychologists concerned with concept formation by Bruner et al. (9), and in regard to emotive word meanings by Osgood et al. (57). The idea that plans form the key part of memory is classically expressed in the work of Bartlett (2), Piaget (61), Newell et al. (51), and Miller et al. (45). In this tradition, a "schema" is typically a combination of a plan and denotative data related to that plan. (For attempts to extend some of these approaches and to relate them to computer programs, see references 55, 66, and 71.)

It might be felt that the two assumptions cited are contradictory, that the cognitive medium must be either associative links or attributes and plans (cf. reference 13). However, Newell, Shaw, and Simon, attempting to model cognitive processing in a computer, developed a "language" (IPL) in which associative links, attributes, and plans are all homogeneously representable as data. IPL and later list-processing languages provide these, respectively, in the form of lists (items connected by undifferentiated associations), description lists (items connected by labeled associations, thereby forming attributes with values), and routines (equivalent to plans). (For a description of IPL see refer-

ence 52.) By constructing a memory model and program in one of these computer languages, it is possible, taking advantage of the substantial foundation of design and development existing in that language, to use associations, attributes, and plans freely as building blocks. Thus, in the programs called BASE-BALL (27), SAD-SAM (41), and STUDENT (6) the meanings of certain English words were in part stored as factual information, in part as plans. That this same flexibility prevails in human cognitive structure is also affirmed by sophisticated learning theorists (58).

Therefore, the issue with which a semantic model has to come to grips is not whether to use plans, attributes, *or* simply associations, but rather what particular *sorts* of these are to be used to represent word meanings, and exactly how all of them are to be interlinked.

However, while computer programs *allow* elaborate data structures, very few programs have been much concerned with the structure of long-term memory as such. There are exceptions: part of Simmons' "Synthex" project (74) constituted a thorough exploration of a straightforward approach, namely a memory consisting of verbatim text (bolstered by a complete word index). Simmons demonstrated that such a memory can be used to retrieve possibly relevant statements but not in general to answer questions by inference. Questions formulated within a cognitive orientation different from the one which the input text itself employed are difficult to answer reliably with such a memory. This points up a major goal for a model of semantic memory: the ability to use information input in one frame of reference to answer questions in another, or, what is the same thing, to *infer* from the memory as well as to retrieve parts of it verbatim.

Programs by Green et al. (27) and by Lindsay (41) explored the idea of using a memory organized as a single predefined hierarchy. Green's program showed that such a memory can be interrogated with natural-language questions, and Lindsay's demonstrated that this kind of memory organization can provide certain inference-making properties as long as information is confined to a single subject like a family tree. However, this kind of organization becomes uncomfortably rigid as larger amounts of material are considered and is clearly not a general enough organization for the diverse knowledge people know and utilize.

Actually, most simulation programs (including those of Green and Lindsay) have not been primarily concerned with long-term memory at all but rather with cognitive processing. (For surveys of simulation programs see reference 22 and especially reference 72. See also references 3, 6, 47, 48, 67, 75.) Raphael's SIR program (Chapter 2 of the present volume), creates a small specialized memory from input English sentences, but again is not primarily concerned with memory per se. Thus, the problems of what is to be contained in an over-all, humanlike permanent memory, what format this is to be in, and how this memory is to be organized have not been dealt with in great generality in prior simulation programs. Reitman's investigations of certain features of such memory structures constitute something of an exception (see Chapter 8 of reference 72). For a good survey of data bases used in question-answering programs, see reference 74.

In sum, relatively little work has been done toward simulating really general and large memory structures, especially structures in which newly input symbolic material would typically be put in relation to large quantities of previously stored information about the same kinds of things.

Further advances in simulating problem-solving and game playing (72), as well as language performance, will surely require programs that develop and interact with large memories.

4.1.3 Memory in Linguistic Theory

Current linguistic theories have minimized the role of a permanent memory even more than simulation programs. Transformational and, more generally, all "generation grammar" linguistics analyze language as the application of formal rules. These rules draw minimally on a lexicon (which amounts to a memory for various properties of words). In pp. 120ff. of Chomsky's work (11) as well as in the thesis of Lakoff (38), there are several proposals for expanding the role of such a lexicon; Katz et al. (31, 32) have suggested how a lexicon can be expanded to include semantic information. In addition, Lamb (39, see also reference 69) allocates one "level" in his "stratificational" view of language to semantic units (sememes) and asserts that these should be discovered by the same procedures that linguists have used to isolate phonemes.

However, in none of these cases has any real effort been made actually to set up a quantity of semantic material and see if it can be used. This is partly because linguists feel that what a person actually does with language is outside their jurisdiction. Chomsky, for instance, specifically divorces his theoretical model from considerations of how people actually deal with language, by insisting that he is modeling a completely abstract linguistic "competence," not the concrete performance of *any* one person, even an ideal one. Thus, "a generative grammar is not a model for a speaker or a hearer. It attempts to characterize in the most neutral possible terms the knowledge of the language that provides the basis for actual use of language by a speaker-hearer." However, this disclaimer is generally followed by an assertion to the effect that "no doubt, a reasonable model of language use will incorporate, as a basic component, the generative grammar that expresses the speaker-hearer's knowledge of the language . . ." (both quotes are from reference 11, p. 9. For an explicit attempt to clarify the relation of Chomsky's work to actual language performance, see reference 45).

Since transformational grammar is a powerful and relatively well-developed body of theory, Chomsky's assertion that such a grammar will be a "basic component" of a "reasonable model" is a strong one, and one that is now generating much psycholinguistic research (reference 40).

Given a familiarity with Chomsky's theoretical framework, it will be useful to ask how a model of memory should relate to it. The answer depends on whether a person's memory for semantic information, as conceived by linguists, is separate from his memory for other sorts of things, such as visually perceived facts, or whether, in contrast, it is part of a general memory which includes these.

If one assumes that semantic memory is strictly limited and separate from other memory, then the former may be allocated to the position expressed by Katz and Postal (32), who say:

The syntactic component is *fundamental* in the sense that the other two components both operate on its out-put. That is, *the syntactic component is the generative source* in the linguistic description. This component generates the abstract formal structures underlying actual sentences. . . . In such a tripartite theory of linguistic descriptions, certain *psychological claims* are made about the speaker's capacity to communicate fluently. The fundamental claim is that the fluent speaker's ability to use and understand speech involves a *basic* mechanism that enables him to construct the formal syntactic structures underlying the sentences which these utterances represent, and two *subsidiary* mechanisms: one that associates a set of meanings with each formal syntactic structure and another that maps such structures into phonetic representations, which are, in turn, the input to his speech apparatus (pp. 1-2, italics mine).

Several computer programs have been written that minimize or bypass the role of semantic knowledge in language. These programs generate sentences that are syntactically grammatical but whose meanings are either random (78) or random permutations of the "dependency" constraints imposed by an input text (34, 35).

On the other hand, if one assumes that memory for semantic material is no different from memory for any other kind of conceptual material, then this memory must take on a much more important role in language. Here it will be assumed that humans, in using language, draw upon and interact with the same memory in which their nonlinguistic information is stored. Under this assumption semantic memory is simply general memory and hence must be flexible enough to hold anything that can be stated in language, sensed in perception, or otherwise known and remembered. In particular, this includes facts and assertions as well as just objects and properties.

Further, under this assumption the semantic component becomes the primary factor in language rather than a "secondary" one subordinate to a separate syntactic component. To consider language production in this light is to put the intended message of the language in control of its format and to see

4.2 The Memory Model

4.2.1 Overview of the Model

The memory model consists basically of a mass of *nodes* interconnected by different kinds of *associative links*. Each node may for the moment be thought of as named by an English word, but by far the most important feature of the model is that a node may be related to the meaning (concept) of its name word in one of two ways. The first relates directly; i.e., its associative links may lead directly into a configuration of other nodes that represents the meaning of its name word. A node that does this is called a *type* node. In contrast, the second kind of node in the memory refers *indirectly* to a word concept by having one special kind of associative link that points to that concept's type node. Such a node is referred to as a *token node*, or simply *token*, although this usage implies more than is generally meant by a "token," since, within the memory model, a token is a permanent node. For any one word meaning there can be exactly one and only one type node in the memory, but there will in general be *many* token nodes scattered throughout the memory, each with a pointer to the same unique type node for the concept. To see the reason for postulating both type and token nodes within the memory, it will be useful to reflect briefly on the way words are defined in an ordinary dictionary.

To define one word, the dictionary builder always utilizes tokens of other words. However, it is not sufficient for the reader to consider the meaning of the defined word as simply an unordered aggregation of pointers to the other word concepts used in its definition. The configuration of these word concepts is crucial; it modifies the meanings of the individual word concepts that make up its parts and at the same time creates a new gestalt with them, which represents the meaning of the word being defined. In the memory model, ingredients used to build up a concept are represented by the token nodes naming other concepts, while the configurational meaning of the concept is represented by the particular structure of interlinkages connecting those token nodes to each other. It will be useful to think of the configuration of interlinked token nodes that represents a single concept as comprising one *plane* in the memory. Each and every token node in the entire memory lies in some such plane and has both its special associative link pointing "out of the plane" to its type node *and* other associative links pointing *within* the plane to other token nodes comprising the configuration. In short, token nodes make it possible for a word's meaning to be built up from other word meanings as ingredients and at the same time to modify and recombine these ingredients into a new configuration. Although we will not describe the detailed structure of a plane until part 4.2.2, it will be useful for understanding the model's over-all organization to examine Fig. 4-1 at this point.

Figure 4-1a illustrates the planes of three word concepts, corresponding to three meanings of "plant." The three circled words, "plant," "plant2," and

the reading of text as a continuous interaction between concepts that the text is currently discussing, the reader's general knowledge of the same concepts (part of which has been acquired through nonlinguistic sources), and what has already been stated about those concepts in the same text (or elsewhere by the same author). Making this kind of three-way interaction natural is therefore a chief aim of the model to be developed here.

This means that the memory model will correspond less to the proposed semantic lexicons of transformational theory than to what is called "deep structure." Thus, when this memory model is used in a program simulating language production, the program will contain something corresponding to transformational rules but nothing corresponding to phrase-structure rules. The reason for this is that the correspondents to phrase structure rules have been incorporated into the conventions specifying the structure of the memory itself (and there broadened almost to triviality). What remains of such rules would be relevant to a learning program, since this would involve building up new parts of the memory, but is not relevant to a program designed simply to use the memory and to express facts it implies in English text.

In other words, it is being proposed that, in people, language is never torn down into the "immediate constituents" that are utilized in rules of the familiar S → NP + VP sort. Instead, language is remembered, dealt with in thought, and united to nonlinguistic concepts in a form that looks like the *result* of phrase structure rules — what Chomsky calls the "base phrase marker" or "basis" of a sentence (reference 11, p. 17). The memory structure will differ from such a basis, or set of bases, in that it will not be divided into small structures, each associated with one sentence, but rather will be one enormous interlinked net. When part of this net is to be expressed in English text, division into sentences will be made by the text producer as convenient, rather than before this text producer begins to work.

While the memory model to be described corresponds most closely to the deep structures in transformational theory, it must at the same time serve the role that transformationalists allocate to a lexicon. The same memory structure to which language adds information during intake and from which it retrieves it during output is also used to interpret language that is read or heard.

The foregoing indicates in general terms the relation of the semantic memory model to linguistic theory, to other simulation programs, and to some common semantic notions. The next section explains the model itself as presently formalized in a computer program. The third section describes this program and its results. The fourth discusses a method for using the memory model to study how people understand sentences and introduces a set of data gathered in this way. The fifth, sixth, and seventh analyze these data, again relying primarily on the memory model, and the final section considers changes of the model that now seem indicated, as well as some implications of the model for a theory of human memory.

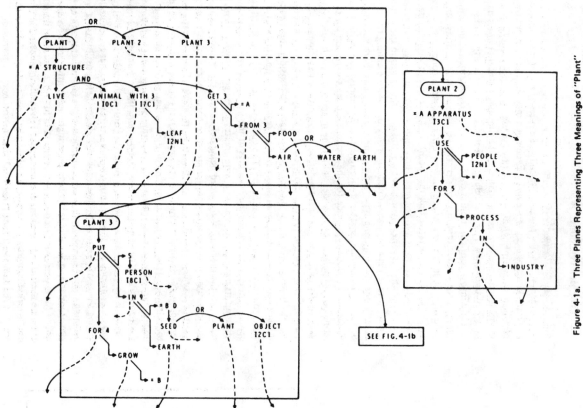

Figure 4-1a.   Three Planes Representing Three Meanings of "Plant"

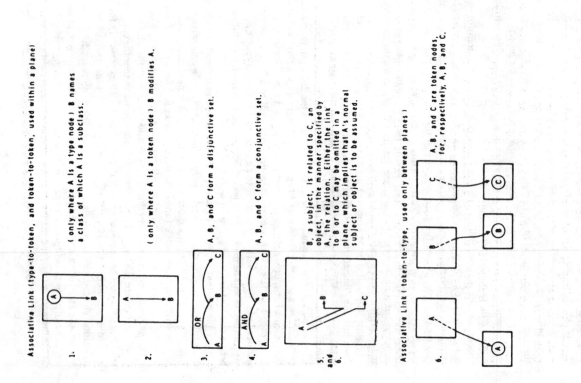

Figure 4-1.   Sample Planes from the Memory

"plan'3," placed at the heads (upper left-hand corners) of the three planes, represent type nodes; every other word shown in the Fig. 4-1a planes represents a resent type nodes. The nonterminated arrows from tokens indicate that each has its special pointer leading out of its plane to its type definition, i.e., to a type node standing at the head of its own plane somewhere else in the memory. Each of these planes, in turn, is itself entirely made up of tokens, except for the type word that heads it. Figure 4-1b illustrates one of these planes. Therefore, the over-all structure of the complete memory forms an enormous aggregation of planes, each consisting entirely of token nodes except for its "head" node, which is always a type node.

Now, what is the full content of a word concept in such a memory? Let us define a *full word concept*, as distinguished from its plane or "immediate definition," so as to include *all* the type and token nodes one can get to by starting at the initial type node, or patriarch, and moving first within its immediate definition plane to all the token nodes found there, then on "through" to the type nodes named by *each* of these nodes, then on to all the token nodes in each of *their* immediate definition planes, and so on until every token and type node that can be reached by this process has been traced through at least once.

Thus one may think of a full concept analogically as consisting of all the information one would have if he looked up what will be called the "patriarch" word in a dictionary, then looked up every word in each of its definitions, then looked up every word found in each of these, and so on, continually branching outward until every word he could reach by this process had been looked up once. However, since a word meaning includes structure as well as ingredients, one must think of the person doing the looking up as also keeping account of all the relationships in which each word encountered by him had been placed by all earlier definitions.

To summarize, *a word's full concept is defined in the memory model to be all the nodes that can be reached by an exhaustive tracing process, originating at its initial, patriarchical type node, together with the total sum of relationships among these nodes specified by within-plane, token-to-token links*.

Our thesis is that such a memory organization will be useful in performing semantic tasks and also constitute a reasonable description of the general organization of human memory for semantic material.

To illustrate the latter point immediately: Suppose that a subject were asked to state everything he knows about the concept "machine." Each statement he makes in answer is recorded, and when he decides he is finished, he is asked to elaborate further on each thing he has said. As he does so, these statements in turn are recorded, and upon his "completion" he is asked if he cannot elaborate further on each of these. In this way the subject clearly can be kept talking for several days, if not months, producing a voluminous body of information. This information will start off with the more "compelling" facts about machines, such as that they are usually man-made, involve moving parts, and so on, and will proceed "down" to less and less inclusive facts, such as the fact that typewriters are machines, and then eventually will get to much more remote information about machines, such as the fact that a typewriter has a stop which prevents its carriage from flying off each time it is returned. We are suggesting that this information can all usefully be viewed as part of the subject's concept of "machine." The order in which such a concept tends to be brought forth from general, inclusive facts to obscure or less and less closely related ones, suggests that the information comprising a word concept in the subject's memory is differentially accessible, forming something that may be viewed as a hierarchy beneath the patriarch word. Our memory model's general organization is designed to make a full concept exactly this sort of hierarchically ordered, extensive body of information. The model differs from the memory involved in this example in that we primarily wish to model recognition memory, not recall. Thus, we should actually present the subject with yes-no questions about facts pertaining to machines, rather than have him produce them. However, this could only increase the amount of information involved in a concept and wouldn't change the subject's feeling that some facts are "closer to the top" in the full concept of "machine" than are others.

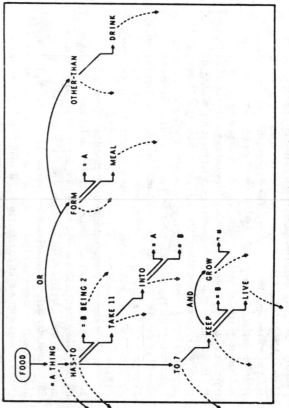

FOOD: 1. That which living being has to take in to keep it living and for growth. Things forming meals, especially other than drink

Figure 4-1b. The Plane Representing "Food"

Clearly a subject has hierarchical concepts similar to that for "machine" for innumerable other word-concepts, so that the over-all amount of information in his memory seems almost unlimited. The sheer quantity of information involved in such concepts argues strongly that both the human subject's memory and our model thereof contain as little redundancy as possible and that it contain stored facts only when these cannot otherwise be generated or inferred. In this regard we note that the information a subject has as the meaning of "machine" will include all the information he has as the meaning of "typewriter," among other things, and there is no need to restate the information constituting his concept of "typewriter" each time it occurs as part of the concept named by some other word, such as "machine," "office," and so on. In short, a word concept like "machine" seems to be made up in large part of a particular, ordered arrangement of other word concepts, such as "typewriter," "drill press," and so on.

Again, a large memory structured as outlined capitalizes on this redundancy by running the pointer from each and every token node for a word meaning to the *same* type node. Recall that in such a memory any given type node will have many token nodes, located in various other planes, all pointing to it, and *its* full concept may well contain token nodes pointing *back* to the type node that heads one of these planes. In other words, there is no restriction to prevent reentries or loops within a full concept, so that all routines that search through or process concepts in the memory must take account of these possibilities.

Viewed most abstractly, the memory model forms simply a large, very complex network of nodes and one-way associations between them. Most important, in such a model of semantic memory there is no predetermined hierarchy of superclasses and subclasses; *every* word is the patriarch of its own separate hierarchy *when some search process starts with it.* Similarly, every word lies at various places down within the hierarchies of (i.e., is an ingredient in) a great many other word concepts, when processing starts with them. Moreover, there are no word concepts as such that are "primitive." Everything is simply defined in terms of some ordered configuration of other things in the memory.

A memory organized in this fashion is incomplete, in that other kinds of human information storage and processing — spatio-visual imagery and reasoning, for example — would seem to require other sorts of stored information. It is conceivable that spatio-visual memory is stored in some completely different kind of structure from semantic information. However, it seems at least as reasonable to suppose that a single store of information underlies both "semantic" memory and "spatio-visual" memory: their difference being not in the structure of the information store, but rather in the way that the static information of that store is used. For example, suppose that a person's visual information is stored in the same interlinked network of nodes that we suggest underlies his language processing, but that he also has the ability to generate

visual imagery to represent this information directly, in order to reason spatially (reference 26). Conceiving of spatial reasoning in this way, with properties abstracted out of actual visual images for purposes of storage, would seem necessary to provide for the flexibility and freedom with which people are able to visually remember, imagine, etc.

Similarly, the ability to recognize objects perceived through the senses would require at least some additional kinds of linkage within a general network memory such as this one we are discussing. But, a network containing one-way associative links from an object's name to the set of properties of that object (as ours does now) would seem already to contain all the *nodes* needed to recognize a particular object given its sensed properties. What would additionally be required to perform perceptual recognition would be reverse links in the memory, plus a processor able to utilize these links for deciding which object a given stimulus array represented (21). A very close interaction between exposure to words and perceptual functioning in people has been thoroughly established (8, 15). Thus, again, it seems logical to suppose that the same static store of information that underlies semantic reasoning may underlie perception rather than that they rely on separate memory structures, even though such a memory would then have to be richer in interlinkages than that we shall utilize here.

These and other possible additional functions with a network memory are purely speculative at the present time, and will not be discussed further in the present work. (On a possible relation of the present program to the phenomena of perceptual "set," see Quillian et al. (66), pp. 34-36. On the use of spatio-visual imagery in reasoning, see, for example, reference 59.)

4.2.2 Details of the Memory Model

Having established the general structure of the memory model as consisting of "planes," each made up of one type node and a number of token nodes, it is further necessary to determine the format of the nodes themselves and the specific varieties of associative links between nodes to be used within a plane.

The most important constraint determining this arises from our assumption that in order to continue to parallel the properties of human semantic memory the model must be able to link nodes together into configurations that are at least as varied and rich as the ideas expressed in natural language. Hence, simply attempting to represent natural language definitions accurately in the model becomes a very powerful constraint dictating the model's structural properties. Over a lengthy period of attempts to encode English text into such network representations, it has always been found necessary to have available several different kinds of associative links rather than the simple undifferentiated associations assumed in most classical psychological studies of word association. At the same time the model must represent all information in a form sufficiently provide a way to take any *two* tokens and relate them by any third token, which by virtue of this use becomes a relationship.

Stated this way, it appears that the semantic model amounts in structure to a kind of parsing system and that encoding dictionary definitions into it is in part, at least, similar to parsing these definitions.

This is true, and what appears on one plane of the memory model has many points of correspondence with what Chomsky calls a "deep structure." In particular, the ternary relations formed by our subject-object links resemble the structure of what were called "kernel" sentences. However, our use of terms like "subject," "object," and "modifier" does not always correspond to that of linguistics, and also a plane encodes the meaning of a number of sentences, whereas a deep structure is explicitly limited to the representation of what can be represented in a single sentence (reference 11, pp. 138f). Also the correspondence, insofar as it exists, is between one of our planes and one of Chomsky's deep structures, not between a plane and a generative grammar. A generative grammar is an attempt to state explicitly *when and how* structural information can be related to sentences, whereas the job of a person encoding dictionary definitions into our memory model is simply to *get* a representation of their structures, i.e., to go ahead and *use* his language-processing abilities rather than to describe these. Hence our coder *does* transformations rather than describe them.

As to the nature of the nodes themselves, it will be assumed that these correspond not in fact to words, to sentences, or to visual pictures, but instead to what we ordinarily call "properties." As indicated earlier, this assumption is now common in work on concepts (30), because properties provide a more elemental and hence more flexible medium than visual pictures or words, and because either a mental picture or a language concept may be thought of as some bundle of properties (attribute values) and associations among them.

Thus, the nodes of the memory model actually correspond more to properties than to words, even though they may be expressed with words. Representing a property requires the name of something that is variable, an attribute, plus some value or range of values of that attribute. This feature is achieved in the memory model by the fact that every token is considered to have appended to it a specification of its appropriate amount or intensity in the particular concept being defined. Omitting this specification from a token (which is generally what is done) means that no restriction is placed on the total range of variation in amount of intensity open to the attribute. On the other hand, whenever such specification does appear overtly with a token node, it consists principally of numerical values, stating how the node's total possible range of amount or intensity *is* restricted. These values allow encoding restrictions to a fineness of nine gradations, i.e., permit nine degrees of "absolute discrimination" to be represented (44). The exact rationale for this kind of specification "tag" has been described elsewhere (64, 65), along with that of the other two tags, repre-

standardized to allow processing by rules that can be specified explicitly, else it will be no more manageable as a theory of memory than is English itself. (See reference 74 for the most thorough attempt to use English text itself as a computer's store of information on which to base the performance of complex tasks.) The representation now used in the memory model therefore lies at a level somewhere between the freedom of English itself and the standardization of, say, symbolic logic. In the memory model, complex configurations of labeled associations must be built up to represent the meaning inherent in dictionary definitions adequately. These are the structures we have called planes.

The attempt to get the meaning of English definitions accurately represented as planes of nodes within the memory model constitutes one major constraint on its structure. A second is provided by the attempt to write programs that can do something interesting by using this memory. To some degree these two constraints on the model balance one another: The first urges elaboration and complexity to represent the meaning of definitions accurately, while the second urges that the model be as simple and standardized as possible to make processing feasible.

As stated, the relational complexity built up in an English definition is always represented in the memory by a configuration of token nodes linked together to form one "plane." Each token in a plane is linked to its type node (which lies out of the plane) by a kind of association that was shown in Fig. 4-1 as a dashed line, while it is related to other token nodes (in the plane) by one or more of the six distinct kinds of associative link listed in the key to Fig. 4-1. In encoding dictionary definitions, these intraplane links are used, respectively, as follows:

Link

1. Dictionary definitions require the use of the subclass-to-superclass pointer whenever they define a word by stating the name of some larger class of which it is a subclass. For example, in the dictionary definition of "plant" shown in Fig. 4-1a, the word's third meaning is said to be a subclass of the class of "putting."

2. Any word or phrase used adjectively or adverbially dictates use of the modification pointer.

3. The multiple meanings of a word, and any phrase such as "air, earth, or water," require the formation of a disjunctive set.

4. Any phrase like "old, red house," or "old house with a red porch" requires that the modifiers of "house" be formed into a conjunctive set.

5-6. Together these two links form the open-ended category, by means of which all the remaining kinds of relationships are encoded. This is necessary because in natural language text almost *anything* can be considered as a relationship, so that there is no way to specify in advance what relationships are to be needed (67). This means that a memory model must senting, respectively, the "number" and the "criteriality" of a token (9), that are available in the model. Here it will only be noted that in encoding dictionary definitions all grammatical inflections, along with all words like "a," "six," "much," "very," "probably," "not," "perhaps," and others of similar meaning, do not become nodes themselves but instead dictate that various range-restricting tags be appended to the token nodes of certain other words. Removing all inflections during encoding permits all nodes in the memory model to represent canonical forms of words; this is of importance in reducing the model's over-all size and in locating conceptual similarities within it (see Section 4.3).

Certain other words are also dropped during the encoding process; e.g., "and," "or," "is," "which," "there," and "that," these being interpreted either directly as relationships that are basic structural aspects of the model or else as *directions* to the coder about how he is to form the plane structure, i.e., as specifications for how the configurations of tokens on a plane are to be structured. Similarly, punctuation shows up only in the associative structure of the model.

All pronouns, as well as *all* words used to refer again to something mentioned previously in the definition, are replaced in the model by explicit references to the earlier nodes. (In Fig. 4-1 such referencing is being done by =A and =B, where some higher token node in the plane has been designated temporarily to be A or B by giving it a *prefix* of =A or =B. A more recent version of the loading program also allows referring to *any* token node in any plane, by a sort of "indirect addressing" feature.) This ability to, in essence, reuse tokens repeatedly in a plane, perhaps modifying them slightly each time, is extremely important in making the model correspond to humanlike memory. In the course of coding many words into the current and earlier network representations, I have come to believe that the greatest difference between dictionary entries and the corresponding semantic concepts that people have in their heads is that, while dictionary makers try hard to specify all the *distinctions* between separate meanings of a word, they make only a very haphazard effort to indicate what these various meanings have in *common* conceptually. Although they may not be aware of it, there is a very good reason for this seeming oversight: The best the dictionary maker has available for showing common elements of meaning is an outlinelike format, in which meanings that have something in common are brought together under the same heading. However, as anyone who has ever reorganized a paper several times will realize, an outline organization is only adequate for *one* hierarchical grouping, when in fact the common elements existing between various meanings of a word call for a complex cross classification. In other words, the common elements within and between various meanings of a word are many, and any one outline designed to get some of these together under common headings must at the same time necessarily separate other

common elements, equally valid from some other point of view. Making the present memory network a general graph rather than a tree (the network equivalent of an outline) and setting up tokens as distinct nodes makes it possible to loop as many points as necessary back into any single node and hence in effect to show any and every common element within and between the meanings of a word. The =A notation causes the network-building program to create such a link.

In all this, it is clear that not only dictionary definitions but also much of the everyday knowledge of the person doing the coding are being tapped and represented in the memory model being built up. For instance, the reader will already have noticed that a numeral is suffixed to the end of some words (a "1" is to be assumed whenever no such numeral appears). This is simply because it is convenient to have each sense of a word named distinctly within the memory in order to be able to use these in building other configurations. This means that a person building such configurations for input to the model must always *decide* which possible sense is intended for every token and use the appropriate suffix.

4.2.3 The Parameter Symbols S, D, and M

In an attempt to encode dictionary definitions it was found that the memory must provide a mechanism for stating that certain nodes in the immediate definition plane of a type node are variable parameters. A value for one of these parameters will be provided only when the word in whose concept the parameter symbol appears is used in text. Other words within that surrounding text will then form certain parts of the current word's concept; the parameter symbols tell how. To accomplish this, parameter symbols are of three kinds, corresponding to certain ways in which other words in text may be related to the word to which the parameter symbols belong: S is the parameter symbol whose value is to be any word related to the present word as its subject; D is the parameter symbol whose value is to be any word related to the present word as its direct object; and M is the parameter symbol whose value is to be any word that the present word directly modifies.

To include a parameter symbol in a word's definition plane is therefore to state where within that concept related subjects, objects, and modificands are to be placed, if one or more of these is provided by text in which the present word is used. For example, when the verb "to comb" is defined by the phrase, "to put a comb through (hair), to get in order," this definition is saying that, when used in text, the verb "to comb" is likely to have an object, which is then to be integrated into its meaning in a certain place, viz., as the object of the node "through." In coding the above definition of "to comb," the object parameter symbol D would be used as a sort of "slot" to hold a place for this object until "comb" is actually used in text. It is important not to confuse the sense in which D refers to some object of "comb" and the sense in which there are object links within a plane. D *always refers to an object of the word in whose defining plane it appears*, while its placement in that plane – indicated by the kind of link from some other token node to it – is another matter. For example, in Fig. 4-1a, in the plane for "plant3," the symbol D (which happens also to have been labeled by =B) has been placed as the *subject* of "in9," but *it is still a D*, because it refers to any direct object of the verb "to plant." The symbol D specifies that any such object of "plant" is to be integrated into the meaning of "plant3" at the place where the D is placed.

A dictionary definition, in addition to stating where within a concept particular sorts of parameter-value information is to be "placed," may offer one or more *clue words* about what such information is likely to be. Thus, in our definition of "to comb" we are told that its direct object is likely to be "hair."

Clue words play several roles in the memory model, one of which corresponds approximately to the role transformational linguists ascribe to "selectional restrictions." In other words, the material comprising a full word concept in the memory model can be viewed as consisting of two sorts of information: On the one hand there is information about the content of the concept itself; on the other there is information about what that concept is likely to combine with when the word is used in text. This latter information is represented by the clue words associated with its parameter symbols. It is significant that this same distinction has been identified in verbal association studies, the associations that subjects give to words being divided into paradigmatic (content information), and syntagmatic (parameter clue information) (17). Ervin (19) has shown that the ratio of content associations to syntagmatic associations given by young children steadily increases with age.

In the versions of the memory model used in the programs to be described in this chapter, clue words have been sought and coded only reluctantly; both they and the parameter symbols having initially been included only because the sort of information comprising them was embarrassingly present in some dictionary definitions. However, it turns out that parameter symbols of some kind play a very crucial role in any such memory, because they make it possible to recognize that two different ways of stating the same thing are in fact synonymous.*

As a final point, we note that the model's *range* readings on tags, together with its ability to form disjunctive sets of attributes, provide it with a ready facility for representing information having a great deal of vagueness. This is essential. It is the very vagueness of the meaning of most language terms that makes them useful; indeed, speech as we know it would be completely impossible if, for instance, one had to specify exactly which machines he had reference

*This subject is developed more fully in Quillian's dissertation. [Editor's note.]

to every time he said "machine," and similarly for any other term whose meaning contains some ambiguity.

To summarize, the memory model, together with the process by which dictionary information is encoded into it, are such that what begins as the English definition of a word seems better viewed after encoding as a complexly structured bundle of attribute values – a full concept, as defined above – whose total content typically extends to an enormous size and complexity throughout the memory. Over all, the memory is a complex network of attribute-value nodes and labeled associations between them. These associations create both within-plane and between-plane ties, with several links emanating out from the typical token node and many links coming into almost every type node.

4.3   Use of the Memory Model in a Simulation Program

4.3.1 The Task of the Program

In selecting a task to perform with a model memory, one thinks first of the ability to understand unfamiliar sentences. It seems reasonable to suppose that people must necessarily understand new sentences by retrieving *stored* information about the meaning of isolated words and phrases and then combining and perhaps altering these retrieved word meanings to build up the meanings of sentences. Accordingly, one should be able to take a model of stored semantic knowledge and formulate rules of combination (cf. the "projection rules," reference 32) that would describe how sentence meanings get built up from stored word meanings.

It further seems likely that if one could manage to get even a few word meanings adequately encoded and stored in a computer memory and a workable set of combination rules formalized as a computer program, he could then bootstrap his store of encoded word meanings by having the computer itself "understand" sentences that he had written to constitute the definitions of *other* single words (64). That is, whenever a new, as yet uncoded, word could be defined by a sentence using only words whose meanings had already been encoded, then the representation of this sentence's meaning, which the machine could build up by using its previous knowledge together with its combination rules, would be the appropriate representation to *add* to its memory as the meaning of the new word. Unfortunately, two years of work on this problem led to the conclusion that the task is much too difficult to execute at our present stage of knowledge. The processing that goes on in a person's head when he "understands" a sentence and incorporates its meaning into his memory is very large indeed, practically all of it being done without his conscious knowledge.

As an example, consider the sentence, "After the strike, the president sent him away." One understands this sentence easily, probably without realizing that he has had to look into his stored knowledge of "president" to resolve a multiple meaning of the word "strike." (Consider, e.g., the same sentence with the word "umpire" substituted for "president." Such a decision in favor of one meaning of a word that has more than one possible meaning will hereafter be referred to as "disambiguation" of that word. See, e.g., reference 73.) Just *what* subconscious processing is involved in unearthing and using the fact that presidents more typically have something to do with labor strikes than with strikes of the baseball variety is by no means obvious, and a good part of this chapter is devoted to stating one way by which this can be accomplished, given that it has been decided that "president" is the correct word to attend to. Sentence understanding involves a great number of such, at present, poorly understood processes; the second half of this chapter will be devoted to developing and using a method of studying how people perform that process, preliminary, we hope, to an eventual simulation program to do so. Meanwhile, the two language functions performed by the present program are far humbler than sentence understanding, although, as will become apparent, one of them is a crucial part of sentence understanding.

The first of these functions is to compare and contrast two word concepts: Given any two words whose meanings are encoded in the memory model, the program must find the more compelling conceptual similarities and contrasts between their meanings. Since, in the usual case, each of the two words to be compared will have several possible meanings, the program is also to specify, for each semantic similarity or contrast it finds, just *which* meaning of each word is involved. This is one step toward the disambiguation of semantic ambiguity in the text. The second major task of the program is to express all the similarities and contrasts found between the two compared words in terms of understandable, though not necessarily grammatically perfect, sentences.

The above tasks are only a part of what apparently is involved in sentence understanding; yet their performance in a fashion comparable to human performance still calls for a basic degree of semantic horse sense, in which up to now computers have been conspicuously lacking and which apparently must be based on an extensive and expressively rich store of conceptual knowledge. Thus, being able to get a computer to perform these tasks indicates to some degree the plausibility of the semantic memory model used.

In briefest form, the program we have developed is used as follows:

1. The experimenter selects a group of words whose definitions are to provide the total store of information in the memory model during a given series of tests.

2. He looks up each of these words in some ordinary dictionary.

3. He encodes each of the definitions given for each word into the specified format and loads them into the machine with a program that combines them into a single network of token and type nodes and associative links — the machine's model of a human memory.

4. He is then free to select arbitrarily any pair of words in the store and to ask the program to compare and contrast the meanings of those two words (requiring that its answers be expressed in sentences).

5. He may then give some fluent speaker the same pair of words, asking him also to compare and contrast them.

6. He compares the sentences the program generates to those the human has produced and, more importantly, considers whether or not the machine's output is one that might reasonably have been produced by a subject.

If this procedure reveals any changes which the experimenter would like to see in the program's performance, he must then revise either some part of the program, some part of the memory structure or content, or all of these, and test further on new examples to see if the program now operates in a manner closer to what he desires. Repetitions of this kind of test-correct-retest cycle constitute the essence of the simulation method; however, it is important to realize that for the purpose of developing a theory of memory, the result of this development process should *not* be thought of as the computer output which the program will now produce but rather as what now may or may not have become clear about the characteristics of workable concept-like memories. Most of the characteristics of which we are aware are incorporated in the model as already described; alterations of this which now seem indicated will be discussed in Section 4.5.

The present program is designed to compare and contrast the meaning of any two word concepts in the memory store and then to generate English text to express each of its findings. This is *not* the same task as merely using the two words in sentences — a vastly simpler job for which one need not even consider the semantic concepts associated with the words (78).

4.3.2 Locating Intersection Nodes

The actual processing system is made up of three separate programs. The first of these transforms input data (definitions that have been encoded as described in the preceding section) into IPL form and interlinks these to form the total memory model. This program will not be considered further here. The second program compares and contrasts the two given word concepts. It outputs anything found, but in a form expressed in the memory model's own internal language of nodes and links. The third program takes these findings, one at a time, and for each generates English text sufficient to express its meaning. Thus, this third program states (in a sort of "me Tarzan, you Jane" style of English) each similarity or contrast of meaning that the second program has found between the two given words.

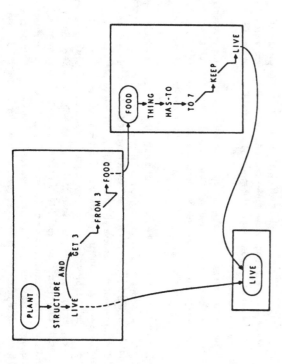

Figure 4-2a. Two Paths Direct from Plant to Live

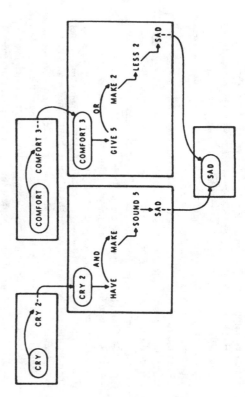

Figure 4-2b. A Path from "Cry" and a Path from "Comfort" which Reach the Same (i.e., an Intersection) Node

It is in the operation of the second program, the comparing and contrasting of two concepts, that the interlocking, token-type structure of the over-all memory begins to pay off. For to do this it is no longer necessary in such a memory to line up some representation of each of the two concepts side by side and try to compare them. Instead, the entire investigation is simply a matter of searching for points in the memory at which the two *full* concepts intersect (full concept was defined in Section 4.2). To see how this is accomplished, recall that the entire memory is a network of nodes and connecting links. Beginning with the two nodes that the program is given to compare (the two patriarch words), this program works alternately on one full word concept and then the other, moving out node by node along the various tokens and types within each. While it will be convenient to visualize this as creating two slowly expanding spheres of activated nodes around each patriarch, actually there is no spatial significance to the expansion of a concept; the nodes in one concept may be located anywhere in the memory model.

The program simulates the gradual activation of each concept outward through the vast proliferation of associations originating from each patriarch, by moving out along these links, tagging each node encountered with a special two-part tag, the "activation tag." Part of this tag always names the patriarch from which the search began, i.e., the name of the concept within which the current node has been reached. Now, the program detects any intersection of meaning between the two concepts simply by asking, every time a node is reached, whether or not it already contains an activation tag naming the *other* patriarch, i.e., showing that this node has previously been reached in the tracing out of the other concept. If there is no such tag, the program next checks to see if there is already an activation tag naming the *current* patriarch, i.e., indicating that this node has been reached previously in tracing out this same concept. If so, the program must take account of this, to inhibit retracing out from the node again and hence repeating its effort, perhaps getting into a loop. Only if neither of these tags is found is the node tagged, and further search leading to the nodes to which *it* points is considered legitimate.

The second part of each activation tag is the name of the "immediate parent" of the current node, i.e., the node at which the associative link leading *directly* to it originated. Thus, the "activated" areas of the memory are turned from a one-way into a two-way network, and, whenever a tag from the opposite patriarch is found, these immediate-parent parts of activation tags permit the program to trace back "up" from the intersection node to the two patriarchs. This produces two *paths*, except when the intersection node *is* one of the patriarchs, in which case only a single path is needed, leading from one patriarch directly to the other.

Examples of such paths and pairs of paths occur in Figs. 4-2a and 4-2b, respectively. The paths from a patriarch to an intersection node produced by the second program should not be confused with the "activation" it makes from each patriarch. While this activation is equivalent to an expanding "sphere," a path is only one particular "line" from the center of the sphere to some point within it, one at which it intersects the other full concept's "sphere."

Expanding the two concepts alternately is extremely important; in effect this converts both concepts into searchers for each other and gives both the maximal number of targets to look for at any given stage of the search.

4.3.3 Making Inferences and Expressing Findings in English

The third program, which generates a piece of text to express each path given it by the second program, produces output of the sort illustrated in Table 4-1. (In this table the paths that the third program has been given to work on are omitted, while the paths for Examples 1 and 2 are those of Fig. 4-2.)

The most important point about the sentence producer is that there seems to be excellent justification for considering it, when taken in conjunction with the first two programs, as an inference maker rather than just a retriever of information. From a relatively small amount of input data, the over-all program will derive a very large number of implicit assertions indeed, and make each such assertion explicit in the form of English text. As an example of an interesting type of "inferential" behavior, consider the output shown in Table 4-1 as Example 2-B. The path expressed by this output is the longer of the two shown in Fig. 4-2a. As can be seen from a study of Fig. 4-2b, this kind of performance is made possible by the fact that the memory model interconnects related information that has been input from a great many different definitions, so that in order to answer some particular question the search program can trace out a "plane-hopping" path. While a path lying completely within one plane (except for its terminal points) amounts only to a representation of some piece of the information put into the memory, a "plane-hopping" path represents an idea that was implied by, but by no means directly expressed in, the data that were input.

By analogy, suppose we fed a machine "A is greater than B," and "B is greater than C." If then, in answer to the question "what is A greater than?" the machine responded "B," we would not want to call this an inference, but only a "retrieval." However, if it went on to say, "A is also greater than C," then we would say that it had made a simple inference. The kind of path that we have been calling "plane-hopping" is exactly the representation of such an inference, since it combines information input in one definition with that input in another. But the fact that our planes are not simple propositions but rather sizable configurations, every node of which provides the possibility of branching off to another plane means that the number of "inferential" paths becomes very large as paths of any appreciable length are considered. Moreover, the possibility that a path may contain fragments from several planes seems to indicate clearly that

the inferences need not be at all simple, although we do not yet have actual computer output with which to demonstrate this very conclusively.

Assuming a "complete" semantic memory — one in which every word used in any definition also has a definition encoded — a concept fans out very rapidly from its patriarch. It appears that in such a full memory model the average node would branch to at least three other nodes, considering both its ties to tokens and to its type, if it is itself a token. This means that the average number of paths of, say, up to ten nodes in length emanating from any type node would be over 88,000, each of which would require at least one unique sentence to express. This is to be compared to 2046 paths emanating from such a type node if no token-to-type links are available.

Another way to look at the potential of a memory store such as the theory specifies is to compute what the present programs could generate if one could get the definitions of say, 850 words encoded and stored in a memory model. There would then be 360,000 word pairs to ask it about. Since at a conservative estimate a memory model of this size would provide ten nontrivial semantic connections, and hence sentences or sentence sets, between the average word pair, the present programs would have the capability to generate well over 3,500,000 short batches of text to express this total conceptual knowledge, ignoring all that information present only in longer paths. The definitions of 850 words comprise far more information than can be modeled in the core of today's computers, even though an efficient packing scheme might greatly increase the storable amount. Nevertheless, calculations such as these seem relevant in evaluating the potential of the model as a general theory of long-term conceptual memory.

While a path represents an idea, it is up to the sentence-producing program to get that idea expressed in English. Thus this program must check a path for restriction tags and other features which make it necessary to insert words such as "not" or "among other things" into the sentence generated to express its meaning.

In attempting to express the meaning of a path, this program also deletes, rearranges, and adds words to those given in the path. It works not only with nodes mentioned in the path itself but sometimes looks *around* these nodes in the memory model to retrieve additional information and to check on things it considers saying. For instance, in Example 2-B the word "air," although not in the path being expressed, was retrieved to produce legitimate English.

In expressing a complex path, such as that of Fig. 4-2a, this text-producing program realizes when the capability of its sentence grammar is being exceeded and starts a new sentence (see e.g., Example 7-C-1 of Table 4-1.) Unfortunately it does this rather often, and a more powerful program clearly would be one which instead of the two sentences shown as Examples 3-A-1 and 3-A-2 would output the single sentence: "A plant is not an animal but a man is." Some of

Table 4-1. Example Output from the Current Program
(Paths have been omitted, but see Fig. 4-2)

Example 1. Compare: CRY, COMFORT
  A. Intersect: SAD
    (1) CRY2 IS AMONG OTHER THINGS TO MAKE A SAD SOUND.*
    (2) TO COMFORT3 CAN BE TO MAKE2 SOMETHING LESS2 SAD.
    (Note that the program has selected particular meanings of "cry" and "comfort" as appropriate for this intersection. The path on which this output is based is shown in Fig. 4-2b.

Example 2. Compare: PLANT, LIVE
  A. 1st Intersect: LIVE
    (1) PLANT IS A LIVE STRUCTURE.
  B. 2nd Intersect: LIVE
    (1) PLANT IS STRUCTURE WHICH GET3-FOOD FROM AIR. THIS FOOD IS THING WHICH BEING2 HAS-TO TAKE INTO ITSELF TO7 KEEP LIVE.
    (The paths which these two replies express are shown in Fig. 4-2a.)

Example 3. Compare: PLANT, MAN
  A. 1st Intersect: ANIMAL
    (1) PLANT IS NOT A ANIMAL STRUCTURE.
    (2) MAN IS ANIMAL.
  B. 2nd Intersect: PERSON
    (1) TO PLANT3 IS FOR A PERSON SOMEONE TO PUT SOMETHING INTO EARTH.
    (2) MAN3 IS PERSON.
    (Here the program is treating "person" as an adjective modifier of "someone.")

Example 4. Compare: PLANT, INDUSTRY
  A. 1st Intersect: INDUSTRY
    (1) PLANT2 IS APPARATUS WHICH PERSON USE FOR 5 PROCESS IN INDUSTRY.

Example 5. Compare: EARTH, LIVE
  A. 1st Intersect: ANIMAL
    (1) EARTH IS PLANET OF7 ANIMAL.
    (2) TO LIVE IS TO HAVE EXISTENCE AS7 ANIMAL.

Example 6. Compare: FRIEND, COMFORT
  A. 1st Intersect: PERSON
    (1) FRIEND IS PERSON.
    (2) COMFORT CAN BE WORD TO4 PERSON.

Example 7. Compare: FIRE, BURN
  A. 1st Intersect: BURN
    (1) FIRE IS CONDITION WHICH BURN.
  B. 2nd Intersect: FIRE
    (1) 'TO BURN2 CAN BE TO DESTROY2 SOMETHING BY4 FIRE.
  C. 3rd Intersect: BURN
    (1) FIRE IS A FLAME CONDITION. THIS FLAME CAN BE A GAS TONGUE4. THIS GAS IS GAS WHICH BURN.
    (The sentence producer starts a new sentence whenever it needs to say something more about something it has used adjectively.)

Example 8. Compare: BUSINESS, COMFORT
  A. 1st Intersect: PERSON
    (1) BUSINESS IS ACT3 WHICH PERSON DO.
    (2) COMFORT2 IS CONDITION3 WHICH PERSON HAVE NEED4.
    (The code contains information indicating that "person" should be plural here, but the sentence producer does not yet make use of this information.)

Example 9. Compare: MAN, BUSINESS
  A. 1st Intersect: PERSON
    (1) MAN3 IS PERSON.
    (2) BUSINESS CAN BE ACTIVITY WHICH PERSON MUST DO WORK2.
    (Something wrong here. I believe a miscoding in the input data.)
  B. 2nd Intersect: GROUP
    (1) MAN2 IS MAN AS9 GROUP.
    (2) BUSINESS2 IS QUESTION3 FOR ATTENTION OF GROUP.

Example 10. Compare: MAN, LIVE
  A. 1st Intersect: ANIMAL
    (1) MAN IS ANIMAL
    (2) TO LIVE IS TO HAVE EXISTENCE AS7 ANIMAL.
  B. 2nd Intersect: LIVE
    (1) MAN IS A LIVE + BEING2.

*"AMONG OTHER THINGS" and "CAN BE" are canned phrases which the program inserts when the next thing it is going to mention is one out of a set of things recorded in its memory. At one point, the program was programmed to insert "AMONG OTHER THINGS" *whenever* it was about to assert one fact out of such a set. We expected this to make its output have a proper, scientifically cautious ring. However, where it had been saying (rather cloddishly, we felt), "TO CRY IS TO MAKE A SAD SOUND," it now said: "TO CRY, AMONG OTHER THINGS, IS, AMONG OTHER THINGS, TO MAKE, AMONG OTHER THINGS, A, AMONG OTHER THINGS, SAD SOUND." In short, it turns out that if the program is really made to hedge whenever it knows more than it is going to say, one sits around the console all day waiting for it to get around to saying anything. This may not be such a bad simulation of certain individuals, but wasn't what we had had in mind. Thus, the program is now severely restricted as to just when it can hedge. Science marches on!

the minor improvements of this single sentence over the two which the program now produces would not be difficult to program, but the unification of the two paths into one is a bit more complicated. Clearly, the sentence-generation program involves something very close to what Chomsky calls "transformations."

In summary, the operation of the sentence producer has little in common with other sentence-generation programs, and in fact its whole philosophy is contradictory to a good part of the spirit of modern linguistics, which attempts to treat syntactic facts in isolation from semantic ones. The program is also de-in Table 4-1. The larger the memory model, the greater the number of search branches that remain active, so that the search program becomes able to unearth a great many more semantic connections at a relatively shallow depth beneath any two patriarchs. This ultimately can only improve the program's performance, although it may also require that more concern be given to directing searches than has so far been the case. At present, but for one exception, a search just "progressively proliferates" along all possible branches from the two patriarchs until it has covered a given number of nodes, e.g., 400.

The one exception to this blind, "breadth first," search occurs whenever two concepts are found to intersect on a word used prepositionally, such as "for5" in the concept "plant2." Instead of treating this as a substantive semantic intersection, the search program merely concentrates an immediate burst of search activity out from the two tokens of the preposition. The reasoning here is simply that, while a match on such a word is not in itself sufficient to be treated as a significant conceptual similarity, it is a good bet to examine immediately the subjects, objects, and modifiers of such prepositions rather than continue the usual search schedule, which normally would not get to these nodes for some time. Unfortunately there is not yet enough evidence available to assess the value of this search heuristic, since its effectiveness, if any, will not show up until the memory model is relatively large.

4.4* The Memory Model as Basis for a Theory of How People Comprehend Language

Sections 4.1 to 4.3 demonstrate that the memory model, once built, can support simulation of a relatively simple type of language behavior. However, this memory model had to be laboriously created by a human "coder." A detailed study of the way in which one such coder encodes seven sentences of English text into the data format of the memory model has been omitted here because of space limitations. The aim of this study is to develop some theoretical understanding of how a person may comprehend text.

As stated earlier, encoding of text into the memory model format is not a procedure for which complete algorithmic rules are available but rather one that depends heavily upon the coder developing his own understanding of what the text means. Whenever a coder represents the meaning of some

*Because this book is concerned more with the art of obtaining semantic behavior in computers and less with the development of theories of human semantic behavior, the editor asked Quillian to condense the four chapters of his dissertation that describe experiments in that area. This section summarizes his results of that investigation; further details were given in Chapters IV-VII and several appendixes of the original dissertation. Quillian informed me that since the thesis was completed he has made substantial progress on his theory of encoding and has developed a text-understanding program that achieves some success in encoding. [Editor's note.]

---

signed in complete contradiction to the subordinate place for semantic information that the formulation of Katz and Postal (quoted on p. 221) would seem to imply for a performance model. As a theory, the program implies that a person first has something to say, expressed somehow in his own conceptual terms (which is what a "path" is to the program), and that all his decisions about the syntactic form that a generated sentence is to take are then made *in the service of* this intention. The sentence producer works entirely in this fashion, figuring out grammatical properties of sentences only as these are needed to solve the problem of expressing a path given to it by the search program.

The programs were tested only on very small memory models, built from no more than 50 or 60 definitions (about 5,000 IPL cells), and on only a few such memories (see Table 4-2).

Table 4.2. Words with Definitions Encoded for Use in Model Memories

(Note: Computer memory limitations have so far required that definitions of no more than twenty of these words be used to constitute a model memory during a given series of word comparisons. Since this paper was written, almost all of the 850 words of basic English have been encoded, but not yet run in the program.)

instrument	flame	country	leather
insurance	experience	desire	land
invent	fact	sex	kiss
interest	comfort	plant	know
iron	cloth	family	laugh
ice	cause	meal	light
idea	attack	animal	language
friend	argue	food	law
develop	business	man	lead
event	burn	live	jelly
earth	build	level	journey
exist	bread	lift	jump
drink	behave	letter	judge
fire	cry	learn	

A small total memory implies that most branches of the proliferating search of a concept are always getting cut short upon reaching a type node for which no definition has yet been encoded. One of the most surprising findings from running the program has been that even with this relative paucity of over-all information, the program almost invariably succeeds in finding some intersections of meaning. Actually, Table 4-1 lists only a selected sample of the program's output for each compared pair of words; there are usually five or six pairs of sentences generated for each problem pair given to it, although most of these are only trivial variations of a couple of basic sentences, such as those segment of text in the format of the model, relationships and features of this meaning that were not explicit in the text itself must be made explicit. This provides a methodological advantage in studying how a coder-subject comprehends text, since certain parts of the coder's otherwise covert "understanding" of the text become externalized and available for observation during coding.

As our coder-subject encoded the seven sentences, she was also required to describe into a tape recorder a running account of the steps she took and of the reasoning she carried out. This verbal protocol has been analyzed for use in developing the theoretical picture of how the process of text understanding may in fact proceed, at least for this one subject.

What does it mean to say that a reader or coder "understands" a piece of text? It seems clear that understanding text includes recognizing the structure of relations between words of the text (as in parsing it), recognizing the referent words of pronouns and of other words used anaphorically, and recognizing the appropriate sense intended for all words with multiple meanings. I take it that the over-all effect of these processes is to encode the text's meaning into some form more or less parallel to that in which the subject's general knowledge is stored, so that its meaning may be compared to that knowledge and perhaps added to it.

There are great methodological difficulties in attempting to study how people understand sentences. The Fifth Annual Report of the Center for Cognitive Studies of Harvard (reference 23) states:

To "explain" speech perception we must propose a device whose input would be the acoustic speech signal and whose output would be the meaning that native speakers retrieve from that acoustic signal. *Without a satisfactory semantic theory, we cannot even specify the output of such a device* (p. 16, italics mine).

The methodological importance of a semantic memory model for a study of understanding stems from the fact that it *does*, to some extent, provide a way to make a reader's "output" not only specifiable, but also visible. That is, a coder who is encoding is taking English text as "input" and then giving as "output" a plane representing the meaning of the text. In this plane a great many of the direct results of his process of understanding the text are represented overtly. In particular, in such a plane the results of the coder's parsing of the text, of his disambiguation of its words' multiple meanings, and of his identification of its anaphoric references, can all be identified. For the researcher this means that he is able to *observe*, for a subject performing a process very much like "understanding," not only an input – the text – but also an output – the representation the subject builds to represent its meaning. To my knowledge there is no other representation existing that permits this in any such comprehensive, economical manner.

While the encoding process is of course not identical to the covert processing that constitutes the understanding of the same text during normal reading, it is at least very heavily dependent upon such understanding, and is in some ways a slowed-down, overt version of it. And it is precisely such a slowed-down version that is needed to investigate the understanding process. Having a recorded protocol of this slowed-down version, we can study the encoding process in the same way that other cognitive processes, such as playing chess, have been studied, and apply part of what has been learned from those analyses to the problem of text understanding. Of course we do not suppose that the step-by-step verbal protocol generated by the coder-subject is identical or even very close to her actual thought processes. However, the two are certainly related, with the protocol revealing various reasoning procedures, logical steps, and her general sequence of operations. All of these are otherwise obscure.

In building a theoretical picture of the text-understanding process from our analysis of this protocol, we assume that text understanding operates on the basis of selective interaction between the text being read and the coder's general over-all memory. It is further assumed that her memory has essentially the same structure as that of our model, and also that the task the text understander faces is to recode the meaning of the text into some similar form so that she can compare it with and perhaps incorporate it into her general memory.

Specifically, the following four steps were taken in this study of the text-understanding process:

1. The total *possible* moves toward comprehension of one of the seven sentences were enumerated, to show the size of the "problem space" these afford the reader-coder. That is, all the *possible* choices facing the understander of this sentence were enumerated, in the same way that possible moves facing a chess player at any given position may be enumerated. This problem space turns out to be very large indeed, with hundreds of thousands of ways available to the reader for combining the separate words of a sentence. A very substantial part of it is due to lexical ambiguity, so that the elimination of such ambiguity is one key step a reader must take toward understanding the sentence.

2. It was then demonstrated experimentally that a computer program, given an appropriate version of the memory model, could go some distance toward effectively resolving the lexical ambiguities of these sentences. In this experiment 19 ambiguous words were considered; of these the program correctly disambiguated 12, left 4 ambiguous, and incorrectly disambiguated 3. This program operated *solely* on the basis of semantic considerations, with no syntactic analysis at all. However, improving its level of performance until it compares with human capability will not be possible unless and until a program *does* also make some use of syntax.

3. A step-by-step characterization of what the coder-subject does during the protocol was undertaken. The main conclusion from this is that the understanding process seems to divide naturally into episodes, created because the coder-subject "bites off" small *segments* of a sentence for intensive processing as she reads it.

4. The particular segmenting of text done by our subject was then analyzed to suggest a way that syntactic processing of text by a reader may guide, and be guided by, his semantic processing of it. *We argue that the same kind of search for semantic intersections carried out by the program described in Section 4.3 must be a key process in this semantic processing.* Several ways to extend and strengthen such search processes in order to adapt them for use in understanding text can also be proposed. Assuming such a continuous interaction between syntactic analysis and semantic processing, a tentative theoretical view of how text understanding may proceed was constructed.

4.5 Some Final Implications and Relations to Linguistic Theory

A tentative theory of the general structure of long-term memory has now been explored in three ways: First, a model of such memory has been utilized in a computer program to simulate human performance on a semantic task. Second, the memory model has been combined with the techniques of protocol collection to produce a methodology for gathering data relevant to how a subject understands text. Third, this subject's internal semantic memory has been assumed to be structured and used as is the memory model, and the implications of this assumption have been utilized to explain the subject's performance and to develop a tentative theory of how text is understood.

4.5.1 Improvements of the Model*

In the model as presented so far, modification of a concept has been encoded by attaching a link labeled "modifier" to a token for the concept to be modified. This modifier link leads to some other node which forms the head of the modifying structure. (In IPL terms, the token node is given an attribute whose name is "modifier" and whose value is the top node of the modifying structure.) In a case where the modifying structure is a prepositional phrase modifying a noun or a verb, it now appears that it would be much better simply to label the modifying link with the preposition itself and run this link from the token node to be modified to the object of the preposition. This would eliminate the link labeled "modifier" and hence would reduce the size of the over-all model. More importantly, it would permit a search (activation of a full concept in the memory) to be directed more readily. Such

*Alterations discussed in this section are being incorporated into a new version of the memory model and program now being developed in conjunction with Dr. D. G. Bobrow.

direction is required in connection with the parsing of prepositional phrases.

In general, it appears that labeling links with words themselves, and especially with prepositions, instead of with predefined linkage names, such as "modifier," is a development worth further exploration. The use of prepositions to label links between tokens in the model would seem to go along with another change, the need for which is pointed up in reference 24. This work, although motivated by purely grammatical considerations, indicates convincingly that the parameter symbols S, D, and M, as conceived in the model so far, are not adequate to achieve the "carrying" of information into alternate forms. Briefly, the examples given in this work and those by Fillmore (24) raise issues of the following sort: Suppose the verb "to swarm" were given the definition: "for (bees, ants, etc.) to cluster in some area." As this definition has been encoded, the parenthesized phrase becomes a parameter symbol S, representing whatever the subject of "swarm" is in some sentence or plane where it occurs. Suppose, however, that we now encounter the sentence: "The gardens swarm with bees." If the subject of "swarm" in this sentence is treated as a value for the parameter symbol S, it will mean that "the gardens cluster in some area." This misinterpretation is due to the fact that S is too gross and undifferentiated a notion, and Fillmore's examples indicate that our S's, D's, and perhaps M's must be subdivided into more precise categories. Fillmore proposes syntactic terms such as "ergative," "agentive," and "locative," as more precise categories which should replace the grosser notions of subject (S) and object (D).

We know that the kinds of parameter symbols utilized in the memory must have a clear-cut correspondence to the kinds of intertoken links used in it. It would appear that using prepositions to label intertoken links refines the memory's ability to differentiate these relationships in a way that matches the more differentiated parameter symbols that Fillmore shows a need for. In this regard, it appears that, whenever possible, prepositions should be used as links between verbs and their subjects and objects, thereby replacing (↘) and (↙). For example, the definition of "swarm" given above might be rewritten before encoding to say: " 'swarming' is clustering in (some area) by (bees, ants)." During encoding, *both* parenthesized phrases in this definition would then become parameter symbols, perhaps called, respectively, the "ergative" (E) and the "locative" (L). Then the sentence, "the gardens swarm with bees," would be interpreted by taking "gardens" as the value of L, rather than of the grosser S. Once this was done, the kind of misinterpretation described would be avoided.

To refine the memory by using more differentiated intertoken links and parameter symbols is to move it to a level of specificity one step further from natural language than it has been. (And from the usual specificity of transformational structures; as one questioner at Fillmore's presentation put it, his examples concern the "deep, deep structure" of language.) To move the code further from natural language appears to put more burden on whatever processes translate back and forth between the model's representation and natural language, e.g., the sentence producing routines of our Chapter III program, and the coder (or eventual program) that encodes textual material into the model's representation. However, the opposite may in fact be the case; Fillmore suggests what may be *more* general generation rules based on his "deep, deep" structures, and, on the encoding or "understanding" side, more precisely differentiated parameter symbols may be *easier* to select values for than are the grosser categories S, D, and M. For example, for the sentence stated, consider intersecting "garden," taken as one patriarch, with the total set of clue words: "bees," "ants," and "area," taken together as the other patriarch set. It would appear that an intersection program could easily select the matching member of this set, "area," and hence the correct parameter for "garden" to fill. Turning the sentence around ("bees swarm in the garden,") would not effect the "understanding" achieved and would hardly even change the process by which it was achieved, since the essential part of this process is the semantic intersecting, rather than syntactic analysis.

Another change in the model relates to its ability to represent ambiguity easily. A coding convention which the reader may have noticed to be a departure from ordinary grammatical procedure was to make some prepositions which modify a verb the object of that verb. This was done to allow indirect objects and other nouns to be made the subject of the preposition, and hence permit certain fine distinctions of meaning to be encoded. For example, consider a sentence like "I threw the man in the ring." This sentence can mean: (a) "While in the ring I threw the man," (b) "I threw the man who was in the ring," or (c) "I threw the man into the ring." The encodings corresponding to these three meanings are shown in Fig. 4-3, parts A, B, and C, respectively.

Presented in this way the distinctions of meaning between (a), (b), and (c) are clear, and the encodings logical, even though using a prepositional phrase as an object of a verb (in c) is contrary to usual practice. However, when such a sentence is encountered in text it is often impossible to decide which of its meanings is intended. It turns out, moreover, that coders are most unreliable and unhappy about making this distinction, even in cases in which one meaning does seem clearly indicated.

Thus it would appear that our coders at least mentally encode most cases of this kind in some form that leaves it ambiguous as to which exact meaning is intended. In order to be ambiguous on this matter in the code as it stands the coder must set up all the alternate forms, A, B, and C, and then group these into a disjunctive set. In the program now under development all meanings strictly like (c) will be encoded in the form of A, while all meanings strictly

"I THREW THE MAN IN THE RING"

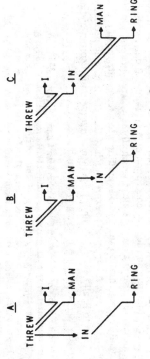

Figure 4-3. Encoding of Three Meanings of a Sentence

like (a) will be encoded as modifiers of the subject ("I" in the above example). This eliminates forms of type C and brings the code more in line with standard terminology. More importantly, however, a new parenthesis notation is being added that will allow a phrase like "in the ring" to modify the entire remainder of the sentence while remaining uncommitted as to just which sub-element it modifies and hence which precise interpretation is intended. Thus the ambiguous form will be easily represented, while the finer distinctions will require slightly more structure. This clearly will increase the psychological verisimilitude of the model and provide a more useful representation. Considerations of this kind, incidentally, cast doubt on efforts to recode natural language into symbolic logic and also suggest that programs attempting to process natural language have their greatest hope of success if they are kept as close as possible to human methods and representations.

4.5.2 Implications for the Relationship of Transformational Grammars to Psychological Performance Models

The viewpoint that emerges from this research conflicts at several points with the relationship that has been said to exist between current linguistic theories and performance models, especially insofar as these involve semantics. The rest of this section will be devoted to clarifying this relationship as it appears once a semantic memory is assumed to be part of the mechanism or organism that deals with natural language.

In the first place, we do not believe that performance theories or computer models can ignore or put off semantics, as most language-processing programs so far have done, and yet hope to achieve success. Whether a program is intended to parse sentences, to translate languages, or to answer natural-language questions, if it does not take account of semantic facts both early and often, I do not think it has a chance of approaching the level of human competence.

Correspondingly, any theory of language, such as that prescribed by Katz et al. (31, 32), which asserts that semantic processing is in any sense temporally or logically subordinate to syntactic processing, would seem to be of very dubious value in performance models.

Secondly, it has already been pointed out that the normal mechanism for understanding language, as we see it, need not refuse to process any sentence because the sentence is "semantically anomalous." This is because the memory model provides a natural measure of the relative semantic similarity between one full concept and any others, and hence allows an understanding process to select the best available interpretation for any given word string instead of first insisting that that string meet previously anticipated conditions in order to be semantically interpretable. Viewing the process of language understanding in this way eliminates the embarrassing necessity to say that people must interpret an "anomalous" sentence by some mysterious process based on the sentence's "direct analogy to well-formed sentences" (reference 11, p. 149). Positing such a semantic memory thus makes the judgment as to what constitutes a semantically anomalous sentence arbitrary – as, incidentally, it has always seemed to many people anyhow. For example, Katz and Postal's assertion that the sentence, "the paint is silent," cannot be understood by the normal rules of language interpretation (reference 32, p. 25) is not easy to accept.

It has also been noted that positing a semantic memory seems to abrogate the need in a performance model for the phrase-structure component of a transformational grammar, that a set of rules corresponding to the transformational component is all that our program employs to generate sentences.

Another of the unquestioned tenets of transformational linguistics is that a single grammar should be considered to underlie both the production and the understanding of sentences. This notion, if feasible, would provide a great simplification of abstract linguistic theory and seems to be almost universally accepted among transformational linguists (note, e.g., the constant reference to an undifferentiated "speaker-hearer" in reference 11).

However, it seems clear that while generative grammars are very natural parts of a sentence-production mechanism, these same grammars raise immediate problems when one attempts to base a parsing or understanding program on them. To parse according to such a grammar must involve a series of trial matching operations, and the tree of possible matches, even if pruned by heuristics, as has been suggested, seems inevitably destined to make it more difficult to parse and hence to understand sentences with any given grammar than it is to produce them with that same grammar. This is blatantly opposite to the facts about people: A child can understand more complex sentences than he can generate, a student in a foreign language finds it easier to understand or read correct sentences than to speak them, and a person can read language faster than he can compose it.

In spite of these contradictory facts, the assumption that a single grammar is the best way to explain the competence both of a speaker and of a hearer is widely held. To explain a grammar's use in understanding, Miller and Chomsky (reference 45, p. 465) have adopted a version of the "analysis-by-synthesis" theory apparently first put forward by Halle and Stevens for phonemics in 1959 (see also reference 42).

The key assumption of the analysis-by-synthesis theory is that in order to understand language one essentially must re-create the generation process by which that language was created. This re-creation is thought to rely upon the grammar and to be guided by cues in the given text. The re-creation is continuously checked and corrected by testing tentative steps of generation against further text. Hence, from this viewpoint, to understand text is to locate all the steps that, given the same grammar, might have generated it.*

This analysis-by-synthesis model follows naturally from assuming that all language competence is to be explained in terms of a single basic set of *rules*, to be called the grammar. On the other hand, if the understanding of text is viewed as the creation of some mental symbolic *representation*, such as that comprising the memory model, then *there is little reason to suppose that a reader or hearer must retrace the steps by which a sentence might have been generated in order to understand it*. The relationship between producing and understanding a given piece of language lies only in the single message content underlying both, not in the processes for moving between English and that message content.

For instance, suppose a bundle of facts $x_1, x_2, \ldots, x_n$ modify object y. Speaker A knows this, and wishes to tell hearer B. To do so he must utilize some way of turning the conceptual connections that represent this information in his head into natural language. For this he has many choices: how many sentences to use; which x's to make into adjectives of y, which ones into predicate nominatives, and which ones into prepositional phrases; whether to use passive sentences, subordinate clauses, rhetorical questions, and so on. However, to obtain an adequate conception of A's meaning, B only needs somehow to arrive at a mental state in which all the x's are represented in his cognitive representation and linked as modifiers to a representation of y. The question of how A happened to *express* each of these facts is of no necessary concern to B; all he must obtain is some mental *representation* corresponding roughly to that which A is trying to communicate.

*From this sort of conception Chomsky has been led to a heavily a priori, anti-environmental theory of language acquisition (11). His reasoning seems to be: A person can understand a very wide range of sentence structures, yet he can only understand what he also could have generated. Therefore, the person must be born with a very high-powered but latent generation grammar and must somehow be able to actualize a latent rule of this grammar whenever it is needed in order to understand some sentence containing an unfamiliar syntactic complication.

Since much of the information that is in A's language can therefore be ignored by B, the tests that he must apply to extract from A's speech what he needs to know clearly can be much simpler than the tests he would have to apply to regenerate B's sentence-generation process fully. In other words, it appears, both from thinking about the problem in terms of a semantic memory model and from the obvious facts about the relative difficulty of understanding language versus producing it, that the process by which a person understands language is most likely "primary" in the sense that it does not rely on any generative grammar or sentence production process. Rather than understanding language by relating it to how a generation grammar would allow the same text to be produced, the understanding process is an autonomous process of its own.

To view a person's understanding of language as a separate problem, independent of any generation grammar, is of course not to say that an understander can ignore the facts of sentence structure — even though people can in fact understand text whose sentence structure is incorrect, wildly distorted, and so on — but merely that a generative grammar need not be in any sense a "component" of the understander's language processor.

Once the domain that a generative grammar has to account for is thus restricted to sentence production, it becomes unnecessary to think of the grammar as a single set of rules that will generate *all* constructions of English. Nine years after the publication of *Syntactic Structures* (Chomsky, 1957) no one has succeeded in building a general generative grammar for all of English. This alone is no condemnation of his proposals, but it does seem much more reasonable to hope for a grammar capable of accounting for how any given idea may be expressed in *some* stretch of acceptable English text. Then, to get this grammar to express the same thought in some other style, i.e., in different sentence structure(s), a higher-level rule could perhaps be written which would alter the grammar itself. This would provide a mechanism similar to that in a person, in that it could express itself in text of some style and perhaps change that style for various occasions but would not simultaneously contain rules capable of producing English of *all* possible styles.

The situation here parallels that for speech accents. Many Americans can approximate a Southern accent, or an Irish or German or French one, but no one can simultaneously speak with all these accents. The task of formulating a single phonological grammar adequate to generate speech in all accents at once clearly is unnecessarily difficult, if even possible. Similarly, it seems unreasonable to seek a grammar that will generate English sentences of all possible styles at once.

The requirement that a generative grammar be universal across all of a natural language's styles of expression *cannot* be escaped as long as the

grammar is considered to underlie sentence understanding as well as sentence production, for an intelligent native speaker has the competence to understand almost any grammatically acceptable sentence style. However, this situation changes as soon as the grammar's job is restricted to language production and language understanding is attacked as a separate problem.

In summary, therefore, the implications of assuming a semantic memory for what we might call "generative psycholinguistics" are: that dichotomous judgments of semantic well-formedness versus anomaly are not essential or inherent to language performance; that the transformational component of a grammar is the part most relevant to performance models; that a generative grammar's role should be viewed as restricted to language production, whereas sentence understanding should be treated as a problem of extracting a cognitive representation of a text's message; that until *some* theoretical notion of cognitive representation is incorporated into linguistic conceptions, they are unlikely to provide either powerful language-processing programs or psychologically relevant theories.

Although these implications conflict with the way others have viewed the relationship of transformational grammars to semantics and to human performance, they do not eliminate the importance of such grammars to psychologists, an importance stressed in, and indeed largely created by, the work of Chomsky. It is precisely because of a growing interdependence between such linguistic theory and psychological performance models that their relationship needs to be clarified.

Bibliography

1. Banerji, R. B., *A Language for the Description of Concepts*, unpublished dittoed paper, Systems Research Center, Case Inst. of Technology, Cleveland, 1964.

2. Bartlett, F. C., *Remembering, a Study in Experimental and Social Psychology*, Cambridge University Press, Cambridge, England, 1932.

3. Baylor, G. W., and Simon, H. A., "A Chess Mating Combination Program," *Proc. SJCC*, Spartan Press, Baltimore, Md., 1966.

4. Berkeley, E. C., and Bobrow, D. G., (eds.) *The Programming Language LISP: Its Operation and Applications*, Information International, Inc., Cambridge, Mass., 1964.

5. Bobrow, D. G., "Syntactic Analysis of Language by Computer – a Survey," *Proc. FJCC*, Spartan Press, Baltimore, Md., 1963.

6. Bobrow, D. G., *Natural Language Input for a Computer Problem Solving System*. Unpublished Ph.D. dissertation, M.I.T., 1964, also Project MAC, Report TR-1, 1964, Chapter 3 of the present volume is a slightly revised version.

7. Bobrow, D. G., and Teitelman, W., "Format-Directed List Processing in LISP," Bolt, Beranek and Newman Report 1366, Cambridge, Mass., 1966.

8. Bruner, J. S., "On Perceptual Readiness," *Psych. Rev.*, Vol. 64, 1957.

9. Bruner, J. S., Goodnow, J. J., and Austin, C. A., *A Study of Thinking*, John Wiley, New York, 1956.

10. Bruner, J. S., and Minturn, A. L., "Perceptual Identification and Perceptual Organization," *J. Gen. Psych.*, Vol. 53, 1955.

11. Chomsky, N., *Aspects of the Theory of Syntax*, The M.I.T. Press, Cambridge, Mass., 1965.

12. Chomsky, N., and Miller, G. A., "Introduction to the Formal Analysis of Natural Languages, Luce, D. R., Bush, R. R., and Galanter, E. (eds.), *Handbook of Mathematical Psychology, Vol. II*, John Wiley, New York, 1963.

13. Chomsky, N., Review of Skinner, B. F., "Verbal Behavior," *Language*, Vol. 35, 1959.

14. Cliff, N., "Adverbs as Multipliers," *Psych. Rev.*, Vol. 66, 1959.

15. Creelman, M. B., *The Experimental Investigation of Meaning*, Springer, New York, 1966.

16. Darlington, J., "Translating Ordinary Language into Symbolic Logic." Memo. MAC-M-149, Project MAC, M.I.T., Cambridge, Mass., 1962.

17. Deese, J., "On the Structure of Associative Meaning," *Psych. Rev.*, Vol. 69, 1962.

18. De Groot, A. D., *Thought and Choice in Chess*, Mouton and Co., The Hague, 1965.

19. Ervin, S. M., "Changes with Age in the Verbal Determinants of Word Association," *Am. J. Psych.*, Vol. 74, 1961.

20. Feigenbaum, E. A., and Simon, H. A., "Performance of a Reading Task by an Elementary Perceiving and Memorizing Program," *Behavioral Science*, Vol. 8, 1963.

21. Feigenbaum, E. A., "An Information Processing Theory of Verbal Learning," Report P-1817, RAND Corp., Santa Monica, Calif., 1959.

22. Feigenbaum, E. A., and Feldman, J. (eds.), *Computers and Thought*, McGraw-Hill, New York, 1963.

23. *Fifth Annual Report, the Center for Cognitive Studies, 1964-65*. The Center for Cognitive Studies, Harvard University, Cambridge, Mass., 1965.

24. Fillmore, C. J., "A Proposal Concerning English Prepositions," paper presented at M.I.T., Cambridge, Mass., April 1966.

25. *Funk and Wagnalls' New "Standard" Dictionary of the English Language*, Funk and Wagnalls, New York, 1959.

26. Gelernter, H., Hansen, J. R., and Loveland, D. W., "Empirical Explorations of the Geometry-Theorem Proving Machine," *Proc. WJCC*, Vol. 17, 1960.

27. Green, Jr., B. F., et al., "Baseball: An Automatic Question Answerer," *Proc. WJCC*, Vol. 19, 1961.

28. Halle, M., and Stevens, K. N., "Speech Recognition: A Model and a Program for Research," in Fodor, J. A., and Katz, J. J. (eds.), *The Structure of Language: Readings in the Philosophy of Language*, Prentice-Hall, Englewood Cliffs, N.J., 1964.

29. Hays, D. G. (ed.), *Readings in Automatic Language Processing*, Elsevier, New York, 1966.

30. Hunt, E. B., *Concept Learning: An Information Processing Problem*, John Wiley, New York, 1966.

31. Katz, J. J., and Fodor, J. A., "The Structure of a Semantic Theory," *Language*, Vol. 39, 1963.

32. Katz, J. J., and Postal, P. M., *An Integrated Theory of Linguistic Descriptions*, The M.I.T. Press, Cambridge, Mass., 1964.

33. Kelly, G., *The Psychology of Personal Constructs*, Vol. I, W. W. Norton, New York, 1955.

34. Klein, S., "Automatic Paraphrasing in Essay Format," SP-1602/001/00, System Development, Santa Monica, Calif., 1964.

35. Klein, S., and Simmons, R. F., "Syntactic Dependence and the Computer Generation of Coherent Discourse," *Mechanical Translation*, Vol. 7, 1963.

36. Kuno, S. K., "Multiple-Path Syntactic Analyzer," *Mathematical Linguistics and Automatic Translation*, Report NSF-8, Computation Laboratory, Harvard University, Cambridge, Mass., 1963.

37. Kuno, S. K., "The Predictive Analyzer," Communications of the Association for Computing Machinery, Vol. 8, 1965, reprinted reference 28.

38. Lakoff, G., "On the Nature of Syntactic Irregularity," *Mathematical Linguistics and Automatic Translation*, Report NSF-16, Computation Laboratory, Harvard University, Cambridge, Mass., 1965.

39. Lamb, S., "The Sememic Approach to Structural Semantics," Romney, K. A., and D'Andrede (eds.), Transcultural studies in cognition, *Am. Anthropologist*, Vol. 66, Part 2, 1964.

40. Lane, H., and Schneider, B., "Some Discriminative Properties of Syntactic Structures," *Verbal Learning and Verbal Behavior*, Vol. 2, 1963.

41. Lindsay, R. K., "Inferential Memory as the Basis of Machines which Understand Natural Language," Feigenbaum, E., and Feldman, J. (eds.), *Computers and Thought*, McGraw-Hill, New York, 1963.

42. Matthews, G. H., "Analysis by Synthesis of Sentences in a Natural Language," *First International Conference on Machine Translation and Applied Language Analysis*, Her Majesty's Stationery Office, London, 1962.

43. McCarthy, J., et al., *LISP 1.5 Programmer's Manual*, The M.I.T. Press, Cambridge, Mass., 1963.

44. Miller, G. A., "The Magical Number Seven, Plus or Minus Two: Some Limits on our Capacity for Processing Information," *Psych. Rev.*, Vol. 63, 1956.

45. Miller, G. A., and Chomsky, N., "Finite Models of Language Users," in Luce, R. D., Bush, R. L., and Glanter, E. (eds.), *Handbook of Mathematical Psychology*, Vol. II, John Wiley, New York, 1963.

46. Miller, G. A., Galenter, E., and Pribam, K. H., *Plans and the Structure of Behavior*, Holt, New York, 1960.

47. Minsky, M., "Steps Toward Artificial Intelligence," *Proc. IRE*, Vol. 49, No. 1, 1961, also in reference 22.

48. Minsky, M., "A Selected Descriptor-Indexed Bibliography to the Literature on Artificial Intelligence," in reference 22.

49. Newell, A. (ed.), "IPL-V Programmer's Reference Manual," Memorandum RM-3739-RC, RAND Corp., Santa Monica, Calif., 1963.

50. Newell, A., Shaw, J. C., and Simon, H. A., "The Processes of Creative Thinking," in H. E. Gruber, Terrell, G., and Wertheimer, M. (eds.), *Contemporary Approaches to Creative Thinking*, Atherton Press, New York, 1962.

51. Newell, A., Shaw, J. C., and Simon, H. A., "Chess Playing Programs and the Problem of Complexity," *IBM J. Research and Development*, Vol. 2, 1958.

52. Newell, A., and Simon, H. A., "Computers in Psychology," in Luce, R. D., Bush, R., and Galanter, E. (eds.), *Handbook of Mathematical Psychology*, Vol. 1, John Wiley, New York, 1963.

53. Newell, A., and Simon, H. A., "An Example of Human Chess Play in the Light of Chess Playing Programs," Carnegie Inst. Tech., Pittsburgh, Pa., 1964 (dittoed).

54. Ogden, C. K., *The General Basic English Dictionary*, W. W. Norton, New York, 1942.

55. Olney, J., "Building a Concept Network for Retrieving Information from Large Libraries: Part I," TM-634/001/11, System Development Corp., Santa Monica, Calif., 1962.

56. Olney, J. C., "Some Patterns Observed in the Contextual Specialization of Word Senses," *Information Storage and Retrieval*, Vol. 2, 1964.

57. Osgood, E. C., Suci, G. J., and Tannenbaum, P. H., *The Measurement of Meaning*, University of Illinois Press, Urbana, Ill., 1957.

58. Osgood, C. E., "On Understanding and Creating Sentences," *Am. Psychologist*, Vol. 18, 1965.

59. Paige, J. J., and Simon, H. A., "Cognitive Processes in Solving Algebra Word Problems," in Kleinmuntz, B. (ed.), *Problem Solving: Research, Method and Theory*, John Wiley, New York, 1966.

60. Petrick, S. R., "A Recognition Procedure for Transformational Grammars," unpublished Ph.D. thesis, M.I.T., 1965.

61. Piaget, J., *The Psychology of Intelligence*, translated by M. Cook and D. E. Berlyne, Routledge and Kegan Paul, London, England, 1950.

62. Quillian, R., "A Design for an Understanding Machine," paper presented at a colloquium: *Semantic Problems in Natural Language*, King's College, Cambridge, England, September 1961.

63. Quillian, R., "A Revised Design for an Understanding Machine," *Mechanical Translation*, Vol. 7, 1967.

64. Quillian, R., "A Semantic Coding Technique for Mechanical English Paraphrasing," Internal memorandum of the Mechanical Translation Group, Research Laboratory of Electronics, M.I.T., Cambridge, Mass., August 1962.

65. Quillian, R., "A Notation for Representing Conceptual Information: An Application to Semantics and Mechanical English Paraphrasing," SP-1395, System Development Corp., Santa Monica, Calif., 1963.

66. Quillian, R., Wortman, P., and Baylor, G. W., "The Programmable Piaget: Behavior from the Standpoint of a Radical Computerist." Unpublished dittoed Paper, Carnegie Inst. Tech., Pittsburgh, Pa., 1965.

67. Raphael, B., "A Computer Program Which 'Understands,'" *Proc. AFIPS*, 1964, *FJCC* (see also Chapter 2 of the present volume).

68. Razran, G. H. S., "A Quantitative Study of Meaning by a Conditioned Salivary Technique (Semantic Conditioning)," *Science*, Vol. 90, 1939.

69. Reich, P. A., "A Stratificational Theory of Language Acquisition," Working Paper No. 4 (IP-4), Dept. of Psychology and Mental Health Research Institute, University of Michigan, Ann Arbor, Mich., 1966.

70. Reid, L. S., Henneman, R. H., and Long, E. R., "An Experimental Analysis of Set: The Effect of Categorical Restriction," *Am. J. Psych.*, Vol. 73, 1960.

71. Reiss, R. F., "An Abstract Machine Based on Classical Association Psychology," Technical memorandum, Librascope Division, General Precision, Inc., Glendale, Calif., 1961.

72. Reitman, W. R., *Cognition and Thought: An Information Processing Approach*, John Wiley, New York, 1965.

73. Rubenstein, H., "Problems in Automatic Word Disambiguation," paper presented at a conference on Computer-Aided Semantic Research, Las Vegas, Nev., December 1965.

74. Simmons, R. F., "Synthetic Language Behavior," *Data Processing Management*, Vol. 5, 1963.

75. Simon, H. A., and Feigenbaum, E. A., "An Information-Processing Theory of Some Effects of Similarity, Familiarization, and Meaningfulness in Verbal Learning," *J. Verbal Learning and Verbal Behavior*, Vol. 3, 1964.

76. Simon, H. A., and Kotovsky, J., "Human Acquisition of Concepts for Sequential Patterns," *Psych. Rev.*, Vol. 70, 1963.

77. Skinner, B. F., *Verbal Behavior*, Appleton Century Crofts, New York, 1957.

78. Yngve, V. H., "A Model and an Hypothesis for Language Structure," *Proc. of the American Philosophical Society*, Vol. 104, No. 5, 1960.

79. Yngve, V. H., *COMIT Programmers' Reference Manual*, The M.I.T. Press, Cambridge, Mass., 1961.

WHAT'S IN A LINK:

Foundations for Semantic Networks

William A. Woods
*Bolt Beranek and Newman
Cambridge, Massachusetts*

I. INTRODUCTION

This chapter is concerned with the theoretical underpinnings for semantic network representations of the sort dealt with by Quillian (1968,1969), Rumelhart, Lindsay, & Norman (1972), Carbonell & Collins (1973), Schank (1975), Simmons (1973), etc. (I include Schank's conceptual dependency representations in this class although he himself may deny the kinship.) I am concerned specifically with understanding the semantics of the semantic network structures themselves, i.e., with what the notations and structures used in a semantic network can mean, and with interpretations of what these links mean that will be logically adequate to the job of representing knowledge. I want to focus on several issues: the meaning of "semantics", the need for explicit understanding of the intended meanings for various types of arcs and links, the need for careful thought in choosing conventions for representing facts as assemblages of arcs and nodes, and several specific difficult problems in knowledge representation--especially problems of relative clauses and quantification.

I think we must begin with the realization that there is currently no "theory" of semantic networks. The notion of semantic networks is for the most part an attractive notion which has yet to be proven. Even the question of what networks have to do with semantics is one which takes some answering. I am convinced that there is real value to the work that is being done in semantic network representations and that there is much to be learned from it. I feel, however, that the major discoveries are yet to be made and what is currently being done is not really understood. In this chapter I would like to make a start at such an understanding.

I will attempt to show that when the semantics of the notations are made clear, many of the techniques used in existing semantic networks are inadequate for representing knowledge in general. By means of examples, I will argue that if semantic networks are to be used as a representation for storing human verbal knowledge, then they must include mechanisms for representing propositions without commitment to asserting their truth or belief. Also they must be able to represent various types of intensional objects without commitment to their existence in the external world, their external distinctness, or their completeness in covering all of the objects which are presumed to exist. I will discuss the problems of representing restrictive relative clauses and argue that a commonly used "solution" is inadequate. I will also demonstrate the inadequacy of certain commonly used techniques which purport to handle quantificational information in semantic networks. Three adequate mechanisms will be presented, one of which to my knowledge has not previously been used in semantic nets. I will discuss several different possible uses of links and some of the different types of nodes and links which are required in a semantic network if it is to serve as a medium for representing knowledge.

The emphasis of this chapter will be on problems, possible solution techniques, and necessary characteristics of solutions, with particular emphasis on pointing out nonsolutions. No attempt will be made to formulate a complete specification of an adequate semantic network notation. Rather, the discussion will be oriented toward requirements for an adequate notation and the kind of explicit understanding of what one intends his notations to mean that are required to investigate such questions.

II. WHAT IS SEMANTICS?

First we must come to grips with the term "semantics". What do semantic networks have to do with semantics? What is semantics anyway? There is a great deal of misunderstanding on this point among computational linguists and psychologists. There are people who maintain that there is no distinction between syntax and semantics, and there are others who lump the entire inference and "thought" component of an AI system under the label "semantics". Moreover, the philosophers, linguists, and programming language theorists have notions of semantics which are distinct from each other and from many of the notions of computational linguists and psychologists.

What I will present first is my view of the way that the term "semantics" has come to be associated with so many different kinds of things, and the basic unity that I think it is all about. I will attempt to show that the source of many confusing claims such as "there is no difference between syntax and semantics" arise from a limited view of the total role of semantics in language.

A. The Philosopher and the Linguist

In my account of semantics, I will use some caricatured stereotypes to represent different points of view which have been expressed in the literature or seem to be implied. I will not attempt to tie specific persons to particular points of view since I may thereby make the error of misinterpreting some author. Instead, I will simply set up the stereotype as a possible point of view which someone might take, and proceed from there.

First, let me set up two caricatures which I will call the Linguist and the Philosopher, without thereby asserting that all linguists fall into the first category or philosophers in the second. Both, however, represent strong traditions in their respective fields. The Linguist has the following view of semantics in linguistics: he is interested in characterizing the fact that the same sentence can sometimes mean different things, and some sentences mean nothing at all. He would like to find some notation in which to express the different things which a sentence can mean and some procedure for determining whether a sentence is "anomalous" (i.e., has no meanings). The Philosopher on the other hand is concerned with specifying the meaning of a formal notation rather than a natural language. (Again, this is not true of all philosophers—just our caricature.) His notation is already unambiguous. What he is concerned with is determining when an expression in the notation is a "true" proposition (in some appropriate formal sense of truth) and when it is false. (Related questions are when it can be said to be necessarily true or necessarily false or logically true or logically false, etc.) Meaning for the Philosopher is not defined in terms of some other notation in which to represent different possible interpretations of a sentence, but he is interested in the conditions for truth of an already formal representation.

Clearly, these caricatured points of view are both parts of a larger view of the semantic interpretation of natural language. The Linguist is concerned with the translation of natural languages into formal representations of their meanings, while the Philosopher is interested in the meanings of such representations. One cannot really have a complete semantic specification of a natural language unless both of these tasks have been accomplished. I will, however, go further and point out that there is a consideration which the philosophers have not yet covered and which must be included in order to provide a complete semantic specification.

B. Procedural Semantics

While the types of semantic theories that have been formulated by logicians and philosophers do a reasonable job of specifying the semantics of complex constructions involving quantification and combination of predicates with operators of conjunction and negation, they fall down on the specification of the semantics of the basic "atomic" propositions consisting of a predicate and specifications of its arguments--for example, the specification of the meanings of elementary statements such as "snow is white" or "Socrates is mortal". In most accounts, these are presumed to have "truth conditions" which determine those possible worlds in which they are true and those in which they are false, but how does one specify those truth conditions? In order for an intelligent entity to know the meaning of such sentences it must be the case that it has stored somehow an effective set of criteria for deciding in a given possible world whether such a sentence is true or false. Thus it is not sufficient merely to say that the meaning of a sentence is a set of truth conditions--one must be able to specify the truth conditions for particular sentences. Most philosophers have not faced this issue for atomic sentences such as "snow is white."

Elsewhere I have argued (Woods, 1967, 1973a) that a specification of truth conditions can be made by means of a procedure or function which assigns truth values to propositions in particular possible worlds. Such procedures for determining truth or falsity are the basis for what I have called "procedural semantics" (although this interpretation of the term may differ slightly from that which is intended by other people who have since used it). This notion has served as the basis of several computer question-answering systems (Woods, Kaplan, & Nash-Webber, 1972; Woods, 1973b; Winograd, 1972).

The case presented above is a gross oversimplification of what is actually required for an adequate procedural specification of the semantics of natural language. There are strong reasons which dictate that the best one can expect to have is a partial function which assigns true in some cases, false in some cases, and fails to assign either true or false in others. There are also cases where the procedures require historical data which is not normally available and therefore cannot be directly executed. In these cases their behavior must be predicted on the basis of more complex inference techniques. Some of these issues are discussed more fully by Woods (1973a).

C. Semantic Specification of Natural Language

You now have the basics of my case for a broader view of the role of semantics in natural language. The outline of the picture goes like this:

There must be a notation for representing the meanings of sentences inside the brain (of humans or other intellects) that is not merely a direct encoding of the English word sequence. This must be so, since (among other reasons) what we understand by sentences usually includes the disambiguation of certain syntactic and semantic ambiguities present in the sentence itself.

The linguist is largely concerned with the process for getting from the external sentence to this internal representation (a process referred to as "semantic interpretation"). The philosopher is concerned with the rules of correspondence between expressions in such notations and truth and falsity (or correctness of assertion) in the real or in hypothetical worlds. Philosophers, however, have generally stopped short of trying to actually specify the truth conditions of the basic atomic propositions "inferences" have come to be used for the entire process. It is easy then to start incorrectly referring to the entire thought process as "semantics". One may properly use the term "semantic inferences" to refer to inferences that cross the boundary between symbol and referent, but one should keep in mind that this does not imply that all steps of the process are "semantic".

At the opposite extreme, there are those who deny any difference in principle between syntax and semantics and claim that the distinction is arbitrary. Again, the misconception arises from a limited view of the role of semantics. When semantics is used to select among different possible parsings of a sentence by using selectional restrictions on so-called semantic features of words, there is little difference between the techniques usually used and those used for checking syntactic features. In another paper (Woods, 1973a) I make the case that such techniques are merely approximations of the types of inferences that are really required, and that, in general, semantic selectional restrictions need to determine the referent of a phrase and then make inferences about that referent (i.e., they involve semantic inferences as I defined the term above). The approximate technique usually used, however, requires no special mechanism beyond what already exists in the syntax specification, and when taken as the paradigm for "semantic inferences" can lead to the false conclusion that semantics is no different from syntax. Likewise, if the representation constructed by a parser purports to be a semantic representation, with no intervening purely syntactic representation, then one might argue that the techniques used to produce it are syntactic techniques and therefore there is nothing left to be semantics.

As we have pointed out, however, a semantic specification requires more than the transformation of the input sentence into a "semantic" representation. The meanings of these representations must be specified also. Recall that semantics refers to the correspondence between linguistic expressions and the things that they denote or mean. Thus although it may be difficult to isolate exactly what part of a system is semantics, any system which understands sentences and carries out appropriate actions in

in their systems, dealing mainly with the specification of the meanings of complex expressions in terms of the meanings of elementary ones. Researchers in artificial intelligence are faced with the need to specify the semantics of elementary propositions as well as complex ones and are moreover required to put to the test the assembly of the entire system into a working total --including the interface to syntax and the subsequent inference and "thought" processes. Thus the researcher in artificial intelligence must take a more global view of the semantics of language than either the linguist or the philosopher has taken in the past. The same, I think, is true of psychologists.

D. Misconceptions about Semantics

There are two misconceptions of what semantics is about (or at least misuses of the term) which are rather widely circulated among computational linguists and which arise I think from a limited view of the role of semantics in language. They arise from traditional uses of the term which, through specialized application, eventually lose sight of what semantics is really about. According to my dictionary, semantics is "the scientific study of the relations between signs or symbols and what they denote or mean". This is the traditional use of the term and represents the common thread which links the different concerns discussed previously. Notice that the term does not refer to the things denoted or the meanings, but to the *relations* between these things and the linguistic expressions which denote them.

One common misuse of the term "semantics" in the fields of computational linguistics and artificial intelligence is to extend the coverage of the term not only to this relation between linguistic form and meaning, but to all of the retrieval and inference capabilities of the system. This misuse arises since for many tasks in language processing, the use of semantic information necessarily involves not only the determination of the object denoted, but also some inference about that object. In absence of a good name for this further inference process, terms such as "semantic response to them is somehow completing this connection. For systems which do not extend beyond the production of a so-called semantic representation, there may or may not be a semantic component included, and the justification for calling something semantic may be lost. Again, if one takes the production of such "semantic" representations as the paradigm case for what semantics is, one is misunderstanding the meaning of the term.

E. Semantics of Programming Languages

Before proceeding it is probably worth pointing out that the use of the term "semantics" by programming language theorists has been much closer to the tradition of the logicians and the philosophers and less confused than in computational linguistics. Programming language theory is frequently used as a paradigm for natural language semantics. Programming languages, however, do not have many of the features that natural languages do and the mechanisms developed there are not sufficient for modeling the semantics of natural language without considerable stretching.

The programming language theorists do have one advantage over the philosophers and linguists in that their semantic specifications stand on firmer ground since they are defined in terms of the procedures that the machine is to carry out. It is this same advantage which the notion of procedural semantics and artificial intelligence brings to the specification of the semantics of natural language. Although in ordinary natural language not every sentence is overtly dealing with procedures to be executed, it is possible nevertheless to use the notion of procedures as a means of specifying the truth conditions of declarative statements as well as the intended meaning of questions and commands. One thus picks up the semantic chain from the philosophers at the level of truth conditions and completes it to the level of formal specifications of procedures. These can in turn be characterized by their operations on real machines and can be thereby anchored to physics. (Notice that the notion of procedure shares with the notion of meaning that elusive quality of being impossible to present except by means of alternative representations. The procedure itself is something abstract which is instantiated whenever someone carries out the procedure, but otherwise, all one has when it is not being executed is some representation of it.)

III. SEMANTICS AND SEMANTIC NETWORKS

Having established a framework for understanding what we mean by semantics, let us now proceed to see how semantic networks fit into the picture. Semantic networks presumably are candidates for the role of internal semantic representation--i.e., the notation used to store knowledge inside the head. Their competitors for this role are formal logics such as the predicate calculus, and various representations such as Lakoff-type deep structures, and Fillmore-type case representations. (The case representations shade off almost imperceptibly into certain possible semantic network representations and hence it is probably not fruitful to draw any clear distinction.) The major characteristic of the semantic networks that distinguishes them from other candidates is the characteristic notion of a link or pointer which connects individual facts into a total structure.

A semantic network attempts to combine in a single mechanism the ability not only to store factual knowledge but also to model the associative connections exhibited by humans which make certain items of information accessible from certain others. It is possible presumably to model these two aspects with two separate mechanisms such as for example, a list of the facts expressed in the predicate calculus or some such representation, together with an index of associative connections which link facts together. Semantic network representations attempt instead to produce a single representation which by virtue of the way in which it represents facts (i.e., by assemblies of pointers to other facts) automatically provides the appropriate associative connections. One should keep in mind that the assumption that such a representation is possible is merely an item of faith, an unproven hypothesis used as the basis of the methodology. It is entirely conceivable that no such single representation is possible.

A. Requirements for a Semantic Representation

When one tries to devise a notation or a language for semantic representation, one is seeking a representation which will precisely, formally, and unambiguously represent any particular interpretation that a human listener may place on a sentence. We will refer to this as "logical adequacy" of a semantic representation. There are two other requirements of a good semantic representation. One is that beyond the requirement of logical adequacy, there must be an algorithm or procedure for translating the original sentence into this representation and the other is that there must be algorithms which can make use of this representation for the subsequent inferences and deductions that the human or machine must perform on them. Thus one is seeking a representation which facilitates translation and subsequent intelligent processing, in addition to providing a notation for expressing any particular interpretation of a sentence.

B. The Canonical Form Myth

Before continuing, let me mention one thing which semantic networks should not be expected to do: that is to provide a "canonical form" in which all paraphrases of a given proposition are reduced to a single standard (or canonical) form. It is true that humans seem to reduce input sentences into some different internal form that does not preserve all of the information about the form in which the sentence was received (e.g., whether it was in the active or the passive). A canonical form, however, requires a great deal more than this. A canonical form requires that *every* expression equivalent to a given one can be reduced to a single form by means of an effective procedure, so that tests of equivalence between descriptions can be reduced to the testing of identity of canonical form. I will make two points. The first is that it is unlikely that there could be a canonical form for English, and the second is that for independent reasons, in order to duplicate human behavior in paraphrasing, one would still need all of the inferential machinery that canonical forms attempt to avoid.

Consider first the motivation for wanting a canonical form. Given a system of expressions in some notation (in this case English, or more specifically an internal semantic representation of English) and given a set of equivalence-preserving transformations (such as paraphrasing or logical equivalence transformations) which map one expression into an equivalent expression, two expressions are said to be equivalent if one can be transformed into the other by some sequence of these equivalence transformations. If one wanted to determine if two expressions $e1$ and $e2$ were equivalent, one would expect to have to search for a sequence of transformations that would produce one from the other—a search which could be nondeterministic and expensive to carry out. A canonical form for the system is a computable function c which transforms any expression e into a unique equivalent expression $c(e)$ such that for any two expressions $e1$ and $e2$, $e1$ is equivalent to $e2$, if and only if $c(e1)$ is equal to $c(e2)$. With such a function, one can avoid the combinatoric search for an equivalence chain connecting the two expressions and merely compute the corresponding canonical forms and compare them for identity. Thus a canonical form provides an improvement in efficiency over having to search for an equivalence chain for each individual case (assuming that the function c is efficiently computable).

A canonical form function is, however, a very special function, and it is not necessarily the case for a given system of expressions and equivalence transformations that there is such a function. It can be shown for certain formal systems [such as the word problem for semigroups (Davis, 1958)] that there can be no computable canonical form function with the above properties. That is, in order to determine the equivalence of a particular pair of expressions $e1$ and $e2$ it may be necessary to actually search for a chain of equivalence transformations that connects these two particular expressions, rather than performing separate transformations $c(e1)$ and $c(e2)$ (both of which know exactly where to stop) and then compare these resulting expressions for identity. If this can be the case for formal systems as simple as semigroups, it would be foolhardy to assume lightly that there is a canonical form for something as complex as English paraphrasing.

brother, sister, etc. The data structure chosen is a logically minimal representation of a family unit consisting of a male and female parent and some number of offspring. Concepts such as aunt, uncle, and brother-in-law are not represented explicitly in the structure but are rather implicit in the structure and questions about unclehood are answered by checking brothers of the father and brothers of the mother. What does such a system do, however, when it encounters the input "Harry is John's uncle"? It does not know whether to assign Harry as a sibling of John's father or his mother. Lindsay had no good solution for this problem other than the suggestion to somehow make both entries and connect them together with some kind of a connection which indicates that one of them is wrong. It seems that for handling "vague" predicates such as uncle, i.e., predicates which are not specific with respect to some of the details of an underlying representation, we must make provision for storing such predicates directly (i.e., in terms of a concept of uncle in this case), even though this concept may be defined in terms of more "basic" relationships (ignoring here the issue that there may be no objective criterion for selecting any particular set of relationships as basic).

If we hope to be able to store information at the level of detail that it may be presented to us in English, then we are compelled to surrender the assumptions of logical minimality in our internal representation and provide for storing such redundant concepts as "uncle" directly. We would not, however, like to have to store all such facts redundantly. That is, given a Lindsay-type data base of family units, we would not want to be compelled to store explicitly all of the instances of unclehood that could be inferred from the basic family units. If we were to carry such a program to its logical conclusion, we would have to store explicitly all of the possible inferable relations, a practical impossibility since in many cases the number of such inferables is effectively infinite. Hence the internal structure which we desire must have some instances of unclehood stored directly and others left to be deduced from more basic family relationships, thus demolishing any hope of a canonical form representation.

Now, for the second point. Quite aside from the possibility of having a canonical form function for English, I will attempt to argue that one still needs to be able to search for individual chains of inference between pairs of expressions $e1$ and $e2$ and thus the principal motivation for wanting a canonical form is superfluous. The point is that in most cases where one is interested in some paraphrase behavior, the paraphrase desired is not one of full logical equivalence, but only of implication in one direction. For example, one is interested in whether the truth of some expression $e1$ is implied by some stored expression $e2$. If one had a canonical form function, then one could store only canonical forms in the data base and ask simply whether $c(e1)$ is stored in the data base without having to apply any equivalence transformations in the process. This is, however, just a special case. It is rather unlikely that what we have in the data base is an expression exactly logically equivalent to $e1$ (i.e., some $e2$ such that $e2$ implies $e1$ and $e1$ implies $e2$). Rather, what we expect in the typical case is that we will find some $e2$ that implies $e1$ but not vice versa. For this case, we must be able to find an inference chain as part of our retrieval process. Given that we must devise an appropriate inferential retrieval process for dealing with this case (which is the more common), the special case of full equivalence will fall out as a consequence; thus the canonical form mechanism for handling the full equivalence case gives no improvement in performance and is unnecessary.

There is still benefit from "partially canonicalizing" the stored knowledge (the term is reminiscent of the concept of being just a little bit pregnant). This is useful to avoid storing multiple equivalent representations of the same fact. There is, however, little motivation for making sure that this form does in fact reduce all equivalent expressions to the same form (and as I said before, there is every reason to believe that this may be impossible).

Another argument against the expectation of a canonical form solution to the equivalence problem comes from the following situation. Consider the kinship relations program of Lindsay (1963). The basic domain of discourse of the system is family relationships such as mother, father,

C. Semantics of Semantic Network Notations

When I create a node in a network or when I establish a link of some type between two nodes, I am building up a representation of something in a notation. The question that I will be concerned with in the remainder of this chapter is what do I mean by this representation. For example, if I create a node and establish two links from it, one labeled SUPERC and pointing to the "concept" TELEPHONE and another labeled MOD and pointing to the "concept" BLACK, what do I mean this node to represent? Do I intend it to stand for the "concept" of a black telephone, or perhaps I mean it to assert a relationship between the concepts of telephone and blackness--i.e., that telephones are black (all telephones?, some telephones?). When one devises a semantic network notation, it is necessary not only to specify the types of nodes and links that can be used and the rules for their possible combinations (the syntax of the network notation) but also to specify the import of the various types of links and structures--what is meant by them (the semantics of the network notation).

D. Intensions and Extensions

To begin, I would like to raise the distinction between intension and extension, a distinction that has been variously referred to as the difference between sense and reference, meaning and denotation, and various other pairs of terms. Basically a predicate such as the English word "red" has associated with it two possible conceptual things which could be related to its meaning in the intuitive sense. One of these is the set of all red things--this is called the *extension* of the predicate. The other concept is an abstract entity which in some sense characterizes what it means to be red, it is the notion of *redness* which may or may not be true of a given object; this is called the *intension* of the predicate. In many philosophical theories the intension of a predicate is identified with an abstract function which applies to possible worlds and assigns to any such world a set of extensional objects (e.g., the intension of "red" would assign to each possible world a set of red things). In such a theory, when one wants to refer to the concept of redness, what is denoted is this abstract function.

E. The Need for Intensional Representation

The following quotation from Quine (1961) relating an example of Frege should illustrate the kind of thing that I am trying to distinguish as an internal intensional entity:

The phrase "Evening Star" names a certain large physical object of spherical form, which is hurtling through space some scores of millions of miles from here. The phrase "Morning Star" names the same thing, as was probably first established by some observant Babylonian. But the two phrases cannot be regarded as having the same meaning; otherwise that Babylonian could have dispensed with his observations and contented himself with reflecting on the meanings of his words. The meanings, then, being different from one another, must be other than the named object, which is one and the same in both cases. (Quine, 1961, p. 9).

In the appropriate internal representation, there must be two mental entities (concepts, nodes, or whatever) corresponding to the two different intensions, morning star and evening star. There is then an assertion about these two intensional entities that they denote one and the same external object (extension).

In artificial intelligence applications and psychology, it is not sufficient for these intensions to be abstract entities such as possibly infinite sets, but rather they must have some finite representation inside the head as it were, or in our case in the internal semantic representation.

F. Attributes and Values

Much of the structure of semantic networks is based on,

or at least similar to, the notion of attribute and value which has become a standard concept in a variety of computer science applications and which was the basis of Raphael's SIR program (Raphael, 1964)--perhaps the earliest forerunner of today's semantic networks. Facts about an object can frequently be stored on a "property list" of the object by specifying such attribute-value pairs as HEIGHT : 6 FEET, HAIRCOLOR : BROWN, OCCUPATION : SCIENTIST, etc. (Such lists are provided, for example, for all atoms in the LISP programming language.) One way of thinking of these pairs is that the attribute name (i.e., the first element of the pair) is the name of a "link" or "pointer" which points to the "value" of the attribute (i.e., the second element of the pair). Such a description of a person named John might be laid out graphically as:

JOHN   HEIGHT   6 FEET
        HAIRCOLOR   BROWN
        OCCUPATION SCIENTIST

Now it may seem the case that the intuitive examples which I just gave are all that it takes to explain what is meant by the notion of attribute-value pair, and that the use of such notations can now be used as part of a semantic network notation without further explanation. I will try to make the case that this is not so and thereby give a simple introduction to the kinds of things I mean when I say that the semantics of the network notation need to be specified.

The above examples seem to imply that the thing which occurs as the second element of an attribute-value pair is the *name* or at least some unique handle on the value of that attribute. What will I do, however, with an input sentence "John's height is greater than 6 feet?" Most people would not hesitate to construct a representation such as:

JOHN   HEIGHT (GREATERTHAN 6 FEET)

Notice, however, that our interpretation of what our

network notations mean has just taken a great leap. No longer is the second element of the attribute-value pair a name or a pointer to a value, but rather it is a predicate which is asserted to be true of the value. One can think of the names such as 6 FEET and BROWN in the previous examples as special cases of identity predicates which are abbreviated for the sake of conciseness, and thereby consider the thing at the end of the pointer to be always a predicate rather than a name. Thus there are at least two possible interpretations of the meaning of the thing at the end of the link--either as the name of the value or as a predicate which must be true of the value. The former will not handle the (GREATERTHAN 6 FEET) example, while the latter will.

Let us consider now another example--John's height is greater than Sue's." We now have a new set of problems. We can still think of a link named HEIGHT pointing from JOHN to a predicate whose interpretation is "greater than Sue's height", but what does the reference to Sue's height inside this predicate have to do with the way that we represented John's height? In a functional form we would simply represent this as HEIGHT(JOHN) > HEIGHT(SUE), or in LISP type "Cambridge Polish" notation,

(GREATER (HEIGHT JOHN)(HEIGHT SUE))

but that is departing completely from the notion of attribute-value links. There is another possible interpretation of the thing at the end of the HEIGHT link which would be capable of dealing with this type of situation. That is, the HEIGHT link can point from JOHN to a node which represents the intensional object "John's height". In a similar way, we can have a link named HEIGHT from SUE to a node which represents "Sue's height" and then we can establish a relation GREATER between these two intensional nodes. (Notice that even if the heights were the same, the two intensional objects would be different, just as in the morning star/evening star example.) This requires a major reinterpretation of the semantics of our notation and a new set of conventions for how we set up networks. We must now introduce a new intensional node at the end of each attribute link and then between the node and other nodes. If we are to mix the two notations together as in:

```
JOHN    HEIGHT    6 FEET
        HIT       MARY
```

then we need either to provide somewhere an indication that these two links are of different types and therefore must be treated differently by the procedures which make inferences in the net, or else we need to find a unifying interpretation such as considering that the "attribute" HEIGHT is now really an abbreviation of the relation "height of equals" which holds between JOHN and (the node?) 6 FEET. It is not sufficient to leave it to the intuition of the reader, we must know how the machine will know to treat the two arcs correctly.

If we use Church's lambda notation, which provides a convenient notation for naming predicates and functions constructed out of combinations or variations of other functions (this is used, for example, as the basic function specification notation in the LISP programming language), we could define the meaning of the height link as the relation (LAMBDA (X Y) (EQUAL (HEIGHT X) Y)). By this we mean the predicate of two arguments X and Y which is true when and only when the height of X is equal to Y. Thus a possible unifying interpretation of the notation is that the link is always the name of a relation between the node being described and the node pointed to, (providing that we reinterpret what we meant by the original link named HEIGHT). Whatever we do, we clearly need some mechanism for establishing relations between nodes as facts (e.g., to establish the above GREATER relation between the nodes for John's height and Sue's height).

H. Relations of More Than Two Arguments

In the example just presented, we have used a link to assert a relation between two objects in the network corresponding to the proposition that John hit Mary. Such

establish predicates as facts that are true about such intensional objects. It also raises for us a need to somewhere indicate about this new node that it was created to represent the concept of John's height, and that the additional information that it is greater than Sue's height is not one of its defining properties but rather a separate assertion about the node. Thus a distinction between defining and asserted properties of the node become important here. In my conception of semantic networks I have used the concept of an EGO link to indicate for the benefit of the human researcher and eventually for the benefit of the system itself what a given node is created to stand for. Thus the EGOs of these two nodes are John's height and Sue's height respectively. The EGO link represents the intensional identity of the node.

G. Links and Predication

In addition to considering what is at the end of a link, we must also consider what the link itself means. The examples above suggest that an attribute link named Z from node X to Y is equivalent to the English sentence "the Z of X is Y" or functionally $Z(X)=Y$ or (in the case where Y is a predicate) $Y(Z(X))$, (read Y of Z of X). Many people, however, have used the same mechanism and notation (and even called it attribute-value pairs) to represent arbitrary English verbs by storing a sentence such as "John hit Mary" as a link named HIT from the node for John to the node for Mary, as in the structure:

```
JOHN    HIT    MARY
```

and perhaps placing an inverse link under Mary:

```
MARY    HIT*    JOHN
```

If we do this, then suddenly the semantics of our notation has changed again. No longer do the link names stand for attributes of the node, but rather arbitrary relations a method of handling assertions has a number of disadvantages, perhaps the simplest of which is that it is constrained to handling binary relations. If we have a predicate such as the English preposition "between" (i.e., LAMBDA (X Y Z) (Y is between X and Z)), then we must invent some new kind of structure for expressing such facts. A typical, but not very satisfying, notation which one might find in a semantic network which uses links for relations is something like:

$$Y \quad \text{LOCATION} \quad (\text{BETWEEN1 } X \text{ } Z)$$

usually without further specification of the semantics of the notation or what kind of thing the structure (BETWEEN X Z) is. For example, is it the name of a place? In some implementations it would be exactly that, in spite of the fact that an underlying model in which there is only one place between any given pair of places is an inadequate model of the world we live in. Another possible interpretation is that it denotes the range of places between the two endpoints (this interpretation requires another interpretation of what the LOCATION link means-- the thing at the end is no longer a name of a place but rather a set of places, and the LOCATION link must be considered to be implicitly existentially quantified in order to be interpreted as asserting that the location is actually one of those places and not all).

Given the notion which we introduced previously that interprets the thing at the end of the link as a predicate which must be true of the location, we have perhaps the best interpretation--we can interpret the expression (BETWEEN X Z) at the end of the link as being an abbreviation for the predicate (LAMBDA (U) (BETWEEN X U Z)), i.e., a one place predicate whose variable is U and whose values of X and Z are fixed to whatever X and Z are.

Although this representation of the three-place predicate "between" (when supplied with an appropriate interpretation of what it means) seems plausible, and I see no major objections to it on the grounds of logical inadequacy, one is left with the suspicion that there may be some predicates

of more than two places which do not have such an intuitively satisfying decomposition into links connecting only two objects at a time. For example, I had to introduce the concept of location as the name of the link from Y to the special object (BETWEEN X Z). In this case, I was able to find a preexisting English concept which made the creation of this link plausible, but is this always the case? The account would have been much less satisfying if all I could have produced was something like:

$$X \quad \text{BETWEEN1} \quad (\text{BETWEEN2 } Y \text{ } Z)$$

with an explication of its semantics that (BETWEEN2 Y Z) was merely some special kind of entity which when linked to X by a BETWEEN1 link represented the proposition (BETWEEN X Y Z). It may be the case that all predicates in English with more than two arguments have a natural binary decomposition. The basic subject-predicate distinction which seems to be made by our language gives some slight evidence for this. It seems to me, however, that finding a natural binary decomposition for sentences such as "John sold Mary a book" (or any of Schank's various TRANS operations) is unlikely.

I. Case Representations in Semantic Networks

Another type of representation is becoming popular in semantic networks and handles the problem of relations of more than one argument very nicely. This representation is based on the notion of case introduced by Fillmore (1968). Fillmore advocates a unifying treatment of the inflected cases of nominals in Latin and other highly inflected languages and the prepositions and positional clues to role that occur in English and other largely noninflected languages. A *case* as Fillmore uses the term is the name of a particular role that a noun phrase or other participant takes in the state or activity expressed by the verb of a sentence. In the case of the sentence "John sold Mary a book" we can say that John is the *agent* of the action, Mary is the *recipient* or *beneficiary* of the action, and the book is the *object* or *patient* of the action (where I have taken arbitrary but typical names for the case roles involved for the sake of illustration). When such a notation is applied to semantic network representations, a major restructuring of the network and what it means to be a link takes place. Instead of the assertion of a fact being carried by a link between two nodes, the asserted fact is itself a node. Our structure might look something like:

```
SELL
    AGT     JOHN
    RECIP   MARY
    PAT     BOOK
```

(ignoring for the moment what has happened to turn "a book" into BOOK or for that matter what we mean by JOHN and MARY--we will get into that later). The notation as I have written it requires a great deal of explanation, which is unfortunately not usually spelled out in the presentation of a semantic network notation. In our previous examples, the first item (holding the position where we have placed SELL above) has been the unique name or "handle" on a node, and the remaining link-value pairs have been predicates that are true of this node. In the case above, which I have written that way because one is likely to find equivalent representations in the literature, we are clearly not defining characteristics of the general verb "sell", but rather setting up a description of a particular instance of selling. Thus to be consistent with our earlier format for representing a node we should more properly represent it as something like:

```
S13472
    VERB    SELL
    AGT     JOHN
    RECIP   MARY
    PAT     BOOK
```

where S13472 is some unique internal handle on the node representing this instance of selling, and SELL is now the internal handle on the concept of selling. (I have gone through this two-stage presentation in order to emphasize that the relationship between the node S13472 and the concept of selling is not essentially different at this level from the relationship it has to the other nodes which fill the cases.)

J. Assertional and Structural Links

Clearly the case structure representation in a semantic network places a new interpretation on the nodes and arcs in the net. We still seem to have the same types of nodes that we had before for JOHN, MARY, etc., but we have a new type of node for nodes such as S13472 which represent assertions or facts. Moreover, the import of the links from this new type of node is different from that of our other links. Whereas the links which we discussed before are assertional, i.e., their mere presence in the network represents an assertion about the two nodes that they connect, these new link names, VERB, AGT, RECIP, PAT, are merely setting up parts of the proposition represented by node S13472, and no single link has any assertional import by itself; rather these links are definitional or structural in the sense that they constitute the definition of what node S13472 means.

Now you may argue that these links are really the same as the others, i.e., they correspond to the assertion that the agent of S13472 is JOHN and that S13472 is an instance of selling, etc. just like the "hit" link between John and Mary in our previous example. In our previous example, however, the nodes for John and for Mary had some a priori meanings independent of the assertion of hitting that we were trying to establish between them. In this case, S13472 has no meaning other than that which we establish by virtue of the structural links which it has to other nodes. That is, if we were to ask for the ego of the node S13472, we would get back something like "I am an instance of John selling a book to Mary" or "I am an instance of selling whose agent is John, whose recipient is Mary and whose patient is a book." If we were to ask for the ego of JOHN, we would get something like "I am the guy who works in the third office down the hall, whose name is John Smith, etc." The fact which I am trying to assert with the "hit" link is not part of the ego of JOHN or else I would not be making a new assertion.

This difference between assertional and structural links is rather difficult for some people to understand, and is often confused in various semantic network representations. It is part of the problem that we cited earlier in trying to determine whether a structure such as:

```
N12368        TELEPHONE
SUPERC
MOD           BLACK
```

is to be interpreted as an intensional representation of a black telephone or an assertion that telephones are black. If it is to be interpreted as an intensional representation of the concept of a black telephone, then both of these links are structural or definitional. If on the other hand, it is to be interpreted as asserting that telephones are black, then the first link is structural while the second is assertional. (The distinction between structural and assertional links does not take care of this example entirely since we still have to worry about how the assertional link gets its quantificational import for this interpretation, but we will discuss this problem later.)

The above discussion barely suffices to introduce the distinction between structural and assertional links, and certainly does not make the distinction totally clear. Moreover, before we are through, we may have cause to repudiate the assumption that the links involved in our non-case representation should be considered to have assertional import. Perhaps the best way to get deeper into the problems of different types of links with different imports and the representation of intensional entities is to consider further some specific problems in knowledge representation.

IV. PROBLEMS IN KNOWLEDGE REPRESENTATION

In previous sections I hope that I have made the point that the same semantic network notations could be used by

different people (or even by the same person at different times for different examples) to mean different things, and therefore one must be specific in presenting a semantic network notation to make clear what one means by the notations which one uses (i.e., the semantics of the notation). In the remainder of this chapter, I would like to discuss two difficult problems of knowledge representation and use the discussion to illustrate several additional possible uses of links and some of the different types of nodes and links which are required in a semantic network if it is to serve as a medium for representing human verbal knowledge. The specific problems which I will consider are the representation of restrictive relative clauses and the representation of quantified information.

A. Relative Clauses

In attaching modifiers to nodes in a network to provide an intensional description for a restricted class, one often requires restrictions which do not happen to exist in the language as single-word modifiers but have to be constructed out of more primitive elements. The relative clause mechanism permits this. Anything that can be said as a proposition can be used as a relative clause by leaving some one of its argument slots unfilled and using it as a modifier. (We will be concerned here only with restrictive relative clauses and not those which are just parenthetical comments about an already determined object.) Let me begin my discussion of relative clauses by dispensing with one inadequate treatment.

The Shared Subpart Fallacy: A mechanism which occasionally surfaces as a claimed technique for dealing with relative clauses is to take simply the two propositions involved, the main clause and the relative clause, and represent the two separately as if they were independent propositions. In such a representation, the sentence "The dog that bit the man had rabies" would look something like that in Fig. 1. The point of interest here is not the names of the links (for which I make no claims) nor the type of representation (case oriented, deep conceptual, or whatever), but simply the fact that the only relationship between the two propositions is that they share the same node for dog. There are a number of problems with this representation: First, since there is no other relationship between the two sentences except sharing of a node (which is a symmetric relationship) there is no indication of which is the main clause and which is the relative clause. That is, we would get the same internal representation for the sentence "The dog that had rabies bit the man."

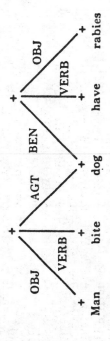

Fig. 1. A shared subpart representation.

Another difficulty is that there is nothing to indicate that the two sentences go together at all in a relative clause relationship. It is possible that on two different occasions we were told about this dog. On one occasion that he had rabies and on another that he bit a man. Then the presence of the two propositions in our data base both sharing the same node for dog would give us a structure identical to that for the example sentence. Now there is a subtle confusion which can happen at this point which I would like to try to clarify. You may say to me, "So what is the problem? Suppose I tell you about this dog and suppose I have told you the two facts at different times, then it is still true that the dog that bit the man has rabies." How do I answer such an argument? On the face of it it seems true. Yet I maintain that the argument is fallacious and that it results from too shallow a treatment of the issues. The crux of the matter I think rests in the notion of which dog we are talking about. Unfortunately, this issue is one that gets omitted from almost all such discussions of semantic networks. If the two facts were told to me at different times, how did I know that they

were about the same dog? (Without further explication of the semantics of the network notation, it is not even clear that we are talking about a particular dog and not about dogs in general.) It is exactly in order to relate the second fact to the first that we need the relative clause mechanism. In the next section we will consider the problem in more detail.

The Transient-Process Account: Quillian[1] once made the observation that a portion of what was in an input sentence was essentially stage directions used to enable the understanding process to identify an appropriate internal concept or node and the rest of the utterance was to be interpreted as new information to be added somehow to the network (and similar observations have been made by others). This gives an attractive account of the relative clause problem above. We interpret the relative clause not as something to be added to the network at all, but rather as a description to be used by the understander to determine which dog is in question. After this, we can forget about the relative clause (it has served its usefulness) and simply add this the new information to the network. We might call this the "transient-process account". Under this account, if I was told about a dog that bit a man and later told that the dog that bit the man had rabies, then I would simply use the relative clause to find the internal concept for the dog that bit the man, and then add the new information that the dog had rabies. What's wrong with that account? Doesn't that explain everything?

Well, no. First, it simply evades the issue of representing the meaning of the sentence, focusing instead on the resulting change in memory contents. It says essentially that the role of the relative clause is a temporary and transient one that exists only during the processing of the utterance and then goes away. But you say, "well, isn't that a plausible account, does not that take care of the problem nicely, who says you have to have a representation of the original sentence anyway?"

---

[1]Personal communication.

determined by the relative clause does not previously exist and something must be created in the semantic network which will continue to exist after the process is finished. This thing must have an internal representation which preserves the information that it is an object determined by a relative clause.

A second argument against the transient process account is that even for sentences where nothing needs to remain in memory after the process has completed (because the relative clause has been used to locate a preexisting node), something needs to be extracted from the input sentence which describes the node to be searched for. In our previous example something like the proposition "the dog bit the man" needs to be constructed in order to search for its instances, and the process must know when it finds such an instance that it is the dog that is of interest and not the man. This specification of the node to be searched for is exactly the kind of thing which a semantic interpretation for the noun phrase "the dog that bit the man" should be. Thus even when no permanent representation of the relative clause needs to remain after the understanding process has completed, something equivalent to it still needs to be constructed as part of the input to the search process. The transient process account does not eliminate the need for such a representation, and the issue of whether a complete representation of the entire sentence (including the relative clause) gets constructed and sent off to the understanding process as a unit or whether small pieces get created and sent off independently without ever being assembled into a complete representation is at this point a red herring. The necessary operations which are required for the search specification are sufficient to construct such a representation, and whether it is actually constructed or whether parts of it are merely executed for effect and then cast away is a totally separate question.

A third argument against the transient process account, which should have become apparent in the above discussion, is that it is not an account at all, but merely a way of avoiding the problem. By claiming that the relative clause is handled during the transient process we have merely pushed the problem of accounting for relative clauses off onto the person who attempts to characterize the

Let's start from the first question--yes, it is a plausible account of the interpretation of *many* sentences, including this one in the context I just set up, and it may also be a correct description of what happens when humans process such sentences. It does not, however, take care of all occurrences of relative clauses. What about a situation when I read this sentence out of context and I haven't heard about the dog before? Then my processing must be different. I must infer that there must be a dog that I do not know about, perhaps create a new node for it, and then assert about this new node that it has rabies. Clearly also I must associate with this new node that it is a dog and that it bit a man. How then do I keep these two different types of information separate--the information which designates what I set the node up to stand for and that which the sentence asserted about it. We're back to the same problem. We need to distinguish the information that is in the relative clause from that in the main clause.

One possible way would be the use of an EGO link which points to a specification of what the node represents. Using such a link, when one creates the new node for the dog which bit the man, one would give the new node an EGO link which in essence says "I am the node which represents the dog that bit the man." When one then adds information to this node asserting additional facts about it, the original motivation for creating the node in the first place is not forgotten and the difference between the sentences "The dog that bit the man had rabies" and "The dog that had rabies bit the man" would lie in whether the facts about biting or about rabies were at the end of the EGO link. (There are a number of other questions which would require answers in order to complete the specification of the use of EGO links for this purpose--such as whether the propositions at the end of the EGO link are thereby made indirectly available as properties of this node or whether they are redundantly also included in the same status as the additional asserted · properties which come later. We will not, however, go into these issues here.)

The above argument should have convinced you that the simple explanation of using relative clauses always only to identify preexisting nodes does not cover all of the cases. For certain sentences such as the above example, the object understanding process. We have not accounted for it or solved it.

B. Representation of Complex Sentences

Let us return to the question of whether one needs a representation of the entire sentence as a whole or not. More specifically, does one need a representation of a proposition expressed about a node which itself has a propositional restriction, or can one effectively break this process up in such a way that propositions are always expressed about definite nodes? This is going to be a difficult question to answer because there is a sense in which even if the answer is the former, one can model it with a process which first constructs the relative clause restricted node and then calls it definite and represents the higher proposition with a pointer to this new node. The real question, then, is in what sense is this new node definite? Does it always refer to a single specific node like the dog in our above example, or is it more complicated than that? I will argue the latter.

C. Definite and Indefinite Entities

Consider the case which we hypothesized in which we had to infer the existence of a heretofore unknown dog because we found no referent for "the dog that bit the man". This new node still has a certain definiteness to it. We can later refer to it again and add additional information, eventually fleshing it out to include its name, who owns it, etc. As such it is no different from any other node in the data base standing for a person, place, thing, etc. It got created when we first encountered the object denoted (or at least when we first recognized it and added it to our memory) and has subsequently gained additional information and may in the future gain additional information still. We know that it is a particular dog and not a class of dogs and many other things about it.

Consider, however, the question "Was the man bitten by a dog that had rabies?" Now we have a description of an indefinite dog and moreover we have not asserted that it exists but merely questioned its existence. Now you may first try to weasel out of the problem by saying something like, "Well, what happens is that we look in our data base for dogs that have rabies in the same way that we would in the earlier examples, and finding no such dog, we answer the question in the negative." This is another example of pushing the problem off onto the understanding process; it does not solve it or account for it, it just avoids it (not to mention the assumption that the absence of information from the network implies its falsity).

Let us consider the process more closely. Unless our process were appropriately constructed (how?) it would not know the difference (at the time it was searching for the referent of the phrase) between this case and the case of an assertion about an unknown dog. Hence the process we described above would create a new node for a dog that has rabies unless we block it somehow. Merely asking whether the main clause is a question would not do it, since the sentence "Did the dog that bit the man have rabies?" still must have the effect of creating a new definite node. (This is due to the effect of the presupposition of the definite singular determiner "the" that the object described must exist.) Nor is it really quite the effect of the indefinite article "a", since the sentence "a dog that had rabies bit the man" should still create a definite node for the dog. We could try conditions on questioned indefinites. Maybe that would work, but let me suggest that perhaps you do not want to block the creation of the new node at all but rather simply allow it to be a different type of entity, one whose existence in the real world is not presupposed by an intensional existence in the internal semantic network.

If we are to take this account of the hypothetical dog in our question, then we have made a major extension in our notion of structures in a semantic network and what they mean. Whereas previously we construed our nodes to correspond to real existing objects, now we have introduced a new type of node which does not have this assumption. Either we now have two very different types of nodes (in which case we must have some explicit indicator or other mechanism in the notation to indicate the type of every node) or else we must impose a unifying interpretation. If we have two different types of nodes, then we still have the problem of telling the process which constructs the nodes which type of node to construct in our two examples.

One possible unifying interpretation is to interpret every node as an intensional description and assert an explicit predicate of existence for those nodes which are intended to correspond to real objects. In this case, we could either rely on an implicit assumption that intensional objects used as subjects of definite asserted sentences (such as "the dog that bit the man had rabies") must actually exist, or we could postulate an inferential process which draws such inferences and explicitly asserts existence for such entities.

Since the above account of the indefinite relative clause in our example requires such a major reinterpretation of the fundamental semantics of our network notations, one might be inclined to look for some other account that was less drastic. I will argue, however, that such internal intensional entities are required in any case to deal with other problems in semantic representation. For example, whenever a new definite node gets created, it may in fact stand for the same object as some other node which already exists, but the necessary information to establish the identity may only come later or not at all. This is a fundamental characteristic of the information that we must store in our nets. Consider again Frege's morning star / evening star example. Even such definite descriptions, then, are essentially intensional objects. (Notice as a consequence that one cannot make negative identity assertions simply on the basis of distinctness of internal semantic representations.)

Perhaps the strongest case for intensional nodes in semantic networks comes from verbs such as "need" and "want". When one asserts a sentence such as "I need a wrench", one does not thereby assert the existence of the object desired. One must, however, include in the representation of this sentence some representation of the thing needed. For this interpretation, the object of the verb "need" should be an intensional description of the needed item. (It is also possible for the slot filler to be a node designating a particular entity rather than just a description, thus giving rise to an ambiguity of

interpretation of the sentence. That is, is it a particular wrench that is needed, or will any wrench do?)

D. Consequences of Intensional Nodes

We conclude that there must be some nodes in the semantic network which correspond to descriptions of entities rather than entities themselves. Does that fix up the problem? Well, we have to do more than just make the assumption. We have to decide how to tell the two kinds of nodes apart, how we decide for particular sentences which type to create, and how to perform inferences on these nodes. If we have nodes which are intensional descriptions of entities, what does it mean to associate properties with the nodes or to assert facts about the nodes. We cannot just rely on the arguments that we made when we were assuming that all of the nodes corresponded to definite external entities. We must see whether earlier interpretations of the meanings of links between nodes still hold true for this new expanded notion of node or whether they need modification or reinterpretation. In short we must start all over again from the beginning but this time with attention to the ability to deal with intensional descriptions.

Let me clarify further some of the kinds of things which we must be able to represent. Consider the sentence "Every boy loves his dog." Here we have an indefinite node for the dog involved which will not hold still. Linguistically it is marked definite (i.e, the dog that belongs to the boy), but it is a variable definite object whose reference changes with the boy. There are also variable entities which are indefinite as in "Every boy needs a dog." Here we plunge into the really difficult and crucial problems in representing quantification. It is easy to create simple network structures that model the logical syllogisms by creating links from subsets to supersets, but the critical cases are those like the above. We need the notion of an intensional description for a variable entity.

To summarize, then, in designing a network to handle intensional entities, we need to provide for definite entities that are intended to correspond to particular entities in the to represent the assertion that John loves Sally. Here we have a situation of the same link names meaning different things depending on the nodes which they are connected to.

Without some explicit indication in the network notation that the two nodes are of different types, no mechanical procedure operating on such a network would be able to handle these links correctly in both cases. With an explicit indication of node type and an explicit definition that the meaning of an arc depends on the type of the node to which it is connected (and how), such a procedure could be defined, but a network notation of this sort would probably be confusing as an explanatory device for human consumption. This is functionally equivalent, however, to an alternative mechanism using a dual set of links with different names (such as R-AGT and AGT, for example) which would make the difference explicit to a human reader and would save the mechanical procedure from having to consult the type of the link node to determine from import of the link. Notice that in either case we are required to make another extension of the semantics of our network notation since we have two different kinds of links with different kinds of import. The ones which make statements about possible slot fillers have assertional import (asserting facts about the predicate LOVE in this case) while the ones that make up the parts of the proposition, which incidentally may itself not be asserted but only part of some intensional representation).

We conclude that the difference between the specification of possible slot fillers for a predicate as part of the information about the predicate and the specification of particular slot fillers for particular instances of the predicate requires some basic distinction in our semantic network notation. One is left with several questions as to just how this distinction is best realized (for example does one want a dual set of link names--or is there a preferable notation?). For the moment, however, let us leave those questions unexplored along with many issues that we have not begun to face and proceed with another problem of knowledge representation that imposes new demands on the interpretations of links and the conventions for representing facts in semantic networks.

real world, indefinite entities which do not necessarily have corresponding entities in the real world, and definite and indefinite variable entities which stand in some relation to other entities and whose instantiations will depend on the instantiations of those other entities.

E. Functions and Predicates

Another question about the interpretation of links and what we mean by them comes in the representation of information about functions and predicates. Functions and predicates have a characteristic that clearly sets them apart from the other types of entities which we have mentioned (with the possible exception of the variable entity which depends on others)--namely, they take arguments. Somewhere in the internal representation of an entity which is a function or a predicate there must be information about the arguments which the function or predicate takes, what kinds of entities can fill those arguments, and how the value of the function or the truth of the predicate is determined or constrained by the values of the arguments. There is a difference between representing the possible entities that can serve as arguments for a predicate and expressing the assertion of the predicate for particular values or classes of values of those arguments. Unfortunately this distinction is often confused in talking about semantic networks. That is, it is all too easy to use the notation:

```
LOVE
    AGT      HUMAN
    RECIP    HUMAN
```

to express constraints on the possible fillers for the arguments of the predicate and to use the same link names in a notation such as:

```
S76543
    VERB     LOVE
    AGT      JOHN
    RECIP    SALLY
```

F. Representing Quantified Expressions

The problem of representing quantified information in semantic networks is one that few people have faced and even fewer handled adequately. Let me begin by laying to rest a logically inadequate way of representing quantified expressions which unfortunately is the one most used in implemented semantic networks. It consists of simply tagging the quantifier onto the noun phrase it modifies just as if it were an adjective. In such a notation, the representation for "every integer is greater than some integer" would look something like:

```
S11113
    VERB    GREATER
    ARG1    D12345
    ARG2    D67890

D12345
    NOUN    INTEGER
    MOD     EVERY

D67890
    NOUN    INTEGER
    MOD     SOME
```

Now there are two possible interpretations of this sentence depending on whether or not the second existential quantifier is considered to be in the scope of the universal quantifier. In the normal interpretation, the second integer depends on the first and the sentence is true, while a pathological interpretation of the sentence is that there is some integer which every integer is greater than. (Lest you divert the issue with some claim that there is only one possible interpretation taking the quantifiers in the order in which they occur in the sentence consider a sentence such as "Everybody jumped in some old car that had the keys in it", in which the normal interpretation is the opposite.) Since our semantic network notation must provide a representation for whichever interpretation we decide was meant, there must be some way to distinguish the difference. If anything, the representation we have given seems to suggest the interpretation in which there is some integer that every integer is greater than. If we take this as the interpretation of the above notation, then we need another representation for the other (and in this case correct) interpretation--the one in which the second integer is a variable entity dependent on the first.

To complicate matters even further, consider the case of numerical quantifiers and a sentence such as "three lookouts saw two boats". There are three possible interpretations of the quantifiers in this case. In the one that seems to correspond to treating the quantifier as a modifier of the noun phrase, we would have one group of three lookouts that jointly participated in an activity of seeing one group of two boats. There is, however, another interpretation in which each of three lookouts saw two boats (for an unknown total number of boats between 2 and 6 since we are not told whether any of them saw the same boats as the others) and still another interpretation in which each of two boats was seen by three men. We must have a way in our network notation to represent unambiguously all three of these possible interpretations. Quillian's (1968) suggestion of using "criterialities" on the arcs to indicate quantification will fail for the same reasons unless some mechanism for indicating which arguments depend on which others is inserted.

Before proceeding to discuss logically adequate ways of dealing with quantification, let me also lay to rest a borderline case. One might decide to represent the interpretation of the sentence in which each of three men saw two boats, for example, by creating three separate nodes for the men and asserting about each of them that he saw two boats. This could become logically adequate if the appropriate information were indicated that the three men were all different (it is not adequate to assume that internal nodes are different just because they are different nodes--recall the morning star/evening star example) and if the three separate facts are tied together into a single fact somewhere (e.g., by a conjunction) since otherwise this would not be an expression of a single fact (which could be denied, for example). This is, however, clearly not a reasonable representation for a sentence such as "250 million people live in the United States", and would be a logical impossibility for representing universally quantified expressions over sets whose cardinality was not known.

A variant of this is related to the transient process account. One might argue that it is not necessary to represent a sentence such as "Every boy has a dog" as a unit, but one can simply add an assertion to each internal node representing a boy. To be correct, however, such an account would require a network to have perfect knowledge (i.e., an internal node for every boy that exists in the world), a practical impossibility. We cannot assume that the entities in our network exhaust those that exist in the world. Hence we must represent this assertion in a way that will apply to future boys that we may learn about and not just to those we know about at this moment. To do this we must be able to store an intensional representation of the universally quantified proposition.

Quantifiers as Higher Operators: The traditional representation of quantifiers in the predicate calculus is that they are attached to the proposition which they govern in a string whose order determines the dependency of the individual variables on other variables. Thus the two interpretations of our first sentence are:

$$(\forall X/integer) \quad (\exists Y/integer) \quad (GREATER\ X\ Y)$$

and

$$(\exists Y/integer) \quad (\forall X/integer) \quad (GREATER\ X\ Y)$$

where I have chosen to indicate explicitly in the quantifier prefix the range of quantification of the variable (see Woods, 1967) for a discussion of the advantages of doing this—namely the uniform behavior for both universal and existential quantifiers). In the question-answering systems that I have constructed, including the LUNAR system, I have used a slightly expanded form of such quantifiers which uniformly handles numerical quantifiers and definite determiners as well as the classical universal and existential quantifiers. This formulation treats the quantifiers as higher predicates which take as arguments a variable name, a specification of the range of quantification, a possible restriction on the range, and the proposition to be quantified (which includes a free occurrence of the variable

of quantification and which may be already quantified by other quantifiers). In this notation, the above two interpretations would be represented as:

(FOR EVERY X / INTEGER : T ; (FOR SOME Y / INTEGER : T ; (GREATER X Y)))

and

(FOR SOME Y / INTEGER : T ; (FOR EVERY X / INTEGER : T ; (GREATER X Y)))

where the component of the notation following the ";" in these expressions is a proposition which restricts the range of quantification (in this case the vacuously true proposition T) and the component following the ";" is the proposition being quantified. This type of higher-operator representation of quantification can be represented in a network structure by creating a special type of node for the quantifier and some special links for its components. Thus we could have something like:

```
S39732
         TYPE          QUANT
         QUANT-TYPE    EVERY
         VARIABLE      X
         CLASS         INTEGER
         RESTRICTION   T
         PROP          S39733

S39733
         TYPE          QUANT
         QUANT-TYPE    SOME
         VARIABLE      Y
         RESTRICTION   T
         PROP          S39734

S39734
         TYPE          PROPOSITION
         VERB          GREATER
         ARG1          X
         ARG2          Y
```

This is essentially the technique used by Shapiro (1971), who is one of the two people I know of to suggest a logically adequate treatment of quantifiers in his nets. (The other one is Martin Kay, whose proposal we will discuss shortly.) This technique has an unpleasant effect, however, in that it breaks up the chains of connections from node to node that one finds attractive in the more customary semantic network notations. That is, if we consider our sentence about lookouts and boats, we have gone successively from a simple-minded representation in which we might have a link labeled "see" which points from a node for "lookout" to one for "boats", to a case representation notation in which the chain becomes an inverse agent link from "lookout" to a special node which has a verb link to "see" and a patient link to "boats", and finally to a quantified representation in which the chain stretches from "lookout" via an inverse CLASS link to a quantifier node which has a PROP link to another quantifier node which has a CLASS link to "boats" and a PROP link to a proposition which has a VERB link to "see". Thus our successive changes in the network conventions designed to provide them with a logically adequate interpretation are carrying with them a cost in the directness of the associative paths. This may be an inevitable consequence of making the networks adequate for storing knowledge in general, and it may be that it is not too disruptive of the associative processing that one would like to apply to the memory representation. On the other hand it may lead to the conclusion that one cannot accomplish an appropriate associative linking of information as a direct consequence of the notation in which it is stored and that some separate indexing mechanism is required.

Other Possible Representations: There are two other possible candidates for representing quantified information, one of which to my knowledge has not been tried before in semantic networks. I will call them the "Skolem function method" and the "lambda abstraction method", after well-known techniques in formal logic.

Skolem Functions: The use of Skolem functions to represent quantified expressions is little known outside the field of mechanical theorem proving and certain branches of formal logic, but it is a pivotal technique in resolution theorem proving and is rather drastically different from the customary way of dealing with quantifiers in logic. The technique begins with a quantified expression containing no negative operators in the quantifier prefix (any such can be removed by means of the transformations exchanging "not every" for "some not" and "not some" for "every not"). It then replaces each instance of an existentially quantified variable with a functional designator whose function is a unique function name chosen for that existential variable and whose arguments are the universally quantified variables in whose scopes the existential variable lies. After this the existential quantifiers are deleted and, since the only remaining variables are universally quantified, the universal quantifiers can be deleted and free variables treated as implicitly universally quantified. The expression $(\forall x)(\exists y)(\forall z)(\exists w) P(x,y,z,w)$, for example, becomes $P(x,f(x),z,g(x,z))$, where f and g are new function names created to replace the variables y and w.

Notice that the arguments of the functions f and g in the result preserve the information about the universally quantified variables on which they depend. This is all the information necessary to reconstruct the original expression and is intuitively exactly that information which we are interested in to characterize the difference between alternative interpretations of a sentence corresponding to different quantifier orderings--i.e., does the choice of a given object depend on the choice of a universally quantified object or not? Thus the Skolem function serves as a device for recording the dependencies of an existentially quantified variable. An additional motivating factor for using Skolem functions to represent natural language quantification is that the quantification operation implicitly determines a real function of exactly this sort, and there are places in natural language dialogs where this implicit function appears to be referenced by anaphoric pronouns outside the scope of the original quantifier (e.g., in "Is there someone here from Virginia? If so, I have a prize for him", the "him" seems to refer to the value of such a function). We can obtain a semantic network notation based on this Skolem function analogy by simply including with every existentially quantified object a link which points to all of the universally quantified objects on which this one depends. This is essentially the technique proposed by Kay (1973).

It must be pointed out that one difficulty with the Skolem function notation which accounts for its little use as a logical representation outside the theorem proving circles is that it is not possible to obtain the negation of a Skolem form expression by simply attaching a negation operator to the "top". Rather, negation involves a complex operation which changes all of the universal variables to existential ones and vice versa and can hardly be accomplished short of converting the expression back to quantifier prefix form, rippling the negation through the quantifier prefix to the embedded predicate and then reconverting to Skolem form. This makes it difficult, for example, to store the denial of an existing proposition. It seems likely that the same technique of explicitly linking the quantified object to those other objects on which it depends might also handle the case of numerically quantified expressions although I am not quite sure how it would all work out--especially with negations.

Lambda Abstraction: We have already introduced Church's lambda notation as a convenient device for expressing a predicate defined by a combination or a modification of other predicates. In general, for any completely instantiated complex assemblage of predicates and propositions, one can make a predicate of it by replacing some of its specific arguments with variable names and embedding it in a lambda expression with those variables indicated as arguments. For example, from a sentence "John told Mary to get something and hit Sam" we can construct a predicate (LAMBDA (X) John told Mary to get something and hit X) which is true of Sam if the original sentence is true and may be true of other individuals as well. This process is called "lambda abstraction".

Now one way to view a universally quantified sentence such as "all men are mortal" is simply as a statement of a relation between a set (all men) and a predicate (mortal) --

namely that the predicate is true of each member of the set (call this relation FORALL). By means of lambda abstraction we can create a predicate of exactly the type we need to view every instance of universal quantification as exactly this kind of assertion about a set and a predicate. For example, we can represent our assertion that every integer is greater than some integer as an assertion of the FORALL relation between the set of integers and the predicate

(LAMBDA (X) (X is greater than some integer))

and in a similar way we can define a relation FORSOME which holds between a set and a predicate if the predicate is true for some member of the set, thus giving us a representation:

(FORALL INTEGER (LAMBDA (X)
  (FORSOME INTEGER (LAMBDA (Y)
    (GREATER X Y)))))

which can be seen as almost a notational variant of the higher-operator quantifier representation. Notice that the expression (LAMBDA (Y) (GREATER X Y)) is a predicate whose argument is Y and which has a free variable X. This means that the predicate itself is a variable entity which depends on X--i.e., for each value of X we get a different predicate to be applied to the Ys.

The use of this technique in a semantic network notation would require a special type of node for a predicate defined by the lambda operator, but such a type of node is probably required anyway for independent reasons (since the operation of lambda abstraction is an intellectual operation which one can perform and since our semantic network should be able to store the results of such mental gymnastics). The structure of the above expression might look like:

```
S12233
TYPE     PROPOSITION
VERB     FORALL
CLASS    INTEGER
PRED     P12234
```

distinctness, or their completeness in covering all of the objects which are presumed to exist in the world. I have also pointed out the logical inadequacies of almost all current network notations for representing quantified information and some of the disadvantages of some logically adequate techniques.

I have not begun to address all of the problems that need to be addressed, and I have only begun to discuss the problems of relative clauses and quantificational information. I have not even mentioned other problems such as the representation of mass terms, adverbial modification, probabilistic information, degrees of certainty, time, and tense, and a host of other difficult problems. All of these issues need to be addressed and solutions integrated into a consistent whole in order to produce a logically adequate semantic network formalism. No existing semantic network comes close to this goal.

I hope that by focusing on the logical inadequacies of many of the current (naive) assumptions about what semantic networks do and can do, I will have stimulated the search for better solutions and flagged some of the false assumptions about adequacies of techniques that might otherwise have gone unchallenged. As I said earlier, I believe that work in the area of knowledge representation in general, and semantic networks in particular, is important to the further development of our understanding of human and artificial intelligence and that many essentially correct facts about human performance and useful techniques for artificial systems are emerging from this study. My hope for this chapter is that it will stimulate this area of study to develop in a productive direction.

```
P12234
   TYPE        PREDICATE
   ARGUMENTS   (X)
   BODY        S12235

S12235
   TYPE        PROPOSITION
   VERB        FORSOME
   CLASS       INTEGER
   PRED        P12236

P12236
   TYPE        PREDICATE
   ARGUMENTS   (Y)
   BODY        S12237

S12237
   TYPE        PROPOSITION
   VERB        GREATER
   ARG1        X
   ARG2        Y
```

V. CONCLUSION

In the preceding sections, I hope that I have illustrated by example the kinds of explicit understanding of what one intends various network notations to mean that must be made in order to even begin to ask the questions whether a notation is an adequate one for representing knowledge in general (although for reasons of space I have been more brief in such explanations in this chapter than I feel one should be in presenting a proposed complete semantic network notation). Moreover, I hope that I have made the point that when one does extract a clear understanding of the semantics of the notation, most of the existing semantic network notations are found wanting in some major respects--notably the representation of propositions without commitment to asserting their truth and in representing various types of intensional descriptions of objects without commitment to their external existence, their external

REFERENCES

Carbonell, J. R., & Collins, A. M. Natural semantics in artificial intelligence. *Proceedings of Third International Joint Conference on Artificial Intelligence*, 1973, 344-351. (Reprinted in the *American Journal of Computational Linguistics*, 1974, *1*, Mfc. 3.)

Davis, M. *Computability and unsolvability*. New York: McGraw-Hill, 1958.

Fillmore, C. The case for case. In Bach and Harms (Eds.), *Universals in linguistic theory*, Chicago, Ill.: Holt, 1968.

Kay, M. The MIND system. In R. Rustin (Ed.) *Natural language processing*. New York: Algorithmics Press, 1973.

Lindsay, R. K. Inferential memory as the basis of machines which understand natural language. In E. A. Feigenbaum & J. Feldman (Eds.), *Computers and thought*. New York: McGraw-Hill, 1963.

Quillian, M. R. Semantic memory. In M. Minsky (Ed.), *Semantic information processing*. Cambridge, Mass.: MIT Press, 1968.

Quillian, M. R. The teachable language comprehender. *Communications of the Association for Computing Machinery*, 1969, *12*, 459-475.

Quine, W. V. *From a logical point of view.* (2nd Ed., rev.) New York: Harper, 1961.

Raphael, B. A computer program which 'understands'. *AFIPS Conference Proceedings*, 1964, *26*, 577-589.

Rumelhart, D. E., Lindsay, P. H., & Norman, D. A. A process model for long-term memory. In E. Tulving & W. Donaldson (Eds.), *Organization of memory*. New York: Academic Press, 1972.

Schank, R. C. *Conceptual information processing*. Amsterdam: North-Holland, 1975.

Shapiro, S. C. A net structure for semantic information storage, deduction, and retrieval. *Proceedings of the Second International Joint Conference on Artificial Intelligence*, 1971, 512-523.

Simmons, R. F. Semantic networks: Their computation and use for understanding English sentences. In R. C. Schank & K. M. Colby (Eds.), *Computer models of thought and language*. San Francisco, Ca.: Freeman, 1973.

Winograd, T. *Understanding natural language*. New York: Academic Press, 1972.

Woods, W.A. Semantics for a Question-Answering System. Ph.D. Thesis, Division of Engineering and Applied Physics, Harvard University, 1967. (Also in Report NSF-19, Harvard Computation Laboratory, September 1967. Available from NTIS as PB-176-548.)

Woods, W.A. Meaning and machines. *Proceedings of the International Conference on Computational Linguistics*, Pisa, Italy, August 1973(a).

Woods, W.A. Progress in natural language understanding: An application to lunar geology. *AFIPS Conference Proceedings*, 1973(b), *42*, 441-450.

Woods, W.A. Syntax, semantics, and speech, presented at IEEE Symposium on Speech recognition, Carnegie-Mellon University, April 1974.

Woods, W. A., Kaplan, R. M., & Nash-Webber, B. The lunar sciences natural language information system: final report. BBN Report No. 2378, June 1972.

A Spreading-Activation Theory of Semantic Processing

Allan M. Collins
*Bolt Beranek and Newman Inc.,
Cambridge, Massachusetts*

Elizabeth F. Loftus
University of Washington

This paper presents a spreading-activation theory of human semantic processing, which can be applied to a wide range of recent experimental results. The theory is based on Quillian's theory of semantic memory search and semantic preparation, or priming. In conjunction with this, several of the misconceptions concerning Quillian's theory are discussed. A number of additional assumptions are proposed for his theory in order to apply it to recent experiments. The present paper shows how the extended theory can account for results of several production experiments by Loftus, Juola and Atkinson's multiple-category experiment, Conrad's sentence-verification experiments, and several categorization experiments on the effect of semantic relatedness and typicality by Holyoak and Glass, Rips, Shoben, and Smith, and Rosch. The paper also provides a critique of the Smith, Shoben, and Rips model for categorization judgments.

Some years ago, Quillian[1] (1962, 1967) proposed a spreading-activation theory of human semantic processing that he tried to implement in computer simulations of memory search (Quillian, 1966) and comprehension (Quillian, 1969). The theory viewed memory search as activation spreading from two or more concept nodes in a semantic network until an intersection was found. The effects of preparation (or priming) in semantic memory were also explained in terms of spreading activation from the node of the primed concept. Rather than a theory to explain data, it was a theory designed to show how to build human semantic structure and processing into a computer.

This research was supported by the National Institute of Education, U.S. Department of Health, Education, and Welfare, Project 1-0420, under Contract OEC-1-71-0100(508) with Bolt Beranek and Newman Inc. Revision of the paper was supported by a grant from the John Simon Guggenheim Memorial Foundation to the first author. We would like to thank Stephen Woods, Colin MacLeod, Mark L. Miller, and the reviewers for their comments on previous drafts of this paper.

Requests for reprints should be sent to Allan M. Collins at Bolt Beranek and Newman Inc., 50 Moulton Street, Cambridge, Massachusetts 02138.
[1] Quillian's theory of priming appeared in the unpublished version of the 1967 paper (i.e., CIP Paper No. 79, Carnegie Institute of Technology, 1965).

Since the theory was proposed, there have been a number of experiments investigating retrieval and priming in semantic memory. In the present paper, we attempt to show how an elaboration of Quillian's basic theory can account for many of the results. In the first section, we briefly review the original theory while trying to correct a number of the common misunderstandings concerning it. In the second section, we extend the theory in several respects, and in the third section show how the extended theory deals with some recent experimental findings. In the fourth section we compare the theory to the model of Smith, Shoben, and Rips (1974).

QUILLIAN'S THEORY OF SEMANTIC MEMORY

The fact that Quillian's theory was developed as a program for a digital computer imposed certain constraints on the theory, which Quillian felt were psychologically unrealistic. We will recount the theory as he proposed it, and then elaborate the theory in psychological terms. The theory made a number of assumptions about structure and processing in human semantic memory. A brief discussion of these assumptions follows.

People's concepts contain indefinitely large amounts of information. Quillian used the example of a machine. If one asks people to tell everything they know about machines, they will start off giving obvious properties, for example, that machines are man-made and have moving parts. But soon people run out of obvious facts and begin giving facts that are less and less relevant, for example, that a typewriter is a machine or even that the keys on the IBM electric typewriters select the position of a ball that strikes the ribbon against the paper. The amount of information a person can generate about any concept in this way seems unlimited.

In these terms concepts correspond to particular senses of words or phrases. For example, not only is the noun "machine" a concept, but the verb "to machine" is a concept; the "particular old car I own" is a concept; even the notion of "driving a car" is a concept; even the notion of "what to do if you see a red light" has to be a concept. Thus, people must have a very large number of concepts, and concepts must have very complicated structures.

A concept can be represented as a node in a network, with properties of the concept represented as labeled relational links from the node to other concept nodes. These links are pointers, and usually go in both directions between two concepts. Links can have different *criterialities*, which are numbers indicating how essential each link is to the meaning of the concept. The criterialities on any pair of links between two concepts can be different; for example, it might be highly criterial for the concept of a typewriter that it is a machine, and not very criterial for the concept of machine that one kind is a typewriter. From each of the nodes linked to a given node, there will be links to other concept nodes and from each of these in turn to still others. In Quillian's theory, the full meaning of any concept is the whole network as entered from the concept node.

The links are not simply undifferentiated links, but must be complicated enough to represent any relation between two concepts. In the original theory, Quillian proposed five different kinds of links: (a) superordinate ("isa") and subordinate links, (b) modifier links, (c) disjunctive sets of links, (d) conjunctive sets of links, and (e) a residual class of links, which allowed the specification of any relationship where the relationship (usually a verb relationship) itself was a concept. These different kinds of links could be nested or embedded to any degree of depth, so that the format was designed to be flexible enough to express anything, however vague or specific, that can be expressed in natural language.

The search in memory between concepts involves tracing out in parallel (simulated in the computer by a breadth-first search) along the links from the node of each concept specified by the input words. The words might be part of a sentence or stimuli in an experimental task. The spread of activation constantly expands, first to all the nodes linked to the first node, then to all the nodes linked to each of these nodes, and so on. At each node reached in this process, an activation tag is left that specifies the starting node and the immediate predecessor. When a tag from another starting node is encountered, an *intersection* between the two nodes has been found.[2] By following the tags back to both starting nodes, the *path* that led to the intersection can be reconstructed.

When an intersection has been found, it is necessary to *evaluate* the path to decide if it satisfies the constraints imposed by syntax and context. The complicated kinds of decision rules that are invoked for comprehension of sentences in this evaluation phase are described in Quillian (1969). For categorization tasks these rules are described by Collins and Quillian (1972b) and in the next section of this paper. As an example, in a phrase such as "the fall leaves," a path found between the concept "to fall" and the

[2] There can be intersections with more than two starting nodes, but we have limited our discussion in this paper to the case of two nodes (as did Quillian, 1966, initially). The basic assumptions in Quillian's theory and our elaboration can apply to intersections with more than two starting nodes, but this leads to complications in the evaluation of intersections. Some of these were discussed by Quillian (1969) in regard to comprehension, but for the experiments considered in this paper, only the case of two starting nodes needs to be considered.

that we will discuss it at length in conjunction with the spreading activation theory's explanation of the Rips et al. (1973) results.

Another common misconception of Quillian's theory shows up in Juola and Atkinson's (1971) work on categorization judgments. In a categorization task, response time is measured for a subject to decide whether or not a particular instance (e.g. "car") is a member of one or more categories (e.g. "flower" or "vehicle"). Juola and Atkinson assume that in Quillian's theory the memory search to make a categorization judgment proceeds from the instance to the category. In fact, the wording in Collins and Quillian (1969) mistakenly gives that impression. But Quillian's theory (1966, 1969) assumes the search proceeds from both the instance and category in parallel. However, if one or the other is presented first, this gives the search from that node a head start, which is the notion of priming. Juola and Atkinson's experiment involves priming in a complicated way, which we will discuss below.

Anderson and Bower (1973) reject a Quillian-like model of a parallel search, while acknowledging that their data are compatible with "a parallel model whose search rate is slower in proportion to the number of paths that must be searched" (p. 371). Anderson and Bower's argument implies wrongly that Quillian has made the independence assumption for his parallel search. An independent parallel search is like a race where the speed of each runner is independent of the other runners. This is a common assumption in psychology, because it makes it possible to assign an upper bound to reaction time (see Sternberg, 1966). But there is no difficulty for Quillian's theory if the parallel search rate depends on the number of paths searched. Hence, Anderson and Bower's data are perfectly compatible with Quillian's parallel search.

The above discussion, then, shows what Quillian's theory is *not*, or at least some of what it is not. Several other misconceptions are discussed in Collins and Quillian (1972b), in particular the notion that Quil-

"hands," and "warts" are all linked directly to the concept "human," these links need not be in any sense equal. The same is true for the links between "bird" and its exemplars, such as "robin," "chicken," or "penguin." Rips et al. (1973) suggest that intermediate nodes are necessary for a network model to explain the reaction time differences they find in categorizing different birds. This makes the mistaken assumption that all links are equally criterial or accessible in any network model. It turns out, however, that differences in links are crucial to many different aspects of human semantic processing as Carbonell and Collins (1973) point out in their discussion of importance (or criteriality) tags.

A related implication of the Rips et al. (1973) paper and also a more recent paper of Smith et al. (1974) is that network models can account for data that network models cannot. A feature model posits that a concept consists of a set of values on a large number of semantic dimensions (e.g., animateness, color, etc.). What is strange about this argument is that network models were developed as a method of representing features in a computer. Any process that can be represented in a feature model is representable in a network model; in particular, the Smith et al. model itself could be implemented in a semantic network (Hollan, 1975). In fact, network models are probably *more* powerful than feature models, because it is not obvious how to handle inferential processing or embedding in feature models.

Smith et al. (1974) argued in favor of feature models because their data for comparison of concepts seemed to fit a feature comparison process. What should be emphasized about Quillian's theory is that the parallel search would inevitably lead to just such a feature comparison process, though the process would take place over a period of time as different connections are found. One way that Quillian's theory is different from the Smith et al. models is that superordinate connections are treated as the same or different (e.g., they exist), would also be found and evaluated. The distinction between these two theories is so crucial

concept "tree leaf" would be rejected as a wrong interpretation, because syntax requires a participial form of "fall" to fit that interpretation. If a path found is rejected, other paths are considered in the order in which they are found.

Priming (or preparation) involves the same tracing process that was described for memory search. When a concept is primed, activation tags are spread by tracing an expanding set of links in the network out to some unspecified depth. When another concept is subsequently presented, it has to make contact with one of the tags left earlier to find an intersection. One of the non-obvious implications of this view of priming is that links as well as nodes will be primed. This is because Quillian treated links themselves as concepts (see above). Thus priming a node such as "red" will prime the links involving the relation "color" throughout the network. This provides a very powerful context mechanism.

Common Misinterpretations of Quillian's Theory

There is a rich variety of misinterpretations of Quillian's theory, many of them deriving from Collins's (Collins & Quillian, 1969, 1970a, 1970b) simplifications of the theory. The problem arose because Collins and Quillian were investigating specific aspects of the theory and only described enough of the theory to motivate a particular experiment. In turn experimenters made interpretations of these simplified versions, which did not fit with the theory as described elsewhere (Bell & Quillian, 1971; Quillian, 1966, 1969).

Perhaps the most prevalent misinterpretation of Quillian's theory concerns the idea of cognitive economy (Anderson & Bower, 1973; Conrad, 1972). In this regard, it is important to distinguish the strong theory of cognitive economy, which Conrad takes issue with in her attack on Collins and Quillian (1969), and the weak theory of cognitive economy, which Collins and Quillian were testing (though they did not spell it out clearly enough). As Conrad (1972) states, she rejects the "hypothesis that all proper-

ties are stored only once in memory and must be retrieved through a series of inferences for all words except those that they most directly define" (p. 153). This is a statement of the strong theory of the Collins and Quillian economy. Undoubtedly the Collins and Quillian (1969) paper gave rise to this notion, but the authors cautioned against making that interpretation of the theory. As they said, "people surely store certain properties at more than one level in the hierarchy" (p. 242), and they cited the maple leaf as an example of this general rule.

The strong theory requires erasing information whenever it applies at a more general level. If a person learns a robin can fly and then later that birds fly, the strong theory implies that "flying" must be erased from "robin." The weak theory of cognitive economy merely assumes that every time one learns that X is a bird, one does not at that time store all the properties of birds with X in memory. Thus, an inference will be necessary to decide that X can fly, unless one encounters this fact directly. Hence, Collins and Quillian, in testing the weak theory of cognitive economy, picked instances where people were not likely to have encountered the general property with the specific instance (e.g., "A wren can fly"). The point of the experiment was to test whether it was possible to measure inference time, when the weak theory of cognitive economy implies that an inference is likely to be necessary for most subjects.

Another assumption sometimes made about Quillian's theory is that all links are equal (Anderson & McGaw, 1973; Rips, Shoben, & Smith, 1973; Wilkins, Note 1). In Quillian's original theory, there were criteriality tags on links, as we described earlier. In Collins and Quillian (1969, 1972b) links were assumed to have differential accessibility (i.e., strength or travel time). The accessibility of a property depends on how often a person thinks about or uses a property of a concept. Whether criteriality and accessibility are treated as the same or different is a complex issue, but network models allow them to be treated either way. Thus for example, even though "lungs,"

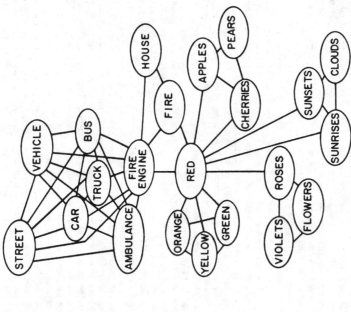

FIGURE 1. A schematic representation of concept relatedness in a stereo-typical fragment of human memory (where a shorter line represents greater relatedness).

lian's theory of memory is rigidly hierarchical, which Anderson and Bower (1973, p. 379) still believe, and Schaeffer and Wallace's (1970) argument that Quillian's theory predicts it will always take less time to compare concepts that are close together in the semantic network. We will return to some of these same papers below, in order to describe how the extended version of Quillian's theory accounts for some of the results these experimenters have used to reject Quillian's theory.

THE EXTENDED THEORY

In order to deal with the specific experimental results that have appeared in recent years, several more processing and structural assumptions must be added to the basic Quillian theory. These do not merely elaborate the theory, but merely elaborate it in such a way that it can be applied to the kinds of experiments on semantic memory that have been performed recently. The elaboration may itself be wrong, so our mistakes should not be held against Quillian's theory.

Local Processing Assumptions

There are four local processing assumptions in the extended theory. These four assumptions transform the theory from computer terms to quasi-neurological terms, a la Pavlov. But all the assumptions of the original theory should be preserved despite the transformation, except that activation tags are to be considered as source-specific activation (i.e., activation that is traceable to its node of origin).

1. When a concept is processed (or stimulated), activation spreads out along the paths of the network in a decreasing gradient. The decrease is inversely proportional to the accessibility or strength of the links in the path. Thus, activation is like a signal from a source that is attenuated as it travels outward.

2. The longer a concept is continuously processed (either by reading, hearing, or rehearsing it), the longer activation is released from the node of the concept at a fixed rate. Only one concept can be actively processed at a time, which is a limita-

tion imposed by the serial nature of the human central process (Collins & Quillian, 1972b). This means that activation can only start out at one node at a time. But it continues in parallel from other nodes that are encountered as it spreads out from the node of origin.

3. Activation decreases over time and/or intervening activity. This is a noncommittal assumption that activation goes away gradually by some mechanism. Assumptions 2 and 3 impose a limitation on the amount of activation that can be allocated in priming more than one concept, because the more concepts that are primed, the less each will be primed.

4. With the assumption that activation is a variable quantity, the notion of intersection requires a threshold for firing. The assumption is that activation from different sources summates and that when the summation at the point of intersection reaches threshold, the path in the network producing the intersection will be evaluated.

Global Assumptions About Memory Structure and Processing

There are three assumptions in the extended theory concerned with the global structure of memory and its processing. These are generalizations of Loftus's (Note 2) arguments that semantic memory is organized primarily into noun categories and that there is a "dictionary" (or lexical memory) separate from the conceptual network.

5. The conceptual (semantic) network is organized along the lines of semantic similarity. The more properties two concepts have in common, the more links there are between the two nodes via these properties and the more closely related are the concepts. This means that different vehicles or different colors will all be highly interlinked through their common properties. This also implies that red things (e.g., fire engines, cherries, sunsets, and roses) are not closely interlinked, despite the one property they have in common. In these terms semantic relatedness is based on an aggre-

gate of the interconnections between two concepts.[3]

Figure 1 illustrates this aggregate notion of concept relatedness for a hypothetical human memory. (It is the kind of diagram that the scaling techniques of Rips et al., 1973, would produce.) In the figure the various vehicles are shown as closely related, because of the numerous individual connections that are assumed to exist between them. Conversely, the concepts associated with "red" are shown as less related, because of the presumed paucity of interconnections between them.

From the assumption that memory is organized according to semantic similarity, to-

[3] Semantic relatedness is a slightly different notion from semantic distance, though the two terms are sometimes used interchangeably. Semantic distance is the distance along the shortest path, and semantic relatedness (or similarity) is an aggregate of all the paths. Two concepts may be close in distance, say by a path through "red," and still not be closely related because that is the only path. Our use of close to refer to both relationships is admittedly confusing. In this paper we shall use close to refer to relatedness or similarity, though in some tasks (Quillian, 1966) it is only distance that matters.

gether with earlier assumptions, it follows that if "vehicle" is primed, activation at any type of vehicle will accumulate from many neighboring nodes. That is to say, to the degree that "fire engine" is primed by "vehicle," it will in turn prime "ambulance," "truck," "bus," etc., and each of these in turn will prime the others. On the other hand, if "red" is primed, the activation that spreads to "fire engine" will not prime "cherries," "roses," or "sunsets" to any great extent, because there are so few connections between these concepts. Instead, "fire engine" will tend to prime other vehicles, and "cherries" to prime other fruits. Hence, the same amount of activation will be diffused among a greater number of concepts.

6. The names of concepts are stored in a lexical network (or dictionary) that is organized along lines of phonemic (and to some degree orthographic) similarity. The links from each node in the lexical network are the phonemic properties of the name, specified with respect to their position in the word. The properties stored about names are assumed to be the properties that Brown and McNeill (1966) found people could identify about words on the "tip of their tongue." Each name node in the lexical network is connected to one or more concept nodes in the semantic network.

7. Loftus's (Note 2) data lead to the further assumption that a person can control whether he primes the lexical network, the semantic network, or both. For example, a person can control whether to prime (a) words in the lexical network that sound like "bird," (b) concepts in the semantic network related to "bird," or (c) words in the lexical network corresponding to the concepts in (b). This control over priming can be thought of in terms of summation of diffuse activation for an entire network (perhaps in a particular part of the brain) and source-specific activation released from a particular node. Thus, (a) would derive from activation of the lexical network together with the word "bird," (b) would derive from activation of the semantic network together with the concept "bird," and (c) would derive from activation of both networks together with the concept "bird."

Assumptions About Semantic Matching Process

There are a number of assumptions about the decision process for evaluating whether or not two concepts match semantically. This is a fundamental process that occurs in many aspects of language processing, such as matching referents, assigning cases, and answering questions (Collins & Quillian, 1972b; Collins, Warnock, Aiello, & Miller, 1975). Categorization tasks, which ask "Is X a Y?" (where X and Y are concepts) directly investigate this process. The decision process described here is a more explicit and somewhat revised version of the process postulated by Collins and Quillian (1972b), with additions to encompass the results of Holyoak and Glass (1975).

8. In order to decide whether or not a concept matches another concept, enough evidence must be collected to exceed either a positive or a negative criterion. The evidence consists of various kinds of intersections that are found during the memory search. Evidence from different paths in memory sum together. Positive and negative evidence act to cancel each other out, as shown by dialogue excerpts in Carbonell and Collins (1973). Failure to reach either criterion before running out of relevant evidence leads to a "don't know" response (Collins et al., 1975). This process is essentially the Bayesian decision model that is common in the reaction time literature (see, for example, Fitts, 1966; Stone, 1960).

There are a number of different kinds of paths between the two concepts that constitute positive or negative evidence. Any of these types of evidence might contribute to a particular decision. The different types are listed in Table 1 and described below in Assumptions 9–13.

9. If the memory search finds that there is a superordinate (or a negative superordinate) connection from X to Y, that fact alone can push the decision over the positive (or negative) criterion. Superordinate links act like highly criterial property links (see below). For example, it is conclusive positive evidence that a mallard is a bird, if superordinate links are found between "mallard" and "duck" and between "duck" and "bird." Similarly, if a negative superordinate link is found between "bat" and "bird," it is conclusive evidence that a bat is not a bird.

10. If the memory search finds properties on which X and Y match (i.e., common properties), this is positive evidence proportional to the criteriality of the property for Y. If the memory search finds properties on which X and Y mismatch (i.e., distinguishing properties), this is negative evidence proportional to the criteriality of the property for Y. There is an asymmetry in the weighing of positive and negative evidence in a property comparison, because a mismatch on just one fairly criterial property can lead to a negative decision, whereas most of the highly criterial properties must match in order to reach a positive decision (Collins & Quillian, 1972b).

It is important to note that property comparisons and superordinate connections sum together in reaching either criterion as the memory search finds them. Thus, distinguishing properties make it harder to reach the positive criterion when there is a superordinate connection and therefore slow down the process.

As an example of property comparison, suppose there is no superordinate connection in a particular person's memory between "mink" and "farm animal" and between "cat" and "farm animal." Then the decision as to whether minks or cats are farm animals might be based on a comparison of the properties of minks or cats on one hand, and farm animals on the other. The most criterial properties of farm animals are presumably being animate and being kept on farms, but other less criterial properties include being domesticated, being raised for some purpose, or being kept in barns or outside. How a particular person would weigh the various properties of minks and cats to decide whether they are farm animals would vary from person to person (our intuition is that minks are farm animals and cats are not, even though both have the two most criterial properties of farm animals—what Smith et al., 1974, called defining properties). This decision strategy is similar to that proposed by Smith et al., as we will discuss later.

11. The Wittgenstein strategy is a variant of the property comparison strategy. It is postulated on the basis of Wittgenstein's (1953) observation that to decide whether something is a game (for example, frisbee), a person compares it to similar instances that are known to be games. Our assumption is that if any properties of X are found that match properties of another instance whose superordinate is Y, these constitute positive evidence. Similarly, any distinguishing properties constitute negative evidence. In the Wittgenstein strategy, unlike the property comparison strategy, matching properties count just as much toward a positive decision as distinguishing properties count toward a negative decision.

To illustrate the Wittgenstein strategy, Collins and Quillian (1972b) pointed out that in deciding whether a stagecoach is a vehicle, it might be compared to a car. The many properties that a stagecoach has in common with a car constitute strong positive evidence that a stagecoach is a vehicle. But notice that a stagecoach does not have a motor, which is highly criterial for being a car. Though this is strong evidence that a stagecoach is not a car, it is only weak evidence that it is not a vehicle. This illustrates how the same evidence is weighed differently in the property comparison strategy and the Wittgenstein strategy. The

TABLE 1

TYPES OF PATHS FOUND IN MEMORY THAT CONSTITUTE POSITIVE OR NEGATIVE EVIDENCE

Positive evidence	Negative evidence
Superordinate connection	Negative superordinate connection
Property comparison, matching property	Property comparison, distinguishing property
Wittgenstein strategy, matching property	Wittgenstein strategy, distinguishing property
	Mutually exclusive subordinates
	Counterexamples

final decision that a stagecoach is a vehicle might depend both on matching properties between a stagecoach and vehicles in general (conveyance, motion, etc.) and matching properties between a stagecoach and particular vehicles like a car (seats, doors, etc.). Thus the property comparison strategy and the Wittgenstein strategy might combine to determine a person's response.

12. The mutually exclusive subordinates strategy was necessary for programming a computer to answer questions (Collins et al., 1975). Holyoak and Glass (1975) argue that this strategy accounts for some of their reaction time data (they call it a contradiction). The assumption is that if two concepts have a common superordinate with mutually exclusive links into the common superordinate, then this constitutes strong negative evidence, almost comparable to a negative superordinate link.

For example, if the question is whether a mallard is an eagle, the fact that a mallard is a duck and ducks and eagles are mutually exclusive kinds of birds is rather conclusive evidence that a mallard is not an eagle. Though Holyoak and Glass (1975) do not mention it, the mutually exclusive restriction is necessary. For example, the fact that Mike Mansfield is a politician does not exclude him from being a lawyer. Although "politician" and "lawyer" are both occupational roles, they are not mutually exclusive and in fact most politicians are lawyers. But lacking specific information to the contrary, people may make a default assumption of mutual exclusivity when two concepts have a common superordinate.

13. Counterexamples also can be used as negative evidence. This strategy derives from Holyoak and Glass (1975), who argue that statements of the kind "All birds are canaries" are disconfirmed by finding a counterexample, such as "robin." If the question is of the form "Is X a Y?" and there is a superordinate link from Y to X, then finding a counterexample involves finding a Z that also has X as superordinate and is mutually exclusive from Y. This is conclusive evidence that X is not always a Y.

Holyoak and Glass (1975) discuss counterexamples in the context of the universal quantifier "all," but the same process would occur for a question of the kind "Is a marsupial a kangaroo?" In such a case, retrieving a counterexample (such as a wallaby) can be used to determine that kangaroos are a subset of marsupials and not equivalent (e.g., "automobiles" and "cars" are equivalent concepts).

Though these five kinds of evidence (Assumptions 9-13) are the only ones we have postulated for the semantic matching process seen in categorization tasks, there may be other kinds of evidence of this sort. We should stress that there are many other kinds of evidence people use for answering more complicated questions (Collins et al., 1975). It is beyond the scope of this paper, however, to consider all the different ways people use evidence to make semantic decisions.

RECENT EXPERIMENTS

In this section, we discuss how the theory deals with some different kinds of recent experiments. The four types of studies to which we apply the theory are (a) several production experiments by Loftus (Freedman & Loftus, 1971; Loftus, 1973a, 1973b, Note 2); (b) Juola and Atkinson's (1971) multiple-category experiment; (c) the Conrad (1972) sentence-verification experiment; and (d) several categorization experiments on the effects of semantic relatedness and typicality (Holyoak & Glass, 1975; Rips et al., 1973; Rosch, 1973; Smith et al., 1974). We intend to deal with the major kinds of available findings to which the Quillian theory has not yet been applied. Our objective is to show how a spreading-activation theory can handle these results, not to consider all the possible alternative explanations of the experiments.

Production Experiments of Loftus

There are several Loftus experiments we want to discuss in terms of the spreading-activation theory. The first of these is an experiment by Freedman and Loftus (1971), in which subjects had to produce an instance of a category that began with a given letter or was characterized by a given adjective. For example, subjects might be asked to name a fruit that begins with the letter A or a fruit that is red. On some trials the category was shown first and on some trials second. Hence, this was a priming experiment in that one concept was activated before the other. Reaction time was measured from the onset of the second stimulus.

Our concern is with the finding that subjects were faster when the category (e.g., "fruit") was given first than when either the letter or the adjective was given first. This basic result was later replicated even for cases in which the instance named was a more frequent associate to the adjective than to the category noun (e.g., "lemon" is a closer associate of "sour" than of "fruit").

The explanation in terms of the theory is as follows: When a noun, such as "fruit," is presented first, the activation spreads to nodes connected to "fruit," among which are instances such as "apple," "pear," "peach," "orange," and "lemon." But these concepts are all highly interlinked with each other (though some, such as "orange" and "lemon," are more closely interlinked than others). Thus, the total amount of activation is spread among a relatively small number of closely interlinked concepts (see Assumption 5). However, when an adjective or letter is presented first, say "red" or "A," the activation spreads to a much wider set of concepts, which are not particularly interlinked with each other. Thus, the large variety of different things that are red or that start with the letter A will receive relatively little priming when the adjective or letter are given first. Because priming the noun leads to a greater accumulation of activation on the instances, these are closer to their threshold for firing, so that it takes less stimulation, and hence less time, to trigger an intersection when the second stimulus is presented.

Freedman and Loftus (1971) explained their finding in terms of entering the category when a noun is presented and entering a cluster within the category when the adjective or letter is presented. Thus if the noun is presented first, the subject can enter the category immediately and need only choose the correct cluster when the adjective or letter is presented. But if the adjective or letter is presented first, the subject must wait until the category is presented, because the cluster is specific to that category. (However, Loftus, Note 2, has revised this explanation for the letter stimulus in her dictionary-network model.)

The Freedman and Loftus explanation is not altogether different from the explanation offered here, though our theory is less rigidly hierarchical. The rigid hierarchy gets into trouble with errors such as one we encountered where a subject produced "Ben Franklin," given the stimulus pair "president" and "F," although he later recognized his mistake. In an activation theory, "Franklin" is a very likely intersection starting at "president" and "F," because he is so closely linked with the concept, "president," and some of its foremost instances, such as "Washington." Such a wrong intersection was likely in this case because the correct answer (prior to Ford) was "Fillmore," who is rather inaccessible and unlikely to be found quickly enough to preclude finding "Franklin." Once such an intersection is found, it is only by evaluating the connection between "president" and "Franklin," that it can be rejected (see Assumptions 8-13). It is a general problem of category-search models that they cannot deal with such errors.

Perhaps the major advantage of the spreading-activation theory over the Freedman and Loftus (1971) explanation is in tying their result to a parallel result in a quite different experiment by Loftus (1973b). In a categorization experiment, Loftus found that the direction of the association between the category and the instance determined whether subjects were faster when given the category first or the instance first. In the experiment she used four kinds of category-instance pairs: (a) pairs where both the category and instance evoked the other with high frequency (e.g., "tree-oak"); (b) pairs where the category evoked activation available to the semantic network if both are primed (hence he will be slower on noun-adjective trials if he primes both).

As can be seen in Figure 2, the subject is much slower on noun-adjective trials than on noun-letter trials in the blocked condition. This is accounted for by the fact that an intersection on a noun-adjective trial occurs in the semantic network and requires the further step of retrieving the corresponding name in the lexical network. On the other hand, the intersection on a noun-letter trial occurs at the name in the lexical network. Therefore, the name does not then need to be retrieved.

The second result that shows up the difference between adjectives and letters was predicted by Loftus from the dictionary-network model. In this experiment (Loftus & Cole, 1974) subjects saw three stimuli, ordered either noun, adjective, letter or noun, letter, adjective. For example, the three stimuli might be "animal," "small," and "mouse." The prediction was that the subject should be faster when the adjective is presented before the letter, and this was the result found. The reasoning is as follows: When the adjective appears before the letter, activation will spread from a small set of instances in the semantic network to the lexical network where the intersection occurs, since the letter can be expected just as in the blocked condition. When the letter is presented before the adjective, activation will spread from a small set of instances in the lexical network back to the semantic network where an intersection with the adjective will occur. Then the subject must return again to the lexical network to retrieve the name, so there is an extra transit necessary in this condition.

Loftus has also run a series of experiments in which subjects were asked to produce a member of a category and a short time later asked to produce a different member of that category (Loftus, 1973b; Loftus, Senders, & Turkletaub, 1974; Loftus & Loftus, 1974). This was accomplished by show-

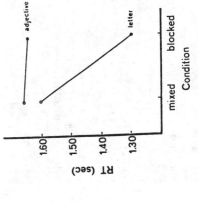

FIGURE 2. Reaction time for noun-adjective and noun-letter stimuli in mixed and blocked conditions (from Loftus, Note 2).

presentation of the category name and the restricting letter if the subject knows a letter is coming. (p. 13)

This is essentially the spreading-activation explanation, if the dictionary is taken to be a lexical network. Rather than saying that "the subject traces some number of pathways," which suggests a conscious tracing process, the present theory would say that activation spreads along some number of pathways, because the subject has activated the lexical network in addition to the semantic network (see Assumption 7). Hence, in the present explanation, the subject's control is reduced to diffusely activating whole networks rather than specific pathways (in addition to the specific nodes activated by the stimuli in the experiment). The difference in the results for the noun-letter trials in the two conditions then depends on whether the subject primes both networks (as in the blocked condition) or only the semantic network (as in the mixed condition). The reason he only activates the semantic network in the mixed condition may be either because of a principle of least effort (hence he could speed up his reaction time if he tried) or because there is less

the instance with high frequency, but the instance evoked the category with low frequency (e.g., "seafood-shrimp"); (c) pairs where the category evoked the instance with low frequency, but the instance evoked the category with high frequency (e.g., "insect-butterfly"); and (d) pairs where both the category and instance evoked the other with low frequency (e.g., "cloth-orlon"). When the category was presented before the instance, reaction time for Conditions (a) and (b) was approximately equal and significantly faster than for Conditions (c) and (d). However, when the instance was presented first, reaction time for Conditions (a) and (c) was approximately equal and significantly faster than for Conditions (b) and (d). That is to say, subjects are fast when the category is presented first, if the category evokes the instance with high frequency, and subjects are fast when the instance is presented first, if the instance evokes the category with high frequency. The spreading-activation theory explains the pattern of reaction times in the following way, assuming that production frequency is a measure of the strength or accessibility of the path from one concept to another. When the first concept (i.e., the one presented first) evokes the second with a relatively high frequency, this means that more activation spreads to the second, and it takes less time to reach the threshold for an intersection. Thus, the amount the first concept primes the second concept determines the reaction time.

By comparing this experiment with the Freedman and Loftus (1971) study, it can be seen that the two results are exactly parallel. Based on our structural assumptions, "fruit" primes "apple" more than "red" or the letter "A" primes "apple" in the Freedman and Loftus study. Hence, the shorter reaction time occurs when "fruit" or "A" is presented first. Similarly in the Loftus (1973b) study, when the category primes the instance most highly, the shortest reaction times occur when the category is presented first. But when the instance primes the category most highly, the shortest reaction times occur when the instance

is presented first. A spreading-activation explanation is quite compelling to account for the Loftus (1973b) results, and the theory offered here encompasses the order effect in both the Loftus study and the earlier Freedman and Loftus experiment within a single framework.

Recently Loftus (Note 2) has found two different ways in which presenting a letter acts differently from presenting an adjective, in variations of the Freedman and Loftus paradigm. This has led her to the development of a dictionary-network model, which we will translate into spreading-activation terms. The first difference between presenting a letter and an adjective appeared when Grober and Loftus (1974) compared reaction time in two conditions: one where noun-adjective (e.g., "fruit-red") and noun-letter (e.g., "fruit-A") trials were randomly intermixed, and one where noun-adjective and noun-letter trials were separated into blocks. In all cases the noun preceded the adjective or letter. The results of this experiment are shown in Figure 2. It is clear that when the subject knows a letter is coming, he can prepare for it. But in the mixed condition, the subject apparently prepares for either kind of trial the same way he prepares for an adjective trial, since adjective trials take the same amount of time in either case. The theory's description of semantic processing on the adjective trials is the same as that given earlier for the Freedman and Loftus (1971) experiment, with the amendment that only the semantic network and not the lexical network would be diffusely primed before the adjective is presented. When an intersection is found in the semantic network, then the subject must retrieve the name from the lexical network.

Loftus (Note 2) described what must happen on noun-letter trials in the blocked condition as follows:

The first step of the process is entering the category. The next step is a quasi-parallel simultaneous search towards the Dictionary. That is to say, the subject traces some number of pathways leading from category instances to the Dictionary representations of those instances. This step can be started during the interval between the ing a category-letter pair (e.g., "fruit-P"), which asked the subject for an appropriate instance, then, following 0, 1, or 2 intervening items, showing the same category paired with a different letter (e.g., "fruit-A"), which asked for a different instance. The general finding is that reaction time for the second instance is shorter than reaction time for the first instance and increases monotonically with the number of intervening items. For example, in Loftus (1973a) a subject's baseline time to name a fruit beginning with the letter "P" was 1.52 sec. However, it took him 1.22 sec to produce the same response if he had named a different fruit on the previous trial and 1.29 sec to produce the response if he had named a different fruit two trials back.

The spreading-activation theory predicts these results by assuming that when an item is processed, other items are activated to the extent that they are closely related to that item. That is, retrieving one category member produces a spread of activation to other category members, facilitating their later retrieval. The assumption (Assumption 3) that activation decreases over time or trials predicts the lag effect.

Meyer and Schvaneveldt (Meyer, 1973; Meyer & Schvaneveldt, 1971; Schvaneveldt & Meyer, 1973; Meyer, Schvaneveldt, & Ruddy, Note 3) have also shown that the time to retrieve information from memory is faster if related information has been accessed a short time previously. Their paradigm is somewhat different. Subjects were required to classify letter strings as words or nonwords. The general finding was that the response time to classify a letter string as a word is faster if the subject has just classified a semantically similar word as opposed to a semantically dissimilar word. Thus, for example, the time it takes to classify "butter" as a word is faster if "butter" is preceded by "bread" than if it is preceded by "nurse." Their results have led Meyer and Schvaneveldt to an explanation in terms of spreading activation and illustrate the widely different paradigms that such a theory can encompass.

Juola and Atkinson's Study with Multiple Categories

An increase in reaction time with multiple categories has been found by Juola and Atkinson (1971) in a task where subjects had to decide whether a stimulus word belonged to one of a specified number (1-4) of previously specified (target) categories. They compared this task with one where subjects decided if the stimulus word was the same as one of a variable number (1-4) of target words. Their experiment was designed to distinguish between two kinds of models, one they attribute to Landauer and Freedman (1968) and one they attribute to Collins and Quillian (1970a). In most respects, their results fit the model they derived from Landauer and Freedman, but since the spreading-activation theory provides an alternative explanation for their results, we want to compare their two models with our theory.

The model Juola and Atkinson (1971) derived from Landauer and Freedman (1968) is very similar to what Landauer and Meyer (1972) call the "category-search model." It assumes that the subject searches through instances of the categories in memory seeking a match for the stimulus word. Such a model predicts that as the number of categories or words in the memory set increases, reaction time for the category-matching task should increase at a greater slope than reaction time for the word-matching task. This is because each additional target category adds more instances that must be searched, whereas each additional target word only adds one, the word itself. This result was essentially what Juola and Atkinson found.

The model they ascribed to Collins and Quillian (1970a) assumed that subjects perform the category-matching task by retrieving their stored category for the stimulus word and comparing this to the given categories to see if it matches one of them. This model would predict that the slope for the two tasks should be about the same, and the intercept for the category-matching task should be greater than for the word-matching task. Their results clearly reject this

model. Although attributed to Collins and Quillian, this model is quite different from Quillian's theory, because the semantic search in Quillian's (1966) theory is assumed to spread in parallel from both categories and instances. When the categories are given first, as in Juola and Atkinson's experiment, then activation would spread out from the categories before the instance even appeared.

In order to explain our interpretation of Juola and Atkinson's results, it is necessary to describe their procedure in more detail. They chose 10 large categories and 12 common instances from each category as stimuli. This makes a total of 120 instances in all. In the word-matching task, they presented from 1 to 4 of the 120 instances as targets on each trial. In the category-matching task, they presented from 1 to 4 of the 10 categories as targets on each trial. In both cases the same set of 120 instances were chosen from the same set of 120 instances. In the word-matching task, then, the discrimination necessary to categorize the stimulus was between one of the target words or a word that had not occurred as a target for a large number of trials (on the average about 24 trials earlier). In the category-matching task, however, the discrimination was between a word in one of the target categories and a word in one of the categories from a recent trial (on the average about 2 trials earlier). The discrimination, therefore, was rather easy in the word-matching task and quite difficult in the category-matching task.

What we think must be happening in the task is that the discrimination between positive and negative responses is made (at least partly) on the basis of activation level. In the category-matching task, as the number of categories increases, the amount of activation allocated to each category decreases (see Assumptions 2 and 3). Furthermore, activation will be left over from previous trials on the categories corresponding to negative instances, though it will have partly decayed (Assumption 3). For example, suppose "tree" was a target category on a particular trial and "body part" was not,

but "body part" was a target on a previous trial. Then "tree" will have a higher activation level than "body part," but the difference will not be very large because "body part" was presented so recently. If a positive instance such as "oak" is presented, it will intersect with "tree"; if a negative instance such as "arm" is presented, it will intersect with "body part." The less activation on "tree," which depends on how many other targets there are, the harder it is to discriminate that it is in fact a target or that "body part" is not a target. The more difficult the discrimination is, the longer it takes to make, and thus there will be a fairly large effect of the size of the target set on reaction time.

In the word-matching task, however, the difference in activation level as the number of targets is varied will not be so critical a factor. This is because the absolute difference between the activation level of targets and nontargets is so much greater in the word-matching task, given Juola and Atkinson's experimental procedure. That is to say, each nontarget was presented as a target so many trials previously (approximately 24) that the activation level for a nontarget would have decayed (Assumption 3) to a very low activation level as compared to any target. Hence, the large absolute difference in activation levels between targets and nontargets makes the differences due to target-set size relatively unimportant.

In conclusion, the spreading-activation theory's explanation of Juola and Atkinson's (1971) results is that the effect of differences in activation level due to target-set size matter more when the discrimination is difficult and matter less when the discrimination is easier. Furthermore, as Juola and Atkinson point out, there are two aspects of their data (namely, the fact that the data for positive responses are not linear, and the marked recency effects in the serial position curves) that fit much better with a parallel model, such as spreading-activation theory, than they do with a serial model, such as the one they derive from Landauer and Freedman (1968).

There are two implications of this view that could be tested fairly easily. One is that reaction time to decide that an instance such as "arm" is a negative instance will depend on the recency with which "body part" was presented as a target category. The more recent its presentation, the longer it will take to say "no." A more global implication is simply that the slope of the curve with respect to target size depends on those factors that affect the difficulty of discrimination, such as the recency with which negative instances occurred as targets (and probably as nontargets as well). This has important implications for the memory-search literature as a whole.

Conrad's Study

Using a true–false reaction time technique for sentences (e.g., the task is to decide whether "A salmon can eat" is true or false), Conrad (1972) found results which she interpreted as contradictory to Quillian's (1966, 1969) theory of semantic processing. In fact, the results of her study are quite close to what Quillian's theory would predict given Conrad's methodology.

In her first experiment, which was like the Collins and Quillian (1969) study, Conrad selected 2-level and 3-level hierarchies from the common culture (e.g., salmon → fish → animal) and properties associated with the objects at different levels. Then she constructed sentences with instances, such as "salmon," from the lowest level and properties from all three levels. The results Collins and Quillian found were that the property was farther removed from the instance in the hierarchy. The reason for the increases in reaction time according to spreading-activation theory is that as the instance and property are farther apart in the hierarchy, it takes activation longer to spread between them and to trigger an intersection (and perhaps to evaluate the path found as well). Unlike Collins and Quillian (1969), Conrad (1972) broke down the properties in her sentences into three groups on the basis of the frequency (high, medium, low) with which people generated each property, given

the different objects in the hierarchies. Another difference from Collins and Quillian's study is that she collected data over 5 days by repeating all the sentences each day.

The results of her first experiment were generally in the same direction as the increases in reaction time that Collins and Quillian found when the property was farther removed from the instance in the hierarchy. There was one reversal in her data out of nine comparisons, and this occurred for the high-frequency properties, where it was not unexpected given the weak theory of cognitive economy (as we will argue below). However, the increases she found were much smaller on the average than those of Collins and Quillian. The weak theory of cognitive economy predicts that people store a property with whatever instance it is linked to in a sentence, so Conrad's repetition of sentences over 5 days should lead to the smaller reaction time increases she found. This is because an inference necessary on the first day would be less likely on the second day, and so on. Conrad, in fact, reports a large Level × Day interaction.

In general, Conrad found that the higher the frequency of the property, the smaller the increases between levels. Given the weak theory of cognitive economy, we would expect that high-frequency properties are more likely to be stored at several levels in the hierarchy, because they are more likely to be encountered in contexts involving specific instances. For example, "leaves" are more likely to be stored as a property with particular types of trees (such as "maple" and "oak") than is "bark," because leaves are a higher frequency property. Thus, the effect of property frequency found by Conrad is consistent with the weak theory.

Conrad (1972) argued that Collins and Quillian's (1969) results could be explained by a confounding of property level and property frequency. Her argument was that the sentences Collins and Quillian used may have been based on high-frequency properties for Level 1 sentences (e.g., "A salmon is pink"), moderate-frequency properties for Level 2 sentences (e.g., "A salmon has fins"), and low-frequency properties for

Level 3 sentences (e.g., "A salmon can eat"). To support her argument, she showed that if one plots her reaction time data in the above way, one obtains approximately the same slope as Collins and Quillian did, whereas if one plots the slope for low-, medium-, or high-frequency properties separately, one obtains much smaller slopes.

However, there are two weaknesses in Conrad's argument. First, she did not use her frequency data to evaluate systematically the frequency of the properties in Collins and Quillian's sentences, so her conjecture about such a confounding has no empirical basis. Collins and Quillian (1969) did obtain subject ratings of importance of the property for the relevant level concept, which should correlate with Conrad's frequency measure. These ratings averaged 1.90 for Level 1 sentences, 1.92 for Level 2 sentences, and 2.16 for Level 3 sentences (based on a 5-point scale, where 1 = very important and 5 = not important). These are small differences and certainly do not support the notion that the slope between Level 1 and Level 2 sentences was due to the confounding Conrad hypothesized. The difference between Level 3 sentences and the others may have contributed to the greater slope that Collins and Quillian found, but even that is doubtful. For those subjects who had sentences with all 3 levels, the slope was actually larger (approximately 100 msec rather than 75 msec), but this was offset by a group of subjects who were slower overall and saw only Level 1 and 2 sentences. So the latter group acted to cancel out any exaggeration of the slope due to the lower importance of Level 3 properties.

Second, the comparison Conrad (1972) made in plotting her data against Collins and Quillian's data compared data based on five responses to the same sentence with data based on one response to a sentence. As indicated above, the weak theory of cognitive economy predicts that repetition of a sentence makes an inference less likely and should reduce the slopes in the way Conrad found. A fairer comparison would be between her data on the first day and Collins

and Quillian's data. But even that comparison has the problem that she may well have included sentences of the kind, "A maple has leaves," where the property is a general property of trees, but where most people would store it as a property of maples as well. This suggests that the fairest comparison is between Collins and Quillian's data and her data on the first day for low-frequency properties, where the properties were least likely to be stored at more than one level. But we cannot make this comparison because she did not break down her data by days. In conclusion, the differences between the two experiments and the fact that the only relevant data do not particularly support the conjecture about a confounding of property level and property frequency make Conrad's argument rather tenuous.

It was Conrad's second experiment that appears more damaging to Quillian's theory, but here she made a crucial methodological change. She presented the object 1 sec before the property, and this turned the experiment into a priming study. In the study she presented properties true of the highest level nodes, together with objects (e.g., "salmon," "fish," or "animal") at different levels in the hierarchy. Therefore, she predicted from Quillian's theory that the lower level objects, such as "salmon," would take activation longer to confirm, since it would take activation longer to spread between lower level objects and higher level properties. But by presenting the object 1 sec before the property and by using only high-level properties, she made it possible for her subjects to prepare during the interval by priming the object's superordinates. For example, if a subject saw "salmon," his best strategy was to retrieve the superordinates, "fish" and "animal," because the property to appear would be a high-level property, such as "eating." In these circumstances, there is little reason to expect systematic differences between objects such as "salmon," "fish," and "animal." Thus, this particular experiment had real methodological problems as a test of Quillian's theory, and it is weaker evidence *against* spreading-activation theory than her first experiment is evidence for the theory.

Effects of Typicality and Semantic Relatedness in Categorization Tasks

In recent experiments, Rips et al. (1973), Rosch (1973), and Smith et al. (1974) have shown that reaction time in a categorization task corresponds very closely to ratings of how typical the instance is of the category. For example, robins and sparrows are considered typical birds whereas chickens and geese are not. The effect of typicality on reaction time is quite large even when frequency of the particular instances in the language is controlled. Like Smith et al., we would argue that the typicality effect is one more manifestation of the fact that semantic similarity speeds up positive decisions and slows down negative decisions. Such an effect has been found repeatedly (Collins & Quillian, 1969, 1970a, 1972b; Schaeffer & Wallace, 1969, 1970; Wilkins, 1971). While Landauer and Meyer (1972) argued that the evidence for similarity effects at that time was either questionable or artifactual, the evidence now seems so overwhelming that any viable theory must account for them. They are very damaging to the category-search model.

There are two reasons why spreading-activation theory predicts that atypical instances will take longer to categorize than typical instances. The most important reason derives from the way evidence is aggregated (see Assumptions 8–13). Because different connections that are found are combined as evidence, distinguishing properties can slow down a positive decision based on a superordinate connection or on matching properties. For example, the decision that a chicken is a bird (i.e., an atypical instance) might be made on the basis of a superordinate connection from "chicken" to "bird," which people learn because chickens are frequently referred to as birds. But the fact that people eat chickens, that they are raised on farms, and that they are rather large are all properties that distinguish chickens from most birds. If these distinguishing properties are found during the

memory search, as some are likely to be, they act to slow down the positive decision, because they are negative evidence. Similarly, matching properties can slow down a negative decision. For example, the decision that a goose is not a duck might be made on the basis of the difference in their necks (a distinguishing property) or simply because they are stored as mutually exclusive kinds of birds (see Assumption 12), but the matching properties that are found (e.g., their affinity to ponds, their webbed feet, their large size) will slow down the decision that they are different. The argument here is similar to that of Smith et al. (1974), which we will discuss in comparing the two theories.

The second reason for the typicality effects relates to those cases where a superordinate connection is found. As we indicated earlier, superordinate links differ in accessibility (or strength), and accessibility depends on use. If a person frequently uses the link that a robin is a bird, and less frequently uses the link that a chicken is a bird (assuming approximately equal frequency for chickens and robins), then the accessibility of "bird" from "robin" will be greater than from "chicken." Because of this, according to the theory, negative judgments are slower when the two concepts are more closely related semantically. The explanation for this reversal according to the theory (and to Holyoak and Glass) is that people make these decisions not on the basis of distinguishing properties (though some might be considered), but because they are stored as mutually exclusive subordinates (Assumption 12). Generation frequency in this case is a measure of the strength of the connection between the two concepts and therefore of how long it will take to find the contradiction between the two mutually exclusive concepts.

The second finding of Holyoak and Glass (1975) involves sentences where people reject the sentence by finding a counterexample (Assumption 13). For example, "All animals are birds," can be rejected by finding another kind of animal, such as a mammal. In this case Holyoak and Glass varied

the production frequency of the predicate noun (e.g., "birds") independently of the production frequency of the counterexample (e.g., "mammals"). Their finding was that reaction time depended not on the production frequency of the predicate noun (which is a measure of the semantic relatedness of the concepts in the sentence) but on the frequency of producing a counterexample. Here again where a decision strategy that is not based on distinguishing properties is appropriate, the reaction time data do not depend on the semantic relatedness of the two concepts.

The importance of these two findings by Holyoak and Glass (1975), in our view, is that they demonstrate that different kinds of evidence can be involved in making categorization judgments. This suggests that approaches such as that of Meyer (1970) and Smith et al. (1974), which try to formulate a single strategy for making such judgments, will inevitably fail.

RELATION OF THE THEORY TO THE MODEL OF SMITH, SHOBEN, AND RIPS

Quillian's (1966, 1969) theory was a forerunner of a number of global theories of semantic processing based on network representations, in particular those of Anderson and Bower (1973), Norman and Rumelhart (1975), and Schank (1972). These theorists have made important advances on the Quillian theory (especially in the representation of acts and causes) which in no way contradict the basic thrust of Quillian's theory. There are some differences between these theories and Quillian's, but the basic intent of this paper is to deal with those aspects of semantic processing where the model of Smith et al. (1974) is the major competitor to Quillian's theory.

Unlike the various network models, the model of Smith et al. represents concepts as bundles of semantic features. Their model has the virtues of being quite clear and explicit, and it agrees quite well with the reaction time data for categorization judgments, except for the Holyoak and Glass (1975) results. Because it is such an initially compelling model, we want to emphasize how it differs from spreading-activation

all the connections found will constitute negative evidence, and subjects will be quite fast to reach the negative criterion in such cases. This too is similar to the explanation in the Smith et al (1974) model.

Recently, Holyoak and Glass (1975) have isolated two different cases where semantic relatedness or typicality does not produce the usual effect on reaction time for negative judgments. One case arises when the decision depends on what they call a contradiction and what we have called mutually exclusive subordinates. The other case arises when the decision depends on a counterexample.

In the first case, Holyoak and Glass found that people are faster to reject sentences such as "All fruits are vegetables" or "Some chairs are tables" than sentences such as "All fruits are flowers" or "Some chairs are beds." In these four sentences the two nouns are mutually exclusive subordinates. The difference between the sentences is that "vegetables" and "tables" are generated with high frequency, while "flowers" and "beds" are generated with low frequency, when subjects are given the frame "All fruits are ..." or "Some chairs are ..." and asked to produce a false sentence. This difference is in the opposite direction of the usual finding that negative judgments are slower when the two concepts are more closely related semantically. The explanation for this reversal according to the theory (and to Holyoak and Glass) is that people make these decisions not on the basis of distinguishing properties (though some might be considered), but because they are stored as mutually exclusive subordinates (Assumption 12).

The way evidence is aggregated in the theory also explains the common finding (Collins & Quillian, 1970a, 1972b; Holyoak & Glass, 1975; Rips et al., 1974) that people are fast to decide that semantically unrelated concepts are different (e.g., that a book is not a dog). In comparing such concepts, there are not likely to be any superordinate connections, and almost all property connections will involve distinguishing rather than matching properties. Therefore, almost theory and point out what we think are its inherent difficulties.

In the model of Smith et al. (1974), the meaning of a concept is assumed to be represented by semantic features of two kinds: defining features and characteristic features. Defining features are those that an instance must have to be a member of the concept, and the model assumes that features can be more or less defining. Characteristic features are those that are commonly associated with the concept, but are not necessary for concept membership. For example, "wings" might be a defining feature of "birds" and "flying" a characteristic feature, since all birds have wings but not all fly. In a categorization task, the model assumes that one concepts are first compared in Stage 1 with respect to all their features, both characteristic and defining. If the match is above a positive criterion, the subject answers "yes"; if it is below a negative criterion, the subject answers "no"; and if it is in-between, the subject makes a second comparison in Stage 2 based on just the defining features. If the instance has all the defining features of the category, the subject says "yes" and otherwise says "no." If the subject can decide in Stage 1, his reaction time will be faster than if he decides in Stage 2.

There are several minor differences between the model of Smith et al. (1974) and the spreading-activation theory that could be minimized by slightly changing their model. The difference in wording between comparing features in their model and finding links between features in our theory is really a nondifference. But the distinction between defining and characteristic features has the inherent difficulty, pointed out through the ages, that there is no feature that is absolutely necessary for any category.⁴ For example, if one removes the wings from a bird, it does not stop being a bird. Furthermore, we doubt if people can make consistent de-

⁴ There is for living things a biologist's taxonomy, which categorizes objects using properties that are not always those most apparent to the layman. Thus, there are arbitrary, technical definitions that are different from the layman's ill-defined concepts, but this is not true in most domains. There is no technical definition of a game, a vehicle, or a country that is generally accepted.

cisions as to whether a feature is defining or characteristic, either from time to time or from one person to another. Smith et al. recognized that features are more or less defining (or criterial), but they were forced into making the artificial distinction between defining and characteristic features. Still, the model could be revised to work without the two stages and make essentially the same reaction time predictions.

The revision is as follows: If features are compared over time, as in Quillian's (1966) theory, then as the process goes on longer, more features will be compared (assuming features have different accessibilities). The comparison process can have a positive criterion and a negative criterion just as before, and features can be weighted by their criteriality. If the match at any point in time is above the positive criterion, the subject says "yes"; if the match falls below the negative criterion, the subject says "no"; and otherwise he goes on comparing features. Finally, if he is running out of relevant information, he says "I don't know." This is simply the Bayesian decision model described in Assumption 9 of the extended theory, where the evidence consists of matching and mismatching features as in the property comparison of Assumption 11.

Thus, we agree that a decision process similar to the one that Smith et al. (1974) postulate does occur for some categorization decisions. But there is a fundamental disagreement, because they argue that all categorizations judgments are made by comparing features of the instance and category, whereas we argue that people use whatever evidence they find, including superordinate links.

Because they exclude the use of superordinate links, the model of Smith et al. has several inherent difficulties. The most obvious is the assumption that even when people have superordinate information stored, they do not use it. While most people may not have learned some superordinate relations (e.g., that a beaver is a mammal, or a sled is a vehicle), there are many they have learned (e.g., that a wren is a bird, and a beaver is an animal). Why would they not

use such information if it is stored? How in fact can they avoid using it? It is an unlikely model which postulates that people use information that is less relevant to make a decision, instead of information that is more relevant.

Another obvious difficulty with the Smith et al. (1974) model is that people seldom know the defining properties of concepts. For example, consider whether a whale is a mammal, a sponge is an animal, a bat is a bird, or a wren is a sparrow. In the Smith et al. model, these difficult (and slow) decisions would be made in Stage 2 on the basis of defining properties. But people generally have no idea what the defining properties of a mammal, an animal, a bird, or a sparrow are. Even if they know that one of the most criterial properties for being a mammal is that it bears its young alive, it seems highly unlikely that they know whether whales (or beavers for that matter) bear their young alive. Neither of the authors has any idea what properties of a sponge make it an animal, but if asked in an experiment whether a sponge was an animal, we would answer "yes," and we would be comparatively slow about it. The reason we would answer "yes" is simply that we were told at one time that a sponge is an animal. We were also told that a bat is not a bird, and if we had not been told, we fear we might have responded "yes" if asked whether a bat is a bird in a categorization experiment. The decision that a wren is not a sparrow would be made because they are mutually exclusive kinds of birds (See assumption 12). They are both small songbirds, and it is hard to believe that many people know what the defining features of a sparrow are that a wren does not have. The fact that there are cases where people must use superordinate information to make correct categorization judgments makes it unlikely that they do not use such information in other cases where they could make the decision simply by matching features or properties. This is one of the strongest arguments for a hybrid theory.

We would like to close this section by raising the question of why one should adopt such a complicated theory when the Smith

et al. (1974) model is simpler and predicts the reaction time data quite well. We have tried to stress the inherent difficulties that their model has in ignoring on defining properties. Experimental tests can probably be devised that will show up those difficulties. We will suggest one such test, but first we might point out that the results of the Loftus (1973b) categorization experiment described earlier do not fit the Smith et al. model very well. If a person is merely comparing features between the instance and the category, then it should not matter whether the instance or category is presented first. It is the asymmetry in the superordinate connections that predicts the asymmetry Loftus found in reaction time, and it is hard to imagine how one could have an asymmetry of that kind in comparing features of two concepts.

One experiment that might show difficulties with the Smith et al. (1974) model is a categorization task. The categories and instances used are based on their multidimensional scaling of birds and animals on the one hand, and mammals and animals on the other. As both Collins and Quillian (Note 4) and Rips et al. (1973) report, subjects are faster at deciding that bird names are in the category "bird" than in the category "animal," whereas they are slower at deciding that mammal names are in the category "mammal" than in the category "animal." Collins and Quillian argue that this is the way people learn the superordinates: that pigeons are birds and lions are animals. Smith et al. argue that it is based on shared features, and they show by their scaling solution that most birds are closer to "bird" than to "animal," and most mammals are closer to "animal" than to "mammal." But there are several bird names that are closer to "animal" than to "bird" (in particular, "goose," "chicken," and "duck"; "pigeon" is equidistant), and there are several mammal names that are closer to "mammal" than "animal" (in particular, "deer," "bear," and "lion"; "horse" is equidistant). We would predict that even for those instances the above pattern would hold, whereas a pure feature-matching theory, such as the Smith et al. model, makes the opposite prediction. So this is a possible test of the two theories. There are undoubtedly many other tests.

Finally, we want to explain why we have been led to such a complicated theory. In trying to write computer programs that answer different types of questions, it becomes apparent that any decision procedure that gives correct answers must be flexible enough to deal with many different configurations of knowledge in memory. This is because people have incomplete knowledge about the world (see Collins et al., 1975), and they often do not have stored particular superordinate links or criterial properties. Any realistic data base for a computer system will have this same kind of incomplete knowledge. Therefore, perhaps our strongest criticism of the Smith et al. (1974) model is that it breaks down when people lack knowledge about defining features.

While at one level this is a complicated theory, at another level it is a simpler theory than the Smith et al. model. By viewing superordinate links as highly criterial properties, the theory becomes a simple Bayesian model. It is only in specifying the particular configurations of knowledge that constitute positive or negative evidence that the Bayesian process that the theory becomes complicated. The difference between the two theories is that the Smith et al. model allows only one kind of evidence (matching or mismatching features), whereas the theory presented here allows other kinds of evidence as well. Thus the theory encompasses a revised version of the Smith et al. model as a special case of a more general procedure.

CONCLUSION

We have extended Quillian's spreading-activation theory of semantic processing in order to deal with a number of experiments that have been performed on semantic memory in recent years. The result is a fairly complicated theory with enough generality to apply to results from many different experimental paradigms. The theory can also be considered as a prescription for building human semantic processing in a computer, though at what level many details are omitted

about decision strategies for different judgments that arise in language processing (see Carbonell & Collins, 1973; Collins et al., 1975; Quillian, 1969). We would argue that the adequacy of a psychological theory should no longer be measured solely by its ability to predict experimental data. It is also important that a theory be sufficiently powerful to produce the behavior that it purports to explain.

REFERENCE NOTES

1. Wilkins, A. J. *Categories and the internal lexicon.* Paper presented at the meeting of the Experimental Psychology Society, Oxford, England, 1972.

2. Loftus, E. F. *How to catch a zebra in semantic memory.* Paper presented at the Minnesota Conference on Cognition, Knowledge, and Adaptation, Minneapolis, 1973.

3. Meyer, D. E., Schvaneveldt, R. W., & Ruddy, M. G. *Activation of lexical memory.* Paper presented at the meeting of the Psychonomic Society, St. Louis, 1972.

4. Collins, A. M., & Quillian, M. R. *Categories and subcategories in semantic memory.* Paper presented at the meeting of the Psychonomic Society, St. Louis, 1971.

REFERENCES

Anderson, J. R., & Bower, G. H. *Human associative memory.* Washington, D.C.: V. H. Winston, 1973.

Anderson, R. C., & McGaw, B. On the representation of meanings of general terms. *Journal of Experimental Psychology,* 1973, *101,* 301–306.

Bell, A., & Quillian, M. R. Capturing concepts in a semantic net. In E. L. Jacks (Ed.), *Associative information techniques.* New York: American Elsevier, 1971.

Brown, R. W., & McNeill, D. The "tip of the tongue" phenomenon. *Journal of Verbal Learning and Verbal Behavior,* 1966, *6,* 325–337.

Carbonell, J. R., & Collins, A. M. Natural semantics in artificial intelligence. *Proceedings of the Third International Joint Conference on Artificial Intelligence,* 1973, 344–351.

Collins, A. M., & Quillian, M. R. Retrieval time from semantic memory. *Journal of Verbal Learning and Verbal Behavior,* 1969, *8,* 240–248.

Collins, A. M., & Quillian, M. R. Does category size affect categorization time? *Journal of Verbal Learning and Verbal Behavior,* 1970, *9,* 432–438. (a)

Collins, A. M., & Quillian, M. R. Facilitating retrieval from semantic memory: The effect of repeating part of an inference. *Acta Psychologica,* 1970, *33,* 304–314. (b)

Collins, A. M., & Quillian, M. R. Experiments on semantic memory and language comprehension.

In L. W. Gregg (Ed.), *Cognition in learning and memory.* New York: Wiley, 1972. (a)

Collins, A. M., & Quillian, M. R. How to make a language user. In E. Tulving & W. Donaldson (Eds.), *Organization of memory.* New York: Academic Press, 1972. (b)

Collins, A., Warnock, E. H., Aiello, N., & Miller, M. L. Reasoning from incomplete knowledge. In D. G. Bobrow & A. Collins (Eds.), *Representation and understanding: Studies in cognitive science.* New York: Academic Press, 1975.

Conrad, C. Cognitive economy in semantic memory. *Journal of Experimental Psychology,* 1972, *92,* 149–154.

Fitts, P. M. Cognitive aspects of information processing: III. Set for speed versus accuracy. *Journal of Experimental Psychology,* 1966, *71,* 849–857.

Freedman, J. L., & Loftus, E. F. Retrieval of words from long-term memory. *Journal of Verbal Learning and Verbal Behavior,* 1971, *10,* 107–115.

Grober, E., & Loftus, E. F. Semantic memory: Searching for attributes versus searching for names. *Memory & Cognition,* 1974, *2,* 413–416.

Hollan, J. D. Features and semantic memory: Set-theoretic or network model? *Psychological Review,* 1975, *82,* 154–155.

Holyoak. K. J., & Glass, A. L. The role of contradictions and counterexamples in the rejection of false sentences. *Journal of Verbal Learning and Verbal Behavior,* 1975, *14,* 215–239.

Juola, J. F., & Atkinson, R. C. Memory scanning for words versus categories. *Journal of Verbal Learning and Verbal Behavior,* 1971, *10,* 522–527.

Landauer, T. K., & Freedman, J. L. Information retrieval from long-term memory: Category size and recognition time. *Journal of Verbal Learning and Verbal Behavior,* 1968, *7,* 291–295.

Landauer, T. K., & Meyer, D. E. Category size and semantic memory retrieval. *Journal of Verbal Learning and Verbal Behavior,* 1972, *11,* 539–549.

Loftus, E. F. Activation of semantic memory. *American Journal of Psychology,* 1973, *86,* 331–337. (a)

Loftus, E. F. Category dominance, instance dominance, and categorization time. *Journal of Experimental Psychology,* 1973, *97,* 70–74. (b)

Loftus, E. F., & Cole, W. Retrieving attribute and name information from semantic memory. *Journal of Experimental Psychology,* 1974, *102,* 1116–1122.

Loftus, E. F., Senders, J. W., & Turkletaub, S. Retrieval of phonetically similar and dissimilar category members. *American Journal of Psychology,* 1974, *87,* 57–64.

Loftus, G. R., & Loftus, E. F. The influence of one memory retrieval on a subsequent memory retrieval. *Memory & Cognition,* 1974, *2,* 467–471.

Meyer, D. E. On the representation and retrieval of stored semantic information. *Cognitive Psychology,* 1970, *1,* 242–300.

Meyer, D. E. Correlated operations in searching stored semantic categories. *Journal of Experimental Psychology,* 1973, *99,* 124–133.

Meyer, D. E., & Schvaneveldt, R. W. Facilitation in recognizing pairs of words: Evidence of a dependence between retrieval operations. *Journal of Experimental Psychology,* 1971, *90,* 227–234.

Norman, D. A., & Rumelhart, D. E. *Explorations in cognition.* San Francisco: W. H. Freeman, 1975.

Quillian, M. R. A revised design for an understanding machine. *Mechanical Translation,* 1962, *7,* 17–29.

Quillian, M. R. *Semantic memory.* Unpublished doctoral dissertation, Carnegie Institute of Technology, 1966. (Reprinted in part in M. Minsky [Ed.], *Semantic information processing.* Cambridge, Mass.: M.I.T. Press, 1968.)

Quillian, M. R. Word concepts: A theory and simulation of some basic semantic capabilities. *Behavioral Science,* 1967, *12,* 410–430.

Quillian, M. R. The Teachable Language Comprehender: A simulation program and theory of language. *Communications of the ACM,* 1969, *12,* 459–476.

Rips, L. J., Shoben, E. J., & Smith, E. E. Semantic distance and the verification of semantic relations. *Journal of Verbal Learning and Verbal Behavior,* 1973, *12,* 1–20.

Rosch, E. On the internal structure of perceptual and semantic categories. In T. E. Moore (Ed.), *Cognitive development and acquisition of language.* New York: Academic Press, 1973.

Schaeffer, B., & Wallace, R. Semantic similarity and the comparison of word meanings. *Journal of Experimental Psychology,* 1969, *82,* 343–346.

Schaeffer, B., & Wallace, R. The comparison of word meanings. *Journal of Experimental Psychology,* 1970, *86,* 144–152.

Schank, R. C. Conceptual dependency: A theory of natural language understanding. *Cognitive Psychology,* 1972, *3,* 552–631.

Schvaneveldt, R. W., & Meyer, D. E. Retrieval and comparison processes in semantic memory. In S. Kornblum (Ed.), *Attention and performance IV.* New York: Academic Press, 1973.

Smith, E. E., Shoben, E. J., & Rips, L. J. Comparison processes in semantic memory. *Psychological Review,* 1974, *81,* 214–241.

Sternberg, S. High-speed scanning in human memory. *Science,* 1966, *153,* 652–654.

Stone, M. Models of choice-reaction time. *Psychometrika,* 1960, *25,* 251–260.

Wilkins, A. J. Conjoint frequency, category size, and categorization time. *Journal of Verbal Learning and Verbal Behavior,* 1971, *10,* 382–385.

Wittgenstein, L. *Philosophical investigations* (G. E. M. Anscombe, trans.). Oxford: Blackwell, 1953.

(Received November 4, 1974)

A Spreading Activation Theory of Memory

JOHN R. ANDERSON

Department of Psychology, Carnegie–Mellon University, Pittsburgh, Pennsylvania 15213

The ACT theory of factual memory is presented. According to this theory, information is encoded in an all-or-none manner into cognitive units and the strength of these units increases with practice and decays with delay. The essential process to memory performance is the retrieval operation. It is proposed that the cognitive units form an interconnected network and that retrieval is performed by spreading activation throughout the network. Level of activation in the network determines rate and probability of recall. With these assumptions in place, the ACT theory is shown to predict interference results in memory, judgements of associative relatedness, impact of extensive practice on memory, the differences between recognition and recall, effects of elaborative processing, and effects of reconstructive recall.

A simple observation about human experience is that we encounter various facts and retain them for varying periods of time. There has probably been more research in experimental psychology studying the many aspects of retention than any other topic. This research has indicated that there are many variables relevant to understanding this retention phenomenon besides the obvious ones of amount of initial study and passage of time. The purpose of this paper is to discuss some of the more important variables in terms of the ACT theory (Anderson, 1976, 1983). This is a theory which represents knowledge in a network and which has its memory processes defined on that network. It will be shown that many memory phenomena can be understood in terms of the network structures that encode the to-be-recalled facts and the network structures which surround these fact encodings. It will also be shown that the memory process of spreading activation plays a key role in explaining these phenomena.

Preparation of this paper and the research described herein was supported by NSF grant BNS78-17463. I am grateful to Matt Lewis, Lynne Reder, and Miriam Schustack for their comments on the manuscript and to the members of the ACT research group (Gary Bradshaw, Bill Jones, Matt Lewis, Peter Pirolli, and Jeff Shrager) for their discussions relevant to the paper.

This paper considers a wide variety of memory phenomena, but only a fraction of the phenomena that have been documented in experimental research on memory. The criterion in choosing phenomena has been to find ones that nicely illustrate the explanatory power of the ACT spreading activation mechanism operating on a memory network. (This is not to say that I have ignored data that contradict ACT; rather, I have argued elsewhere that seemed irrelevant). While the paper will detail other aspects of the ACT memory theory, this will only be to set the stage for discussion of spreading activation.

The first part of this paper will set forth the principles of the ACT theory of fact memory (Anderson, 1983). This theory has undergone some significant modifications since it was set forth by Anderson (1976). Using the three-stage organization proposed by Melton (1963), the ACT theory can be divided into principles concerning initial encoding, principles concerning storage, and principles concerning retrieval. The presentation of the ACT theory will be divided according to this categorization. With this theory in place I will apply it to explain a number of memory phenomena.

The Cognitive Unit

Before we can specify the processes of memory it is necessary to say something about the units that these memory processes operate on. In the ACT theory as developed by Anderson (1976), these units were individual associative links where a set of links made up a proposition. There has been a considerable literature now addressed to the issue of whether whole propositions might better be considered the units of memory (e.g., Anderson & Bower, 1973, 1980; Goetz, Anderson, & Schallert, 1981; Graesser, 1978; Jones, 1978; Kintsch, 1974). In the interest of getting on with the major points of this paper, I will not review the considerations but simply state that in the current ACT theory the units of memory are larger structures like the proposition (but see Anderson, 1980, for a discussion).

We use the term *cognitive units* to refer to the units of memory in the current ACT theory. A cognitive unit consists of a *unit node* plus a set of *elements*. For instance, a proposition is a cognitive unit where the elements are the relation and arguments of a proposition and the unit node is the proposition itself. There are clear similarities between my use of a "unit node" and Estes (1972) use of control nodes, Mandler's (1967), Miller's (1956), Simon's (1974), and Wickelgren's (1979) use of chunks, to name just a few of the predecessors to this idea. Cognitive units can be organized hierarchically as when one proposition occurs as a subproposition of another. While propositions are cognitive units, I do not mean to imply that they are the only type of cognitive unit. I have argued elsewhere (Anderson, 1983) that images and temporal strings (e.g., of words) can also be cognitive units. The points of this paper will not depend critically on whether we assume that this material is encoded as propositions, strings, images, or whatever. For present purposes the encoding can be considered to be the "generic" cognitive unit. Whatever the character of the cognitive unit, it can be represented in network form with the unit node connected to the elements.

An essential feature of a cognitive unit is that it is limited in the number of elements that it can contain. Currently, I have been working with a limitation set at five elements. This means that it is reasonable to consider a paired associate or simple sentence to be encoded by a cognitive unit but that it is not reasonable to consider a paragraph or 30-word list as encoded by a single cognitive unit.

Cognitive units gather their functional significance because they are the units of encoding and retrieval. When part of a cognitive unit is formed in long-term memory, all of it is encoded. Similarly, when part of a cognitive unit is retrieved from long-term memory, all of it is. For instance, when a proposition consisting of subject, verb, and object is formed, all three elements will be encoded in the unit, not just one or two.

Encoding

When a cognitive unit is created, either to record some external event or the result of some internal computation, a transient copy of it is placed in working memory. The basic encoding assumption of the ACT theory is that there is a probability that a transient working memory structure will be turned into a permanent long-term memory *trace*. This encoding assumption is spectacularly simple. The probability is constant over many manipulations. For instance, it does not vary with intention or motivation to learn, consistent with the ample research indicating that intention and motivation are irrelevant if processing is kept constant (e.g., Nelson, 1976; Postman, 1964).

Also, the probability of forming a long-term memory trace does not vary with the duration of residence in working memory. This is consistent with research (e.g., Nelson, 1977; Woodward, Bjork & Jongeward, 1973; Horowitz & Newman, 1969) that fails to find much effect of study time when the information is not being actively processed during study. However, probability of recall is found to increase with repetition even if that repetition is back to back

(Horowitz & Newman, 1969). One would suppose that a second presentation of an item has some chance of creating a new working memory copy. It is also worth noting here the results of Loftus (1972) with respect to picture memory: duration of a fixation on a picture part has no effect on its probability of recall but number of fixations on that part does.

The ACT theory is also quite straightforward about the impact of additional learning opportunities once a trace has been established: all traces have a strength associated with them. The first successful trial establishes the trace with a strength of one unit. Each subsequent trial increases the strength by one unit. Strength of a trace will be important to determining its probability and speed of retrieval. Thus, ACT clearly makes the prediction that overlearning will increase the probability of retention and speed of retrieval—predictions which are equally clearly confirmed.

Retention

According to the ACT theory, traces once formed are not lost but the strength of a trace can decay. Based on data summarized by Wickelgren (1976) and data of our own we assume that trace strength S is a power function of time with the form

$$S = t^{-b}   (1)$$

where t is measured from the point at which the trace was created in working memory and the exponent b has a value on the interval 0 to 1. The function has a strange value at $t = 0$, namely infinity. However, the strength value is only relevant to performance when the trace is out of working memory and must be retrieved (i.e., at times after $t = 0$). I regard this decay function as reflecting a fundamental fact about the system incapable of any further theoretical unpacking short of getting into the physiological character of the system (e.g., see Eccles' (1972) discussion of neural effects of use and disuse). Such a power function is to be contrasted with a exponential function (e.g., $S = a^t$) where $a < 1$. Such exponential functions would produce much more rapid forgetting than is empirically observed.

One of the interesting issues is what the retention function is like for a trace which has had multiple strengthenings. I will simply assume that its total strength is the sum of the strengths remaining from the individual strengthenings

$$S = \sum_i t_i^{-b}   (2)$$

where t_i is the time since the ith strengthening. Evidence for this assumption will be given later when I discuss effects of extensive practice.

Retrieval

To explain the retrieval process in ACT it is necessary to explain more fully the concept of working memory. Working memory contains the information currently available to the system for processing and so combines encoding of information about the current environment, inferences, current goal information, and traces from long-term memory. Since working memory contains traces from long-term memory and since new traces in working memory may be permanently encoded in long-term memory, working memory and long-term memory overlap in terms of their contents. Working memory elements are active to varying degrees. The continuous nature of activation (in contrast to the 1976 ACT) means that membership in working memory is a matter of degree. Less active working memory elements are processed less rapidly, for instance, in a recognition task.

A spreading activation process determines the level of activity in long-term memory. At any point in time certain working memory elements are sources of activation—either because they are encodings of perceptual events or because they are currently being processed. Activation can spread from these elements to associated elements in the network of elements and units. As soon as source drops from attention, its activation begins to decay, as does the activation of the network supported by spread from it. Some of the best evidence for this activation analysis of memory is what the accumulating evidence for an automatic process that makes information available on the basis of an associative relatedness (e.g., Fischler, 1977; Meyer & Schvaneveldt, 1976; Neely, 1977; Warren, 1972, 1977). Much of this research uses a priming methodology and has been concerned with semantic memory although similar effects have been shown in episodic memory (McKoon & Ratcliff, 1979). One does not think of the typical priming paradigms, such as naming, lexical decision, or Stroop tasks, as memory tasks of the same character as paired-associate recall or sentence recognition. Nonetheless, the claim made here is that the same spreading activation mechanism is involved in memory retrieval. The evidence for the claim is the coherence with which a wide variety of memory phenomena can be interpreted in terms of this mechanism. A basic purpose of this paper is to document this theoretical coherence.

It is assumed that if a trace has level of activation A converging on it, the time to retrieve that trace will behave as an exponential with rate parameter A. In the typical memory experiment, retrieving a trace amounts to processing to the point where some simple recall or recognition task can be performed. This means that retrieval time in an experiment should be of the form

$$RT = I + 1/A   (3)$$

where I is the intercept. It is also assumed that there is a cutoff time K such that if the trace is not processed by then, there will be a retrieval failure. Since rate of retrieval is an exponential function of activation level, probability of successful recall should obey a function of the form

$$PR = 1 - e^{-AK}.   (4)$$

The cutoff means that the previous equation (3) for mean reaction time needs to be amended because the long times are edited out by the cutoff time. Mean time for successful retrievals will be

$$RT = I + 1/A - Ke^{-K/A}/(1 - e^{-KA})   (5)$$

where the third factor is the correction. The form of the correction derives from the underlying assumption of exponential processing times.

The probabilistic retrieval process implies that we should see some mixture of recall of an item and failure to recall it if repeated memory tasks are administered. This is observed (Estes, 1960; Goss, 1965; Jones, 1962). It is also observed that an item successfully recalled on one trial has a greater probability of recall on a second trial. The above analysis would appear to imply independence of recall, but there are a number of explanations for this observed nonindependence. First, the above is only an analysis of retrieval and ignores the all-or-none encoding phenomena which will produce nonindependence among successive recalls. Second, nonindependence would be produced by the successful trial providing a strengthening experience and so increasing the level of activation for the second test. Third, nonindependence could be produced by item selection effects if there were considerable variation among items in the level of activation they could achieve (Underwood & Keppel, 1962).

Computation of asymptotic levels of activation. A schematic retrieval situation is illustrated in Figure 1. I assume that the subject is focusing on an encoding of some event or stimulus (e.g., a sentence) and this is the source of activation. In Figure 1, I have a pair of units focused in working memory and their elements. These elements are also part of units in long-term memory, as is indicated by the associative links going to long-term memory units. The elements of long-term memory are also interassociated with other units, some of which are illustrated in Figure 1. Activation can spread from the elements of focused units throughout the long-term memory structure. These elements of focused working-memory units are referred to as *sources of activation*. The amount of activation they emit is a function of their strength.

A pattern of activation in long-term memory is set up in response to the input of activation from the focused units. The elements and units are the nodes in this activation pattern. Basically, if a node n_u receives activation a_{1u} to a_{iu} from nodes n_1 to n_i, its level of activation is $\sum a_{iu}$. The activation that node n_x sends to nodes n_1 to n_i is determined by the strength s_1 to s_i of each node and the activation level of node n_x. If its level of activation is a_x, the amount of activation it sends to node n_k is $l a_x s_k/\sum s_j$ where l is the loss in activation and $s_k/\sum s_j$ is the *relative strength* of node n_k from n_x. Let $f_{xy} = l s_k/\sum s_j$ for all nodes j connected to n_x and 0 otherwise. This means that the level of activation of node y is

$$a_y = \sum_r f_{ry} a_r + c_y \quad (6)$$

where c_y is 0 unless y is a focused element, in which case c_y is the amount of activation coming from this source. Thus, if we have

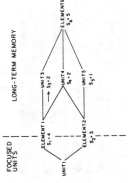

FOCUSED UNIT NODES IN WORKING MEMORY

CONNECTED ELEMENTS AND UNITS IN LONG-TERM MEMORY

Fig. 1. A schematic representation of the structure of memory relevant to retrieval dynamics. Several units and their elements are active in working memory and activation spreads from these elements through the long-term memory network.

a network of m nodes, we have m simultaneous equations with variables a_1-a_m which we can solve to find the pattern of activation set up by a particular set of focused elements in working memory. While it undoubtedly takes some time for the network structure to reach this asymptotic pattern of activation, I will assume that it is relatively small compared to other processing times and can be ignored. (See Anderson, 1983, for a discussion of the circumstances under which a stable pattern of activation will be achieved and the time to achieve this pattern.) This is in keeping with a suggestion by Wickelgren (1976b) for rapid spread of activation. Recently, Ratcliff & McKoon (1981) have found evidence to support this assumption.

Because of the loss factor l in the above equations, there is a bound on the total amount of activation that will be "pumped" into the network from a source. This is part of what guarantees that the network will move to a stable asymptotic pattern. If the source nodes provide A units of activation, the total activation of all nodes in the asymptotic pattern will be $A/(1 - l)$. This asymptotic amount of activation is distributed among the nodes in the network with nodes getting more activation to the degree they are closely and strongly connected to sources of activation.

Note that this scheme also allows activation to reverberate back. That is, if node 1 connects to node 2, activation from node 1 will spread to node 2 and activation from node 2 will spread back to node 1. Contrary to many people's intuitions, these reverberatory possibilities do not change expectations about a stable asymptotic pattern of activation.

As a small example, consider the network in Figure 2 where we denote the strengths of the long-term memory nodes by s_i and their activation levels by a_i. Let us consider the activation level of element 1 which we denote by a_1. It is part of the focused unit 1 and so will be a source of activation proportional to its strength. Since its strength is 4, it will receive four units of ac-

is that one needs to specify all of the long-term memory network connected at any distance to the working memory elements to derive precise predictions about activation patterns. However, the impact of distant structure is minimal and one's derivations will be quite accurate assuming only the proximal network structure (see Anderson, 1983).

Another approximating assumption that can be made in computation is to assume that activation will only flow forward from the working memory elements and not reverberate backwards. Under this assumption, derivations become quite direct. Consider the analysis of Figure 2 under these assumptions. In the example, half of the four measures of activation from element 1 go to unit 3 and the other half to unit 4. Similarly, two thirds of the three measures of activation from element 2 will go to unit 4 and one third to unit 5. This means that $2l$ measures of activation will go to unit 3, $4l$ measures to unit 4, and $1l$ measure to unit 5. This clearly preserves the ordering of the three units as obtained from the more exact derivation.

Basically, the view of activation is one in which activation reverberates throughout the network, setting up a stable pattern of activation that reflects how closely connected various nodes are to elements of focused units.

Effects of node strength. Under this view, the critical factor determining retrieval dynamics is the strength of the individual nodes. The strength of a node is a function of its frequency of exposure. The strength of the elements of focused units determines the amount of activation they can emit into the network. Also, more activation is sent down the paths leading to the stronger nodes. Thus, more activation will accumulate in those parts of the network that have stronger nodes.

Note that frequency of exposure to facts involving a concept will increase the concept's strength and so influence the amount of activation it can emit. On the other hand, learning additional facts about a concept

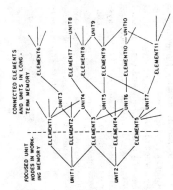

FOCUSED UNITS

LONG-TERM MEMORY

Fig. 2. A simple schematic network structure for illustrating the computation of asymptotic levels of activation.

tivation from itself (the c_u in Eq. 6). Element 1 is also connected to unit 3 and unit 4 and so will receive activation from them. The relative strength of element 1 to all the elements out of unit 3 is $4/9$. Similarly, its relative strength of element 4 is $4/9$. I assume that the activation of unit 3 less a loss factor l, is sent out to all the attached nodes according to their relative strengths. The level of activation of unit 3 is a_3. Therefore, element 1 receives $4/9 l a_3$ activation from unit 3. Similarly, it receives $1/5 l a_4$ activation from unit 4. The activation of element a_1 is the sum of its self-activation and the activation from units 3 and 4, that is, $4 + 4/9 l a_3 + 1/5 l a_4$. Thus, we can express the activation patterns in this network by the simultaneous equations

$$
\begin{aligned}
a_1 &= 4 + .44 l a_3 + .33 l a_4 \\
a_2 &= 3 + .25 l a_4 + .38 l a_5 \\
a_3 &= .5 l a_1 + .4 l a_6 \\
a_4 &= .5 l a_1 + .67 l a_2 + .4 l a_6 \\
a_5 &= .33 l a_2 + .2 l a_6 \\
a_6 &= .55 l a_3 + .42 l a_4 + .62 l a_5 .
\end{aligned}
\quad (7)
$$

Supposing the loss factor l is .8, these equations can be solved as $a_1 = 7.97$, $a_2 = 5.32$, $a_3 = 5.16$, $a_4 = 7.99$, $a_5 = 2.41$, and $a_6 = 6.15$. Given this pattern of activation, unit 4 should clearly be retrieved faster than unit 3 which should be retrieved faster than unit 5.

One of the problems in using this model

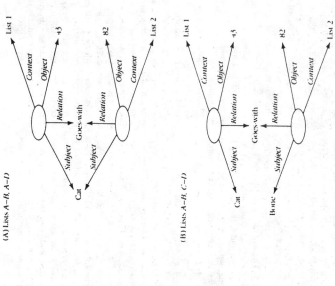

FIG. 3. (A) Network representation for the typical interference condition of a paired-associate paradigm; (B) network representation for the typical control condition of a paired-associate paradigm.

will create competitors to take strength away from existing facts. Thus, we see additional knowledge has both beneficial and harmful effects. Much of this paper is concerned with understanding these mixed effects of more knowledge.

Activation and temporal data. An important distinction between this version of spreading activation and others (Anderson, 1976; Collins & Quillian, 1972; Collins & Loftus, 1975) is that the factor that determines processing times is not time for activation to spread but rather asymptotic level of activation. Asymptotic level of activation affects processing time through ACT's pattern matcher for productions. Although we will not consider in detail the characteristics of ACT's production system, it is the case that any long-term memory fact can affect behavior (as in the generation of a memory report) only by being matched to part of the condition of a production. It is assumed that the production pattern matcher matches more rapidly those facts which are most active.

There are a number of reasons for believing that the important factor is asymptotic level of activation and not time for activation to spread. There are data (Ratcliff & McKoon, 1981; Schustack, 1981; Warren, 1977) which suggest that priming effects due to activation do not have a significant rise time and that the only important factor is overall level of activation. There are data from my laboratory (see Anderson, 1983) that show that fan does not interact with memory complexity and distance but it does interact with complexity of patterns being searched for. This is what one would expect if time to activate a structure was minimal (so distance and complexity were not important) but time to match a pattern was significant.

Summary

So, to recapitulate, experience establishes a network of nodes connected by links of varying strengths. This network consists of cognitive units (e.g., propositions) encoding various facts. At any point in time certain nodes are sources of activation. The levels of activation of the nodes in the network reflect their degree of association to the source nodes. When the source nodes change, spreading activation rapidly adjusts the levels of activation to achieve a new asymptotic pattern. The speed with which information in any part of the network can be processed is a function of its level of activation.

INTERFERENCE

The analysis of interference effects in memory has been very influential in the development of the ACT theory. Much of the traditional research on interference has been based on a paired-associate paradigm with a recall measure, and it is this paradigm that I would like to discuss first.

The Classic Paired-Associate Paradigm

A frequent contrast in discussion of interference is between the A–B, A–D condition and the A–B, C–D condition. In the first condition, the subject learns two lists composed of paired associates where the two lists involve same stimuli (A's) but different responses (B's and D's). In the second condition, the lists involve different stimuli (A's, C's) and different responses (B's, D's). The different network representations for the two lists are illustrated in Figure 3.

When a stimulus is presented at the time of test, we assume that it and the list context are elements of a focused unit—for instance, a unit encoding the fact that the stimulus is being presented in the current context. Therefore, these elements serve as sources of activation. The response will be retrieved if (a) a trace connecting stimulus, response, and context has been formed, and (b) it can be retrieved within the cutoff time. Let S^+ be the strength of the trace, S_s be the strength of all other traces connected to the stimulus, and S_c be the strength of all other traces connected to the context. Let A_s be the activation from the stimulus and A_c be the activation from the context. Then, ignoring interactions due to activa-

tion flowing backward, the activation converging on the trace from the stimulus and context will be

$$A = A_s(S^+/(S^+ + S_s)) + A_c(S^+/(S^+ + S_c)). \qquad (8)$$

Probability of recall will increase with A as implied by the earlier equation (4). From Equation (8) we see that as the competing strengths (S_s, S_c) increase we will need more target strength (S^+) to maintain the same level of activation. From this observation derive the basic predictions of negative transfer and retroactive interference. To achieve the same level of performance on the second list in the A–B, A–D paradigm, as in the A–B, C–D, extra study will be required in the interference condition to increase its trace's strength to compensate for the strength of the competing first-list trace connected to the stimulus. This is the prediction of negative transfer. In a retest of list 1 after list 2, the relative strength of the list 1 trace in the interference condition will be reduced by the competing list 2 trace and so lower recall will be observed. This is the prediction of retroactive interference.

The Problem of Proactive Interference

One of the proactive interference paradigms has been difficult to explain in the

ACT framework. This is the two-list para-digm that contrasts A–B, A–D list with the A–B, C–D control. Proactive interference *in this paradigm refers to the fact that a re-test of the second list (at a delay) is worse if it had been in an interfering relation to the first list* (ie., retention of A–D is worse than C–D). This is true even though the second lists (A–D or C–D) are brought to the same level of recall before the retention interval. I will assume that if the control and interfer-ence conditions had the same level of recall at the beginning of the retention interval, they had the same level of activation. The activation in the control (noninterference) case is

$$A_N = A_s \frac{S_N}{K + S_N} + A_c' \frac{nS_1 + nS_S}{nS_1 + S_S}$$
$$= A_s \frac{S_N}{K + S_N} + A_c' \frac{S_S}{S_1 + S_S} \quad (9)$$

where A_s is the activation from the stimu-lus, A_c the activation from the context, S_S the strength of the second list trace, S_1 the strength of the first list trace, K the strength of prior associations to the stimulus, and n the number of items in a list. A_c' is A_c/n and reflects the contextual contributions to each list element. The activation in the in-terference case is

$$A_1 = A_s \frac{S_1}{K + S_1 + S_1} + A_c' \frac{S_1}{S_1 + S_S} \quad (10)$$

where the only differences are that the strength of the second list trace, S_1, must be larger than S_N to compensate for the inter-ference of the first list trace from the stimu-lus. Note that it is assumed in both cases that there is interference of the first list from the context. At a delay the activation formulas become

$$A_N' = A_s \frac{d_2 S_N}{K + d_2 S_N} + A_c' \frac{d_2 S_N}{d_1 S_1 + d_2 S_N} \quad (11)$$

$$A_1' = A_s \frac{d_2 S_1}{K + d_1 S_1 + d_2 S_1} + A_c' \frac{d_2 S_1}{d_1 S_1 + d_2 S_1} \quad (12)$$

where it is assumed that the activations (A_s, A_c) do not change with time and the decay in prior strength (K) is also negligi-ble. The decay (d_1) in the first list strength is smaller than the decay (d_2) in the second list strength, that is, $d_1 > d_2$. These as-sumptions about decay of strength are im-plied by the power law retention functions. Under a wide range of reasonable parame-ter assumptions, although not under all pos-sible parameter assumptions, it can be shown that $A_N = A_1$ implies $A_N' < A_1'$. To take an example, suppose $A_s = 1$, $A_c' = 1$, $d_1 = .75$, $d_2 = .5$, $K = 1$, $S_1 = 1$, and $S_N = 1$. Then $A_N = 1$; to get $A_1 = 1$ it is necessary to set $S_1 = \sqrt{2}$. Under these pa-rameter assumptions, $A_N' = .733$ and $A_1' = .773$. That is, there is more activation at a delay in the interference condition.

Thus, it can be shown that ACT predicts just the opposite of proactive interference. Interestingly, despite the traditional belief, proactive inhibition has seldom been shown in a contrast of an A–B, A–D paradigm with an A–B, C–D paradigm. Most experi-ments that have brought the control and in-terference conditions to the same learning criterion have contrasted a one-list control with a two-list interference (e.g., Koppen-aal, 1963; Ceraso & Henderson, 1965; Houston, 1969; Postman, Stark, & Fraser, 1968). In fact, in our own laboratory we have confirmed ACT's prediction of proac-tive facilitation in the A–B, A–D versus A–B, C–D contrast and have shown proac-tive inhibition in the A–B, A–D versus C–D contrast. For instance, in one experi-ment each list in each condition involved 20 word–number pairs (a methodology similar to Anderson, 1981a). We looked at retention of the last list a week later after bringing it to 90% initial learning in all conditions. The retention of A–D in the A–B, A–D condi-tion was 70%, the retention of C–D in the A–B, C–D condition was 63%, and reten-tion of C–D in the single-list paradigm was 81%. It should be emphasized that these re-sults were obtained in an unpaced MMFR test. The ACT predictions about the order-ing of these paradigms only apply in this sit-uation. List discrimination problems might well produce poorer performance in a A–B, A–D paradigm than a A–B, C–D paradigm when a paced, nonMMFR test is used.

Our history in this effort was that we started from the traditional wisdom that proactive interference could be obtained in the contrast between A–B, A–D and A–B, C–D paradigms. Starting with HAM (An-derson & Bower, 1973) and then ACT (An-derson, 1976), it was observed that these theories could not predict proactive inter-ference when the two lists were trained to the same criterion. Our first response was to try to explain proactive interference away as an experimental artifact (e.g., An-derson & Bower, 1973), and we engaged in a series of experiments to confirm these at-tempted explanations. The outcome of these experiments was the discovery of fail-ure to confirm an interfering relationship. Subsequently, a search of the literature in-dicated that most demonstrations of proac-tive interference involved contrasting a sin-gle list with a two-list paradigm. Indeed, Postman, Stark, and Burns (1974) and Post-man and Gray (1977) report failure to find proactive interference comparing the two two-list paradigms in an unpaced MMFR test. The demonstrations of poorer second-list retention in the A–B, A–D paradigm have involved paced nonMMFR tests (Postman & Gray, 1977; Underwood & Ekstrand, 1967).

Cumulative Proactive Interference

To restate the conclusion of the previous section, proactive interference (PI) seems to be obtained only comparing two lists with single lists. In this case, the contrast seems a special case of the cumulative PI design (e.g., Greenberg & Underwood, 1950; Keppel, Postman, & Zavortink, 1964; Postman & Keppel, 1977; Underwood, 1957) where it is found that retention deteri-orates for successive unrelated lists. The typical design involves having subjects learn one list one day, having them return the next day to recall the previous day's list and then learn a second list, repeating this pattern over days. The ACT analysis, with certain assumptions about context, does predict cumulative PI. The following are the equations for activation for the first and second lists immediately and at delay.

$$A_1 = A_s \frac{S_1}{K + S_1} + A_c' \frac{S_1}{S_1} \quad (13)$$

$$A_2 = A_s \frac{S_2}{K + S_2} + A_c' \frac{S_2}{d_1 S_1 + S_2} \quad (14)$$

$$A_1' = A_s \frac{d_1 S_1}{K + d_1 S_1} + A_c' \frac{d_1 S_1}{d_1 S_1} \quad (15)$$

$$A_2' = A_s \frac{d_1 S_2}{K + d_1 S_2} + A_c' \frac{d_1 S_2}{d_2 S_1 + d_1 S_2} \quad (16)$$

where S_1 is the strength of the first list trace, S_2 the strength of the second list trace, d_1 the decay after 24 hours, and d_2 the decay after 48 hours. Assuming a power law for decay, we have $d_n = r^{-t}$ where t will be the number of hours. Then we can derive the expression for the nth list in a cu-mulative PI design.

$$A_n = A_s \frac{S_n}{K + S_n}$$
$$+ A_c' \frac{S_n}{\sum_{i=1}^{n} S_i(t(n - i)24)^{-t}} \quad (17)$$

$$A_n' = A_s \frac{d_1 S_n}{K + d_1 S_n}$$
$$+ A_c' \frac{d_1 S_n}{\sum_{i=1}^{n} S_i(t(n - i + 1)24)^{-t}} \quad (18)$$

The essential observation is that the num-ber of interfering contextual associations increases with number of lists. Therefore, greater trace strength will be required to achieve the same level of activation, that is, $S_n > S_{n-1}$. It can also be shown under a wide range of plausible parameter values that if $A_n = A_{n-1}$ then $A_n' < A_{n-1}'$. This is because with each successive trial (1) a larger portion of the activation comes from *the stimulus which decays rapidly*, and (2) *the decay of the interfering associations from the context slows down.*

As an illustration, we considered the case where $A_s = 5$, $A'_s = 1$, $K = 10$, and the exponent for decay $d = .5$. Setting $S_1 = 2$, we got $A_1 = 1.8$. To get $A_2 = 1.8$, we had to set $S_2 = 2.3$ and similarly $S_3 = 2.6$, $S_4 = 2.9$, and $S_5 = 3.1$. Then we calculated the activation at delay: $A'_1 = 1.11$, $A'_2 = .84$, $A'_3 = .73$, $A'_4 = .69$, $A'_5 = .65$. We set K in equation (11) at 1 and got the following probabilities of recall for successive lists at a 24-hour delay: .67, .57, .52, .50, and .48. Thus, the explanation of cumulative proactive interference may lie in increasing contextual interference.

This analysis implies that there should not be cumulative proactive interference to the extent that one could create a novel context for each study. We performed a modest context manipulation experiment to put this prediction to test. Subjects learned three lists of 20 paired associates, either from a computer in a windowless cubicle or from a human experimenter in a windowed seminar room. As in the classic paradigm for cumulative PI, list n was learned on day n to a 95% recall criterion and tested for retention on day $n + 1$. We used all $2^3 = 8$ sequences of contexts for the three lists, each sequence with 10 subjects. We counterbalanced for any effect of a particular context on learning.

Averaged over sequences, performance was 87.6% on list 1, 86.1% on list 2, and 82.3% on list 3. Thus, there is only a modest buildup of PI which tempers one's expectations about effects of context change. Nonetheless, retention was 88.4% for list 1 when context was changed from list 1 versus 83.9% when it was the same. Similarly, it was 84.5% for list 3 when context was changed from list 1 and 2 versus 78.3% when it was unchanged. The combined differences reach the conventional level for statistical significance, $t_{108} = 2.31$; $p < .05$. There is very little PI over the three tests

in a changed context—87.6% for list 1, 88.4% for list 2, and 84.5% for list 3. On the other hand, the PI is fairly clear when context does not change—87.6%, 83.9%, and 78.3%. This analysis of cumulative PI implies that it results from contextual interference and not stimulus-specific interference. This is consistent with conclusions of Wickens, Moody, and Dow (1981) that PI is due to interference on response set or list differentiation.

In summary, this theory is consistent with the major trends of traditional research on interference. Before going on to consider two other topics, I would like to consider two other subissues about interference because they serve to lay the groundwork for subsequent analyses. These are interference effects on reaction-time measures and effects of network integration on interference.

Reaction Time and Interference

In the ACT framework, reaction time should be a purer measure of interference than percent recall. This is because percent recall reflects both the formation of links, which is not subject to interference, and retrieval, which is. In contrast, reaction time reflects only the retrieval of those links formed. It is also the case that after neurasymptotic levels are achieved in percent recall, reaction time will continue to reflect interference effects. Figure 4 displays data from a paired-associate paradigm (Anderson, 1981a). Subjects were given eight trials of study test on list 1, then eight trials on list 2, then four trials of retest of list 1, and then four more trials of retest on list 2. For the interference subjects, the two lists were in an A–B, A–D relation; for the control subjects, they were in a A–B, C–D relation. We have plotted reaction time against accuracy. Note that there are separate functions for interference and control, both of which can be approximated by straight line relationships. However, the interference function is above the control function, indicating that when the two conditions have been equated for percent recall, the

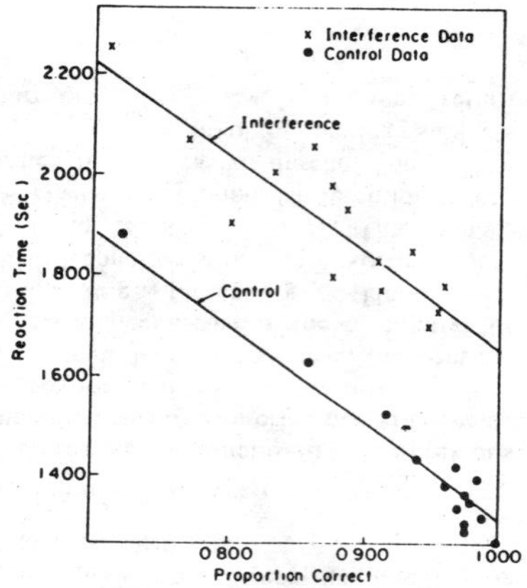

interference condition is at a disadvantage with respect to reaction time. This is consistent with the ACT claim that reaction time is a more sensitive indicant of interference.

Many of the reaction-time experiments we have done have involved subjects recognizing whether they saw particular sentences. In one experiment (Anderson, 1976) we had subjects recognize whether they had studied location–subject–verb sentences such as *In the winery the fireman slept*. We manipulated independently whether subjects studied one or two facts about subject, verb, and object. Table 1 reproduces the results from that experiment classified according to the number of facts studied about each concept. Data are also presented for foil sentences which were created from the same words as the target sentences but were in novel combinations. As can be seen, reaction time increases as number of facts increase on any of the three dimensions. This increase in reaction time has been referred to as the *fan effect* because more facts increase the fan of propo-

sitional associations leading from a concept. Increasing the number of facts on any dimension will reduce the amount of activation converging on the memory trace.

It is interesting that the foil items also show this fan effect. The general proposal that we (Anderson, 1976; 1983; King & Anderson, 1976) have advanced for recognition of foils is that subjects wait a period of time and reject the sentence if they fail to retrieve a matching trace. The amount of time a subject waits is adjusted to reflect the fan of the probe. This is essential for a waiting strategy to work since the subject must allow enough time to elapse for the positive probes to be recognized. Note that subjects take somewhat longer to reject foils. They would have to wait longer than normal target time to make sure the probe was not a target.

Effects of Network Integration

One of the results that has been shown in the interference literature (e.g., Postman & Gray, 1977; Postman & Parker, 1970) is that interference is diminished in an A–B, A–D paradigm if the subject makes an effort to maintain B responses during A–D learning. The consequence of maintaining the two responses should be to integrate them together. Figure 5 illustrates in very simplified network terms the single list condition (a), the two-list nonintegrated condition (b), and the two-list integrated condition (c). Assuming that one unit of activation is flowing into the A stimulus and that all nodes are of equal strength, it is possible to calculate the levels of network activation given the earlier model. Assuming a loss of .8 in spread in equations like those in (8) on page 6, 2.22 units will accumulate at D in the single-list condition, 1.11 in the nonintegrated condition, and 1.43 in the integrated condition. Thus, ACT does predict a benefit of such integrating structure. As we will see in the discussion of elaborative processing, this is just the tip of the iceberg in terms of the memory phenomena that can be accounted for in terms of such network integration.

Fig. 4. Plot of reaction time as a function of percent recall for interference condition and control condition from Anderson (1981a).

TABLE I

LOCATION–SUBJECT–VERB EXPERIMENT (*In the church the sailor sang*)—MEAN REACTION TIMES AND ERROR RATES (IN PARENTHESES)

Targets

	L = 1			L = 2		
	V = 1	V = 2	Mean	V = 1	V = 2	Mean
S = 1	1220 (.034)	1183 (.017)	1202 (.026)	1297 (.046)	1402 (.086)	1350 (.066)
S = 2	1232 (.069)	1421 (.080)	1327 (.075)	1358 (.046)	1500 (.082)	1429 (.064)
Mean	1226 (.052)	1302 (.049)	1264 (.051)	1328 (.046)	1451 (.084)	1390 (.065)

Foils

	L = 1			L = 2		
	V = 1	V = 2	Mean	V = 1	V = 2	Mean
S = 1	1323 (.029)	1387 (.035)	1355 (.032)	1404 (.034)	1469 (.023)	1437 (.029)
S = 2	1320 (.028)	1371 (.028)	1346 (.028)	1488 (.023)	1511 (.063)	1500 (.043)
Mean	1322 (.029)	1379 (.031)	1351 (.030)	1446 (.029)	1490 (.043)	1468 (.036)

JUDGMENTS OF ASSOCIATIVE RELATEDNESS

The discussion to date has assumed that activation makes information available for inspection by other procedures. Thus, activation determines the amount of cognitive resources available to process information. In addition to this role, level of activation can also provide information in and of itself. The more active a particular part of the network is, the more it must be related to the current context. Level of activation does not tell us how the network is related, but it does provide information about degree of relation. There is evidence that information about level of activation is available relatively immediately, and is used by subjects to facilitate certain types of memory judgments.

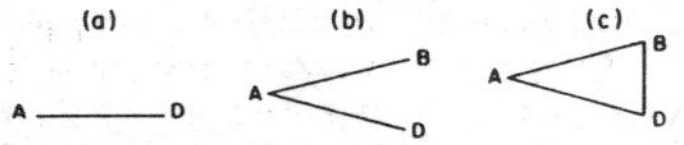

Rejection of Foils

The experiment by Glucksberg and McCloskey (1981) nicely illustrates the use of information about associative relatedness. They had subjects study affirmative facts such as *John has a pencil*, negative facts such as *Bill doesn't have a shovel* and "don't know" facts such as *It is unknown whether Fred has a chair*. Then subjects had to judge of various statements whether they were true or false or whether their truth was unknown. An interesting comparison involves the speed with which subjects can judge that they do not know something when they have explicitly learned that they do not know (e.g., *Fred has a chair*), and their speed in cases where their lack of knowledge is only implicit (e.g., *Bill has a*

FIG. 5. (a) Schematic representation of a paired associate without interference; (b) representation of two interfering and unintegrated paired associates; (c) representation of two interfering but integrated paired associates.

pencil). Subjects are faster in the implicit case. In this case, subjects can monitor for an intersection of activation between subject and predicate at a trace. If no such locus of high activation appears, subjects can use this low level of activation as evidence that subject and predicate are unrelated and so conclude that the sentence is not known. In the explicit case, however, the "don't know" fact creates a locus of high activation which the subject must explicitly reject. Apparently it is easier to use the low level of activation as a basis for a response than it is to explicitly retrieve the "don't know" tag.

The experiment by Shoben, Wescourt, and Smith (1978) is another example that illustrates the importance of level of activation to rejection of foils in a sentence recognition task. One type of foil involved sentences that were true but not studied (e.g., *Tigers have stripes*), and the other type involved sentences that were false and not studied (e.g., *Tigers have fingers*). Subjects were slower and made many more errors at rejecting the true foils, suggesting that subjects were sometimes responding just to the high activation created by intersection of subject and predicate.

Thematic Judgments

The experiments of Reder and Anderson (1980) and Smith, Adams, and Schorr (1978) are examples of situations where subjects can use this strategy of activation monitoring to make positive judgments. These researchers had subjects study a set of facts about a person that all fell under some theme such as going to the circus. So a subject might study

Marty laughed at the clown.
Marty ate cotton candy.
Marty cheered the trapeze artist.

Subjects were transferred to a fact recognition situation where they had to recognize these facts about the individual and reject facts from different themes (e.g., *Marty waited for the train*). The number of such facts studied about a person was varied.

Based on the research on the fan effect one might expect recognition time to increase with the number of facts studied about the individual. However, the material in the typical fan experiment is not thematically integrated as is this material. In these experiments, recognition time did not depend on how many facts a subject studied about the individual.

Reder and Anderson postulated on the basis of data from Reder (1979) that subjects were actually judging whether a probe fact came from the theme or not and that subjects were not carefully inspecting to see if the fact about the individual was studied. To test this idea, we examined what happened when the foils were other predicates consistent with the theme. So if the subject has studied

Marty laughed at the clowns.

a foil might be

Marty liked the animal trainer.

In this situation subjects took much longer to make their verifications and the fan effect reemerged.

We proposed that subjects set up a representation such as that in Figure 6. We assumed that thematically related predicates are already associated to a theme-node like circus. We assume that subjects create a subnode to represent same-theme facts about a person. This subnode is associated to the theme and to the individual theme predicates. We have represented two such theme nodes in the figure and two subnodes. Reder and Anderson manipulated whether subjects studied one or two themes in that study and found evidence that subjects organized knowledge by subnode according to theme. Specifically, we found that subjects were slowed in their judgments of facts in one theme by the addition of another theme but not affected by the number of facts associated with that other theme. Recently, Reder and Ross (1983) extended this finding to the contrast between two and three themes. This is what would be predicted on the basis of Figure 6.

TABLE 2
LEVEL OF ACTIVATION OF VARIOUS NODES IN
FIGURE 6 UNDER VARIOUS CONDITIONS

	Number of facts about target theme	
	1	3
1. Target trace in the presence of the target		
Number of facts about other theme 0	7.78	6.83
1	7.26	6.57
3	7.24	6.56
2. Subnode in the presence of the target		
Number of facts about other theme 0	7.06	7.49
1	5.59	6.29
3	5.50	6.22
3. Subnode in the presence of a related foil		
Number of facts about other theme 0	5.30	5.94
1	4.07	4.88
3	4.00	4.81
4. Subnode in the presence of an unrelated foil		
Number of facts about other theme 0	1.40	1.42
1	.70	.75
3	.66	.71

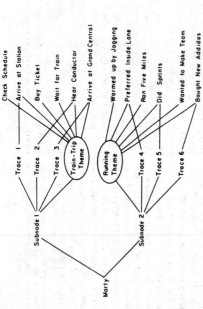

FIG. 6. Network representation for the Reder and Anderson experiments. Facts about Marty are organized into two subnodes according to theme.

Additional themes create a fan out of the person node but the number of facts associated to the second subnode should have little or no impact on the amount of activation intersecting between person and predicate.

In Reder and Anderson we proposed that in the presence of unrelated foils subjects simply retrieved the subnode while in the presence of related foils they had to retrieve the target trace. We were somewhat vague about how a subject might retrieve the subnode and evaluate it, but in the context of the current framework there is an easy explanation. Subjects could respond to the level of activation of the subnode. A high level of activation intersecting from the person and the predicate would be evidence that the subnode was thematically relevant.

Calculation of activation patterns. I have calculated what the activation patterns would be for the Anderson and Reder experiments, assuming a representation like that in Figure 6. In doing so, I set the amount of activation from the predicate (which for simplicity is represented by a single node) to be ten and from the person node to be one since I expected more activation from the multiple familiar concepts of the predicate. The conditions of the Anderson and Reder experiment can be classified according to the number of things learned about the tested dimension (1 or 3) and the number of things about the untested dimension (0, 1, or 3). I calculated the pattern of activation in each of these situations. For each of these conditions, Table 2 reports the level of activation of the trace for targets and also the level of activation of the subnode in the presence of a target, a related foil, and an unrelated foil.

Note that the activation of the target trace decreases with the number of facts in the same theme as the probe, decreases when there is a second theme, but shows very little variation of one versus three facts in the nontested theme. This is precisely the fan effect reported by Reder and Anderson when related foils were used. Thus it appears, as hypothesized for the related-foil condition, that activation of the trace is controlling judgment time.

It was hypothesized that when foils were unrelated, level of activation of the subnode and not of the trace would control judgment time. The subnode actually shows a reverse fan effect in Table 2 when a target is presented as a probe—greater activation when there are three facts. This is because there are more paths converging on the subnode in this case. Although these additional paths may not be direct routes from sources of activation to the subnode, they are nonetheless indirect routes. Thus, presented with *Marty arrived at the station,* activation can spread from *arrive at station* to the train theme to *hear conductor* to subnode 1. Also note that the subnode has a high level of activation in the presence of a related foil. Although this level is not as high as for a target, it is sufficiently high to cause trouble for a scheme of responding to level of activation as a basis for discriminating between targets and related foils. Reder and Anderson (1980) and Smith et al. (1978) both report no fan effects in the presence of unrelated foils. If subjects were responding purely on the basis of level of activation, there should be a reverse fan effect as Table 2 indicates. Reder and Ross (1983) speculated that the subjects adopt a mixed strategy in this case, sometimes responding to subnode activations and sometimes responding to the trace. The direct and reverse fan effects would then tend to cancel themselves out. Consistent with this hypothesis, Reder and Ross showed that when subjects are explicitly instructed to respond on a thematic basis (i.e., either accept studied sentences or unstudied but related sentences) they do show a reverse fan effect. Reder and Ross also found subjects slower to accept unstudied related sentences than studied sentences in these thematic judgment conditions. This is to be expected from Table 2 because in the presence of related foils (which are the same as Reder and Ross's related, nonstudied targets) there is a lower level of activation of the subnode than in the presence of targets.

Refocusing on Subnodes

The activation patterns were calculated in the previous section under the assumption that the subject spreads activation from the person node like Marty in Figure 6. In these calculations the activation from *Marty* is broken up twice before getting to the target predicate. It is divided once between the two subnodes and once among the facts attached to the subnode. This implies that the activation level of the traces should be no different if six facts were attached to one subnode than if the six facts were divided between two subnodes. In both cases, one sixth of the activation reaches the subnode. In fact, however, there is evidence (Reder & Anderson, 1980; McCloskey & Bigler, 1980) that subjects are faster in the two subnode condition.

These and other results (Anderson, 1976; Anderson & Paulson, 1978) lead to the second aspect of the subnode model, the refocusing process. Even in cases where subjects must retrieve the specific fact, subjects can use level of activation of the subnode to refocus their activation. They select the most active subnode and make that the source of activation rather than the original node. This is a two stage process; first the subnode is selected and then activation spreading from the subnode enables identification of the target fact. Since activation spreads rapidly, the time for the subnode selection should be relatively brief. This subnode-plus-refocusing model explains the low estimate of strength of prior associations that we have obtained in some previous experiments (e.g., Lewis & Anderson, 1976; Anderson, 1981). As suggested in Anderson (1976), subjects may create an experimental subnode and use contextual associations to focus on it. This would protect them from the interference of prior associations. This model also offers a reason why we may be faster at retrieving information about familiar concepts. Presumably such concepts have a well-developed and perhaps hierarchical subnode structure which can be used to focus the retrieval process on a relatively small subset of the facts known about that concept.

Summary

This section has reviewed how subjects can use judgments of associative relatedness to avoid direct retrieval. When such judgments are implemented in the subnode-plus-refocusing model they can eliminate interfering fan effects and even produce positive fan effects. This subnode focusing strategy will only work when the subnode can reliably be activated above the level of other subnodes. This is presumably why it is not to the advantage of the system to create a subnode for each fact. There must be enough facts converging on the subnode with enough associative interconnections to guarantee the subnode a high level of activation in the presence of a related fact.

PRACTICE

People get better at remembering facts by practicing them and it should come as no surprise that ACT predicts this basic fact of memory. However, the serious issue is whether the ACT theory can predict the shape of the improvement function and how this varies with factors such as fan.

Accumulation of Strength with Practice

ACT makes some fairly interesting predictions about the cumulative effects of extensive but widely distributed practice. By widely distributed I am referring to practice at intervals on the order of 24 hours. The reason for looking at such wide spacings is to avoid complications due to diminished effects of massed presentations. ACT does not really have an analysis of spacing effects except to note that it can implement the encoding variability explanation (see Anderson, 1976, for how). However, an assumption of the following analysis of practice is that each unit of practice is as effective as the next. By looking at widely spaced units this assumption becomes plausible. In the analyses to follow I will designate the cumulative impact of multiple massed practices per day as one unit of strength. Given this scaling of strength, I will be concerned with the accumulation of strength over the multiple days which are spaced.

With spaced repetitions the strength of a trace will just be a sum of the individual strengthenings. However, because of the delay between repetitions. it will not be simply a linear function of number of repetitions. We can assume that the early strengthenings have considerably decayed by the time of the nth strengthening. Assuming n spaced repetitions each t time units apart, the total strength of a trace after the nth strengthening. and just before the $n + 1$st, will be (by Eq. 2)

$$S = \sum_{i=1}^{n} s(ti)^{-b} \qquad (19)$$

assuming the power law function for decay where s is the strength of each repetition and $b(<1)$ is the exponent of the power function. It can be shown (Anderson, 1982) that this sum is closely approximated as

$$S = d(n)^{+c} - a \qquad (20)$$

where $c = 1 - b$, $d = sr^{-b}/(1 - b)$, and $a = (1 + b)sr^{-b}/2(1 - b)$. Thus, strength approximately increases as a power function of practice. As we will see, this power function prediction corresponds to a good deal of data. However, before presenting this data, it is necessary to consider the impact of this strength accumulation on spreading activation.

Effects of Extensive Practice

A set of experiments was conducted to test the prediction given earlier about a power law increase in the strength of a trace with practice. In these experiments, subjects were given extensive practice (i.e., hundreds of trials over many days). In one experiment subjects studied subject–verb–object sentences of the form *The lawyer hated the doctor.* After studying these sentences they were transferred to a sentence recognition paradigm in which they had to discriminate these sentences from foil sentences made of the same words as the target sentence but in new combinations. There were 25 days of tests. Each day subjects were tested on each sentence 12 times in one group or 24 times in the other group. There was no difference between these two groups (which is consistent with earlier remarks about massing of practice), so these two groups will be treated as one in the analysis.

There were two types of sentences—*no fan* sentences made from words that appeared in only one sentence and *fan* sentences made from words that appeared in two sentences. Figure 7 shows the change in reaction time with practice (number of days). The functions that are fit to the data in Figure 7 are of the form $T = K + AP^{-b}$ where K is an intercept not affected by strengthening, $K + A$ is the time on day 1, P is the amount of practice (measured in days), and the exponent b is the rate of improvement. It turns out that this data can be fit assuming different values of A for the fan and no fan and keeping K and b constant. The equations are

$$T = .36 + .77(P - \tfrac{1}{2})^{-.36} \qquad \text{for no fan (21)}$$
$$T = .36 + 1.15(P - \tfrac{1}{2})^{-.36} \qquad \text{for fan. (22)}$$

The value $P - \tfrac{1}{2}$ appears in these equations as this is the average practice on a day P.

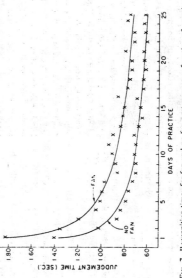

FIG. 7. Recognition times for fan and no fan sentences as a function of practice.

One implication of these equations is that the fan effect diminishes with practice. They also imply that the fan effect never disappears. After P days the fan effect is $.38(P - \frac{1}{2})^{-.38}$ according to these equations. Hayes-Roth (1977) reported data on practice from which she concluded that the fan effect disappeared after 10 days and 100 practice trials. However, this is not what these equations imply and Figure 7 shows that there still is a fan effect after 25 days and 600 trials. Perhaps the Hayes-Roth conclusion was a case of erroneously accepting the null hypothesis.

Earlier, I showed that strength increased as a power function of practice. Now I will show that this implies that reaction time should decrease as a power function. Recall that the amount of activation sent to a trace from a concept is a product of the activation emitted from the concept and the strength of that trace relative to competing traces. The activation emitted by a concept is a function of its strength. Let I be the prior strength of a concept. Then the strength of the concept after P days of practice will be

$$I' + AP^{cr} \qquad (23)$$

where $I' = I - a$, $A = d$, and $P = n$ from Equation (20) earlier. In this we are assuming that the prior strength of I maintains a stable value over the experiment. Again drawing on an assumption about the ineffectiveness of mass practice, I will assume the strength of the concept to be equal for fan and no-fan concepts.

The relative strength of one of n experimental facts attached to a concept will be $1/n$ where I am making the assumption that subjects can completely filter out by a subnode structure any interference from preexperimental associations. This implies that the activation converging on the trace will be

$$\frac{3}{n}(I' + AP^{cr}) \qquad (24)$$

where the 3 reflects the fact that activation is converging from 3 concepts (subject, verb, object).

According to the earlier retrieval assumptions, recognition time will be a function of the inverse of this quantity or

$$\frac{n}{3(I' + AP^{cr})} = \frac{nA'P^{-r}}{[I'/AP^{cr} + 1]} \qquad (25)$$

where $A' = A/3$. To the extent that I, prior strength of the concept, is small relative to the impact of the massive experimental practice this function becomes

$$nA'P^{-r} \qquad (26)$$

and total reaction time is predicted to be of the form

$$K_1 + A''P^{-r} \qquad (27)$$

where K_1 is the intercept not affected by general practice and not retrieval of the strength of traces of concepts and $A'' = nA' + K_2$. The quantity K_2 reflects that part of the improvement that is due to general practice and, I assume, is improving at the same rate as memory retrieval. In general, even Equation (25) above, with a significant I factor, will yield a good fit to such a power function. Thus, we would expect the data in Figure 7 to be fit well by a power function. Note also that according to the ACT analysis, these functions should only vary in the parameter A'' and not in intercept K_1 or exponent c. The A'' will increase with n, the number of studied facts. As the reader can confirm from Figure 7, we get a good fit to the data based on these assumptions.

Interaction Between Practice and Prior Familiarity

One basic consequence of this increase in concept strength is that subjects can remember more facts about frequent concepts and retrieve facts of similar relative strength more rapidly. Anderson (1976) reported that subjects can retrieve facts about

more familiar people (e.g., Ted Kennedy is a senator) more rapidly than facts about less familiar people (Birch Bayh is a senator—experiment done when B. B. was still a senator). Anderson (1981b) noted that there are serious issues about whether pairs of facts like these are equated in terms of other properties. In that research report, I had subjects learn new facts about familiar or unfamiliar people and tried to control such things as degree of learning for these new facts. Still we found subjects at an advantage both in learning and retrieving new facts about the familiar person.

We recently performed an experiment in which we compared time to verify sentences studied in the experiment such as *Ted Kennedy is in New York* with other sentences studied such as *Bill Jones is in New Troy*. We found that subjects were initially more rapid at verifying the experimental facts about the familiar concepts, consistent with Anderson (1981b). However, we also looked at the effects of fan and practice on these verification times. Figure 8 shows what happened to the effects of fan

and familiarity over nine days of practice. As can be seen, the effects of fan largely maintained themselves over the period while the effects of familiarity diminished. This is what would be predicted on the basis of Equation (24). As practice P increases, the effect of prior familiarity I diminishes dramatically.

The functions fit to the data are of the form $a + b/(I + P^c)$ where a is the asymptote, b is the retrieval time parameter, I is prior strength and strength accumulated in original learning, P is the independent variable (number of days), and c is the exponent controlling growth of strength. The quantity P^c reflects the strength after P days. One value of a was estimated for all four conditions; this is .36 seconds. Separate values of b were estimated for the no fan (1.42 sec) and fan conditions (1.94 sec). Separate values of K were estimated for the familiar material (.88) and the unfamiliar material (.39). Finally a single parameter for c was estimated for all four conditions; this was .31.

On day 10, subjects were asked to learn some new facts of different form (e.g., Bill Jones hated the doctor) about the *old people* studied in the experiment plus some *new people* not yet studied. Some of the new people were familiar famous names and others were unfamiliar. After learning these new facts, the subjects went through one session of verification for these. There was no difference in the time they took to recognize the new facts about old familiar or new familiar people. In both cases, they took .96 seconds. They were still longer to recognize new facts about the old unfamiliar people (1.00 sec). Thus, the practice had not completely eliminated the differences between familiar and unfamiliar. However, they took longest to recognize facts about the new unfamiliar people (1.06 sec). So, the practice had increased the capacity of the unfamiliar nodes.

Summary

This section has reviewed the consequence of increased node strength with

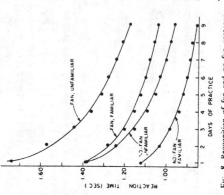

Fig. 8. Recognition of fan and no fan sentences about familiar and unfamiliar concepts as a function of practice.

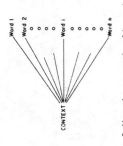

Fig. 9. Network representation of the word-context associations for a single list.

practice. Reaction times decrease and fan effects decrease for stronger nodes which can emit greater activation. However, the data reported here show that the basic pattern of results do not change.

RECOGNITION VERSUS RECALL

The basic difference between the recall and the recognition paradigm is quite straightforward under the ACT analysis. In the recognition paradigm, parts of a trace are presented and the subject is asked whether he recognizes their combination. In the recall paradigm the subject is also asked to retrieve other components of the trace. In ACT, activation converges on the trace from all presented components. If there is sufficient activation the trace becomes available. In a recognition task the subject simply says that he recognizes the test probe. In a recall task the subject retrieves part of the trace according to task specifications. It is typical to present more of the trace in a recognition paradigm. For instance, in paired-associate learning both stimulus and response are typically presented in a recognition test but only the stimulus is presented in a recall test. However, it is possible to do a recognition test by simply presenting a stimulus. One would expect a high conditional probability between success at recognizing the stimulus and success at recalling the response, and indeed there is (Martin, 1967). Under the ACT analysis, recognition is typically better than recall because more of the trace is typically presented, not because of any inherent superiority of recall over recognition.

Paired-Associate Recognition

One of the interesting analyses of recognition versus recall is that of Wolford (1971). He showed that, correcting for guessing, recognition of a paired associate could be predicted by the probabilities of forward and backward recall. His model was basically that a paired associate could be recognized if the subject could retrieve the response from the stimulus or the stim-ulus from the response. Let P_f and P_b be these two probabilities of recall. On the assumption that the two directions of recall are independent, Wolford derived, for corrected recognition P_r, the equation

$$P_r = P_f + (1 - P_f)P_b. \quad (28)$$

Under the ACT theory, the subject is not viewed as performing two independent retrievals in recognition but rather converging activation from the two sources. This is an important way in which the current ACT differs from the earlier ACT (Anderson, 1976) and its predecessor, HAM (Anderson & Bower, 1973). Nonetheless, ACT predicts the relationship documented by Wolford. We may assume that an amount of activation A_S comes from the stimulus and an amount A_R from the response. This means that we have the following equations for forward recall, backward recall, and recognition

$$P_f = 1 - e^{-CA_s} \quad (29)$$
$$P_b = 1 - e^{-CA_R} \quad (30)$$
$$P_r = 1 - e^{-C(A_s + A_R)} \quad (31a)$$
$$= 1 - e^{(-CA_s)}(e^{-CA_R}) \quad (31b)$$
$$= 1 - (1 - P_f)(1 - P_b) \quad (31c)$$
$$= P_f + (1 - P_f)P_b. \quad (31d)$$

The above analysis assumes that the probability of forming the trace is one and all failures of recall derive from failures of retrieval. If there is some probability of failing to encode the trace, the ACT analysis would predict that probabilities of forward and backward recall would overpredict probability of recognition. This is because forward and backward recall would no longer be independent. While Wolford found no evidence at all for nonindependence, other researchers (e.g., Wollen, Allison, & Lowry, 1969) have found evidence for a weak nonindependence.

Word Recognition

Another major domain where recall and recognition have been contrasted is memory for single words. A subject is presented with a list of such words and then must either recall (typically free recall) or recognize them. Recognition performance can be much higher than recall performance in such experiments. According to the framework set forth by Anderson (1972) and Anderson and Bower (1974), it is assumed that the subject forms traces linking the words to the various contextual elements. Although the contextual elements are undoubtedly more complex, the contextual factor is often represented as an association between the word and a single context element. This simplified situation is illustrated in Figure 9 where each line corresponds to a trace. Under this model, recognition involves retrieving the context from the word and verifying that it is indeed a list context. Direct recall involves retrieving list words from the list context. However, because of the high fan out of the context, the subject will have limited success at this. Thus, an auxiliary process involves using various strategies to generate words which can then be recognized. Because of this feature, this has been called the generate–recognize model of recall. For a review of relevant positive evidence see Anderson and Bower (1973) or Kintsch (1970). The major challenge to this analysis has come from various experiments showing contextual effects. These results will be reviewed in the next subsections.

The basic assumptions of the generate–recognize model are consistent with the current framework. The current framework makes it clear that recognition is better than recall because of the difference in fan out of the context node versus word nodes. If the same word appeared in multiple contexts we might expect this situation to be reversed and, indeed, Anderson and Bower (1972a, 1974) present evidence that recognition performance degrades as a word appears in multiple contexts.

Effects of Encoding Context

A large number of studies have been performed that display an effect of encoding context on both recognition and recall (e.g., Flexser & Tulving, 1978; Tulving & Thomson, 1971; Watkins & Tulving, 1975). These experiments are said to illustrate the encoding specificity principle that memory for an item is specific to the context in which it was studied. The experiment by Tulving and Thomson (1971) is a useful one to consider. They had subjects study items (e.g., black) either in isolation, in the presence of a strongly associated encoding cue (e.g., white), or in the presence of a weakly associated encoding cue (e.g., train). The strong and weak cues were selected from association norms. Orthogonal with this variable, subjects were tested for recognition of the word in one of these same three contexts. Recognition was best when study context matched test context.

We have explained these results in terms of selection of word senses (Reder, Anderson, & Bjork, 1974; Anderson & Bower; 1974) or in terms of elaborative encodings (Anderson, 1976). These explanations still hold in the current ACT framework. Figure 10 illustrates the network structure assumed in this explanation for the case of study with a weak encoding cue. The basic idea is that a to-be-recalled word like black has multiple senses. In this case we have black illustrated with two senses, black1 and black2. Attached to black1 is a weak associate train and attached to black2 is a strong associate white. The oval nodes in Figure 10 are the traces encoding these as-

Fig. 11. A representation of the relevant memory structures for the Light and Carter-Sobell experiments.

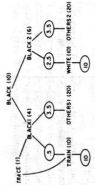

Fig. 10. A representation of the relevant network structure in the encoding specificity experiments. The numbers associated with the nodes are the strengths associated with the spreading activation analysis on p. 6.

ceives the greatest activation from *train* and *black*. In Figure 10 this will be *black1* which lies at the intersection of *train* and *black*. Thus, there are two "waves" of activations. The first determines the sense of the words and the second spreads activation from the word senses to retrieve the trace. It is this same double activation process that is used in selecting a subnode.

Evidence for Multiple Sense Nodes

While one can explain the encoding specificity result assuming multiple senses as in Figure 10, it is not really necessary to assume multiple senses to explain the basic effect that recognition is higher if the study context is presented at test. To see this, note in Figure 10 that the study context, *train*, is associated to the trace. This means that there will be more activation converging at the trace at test if *train* is presented again, independent of any sense selection.[1] However, there are a number of additional results that indicate the need for the multi-sense-node explanation. One is that it has been found (Reder, et al. 1974; Tulving & Thomson, 1973; Watkins & Tulving. 1975) that recognition is worse in a test context that promotes selection of the wrong sense than a neutral test context that just fails to present any encoding word. For instance, after studying *train–black* subjects are worse in recognition of *black* in the context *white–black* than when *black* is presented alone. Thus, it is not just the absence of *train* that hurts recognition. It is the presence of another context that actively selects against the original interpretation.

sociations. The oval nodes in Figure 10 leading to others1 and others2 represent other unidentified associations. Similarly, the nodes at the bottom attached to *train* and *white* represent other unidentified associations. For simplicity, I have only represented the multiple senses attached to *black*.

At first blush. people often have the intuition that there is only one sense for a word like *black*. However, there are a number of distinct if similar senses. In the presence of *white*, one is likely to come up with senses of *black* that refer to a prototypical color or race of people. In the presence of *train* one is likely to come up with the sense associated with soot or the glistening black of a polished toy train.

I assume that the encoding context determines the sense of the word chosen and that a trace is formed involving that sense and, perhaps, the encoding context. When the subject is tested, context will again determine the sense chosen and activation will spread from the chosen sense. Probability of recognition will be greater when the same sense is chosen because activation will be spreading from a sense node directly attached to the trace.

It should be noted that the choice of a sense for the word can also be accomplished by means of spreading activation. That is, the sense of *black* chosen when train-black is presented is the one that re-

The multiple sense representation is important for understanding the results of Light and Carter-Sobell (1970). They had subjects study a pair like *raspberry–jam* with *jam* as the target and then tested subjects with *raspberry–jam*, or *strawberry–jam* which tapped the same sense of that word, or *log–jam* which tapped a different sense. They found the three conditions were in this order in terms of decreasing level of recall. Figure 1 shows a schematic of the memory representation for their experiment. I constructed sets of equations like those given in (14) to derive the patterns of network activation when various cues were presented to serve as sources of activation. The predictions were derived under the assumption that all links have equal relative strength where multiple links emanate from a node. I also assumed in these calculations that one unit of activation would spread both from the context word and from the selected sense of the target word. Presented with *raspberry* and *jam* were 1.65 units of activation accumulating at the trace. Cued with *strawberry* and *jam*, 1.26 units were accumulated at the trace. Finally, cued with *log* and *jam*, .29 units accumulated at the trace. This corresponds to the ordering found by Light and Carter-Sobell. The difference between *raspberry–jam* versus *strawberry–jam* is a result of the fact that *raspberry* is directly connected to the trace. The difference between *strawberry–jam* versus *log–jam* is due to the difference between the two senses selected.[2]

Recognition Failure

Experiments such as those reported by Tulving and Thomson (1973) and by Watkins and Tulving (1975) are thought to be damaging for the generate–recognize models. In a typical example of these ex-

periments, subjects study a word with a weak associate, are then asked to recognize it in the context of a strong associate, and are then asked to recall it in the context of the old weak associate. In these cases it is often found that recall is superior to recognition and that many words are not recognizable but can be recalled. The phenomenon of recallable words not being recognized is called *recognition failure* and it is sometimes interpreted as disproving generate–recognize models. This is because recognition is one of the subprocesses in the generate–recognize model of recall so recognition of a word is a precondition for its recall. However, the activation patterns set up in ACT for the strong-associate recognition condition are very different than the activation patterns set up in the weak-associate recall condition. Therefore, there is no reason to assume that the recognition should be predictive of recall. We would only expect recognition to be predictive of recall in the same context.

I used Figure 10 to calculate how much activation should converge on the trace in these two conditions. My calculations were performed under the assumption that active nodes (representing presented words) would send out one unit of activation each. Thus, when the target and the strong cue are presented, I assumed nodes *white* and *black2* would be active and send out one unit of activation each. In this case, .24 units of activation converge on the trace. When just *train* (the weak cue) is presented and activated, .88 units of activation are expected to converge. So in point of fact, the weak associate is a better prompt for the memory trace than is the target and strong cue. This is because *train* is directly con-

[1] Past versions of the generate–test model assumed that there was no contribution of the trace except in terms of sense selection. However, in this model the context word can be just as important a source of activation as the target word. In fact, there are some results that suggest it might be a more important source (Bartling & Thompson, 1977; Rabinowitz, Mandler, & Barsalou, 1977). To the extent that it is the more important source, encoding specificity results should occur even for those words that truly have a single sense (Tulving & Watkins, 1977).

[2] Underwood & Humphreys (1979) have basically replicated the results of Light and Carter-Sobell, but they argue that the magnitude of the results do not justify the multiple-sense interpretation. It is hard to make clear predictions about the magnitude of the effect.

nected to the trace while *white* and *black2* are not. This analysis is consistent with the research and ideas of Rabinowitz, Mandler, and Barsalou (1977) and of Bartling and Thompson (1977) who showed that a considerable asymmetry existed between the forward recall of the target in response to the weak associate cue versus the opposite backward recall of the weak associate in response to the target cue with backward recall much lower. Rabinowitz et al. also noted a much reduced incidence of recognition failure when recognition was conditionalized on backward rather than forward recall.

One of the phenomena that has captured considerable attention (e.g., Flexser & Tulving, 1978; Wiseman & Tulving, 1975) is the relationship that occurs across experiments between probability of recognition conditional on recall $P(\text{Rn/Rc})$ and unconditional recognition $P(\text{Rn})$.

$$p(\text{Rn/Rc}) = p(\text{Rn}) + c[p(\text{Rn}) - p(\text{Rn})^2] \tag{32}$$

where c has been estimated to be .5. This indicates that the probability of recognition conditional on recall is only marginally superior to the unconditional probability of recognition. Under the current framework we would predict that, if the trace has been formed, the probability of retrieving the trace from the cue is independent of the probability of retrieving it from the target. The reason there is not complete independence is that if there was no trace formed, there will be failure of recall in both cases. This is substantially the explanation of the function offered by Flexser and Tulving (1978).

Summary

According to the current ACT analysis, the difference between recognition and recall is one of the number and directness of the sources of activation. Context affects recall and recognition by providing sources of activation. Recognition will only be pre-dictive of recall in the same context. It makes no more sense to talk about recognition conditional on recall when the contexts are different than it does to talk about conditional measure when the targets are changed. In different contexts different activation patterns will be set up just, as different contexts will be set up when the subject is asked to recognize different words. It is an interesting question to what extent differences in activation patterns instantiate what Tulving means by encoding specificity.

ELABORATIVE PROCESSING

One of the most potent manipulations that can be performed in terms of increasing a subject's memory for material is to have the subject elaborate on the to-be-remembered material (see Anderson & Reder, 1979; Anderson, 1980b for reviews). As Anderson and Reder argue, much of the research under the rubric of "depth of processing" (see Craik & Lockhart, 1972; Cermak & Craik, 1979, for a current survey) can be understood in terms of elaborative processing. That is, instructions which are said to promote "deeper processing" of the input can often be viewed as encouraging the subject to engage in more elaborative processing of the input. The phrase *elaborative processing*, though, is not much more technically precise than is the much lamented term *depth of processing* (Nelson, 1977). What I would like to do is spell out some of the ways elaboration can occur within this ACT framework. There are three basic ways that elaborations can improve recall. The first, and weakest, occurs when study elaborations serve to redirect activation away from interfering paths and towards the target path. (This is related to the concept of network integration discussed earlier.) The second occurs when subjects spread activation at test from additional concepts which were not in the probe but were part of the elaboration at study. Basically, this involves elaborating on the probe at test to try to generate additional

concepts from which to spread activation. The third method involves using inferential methods to reconstruct from the elaborations that can be retrieved at test what the target trace must have been. I will go through each of these uses of elaboration in turn.

Redirecting Activation

To illustrate the first possibility, let us consider an example of elaboration given in Anderson (1976). One subject who was asked to memorize the paired associate *dog –chair* generated the following elaboration.

> The dog loved his masters. He also loved to sit on the chairs. His masters had a beautiful black velvet chair. One day he climbed on it. He left his white hairs all over the chair. His masters were upset by this. They scolded him.

Figure 12 illustrates this elaboration in approximate network form proposed in Anderson (1976). Note that the impact of this elaboration is to introduce multiple paths between *dog* and *chair*. There are two effects of this structure. First, it redirects activation that would go directly from *dog* to *chair* to other parts of the elaborative structure and this activation will only arrive at *chair* in a less direct and dissipated form. On the other hand, this activation is also being taken away from the prior facts. For example, activation is taken away from the prior associates to spread to *master* and some of the activation arriving at *master* spreads on to *dog*. Thus, the experimental fan out of *dog* somewhat dissipates direct activation of *chair* but somewhat redirects activation toward *chair*. We used the net-

work in Figure 12 to see what the overall effect would be. Again we solved for the asymptotic patterns of activation using equations such as (7). We assumed the total strength of the prior nodes attached to *dog* was nine and the strength of all experimental nodes was one. In this case, inputting one unit of activation at *dog*, .19 units arrived at *chair*. In contrast, when there was a single experimental path from *dog* to *chair*, only .12 units arrived at *chair*. Clearly, whether the elaborated structure will be better will depend on the specifics of the elaboration, but this example at least illustrates that it is possible that an elaborated structure can result in greater activation of the target trace.

A question that naturally arises about such elaborations is how the subject discriminates between target traces and elaborations. For instance, how is it that the subject knows it was the *dog–chair* that he studied and not *dog–master*? It is assumed that part of a trace is a tag indicating whether it is an encoding of a study event or part of a subject elaboration. Reder (personal communication), who had subjects explicitly generate elaborations of text, found her subjects very good at discriminating what they explicitly studied from what they generated as elaboration. However, to whatever extent subjects do lose these tags and to whatever extent they are willing to venture guesses in the absence of such tags, we would see inferential and semantic intrusions and false alarms.

In some experiments (e.g., Bransford, Barclay & Franks, 1972; Owens, Bower, & Black, 1979; Sulin & Dooling, 1974; Thorn-

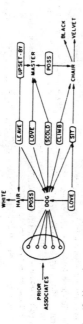

FIG. 12. Network representation of the elaborative structure generated to connect the pair *dog–chair*.

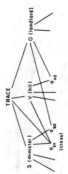

Fig. 13. Network representation of a subject-verb-object trace and the overlapping network of associations among the concepts. One of the intersecting concepts has been included in the trace.

dyke, 1977), false acceptance of inferentially related foils is almost as high as acceptance of presented targets. I doubt that these very high false alarm rates can be attributed to loss of tags. This is because of Reder's evidence that subjects are quite good at distinguishing elaborations from studied material. Also, it seems improbable that subjects would have explicitly generated all these inferences. A better explanation of these intrusions and false alarms involves the notion of reconstructive recall which I will discuss later in this section.

People have commented on the superficial contradiction between the fan analysis (which claims that the greater the number of experimental paths leading from a concept, the poorer the memory) and this elaborative analysis (which says the greater the number of experimental paths the better the memory). To help clarify the situation I (Anderson, 1980b) have coined the terms *irrelevant fan* and *relevant fan*. In the typical fan experiment, we are creating irrelevant fan in that the paths lead away from each other. In Figure 12 we have relevant fan in that the various paths leading from *dog* converge back on *chair*.

Elaborative Sources of Activation

There are other more powerful advantages to the structure in Figure 12 than its ability to direct more activation to the target. The subject can use any of the retrieved elaborations as additional sources for activating the target. So if the subject recalled his elaboration *The dog loved his master*, he can use *master* as another point from which to spread activation to the target structure. That is, the subject need not confine himself to spreading activation from the presented word. He can retrieve concepts used in the elaboration, focus on these, and spread activation from them.

Configural cueing. The research on configural cueing of sentence memory can be understood in terms of this elaborative analysis. Anderson and Bower (1972b) had subjects study sentences such as

The minister hit the landlord

and then cued subjects for memory of the objects of the sentence with prompts such as

The minister ____ the ____
The ____ hit the ____
The minister hit the ____

When the instructions to the subject were just to study the sentences and when the subjects presumably studied the sentences passively, the experiments uncovered the relationship between recall to the three cues

$$P(SV) \leq P(S) + (1 - P(S))P(V). \quad (33)$$

On the other hand, when subjects were asked to generate meaningful continuations to the sentences, the relationship obtained was

$$P(SV) > P(S) + (1 - P(S))P(V). \quad (34)$$

Subsequent research by Foss & Harwood (1975), Jones (1980), and Anderson (1976) has confirmed that whether one gets the first or second relationship depends on how much subjects process the meaning of these sentences. The research caused a minor flap about whether or not there are configural cues in memory, but the basic results fall out quite neatly in the current framework and in such a way that the configural issue is blurred.

If subjects generate no elaborations, ACT predicts relationship (33) between probability of recall to the configural SV cue and the single-word S or V cue. Subject and verb contribute independent and additive activations to the trace. As we noted in the analysis of Wolford's recognition paradigm (p. 19) the effect of summing activation from cues C_1 and C_2 is to produce a level of activation that gives us the relation between probabilities of recall

$$P(C_1 \text{ \& } C_2) = P(C_1) + (1 - P(C_1))P(C_2). \quad (35)$$

One can get the inequality in Equation (33) to the extent where a trace is not formed. That is, let $P^*(C)$ be the probability of reviving the trace from cue C conditional on the trace being formed and let $P(C)$ be the unconditional probability of trace retrieval. Let a be the probability of trace formation. Then

$$P(C_1) = aP^*(C_1) \quad (36)$$
$$P(C_2) = aP^*(C_2) \quad (37)$$
$$P(C_1 \text{ \& } C_2) = a[P^*(C_1) + (1 - P^*(C_1))P^*(C_2)] \quad (38)$$
$$< aP^*(C_1) + (1 - aP^*(C_1)aP^*(C_2) \quad (39)$$
$$= P(C_1) + (1 - P(C_1))P(C_2). \quad (40)$$

The advantage of the subject and verb cue under meaningful processing instructions can be explained if these instructions cause the subject to process the sentence elaboratively. A schematic memory structure for such a sentence showing the effect of elaborations is illustrated in Figure 13. There is a trace interconnecting the subject (minister), verb (hit), and object (landlord). The assumption is that under meaningful processing instructions, the subject will retrieve one or more schemata for elaboration. So, he might retrieve *people hit people with hand-held objects*. This would lead to the elaboration that the minister hit the landlord with an object and that he held the object. This elaboration process can continue by retrieving another schema. Suppose the subject can recall a movie where a minister carried a wooden cross when confronting the devil. This would lead to the elaborations that the hitting instrument was a wooden cross and that the landlord was the devil. (Actually, one subject given this sentence did continue it *with a cross*—but I have no idea about the exact elaborative processes that led her to this continuation). Figure 13 indicates some of the impact of such elaborative activity by including *cross* in the trace for the sentence.

Such elaborative encoding by itself will not produce configural effects. If activation spreads from S, or from V, or from both, the same prediction holds for the structure in Figure 13 about amount of activation of the trace and probability of recall, as when cross is not part of the trace. Basically, S and V make independent contributions to the overall pattern of activation. When presented together their contributions are just summed.

However, suppose that the subject at test also tried to elaborate with associates of the presented items and that he selected some associates of the words, and spread activation from these as well as from the presented word. In the presence of S or V alone he has a poor probability of regenerating the old associate. However, presented together there is a good probability that the old associate will be at the intersection of activation of these two words, have the highest activation, and so be selected. In that case, the subject could use this associate as an additional source of activation to converge on the trace and boost his recall over what we would expect on the basis of the single word cue.

The basic idea here is that, if the subject can recreate at test the elaborative activities he engaged in at study he can boost his recall. If the subject chooses as elaborations the most strongly activated associates of the probe, there is a chance that test associates will overlap with study associates. The probability and degree of overlap will vary with the number of terms in the test probe. This is basically the "semantic triangulation" explanation proposed by Anderson and Bower (1972b) or the sense selection explanation proposed by Anderson (1976) *where it is assumed that elaboration selects a particular word sense.* Anderson and Bower (1973) showed heightened object recall conditional on a subject's ability to regenerate the old continuation and Anderson (1976) showed heightened object recall conditional on ability to recognize the sense of the subject or verb.

Configurally related sentence cues. A similar analysis can be made of the experiment of Anderson and Ortony (1975) who had subjects study sentences such as

A. Nurses are often beautiful.
B. Nurses have to be licensed.
C. Landscapes are often beautiful.

and cued subjects for recall with a term like *actress*. They point out that *nurses* has two interpretations, one as a female person and the other as a profession. Similarly, *beautiful* has two interpretations, one appropriate to women and one appropriate to landscapes. In the case of A, *actress* is appropriate to the selected senses of *nurse* and *beautiful*, but it is not in the case of B or C. They were interested in the relationships among the probability that *actress* evokes recall of sentence A, the probability of it evoking recall of sentence B, and the probability of it evoking recall of sentence C. Referring to these three probabilities as *t*, *s*, and *p*, they observed the following: $t > s + (1-s)p$. This was interpreted as contrary to associative theory.

Figure 14 shows the network schematics for situations A, B, and C. In each case, we have assumed that concepts at the intersection of subject and predicate are chosen for inclusion in the trace elaboration. As an example, for case A we have chosen *glamour* at the intersection of *nurse* and *beautiful*. The word *glamour* is also closely associated to *actress* and hence *actress* is closely associated to the trace. In contrast, the elaborations at the intersection of the subject and predicate in B and C are not closely associated to *actress* and hence ac-

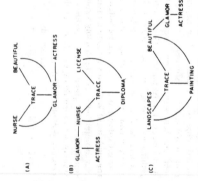

FIG. 14. Network representation for the three conditions of the Anderson and Ortony experiment.

tress is not closely associated to the trace. Thus, we would expect out of this associative analysis just what Anderson and Ortony found—much greater recall of the sentence with the *actress* cue in case A.

Generation of Elaborations

An important issue about elaborations concerns how they are generated. Anderson (1976) proposed that they could be generated by inferential productions. I still believe this to be plausible in some circumstances, but a more important mechanism involves analogy to prior knowledge structures and this is the mechanism that I would like to develop here. With this mechanism it is possible to explain how memory elaboration and memory reconstruction can be combined to yield enhanced memory performance. The mechanism provides an explanation for Bartlett's (1932) observation that memory often depends critically on a match between the interpretive activities at study and the interpretive activities at test.

The details of this elaborative mechanism are described in Anderson (1983), but the basic idea is that the subject has stored in long-term memory sets of events which can

serve as analogs for elaborating the current event. I call these event sets *schemata*. For instance, the *chair* story in Figure 12 may have been based on one or more event sets in the subject's life. This elaboration notion can be made more powerful if the elaboration the subject generates is an interweaving of more than one event set. To consider a new example, suppose the subject is given as a to-be-remembered sentence

The janitor chased the cat.

and has in memory the schemata

A. The janitor found the rat in the basement.
   The janitor chased the rat.
   He killed the rat.
B. The dog chased the cat.
   He cornered the cat.
   The cat scratched him.

These schemata can be actual events in the subject's life (indeed, they are events in mine). Combined together we can construct the elaboration

The janitor found the cat in the basement.
The janitor chased the cat.
The janitor cornered the cat.
The cat scratched him.
The janitor killed the cat.

This elaboration is generated from the original memory by simple substitution of terms to achieve compatibility with the target trace. In the first case, *cat* is substituted for *rat*, and in the second case, *janitor* for *dog*. The schemata do not have to be encodings of specific events. They can also be more general event characterizations as envisioned in some of the current work on schemata.

Inferential Reconstruction

So far we have a mechanism for generating elaborations at study. This can be useful in numerous ways as already discussed. However, these schemata become much more powerful when we consider their potential use at recall. Suppose the subject was not able to remember the target sentence and was only able to remember two of his elaborations.

The janitor cornered the cat.
The janitor killed the cat.

The subject can apply the same elaborative process to these sentences as he applied to the original studied sentence. Suppose that the subject is able to reevoke the *dog chasing cat* schema from *The janitor cornered the cat* and generate an elaboration based on it. Then he might infer that the study sentence was one of the sentences he generated by elaborating with the schema, that is, either *The janitor chased the cat* or *The cat scratched the janitor*. In this situation the subject would have a fair probability of an inferential intrusion but also a fair probability of a correct recall. If the subject were also able to recall the rat-chasing schema and elaborate with it he would be in a stronger position. He could infer from these elaborations that the studied sentence might have been *The janitor chased the cat* or *The janitor found the cat in the basement*. Intersecting this with the elaborations from the other schema, the subject would have strong circumstantial evidence that what he had really seen was *The janitor chased the cat*.

The above example illustrates the basic processes underlying the phenomenon of *inferential redundancy*. At recall, the subject can use those study elaborations he can recall to infer what schemata he must have been using at study. He can then use these schemata to elaborate on the study elaborations and use the intersection of these test elaborations to infer what the original sentence had been. This is a very important role for prior knowledge.

As we noted above, the subject may have to select from a number of possible inferred candidates for the target trace. This can produce a high rate of false alarm and intrusion. However, the subject need not be at chance in choosing among the alternatives. He can try to recognize the alternative he generates. That is, when he spreads activation from *janitor* it may not have been enough to activate the trace. However, when he elaborates *The janitor chased the cut* as a candidate and spreads activation from *janitor*, *chased*, and *cut*, this may raise the activation level to the point where the original study trace is available.

The subject may also use statistical properties of the study material to reject various candidate sentences. Thus, he may know that none of the study sentences involved locations and so on this basis reject a sentence such as *The janitor found the cat in the basement*.

Experimental evidence. A clear prediction is that manipulations which increase the use of elaborations should increase both the level of recall and of intrusion. Experiments consistent with this prediction are reviewed by Anderson and Reder (1979). For instance, the prediction was nicely confirmed in the experiments of Owens et al. (1979) who found that providing subjects with thematic information increased both the level of recall and of intrusion. One of their examples involved having subjects study a story about a coed with or without the knowledge that she had an unwanted pregnancy. Presumably, the effect of this additional information is to increase the likelihood of evoking pregnancy-related schemata. So, when one of the target sentences read

The doctor said, ''My expectations are confirmed.''

subjects could embellish this with their schema for a doctor telling a woman that she is pregnant. The effect of this embellishment would be to increase memory for the target sentence but also to increase the likelihood that subjects would intrude other elements from this schema such as

The doctor told Nancy that she was pregnant.

We can understand the influence of the Owens et al. priming manipulation in terms of the spreading activation theory that we have developed. Recall that schemata are data structures in memory that have to be retrieved themselves before they can be used for embellishments. Thus, the statement

The doctor said, ''My expectations are confirmed.''

would spread some activation to the doctor-tells-woman-she's-pregnant schema but not much. On the other hand, with the pregnancy concept already active, considerably more activation would converge on this schema, making its selection for elaboration more likely.

This same consideration can explain the effect of pretest instructions such as those given by Sulin and Dooling (1974). They told subjects only at test that a passage they had read about ''Carol Harris'' was really about Helen Keller. This produced a large increase in subjects' willingness to accept foils such as

She was deaf, dumb, and blind.

The impact of identifying Carol Harris with Helen Keller should be to spread activation to the Helen Keller facts and thus strongly influence the elaborations that subjects generate at test. As a consequence, their elaborations will contain the candidate sentence which may then be falsely accepted.

This idea, that contextual information can influence the elaboration process, explains the powerful interaction that we obtained in Schustack and Anderson (1979). There we presented subjects with 42 short historical passages for study and then tested their recognition memory for sentences taken from these passages. We provided subjects with analogies for the referents of these passages either at study or at test. For instance, it might be pointed out to the subjects that the passage about Yoshida Ichiro had strong analogies to what they knew about Lyndon Johnson. We found that subjects' memory for this material was greatly improved but only if the same analogy was presented at study as at test. Thus, it was important that subjects' study elaborations and test elaborations both take advantage of information to be found with the Lyndon Johnson schema.

The notion of fluctuations in schema availability also helps to explain an interest-ing result reported by Bower, Black, and Turner (1979). They had subjects study 1, 2, or 3 stories that constituted variations on the same general theme. For instance, stories could be about visiting a doctor, visiting a dentist, or visiting a chiropractor. Bower et al. found an increased tendency, the more stories the subject had studied, to intrude theme-related inferences and to false alarm to such inferences. With each story studied, the subject would have another opportunity to rehearse and strengthen the elaborative schemata. He would also have in memory these earlier stories which could themselves serve as elaborative schema. Therefore, these schemata for making theme-related inferences would be more available the more stories that had been studied.

Summary

This section has considered the various ways activation influences the generation of elaborations and their use. It was argued that spread of activation determined which schemata were chosen for elaboration both at study and at test. Elaborations can influence recall by redirecting activation towards the to-be-recalled material, providing additional sources of activation, and providing a means for reconstructing what had been studied. Many of the interesting interactions in memory can be understood as depending on activation selecting the right schemata for elaboration.

CONCLUSIONS

We have reviewed some of the memory phenomena that can be understood in terms of the spreading activation mechanism of the current ACT theory (Anderson, 1976). Many of these phenomena had been thought to be difficult for the old ACT (Anderson, 1976) or its predecessor, HAM (Anderson and Bauer, 1973). It is worth noting the features of the new ACT that enable it to deal with these formerly troublesome phenomena. Most fundamentally, activation is a continuously varying quan-tity. This enables it to produce more subtle behavior than was possible with the all-or-none mechanisms of the former ACT or HAM. Because activation can sum and varies with associative distance and strength, level of activation of a node is sensitive to the particular configuration of activation sources. This enables ACT to produce some of the phenomena in the memory literature that depend on the context of study and test.

REFERENCES

ANDERSON, J. R. FRAN: A simulation model of free recall. In G. H. Bower (Ed.), *The Psychology of Learning and Motivation.* New York: Academic Press, 1972. Vol. 5.

ANDERSON, J. R. *Language, Memory, and Thought.* Hillsdale, N.J.: Erlbaum, 1976.

ANDERSON, J. R. Concepts, propositions, and schemata: What are the cognitive units? *Nebraska Symposium of Motivation,* 1980, 28, 121–162. (a)

ANDERSON, J. R. *Cognitive Psychology and its Implication.* San Francisco: Freeman, 1980. (b)

ANDERSON, J. R. Interference: The relationship between response latency and response accuracy. *Journal of Experimental Psychology: Human Learning and Memory,* 1981, 7, 326–343. (a)

ANDERSON, J. R. Effects of prior knowledge on memory for new information. *Memory & Cognition,* 1981, 9, 237–246. (b)

ANDERSON, J. R. Acquisition of cognitive skill. *Psychological Review,* 1982, 89, 369–406.

ANDERSON, J. R. *The Architecture of Cognition.* Cambridge, Mass.: Harvard Univ. Press, 1983.

ANDERSON, J. R., & BOWER, G. H. Recognition and retrieval processes in free recall. *Psychological Review,* 1972, 79, 97–123. (a)

ANDERSON, J. R., & BOWER, G. H. Configural properties in sentence memory. *Journal of Verbal Learning and Verbal Behavior,* 1972, 11, 594–605. (b)

ANDERSON, J. R., & BOWER, G. H. *Human Associative Memory.* Washington, D.C.: Winston, 1973.

ANDERSON, J. R., & BOWER, G. H. Interference in memory for multiple contexts. *Memory & Cognition,* 1974, 2, 509–514.

ANDERSON, J. R., & BOWER, G. H. *Human Associative Memory: A Brief Edition.* Hillsdale, N.J.: Erlbaum, 1980.

ANDERSON, J. R., & PAULSON, R. Representation and retention of verbatim information. *Journal of Verbal Learning and Verbal Behavior,* 1977, 16, 439–451.

ANDERSON, J. R., & REDER, L. M. An elaborative processing explanation of depth of processing. In

L. S. Cermak & F. I. M. Craik (Eds.), *Levels of Processing in Human Memory*. Hillsdale. N.J.: Erlbaum, 1979.

ANDERSON, R. C., & ORTONY, A. On putting apples into bottles—A problem of polysemy. *Cognitive Psychology*, 1975, 7, 167–180.

BARTLETT, F. C. *Remembering: A Study in Experimental and Social Psychology*. Cambridge: Cambridge Univ. Press, 1932.

BARTLING, C. A., & THOMPSON, C. P. Encoding specificity: Retrieval asymmetry in the recognition failure paradigm. *Journal of Experimental Psychology: Human Learning and Memory*, 1977, 3, 690–700.

BRANSFORD, J. D., BARCLAY, J. R., & FRANKS, J. J. Sentence memory: A constructive versus interpretive approach. *Cognitive Psychology*, 1972, 3, 193–209.

BOWER, G. H., BLACK, J. B., & TURNER, T. J. Scripts in memory for text. *Cognitive Psychology*, 1979, 11, 177–220.

BROADBENT, D. E. *Perception and Communication*. Elmsford, N.Y.: Pergamon, 1958.

CERASO, J., & HENDERSON, A. Unavailability and associative loss in RI and PI. *Journal of Experimental Psychology*, 1965, 70, 300–305.

CERMAK, L. S., & CRAIK, F. I. M. *Levels of Processing in Human Memory*. Hillsdale, N.J.: Erlbaum, 1979.

COLLINS, A. M., & LOFTUS, E. F. A spreading-activation theory of semantic processing. *Psychological Review*. 1975, 82, 407–428.

COLLINS, A. M., & QUILLIAN, M. R. Experiments on semantic memory and language comprehension. In L. Gregg (Ed.), *Cognition and Learning*. New York: Wiley, 1972.

CRAIK, F. I. M., & LOCKHART, R. S. Levels of processing: A framework for memory research. *Journal of Verbal Learning and Verbal Behavior*, 1972, 11, 671–684.

CRAIK, F. I. M., & WATKINS, M. J. The role of rehearsal in short-term memory. *Journal of Verbal Learning and Verbal Behavior*, 1973, 12, 599–607.

ECCLES, J. C. Possible synaptic mechanisms subserving learning. In A. G. Karczmar & J. C. Eccles (Eds.), *Brain and Human Behavior*. New York: Springer-Verlag, 1972.

ESTES, W. K. Learning theory and the new "mental chemistry." *Psychological Review*, 1960, 67, 207–223.

ESTES, W. K. An associative basis for coding and organization. In A. W. Melton & E. Martin (Eds.), *Coding processes in human memory*. Washington: Winston, 1972.

FISCHLER, I. Semantic facilitation without association in a lexical decision task. *Memory and Cognition*, 1977, 5, 335–339.

FLEXSER, A. J., & TULVING, E. Retrieval independ-

dence in recognition and recall. *Psychological Review*, 1978, 85, 153–172.

FOSS, D. J., & HARWOOD, D. A. Memory for sentences: Implications for human associative memory. *Journal of Verbal Learning and Verbal Behavior*, 1975, 14, 1–16.

GLUCKSBERG, S., & McCLOSKEY, M. Decisions about ignorance: Knowing that you don't know. *Journal of Experimental Psychology: Human Learning and Memory*, 1981, 7, 311–325.

GOETZ, E. T., ANDERSON, R. C., & SCHALLERT, D. L. The representation of sentences in memory. *Journal of Verbal Learning and Verbal Behavior*, 1981. 20, 369–385.

GOSS, A. E. Manifest strengthening of correct responses of paired-associates under postcriterion zero percent occurrence of response members. *Journal of General Psychology*, 1965, 72, 135–144.

GRAESSER, A. C. Tests of a holistic chunking model of sentence memory through analyses of noun intrusions. *Memory and Cognition*, 1978, 6, 527–536.

GREENBERG, R., & UNDERWOOD, B. J. Retention as a function of stage of practice. *Journal of Experimental Psychology*. 1950, 40, 452–457.

HAYES-ROTH, B. Evolution of cognitive structures and processes. *Psychological Review*. 1977, 84, 260–278.

HOROWITZ, L. M., & NEWMAN, W. An interrupted stimulus can facilitate PA learning. *Journal of Verbal Learning and Verbal Behavior*. 1969, 8, 219–224.

HOUSTON, J. P. Proactive inhibition and undetected retention interval rehearsal. *Journal of Experimental Psychology*, 1969, 82, 511–514.

JONES, G. V. Tests of a structural theory of the memory trace. *British Journal of Psychology*, 1978, 69, 351–367.

JONES, G. V. Interaction of intrinsic and extrinsic knowledge in sentence recall. *Attention and Performance VIII*. Hillsdale, N.J.: Erlbaum, 1980.

JONES, J. E. All-or-none versus incremental learning. *Psychological Review*, 1962, 69, 156–160.

KEPPEL, G., POSTMAN, L., & ZAVORTINK, B. Studies of learning to learn: VIII. The influence of massive amounts of training upon the learning and retention of paired-associate tests. *Journal of Verbal Learning and Verbal Behavior*, 1968, 7, 790–796.

KING, D. R. W., & ANDERSON, J. R. Long term memory search: An intersecting activation process. *Journal of Verbal Learning and Verbal Behavior*. 1976, 15, 587–605.

KINTSCH, W. Models for free recall and recognition. In D. A. Norman (Ed.), *Models of Human Memory*. New York: Academic Press, 1970. Pp. 307–373.

KINTSCH, W. *The Representation of Meaning in Memory*. Hillsdale. N.J.: Erlbaum, 1974.

KOPPENAAL, R. J. Time changes in the strengths of A–B, A–C lists: Spontaneous recovery? *Journal of Verbal Learning and Verbal Behavior*, 1963, 2, 310–319.

LEWIS, C. H., & ANDERSON, J. R. Interference with real world knowledge. *Cognitive Psychology*, 1976, 8, 311–335.

LIGHT, L. L., & CARTER-SOBELL, L. Effects of changed semantic context on recognition memory. *Journal of Verbal Learning and Verbal Behavior*, 1970, 9, 1–11.

LOFTUS, G. R. Eye fixations and recognition memory for pictures. *Cognitive Psychology*, 1972, 3, 525–551.

McCLOSKEY, M., & BIGLER, K. Focused memory search in fact retrieval. *Memory & Cognition*, 1980, 8, 253–264.

McKOON, G., & RATCLIFF, R. Priming in episodic and semantic memory. *Journal of Verbal Learning and Verbal Behavior*, 1979, 18, 463–480.

MANDLER, G. Organization and memory. In K. W. Spence & J. A. Spence (Eds.), *The Psychology of Learning and Motivation*. New York: Academic Press, 1967, 328–372. Vol. 1.

MARTIN, E. Relation between stimulus recognition and paired-associate learning. *Journal of Experimental Psychology*, 1967, 74, 500–505.

MELTON, A. W. Implications of short-term memory for a general theory of memory. *Journal of Verbal Learning and Verbal Behavior*. 1963, 2, 1–21.

MEYER, D., & SCHVANEVELDT, R. Meaning, memory, and mental processes. *Science*, 1976, 192, 27–33.

MILLER, G. A. The magical number seven, plus or minus two: Some limits on our capacity for processing information. *Psychological Review*, 1956, 63, 81–97.

NEELY, J. H. Semantic priming and retrieval from lexical memory: Roles of inhibitionless spreading activation and limited-capacity attention. *Journal of Experimental Psychology: General*, 1977, 106, 226–254.

NELSON, T. O. Reinforcement and human memory. In W. K. Estes (Ed.), *Handbook of Learning and Cognitive Processes*. Hillsdale, N.J.: Erlbaum, 1976. Vol. 3.

NELSON, T. O. Repetition and depth of processing. *Journal of Verbal Learning and Verbal Behavior*, 1977, 16, 151–172.

OWENS, J., BOWER, G. H., & BLACK, J. B. The "soap opera" effect in story recall. *Memory and Cognition*, 1979, 7, 185–191.

POSTMAN, L. Short-term memory and incidental learning. In A. W. Melton (Ed.), *Categories of Human Learning*. New York: Academic Press, 1964.

POSTMAN, L., & GRAY, W. Maintenance of prior associations and proactive inhibition. *Journal of Experimental Psychology: Human Learning and Memory*, 1977, 3, 255–263.

POSTMAN, L., & KEPPEL, G. Conditions of cumulative proactive inhibition. *Journal of Experimental Psychology: General*, 1977, 106, 376–403.

POSTMAN, L., & PARKER, J. F. Maintenance of first-list associations during transfer. *American Journal of Psychology*, 1970, 83, 171–188.

POSTMAN, L., STARK, K., & BURNS, S. Sources of proactive inhibition on unpaced tests of retention. *American Journal of Psychology*, 1974, 87, 33–56.

POSTMAN, L., STARK, K., & FRASER, J. Temporal changes in interference. *Journal of Verbal Learning and Verbal Behavior*, 1968, 7, 672–694.

RABINOWITZ, J. C., MANDLER, G., & BARSALOU, L. W. Recognition failure: Another case of retrieval failure. *Journal of Verbal Learning and Verbal Behavior*, 1977, 16, 639–663.

RATCLIFF, R., & McKOON, G. Does activation really spread? *Psychological Review*, 1981, 88, 454–457.

REDER, L. M. The role of elaborations in memory for prose. *Cognitive Psychology*, 1979, 11, 221–234.

REDER, L. M., & ANDERSON, J. R. A partial resolution of the paradox of interference: The role of integrating knowledge. *Cognitive Psychology*, 1980, 12, 447–472.

REDER, L. M., & ROSS, B. H. Integrated knowledge in different tasks: Positive and negative fan effects. *Journal of Experimental Psychology: Learning, Memory and Cognition*. 1983, 9, 55–72.

REDER, L. M., ANDERSON, J. R., & BJORK, R. A. A semantic interpretation of encoding specificity. *Journal of Experimental Psychology*, 1974, 102, 648–656.

SCHUSTACK, M. W., & ANDERSON, J. R. Effects of analogy to prior knowledge on memory for new information. *Journal of Verbal Learning and Verbal Behavior*, 1979, 18, 565–583.

SHOBEN, E. J., WESCOURT, K. T., & SMITH, E. E. Sentence verification, sentence recognition, and the semantic-episodic distinction. *Journal of Experimental Psychology: Human Learning and Memory*, 1978, 4, 304–317.

SIMON, H. A. How big is a chunk? *Science*, 1974, 183, 482–488.

SMITH, E. E., ADAMS, N., & SCHORR, D. Fact retrieval and the paradox of interference. *Cognitive Psychology*, 1978, 10, 438–464.

SULIN, R. A., & DOOLING, D. J. Intrusion of a thematic idea in retention of prose. *Journal of Experimental Psychology*, 1974, 103, 255–262.

THORNDYKE, P. W. Cognitive structures in comprehension and memory of narrative discourse. *Cognitive Psychology*, 1977, 9, 77–110.

TULVING, E., & THOMSON, D. M. Retrieval processes in recognition memory: Effects of associative context. *Journal of Experimental Psychology*. 1971, 87, 116–124.

TULVING, E., & THOMSON, P. M. Encoding specificity and retrieval processes in episodic memory. *Psychological Review.* 1973, **80**, 352–373.

TULVING, E. & WATKINS, O. C. Recognition failure of words with a single meaning. *Memory and Cognition.* 1977, **5**, 513–522.

UNDERWOOD, B. J. Interference and forgetting. *Psychological Review.* 1957, **64**, 49–60.

UNDERWOOD, B. J., & EKSTRAND, B. R. Studies of Distributed Practice: XXIV Differentiation and Proactive Inhibition. *Journal of Experimental Psychology.* 1967, **74**, 574–580.

UNDERWOOD, B. J. & HUMPHREYS, M. Content change and the role of meaning in word recognition. *American Journal of Psychology.* 1979, **92**, 577–609.

UNDERWOOD, B. J., & KEPPEL, G. One trial learning? *Journal of Verbal Learning and Verbal Behavior.* 1962, **1**, 1–13.

WARREN, R. E. Stimulus encoding and memory. *Journal of Experimental Psychology.* 1972, **94**, 90–100.

WARREN, R. E. Time and the spread of activation in memory. *Journal of Experimental Psychology: Learning and Memory.* 1977, **3**, 458–466.

WATKINS, M. J., & TULVING, E. Episodic memory: When recognition fails. *Journal of Experimental Psychology: General.* 1975, **104**, 5–29.

WICKENS, D. D., MOODY, M. J., & DOW, R. The nature of timing of the retrieval process and of interference effects. *Journal of Experimental Psychology: General.* 1981, **110**, 1–20.

WICKELGREN, W. A. The long and the short of memory. *Psychological Bulletin.* 1973, **80**, 425–438.

WICKELGREN, W. A. Single-trace fragility theory of memory dynamics. *Memory and Cognition.* 1974, **2**, 775–780.

WICKELGREN, W. A. Memory storage dynamics. In W. K. Estes (Ed.), *Handbook of Learning and Cognitive Processes.* Hillsdale, N.J.: Erlbaum, 1976. Vol. 4 (a)

WICKELGREN, W. A. Network strength theory of storage and retrieval dynamics. *Psychological Review.* 1976, **83**, 466–478. (b)

WICKELGREN, W. A. Chunking and consolidation: A theoretical synthesis of semantic networks, configuring in conditioning, S-R versus cognitive learning, normal forgetting, the amnesic syndrome, and the hippocampal arousal system. *Psychological Review.* 1979, **86**, 44–60.

WISEMAN, S., & TULVING, E. Encoding specificity: Relation between recall superiority and recognition failure. *Journal of Experimental Psychology: Human Learning and Memory.* 1976, **2**, 349–361.

WOLFORD, G. Function of distinct associations for paired-associate performance. *Psychological Review.* 1971, **73**, 303–313.

WOLLEN, K., ALLISON, T., & LOWRY, D. Associative symmetry versus independent association. *Journal of Verbal Learning and Verbal Behavior.* 1969, **8**, 283–288.

WOODWARD, A. E., BJORK, R. A., & JONGEWARD, R. H. Recall and recognition as a function of primary rehearsal. *Journal of Verbal Learning and Verbal Behavior.* 1973, **12**, 608–617.

(Received February 24, 1982)

Frames, Scripts, and Schemas

Semantic networks evolved into even more structured representations. In a classic paper, Minsky extended the idea of a concept in a semantic network into the notion of a large organized data structure, or *frame*, embedded in a *frame system*. Each frame contains *slots*, which accept only certain input values, and which frequently have *default values* to use if there are no input values. The frame for a bedroom, for example, has a slot for a bed, which can be instantiated by any object playing the role of a bed, and also has as a default value the prototypical bed. Frames are essentially models of parts of the world; to understand input information is to determine which frame, or configuration of frames, best fits the input.

At roughly the same time that Minsky was developing his notion of frames, Schank and his colleagues were developing a variety of representational formalisms. Two of these formalisms are described in the selection presented here, which comprises the first three chapters of Schank's and Abelson's influential book. Schank developed a set of *primitive acts* that he thought could be used to represent all actions (or verb concepts). On top of this system of primitive acts, Schank and Abelson developed the notion of *scripts*, an important variation on Minsky's frame. A script is used to represent a stereotypical action sequence; the classic example is the *restaurant* script (which is presented in the current selection).

The selection by Rumelhart, Smolensky, McClelland, and Hinton attempts to show how a connectionist architecture can account for the same phenomena as can frames and scripts. According to Rumelhart and colleagues, a frame or script is not a single, prestored object; rather, such representations emerge when needed from the interaction of a large number of simpler processing elements, all working in concert. This approach, the authors argued, provides a "schema" more flexible than that offered by the conventional, symbolic architecture.

The Psychology of Computer Vision
(Chapter 6)

A FRAMEWORK FOR REPRESENTING KNOWLEDGE

Marvin Minsky

6.1 FRAMES

It seems to me that the ingredients of most theories both in artificial intelligence and in psychology have been on the whole too minute, local, and unstructured to account—either practically or phenomenologically—for the effectiveness of common sense thought. The "chunks" of reasoning, language, memory, and "perception" ought to be larger and more structured, and their factual and procedural contents must be more intimately connected in order to explain the apparent power and speed of mental activities.

Similar feelings seem to be emerging in several centers working on theories of intelligence. They take one form in the proposal of Papert and myself[1] to substructure knowledge into "microworlds"; another form in the "problem-spaces" of Newell and Simon;[2] and yet another in new, larger structures that theorists like Schank,[3] Abelson,[4] and Norman[5] assign to linguistic objects. I see all these as moving away from the traditional attempts both by behavioristic psychologists and by logic-oriented students of artificial intelligence in attempts to represent knowledge as collections of separate, simple fragments.

I try here to bring together several of these issues by pretending to have a unified, coherent theory. The paper raises more questions than it answers, and I have tried to note the deficiencies of the theory.

Here is the essence of the theory: When one encounters a new situation (or makes a substantial change in one's view of the present problem) one selects from memory a substantial structure called a frame. This is a remembered framework to be adapted to fit reality by changing details as necessary.

A *frame* is a data-structure for representing a stereotyped situation, like being in a certain kind of living room, or going to a child's birthday party. Attached to each frame are several kinds of information. Some of this information is about how to use the frame. Some is about what one can expect to happen next. Some is about what to do if these expectations are not confirmed.

We can think of a frame as a network of nodes and relations. The "top levels" of a frame are fixed, and represent things that are always true about the supposed situation. The lower levels have many *terminals*—"slots" that must be filled by specific instances or data. Each terminal can specify conditions its assignments must meet. (The assignments themselves are usually smaller "subframes.") Simple conditions are specified by markers that might require a terminal assignment to be a person, an object of sufficient value, or a pointer to a sub-frame of a certain type. More complex conditions can specify relations among the things assigned to several terminals.

Collections of related frames are linked together into *frame systems*. The effects of important actions are mirrored by transformations between the frames of a system. These are used to make certain kinds of calculations economical, to represent changes of emphasis and attention, and to account for the effectiveness of "imagery."

For visual scene analysis, the different frames of a system describe the scene from different viewpoints, and the transformations between one frame and another represent the effects of moving from place to place. For nonvisual kinds of frames, the differences between the frames of a system can represent actions, cause-effect relations, or changes in metaphorical viewpoint. Different frames of a system share the same terminals; this is the critical point that makes it possible to coordinate information gathered from different viewpoints.

Much of the phenomenological power of the theory hinges on the inclusion of expectations and other kinds of presumptions. A frame's terminals are normally already filled with "default" assignments. Thus, a frame may contain a great many details whose supposition is not specifically warranted by the situation. These have many uses in representing general information, most-likely cases, techniques for bypassing "logic," and ways to make useful generalizations.

The default assignments are attached loosely to their terminals, so that they can be easily displaced by new items that better fit the current situation. They thus can serve also as "variables" or as special cases for "reasoning by example," or as "textbook cases," and often make the use of logical quantifiers unnecessary.

The frame systems are linked, in turn, by an information retrieval network. When a proposed frame cannot be made to fit reality—when we cannot find terminal assignments that suitably match its terminal marker conditions—this network provides a replacement frame. These interframe structures make possible other ways to represent knowledge about facts, analogies, and other information useful in understanding.

Once a frame is proposed to represent a situation, a matching process tries to assign values to the terminals of each frame, consistent with the markers at each place. The matching process is partly controlled by information associated with the frame (which includes information about how to deal with surprises) and partly by knowledge about the system's current goals. There are important uses for the information obtained when a matching process fails. I will discuss how it can be used to select an alternative frame that better suits the situation.

Apology! The schemes proposed herein are incomplete in many respects. First, I often propose representations without specifying the processes that will use them. Sometimes I only describe properties the structures should exhibit. I talk about markers and assignments as though it were obvious how they are attached and linked; it is not.

Besides the technical gaps, I will talk as though unaware of many other important kinds of problems. I simplify many issues related to "under-standing" that really need much deeper analysis. I often treat statically things that probably require procedural representations. I do not claim that the ideas proposed here are enough for a complete theory, but only that the frame-system scheme may help explain a number of phenomena of human intelligence. The frame idea itself is not particularly original—it is in the tradition of the "schema" of Bartlett and the "paradigms" of Kuhn; the idea of a frame system is probably more novel.

6.1.1 Local and Global Theories for Vision

For there exists a great chasm between those, on the one side, who relate everything to a single central vision, one system more or less coherent or articulate, in terms of which they understand, think and feel—a single, universal, organizing principle in terms of which alone all that they are and say has significance—and, on the other side, those who pursue many ends, often unrelated and even contradictory, connected, if at all, only in some de facto way, for some psychological or physiological cause, related by no moral or esthetic principle....

—Berlin, I.: "The Hedgehog and the Fox," 1953

When we enter a room we seem to see the entire scene at a glance. But seeing is really an extended process. It takes time to fill in details, collect evidence, make conjectures, test, deduce, and interpret in ways that depend on our knowledge, expectations and goals. Wrong first impressions have to be revised. Nevertheless, all this proceeds so quickly and smoothly that it seems to demand a special explanation.

Some people dislike theories of vision that explain scene analysis largely in terms of discrete, serial, symbolic processes. They feel that although programs built on such theories may indeed seem to "see," they must be too slow and clumsy for a nervous system to use. But the alternative usually proposed is some extreme position of "holism" that never materializes into a technical proposal. I will argue that it is indeed possible for essentially serial symbolic mechanisms to explain much of the phenomenology of the apparent instantaneity and completeness of visual experience.

Some early Gestalt theorists tried to explain a variety of visual phenomena in terms of global properties of electrical fields in the brain. This idea did not come to much.[6] Its modern counterpart, a scattered collection of attempts to use ideas about integral transforms, holograms, and interference phenomena, has done no better. In spite of this, most thinkers outside (and some inside) the symbolic processing community still believe that only through some sort of field-like global parallel process could the required speed be attained.

While my theory is thus addressed to basic problems of Gestalt psychology, the method is fundamentally different. In both approaches, one wants to explain the structuring of sensory data into wholes and parts. Gestalt theorists hoped this could be based primarily on the operation of a few general and powerful principles; but these never crystallized effectively and the proposal lost popularity. In my theory the analysis is based on the interactions between sensations and a huge network of learned symbolic information. While ultimately those interactions must themselves be based also on a reasonable set of powerful principles, the performance theory is separate from the theory of how the system might originate and develop.

6.1.2 Parallelism

Would parallel processing help? This is a more technical question than it might seem. At the level of detecting elementary visual features, texture elements, stereoscopic and motion-parallax cues, it is obvious that parallel processing might be useful. At the level of grouping features into objects, it is harder to see exactly how to use parallelism, but one can at least conceive of the aggregation of connected "nuclei,"[7] or the application of boundary line constraint semantics,[8a] performed in a special parallel network.

At "higher" levels of cognitive processing, however, I suspect funda-mental limitations in the usefulness of parallelism. Many "integral" schemes were proposed in the literature on "pattern recognition" for parallel operations on pictorial material—perceptrons, integral transforms, skeletonizers, and so forth. These mathematically and computationally interesting schemes might quite possibly serve as ingredients of perceptual processing theories. But as ingredients only! Basically, "integral" methods work only on isolated figures in two dimensions. They fail disastrously to cope with complicated, three-dimensional scenery. Why?

In complex scenes, the features belonging to different objects have to be correctly segregated to be meaningful; but solving this problem—which is equivalent to the traditional Gestalt "figure-ground" problem—presupposes solutions for so many visual problems that the possibility and perhaps even the desirability of a separate recognition technique falls into question, as noted by Minsky and Papert.[9] In three dimensions the problem is further confounded by the distortion of perspective and by the occlusions of parts of each figure by its own surfaces and those of other figures.

The new, more successful symbolic theories use hypothesis formation and confirmation methods that seem, on the surface at least, more inherently serial. It is hard to solve any very complicated problem without giving essentially full attention, at different times, to different subproblems. Fortunately, however, beyond the brute idea of doing many things in parallel, one can imagine a more serial process that deals with large, complex, symbolic structures as units! This opens a new theoretical "niche" for performing a rapid selection of large substructures; in this niche our theory hopes to find the secret of speed, both in vision and in ordinary thinking.

6.1.3 Artificial Intelligence and Human Problem Solving

In this essay I draw no boundary between a theory of human thinking and a scheme for making an intelligent machine; no purpose would be served by separating these today since neither domain has theories good enough to explain—or to produce—mental imagery. There is, however, a difference in professional attitudes. Workers from psychology inherit stronger desires to minimize the variety of assumed mechanisms. I believe this leads to attempts to extract more performance from fewer "basic mechanisms" than is reasonable. Such theories especially neglect mechanisms of procedure control and explicit representations of processes. On the other side, workers in artificial intelligence have perhaps focused too sharply on just such questions. Neither have given enough attention to the structure of knowledge, especially procedural knowledge.

It is understandable why psychologists are uncomfortable with complex proposals not based on well established mechanisms. But I believe that parsimony is still inappropriate at this stage, valuable as it may be in later phases of every science. There is room in the anatomy and genetics of the brain for much more mechanism than anyone today is prepared to propose, and we should concentrate for a while more on sufficiency and efficiency rather than on necessity.

Up to a few years ago, the primary goal of AI work on vision had to be sufficiency: to find any way at all to make a machine analyze scenes. Only recently have we seen the first signs of adequate capacity to aggregate features and cues correctly into parts and wholes. I cite especially the sequence of work of Roberts,[10] Guzman,[7] Winston,[8b] Huffman,[11] Clowes,[12] Shirai,[13] Waltz,[8a] Binford and Horn,[14] Nevatia and Binford,[15] and Binford and Agin[16] to indicate some steps toward adequate analyses of figure-ground, whole-part, and group-structuring issues.

Although this line of development is still primitive, I feel it is sound enough that we can ask it to explain not only the brute performance of vision but also some of its speed and smoothness. Some new issues confront our theory when we turn from sufficiency to efficiency: How can different kinds of "cues" lead so quickly to identifying and describing complex situations? How can one one make changes in case of error or if new evidence is found? How does one resolve inconsistencies? How can position change without recomputing everything? What about moving objects? How does the vision process exploit knowledge associated with general, nonvisual activities? How does one synthesize the information obtained from different viewpoints? How can the system exploit generally correct expectations about effects of contemplated actions? Can the theory account for the phenomenological effects of imagery, the self-directed construction and manipulation of imaginary scenes?

Very little was learned about such matters in the main traditions of behavioral or of perceptual psychology; but the speculations of some earlier psychologists, particularly of Bartlett,[17] have surely found their way into this essay. In the more recent tradition of symbolic information processing theories, papers like those of Newell[18,19] and Pylyshyn[20] take larger technical steps to formulate these issues.

6.1.4 Tracking the Image of a Cube

But in the common way of taking the view of any opake object, that part of its surface, which fronts the eye, is apt to occupy the mind alone, and the opposite, nay even every other part of it whatever, is left unthought of at that time: and the least motion we make to reconnoitre any other side of the object, confounds our first idea, for want of the connexion of the two ideas, which the complete knowledge of the whole world would naturally have given us, if we had considered it the other way before.

—Hogarth, W.: The Analysis of Beauty, in "Hogarth Essays," 1955

I begin by developing a simplified frame system to represent the perspective appearances of a cube. Later I will adapt it to represent the insides of rooms and to acquiring, using, and revising the kinds of information one needs to move around within a house.

In the tradition of Guzman and Winston, I begin by assuming that the result of looking at a cube is a structure something like that in Fig. 6.1. The substructures A and B represent details or decorations on two faces of the cube. When we move to the right, face A disappears from view, while a new that all of them are normally necessary or that just one of each variety is adequate. It all depends.

I am not proposing that this kind of complicated structure is recreated every time one examines an object. I imagine instead that a great collection of frame systems is stored in permanent memory, and one of them is evoked

when evidence and expectation make it plausible that the scene in view will fit it. How are they acquired? I will propose that if a chosen frame does not fit well enough, and if no better one is easily found, and if the matter is important enough, then an adaptation of the best one so far discovered will be constructed and remembered for future use.

Do we build such a system for every object we know? That would seem extravagant. More likely, I would think, one has special systems for important objects but also a variety of frames for generally useful "basic shapes"; these are composed to form frames for new cases.

The different frames of a system resemble the multiple "models" described in Guzman[21] and Winston.[8b] Different frames correspond to different views, and the names of pointers between frames correspond to the motions or actions that change the viewpoint. Later I discuss whether these views should be considered as two- or as three-dimensional.

Each frame has terminals for attaching pointers to substructures. Different frames can share the same terminal, which can thus correspond to the same physical feature as seen in different views. This permits us to represent, in a single place, view-independent information gathered at different times and places. This is important also in nonvisual applications.

The matching process which decides whether a proposed frame is suitable is controlled partly by one's current goals and partly by information attached to the frame; the frames carry terminal markers and other constraints, while the goals are used to decide which of these constraints are currently relevant. Generally, the matching process could have these components:

1. A frame, once evoked on the basis of partial evidence or expectation, would first direct a test to confirm its own appropriateness, using knowledge about recently noticed features, loci, relations, and plausible subframes. The current goal list is used to decide which terminals and conditions must be made to match reality.

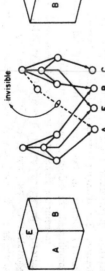

Fig. 6.3

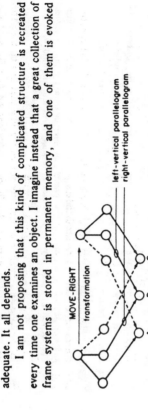

Fig. 6.1

face decorated with C is now seen. If we had to reanalyze the scene from the start, we would have to

1. lose the knowledge about A
2. recompute B
3. compute the description of C

But since we know we moved to the right, we can save B by assigning it also to the "left face" terminal of a second cube frame. To save A—just in case!—we connect it also to an extra, invisible face-terminal of the new cube-schema as in Fig. 6.2.

If later we move back to the left, we can reconstruct the first scene without any perceptual computation at all: just restore the top-level pointers to the first cube frame. We now need a place to store C; we can add yet another invisible face to the right in the first cube frame! (See Fig. 6.3.) We could extend this to represent further excursions around the object. This would lead to a more comprehensive frame system, in which each frame represents a different "perspective" of a cube. In Fig. 6.4 there are three frames corresponding to 45-degree MOVE-RIGHT and MOVE-LEFT actions. If we pursue this analysis, the resulting system can become very large; more complex objects need even more different projections. It is not obvious either

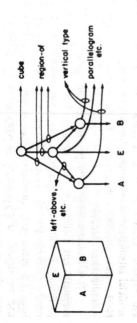

Fig. 6.2

the relations between parts of two-dimensional views? Let us separate, at once, the two issues: is imagery symbolic? and is it based on two-dimensional fragments? The first problem is one of degree; surely everyone would agree that at some level vision is essentially symbolic. The quarrel would be between certain naive conceptions on one side—in which one accepts seeing either as picture-like or as evoking imaginary solids—against the confrontation of such experimental results of Piaget and Inhelder[22] and others in which many limitations that one might fear would result from symbolic representations are shown actually to exist!

Thus we know that in the art of children (and, in fact, in that of most adult cultures) graphic representations are indeed composed from very limited, highly symbolic ingredients. See, for example, Chap. 2 of Gombrich.[23] Perspectives and occlusions are usually not represented "realistically" but by conventions. Metrical relations are grossly distorted; complex forms are replaced by signs for a few of their important features. Naive observers do not usually recognize these devices, and maintain that they do "see and manipulate pictorial images" in ways that, to them, could not conceivably be accounted for by discrete descriptions.

As for our second question, the issue of two vs. three dimensions evaporates at the symbolic level; the very concept of dimension becomes inappropriate. Each particular symbolic representation of an object serves some goals well and others poorly. If we attach the relation labels *left-of*, *right-of*, and *above* between parts of the structure, say, as markers on pairs of terminals, certain manipulations will work out smoothly; for example, some properties of these relations are "invariant" if we rotate the cube while keeping the same face on the table. Most objects have "permanent" tops and bottoms. But if we turn the cube on its side such predictions become harder to make; people have great difficulty keeping track of the faces of a six-colored cube if one makes them roll it around in their mind.

If one uses instead more "intrinsic" relations like *next-to* and *opposite-to*, then turning the object on its side disturbs the "image" much less. In Winston we see how systematic replacements (e.g., of "left" for "behind," and "right" for "in-front-of") can simulate the effect of spatial rotation.

Hogarth did not take a position on the symbolic issue, but he did consider good imagery to be an acquired skill and scolds artists who give too little time to perfecting the ideas they ought to have in their minds of the objects in nature. He recommends that

[he who will undertake the acquisition of] perfect ideas of the distances, bearings, and oppositions of several material points and lines in even the most irregular figures, will gradually arrive at the knack of recalling them into his mind when the objects themselves are not before him—and will be of infinite service to those who invent and draw from fancy, as well as to enable those to be more correct who draw from the life.

—Hogarth, W.: The Analysis of Beauty, in "Hogarth Essays," 1955

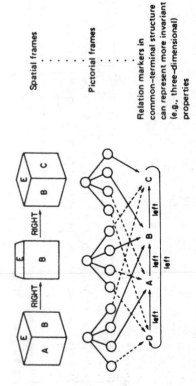

Spatial frames

Pictorial frames

Relation markers in common-terminal structure can represent more invariant (e.g., three-dimensional) properties

Fig. 6.4

2. Next it would request information needed to assign values to those terminals that cannot retain their default assignments. For example, it might request a description of face C, if this terminal is currently unassigned, but only if it is not marked "invisible." Such assignments must agree with the current markers at the terminal. For example, in assigning face C, one might already have markers for such constraints or expectations as:

Right-middle visual field
Must be assigned
Should be visible; if not, consider moving right
Should be a cube-face subframe
Share left vertical boundary terminal with face B
If failure, consider box-lying-on-side frame
Same background color as face B

3. Finally, if informed about a transformation (e.g., an impending motion) it would transfer control to the appropriate other frame of that system.

Within the details of the control scheme are opportunities to embed many kinds of knowledge. When a terminal-assigning attempt fails, the resulting error message can be used to propose a second-guess alternative. Later I will suggest using these to organize memory into a similarity network as proposed by Winston.[8b]

6.1.5 Is Vision Symbolic?

Can one really believe that a person's appreciation of three-dimensional structure can be so fragmentary and atomic as to be representable in terms of

Thus, deliberate self-discipline in cataloguing relations between points on opposing surfaces is, he thinks, a key to understanding the invariant relations between the visible and invisible parts; they supply the information needed to imagine oneself within the interior of the object, or at other unexperienced locations; he thus rejects the naive image idea.

Some people believe that we solve spatial problems by maintaining in one's head, somehow, the analog of a three-dimensional structure. But even if one somehow could assemble such a model there would remain, for the "mind's eye," most of the old problems we had for the real eye as well as the new and very hard problem of assembling—from two-dimensional data—the hypothetical imaginary solid.

Although these arguments may seem to favor interconnected two-dimensional views for aggregation and recognition, I do not consider these satisfactory for planning or for manipulative activities. Another representation, still symbolic but in terms of basic solid forms, would seem more natural. Thus a telephone handset could be described in terms of two modified spherical forms connected by a curved, rectangular bar. The problem of connecting two or more qualitatively different ways to represent the same thing is discussed, but not solved, in a later section.

6.1.6 Seeing a Room

Visual experience seems continuous. One reason is that we move continuously. A deeper explanation is that our "expectations" usually interact smoothly with our perceptions. Suppose you were to leave a room, close the door, turn to reopen it, and find an entirely different room. You would be shocked. The sense of change would be almost as startling as if the world suddenly changed before your eyes.

A naive theory of phenomenological continuity is that we see so quickly that our image changes as fast as does the scene. Below I press an alternative theory: the changes in one's frame-structure representation proceed at their own pace; the system prefers to make small changes whenever possible; and the illusion of continuity is due to the persistence of assignments to terminals common to the different view frames. Thus, continuity depends on the confirmation of expectations which in turn depends on rapid access to remembered knowledge about the visual world.

Just before you enter a room, you usually know enough to "expect" a room rather than, say, a landscape. You can usually tell just by the character of the door. And you can often select in advance a frame for the new room. Very often, one expects a certain particular room. Then many assignments are already filled in.

The simplest sort of room-frame candidate is like the inside of a box. Following our cube-model, the room-frame might have the structure shown in Fig. 6.5 at its top level.

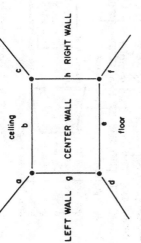

Fig. 6.5

One has to assign to the frame's terminals the things that are seen. If the room is familiar, some are already assigned. If no expectations are recorded already, the first priority might be locating the principal geometric landmarks. To fill in LEFT WALL one might first try to find edges a and d and then the associated corners ag and gd. Edge g, for example, is usually easy to find because it should intersect any eye-level horizontal scan from left to right. Eventually, ag, gb, and ba must not be too inconsistent with one another because they are the same physical vertex.

However the process is directed, there are some generally useful knowledge-based tactics. It is probably easier to find edge e than any other edge, because if we have just entered a normal rectangular room, then we may expect that

Edge e is a horizontal line.
It is below eye level.
It defines a floor-wall texture boundary.

Given an expectation about the size of a room, we can estimate the elevation of e, and vice versa. In outdoor scenes, e is the horizon and on flat ground we can expect to see it at eye level. If we fail quickly to locate and assign this horizon, we must consider rejecting the proposed frame: either the room is not normal or there is a large obstruction.

The room-analysis strategy might try next to establish some other landmarks. Given e, we next look for its left and right corners, and then for the verticals rising from them. Once such gross geometrical landmarks are located, we can guess the room's general shape and size. This might lead to selecting a new frame better matched to that shape and size, with additional markers confirming the choice and completing the structure with further details.

Of course a competent vision system has to analyze the scene not merely as a picture, but also in relation to some sort of external space-frame. For vision to proceed smoothly when one is moving around, one has to know where each feature "is," in the external world of mobility, to compensate for transformations induced by eye, head, and body motions, as well as for gross locomotion. I discuss this in Sec. 6.5.

6.1.7 Scene Analysis and Subframes

If the new room is unfamiliar, no preassembled frame can supply fine details; more scene analysis is needed. Even so, the complexity of the work can be reduced, given suitable subframes for constructing hypotheses about substructures in the scene. How useful these will be depends both on their inherent adequacy and on the quality of the expectation process that selects which one to use next. One can say a lot even about an unfamiliar room. Most rooms are like boxes, and they can be categorized into types: kitchen, hall, living room, theater, and so on. One knows dozens of kinds of rooms and hundreds of particular rooms; one no doubt has them structured into some sort of similarity network for effective access. This will be discussed later.

A typical room-frame has three or four visible walls, each perhaps of a different "kind." One knows many kinds of walls: walls with windows, shelves, pictures, and fireplaces. Each kind of room has its own kinds of walls.

A typical wall might have a 3 X 3 array of region-terminals given by combinations of (left-center-right) and (top-middle-bottom) so that wall objects can be assigned qualitative locations. One would further want to locate objects relative to geometric interrelations in order to represent such facts as "Y is a little above the center of the line between X and Z."

In three dimensions, the location of a visual feature of a subframe is ambiguous, given only eye direction. A feature in the middle of the visual field could belong either to a Center Front Wall object or to a High Middle Floor object; these attach to different subframes. The decision could depend on reasoned evidence for support, on more directly visual distance information derived from stereo disparity or motion-parallax, or on plausibility information derived from other frames. A clock would be plausible only on the wall-frame while a person is almost certainly standing on the floor.

I do not imagine the boundaries of spatial frame cells to be constrained by accurate metrical dimensions. Each cell terminal would specify the (approximate) location of a typically central place in that cell, and some comparative size range. We expect correct topological constraints; a left-wall-edge must agree to stay to the left of any object assigned to lie flat against that wall. The process of "matching" a scene to an acceptable subset of all such constraints may result in a certain degree of "strain," as a cell is expanded (against its size-range specification) to include the objects proposed for its interior. The tolerance of such strains should depend on constraint priorities that in turn should depend on one's current purpose, past experience, and so forth. I repeat: the richness of visual experience does not support, at this stage, a drive toward the most elegant and parsimonious theory.

6.1.8 Perspective and Viewpoint Transformations

In sum, at Substage IIIB (age 8 or 9, typically) the operations required to coordinate perspectives are complete, and in the following quite independent forms. First, to each position of the observer there corresponds a particular set of left-right, before-behind relations between the objects.... These are governed by the projections and sections appropriate to the visual plane of the observer (perspective). During this final substage the point to point nature of the correspondence between position and perspective is discovered. Second, between each perspective viewpoint valid for a given position of the observer and each of the others, there is also a correspondence expressed by specific changes of left-right, before-behind relations, and consequently by changes of the appropriate projections and sections. It is this correspondence between all possible points of view which constitutes co-ordination of perspectives .. though as yet only in a rudimentary form.

—Piaget, J., and Inhelder, B.: "The Child's Conception of Space," 1956

When we move about a room, the shapes of things change. How can these changes be anticipated, or compensated, without complete reprocessing? The results of eye and head rotation are simple: things move in the visual field but keep their shapes; but changing place causes large shape changes that depend both on angle and on distance relations between the object and observer. The problem is particularly important for fast-moving animals because a model of the scene must be built up from different, partially analyzed views. Perhaps the need to do this, even in a relatively primitive fashion, was a major evolutionary stimulus to develop frame systems, and later, other symbolic mechanisms.

Given a box-shaped room, lateral motions induce orderly changes in the quadrilateral shapes of the walls as in Fig. 6.6. A picture-frame rectangle, lying

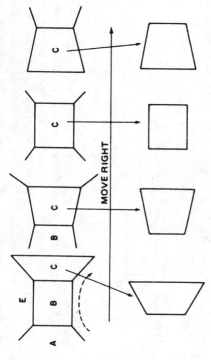

MOVE RIGHT

Fig. 6.6

flat, we assume that an ellipse on a left wall is a left-ellipse, expect it to transform the same way as the left wall, and are surprised if the prediction is not confirmed.

Is it plausible that a finite, qualitative symbolic system can represent perspective transformations adequately? People in our culture are chronically unrealistic about their visualization abilities, e.g., to visualize how spatial relations will appear from other viewpoints. We noted that people who claim to have clear images of such configurations often make qualitative errors in describing the rotations of a simple multicolored cube. And even where we are actually able to make accurate metrical judgements we do not always make them; few people are disturbed by Huffman's "impossible" pyramid, shown in Fig. 6.9. This is not a perspective of any actual truncated pyramid; if it were, the three edges when extended would all meet at one point. In well-developed skills, no doubt, people can routinely make more precise judgements, but this need not require a different mechanism. Where a layman uses 10 frames for some job, an expert might use 1000 and thus get the appearance of a different order of performance.

In any case, to correctly anticipate perspective changes in our systems, the top-level transformation must induce appropriate transforms in the subframe systems. To a first approximation, this can be done simply by using the same transformation names. Then a "move-right" action on a room frame would induce a "move-right" action on objects attached to the wall subframes (and to their subframes).

I said "first approximation" because this scheme has a serious bug. If you stand near a left wall and walk forward, the nearby left-wall objects suffer a large "move-right" transform, the front wall experiences a "move closer" transform, and the right wall experiences a small "move left" transform. So matters are not so simple that it is always sufficient merely to transmit the motion name down to lower levels.

6.1.9 Occlusions

When we move to the right, a large object in the center foreground will probably occlude any further-away object to its visual left. When a motion is planned, one should be able to anticipate some of these changes. Some objects should become invisible and other objects should appear. Our prototype cube system has no occlusion problem because the scene is completely convex; the disappearance of an entire side and its contents is easily handled at the top level. But in a room, which is basically concave, the subobjects of different terminals can occlude one another. We consider two extreme strategies:

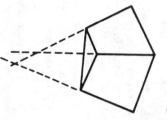

Fig. 6.9

flat against a wall, should transform in the same way as does its wall. If a "center rectangle" is drawn on a left wall it will appear to project out because one makes the default assumption that any such quadrilateral is actually a rectangle, and hence it must lie in a plane that would so project. In Fig. 6.7(a), both quadrilaterals could "look like" rectangles, but the one to the right does not match the markers for a "left rectangle" subframe (these require, e.g., that the left side be longer than the right side). That rectangle is therefore represented by a center-rectangle frame and seems to project out as though parallel to the center wall.

Thus we must not simply assign the label "rectangle" to a quadrilateral but to a particular frame of a rectangle system. When we move, we expect whatever space transformation is applied to the top-level system will be applied also to its subsystems as suggested in Fig. 6.7(b). Similarly the sequence of elliptical projections of a circle contains congruent pairs that are visually ambiguous as shown in Fig. 6.8. But because wall objects usually lie

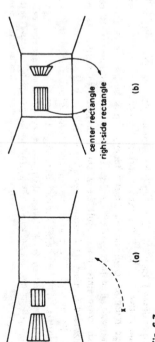

center rectangle

right-side rectangle

(a)

(b)

Fig. 6.7

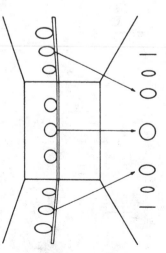

Two figures are congruent, but transform differently.

Fig. 6.8

sensation, or anticipates it by his imagination. These faculties may mimic or copy the perceptions of the senses; but they never can entirely reach the force and vivacity of the original sentiment... The most lively thought is still inferior to the dullest sensation.

—Hume, D.: An Enquiry Concerning Human Understanding

A theory of seeing should be also a theory of imagining. In our concept both have the same end results: assignments to terminals of frames. Everyone will agree with Hume that there are differences between vision and imagery. Hume theorizes that this is because vision is immediate and direct, whereas imagery is derived from recombinations of memories of direct "impressions" and that some of the force is lost, somehow, in the storage, retrieval, and computation. I propose instead that seeing seems more vivid than imagining because its assignments are less flexible: they more firmly resist the attempts of other processes to modify them. If you try to change the description of a scene actually projected on your retinae, your vision system is likely simply to change it right back. There is no correspondingly rigid constraint on phantasies.

However, even "seen" assignments are not completely inflexible; anyone can learn to mentally reverse the interpretation of a skeleton-cube drawing. So-called "ambiguous" figures are those that are easy to describe in different ways. Changing a frame for such a purpose amounts to a change in "descriptive viewpoint," one in which the action or transformation is symbolic rather than physical; in any case, we are told that there are mental states in which phantasies are more inflexible than "direct impressions" and even, sometimes, more "vivid."

6.1.11 Default Assignment

While both seeing and imagining result in assignments to frame terminals, imagination leaves us wider choices of detail and variety of such assignments. I conjecture that frames are never stored in long-term memory with unassigned terminal values. Instead, what really happens is that frames are stored with weakly bound default assignments at every terminal! These manifest themselves as often useful but sometimes counterproductive stereotypes.

Thus if I say, "John kicked the ball," you probably cannot think of a purely abstract ball, but must imagine characteristics of a vaguely particular ball; it probably has a certain default size, default color, default weight. Perhaps it is a descendant of one you first owned or were injured by. Perhaps it resembles your latest one. In any case your image lacks the sharpness of presence because the processes that inspect and operate upon the weakly bound default features are very likely to change, adapt, or detach them.

Such default assignments would have subtle, idiosyncratic influences on the paths an individual would tend to follow in making analogies, generalizations, and judgments, especially when the exterior influences on such choices are weak. Properly chosen, such stereotypes could serve as a storehouse of

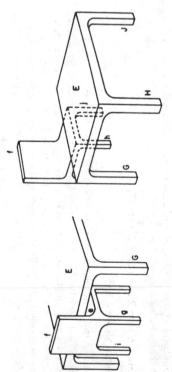

Fig. 6.10

Local assemblies: Just as for the different views of a single object, occlusions of a familiar assembly could be handled by a special frame system for that configuration; e.g., a chair and table as in Fig. 6.10. If we apply the same perspective transformations to such a "niche-frame" that we apply to its superiors, then to a first approximation, occlusions between the objects are handled automatically.

This works for compact, familiar subgroups of objects but cannot handle the details of occlusions between elements of the niche and other things in the room. For engineering applications the scheme's simplicity would not outweigh its frequent errors. As a theory of human performance, it might be good enough. A trained artist or draftsman can answer such questions better, but such activities proceed slowly and need not be explained by a first-order theory concerned mainly with speed.

Global occlusion system: A more radical scheme would make all perspective frames subsidiary to a central, common, space-frame system. The terminals of that system would correspond to cells of a gross subjective space, whose transformations represent, once-and-for-all, facts about which cells occlude others from different viewpoints.

If there were such a supersystem, would it be learned or innate? The context of the Piaget-Inhelder quotation presents evidence that complete coordination structures of this sort are not available to children in their first decade.

6.1.10 Imagery and Frame Systems

Everyone will readily allow that there is a considerable difference between the perceptions of the mind, when a man feels the pain of excessive heat, or the pleasure of moderate warmth, and when he afterwards recalls to his memory this formalisms into "universal" ones, but it might be hard to do this in ways easy to develop or practical to use.

It appears that only with the emergence of Piaget's "formal" stage (for perspective, not usually until the second decade) are children reliably able to reason *about*, rather than *with* transformations. Nor do such capacities appear at once, or synchronously in all mental activities. To get greater reasoning power—and to be released from the useful but unreliable pseudologic of manipulating default assignments—one must learn the equivalent of operating on the transformations themselves. (One needs to get at the transformations because they contain knowledge needed for more sophisticated reasoning.) In a computational model constructed for artificial intelligence, one might try to make the system read its own programs. An alternative is to represent (redundantly) information about processes some other way. Workers on recent "program-understanding" programs in our laboratory have usually decided, for one reason or another, that programs should carry "commentaries" that express more directly their intentions, prerequisites, and effects; these commentaries are (at present) usually written in specialized sublanguages.

This raises an important point about the purpose of our theory. "Schematic" thinking, based on matching complicated situations against stereotyped frame structures, must be inadequate for some aspects of mental activity. Obviously mature people can to some extent think about, as well as use their own representations. Let us speculatively interpret "formal operations" as processes that can examine and criticize our earlier representations (be they frame-like or whatever). With these we can begin to build up new structures to correspond to "representations of representations." I have no idea what role frame systems might play in these more complex activities.

The same strategy suggests that we identify (schematically, at least) the direct use of frames with Piaget's "concrete operations." If we do this then I find Piaget's explanation of the late occurrence of "formal thinking" paradoxically reassuring. In first trying to apply the frame-system paradigm to various problems, I was disturbed by how well it explained some things and how poorly others. But it was foolish to expect any single scheme to explain very much about thinking. Certainly one cannot expect to solve all the problems of sophisticated reasoning within a system confined to concrete operations—if that indeed amounts to the manipulation of stereotypes.

6.2 LANGUAGE, UNDERSTANDING, AND SCENARIOS

6.2.1 Words, Sentences, and Meanings

The device of images has several defects that are the price of its peculiar excellences. Two of these are perhaps the most important: the image, and particularly the visual image, is apt to go farther in the direction of the individualization of situation than is biologically useful; and the principles of the

---

valuable heuristic plan-skeletons; badly selected, they could form paralyzing collections of irrational biases. Because of them one might expect, as reported by Freud, to detect evidences of early cognitive structures in "free association" thinking.

6.1.12 Frame-Systems and Piaget's Concrete Operations

What, in effect, are the conditions for the construction of formal thought? The child must not only apply operations to objects—in other words, mentally execute possible actions on them—he must also "reflect" those operations in the absence of the objects which are replaced by pure propositions. This "reflection" is thought raised to the second power. Concrete thinking is the representation of a possible action, and formal thinking is the representation of a representation of possible action.

It is not surprising, therefore, that the system of concrete operations must be completed during the last years of childhood before it can be "reflected" by formal operations. In terms of their function, formal operations do not differ from concrete operations except that they are applied to hypotheses or propositions [whose logic is] an abstract translation of the system of "inference" that governs concrete operations.

—Piaget, J.: "Mental Imagery in the Child: A Study of the Development of Imaginal Representation," 1971

I think there is a similarity between Piaget's idea of a concrete operation and the effects of applying a transformation between frames of a system. What kinds of superficially "logical" operations are easy to perform with frames by using loosely attached default assignments? It should be easy, for example, to find the transitivity of instantiation of subframes; thus surface syllogisms of the form

All A's are B's and All B's are C's
⇒
All A's are C's

would occur in the natural course of substituting acceptable subframes into marked terminals of a frame. (I do not mean that the generalization itself is asserted, but only that its content is applied to particular cases because of the transitivity of instantiation of subframes.) One would expect, then, to also find the same belief in

Most A's are B's and Most B's are C's
⇒
Most A's are C's

even though this is sometimes false, as some adults have learned.

I do not understand the limitations of what can be done by simple processes working on frames. One could surely invent some "inference-frame technique" that culd be used to rearrange terminals of other frames so as to simulate deductive logic. As in other aspects of the theory of computation, we often find tricky encoding operations to transform these apparently limited combination of images have their own peculiarities and result in constructions which are relatively wild, jerky and irregular, compared with the straightforward unwinding of a habit, or with the somewhat orderly march of thought.

—Bartlett, F. C.: "Remembering: A Study in Experimental and Social Psychology," 1932 (revised, 1961)

The concepts of frame and default assignment seem helpful in discussing the phenomenology of "meaning." Chomsky[24] points out that such a sentence as

a. "colorless green ideas sleep furiously"

is treated very differently than the nonsentence

b. "furiously sleep ideas green colorless"

and suggests that because both are "equally nonsensical," what is involved in the recognition of sentences must be quite different from what is involved in the appreciation of meanings.

There is no doubt that there are processes especially concerned with grammar. Since the meaning of an utterance is "encoded" as much in the positional and structural relations between the words as in the word choices themselves, there must be processes concerned with analyzing those relations in the course of building the structures that will more directly represent the meaning. What makes the words of (a) more effective and predictable than (b) in producing such a structure—putting aside the question of whether that structure should be called semantic or syntactic—is that the word-order relations in (a) exploit the (grammatical) conventions and rules people usually use to induce others to make assignments to terminals of structures. This is entirely consistent with grammar theories. A generative grammar would be a summary description of the exterior appearance of those frame rules—or their associated processes—while the operators of transformational grammars seem similar enough to some of our frame transformations.

But one must also ask: to what degree does grammar have a separate identity in the actual working of a human mind? Perhaps the rejection of an utterance (either as nongrammatical, as meaningless, or most important, as not understood) indicates a more complex failure of the semantic process to arrive at any usable representation; I will argue now that the grammar-meaning distinction may illuminate two extremes of a continuum, but obscures its all-important interior.

We certainly cannot assume that "logical" meaninglessness has a precise psychological counterpart. Sentence (a) can certainly generate an image! The dominant frame (in my case) is that of someone sleeping; the default system assigns a particular bed, and in it lies a mummy-like shape-frame with a translucent green color property. In this frame there is a terminal for the character of the sleep—restless, perhaps—and "furiously" seems somewhat inappropriate at that terminal, perhaps because the terminal does not like to accept anything so "intentional" for a sleeper. "Idea" is even more disturbing, because a person is expected, or at least something animate. I sense frustrated

procedures trying to resolve these tensions and conflicts more properly, here or there, into the sleeping framework that has been evoked.

Utterance (b) does not get nearly so far because no subframe accepts any substantial fragment. As a result no larger frame finds anything to match its terminals, hence finally, no top level "meaning" or "sentence" frame can organize the utterance as either meaningful or grammatical. By combining this "soft" theory with gradations of assignment tolerances, I imagine one could develop systems that degrade properly for sentences with "poor" grammar rather than none; if the smaller fragments—phrases and subclauses—satisfy subframes well enough, an image adequate for certain kinds of comprehension could be constructed anyway, even though some parts of the top level structure are not entirely satisfied. Thus, we arrive at a qualitative theory of "grammatical:" if the top levels are satisfied but some lower terminals are not we have a meaningless sentence; if the top is weak but the bottom solid, we can have an ungrammatical but meaningful utterance.

I do not mean to suggest that sentences must evoke visual images. Some people do not admit to assigning a color to the ball in "he kicked the ball." But everyone admits (eventually) to having assumed, if not a size or color, at least some purpose, attitude, or other elements of an assumed scenario. When we go beyond vision, terminals and their default assignments can represent purposes and functions, not just colors, sizes and shapes.

6.2.2 Discourse

Linguistic activity involves larger structures than can be described in terms of sentential grammar, and these larger structures further blur the distinctness of the syntax-semantic dichotomy. Consider the following fable, as told by W. Chafe.[25]

There was once a Wolf who saw a Lamb drinking at a river and wanted an excuse to eat it. For that purpose, even though he himself was upstream, he accused the Lamb of stirring up the water and keeping him from drinking ...

To understand this, one must realize that the Wolf is lying! To understand the key conjunctive "even though" one must realize that contamination never flows upstream. This in turn requires us to understand (among other things) the word "upstream" itself. Within a declarative, predicate-based "logical" system, one might try to axiomatize "upstream" by some formula like:

A upstream B

[Event T, Stream muddy at A]
⇒
[Exists [Event U, Stream muddy at B]]

Later U, T

But an adequate definition would need a good deal more. What about the fact that the order of things being transported by water currents is not ordinarily changed? A logician might try to deduce this from a suitably intricate set of "local" axioms, together with appropriate "induction" axioms. I propose instead to represent this knowledge in a structure that automatically translocates spatial descriptions from the terminals of one frame to those of another frame of the same system. While this might be considered to be a form of logic, it uses some of the same mechanisms designed for spatial thinking.

In many instances we would handle a change over time, or a cause-effect relation, in the same way as we deal with a change in position. Thus, the concept *river-flow* could evoke a frame-system structure something like that shown below, where S1, S2, and S3 are abstract slices of the flowing river shown in Fig. 6.11. In my default system the Wolf is at the left, the Lamb at the right, and S1, S2, and S3 flow past them. In the diagram, presume that the S's cannot be seen unless they are directly next to either the wolf or the lamb. On reflection, my imaginary currents usually flow from left to right, and I find it some effort to use reversed versions. Perhaps they all descend from copies of the same protosystem.

The time (and not coincidentally, current) transformation represents part of our understanding of the effects of the flow of the river. If the terminal S3 is the mud effect produced by the Lamb, the frame system causes the mud effect to become invisible and not near the Wolf. Thus, he has no valid reason to complain. A more detailed system could have intermediate frames; none of them is the Wolf contaminated.

There are many more nuances to fill in. What is "stirring up" and why would it keep the wolf from drinking? One might normally assign default floating objects to the S's, but here S3 interacts with "stirring up" to yield something that "drink" does not find acceptable. Was it "deduced" that

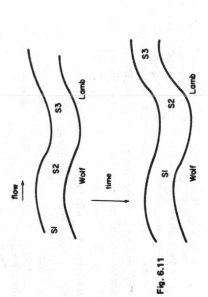

Fig. 6.11

stirring river-water means that S3 in the first frame should have "mud" assigned to it; or is this simply the default assignment for stirred water? The meaning of "eat" ought to be understood, too. In children's stories, being eaten is a bad way to disappear, but it is not always irreversible.

Almost any event, action, change, flow of material, or even flow of information can be represented to a first approximation by a two-frame generalized event. One can have slots for agents, tools, side-effects, preconditions, generalized trajectories, just as in the "trans" verbs of "case grammar" theories.

To see if one has understood an event or action, one can try to build an appropriate instantiated frame-pair. If one stores the important parts of the new construct so that it can be retrieved under similar conditions, one should understand it faster the next time. Thus the relation between understanding and learning should be very intimate.

But in representing changes by simple "before-after" frame-pairs, one may have to pay a price for the convenience of using implicit representation: it will not make it easy to do planning or abstract reasoning. The problem is that with implicit representation, there is no convenient place to attach properties of, or information about, the transformation. As a second approximation, we could label pairs of nodes that point to corresponding terminals, obtaining structure like the "comparison-notes" in Winston,[8] or we might place at the top of the frame system information describing the differences more abstractly. Something of this sort will be needed eventually.

This is perhaps a good point to mention the work of R. Schank on "conceptual dependency",[26] he attempts to construct representations of the meanings of such diverse assertions as "Sam believes that John is a fool" (in which the thing that Sam believes is not an object but requires a "conceptualization"), or "Q: Do you want a piece of chocolate? A: No. I just had an ice cream cone" (in which understanding requires representing details of a complex notion of satiation).

Schank proposes a small collection of "basic conceptualizations" and relations between them from which to build representations for any meaning. I find it hard to decide how adequate these are. How well, for example, could they describe flows? His schemes include an idea of "conceptual cases," which resemble some of our frame-terminals. (See Sec. 6.2.8.) His representation scheme is quite different from mine, at least on the surface, in that, e.g., he attempts to represent the effects of actions more abstractly than as a before-after transformation pair. It remains to be seen, for example, how a single abstract concept of cause (or even several) would be used in a functioning "belief system." It certainly would not be enough to characterize causality only in terms of one condition or action being necessary for another to happen. Putting details aside, what is important, I think, is that Schank has made a strong start on an important and neglected area of epistemology and, once this area develops some performance tests, it should yield good knowledge-representation methods.

The work of Y. Wilks[27] on "preference semantics" also seems rich in ideas about ways to build frame-like structures out of simpler ones, and his preference proposals embody specific ways one might represent default assignments and procedures for making them depend on larger aspects of a discourse than mere sentences. Wilks' system is interesting also in demonstrating, I think, ways in which one can get some useful informal reasoning or pseudodeduction as a product of the template building and instantiation processes without an elaborate formal logical system or undue concern with consistency.

R. P. Abelson[4] has worked toward representing even more extended activities. Beginning with elements like Schank's, he works out schemes in which the different concepts interact, arriving at intricate scripts—skeletonized scenarios of elaborate belief systems, attempting even to portray such interactions as one's image of the role he plays in another person's plans.

D. McDermott[28] discusses many issues related to knowledge representations. In his scheme for plausible inference, statements are not simply accepted, but are subjected to a process of "doubting" and "believing"; in effect, things assumed by default (or plausibility) are retained with mechanisms for revising those beliefs when later, dependent assumptions run into problems. McDermott is particularly attentive to the problems involved in recovery from the errors any such system is forced to make in the course of informal, common sense inference.

6.2.3 Meaning-Structure of a Discourse

Words . . . can indicate the qualitative and relational features of a situation in their general aspect just as directly as, and perhaps even more satisfactorily than, they can describe its particular individuality. This is, in fact, what gives to language its intimate relation to thought processes. For thinking, in the proper psychological sense, is never the mere reinstatement of some suitable past situation produced by a crossing of interests, but is the utilization of the past in solution of difficulties set by the present. . . . Equally, nobody ever thinks who, being challenged, merely sets up an image from some more or less relevant situation, and then finds for himself a solution, without in any way formulating the relational principle involved.

—Bartlett, F. C.: "Remembering: A Study in Experimental and Social Psychology," 1932 (revised, 1961)

"Case grammar" sentence-analysis theories such as those of Fillmore[29] and Celce-Murcia[30] involve structures somewhat like frames. Centered mainly around the verb, parts of a sentence are used to instantiate a sort of verb frame in accord with various uses of prepositions. I agree that this surely is a real phenomenon; sentences are built around verbs, so it makes sense to use verb-centered frame-like structures for analyzing sentences.

In more extended discourse, however, I think that verb-centered structures often become subordinate or even disappear. The topic or "theme" of a paragraph is as likely to be a scene as to be an action, as likely to be a characterization of a person as to be something he is doing. Thus in understanding a discourse, the synthesis of a verb-structure with its case

assignments may be a necessary but transient phase. As sentences are understood, the resulting substructures must be transferred to a growing "scene frame" to build up the larger picture. An action that is the chief concern of one sentence might, for example, become subsidiary to a characterization of one of the actors in a larger story-frame.

I am not proposing anything like "verbs describe local (sentential) structures and nouns describe global (paragraphic) structures"—although that might be a conceptually useful first approximation. Any concept can be invoked by all sorts of linguistic representations. It is not a matter of nouns or verbs. The important point is that we must not assume that the transient semantic structure built during the syntactic analysis (what language theorists today call the "deep structure" of a sentence) is identical with the larger (and "deeper") structure built up incrementally as each fragment of a coherent linguistic communication operates upon it!

I do not want this emphasis on topical or thematic superframes to suggest a radical confrontation between linguistic vs. nonlinguistic representations. Introspectively, a substantial portion of common sense thinking and reasoning seem to resemble linguistic transformations and other manipulations. The frames associated with word senses, be they noun, verb or whatever, are surely centers for the concentrated representation of vital knowledge about how different things are related, how they are used, and how they transform one another. Practically, there would be large advantages in having mechanisms that could use these same structures both for thinking and for communicating.

Let us imagine a frame-oriented scenario for how coherent discourse might be represented. At the start of a story, we know little other than that it will be a story, but even this gives us a start. A conventional frame for "story" (in general) would arrive with slots for setting, protagonists, main event, moral, etc. Indeed, the first line of a properly told story usually helps with the setting; the wolf and lamb story immediately introduces two antagonists, places them by the river (setting), and provides the wolf with a motive. The word "excuse" somehow prepares us for the likelihood of the wolf making false statements.

Each sentential analysis need be maintained only until its contents can be used to instantiate a larger structure. The terminals of the growing meaning-structure thus accumulate indicators and descriptors, which expect and key further assignments. A terminal that has acquired a "female person" marker will reject "male" pronominal assignments using, I suppose, the same sorts of considerations that resist assignment of tables and chairs to terminals of wall frames. As the story proceeds, information is transferred to superframes whenever possible, instantiating or elaborating the scenario. In some cases we will be lucky enough to attach a whole subframe, for example, a description of the hero, to a single terminal in the superframe. This could happen if a terminal of the "story" superframe matches a top level indicator on the current sentence-frame. Other sentences might produce relations constraining pairs of already existing terminals. But what if no such transfer can be made because the listener expected a wrong kind of story and has no terminals to receive the new structure?

We go on to suppose that the listener actually has many story frames, linked by the kinds of retrieval structures discussed later on. First we try to fit the new information into the current story frame. If we fail, we construct an error comment like "there is no place here for an animal." This causes us to replace the current story frame by, say, an animal-story frame. The new assignments to terminals may all survive, if the new story frame has the same kinds of terminals. But if many previous assignments do not so transfer, we must get another new story frame. If we fail, we must either construct a basically new story frame—a major intellectual event, perhaps—or just give up and forget the assignments. (Presumably that is the usual reaction to radically new narrative forms! One does not learn well if the required jumps are too large: one cannot really understand animal stories until one possesses the conventional personality frames for the wolf, pig, fox, etc.)

Thus a discourse assembles a network of instantiated frames and subframes. Attributive or descriptive information can often be represented by simple substructures, but actions, temporal successions, explanations and other complicated things surely need more elaborate attachments. We must recognize that profoundly hard questions, central to epistemology as well as to linguistics, are entrained in this problem of how to merge information from different sources and subframes. The next few sections raise more questions about these than they begin to answer.

6.2.4 Language Translation

Translation affords an opportunity to observe defaults at work. In translating the story about the wolf and the lamb from English to Japanese, according to Chafe, it is required to mention the place on the river where the actors stand, although it is not required in English. In English one must cite the time—if only by saying "Once...." In Japanese, it is customary to characterize the place, as well as the time, even if only by a nonspecific "In a certain place...."

I think both place and time are required, in the deeper meaning frames of people who think much as we do whatever natural language they speak! Hence, default assignments for both would be immediately available to the translator if he understood the sentence at all. Good simultaneous translators proceed so rapidly that one wonders how much they can really understand before speaking; our theory makes this less of an issue because if the proper frame is retrieved in the course of partial understanding, its default assignments are available instantly, before the more complex assignment negotiations are completed.

A translation of "The Wolf and Lamb" into Japanese with acceptable surface structure might be, according to Chafe,

Once certain place in river at water drinking be child-sheep saw one animal wolf was and that wolf that child-sheep eat for excuse make-want-seeming was....

It is more natural, in Japanese, to say what the Lamb was drinking than just to say he was drinking. Here is one way that language affects thinking: each such linguistic convention focuses special attention on filling certain terminals. If water is the usual thing to drink in one's culture, then water is the default assignment for what is being drunk. When speech production requires such an assignment in a sentence-output frame, that default will normally be assumed. Of course, one should be even more certain of water if the drinking is done beside a river; this needs some machinery for relating drinking and river stereotypes. It seems clear that if there is a weakly bound drinkable-fluid slot in one frame, and a strongly bound drinkable fluid in the subframe to be attached, the latter should dislodge the former. Thus, even if our listener usually drinks wine, he should correctly imagine the lamb drinking water.

6.2.5 Active Vs. Passive

In our traditional "folk phenomenology," seeing and imagining are usually seen as "passive" and "active." It is tempting to exploit this viewpoint for vision:

In seeing, one analyzes a scene by assembling and instantiating frames, generally without much choice because of the domination of the need to resolve "objective" visual evidence against the need for a consistent and plausible spatial scene-description.

In imagining, we have much more choice, for we are trying to assemble and instantiate frames to represent a "scene" that satisfies internally chosen—hence changeable—goals.

In language, a similar contrast is tempting:

In listening (which includes parsing) one has little choice because of the need to resolve the objective word string into a structure consistent with grammar, context, and the (assumed) intention.

In speaking, we have much more choice, because there are so many ways to assemble sentence-making frames for our chosen purpose, be it to inform, convince, or mislead.

However, these are dangerous oversimplifications; things are often quite the other way around! Speaking is often a straightforward encoding from a semantic structure into a word sequence, while listening often involves extensive and difficult constructions—which involve the totality of complexities we call understanding.

Consider the analogy between a frame for a room in a visual scene and a frame for a noun phrase in a discourse. In each case, some assignments to terminals are mandatory, while others are optional. A wall need not be decorated, but every moveable object must be supported. A noun phrase need not contain a numerical determiner, but it must contain a noun or pronoun equivalent. One generally has little choice so far as surface structure is concerned: one must account for all the words in a sentence and for all the major features of a scene. However, surface structure is not everything in vision or in language. One has unlimited options about incorporating consequences of context and knowledge into semantic structure. An object has not only a visual form, but a history. Its presence has usually a cause and often some other significance—perhaps as a clue in a puzzle, or as a symbol of a changing relationship.

Any sentence can be understood in many ways. I emphasize that I am not talking of the accidental (and relatively unimportant) ambiguities of parsing, but of the purposeful variations of interpretation. Just as any room can be seen from different physical viewpoints, so any assertion can be "viewed" from different representational viewpoints as in the following, each of which suggests a different structure:

He kicked the ball.
The ball was kicked.

or even

There was some kicking today.

Because these variations formally resemble the results of the syntactic, active-passive operations of transformational grammars, one might overlook their semantic significance. We select one or the other in accord with thematic issues—on whether one is concerned with what "he" did, with finding a lost ball, with who damaged it, or whatever. One answers such questions most easily by bringing the appropriate entity or action into the focus of attention by evoking a frame primarily concerned with that topic.

In the traditional view of transformational linguistics, these alternate frames have no separate existence but are only potential derivatives from a single deep structure. There is an advantage to supposing their separate existence in long term memory: we could attach specific knowledge to each about how it should be used. However, as language theorists rightly point out, there are systematic regularities which suggest that such "transformations" are nearly as readily applied to unfamiliar verbs with the same redirections of concern; this makes separate existence less plausible. I have the impression that transformational theorists tend to believe in some special central mechanisms for management of such changes of "semantic perspective," even though, I should think, the variety of idiosyncracies attached to individual words makes this technically difficult. A theory more in the spirit of this essay would suggest that whenever one encounters an unfamiliar usage (or an unfamiliar word) he applies some matching process to guess—rightly or wrongly—which familiar usage it resembles, and then adapts the existing attention-transformation system for that word. I cannot see what kind of experiment might distinguish between these conjectures, but I still feel that the distinction is important.

Some readers might object that things should not be so complicated—that we need a simpler theory if only to explain how people understand sentences so quickly. One must not forget that it often takes minutes, hours, or forever, to understand something.

6.2.6 Scenarios

Thinking ... is biologically subsequent to the image-forming process. It is possible only when a way has been found of breaking up the "massed" influence of past stimuli and situations, only when a device has already been discovered for conquering the sequential tyranny of past reactions. But though it is a later and a higher development, it does not supercede the method of images. It has its own drawbacks. Contrasted with imaging it loses something of vivacity, of vividness, of variety. Its prevailing instruments are words, and, not only because these are social, but also because in use they are necessarily strung out in sequence, they drop into habit reactions even more readily than images do. [With thinking] we run greater and greater risk of being caught up in generalities that may have little to do with actual concrete experience. If we fail to maintain the methods of thinking, we run the risks of becoming tied to individual instances and of being made sport of by the accidental circumstances belonging to these.

—Bartlett, F. C.: "Remembering: A Study in Experimental and Social Psychology," 1932, (revised, 1961)

We condense and conventionalize, in language and thought, complex situations and sequences into compact words and symbols. Some words can perhaps be "defined" in elegant, simple structures, but only a small part of the meaning of "trade" is captured by

first frame   second frame

A has X   B has Y   →   B has X   A has Y

Trading normally occurs in a social context of law, trust, and convention. Unless we also represent these other facts, most trade transactions will be almost meaningless. It is usually essential to know that each party usually wants both things but has to compromise. It is a happy but unusual circumstance in which each trader is glad to get rid of what he has. To represent trading strategies, one could insert the basic maneuvers right into the above frame-pair scenario: in order for A to make B want X more (or want Y less) we expect him to select one of the familiar tactics:

Offer more for Y.
Explain why X is so good.
Create favorable side-effect of B having X.

Disparage the competition.
Make B think C wants X.

These only scratch the surface. Trades usually occur within a scenario tied together by more than a simple chain of events each linked to the next. No single such scenario will do; when a clue about trading appears it is essential to guess which of the different available scenarios is most likely to be useful.

Charniak's thesis[31] studies questions about transactions that seem easy for people to comprehend yet obviously need rich default structures. We find in elementary school reading books such stories as:

Jane was invited to Jack's birthday party.
She wondered if he would like a kite.
She went to her room and shook her piggy bank.
It made no sound.

Most young readers understand that Jane wants money to buy Jack a kite for a present but that there is no money to pay for it in her piggy bank. Charniak proposes a variety of ways to facilitate such inferences—a "demon" for *present* that looks for things concerned with *money*, a demon for "piggy bank" which knows that shaking without sound means the bank is empty, etc. But although *present* now activates *money*, the reader may be surprised to find that neither of those words (nor any of their synonyms) occurs in the story. "Present" is certainly associated with "party" and "money" with "bank," but how are the longer chains built up? Here is another problem raised in Charniak. A friend tells Jane:

He already has a kite.
He will make you take it back.

Take which kite back? We do not want Jane to return Jack's old kite. To determine the referent of the pronoun "it" requires understanding a lot about an assumed scenario. Clearly, "it" refers to the proposed new kite. How does one know this? (Note that we need not agree on any single explanation.) Generally, pronouns refer to recently mentioned things, but as this example shows, the referent depends on more than the local syntax.

Suppose for the moment we are already trying to instantiate a "buying a present" default subframe. Now, the word "it" alone is too small a fragment to deal with, but "take it back" could be a plausible unit to match a terminal of an appropriately elaborate buying scenario. Since that terminal would be constrained to agree with the assignment of "present" itself, we are assured of the correct meaning of it in "take X back." Automatically, the correct kite is selected. Of course, that terminal will have its own constraints as well; a subframe for the "take it back" idiom should know that "take X back" requires that:

X was recently purchased.
The return is to the place of purchase.
You must have your sales slip.
Etc.

If the current scenario does not contain a "take it back" terminal, then we have to find one that does and substitute it, maintaining as many prior assignments as possible. Notice that if things go well the question of it being the old kite never even arises. The sense of ambiguity arises only when a "near miss" mismatch is tried and rejected.

Charniak's proposed solution to this problem is in the same spirit but emphasizes understanding that because Jack already has a kite, he may not want another one. He proposes a mechanism associated with "present":

a. If we see that a person P might not like a present X, then look for X being returned to the store where it was bought.
b. If we see this happening, or even being suggested, assert that the reason why is that P does not like X.

This statement of "advice" is intended by Charniak to be realized as a production-like entity to be added to the currently active data-base whenever a certain kind of context is encountered. Later, if its antecedent condition is satisfied, its action adds enough information about Jack and about the new kite to lead to a correct decision about the pronoun.

Charniak in effect proposes that the system should watch for certain kinds of events or situations and inject proposed reasons, motives, and explanations for them. The additional interconnections between the story elements are expected to help bridge the gaps that logic might find it hard to cross, because the additions are only "plausible" default explanations, assumed without corroborative assertions. By assuming (tentatively) "does not like X" when X is taken back, Charniak hopes to simulate much of ordinary "comprehension" of what is happening. We do not yet know how complex and various such plausible inferences must be to get a given level of performance, and the thesis does not answer this because it did not include a large simulation. Usually he proposes terminating the process by asserting the allegedly plausible motive without further analysis unless necessary. To understand why Jack might return the additional kite it should usually be enough to assert that he does not like it. A deeper analysis might reveal that Jack would not really mind having two kites but he probably realizes that he will get only one present; his utility for two different presents is probably higher.

6.2.7 More Complex Scenarios

The meaning of a child's birthday party is very poorly approximated by any dictionary definition like "a party assembled to celebrate a birthday," where a party would be defined, in turn, as "people assembled for a celebration." This lacks all the flavor of the culturally required activities. Children know that the "definition" should include more specifications, the particulars of which can normally be assumed by way of default assignments:

DRESS ...... SUNDAY BEST.
PRESENT ..... MUST PLEASE HOST.
         MUST BE BOUGHT AND GIFT-WRAPPED.
GAMES ...... HIDE AND SEEK. PIN TAIL ON DONKEY.
DECOR ..... BALLOONS. FAVORS. CREPE-PAPER.
PARTY-MEAL . CAKE. ICE-CREAM. SODA. HOT DOGS.
CAKE .... CANDLES. BLOW-OUT. WISH. SING BIRTHDAY
         SONG.
ICE-CREAM .. STANDARD THREE-FLAVOR.

These ingredients for a typical American birthday party must be set into a larger structure. Extended events take place in one or more days. A Party takes place in a Day, of course, and occupies a substantial part of it, so we locate it in an appropriate day frame. A typical day has main events such as

Get-up   Dress   Eat-1   Go-to-Work   Eat-2   ...

but a School-Day has more fixed detail:

Get-up   Dress
Eat-1   Go-to-School   Be-in-School
     Home-Room   Assembly   English   Math (arrgh)
     Eat-2   Science   Recess   Sport
     Go-Home   Play
     Eat-3   Homework   Go-to-Bed

Birthday parties obviously do not fit well into school-day frames. Any parent knows that the Party-Meal is bound to Eat-2 of its Day. I remember a child who did not seem to realize this. Absolutely stuffed after the Party-Meal, he asked when he would get Lunch.

Returning to Jane's problem with the kite, we first hear that she is invited to Jack's Birthday Party. Without the party scenario, or at least an invitation scenario, the second line seems rather mysterious:

She wondered if he would like a kite.

To explain one's rapid comprehension of this, I will make a somewhat radical proposal: to represent explicitly, in the frame for the party scenario's structure, pointers to a collection of the most serious problems commonly associated with it:

Y must get P for X .... Choose P!
X must like P .... Will X like P?

Buy P .... Where to buy P?
Get money to buy P ... Where to get money?
Y must dress up ..... What should Y wear?

The reader is free to wonder, with the author, whether this solution is acceptable. The question, "Will X like P?" certainly matches "She wondered if he would like a kite?" and correctly assigns the kite to P. But is our world regular enough that such question sets could be precompiled to make this mechanism often work smoothly? I think the answer is mixed. We do indeed expect many such questions; we surely do not expect all of them. But surely "expertise" consists partly in not having to realize *ab initio*, what are the outstanding problems and interactions in situations. Notice, for example, that there is no default assignment for the present in our party-scenario frame. This mandates attention to that assignment problem (and prepares us for a possible thematic concern; at least it does for me). In any case, we probably need a more active mechanism for understanding *wondered* that can apply the information currently in the frame to produce an expectation of what Jane will think about.

The third line of our story, about shaking the bank, should also eventually match one of the present-frame questions, but the unstated connection between Money and Piggy-Bank is presumably represented in the piggy-bank frame, not the party frame, although once it is found it will match our Get-Money question terminal. The primary functions and actions associated with piggy banks are Saving and Getting-Money-Out, and the latter has three principal methods:

1. Using a key. Most piggy banks don't offer this option.
2. Breaking it. Children hate this.
3. Shaking the money out or using a thin slider.

In the fourth line does one know specifically that a silent Piggy Bank is empty, and hence out of money (I think, yes) or does one use general knowledge that a hard container which makes no noise when shaken is empty? I have found quite a number of people to prefer the latter. Logically the "general principle" would suffice, but I feel that this misses the important point that a specific scenario of this character is engraved in every child's memory. The story is instantly intelligible to most readers. If more complex reasoning from general principles were required this would not be so, and more readers would surely go astray.

It is all too easy to find even more complex problems:

A goat wandered into the yard where Jack was painting. The goat got the paint all over himself. When Mother saw the goat she asked, "Jack, did you do that?"

There is no one word or line, which is the referent of "that." It seems to refer, as Charniak notes, to "cause the goat to be covered with paint."

Finally, just as there are familiar "basic plots" for stories, there must be basic superframes for discourses, arguments, narratives, and so forth. As with sentences, we should expect to find special linguistic indicators for operations concerning these larger structures; we should move beyond the grammar of sentences to try to find and systematize the linguistic conventions that, operating across wider spans, must be involved with assembling and transforming scenarios and plans.

6.2.8 Questions, Systems, and Cases

Questions arise from a point of view—from something that helps to structure what is problematical, what is worth asking, and what constitutes an answer (or progress). It is not that the view determines reality, only what we accept from reality and how we structure it. I am realist enough to believe that in the long run reality gets its own chance to accept or reject our various views.

—Newell, A.: Artificial Intelligence and the Concept of Mind, in R. C. Schank and K. M. Colby (eds.), "Computer Models of Thought and Language," 1973

Examination of linguistic discourse leads thus to a view of the frame concept in which the "terminals" serve to represent the questions most likely to arise in a situation. To make this important viewpoint more explicit, I will spell out this reinterpretation:

A Frame is a collection of questions to be asked about a hypothetical situation; it specifies issues to be raised and methods to be used in dealing with them.

The terminals of a frame correspond perhaps to what Schank[32] calls "conceptual cases," although I do not think we should restrict them to so few types as Schank suggests. To understand a narrated or perceived action, one often feels compelled to ask such questions as

What caused it? (agent)
What was the purpose? (intention)
What are the consequences? (side effects)
Who does it affect? (recipient)
How is it done? (instrument)

The number of such "cases" or questions is problematical. While we would like to reduce meaning to a very few "primitive" concepts—perhaps in analogy to the situation in traditional linguistic analysis—I know of no reason to suppose that that goal can be achieved. My own inclination is to side with such workers as Martin,[33] who look toward very large collections of "primitives," annotated with comments about how they are related. Only time will tell which is better.

For entities other than actions one asks different questions; for thematic topics the questions may be much less localized, e.g.,

How can I find out more about this?
How will it help with the "real problem?"

Charniak does not permit himself to make a specific proposal to handle this kind of problem, remarking only that his "demon" model would need a substantial extension to deal with such a poorly localized "thematic subject." Consider how much one has to know about our culture to realize that *that* is not the goat-in-the-yard but the goat-covered-with-paint. Charniak's thesis—basically a study rather than a debugged system—discusses issues about the activation, operation, and dismissal of expectation and default-knowledge demons. Many of his ideas have been absorbed into this essay.

I wish I could present a working hierarchy of how these different kinds of frameworks could be classified and organized into a system. In order of "scale," among the ingredients of such a structure there might be these kinds of levels:

Surface syntactic frames: Mainly verb cases. Prepositional and word-order indicator conventions.

Surface semantic frames: Deep syntactic frames perhaps. Action-centered meanings of words. Qualifiers and relations concerning participants, instruments, trajectories and strategies, goals, consequences and side-effects.

Thematic frames: Topics, activities, portraits, setting. Outstanding problems and strategies commonly connected with topic.

Narrative frames: Stories, explanations, and arguments. Conventions about foci, protagonists, plots, development, etc., with the purpose of causing the listener to construct a new Thematic Frame in his own mind.

In spite of this tentative character, I will try to summarize my image of language understanding, as somewhat parallel to seeing.

The key words and ideas of a discourse evoke substantial thematic or scenario structures, drawn from memory with rich default assumptions. The individual statements of a discourse lead to temporary representations—which seem to correspond to what contemporary linguists call "deep structures"—which are then quickly rearranged or consumed in elaborating the growing scenario representation.

A single sentence can assign terminals, attach subframes, apply a transformation, or cause a gross replacement of a high level frame (because a proposed assignment no longer fits well enough). A pronoun is comprehensible (only) when general linguistic conventions, interacting with defaults and specific indicators, determine a terminal or subframe of the current scenario.

In vision the transformations usually have a simple group-like structure, in language we can expect more complex, less regular systems of frames. Nevertheless, because time, cause, and action are so important to us, we often use sequential transformation pairs that replace situations by their temporal or causal successors.

Because syntactic structural rules direct the selection and assembly of the transient sentence frames, linguistic findings should help us understand how our frame systems are constructed. One might look for such structures specifically associated with assigning terminals, selecting emphasis or attention viewpoints (transformations), inserting sentential structures into thematic structures, and changing gross thematic representations.

In a "story" one asks what is the topic, what is the author's attitude, what is the main event, who are the protagonists and so on. As each question is given a tentative answer the corresponding subframes are attached and the questions they ask become active in turn.

The "markers" I proposed for vision frames become more complex in this view. If we adopt for the moment Newell's larger sense of "view", it is not enough simply to ask a question; one must indicate how it is to be answered. Thus a terminal should also contain (or point to) suggestions and recommendations about how to find an assignment. "Default" assignments then become the simplest special cases of such recommendations, and one certainly could have a hierarchy in which such proposals depend on features of the situation, perhaps along the lines of Wilks' "preference" structures.[27]

It is tempting to imagine varieties of frame systems that span from simple template-filling structures to implementations of the "views" of Newell—with all their implications about coherent generators of issues to be concerned with, ways to investigate them, and procedures for evaluating proposed solutions. But as I noted in Sec. 6.1.12, I feel uncomfortable about any superficially coherent synthesis in which one expects the same kind of theoretical framework to function well on many different levels of scale or concept. We should expect very different question-processing mechanisms to operate on our low-level stereotypes and on our most comprehensive strategic overviews.

6.3 LEARNING, MEMORY, AND PARADIGMS

To the child, nature gives various means of rectifying any mistakes he may commit respecting the salutary or hurtful qualities of the objects which surround him. On every occasion his judgements are corrected by experience; want and pain are the necessary consequences arising from false judgement; gratification and pleasure are produced by judging aright. Under such masters, we cannot fail but to become well informed; and we soon learn to reason justly, when want and pain are the necessary consequences of a contrary conduct.

In the study and practice of the sciences it is quite different; the false judgements we form neither affect our existence nor our welfare; and we are not forced by any physical necessity to correct them. Imagination, on the contrary, which is ever wandering beyond the bounds of truth, joined to self-love and that self-confidence we are so apt to indulge, prompt us to draw conclusions that are not immediately derived from facts..."

—Lavoisier, A.: "Elements of Chemistry," 1952

How does one locate a frame to represent a new situation? Obviously, we cannot begin any complete theory outside the context of some proposed global scheme for the organization of knowledge in general. But if we imagine working within some bounded domain we can discuss some important issues:

Expectation: How to select an initial frame to meet some given conditions?

Elaboration: How to select and assign subframes to represent additional details?

Alteration: How to find a frame to replace one that does not fit well enough?

Novelty: What to do if no acceptable frame can be found? Can we modify an old frame or must we build a new one?

Learning: What frames should be stored, or modified, as a result of the experience?

In popular culture, memory is seen as separate from the rest of thinking; but finding the right memory—it would be better to say: finding a *useful* memory—needs the same sorts of strategies used in other kinds of thinking! We say someone is "clever" who is unusually good at quickly locating highly appropriate frames. His information retrieval systems are better at making good hypotheses, formulating the conditions the new frame should meet, and exploiting knowledge gained in the "unsuccessful" part of the search. Finding the right memory is no less a problem than solving any other kind of puzzle!

Because of this, a good retrieval mechanism can be based only in part upon basic "innate" mechanisms. It must also depend largely on (learned) knowledge about the structure of one's own knowledge! Our proposal will combine several elements—a pattern matching process, a clustering theory, and a similarity network.

In seeing a room, or understanding a story, one assembles a network of frames and subframes. Everything noticed or guessed, rightly or wrongly, is represented in this network. We have already suggested that an active frame cannot be maintained unless its terminal conditions are satisfied. We now add the postulate that even the satisfied frames must be assigned to terminals of superior frames. This applies, as a special case, to any substantial fragments of "data" that have been observed and represented.

Of course, there must be an exception! We must allow a certain number of items to be attached to something like a set of "short term memory" registers. But the intention is that very little can be remembered unless embedded in a suitable frame. This, at any rate, is the conceptual scheme; in particular domains we would of course admit other kinds of memory "hooks" and special sensory buffers.

6.3.1 Requests to Memory

We can now imagine the memory system as driven by two complementary needs. On one side are items demanding to be properly represented by being embedded into larger frames; on the other side are incompletely-filled frames demanding terminal assignments. The rest of the system will try to placate these lobbyists, but not so much in accord with "general principles" as in accord with special knowledge and conditions imposed by the currently active goals.

When a frame encounters trouble—when an important condition cannot be satisfied—something must be done. We envision the following major kinds of accomodation to trouble.

Matching: When nothing more specific is found, we can attempt to use some "basic" associative memory mechanism. This will succeed by itself only in relatively simple situations, but should play a supporting role in the other tactics.

Excuse: An apparent misfit can often be excused or explained. A "chair" that meets all other conditions but is much too small could be a "toy."

Advice: The frame contains explicit knowledge about what to do about the trouble. Below, we describe an extensive learned "similarity network" in which to embed such knowledge.

Summary: If a frame cannot be completed or replaced, one must give it up. But first one must construct a well-formulated complaint or summary to help whatever process next becomes responsible for reassigning the subframes left in limbo.

In my view, all four of these are vitally important. I discuss them in the following sections.

6.3.2 Matching

When replacing a frame, we do not want to start all over again. How can we remember what was already "seen?" We consider here only the case in which the system has no specific knowledge about what to do and must resort to some "general" strategy. No completely general method can be very good, but if we could find a new frame that shares enough terminals with the old frame, then some of the common assignments can be retained, and we will probably do better than chance.

The problem can be formulated as follows: let E be the cost of losing a certain already assigned terminal and let F be the cost of being unable to assign some other terminal. If E is worse than F, then any new frame should retain the old subframe. Thus, given any sort of priority ordering on the terminals, a typical request for a new frame should include:

1. Find a frame with as many terminals in common with [a, b, ..., z] as possible, where we list high priority terminals already assigned in the old frame.

But the frame being replaced is usually already a subframe of some other frame and must satisfy the markers of its attachment terminal, lest the entire structure be lost. This suggests another form of memory request, looking upward rather than downward:

2. Find or build a frame that has properties [a, b, ..., z]

If we emphasize differences rather than absolute specifications, we can merge (1) and (2):

3. Find a frame that is like the old frame except for certain differences [a, b, ..., z] between them.

One can imagine a parallel-search or hash-coded memory to handle (1) and (2) if the terminals or properties are simple atomic symbols. (There must be some such mechanism, in any case, to support a production-based program or some sort of pattern matcher.) Unfortunately, there are so many ways to do this that it implies no specific design requirements.

Although (1) and (2) are formally special cases of (3), they are different in practice because complicated cases of (3) require knowledge about differences. In fact (3) is too general to be useful as stated, and I will later propose to depend on specific, learned, knowledge about differences between pairs of frames rather than on broad, general principles.

It should be emphasized again that we must not expect magic. For difficult, novel problems a new representation structure will have to be constructed, and this will require application of both general and special knowledge. The paper of Freeman and Newell[34] discusses the problem of design of structures. That paper complements this one in an important dimension, for it discusses how to make a structure that satisfies a collection of functional requirements—conditions related to satisfying goals—in addition to conditions on containment of specified substructures and symbols.

6.3.3 Excuses

We can think of a frame as describing an "ideal." If an ideal does not match reality because it is "basically" wrong, it must be replaced. But it is in the nature of ideals that they are really elegant simplifications; their attractiveness derives from their simplicity, but their real power depends upon additional knowledge about interactions between them! Accordingly we need not abandon an ideal because of a failure to substantiate it, provided one can explain the discrepancy in terms of such an interaction. Here are some examples in which such an "excuse" can save a failing match:

Occlusion: A table, in a certain view, should have four legs, but a chair might occlude one of them. One can look for things like T-joints and shadows to support such an excuse.

Functional variant: A chair-leg is usually a stick, geometrically; but more important, it is functionally a support. Therefore, a strong center post, with an adequate base plate, should be an acceptable replacement for all the legs. Many objects are multiple purpose and need functional rather than physical descriptions.

Broken: A visually missing component could be explained as in fact physically missing, or it could be broken. Reality has a variety of ways to frustrate ideals.

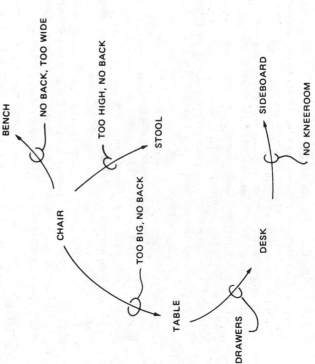

Fig. 6.12

Winston's thesis[8b] proposes a way to construct a retrieval system that can represent classes but has additional flexibility. His retrieval pointers can be made to represent goal requirements and action effects as well as class memberships. Because the idea is not well-known, I will explain it by elaborating an example sketched in his thesis:

What does it mean to expect a chair? Typically, four legs, some assortment of rungs, a level seat, an upper back. One expects also certain relations between these "parts." The legs must be below the seat, the back above. The legs must be supported by the floor. The seat must be horizontal, the back vertical, and so forth.

Now suppose that this description does not match; the vision system finds four legs, a level plane, but no back. The "difference" between what we expect and what we see is "too few backs." This suggests not a chair, but a table or a bench.

Winston proposes pointers from each description in memory to other descriptions, with each pointer labelled by a difference marker. Complaints about mismatch are matched to the difference pointers leaving the frame and thus may propose a better candidate frame. Winston calls the resulting structure a similarity network. (See Fig. 6.12.)

Parasitic contexts: An object that is just like a chair, except in size, could be (and probably is) a toy chair. The complaint "too small" could often be so interpreted in contexts with other things too small, children playing, peculiarly large "grain," and so forth.

In most of those examples, the kinds of knowledge to make the repair—and thus salvage the current frame—are "general" enough usually to be attached to the thematic context of a superior frame. In the remainder of this essay, I will concentrate on types of more sharply localized knowledge that would naturally be attached to a frame itself for recommending its own replacement.

6.3.4 Advice and Similarity Networks

The justification of Napoleon's statement—if, indeed he ever made it—that those who form a picture of everything are unfit to command, is to be found in the first of these defects. A commander who approaches a battle with a picture before him of how such and such a fight went on such and such an occasion, will find, two minutes after the forces have joined, that something has gone awry. Then his picture is destroyed. He has nothing in reserve except another individual picture and this also will not serve him for long. Or it may be that when his first pictured forecast is found to be inapplicable, he has so multifarious and pressing a collection of pictures that equally he is at a loss what practical adjustment to make. Too great individuality of past reference may be very nearly as embarrassing as no individuality of past reference at all. To serve adequately the demands of a constantly changing environment, we have not only to pick items out of their general setting, but we must know what parts of them may flow and alter without disturbing their general significance and functions.

—Bartlett, F. C.: "Remembering: A study in Experimental and Social Psychology," 1932 (revised 1961)

In moving about a familiar house, we already know a dependable structure for "information retrieval" of room frames. When we move through Door D, in Room X, we expect to enter Room Y (assuming D is not the exit). We could represent this as an action transformation of the simplest kind, consisting of pointers between pairs of room frames of a particular house system.

When the house is not familiar, a "logical" strategy might be to move up a level of classification: when you leave one room, you may not know which room you are entering, but you usually know that it is some room. Thus, one can partially evade lack of specific information by dealing with classes—and one has to use some form of abstraction or generalization to escape the dilemma of Bartlett's commander.

In some sense the use of classes is inescapable; when specific information is unavailable, one turns to classes as a "first-order" theory underlying any more sophisticated model. Fortunately, it is not necessary to use classes explicitly; indeed, that leads to trouble! While "class," taken literally or mathematically, forces one into an inclusion-based hierarchy, "concepts" are interrelated in different ways when in different contexts, and no single hierarchical ordering is generally satisfactory for all goals. This observation holds also for procedures and for frames. We do not want to be committed to an inflexible, inclusion-oriented classification of knowledge.

Winston proposes, incidentally, that a machine might spend idle time in an orderly comparison of various models in memory with one another. Whenever it finds few important differences between a pair, it inserts difference pointers for them.

But difference information becomes available also in any attempt to match a situation with memory, as successive attempts yield models that are generally similar but have specific, describable differences. Thus, instead of wasting this information one can use it to make the similarity network structure grow in the course of normal use of memory. If this pointer-building procedure is sensible about recording differences "relevant" to achieving goals, the result will be so much the more useful, and we have a mechanism for learning from experience.

Is a similarity network practical? At first sight, there might seem to be a danger of unconstrained growth of memory. If there are N frames, and K kinds of differences, then there could be as many as $K \times N \times N$ interframe pointers. One might fear the following consequences:

1. If N is large, say 10^7, then $N \times N$ is very large—of the order of 10^{14}—which might be impractical, at least for human memory.
2. There might be so many pointers for a given difference and a given frame that the system will not be selective enough to be useful.
3. K itself might be very large if the system is sensitive to many different kinds of issues.

Actually, none of these problems seem really serious in connection with human memory. According to contemporary opinions (admittedly, not very conclusive) about the rate of storage into human long-term memory there are probably not enough seconds in a lifetime to cause a saturation problem.

In regard to (2), most pairs of frames that make up the $N \times N$ term should be so different that no plausible comparison mechanism should consider inserting any pointers at all between them. As Winston notes, only a "near miss" is likely to be of much value. Certainly, excessive reliance on undiscriminating differences will lead to confusion.

So the real problem, paradoxically, is that there will be too few connections! One cannot expect to have enough time to fill out the network to saturation. Given two frames that should be linked by a difference, we cannot count on that pointer being there; the problem may not have occurred before. However, in the next section we see how to partially escape this problem.

6.3.5 Clusters, Classes, and a Geographic Analogy

Though a discussion of some of the attributes shared by a number of games or chairs or leaves often helps us to learn how to employ the corresponding term, there is no set of characteristics that is simultaneously applicable to all members of

---

the class and to them alone. Instead, confronted with a previously unobserved activity, we apply the term "game" because what we are seeing bears a close "family resemblance" to a number of the activities we have previously learned to call by that name. For Wittgenstein, in short, games, chairs, and leaves are natural families, each constituted by a network of overlapping and crisscross resemblances. The existence of such a network sufficiently accounts for our success in identifying the corresponding object or activity.

—Kuhn, T.: "The Structure of Scientific Revolutions," 1970

To make the similarity network act more "complete," consider the following analogy. In a city, any person should be able to visit any other; but we do not build a special road between each pair of houses; we place a group of houses on a "block." We do not connect roads between each pair of blocks; but have them share streets. We do not connect each town to every other; but construct main routes, connecting the centers of larger groups. Within such an organization, each member has direct links to some other individuals at his own "level," mainly to nearby, highly similar ones; but each individual has also at least a few links to "distinguished" members of higher level groups. The result is that there is usually a rather short sequence between any two individuals, if one can but find it.

To locate something in such a structure, one uses a hierarchy like the one implicit in a mail address. Everyone knows something about the largest categories, in that he knows where the major cities are. An inhabitant of a city knows the nearby towns, and people in the towns know the nearby villages. No person knows all the individual routes between pairs of houses; but, for a particular friend, one may know a special route to his home in a nearby town that is better than going to the city and back. Directories factor the problem, basing paths on standard routes between major nodes in the network. Personal shortcuts can bypass major nodes and go straight between familiar locations. Although the standard routes are usually not quite the very best possible, our stratified transport and communication services connect everything together reasonably well, with comparatively few connections.

At each level, the aggregates usually have distinguished foci or capitols. These serve as elements for clustering at the next level of aggregation. There is no nonstop airplane service between New Haven and San Jose because it is more efficient overall to share the "trunk" route between New York and San Francisco, which are the capitols at that level of aggregation.

As our memory networks grow, we can expect similar aggregations of the destinations of our similarity pointers. Our decisions about what we consider to be primary or "trunk" difference features and which are considered subsidiary will have large effects on our abilities. Such decisions eventually accumulate to become epistemological commitments about the "conceptual" cities of our mental universe.

The nonrandom convergences and divergences of the similarity pointers, for each difference **d**, thus tend to structure our conceptual world around

acquisition of new centers is in large measure forced upon us from the outside: by the words available in one's language; by the behavior of objects in one's environment; by what one is told by one's teachers, family, and general culture. Of course, at each step the structure of the previous structure dominates the acquisition of the latter. But in any case such forms and clusters should emerge from the interactions between the world and almost any memory-using mechanism; it would require more explanation were they not found!

6.3.6 Analogies and Alternative Descriptions

We have discussed the use of different frames of the same system to describe the same situation in different ways: for change of position in vision and for change of emphasis in language. In the wolf and lamb episode, for example, two frames are used in a before-after situation pair. Sometimes, in "problem-solving," we use two or more descriptions in a more complex way to construct an analogy or to apply two radically different kinds of analysis to the same situation. For hard problems, one "problem space" is usually not enough!

Suppose your car battery runs down. You believe that there is an electricity shortage and blame the generator.

The generator can be represented as a mechanical system: the rotor has a pulley wheel driven by a belt from the engine. Is the belt tight enough? Is it even there? The output, seen mechanically, is a cable to the battery or whatever. Is it intact? Are the bolts tight? Are the brushes pressing on the commutator?

Seen electrically, the generator is described differently. The rotor is seen as a flux-linking coil, rather than as a rotating device. The brushes and commutator are seen as electrical switches. The output is current along a pair of conductors leading from the brushes through control circuits to the battery.

We thus represent the situation in two quite different frame-systems. In one, the armature is a mechanical rotor with pulley, in the other it is a conductor in a changing magnetic field. The same—or analogous—elements share terminals of different frames, and the frame-transformations apply only to some of them.

The differences between the two frames are substantial. The entire mechanical chassis of the car plays the simple role, in the electrical frame, of one of the battery connections. The diagnostician has to use both representations. A failure of current to flow often means that an intended conductor is not acting like one. For this case, the basic transformation between the frames depends on the fact that electrical continuity is in general equivalent to firm mechanical attachment. Therefore, any conduction disparity revealed by electrical measurements should make us look for a corresponding disparity in the mechanical frame. In fact, since "repair" in this universe is synonymous with "mechanical repair," the diagnosis must end in the mechanical frame.

1. the aggregation into d-clusters
2. the selection of d-capitols

Note that it is perfectly all right to have several capitols in a cluster, so that there need be no one attribute common to them all. The "crisscross resemblances" of Wittgenstein are then consequences of the local connections in our similarity network, which are surely adequate to explain how we can feel as though we know what is a chair or a game—yet cannot always define it in a "logical" way as an element in some class-hierarchy or by any other kind of compact, formal, declarative rule. The apparent coherence of the conceptual aggregates need not reflect explicit definitions, but can emerge from the success-directed sharpening of the difference-describing processes.

The selection of capitols corresponds to selecting stereotypes or typical elements whose default assignments are unusually useful. There are many forms of chairs, for example, and one should choose carefully the chair-description frames that are to be the major capitols of chair-land. These are used for rapid matching and assigning priorities to the various differences. The lower priority features of the cluster center then serve either as default properties of the chair types or, if more realism is required, as dispatch pointers to the local chair villages and towns. Difference pointers could be "functional" as well as geometric. Thus, after rejecting a first try at "chair" one might try the functional idea of "something one can sit on" to explain an unconventional form. This requires a deeper analysis in terms of forces and strengths. Of course, that analysis would fail to capture toy chairs, or chairs of such ornamental delicacy that their actual use would be unthinkable. These would be better handled by the method of excuses, in which one would bypass the usual geometrical or functional explanations in favor of responding to contexts involving art or play.

It is important to reemphasize that there is no reason to restrict the memory structure to a single hierarchy; the notions of "level" of aggregation need not coincide for different kinds of differences. The d-capitols can exist, not only by explicit declarations, but also implicitly by their focal locations in the structure defined by convergent d-pointers. (In the Newell-Simon GPS framework, the "differences" are ordered into a fixed hierarchy. By making the priorities depend on the goal, the same memories could be made to serve more purposes; the resulting problem-solver would lose the elegance of a single, simply-ordered measure of "progress," but that is the price of moving from a first-order theory.)

Finally, we should point out that we do not need to invoke any mysterious additional mechanism for creating the clustering structure. Developmentally, one would assume, the earliest frames would tend to become the capitols of their later relatives, unless this is firmly prevented by experience. For, each time the use of one stereotype is reasonably successful, its centrality is reinforced by another pointer from somewhere else. Otherwise, the

Eventually, we might locate a defective mechanical junction and discover a loose connection, corrosion, wear, or whatever.

Why have two separate frames, rather than one integrated structure to represent the generator? I believe that in such a complex problem one can never cope with many details at once. At each moment one must work within a reasonably simple framework. I contend that any problem that a person can solve at all is worked out at each moment in a small context and that the key operations in problem solving are concerned with finding or constructing these working environments.

Indeed, finding an electrical fault requires moving between at least three frames: a visual one along with the electrical and mechanical frames. If electrical evidence suggests a loose mechanical connection, one needs a visual frame to guide himself to the mechanical fault.

Are there general methods for constructing adequate frames? The answer is both yes and no! There are some often-useful strategies for adapting old frames to new purposes; but I should emphasize that humans certainly have no magical way to solve all hard problems! One must not fall into what Papert calls the Superhuman-Human Fallacy and require a theory of human behavior to explain even things that people cannot really do!

One cannot expect to have a frame exactly right for any problem or expect always to be able to invent one. But we do have a good deal to work with, and it is important to remember the contribution of one's culture in assessing the complexity of problems people seem to solve. The experienced mechanic need not routinely invent; he already has engine representations in terms of ignition, lubrication, cooling, timing, fuel mixing, transmission, compression, and so forth. Cooling, for example, is already subdivided into fluid circulation, air flow, thermostasis, etc. Most "ordinary" problems are presumably solved by systematic use of the analogies provided by the huge network of these structures. The huge network of knowledge, acquired from school, books, apprenticeship or whatever, is interlinked by difference and relevancy pointers. No doubt the culture imparts a good deal of this structure by its conventional use of the same words in explanations of different views of a subject.

What about interactions that cross many of these boundaries? A Gestalt philosopher might demand some kind of synthesis in which one sees the engine as a whole. But before we demand a general solution, we should remind ourselves that for faults that stem from three-or-more interacting elements, a human auto mechanic will diagnose them, if at all, only after expensive, exhaustive replacement of many innocent components. Thus, the desire for complete synthesis is probably a chimera, and should not be a theoretical requirement. To be sure, there must indeed be some structure linking together the different conceptual engine frames. But this, too, may be relatively simple. Perhaps one must add a fourth engine-superframe whose terminals point to the various electrical, mechanical, and visual representation frames and are themselves interconnected by pointers describing when and how the different subframes are to be used. Presumably every complicated system that is "understood" contains some superframe structures that direct the utilization of subframes.

Incidentally, it is tempting in our culture to believe that a larger view is taken in our subconscious minds. As Poincaré observes, one often comes upon a sudden illumination after a period of conscious formulation, followed by a much longer period of nonconscious activity. I read his further discussion as proposing that the unconscious activity is a combinatorial heuristic search in which the chance of success depends mainly on the quality of the ingredients introduced by the preliminary conscious analysis; these elements are combined in different ways until a configuration is reached that passes some sort of test.

I have spoken of the feeling of absolute certitude accompanying the inspiration...; often this feeling deceives us without being any the less vivid, and we only find it out when we seek to put on foot the demonstrations. I have especially noticed this fact in regard to ideas coming to me in the morning or evening in bed while in a self-hypnagogic state.

—Poincaré, H.: "The Foundations of Science," 1946

The inspirational product is thus not a fully detailed solution but a "point of departure" or plan, brought to consciousness because it has passed some sort of threshold of "esthetic sensibility."

On this last point Poincaré does indeed seem to subscribe to a holistic conception for he characterizes "elegant" mathematical entities as those "whose elements are so harmoniously disposed that the mind can embrace their totality while realizing the details." It remains to be seen whether the filters that admit new descriptive combinations to the status of fully conscious attention require a complex, active analysis or can be explained by simpler matching and retrieval operations. (It is an unhappy fact that mathematicians have not contributed much to understanding the mechanisms of problem-solving, with the exception of Poincaré, Polya, and a few others. I wonder if this is not largely due to their attachment to the concept of "elegance," passed from one generation to the next as an intangible quality, worshipped but not explained or analyzed.) In any case, I see no reason to suppose that the unconscious is distinguished either along the dimension of massive parallel computation or by extraordinary holistic synthesis. A more plausible function would seem to be rapid, shallow exploration using material prepared by earlier analysis. The unconscious aspect might only reflect the lack of "annotation" and record-keeping that would make the process otherwise accessible to review and analysis. But the question about the complexity of the acceptance filter certainly still stands.

6.3.7 Summaries: Using Frames in Heuristic Search

Over the past decade, it has become widely recognized how important are the details of the representation of a "problem space"; but it was not so well recognized that descriptions can be useful to a program, as well as to the person writing the program. Perhaps progress was actually retarded by ingenious schemes to avoid explicit manipulation of descriptions. Especially in "theorem-proving" and in "game-playing" the dominant paradigm of the past might be schematized as follows:

The central goal of a theory of problem-solving is to find systematic ways to reduce the extent of the search through the problem space.

Sometimes a simple problem is indeed solved by trying a sequence of "methods" until one is found to work. Some harder problems are solved by a sequence of local improvements, by "hill-climbing" within the problem space. But even when this solves a particular problem, it tells us little about the problem-space; hence yielding no improved future competence. The best-developed technology of heuristic search is that of game-playing using tree-pruning, plausible-move generation, and terminal-evaluation methods. But even those systems that use hierarchies of symbolic goals do not improve their understanding or refine their representations. I now propose a more mature and powerful paradigm:

The primary purpose in problem solving should be better to understand the problem space, to find representations within which the problems are easier to solve. The purpose of search is to get information for this reformulation, not—as is usually assumed—to find solutions; once the space is adequately understood, solutions to problems will more easily be found.

In particular, I reject the idea that the value of an intellectual experiment should be assessed along the dimension of success–partial success–failure, or in terms of "improving the situation" or "reducing a difference." An application of a "method," or a reconfiguration of a representation can be valuable if it leads to a way to improve the strategy of subsequent trials. Earlier formulations of the role of heuristic search strategies did not emphasize these possibilities, although they are implicit in discussions of "planning."

How can the new paradigm be combined with the classical minimax strategy? In a typical episode, one is located at a certain node A in the search tree, and examines two or more possible moves, say, B and C. Each of these is somehow evaluated to yield values V(B) and V(C). Then these are somehow combined to yield a score

$$S(A) = Mm[V(B), V(C)]$$

where Mm is some function that takes two numbers and yields one. In effect, Mm has to summarize the results of all the search below A and compress them into a single numerical quantity to represent the value of being at node A. Now, what is the purpose of this? If one were able to search the entire game-tree, we could use S at each node to decide which move is best to make.

Since we cannot search the whole tree, we need information about what next to explore; we want S to tell the move generator what kinds of moves to consider. But if S is a mere number, this is unsuitable for much reasoning or analysis.

If S(B) has a low value, we can assume that B is a bad position. But if we want the move generator not to make the "same kind of mistake" again, the message must contain some additional clue about why B is weak—or better, what to do about it. So we really need a summary explanation of what was found in the search; and since we are in a tree we need further to summarize such summaries recursively.

There is a problem here we might call "summary-divergence." If the summary of the situation at A contains (in general) any explicit mention of B and C, then any recursive description scheme is in danger of containing an explicit copy of the entire move-tree; then to answer a question one might have nearly as bad a time searching the summary as the game-tree itself. One way to prevent this is simply to limit the size of the summary. However, we can avoid such drastic knowledge-destruction; in a frame-description, the important features and relations at the top levels can serve as summaries while the lower-level subsidiary descriptions can be accessed only if necessary. How much of the whole analysis tree remains in long term memory, and how much is left as garbage after the move is made would depend on other aspects of how the game-player uses his general experience.

How are the summaries to be made? Again, the frame idea suggests a flexible approach. Instead of demanding a rigid format, we could build up a collection of ad hoc "summary" frames, each evoked when their terminals fit subordinate descriptions and its frame-markers match the current goals. Thus each does its job when appropriate. For example, one might have a variety of "fork" frames. If a Knight lands on a square that threatens both check and rook capture, a fork frame is activated by its condition that in each of only two plausible moves, the unmoved piece is lost. Once this frame is activated it can make a specific recommendation, perhaps that the generator for the forked player see if a previously available move can apply the additional defense to the forking square.

6.3.8 Frames as Paradigms

Until that scholastic paradigm [the medieval "impetus" theory] was invented, there were no pendulums, but only swinging stones, for scientists to see. Pendulums were brought into the world by something very like a paradigm-induced gestalt switch.

Do we, however, really need to describe what separates Galileo from Aristotle, or Lavoisier from Priestly, as a transformation of vision? Did these men really see different things when looking at the same sorts of objects? Is there any legitimate sense in which we can say they pursued their research in different worlds?

[I am] acutely aware of the difficulties created by saying that when Aristotle and Galileo looked at swinging stones, the first saw constrained fall, the

These might seem simpleminded, but if the new problem is not too radically different from the old ones, then they have a good chance to work, especially if one picks out the right first-order approximations. If the new problem is radically different, one should not expect any learning theory to work well. Without a structured cognitive map—without the "near misses" of Winston, or a cultural supply of good training sequences of problems—we should not expect radically new paradigms to appear magically whenever we need them.

What are "kinds of interactions," and what are "debugging techniques"? The simplest, perhaps, are those in which the result of achieving a first goal interferes with some condition prerequisite for achieving a second goal. The simplest repair is to reinsert that prerequisite as a new condition. There are examples in which this technique alone cannot succeed because a prerequisite for the second goal is incompatible with the first. Sussman presents a more sophisticated diagnosis and repair method that recognizes this and exchanges the order of the goals. Goldstein considers related problems in a multiple description context.

If asked about important future lines of research on artificial or natural intelligence, I would point to the interactions between these ideas and the problems of using multiple representations to deal with the same situation from several viewpoints. To carry out such a study, we need better ideas about interactions among the transformed relationships. Here the frame-system idea by itself begins to show limitations. Fitting together new representations from parts of old ones is clearly a complex process itself, and one that could be solved within the framework of our theory (if at all) only by an intricate bootstrapping. This, too, is surely a special skill with its own techniques. I consider it a crucial component of a theory of intelligence.

6.4 CONTROL

I have said little about the processes that manipulate frame systems. This is not the place to discuss long-duration management of thought involving such problems as controlling a large variety of types of goals, sharing time between chronic and acute concerns, or regulating allocation of energy, storage, and other resources.

Over much smaller time spans (call them episodes) I imagine that thinking and understanding, be it perceptual or problem-solving, is usually concerned with finding and instantiating a frame. This breaks large problems down into many small jobs to be done and raises all the usual issues about heuristic programming, the following for example:

Top-down or lateral: Should one make a pass over all the terminals first, or should one attempt a complete, detailed instantiation of some supposedly most critical one? In fact, neither policy is uniformly

second a pendulum. Nevertheless, I am convinced that we must learn to make sense of sentences that at least resemble these.

—Kuhn, T.: "The Structure of Scientific Revolutions," 1970

According to Kuhn's model of scientific evolution "normal" science proceeds by using established descriptive schemes. Major changes result from new "paradigms," new ways of describing things that lead to new methods and techniques. Eventually there is a redefining of "normal."

Now while Kuhn prefers to apply his own very effective redescription paradigm at the level of major scientific revolutions, it seems to me that the same idea applies as well to the microcosm of everyday thinking. Indeed, in that last sentence quoted, we see that Kuhn is seriously considering the paradigms to play a substantive rather than metaphorical role in visual perception, just as we have proposed for frames.

Whenever our customary viewpoints do not work well, whenever we fail to find effective frame systems in memory, we must construct new ones that bring out the right features. Presumably, the most usual way to do this is to build some sort of pair-system from two or more old ones and then edit or debug it to suit the circumstances. How might this be done? It is tempting to formulate it in terms of constructing a frame-system with certain properties. This appears to simplify the problem by dividing it into two stages: first formulate the requirements and then solve the construction problem.

But that is certainly not the usual course of ordinary thinking! Neither are requirements formulated all at once, nor is the new system constructed entirely by deliberate preplanning. Instead we recognize unsatisfied requirements, one by one, as deficiencies or "bugs," in the course of a sequence of modifications made to an unsatisfactory representation.

I think Papert[35,36] is correct in believing that the ability to diagnose and modify one's own procedures is a collection of specific and important "skills." Debugging, a fundamentally important component of intelligence, has its own special techniques and procedures. Every normal person is pretty good at them or otherwise he would not have learned to see and talk! Although this essay is already speculative, I would like to point here to the theses of Goldstein[37] and Sussman[38] about the explicit use of knowledge about debugging in learning symbolic representations. They build new procedures to satisfy multiple requirements by elementary but powerful techniques:

1. Make a crude first attempt by the first order method of simply putting together procedures that separately achieve the individual goals.
2. If something goes wrong, try to characterize one of the defects as a specific (and undesirable) kind of interaction between two procedures.
3. Apply a "debugging technique" that, according to a record in memory, is good at repairing that specific kind of interaction.
4. Summarize the experience to add to the "debugging techniques library" in memory.

In the "productions" of Newell and Simon,[2] the control structure is implicit in the sequential arrangement (in some memory) of the local behavior statements. In systems like the CONNIVER language[39] there are explicit higher-level control structures, but a lot still depends on which production-like assertions are currently in active memory and this control is not explicit. Both systems feature a high degree of local procedural control. Anything "noticed" is matched to an "antecedant pattern" which evokes another subframe, attaches it, and executes some of its processes.

There remains a problem. Processes common to many systems ought to be centralized, both for economy and for sharing improvements that result from debugging. Too much autonomy makes it hard for the whole system to be properly responsive to central, high level goals.

The next section proposes one way such conflicts might possibly be resolved. A frame is envisioned as a "packet" of data and processes and so are the high level goals. When a frame is proposed, its packet is added to the current program "environment" so that its processes have direct access to what they need to know, without being choked by access to the entire knowledge of the whole system. It remains to be seen how to fill in the details of this scheme and how well it will work.

I should explain at this point that this manuscript took shape, over more than a year, in the form of a file in the experimental ARPA computer network—the manuscript resided at various times in two different M.I.T. computers and one at Stanford, freely accessible to students and colleagues. A graduate student, Scott Fahlman, read an early draft before it contained a control scheme. Later, as part of a thesis proposal, Fahlman presented a control plan that seemed substantially better than my own, which he had not seen, and the next section is taken from his proposal. Several terms are used differently, but this should cause no problem.

Frame Verfication
by Scott Fahlman

"I envision a data base in which related sets of facts and demons are grouped into packets, any number of which can be activated or made available for access at once. A packet can contain any number of other packets (recursively), in the sense that if the containing packet is activated, the contained packets are activated as well, and any data items in them become available unless they are specifically modified or cancelled. Thus, by activating a few appropriate packets, the system can create a tailor-made execution environment containing only the relevant portion of its global knowledge and an appropriate set of demons. Sometimes, of course, it will have to add specific new packets to the active set in order to deal with some special situation, but this inconvenience will be far less than the burden of constantly tripping over unwanted knowledge or triggering spurious demons.

good. One should usually "look before leaping," but there must be pathways through which an interesting or unexpected event can invoke a subframe to be processed immediately.

Central control: Should a frame, once activated, "take over" and control its instantiation, or should a central process organize the operation. Again, no uniform strategy is entirely adequate. No "demon" or other local process can know enough about the overall situation to make good decisions; but no top-level manager can know enough details either.

Perhaps both issues can be resolved by something involving the idea of "back-off" proposed to me by William Martin in contrast to "back-up" as a strategy for dealing with errors and failures. One cannot either release control to subsidiaries or keep it at the top, so we need some sort of interpreter that has access both to the top level goals and to the operation of the separate "demons." In any case, one cannot ask for a uniform strategy; different kinds of terminals require different kinds of processes. Instantiating a wall terminal of a room-frame invites finding and filling a lower level wall subframe, while instantiating a door terminal invites attaching another room frame to the superior house frame. To embed in each frame expectations about such matters, each terminal could point to instructions for the interpreter about how to collect the information it needs and how to complain about difficulties or surprises.

In any case, the frame-filling process ought to combine at least the components of decision tree and demon activation processes: in a decision tree control depends on results of tests. A particular room frame, once accepted, might test for a major feature of a wall. Such tests would work through a tree of possible wall frames, the tree structure providing a convenient nonlinear ordering for deciding which default assignments can remain and which need attention.

In a demon model, several terminals of an evoked frame activate "demons," for noticing things. A round object high on a center wall (or elliptical on a side wall) suggests a clock, to be confirmed by finding an appropriate number, mark, or radial line. If not so confirmed, the viewer would have "seen" the clock but would be unable to describe it in detail. An eye-level trapezoid could indicate a picture or a window; here further analysis is usually mandatory.

The goal of seeing is not a fixed requirement to find what is out there in the world; it is subordinate to answering questions by combining exterior visual evidence with expectations generated by internal processes. Nevertheless, most questions require us in any case to know our orientation with respect to our immediate surroudings. Therefore a certain amount of "default" processing can proceed without any special question or goal. We clearly need a compromise in which a weak default ordering of terminals to be filled is easily superseded when any demon encounters a surprise.

"The frame begins the verification process by checking any sample features that it already has on hand—features that arrived in the first wave or were obtained while testing previous hypotheses. Then, if the hypothesis has not already been accepted or rejected, the frame begins asking questions to get more information about features of the sample. The nature of these questions will vary according to the problem domain: A doctor program might order some lab tests. A vision program might look more closely. Sometimes a question will recursively start another recognition process: 'This might be a cow—see if that part is an udder.'

"The order in which the questions are asked is determined by auxiliary information in the frame. This information indicates which features are the most critical in the verification at hand, how these priorities might be affected by information already present, and how much each question will cost to answer. As each new feature of the sample is established, its description is added to a special packet of information about the sample, along with some indication of where the information came from and how reliable it is. This packet can be taken along if the system moves to another hypothesis. Sometimes unsolicited information will be noticed along the way; it, too, is tested and thrown into the pot.

"Of course, the system will practically never get a perfect match to any of its ideal exemplars. Auxiliary frame information will indicate for each expected type of violation whether it should be considered trivial, serious, or fatal (in the sense that it decisively rules out the current frame). Continuously variable features such as size, body proportions, or blood pressure will have a range of normal variation indicated, along with a mapping from other ranges into seriousness values. Sometimes a feature will provide no real evidence for or against a hypothesis, but can be explained by it; this, too, is noted in the frame. If there are striking or conspicuous features in the sample (antlers, perhaps) that are not mentioned in the current frame, the system will usually consider these to be serious violations; such features are evaluated according to information stored in a packet associated with the feature, since the hypothesis frame clearly cannot mention every feature not present in the exemplar.

"Occasionally a feature will have a strong confirming effect: If you see it, you can stop worrying about whether you are in the right place. Usually, though, we will not be so lucky as to have a decisive test. The normal procedure, then, is to gather in sample features until either some satisfaction level is reached and the hypothesis is accepted or until a clear violation or the weight of several minor violations sends the system off in search of something better. (My current image of the satisfaction level is as some sort of numerical score, with each matched feature adding a few points and each trivial mismatch removing a few. Perhaps some more complex symbolic scheme will be needed for this, but right now I do not see why.) The satisfaction level can vary considerably, according to the situation: The most cursory glance will convince me that my desk is still in my office, while a unicorn or a thousand dollar bill will rate a very close inspection before being accepted.

"Sometimes the sample will appear to fit quite well into some category, but there will be one or two serious violations. In such a case the system will consider possible excuses for the discrepancies: Perhaps the cow is purple because someone has painted it. Perhaps the patient doesn't have the expected high blood pressure because he is taking some drug to suppress it. If a discrepancy can be satisfactorily explained away, the system can accept the hypothesis after all. Of course, if the discrepancies suggest something else, the system will try that first and resort to excuses only if the new hypothesis is no better. Sometimes two categories will be so close together that they can only be told apart by some special test or by paying particular attention to some otherwise insignificant detail. It is a simple enough matter for both of the frames to include a warning of the similarity and a set of instructions for making the discrimination. In medicine, such testing is called differential diagnosis.

"Note that this use of exemplars gives the system an immense flexibility in dealing with noisy, confused, and unanticipated situations. A cow may formally be a large quadruped, but our system would have little trouble dealing with a three-legged cow amputee, as long as it is a reasonably good cow in most other respects. (A missing leg is easy to explain; an extra one is somewhat more difficult.) If the system is shown something that fits none of its present categories, it can at least indicate what the sample is close to, along with some indication of the major deviations from that category. A visual system organized along these lines might easily come up with 'like a person, only 80 feet tall and green' or 'a woman from the waist up and a tuna fish from the waist down.' Under certain circumstances, such descriptions might serve as the nuclei of new recognition frames representing legitimate, though unnamed, conceptual categories.

"An important feature of recognition frames (and of the recognition categories they represent) is that they can be organized into hierarchies. The system can thus hypothesize at many levels, from the very general to the very specific: An animal of some sort, a medium-sized quadruped, a dog, a collie, Lassie. Each level has its own recognition frame, but the frames of the more specific hypotheses include the information packets of the more general frames above them; thus, if the system is working under the 'dog' frame, the information in the 'animal' frame is available as well. A specific frame may, of course, indicate exceptions to the more general information: The 'platypus' frame would include the information in 'mammal,' but it would have to cancel the parts about live birth of young. Often a general frame will use one of the specific cases below it as its exemplar; 'mammal' might simply use 'dog' or 'cow' as its exemplar, rather than trying to come up with some schematic model of an ideal nonspecific mammal. In such a case, the only difference between hypothesizing 'mammal' and 'cow' would be a somewhat greater reluctance to move to another mammal in the latter case; the system would test the same things in either case.

"Note that there can be many different hierarchical networks, and that these can overlap and tangle together in interesting ways: A komodo dragon is taxonomically a reptile, but its four-legged shape and its habits are closer to a dog's than to a snake's. How to represent these entanglements and what to do about them are problems that will require some further thought. Some frames are parasitic: Their sole purpose is to attach themselves to other frames and alter the effects of those frames. (Perhaps 'viral' would be a better term.) 'Statue-of' might attach to a frame like 'cow' to wipe out its animal properties of motion and material (beef), while leaving its shape properties intact. 'Mythical' could be added to animal to make flying, disappearance, and the speaking of riddles in Latin more plausible, but actual physical presence less so. Complications could be grafted onto a disease using this mechanism. There is nothing to prevent more than one parasite at a time from attaching to a frame, as long as the parasites are not hopelessly contradictory; one could, for instance, have a statue of a mythical animal."

6.5 SPATIAL IMAGERY

6.5.1 Places and Headings

We normally imagine ourselves moving within a stationary spatial setting. The world does not recede when we advance; it does not spin when we turn! At my desk I am aware of a nearby river whose direction I think of as north although I know that this is off by many degrees, assimilated years ago from a truer north at another location on the same river. This sense of direction permeates the setting; the same "north" is constant through one's house and neighborhood, and every fixed object has a definite heading.

Besides a heading, every object has a place. We are less positive about the relations between places from one room to another. This is partly because heading is computationally simpler but also because (in rectangular rooms) headings transfer directly whereas "place" requires metric calculations.

In unfamiliar surroundings, some people deal much less capriciously than others with headings. One person I know regularly and accurately relates himself to true compass direction. He is never lost in a new city. Only a small part of this is based on better quantitative integration of rotations. He uses a variety of cues—maps, shadows, time-of-day, major landmarks (even glimpsed from windows), and so forth. It seems at first uncanny, but it doesn't really require much information. The trick is to acquire effective habits of noticing and representing such things.

Once acquired, headings are quite persistent and are difficult to revise when one tries to make "basic" changes. When I finally understood the bend in the river, it did not seem worth the effort to rebuild my wrong, large-scale spatial model. Similarly, I spent years in Boston before noticing that its "Central Park" has five sides. A native of rectangular Manhattan, I never repaired the thoroughly non-Euclidean nonsense this mistake created; there is simply no angular sector space in it to represent Boston's North End.

Such difficulties suggest that we use gross, global frames of reference as well as smaller, local structures. The difficulty of rearrangement suggests that the local frames are not complete, transformable, structures but depend on their attachment to "global frames" to deduce inter-object relationships. Below I discuss some implications of using global reference systems; in principle this suggests more powerful and general processes for rearranging parts of complicated images, but in practice people seem quite limited at this, especially when operating under time constraints.

6.5.2 A Global Space Frame System?

I do not like the following model very much, but something of its sort seems needed. A global space frame (GSF for short) is a fixed collection of "typical locations" in an abstract three-dimensional space, and copies of it are used as frameworks for assembling components of complex scenes. One might imagine such a skeleton as a five-by-five horizontal array of "places," each with three vertical levels. The central cells represent zones near the center of interest, while the peripheral cells have to represent everything else. (In effect, one always imagines himself within this universal ghost room in which one's current real environment is also embedded.) Actually, people probably use skeletons more complicated and less mathematically regular than this, emphasizing easily accessible volumes near the hands and face to represent space in ways more directly related to manipulative access than to a uniform physical geometry.

The GSF is associated with a system of view frames; each view frame describes the visual appearance of the GSF from a different observer viewpoint. The system is thus both Copernican and Ptolemaic; the embedding of the current scene in the GSF skeleton does not change when the observer moves, but each viewpoint gives the scene a distinctive appearance because the observer's location (or, rather, his belief about his location) activates an appropriate view-frame.

The view-frame corresponding to any particular place is derived by projecting the GSF cells toward that place; this yields an array of view lists—each of which is an ordered list of those cells of the GSF that would intersect some certain ray emitted from the observer's eye. Thus a view frame is like an ordinary scene frame except that its elements are derived from the GSF skeleton rather than from specific visual features and relations of any particular scene. While view lists correspond to retinal regions, we think of them as three-dimensional zones extending in some general direction out to distant space.

tempting: why not abandon the whole visual frame-system idea and build "3-D" object-frames that map directly into space locations? Then an object-frame could represent almost directly a symbolic three-dimensional structure and the GSF system could automatically generate different view-frames for the object.

For a computer system, this might work very well. For a psychological model, it leaves too many serious problems: How can we deal with translations, rotations, and scale-changes; how do we reorient substructures? A crude solution, for rotations, is to have for each object a few standard views such as embeddings of different sizes and orientations. Before rejecting this outright, note that it might be entirely adequate for some kinds of performance and for early stages of development of others.

But in "adult" imagery, any object type can be embedded in so many different ways that some more general kind of transformation-based operation seems needed. The obvious mathematical solution, for purposes of relocation and scaling, is to provide some kind of intermediate structure: each object-frame could be embedded in a relocatable, "portable" mini-GSF that can be rotated and attached to any global GSF cell, with an appropriate "view note" specifying how the prototype figure was transformed.

Providing such a structure entails more than merely complicating the embedding operation. It also requires building a "uniform structure" into the GSF, straightening out the early, useful, but idiosyncratic exaggerations of the more familiar parts of near-body space. Attractive as such a model might be, I simply do not believe one is ever actually realized in people. People are not very good at imagining transformed scenes; I quoted Hogarth's account of the very special training required, and I noted Piaget's observation that even moderate competence in such matters seems not to mature before the second decade.

We thus have a continuum of spatial mechanism theories to consider. I will not pick any particular point in this spectrum to designate as "the theory." This is not entirely because of laziness; it is important to recognize that each individual probably has to develop through some sequence of more-and-more sophisticated such mechanisms. Before we can expect to build a theory consistent with developmental phenomena, we will have to understand better which mechanisms can suffice for different levels of image-manipulation performance. And we certainly need to see a much more complete psychological portrait of what people really do with spatial-visual imagery.

Since we have come so close to building a three-dimensional analog mechanism, why not simply do that in some more elegant and systematic way? Although this is a popular proposal, no one has moved past the early, inadequate Gestalt models to suggest how a practical scheme might function. The neuronal construction of a non-symbolic three-dimensional representation system is imaginable, but the problems of

Occlusions are explained or imagined in terms of view-list orderings; one expects not to see all of an object that comes later on a view list than does another object. (Similarly, earlier objects are obstacles to manipulating later ones.) In memory matching, occluded view-list cells should relax the matching constraints on corresponding terminals.

To absorb visual information from multiple viewpoints, we need some sort of "indirect address" scheme in which visual features are assigned to view frames through the GSF skeleton; here is a first-order sketch of such a scheme:

Seeing: A variety of types of visual "features" are detected by retinal or post-retinal "feature demons." Each detected feature is automatically associated with the view direction of the current view list corresponding to its location in the visual field.

Frame-activation: At the same moment, some object frame or expectation is tentatively assigned to some of the GSF cells in the current view list for that direction. This means that each terminal of that frame is associated with the view direction of some active view list. (In other words, scene frame terminals contain spatial-location information by pointing to GSF places. [See below.]) Different scene frames of the same system are selected according to the current view frame. The headings of objects must be appropriately transformed.

Instantiation: When looking in a certain direction we (a) expect to see certain visual features in certain cells, as suggested by the active scene frame, and (b) actually see certain features in certain visual regions. So it is natural to propose a first-order vision theory in which each marker of each terminal actually specifies the signature—and also the proposed GSF location-cell—of some class of visual feature-demons. The observer can also be represented within the system as an object, allowing one to imagine himself within a scene but viewed from another location.

Given all this it is easy to obtain the information needed to assign terminals and instantiate frames. All the system has to do is match the "perceptual" [feature-demon, view-list] pairs to the "schematic" [marker, GSF-cell] pairs. If object-frame terminals could be attached directly to GSF locations and if these were automatically projected into view-lists, these would eliminate almost all need to recompute representations of things that have already been seen from other viewpoints.

6.5.3 Embedding Complications

In our first formulation, the terminals of a vision frame were understood to be in some way associated with cells of the GSF skeleton. The idea is help to realize multiple memory frames with common terminals—since this is a similar (and simpler) problem. Other visual memory needs demand ways to file assignment sets in long term memory; one wants representations of one's home, nesting area, predation regions, mate, enemies, and "bad places." It would be of value to develop a reliable global orientation within one's territory, if one is that kind of animal.

While the needs of vision point toward frame-like symbol manipulation, they do not so clearly point toward processes in which one makes hypothetical internal substitutions, i.e., imagination. But those operations would be useful in any problem-solving activity that requires planning.

We should consider individual as well as evolutionary development. In an "adult" system one's current view-frame depends on where one thinks his feet are; and this requires accumulating rotations due to body posture, head rotation, and eye-direction. It would be no surprise to find "innate" hardware, perhaps in the frontal visual cortex, through which such postural parameters operate to readdress the signatures of visual feature demons; the innateness hypothesis is supported by the good visual-motor coordination seen in the early infancy of many vertebrates. On the other hand, men could do with less preprogramming, given enough other mechanism to make this evolution within the individual reasonably certain.

Although the "adult" system is Copernican we would expect to find, in babies, more self-centered schemata. Perhaps the infant begins with a system centered around the face (rather than the feet), whose primary function is to relate vision to arm-motions; next one would expect a crude locomotor body image; only much later emerges the global system with a "permanent" sense of heading and within which the "observer" can freely move. This evolution from head through body to space-centered imagery would certainly be very laborious, but the infant has plenty of time. Perhaps one could study such a process, in microcosm, by seeing how people acquire the skill required for map-navigation. At first, one has to align the map with the scene; later this seems less necessary. The trick seems to involve representing both the scene and the map, alike, with respect to an internally defined reference direction for (say) North. Of course, part of this new skill involves improving one's collection of perspective transforms for irregular shapes of landmarks as one's viewpoint moves through extremes of obliquity.

In any case, the question is not to decide between "innate" and "developmental" models but to construct better scenarios of how intermediate systems would operate. The relative helplessness of the infant human does not mean he lacks the innate spatiomotor machinery of the infant horse, but perhaps only that its availability is "purposefully" delayed until the imagery prerequisites are also available for building the more complex system.

6.5.5 Metric and Quantitative Issues

Most people in our culture feel a conflict between (a) explaining thinking in terms of discrete symbolic descriptions and (b) the popular phenomenology in

constructing hypothetical solids and surfaces within it bring us right back to the same computationally nontrivial—and basically symbolic—issues. And the equivalent of the instantiated view-list has to be constructed in any case, so far as I can see, so that the value of an intermediate, analog space model remains somewhat questionable.

6.5.4 Evolution

Our frame theory assumes a variety of special mechanisms for vision and symbolic manipulation. I doubt that much of this arises from "self-organizing" processes; most of it probably depends on innately provided "hardware." What evolutionary steps could have produced this equipment? The arguments below suggest that the requirements of three-dimensional vision may have helped the evolution of frame-like representations in general.

In the early steps of visual evolution, the most critical steps must have concerned the refinement of specific feature detectors for use in nutrition, reproduction, and defense. As both vision and mobility grew more sophisticated, it became more important to better relate the things that are seen to their places in the outer world—to locations that one can reach or leap at. Especially, one needs the transformations that compensate for postural changes. These problems become acute in competitive, motion-rich situations. In predation or flight, there is an advantage in being able to coordinate information obtained during motion; even if vision is still based on the simplest feature-list recognition scheme, there is an advantage in correct aggregation of different features seen at different times.

Many useful "recognition" schemes can be based on simple, linear, horizontal ordering of visual features. One can get even more by using similar data from two motion-related views, or by using changes (motion parallax) in a moving view. Since so much can be done with such lists, we should look (1) for recognition schemes based on matching linear memory frames to parts of such ordered sets and (2) for aggregation schemes that might serve as early stages in developing a coarse ground-plan representation. One would not expect anything like a ground plan at first; initially one would expect an egocentric polar representation, relating pairs of objects, or relating an object to some reference direction such as the sun. We would not expect relational descriptions, sophisticated figure-ground mechanisms, or three-dimensional schemata at early stages. (I know of no good evidence that animals other than humans ever develop realistic ground plans; although other animals' behavior can appear to use them, there may be simpler explanations.)

The construction and use of a ground plan requires evolution of the very same motion transformations needed to assign multiple view data to appropriate cells. For a theory of how these in turn might develop we need to imagine possible developmental sequences, beginning in egocentric angular space, that at every stage offer advantages in visual-motor performance. Among such schemata, I would expect to find some structures that would also magnitude. Consider three objects A, B, and C tentatively assigned, in that order, to a center wall of a room. If we move right and now find B to the left of A, we can reassign B to the foreground. There is even more information in crude judgments of apparent movement, which can be interpreted as (inverse) order of distance from the observer's line of motion.

One thus hardly ever needs quantitative precision; differential measurements are fine for nearby objects while correspondingly gross judgments suffice for objects at grossly different ranges. For most practical purposes it is enough to notice just a few relations between an object and its neighbors. The number of noticed relations need not even grow faster than the number of objects: if two objects are near opposite walls, then this fact is directly represented in the top-level room frame, and one rarely needs to know more; if two objects are close together, there is usually a smaller frame including both, which gives more information about their relation. So we would (correctly) expect people to find it hard to recall spatial relations between objects in distinct subframes because reconstruction through chaining of several frames needs information that is not usually stored—and would be tedious and inaccurate in any case.

There are some substantial objections to the GSF scheme. It is in the nature of perspective that each nearby cell will occlude a number of faraway cells, and the cell-boundary occlusions are so irregular that one would not be able to tell just which parts of a faraway object will be occluded. (So the view-list idea does not work very well, but so far as human imagery is concerned, people have similar problems.) To improve the predictive quality of the system, the view lists could be elaborated to view structures for representing spatial relations more complex than simple "nearer-further." The metrical quality of the system could be dramatically improved, I think, by using "symbolic interpolation": consider together or sequentially two or more view-lists from nearby locations, and compromise between predictions that do not agree. One can thus better estimate the exact boundary of an occlusion by finding out which motions would make it certainly occur.

This idea of interpolation—or, in its simplest form, superposition—may often offer a way to improve the accuracy of an otherwise adequate strategy. If one averages—or otherwise summarizes—the predictions of two or more standard views, one obtains predictions of intermediate views that are better than one might imagine. Thus the calculations for body-image management (which one might suppose require complex vector and matrix transformations) might very well be handled by summing the expectations or predictions from the nearest "stereotype postures"—provided that the latter are reasonably adequate by themselves. It is tempting to generalize this to abstract activities, e.g., processes that can make symbolic use of multiple representations.

Another area in which quantitative methods seem important, at least on the surface, is in memory retrieval. One needs mechanisms for controlling the allowed range-of-variation of assignments. Does one demand "best match,"

which the inner world seems continuously colored by magnitudes, intensities, strengths and weaknesses—entities with the properties of *continua*. Introspection or intuition is not very helpful in this area. I am convinced that the symbolic models are the more profound ones and that, perhaps paradoxically to some readers, continuous structures are restrictive and confining. We already illustrated this point in the discussion of evaluation functions in chess. To be sure, continuous variables (and "analog machinery") could be helpful in many applications. There would be no basic problem in adding magnitudes, probabilities, utility theories, or comparable mathematical gadgets. On the other side, naive analysts underrate the power of symbolic systems. Perhaps we tend to reject the idea of symbolic descriptions because of our sense of "continuous awareness"—would we not notice any hypothetical processes in which one symbolic description is abruptly dissolved and replaced by another?

There would be no actual power in such a continuous awareness; for only a process that can reflect on what it has done—that can examine a record of what has happened—can have any consequences. Just as our ability to debug a computer program depends on the character and quality of traces and records, self-consciousness itself must depend on the quality and character of one's summaries of his own recent states. The "phenomenological" smoothness or roughness of a sequence of mental states would then reflect only the style of description used in the representation of that sequence.

Many psychologists feel that the experiments of Shepard on matching rotated objects indicate that humans perform continuous operations upon picture-like images.[40] In that experiment it was shown that the time it takes for a person to decide whether two pictures show rotations of the same object increases linearly with the angle of rotation between them. But a time-linear experimental result does not imply that an analog, non-symbolic process is involved. Equally natural explanations include

A large number of quasi-independent activities, or

A transformational structure that is incremental.

So Shepard's result might suggest that a person has no frame transformations for accurate large rotations of unfamiliar objects; he has to apply many small, incremental changes. Essentially this same proposal is worked out in some detail elsewhere and I will not describe my own version here.

In a computer-based robot, one certainly could use metric parameters to make exact perspective calculations. But in a theory of human vision, I think we should try to find out how well our image abilities can be simulated by "qualitative," symbolic methods. People are very poor at handling magnitudes or intensities on any absolute scale; they cannot reliably classify size, loudness, pitch, and weight into even so many as ten reliably distinct categories. In comparative judgments, too, many conclusions that might seem to require numerical information are already implied by simple order, or gross order of does one require a threshold of fit, or what? No one policy will work well. Consider a request of the form

"Pick up the big red block."

To decide what is "biggest," one has to compare different dimensions. Rather than assign a fixed procedure—which might work in simple problems—one should refer to the current problem-goal. If one is concerned with weight, then biggest = heaviest should work. If one is propping up a window, then biggest = largest dimension—that is, longest—is appropriate. The situation is more complex with unspecified selection, as in

"Pick up a big red block."

but the same principles apply: divide the world into classes appropriate to the micro-world we are in and then pick one from that class that best fits "big." Normally "big" means biggest, but not in a context that refers also to "enormous" blocks. Again, one must choose from one's collection of clustering methods by using the goal-micro-world context. But here, again, the quantitative aspects should be on tap, not on top, or else the outstandingly important aspects of each domain will not be captured. McDermott[28] discusses many issues about discrete representation of spatial structures in his thesis.

This essay contains quite a few different arguments against quantitative models. Perhaps I should explain the general principle upon which they are based, since I see that separately they are not very compelling. Thesis: the output of a quantitative mechanism, be it numerical, statistical, analog, or physical (nonsymbolic), is too structureless and uninformative to permit further analysis. Number-like magnitudes can form the basis of decisions for immediate action, for muscular superpositions, for filtering and summing of stimulus features, and so forth. But each is a "dead end" so far as further understanding and planning is concerned, for each is an evaluation and not a summary. *A number cannot reflect the considerations that formed it.* Thus, although quantitative results are useful for immediate purposes, they impose a large cost on further and deeper development.

This does not mean that people do not, or even that they should not, use such methods. But because of the block they present to further contemplation, we can predict that they will tend to be focused in what we might call terminal activities. In large measure, these may be just the activities most easily seen behavioristically and this might account in part for the traditional attraction of such models to workers in the behavioristic tradition. The danger is that theories based upon them—response probabilities, subjective probabilities, reinforcement schedule parameters—are not likely to be able to account for sophisticated cognitive activities. As psychological theories they are very likely to be wrong.

At times I may have overemphasized ways in which other kinds of first-order models can be satisfactory. This may be an overreaction to some holism-oriented critics who showed (but did not notice) that if you can always notice one more feature of a situation, then you can make yourself believe that you have already noticed an infinite number of them. On the other side I may have overreacted against colleagues who ignore introspective phenomenology too thoroughly or try to explain behavior in terms of unstructured elementary fragments. While any theory must "reduce" things to simpler elements, these need not be identifiable with behaviorally observable units of learning or doing.

REFERENCES

1. Minsky, Marvin, and Seymour Papert: Progress Report on Artificial Intelligence, *M.I.T. Artificial Intelligence Laboratory Memo 252*, 1972.

2. Newell, Allen, and Herbert Simon: "Human Problem Solving," Prentice-Hall, Englewood Cliffs, N.J., 1972.

3. Schank, R. C.: Identification of Conceptualizations Underlying Natural Language, in R. C. Schank and K. M. Colby (eds.), "Computer Models of Thought and Language," W. H. Freeman, San Francisco, 1973.

4. Abelson, R. P.: The Structure of Belief Systems, in R. C. Schank and K. M. Colby (eds.), "Computer Models of Thought and Language," W. H. Freeman, San Francisco, 1973.

5. Norman, Donald: Memory, Knowledge and the Answering of Questions, in R. L. Solso (ed.), "Contemporary Issues in Cognitive Psychology: The Loyola Symposium," V. H. Winston & Sons, Washington, D.C., 1973.

6. Koffka, K.: "Principles of Gestalt Psychology," Harcourt, Brace, New York, 1935; Harcourt Brace Jovanovich, 1963.

7. Guzman, Adolfo: "Computer Recognition of Three-dimensional Objects in a Visual Scene," Ph.D. thesis, MAC-TR-59, Project MAC, Massachusetts Institute of Technology, Cambridge, Mass., 1968.

8a. Waltz, David: "Generating Semantic Descriptions from Drawings of Scenes with Shadows," Ph.D. thesis, Massachusetts Institute of Technology, Cambridge, Mass., 1972 (included as Chap. 2 of this book).

8b. Winston, Patrick H.: "Learning Structural Descriptions from Examples," Ph.D. thesis, Massachusetts Institute of Technology, Cambridge, Mass., 1970 (included as Chap. 5 of this book).

9. Minsky, Marvin, and Seymour Papert: "Perceptrons," The M.I.T. Press, Cambridge, Mass., 1969.

10. Roberts, L. G.: Machine Perception of Three-Dimensional Solids, in J. T. Tippet et al. (eds.), "Optical and Electro-Optical Information Processing," pp. 159-197, The M.I.T. Press, Cambridge, Mass., 1965.

11. Huffman, David: Impossible Objects as Nonsense Sentences, in B. Meltzer and D. Michie (eds.), "Machine Intelligence 6," Edinburgh University Press, Edinburgh, Scotland, 1971.

12. Clowes, Maxwell: On Seeing Things, *Artif. Intel.*, 2(1):79-116 (1971).

13. Shirai, Yoshiaki: A Context Sensitive Line Finder for Recognition of Polyhedra, *Artif. Intel.*, 4(2):95-120 (1973) (included as Chap. 3 of this book).

14. Binford, T. O., and B. K. P. Horn: "The Binford-Horn Line Finder," *M.I.T. Artificial Intelligence Laboratory Working Paper 16*, 1971.

15. Nevatia, R., and T. O. Binford: Structured Descriptions of Complex Objects, *3d Intern. J. Conf. Artif. Intel.*, Stanford Research Institute Publications Department, Menlo Park, Calif., pp. 641-657, 1973.

16. Binford, T. O., and G. J. Agin: Computer Description of Curved Objects, *3d Intern. J. Conf. Artif. Intel.*, Stanford Research Institute Publications Department, Menlo Park, Calif., pp. 629–640, 1973.

17. Bartlett, F. C.: "Remembering: A Study in Experimental and Social Psychology," The University Press, Cambridge, England, 1932, 1961.

18. Newell, Allen: Artificial Intelligence and the Concept of Mind, in R. C. Schank and C. M. Colby (eds.), "Computer Models of Thought and Language," W. H. Freeman, San Francisco, 1973.

19. Newell, Allen: "Productions Systems: Models of Control Structures, Visual Information Processing," Academic Press, New York, 1973.

20. Pylyshyn, Z. W.: What the Mind's Eye Tells the Mind's Brain, *Psych. Bull.*, 80(1):1–24 (1973).

21. Guzman, Adolfo: "Some Aspects of Pattern Recognition by Computer," M.S. thesis, MAC-TR-37, Project MAC, Massachusetts Institute of Technology, Cambridge, Mass., 1967.

22. Piaget, Jean, and B. Inhelder: "The Child's Conception of Space," The Humanities Press, New York, 1956.

23. Gombrich, E. H.: "Art and Illusion," Pantheon Books, New York, 1969.

24. Chomsky, N.: "Syntactic Structures," Mouton, The Hague, Netherlands, 1957.

25. Chafe, D. W.: Contrastive Semantics Project, *First Technic Report*, Department of Linguistics, University of California, Berkeley, 1972.

26. Schank, R. C.: Conceptual Dependency: A Theory of Natural Language Understanding, *Cognit. Psych.*, 3(4):557–631 (1972).

27. Wilks, Y.: Preference Semantics, *Artificial Intelligence Center AIM* 206, Stanford University, Stanford, Calif., 1973.

28. McDermott, Drew: "Assimilation of New Information by a Natural Language Understanding System," M.S. thesis, AI-TR-291, Artificial Intelligence Laboratory, Massachusetts Institute of Technology, Cambridge, Mass., 1974.

29. Fillmore, C. J.: The Case for Case, in E. W. Bach and R. H. Harms (eds.), "Universals in Linguistic Theory," Holt, Rinehart & Winston, New York, 1968.

30. Celce-Murcia, M.: Paradigms for Sentence Recognition, Department of Linguistics, University of California at Los Angeles, Los Angeles, 1972.

31. Charniak, E.: "Toward a Model of Children's Story Comprehension," Ph.D. thesis, AI-TR-266, Artificial Intelligence Laboratory, Massachusetts Institute of Technology, Cambridge, Mass., 1974.

32. Schank, R. C.: The Fourteen Primitive Actions and Their Inferences, *Artificial Intelligence Center AIM* 183, Stanford University, Palo Alto, Calif., 1972.

33. Martin, William: Memos on the OWL System, Project MAC, Massachusetts Institute of Technology, 1974.

34. Freeman, P., and A. Newell: A Model for Functional Reasoning in Design, *Proc. 2d Intern. Conf. Artif. Intel.*, London, 1971.

35. Papert, S.: Teaching Children to Be Mathematicians vs. Teaching about Mathematics, *Int. J. Math. Educ. Sci. Technol.*, 3:249–262(1972).

36. Minsky, M.: Form and Content in Computer Science, *J.A.C.M.* (Jan. 1972).

37. Goldstein, Ira: "Understanding Simple Picture Programs," Ph.D. thesis, AI-TR-294, Artificial Intelligence Laboratory, Massachusetts Institute of Technology, Cambridge, Mass., 1974.

38. Sussman, G. J.: "A Computational Model of Skill Acquisition," Ph.D. thesis, AI-TR-297, Artificial Intelligence Laboratory, Massachusetts Institute of Technology, Cambridge, Mass., 1973.

39. McDermott, Drew, and Gerald Sussman, The CONNIVER Reference Manual, *M.I.T. Artificial Intelligence Laboratory Memo* 259A, 1972.

40. Shepard, R. N. and B. Metzler: Mental Rotation of Three-Dimensional Objects, *Science*, 171:701–703, 1971.

SCRIPTS, PLANS, GOALS, AND UNDERSTANDING

R.C. Schank & R.P. Abelson

(Chapters 1 - 3)

1 Introduction

1.1 What this book is about

This book reflects a convergence of interests at the intersection of psychology and artificial intelligence. What is the nature of knowledge and how is this knowledge used? These questions lie at the core of both psychology and artificial intelligence. The psychologist who studies 'knowledge systems' wants to know how concepts are structured in the human mind, how such concepts develop, and how they are used in understanding and behavior. The artificial intelligence researcher wants to know how to program a computer so that it can understand and interact with the outside world. The two orientations intersect when the psychologist and the computer scientist agree that the best way to approach the problem of building an intelligent machine is to emulate the human conceptual mechanisms that deal with language. There is no way to develop adequate computer 'understanding' without providing the computer with extensive knowledge of the particular world with which it must deal. Mechanistic approaches based on tight logical systems are inadequate when extended to real-world tasks. The real world is messy and often illogical. Therefore artificial intelligence (henceforth AI) has had to leave such approaches behind and become much more psychological (cf. Schank and Colby, 1973; Bobrow and Collins, 1975; Boden, 1976). At the same time, researchers in psychology have found it helpful to view people as 'information processors' actively trying to extract sense from the continual flow of information in the complicated world around them. Thus psychologists have become more interested in machine models of real-world knowledge systems. The name 'cognitive science' has been used to refer to this convergence of interests in psychology and artificial intelligence (Collins, 1976).

This working partnership in 'cognitive science' does not mean that psychologists and computer scientists are developing a single comprehensive theory in which people are no different from machines. Psychology and artificial intelligence have many points of difference in methods and goals. Intellectual history, like political history, is full of shifting alliances between different interest groups. We mention this because for many commentators, the blood quickens when computers and human beings are associated in any way. Strong claims for similarity (e.g., Newell and Simon, 1972) are countered by extravagant alarms (e.g. Weizenbaum, 1976). Enthusiasts and horrified skeptics rush to debate such questions as whether a computer could ever be in love. We are not interested in trying to get computers to have feelings (whatever that might turn out to mean philosophically), nor are we interested in pretending that feelings don't exist. We simply want to work on an important area of overlapping interest, namely a theory of knowledge systems. As it turns out, this overlap is substantial. For both people and machines, each in their own way, there is a serious problem in common of making sense out of what they hear, see, or are told about the world. The conceptual apparatus necessary to perform even a partial feat of understanding is formidable and fascinating. Our analysis of this apparatus is what this book is about.

pegged specifically to a particular type of real-world content. Where generalizing is possible, we will attempt to take advantage of it, but we will not try to force generality where it seems unnatural.

In order to adopt this attitude, we have set some boundaries on the type of knowledge we will to consider. Our focus will be upon the world of psychological and physical events occupying the mental life of ordinary individuals, which can be understood and expressed in ordinary language. Our knowledge systems will embody what has been called 'naive psychology' (Heider, 1958) – the common sense (though perhaps wrong) assumptions which people make about the motives and behavior of themselves and others – and also a kind of 'naive physics', or primitive intuition about physical reality, as is captured in Conceptual Dependency (CD) theory (Schank, 1972, 1975). This book goes well beyond CD theory, however. That theory provides a meaning representation for events. Here we are concerned with the intentional and contextual connections between events, especially as they occur in human purposive action sequences. This new stratum of conceptual entities we call the Knowledge Structure (KS) level. It deals with human intentions, dispositions, and relationships. While it is possible computers cannot actually experience such intentions and relationships, they can perfectly well be programmed to have some understanding of their occurrence and significance, thus functioning as smart observers. If our theory is apt, it will provide a model of the human observer of the human scene; it will also explain how to construct a computer observer of the human scene, and lead to the eventual building of a computer participant in the human world.

Often our emphasis will be on the nature of potential understanding of two or three sentences, story fragments, or longer stories. These provide a straightforward and helpful way to pose the major issues. Lurking beneath the surface, however, is an interest in the ingredients of personal belief systems about the world, which dispose people toward alternative social, religious, or political actions. One of us has a major interest in belief systems and ideologies (Abelson, 1973). This book is not directly addressed to that interest, but the concepts developed are a major part of that total effort.

What we will not present in this book is a general apparatus for attempting to represent any and all knowledge. We give no information retrieval methods of interest to library scientists. The reader with a passion for mathematics and/or logic will be disappointed. Likewise, anyone wondering, for example, whether we could get a computer to play squash or roll pasta dough should not wait with

1.2 Knowledge: Form and Content

A staggering amount of knowledge about the world is available to human beings individually and collectively. Before we set out on a theory of knowledge systems, we ought to ask ourselves: knowledge about what? We must be wary of the possibility that knowledge in one domain may be organized according to principles different from knowledge in another. Perhaps there is no single set of rules and relations for constructing all potential knowledge bases at will. A desire for generality and elegance might inspire a theorist to seek a 'universal' knowledge system. But if you try to imagine the simultaneous storage of knowledge about how to solve partial differential equations, how to smuggle marijuana from Mexico, how to outmaneuver your opponent in a squash game, how to prepare a legal brief, how to write song lyrics, and how to get fed when you are hungry, you will begin to glimpse the nature of the problems.

Procedures for intelligently applying past knowledge to new experience often seem to require common sense and practical rules of thumb in addition to, or instead of, formal analysis (Abelson, 1975). The prospects for the general theorist to cope with all the varied applications of common sense are especially dismal. Nevertheless, many artificial intelligence researchers take a generalist point of view. It is in the best tradition of mathematics (in which computer scientists are generally well trained) that great power is gained by separating form and content: the same system of equations may account for a great many apparently disparate phenomena. It is also a central tenet in computer science that generality is highly desirable. Turing's (1936) original principle of the general purpose machine has often been embraced as though the computer were (or soon would be) in practice a general purpose machine. The field of artificial intelligence is full of intellectual optimists who love powerful abstractions and who strive to develop all-embracing formalisms.

It is possible to be somewhat more pragmatic about knowledge, however. The five-year-old child learning to tie shoelaces need not in the process be learning anything whatsoever about mathematical topology. There is a range of psychological views on the nature of knowledge, and we shall say a little more about this in the next section. For now, we simply note that we will take a pragmatic view. We believe that the form of knowledge representation should not be separated too far from its content. When the content changes drastically, the form should change, too. The reader will encounter plenty of abstractions in this book, but each set of them will be bated breath. The geometry of bouncing balls, the 'feel' of dough texture, and many other aspects of human activities involve knowledge falling outside of our present boundaries. This is because (among other reasons) visual and kinesthetic processes cannot readily be represented in verbal form. However, a great deal of the human scene can be represented verbally, and we have no lack of things to work on.

1.3 Traditional Points of View

We have mentioned that our task lies at the intersection of psychology (more specifically, cognitive psychology and cognitive social psychology) and artificial intelligence. Since we are concerned with verbally expressible knowledge, there is also an overlap with linguistics. When one tries to work in a disciplinary intersection, one inevitably comes into conflict with the traditional standards, habits, and orientations of the parent disciplines. This is especially true when the disciplines correspond to university departments, breeding suspicion of out-groups (cf. Campbell, 1969). Here we briefly sketch some of these conflicts, which we have resolved somewhat differently from others working at the same intersection.

Psychology is a heterogeneous discipline. The major subdivisions are developmental, clinical, cognitive and social psychology, and psychobiology. It is surprising to the non-psychologist but familiar to all but the youngest generation of psychologists that cognitive psychology is a relatively new branch of study. American experimental psychology was dominated for so long by behaviorism – roughly, from 1935 to 1960 – that the study of mental processes lay almost entirely dormant while other branches of psychology were developing rapidly. Since mental events could not be observed directly, there was scientific resistance toward relying on them to explain anything, whatever the scientist's common sense might tell him. Introspective evidence was not regarded as objectively trustworthy.

Since 1960, there has been an enormous surge of careful experimental work on mental phenomena. Skinner notwithstanding, hu-

man psychology could not seem to do without cognitive processes. Nevertheless, the methodological caution of the behaviorists was carried over into this resurgence. Acceptable scientific procedure called for quantitative response measurements such as accuracy of recall or choice reaction time when subjects were confronted with well-controlled stimulus tasks. In the verbal domain, stimulus control usually entailed repetitive trials on isolated verbal materials, deliberately avoiding meaningful connotations in the experimental situation. While recent experimental materials have not been as trivial as the old-fashioned nonsense syllables, neither have they been genuinely meaningful or even necessarily plausible. Experimental tasks are often unusual and/or unnatural in relation to tasks encountered daily by people in using language. For example, in a well-known experiment by Foss and Jenkins (1973), subjects listened to 48 sentences such as 'The farmer placed the straw beside the wagon', with instructions to press a key the instant they first heard the phoneme 'b'. In another well-known series of experiments by Anderson and Bower (1973), subjects heard 32 unrelated sentences such as 'In the park, the hippie kissed the debutante', 'In the bank, the tailor tackled the lawyer', etc., and an hour later were asked to recall as many of them as they could. The artificiality of tasks such as the latter led Spiro (1975) to remark tartly,

Why should a research subject integrate the to-be-remembered information with his or her other knowledge? The role the information will play in his or her life can be summarized as follows: take in the information, hold it for some period of time, give it back to the experimenter in as close to the original form as possible, and then forget it forever. The information cannot be perceived as anything but useless to the subject in his or her life (given the common employment of esoteric or clearly fictional topics as stimulus materials). The information, even when not clearly fictional, is probably not true. In any case, the subject knows that the relative truth of the information has nothing to do with the purpose of the experiment. (p.11)

In complaining about the lack of meaningful context in experiments such as these, it is no doubt unfair to present them out of their context. The experimenters had serious purposes, and the data were of some interest. But since our needs are for a set of interrelated constructs to explain the process of natural understanding of connected discourse, this style of experimentation is both too unnatural and too slow. There has been a gradual increase in research with connected discourse as stimulus material (e.g., Bransford and Johnson, 1972; Kintsch, 1974; Frederiksen, 1975; Thorndyke, 1977) put them. (Actually Chomsky would deny that he works on generation. Transformationalists prefer to think of themselves as working on an abstract formalism with no process notions present at all.)

Linguists have almost totally ignored the question of how human understanding works. Since human understanding this seems odd at best. Some 'computational linguists', (e.g. Friedman, 1969 and Kay, 1973) have attacked the problem. However, they have followed linguistic tradition and consequently have maintained one of the fundamental flaws of linguistics in their work. They have divided the problem into linguistic and non-linguistic parts, a division that holds up no better for understanding than it does for generation.

Artificial intelligence has a somewhat more congenial recent history. The field is relatively new, and its early efforts were predominantly oriented toward getting computers to solve logical and mathematical problems (e.g. Newell, Shaw and Simon, 1957; Minsky, 1961; Feigenbaum and Feldman, 1963; Nilsson, 1971), and to play games such as checkers (Samuel, 1963) and chess (Bernstein et al, 1958; Newell, Shaw and Simon, 1958) intelligently. Early efforts to have computers deal with natural language were marked either by drastic failure (as in the case of mechanical translation from one language to another) or drastic oversimplification in the admissible vocabulary (Green et al, 1961) and grammar (Abelson, 1963; Colby and Gilbert, 1964), or by programming tricks producing smooth locutions which made the computer seem smarter than it actually was (Weizenbaum, 1966).

It has nevertheless been consistently regarded as important that computers deal well with natural language. In practical terms, such a development would mean that anyone could interact with a computer without learning a programming language or some special code to communicate about a special problem, whether it be library or consumer information, travel and ticket reservations, suggestions about home repairs, crop protection, first aid, etc. Computerized teaching programs would not have to be restricted to giving multiple-choice tests of the student's knowledge, but could interpret and respond intelligently to free-form answers and questions from the student. None of these high-sounding things are possible, of course, unless the computer really 'understands' the input. And that is the theoretical significance of these practical questions – to solve them requires no less than articulating the detailed nature of 'understanding'. If we understood how a human understands, then we might know how to make a computer understand, and vice versa.

but the field is still marked with a very cautious theoretical attitude. We are willing to theorize far in advance of the usual kind of experimental validation because we need a large theory whereas experimental validation comes by tiny bits and pieces. Our approach, in the artificial intelligence tradition, is discussed in Section 1.6.

If the research properties of experimental cognitive psychology are often unduly restrictive, the traditions in the field of linguistics are even more restrictive. Linguistics has concerned itself with the problem of how to map deep representations into surface representations (see Chomsky, 1965). After a long obsession with syntactically dominated deep representations, recent work in linguistics has oriented deep representations much more towards considerations of meaning (Lakoff, 1971; Clark, 1974). Despite this reorientation linguists have managed to miss the central problems.

Two fundamental problems stand out: How do people map natural language strings into a representation of their meaning? How do people encode thoughts into natural language strings? Because of a purported interest in the purely formal properties of language, linguists have consciously avoided both of these naturalistic problems. The second question seems, on the surface, to be closer to a linguist's heart. But linguists treat generation as a problem of determining whether a string is grammatical, i.e., whether it can be generated by the grammar they have set up. A grammar that generates natural language strings would be interesting and useful of course, if, and this is a big 'if', it started at the node S (for sentence). People, on the other hand, start with an already well-formed idea (or the beginnings of an idea) that they want to express. Linguists thus wind up concerning themselves with considerations of semantics at the level of 'Can I say this string? Will it mean something'? People already know what they want to say and that it is meaningful.

Two remedies for this linguistic notion of semantics come to mind. For the generation problem the obvious solution is to start the process earlier. How do people get thoughts to express? Linguists explicitly consign this question to other disciplines; yet it is an important part of the generation process, and one which when treated as a linguistic question completely changes the process under investigation. The other remedy is to apply such semantic considerations as 'Does this string mean something?' to the problem of understanding what someone else has said. Questions of how strings can be meaningfully interpreted belong to the domain of understanding, not generation, where Chomsky (1965, 1971) has repeatedly pels the reader toward an interpretation. The reader brings a large repertoire of knowledge structures to the understanding task. Elsewhere these structures have been called 'frames' (Minsky, 1975) and 'schemata' (Rumelhart, 1976). Rumelhart puts the matter very well when he says, 'The process of understanding a passage consists in finding a schema which will account for it.'

Interestingly, the idea of the schema in the interpretation of human events has a long tradition in social psychology. American social psychology had its roots in Gestalt psychology, and therefore did not succumb to the excesses of behaviorism the way human experimental psychology did. The phenomenology of mental life maintained a central role, largely through the towering influence of Kurt Lewin in the 1940's. Lewin (1936) wrote about human goal strivings in terms of internal images people had of their 'life spaces'. Since then a long succession of social psychologists have appealed to structured ideational kernels of the way people supposed the world to be organized: Heider's (1946, 1958) 'balance principle' and 'naive psychology'; Festinger's (1957) 'cognitive dissonance theory'; Abelson and Rosenberg's (1958) 'psycho-logic'; Kelley's (1967) and Jones and Davis' (1966) 'attribution theory', and many more. The terminology of the 'schema' is very much active in the 1970's (cf. Kelley, 1971; Tesser, 1977), even in areas well beyond social psychology (Rumelhart, 1975; Bobrow and Norman, 1975; Rumelhart and Ortony, 1976). The second author's orientations in the present book can be traced back to earlier excursions into 'hot cognition' (Abelson, 1963), 'individual belief systems' (Abelson and Carroll, 1965), and 'implicational molecules' (Abelson and Reich, 1969).

There is a very long theoretical stride, however, from the idea that highly structured knowledge dominates the understanding process, to the specification of the details of the most appropriate structures. It does not take one very far to say that schemas are important: one must know the content of the schemas. To be eclectic here is to say nothing. If one falls back on the abstract position that only form is important, that the human mind is capable of developing knowledge structures of infinitely varied content, then one sacrifices the essence of the structure concept, namely the strong expectations which make reality understandable. In other words, a knowledge structure theory must make a commitment to particular content schemas.

The commitment to particular content is a policy we follow consistently throughout the book. Whether we are talking of scripts, plans,

In the last several years there have been two clusters of developments in artificial intelligence which are miles ahead of previous efforts. First, there is a new generation of programs for 'parsing' sentences (in English and other languages) – that is, for deciding the proper features (such as what part of speech) to assign to each word in a sentence. The approaches of Woods (1970), Winograd (1972), Riesbeck (1975) and Marcus (1975) differ in the relative priority they give to syntactic or semantic features in parsing, but all agree that semantic features are considerably more important than linguists had generally been willing to acknowledge. Second, there has been increasing recognition that context is of overwhelming importance in the interpretation of text. Implicit real-world knowledge is very often applied by the understander, and this knowledge can be very highly structured. The appropriate ingredients for extracting the meaning of a sentence, therefore, are often nowhere to be found within the sentence.

There are several famous illustrations of this latter point. Collins and Quillian's (1972) is:

1 The policeman held up his hand and stopped the car.

Somehow in understanding this sentence we effortlessly create a driver who steps on a brake in response to seeing the policeman's hand. None of these intermediate links are mentioned in sentence (1). Another example, (from Abelson, 1969) is:

2 I went to three drugstores this morning.

Very innocently, the concept that the person must not have found what he wanted in the first two drugstores is implied, otherwise why would he have gone to three? This kind of implicit inference is very common – and of course can be wrong, but it is intrinsic to natural understanding that useful, fallible presumptions creep in.

Perhaps the simplest example of implicit inferences can be seen in a simple sentence such as (from Schank, 1972):

3 I like apples.

The speaker is talking about 'eating' but this is not explicitly mentioned. And why should it be? The speaker, unless he is deliberately trying to fool his listener, knows that the listener knows what action is being implicitly referenced. These examples were constructed with a point in mind, but are not really unusual. In all of them, and in many, many other examples to be found in this book, more is at issue than 'semantics'. It is 'pragmatics', the way things usually work – not how they might conceivably work – which most often im-

These two rules have forced us to look for one economical form for representing meaning. In doing so, we have invented the initial framework:

C The meaning propositions underlying language are called conceptualizations. A conceptualization can be active or stative.

D An active conceptualization has the form:
Actor Action Object Direction (Instrument)

E A stative conceptualization has the form:
Object (is in) State (with Value)

The form that we postulate for conceptualizations has led us to the principle of primitive actions. That is, because a conceptualization is defined as an actor doing something to an object in a direction, we have had to determine just what an actor can do. Clearly, Principle A forces us to look closely at actions that seem similar to see if we can extract the essence of their similarity. Principle B forces us to make explicit whatever differences there might be between two actions and to express them accordingly. For example, two verbs in a language may share a similar primitive element (as 'give' and 'take' share the primitive element **TRANSFER of POSSESSION**) but also have differences. The best representation for our purposes for a given verb then, will be the primitive element it shares with other verbs, plus the explicitly stated concepts that make it unique. As it happens, these explicitly stated concepts also turn out to share similar elements with other verbs, so that often a verb is represented as a particular combination of primitive actions and states none of which are unique to that verb, but whose combination is entirely unique. (Many verbs are represented entirely by states with no primitive act used at all.)

The primitive acts of Conceptual Dependency are:

ATRANS The transfer of an abstract relationship such as possession, ownership or control. Thus, one sense of 'give' is:
ATRANS something to someone else; a sense of 'take' is:
ATRANS something to oneself. 'Buy' is made up of two conceptualizations that cause each other, one an **ATRANS** of money, the other an **ATRANS** of the object being bought.

---

goals, themes, etc., we try whenever feasible to lay out the particulars of members of these conceptual categories. This is the same policy as was followed by the first author in developing Conceptual Dependency theory (Schank, 1972) to describe individual actions.

There has been much debate over whether the conceptual primitives of CD theory are the 'right' primitives, and some criticism that the theory is ad hoc. For many purposes, however, the important criterion is whether the theory is useful. Further, we would argue that any theory proposed as a replacement will have to come to grips with the same content issues as CD theory, and will more than likely end up with much the same primitives (as did Norman and Rumelhart (1975) for example). Indeed, the systematic linguistic exploration by Jackendoff (1976) of candidates for primitives seems to point in this direction.

We anticipate that there will be similar debate about the primitives we will propose in this book for higher-level knowledge structures. We will not be dogmatic about particular primitives, however, knowing that revisions in our scheme will no doubt be necessary as psychological validations and unanticipated theoretical considerations come along.

1.4 Conceptual Dependency Theory

In order to understand what follows in this book it is helpful to have a rudimentary exposure to Conceptual Dependency Theory. The theory has been described at length elsewhere (see especially Schank, 1975); we need not go into it in much detail here.

Conceptual Dependency (henceforth CD) is a theory of the representation of the meaning of sentences. The basic axiom of the theory is:

A For any two sentences that are identical in meaning, regardless of language, there should be only one representation.

The above axiom has an important corollary that derives from it.

B Any information in a sentence that is implicit must be made explicit in the representation of the meaning of that sentence.

MTRANS The transfer of mental information between animals or within an animal. We partition memory into two pieces: The **CP** (conscious processor where something is thought of), and the **LTM** (long term memory where things are stored). The various sense organs can also serve as the originators of an **MTRANS**. Thus, 'tell' is **MTRANS** between people, 'see' is **MTRANS** from eyes to **CP**, 'remember' is **MTRANS** from **LTM** to **CP**, 'forget' is the inability to do that, 'learn' is the **MTRANS**ing of new information to **LTM**.

MBUILD The construction by an animal of new information from old information. Thus, 'decide', 'conclude', 'imagine', 'consider', are common examples of **MBUILD**.

SPEAK The actions of producing sounds. Many objects can **SPEAK**, but human ones usually are **SPEAK**ing as an instrument of **MTRANS**ing. The words 'say', 'play music', 'purr', 'scream' involve **SPEAK**.

ATTEND The action of attending or focusing a sense organ towards a stimulus. **ATTEND** ear is 'listen', **ATTEND** eye is 'see' and so on. **ATTEND** is nearly always referred to in English as the instrument of **MTRANS**. Thus, in Conceptual Dependency, 'see' is treated as **MTRANS** to **CP** from eye by instrument of **ATTEND** eye to object.

Some set of primitive ACTs is essential for representing meanings, especially if sentences that have the same meaning are going to be represented in only one way. The ACTs presented here are not category names for verbs. They are the elements of action. An analogous situation is the formation of compounds from the elements in chemistry.

The use of such primitives severely reduces the inference problem (see Schank, 1975), since inference rules need only be written once for any ACT rather than many times for each verb that references that ACT. For example, one rule is that if you **MTRANS** something to your LTM, then it is present there (i.e., you know it). This is true whether the verb of **MTRANS**ing was 'see', 'hear', 'inform', 'memorize', or whatever. The inference comes from the ACT rather than the verb.

PTRANS The transfer of the physical location of an object. Thus, 'go' is **PTRANS** oneself to a place; 'put' is **PTRANS** of an object to a place.

PROPEL The application of a physical force to an object. **PROPEL** is used whenever any force is applied regardless of whether a movement (**PTRANS**) took place. In English, 'push', 'pull', 'throw', 'kick', have **PROPEL** as part of them. 'John pushed the table to the wall' is a **PROPEL** that causes a **PTRANS**. 'John threw the ball' is **PROPEL** that involves an ending of a **GRASP** ACT at the same time. Often words that do not necessarily mean **PROPEL** can probably infer **PROPEL**. Thus, 'break' means to **DO** something that causes a change in physical state of a specific sort (where **DO** indicates an unknown ACT). Most of the time the ACT that fills in the **DO** is **PROPEL** although this is certainly not necessarily the case.

MOVE The movement of a body part of an animal by that animal. **MOVE** is nearly always the ACT in an instrumental conceptualization for other ACTs. That is, in order to throw, it is necessary to **MOVE** one's arm. Likewise **MOVE** foot is the instrument of 'kick' and **MOVE** hand is often the instrument of the verb 'hand'. **MOVE** is less frequently used noninstrumentally, but 'kiss', 'raise your hand', 'scratch' are examples.

GRASP The grasping of an object by an actor. The verbs 'hold', 'grab', 'let go', and 'throw' involve **GRASP** or the ending of a **GRASP**.

INGEST The taking in of an object by an animal to the inside of that animal. Most commonly the semantics for the objects of **INGEST** (that is, what is usually **INGEST**ed) are food, liquid, and gas. Thus, 'eat', 'drink', 'smoke', 'breathe', are common examples on **INGEST**.

EXPEL The expulsion of an object from the body of an animal into the physical world. Whatever is **EXPEL**ed is very likely to have been previously **INGEST**ed. Words for excretion and secretion are described by **EXPEL**, among them, 'sweat', 'spit', and 'cry'.

In the original development of Conceptual Dependency theory, we spent most of our effort on representation of verbs and states. The bulk of Chapter 3 is one answer to the question of how to represent nouns. How does one represent a restaurant? Is it 'a place where people eat'? Or 'a place you go to eat where someone serves you and you pay'? How far do you go in such a representation? Scripts, although invented to handle a different but related problem, form the basis of the answer to the representation of certain complex nouns as well. How to represent concrete nouns is discussed briefly when we deal with memory in the next section.

Other researchers in artificial intelligence have much discussed the primitive actions that we have developed. Many of them seem to adopt one or more of them for their purposes, while usually rejecting either the rest of the set or the principle that it is necessary to represent sentences at the level of primitive actions each and every time. The most often heard suggestion is that one should only 'break down words into primitives when necessary'.

When is it necessary to break down a sentence into its minimal meaning units? The answer is simple enough: only when you need to exploit the 'meaning' itself. It is not necessary for word association tasks, for microworlds where there is little or no ambiguity or overlap in meaning, or for simple retrieval tasks where the meaning of the elements dealt with is not needed.

If you need to know the meaning of what you are dealing with, then it is necessary to look at the elements that make up that meaning. The only argument to this can be an argument based upon when you break down a sentence, not if you break down a sentence.

The 'when' question seems clear enough to us, although others differ with our position. Since memory ideally stores information in only one way, any pattern matching that needs to be done against information stored in memory requires a canonical form for the information. That is, information in memory must be stored in something like the primitive terms of Conceptual Dependency, and likewise the inference processes that are part of memory must be in those terms.

Should the breakdown into primitives occur after parsing ('when necessary'), or during parsing (assuming it is always necessary)? A good parser should exploit the meaning of a sentence. In understanding it seems doubtful that people first do a syntactic analysis without recourse to meaning and than look at the meaning. People understand as they go. Our parser (Riesbeck, 1975) has been quite

---

Conceptualizations that are attribute-value statements make use of a large number of SCALES. These scales run between boundaries which by convention are labeled -10 to 10. Scales are useful for indicating changes in state. Some of the scales we use, with their boundaries and some steps in between, are indicated below. In current applications of Conceptual Dependency Theory, it has not been necessary to undertake a serious quantitative scaling of relative points along the -10 to 10 continuum. At present, the occasional numerical references are only used suggestively.

HEALTH (dead, diseased, under the weather, tolerable, in the pink)

ANTICIPATION (terrified, nervous, hoping, confident)

MENTAL STATE (broken, depressed, all right, happy, ecstatic)

PHYSICAL STATE (end of existence, damaged, OK, perfect)

AWARENESS (dead, unconscious, asleep, awake, keen)

The symbol $\Leftarrow$ denotes causality. Some example sentences and their representations are:

John killed Mary.

John **DO**
$\Uparrow$
Mary **HEALTH**(-10)

John kicked Mary.

John **PROPEL** foot to Mary
$\Uparrow$
foot(John) **BE PHYSICAL CONTACT**(Mary)

John told Mary that Bill was happy.

John **MTRANS**(Bill **BE MENT.ST**(5)) to Mary

John read a book.

John **MTRANS**(information) to **LTM**(John) **from** book
inst(John **ATTEND** eyes to book)

successful using predictions that it generates based upon the kinds of meanings that it expects. Since it is hard to find a case when such breakdown is not necessary (in a real and complex system), we see little choice but to 'break down the words' every time.

One exception to this has occurred as a result of this book. In Chapters 4-7, various Knowledge Structures are introduced as an adjunct to Conceptual Dependency. We are beginning to find that it is sometimes better to parse directly into our Knowledge Structure representation rather than going by way of Conceptual Dependency. Thus, for example, the word 'want', which seemed primitive enough but was not so treated in Conceptual Dependency, is primitive in Knowledge Structures. It is reasonable with such words to go directly to where we want to be, thus bypassing Conceptual Dependency. This is, in fact, a complaint sometimes made about our work, namely that at the highest memory levels it will be necessary to reorganize information at places other than the primitive actions and thus we will have to 'unbreak down' again. The Knowledge Structure representation that we develop should answer this complaint.

1.5 Memory

Before we get into the substance of this book, it is worthwhile to introduce one more issue, namely memory. For a long time, the problems of natural language processing seemed to be separate from the problems of memory. Recently, Quillian (1968), Anderson and Bower (1973), Rieger (1975), Norman and Rumelhart (1975), and others have made it quite clear that memory and language are inextricably bound together. However, while the importance of dealing with memory has been generally agreed upon, the form that memory takes is still at issue. This book is, in a sense, entirely about memory. We are arguing here for certain theoretical entities that must form the basis of human memory organization.

The form of memory organization upon which our arguments are based is the notion of episodic memory. An episodic view of memory claims that memory is organized around personal experiences or episodes rather than around abstract semantic categories. If

memory is organized around personal experiences then one of the principal components of memory must be a procedure for recognizing repeated or similar sequences. When a standard repeated sequence is recognized, it is helpful in 'filling in the blanks' in understanding. Furthermore much of the language generation behavior of people can be explained in this stereotyped way.

Other proposals for memory organization have stressed the more scholastic notion of semantic memory. Briefly, semantic memory is a memory for words that is organized in a hierarchical fashion using class membership as the basic link. For example, 'canary' is linked to 'bird' and 'bird' to 'animal' in a hierarchical tree.

We can see at once that such an organization will not work for verbs, nor for nouns that are abstract nor for nouns that do not submit easily to standard categories (such as 'teletype'). Even if other semantic links besides class membership are used, such an organization implies that propositions are stored by linking them to the words with which they are expressed. This is not possible in the conceptual, non-word-oriented system that we have described. We could overcome this difficulty by organizing concepts in networks but the complexity of the possible combination of elemental concepts makes this extremely cumbersome. There are other difficulties as well.

An episodic memory, on the other hand, is organized around propositions linked together by their occurrence in the same event or time span. Objects are most commonly defined by their place in a sequence of propositions describing the events associated with an object for an individual. A trip is stored in memory as a sequence of the conceptualizations describing what happened on the trip. Some of the conceptualizations will be marked as salient and some will have been forgotten altogether.

Nominal concepts (concrete nouns) fit in this view with a two-part definition. The first and primary part is a functional definition that attempts to generalize the salient events over particular episodes in which the noun has occurred. The complete functional definition of a given noun lists all distinguishable occurrences of that noun present in memory. The second part is a physical description of one particular member of the class that is being defined.

For a 'spoon,' for example, the definition in memory lists the general usage for a spoon first (e.g., a thing that you PTRANS into mushy or liquid objects in order to PTRANS that object to your mouth so as to INGEST it). All interesting specific instances would also be stored

1.6 The Methodology of AI

Although the work we describe in this book is intended to lead towards the eventual computer understanding of natural language, it is not necessary to have much familiarity with computers in order to understand what we are saying. This fact is, or ought to be, true of nearly all clearly written work in artificial intelligence (AI). The computer is used in AI research as an omnipotent, but very dull and plodding, god. Under this view, it sometimes seems unnecessary to actually write the program that embodies the theory. One only need show the process in convincing enough detail. This is what one imagines. However, the reality is somewhat different – researchers actually do write programs.

Whenever an AI researcher feels he understands the process he is theorizing about in enough detail, he then begins to program it to find out where he was incomplete or wrong. It is the rare researcher who can detail a theory, program it, and have the program work right away. The time between the completion of the theory and the completion of the program that embodies the theory is usually extremely long. In modelling such complex processes as comprehension of language, there are more things to keep track of than a human trying to be conscious of each variable can manage. Understanding at such a level of complexity is a relatively subconscious process in everyday life.

What AI has to contribute to psychology is exactly this experience with modelling processes. An AI researcher asks what the input is and what the output is for every subprocess he deals with. In asking these questions he recognizes, at the very least, the nature and number of the subprocesses that must make up the entire process he wishes to model.

An analogy can be seen in asking directions from one place to another. If, while in New York, one asks how to get to Coney Island, and is told to take the 'N' train to the last stop, these directions will be adequate only if this improperly specified algorithm can be filled out with a great deal of knowledge about how to walk, pay for subways, get in the train and so on. We call this information a 'script' (detailed in Chapter 3). The point here is that a computer that does not have any prior information would make no sense of this response. It must be given information about: parsing sentences, finding meanings, filling in substeps in a plan, recognizing trains, paying for subways, walking, and so on. An AI researcher is forced to specify each and every detail in a theory that accounts for the abil-

(including, for example, 'The time I was camping and washed my spoon in the sand.'). Last, we would have a physical description of a particular spoon (most likely the kind that you have at home). The over-all organization of memory is a sequence of episodes organized roughly along the time line of one's life. If we ask a man, 'Who was your girlfriend in 1968?' and ask him to report his strategy for the answer, his reply is roughly: 'First I thought about where I was and what I was doing in 1968. Then I remembered who I used to go out with then.' In other words, it really isn't possible to answer such a question by a direct look-up. Lists of 'past girlfriends' do not exist in memory. Such a list must be constructed. The process by which that list is constructed is a search through episodes organized around times and locations in memory.

Of course if we ask someone not about past girlfriends but about past history learned from books, say, 'Who ruled England in 1668?', then the memory search mechanism might not turn out to be episodic. The respondent might conceivably remember when he learned this fact, but it is more likely that such scholastic memories could get divorced from their episodic origins and become organized more 'semantically', as in Collins' (1976) model of book knowledge. The whole question of episodic vs. semantic memory is controversial (cf. Loftus and Loftus, 1976), and our clear preference for the episodic mode is partly a function of the non-scholastic character of the knowledge we are interested in.

Some episodes are reminiscent of others. As an economy measure in the storage of episodes, when enough of them are alike they are remembered in terms of a standardized generalized episode which we will call a script. Thus, rather than list the details of what happened in a restaurant for each visit to a restaurant, memory simply lists a pointer (link) to what we call the restaurant script and stores the items in this particular episode that were significantly different from the standard script as the only items specifically in the description of that episode. This economy of storage has a side effect of poor memory for detail. But such a side effect, we shall argue, is the price of having people able to remember anything at all. Script-based memory is what will enable computers to understand without having their memories filled up so much that search time is horrendously long.

2 Causal Chains

ity to understand such a simple response to a question. We cannot be satisfied by an answer such as 'well, you use your knowledge about subways.' To put it on a computer we must know what form that knowledge takes. How are subways represented in memory? What pieces are where? How are they accessed? When and why are they accessed? What happens before they are accessed? What happens afterwards?

It is the asking and answering of such questions, and then the testing of those answers on a computer, that constitutes AI research. We use those methods in this book and thus our arguments lose some of the traditional psychological flavor of theories. That is, we are not oriented toward finding out which pieces of our theory are quantifiable and testable in isolation. We feel that such questions can wait. First we need to know if we have a viable theory. Viable here means: Will it work on a computer? Can we properly specify each subpart?

Our attitude may be somewhat unsettling to psychologists accustomed to piecemeal experimental testing of theoretical propositions. To them we urge the same patience in judging our work that they use in tolerating the very slow accumulation of knowledge in the experimental tradition. The AI style of research is much more disciplined than it may look. Although running computer programs provides the ultimate test, there are also strong criteria of intuitive necessity and internal consistency in theory formulation. Throughout this book we will often appeal to examples where the human understander readily makes inferences not explicitly available in the text of the example, or perceives something as odd or ridiculous. We persistently ask: what does an understander have to know in order to fill in missing inferences or perceive oddities? Addressing this question leads us to an inductive, rather than experimental, style of psychology, and we feel that this is the more appropriate style for this stage of development in our problem area.

2.1 Understanding Text

Early work in natural language understanding (e.g., Woods, 1970, Winograd, 1972, Schank, 1972) was concerned almost exclusively with individual sentences. Recently there has been a shift of attention towards whole texts (e.g., Wilks 1973, Rumelhart 1975, Schank 1975). On the surface this shift seems simple enough. If one can understand individual sentences, then to understand a text, all one need do is treat it as a set of individual sentences and apply the same methods. Our work would be much simplified if this were the case, but sadly it is not. The meaning of a text is more than the sum of the meanings of the individual sentences that comprise it.

People, in speaking and writing, consistently leave out information that they feel can easily be inferred by the listener or reader. They try to be concise and therein begins the root of the problem.

In wondering how we might go about representing the meaning of a text we came up against the problem of what connections existed implicitly in a text. One of the things that people seem to leave out when they talk are the connectors of the text. For example consider paragraphs (1) and (2):

1 John came over yesterday. Boy, was he mad.
2 John came over yesterday. When Mary saw John she almost died laughing. Boy, was he mad.

In (1) we are expected to figure out that the relationship between the first sentence and the second is that the second was in some way related to the reason for the first. In (2), the second sentence has two parts in it. The second part is implicitly stated to be the result of the first. Similarly, the third sentence is implicitly the result of the second part of the second sentence.

The connectivity here is provided by causality relationships of various types. If the nature of the connectivity of text is causal, then what we need are rules for determining causal relationships between events.

One of the first problems in this search is determining just when causality is present. Although the use of causal words tends 'to point out that some causality relationship is present, often the stated causality is misleading. For example, consider sentence (3):

3 John cried because Mary said she loved Bill.

Sentence (3) is a meaningful, well constructed English sentence. Yet, it is literally quite silly. Certainly John didn't cry because of the event of Mary speaking. What 'speaking' does cause is 'thinking', which can cause 'sadness' which can be a reason for 'crying'. Since people don't really misunderstand sentences such as (3), there is little reason for speakers to worry about their imprecision. However, in designing a theory of understanding, there is a great deal to worry about. Sometimes when people say 'event X caused event Y' they mean it and sometimes they do not. In order to understand we must be able to fill in the gaps left implicit by a speaker. When we hear someone say 'X caused Y', and we know that X could not have caused Y, we react accordingly. We check to make sure the causalities we hear are correct. To model understanding it is necessary to find out precisely what the rules are for this.

The same problem exists with respect to sentences that claim a given event caused a given state. For example, compare the following two sentences:

4 Joe burned his hand because he touched the stove.
5 Joe burned his hand because he forgot the stove was on.

People have no trouble recognizing that (4) means what it says causally and (5) does not. 'Forgetting' does not cause 'burning'. Readers of sentences such as (5) understand that they are called upon to supply the 'real' causality themselves by making an inference. We might expect that they would infer (4) upon reading (5).

Now, a simple theory would claim that this problem is simply resolved. Sentence (5) has a mental event causing a physical state and since mental events do not ordinarily cause physical states, we must infer an intermediate action that will fix it up. This is correct as far as it goes but there are other types of cases. Consider the following sentences:

6 John's leg was broken because Mary tripped him.
7 John leg was broken because Mary knocked over a pile of bricks.

In sentence (6) we are happy with the causality because we know that 'tripping someone' can cause a broken leg. However in (7) there is no such direct connection. Here again, we must infer the real causative event. The 'knocking over' must have propelled the bricks into contact with John's leg. That contact caused the broken leg. As with all inferences, this causality may be incorrect. What is important is that understanders can create such connections when the need arises. The rules that work for this example will be given in the next section.

Thus, statements of causality cannot be taken at face value. If we hear that X caused Y, we must ask if X could cause Y directly and if it cannot we must figure out the intermediate events. This is the principle of causal chaining.

2.2 Causal Types

A very simple causal syntax exists in natural thought, a syntax that can be violated in natural language expression. In the reconstruction of the thought that underlies the utterance, the causal syntax must be rigidly obeyed. To do this, a fairly complex causal semantics, or world knowledge store, must be exploited.

In the physical world, the causal syntax is as follows:

CS1 Actions can result in state changes.

CS2 States can enable actions.

In Conceptual Dependency, CS1 is denoted:

ACT
→r
STATE

and CS2 is represented:

STATE
→E
ACT

The meat of these rules is in their real world application. That is, not any action can result in any state, and not any state can enable any action. Thus, for every primitive action there is associated with it the set of states that it can affect as well as the set of states that are necessary in order to effect it. Since there are only eleven primitive actions this delimitation of world knowledge is easily accomplished.

To see how it all works we return again to sentence (7). In sentence (7) there is one action given – Mary PROPEL Mary; and one state change given – leg(John) BE PHYS.ST(-). For PROPEL, we have a list of the states that can result from PROPEL as well as the set of conditions under which those states can occur. The applicable rules here are:

A PROPEL can result in PHYSICAL CONTACT between the object of the PROPEL and any objects in the location specified in the Directive case.

B PROPEL results in PHYS. ST (-) if one of the objects in the PROPEL is human, if it results in PHYSICAL CONTACT (PHYSCONT) and if the force of the PROPEL is great.

In application, these rules when applied to Mary PROPEL Mary to bricks yield that Mary is in PHYSCONT with bricks. That is, according to the causal rules, Mary could be damaged but not John's leg. It is therefore necessary to hypothesize an action that would have resulted in a PHYS. ST.(-) for John's leg. Using the above rules backwards, we get the hypothetical event:

Something$_1$ PROPEL something$_2$ to leg(John)

This hypothetical event must be derived from some real event as a possible inference in order to make sense of the stated causation. This can be done if it is known that:

If a moveable object is put in PHYS. CONT with the object of a PROPEL then it can become the object of the new PROPEL, where the actor of the new PROPEL is the same as object of original PROPEL.

We can then hypothesize as an inference:

Mary PROPEL bricks to leg(John)

Using the original rules for PROPEL given above, this hypothetical event is causally correct in the sense that the known event could cause it, and the known state could result from it.

The causal chaining inference rules given here are an extremely important part of the understanding process. People, and therefore computers, must have rules like those given above, or they would not be able to understand.

One problem in building causal chaining mechanisms is recognizing when causality considerations occur. Causality need not be expressed directly in English. There exists a class of verbs in English, for example, that have implicit causal connections. Thus in the analysis of sentence (8):

8 John prevented Mary from leaving the room by hitting her.

there is an implicit causality. 'Prevent' means, 'to do something that causes something else not to happen'. According to our causal syntax, the action done resulted in a state that disabled an intended action.

So, one thing we have here is a modification of rule CS2 above which we call rule CS3:

CS3 States can disable actions.

CS3 is represented as:

STATE
→dE
ACTION

The causally correct analysis here then is:

PROPEL(hitting) results in

STATE disable **PTRANS**(leaving the room)

This kind of analysis is important because it makes possible the inference of what is really going on. If we ask the question that derives from the above chain, we get: what **STATE** resulting from a **PROPEL** can disable a **PTRANS**? Many possibilities exist here, for example, unconsciousness.

Another possibility here is that the **STATE** resulted in a **MENTAL STATE** which caused the intended **PTRANS** to no longer be intended. For example, we can imagine Mary being frightened and deciding not to leave the room due to the possibility of being further harmed. We thus have a fourth rule:

CS4 States (or acts) can initiate mental states.

CS4 is represented as:

STATE (or **ACT**)
→I
MENT.ST

A fifth rule occurs here too. In the example above, fear was a reason for a decision. The general rule is

CS5 Mental states can be reasons for actions.

CS5 is represented as:

MENT.ST
→R
ACTION

Using these causal rules it is possible to do three things: First, we can decide what is and is not a causal chain. When we encounter a 'because' type word, we can try to connect together causally the two clauses. If we cannot make the connection because of a causal syntax violation, we postulate some set of unknown states and actions that would correctly complete the chain. These empty conceptualization holders become the primary candidates for inferences.

Second, we can now analyze correctly the conceptual representation of words such as 'prevent', 'help', 'allow', such that their dictionary definition contains implicit causal chains that demand inferences to be made.

Third, and perhaps most important, we now have a way of representing connected text. We shall now explain.

When we think about what makes connected text connected, the answer does not seem obvious. However, if we reverse the question and ask if there is evidence of causal connections in text, the answer seems to be that such evidence is everywhere.

Consider the following story:

9 John was thirsty. He opened a can of beer and went into the den. There he saw a new chair. He sat down in it. Suddenly the chair tilted over and John fell on the floor. His beer spilled all over the chair. When his wife heard the noise she ran into the den. She was very angry that her new chair had been ruined.

Below is a representation of all the events in the above story connected together with the causalities that are implicit in the story. The result is a giant causal chain, that serves to relate together the events and state changes. It is this connectability that makes the story coherent. If we could not construct a causal chain we could probably not understand the story. (We use the following notational devices below: **IR** denotes an initiate followed by a reason where the intermediate mental action has been left out. Similarly **rE** denotes a result followed by an enable with the intermediate state left out. **DO** indicates an unknown action.)

The above representation says, essentially this: John's thirst caused him to decide to **DO** an action that would result in a beer being opened which would enable him to drink it. What we have is: the **THIRST** initiated an **MBUILD** (left out) to open the beer which was the **REASON** that he did the action (whatever it was) that resulted in the beer being open. The beer being open enabled another action (spilling) that happened much later in the sequence of events. (States enable events but the events that are enabled can occur any time after the state is initially present just as long as the state continues to be present.)

Thus, connecting up the actual 'state enables action' and 'action results in state' causalities is what makes sense of a text. A text is disconnected if a causal chain cannot be constructed to represent it.

Furthermore a theory of importance in text can be derived by causal chaining. Events or states that have multiple connections are likely to be highly significant with respect to the text. States or events that lead nowhere are likely to be forgotten.

The basic philosophy here then is this: Once the actual events that took place are determined, understanding is possible. The problem in understanding is how to make explicit that which has been left implicit. Conceptual Dependency was designed to handle that problem at the single thought (or sentence) level. Causal chains handle that problem at the level of interconnected thought (or texts).

2.3 Representation of Causation

We use the following causal links in our representations:

- **r** means an **ACT** results in a **STATE**.
- **E** means a **STATE** enables an **ACT**.
- **I** means a **STATE** or **ACT** initiates a mental **STATE**.
- **R** means a mental **ACT** is the reason for a physical **ACT**.
- **dE** means a **STATE** disables an **ACT**.

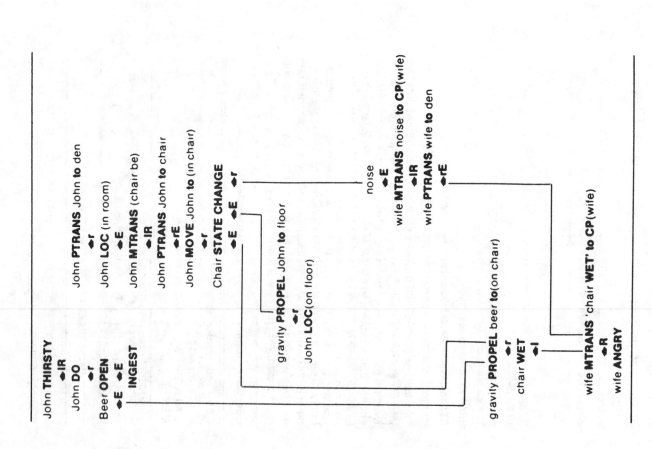

We use two standard abbreviations. These are:

▸rE an **ACT** results in a **STATE** which enables an **ACT**.

▸IR an **ACT** or **STATE** initiates a thought which is the reason for an **ACT**.

These abbreviations serve to leave items implicit when they are of no particular interest at a given time.

While these abbreviations help us focus on the items that interest us without dallying on irrelevant details they can also lead to problems. When we hear

3 John cried because Mary said she loved Bill.

we have an **IR**. It is important first to be able to recognize that John did an **MBUILD** of something sad and this is why he cried. However, if we make no attempt at all to figure out what John was sad about, i.e., what his actual train of thought was, we will miss the very important (though possibly wrong) inference that John loved Mary. This problem becomes more acute the less transparent the reasoning of an individual is.

There is another problem with causal chains in that people often speak of negative events causing things and in a strictly physical world this is rather odd.

That is, the causal chains that we have been presenting here are useful for figuring out chains of causality that are based on physical reality. Thus sentence (10) is easily handled with causal chains:

10 John gave Bill an orange for his cold.

John **ATRANS** orange to Bill

▸rE

Bill **INGEST** orange to **INSIDE**(Bill)

▸r

Bill **HEALTH**(POS change)

Here, as a result of the semantics of causation, we are forced to postulate an **INGEST** action that is rather important to understanding the sentence.

But, when the world is full of intentions that get only partially realized, or plans that go astray, causal chains do not work so simply. A higher level of representation is needed to account for sentences such as (11) and (12):

11 Mary liked John but not enough to agree to go to the motel.

12 John can't go because he hurt his arm.

Our simple causal world needs more information and apparatus to handle these. After Chapters 3, 4, and 5 present such apparatus, we will discuss some modifications to how we deal with causal chains.

What we have developed so far is useful nonetheless. It allows us to deal with physical events. Since we can now infer events that are missing explicitly from a causal chain, the next interesting question is when that is not possible to do. That is, even in the physical world of events and states, people still manage to skip enough intermediate steps in a chain so as to exasperate a naive chain builder. For example, there is nothing wrong with the sequence:

13 John ordered a new suit. He paid the bill with his credit card.

However, a causal chain builder would not be able to discern any obvious connection between the **MTRANS** of order and the **ATRANS** of the suit and the **ATRANS** of the money.

While there is, in fact, a causal chain there, it cannot be derived simply by using the principles of causal chain construction. To build the chain, what we need is knowledge of the social world rather than the physical world we have been discussing. This will be discussed in the next chapter.

2.4 Causal Propensity

We have concentrated thus far on situations with incompletely specified causality, that could be filled in more or less straightforwardly with a single most plausible sequence of conceptualizations. Psychologists have long been interested in the subjectively very compelling nature of certain causal sequences, for example, those arising from **PROPEL** actions (Heider, 1944; Michotte, 1963). A more complicated case of especial interest to psychologists, arises when two distinct causal chains compete as explanations for the outcome of an ambiguous situation.

One type of illustration of such causal ambiguity arises from controversial events in political conflict situations. What causes British troops to arrest Irish Republican Army leaders? The I.R.A. says it is a consequence of a British policy of oppression, and the British say it is a consequence of the I.R.A. practicing violence. What causes South African blacks to riot? The blacks say it is the humiliations of apartheid, and the South African government says it is Communist agitators. In politics, it is very frequent to see a hated group as the causal agent initiating actions which result in bad consequences. Causation is invested in actors perceived to have malevolent intentions. Explanations involving multiple causation are avoided.

Going beyond politics, actors are seen in general as having a certain degree of causal propensity in their appropriate sphere of action. In cases of causal ambiguity, actors who are credited with high causal propensity may tend to take the blame (as does the malevolent enemy), or get the credit (as, say, the professor does for a paper written jointly with a graduate student). Concepts of causal propensity come from whatever knowledge is available about the attitudes and capabilities of actors, and this knowledge can be manipulated by shadings in the verbal descriptions of actors – as every propagandist well knows, or in how closely available knowledge is scanned for clues as to what might have caused a later event. The first point is well illustrated in a subtle study by Bar-Hillel (1975), described in a paper by Tversky and Kahneman (1976) on causal thinking. In the study, the responsibility for a taxicab accident was seen differently depending on the wording of a statistical generalization about the cab company.

Tversky and Kahneman were interested in concepts of probability which do not concern us here, but we can paraphrase the Bar-Hillel study appropriately. Subjects were shown a paragraph describing an accident as below. (The key sentence is underlined here for emphasis).

14 Two cab companies, the Green and the Blue, operate in a city. The vast majority of cabs in the city are Green cabs. One night, a cab was involved in a hit-and-run accident. A witness identified the cab as a Blue cab. The court tested his ability to identify cabs under the appropriate visibility conditions. The witness was correct in most of the cases.

Subjects given this story were asked whether a Green cab or Blue cab was more likely to have caused the accident. Overwhelmingly, subjects choose the Blue cab as more likely. Now consider a variant of the story, which has exactly the same objective likelihood structure as (14), but a different wording of the second sentence:

15 Two cab companies, the Green and the Blue, operate in a city. The vast majority of cab accidents in the city involve Green cabs. One night, a cab was involved in a hit-and-run accident. A witness identified the cab as a Blue cab. The court tested his ability to identify cabs under the appropriate visibility conditions. The witness was correct in most of the cases.

Subjects shown story (15) and asked whether a Blue cab or a Green cab was more likely to have caused the accident, in this case were not so sure, and many chose Green as more likely.

Tversky and Kahneman (1976) explain the objectively unjustified difference in judgements in the two cases as follows: In (14), 'the difference in mere frequencies of Green and Blue cabs cannot be psychologically related to the propensity of any particular cab to be involved in an accident, and it is therefore ignored'. In (15), 'the difference in frequency of accident is interpreted as a difference in accident-proneness and it is therefore utilized'. In other words, the greater frequency of Green cab accidents suggests that Green cabs are dangerous and/or their drivers reckless, and these causal propensities are available to attach themselves to any individual ambiguous case.

Illustrations of a related point about causal propensity is a study by Ross et al. (1976). Subjects were induced to first 'explain' particular events (such as suicide) in the later lives of clinical patients whose case histories they had read; then they were told that the later events were not really known to have happened, but were arbitrarily attached to the cases to create the experimental task. Subjects were then asked, nevertheless, to judge the likelihood that the particular events might really happen (e.g., that the person would really commit suicide). The task of identifying known antecedents to explain a particular event considerably increased average estimates of the event's likelihood, compared to estimates made by people who read the same case history but did not engage in any 'explaining' task. Presumably the explaining task leads subjects to construct reason causations (Section 2.2, rule CS5) flowing from very powerful early mental states, i.e., strong causal propensities.

3 Scripts

3.1 Introduction

How do people organize all the knowledge they must have in order to understand? How do people know what behavior is appropriate for a particular situation? To put it more concretely, how do you know that, in a restaurant, the waitress will get you the food you ask for whereas if you ask her for a pair of shoes, or you ask her for food on a bus she will react as if you had done something odd?

People know how to act appropriately because they have knowledge about the world they live in. What is the nature and form of that knowledge? How is it organized? When is it brought to bear? How is it accessed? What portions of that knowledge are thought about and used, and under what circumstances?

These examples are rather special, but the concept of causal propensity is important, and we shall have more to say about it in Chapter 6. The psychological misuse of causal thinking raises an important general issue for artificial intelligence. In the first study above (like others of similar character) people were misled into treating two statistically equivalent situations differently because of the active wording of (15) which suggests that drivers of Green cabs are generally more reckless or less competent, versus the passive wording of (14) which simply suggests that Green cabs are generally more numerous. In the second study, clinical material scanned under a false assumption about a future event leads to unwarranted exaggeration of particular causal linkages. A computer understanding system might conceivably be designed not to be misled by such nuances, but this would be at the probable expense of considerable computing time and effort.

However, prior experience with similar problems and instructions to think very carefully could also steer people away from errors. In other words, the tendency to make inferential errors is not something true of people and false of machines. Rather, errors occur when systems process rapidly and without much depth, and they can be minimized in systems operating in 'careful mode' (cf. Sussman, 1974). But, carefulness is a luxury which understanding systems may often not be able to afford.

Inferential concepts like causal propensity are 'quick-and-dirty' and thus useful heuristics. They help the understander make rapid sense of causal ambiguities. It is worthwhile, perhaps even mandatory, to program such short-cuts in any real-time computer understanding system, even at the cost of occasional errors. The short-cut principle of causal propensity says that in cases of causal ambiguity, pick the causal chain originating from the generally most causally active actor. Principles such as this enable people to read and understand quickly.

We recognize two classes of knowledge that people bring to bear during the understanding process: general knowledge and specific knowledge. General knowledge enables a person to understand and interpret another person's actions simply because the other person is a human being with certain standard needs who lives in a world which has certain standard methods of getting those needs fulfilled. Thus, if someone asks you for a glass of water, you need not ask why he wants it. Even if he later uses it for a nonstandard but clear purpose - say he throws it in somebody's face and steals that person's watch - you have no trouble interpreting his actions. It is easy to understand what his plan was, and why he needed the water. We may never have observed such a sequence before, but our general knowledge about people and the world they live in allows us to interpret the events we see.

We use specific knowledge to interpret and participate in events we have been through many times. Specific detailed knowledge about a situation allows us to do less processing and wondering about frequently experienced events. We need not ask why somebody wants to see our ticket when we enter a theater, or why one should be quiet, or how long it is appropriate to sit in one's seat. Knowledge of specific situations such as theaters allows us to interpret the remarks that people make about theaters. Consider how difficult it would be to interpret 'Second aisle on your right' without the detailed knowledge about theaters that the patron and the usher both have. It would be rather odd to respond 'What about the second aisle on my right?' or 'Where is my seat?' or 'Is this how I get into the theater?' The usher simply takes the ticket and, assuming you understand and have specific knowledge about theatres, utters his otherwise cryptic remark without any verbal input from you.

The remainder of this chapter deals with the nature and form of such specific knowledge. We shall discuss issues related to general knowledge in Chapter 4.

With stories as well as with isolated utterances, human readers seem to have no trouble in rapidly extracting the features of the situation intended for emphasis by the writer. Consider, for example, the sentence:

1 While giving his order to the waiter at Mamma Leone's one evening, Spillane was approached by the owner, a notorious Mafia figure.

The 'while'-clause functions to set the Leone's restaurant context with its huge store of generalized and specific world knowledge. Nevertheless, the reader does not slow down to work out who 'the waiter' is or how Spillane came to be talking to him, but quickly notes that Spillane is probably at a table, in the act of ordering, in a well-known Italian restaurant.

Such specific knowledge exists in detail for every mentally competent person in the world with respect to every standard situation that he has been in many times. What form does such knowledge take?

We established in Chapter 2 that the directed inference process results in a connected causal chain of events. This causal chain is useful for representing any sequential flow of events. Since certain sequences of events frequently occur in a specific order we must postulate that people have developed special mechanisms to deal with them. That is, there are certain groupings of causal chains that exist in the form of large conceptual units.

We would anticipate that two special mechanisms are needed. First, we must be able to refer to a frequent event sequence in a sketchy manner. An event sequence with ten steps in it may be identifiable from just the first and last of those events. That means we need a special inference capability that can do more than the one described in Chapter 2. It would be a tedious and, most likely, unending process, to try to recover every missing event in a causal chain. So, the first special mechanism must be able to recognize that a script – a standard event sequence – has been mentioned.

Second, we need a mechanism for recovering steps that have been left out of a causal chain. Some of these steps may be needed to understand a given event sequence. We call this mechanism a script applier. It fills in the causal chain between two seemingly unrelated events by referring to the script recognized by the first special mechanism.

These two understanding mechanisms have their counterparts in the generation of language. When someone decides to tell a story that references a script, he recognizes that he need not (and because he would otherwise be considered rather boring, should not) mention every detail of his story. He can safely assume that his listener is familiar with the referenced script and will understand the story as long as certain crucial items are mentioned.

Let us look at some simple stories to see how this can be done:

2 John went to a restaurant. He asked the waitress for coq au vin. He paid the check and left.

3 John got on a bus. He fell asleep. He woke up in New York.

4 John was the quarterback. As time ran down, he threw a 60-yard pass into the end zone. His team won the game.

5 John went to Bill's birthday party. Bill opened his presents. John ate the cake and left.

These stories are understandable because they make reference to frequently occurring scripts. Much more than the three lines given in each story is understood by someone listening to it. A story understander must fill in the parts of each story that were left out. A story understander can do this by implicity or explicitly referring to the referenced script.

Consider stories (6) and (7):

6 John went in to a restaurant. He saw a waitress. He went home.

7 John was walking on the street. He thought of cabbages. He picked up a shoe horn.

The connectivity of stories (6) and (7) is altogether different from that of stories (2)-(5). Stories (2)-(5) make reference to a script. Story (6) seems to reference a script but never quite gets there. By this we mean that the point or main goal of the script cannot safely be inferred. Did John eat or didn't he? You can't tell from this story. That is, in story (6) the events seem disconnected because of uncertainty that the referenced script should actually be instantiated. Story (7) does not reference a script and in any case it makes little sense. Stories need not reference scripts to make sense. Consider story (8):

8a John wanted a newspaper.
 b He found one on the street.
 c He read it.

Although (8) does not reference a script it is understandable. The events in it can be easily connected to each other with information readily obtainable from the story. In order to connect (a) to (b) it is necessary only to hypothesize 'John saw and picked up the newspaper.' One of these conditions is given by the story explicitly and the other is readily inferable. They do not violate necessary conditions or other conditions of the story itself (as discussed in Chapter 2). It is possible to connect (b) to (c) by the inferences that 'find' results in 'have', and 'have' enables 'read'.

Such simple connectivity is present in (2)-(5) only by virtue of the existence of appropriate scripts. Contrast Story (2) with Story (9):

2 John went to a restaurant. He asked the waitress for coq au vin.

9 John went to a park. He asked the midget for a mouse. He picked up the box and left.

In Story (9) we are unprepared for the reference to 'the' midget rather than 'a' midget and 'the' box rather than 'a' box. Further, we are incapable of connecting the last two lines of the story, without a great deal of effort. Story 9 allows us no reference to a standard situation in which midgets, mouses, boxes and parks relate. The story is not understandable, simply by virtue of the fact that we have no world knowledge that serves to connect its pieces. If there were a standard 'mouse buying script' that averred that only midgets in parks sold mice which were always packed in boxes, then we would be able to apply that script to Story 9 and connect the pieces of the story. What scripts do, then, is to provide connectivity.

In Story 2, which is superficially quite similar to Story 9, we get a great deal of connectivity. We are not suprised when 'the' waitress or 'the' check are mentioned. We understand exactly the relationship between asking for coq au vin and paying the check. Further, we assume that John ate coq au vin, that he waited a while before being served, that he looked at a menu, and so on. All this information is brought up by the restaurant script. Further, it is brought up by a particular part or track of the restaurant script, namely the kind of restaurant in which one orders coq au vin. This 'fancy restaurant track' of the restaurant script includes within it the possibility of a maitre d', a wine steward, tablecloths, paying with credit cards, fancy desserts and so on.

Thus the restaurant script must contain a tremendous amount of information that encompasses the enormous variability of what can occur in a restaurant. There must also be a 'fast food restaurant' track, a cafeteria track, etc. in the restaurant script, that includes the entering, ordering and paying scenes, but has a different set of possibilities than the fancy restaurant. In the 'fast food track', paying can occur immediately after ordering and before eating; eating may occur inside or outside the restaurant; the person who takes the order must be approached by the patron rather than going to where the patron is seated.

The presence of such tracks in the restaurant script is indicated by the understandability of stories that make use of those tracks. For example, consider Story (10):

10 John went into the restaurant. John ordered a Big Mac. He paid for it and found a nice park to eat in.

This story is understandable precisely because it calls up the track of the restaurant script that states that you don't have to be inside a fast food restaurant to eat there. However, if a reader does not understand that 'Big Mac' calls up the fast food track, he will have difficulty understanding the story. That is, the same story, with 'coq au vin' substituted for 'Big Mac', would seem rather odd. A story with this substitution would in principle be understandable, but the lack of applicability of available scripts would make it harder (and take more time) for a hearer to understand.

Thus while it is possible to understand a story without using a script, scripts are an important part of story understanding. What they do is let you leave out the boring details when you are talking or writing, and fill them in when you are listening or reading.

We shall now describe a script in more definite terms. A script is a structure that describes appropriate sequences of events in a particular context. A script is made up of slots and requirements about what can fill those slots. The structure is an interconnected whole, and what is in one slot affects what can be in another. Scripts handle stylized everyday situations. They are not subject to much change, nor do they provide the apparatus for handling totally novel situations. Thus, a script is a predetermined, stereotyped sequence of actions that defines a well-known situation. Scripts allow for new references to objects within them just as if these objects had been previously mentioned; objects within a script may take 'the' without explicit introduction because the script itself has already implicitly introduced them.

Stories (2)-(5) all make use of scripts. There are scripts for eating in a restaurant, riding a bus, watching and playing a football game, participating in a birthday party, and so on. These scripts are responsible for filling in the obvious information that has been left out of a story. Of course, it is obvious only to those understanders who actually know and can use the script. For example, these questions might be asked of hearers immediately after respective stories (2)-(5) with the full expectation of an accurate and fast reply.

Q1 What did John eat?

Q2 Where did the bus go?

Q3 What happened to the pass John threw?

Q4 Where did the presents come from?

Every script has associated with it a number of roles. When a script is called for use, i.e., 'instantiated' by a story, the actors in the story assume the roles within the instantiated script. If no actor has been specifically mentioned when a particular script is instantiated, his presence is nonetheless assumed and a default unnamed actor is used in his place. All this happens whenever a script is called up. This explains the use of the definite article in reference to 'the waitress'. She has been implicitly mentioned before by the initial instantiation of the script. (Roles are discussed at greater length in Chapter 6.)

A script must be written from one particular role's point of view. A customer sees a restaurant one way, a cook sees it another way. Scripts from many perspectives are combined to form what might be considered the 'whole view' of the restaurant. Such a 'whole view' is rarely, if ever, needed or called up in actual understanding, although it might well constitute what we may consider to be one's 'concept' of a restaurant.

We have built, at Yale, a computer program called SAM ('Script Applier Mechanism') that understands simple stories about script-based situations. It is described in detail in Chapter 8. Much of what we have to say here about script application has been influenced by our experience with that program. It has been tested most extensively with stories about restaurants. Let us consider the restaurant script in detail.

3.2 The Restaurant Script

The following is a sketch of one track of the restaurant script (the coffee shop track) from the point of view of the customer. Since the particular verbs that might best describe each action may not always fit in a given story that calls up a script, the actions of a script are described in terms of the underlying events that take place. The primitive ACT is the core of each event in the chain of events being effected. One of the scenes (ordering) is given below with a good deal of optional detail. The options to the right provide a single coherent path through the scene; shortcuts and loops are indicated on the left.

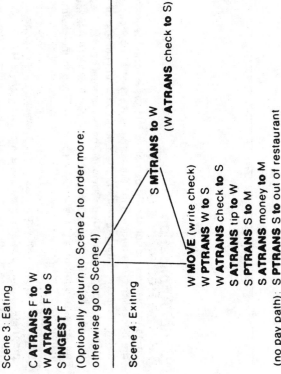

Track: Coffee Shop

Props: Tables
 Menu
 F-Food
 Check
 Money

Roles: S-Customer
 W-Waiter
 C-Cook
 M-Cashier
 O-Owner

Entry conditions: S is hungry.
 S has money.

Results: S has less money
 O has more money
 S is not hungry
 S is pleased (optional)

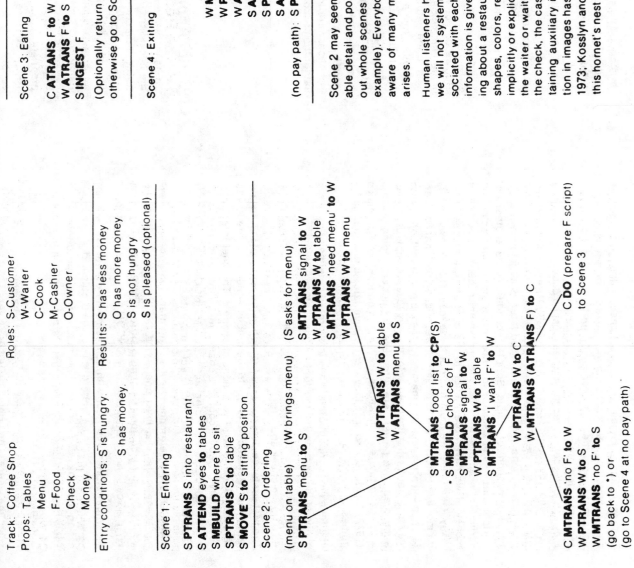

Scene 1: Entering

S **PTRANS** S into restaurant
S **ATTEND** eyes to tables
S **MBUILD** where to sit
S **PTRANS** S to table
S **MOVE** S to sitting position

Scene 2: Ordering

(menu on table)   (W brings menu)   (S asks for menu)
S **PTRANS** menu to S   S **MTRANS** signal **to** W
                                          W **PTRANS** W to table
                                          S **MTRANS** 'need menu' **to** W
                                          W **PTRANS** W to menu

       W **PTRANS** W to table
       W **ATRANS** menu to S

   S **MTRANS** food list **to CP**(S)
 · S **MBUILD** choice of F
   S **MTRANS** signal **to** W
   W **PTRANS** W to table
   S **MTRANS** 'I want F' **to** W

       W **PTRANS** W to C
       W **MTRANS** (**ATRANS** F) **to** C

C **MTRANS** 'no F' **to** W   C **DO** (prepare F script)
W **PTRANS** W to S   to Scene 3
W **MTRANS** 'no F' **to** S
(go back to *) or
(go to Scene 4 at no pay path)

Scene 3: Eating

C **ATRANS** F **to** W
W **ATRANS** F **to** S
S **INGEST** F

(Optionally return to Scene 2 to order more;
otherwise go to Scene 4)

Scene 4: Exiting

                                   S **MTRANS to** W
                                        (W **ATRANS** check **to** S)
W **MOVE** (write check)
W **PTRANS** W **to** S
W **ATRANS** check **to** S
S **ATRANS** tip **to** W
S **PTRANS** S **to** M
S **ATRANS** money **to** M
(no pay path): S **PTRANS** S **to** out of restaurant

Scene 2 may seem very detailed. In fact we have left out considerable detail and possible options in each of the scenes. We have left out whole scenes (the 'wait to be seated by the hostess' scene, for example). Everybody who has been to a restaurant often enough is aware of many more details and can use them if the occasion arises.

Human listeners have available another kind of information which we will not systematically treat, namely imagery (mainly visual) associated with each action in the sequence. Often, descriptive visual information is given with each action in a story, but even if it is not, the listener hearing about a restaurant will typically call to mind impressions of the shapes, colors, relative positions and other properties of objects implicitly or explicitly present in the scene: tables, tablecloths, how the waiter or waitress is dressed, how the food looks (and smells), the check, the cash register, etc. With each action a 'vignette' containing auxiliary information is stored. The nature of the information in images has been the subject of much controversy (Pylyshyn, 1973; Kosslyn and Pomerantz, 1977), and we do not wish to stir up this hornet's nest here.

The restaurant script is a giant causal chain. Although the details have been left out, each action in the above script results in conditions that enable the next to occur. To perform the next act in the sequence, the previous acts must be completed satisfactorily. If they cannot be completed the hitches must be dealt with. Perhaps a new action not prescribed in the straightforward version of the script will be generated in order to get things moving again. This 'prescriptive' behavior, to be discussed later, is an important additional component of scripts. Script preconditions are another important part of the causal sequence in scripts. In the restaurant script, for example, we must inquire whether the main actor has money. If we have no evidence to the contrary, we proceed normally. Otherwise, we must find out if the main actor knows he has no money. If the answer is negative, we must predict that an interference will arise when the main actor tries to pay his bill; otherwise we must predict that the main actor may try to leave without paying. Such predictive powers are often used in understanding. Events with strong future implications are 'kept in mind' – like Charniak's (1972) 'demons' – so that they can resolve later inferential ambiguities.

In a text, new script information is interpreted in terms of its place in one of the paths within the script. Thus in story (2):

2 John went to a restaurant. He asked the waitress for coq au vin. He paid the check and left.

The first sentence describes the first action in scene 1 of the restaurant script. Sentence 2 refers to the crucial action of scene 2, and sentence 3 to the last two actions of scene 4. The final interpretation of story (2) would contain a chain through the restaurant script that included all the principal actions (or MAINCONS, for main conceptualizations) needed to connect the events.

MAINCONS are determined by their importance in a scene. For every scene there is at least one MAINCON. In scene 2 above, the MAINCON is the customer stating his order (MTRANS 'I want F' to W). If a scene is 'instantiated' its MAINCON must have happened.

Most real stories that deal with scripts relate events that are unusual with respect to a standard script. The problem in script application then, besides deciding how much of a script to infer, is to know how to tie together events that are not directly in the script.

Consider story (11):

11 John went to a restaurant. He ordered a hamburger. It was cold when the waitress brought it. He left her a very small tip.

In story (11) the first two sentences describe actions in scenes 1 and 2. Part of the third sentence is in the script as an action of scene 3, but there is also the information that the hamburger is cold. The fourth sentence ('He left her a very small tip') is a modification of the 'S ATRANS tip to W' action of scene 4. The modifier, 'very small' is presumably related to the unexpected information about the 'cold hamburger'. Even an unknowledgable script applier, checking story (11) against the standard restaurant script, could come up with the low-level hypothesis that the small size of the tip must have something to do with the temperature of the hamburger, since these two items of information are the only deviations from the script.

But we do not want our processor to lack knowledge. In slightly more complex examples, adequate understanding requires attention to the nature of deviations from the script. A smart processor can infer from a cold hamburger that the INGEST in scene 3 will not lead to the result of S having pleasure. The concept of a very small tip can be stored with the restaurant script as a reaction to the violation of pleasure. Thus the processor might even infer that a cold hamburger was unsatisfactory by working backwards from its understanding of a small tip. This might be necessary if the food description were ambiguous in desirability, say, a 'very rare steak', rather than a 'cold hamburger'.

3.3 Script Application

To define when a script should be called into play, script headers are necessary. The headers for the restaurant script are concepts having to do with hunger, restaurants, and so on in the context of a plan of action for getting fed. Obviously contexts must be restricted to avoid calling up the restaurant script for sentences that use the word 'restaurant' as a place ('Fuel oil was delivered to the restaurant').

Even if a proper header is encountered, however, it may not be appropriate to call up all the details of a script or even its MAINCONs. This is because script references in stories are often to 'fleeting scripts'.

12 John took a bus to New York.
In New York he went to a museum.
Then he took a train home.

In this example, the names of scripts are mentioned and it is presumed that each script proceeded normally. (Alternatively, it is possible that some abnormal things happened which were considered unworthy of narration by the author of the story. This alternative makes no practical difference except in very special cases.) There is a serious question about what 'proceeded normally' means in terms of what really is stored in the long-term memory of an understanding system.

Here we have the three explicitly stated scripts, **BUS, MUSEUM-GOING**, and **TRAIN**. (From this point, we shall indicate a script name by a $ in front of the name; thus **$BUS** indicates the bus script). It is unlikely that people would fill in the default paths of each of these scripts if exposed to story (12). What is more likely is that they simply remember that the script occurred by establishing a pointer to the entire script. In this manner, the information about the script is available if needed, but memory is not cluttered with gratuitous detail. The story can be stored as a sequence of three pointers.

For a script to be non-fleeting, two of its lines must occur, a header and one other line. When a header is found, requests (as in Riesbeck's (1975) parsing system) are called up that connect possible inputs with events within the script. If such an input is found, then the script is 'instantiated'; that is, a copy of some of its general details is made, with slots filled in by the known properties of the story at hand. The role references are concretized. For example, a reference to 'the bus driver' results in the creation of a token with a pointer to the script role Driver. General information about specific roles such as Driver is stored under role themes, (see Chapter 6) and can be accessed if a role person undertakes some action not already in the script.

The nature of instantiated detail depends upon the story event(s) found after the header is found. Consider this story:

13 John went to a restaurant.
He ordered chicken.
He left a large tip.

The action of ordering calls in the ordering scene of the restaurant script. Since the entering scene lies on the path to ordering, we assume that its main conceptualization has taken place. Then the MAINCONs between ordering and tipping are assumed, as well as the final exit. Consequently our understanding system will treat example (13) as if it had actually been:

14 John went to a restaurant.
  He sat down.
  He read a menu.
  He ordered chicken.
  He ate the chicken.
  He left a large tip.
  He paid the check.
  He left the restaurant.

That is, we fill in, as if we had actually heard them, the events on the default path of the applied script, as long as we are simply filling in the steps between explicitly stated points. Thus, in order to get from 'entering' to 'ordering', it is safe to assume 'sitting' and 'reading'. In order to get from 'ordering' to 'tipping' it is safe to assume 'eating'. Since 'tipping' is a prelude to 'paying' and 'leaving', we also assume 'leaving'. We do not want to assume too many steps when we are told of events that are far apart in the script. Thus, the story, 'John went to a restaurant. He left a large tip.', is considered odd. Do we want to assume that he ate? It is highly likely that John did eat in this story. Nonetheless, we might not want to simply assume it.

So, the rules for dealing with instantiated scripts are directly related to how many steps are left out. Essentially, instantiated scripts are those that make explicit one or more specific steps in the script itself. It is then our job to fill in the surrounding steps that ought to be explicitly inferred and treat them as if they were said.

The rules for activating a script are dependent on certain key concepts or conceptualizations when found in certain contexts. The restaurant context should not be called up simply because an input sentence refers to 'restaurant', but this is not to say that access to the script should be completely suppressed, because script-related information may be useful in later stages of understanding. For example, in 'I met a bus driver in the restaurant', remembering that one of the persons in the story has a role in the bus script may be crucial for interpreting what he might say or do afterwards. (Such role information is discussed further in Chapter 6.)

The conceptualizations which invoke a script are its headers. These headers come in four varieties, which are classified on the basis of how strongly they predict that the associated context will in fact be instantiated.

The first type is called a Precondition Header (PH) because it triggers the script reference on the basis of a main script precondition being mentioned in the text. For example, the sentence 'John was hungry' is a PH for the restaurant script because it is the goal condition for the MAINCON (INGEST food), which is normally assumed to be true when the script is instantiated. A story understander having access to both scripts and plans would make the prediction (a relatively weak one, to be sure) that the restaurant context would come up because this script is known to be a common means of implementing a plan of action for getting fed. A related PH would be an actual statement of the goal the script is normally assumed to achieve, or one from which the goal could easily be inferred. In 'John wanted a Big Mac', or 'John wanted some Italian food', the inference chain to the script precondition is straightforward. Knowledge about the existence of an Italian food subtrack of the restaurant script would make the PH prediction about the probable invocation of that script even more forceful.

A second type of Header making stronger predictions than a PH about the associated context is called an Instrumental Header (IH). An IH commonly comes up in inputs which refer to two or more contexts, of which at least one can be interpreted as a 'instrumental' for the others. For example, in 'John took the subway to the restaurant', both the subway and restaurant contexts would be predicted, since subsequent inputs about either make perfectly good sense. Here, the reference to the restaurant is anticipatory, and the subway is a recognized instrumental means of reaching locales in which more important script goals can be expected to be achieved. In turn, we understand that the restaurant script is in some sense instrumental to the business context in a sentence like 'John went to a business lunch'. An important function of scripts is to provide the background in which more planful activities are carried out.

The notion of a time-place locale for situations leads to the third and most strongly predictive type of header, the Locale Header (LH). Many situations are known to have a 'residence', a place or building where they characteristically go on. Indeed, many organizations have distinctively designed buildings (for example, McDonald's Golden Arches) which signal their script to the public. When an understander reads that an actor is in the proximity of such a residence, or better yet, inside the residence, expectations about the occurrence of the script are correspondingly reinforced. Examples of LH are 'John went to the soccer field' or 'John went into the Museum of Modern Art'. It is important to note that LH's need not be complete sentences: certain kinds of prepositional phrases ('At Leone's, John ordered a hot dog', 'On the bus, John's pocket was picked') are often used as a shorthand to define locale. Sentences like these can usually be paraphrased as a temporal clause of the form 'When X was at locale Y' attached to the main conceptualization.

The conceptual pattern that is being looked for here is X be LOC(script header). This pattern also occurs in places where we do not want to invoke a script. For example in (15):

15 The delivery man brought fifteen boxes of doughnuts to the restaurant. He went inside and spoke to the manager.

Clearly, the delivery man is in the restaurant here, but we do not want to predict that he will now eat (although he might). In (15), we call up the $DELIVERY script first. While the restaurant script can be a subpart of a larger script (such as $TRIP) it must be marked as not being capable of being subsumed by $DELIVERY. This marking calls off the restaurant script initially, but keeps open expectations for subsequent calls to the restaurant script. Thus if we see another scene of the script (e.g., if the delivery man sits down and orders) we must be prepared to initiate the full restaurant script. Thus, script headers can be suppressed by certain contexts.

The fourth kind of header is the Internal Conceptualization Header (ICH). Any conceptualization or role from a script may occur in a text. It will sometimes call the script up and sometimes it will not. The most obvious cases of these alternatives are when a role name (such as waitress) is used in the locale of the role or away from the role (as in 'I went out with a waitress').

A problem occurs when we have a story such as (16):

16 John went to visit his friend Mary who was a waitress. While he was waiting for her, he ordered a hamburger.

The reference to restaurant here is only by inference. However, that inference is enough to set up a possible expectation for the activities of the restaurant script. As we said earlier, two items are really necessary to be certain a script has been invoked. Here, the second item is a conceptualization internal to the script. Its recognition comes from the mention of waitress, plus the recognition of the conceptual sense of 'order' (i.e., the restaurant sense). Only with these two key concepts in context can the script be called.

In order to relate an unexpected sentence to an instantiated script we need to know what kinds of events can cause detours or abrupt endings in scripts. We recognize two broad classes of such events: interferences and distractions. Interferences are states or actions which prevent the normal continuation of a script. There are two types of interferences: obstacles, where some enabling condition for an impending action is missing, and errors, where an action is completed with an unexpected and inappropriate result.

The actor encountering an obstacle may respond by taking corrective action to try to produce the missing enabling condition. Such corrective actions we call prescriptions. Alternatively, the actor may give up, either immediately or after one or more prescriptions fail, and exit from the scene. The actor encountering an error is in a different situation. The usual correctives are loops—repetitions of the action to try to get it to come out right. Often a prescription must accompany the loop. For example, when the waitress brings you a hot dog after you order a hamburger, it is unreasonable merely to order a hamburger again as if nothing had happened. If the error is to be fixed, the standard prescription would be to explain to the waitress (or perhaps argue with her) that you did not order the hot dog. Alternatively, the actor may tolerate an error and proceed through the script anyway. Thus if the waitress brings the wrong order, the customer might either send it back and reorder, or accept the substitute or trade with a friend. Bad errors may of course present obstacles, so that the next action is not even enabled, e.g. if the waitress brings an empty casserole, then the option of eating anyway is removed.

Beyond responding instrumentally to an obstacle or error an actor may often also respond emotionally. He may express frustration, sadness, or anger at obstacles. After certain errors, he may be indignant, after others, amused. These emotional states are all reactions to interferences. They may be intense enough on occasion to abort the initial goal(s) of the script, as when the disgusted customer loses his appetite, and/or they may initiate derivative goals (e.g., punishing the guilty role person, say, by leaving the waitress a very small tip as in story (11)).

Distractions are unexpected states or actions which initiate new goals for the actor, carrying him temporarily or permanently out of the script. By their nature, distractions are not tied to a particular script—any number of things can distract a customer in a restaurant, for example. It is possible for some event to be both an inter-

3.4 Interferences and Distractions

Suppose that a script has been instantiated, and then a sentence comes along which does not relate to anything in the script:

17 John went to a restaurant.
    He ordered veal scallopini.
    The weather was rather poor.

There is no way in which the instantiated script helps the understanding of the third sentence. That unexpected sentence refers to a new topic which might be another script or might not. In any case, the computer or human understander must simply wait to see what comes next.

Often a sentence which does not seem to fit anything directly in an instantiated script can be related to the script indirectly.

18 John went to a restaurant.
    He sat down and signaled the waitress.
    He got mad.
    He left.

In the story above, we must be careful not to assume all of the events on the default path of the restaurant script. The sentence 'He sat down and signaled the waitress' leads us to assume the default entering scene and the beginning of the ordering scene. But on seeing 'He got mad' we must stop processing the script in the normal fashion. At this point we must find out what could have made John mad—was it something within the scriptal context, or in some new context? The answer is inferred via a simple rule about anger, namely that it is ordinarily caused by something some other person either did or did not do. We immediately look at the script to see if some action is called for on the part of another person at this point in the script. The answer is that a waitress should come to John at this point. So we can assume that this did not happen, and that this is why John got mad and left. It is important to remember the point in the script where the exit took place. We do not want to infer the rest of the default path of the script (i.e., that he paid the check before leaving).

The above inference is a weak one. John may have gotten mad about something else. But text is usually presented so as to be understood correctly. That is, people don't intentionally mislead in stories of this kind. If something non-standard had occurred it probably would have been mentioned explicitly. In filling out scripts, we are relatively safe with weak inferences precisely because it is usual for non-standard occurrences to be explicitly mentioned.

ference and a distraction, such as the waitress dropping the soup, which fails to complete the ATRANS of soup to the customer, and which may initiate a new goal of getting the customer's clothes dry.

The above concepts provide a set of questions which a processor can ask when it encounters an unexpected input within a script:

a Does it specify or imply the absence of an enablement for an impending script action? (Obstacle)

b Does it specify or imply that a completed action was done in an unusual manner, or to an object other than the one(s) instantiated in the script? (Error)

c Does it specify an action which can be understood as the corrective resolution of an interference? (Prescription) This question would be activated when an obstacle is inferred from or described directly in the text.

d Does it specify or imply the repetition of a previous action? (Loop) This is activated when an error is inferred from or described directly in the text.

e Does it specify or imply emotional expression by the actor, likely to have been caused by an interference? (Reaction)

f Does it specify or imply that the actor will have a new goal that has nothing to do with the original script? (Distraction)

g Does it specify or imply the motivated abandonment of the script by the main actor? (Abandonment)

If any of the questions a – f are answered in the affirmative, then a detour is established within the script! New expectations will now guide the processing of subsequent inputs. A detour path will be followed until the original script either is reentered or abandoned. Scriptal deviations can thus be handled in a well-structured way.

The identification of inputs as obstacles, errors, etc., often depends upon having scripts available as points of reference. If we were not in a script, we might not recognize certain states as interferences, or if we did, we still might not know with what they were interfering. Compare, for example, the two stories:

19 John went to a restaurant.
He sat down.
He discovered he didn't have his magnifying glass.

20 John went for a walk.
He turned into Main St.
He discovered he didn't have his magnifying glass.

In story (19), it is easy to understand that the magnifying glass might be important because the menu is expected to arrive next. In story (20) we have no clear idea about the significance of the magnifying glass. 'A walk' does not specify enough of a sequence of events to be a script (unless we know John's personal habits). With no anticipated next event, we have no information on why the magnifier might be used.

The detour categories a-f tend to occur in certain standard patterns. One common type of sequence involves successful resolution of an interference:

(Obstacle) – (Prescription) – (Success),
or (Error) – (Loop) – (Success)

These success sequences return processing to the script at the point of the previously blocked action, in the case of an obstacle, or following the previously flawed action, in the case of an error. The category 'Success' may often be implicit, but sometimes it is explicitly marked, and we need to recognize it if it occurs. Consider an elaboration of story (19):

21 John went to a restaurant.
He sat down.
He discovered he didn't have his magnifying glass.
He asked the waitress to read him the menu.
She agreed.

The obstacle in the third sentence by inference relates to the action 'S MTRANS food list to CP(s)' in the Ordering Scene. The normal instrumental action for this is ATTENDing eyes to the menu, and sometimes this ATTEND in turn has an instrumental action, namely GRASPing the magnifying glass in proper position. The enablement of having the glass is here missing. The customer chooses a prescription of a type which is of general utility, namely asking someone else to produce a result difficult to produce oneself. (Prescriptions, like medicines, are sometimes general in their applicability, sometimes specific.) The waitress agrees to his request, returning processing to the script with the action 'W MTRANS food list to CP(S)' anticipated as a substitute for 'S MTRANS food list to CP(S)'.

It was of course possible for the customer to choose to restore the missing enablement rather than to modify the act to be enabled. (These two distinct categories are both generally pertinent in overcoming obstacles.) The fourth sentence might have been, 'He borrowed a magnifying glass from his old friend Moody at the next table', or even, 'He went home to get it.' These prescriptions return processing to the original action, 'S MTRANS food list to S', although the going home alternative has the interesting property that the customer leaves the restaurant. We of course should expect him to return, and it is only by understanding the nature of detour paths that it is possible to realize that leaving the restaurant does not here terminate the script.

Some Obstacle-Prescription pairs are so common that they may come to be recognized as a path of the script itself. In the Ordering scene if S needs a menu but it is not on the table and the waitress doesn't spontaneously bring it, then we have an Obstacle – the enabling menu for knowing the food list is missing. An obvious prescription is to signal the waitress to bring a menu. Anyone who has eaten with any frequency in restaurants knows that this ordinarily works. Therefore it is unnecessary and somewhat odd to use alternative prescriptions – say, searching by yourself for where the menus are kept – unless the primary prescription fails.

Later on in the ordering scene there is a common Error-Loop pair. If the customer orders something which is not available, then from the point of view of the restaurant, he has made an error. The loop which is initiated, namely ordering something else, is virtually unavoidable. Thus we treat it as part of the main script.

Every act in the restaurant (or any other) script is potentially subject to obstacles and errors, each of which suggests its own appropriate prescriptions or loops. A few of these will occur with sufficient frequency that a person repeatedly exposed to the script situation will learn them along with the rest of the script. This is the major way in which scripts grow. In time, he may learn a sizeable number of alternative script paths which were once detours, even to the point of having prescriptive sub-branches to follow if there are anticipated interferences to prescriptions themselves. Indeed, occupational role members must have very elaborate scripts from their situational point of view, e.g., a trial lawyer's conception of the courtroom script. Occasional or new participants in the same situation, or those knowing it only from hearsay, naturally have much simpler scripts. In a child's early experiences in restaurants, for example, there is no appreciation of many of the details we have listed, such as the waitress bringing the check. (Some aspects of a child's learning of scripts are discussed in Chapter 9.) To the extent that experiences in certain situations are different, then, different scripts would be appropriate. When we refer to 'the' restaurant script, therefore, we are relying on those stereotyped details which are culturally consensual.

Returning to our discussion of detours, another common sequence is a chain of attempts to remove a stubborn obstacle:

(Obstacle) – (Prescription) – (Failure) – (Prescription) – (Failure)...

This chain terminates either in a final success, or in a last straw (Failure) – (Abandonment) sequence. In the latter case, control does not return to the script, of course, because the script is terminated.

Failures are prone to elicit emotional reactions, albeit emotional reactions also occur in direct response to obstacles and errors. Reactions in turn may or may not interrupt the instrumental sequence. Thus we might have either:

(Obstacle) – (Prescription) – (Failure) ⌐ (Reaction)
                                       └ (Prescription)...

or

(Obstacle) – (Prescription) – (Failure) – (Reaction) – (Distraction)

The (Reaction) – (Distraction) pair is meant to express those cases where the actor is carried away by his anger, annoyance, etc., initiating some nonscriptal action as a consequence.

Distractions need not occur only as a result of emotional reactions. Indeed, distractions can come from many sources. If the distracting events play out their course within the location of the situational script, then it is likely that control will return to the script at the point it was interrupted. The restaurant script may be said to be 'in abeyance' in the middle of the following story, for example:

22 John was eating in a restaurant.
Suddenly a thief tried to run off with several coats.
The manager tackled the thief.
The police came and arrested the man.
John paid the check and left.

With a script held in abeyance, the problem is to postpone the requests that were looking for completion of the script that was started (here, restaurant). That is, once the distraction scene starts we really do not expect the restaurant script to continue until the substory has ended. Nonetheless, it could continue at any point and requests to handle those inputs must be around.

A peculiar problem, though, is that the distraction substory may take the main actor out of the restaurant (or other script locus), and there is no telling whether or not he will return. One of the authors well remembers a personal experience at a modest restaurant with three friends some years ago. One of our group was not too hungry, and he asked the waiter just for a plate to share some of our spaghetti. The waiter said this would cost $.25 (a princely sum in those days), and we considered this an unreasonable pretension for such a humble place. Indignant, we decided to cancel our orders and leave. However, the waiter maintained that since the cook was already making the food, we were responsible for paying the bill. Now we were really mad, and we refused to pay. Thereupon he telephoned the police and we were led a block away to the station house and held on $200 bail. We were charged with failure to pay our obligation of $5.50, and were threatened with a night in jail. This sobered us, but we still did not want to surrender meekly to the restaurant manager who was standing by awaiting action. Did we return to the restaurant?.... Well, yes and no. We solved our problem by asking if we could have the food as a take-out order. That was agreed, and we went happily home with no extra plate and no extra charge.

Such a 'realistic' story involves the interaction of three scripts in abeyance at once (**$RESTAURANT**, **$PETTY CLAIM**, and **$JAIL HOUSE**), with an unexpected resolution of the interferences in all three.

3.5 Script Interactions

There are several ways in which more than one script can be active at once. In the previous section, we discussed the possibility of a 'script in abeyance', with a distracting script occurring within its boundaries. Another possibility is that the second script does more than merely distract from the first, but actually interferes, preventing the occurrence of normal actions:

23 John was eating in a dining car.
The train stopped short.
John's soup spilled.

The first sentence activates two scripts simultaneously, **$RESTAURANT** and **$TRAIN**. (One could postulate a dining car script that we

would expect someone who eats on dining cars to have. If we had that script here, these problems would not occur for this example).

When two scripts are active at once they compete for incoming items of information. Sometimes the events that fit in one affect the events of the other. The second sentence of (23) is clearly part of the train script. However, it causes a problem that doesn't usually occur in the restaurant script, namely that the table moved suddenly. We cannot expect the restaurant script to contain information about what to do or even what happens when a table moves suddenly. The third sentence (John's soup spilled) must be handled by means other than a script. This is done easily enough (in principle) by inferring the physical effects of a sudden train stop, and knowing that soup spills when moved abruptly. The problem here is the serious effect this sentence has on the restaurant script. It is as if the waiter has done something wrong, such as bringing the wrong order. That is, the customer can, at this point, ask for a replacement. A next sentence such as 'John called the waiter' would have to be handled as an Error-Loop detour path within the restaurant script. Remember that in this example two scripts are active at the same time. Any new item is potentially in either one. Here this means handling the spilling soup as an inference from the train moving and sending information to the instantiated restaurant script that the food is now no good (and perhaps that the customer is now wet). Such new inputs trigger detour paths in the restaurant script that are capable of handling them even though the impetus for them came from outside the script itself.

24 John was wooing his girlfriend in the restaurant.
He asked her for the salt.
Then he asked her for her hand.

In example (24), a similar problem occurs. Here again we have two scripts (**$ROMANCER** and **$RESTAURANT**) active at the same time. The next inputs don't affect each other, but which new input belongs to which script? The problem in this example is obviously not too serious and is quite a bit like semantic ambiguity in the disambiguation of isolated sentences. Resolution is possible as long as there is enough information in the script applier about the requirements of the two scripts. A serious problem occurs when a new event could occur in either of the two scripts. For example, suppose we had 'He asked her for money'. This might fit a path in the wooing script (as in 'he is after her for her money'), or it might be part of the restaurant script (as in the path that handles what to do if you discover you can't pay). This is a case of ambiguity within scripts which we call Scriptal Ambiguity. Often, other knowledge (for example, about John's personal character) will help disambiguate such sentences. If not, future inputs usually will.

An amusing kind of scriptal ambiguity occurs when the players think they are in different scripts, or when two players in a single script each have two different roles, one real and the second a figment of the other person's imagination – as in the following anecdote:

25 A traveling salesman found himself spending the night at home with his wife when one of his trips was unexpectedly canceled. The two of them were sound asleep, when in the middle of the night there was a loud knock at the front door. The wife woke up with a start and cried out, 'Oh, my God! It's my husband!' Whereupon the husband leapt from the bed, ran across the room, and jumped out the window.

If we regard husband-surprising-wife's-lover as a script, then we can readily understand this anecdote as the husband seeming to the wife to be her secret lover, and the wife seeming to the husband to be the spouse of the jealous husband outside. For a script application mechanism to appreciate this duality, it would have to infer one version of the script from the wife's point of view, and a second from the husband's. It would have to understand, in other words, that there can be a script in someone's mind – a personal script – which is at variance with the actual or situational script because of systematic distorting factors.

Of course, in order to really understand the joke in story (25), the listener must apply a rule about personal scripts, namely that in order for a personal script to override serious discrepancies with reality, it must have been very well practiced by the individual. Thus we infer that both husband and wife are well versed in adultery. We will have more to say about personal scripts in Section 3.6.

The concurrent activation of more than one script creates rather complex problems. A slightly less troublesome type of script interaction arises at the boundary where one script leaves off and another begins. Consider this example.

26 John was robbed on the train.
At the restaurant he couldn't pay the check.

In this example, the robbery is an unpredicted event in the train script. The new event does not affect the normal completion of the train script, so we simply have a pointer to the train script (since it is a fleeting script) and a pointer to a robbery script embedded within

it. However, when the next line of the story is seen, it is affected by the earlier robbery script. This is noticed by the entry conditions on a script. In order to perform a role in a script, certain conditions must be met. To take a train ride, one must be able to get to the station and into the train (i.e., the doors of the train must be open at the appropriate time). Further, one must either have a ticket or the money to purchase one (in which case someone must be selling a ticket and one must be able to find him). The entry conditions for a customer in a restaurant are similar to those for a train. Obviously an important entry condition for restaurants is that the customer have the means to pay the check. When a script is begun, it is necessary to check the entry conditions. If an entry condition has been violated it must be noticed immediately upon instantiating the script or when a pointer to that script is created. So in (26), the robbery, from which one must infer John has no money, violates one of the entry conditions of the next script to be activated. This violation sets up an expectation for the no-pay path of the resturant script with a link back to the robbery as the reason for taking this path of the script.

A final script interaction type concerns indeterminacy in script-endings.

27 Yesterday John was in New York.
He went to a restaurant.
He ate a large lobster.
Then he bought a watch.

In (27) we have the problem of recognizing when an active script has been ended and a new script has begun. Once the restaurant script has been instantiated in (27), we expect it to be ended in normal fashion. When a new input comes in that does not normally fit in that script without an ending being perceived, we have a problem. If the new input is something which is unexpected but could possibly occur in a restaurant, (i.e., is a Distraction), should the restaurant script end? If the new input were, 'The waitress did a dance', we would have no reason to end the restaurant script since this could occur in a restaurant, and would not be likely to initiate a customer reaction leading to a PTRANS from the restaurant. The restaurant script would simply be held in abeyance. In the example given in (27), ('Then he bought a watch') we have something that can normally be handled by a script, but that takes place in watch stores and not restaurants. We have to assume that the restaurant script has ended and infer 'He left the restaurant'. This would cause all the normal MAINCONs of the restaurant script to be inferred. The watch-buying event thus serves double duty: it activates a new script at the same time it terminates an instantiated old one. We call this a 'script-ending script'.

Of course, it is conceivable that one could buy a watch in a restaurant. Because of this possibility, with script ending scripts we still keep the requests active from the original script. Thus, if we next encounter 'Then he paid the check', if we have marked our previous inference with a lack of certainty, we can undo what we have inferred and place the 'watch' event inside the restuarant script as a Distraction.

The problem of script-ending scripts is a difficult one, partially because it occurs frequently, and partially because one can never be certain that the right decision has been made. Time span seems to play a role in the decision process too. For example, if 'Then he bought a watch' were (a) 'He bought a watch' or (b) 'He bought a watch an hour later' we have different solutions. In (a) we would probably assume that John was still in the restaurant and in (b) we would feel more certain that the restaurant script was ended because of the time gap.

3.6 Types of Scripts

So far we have examined situational scripts in which 1) the situation is specified; 2) the several players have interlocking roles to follow, and 3) the players share an understanding of what is supposed to happen. The waitress typically does what the customer expects, and the customer typically does what the waitress expects. There is great social economy when both parties know the script because neither party need invest effort deciding what the actions of the other mean and how appropriately to respond. Indeed, it is characteristic of institutionalized public situations with defined goals (the customer eating, the restaurant making money) that the social interactions be stylized. This is one reason why scripts are so common, and so helpful in understanding.

Suppose, however, that one of the parties wants to direct the interaction into channels other than those defined by the situational

script. He may have some Personal Script which he is following, over and above the actions needed to conform to the situational script. The customer for example, may have the goal of making a date with the waitress. If he has pursued such a goal often, then the actions involved may (for him) be very stylized and scriptal. The main path might involve friendly conversation, casual kidding, finding out if she is unattached, displaying interest, and asking when she gets off work. The waitress might or might not respond in the anticipated way. She might be friendly, but misinterpret the motive for the customer's friendly overtures. She might remain aloof and business-like. She might play hard to get.

Personal scripts do not behave in the stylized fashion of situational scripts. All the participants in personal scripts are not necessarily aware of their participation. The seducee, say, or the victim of a swindle is often not aware until the very end of the enactment of the actor's personal script of their participation in it. The personal script exists solely in the mind of its main actor. It consists of a sequence of possible actions that will lead to a desired goal. It is different from a plan (to be discussed in Chapter 4) in that there is no planning involved for the actor in a personal script. He is participating in a sequence of events much like other sequences he has used many times before. He could teach his method to anyone who wanted to know it. There is very little planning involved because he has done this personal script repeatedly.

There is, of course, no limit to the mental projections a person can bring to a situation in the hope of attaining some goal. These are frequently not script-like, but suited ad hoc appropriately to the particular situation. If the customer says to the waitress, 'If you see a tall man with a walrus mustache later this evening, a Mr. Robinson, please tell him that John and Mary found his umbrella', we don't want to try to interpret this request as part of a script. It is unique to this particular situation. Indeed, even if this customer for some reason often says such things to waitresses as part of a peculiar personal script, an understanding system would have great difficulty perceiving this without intimate knowledge of the mental world of this customer. From the standpoint of an artificial intelligence system, therefore, the useful personal scripts to store are those which are common to many individuals, and can therefore be conjectured for new characters in a story. There are many such common personal scripts. They tend to have the character of roles or parts which people assume as the occasion arises, for example, $FLATTERER, $JEALOUS SPOUSE, $GOOD SAMARITAN, etc., or stealthy occupations like $PICKPOCKET or $SPY.

With personal scripts, then, we would in practice restrict our attention to the most common readily inferred type. Often, personal scripts are used in otherwise novel situations, where there are no other scripts around. Interesting interactions occur when more than one script type is around at a time. Here we simply sketch some possible interactions and their properties.

a One actor with a concealed personal script within a situational script.

This is a very common type of interaction. One actor behaves with stylized duplicity, maintaining a public front while pursuing a personal motive. Persistent toadying to superiors in hope of a promotion, the affectation of virtues by political candidates, the rapid-fire friendly conversation of reporters, salesman, con artists and spies – these are all potential examples.

This type of script interaction is different in an important respect from most of the types discussed in previous sections. Here if a story understander is aware of the personal script, he is set to expect certain interferences during the progress of the situational script. This is in contrast to stories such as (16), (21) – (23), (27), in which unexpected or accidental events arise without prior warning. With prior knowedge of a personal script, the understander can prime appropriate questions or requests of both non-scriptal and scriptal input.

b Two or more actors with competing concealed personal scripts within a situational script.

This is an extension of the previous type. It might involve spy and counterspy, or a group of dishonorable thieves in a bank robbery, or any number of other situations of competition and double-cross. Here again the interesting questions for the understander are how the protagonists manage their double roles, and whether either or both of them develops awareness of the other's hidden agenda. The complexities of monitoring the input are much greater than in the previous case, but there are no new conceptual features.

c One or more actors with personal scripts whose nature is known by the other actors.

We have discussed the possibility that a personal script be concealed, but it is not unusual for a personal script even to be known in advance by other players. There are many stylized interactions in which one or both parties know the other to be dissembling, as in polite social invitations known not to be intended. Quite often if the deceit is relatively harmless, the knowing victim will pretend not to

Personal scripts are usually but not always goal-oriented. A personal script also might be followed as a matter of ritual (e.g., SPRAYER), or as an elaborated emotional and behavioral reaction following a situational outcome. An example of the latter would be the SJILTED LOVER who (say) discovers he has been jilted, disbelieves it, confirms it, is furious at his rival, curses all women, feels depressed, gets drunk, and throws himself in the river. This non-goal-oriented type is not quite as interesting from an artificial intelligence point of view as the goal-oriented type, because other individuals do not 'get into the act'. The personal script can be very personal indeed.

Clinical psychologists tend to be interested in very personal scripts. These are the stuff of neuroses, especially when they are activated inappropriately and create interferences in the ongoing social behavior of the individual. Behavior governed by unconscious motivation stems from a script hidden from an individual's conscious self. It is not our task in this volume to pursue such matters, other than to note the potential relevance of the script concept, properly explicated, to the demystification of neurotic behavior. Indeed, a school of clinical psychologists – the 'transactional school' – has already used the term 'script' for use in the analysis of behavior (cf. Steiner, 1975) although their use of it is looser than ours. In any case, we will not try to deal with idiosyncratic or unconscious personal scripts. The knowledge needed to handle their occurrences is too specialized and unparsimonious and is of little use in predicting and understanding actions at the level at which we are interested. Suppose we encounter a story like (28):

28 Mary's friends offered heroin to her. She shot up.

Here the simplest answer to the question, 'Why did Mary shoot up heroin?' is that she wanted to (or that it was her habit), and the next simplest is that her friends persuaded her. Without very specialized additional context, we would not likely assume (say), that she did it because as a child she hated her overbearing older sisters, and now she lets her peers talk her into bad behavior in the hopes that they will all be caught and punished, thus getting even with the sisters and also expressing her own guilt for hating them. This could conceivably be correct, but it is so much explanation based on so little substance that, like syndicated newspaper columns offering psychiatric advice, it puts one off as being gratuitous. Our policy in developing a theory of knowledge structures is to get as far as we can with fairly simple and general constructs.

know, in order to save the face of the other. This is what Goffman (1959) calls the 'face work' of everyday social interaction. Rather complicated patterns of social misrepresentation (both script-like and non-script-like) can occur, and it is not our purpose here to try to trace these. At this stage in the development of script concepts, perhaps we can hope only to cope with very obvious personal-situational script interactions where foreknowledge or discovery of the other's personal script leads immediately to a prescribed action. For example, if a dope peddler discovers that some people acting like customers are in reality members of the dope squad, he will avoid the incriminating rendezvous.

There is one further type of script we recognize, namely the IN-STRUMENTAL SCRIPT. Instrumental scripts are quite like situational scripts in structure, that is, they describe prescribed sequences of actions. However, the kinds of actions they describe, the variability of the ordering, and the use of the script in understanding, differs. Examples of instrumental scripts are **$LIGHTING A CIGARETTE, $STARTING A CAR, $WORKING A KEYPUNCH, $FRYING AN EGG**. There is little variability with instrumental scripts. The order of events is very rigid, and each and every one of the events in the script must be done. There are obviously an extremely large number of instrumental scripts. Every cookbook contains hundreds of them.

There are, of course, situational scripts, in which the variability is about the same as some instrumental scripts. In the coffee shop track of the restaurant script there is little possibility for actions varying. In fact, there is probably more possible variability in frying an egg. The crucial differences between instrumental and situational scripts are with respect to the number of actors, and the overall intention or goal of the script.

Usually, situational scripts take multiple actors, while instrumental scripts have only one participant. Things can and do happen in a situational script that are not expected and are often the point of any story that invokes situational script. For example, a fight in a restaurant is of interest because of its unusualness. The restaurant is just so much context for the story. Barring a bomb going off, we don't expect stories about 'what happened while I was starting my car'. The actions in instrumental scripts are fixed and uninteresting for the most part. Unusual or other interesting events do not usually take place with instrumental scripts as their context. In an instrumental script, nearly the only thing that can be related within it is the failure of the intended goal and what was done to correct it. This

is usually itself a standard prescription. There are only a few things to do when a car doesn't start and they are part of the script as well.

Making the distinction between situational and instrumental scripts enables us to make some choices that facilitate processing. When we instantiate a situational script, we must set up prediction mechanisms that will: be able to handle definite references to characters that have not yet been mentioned (e.g., the waitress); be able to infer the presence of important (or goal) scenes that have not been instantiated (e.g., 'eating' in a restaurant); find the appropriate detour path for unexpected inputs. Most importantly, mechanisms of memory must be set up to remember the unexpected events of the situational script together with the explicit and inferred MAIN-CONS.

An instrumental script has available to it much of this apparatus, but it is unreasonable to bring it to the fore every time that an instrumental script is referenced. We simply don't expect that 'I fried an egg' is the beginning of a story about an interesting thing that happened in the process of egg frying. To bring powerful prediction mechanisms to bear at this point would be a mistake.

Perhaps more important is our treatment of these two script types after they have been processed. We have stated what we would like to remember after having made use of a situational script. What is the analogy with instrumental scripts? It is not unreasonable to expect that, except under very unusual circumstances, we would want to forget the details of an instrumental script and remember only the goal. In fact, it is not implausible to even forget the script entirely, to save memory space and processing time. The reason that this can be done is that an instrumental script can always be rediscovered. If someone is smoking a cigarette, it must have gotten lighted somehow. If, for some reason we ever need to use this fact, it can be inferred and found as easily as if we had been told it.

The three script types described in this chapter can occur together in a juxtaposition that might include them all. For example, John could take Mary to dinner at a restaurant, doing various instrumental scripts along the way (lighting her cigarette, starting the car). However, during the meal he is affecting the personal script of **RO-MANCER**. This affects his behavior every now and then, in what he says, how he walks, what wine he orders, but probably not in that he orders or pays the check (situational) or how he cuts his meat (instrumental).

der comes equipped with thousands of scripts. He uses these scripts almost without thinking.

We will discuss how scripts are acquired in Chapter 9. A simple example will suffice here. One of us (RS) recently bought a new car. My daughter Hana (age 4) was with me when we bought it and asked if I was going to get a new key chain. I asked her what she meant. She replied that when we had gotten our old car in Rhode Island (where it had arrived off the boat 2 years earlier) I had bought a new key chain. This was her only experience with getting a car and already the events in it were a script for her. When you get a new car you get a new key chain. If people are building scripts at such an early age, it seems easy to imagine that the number they possess is great.

3.7 Script-based Understanding

By subscribing to a script-based theory of understanding, we are making some strong claims about the nature of the understanding process. In order to understand the actions that are going on in a given situation, a person must have been in that situation before. That is, understanding is knowledge-based. The actions of others make sense only insofar as they are part of a stored pattern of actions that have been previously experienced. Deviations from the standard pattern are handled with some difficulty.

To illustrate this, consider the following example that recently happened to one of us. I received a phone call from an old friend who lives about 100 miles north of me. He said 'Hi, I'm on I-91'. (The highway that connects our respective cities.) I asked him if he would like to drop by and he said he would. I then asked him where he was exactly so I'd know when to expect him. He answered 'Well let's see, oh there's a sign coming up, it says, wait a minute, Wallingford next, uh, oh there it is, exit 14'. At this point I was totally baffled. I had visions of my friend having lost connection with reality. My 'telephoning before visiting' script did not have room in it for uncertainty about one's location that could be resolved by signs 'coming up'. It took me a while to realize that my friend, being a gadget-oriented person, had a phone installed in his car. What we had was the telephone script mixed with the driving script, a mix that I was quite unfamiliar with.

Of course, people can adapt to situations with which they do not have previous experience. This adaptability comes from knowledge of plans and goals discussed in Chapters 4 and 5. However, even there the point remains the same. People need a great deal of knowledge in order to understand. That knowledge can be of two kinds: specific and general. Scripts are intended to account for the specific knowledge that people have. Most of understanding is script-based.

Understanding then, is a process by which people match what they see and hear to pre-stored groupings of actions that they have already experienced. New information is understood in terms of old information. By this view, man is seen as a processor that only understands what it has previously understood. Our script-based program, SAM, works this way. It thus can be faulted on the basis that anything that it understands was preprogramed into it in gory detail. We will meet other bases for understanding, but we view human understanding as heavily script-based. A human understan-

Schemata and Sequential Thought Processes in PDP Models

D. E. RUMELHART, P. SMOLENSKY, J. L. McCLELLAND and G. E. HINTON

One of our goals for this book is to offer an alternative framework for viewing cognitive phenomena. We have argued that talk at the level of units and activations of units is the preferable way to describe human thought. There is, however, already an established language for discussing cognitive phenomena. In this chapter we wish to address the relationship between some of the key established concepts and our parallel distributed processing models. There are many important concepts from modern cognitive science which must be explicated in our framework. Perhaps the most important, however, is the concept of the *schema* or related concepts such as scripts, frames, and so on. These large scale data structures have been posited as playing critical roles in the interpretation of input data, the guiding of action, and the storage of knowledge in memory. Indeed, as we have argued elsewhere (cf. Rumelhart, 1980), the schema has, for many theorists, become the basic building block of our understanding of cognition. Yet, the PDP language we are proposing is devoid of terms such as schemata, scripts, frames, and so forth. Instead, we have proposed building blocks at a much more microlevel—at the level of units, activations, and similar "low-level" concepts. Interestingly, it was struggling with the concept of the schema and some of its difficulties that led one of us (DER) to an exploration of PDP models to begin with. It was therefore with some priority that we began to develop an interpretation of the schema in the language of parallel distributed processing.[1]

Perhaps the first thought that comes to mind is to map the notion of the schema onto the notion of the unit. This does, indeed, capture some of the important aspects of the schema. In particular, the unit is an element, like the schema, which monitors its inputs searching for a good fit and takes on a value which represents how well its inputs fits its own internal criteria. However, such an identification misses much of what makes the schema a powerful conceptual tool. In particular, there is no analog to the *variable* or *default values*. There is no notion of the internal structure of the schema nor many of the other important aspects of schemata. Moreover, the scale is wrong. Schema theorists talk of schemata for rooms, stories, restaurants, birthday parties, and many other high-level concepts. In our parallel distributed processing models, units do not tend to represent such complex concepts. Instead, units correspond to relatively simple features or as Hinton (1981a) calls them *microfeatures*. If we are to do justice to the concept of the schema, we are going to have to look beyond the individual unit. We are going to have to look for schemata as properties of entire networks rather than single units or small circuits. In the following sections we show how features of networks can capture the important features of schemata. Since our interpretation is clearest in the subset of PDP models that can be characterized as *constraint satisfaction* networks, it will be useful to first describe that class of models and provide a language for talking about their properties.

PARALLEL DISTRIBUTED PROCESSING MODELS AS CONSTRAINT SATISFACTION NETWORKS

It is often useful to conceptualize a parallel distributed processing network as a *constraint network* in which each unit represents a hypothesis of some sort (e.g., that a certain semantic feature, visual feature, or acoustic feature is present in the input) and in which each connection represents constraints among the hypotheses. Thus, for example, if feature B is expected to be present whenever feature A is,

[1] All of the authors have contributed to the ideas expressed in this chapter. Smolensky's slightly different framework is sketched in Chapter 6. Hinton's view of the microstructure of symbols is sketched in J. A. Anderson and Hinton (1981, pp. 29-32), and McClelland (1981) shows how PDP networks can be employed to fill default values (see the discussion in Chapter 1). While we will all agree with the flavor of the current discussion not all of us endorse the exact details.

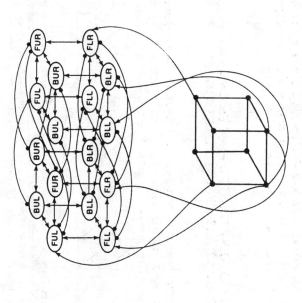

there should be a positive connection from the unit corresponding to the hypothesis that A is present to the unit representing the hypothesis that B is present. Similarly, if there is a constraint that whenever A is present B is expected *not* to be present, there should be a negative connection from A to B. If the constraints are weak, the weights should be small. If the constraints are strong, then the weights should be large. Similarly, the inputs to such a network can also be thought of as constraints. A positive input to a particular unit means that there is evidence from the outside that the relevant feature is present. A negative input means that there is evidence from the outside that the feature is not present. The stronger the input, the greater the evidence. If such a network is allowed to run it will eventually *settle* into a locally optimal state in which as many as possible of the constraints are satisfied, with priority given to the strongest constraints. [2] The procedure whereby such a system *relaxing* into such a state is called *relaxation*. We speak of the system *relaxing* to a solution. Thus, a large class of PDP models, including the interactive activation model of word perception, are constraint satisfaction models which settle on locally optimal solutions through the process of relaxation.

Figure 1 shows an example of a simple 16-unit constraint network. Each unit in the network represents a hypothesis concerning a vertex in a line drawing of a Necker cube. [3] The network consists of two interconnected subnetworks—one corresponding to each of the two global interpretations of the Necker cube. Each unit in each network is assumed to receive input from the region of the input figure—the cube—corresponding to its location in the network. Each unit in the Figure is labeled with a three letter sequence indicating whether its vertex is hypothesized to be front or back (F or B), upper or lower (U or L), and right or left (R or L). Thus, for example, the lower left-hand unit of each subnetwork is assumed to receive input from the lower left-hand vertex of the input figure. The unit in the left-hand network represents the hypothesis that it is receiving input from a lower left-hand vertex in the front surface of the cube (and is thus labeled FLL), whereas the one in the right subnetwork represents the hypothesis that it is receiving input from a lower left vertex in the back surface (BLL).

FIGURE 1. A simple network representing some of the constraints involved in perceiving the Necker cube.

Since there is a constraint that each vertex has a single interpretation, these two units are connected by a strong negative connection. Since the interpretation of any given vertex is constrained by the interpretations of its neighbors, each unit in a subnetwork is connected positively with each of its neighbors within the network. Finally, there is the constraint that there can only be one vertex of a single kind (e.g., there can only be one lower left vertex in the front plane FLL). There is a strong negative connection between units representing the same label in each subnetwork. Thus, each unit has three neighbors connected positively, two competitors connected negatively, and one positive input from the stimulus. For purposes of this example, the strengths of connections have been arranged so that two negative inputs exactly balance three positive inputs. Further, it is assumed that each unit receives an excitatory input from the ambiguous stimulus pattern and that each of these excitatory influences is relatively small. Thus, if all three of a unit's neighbors are on and both of its competitors are on, these effects would entirely cancel out one another; and if there was a small input from the outside, the unit would have a tendency to come on. On the other hand, if fewer than three of its neighbors were on and both of its

[2] Actually, these systems will in general find a locally best solution to this constraint satisfaction problem. It is possible under some conditions to insure that the "globally" best solution is found through the use of stochastic elements and a process of annealing (cf. Chapters 6 and 7 for a further discussion).

[3] J. A. Feldman (1981) has proposed an analysis of the Necker cube problem with a somewhat different network. Although the networks are rather different, the principles are the same. Our intention here is not to provide a serious account of the Necker cube phenomena, but rather to illustrate constraint networks with a simple example.

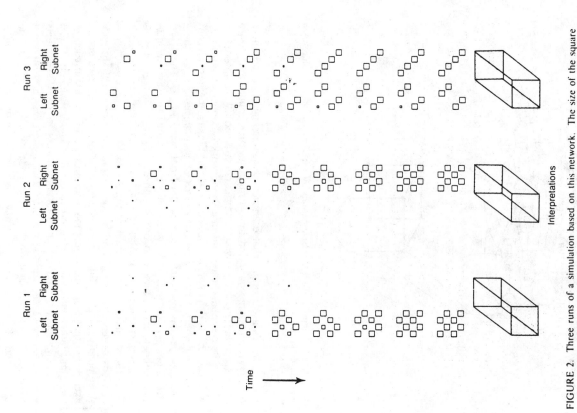

FIGURE 2. Three runs of a simulation based on this network. The size of the square indicates the activation value of each unit. The units are arranged in the shape of the sub-network with each square shown in its position corresponding to the vertex of the cube from which it is receiving input. The states are shown after every second update.

competitors were on, the unit would have a tendency to turn off, even with an excitatory input from the stimulus pattern.

In the last paragraph we focused on the individual units of the networks. However, it is often useful to focus not on the units, but on entire *states* of the network. In the case of binary (on-off or 0-1) units, there is a total of 2^{16} possible states in which this system could reside. That is, in principle, each of the 16 units could have the value either 0 or 1. In the case of continuous units, in which each unit can take on any value between 0 and 1, the system can, in principle, take on any of an infinite number of states. Yet, because of the constraints built into the network, there are only a few of those states in which the system will settle. To see this, consider the case in which the units are updated asynchronously, one at a time. During each time slice, one of the units is chosen to update. If its net input exceeds 0 its value will be pushed toward 1, otherwise its value will be pushed toward 0, using the activation rule from the word perception model:

$$a_j(t+1) = a_j(t) + \begin{cases} net_j(1 - a_j(t)) & net_j > 0 \\ net_j a_j(t) & \text{otherwise.} \end{cases}$$

Here, $a_j(t)$ stands for the activation of unit j at time t, and $net_j(t)$ stands for the net input to unit j at t. $net_j(t)$ is simply the sum of the excitatory and inhibitory influences on unit j:

$$e_j(t) \sum_{i \neq j} w_{ji} a_i(t)$$

where $e_j(t)$ is the external input to unit j at t and w_{ji} is the weight on the connection to unit j from unit i.

Imagine that the system starts with all units off. A unit is then chosen at random to be updated. Since it is receiving a slight positive input from the stimulus and no other inputs, it will be given a positive activation value. Then another unit is chosen to update. Unless it is in direct competition with the first unit, it too will be turned on. Eventually, a coalition of neighboring units will be turned on. These units will tend to turn on more of their neighbors in the same subnetwork and turn off their competitors in the other subnetwork. The system will (almost always) end up in a situation in which all of the units in one subnetwork are fully activated and none of the units in the other subnetwork are activated. That is, the system will end up interpreting the Necker cube as either facing left or facing right. Whenever the system gets into a state and stays there, the state is called a *stable state* or a *fixed point* of the network.

Figure 2 shows the output of three runs of a simulation based on this network. The size of the square indicates the activation value of each

Essentially, the equation says that the overall goodness-of-fit is given by the sum of the degrees to which each pair of units contribute to the goodness plus the degree to which the units satisfy the input constraints. The contribution of a pair of units is given by the product of their activation values times the weights connecting them. Thus, if the weight is positive, each unit wants to be as active as possible—that is, the activation values for these two units should be pushed toward 1. If the weight is negative, then as least one of the units should be 0 to maximize the pairwise goodness. Similarly, if the input constraint for a given unit is positive, then its contribution to the total goodness-of-fit is maximized by being the activation of that unit toward its maximal value. If it is negative, the activation value should be decreased toward 0. Of course, the constraints will generally not be totally consistent. Sometimes a given unit may have to be turned on to increase the function in some ways while decreasing it in other ways. The point is that it is the sum of all of these individual contributions that the system seeks to maximize. Thus, for every state of the system—every possible pattern of activation over the units—the pattern of inputs and the connectivity matrix **W** determines a value of the goodness-of-fit function. The system processes its input by moving upward from state to adjacent state until it reaches a state of maximum goodness. When it reaches such a *stable state* or *fixed point* it will stay in that state and it can be said to have "settled" on a solution to the constraint satisfaction problem or alternatively, in our present case, "settled into an interpretation" of the input.

It is important to see, then, that entirely *local* computational operations, in which each unit adjusts its activation up or down on the basis of its net input, serve to allow the network to converge towards states that maximize a *global* measure of goodness or degree of constraint satisfaction. Hopfield's main contribution to our present analysis was to point out this basic fact about the behavior of networks with symmetrical connections and asynchronous update of activations.

In general, since there are so many states, it is difficult to visualize the goodness-of-fit function over which the system is moving. In the present case, however, we can get a reasonably good image of this landscape. To begin, we can limit our consideration to those states in which a particular unit is either on or off since the system always ends up in such states. We can consider the states arrayed along two dimensions. One dimension corresponds to the number of units turned on in the left subnetwork and the other dimension corresponds to the number of units turned on in the right subnetwork. Thus, at (0,0) we locate the state in which no units are turned on. Clearly, by the above

unit. The units are arranged in the shape of the subnetwork with each square shown in its position corresponding to the vertex of the cube from which it is receiving input. The system begins with a zero activation value on all units—represented by single dots. Then, once each time slice, at most one unit is changed. On each run the system winds up in a state in which each unit has a value of either 0 or 1 (designated by a large square). The first two runs are most typical of the system. In this case, the inputs are low relative to the strength of the constraints among units. When low inputs are involved, the system virtually always winds up either in the state in which all of the units in the left-hand network are turned on and all of the units in the right-hand are off or vice versa. These final stable states correspond to the interpretations of a left-facing and right-facing cube as illustrated in the figure for the first and second run respectively. The third example of the simulation results is much more aberrant and was generated with a high input value. With a high input value, the system can occasionally get a third interpretation of the Necker cube. This is the "impossible" cube with two front faces illustrated in the figure. Thus, of the 2^{16} possible states of the system, only two are ever reached with low input values and only three are ever reached at all. The constraints implicit in the pattern of connections among the units determines the set of possible stable states of the system and therefore the set of possible interpretations of the inputs.

Hopfield (1982) has shown that it is possible to give a general account of the behavior of systems such as this one (with symmetric weights and asynchronous updates). In particular, Hopfield has shown that such systems can be conceptualized as minimizing a global measure which he calls the *energy* of the system through a method of *gradient descent* or, equivalently, maximizing the constraints satisfied through a method of *hill climbing*. In particular, Hopfield has shown that the system operates in such a way as to always move from a state that satisfies fewer constraints to a state that satisfies more constraints, where the measure of constraint satisfaction is given by[4]

$$G(t) = \sum_i \sum_j w_{ij} a_i(t) a_j(t) + \sum_i input_i(t) a_i(t).$$

---

[4] Note, the question of what to call this constraint satisfaction function is difficult. Hopfield uses the negation of this function and, by analogy to thermodynamics, calls it *energy*. This system can thus be said to settle into states of minimum energy. Similarly, Hinton and Sejnowski (Chapter 7) use the same terminology. Smolensky (Chapter 6) has a similar function which he calls *harmony* to emphasize that increasing values correspond to more harmonious accounts of the inputs. In this chapter we have chosen to use the language of constraint satisfaction and call the function G for measure of the goodness-of-fit of the state to its constraints.

equation such a state will have zero goodness of fit. [5] At (8,8) we have the state in which all of the units are turned on. At location (8,0) we have the state in which the units on the left network are all turned on and those on the right network are all off. At position (0,8) we have the state in which those in the left network are all off and those in the right network are all on. Each of those locations contain unique states. Now, consider the location (1,0) in which one unit from the left subnetwork and zero units in the right subnetwork are turned on. There are eight different states, corresponding to the eight different units in the left subnetwork that might have been turned on. In order to plot the goodness-of-fit landscape for this state space, we have plotted only the states at each location of the two-dimensional space with highest goodness-of-fit—i.e., the best state at each location. Figure 3 shows the landscape. In the figure, we are viewing the goodness landscape from about the (0,0) corner, the start state. Thus, the peak to the right corresponds to the goodness of the state in which all of the units in the left subnetwork are turned on and all in the right subnetwork are turned off. The peak at the upper left portion of the -figure

corresponds to the state (0,8). The two peaks in the graph at (8,0) and (0,8) correspond to the two primary interpretations of the Necker cube. It should be clear that if we start a system at (0,0) and allow it to "hill climb" it will almost always end up at one of these two peaks. It might be noted, that there are three smaller peaks right in the middle of the surface. These local peaks are very hard to get to because the system is almost always swept from the start state uphill to one of the two major peaks. It is possible, by having large input values, to reach location (4,4). This peak corresponds to the impossible Necker cube illustrated in the previous figure.

The input to the system can be conceptualized as systematically modifying or *sculpting* the goodness landscape. This effect is illustrated in Figure 4. In this case, the same landscape has been plotted, except the units corresponding to the interpretation of the Necker cube as facing to the left receive more input than the corresponding units on the other subnetwork. (This could perhaps be done by slightly shading that face of the Necker cube.) What we see is a "sloping" goodness surface with the peak associated with the interpretation of the Necker cube as left facing.

To summarize, then, there is a large subset of parallel distributed processing models which can be considered as carrying out their information processing by climbing into states of maximal satisfaction of the

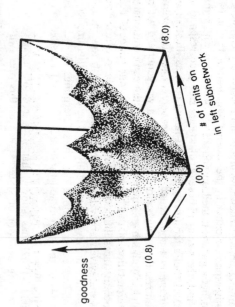

FIGURE 3. The goodness-of-fit surface for the Necker-cube network. The low point at the (0,0) corner corresponds to the start state. The peaks on the right and left correspond to the standard interpretations of the Necker cube, and the peak in the center corresponds to the impossible Necker cube illustrated in the previous figure.

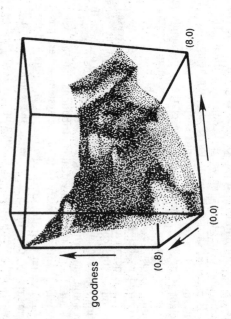

FIGURE 4. The distortions of the goodness landscape when a large input is given to the units corresponding to the front face of a left-facing cube. The figure shows only one major peak corresponding to the view of the left-facing cube.

---

[5] Note, zero goodness-of-fit is *not* the minimum goodness-of-fit attainable. In general, goodness-of-fit can be negative as well as positive. When there is negative goodness-of-fit, the system can always be made better by turning off all of the units.

terms of explicitly specified computer implementations or, similarly, formally specified implementations of the concept. Thus, Minsky (1975) postulated the concept of the frame, Schank and Abelson (1977) focused on the concept of the script, and Bobrow and Norman (1975) and Rumelhart (1975) developed an explicit notion of the schema. Although the details differed in each case, the idea was essentially the same. Perhaps Minsky (1975) was clearest in the motivation:

It seems to me that the ingredients of most theories both in artificial intelligence and in psychology have been on the whole too minute, local, and unstructured to account—either practically or phenomenologically—for the effectiveness of common sense thought. The "chunks" of reasoning, language, memory, and "perception" ought to be larger and more structured, and their factual and procedural contents must be more intimately connected in order to explain the apparent power and speed of mental activities. (p. 211)

Minsky and the others argued that some higher-level "suprasentential" or, more simply, conceptual structure is needed to represent the complex relations implicit in our knowledge base. The basic idea is that schemata are data structures for representing the generic concepts stored in memory. There are schemata for generalized concepts underlying objects, situations, events, sequences of events, actions, and sequences of actions. Roughly, schemata are like models of the outside world. To process information with the use of a schema is to determine which model best fits the incoming information. Ultimately, consistent configurations of schemata are discovered which, in concert, offer the best account for the input. This configuration of schemata together constitutes the *interpretation* of the input.

Different theorists have proposed more or less concrete specifications of the exact nature of these higher-level structures, but somehow none of them has ever really been adequate. None of them ever captured all of the qualitative characteristics that schemata were supposed to have. For example, a schema is supposed to be a kind of generative thing, which is flexible but which can produced highly structured interpretations of events and situations. Many representational formats have been proposed in an attempt to meet these criteria. For example, Rumelhart (1975) chose as a representation for the schema, a notation rich in generative capacity, namely, the rewrite rules from generative linguistics. Although the generativity of the rewrite rules and the idea that the structure is "constructed" in the process of interpretation is well captured by the rewrite rules, the nonprocedural character of such a system seems wrong. Some more active representation seems

constraints implicit in the network. A very useful concept that arises from this way of viewing these networks is that we can describe the behavior of these networks, not only in terms of the behavior of individual units, but in terms of properties of the network itself. A primary concept for understanding these network properties is the *goodness-of-fit landscape* over which the system moves. Once we have correctly described this landscape we have described the operational properties of the system—it will process information by moving uphill toward goodness maxima. The particular maximum that the system will find is determined by where the system starts and by the distortions of the space induced by the input. One of the very important descriptors of a goodness landscape is the set of maxima which the system can find, the size of the region that feeds into each maximum, and the height of the maximum itself. The states themselves correspond to the best possible interpretations, the peaks in the space correspond to a particular maximum, the extent of the foothills or skirts surrounding a particular peak determines the likelihood of finding the peak, and the height of the peak corresponds to the degree that the constraints of the network are actually met or, alternatively, to the goodness of the interpretation associated with the corresponding state.

CONSTRAINT SATISFACTION AND SCHEMATA

In the previous section we recounted a perspective on parallel distributed processing systems. In this section we address, again, the nature of the schema and relate it to constraint satisfaction systems and PDP models. We will proceed by first recounting some of the history of the concept of schemata, then by offering an interpretation of the schema in terms of PDP models, by giving a simple example, and finally showing how the various properties attributed to schemata are, in fact, properties of the PDP networks of the kind we have been discussing.

The schema, throughout its history, has been a concept shrouded in mystery. Kant's (1787/1963) use of the term has been provocative but difficult to understand. Bartlett's (1932) usage has long been decried for its vagueness. Piaget (1952) used the term schema, but it was difficult to come up with a consistent interpretation of Piaget's own views on the matter. Throughout most of its history, the notion of the schema has been rejected by mainstream experimental psychologists as being too vague. As a result, the concept of the schema was largely shunned until the mid-1970s. The concept was then revived by an attempt to offer a more clearly specified interpretation of the schema in necessary. Moreover, the important notions of "default values," variables, and so forth are poorly represented by the rewrite notation. Minsky (1975) and Schank and Abelson (1977) employed passive data structures with slots and explicit default values. These representations are better but are not active and seem to lack the flexibility and generativity that the schema requires. Rumelhart (1977) proposed a representation in which schemata are special kinds of procedures. This view was most completely explicated in Rumelhart (1980). Attempts to build explicit models employing this view, however, have proven unsuccessful. The representation is simply too unwieldy.

It should be clear from the foregoing that there are two distinct ways in which the term schema can be used. On the one hand, it is used to refer to an idea which is common to the work of Kant, Bartlett, Piaget, Minsky, Schank and Abelson, Norman and Bobrow, Rumelhart and Ortony, and many others. This is an idea that has evolved over the years and through the eyes of many different theorists. Many people have sought to clarify and further develop the idea. On the other hand, the term schema is used to refer to one of a large number of instantiations of the general idea of the schema. These explicit schema models are always - only pale representations of the underlying intuitions. Whenever a new instantiation of the schema idea is developed, a new perspective is offered on the underlying idea. What we hope to do in this chapter is to propose an alternative to the conventional representation of the schema and at the same time, through the development of a new perspective on schemata, sharpen the idea and develop a system which better captures our intuitions of the nature of the human information-processing system.

One important feature of schemata proposed by Rumelhart and Ortony (1977) has never actually been included in any implementation of the idea. This involves the nature of variable constraints and the filling of default values. The variable constraints associated with each variable serve two functions. On the one hand, they are important for determining whether a particular candidate is an allowable assignment for a variable and, if the variable remains unfilled, are used in the assignment of a default value. These constraints should not be considered absolute. Rather it was proposed that variable constraints should be considered as distributions of possible values. The nearer to the mode of the distribution, the better the variable filler. Moreover, the mode could itself be considered the default value. Importantly, however, there are interdependencies among the possible slot fillers. If one variable is filled with a particular value then it changes the default for the other variables. It was therefore proposed that the variable constraints (and the fillers of the default values) should be considered *multivariate distributions* in which the default value for a particular

variable is determined by the values filling the other slots. This idea was difficult to integrate with any of the conventional semantic networks or similar representational formats for schemata. As we shall see, this is a central feature of the PDP analog to schemata.

If schemata are to work as a basis for models of cognitive processing, they must be very flexible objects—much more flexible than they really ever have been in any actual implementations. This is a sort of dilemma. On the one hand, schemata are the structure of the mind. On the other hand, schemata must be sufficiently malleable to fit around most everything. None of the versions of schemata proposed to date have really had these properties. How can we get a highly structured schema which is sufficiently rich to capture the regularities of a situation and to support the kinds of inferences that schemata are supposed to support and at the same time is sufficiently pliable to adapt to new situations and new configurations of events?

On our current view, the answer is simple. Schemata are not "things." There is no representational object which is a schema. Rather, schemata emerge at the moment they are needed from the interaction of large numbers of much simpler elements all working in concert with one another. Schemata are not explicit entities, but rather are implicit in our knowledge and are created by the very environment that they are trying to interpret—as it is interpreting them.[6] Roughly, the idea is this: Input comes into the system, activating a set of units. These units are interconnected with one another, forming a sort of constraint satisfaction network. The inputs determine the starting state of the system and the exact shape of the goodness-of-fit landscape. When the system then moves toward one of the goodness maxima, there is little tendency for the system to migrate toward another state.

The states themselves are the product of the interaction among many groups of units. Certain groups, or subpatterns of units tend to act in concert. They tend to activate one another and, when activated, tend to inhibit the same units. It is these coalitions of tightly interconnected units that correspond most closely to what have been called schemata. The stable pattern as a whole can be considered as a particular configuration of a number of such overlapping patterns and is determined by

---

[6] Hofstadter (1979) expresses essentially the same view in his book *Gödel, Escher, Bach* when the Anteater says:

My "symbols" are ACTIVE SUBSYSTEMS of a complex system, and they are composed of lower-level active subsystems . . . They are therefore quite different from PASSIVE symbols, external to the system, such as letters of the alphabet of musical notes, which sit there immobile, waiting for an active system to process them. (p. 324)

An Example

Consider our knowledge of different kinds of rooms. We all have a clear idea of what a typical kitchen or bathroom or living room or office looks like. We know that living rooms have sofas and easy chairs, but they don't usually have ovens or bathtubs and that offices have desks and typewriters, but they don't usually have beds. On the other hand, kitchens, living rooms, and offices might all very well have telephones, carpets, etc. Our default bathroom is very small, our default kitchen is somewhat larger but still probably small relative to our default living room. We chose our knowledge of rooms and types of rooms as the primary example to illustrate the PDP representation of schemata. To begin, we need a constraint network that embodies the constraints implicit in our knowledge of rooms. We built our constraint network in the following way. We chose a set of 40 descriptors of rooms. These descriptors are listed in Table 1. We asked two subjects to imagine an office and then, for each of the 40 descriptors asked if the descriptor was accurate of that office. We then asked subjects to imagine a living room and asked about the 40 descriptors again. We then asked about a kitchen, a bathroom, and a bedroom. After finishing these five types of rooms we asked subjects to imagine another office, etc. We collected a total of sixteen judgments of the 40 descriptors on each of the five room types.[7] This data served as the basis for creating our network. In principle, we could imagine presenting each of these 80 room descriptions to the system and have it

TABLE 1

THE FORTY ROOM DESCRIPTORS

ceiling	walls	door	windows	very-large
large	medium	small	very-small	desk
telephone	bed	typewriter	bookshelf	carpet
books	desk-chair	clock	picture	floor-lamp
sofa	easy-chair	coffee-cup	ashtray	fireplace
drapes	stove	coffeepot	refrigerator	toaster
cupboard	sink	dresser	television	bathtub
toilet	scale	oven	computer	clothes-hanger

[7] This was not designed to be a formal experiment of any kind. Rather it was conceptualized as a method of quickly getting a reasonable data base for building an example. Some slight modifications in the data base were made in order to emphasize certain points in our example.

the dynamic equilibrium of all of these subpatterns interacting with one another and with the inputs. Thus, the maxima in the goodness-of-fit space correspond to interpretations of the inputs or, in the language of schemata, configurations of instantiated schemata. In short, they are those states that maximize the particular set of constraints acting at the moment. Depending on the context and the inputs, the system will be closer to one or another of the peaks in the goodness-of-fit function at the outset and will usually find the closest one. This interpretation, we believe, captures almost all of the important aspects of the schema with a view that is at once more flexible than the previous interpretations and yet highly structured. The degree of structure depends on the tightness of the coupling among the coalitions of units which correspond to the schemata in question. Thus, the language of schemata and schema theories should be considered an approximation to the language of PDP. In those cases in which there are coalitions of units that tend to work together, we have a rather close correspondence to the more conventional notion of a schema. In those cases in which the units are more loosely interconnected, the structures are more fluid and less schema-like. Often, knowledge is structured so that there are relatively tight connections among rather large subsets of units. In these cases, the schema provides a very useful description.

One important difference between our interpretation of schemata and the more conventional ones is that in the conventional story, schemata are stored in memory. Indeed, they are the major *content of memory*. In our case, *nothing stored corresponds very closely to* a schema. What is stored is a set of connection strengths which, when activated, have implicitly in them the ability to generate states that correspond to instantiated schemata. This difference is important—especially with regard to learning. There is no point at which it must be decided to create this or that schema. Learning simply proceeds by connection strength adjustment, according to some simple scheme such as those we discuss in various places in this book. As the network is reorganized as a function of the structure of its inputs, it may come to respond in a more or less schema-like way.

We now turn to an example to illustrate the various aspects of these PDP networks and show that many of those features that prompted the invention of schemata in the first place are present in these networks. At the same time, we show that certain features that are problematic with conventional representations of schemata are better dealt with in the PDP language.

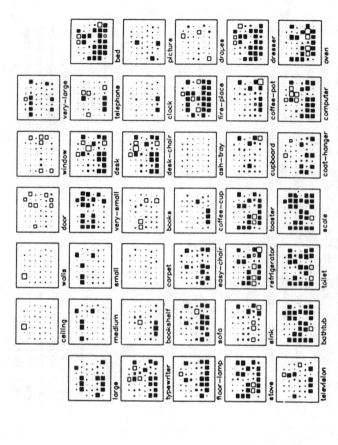

learn according to one or another learning rule we have discussed. Rather than doing that, however, we simply set the weights according to the following equation:

$$w_{ij} = -\ln \frac{p(x_i = 0 \ \& \ x_j = 1)\, p(x_i = 1 \ \& \ x_j = 0)}{p(x_i = 1 \ \& \ x_j = 1)\, p(x_i = 0 \ \& \ x_j = 0)}.$$

This equation is derived from a Bayesian analysis of the probability that unit x_i should be on given unit x_j is on and vice versa (see Hinton & Sejnowski, 1983). Four aspects of the weight equation should be noted:

- If the two units tend to be on and off together (i.e., the probability that $x_i = x_j$ is much greater than the probability that $x_i \neq x_j$), then the weight will be a large positive value.

- If, on the other hand, the probability that the two units take on different values (i.e., $x_i \neq x_j$) is much greater than the probability that they take on the same values (i.e., $x_i = x_j$), then the weight takes on a large negative value.

- If the two units come on and off independently (i.e., if $p(x_i = v_1 \ \& \ x_j = v_2) = p(x_i = v_1)\, p(x_j = v_2)$), then the weight between the two units is zero.

- The weights are symmetric (i.e., $w_{ij} = w_{ji}$).

In addition, each unit has a bias (constant input) which is given by

$$bias_i = -\ln \frac{p(x_i = 0)}{p(x_i = 1)}.$$

Note that if the unit is usually off, it has a negative bias; if it is usually on, it has a positive bias; and if it is equally often on or off, it has a zero bias. [8] The weight matrix estimated by this means is shown in Figure 5. The figure uses the method of Hinton and Sejnowski (Chapter 7) to display the weights. Each unit is represented by a square. The name below the square names the descriptor represented by each square. Within each unit, the small black and white squares represent the weights from that unit to each of the other units in the

FIGURE 5. The figure uses the method of Hinton and Sejnowski (Chapter 7) to display the weights. Each unit is represented by a square. The name below the square names the descriptor represented by each square. Within each unit, the small black and white squares represent the weights from that unit to each of the other units in the system. The relative position of the small squares within each unit indicates the unit with which that unit is connected.

system. The relative position of the small squares within each unit indicates the unit with which that unit is connected. For example, the white square on the lower right-hand portion of the refrigerator units represents the strength of the connection between refrigerator and oven. White squares represent positive connections and black squares represent negative connections. The size of the square represents the strength of the connection. Thus, the fact that the square representing the connection from the refrigerator unit to the stove unit is large and white represents the fact that there is a strong positive weight between the two.

It should be noted that each of the units in this example is a visible unit in the sense that each can directly receive inputs from outside the network. There are no hidden units receiving inputs only from other

---

8 With a finite data base some of the probabilities mentioned in these two equations might be 0. In this case the values of weights are either undefined or infinite. In estimating these probabilities we began by assuming that everything occurs with some very small probability (.00001). In this way the equation led to finite values for all weights.

bathroom, living room, or bedroom, respectively. It is, as previously noted, these maxima that we believe correspond roughly to instantiations of schemata for kitchens, offices, bathrooms, living rooms, and bedrooms. The system receives input in the form of having some of the descriptors clamped from the outside. It then finds the best interpretation of the input through this process of hill climbing. As it climbs, the system "fills in" the relevant descriptors of the scene in question.

In the case of the network we created for this example, there are essentially five maxima—one corresponding to each of the different room types. There are 2^{40} possible binary states in which the system could potentially settle, but, in fact, when it is started by clamping exactly one descriptor, it will only settle into one of five states. This roughly corresponds to the view that this data base contains five schemata defined over the set of 40 descriptors. There are, as we shall see, numerous subschemata which involve subpatterns within the whole pattern.

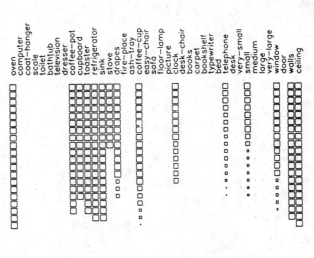

oven
computer
coat-hanger
scale
toilet
bathtub
television
dresser
coffee-pot
cupboard
toaster
refrigerator
sink
stove
drapes
fire-place
ash-tray
coffee-cup
easy-chair
sofa
floor-lamp
picture
clock
desk-chair
books
carpet
bookshelf
typewriter
bed
telephone
desk
very-small
small
medium
large
very-large
window
door
walls
ceiling

FIGURE 6. Five runs of the network from five different starting places. In each case, the unit *ceiling* and one other is clamped on. The clamping of *ceiling* represents information indicating that *room* is the domain of discussion. The other clamped units are *oven*, *desk*, *bathtub*, *sofa*, and *bed* in the five runs. In each case, the system settles on a prototype for the type of room most closely related to the clamped units.

units in the network. We consider this example to be a simplified case. It is possible to imagine hidden units which respond to patterns among the input units. In the general case, we, of course, recognize that hidden units would be required to give different coalitions enough coherence. As we have pointed out elsewhere in the book (cf. Chapter 2 and Chapter 8), multilayer systems containing hidden units are sometimes required to carry out certain computations. In the present instance, however, the existence of hidden units would not change the basic properties of the network which we wish to illustrate. Such higher-level units are not required for the basic schema-like behavior of these networks and, in no case should such a unit be confused with a schema.

It should also be noted that we have chosen a rather high level of abstraction for this example. We have taken such features as *has television* as a *microfeature*. In a more realistic example, we would expect *television* to itself be a particular pattern over a set of units that are used to represent many different varieties of television. There might be many variations on the *television* pattern corresponding to variations among televisions. Moreover, since televisions in bedrooms may be systematically different (perhaps smaller) than televisions in living rooms, we would expect that these correlations would be picked up and there would be a context dependency between the particular version of *television* and the remaining objects in the room. In such a case the units that participate in the representation of television would play the role of a slot in a schema, and the particular pattern of activation on these units would represent the characteristics of the slot filler.

Figure 6 shows several examples of the processing of this network. These runs started by "clamping" one of the descriptors on (that is, by setting the value to 1 and not letting it change) and then letting the system find a goodness-of-fit maximum. In the first example, the descriptor *oven* was clamped on. In such a case, we expect that the system will bring those units most tightly bound to the *oven* unit on and turn off those units negatively correlated to *oven* or other units that it turns on. On the assumption that *oven* is a central feature of the *kitchen* schema, the pattern the system eventually turns on is just that which might be said to correspond to the default or prototype kitchen. The strengths of each of the 40 units is shown along with the "goodness-of-fit" of the state after every 20 updates. The system begins with *oven* and *ceiling* on and then adds *coffee-cup* (weakly), then *sink* and *refrigerator*, concludes that the room is *small*, adds *toaster* and *coffeepot* and finally ends up at a maximum with *ceiling*, *walls*, *window*, *small*, *telephone*, *clock*, *coffee-cup*, *drapes*, *stove*, *sink*, *refrigerator*, *toaster*, *cupboard*, *coffeepot*, and *oven*. In other words, it finds the default or prototype kitchen. Similarly, runs of the system starting with *desk*, *bathtub*, *sofa*, or *bed* clamped lead to goodness maxima corresponding to the prototype or default office,

If it was difficult to visualize the landscape for the case of the Necker Cube model described above with 2^{16} states, it is even more difficult with the 2^{40} states of this example. It is, however, possible to get some idea of the landscape in the region of the maxima by plotting the goodness function over a small subset of the goodness landscape. It should be recalled that the states of a system with 40 units can be considered to be a vector in 40-dimensional space. If, as in the present case, the units have a minimum and maximum value, then each point in the 40-dimensional hypercube is a possible state of the system. The states of the system in which all units are at their minimum or maximum values (the binary states of the system) correspond to the corners of the hypercube. Now, each maximum of our network falls at one corner of this 40-dimensional cube. The intersection of a plane and the hypercube will pick out a two-dimensional subset of all of the possible states of the system. Finally, since three points determine a plane, we chose subsets of three of the maxima and plotted the goodness-of-fit landscape for those states falling on the plane passing through those three points. Figure 7 shows the landscape for the plane passing through the maxima for *bedroom*, *office*, and *kitchen*. Note that there are three peaks on the graph, one corresponding to each of the maxima on the plane. Note also that there are "ridges" connecting the two maxima. These correspond to simple mixtures of *bedroom* and *office* is higher than those connecting *kitchen* to either of the others indicates that *kitchen* is more

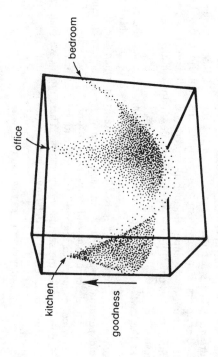

FIGURE 7. The value of the goodness function for the states on the plane passing through the three goodness maxima corresponding to the prototypes for *kitchen*, *bedroom*, and *office*.

oven
computer
coat-hanger
scale
toilet
bathtub
television
dresser
coffee-pot
cupboard
toaster
refrigerator
sink
stove
drapes
fire-place
ash-tray
coffee-cup
easy-chair
sofa
floor-lamp
picture
clock
desk-chair
books
carpet
bookshelf
typewriter
bed
telephone
desk
very-small
small
medium
large
very-large
window
door
walls
ceiling

oven
computer
coat-hanger
scale
toilet
bathtub
television
dresser
coffee-pot
cupboard
toaster
refrigerator
sink
stove
drapes
fire-place
ash-tray
coffee-cup
easy-chair
sofa
floor-lamp
picture
clock
desk-chair
books
carpet
bookshelf
typewriter
bed
telephone
desk
very-small
small
medium
large
very-large
window
door
walls
ceiling

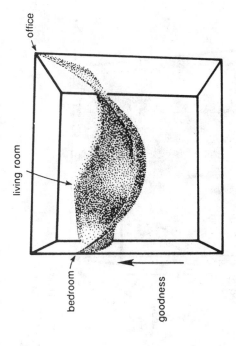

FIGURE 9. The value of the goodness function for the states on the plane passing through the three goodness maxima corresponding to the prototypes for *living-room*, *bedroom*, and *office*.

distinctive from the other two than they are from each other. Figure 8 shows the plane containing *office*, *bedroom*, and *bathroom*. In this case we see that the goodness function sinks much lower between the *office-bedroom* axis and *bathroom*. This occurs because *bathroom* is much more different from the other two than is *kitchen*. In any of these cases, it should be recognized that given the starting configuration of the system it will simply find one of these maxima and thereby find one of these interpretations of the input. By contrast, Figure 9 shows the goodness-of-fit landscape on the plane passing through *bedroom*, *office*, and *living-room*. In order to get a clearer perspective on the surface, the angle of viewing was changed so we are looking at the figure from between *bedroom* and *office*. Clearly, the whole graph is greatly elevated. All points on the plane are relatively high. It is a sort of goodness plateau. These three points are essentially three peaks on a much larger mountain containing all three maxima. Finally, Figure 10 shows the goodness landscape on the plane containing the three most distinct prototypes—*bedroom*, *kitchen*, and *bathroom*. The goodness function dips well below zero in this plane. Mixtures of *kitchens*, *living-rooms*, and *bathrooms* are poor rooms indeed.

It should be mentioned that there are essentially two assumptions that can be made about the input. Under one assumption, inputs are clamped to either their minimum or maximum value and aren't allowed to move. That was the way inputs were treated in the present examples. Other times, it is convenient to imagine that inputs are merely biases feeding input into certain of the units. This is the way inputs were treated in the Necker cube example. These two ways of viewing inputs can be combined by assuming that the case of clamping corresponds to very, very strong biasing. So strong that internal constraints can *never* overcome the external evidence. The case of clamping is simpler, however. In this case there is no distortion of the goodness-of-fit landscape; certain states are simply not available. The system is forced to move through a different part of the state space. In addition to its effects on the region of the state space that is accessible, the input (along with the context) determines where the system begins its processing and therefore, often, which of the maxima it will find. Figure 11 illustrates this point. The figure shows the goodness function on the set of states on the plane passing through the start state, the *bedroom* maximum, and the *kitchen* maximum for two different inputs. In Figure 11A we have clamped the *bed* unit to be on. It should be noted that to move from the start state to the *kitchen* peak in the first case involves climbing through a dip in goodness-of-fit. Since the system strictly goes

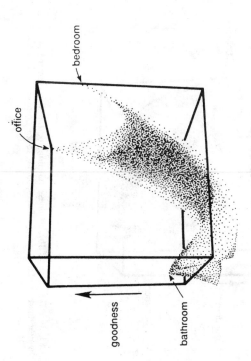

FIGURE 8. The value of the goodness function for the states on the plane passing through the three goodness maxima corresponding to the prototypes for *bathroom*, *bedroom*, and *office*.

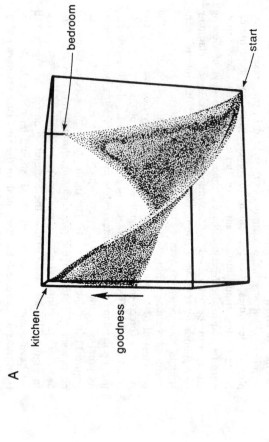

FIGURE 10. The value of the goodness function for the states on the plane passing through the three goodness maxima corresponding to the prototypes for *kitchen*, *bedroom*, and *bathroom*.

"uphill" it will be unable to reach the *kitchen* maximum and will move instead monotonically uphill toward the *bedroom* peak. Similarly, in Figure 11B with *oven* clamped there is a dip separating the start state from the *bedroom* maximum but a monotonically increasing slope flowing into the *kitchen* peak. Figure 11C shows, for comparison, the landscape from the start state when no units are clamped on. In this case, there is no dip separating the start state from either peaks, so the system can move to either maximum.

To summarize, we have argued that the maxima in the goodness-of-fit landscapes of our networks correspond to configurations of instantiated schemata. We have shown how these maxima are determined by coalitions among units and how the inputs determine which of the maxima the system will find. It should be clear that the multivariate distributions proposed by Rumelhart and Ortony are readily captured in the PDP framework. The values of each variable determine what values will be filled in for the other variables. We have yet to show that the kind of PDP system we have been describing really has all of the important properties of schemata. In the following section. we use the present example to illustrate these properties and discuss some of the advantages of our formulation over previous formulations of the schema idea.

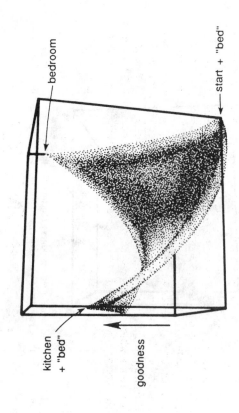

FIGURE 11.

filled in in the processing of the input. Perhaps the best example from our current data base is what might be called the *size slot*. In this case, the *very-large, large, medium, small*, and *very-small* units are all mutually inhibitory. (See the weight matrix in Figure 6). The different maxima have different default values for these slots. The *bathroom* has a default value of *very-small*, the *kitchen* has a default value of *small*, the *bedroom* has a default value of *medium*, the *office* is *large*, and the default *living-room* is *very-large*. Interestingly, when the input contains information that descriptors other than the default descriptors apply, the default size changes as well. For example, Figure 12 shows a case in which *bed* and *sofa* were both clamped. What we get in such a case is a room which might best be described as a large, fancy bedroom. The size variable is filled in to be *large*, it also includes an *easy-chair*, a

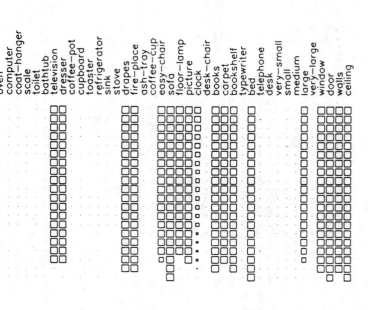

oven
computer
coat-hanger
scale
toilet
bathtub
television
dresser
coffee-pot
cupboard
toaster
refrigerator
sink
stove
drapes
fire-place
ash-tray
coffee-cup
easy-chair
sofa
floor-lamp
picture
clock
desk-chair
books
carpet
bookshelf
typewriter
bed
telephone
desk
very-small
small
medium
large
very-large
window
door
walls
ceiling

FIGURE 12. The output of the room network with *bed, sofa*, and *ceiling* initially clamped. The result may be described as a large, fancy bedroom.

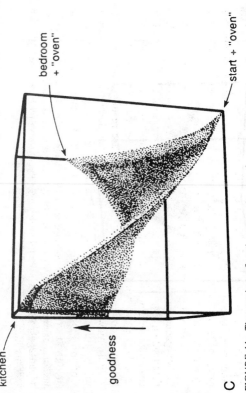

kitchen

bedroom
+ "oven"

start + "oven"

goodness

C

FIGURE 11. The goodness function over the set of states on the plane passing through the start state, the *bedroom* maximum, and the *kitchen* maximum for two different inputs. In *A* we have clamped the *bed* unit to be on. In *B* we have clamped the *oven* unit on. *C* shows the landscape from the start state when no units are clamped on.

Properties of Schemata and Maxima in Constraint Satisfaction Networks

Rumelhart and Ortony (1977; Rumelhart, 1980) have outlined a set of properties which characterize schemata. In this section we consider each of these properties and show how they map onto features of the PDP networks we are now outlining.

Schemata have variables. Essentially, the variables of a schema correspond to those parts of the pattern that are not completely determined by the remainder of the structure of the pattern itself. It is these parts that vary from one situation to another in which, nevertheless, the bulk of the units corresponding to the schema is active. On this account, the binding of a variable amounts to filling in a variable subpattern. Default values represent variable subpatterns that tend to get filled-in in the absence of any specific input. Since patterns tend to complete themselves, default values tend to be automatically filled in by the process of settling into an interpretation. In some cases, there are sets of units that are mutually inhibitory so that only one can be active at a time but any of which could be combined with most other units. Such a set of units can be considered to constitute a *slot* which is *floor-lamp,* and a *fireplace.* Similarly, the setting of the size variable modifies the default values for the other descriptors. In this case, if we set the size variable to *large* we get a bedroom with a *fireplace.*

Schemata can embed. In structural interpretations of schemata, it is useful to think of a schema as a kind of tree structure in which subschemata correspond to subtrees that can fill variable slots. Under our interpretation, subschemata correspond to small configurations of units which cohere and which may be a part of many different stable patterns (and therefore constitute a schema on their own right). Each stable subset of cohering units can be considered a schema. Large schemata will often consist of patterns of coherence among these coherent subsets. There are several instances of this in our example. For example, the *easy-chair* and *floor-lamp* constitute a subschema, the *desk* and *desk-chair,* the *window* and *drapes,* and other similar combinations constitute small schemata that can be either present or absent in several different configurations. Consider, for example, the case of *window* and *drapes.* These two elements almost always appear together and either both appear or neither appear. We will refer to this pattern as the *window* schema. Figure 13 shows the effect of adding *drapes* and/or *window* to the *office* schema. The default value for this schema involves no windows. The highest peak, at the origin of the graph, corresponds to the *office* maximum. One axis corresponds to the amount of *drapes* added to the schema (i.e., to the activation value for the *drapes* unit). The second axis corresponds to the amount of *window* added. The third axis, of course, corresponds to the goodness-of-fit for each of the states. It should be noted that the low points on the graph correspond to those cases in which one of the two units of the window subschema is on and the other is off. The high points on the graph, corresponding to goodness maxima, occur when either neither is on (at the origin) or both of the units are on. The case where neither is on corresponds to a slightly higher peak than when both are on. Thus, the default *office* probably doesn't have a window, but if the input indicates that either one of the units (*window* or *drapes*) is on, turning the other one on is best. To conclude, large schemata such as the *office* schema can be conceptualized as consisting, in part, of a configuration of subschemata which may or may not be present as wholes. Having parts of these subschemata is worse than having either the entire subschema or none of it.

Schemata represent knowledge at all levels. They should represent encyclopedic knowledge rather than definitional information. This amounts to the claim that all coherent subpatterns should be considered schemata as well as the whole stable pattern. It also suggests that knowledge of all sorts should be represented in the interconnections among the constituent units.

Schemata are active processes. This is obviously true of the the PDP system we are describing. They are a kind of organic element which grows and fulfills itself within its environment.

Schemata are recognition devices whose processing is aimed at the evaluation of their goodness-of-fit to the data being processed. This feature is obviously also a part of the idea outlined here. The goodness-of-fit is roughly determined by the height of the peak in goodness space. The processing of the system is aimed toward climbing uphill along the goodness-of-fit gradient. The stable points correspond to local maxima in this space. The height of the peak corresponds to the goodness-of-fit.

Some additional features of our interpretation. There are three major difficulties with the conventional representation of schemata that are naturally overcome in the PDP approach. In the conventional approaches, decisions must be made about which aspects of a given

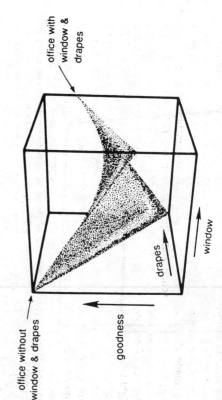

FIGURE 13. The goodness landscape for *office* as a function of the activation value of the *drapes* unit and the *window* unit. The function shows that it is maximum when either both are 0 or both are 1. This pattern of interaction is consistent with the view that the combination *window-drapes* form a subschema.

different chairs might play in the overall room schema. This would also allow the representation to capture the assignment of a particular object to a particular role.

PARALLEL DISTRIBUTED PROCESSING MODELS AND THINKING

In the previous section we offered an interpretation of the schema in terms of the emergent properties of simple PDP networks. From there, we believe that we can make contact with much of the cognitive science literature. There are central issues, however, which remain difficult to describe within the PDP framework. We have particularly in mind here, the process of thinking, the contents of consciousness, the role of serial processes, the nature of mental models, the reason for mental simulations, and the important synergistic role of language in thinking and in shaping our thought. These issues are especially important because these are issues that PDP approaches do not, on first blush, seem to have much to say about. In this section we attack some of those problem areas. We don't claim to have solutions to them, rather we can outline a story that represents our current understanding of these processes. The story is overly simplistic but it does give an idea of where we are in our thinking on these critical issues.

It should be noted here that the account of mental processing we have been developing offers an interesting perspective on the relations between parallel and serial processing. The "parallel" in "parallel distributed processing" is intended to indicate that, as a basic architectural design principle, processing is carried out, in so far as possible, in parallel. Parallel algorithms are employed rather than serial ones. At the same time, however, the "distributed" in "parallel distributed processing" brings a serial component to PDP systems. Since it is patterns of activations over a set of units that are the relevant representational format and since a set of units can only contain one pattern at a time, there is an enforced seriality in what can be represented. A given set of units can, however, be seen as representing a sequence of events. Since we assume that the system is moving toward a maximum goodness solution every time a new input comes into the system, the system operates in the following way. An input enters the system, the system relaxes to accommodate the new input. The system approaches a relatively stable state which represents the interpretation of the input by the system. The system then occupies this state until the stimulus conditions change. When a new input arrives, the system relaxes to a new state. Looking at the system over a short time frame, it is dominated

schema are constant and which are variable. The PDP solution is essentially that all aspects are variable: some aspects are simply more tightly constrained than others. Secondly, in a conventional representation, one has to decide exactly which aspects of the situation are part of the schema and which are not. In our PDP approach, units may cohere more or less strongly to their mates and in this sense be more or less a part of the schema. Finally, on the conventional view a decision must be made about whether a certain set of relationships should be put together to form a schema at all. Again, in the PDP formulation no such decision needs to be made. One can have schemata of varying degrees of existence. The rigidity of the schema is determined by the tightness of bonding among the units that constitute the schema. The tighter the bond, the more strongly the constituent elements activate one another, and the more rigid the structure. The weaker the bonds, the more fluid the structure, and the more easily a system can flow among states. This degree of fluidity depends on the shape of the goodness-of-fit landscape. Tightly rigid schemata have sharp peaks in goodness space; fluid schemata with many variable parts correspond to rounded hilltops. The goodness landscape, in turn, depends on the knowledge base that lies beneath it. If the knowledge is tightly interconstrained so that one part strongly predicts other parts, then we have a rigid schema. We can't easily get just part of it active. If part of it becomes active, the part will pull in the whole and suppress the activity of aspects that are not part of it. On the other hand, if the knowledge is only loosely interrelated, the schema will be a relatively weak organizer of the information and will be a pressure for structuring the input, but it will flow easily from one pattern to another. Moreover, within a schema itself, some aspects will be tightly bound together while other aspects will be only more loosely tied to the body of the schema. Input situations that demand an interpretation that breaks up the tightly bound clusters are going to be more difficult for the system to attain than those that require breaking up much more loosely interconnected elements.

Finally, we point out one way in which these ideas about schemata might be elaborated to overcome one apparent deficiency of the network we have thus far been considering. The network uses a fixed set of units to represent each type of object that might be present in a particular instantiation of a schema. This is clearly an oversimplification since it is often necessary to be able to think about two different instantiations of the same subschema within a larger overall schema—for example, there is often more than one chair in a living room. To capture such situations, it is necessary to imagine that the network may contain several subsets of units, each capable of representing a different possible chair. The subsets would correspond to different roles the by the relaxation process in which all units work cooperatively to "discover" an interpretation of a new input. Looking over a somewhat longer time frame, we see the system as sequentially occupying a series of relatively stable states—one for each change in input. Roughly, if we imagine that the relaxation process takes on the order of a few tenths of a second and that the time spent in essentially the same stable state is on the order of a half of a second or so, we could see events requiring less than about a half second to be essentially a parallel process, and those requiring several seconds to involve a series of such processes and therefore to have a serial component.

The Contents of Consciousness

It isn't necessary for the arguments that follow, but for the sake of concreteness, we suppose that there is a relatively large subset of the total units in the system whose states of activity determine the contents of consciousness. We imagine that the time average of the activities of these units over time periods on the order of a few hundred milliseconds correspond to the contents of consciousness. Since we imagine that our systems must be such that they reach equilibrium in about this amount of time, the contents of consciousness are dominated by the relatively stable states of the system. Thus, since consciousness is on the time scale of sequences of stable states, consciousness consists of a sequence of interpretations—each represented by a stable state of the system. Typically, consciousness contains a single interpretation (i.e., a single pattern representing its inputs) and consists of a sequence of such interpretations. On occasions in which the relaxation process is especially slow, consciousness will be the time average over a dynamically changing set of patterns and thus would be expected to lead to "fuzzy" or unclear phenomenal impressions.

The Problem of Control

One common critique of the kind of model we have sketched so far is that it can't really change without external prodding. Suppose that we are in a fixed stimulus environment. In this case, the system will relax into an interpretation for that environment and stay there. Our conscious experience will be of a fixed interpretation of a fixed stimulus. Until the world changes there is no change to the system nor to the contents of our consciousness. Obviously this is an incorrect

conclusion. How can such a system do something? Perhaps the first thing that comes to mind is that the environment never really is fixed. It is always changing and therefore the contents of our consciousness must always be changing to interpret the current state of affairs. A good example of this might be the movies. We sit in the movies and watch. Our system reaches a sequence of interpretations of the events on the screen. But, since the movie is always continuing, we are driven to continue to interpret it. Surely, what is true of a movie is also true of life—to some extent. This may be part of the story, but it would appear to be rather more passive than we might want. We don't just sit passively by and let the world change and then passively monitor it. Rather we act on the world.

A second answer to the problem of a system fixated on a particular interpretation becomes apparent in realizing that our interpretation of an event often dictates an action which, in turn, changes the environment. The environmental change can then feed back into the system and lead to another interpretation and another action. Figure 14 illustrates how this feedback loop can continuously drive the system from state to state. A paradigm case for this is playing a game. We can imagine that we are playing a game with someone; our input consists of a board configuration, and we settle into a state which includes a specification of a response. It would be quite easy to build a relaxation network that would take as input a description of a current board situation and produce, as part of the state to which it relaxed, a specification of the response. It would simply require that, for each game situation, the system relaxes to a particular state. Certain units of the state represent the action (or class of actions) that should be taken. Upon taking these actions, the opponent makes a play which in turn leads to a new set of constraints to which the system relaxes. In this way, the system can make a sequence of moves. Indeed, as we describe below, we have built such a network that can play tic-tac-toe. Other more complex games, such as checkers or chess require rather more effort, of course, but can, in principle, be dealt with in the same way. Although this is a much more activist view, it is still a "data-driven" view. The system is entirely reactive—given I am in this state, what should I do?

Mental Models

Suppose, for arguments sake, that the system is broken into two pieces—two sets of units. One piece is the one that we have been discussing, in that it receives inputs and relaxes to an appropriate state that includes a specification of an appropriate action which will, in turn, about the state of the world and thereby "predicting" the outcomes of actions.

Now, suppose that the world events did not happen. It would be possible to take the output of the mental model and replace the stimulus inputs from the world with inputs from our model of the world. In this case, we could expect that we could "run a mental simulation" and imagine the events that would take place in the world when we performed a particular action. This mental model would allow us to perform actions entirely internally and to judge the consequences of our actions, interpret them, and draw conclusions based on them. In other words, we can, it would seem, build an internal control system based on the interaction between these two modules of the system. Indeed, as we shall show, we have built a simple two-module model of tic-tac-toe which carries out exactly the process and can thereby "imagine" playing tic-tac-toe. Figure 15 shows the relationships between the interpretation networks, the inputs, the outputs, and the network representing a model of the world and the process of "mental simulations."

Mental Simulations and Mental Practice

One nice feature of this model is that it ties into the idea of mental simulations and learning through mental practice. Performance in the task involves two parts—a system that determines what to do in any given situation and a system that predicts what will happen if any given action is carried out. If we have a reasonably good model of the "world" we could learn from our model the various consequences of our actions—just as if we were carrying them out in the real world. It may very well be that such a feature accounts for the improvement that occurs in mentally practicing complex motor tasks.

Conversations: Actual and Imagined

Imagine a situation in which we had a relaxation network which would take as input a sentence and produce an interpretation of that sentence as well as the specifications for a response to that input. It is possible to imagine how two individuals each with such a network could carry out a conversation. Perhaps, under appropriate circumstances they could even carry out a logical argument. Now, suppose that we don't actually have another participant. but instead have a mental model of the other individual. In that case, we could imagine carrying

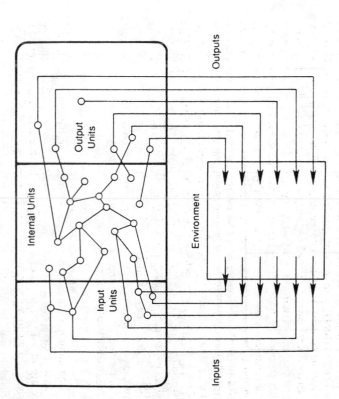

FIGURE 14. The inputs to the PDP system should be considered as partially due to the effects that the output of the system has had on the environment. In this way, the output of the system can drive it from state to state.

change the inputs to the system. The other piece of the system is similar in nature, except it is a "model" of the world on which we are acting. This consists of a relaxation network which takes as input some specification of the actions we intend to carry out and produces an interpretation of "what would happen if we did that." Part of this specification would be expected to be a specification of what the new stimulus conditions would be like. Thus, one network takes inputs from the world and produces actions; the other takes actions and predicts how the input would change in response. This second piece of the system could be considered a mental model of the world events. This second portion, the mental model of the world, would be expected to be operating in any case, in as much as it is generating expectations the linguistic forms pick out aspects of the entire interpretation to emphasize. Once this emphasis has taken place and the new input has been processed, the next state will be strongly affected by the new input and our new interpretation will be shaped, to some extent, by the words we chose to express our first idea. Thus, our thinking about a topic will be, sometimes strongly, affected by the language tools we have for expressing our ideas.

External Representations and Formal Reasoning

If the human information-processing system carries out its computations by "settling" into a solution rather than applying logical operations, why are humans so intelligent? How can we do science, mathematics, logic, etc.? How can we do logic if our basic operations are not logical at all? We suspect the answer comes from our ability to create artifacts—that is, our ability to create physical representations that we can manipulate in simple ways to get answers to very difficult and abstract problems.

The basic idea is that we succeed in solving logical problems not so much through the use of logic, but by making the problems we wish to solve conform to problems we are good at solving. People seem to have three essential abilities which together allow them to come to logical conclusions without being logical. It is these three abilities that have allowed us to accomplish those uniquely human achievements of formal reasoning. These abilities are:

- We are especially good at pattern matching. We seem to be able to quickly "settle" on an interpretation of an input pattern. This is an ability that is central to perceiving, remembering, and comprehending. Our ability to pattern match is probably not something which sets humans apart from other animals, but is probably *the* essential component to most cognitive behavior.

- We are good at modeling our world. That is, we are good at anticipating the new state of affairs resulting from our actions or from an event we might observe. This ability to build up expectations by "internalizing" our experiences is probably crucial to the survival of all organisms in which learning plays a key role.

- We are good at manipulating our environment. This is another version of man-the-tool-user, and we believe that this is perhaps the crucial skill which allows us to think logically, do mathematics and science, and in general build a culture.

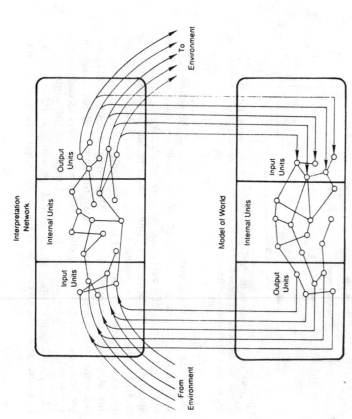

FIGURE 15. The relationships among the model of the world, the interpretation network, the inputs, and the outputs for the purpose of mental simulations.

out a conversation with someone else. We could hold an imaginary argument with someone else and perhaps even be convinced by it! Indeed, this brings up the last move that we wish to suggest. Suppose that we don't have a model of another person at all. Suppose that instead we simply use our one single model to both produce and react to imagined linguistic inputs. This description is, it would seem, consistent with Vygotsky's (1934/1962) view of thinking and is consistent with the introspections about a certain kind of thinking and "internal speech." Note, this does *not* suggest that thinking is simply internal speech. More generally, thinking, as we have argued, involves a sequence of states of consciousness. There are a number of ways of controlling that sequence. One way involves running "mental simulations." Another way involves recycling linguistic inputs. Note, this gives language an interesting, almost Whorfian, role however. Suppose that the interpretation that led to the production of the internal speech was much richer than the linguistic forms could possibly suggest. Thus,

Especially important here is our ability to manipulate the environment so that it comes to represent something. This is what sets human intellectual accomplishments apart from other animals.

Roughly speaking, the view is this: We are good at "perceiving" answers to problems. Unfortunately, this is not a universal mechanism for solving problems and thinking, but as we become more expert, we become better at reducing problem domains to pattern-matching tasks (of the kind best accomplished by PDP models).[9] Thus, chess experts can look at a chess board and "see" the correct move. This, we assume, is a problem strictly analogous to the problem of perceiving anything. It is not an easy problem, but it is one that humans are especially good at. It has proven to be extraordinarily difficult to duplicate this ability with a conventional symbol-processing machine. However, not all problems can be solved by immediately "seeing" the answer. Thus, few (if any) of us can look at a three-digit multiplication problem (such as 343 times 822) and see the answer. Solving such problems cannot be done by our pattern-matching apparatus, parallel processing alone will not do the trick; we need a kind of serial processing mechanism to solve such a problem. Here is where our ability to manipulate our environment becomes critical. We can, quite readily, learn to write down the two numbers in a certain format when given such a problem.

$$\begin{array}{r} 343 \\ 822 \\ \hline \end{array}$$

Moreover, we can learn to see the first step of such a multiplication problem. (Namely, we can see that we should enter a 6 below the 3 and 2.)

$$\begin{array}{r} 343 \\ 822 \\ \hline 6 \end{array}$$

We can then use our ability to pattern match again to see what to do next. Each cycle of this operation involves first creating a representation through manipulation of the environment, then a processing of this (actual physical) representation by means of our well-tuned perceptual apparatus leading to a further modification of this representation.

[9] As we have argued before, it is because experts have such a powerful pattern-matching capability that expert systems that rely only on pattern matching (albeit not nearly as powerful as the human system) are as successful as they are.

By doing this we reduce a very abstract conceptual problem to a series of operations that are very concrete and at which we can become very good. Now this applies not only to solving multiplication problems. It applies as well to solving problems in logic (e.g., syllogisms), problems in science, engineering, etc. These dual skills of manipulating the environment and processing the environment we have created allow us to reduce very complex problems to a series of very simple ones. This ability allows us to deal with problems that are otherwise impossible. This is *real* symbol processing and, we are beginning to think, the primary symbol processing that we are able to do. Indeed, on this view, the external environment becomes a key extension to our mind.

There is one more piece to the story. This is the tricky part and, we think, the part that fools us. Not only can we manipulate the physical environment and then process it, we can also learn to internalize the representations we create, "imagine" them, and then process these imagined representations—just as if they were external. As we said before, we believe that we are good at building models of our environment so that we can anticipate what the world would be like after some action or event takes place. As we gain experience with the world created by our (and others') actions we develop internal models of these external representations. We can thus imagine writing down a multiplication problem and imagine multiplying them together. If the problem is simple enough, we can actually solve the problem in our imagination and similarly for syllogisms. Consider, for example, a simple syllogism: All A are B and no C are B. We could solve this by drawing a circle for A, a larger circle including all of the A's around the first circle to represent the B's, and a third disjoint circle standing for the C's. We could then "see" that no A's are C. Alternatively, we need not actually draw the circles, we can merely imagine them. We believe that this ability to do the problem in our imagination is derivative from our ability to do it physically, just as our ability to do mental multiplication is derivative from our ability to do multiplication with pencil and paper. The argument that external representations play a crucial role in thought (or, say, in solving syllogisms) is sometimes challenged on the ground that we don't really *have* to draw Venn diagrams (or whatever) to solve them since we *can* solve them in our head. We argue that the major way we can do that is to imagine doing it externally. Since this imagination is, we argue, dependent on our experience with such representations externally, the argument that we *can* solve them mentally loses its force against the view that external symbols are important for thought processes. Indeed, we think that the idea that we reason with mental models is a powerful one precisely because it is about this process of imagining an external representation and operating on that.

It is interesting that it is apparently difficult to invent new external representations for problems we might wish to solve. The invention of a new representation would seem to involve some basic insight into the nature of the problem to be solved. It may be that the process of inventing such representations is the highest human intellectual ability. Perhaps simply creating an external representation sufficient to support problem solving of a particular kind is evidence of a kind of abstract thinking outside of the simple-minded view sketched here. That may be, but it seems to us that such representational systems are not very easy to develop. Usually they are provided by our culture. Usually they have evolved out of other simpler such systems and over long periods of time. Newer ones, when they are developed, usually involve taking an older system and modifying it to suit new needs. One of the critical aspects of our school system would seem to be teaching such representational schemes. The insights into the nature of the problem become embedded in the representations we learn to use to solve the problems.

Language plays an especially tricky and interesting role in all of this. Perhaps the internal/external issue is not too important with language. The notion we have here is one of "self-instruction." This follows Vygotsky's (1934/1962) view, we believe. We can be instructed to behave in a particular way. Responding to instructions in this way can be viewed simply as responding to some environmental event. We can also remember such an instruction and "tell ourselves" what to do. We believe that the process of following instructions is essentially the same whether we have told ourselves or have been told what to do. Thus, even here, we have a kind of internalization of an external representational format (i.e., language). We don't want to make too much of this point since we recognize that the distinction between external and internal when we ourselves produce the external representation is subtle at best, but we don't really think it differs too much from the case in which we write something down and therefore create a real, physical, viewable representation. Saying something out loud creates a hearable representation. There are interesting cases in which people talk to themselves (for example, solving difficult problems in noisy environments leads people to literally talk to themselves and instruct themselves on the problems they are solving).

Before leaving this topic, one more important aspect of external representations (as opposed to internal representations) should be noted. External representations allow us to employ our considerable perceptual/motor abilities in solving abstract problems. This allows us to break problems into a sequence of relatively simple problems. Importantly, once an external representation is created, it can be reinterpreted without regard to its initial interpretation. This freedom allows us to discover solutions to problems without "seeing" our way to the end. We can inspect intermediate steps and find alternative solutions which might be better in some ways. In this way, we can discover new features of our representations and slowly extend them and make them more powerful.

Goal Direction in Thinking

Our discussion thus far has left one central issue undiscussed, namely, the role of goals in thought and problem solving. Clearly it is not the case that the same perceptual stimulus always drives the system to react in a consistent way. Rather, our goals or intentions interact with the stimuli (internal and external) that provide the inputs to the thinking process. Further, goals organize whole sequences of thoughts into a coherent problem-solving activity, and the notion that there is a hierarchy of goals is certainly important for understanding these coherent sequences.

While we have not stressed the importance of goals, it is not difficult to see how they could be incorporated into our framework. Goals can be explicitly represented as patterns of activation and can thus provide one source of input to the thinking process. Nor is it difficult to imagine how a PDP network could learn to establish specific subgoal patterns in response to particular superordinate goals and inputs.

Summary

These ideas are highly speculative and detached from any particular PDP model. They are useful, we believe, because they suggest how PDP models can be made to come into contact with the class of phenomena for which they are, on the face of it, least well suited—that is, essentially sequential and conscious phenomena. Even in these cases, however, they lead us to view phenomena in new ways.

An Example

In these last few sections, we have been talking at a very general level. We often find it useful to be concrete about our ideas.

Therefore, to illustrate the notion of thought as mental simulation more concretely, we created two relaxation networks that can be connected together to mentally simulate playing a game of tic-tac-toe. The two networks are very similar. The first is a system which, given a pattern representing the board of a tic-tac-toe game, will relax to a solution state that fills in an appropriate response. The second module is nearly identical to the first; it takes as input a board position and a move and settles to a prediction of the opponent's responding move. In short, it is a "mental model" of the opponent. When the output of the first is fed, as input, to the second and the output to the second is fed, as input, to the first, the two networks can simulate a game of tic-tac-toe.

Figure 16 illustrates the basic structure of the tic-tac-toe playing network. The network consists of a total of 67 units. There are nine units representing the nine possible responses. These are indicated by the nine dots at the top of the figure. There is one unit for each of the nine possible moves in tic-tac-toe. Since only one response is to be made at a time, these units are mutually inhibitory. This is indicated by the heavy black line feeding back from the top plane in the figure to itself. There are a total of 18 units representing the board configuration. These are divided into two groups of nine: one group for the positions of the friendly or player pieces on the board and one group representing the positions of the opponent's pieces. Since if any square is occupied, it is not a possible move, each board unit strongly inhibits its corresponding output unit. This strong inhibition is indicated by the heavy black lines connecting the board units to the response units. In addition to these 9 output units and 18 input units, there is a total of 40 hidden units which detect patterns in the board units and activate the various response alternatives. These 40 units can be divided into eight classes corresponding to the eight possible ways of getting three ×'s or ○'s in a row. In the figure, one of each such category of units is illustrated. The receptive field of each unit is indicated by the line inside the circle representing that unit. Thus, there is one unit for each of the three horizontal lines, one for each of the three vertical lines, and one for each of the two possible diagonal lines. For each of the eight classes of hidden units, there are five different pattern types that different units are responsive to. For example, some units are responsive to empty regions. That is, they respond just in case none of the board units from which it receives inputs is turned on. This is implemented by making them be inhibited by any activity in their receptive field and by giving them a negative threshold. We call this an *empty line detector*. All things being equal, it is better to move into an empty row, column, or diagonal; therefore these units weakly activate their respective output units. At the start of the game these are the only units which are active and therefore the sole criterion for the first move is the number of possible strings of three the square is a member of. Since the center square intersects the largest number, it will usually be chosen by the system for its first move. On later moves, there are other units feeding into the decision, but these units also contribute. Another unit type will respond whenever two or more units of the same kind occur in its regions. This is the kind of unit illustrated in the figure. It receives strong inhibitory input from one set of board units (in this case the opponent's pieces) and excitatory inputs from the other set. It has a rather high positive threshold so that it will not come on until at least two units are on in its row. We call this a *friendly doublet detector*. Whenever this unit comes on it means that the system can make a winning move by playing in that row. Therefore, it is strongly positively connected to its respective output units. If such a move is possible, the system will make it. There are similar units which respond to two or more units from the representation of the opponent's pieces are active in its receptive field. We call this an *opponent doublet detector*. If such a

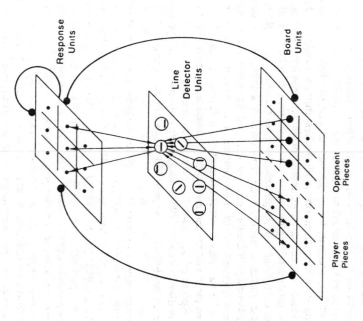

Response Units

Line Detector Units

Board Units

Player Pieces

Opponent Pieces

FIGURE 16. The basic structure of the tic-tac-toe playing network.

response units
friendly pieces
enemy pieces
empty line detectors
friendly singleton detectors
enemy singleton detectors
friendly doubleton detectors
enemy doubleton detectors

FIGURE 17. A sample run of the tic-tac-toe playing network.

unit comes on, it means that the opponent could win by a move in this region, so it excites its response units very strongly as well. Unless there is a winning move somewhere else, the blocking response will become the most active. Finally, there are units which respond to one or more friendly pieces or one or more opponent pieces in an otherwise open line. We call these *friendly singleton* and *opponent singleton detectors*. It is generally good to extend your own singleton or block an opponent's singleton if there is nothing more pressing, so these units also activate their respective output units, only rather more weakly than the units detecting doublets. Thus, the net input arriving at any given unit is the weighted sum of all of these urgencies detected by the hidden units. Because of the direct inhibition from the board units, only those response units corresponding to open squares receive positive input. The mutual inhibition insures that the strongest unit will usually win. In order that this system truly climb in overall goodness-of-fit, all weights are symmetric and the update is done asynchronously at random. This means that when there isn't much difference between the possible response alternatives, a weaker one will sometimes get the upper hand and win the competition. This never happens, however, when a unit is receiving very strong input, as with the case of an open double for a win or to be blocked.

The simplest case is when the system simply is given a board position, settles on a move; is given the next board position incorporating the opponent's response, settles on a move for that position, etc., until a game is finished. This involves only one network and presumably would be the basic modality for the system to run in. Figure 17 shows a sample run of such a situation. The activation levels of each of the 67 units is shown in each column. Successive activation states are shown from left to right. At the start, it should be noted that there is a friendly piece in the center square and two enemy pieces, one in each corner of the upper row. It is the system's move. The system starts with the units corresponding to the board position clamped on and all other units off. The figure shows the strengths for each of the units after every 50 asynchronous updates. By the second time slice, the system is beginning to extract the relevant features of the board position. The five groups of eight units shown in each column following the response units and board position display the line-detector units. Each group of eight is laid out with three units across the top corresponding to the top, middle, and bottom lines from left to right. The second row of the eight corresponds to the left and right diagonals, and the bottom row of each eight corresponds to the left, middle, and right columns. Thus, we see that the system has, by the second time slice, begun to discover that the bottom row is empty, that it has a singleton in the left column, and that the opponent has a singleton in the left column, and

that the opponent has a doubleton in the top row. Then the system discovers a friendly singleton in the middle column, an enemy singleton in the top row, and an enemy singleton in the right column. Based on this, the blocking response in the top-middle position begins to gain strength. As the observation that the opponent has an open double increases in strength, the activation level of the blocking response gains strength even faster. Finally, the strength of a response unit exceeds criterion and the system detects that it has settled on a move. At this point, we assume a motor system (or the like) would be invoked and the move actually made. Upon having made the move, the world has changed and (we can imagine) the opponent makes a response. In this case, a new board position could be presented to the system and the process could begin again.

Here we have a system that can take a board position and decide on a move. When we make our move and present the system with the new board position, it can make its next move, etc., until the game is finished. Here we see a kind of sequential behavior of our relaxation system driven by changes in the outside which are, in turn, the result of the activity of the system itself. Nothing is different; we see that sequential processing results simply from the addition of the systems own responding to the environmental process of generating a sequence of stimuli. This is a very common form of control of sequential behavior and involves no special mechanism. The case of "mental simulations" involves a bit more machinery. We need a "model of the world" to predict the environment's response to any action that might be taken. In the case of tic-tac-toe, this involves a network which models the opponent. In general, the model of the opponent may be arbitrarily different from that used by the system to make its own response. In our case, however, it is sufficient to build an identical network for the opponent. The only difference is that in the opponent's network, the board is interpreted differently: The opponent's board position of the original network setup drives the friendly board position in the model of the opponent, and the friendly board position in the original network drives the opponent board position in the model of the opponent. Figure 18 shows a run of the system "mentally simulating" the play of a game. The state of the units are shown after every 100 updates. First, the state of the original network is shown as it settles on its move, then the state of the model of the opponent is shown as it settles on its move. This continues until the game reaches a conclusion. In this instance, the "simulated player" makes a "mistake" in its response to the system's opening. Successive moves show the system taking advantage of its own mistake and winning the game.

CONCLUSION

We have argued in this book that the analysis of psychological phenomena in terms of units, activations of units, connections among units, and the action of large coalitions of such units leads us to many insights that have not been possible in terms of the language that has recently been more popular in cognitive science. In that sense, we may be perceived as throwing out the insights gained from the more conventional language and concepts. We are not throwing out such insights. In this chapter, we attempt to show the relationship between two such insights and our models. At start, we argue that the concept of the schema has a correspondence in the PDP framework. In particular, we argue that a schema is best viewed as a coalition of units which cohere and that configurations of such coalitions determine the interpretations that the system can attain. These stable states correspond to instantiated configurations of schemata that can be characterized in terms of goodness-of-fit maxima that the system can move into. Such processing systems, we argue, have all of the features of schemata and more. Among the advantages of this view is that the

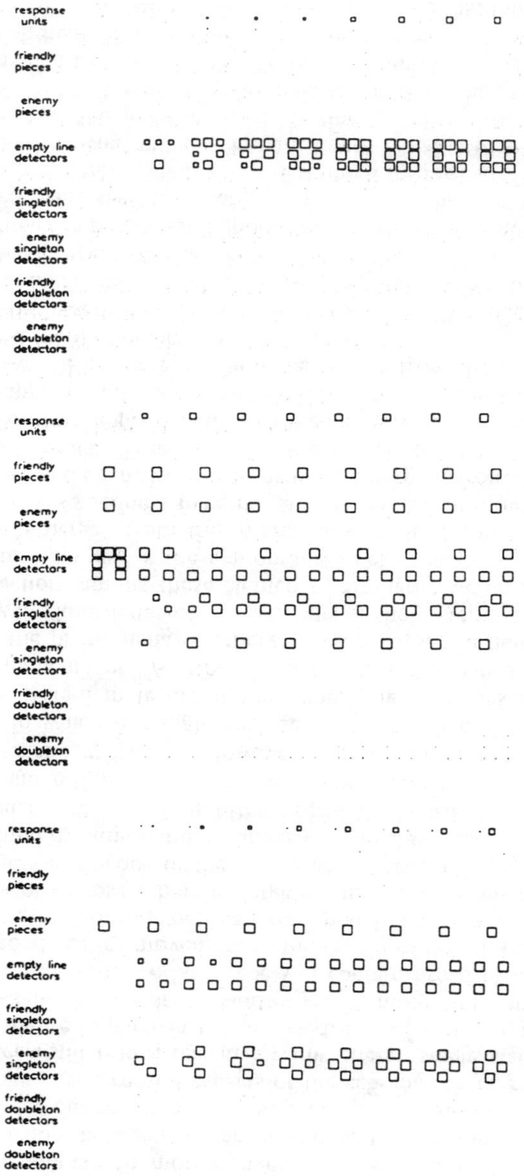

Figure row labels:
response units / friendly pieces / enemy pieces / empty line detectors / friendly singleton detectors / enemy singleton detectors / friendly doubleton detectors / enemy doubleton detectors

response units / friendly pieces / enemy pieces / empty line detectors / friendly singleton detectors / enemy singleton detectors / friendly doubleton detectors / enemy doubleton detectors

response units / friendly pieces / enemy pieces / empty line detectors / friendly singleton detectors / enemy singleton detectors / friendly doubleton detectors / enemy doubleton detectors schema becomes much more fluid and flexible and able to accommodate itself to inputs. In more conventional representations there is a strong distinction between variables and slots and the bulk of the schema. Under our interpretation an aspect of the schema is more or less a variable. Even central aspects of the schema can be missing and the system can still find a reasonably low energy stable state. If very rigid schemata are implicit in the knowledge base, this will show up as narrow peaks in the goodness landscape. If more fluid and variable schemata are required, the landscape will contain broad plateaus which allow for a good deal of movement in the region of the maximum.

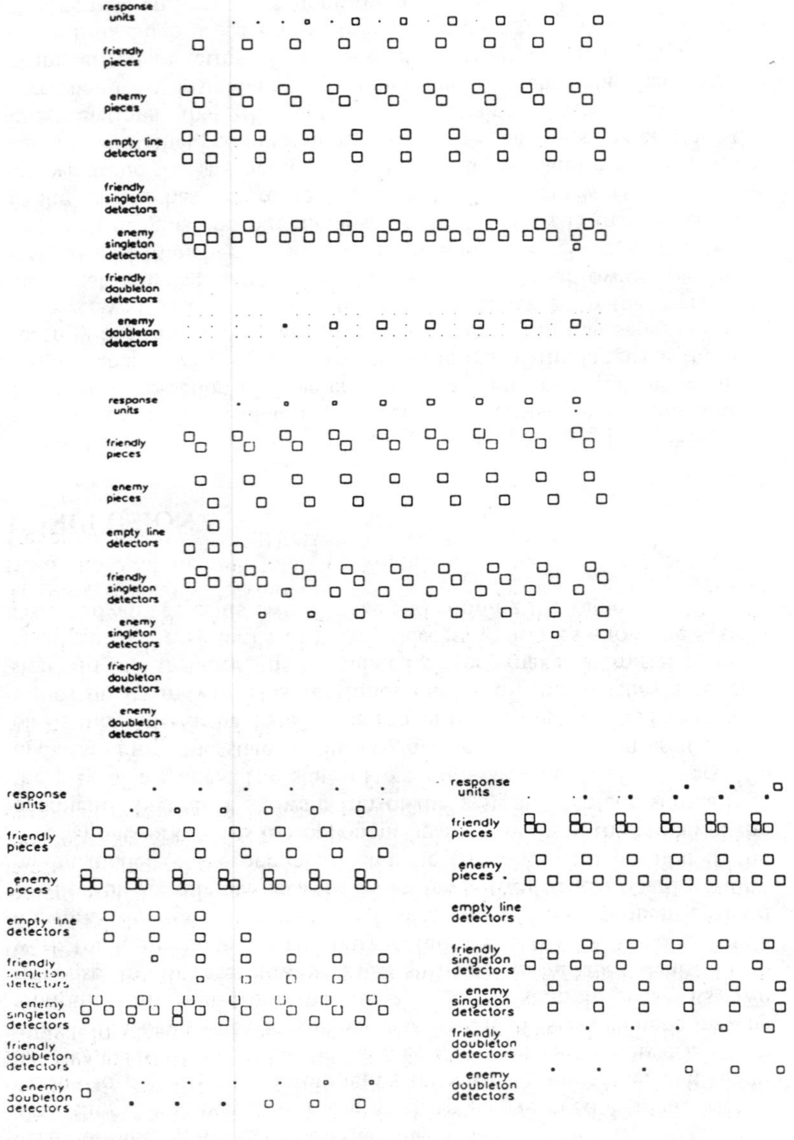

We see the relationship between our models and schema theory as discussed by other researchers as largely a matter of levels of analysis. This is roughly analogous to the relationship between the level of discussion of fluid dynamics and an underlying level of description involving statistical mechanics. It is often useful to theorize at the level of turbulence and different kinds of turbulence, and such a description will do for many purposes. However, we can often run up against phenomena in which our high-level descriptions will not do, we must describe the system in terms of the underlying processes in order to understand its behavior. Another feature of this example is our understanding of the phenomena of emergent properties. Turbulence is not predicted by the knowledge of the elements of the system; it is inherent in the interactions among these elements. Similarly, we do not believe that single-unit activity is the appropriate level of analysis. Properties of networks "emerge" from the interactions of the elements. Indeed, such properties as goodness maxima, etc., are emergent in just this way. In general, we see cognitive phenomena as emergent from the interactions of many units. Thus, we take the symbolic level of analysis to provide us with an approximation to the underlying system. In many cases these approximations will prove useful; in some cases they will be wrong and we will be forced to view the system from the level of units to understand them in detail.

We also discussed the relationship between PDP models and the more conventional sequential processing systems. We believe that processes that happen very quickly—say less than .25 to .5 seconds—occur essentially in parallel and should be described in terms of parallel models. Processes that take longer, we believe, have a serial component and can more readily be described in terms of sequential information-processing models. For these processes, a process description such as a production would, we imagine, provide a useful approximate description. We would caution, however, that when one chooses a formalism such as production systems and attempts to use it not only to describe the conscious sequential processes that occur at this slow time scale, it is important not to fall into the trap of assuming that the

FIGURE 18. The tic-tac-toe system mentally simulating the play of a game.

microstructure of these sequential processes should also be described in the same terms. Production systems have the power of Turing machines and people often attempt to describe phenomena at this faster time scale in terms of the same sequential formalism that seems appropriate for the slower time scale. We believe that it will turn out that this approach is wrong, that the power of the formalism has led us astray. In these cases we suspect that the unit level of analysis will be required.

Finally, we showed how the important notion of mental models and the related notion of mental simulations play important roles in the sequential behavior of a PDP system. We illustrated this point with a system which could use a "model of its opponent" to "mentally simulate" a tic-tac-toe game. We suspect that this process will turn out to be important when we begin to apply our models to temporally extended reasoning and problem-solving tasks.

ACKNOWLEDGMENTS

This research was supported by: Contracts N00014-79-C-0323, NR 667-437 and N00014-85-K-0450, NR 667-548 with the Personnel and Training Research Programs of the Office of Naval Research, by grants from the System Development Foundation, and by a NIMH Career Development Award (MH00385) to the third author.

Mental Models

The term *mental models* has been used in two different senses (see the section on Reasoning in Part 5, *Thinking*). As the term is used in this section, a mental model represents the domain-specific knowledge needed to understand a dynamic system or natural physical phenomena. The physical phenomena are drawn from domains such as electricity, heat, and motion, and the knowledge involved varies from common-sense conceptions to expert understanding. What is particularly important is that the knowledge included in a model allow one to *simulate qualitatively* the phenomenon or system. A person who has a mental model of a door buzzer, for example, can mentally trace the causal sequence of events that occur during the buzzer's operation.

Hayes' paper concerns how common-sense knowledge can be used in reasoning. Hayes provides a way of characterizing the possible states of liquids. He then shows how one can construct transitions between different liquid states (a kind of qualitative simulation), using only a small number of possible transition types to construct a "history" of some event. The paper is a paradigm for research on the representation of common-sense knowledge of the physical world.

The deKleer and Brown paper focuses on a designed, electrical system, rather than on a natural physical phenomenon. The key idea is that one can decompose a complex system (a door buzzer, for example) into a set of component models (switches, coils, and the like), whose characterization is independent of the system in which they are embedded. Then, to construct a qualitative simulation of the system, we must know two things: (1) the topology of connections between the various components (i.e., what is connected to what), and (2) the incremental input–output functions of the various components (e.g., if a particular input to a component increases, what happens to the output). This approach to qualitative modeling has proven influential.

Naive Physics I: Ontology For Liquids

Patrick J. Hayes

Cognitive Science
University of Rochester
Rochester, New York

Here I discovered water—a very different element from the green crawling scum that stank in the garden but. You could pump it in pure blue gulps out of the ground. And you could swing on the pump handle and it came out sparkling like liquid sky. And it broke and ran and shone on the tiled floor, or quivered in a jug, or weighted your clothes with cold. You could drink it, draw with it, froth it with soap, swim beetles across it, or fly it in bubbles in the air. You could put your head in it, and open your eyes, and see the sides of the bucket buckle, and hear your caught breath roar, and work your mouth like a fish, and smell the lime from the ground. Substance of magic—which you could tear or wear, confine or scatter, or send down holes, but never burn or break or destroy.

—From "Cider with Rosie", by Laurie Lee

1 Introduction

This paper is a first essay in "Naive Physics", the attempt to create a formalisation of common-sense knowledge of the physical world. The general background and overall aims are explained in chapter 1, this volume, "The Second Naive Physics Manifesto".

The choice of liquids as a first subject may seem arbitrary and obscure. It was made because liquids have seemed for some time to present some very difficult unsolved problems for formalizers. Liquids have, for example, no definite shape. and they merge and split and move in mysterious ways. As expected, I have been forced to develop many other concepts in order to talk of liquids: geometry, time, change, shape among them. None of these is fully investigated here, but we have made a start. In a sense, since the space of concepts is so richly connected, it probably doesn't matter where one starts: every cluster leads into other clusters.

I use first-order logic as the formal language. However, readers to whom logic is either unfamiliar or unattractive should be able to follow most of the ideas by reading the text and looking at the pictures. The same ideas and concepts could be expressed in any one of many formal languages.

A brief note on the logical language used. We use the full predicate calculus with equality, not just clausal form. We use all the usual connectives, and exclusive *or* (written $\dot{\vee}$), which is often very useful. The usual precedence rules are used: $\sim$ binds more tightly than $\wedge$, $\vee$, or $\dot{\vee}$; these more than $\supset$ or $\equiv$; and quantifiers have the widest scope of all. Brackets or layout will override these conventions. I will assume $\wedge$, $\vee$, and $\dot{\vee}$ to be variadic. Note that $A \dot{\vee} B \dot{\vee} C$ means

$$(A \wedge \sim B \wedge \sim C) \vee (\sim A \wedge B \wedge \sim C) \vee (\sim A \wedge \sim B \wedge C)$$

so that $\dot{\vee}$ is not associative.

Some "higher-order" quantifications will be used: these are to be regarded only as syntactic sugarings of related first-order expressions. Predicate and relation names will be capitalised; constant, variable and function names not. Free variables are understood to be universally quantified with the whole axiom as scope.

The only other syntactic curiosity is restricted quantification, for which we use an epsilon, for example:

$$\forall t \, \epsilon \, l. \; P(t)$$

We assume that the underlying logic has a fairly sophisticated sort structure, so that relations and functions are defined only on particular combinations of sorts of their arguments. I will indicate types informally by the consistent use of special variable names, such as ar for arrivals, le for leavings and h for histories: see Cohn (1983) for a more formal description of the necessary logic.

2 Individuals and Individuation

Every representational formalism I know which has even the glimmerings of a clear semantics, is based on the idea of individual entities and relationships between them. The individuals need not be *physical* individuals; they may be abstract "things" like *the color green* or *the German nation* or *the concept of man* or *the number zero*. They may only exist in some imaginary world, like *the King of France who would be on the throne now if there hadn't been any revolution*: indeed, they may actually *be* an imaginary world, or a state of it. They may be arbitrarily big or arbitrarily small, real or platonic, compact or spread out; still they are *individuals*: separate entities, each not to be confused with any other entity. They partake in relations with other such crisp *individuals*: physical relations such as being inside of, having as color, and abstract relations such as being in 1:1 correspondence with, or bearing an analogy to, or being a physical property.

Many problems in the philosophy of logic turn on the question of how we *identify* individuals: how they are *individuated*. Intuitively, certain properties of a thing serve to distinguish it from other things and to identify it as being the thing that it is, while other properties of the thing are merely properties that it happens to have. Thus, my car is a Malibu, like many other Malibu's, but it has several properties—

its chassis number, its registration plate, the dent in the rear door, etc., which, taken together, I use to identify it as being mine.

To distinguish properties of a thing which are essential to it from properties which are merely properties, in this way, is to espouse what Quine calls *essentialism*. He evidently regards it as incompatible with Science, a view with which we can happily agree, while using essentialism wholeheartedly ourselves.

However, the fundamental criteria for individuating a complex object cannot be such superficial properties as those I have mentioned, for they can change. For example, take my car. If it were stolen, its bodywork and driver's seat repaired, its engine and chassis numbers filed off, and resprayed, then all the properties by which I identify it would be false of it; and yet it would still be my car, the very same Malibu. I think what we have to say here is that it is my car because it has continuously *been* my car through all the intervening history. It was my car when it was stolen, and repairing, respraying, etc., are not operations which destroy the identity of a car: ergo, it is still my car. It still would be my car, indeed, if every single piece of it had been replaced, so that it had no part in common with the car that had been stolen from me. (If I could demonstrate this spatiotemporal continuity to a court, it would I think agree that the car was mine, however altered in appearance it seemed.)

The point of this is to illustrate the fact that spatiotemporal continuity is the criterion for determining the identity of complex assemblies: for these can have parts replaced but still retain their identity.

Consider now *pieces* of solid stuff, like metal bars or wooden blocks. Every solid physical object is either a piece of solid stuff, or else an assembly which is made up of a finite number of other solid physical objects. We can state this formally:

$$\forall x.Solidobject(x) \supset Assembly(x) \tag{1a}$$
$$\vee \; \exists m.Stuff(m) \wedge Rigid(m) \wedge madeof(x) = m$$

$$Assembly(x) \supset \exists x_1,...,x_n.Part(x,x_1) \wedge .... \wedge Part(x,x_n) \tag{1b}$$
$$\wedge \; Solid(x_1) \wedge .... \wedge Solid(x_n)$$

Here, *madeof* is a function between a solid undecomposable physical *thing* and a *substance*. (Substances, like *wood*, can be thought of either as abstract individuals—the essence of woodiness—or as worldly, solid but rather spread-out individuals; all the wood in the world. This latter is the nominalist idea developed by Goodman (1966), according to which our relation *madeof* is thought of as meaning *being-a-part-of* (in a rather different sense from our *part*). The platonist-nominalist division between ways of thinking of substances need not concern us here: it is sufficient for our purpose that substances exist as individuals, and can be quantified over.) It is amusing to try to find counterexamples to (1). A muscle-tendon-bone junction? A bar which is steel at one end but aluminium at the other, with a smooth transition between them? I think we always make a *conceptual* division into well-defined parts, even when exact boundaries (as in muscle-tendon-bone) are hard or impossible to place exactly.

I think that *being the same piece* of stuff is the basic individuating property for solid pieces. Thus, a wooden brick is an object, an individual; and it comprises a certain unique *piece* of wood, distinguishable from other pieces of (the same) wood. The block *is* the piece of wood; and every piece of wood is an object. Notice how this differs from the criterion for individuating an assembly.

These objects, moreover, are fairly *enduring*. They can be destroyed (cutting, crushing, burning . . .) and created (cutting, forging, molding . . .) but only by recognizable actions and events. They do not appear and vanish by accident, casually, without anyone noticing, as it were: the events which mark their creation and destruction are nameable, describable entities. They have a beginning and an end. It is possible to keep track of them.

3 The Problem With Liquids

But for liquids, this is far less plausible. Axiom (1) fails immediately: think of a half-melted triple-decker ice cream cone, for example. We can distinguish water, the generic stuff, from a particular piece of water, just as with solid substances. But the criteria for identifying pieces of water do not seem to be the same as for pieces of solids. Lake Leman, for example, has the Rhone flowing in one end and out the other, so it certainly isn't the same piece of water from day to day, yet we feel it is the same *lake*.

Consider a glass containing 100 cc of water. We could say this *piece of water* was an object. Now we pour 10 cc into another glass: now there are *two* objects, and neither is identical to the first one. Now pour it back: there is one object again. Is it the same object as that with which we began? It would seem so, since it is the same water and the same glass, and it has all the same properties as the former. But then, we have individuals which cease to exist and reappear later, which is rather worrying.

Perhaps we should say that a glass of water is like an assembly, so that we can replace bits by others without changing its identity. After all, we could take a car completely to pieces and then reassemble it, and it would be the same car. And this would let Lake Leman be an object, albeit in a state of continuous overhaul.

But what are the components of these assemblies? Presumably, smaller pieces of water. Presumably then one could say, after pouring the 10 cc back, that the 100 cc contained two *parts*, one of 10 cc and one of 90 cc. Now pour out 20 cc and one of 20 cc back. It now contains another two parts: one of 80 cc and one of 20 cc. None of these four parts is the same as another, so they must *overlap*. Clearly, by repeating this sort of argument one sees that any piece of water must be an assembly of a very large (maybe infinite) number of very small (maybe infinitesimal) pieces, with no structure: a wholly disorganized assembly, like a powder.

Now, this *is* a good way to look at liquids, but it seems overly sophisticated for everyday use, and gives rise to many problems of its own (one can't *see* the separate grains, for example, and this requires an explanation). Moreover, these liquid assemblies, unlike such well-made things as cars, come apart and reassemble at the slightest provocation. It seems hardly possible to keep track of their existence: they can come apart or recombine by accident, as it were.

And in any case, there is another problem, for sometimes we seem to use the other ontology. We can say, this water (in this glass) came out of the tap. But this requires us to treat the water in the glass as a particular *piece* of water, not a mere assembly: for if I pour some water from the sewer into it, then it's the same assembly, having merely grown somewhat (think of adding seat covers to my car): but it's a very different piece of stuff.

Pieces of liquid, then, are objects which give rise to considerable difficulty. It's not clear what they *are*. We will revisit this question in section 10. but before then will try to do without pieces of liquid altogether. It turns out that one can get a long way by talking only about the pieces of space or space–time which contain liquid. and how they can be connected to one another. And this geometric approach gives one good way to individuate liquid objects, as discussed in section 10.

4 Doing Without Liquid Individuals: Containment

The first idea is to avoid talking about *pieces of liquid* altogether, and to refer. rather, to *containers*, which may be full of liquid, to distinguish one piece of liquid from another. More exactly, we will introduce a notion of *contained space* which may contain some liquid. A notion of *quantity* or *amount* is naturally introduced at the same time. In this way we can talk about *the 20 cc of water in this cup or the 10 cc of water in that cup* in a natural way without being committed to the view that such a 20 cc or 10 cc of water *is* an individual thing.

By a *contained space* we will mean some connected volume of three-dimensional-space which has a contiguous rigid boundary (at least) below it and around it. As a first, temporary approximation, we will also assume that the substance comprising the boundary is impermeable and has no leaks. Examples include the inside of a cup or a dish or a jug or a bath; the bed and banks of a lake or a pond; the interior of a paint tin or a petrol can. Notice we distinguish between the *container*, which is a solid object, or part of a solid object, and the *contained space*, which is *not* a physical object but is characterized by a certain capacity and by being in a certain relation to a container.

Let us say that if *c* is a container then *inside(c)* is the space it contains: *inside* is a function from containers to their contained spaces. We will also need to be able to refer to some liquids being in a certain place. If *s* is a contained space and *l* a liquid (in the generic sense—a *liquid stuff* such as water or oil), then we will refer to the *amount of l* in *s*. We assume that there is a function *amount(l,s)* from liquids and contained spaces, to entities called *amounts* which are abstract "quantities". We will assume that the set of amounts is (partially) ordered and has a zero element. *none*. Thus, "there's whisky in the jar" can be represented:

$$amount(whisky, inside(jar)) > none.$$

Notice that we have nowhere spoken of the piece of whisky in the jar as an individual entity: *whisky* here is a generic liquid stuff. We can measure quantities by *measure functions*, which are functions to some *measure space* from quantities. (We will take measure space to be the positive reals for the moment, but there is considerable interest in extending the notion to other structures, such as finite discrete sets, tolerance spaces and catastrophes. This will be discussed more fully elsewhere.) For example, litres is a measure function, and we can write

$$liters(amount(whisky, inside(jar)))=0.83$$

to say there is 0.83 litres of whisky in the jar.

We have to distinguish amounts from numbers in order to allow different measure functions: 0.83 liters is 1.46 pints, for example, and a heaped tablespoonful is about an ounce. We can express general conversions:

$$liters(x) = 1.76 \times pints(x)$$

In any case, it seems a good idea on general grounds to have a prenumerate notion of *quantity*, independent of any quantitative measurement. We also have the axiom :

$$Measurefun(q) \supset q(none) = 0 \qquad (2)$$

(I have deliberately not distinguished between mass and volume. I believe the distinction to be fairly sophisticated. Thus, we could introduce notions of the mass of a given amount of liquid *l*, and the volume of a given amount of liquid *l*, and refuse to have any scales of *amounts*, only masses and volumes. I think something like this is what happens in the heads of kids who learn about density for the first time. It is a difficult concept, requiring a fairly thorough overhauling of one's ontological apparatus. The density of liquid *l* is the ratio of the mass of a given amount of liquid *l* to the volume of the same amount. It is by no means *a priori* obvious that it is independent of the amount. I have observed exactly this difficulty in teaching this concept to a child: he couldn't believe, at first, that the density of a big rock would be the same as that of a little piece of the same material. (His problem had been exacerbated by his having been taught in school that the mass of a body was "the amount of it there is", a description he—quite reasonably—could not distinguish from that of the volume.))

We will need the notion of the *capacity* of a container, i.e. the maximum amount it can contain. It is in fact more convenient to introduce a notion of *amount of space*, and define *capacity(s)*, where *s* is a contained space, to be the amount of space it comprises. We then have the axiom

$$none \leq amount(l,s) \leq capacity(s) \qquad (3)$$

and we can define

$$\neg Full(s,l) \equiv amount(l,s) = capacity(s) \qquad (4)$$

Consider now a lake. This is a contained-space defined by geographical constraints. Lake Leman, for example, is the space contained between the Jura Mountains. Lausanne, the Dent d'Oche, Thonon, and the Rochers de Naye, below the 400-meter contour (more or less). Its container is the surface of the earth under it, i.e. the *lake bed*. I think the only way to describe lakes, rivers and ponds in the present framework is to say that they are contained-spaces which are full of water: that is. the space ends at the surface of the water. To be *in* the lake is then, reasonably, to be immersed in water, while to be *on* the lake is to be immediately above the water and supported by the lake (cf. *on the table*), which seems reasonable. Thus a lake is full by definition.

It might seem that we have essentially resuscitated our original ontology of pieces-of-water under a different name. But not so. For with *this* ontology, Lake Leman is a fixed object in geographical space whereas in the pieces-of-water ontology, it would be constantly changing, since the Rhone flows in one end and out the other; it would be a phenomenon, not an object.

One can make several objections. I will consider two.

1. If the Rhone were to dry up and Lake Leman drain away, we would say the Lake had gone, but the *space* would still be there: so 'Lake Leman' must refer to the water, not the space. No. Because a lake, on our account, is a space full of water. and its top is the surface of the water. Thus, as the lake drained away, we would have its space shrinking and when all the water had gone, so would have the lake. Notice in this connection the distinction between a lake (or a river) and the lake valley (river bed). The latter is a container, the former a contained space. But, in general:

$$capacity(lake) < capacity(inside(lake\text{-}valley)).$$

For rivers, the analogous inequation is the no-flooding condition.

2. Since Lake Leman (for example) is, on our account, merely a *space*, how can it support a boat? Perhaps the water supports the boat. But we want to avoid saying that any particular *piece* of water supports the boat. But, on the other hand, the water in my bath (say) does not support the boat in any way, and we want this to be quite clear. The only way to handle this for now, is to say that, in fact, the *lake* supports the boat: that is, the space supports it. But it only does so *because* it is full of water, so that an empty space would not support a boat. Thus, boats float on lakes and ponds *because* lakes and ponds are full of water.

A naive axiom might be something like this:

$$On(t,su)\& Top(su,s) \& \exists l.Full(s,l) \supset Floatable(t)$$
$$\equiv Supports(s,t) \qquad (5)$$

where *Floatable* is supposed to relate to some (as yet unspecified) theory of buoyancy.

Notice that axiom (5) makes no reference to density. Again I believe a concern for variable density arises only at a very sophisticated level of understanding. It also ignores the way in which floating objects are partly submerged.

All in all, agreeing to swallow some artificiality, the idea of avoiding liquid objects by talking about pieces of space seems to work reasonably well for nicely contained liquid. Before considering other situations liquid can be in, we will develop some apparatus for describing geometrical relationships.

5 Space: Places, Enclosures and Portals

(The concepts outlined in this section really belong in a 'geometry' cluster, and will be described more fully elsewhere. The present account should be taken merely as a sketch.)

Three-dimensional space can be described in a very large number of ways. We can use one of many coordinate systems, for example. Any heuristically adequate description must, however, distinguish the description of the shape of an object, or internal arrangement of a space such as the interior of a room, from the description of where this object or space is located in a larger arrangement or coordinate system. A box has a certain shape—occupies a certain piece of space—independently of where it is in a building (more or less). This point deserves more elaboration, but I mention it here only to emphasize that any kind of global coordinate system is heuristically inadequate: We need a notion of a *piece* of space, and how such pieces can be related and connected to one another. In this section I will develop a theory of such pieces, and how they connect to one another, which is entirely topological, and does not depend upon or use any metric ideas or coordinate system.

A contained space is such a piece which is inside a container. Thus, the inside of a cup is the *same* piece of space, in the same relation to the cup, wherever the cup happens to be. So if the cup is moved across a room, its inside moves with it. If the cup is rotated about a horizontal axis, however, the circumstances inside it are liable to change. Indeed this is generally true, for the global gravity vertical runs through all places. (This vertical direction is obviously of great evolutionary importance, since our bodies have an apparatus of great delicacy whose sole purpose is to detect it: the semicircular canals in the inner ear.) I will therefore distinguish three independent aspects of the spatial disposition of an object: its *shape*, its *position* in some larger spatial framework, and its *orientation* with respect to the gravity vertical. Only the first and last will be of great concern to us. I will assume that such concepts as vertical, top, bottom, horizontal, etc., can be used without further comment: they all refer to the global gravity vertical.

We need to characterize the shape of containers. Intuitively, a container is a solid object which *surrounds* a space, so that there is no way out; or, perhaps, so that the only way out is at the top. So we need the notion of "a way out", which I will call a *portal*: that is, a piece of surface which links two pieces of space and through which objects and material can pass.

There seem to be two different ways to describe this. We can say that a portal is a *common face* of the spaces on either side of it, and is itself free space, i.e. is occupied by no solid lamina. Or we can say that it is a surface through which one can pass from (a point in) one space to (a point in) the other, i.e. such that there is a free-space path from one space to the other which intersects it. (Suitably tightened up, these two definitions are, in fact, equivalent: an intuitively obvious fact which is quite hard to prove.)

These two properties of a portal reflect two fundamentally different approaches to the qualitative description of spatial arrangement and connection, which might be called the space/surface approach and the point/path approach. There are distinct topological theories which arise from each: respectively, homology theory and homotopy theory (see for example Hocking & Young 1961).

From homology theory we borrow the idea of a *face*. A face of a spatial or spatiotemporal entity is a piece of space of one lower dimension which forms part of its boundary. Thus, for example, the surface of a wall of a room is a face of a room: the edge of a tabletop is the face of the tabletop, which is itself a face of the table. We will write $Face(s_1, s_2)$ in formulae.

There is a basic fact which we will make implicit use of: in a space of dimension n, a piece of space of dimension $n-1$ is a face of exactly two pieces of dimension n: it has two sides. (For any $k < n-1$, this fails: a piece of dimension k can be a face of an indefinite number of pieces of dimension $k + 1$. Take $n = 3$, $k = 1$, and consider the spine of a book, for example; or $n = 4$, $k = 2$, and consider a tabletop on which a number of bricks are successively placed and removed in turn.) We can make use of this fact by defining a function *toso* ("the other side of"), such that:

$$Face(f,v) \equiv Face(f, toso(f,v)) \tag{6}$$

$$toso(f, toso(f,v)) = v \tag{7}$$

The function *toso* is, by our discussion above, defined only in suitable dimensions. Thus, if f is a point and v part of a line, then $toso(f,v)$ is the other half of the line. If v is a piece of 3-space or an object, then $toso(f,v)$ is another piece of space.

Let us say that a face f of v is a *Top* (of v) if its surface normal has a positive vertical component, similarly for *Bottom*. Then *toso* reverses direction:

$$Top(f,v) \supset Bottom(f, toso(f,v)) \tag{8}$$

(From which the contraposition also easily follows, so we could replace implication by equivalence.) We will also need:

$$\sim Face(s) \tag{9}$$

A solid object defines a piece of space which it (just) fills. Such a piece of space can however be surfacelike, a lamina, as in a sheet of metal. We will want to say that such an object is the face of the spaces of both sides of it. But we will also want to be able to distinguish such an object from its surfaces, since we will want to be able to say whether or not they are wet. I will distinguish therefore a surface (which may or may not be occupied by an object) from the two *directed surfaces* which are its sides. It is convenient to assume that solid objects (considered as pieces of space) contain their boundaries (faces), but that pieces of free space do not: the former can be seen as closed, the latter open, sets in metric, Euclidean, three-dimensional space, in the sense of topology. We can think of a solid object as having an open interior and a "skin" composed of its faces: laminar objects are "all skin". (The topological foundations of such an intuitive geometry deserve closer attention.)

Let us say that $Int(s_1, s_2)$ if the piece of space s_1 is wholly contained in s_2, and let $space(o)$, where o is an object, be the space occupied by o. Then we can say:

$$s = space(o) \equiv (\forall f. Face(f,o) \supset Int(f,s)) \tag{10}$$

It is convenient to treat *space* as a coercion function in formulae, so that if an expression 'e' naming an object occurs in an argument-place requiring a space or surface, it is taken to mean '$space(e)$'. With this convention, we can often mention objects as though they were pieces of space, writing for example $Int(o_1, o_2)$. We will do this without further comment from time to time. We can define:

$$Free(s) \equiv \; \sim\! \exists o. Int(s,o) \tag{11}$$

and we have

$$Int(s,s) \tag{12a}$$

$$Int(s_1, s_2) \land Int(s_2, s_3) \supset Int(s_1, s_3) \tag{12b}$$

Now consider two (open) pieces of space separated by a connecting face. There are four possibilities. If the face is free then so must both spaces be (for if one were solid then it would contain the face), so the face is a portal. Or just the face might be a laminar object. Or one piece of space might be the space of an object, containing the face, and the other be free. Or both spaces might be full, in which case we have two objects joined along a face (see Figure 1).

$$Face(f,v) \equiv$$
$$Free(f) \land Free(v) \land Free(toso(f,v))$$
$$\lor \, \exists o. f = space(o) \land Free(v) \land Free(toso(f,v))$$
$$\lor \, \exists o. Int(f,o) \land (Free(v) \land toso(f,v) = space(o)$$
$$\lor \, Free(toso(f,v)) \land v = space(o))$$
$$\lor \, \exists o_1, o_2. v = space(o_1) \land toso(f,v) = space(o_2) \land Joined(o_1, o_2, f) \tag{13}$$

$$Joined(o_1,o_2,f) \equiv Face(f,o_1) \wedge Face(f,o_2) \wedge o_1 \neq o_2 \qquad (14)$$

This last case is the only interpenetration we allow:

$$In(s,o_1) \wedge In(s,o_2) \supset Joined(o_1,o_2,s) \dot\vee o_1 = o_2 \qquad (15)$$

We can now, at last, characterize some containers. A closed container, the simplest case, is a solid object o which encloses a space we will call $inside(o)$. (Note that $inside(o)$ is not In the object o, but rather is enclosed by it: an empty glass bottle encloses air but all the space In it is full of glass.) I will not attempt a complete axiomatization of $inside$, but we do have:

$$Closedcontainer(o) \wedge Face(f,inside(o)) \supset In(f,o) \qquad (16)$$

which gives some flesh to the idea of enclosure; and of course

$$Free(inside(o)) \qquad (17)$$

These alone have some interesting consequences. Assume for example $Closedcontainer(ob)$ and $Face(f,inside(ob))$. Then from (16) we can conclude $In(f,ob)$ and hence $\sim Free(f)$, by (11). Now, checking the various cases in (13), applied to f and $inside(ob)$, the first is ruled out; and the last is ruled out by (17)—since if $inside(ob)$ is $space(o_j)$ then it is not $Free$, by (12a) and (11)—and in the third case, the first subcase, which has $inside(ob) = space(o)$, is similarly eliminated. Hence only two cases remain, either:

$$\exists o. \, f = space(o) \wedge Free(inside(ob)) \wedge Free(tosof,inside(ob)))$$

or

$$\exists o. \, In(f,space(o)) \wedge tosof,inside(ob)) = space(o) \wedge Free(inside(ob)))$$

In the first case, since (16) implies that $In(f,ob)$, we have $In(space(o),ob)$, ie $In(o,ob)$. But then, since $In(o,o)$ by (12a), we can conclude from (15) that $Joined(o,ob,o) \dot\vee = ob$. The definition (14) of $Joined$ rules out the first possibility since nothing is a face of itself, so we are obliged to conclude that $o = ob$. A similarly tortuous piece of reasoning, using (15), (6) and (17), establishes that $o = ob$ in the second case also. The first case then has f, the face of the inside, being the object ob, so that ob is a laminar object such as a gas can, while the second case has f being merely a part of ob, which has nontrivial thickness: a solid object with a cavity, like a coconut. And these are exactly the two possible ways to make a closed container.

More interesting are open containers, i.e. those with (at least) one portal. If there is just one, we will call it the top of the container, so that we can say:

$$Opencontainer(o) \supset Free(top(o)) \wedge$$
$$\forall f. \, Face(f,inside(o)) \supset In(f,o) \dot\vee f = top(o) \qquad (18)$$

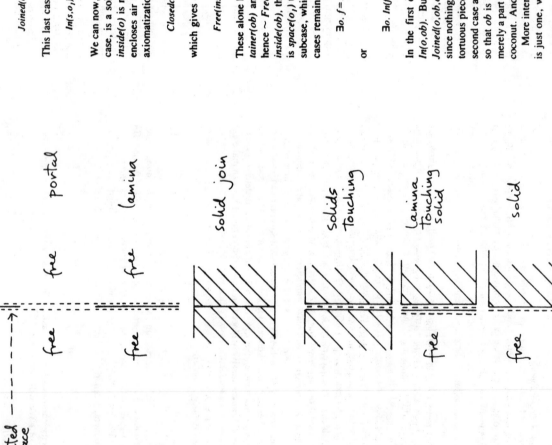

Figure 1. Surfaces and directed surfaces

We could now define some more familiar ideas, for example:

$$Brim(e,o) \equiv Face(e,top(o)) \qquad (19)$$

(This is the first nontrivial use of lower-dimensional Faces). Notice that *top*, unlike *Top* introduced earlier, is independent of orientation. We can define a very useful notion of "right way up" (*Rwu*) by saying:

$$Rwu(o) \equiv Top(top(o),o) \qquad (20)$$

(It is important to realize that *Top*, and hence *Rwu*, are not relations which are intrinsic to an object. Unlike most of what we have considered they are liable to be altered when the object is moved around in space.)

We will also need other kinds of containment, such as leaky containers (those with a portal lower than the top) and channels (like a container, but with portals at both its ends). Unfortunately to describe these adequately requires metric ideas. (For example, a tin with a small hole in the base is a leaky tin, but a tin with the bottom missing isn't a container at all, although it could be a channel.) I will not go into this in detail here. Our use of the function *inside* will be taken to imply that the object defines a space in some way, and we will introduce categories of such objects as we need them. For a start,

$$Container(o) \equiv Closedcontainer(o) \lor (Opencontainer(o) \land Rwu(o)) \qquad (21)$$

Before leaving geometry, we need the notion of a side of a surface. We will define a *directed surface*, $d(f,v)$ where f is part of a face of v. The idea is that such an object is an arbitrarily thin, open, lamina on the v side of the face f. (Since Euclidean space is normal, i.e. Hausdorff and compact, such a lamina *can* be arbitrarily thin.) We extend *toso* by defining

$$toso(d(f,v)) = d(f,toso(f,v)) \qquad (22)$$

then we have

$$toso(toso(d(f,v))) = d(f,v)$$

And if we assert

$$In(d(f,v),v) \qquad (23)$$

then we can easily derive

$$In(toso(d(f,v)), toso(f,v))$$

We will extend *In* to directed faces in the obvious way, so that

$$In(f_1,f_2) \equiv In(d(f_1,v),d(f_2,v)).$$

If o is a solid object and f a face of o, then the directed face $d(f, toso(f,o))$ is an *outer* face of o. If o is a laminar container then we can define an outer directed face of o to be $d(f,toso(inside(o)))$ where f is part of o:

$$Outer(d,o) \equiv \exists f.Face(f,o) \land d=d(f,toso(f,o))$$
$$\lor\ In(f,o) \land d=d(f,toso(f,inside(o))) \qquad (24)$$

The first case is a solid object o, the second a laminar container. We can then say that two objects are *touching* if they share an outer directed face:

$$Touching(o_1,o_2) \equiv \exists d.\ Outer(d,o_1) \land Outer(d,o_2) \qquad (25)$$

i.e. d is an arbitrarily thin free space separating the objects. Notice how this differs from a join along a shared face.

Since a solid object not attached to anything else is, by our definitions, completely surrounded by free space, we can define *surround(o)* to be this space. Thus we have

$$Free(surround(o)) \qquad (26)$$

$$Outer(d,o) \supset In(d,surround(o)) \qquad (27)$$

$$Free(s) \land In(o,s) \supset In(s,surround(o)) \qquad (28)$$

Similarly, if v is a free volume bounded by a solid face f, then the directed face $d(f,v)$ will be called an *inward* face of v:

$$Inward(d,v) \equiv \exists f.\ Face(f,v) \land d=d(f,v) \qquad (29)$$

Figure 1 illustrates the ways in which spaces, surfaces, objects and directed surfaces can be related to one another.

Later we will need to consider edges and surfaces in some detail, and in order to talk of directions on a surface we will need the concept of a *directed edge*. This is, of course, merely the 1-dimensional version of a directed surface, and we will write $d(e,f)$, where e is an edge which is part of the boundary of the piece of surface f. All the above axioms apply unchanged, so that $d(e,f)$ is *In* the surface f. We will use *inward* and *outer* for edges and surfaces also.

However, the full story is more complicated, since directed surfaces themselves, being essentially two-dimensional entities, have edges and hence directed edges.

We must distinguish an edge of a surface from the corresponding edge of the directed surface immediately above it. For example, the latter may be free when the former, being inside a solid surface, is not. One can think of an edge of a directed surface as being an arbitrarily low "fence" on the appropriate side of the underlying surface, and a directed edge of a directed surface is then one side of it be free: this is a "wire" raised on a surface, as in a cloisonné enamel, or a pattern of hedges seen from the air.

Suppose v is a volume of space, f a face of it and e an edge of f. Then $d(e,f)$ is a directed edge which, by (23), is In the surface f. The side of f towards v is $d(f,v)$: $d(e,v)$ is the edge of this side (notice, *not* a directed edge), i.e. the "fence" above the edge e on the v side of the surface f. The *directed edge* of the directed surface $d(e,v)$ corresponding to $d(e,f)$ is $d(d(e,v),d(f,v))$, which we will abbreviate by $d(e,f,v)$.

The situation is illustrated in Figure 2, an inspection of which may help convince the reader of the reasonableness of the following axioms.

$$Face(e,f) \wedge Face(f,v) \supset Face(d(e,v),d(f,v)) \qquad (30)$$

$$toso(d(e,v),d(f,v)) = d(toso(e,f),v) \qquad (31)$$

It follows from these and earlier axioms that the other side of a directed edge of a directed face is what one would expect:

$$
\begin{aligned}
toso(d(e,f,v)) &=_{df} toso(d(d(e,v),d(f,v))) \\
&= d(d(e,v),toso(d(e,v),d(f,v))) \\
&= d(d(e,v),d(toso(e,f),v)) \qquad \text{by (22)} \\
&=_{df} d(e,toso(e,f),v) \qquad \text{by (31)}
\end{aligned}
$$

The identity just proven should be compared to (22).

Notice that, by (23), $d(e,f,v)$ is in $d(f,v)$ and hence in v. Thus if one is on one side of a fence, one is In the airspace above the ground.

Finally, let us briefly consider corners of objects and edges of laminas. If e is a corner of o, then it is a face of two faces of o. In this case we will say that these two faces are each on the other side of e from the other: thus, $toso$ does not distinguish between a line on a surface and a corner, or between convex and concave corners. It would be consistent to say that if e is an edge of a lamina f then $toso(e,f)$ was f itself. (This would be the limiting case as the corner was made sharper.) We will not adopt this convention, however, but will merely say in this case that $toso(e,f)$ is *Free*. Indeed, we can usefully define *Edge* by:

$$Lamina(o) \supset (Edge(e,o) \equiv Face(e,o) \wedge Free(toso(e,o))) \qquad (32)$$

6 The Fifteen States of Liquids

The contained-space ontology seems to work reasonably well for liquids contained safely in bounded volumes. However, as any child knows, this is not the normal condition of liquids, and typically, is a state which requires some care to maintain. Left to themselves, liquids flow and stick to things, and are liable to finish up in a different place from that in which they began. It is not clear whether the ontology which serves for contained fluids can be usefully extended to fluids which are running around loose, or are divided up into fine particles, etc. . . .

Let us try to make a taxonomy of the possible states liquid can be in. I will begin by drawing as many distinctions as possible, thus dividing the space of possibilities up into lots of little boxes (Figure 3).

Liquid can be in *bulk*, or it can be *finely divided* as in a spray, mist, droplets or rainfall. It can be *lazy* or *energetic*. (An object or state or process is *energetic* if it requires effort to maintain; *lazy* otherwise, i.e. if it can "just happen". I believe this distinction is of considerable importance throughout naive physics. For example, water falling is lazy, but flying upwards through the air, as in a fountain, is energetic.) It can be *supported* or *unsupported*. If it is supported, it can be in a space (*inside* some object), or on a surface (i.e. *In* the directed surface on one side of the surface). It can be *moving* or *still*: obviously, still liquid is lazy. Of the 32 logical possibilities, only 15 are physically possible, even allowing such outré possibilities as mist being blown along a tube.

There are a few other possibilities, such as liquid soaked up in a sponge or cloth, or suspended by surface tension across the holes in a metal mesh, or free-floating bubbles, but I shall ignore these. In fact, I shall ignore all except the *lazy bulk* states (the top left hand group in Figure 3) in what follows, in order to keep the presentation to a reasonable length. I do not expect the extension to the remaining states to give rise to any deep problems.

We handled containment, without using liquid objects, by referring to pieces of space which *contain* liquid. A similar device works for wet surfaces. We can use the apparatus of directed surfaces. Let f be a solid face of a free volume v: then to say that f is wet is to say that $d(f,v)$ contains some amount of liquid. It is convenient to use the same function *amount* as before. We can also have a notion of capacity, and can use the same function name;

$$Wetby(d,l) \equiv capacity(d) \geq amount(l,d) > none \qquad (33)$$

Here, we must give the phenomenon a name since it is possible for a surface, unlike a container, to support *more* than its capacity: this is when the liquid flows across the surface.

Our geometry now enables us to make several useful inferences. For example, if one surface touches another wet surface, then the first one will be wet also, since to

	BULK			DIVIDED		
	ON SURFACE	IN SPACE	UNSUPPORTED	ON SURFACE	IN SPACE	UNSUPPORTED
ENERGETIC MOVING	Waves lapping shore (?) jet hitting a surface (?)	Pumped along pipeline.	Waterspout, fountain, jet from hosepipe.		steam or mist blown along a tube (?)	spray, splash, driving rain.
LAZY MOVING	Flowing down a surface, e.g. a sloping roof.	Flowing along a channel, e.g. river.	Falling column of liquid, e.g. pouring from a jug, or waterfall.		Mist rolling down a valley (?)	Rain, shower.
LAZY STILL	Wet surface	Contained, in container		Dew, drops on a surface.	Mist filling a valley (?)	Mist, cloud.

Figure 3. The possible physical states of liquid

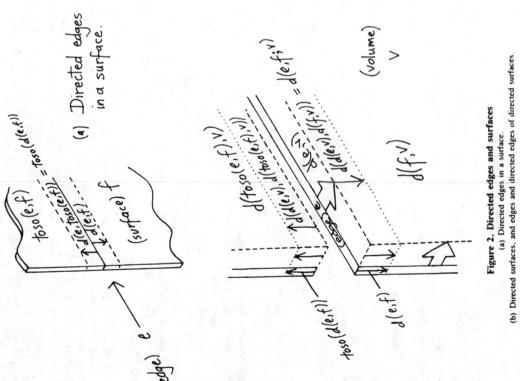

Figure 2. Directed edges and surfaces

(a) Directed edges in a surface.

(b) Directed surfaces, and edges and directed edges of directed surfaces.

touch a surface is to share the intervening directed surface. More exactly, we can easily show that:

$$Touching(o_1,o_2) \land (\exists d.\ Outer(d,o_1) \land Wetby(d.l))$$
$$\supset$$
$$\exists d'.\ Outer(d'.o_2) \land Wetby(d'.l)$$

Similarly, we can, with a little more work, show that an object immersed in liquid is *really* wet, all over. For this we need:

$$In(s_1,s_2) \land Free(s_1) \land Full(s_2,l) \supset Full(s_1,l) \tag{34}$$

Now suppose $In(o,s)$, $Full(s,l)$ and $Outer(d,o)$. Then $In(surround(o),s)$ and $In(d,surround(o))$, by (28) and (27). Hence by (34) (twice), $Full(d,l)$. Thus if someone falls in the lake, he will be as wet as he can get, all over. Finally, it is left as an exercise for the reader to show that if a container is full, then its inside is wet.

Both a wetting and a containment have more structure than we have so far described. If a contained-space contains liquids then there is a surface, which is a horizontal plane (below the *top* of an open container), such that the space below the surface is full (and above it is empty) even though the contained space as a whole is not full. Similarly, if a (directed) face contains liquid, then the chances are that there is a patch of the face which is full and is properly contained in the face. The edge of such a patch is analogous to the surface of the liquid in a container (but has, regrettably, no such tidy property as horizontality). (It is also possible for a surface to be merely damp, all over. I will ignore this possibility for now but it would figure more prominently if we considered mists, spray and rain.)

An open container will spill if the surface of the liquid reaches the edge of its supports, i.e. a free face of it. In both cases, this can happen while the whole space is not yet full, (by tipping an open container, for example). We need a way, therefore, of talking about the full parts of containments and wettings, which we will call a *wet*.

$$amount(l.s) > none \supset$$
$$In(wet(s),s)$$
$$\land\ amount(l,wet(s)) = capacity(wet(s)) = amount(l.s)$$
$$\land\ (contained(s) \supset$$
$$\exists p.Horizontal(p) \land (Top(su,wet(s)) \supset In(su,p))) \tag{35}$$

(This allows, for example, a U-shaped container, in which the liquid has two tops)
Now the spilling criterion can be simply stated: *wet(s)* shares a face with a portal of *s*

The three remaining cases, involving movement and change, cannot be handled by talking only of pieces of space. We need the concept of things that *happen* rather than merely *are*. In the next section I develop some new apparatus for talking

about time and change, which is to a large extent an extension, into the fourth dimension, of the geometric ideas of section 5.

7 Change and Movement: Histories

The now traditional approach to the description of change, due to McCarthy (1959, McCarthy & Hayes 1969), introduces the notion of a time-instant or ''situation''. Relations whose truth-value is time-dependent are made to depend upon the situation as well as their ''static'' arguments. A detailed account of the logic of this technique is in (Hayes 1971). Exactly the same idea underlies the familiar context-as-possible-world style of using such systems as Conniver and the tense logics developed by philosophical logicians (see for example Prior 1968: for the connections between tense-logics and the situation calculus, see McCarthy & Hayes 1969, part 4).

I will here use a rather different approach based on the idea of a *history*. A history differs from a situation in being restricted spatially and extended temporally: it is a connected piece of space-time in which ''something happens'', more or less separate from other such pieces. Histories, unlike situations, have a *shape*: much of this section will be devoted to ways of describing their shape.

Examples of histories include the inside of a room during the afternoon, a horserace and the pouring of water from one cup into another. The idea is that a history shall contain an event, isolating it temporally and spatially from other events. We include the special case in which nothing happens at all.

A *state* (an idea we have already used) is an instantaneous ''slice'' of a history at a certain time-instant. For most histories, there are two distinguished states called the *start* and the *finish*, between which the history exists: if s is a state which is the start of one, then $do(a.s)$ is the state which is the end of it. A state is not a situation, as it has a limited spatial extent and a spatial shape. It is a very thin history.

Almost all the histories we consider in this paper are in a particularly simple class, consisting of a certain piece of space in which something happens for a certain length of time: they are *rectangular*. (Contrast for example a movement through space, which ''slopes'' in space–time.) It makes sense therefore to speak of the place *where* a history takes place: if h is a (rectangular) history then $where(h)$ is that place. Similarly, $when(h)$ is the time-interval during which h takes place. (It is convenient to define $when$ to be the open interval, so that it does not include its endpoints. It often happens that some condition is true throughout a history except at its endpoints, at which transient phenomena take place.)

If h is a history and t a time-instant (we assume a global timescale of some sort with an inequality defined on it), the $h @ t$ (read: h at t) is the ''slice'' of h at t. This is a state, that is, a spatial entity at a particular time. Notice that a state is not merely a place, but has an associated time-value: sometimes we will write a state as a pair $\langle p,t \rangle$ where p is a place or other spatial entity and t a time-instant.

To avoid confusion, one must keep clearly in mind the distinctions between a four-dimensional history or state, a three-dimensional spatial entity (a place, a piece of space or an object), and a time-instant. We can illustrate these diagrammatically as in Figure 4(a), in which the three spatial dimensions have been reduced to two, so that time can be represented as the third dimension. (This is a graphical convention we shall use subsequently.) Spatial entities belong on the space axes, time-instants on the time-axis, and histories and slices in the center of the diagram.

There is a fundamental extensionality axiom:

$$(when(h_1) = when(h_2) \land \forall t \in when(h_1). h_1@t = h_2@t) \supset h_1 = h_2 \qquad (36)$$

Notice however that we do not rule out the possibility that one history could be an episode of two distinct histories, or could be *In* two distinct histories.

Now we are in the real four-dimensional world, purely spatial entities can be seen for the abstractions that they are. There are no objects, only instantaneous states of objects. We will henceforth assume that *all spatial relations apply to slices*, including *Face* and *In*.

Figure 4(b) illustrates some useful relationships between histories. An episode is a proper temporal part of a history. We can define:

$$Episode(h_2, h_1) \equiv begin(h_2) > begin(h_1) \\ \land end(h_2) < end(h_1) \\ \land \forall t \in when(h_2). h_2@t = h_1@t \qquad (37)$$

and clearly we have:

$$start(h) = sl(h, begin(h)) \qquad (38)$$
$$finish(h) = sl(h, end(h)) \qquad (39)$$

The other two relationships are extensions of three-dimensional spatial relationships along the time axis, like the writing in a stick of rock candy. It is convenient to use the same relation names. We have:

$$In(h_2, h_1) \equiv when(h_1) = when(h_2) \\ \land \forall t \in when(h_1). In(h_2@t, h_1@t) \qquad (40)$$

$$Face(h_2, h_1) \equiv when(h_1) = when(h_2) \\ \land \forall t \in when(h_1). Face(h_2@t, h_1@t) \qquad (41)$$

This extension of *Face* and *In* from spatial entities to histories is a generally useful device, and we will use it more generally. If *R* and *f* are any relation or function on spatial entities (objects, pieces of space, pieces of surface) then the use of *R* or *f* applied to histories will be taken to mean that the histories in question are contemporary (have the same *when*) and that *R* holds between corresponding slices, or the value of *f* is that when applied to the contemporary slice throughout:

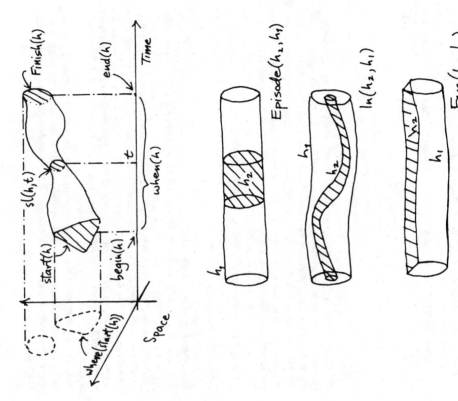

$$R(h_1, \ldots, h_n) \equiv when(h_1) = when(h_2) = \ldots = when(h_n) \\ \land \forall t \in when(h_1). R(h_1@t, \ldots, h_n@t) \qquad (42a)$$

$$f(h_1, \ldots, h_n) = h_0 \equiv when(h_0) = when(h_1) = \ldots = when(h_n) \\ \land \forall t \in when(h_0). f(h_1@t, \ldots, h_n@t) = h_0@t \qquad (42b)$$

Figure 4. Some relationships between histories

This useful convention enables us to succinctly state that certain properties of a spatial entity do not change during a certain time period.

Notice that, although we have introduced *Face* and *In* applied to histories as an abbreviation convention, in fact they are literally true in four-dimensional space, i.e. if $Face(h_2,h_1)$ then h_2 is in fact a (three-dimensional: two spatial dimensions + time) face of h_1 in four-dimensional space. The history of a cube, for example, has six such faces—the histories of its faces in three-dimensional space—and two other faces, the *start* and *finish*: eight in all. (Nonrectangular histories can have somewhat more complicated shapes, however.)

Relations on slices play here the same role that fluents play in the situation calculus. Where one would write $R(o_1, \ldots . o_n,t)$ in the situation calculus, we will write $R(o_1@t, \ldots , o_n@t)$.

A physical object is a three-dimensional entity which has an associated history representing the life-span of the object: a slice of this history (which we will call the *life* of the object), *is* the object at a given time. If the object is rigid, then its shape is constant, so we can (using the convention just introduced) apply shape descriptors to its history. We might for example assert *spherical(h)*, where *h* is the history of a ballbearing. In line with the open-closed distinction for spaces and objects, the history of a solid object (unlike other histories) includes its start and finish: thus, a solid object contains *all* its faces.

A special case which will be useful later is a history during which no change takes place at all. We will call this an *enduring*. Given a three-dimensional entity *o*, and a time-interval *I*, *endure(o,I)* is defined by the following:

$$when(endure(o,I)) = I \tag{43}$$

$$\forall t \in I. \; endure(o,I)@t = \langle o,t \rangle \tag{44}$$

Clearly an enduring is rectangular.

If *f* is some function of spatial entities, then we will say that *f* is *Increasing* in *h* if:

$$Increasing(f,h) \equiv \forall t,t' \in when(h). \; t < t' \supset f(h(@t,t) < f(h(@t') \tag{45}$$

and similarly for *Decreasing*.

8 Histories of Lazy Bulk Liquid

There are five possible lazy bulk histories, shown in Figure 5. The two static ones may be mere endurings, in part: a cup full of liquid, or water spilt on a table, sitting doing nothing for a period. But they may also have less trivial episodes. A cup may be filled or emptied. The wetness on a table may spread, or it may dry up. These changes do not take place randomly, however. A cup will fill only if liquid enters it from somewhere else. Similarly, the three kinds of movement all have ends which are faces through which liquid is passing, and the liquid must go to, or come from, somewhere else. We need to be able to keep track of these comings and goings. Let *f* be a face of *v*: a *leaving* (from *v* through *f*) is a history whose *where* is the directed face $d(f,v)$, and during which liquid passes from *v* into *f*. (*v* may be a volume or a directed surface, the latter corresponding to liquid leaving a surface along its edge.) Similarly an *arriving* (into *v* through *f*) is a history of liquid emerging from *f* into *v*.

It is tempting to say that *toso* of an arriving is a leaving, and vice versa, but this is true only if the face is a portal. A leaving at a solid surface is more complicated, since the liquid stays on the surface. In this case, we can say that the edge of the leaving is itself a leaving into the surrounding directed surface surrounding the leaving. That is, liquid is injected into the surrounding directed face. For this to be possible, we must also allow arrivings and leavings whose *wheres* are directed faces of directed edges. The connections between all these can be stated as:

$$where(h)=d(f,v) \wedge Free(f) \supset (Leaving(h) \equiv Arriving(toso(h))) \tag{46}$$

$$where(h)=d(f,v) \wedge Leaving(h) \wedge \sim Free(f) \supset$$
$$\exists e,h'. \; Face(e,f) \wedge Free(d(e,v))$$
$$\wedge \; where(h')=d(e,f,v)$$
$$\wedge \; when(h')=when(h)$$
$$\wedge \; Leaving(h') \tag{47}$$

In (46) we are using the convention described earlier: in applying the spatial function *toso* to the history *h* we mean to denote a history contemporary with *h* whose every slice is *toso* of the instantaneous slice of *h*. The analogous spatial relationship has had to be spelled out in (47) for lack of a suitable spatial relationship name. It will be convenient to introduce one in what follows. Let us say that if *f* is a solid face of free *v*, and *e* is a face of *f* such that $d(e,v)$ is free, then $d(e,f,v)$ is a *Splat* of $d(f,v)$:

$$Splat(d(e,f,v),d(f,v)) \equiv Free(v) \wedge \sim Free(f) \wedge Free(d(e,v)) \tag{48}$$

Then (47) above can be replaced by :

$$where(h) = d(f,v) \wedge \sim Free(f) \supset$$
$$Leaving(h) \equiv \exists h'. \; Splat(h',h) \wedge Leaving(h') \tag{49}$$

where we rely on the convention to establish contemporaenity of *h* and *h'*, cf. (46).

Arrivings and leavings will be the 'glue' with which we attach other liquid-containing histories to one another.

All the possible lazy bulk histories, their episodes and geometric relationships, are illustrated in Figure 5. Before giving the axioms, I will briefly discuss each case.

A wetting can merely endure: or it can spread (i.e. its *wet* can increase in size) if there is an arriving into it; a spreading will spill iff it reaches a free edge of its support. It can also dry up: this is the only change which does not require an arriving or leaving.

Neither containments nor wettings can appear or disappear suddenly. The three movements can, however: if one pours water from a jug, the column of water appears instantly, and vanishes as suddenly when the pouring stops. Flowings also, we will assume, establish themselves with no time lag and vanish promptly when their supporting conditions fail. This is of course not accurate, but it will serve as a first approximation.

All three movement histories are similar in that they require an arriving at one end and a leaving at the other, the former higher than the latter (because we are assuming laziness), and their direction is from the former to the latter. They are all endurings: there is no change in them during their lifetimes. As wettings and containments contain *amounts* of liquid, so the three movements have associated *rates*; as, we will assume, do arrivings and leavings. We will use a function $rate(l,h)$ which is supposed to take values in some suitable quantity space. The three movements differ only in their shape and support relationships.

To axiomatize all this we start by listing the possible histories.

$$Wetness(h) \wedge \sim Moving(h) \wedge \exists v. where(h) = d(support(h), v)$$
$$\vee (Containment(h) \wedge \sim Moving(h) \wedge where(h) = inside(support(h)))$$
$$\vee (Flowing1(h) \wedge Moving(h) \wedge \exists v. where(h) = d(support(h), v))$$
$$\vee (Flowing2(h) \wedge Moving(h) \wedge where(h) = inside(support(h), v))$$
$$\vee (Falling(h) \wedge Moving(h) \wedge \sim Supported(h))$$

This axiom should really have an antecedent setting out the ''bulk, lazy'' conditions, but this will be omitted here.

Considering now wetnesses, we can say

$$Wetness(h) \supset amount(begin(h)) = amount(end(h)) = none$$
$$\wedge \forall t \in when(h). Wetby(h@t) \qquad (51)$$

(Here we have omitted the 'liquid-stuff' parameter from *amount* and *Wetby*. We will continue to omit this from now on, to make the formulae neater.) Instantaneous wetnesses are impossible:

$$Wetby(h@t) \supset \exists h'. Wetness(h') \wedge Episode(h.h') \qquad (52)$$

Next, the possible episodes of a wetness; another taxonomy:

$$Wetness(h') \wedge Episode(h.h') \equiv$$
$$Merewet(h)$$
$$\vee Drying(h)$$
$$\vee Spreading(h) \qquad (53)$$

Taking these in turn, we have:

$$Merewet(h) \equiv \exists w. Wetby(w) \wedge h = endure(w, when(h)) \qquad (54)$$

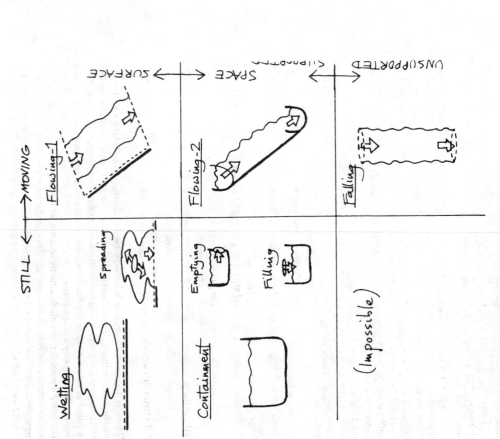

Figure 5. Lazy bulk liquid histories

A containment may merely endure, or it may fill—this needs an arriving—or it may empty, if (and only if) there is a portal below its surface. It is of course possible for a containment to have an arriving and a leaving simultaneously, as Lake Leman has the Rhone flowing in one end and out the other. In this situation, it is both filling and an emptying, at once.

$$Drying(h) \supset Decreasing(amount,h) \tag{55}$$

Notice that *amount* here is a functional parameter.

$$Spreading(h) \supset \exists ar.Arriving(ar) \wedge Inward(ar,h)$$
$$\wedge (Increasing(amount,h)$$
$$\vee \exists le.Leaving(le) \wedge Inward(le,h)) \tag{56}$$

It can't spread unless there is a supply, and either it gets bigger, or pours off th edge somewhere. Notice, *this* is not exclusive choice. Containments are in many ways similar.

$$Containment(h) \supset amount(start(h)) = amount(finish(h)) = none$$
$$\wedge Contained(h \tag{57}$$

(making use of the convention in (42a) for the base case $n=1$)

$$Contained(h@t) \supset \exists h'.Containment(h') \wedge Episode(h,h') \tag{58}$$

The taxonomy of containment episodes:

$$Containment(h') \wedge Episode(h,h') \equiv$$
$$Merecontain(h)$$
$$\vee (Filling(h) \vee Emptying(h)) \tag{59}$$

Notice that fillings and emptyings are not exclusive. Taking each case in turn again:

$$Merecontain(h) \equiv \exists c.Contained(c) \wedge h = endure(c,when(h)) \tag{60}$$

$$Filling(h) \supset \exists ar.Arriving(ar) \wedge Inward(ar,h)$$
$$\wedge (Increasing(amount,h)$$
$$\vee \exists le.Leaving(le) \wedge Inward(le,h)) \tag{61}$$

$$Emptying(h) \supset \exists le.Leaving(le) \wedge Inward(le,h)$$
$$\wedge (Decreasing(amount,h)$$
$$\vee \exists ar.Arriving(ar) \wedge Inward(ar,h)) \tag{62}$$

There is apparently complete symmetry between fillings and emptyings (in fact leavings and arrivings are not exactly dual to one another, as we will see), unlike spreadings and dryings. In fact, a spreading is exactly analogous to a filling, but drying has no counterpart for bulk containment (it would be evaporation), and it is impossible to *empty* a wet surface.

Notice the exclusive-or's in axioms (61) and (62). These entail that in a filling with a leaving, the amount does not increase, and similarly does not decrease in a emptying with a leaving. This is an idealisation which allows baths to overflow and leak, but does not allow one to fill a leaky bath. It means that in an episode which is both a filling and an emptying (and therefore has both a leaving and an arriving), the amount neither increases nor decreases: Lake Leman is a good example.

We know from axiom (47) that liquid cannot leave through a solid face. We need however to state the contrapositive, that it *will* leave through a portal, given the chance. There are three ways: a free edge of a wetness' wet, a free face of a containment's wet, or the free edge of a face of a containment's wet (the edge of an overflowing bath, for example). The first two can be covered together:

$$\sim Moving(h') \wedge Episode(l,h') \supset$$
$$(Face(f,wet(h)) \wedge \sim Top(f,wet(h)) \wedge Free(f)$$
$$\equiv Leaving(d(f,h)) \tag{63}$$

(This uses the convention in (42) heavily. For example, the face f is a history, as are the entities $wet(h)$ and $d(f,h)$: and these are all exactly contemporary with the episode h during which liquid is leaving.)

$$(Containment(h') \vee Flowing2(h')) \wedge Episode(h,h') \supset$$
$$(Face(f,wet(h)) \wedge Face(e,f) \wedge Free(e) \wedge (\sim Free(f) \vee Top(f,h))$$
$$\equiv Leaving(d(e,f,toso(f,h)))) \tag{64}$$

We cannot use *Splat* to shorten axiom (64), since the face f may well be free, as in an overflowing bath.

Now the movements:

$$Movement(h) \supset Arriving(in(h)) \wedge Leaving(out(h))$$
$$\wedge Inward(in(h),h) \wedge Inward(out(h),h)$$
$$\wedge height(in(h)) > height(out(h))$$
$$\wedge direction(h) = \langle in(h),out(h) \rangle \tag{65}$$

in and *out* are the (directed) ends of the movement. We can regard these as Skolem functions: it is handy to have names for these arrivings and leavings. So handy, in fact, that I will use them for spreadings, fillings and emptyings also.

There is not much more to be said about these moving histories, as their only episodes are themselves. It is useful to characterise the shape of fallings.

$$Falling(h) \supset Vertical(direction(h))$$
$$\wedge where(in(h)) = d(top(h),where(h))$$
$$\wedge where(out(h)) = d(bottom(h),where(h)) \tag{66}$$

We can emphasize their simplicity by:

$$Movement(h) \supset h = endure(where(h),when(h)) \tag{67}$$

Notice this entails that the *rate* of a movement history is constant throughout.

Finally, we need to say that these arrivings and leavings are all there are.

$$Arriving(ar) \supset \exists h.\ (Spreading(h) \wedge Inward(ar,h))$$
$$\vee (Filling(h) \wedge Inward(ar,h))$$
$$\vee (Moving(h) \wedge ar=in(h)) \tag{68}$$

$$Leaving(le) \supset \exists le'.\ Leaving(le') \wedge Splat(le.le')$$
$$\vee$$
$$\exists h.(Emptying(h) \wedge Inward(le,h))$$
$$\vee (Moving(h) \wedge le=out(h))$$
$$\vee (Spreading(h) \wedge Inward(le,h)) \tag{69}$$

One could go on, introducing a notion of rate of change of quantity, to relate rate of flow (our rate) and rate of change, but I will ignore this. However, we do need to relate amounts to the sizes of the wet parts of a containment or wetting.

$$Increasing(amount,h) \equiv$$
$$\forall t,t' \in when(h).\ t<t' \supset In(wet(h(a\ t),wet(h(a\ t'))) \tag{70}$$

$$Decreasing(amount,h) \equiv$$
$$\forall t,t' \in when(h).\ t<t' \supset In(wet(h(a\ t'),wet(h(a\ t))) \tag{71}$$

We could, in fact, regard *wet* as a quantity scale, the measure space being the set of pieces of three-dimensional space. The appropriate inequality is of course just *In*. so that axioms (70) and (71) could be written simply as

$$Increasing(amount,h) \equiv Increasing(wet,h)$$
$$Decreasing(amount,h) \equiv Decreasing(wet,h) \tag{72}$$

We have also

$$amount(s) = capacity(s) \equiv et(s)=s \tag{74}$$

which is, in fact, the crux of the matter, as we will see.

9 Some Examples

The theory so far, together with a little extra geometry and analysis (which we will not attempt to formalize) enables one, given a description of a physical setup involving liquids, to infer quite detailed knowledge about the future, past or surroundings of the set-up. In this section we will consider a few examples.

Suppose an open container with no leaks is empty, but at time *t* a falling history begins whose *bottom* is the free top of the container: for example, you turn on the bath tap with the plug in. By axiom (46), this leaving has an arriving on its other side, which is an inward-directed face of the inside of the bath. By axiom (59), there must be a filling inside the bath, so the *amount* of water increases: axiom (61). So long as the tap keeps running, it will go on increasing. Let us suppose that eventually the bath is full, i.e. it contains its capacity. Then, by (74), its *wet* is its inside. But the top of it is a face of its inside, with a free edge: and so by axiom (57) the amount of water in it cannot exceed its capacity, but by axiom (61) it must either increase or there must be a leaving somewhere. (Notice that if the container were closed—a tank being filled along a pipe, say—then the same line of reasoning would insist on there being a leaving which could not possibly occur, by axioms (47) and (16). One can conclude from this contradiction, by *modus tollens*, that the arriving must cease to exist at that time, and hence that the flowing-2 along the supply pipe, etc. (working backwards) must cease also. And this is, of course, exactly what happens, assuming the tank doesn't burst.)

So, the bath will overflow. We can describe this in more detail. *Toso* of the leaving is an arriving. Now there are two cases, depending on whether the bath is a lamina or a more solid affair. If a lamina, this *toso* is in free space, so we have an arriving in free space, which can only (by axioms (68) and (50) and assuming that free space doesn't support anything), be the top of a falling. If the rim of the bath is a corner, however, then *toso* of the leaving is a directed edge along the outside surface of the bath (see axiom (19)): again, by axioms (68) and (50), this can only be the arriving of a flowing-1, or a spreading. Either is possible: the latter if the bath is sunk into a flat floor onto which the water spreads; the former if the outside slopes downwards.

We could follow the water even further, but let us consider another example. There is a horizontal floor which is dry (amount = none) at time *t*, but at some later time is wet. What happened in between? Well, there must be a wetness history *h* surrounding the later moment, by axiom (52). Now, by (51), this wetness's start must be later than *t*, and *h* must have started dry. Its first episode could only have been a spreading, therefore (this requires the "analysis" mentioned earlier: specifically, if $t_1 < t_2$, $f(t_1) = 0$ and $f(t_2) > 0$, then *f* is increasing in $\langle t_1, t_2 \rangle$), and therefore must, by (56), have had an arriving at an edge of it, and by (46) there must have been a leaving on the other side of this. Now this leaving is directed along the surface, and can either be part of a *Splat*, or the *out* of a *flowing-1*, if there is a suitable sloped surface nearby, or of another spreading, or an "edge-type" leaving from an emptying, as described in axiom (64). All of these are possible: a *Splat* could result from something pouring or flowing-2 onto the floor: a flowing-1 could have been, for example, water running down a vertical side of a box: the spreading could have run off the edge of a laminar sheet on the floor: the emptying could have been a leaky paint tin.

As a final example, consider a cup of milk held above a table, which is a horizontal lamina suspended above the floor. There are no other liquids and no other surfaces. The cup is rotated slowly about a horizontal axis: what will happen? At first, nothing. But after a while (this requires more geometry than we have developed), the *top* of the *wet* in the cup will reach the edge of the rim. At that moment,

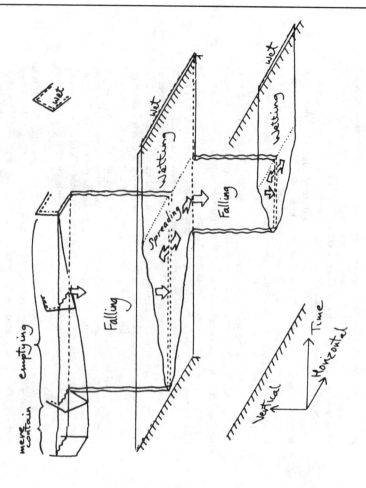

Figure 6. Pouring a cup of milk onto a table

by axiom (64), a leaving history will start and the containment in the cup will enter a leaving episode. Assuming the cup to be a lamina, *toso* of this leaving will, by axiom (46), be an arriving in free space, which can therefore by axioms (68) and (50) only be the top of a falling. Since a falling is vertical and the cup is above the table, the bottom of this falling is part of the surface of the table, directed upwards. Therefore, by (49), the free edge of this part will be a leaving also (Splat), and by (46) will have an arriving on its other side, into the top of the table. This could only be, by axiom (68) a directed face of a spreading or a flowing-1: but the latter is impossible since the table is horizontal, so there must be a spreading on the table top. Although this has taken a while to infer, it takes place instantaneously: the emptying in the cup and the spreading on the table begin at the same instant. As the milk is spreading over the table, the amount of it there is increasing, and the amount in the cup is decreasing. The spreading is therefore expanding across the table, by axiom (72). This configuration may continue until the cup is empty (amount = none), at which time the emptying, and hence the leaving, arriving, falling, leaving, leaving and arriving (working down) must also cease, and the spreading reverts to a mere wetness. Or, the spreading may reach the edge of the table, before the cup runs dry. In this case a leaving comes into existence along the edge, by axiom (63). The spreading may or may not cease to expand (axiom (56)), but in any case there is again an arriving into free space on the other side, and hence, by similar reasoning a falling onto the floor, a splat, and a spreading there. When the cup runs out now both spreadings instantly revert to mere wettings, in which state they will remain unless they become dryings. The whole sequence is illustrated in Figure 6.

Notice incidentally that since, when the cup was full of milk, its inside surface was wet, this state of wetness must have been a slice of a wetness history, by (52) and this wetness history may continue, even though the containment which gave rise to it has vanished. So the inside of the cup will also be wet, in the final state unless it has dried. (If we had quantitative concepts we could say that dryings were always slow, which would ensure that the inside were wet.) Notice also that if the table had been a solid cube instead of a lamina, we could have inferred that the milk, on reaching its top edge, would have flowed-1 down its side before spreading across the floor, not fallen.

The finite taxonomies play a crucial role in this sort of reasoning. Given that an arriving exists in some geometric configuration, for example, axiom (50) will usually enable one to infer what sort of history it has to be a face of, because the configuration will typically be consistent with only one of the possibilities listed here. One reasons by a combination of two inferential processes: establishing the existence of a history (typically an arriving or leaving) because some other one exists; and deciding that a certain history must be of some sort because its properties are incompatible with all the other possibilities, and it must be *one* of them. (The reader may be reminded of the Waltz filtering algorithm here, or of Sherlock Holmes, or of relaxation, or a winner-take-all network.) I believe this taxonomic approach to common-sense reasoning is of fundamental importance.

I do not want to leave the impression that there are no problems. Rain flowing off a roof into a gutter, and a tin with many small leaks, are just two examples which I can see no way to handle reasonably.

10 Liquid Individuals Revisited

We have managed to avoid pieces of liquid, throughout this quite extensive development, by always talking of pieces of space or space-time which *contain* some liquid. One could go further and avoid talking of solid objects, indeed, by using a similar idea of pieces of space filled with solid stuff, but that would be artificial. (However, the idea of *the space occupied by* an object seems to be of general utility.) Unfortunately, we have had to swallow some similar artificialities with liquids, at least in the case of liquids in bulk. It seems somewhat peculiar, for example, to have a *space* supporting, or being supported by, a solid object (as in flotation and containment). And it seems odd to be unable to say, when one glass of water is poured into another, that it is the *same* water in the second glass that was in the first glass. Some of this artificiality can be avoided by carefully allowing fluid objects back into our ontology. The preceding development will not have been wasted, however, since liquid histories can plausibly be the criteria by which we individuate liquid objects, thus neatly avoiding the ontological nightmare discussed in section 3.

The idea, then, is that any history (of a certain kind) actually contains a (single) liquid object, which fills the history and lasts as long as it does. Contrariwise, every liquid object fills some history. For example, Lake Leman is now an object, made of water, with a flat top; and it is this object which supports the boat and is supported by the lake bed. It is a single individual object even though of different molecules from one week to the next: it is individuated by its history, its spatiotemporal 'position'. Similarly, a glassful of water is the same object while the glass is being filled, although its size is increasing; and it ceases to exist when the water is emptied out into another glass. A bath being filled and emptied contains a single, unique liquid object—*the* bathwater. A river is an object, similarly, as is Niagara Falls, or the puddle of milk on the floor.

Looked at in this way, then, all the preceding discussion has really been about liquid objects, how they relate to one another and to solid objects in space, and how they can be created and destroyed. We have overcome the ontological nightmare by analyzing in some detail how to keep track of liquid objects.

This idea of liquid objects coexisting with histories still does not allow us to say that the water in this glass used to be in that glass, or that this water came out of the tap. For liquid objects are not identified by being the same piece of liquid (like pieces of solid stuff), but by spatiotemporal continuity (like assemblies: in fact we can explain liquids as limiting cases of powders, which can actually be regarded as unorganized assemblies). In order to express these assertions we need a different sort of liquid individual: *a piece of liquid*. This is meant to be a particular collection of molecules, a piece of stuff.

A given liquid object may or may not be a piece of liquid, and a piece of liquid may or may not be a liquid object. For example, a river is not a piece of liquid, but some water in a glass is. While we are pouring water from one glass into another, there is one piece of liquid present, the same one that there was when it was contained in the first glass, but there are three liquid objects: one, shrinking, in the top glass, and another, growing, in the bottom glass; and a falling. None of these four individuals is the same as another.

We can summarize the criteria for individuating pieces of liquid by considering spatial boundaries. Any history consisting of a piece of space and a time interval such that no liquid crosses the boundary of the space during the interval, defines a piece of liquid, viz. all the liquid in the space during that interval. Notice that we do not require that the ''piece'' be spatially connected. It is convenient also to have a notion of one piece of liquid (or of stuff in general) being *part* of another.

Consider a glass of water and a glass of ink being mixed in a third glass to get colored water. There are three containment histories here, defining three liquid objects. But we can also say that *the* water and ink from the first two glasses were pieces of liquid which are now part of the piece of liquid which coincides with the final liquid object: for, consider a volume enclosing all three glasses but no other liquid, and consider the piece of liquid it contained: the water and the ink were parts of this piece, and it is the same piece at the end of the history (in which all three containments, and the intervening pourings, traversals, etc., are enclosed) as it was at the beginning, so they are still part of it.

We can use the notions of arrivings and leavings, introduced earlier, to specify this no-boundary-crossing criterion. Let us say that a history is *closed* if no face of it is an arriving or leaving. Then a closed history containing liquid defines a piece of liquid.

Pieces of liquid, unlike liquid objects, are eternal. Consider pouring a glass of water into a lake. The liquid object which was in the glass ceases to exist: but the piece of water is now part of the lake. (To see this, imagine a surface enclosing a glass and the lake, and consider *the* piece of water inside this surface during the pouring.) *It* still exists, although one would be very hard put to separate it out again. Such ''separability'' is irrelevant to the identity of a piece of liquid.

This ontology of pieces of liquid is very much more sophisticated than the earlier one of liquid objects. To handle it well requires one to reason in terms of *imaginary* surfaces in space, for a start. Conservation of amount is a trivial consequence of this ontology. (For example, if I pour water from one glass into another, it is the *same* piece of water, so of course it must be the same amount, if—as we should—we make *amount* a function of pieces of liquid rather than liquid objects.) We know from the work of Piaget that conservation arises quite late in childrens' development. This may, I suggest, be due to the preconservation child not having access to this more sophisticated ontology for mass terms. Conservation is far less obvious for liquid objects: indeed, I cannot see any very plausible way of expressing it without some very involved assumptions about rates of flow.

We must now be careful in using equality. Consider (again) a cup full of water.

taken as asserting *both* that $\lambda x \cdot x = p$ is true of the enduring object o, but in a time-dependent way (i.e. is a fluent), *and* that $\lambda x \cdot o = x$ is true of the enduring object p, but similarly. After the equation becomes false, both o and p still exist, but they have separated.

This phenomenon is not, in fact, special to liquids. It occurs wherever different, rival criteria of individuation are simultaneously in use. My car, for example, is at any instant the same as a particular collection of components: but this identity is time-dependent. A description such as "the regulator that used to be in my car before I had it replaced" uses both ways of individuating "car", as an enduring assembly and a contingent collection of parts.

It may strike the reader, as it did me at first, that this all seems extremely unnatural. After all, the water in a glass is what it is: how can it be two different things at the same time? Surely, one feels, this baroque way of speaking must be an artifact: in the actual real world, things just *are*. But I now believe that such naive ontological realism is unfounded. In the *actual* real world, there are no *a priori* individuals at all. The universe can be conceptualized as a continuum, perhaps a huge quantum-mechanical wave function. Divisions of it into conceptual individuals are made by us, by our language, not by nature. And then of course, there is no reason at all why we may not carve up the universe's space–time fabric into overlapping pieces, if it is convenient to do so.

11 Further Works

The theory of liquids developed in sections 4 to 9, although I think quite useful, is by no means fully satisfactory and represents only an initial foray. I believe the geometric ideas, especially the concept of *Face* and of *d* (direction), and the basic approach of using histories to describe change, are likely to survive subsequent developments. The rest is less secure, however, and there are many problems. These will be made clearer only by attempting to extend the theory to a wider range of concepts. Some obvious directions are:

1. The introduction of metric ideas into the geometry, and the development of a suitable topology.
2. An account of shape and a theory of the deformability of liquid objects.
3. The introduction of non-lazy histories such as fountains and splashes (including an account of pressure, force and impact: for example, a *Splat* is usually an impact on the non-free face, hence the name).
4. A theory of liquid flow based on the idea of a path or trajectory *along which* liquid can flow: this would be based on homotopic ideas, as the account here is based on homological ideas.
5. An account of rates and rates of change (which should be linked with metric ideas, so that liquid will flow only *slowly* through a small hole or across a surface).
6. A more detailed account of the interrelations between solid and liquid surfaces: for example, how flotation and lubrication work

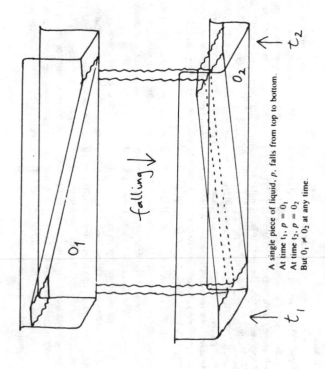

A single piece of liquid, p, falls from top to bottom.
At time t_1, $p = o_1$
At time t_2, $p = o_2$
But $o_1 \neq o_2$ at any time.

Figure 7. Liquid objects and pieces of liquid

This is a liquid object (filling a containment), and it is also a piece of liquid. We might say that $o = p$, where o denotes the liquid object and p the piece of liquid: for these are both the same object. However, this equality may change in the course of time. If part of the water is poured out of the cup into another, then we have the *same* liquid object in the first cup, but a different piece of water (part of the original piece), say p'. If now the rest of the water is poured into the second cup, this contains a *new* liquid object, o' say, which is the same thing as the *original* piece of water p (see Figure 7).

Liquid objects endure through time, as do pieces of liquid. It always makes sense to equate two liquid-object expressions, or two piece-of-liquid expressions, independently of time. But since the criteria for individuating such objects are different, it makes sense to equate a liquid-object expression and a piece-of-liquid expression only during a time-period when these criteria agree. Such an equality *must* be understood as temporary, as liable to change in truth-value.

This phenomenon is more complicated than the case of an object ceasing to have a certain time-dependent property, as when a person ceases to be mayor. Unlike this familiar case (which can be adequately handled by the state- or situation-variable idea), we have here a strange symmetry. The equation $o = p$ can be equally validly

I hope to investigate some of these in subsequent work, as well as other areas of naive physics altogether. Finally, I am grateful to Ray Turner for pointing out that to establish the consistency of a large axiom system may not be an altogether trivial task.

Acknowledgments

This paper, with minor changes, originally appeared as Memo 35 of the Institut pour les Etudes Semantiques et Cognitives, Universite de Geneve. It was written while the author was visiting the Institut in 1978.

The early development of some of these ideas was supported by the U.K. Science Research Council on grant number B/RG/61198. I would also like to thank the Dalle Molle foundation and the University of Geneva for financial support, and the Directrice of the Institut, Mme M. King, for inviting me to visit. Maggie King, Mimi Sinclair, Henri Wermus and Giuseppe Trautteur gave me many useful ideas and criticisms. Bob Welham and Jerry Hobbs made many useful criticisms and suggestions. Finally, I would like to thank my wife, Jackie Hayes, for her support, for being a never failing source of reliable intuitions., for much constructive criticism, and for not complaining at retyping the manuscript four times because of my mistakes.

References

Cohn, T. (1983) Improving the Expressiveness of Many-Sorted Logic. *Proc. AAAI*, Washington, D.C.

Goodman, N. (1966). *The structure of appearance*. New York: Bobbs Merrill.

Hayes, P. (1971). A logic of actions. *Machine intelligence 6*. Edinburgh: Edinburgh University Press.

Hocking, J., & Young, G. (1961). *Topology*. Boston: Addison-Wesley.

McCarthy, J. (1959). Situations, actions & causal laws. (Memo 2). Stanford University, Stanford A.I. Project.

McCarthy, J. & Hayes, P. (1969). Some philosophical problems from the standpoint of artificial intelligence. *Machine Intelligence 4*. Edinburgh: Edinburgh University Press.

Prior, A. N. (1968). *Past, present & future*. Oxford: Clarendon Press.

Assumptions and Ambiguities in Mechanistic Mental Models

Johan de Kleer
John Seely Brown
Xerox Palo Alto Research Center

INTRODUCTION

Our long-range goal is to develop a model of how one acquires an understanding of mechanistic devices such as physical machines, electronic and hydraulic devices, or reactors. We focus on two aspects of this problem. First, we lay out a framework for investigating the structure of people's mental models of physical devices, which we call *mechanistic mental models*. This involves developing a precise notion of a qualitative simulation and the kinds of "work," one expects it to do. The concept of qualitative simulation derives from the common intuition of "simulating the machine in the mind's eye." One of the goals of this chapter is to put this common intuition on a more solid theoretical base.

Although one would intuitively expect qualitative simulations to be simpler than quantitative simulations of a given device, they turn out to be equally complex, but in a different way. Their complexities are not readily apparent from protocols of subjects reasoning about a mechanistic device, a fact that we account for in the latter part of the chapter. These complexities arise, in part, from the fact that devices may appear nondeterministic and underconstrained when the quantities and forces involved in their makeup are viewed solely from a qualitative perspective. Therefore, if the qualitative simulation of the device is to behave deterministically, additional knowledge and reasoning must be used to further constrain or disambiguate these "apparent" ambiguities. Thus, the second aspect of this research investigates the kinds of ambiguities that arise when a device is analyzed qualitatively, and explores the various techniques and knowledge sources that can be used to circumvent or resolve them.

It is surprisingly difficult to construct mental models of a device, if these models are to be capable of predicting the consequences of events that have not already been considered during the creation of the model. Thus, the process for constructing a good mental model involves a different kind of problem-solving than the process for "running" the resultant mental model; a distinction that we find crucial to understanding how people use mental models. In fact, simply clarifying the differences between the work involved in constructing a qualitative simulation—a process we call *envisioning*—and the work involved in simulating the result of this construction—a process we call *running*[1]—turn out to have both theoretical and practical ramifications.

The first two sections of the chapter provide an outline of a theory of qualitative simulation. The last section explores some of the psychological implications of this theory. We discuss several kinds of learning and illustrate how people might learn "ideal" models by making successive refinements to their nonrobust, initial models, making explicit the hidden assumptions in them. We also discuss two ways to use nonideal models to explain how something works: first, to provide a framework for embedding models within models and, second, to sequence a collection of models that converge on an ideal understanding of the device.

QUALITATIVE SIMULATIONS

A Basis for Mechanistic Mental Methods

Complex devices, such as machines, are built from combinations of simpler devices (components). Let us assume we know the behaviors of the components, as well as the way in which they are connected to form the composite device. The behaviors of the components are described qualitatively, with the quantities of importance to the operation of the device described by qualitative values such as "going up" or "going down," "high," or "low." The qualitative simulation presents the interesting events in the functioning of the machine in their causal order. Figure 8.1 illustrates a conventional door-buzzer (for the moment we will ignore the push button that activates the buzzer) which we will use as one of our main examples throughout the chapter. The buzzer is a simple device, but one complex enough to explore ideas of qualitative simulation (see de Kleer & Brown, 1981, for a more detailed description). The buzzer's qualitative simulation might be expressed as: *The clapper-switch of the buzzer closes, which causes the coil to conduct a current, thereby generating an electromagnetic field which in turn pulls the clapper arm away from the switch contact, thereby opening the switch, which shuts off the magnetic field, allowing the clapper arm to return to its closed position, which then starts the whole process over again.*[2]

---

[1] In some of our earlier papers we referred to this process as *envisionment*.

[2] The repetitive opening and closing of the switch (i.e., its vibration) produces an audible sound.

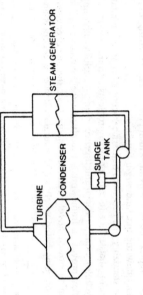

FIG. 8.2. Steam plant.

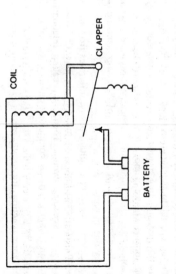

FIG. 8.1. Buzzer.

will produce very little more than what is already explicitly represented in the functional representation produced by the first kind of simulation.[4]

We need to distinguish four related notions which form the basic distinctions for a theory of qualitative reasoning. The most basic, *device topology*, is a representation of the structure of the device (i.e., its physical organization). For example, the steam plant consists of a steam generator, turbine, condenser, their connecting pipes, etc. The second, *envisioning*, is an inference process which, given the device's structure, determines its function. The third, *causal model*, describes the functioning of the device (i.e., a description of how the device's behavior results from its constituent components which is stated in terms of how the components causally interact). The last is the *running* of the causal model to produce a specific behavior for the device, by giving a chain of events each causally related to the previous one. Thus, both the structure and functioning of a device are represented by some knowledge representation scheme (device topology and causal model, respectively), with the former being the input to the envisioning process and the latter being its output, which, in turn, is then used in the running. The two examples of qualitative simulation presented earlier are ambiguous as to whether they refer to the envisioning, the causal model, or the running.

Determining the functioning of a device solely from its structure, i.e., envisioning, often requires some very subtle reasoning. The task, in essence, is to figure out how the device works given only its structure, and the knowledge of some basic principles. Structure describes the physical organization of the device, namely its constituent components and how they are connected, but it does not describe how the components function in the particular device. (That is one of the end results that the envisioning process is trying to discover.) The "behaviors" of each component are described in a manner that is independent of the

<hr>

[4]Note that this latter kind of simulation is just one of the kinds of inference mechanisms that can use or "interpret" the functional representation. Others can inspect it in order to answer such questions as "Could *x* cause *y* to happen?"

Qualitative simulation does not account for all of the kinds of qualitative reasoning that are possible about the device. In particular, it does not account for those aspects of a component's behavior which are "noncausal" or more "constraint-like." A complete qualitative *analysis* would consist of more parts. The first, of which we just gave an example, identifies the path of causal action in the device's functioning, and a second identifies the support which enables the causal action path to exist. However, in this chapter we are primarily concerned with qualitative *simulation*, which only concerns the first. For example, a qualitative simulation of the steam plant illustrated in Fig. 8.2 might be: "*The heat input to the steam generator causes the production of steam which is carried through the pipe to the turbines causing the turbines to turn...*" Although this simulation details the causal action of the plant, it does not make the inference that the water is conserved in the system because no single component loses water. These more constraint-like arguments, although they are qualitative, are part of the support structure[3] for the causal action, and thus not discussed here.

The simplicity of the qualitative simulation as expressed in the preceding two examples is deceptive. Qualitative simulation encompasses a variety of ideas which need to be carefully differentiated. For example, we must distinguish simulation as a process from the results of that process. A simulation process operates on a representation describing the device, producing another representation that describes how the device functions. One source of confusion is that this latter representation can likewise be "interpreted" or simulated, but doing so

<hr>

[3]Roughly speaking, the biasing network of a transistor is another example of a support structure because it *enables* the transistor to amplify but does not itself play a active role in the amplification. However, this kind of support seems to be a different kind of support than the one mentioned in the steam plant. This suggests that the action-support distinction may turn out to be independent from the cause-constraint distinction although action more commonly requires causal reasoning while support more commonly requires constraint-like reasoning.

but fails to state any rationale for these causal connections. Because it is impossible to tell, a priori, whether the component models lead to unique behavior, the problem-solver must entertain the possibility that the structural evidence is underconstraining. Therefore the envisioning must take into account the possibility that one structure may lead to multiple possible functionings among which the envisioning cannot, in principle, distinguish.

The problem-solving methods for envisioning that we have investigated are based on the two techniques of relaxation and propagation. (In this brief discussion of the methods, we will ignore the added complexity introduced by the possibility of nonunique outcomes; both methods can be extended to deal with it.) The method under consideration in this chapter is that of propagation, because relaxation, even qualitative relaxation,[5] has the disadvantage of failing to identify the causal relationships (and thus also the mechanisms producing them) of the device's behavior. To solve by propagation, one starts with a single, noncausally produced event (e.g., an input or a state in disequilibrium), then examines the nearby components to determine what events resulted, and repeats the procedure indefinitely. This technique has the advantage of automatically constructing the causal relationships between events, and at the same time identifying the mechanisms of the causal relationships. However, because its method is to proceed locally, without referencing global effects, it often produces multiple behaviors, only one of which is possible.

"Running," the resulting causal model is closest to the original psychological intuition of "simulating the machine in the mind's eye." By running the model, one, in essence, does a straight-forward simulation of the machine; the running itself does not have to determine or "prove" the causal or temporal ordering of events, as the envisioning process already has done so, and encoded the information in the causal model which serves as the input data for the running process.

The simplicity and elegance of the running process is the result of the complex problem-solving (i.e., envisioning) that constructed it. Our intuition that "simulation in the mind's eye" is simple is manifested by this running process. However, that sense of simplicity is deceptive, for the running is not possible without the more complex problem-solving which preceded it, removing all the ambiguities about how the machine might function.

Understandably, the problems that arise in constructing causal models and the mechanisms that suffice in solving these problems become important for cognitive psychology and artificial intelligence. For psychology, it is important because they provide a framework for analyzing the "competency" involved in determining how a novel machine functions. Inasmuch as envisioning is restricted to being based solely on structural evidence, it becomes an interesting

[5]Qualitative relaxation begins by assigning all possible qualitative values to all the interacting quantities and then repeatedly applies all the local component models to restrict the values for each quantity it references.

particular context in which the component is embedded (i.e., context-free). These behaviors form a component model (or schema) which characterizes all the potential behaviors of the component, and the envisioning process instantiates a specific behavior for each component from these models. These component models are the basic principles which the envisioning process draws upon to derive the functioning from the structure.

We will discuss these component models in detail in the following section, but a simple example from the steam plant will help clarify the point for this discussion. The specific behavior of the pipe connecting the boiler and turbine might be that the contents flow from right to left. This certainly is an inadequate component model for the pipe throughout the entire model as the contents flow from left to right in the pipes from the condenser to the boiler. A possible component model for the pipe, overall, is "the contents will flow from the high-pressure end to the low-pressure end; and if these pressures are the same, nothing will flow." This component model for pipes works for every pipe in the steam plant. To determine the functioning of the overall device, each component's model must be examined and an individual, specific behavior instantiated for it. Thus, the functioning of the entire device is determined, in part, by "gluing together" the specific behaviors of all of its components. The problem for envisioning is determining for each component which behavior is actually manifested given all the possible behaviors its model characterizes.

What makes the problem-solving effort involved in the structure-to-function inference process difficult is that the behavior of the overall device is constrained, not only by local interactions of its component behaviors, but also by global interactions. Therefore, in principle, the behavior models of the components which are specified qualitatively may not provide enough information to identify the correct functioning of the device. For example, if values are described qualitatively, fine-grained distinctions cannot be made, such as, whether one force is stronger than another. Thus, in the case of the buzzer, the envisioning may not be able to determine whether the force of the magnetic field is stronger than the restoring force of the spring. Which of the forces is the greater may, in fact, be crucial to the functioning of the device. Also, because the primitives used for constructing simulations are the component models, they are, by definition, local and hence cannot reference or utilize aspects of global behaviors. For example, the buzzer makes noise because it oscillates, but oscillation is a property of the combination of the models of the components on the feedback path, not of any one in particular.

In order to describe how the resultant behavior derives from the behaviors of the constituents, first, each important event in the overall behavior must be causally related to preceding events. Then, each causal relationship must be explained by some fragment of the component model of one of its components. The first example we gave, describing Fig. 8.1, is, at best, an abridged description of the buzzer's function. It causally relates each event to the preceding one.

inference strategy in its own right for artificial intelligence applications, especially given the desire for artificial intelligence systems to be robust, i.e., to be able to deal with novel situations. The resulting models are more likely to be void of any implicit assumptions or built-in presuppositions based on how the device was intended to behave.

Let us now consider the major ingredients of the envisioning process.

Device Topology and Class-Wide Assumptions

We have developed a language of primitives for expressing and defining the structure of a machine. A machine consists of constituents. Some of these constituents represent parts which themselves can be viewed as smaller machines (e.g., resistors, valves, boilers). Other constituents represent connections (e.g., pipes, wires, cables) through which the parts communicate by transmitting information. These connections can be thought of as conduits through which "stuff" flows, its flow captured by conduit laws, which are explained later. We call the representation of the machine in these terms its *device topology*.

As illustrated in Fig. 8.3, the parts of the buzzer are the spring-loaded clapper with an attached switch, the coil, and the battery. The conduits of the buzzer are three wires and a magnetic field. The clapper is connected electrically between the battery and the coil, and the "stuff" that flows in these wires is electrical charge. The clapper is also connected to a magnetic field, a very different kind of conduit than wire.

Assumptions are embodied in the identification of the important constituents of the machine, in their models, and in the physics of the conduits. Some of these assumptions are idiosyncratic to a particular constituent or device, but others apply to a wide class of devices. For example, the above buzzer explanation ignores any currents the magnetic field of the coil might induce; this assumption

is valid for most electro-mechanical devices. Similarly, for most electro-mechanical devices, one can assume that electrical charges (or current) flows instantaneously in the wires. We call such assumptions *class-wide assumptions*. They form a kind of universal resolution for the "microscope" being used to study the physical model.

We use this microscope to view behavior, focusing only on certain aspects of the behavior and then only to a certain level of precision. Because we use the same microscope to view the behaviors of all the devices of a certain class (e.g., elctro-mechanical), it makes the same basic assumptions for each. Although, depending on one's philosophical position, it may be possible to employ an assumption-free microscope, certainly the microscope used for qualitative modeling is not. We introduce the notion of class-wide assumptions to distinguish them from assumptions that apply to only one particular device: the latter, though, plays a major role later in this paper.

Conduit Laws

The conduits contain stuff (e.g., water, oil, steam, electrons, etc.) which mediates the interactions between components. (See Williams, Hollan, & Stevens, this volume for a discussion of "stuff.") The physics of these conduits explains how this stuff communicates information. The stuff can be modeled as a set of identical objects, each of which obeys a rigidly defined set of rules. For example, in the lemming metaphor (Gentner & Gentner, this volume) for current flow, the running lemmings represent flowing current and the battery supplies the noise (impetus) to urge the lemmings to move. These mythical objects, though not necessarily representative of actual objects, serve to give a causal account of the transfer of *information* in the connections. In this chapter we will not concern ourselves with accounting for this transfer, and will instead rely solely on its existence so that we can speak simply of conduits transferring information between components.

The brevity of the discussion here belies the importance of the qualitative physics of stuff in conduits. The choice of the physics for the conduits has enormous influence on the models for the components; they too are subject to the same physics, being processors and manipulators of the stuff in the conduits. In this chapter we utilize an oversimplified account of stuff. To prevent later confusion, however, we must make two important observations. First, although in the functioning of the machine all the conduits contain stuff, all of which may be flowing, at any given time only *some* of that stuff contributes to the causal action. And second, the communication of information within a conduit does not necessarily mean that stuff is flowing in it. For example, the introduction of a quantity of water in one end of a pipe will almost instantaneously increase the pressure at the far end of the pipe even though it might be a very long time (if ever) before the quantity of water moves to the far end of the pipe.

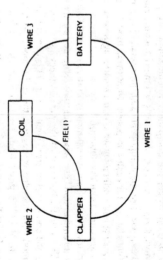

FIG. 8.3. Device topology of the buzzer.

We assume that the behavior of the objects in the conduits can be summarized as a collection of attributes (e.g., pressure, velocity, current, voltage, volume). These attributes are a collective description of the objects in the conduits. When a conduit connects two components, both components have direct access to the values of the attributes in the conduit. Each component is modeled by rules that monitor the attribute values in some of the conduits connected to it and, which can change the state of the component accordingly, thereby affecting other conduits connected to it. These behavioral rules form the essence of a component model.

Component Models

In order to explore the ramifications of these ideas, a formalism for rules comprising a component model must be developed. The formalism will provide a common language for expressing the model of a component. Also, the existence of a formalism should remove any potential ambiguities about the component models and make it easier to study the simulation and problem-solving processes which use them. A component model characterizes all the potential behaviors that the component can manifest. It does not, however, specify which ports or conduits connected to them are the inputs, and which are the outputs; very often that can only be determined in the broader context of how a particular component is used in the overall device.[6]

A component's behavior is typically divided into a number of distinct regions or states within which its behavior is relatively simple. For example, a switch has two states, "on," and "off," each of which specifies radically different, but simple, behaviors. The behavior of each state is described by a definition part and a transition part; the definition part describes how the attributes of the connecting conduits interrelate, and the transition part describes how attribute values of the connecting conduits can change the state of behavior of the component.

The transition part is a collection of conditions on attribute values along with their resulting effect on the state of the component. The definition part is a collection of qualitative equations on attribute values which define what it means to be in that state. This definition part can be used to determine the consequences of a component being in a given state. If the envisioning process knows a component is in a particular state, it can use the definition part to infer the new values of attributes in some of its connecting conduits and thus to determine the component's behavior. The definition part can also be used as a criterial test to determine whether a component is in that state. This is done by determining

whether the definition attribute equations of a hypothetical state hold in the particular behavioral context. (The utility of this second use though, will not become evident until assumptions are introduced.)

The general form of a component model is as follows:

⟨component⟩ : ⟨state1⟩:
    ⟨definition-part⟩,
    ⟨transition-part⟩.
  ⟨state2⟩:
    ⟨definition-part⟩,
    ⟨transition-part⟩.
  . . .

The definition part is a sequence of "⟨attribute⟩ $\Leftarrow$ ⟨value⟩" or "⟨attribute⟩ $\Leftrightarrow$ ⟨attribute⟩." (For more complex examples, this simple definition of the attribute equation would have to be extended, but it suffices for this chapter.) The transition part is a sequence of "IF ⟨attribute-test⟩ CAUSES: ⟨transition⟩." Note that the only attributes a model may reference are those of the conduits attached to the component and the only state that may be referenced is the component's own.

In this example, fields are described by the single attribute of field strength (indicated by an "F") and wires are described by the single attribute of current flow (indicated by an "I"). Figure 8.4 diagrams the attributes corresponding to the conduits of Fig. 8.3. One possible set of specific models for the buzzer is:

CLAPPER : OPEN:
    $I1 \Leftarrow 0, I2 \Leftarrow 0$
    IF F1 = 0 CAUSES: clapper will become CLOSED.
  CLOSED:
    $I1 \Leftarrow 1, I2 \Leftarrow 1$
    IF F1 = 1 CAUSES: clapper will become OPEN.

COIL : ON:
    $F1 \Leftarrow 1$
    IF I2 = 0 CAUSES: coil will become OFF
    IF I3 = 0 CAUSES: coil will become OFF.
  OFF:
    $F1 \Leftarrow 0$
    IF I2 = 1 CAUSES: coil will become ON
    IF I3 = 1 CAUSES: coil will become ON.

BATTERY: $I1 \Leftrightarrow I3$.

(Model 1)

Note that we also introduce the idea of qualitative time. The statements "will become" do not make quantitative discriminations. If two component models were simultaneously to cause state transitions, the simulator, by itself, would not

[6]Determining which conduit(s) is (are) actually functioning as the input may seem obvious but for n-conduit devices (where n > 2), such as transistors such determination can be problematic without recourse to a global analysis of the overall device.

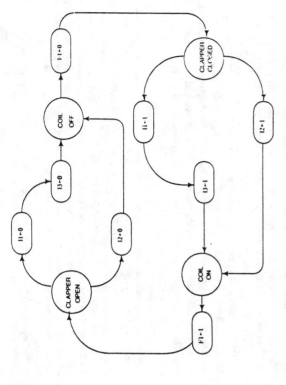

FIG.8.5.   Causation in the buzzer.

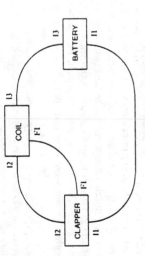

FIG. 8.4.   Attribute topology of the buzzer.

be able to determine which necessarily happens first. Additional information or additional inference machinery would be required, as will be discussed later.

Causal Model

These models can now be used by the envisioning process to determine the behavior of the buzzer and construct its causal model. The envisioning problem-solving process consists of a propagation phase followed by a filtering phase (which is discussed later). The first phase of envisioning is very much like a simulation, albeit a very specialized one. Intuitively, this first phase consists simply of starting with particular values for the conduit attributes, and then, using the component models repetitively, deducing the changes in other conduit attributes and component states. This view, however, does not illustrate the power of envisioning as it suggests the result is simply a historical trace of attribute values over time.

Each application of a component model derives value(s) for unknown attribute values from known ones. This relationship between antecedents and consequences establishes a primitive causal connection between causes (antecedents) and effects (consequences). Thus, envisioning is simply a kind of composition process that glues together primitive causal connections by attaching the effects of one primitive to the causes of another. The particular attribute values become secondary, bringing the rules and their relationships (i.e., the causality) to the forefront. This is best illustrated by the diagram shown in Fig. 8.5. Because the causal model identifies which attributes cause component behavior and which attributes are caused by component rules, it distinguishes the inputs and outputs of each component.[7]

Each node in the diagram represents a component model applied to some particular attribute values. Each edge in the diagram represents the results of a piece of one component's model affecting some component state or conduit attribute. Consequently, the result of the envisioning is an explicit representation of the causality inherent in the device's function.

Each edge in Fig. 8.5 corresponds to the application of only a piece of a component model. For example, the edge from COIL ON to F1 ⇐ 1 corresponds to the piece of the component model:

COIL: ON:
    F1 ⇐ 1

The essential character of envisioning is that it converts one kind of description into another, primitive structural pieces into behavioral ones. The causal model of Fig. 8.5 is much more than a simple dependency graph of effects and causes— it also identifies the structural mechanism which connects each effect to its causes. Thus Fig. 8.5 represents the connection between the buzzer's structure and its function.

The necessity of establishing, a principled connection between structure and function was one of the motivations for the choice of the model syntax intro-

---

[7]Again, note that for more complex components, determining the inputs and outputs can be problematic. For example, it is not necessarily true that the conduit that is first "activated" is the component's input, especially if the overall device has feedback paths.

duced in the previous section. Consider another model for the buzzer, one which does not obey our syntax:

CLAPPER : OPEN:
    coil will become ON.
  CLOSED:
    coil will become OFF.

COIL : ON:
    clapper will become OPEN.
  OFF:
    clapper will become CLOSED.

(Model 2)

This model, with its clapper and coil component models, produces the same state transition behavior as that indicated in Fig. 8.5. However, it provides little useful information on how its functioning relates to the structure, let alone on how it could be derived from the structure. For example, it cannot explain the means by which the clapper affects the coil. Syntax alone, however, is insufficient to gain all the important properties we want a causal model to possess.

Most devices (unlike the buzzer) have interesting external inputs. For example, an engine typically has a throttle, which serves as an external input to the machine. Different input values can cause different behaviors, and thus different causal paths. These different causal "stories" will often show marked similarity, as the behaviors were produced by the same structure. We consider all stories produced by the different values of inputs to be all part of the causal model. This causal model usually consists of only a small set of stories because most of the input values produce duplicate causal paths with only the attribute values varying. For example, between the minimum throttle setting at which the engine runs and the maximum throttle setting at which it disintegrates, the causality of an engine does not change.

Constraints on the Formulation of Causal Models

In order for a simulation of a fixed resolution to be the most useful or "valid," thus maximizing the work realizable by the simulation, the simulation must satisfy constraints beyond those imposed by the formalism for component models. Both establishing and satisfying these constraints turns out to be a far more complex and subtle issue than it first appears. However, the cost of not satisfying them would be great because running the causal model produced by the envisioning process for any previously untested case would be unreliable. Ideally a simulation should be *consistent*, *corresponding*, and *robust*.

A *consistent* causal model is free of internal contradictions: No two component models may specify different values for the same attribute for any single

composite state of the device. Consistency can be defined analogously for component models.[8]

The *correspondence* constraint specifies that the causal model must be faithful to the behavior of the actual device under examination. The resolution established by the class-wide assumptions defines an abstraction map from the actual physical object to the structure upon which the envisioning operates. The actual physical structure is, so to speak, operated on by nature producing some behavior. The representation of the structure is operated on by the envisioning to produce a description of the device's behavior. Another description of the device's behavior is gotten by describing the observed behavior. For a causal model to be *corresponding*, these two behaviors, one derived through an envisioning and the other derived through observing the actual system, must be the same.

Correspondence is not quite enough to establish robustness. For example, if the device experiences unusual operating conditions the causal model may no longer correspond. Unusual operating conditions can result from unexpected inputs or from unexpected failures in the components. For a causal model to be *robust* it also must be useful in unusual situations. In particular, we would like the envisioning to produce a causal model that satisfies the correspondence constraint even when the device's structure is perturbed. For example, suppose we had a machine consisting of four parts, one of which was faulted; *robustness* stipulates that by substituting the faulty component model for the correct one (i.e., the perturbation), the causal model produced for the overall device must represent the behavior of the actual faulted system. The main way to achieve the robustness of the causal model is to have the component models, themselves, be robust.[9]

Unfortunately, it is very difficult to tell whether the component models used in the envisioning are robust or not. To help solve this difficulty we introduce esthetic principles which can be used to identify particular sources of nonrobustness and which can also provide guidance in the choice and construction (i.e., learning) of component models. Our central esthetic is the no-function-in-struc-

---

[8] Actually, a rigorous definition for a component model being consistent is beyond the scope of this chapter. First, in order for the definition of consistency to have any force, we need to add a restriction that there be only one model for each component. Without this restriction, any set of rules specifying the behavior of a component could be consistent by just segregating them into different models for the same component. Second, one has to carefully decide what aspects of the "outside world" can or need to be considered. For example, if a model has an internal contradiction in an unrealizable state is it consistent? Similarly, if syntactically different attributes asserted in a state definition become dependent as a consequence of the physics of the environment (e.g., voltage and current) and through that dependency their values become contradictory, is the model, by itself, consistent?

[9] We assume that the envisioning process itself is error-free and complete (i.e., that it makes all possible deductions).

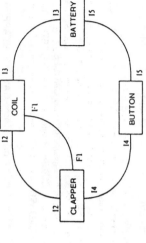

FIG. 8.6. Attribute topology of the buzzer with button.

SWITCH : OPEN:

    I4 ⇐ 0, I5 ⇐ 0

    IF BUTTON = PUSHED

        CAUSES: switch will become CLOSED.

    CLOSED:

    I4 ⇐ 1, I5 ⇐ 1

    IF BUTTON = RELEASED

        CAUSES: switch will become OPEN

                         (Model 3)

Although the causal model produced by the original model set (Model 1) was consistent and corresponding, this new model set (Model 1 amended with Model 3) is neither. To see this, we must use the definition parts both imperatively (as specifying what consequences follow from being in a particular state) and criterially (as a test to determine whether a component is in a particular state). Consider the case where the switch is closed. Used imperatively, the definition part of the switch model indicates that current flows. Using the definition parts of the clapper states criterially (from Model 1), the clapper cannot be in state open as that state predicts no current flow and therefore the clapper must be closed. Thus the model set predicts that if the switch is closed the clapper is always open, which is contrary to the observed facts. To avoid this difficulty, a better switch model would be:

SWITCH : OPEN:

    I4 ⇐ 0, I5 ⇐ 0

    IF BUTTON = PUSHED

        CAUSES: switch will become CLOSED.

    CLOSED:

    I4 <=> I5

    IF BUTTON = RELEASED

        CAUSES: switch will become OPEN.

                         (Model 4)

ture principle. This principle states that the rules for specifying the behavior of any constituent part of the overall device can in no way refer, even implicitly, to how the overall device functions. Thus every part of the same type must be modeled in the same way. One consequence of this principle is that component models may only reference attributes of adjoining conduits (i.e., a locality principle). For example, the component model for the battery (see Fig. 8.3) may only reference information in WIRE1 and WIRE3; it may not reference the internal state of the coil or clapper. Localness, however, does not guarantee that the no-function-in-structure principle holds. The clapper-switch model (Model 1) presented earlier violates this principle (as we see in the next section) in that it presumes itself connected in a loop with the battery.

Motivations and Consequences of the Constraints[10]

These three constraints, consistency, correspondence, and robustness, are important for nearly all applications of qualitative simulations. Consistency, for example, is crucial, because without it the causal model may not be able to predict any behavior at all for the device. Having consistent component models enables the envisioning to attribute any discovered contradictions to some assumption it made while locally propagating behaviors of components. As we discuss later, the ability to make and then later retract assumptions is the crux of envisioning.

Robustness is the most subtle constraint and is also the most difficult to satisfy. In order to appreciate its importance, consider the operator of a nuclear power-plant that has just suffered a serious casualty where he cannot physically go and safely observe its internal state. Indeed, he must use his own mental model of the reactor's functioning in order to hypothesize and test what state the system is actually in, given the available (often scanty) external evidence. If his mental, causal model is predicated on some implicit assumption that holds for the correct functioning of the reactor, but not for the particular faulted reactor, then as he "runs" his model under his current hypothesis, its behavior need not (and probably will not) correspond to the behavior of the faulted reactor. This will lead him either to reject a correct hypothesis or accept an incorrect one. If his model is sufficiently nonrobust, it can become so nonrepresentative of the actual faulted reactor that the faulted reactor becomes cognitively "impenetrable" to the operator.

In order to illustrate these constraints, consider the previous buzzer model which has been artificially perturbed through the seemingly innocuous addition of a button which acts as a switch to turn the buzzer on and off (see Fig. 8.6).

---

[10]This section is rather technical and may be skipped on initial reading.

In Model 4, the rules for the closed state are now satisfactory, but problems remain with the open state. Imperatively, the definition part of the switch model says no current can flow in the wires connected to it. Using the definition parts of the clapper states criterially (from Model 1), the clapper therefore cannot be closed and must be open. Thus the model set predicts that if the switch is open, the clapper is open, which is still contrary to the observed facts. Furthermore, the coil model (from Model 1) says that if there is no current the coil must (or will) be off and thus the clapper will close. This next state is inconsistent because the clapper says the current is flowing and the switch says it is not. No modification of the switch model will resolve these violations of consistency and correspondence. The problem lies with the lack of robustness in the clapper.

A similar example can be used to illustrate the need for robustness in handling casualties or troubleshooting devices. The troubleshooter, in order to identify a faulty component, must be able to correctly hypothesize the consequences of perturbations in the component models of the device. Let us use the buzzer model as an extreme example, and suppose that the troubleshooter wanted to hypothesize the consequences of a dead battery:

BATTERY : $I_1 \Leftarrow 0$, $I_3 \Leftarrow 0$.   (Model 5)

As with the button model above, when this model is used by the envisioning, the envisioning generates an internal contradiction implying that it cannot be used to predict any behavior for the buzzer, let alone to compare the hypothetical behavior with the observed symptoms. The nonrobust model, Model 1 amended with Model 4, presumes the correct functioning of the faulty part (the battery) in one of its neighbors (the clapper-switch). Usually, this results in making the perturbed simulation nonrepresentative of the actual facts, but sometimes, as is the case here, the perturbed simulation is simply inconsistent. Also, in actuality a dead battery is typified by a closed clapper-switch with no current flowing through it—a direct contradiction with the component model itself. The model for the clapper stated current would flow if it was closed, whereas in actual fact it should state that current would flow if there was current available to flow.

In this chapter we do not discuss the procedure by which the faulty component might be identified. The form of robustness we have defined merely insures that, for any faulty component (with a known model), envisioning can construct a corresponding causal model. A far stronger form of robustness is that this causal model be identifiable from studying the differences between the device's actual and correct behaviors. The identification process imputes unexpected behaviors to possible causes, and the causal model produced by the envisioning provides the groundwork for this because it can also be used to relate effects to causes. This is discussed further in the section on troubleshooting.

Robustness is far more likely to be a problem for a mechanistic mental model than for a numerical simulation tool (e.g., SPICE [Nagel & Pederson, 1973]). In a simulation tool the component models provided by the tool designer are apt to be "context free" as he does not know what composite devices will be constructed from his components and thus cannot embed implicit assumptions into the component models about how the composite device functions. Also, the bottom-up analysis style of a designer using a simulation tool makes it easier for him to maintain a clean separation between structure and function in his own model. However, in the cognitive science arena, we are more interested in the *synthesis* process, the kind that one is likely to go through in an attempt to construct an understanding of an already-designed artifact. Here, a person is much more likely to let his partial understanding of how the device functions impact the way he thinks about (i.e., models) the particular components.

Much of the discussion has proceeded as if a person has a model of a device, when in fact he will usually continually improves his understanding or model of a system by changing the component models, altering the device topology, and inventing new physics for the objects in the conduits. But improvement (or learning) needs to be driven by tests or "critics"; the consistency, correspondence and robustness constraints intend to provide the basis for such criticism.

AMBIGUITIES, ASSUMPTIONS AND MECHANISMS

Origin of Ambiguities

The apparent simplicity in the movement from structure to function for the buzzer example (Fig. 8.3 to Fig. 8.5) is somewhat misleading. In this example, every step in the simulation was uniquely predicted by the preceding ones and thus the causal mechanism was trivial to construct. This is not a usual case—usually one event can cause many others and it is extremely difficult to identify which of the possibilities will actually happen. A more robust model of the buzzer has several such ambiguities. For example, there is no way we can tell from the structural description of Fig. 8.3 whether the magnetic field is necessarily strong enough to lift the clapper against the restoring force of the spring. This is a particularly easy ambiguity to resolve if we assume the purpose of the buzzer is to make a noise. In particular, if the magnetic force is insufficient to overcome the restoring force it will never be able to lift the clapper and hence never make a noise.

To illustrate the ambiguity of whether the field has sufficient strength, let us consider a slightly more accurate model for the clapper:

CLAPPER : OPEN:

$I_1 \Leftarrow 0$, $I_2 \Leftarrow 0$

IF F1 < spring-force CAUSES:

CLAPPER will become CLOSED.

CLOSED:

$I_1 \Leftarrow 1$, $I_2 \Leftarrow 1$

IF F1 > spring-force CAUSES: CLAPPER will become

OPEN.

(Model 6'')

In general, ambiguities originate from the fact that the information available to the qualitative analysis underdetermines or partially characterizes the actual behavior of the overall device. There are three reasons for this underdetermination. The first and most obvious is that the quantities referenced by the component models are qualitative and thus fine-grained distinctions cannot be made between the attribute values or component states. This is the origin of the ambiguity illustrated between Fig. 8.5 and 8.7. Second, because the implicit time progression in the simulation is qualitative, it is not always possible to determine the actual ordering of events. And the third reason, not directly related to the qualitative nature of the models, comes from the limitations on the kinds of information captured by the models. Because envisioning is trying to identify a global flow of action by gluing together local cause-effect rules of the component models, a component model encodes only those aspects of the component's behavior that can be used in such a fashion. However, our understanding of a given component often involves knowledge that is not (or, perhaps, cannot be) encoded in such mechanistic rules. For example, in modeling the internal operation of a pump we know from the laws of physics that fluid is conserved in passing through the pump. But, because this piece of knowledge is a *constraint* and cannot be represented by any cause-effect rule, it can lead to a given component model being underdetermined.

Origin of Assumptions

In the previous buzzer example, because of the qualitative nature of the attribute values, the envisioning process cannot determine whether the spring is stronger than the magnetic field. In this impasse, it is forced to consider two hypothetical situations: one in which it *assumes* the spring is stronger than the magnetic field (Fig. 8.5) and one in which it *assumes* the spring is weaker than the field (Fig. 8.7).

Inasmuch as qualitative analysis is inherently ambiguous, any algorithm that implements it will, in general, not be able to discover a unique causal description for the device's functioning. Because envisioning presumes that there is a unique description, the consequences of these ambiguities are manifested as impasses during the envisioning process. These impasses occur when it cannot evaluate a condition in a transition part to determine whether a transition occurs or invoke an attribute equation in a definition part to determine the value of an unknown attribute. In order to proceed around impasses, the envisioning must introduce assumptions about the truth or falsity of conditions or about the values of unknown attributes.

The buzzer example illustrates an impasse that arises from being unable to determine whether a transition condition holds. In this impasse the envisioner introduces an assumption that the condition ''F1 > spring force'' is true, and then proceeds to analyze the new resulting state. Of course, the resulting causal

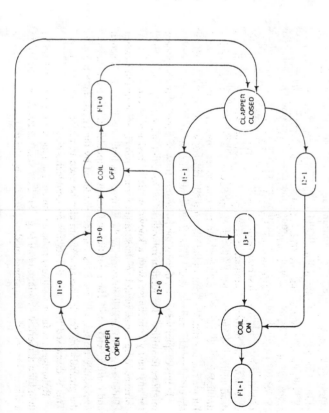

FIG. 8.7. A noiseless causal model.

With the information provided in Model 1 amended with that of Model 6 there is no way to tell whether the buzzer will make a noise (i.e., vibrate). At best we can come up with two possible functionings for the buzzer, that it will be silent, or that it will make noise. Neither alternative can be chosen, though, without violating the no-function-in-structure principle (by referencing the buzzer's overall function to see if it makes noise).

Thus the result of an envisioning can be a collection of different causal models, each with its own underlying assumptions. In the case under consideration, two causal models are produced. The first one assumes the spring can overcome the field and is illustrated by Fig. 8.5, and the second, illustrated by Fig. 8.7, assumes it cannot. The two causal models show marked similarity. Because Fig. 8.7 is so similar to Fig. 8.5, we could just collapse the two by annotating two of the edges as being dependent on an assumption. Such a simple merging is usually not possible because the causal models under different sets of assumptions will not usually be so similar to each other. In order to determine the correct functioning of the device, the correct set of assumptions must be selected.

---

[11]Because this model is oversimplified, we could have used purely syntactic techniques to resolve the ambiguities discussed in this section.

model will then contain two accounts of the device's functioning: one in which the transition takes place and one in which it does not.

The second kind of impasse results when the envisioning stops because it cannot discover all of the necessary attribute values to use an attribute equation of a definition part imperatively, thus leaving some attributes unknown. This type of impasse does not occur with our buzzer model. Although this type is far more difficult to deal with, there are some heuristic strategies to circumvent such impasses. The basic one is to choose attributes and their values that will allow the envisioning to continue tracing an unbroken path of possible causal action. The choice of attribute must be one at the "boundary" between where conduit attributes are known and unknown, such that the assumed attribute values will combine with other known attributes to lead to the discovery of new values. In this way the assumption will never break the tracing of the potential causal path, because the assumption, itself, will never be the sole cause for an effect.

The difficulty with the above assumption-introduction strategy is that, even after the unknown attributes have been selected, the envisioner still needs to choose a value for it. One must appeal to some other source of knowledge. The analysis of complex devices can be decomposed into two relatively independent parts. The first concerns itself with what the attribute values are when the machine is "at rest" (i.e., at equilibrium) and the second with how disturbances from that equilibrium propagate through the device. Envisioning is the most useful for this latter type of analysis inasmuch as it provides a causal account of how the disturbance propagates through the device. Because the analysis is concerned with disturbances from equilibrium originating from some localized signal it can be fairly reliably assumed that those disturbances which have been discovered causally dominate those which have not. The strategy is, until proven otherwise, to *temporarily assume* that unknown attributes have negligible value. This is best illustrated by an example.

The flow rate of water through a constricted pipe is proportional to the difference in pressure between the ends of the pipe. The envisioner may discover that the pressure rises at one end of the pipe but may be unable to determine the change in flow through it because the pressure change at the other end is unknown. In this case, the impasse can be resolved by assuming the pressure change at the other end of the pipe is negligible. The attribute equation for the pipe can then be applied to determine the flow through the pipe. Note that the pressure change at the far end of the pipe has not yet been discovered and thus is not propagated. the impasse is circumvented by proceeding *as if* it were negligible compared to currently known values. This pressure change remains to be discovered, perhaps as a consequence of making the assumption in the first place.

Some impasses also result purely from the fact that the envisioning process itself proceeds locally. These impasses appear indistinguishable from those discussed. but unlike assumptions which arise from the inherent ambiguity of

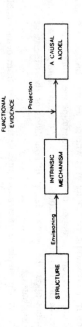

FIG. 8.8. Intrinsic mechanism.

qualitative analysis, these assumptions are often resolved by the conclusion of the analysis. Locality in the envisioner leads to both kinds of assumptions, and both can be resolved. For assumptions which originate from unevaluable transition conditions, the envisioner may discover better values for the attributes and hence directly determine whether the condition holds. It may also be discovered that the new state is inherently contradictory in which case the condition cannot hold. Assumptions of the second type can only be resolved indirectly. The assumption that some unknown attribute is negligible may lead to an immediate contradiction. In such cases, the alternate causal path which provided the contradictory value assigns a value to the unknown attribute so the impasse does not recur as a result of the contradiction.

The introduction of assumptions forces some redefinition of consistency, correspondence and robustness. But because their redefinitions will not alter the basic concepts of these constraints, we do not discuss them.

The Intrinsic Mechanism

In general, external evidence is required to resolve the ambiguities by either verifying or rejecting the various assumptions created by the envisioning process. This external information is functional (behavioral) in nature, thereby requiring an additional kind of problem-solving in order to use it to resolve the assumptions. As we have discussed in the case of the buzzer, the external evidence that is needed is that "the buzzer makes noise." Before expanding this point, we need to introduce the notion of an *intrinsic mechanism* of a device as being a description of all the potential causal models of the device that are produced by the envisioning.[12] The intrinsic mechanism represents the essential character of the device's operation. The external evidence then selects the one causal model of the intrinsic mechanism under which the machine actually operates. This selection process is called *projection* (see Fig. 8.8).

---

[12]Issues concerning whether a device has a unique intrinsic mechanism. whether it depends on the resolution of the analysis, or whether it simply depends on the calculus as opposed to the resolution, need not concern us here but will be discussed in a later paper.

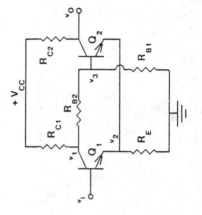

FIG. 8.10. Schematic of Schmitt Trigger.

knows what the Schmitt Trigger is supposed to do. The three other causal models are possible, but implausible in normal circuits. However, were the engineer to design a Schmitt Trigger, or to troubleshoot one, he would have to be aware of the other possibilities.

The projection of external evidence on intrinsic mechanisms can be difficult because the external evidence may be given in entirely different terms from those describing intrinsic mechanisms. The external evidence may be "it makes noise," "it oscillates," "it has a snapping action," or "it latches." The intrinsic mechanism may be more of the form "the spring causes the clapper to close" or "the rising voltage triggers the monostable." This functional evidence varies with how closely it is related to the representational primitives of the intrinsic mechanism. At one end of the scale, the functional evidence makes specific reference to branch points (e.g., whether or not the magnetic field lifts the clapper), whereas at the other end of the scale it refers to aspects of the intrinsic mechanism's operation (e.g., "it oscillates" or "it makes noise"). The closer the kind of evidence is to the branch points of the intrinsic mechanism, the easier the problem-solving will be in projecting it and thereby selecting the actual functioning of the correctly working device.

The subject of the projection problem-solving is the translation of the functional evidence into a vocabulary that is directly related to the intrinsic mechanism. This requires the invention and development of a technical vocabulary of mechanism and function. One simple projection is to have a special kind of simulator which constantly monitors the progress of the simulation and explicitly rejects any collections of assumptions which already manifest behavior inconsistent with the functional evidence. In this way projection can be done very efficiently.

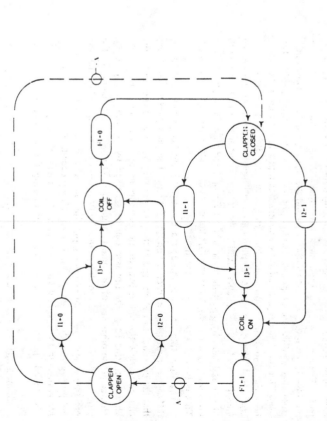

FIG. 8.9. Intrinsic mechanism for buzzer.

We represent the intrinsic mechanism as a structure that has each causal model maximally collapsed upon the others. Figure 8.9 is a simple example which diagrams the intrinsic mechanism for the buzzer consisting of the causal models of Figs. 8.5 and 8.7. The dashed lines indicate that an assumption must be introduced whose validity will determine whether this edge is in force or not. This representation is similar in some ways to Rieger and Grinberg's (1977, 1978) and encompasses all possible behaviors of the machine.

An example of a more complex intrinsic mechanism is that of a Schmitt Trigger (Fig. 8.10). (The electrical models used to analyze it are not presented here [see de Kleer, 1979].) Of importance is how an intrinsic mechanism (see Fig. 8.11) with multiple competing assumptions might be represented. The Schmitt Trigger's intrinsic mechanism contains three interdependent assumptions: to include P1, to include P2, and to include P3. Of the six apparent possibilities only four are realizable: both P1 and P2, both P1 and P3, P2 alone, and P1 alone. The intrinsic mechanism illustrated in Fig. 8.11 thus encodes four different causal models for the circuit. Any electrical engineer would know that assumptions P1 and P3 select the correct causal model, but only because he

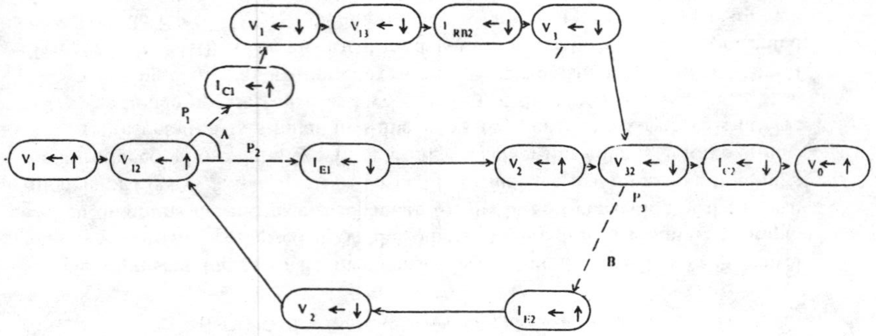

IMPLICATIONS OF THE THEORY

In the previous sections we have detailed a partial theory of qualitative simulation, a technique for reasoning about physical machines. Although the conceptual distinctions we have introduced have emerged primarily from building various kinds of qualitative simulations, we believe that many of these distinctions may be useful for investigating human performance.[13] In this section we will discuss some of the potential psychological implications of the theory by indicating how it could account for some of the apparent phenomena produced by people reasoning about machines. We have not performed any experiments per se, and thus most of the following accounts are speculative. However, by presenting some of these accounts we hope to show the power that a theoretical account can provide, to further clarify our own notions of mechanistic mental models for the reader, and to provide conjectures for future investigation and experiment.

Troubleshooting

The task of troubleshooting is, in many ways, the inverse of envisioning. The troubleshooter needs to move from known function to unknown structure, whereas the envisioning moves from known structure to unknown function. If a fault has in some way perturbed the structure of the device, the troubleshooter, even though he may have complete access to the behavior of the faulted device, no longer has total information about its structure (because, for example, a fault that opened a diode's junction might not, of course, be directly observable). The troubleshooter asks the question, "What could have caused this (symptomatic) overall behavior?" rather than, "What behavior do all these local component behaviors produce when connected in this way?" This troubleshooting process, like that of envisioning, entails extensive problem solving in order to resolve ambiguities. For the troubleshooter, the ambiguities lie in determining which of the many possible causes for a given symptom is the actual one.

A great deal of troubleshooting expertise concerns associating patterns, often generalized, of symptoms with causes. Our theory says very little about this. On the other hand, the troubleshooter must often also utilize his understanding of device functioning to determine the fault, and for this task our theory has more to say. The distinction between the intrinsic mechanism and the correct causal

---

[13]Indeed, many of the simulations we built were at least guided by intuitions about how we, the authors, reasoned about complex systems. Nevertheless, the main motivation for our doing this work was to better understand the subtleties of qualitative simulations; it was not to build a theory grounded on psychological data.

FIG. 8.11. Intrinsic mechanism for Schmitt Trigger. A voltage between two nodes is indicated by two subscripts; V_{12} represents the voltage from node I to 2. The current is labeled as "I" with a subscript indicating the component, or in the case of transistors with a terminal label and a transistor number. Thus I_{C1} represents the current in the collector of transistor Q_1.

Three Kinds of Learning

We can distinguish three forms of learning in which one might engage while acquiring an understanding of a new machine. The first kind of learning involves establishing a connection between the structure of the device and its function. The second involves making the structure-function connection more robust by making implicit assumptions explicit. And, the third type of learning is the "caching," or the storing, of the results of the projection problem-solving on the intrinsic mechanism.

A learner trying to acquire a deep understanding of a particular device will be likely to employ all three types of learning. Early in the learning process he is either given or infers some collection of component models, and from these primitives he synthesizes, via the envisioning process, a connection between the structure and function of the device. Synthesizing this connection is also known as "constructing a mechanistic mental model of the device."[15] Being preliminary, his mental model invariably includes many implicit assumptions, which may or may not be correct. As the learning progresses, he identifies and makes explicit these assumptions. His progress is motivated by discovering violations to the consistency, correspondence and robustness constraints. He might notice the latter of the three by encountering situations where his mental model fails to explain the behavior of the system (as when the system is experiencing a given fault or casualty), or by examining the consequences of hypothetical modifications to his model and thus finding that it becomes self-contradictory. Every time such violations happen the learner has the chance to identify an underlying or implicit assumption in one of his component models. Thus the impetus for this second type of learning is to increase the robustness of his mental model by making its *implicit* assumptions *explicit*. But, as we saw in the case of the buzzer, this evolution invariably creates new ambiguities for the envisioning process which then must get resolved by the *explicit* use of external functional evidence, which entails a third kind of learning.

[15]This view of a mental model as establishing a principled connection between the structure of the device and its causal model helps us better understand the subtleties of using a simulator in computer-based training and educational systems. In particular, what has often been ignored in the design of training simulators is that a student using a simulator, even one that animates the state changes that a device goes through, must still construct his own causal model for these state transitions from his underlying component models. Thus he must do several tasks simultaneously: infer or refine the component models, if he doesn't already have satisfactory ones; select the appropriate parts of each; and then connect these parts so as to capture the causality of the system. In other words, he must, metaphorically speaking, parse the surface structure events as portrayed by the training simulator into a deep structure causal model of the device. Without knowing the ingredients of causal model and without knowing, at least, a hypothetical process for constructing it, the designer will have difficulty determining how to animate the simulator (or augment it with a "coach") so to facilitate and disambiguate the student's understanding of causal *process*. See the STEAMER and SOPHIE projects for examples of the use of training simulators (Williams, Hollan, & Stevens, 1981) and (Brown, Burton, & de Kleer, 1982).

model suggests a possible solution to the long-standing issue of why people find some faults so much harder to troubleshoot than others. The difficulty of a fault is determined by how much effort needs to be expended to locate it. For many faults this difficulty is directly related to how much the perturbation in structure (i.e., the fault) perturbs the function. Before this statement can have any predictive value, however, there needs to be a way to measure how much the fault perturbs function, i.e., a metric on the causal model (function) space.[14] In general this is difficult to do, but the intrinsic mechanism view provides at least a language for discussing the degree of perturbation. In particular, three cases can be discerned for characterizing how much a fault has perturbed the correct functioning of the device.

The first and simplest case is where the function of the perturbed device is basically unchanged, meaning that the "perturbed" causal model is identical to the one of the correctly working device. Two examples containing such an occurrence would be an amplifier that wasn't producing its expected output power rating and an engine with a partially clogged fuel line whose rate of revolution was lower than expected. In all cases where the functioning remains unchanged, the original causal model can be consulted to identify which components could cause the changed outputs. Accordingly, finding this kind of fault should be relatively straightforward.

In the second case, the function of the perturbed device violates the correct causal model, but is still contained in the intrinsic mechanism. In this situation the troubleshooter can apply a two-phase strategy: first do a differential diagnosis on the intrinsic mechanism, and second, consult the resulting perturbed causal model to identify which components could cause the changed outputs as in the previous case. An example of this might occur in a high-gain amplifier. High-gain amplifiers are susceptible to undesirable positive-feedback; and designers choose particular component values to avoid it. Positive feedback, although it is part of the *intrinsic* mechanism, is not a part of the intended causal model. Thus, if the device exhibits the symptom of positive feedback, this two-phase strategy, being used as a heuristic, will localize the fault.

The last case is conjectured to be the most difficult. Here, the fault so perturbs the function that the function is not even part of the intrinsic mechanism. In this case, unless the symptom is of some known type, the troubleshooter faces a prohibitively explosive combinatorial number of searches, hypothesizing each fault and envisioning its consequences. Even worse, the envisioning process cannot utilize external evidence such as teleology and design because the faulted device will not necessarily manifest the intended teleology.

[14]If the fault produces recognizable symptoms, the fault is often easy to locate independent of what it does to the function. For example, the causes for catastrophic faults where smoke or fire comes out of the machine is often easily identifiable structurally.

As the primitives or component models of a device get stripped of their implicit assumptions about the functioning of the overall device, the problem-solving work performed by projection increases. The third form of learning concerns a technique for preserving this "work" so that it can be called upon only when needed and otherwise remains transparent. In essence, one can cache the results of projection (namely problem-solving) by recording what aspects of the component models were actually used in the device's correct causal model. From this knowledge he can synthesize new idiosyncratic component models which make explicit just those aspects, thereby eliminating the genesis of any ambiguities. Using only these idiosyncratic primitives, he can then "re-envision" the machine extremely efficiently. But what makes these models different from the nonrobust versions with which the learner started out? The difference is that now these idiosyncratic models can be linked with their embedded assumptions, which act as caveats, whereas the nonrobust models did not articulate their assumptions. If these caveats are violated, then the learner invokes the original models. For a somewhat artificial example, let us revisit the buzzer. Were we to start the envisioning process on this device using the more robust, second set of component models, we would discover two possible causal models, one with the buzzer oscillating and the other with the clapper always closed. By using the external evidence that the buzzer always makes a noise (when properly working), we would know which of these two models was in force. We could then safely use a highly simplified model of the clapper switch (as in Model 1) and efficiently re-envision the buzzer. In general, a particular device uses only a small subset of a component's rules when the overall device is functioning correctly, and the learner can identify this small subset (once he has identified the correct causal mechanism) and mold it into a simpler, but idiosyncratic, component model along with the appropriate functional caveats.[16]

One of the consequences of these three kinds of learning is that the phenomenological accounts of expert's and novice's behavior are not likely to *appear* very different for any one task. The novice unwittingly embeds assumptions about how the device is intended to function in his component models. He holds these assumptions implicitly, meaning that he cannot articulate them. The expert's explanations of how the device works uses models much like the novice's in that they contain implicit assumptions; the difference, of course, is that the expert can recover the assumptions, as well as the more robust component models when needed. This ability to recover these assumptions stems, in part, from having explicitly reasoned through and resolved the ambiguities.

Explanations

The above discussion concerning this third kind of learning suggests that nonrobust component models can be used in another important role, that of explanation. In particular, it is important to realize that the explainer often purposely violates the no-function-in-structure principle. In explaining how a device works, one wants to construct a *sequence* of explanations, commencing with one built around component models that have the not-easily-understood aspects of the device's functioning implicitly embedded in them. That is, it is often pedagogically expedient to let an "explanation" presuppose part of what it is trying to explain. By using highly simplified primitives (component models), the correct causal model or running process can be more easily communicated. Furthermore, from the learner's perspective, the simply constructed, but correct causal model can serve as a cognitive framework for organizing forthcoming refinements derived from models with fewer implicit assumptions (and thus fewer violations to the no-function-in-structure principle).

Thus, an "ideal" explanatory sequence would start with a set of component models that enabled the envisioning process to produce an intrinsic mechanism identical to that of the desired causal model (meaning the qualitative simulation would encounter no ambiguities). Further explanations would then refine these component models, so that none of them contained implicit assumptions. The resulting sequence of "explanations" would eventually lead the learner to converge on an intrinsic mechanism built around robust component models, where each new element of the sequence articulated an implicit assumption, produced and resolved a new ambiguity, and grew a new link in a path (or set of links) in the intrinsic mechanism representation. Note that all such refinements necessarily would produce only additions to the initial causal model; no radical reformulation of its organization would ever be necessary, which is why choosing models that produce the correct causal model can serve as such a powerful backbone for an explanation sequence. Of course, depending on the device, the correct causal model might be too complex to easily grasp. This suggests changing the resolution of the models and using hierarchical or embedded component models, a topic to be discussed in the multiple models section.

Impediments to Learning

A learner's impediment to his own robust understanding is his tacit application of external evidence to the choice of component models or to the envisioning process itself. By knowing that the buzzer actually makes noise, a learner may have started with a component model for the clapper in which the magnetic field was always strong enough to lift the clapper. The resulting mental model would be useless for predicting the cause of a faulty behavior (stemming, in reality,

---

[16]A variant of this form of learning involves augmenting the technical functional vocabulary so as to facilitate the projection actually reasoned through for the case at hand. This technical vocabulary is useful for any device which instantiates this mechanism, not just the particular device under study. For a related discussion, see diSessa (this volume) on the growth of phenomenological primitives.

The Conflict Between Making Assumptions Explicit and Simplifying Problem Solving

The desire for more robust models conflicts with the desire for simpler problem solving. Making the implicit assumptions explicit leads to more ambiguities, for whose solution more external, general purpose problem solving is needed. This seems somewhat paradoxical: As one gets more exposure to devices, and hence has component models with fewer hidden assumptions, understanding the next new device becomes harder, rather than easier. That is, the more experience one has understanding devices, the harder it is to construct an understanding of another device which is built out of the same components. A mitigating factor is that, as the learner's familiarity with the domain and machine increases, he will develop a more powerful technical vocabulary describing functional notions, which in turn will make his projection problem-solving simpler. Indeed, electrical engineers have an extensive vocabulary, one sufficiently powerful that often just by knowing that a device satisfies one functional predicate (e.g., the Schmitt Trigger involves hysteresis), the engineer can disambiguate all potential interpretations of how it works.

Multiple Models

In reasoning about a particular physical device, a human appears to use multiple models for the same constituent component. Williams, Hollan and Stevens (this volume) present protocols of a subject using multiple models for a heat exchanger. The phenomenology of using multiple models can arise from diverse sources and often what appears as multiple models may be instead the result of a single envisioning model. Multiple models is a very amorphous subject and one to which we cannot do justice in this brief discussion. We hope that this discussion raises some interesting distinctions for further progress in this area. An important presupposition we make in this section is that the subject's model is, to some extent, derived from studying the device and not solely from being told about the device's operation.

The task of discovering which component models the subject is using is a difficult one. It requires working backwards from the subject's explanations, his "simulations in the mind's eye." Recall, however, that running processes is relatively simple, as the causal models upon which they are based encode most of the necessary problem-solving work. This means that the facets of the component models actually reported or "seen" in the running are likely to be only a small fragment of the model which the envisioning used to construct the causal model originally. This means that the subject might manifest having two different models for a component. Although phenomenologically these two models might be different, they are just different facets of the same more complete

from a weak battery), because it would predict that the clapper would rise regardless of how weak the battery was.

Figure 8.12 represents some of the ways external evidence can be implicitly (and undesirably) projected onto the choice of structure and the envisioning process. For any given device, the learner implicitly projects functional evidence onto the structure, thereby producing hidden assumptions in the component models. For robustness, the learner should project the evidence explicitly onto the intrinsic mechanism, and thereby resolve the explicit assumptions. The goal of the learning process is acquiring a more robust understanding, as illustrated in Fig. 8.8.

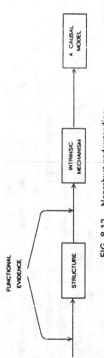

FIG. 8.12. Nonrobust understanding.

The Limits of Learning

The learning process is open-ended: A learner can never be sure that he has identified every implicit assumption. A practice in physics is to identify and then presume them for every device in the class. These class-wide assumptions provide an elegant way of being reasonably sure that, except for a certain known set of assumptions, the no-function-in-structure principle has not been violated.

Although there is no definitive test of whether important implicit assumptions remain unidentified, one thing is certain about a set of component models for which all implicit assumptions have been eliminated: Every possible behavior of a real machine with the same structure must be consistent with one of the ambiguities produced by the envisioning using that model set. For example, the earlier buzzer analysis contained an ambiguity about whether the clapper would rise. It is possible to design two different buzzers with the same structure as shown in Fig. 8.3 one of which is silent and one of which buzzes. It would be very desirable that the converse hold; that is, every possible ambiguity predicted by the envisioning be manifested by some actual machine with the same structure. The extent to which this latter condition holds determines how informative the intrinsic mechanism is, especially for the purposes of how it is used in troubleshooting.

(underlying) model. A strategy is needed to uncover when the phenomenological accounts stem from a single model or multiple models.

One potential strategy for probing the underlying models is to query the subject about the ambiguities produced when the models abstracted from his running process (by the experimenter) are used in envisioning. The aim of this strategy is to force the learner to articulate the ambiguities and problem-solving episodes that were involved in his constructing the running, but which were not evident in the running process, itself. Another strategy is to ask the subject to analyze different devices built from the same primitive components.

The difference in the way models are manifested in the envisioning and in the running can make it appear as if there are multiple models when, in fact, one is just a derivative of the other. It is important to note that the simpler model might actually contradict the model from which it is derived, because the simpler model may not incorporate boundary conditions automatically presumed in the running. However, this simpler model will not contradict its "parent" model if it incorporates the assumptions underlying the correct causal model.

The more interesting cases occur when multiple models are used in envisioning (as opposed to when they appear to be used in the running). As we saw in the earlier section on learning, the learner's component models evolve as he better understands the given device. Thus, there is the possibility that the subject learned during the envisioning process, and consequently revised one of his component models. A subject's protocol might then reveal two models: the model before his learning episode and the new model constructed as its result. The final running need not refer to the earlier model, but the protocol might indicate some reasoning based on the earlier one. The learning episode that occurred, separating the two models, was probably precipitated by violations of the consistency or correspondence constraints (e.g., a disagreement with some known aspect of the device's global behavior).

A component model is simply a description of the input-output behavior of the particular component. The model's rules make no reference to *how* the component achieves this input-output behavior. For example, the model of the clapper does not explain the mechanism by which the field moves the clapper. However, one can, recursively, view a component as a composite device. Each component in turn consists of internal subcomponents and subconduits. These subconstituents also have models, which we call the *embedded* models of the original component. The input-output behavior of a component is explained by these embedded models. In the example of the clapper, the embedded models may describe the flow of information in magnetic fields and the effects of magnetic forces on materials. Were a more detailed analysis required during the envisioning process, it might be necessary to reference such embedded models. The situation is analogous for conduits: a conduit may be modeled by its own device topology which explains how the conduit transmits information.

Embedding leads to different kinds of multiple models. The simplest is the original model and its expansion through the inclusion of its embedded submodels. Usually, however, only one of the embedded submodels is needed to resolve a particular difficulty in the envisioning. Thus, there may exist multiple models of the component, each expanded through an embedded model that explains the component's behavior for a given situation. These differing models may manifest themselves for different states of the same component or for different occurrences of the same component type in the device. These different models often appear to contradict each other, as different expansions of the same model may predict different behaviors. But this contradiction is in appearance only, because each expansion is made under some specific assumption and it is those *assumptions* that are contradictory, not the models.

What may at first appear to be multiple models may be the result of different kinds of inferences on the same consistent component model. However, people certainly use multiple models in problem solving in ways not accounted for earlier. For example, if the multiple models do not contradict each other predicting the same results, or noninterfering results (e.g., results on different conduits), then they may be considered as one single consistent model for the purposes of our theory. However, differences in the "style" (e.g., constraint vs. mechanistic) of component models may motivate considering two consistent models as distinct (see Stevens & Collins, 1980). The consistency constraint explicitly rules out multiple contradictory models, even though the latter can be, of course, extremely useful in learning new devices and components, because they form a dialectic which the learner can use to form new models. Often multiple contradictory models arise through consideration of different embedded models. Their boundary conditions, however, can be overgeneralized so that the different expanded models actually do contradict each other. Unfortunately, our theory has no mechanism to handle or to profit from this situation; nor does it say anything about multiple device topologies.

Multiple component models, of course, lead to multiple device models (causal models). But these causal models are multiple only because one of the device's constituent components has multiple models. The multiple causal models do, however, identify the consequences of the different component models and therefore can play a important role in a dialectic process by revealing some of the entailments of the different choices for component models.

Methodological Considerations

The processes discussed in this chapter are not meant to be a complete or accurate account of how people acquire an understanding about physical mechanisms. Rather, the primary purpose of this research is to identify some of the underlying knowledge states and interpretive processes for those states that a constructive theory of mechanistic models must eventually account for. In addition, the resulting technical distinctions and corresponding vocabulary help extend an ontology that the empirical psychologist can use for perceiving and describing subtleties in a subject's behavior.

There is much evidence that suggests that the major mode humans use to "understand" a complex device whose functionality is already understood. Although it may have been relatively simple for us to build an "understander" based on pattern recognition of structural schemata, it would have deflected us from our goal of understanding how a subject can construct a mechanistic mental model as opposed to understanding how he recognizes the instantiation of one. Although recognition rules or structural schemata may speed the discovery process, their origin must be accounted for and their limitations understood.[17]

In order to construct a learning theory having generality or validity, we need to follow some methodological constraints (or principles). If we need to add a new rule every time we encounter a machine we can't recognize, our learning theory would be of little use. We must impose some a priori constraints on the nature of our rules. For example, a preferable set of rules would be one that was guaranteed to recognize all members of a specific class without needing to add any more rules. Another preferable set would be one which only needed rules added under a very specific set of conditions and then, only need a limited number. We choose to employ the meta-theoretic constraint of using no recognition rules, and, instead, demand that the theory be able to construct its own recognition schemata. Of course, the necessity for some external evidence (perhaps provided by the structural recognition rules) is inevitable, but by taking this approach we develop a deeper understanding of the capabilities of qualitative simulation and of the kinds of information external evidence must provide.

ACKNOWLEDGMENTS

We would like to thank Allan Collins and Bob Lindsay for their tremendous help with this paper. Various discussions with Mike Williams and Kurt VanLehn clarified many of the ideas. We also wish to thank Jackie Keane for drawing the figures. Rachel Rutherford and Eric Larson helped edit early drafts.

[17]In an earlier paper (Brown, Collins, & Harris, 1978) we explored the notion of augmenting device-recognition schemata with explicit information about the consequences of generic faults in the component models or plan fragments. The work reported on in this paper, grew, in part, out of our realization of the inherent brittleness of understanding devices and faults with such recognition schemes, although for a fixed class of devices that recognition scheme has its merits.

REFERENCES

Brown, J. S., Collins, A., & Harris, G. Artificial intelligence and learning strategies. In H. O'Neil (Ed.), *Learning strategies.* N.Y.: Academic Press, 1978.

Brown, J. S., Burton, R. R., & de Kleer, J. Pedagogical, natural language and knowledge engineering techniques in SOPHIE I, II, and III. In S. Derek & J. S. Brown (Eds.), *Intelligent tutoring systems,* N.Y.: Academic Press, 1982.

de Kleer, J. Causal and teleological reasoning in circuit recognition. *Artificial Intelligence Laboratory,* Technical Report-529, Cambridge, Mass.: M.I.T., 1979.

de Kleer, J., & Brown, J. S. Mental models of physical mechanisms and their acquisition. In J. R. Anderson (Ed.), *Cognitive skills and their acquisition.* Hillsdale, N.J.: Lawrence Erlbaum Associates, 1981.

Nagel, L. W., & Pederson, D. O. Simulation program with integrated circuit emphasis. *Proc. of the 16th Midwest Symposium Circuit Theory,* Waterloo, Canada, April 1973.

Rieger, C., & Grinberg, M. The declarative representation and procedural simulation of causality in physical mechanisms. *Proc. of the Fifth International Joint Conference on Artificial Intelligence,* 1977, 250–255.

Rieger, C., & Grinberg, M. A system for cause-effect representation and simulation in computer aided design. *Proc. of the IFIP Working Conference on Artificial Intelligence and Pattern Recognition in Computer-Aided Design.* North Holland, 1978.

Stevens, A. L., & Collins, A. Multiple conceptual models of a complex system. In R. Snow, P. Federico, & W. Montague (Eds.), *Aptitude, learning and instruction, Vol. 2,* Hillsdale, N.J.: Lawrence Erlbaum Associates, 1980.

Williams, M., Hollan, J., & Stevens, A. An overview of STEAMER: An advanced computer assisted instructional system for propulsion engineering. *Behavior Research Methods and Instrumentation,* 1981, *13*(2), 85–90.

Chapter 3

Categorization

Similarity and Analogy

Categories are our main way of dividing the world into manageable units—units such as *dog, tulip, chair, boat, lightbulb,* and so on. In the classical view, categorization was thought to be based on defining features. That is, we determined that an object was a member of a category by ensuring that it contained some critical feature(s) common to all members of the category. This classical view of categories has largely been replaced by a view that emphasizes similarity: An object is a member of a category if it is sufficiently similar to known members of the category, or to a prototype of the category (see Smith, E. E. & Medin, D. L. (1981). *Categories and Concepts*. Harvard University Press).

The Tversky paper provides detailed support for the idea that categorizing an object amounts to determining its similarity to other members of the category. Tversky uses axiomatic considerations about similarity to derive a rule that states that the similarity of any two objects increases with the number of features the two objects have in common, and decreases with the number of features that are distinct to either object. He then uses this similarity rule to predict how readily various objects can be categorized.

Gentner's paper extends the notion of similarity to construct a structure-mapping, theory of analogy. Gentner focuses on *structural* similarity, rather than on *literal* similarity. She argues that the strength of an analogical match does not depend on the overall degree of featural overlap. Rather, only certain features matter for analogical similarity: Those that specify relations into which the object enters, as opposed to those that specify simple properties of the object. Gentner uses these ideas about analogical similarity to provide interpretation rules for analogy.

Features of Similarity

Amos Tversky
Hebrew University
Jerusalem, Israel

The metric and dimensional assumptions that underlie the geometric representation of similarity are questioned on both theoretical and empirical grounds. A new set-theoretical approach to similarity is developed in which objects are represented as collections of features, and similarity is described as a feature-matching process. Specifically, a set of qualitative assumptions is shown to imply the contrast model, which expresses the similarity between objects as a linear combination of the measures of their common and distinctive features. Several predictions of the contrast model are tested in studies of similarity with both semantic and perceptual stimuli. The model is used to uncover, analyze, and explain a variety of empirical phenomena such as the role of common and distinctive features, the relations between judgments of similarity and difference, the presence of asymmetric similarities, and the effects of context on judgments of similarity. The contrast model generalizes standard representations of similarity data in terms of clusters and trees. It is also used to analyze the relations of prototypicality and family resemblance.

Similarity plays a fundamental role in theories of knowledge and behavior. It serves as an organizing principle by which individuals classify objects, form concepts, and make generalizations. Indeed, the concept of similarity is ubiquitous in psychological theory. It underlies the accounts of stimulus and response generalization in learning, it is employed to explain errors in memory and pattern recognition, and it is central to the analysis of connotative meaning.

Similarity or dissimilarity data appear in different forms: ratings of pairs, sorting of objects, communality between associations,

This paper benefited from fruitful discussions with Y. Cohen, I. Gati, D. Kahneman, L. Sjöberg, and S. Sattath.

Requests for reprints should be sent to Amos Tversky, Department of Psychology, Hebrew University, Jerusalem, Israel.

errors of substitution, and correlation between occurrences. Analyses of these data attempt to explain the observed similarity relations and to capture the underlying structure of the objects under study.

The theoretical analysis of similarity relations has been dominated by geometric models. These models represent objects as points in some coordinate space such that the observed dissimilarities between objects correspond to the metric distances between the respective points. Practically all analyses of proximity data have been metric in nature, although some (e.g., hierarchical clustering) yield tree-like structures rather than dimensionally organized spaces. However, most theoretical and empirical analyses of similarity assume that objects can be adequately represented as points in some coordinate space and that dissimilarity behaves like a metric dis-tance function. Both dimensional and metric assumptions are open to question.

It has been argued by many authors that dimensional representations are appropriate for certain stimuli (e.g., colors, tones) but not for others. It seems more appropriate to represent faces, countries, or personalities in terms of many qualitative features than in terms of a few quantitative dimensions. The assessment of similarity between such stimuli, therefore, may be better described as a comparison of features rather than as the computation of metric distance between points.

A metric distance function, δ, is a scale that assigns to every pair of points a nonnegative number, called their distance, in accord with the following three axioms:

Minimality:

$$\delta(a,b) \geq \delta(a,a) = 0.$$

Symmetry:

$$\delta(a,b) = \delta(b,a).$$

The triangle inequality:

$$\delta(a,b) + \delta(b,c) \geq \delta(a,c).$$

To evaluate the adequacy of the geometric approach, let us examine the validity of the metric axioms when δ is regarded as a measure of dissimilarity. The minimality axiom implies that the similarity between an object and itself is the same for all objects. This assumption, however, does not hold for some similarity measures. For example, the probability of judging two identical stimuli as "same" rather than "different" is not constant for all stimuli. Moreover, in recognition experiments the off-diagonal entries often exceed the diagonal entries; that is, an object is identified as another object more frequently than it is identified as itself. If identification probability is interpreted as a measure of similarity, then these observations violate minimality and are, therefore, incompatible with the distance model.

Similarity has been viewed by both philosophers and psychologists as a prime example of a symmetric relation. Indeed, the assumption of symmetry underlies essentially all theoretical treatments of similarity. Contrary to this tradition, the present paper provides empirical evidence for asymmetric similarities and argues that similarity should not be treated as a symmetric relation.

Similarity judgments can be regarded as extensions of similarity statements, that is, statements of the form "a is like b." Such a statement is directional; it has a subject, a, and a referent, b, and it is not equivalent in general to the converse similarity statement "b is like a." In fact, the choice of subject and referent depends, at least in part, on the relative salience of the objects. We tend to select the more salient stimulus, or the prototype, as a referent, and the less salient stimulus, or the variant, as a subject. We say "the portrait resembles the person" rather than "the person resembles the portrait." We say "the son resembles the father" rather than "the father resembles the son." We say "an ellipse is like a circle," not "a circle is like an ellipse," and we say "North Korea is like Red China," rather than "Red China is like North Korea."

As will be demonstrated later, this asymmetry in the choice of similarity statements is associated with asymmetry in judgments of similarity. Thus, the judged similarity of North Korea to Red China exceeds the judged similarity of Red China to North Korea. Likewise, an ellipse is more similar to a circle than a circle is to an ellipse. Apparently, the direction of asymmetry is determined by the relative salience of the stimuli; the variant is more similar to the prototype than vice versa.

The directionality and asymmetry of similarity relations are particularly noticeable in similies and metaphors. We say "Turks fight like tigers" and not "tigers fight like Turks." Since the tiger is renowned for its fighting spirit, it is used as the referent rather than the subject of the simile. The poet writes "my love is as deep as the ocean," not "the ocean is as deep as my love," because the ocean epitomizes depth. Sometimes both directions are used but they carry different meanings. "A man is like a tree" implies that man has roots; "a tree is like a man" implies that the tree has a life history. "Life is like a play" says that people play roles. "A play is like life" says that a play can capture the essential elements of human life. The relations between the interpretation of metaphors and the assessment of similarity are briefly discussed in the final section.

The triangle inequality differs from minimality and symmetry in that it cannot be formulated in ordinal terms. It asserts that one distance must be smaller than the sum of two others, and hence it cannot be readily refuted with ordinal or even interval data. However, the triangle inequality implies that if a is quite similar to b, and b is quite similar to c, then a and c cannot be very dissimilar from each other. Thus, it sets a lower limit to the similarity between a and c in terms of the similarities between a and b and between b and c. The following example (based on William James) casts some doubts on the psychological validity of this assumption. Consider the similarity between countries: Jamaica is similar to Cuba (because of geographical proximity); Cuba is similar to Russia (because of their political affinity); but Jamaica and Russia are not similar at all.

This example shows that similarity, as one might expect, is not transitive. In addition, it suggests that the perceived distance of Jamaica to Russia exceeds the perceived distance of Jamaica to Cuba, plus that of Cuba to Russia—contrary to the triangle inequality. Although such examples do not necessarily refute the triangle inequality, they indicate that it should not be accepted as a cornerstone of similarity models.

It should be noted that the metric axioms, by themselves, are very weak. They are satisfied, for example, by letting $\delta(a,b) = 0$ if $a = b$, and $\delta(a,b) = 1$ if $a \neq b$. To specify the distance function, additional assumptions are made (e.g., intradimensional subtractivity and interdimensional additivity) relating the dimensional structure of the objects to their metric distances. For an axiomatic analysis and a critical discussion of these assumptions, see Beals, Krantz, and Tversky (1968), Krantz and Tversky (1975), and Tversky and Krantz (1970).

In conclusion, it appears that despite many fruitful applications (see e.g., Carroll & Wish, 1974; Shepard, 1974), the geometric approach to the analysis of similarity faces several difficulties. The applicability of the dimensional assumption is limited, and the metric axioms are questionable. Specifically, minimal-ity is somewhat problematic, symmetry is apparently false, and the triangle inequality is hardly compelling.

The next section develops an alternative theoretical approach to similarity, based on feature matching, which is neither dimensional nor metric in nature. In subsequent sections this approach is used to uncover, analyze, and explain several empirical phenomena, such as the role of common and distinctive features, the relations between judgments of similarity and difference, the presence of asymmetric similarities, and the effects of context on similarity. Extensions and implications of the present development are discussed in the final section.

Feature Matching

Let $\Delta = \{a,b,c,\ldots\}$ be the domain of objects (or stimuli) under study. Assume that each object in Δ is represented by a set of features or attributes, and let A,B,C denote the sets of features associated with the objects a,b,c, respectively. The features may correspond to components such as eyes or mouth; they may represent concrete properties such as size or color; and they may reflect abstract attributes such as quality or complexity. The characterization of stimuli as feature sets has been employed in the analysis of many cognitive processes such as speech perception (Jakobson, Fant, & Halle, 1961), pattern recognition (Neisser, 1967), perceptual learning (Gibson, 1969), preferential choice (Tversky, 1972), and semantic judgment (Smith, Shoben, & Rips, 1974).

Two preliminary comments regarding feature representations are in order. First, it is important to note that our total data base concerning a particular object (e.g., a person, a country, or a piece of furniture) is generally rich in content and complex in form. It includes appearance, function, relation to other objects, and any other property of the object that can be deduced from our general knowledge of the world. When faced with a particular task (e.g., identification or similarity assessment) we extract and compile from our data base a limited list of relevant features on the basis of which we perform the required task. Thus, the representation of an object as a collection of features is viewed as a product of a prior process of extraction and compilation.

Second, the term *feature* usually denotes the value of a binary variable (e.g., voiced vs. voiceless consonants) or the value of a nominal variable (e.g., eye color). Feature representations, however, are not restricted to binary or nominal variables; they are also applicable to ordinal or cardinal variables (i.e., dimensions). A series of tones that differ only in loudness, for example, could be represented as a sequence of nested sets where the feature set associated with each tone is included in the feature sets associated with louder tones. Such a representation is isomorphic to a directional unidimensional structure. A nondirectional unidimensional structure (e.g., a series of tones that differ only in pitch) could be represented by a chain of overlapping sets. The set-theoretical representation of qualitative and quantitative dimensions has been investigated by Restle (1959).

Let $s(a,b)$ be a measure of the similarity of a to b defined for all distinct a, b in Δ. The scale s is treated as an ordinal measure of similarity. That is, $s(a,b) > s(c,d)$ means that a is more similar to b than c is to d. The present theory is based on the following assumptions.

1. *Matching:*

$$s(a,b) = F(A \cap B, A - B, B - A).$$

The similarity of a to b is expressed as a function F of three arguments: $A \cap B$, the features that are common to both a and b; $A - B$, the features that belong to a but not to b; $B - A$, the features that belong to b but not to a. A schematic illustration of these components is presented in Figure 1.

2. *Monotonicity:*

$$s(a,b) \geq s(a,c)$$

whenever

$$A \cap B \supset A \cap C, \quad A - B \subset A - C,$$

and

$$B - A \subset C - A.$$

Moreover, the inequality is strict whenever either inclusion is proper.

That is, similarity increases with addition of common features and/or deletion of distinctive features (i.e., features that belong to one object but not to the other). The monotonicity axiom can be readily illustrated with block letters if we identify their features with the component (straight) lines. Under this assumption, E should be more similar to F than to I because E and F have more common features than E and I. Furthermore, I should be more similar to F than to E because I and F have fewer distinctive features than I and E.

Any function F satisfying Assumptions 1 and 2 is called a *matching function*. It measures the degree to which two objects—viewed as sets of features—match each other. In the present theory, the assessment of similarity is described as a feature-matching process. It is formulated, therefore, in terms of the set-theoretical notion of a matching function rather than in terms of the geometric concept of distance.

In order to determine the functional form of the matching function, additional assumptions about the similarity ordering are introduced. The major assumption of the theory (independence) is presented next; the remaining assumptions and the proof of the representation theorem are presented in the Appendix. Readers who are less interested in formal theory can skim or skip the discussion of the representation theorem.

Let Φ denote the set of all features associated with the objects of Δ, and let X,Y,Z,...etc. denote collections of features (i.e., subsets of Φ). The expression $F(X,Y,Z)$ is defined whenever there exists a, b in Δ such that $A \cap B = X$,

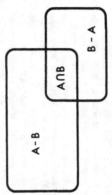

Figure 1. A graphical illustration of the relation between two feature sets.

$A - B = Y$, and $B - A = Z$, whence $s(a,b) = F(A \cap B, A - B, B - A) = F(X,Y,Z)$. Next, define $V \simeq W$ if one or more of the following hold for some X,Y,Z: $F(V,Y,Z) = F(W,Y,Z)$, $F(X,V,Z) = F(X,W,Z)$, $F(X,Y,V) = F(X,Y,W)$.

The pairs (a,b) and (c,d) are said to *agree* on one, two, or three components, respectively, whenever one, two, or three of the following hold: $(A \cap B) \simeq (C \cap D)$, $(A - B) \simeq (C - D)$, $(B - A) \simeq (D - C)$.

3. Independence: Suppose the pairs (a,b) and (c,d), as well as the pairs (a',b') and (c',d'), agree on the same two components, while the pairs (a,b) and (a',b'), as well as the pairs (c,d) and (c',d'), agree on the remaining (third) component. Then

$$s(a,b) \geq s(a',b') \text{ iff } s(c,d) \geq s(c',d').$$

To illustrate the force of the independence axiom consider the stimuli presented in Figure 2, where

$A \cap B = C \cap D$ = round profile = X,
$A' \cap B' = C' \cap D'$ = sharp profile = X',
$A - B = C - D$ = smiling mouth = Y,
$A' - B' = C' - D'$ = frowning mouth = Y',
$B - A = B' - A'$ = straight eyebrow = Z,
$D - C = D' - C'$ = curved eyebrow = Z'.

By independence, therefore,

$s(a,b) = F(A \cap B, A - B, B - A)$
$= F(X,Y,Z) \geq F(X',Y,Z)$
$= F(A' \cap B', A' - B', B' - A')$
$= s(a',b')$

if and only if

$s(c,d) = F(C \cap D, C - D, D - C)$
$= F(X,Y,Z') \geq F(X',Y,Z')$
$= F(C' \cap D', C' - D', D' - C')$
$= s(c',d')$.

Thus, the ordering of any two components (e.g., X,Y vs. X',Y') is independent of the fixed level of the third factor (e.g., Z or Z').

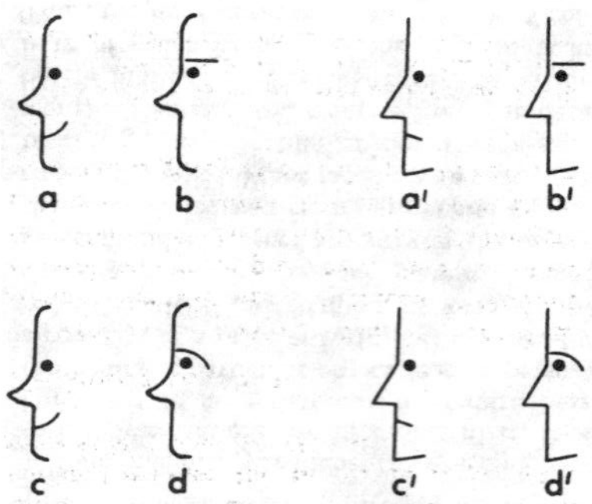

Figure 2. An illustration of independence.

It should be emphasized that any test of the axioms presupposes an interpretation of the features. The independence axiom, for example, may hold in one interpretation and fail in another. Experimental tests of the axioms, therefore, test jointly the adequacy of the interpretation of the features and the empirical validity of the assumptions. Furthermore, the above examples should not be taken to mean that stimuli (e.g., block letters, schematic faces) can be properly characterized in terms of their components. To achieve an adequate feature representation of visual forms, more global properties (e.g., symmetry, connectedness) should also be introduced. For an interesting discussion of this problem, in the best tradition of Gestalt psychology, see Goldmeier (1972; originally published in 1936).

In addition to matching (1), monotonicity (2), and independence (3), we also assume solvability (4), and invariance (5). Solvability requires that the feature space under study be sufficiently rich that certain (similarity) equations can be solved. Invariance ensures that the equivalence of intervals is preserved across factors. A rigorous formulation of these assumptions is given in the Appendix, along with a proof of the following result.

Representation theorem. Suppose Assumptions 1, 2, 3, 4, and 5 hold. Then there exist a similarity scale S and a nonnegative scale f such that for all a,b,c,d in Δ,

(i) $S(a,b) \geq S(c,d)$ iff $s(a,b) \geq s(c,d)$;

(ii) $S(a,b) = \theta f(A \cap B) - \alpha f(A - B) - \beta f(B - A)$, for some $\theta, \alpha, \beta \geq 0$;

(iii) f and S are interval scales.

The theorem shows that under Assumptions 1–5, there exists an interval similarity scale S that preserves the observed similarity order and expresses similarity as a linear combination, or a contrast, of the measures of the common and the distinctive features. Hence, the representation is called the *contrast model.* In parts of the following development we also assume that f satisfies feature additivity. That is, $f(X \cup Y) = f(X) + f(Y)$ whenever X and Y are disjoint, and all three terms are defined[1].

Note that the contrast model does not define a single similarity scale, but rather a family of scales characterized by different values of the parameters θ, α, and β. For example, if $\theta = 1$ and α and β vanish, then $S(a,b) = f(A \cap B)$; that is, the similarity between objects is the measure of their common features. If, on the other hand, $\alpha = \beta = 1$ and θ vanishes then $-S(a,b) = f(A - B) + f(B - A)$; that is, the dissimilarity between objects is the measure of the symmetric difference between the respective feature sets. Restle (1961) has proposed these forms as models of similarity and psychological distance, respectively. Note that in the former model ($\theta = 1$, $\alpha = \beta = 0$), similarity between objects is determined only by their common features, whereas in the latter model ($\theta = 0$, $\alpha = \beta = 1$), it is determined by their distinctive features only. The contrast model expresses similarity between objects as a weighted difference of the measures of their common and distinctive features, thereby allowing for a variety of similarity relations over the same domain.

The major constructs of the present theory are the contrast rule for the assessment of similarity, and the scale f, which reflects the salience or prominence of the various features. Thus, f measures the contribution of any particular (common or distinctive) feature to the similarity between objects. The scale value $f(A)$ associated with stimulus a is regarded, therefore, as a measure of the overall salience of that stimulus. The factors that contribute to the salience of a stimulus include intensity, frequency, familiarity, good form, and infor-

national content. The manner in which the scale f and the parameters (θ, α, β) depend on the context and the task are discussed in the following sections.

Let us recapitulate what is assumed and what is proven in the representation theorem. We begin with a set of objects, described as collections of features, and a similarity ordering which is assumed to satisfy the axioms of the present theory. From these assumptions, we derive a measure f on the feature space and prove that the similarity ordering of object pairs coincides with the ordering of their contrasts, defined as linear combinations of the respective common and distinctive features. Thus, the measure f and the contrast model are derived from qualitative axioms regarding the similarity of objects.

The nature of this result may be illuminated by an analogy to the classical theory of decision under risk (von Neumann & Morgenstern, 1947). In that theory, one starts with a set of prospects, characterized as probability distributions over some consequence space, and a preference order is assumed to satisfy the axioms of the theory. From these assumptions one derives a utility scale on the consequence space and proves that the preference order between prospects coincides with the order of their expected utilities. Thus, the utility scale and the expectation principle are derived from qualitative assumptions about preferences. The present theory of similarity differs from the expected-utility model in that the characterization of objects as feature sets is perhaps more problematic than the characterization of uncertain options as probability distributions. Furthermore, the axioms of utility theory are proposed as (normative) principles of rational behavior, whereas the axioms of the present theory are intended to be descriptive rather than prescriptive.

The contrast model is perhaps the simplest form of a matching function, yet it is not the only form worthy of investigation. Another

---

[1] To derive feature additivity from qualitative assumptions, we must assume the axioms of an extensive structure and the compatibility of the extensive and the conjoint scales; see Krantz et al. (1971, Section 10.7).

matching function of interest is the *ratio model*,

$$S(a,b) = \frac{f(A \cap B)}{f(A \cap B) + \alpha f(A-B) + \beta f(B-A)}, \quad \alpha, \beta \geq 0,$$

where similarity is normalized so that S lies between 0 and 1. The ratio model generalizes several set-theoretical models of similarity proposed in the literature. If $\alpha = \beta = 1$, $S(a,b)$ reduces to $f(A \cap B)/f(A \cup B)$ (see Gregson, 1975, and Sjöberg, 1972). If $\alpha = \beta = \frac{1}{2}$, $S(a,b)$ equals $2f(A \cap B)/(f(A) + f(B))$ (see Eisler & Ekman, 1959). If $\alpha = 1$ and $\beta = 0$, $S(a,b)$ reduces to $f(A \cap B)/f(A)$ (see Bush & Mosteller, 1951). The present framework, therefore, encompasses a wide variety of similarity models that differ in the form of the matching function F and in the weights assigned to its arguments.

In order to apply and test the present theory in any particular domain, some assumptions about the respective feature structure must be made. If the features associated with each object are explicitly specified, we can test the axioms of the theory directly and scale the features according to the contrast model. This approach, however, is generally limited to stimuli (e.g., schematic faces, letters, strings of symbols) that are constructed from a fixed feature set. If the features associated with the objects under study cannot be readily specified, as is often the case with natural stimuli, we can still test several predictions of the contrast model which involve only general qualitative assumptions about the feature structure of the objects. Both approaches were employed in a series of experiments conducted by Itamar Gati and the present author. The following three sections review and discuss our main findings, focusing primarily on the test of qualitative predictions. A more detailed description of the stimuli and the data are presented in Tversky and Gati (in press).

Asymmetry and Focus

According to the present analysis, similarity is not necessarily a symmetric relation. Indeed, it follows readily (from either the contrast or the ratio model) that

$$s(a,b) = s(b,a) \text{ iff } \alpha f(A-B) + \beta f(B-A)$$
$$= \alpha f(B-A) + \beta f(A-B)$$
$$\text{iff } (\alpha - \beta)f(A-B) = (\alpha - \beta)f(B-A).$$

Hence, $s(a,b) = s(b,a)$ if either $\alpha = \beta$, or $f(A-B) = f(B-A)$, which implies $f(A) = f(B)$, provided feature additivity holds. Thus, symmetry holds whenever the objects are equal in measure ($f(A) = f(B)$) or the task is nondirectional ($\alpha = \beta$). To interpret the latter condition, compare the following two forms:

(i). Assess the degree to which a and b are similar to each other.
(ii). Assess the degree to which a is similar to b.

In (i), the task is formulated in a nondirectional fashion; hence it is expected that $\alpha = \beta$ and $s(a,b) = s(b,a)$. In (ii), on the other hand, the task is directional, and hence α and β may differ and symmetry need not hold.

If $s(a,b)$ is interpreted as the degree to which a is similar to b, then a is the subject of the comparison and b is the referent. In such a task, one naturally focuses on the subject of the comparison. Hence, the features of the subject are weighted more heavily than the features of the referent (i.e., $\alpha > \beta$). Consequently, similarity is reduced more by the distinctive features of the subject than by the distinctive features of the referent. It follows readily that whenever $\alpha > \beta$,

$$s(a,b) > s(b,a) \text{ iff } f(B) > f(A).$$

Thus, the focusing hypothesis (i.e., $\alpha > \beta$) implies that the direction of asymmetry is determined by the relative salience of the stimuli so that the less salient stimulus is more similar to the salient stimulus than vice versa. In particular, the variant is more similar to the prototype than the prototype is to the variant, because the prototype is generally more salient than the variant.

Similarity of Countries

Twenty-one pairs of countries served as stimuli. The pairs were constructed so that one element was more prominent than the other element (e.g., Red China–North Vietnam, USA–Mexico, Belgium–Luxemburg). To verify this relation, we asked a group of 69 subjects[1] to select in each pair the country they regarded as more prominent. The proportion of subjects that agreed with the a priori ordering exceeded ⅔ for all pairs except one. A second group of 69 subjects was asked to choose which of two phrases they preferred to use: "country a is similar to country b," or "country b is similar to country a." In all 21 cases, most of the subjects chose the phrase in which the less prominent country served as the subject and the more prominent country as the referent. For example, 66 subjects selected the phrase "North Korea is similar to Red China" and only 3 selected the phrase "Red China is similar to North Korea." These results demonstrate the presence of marked asymmetries in the choice of similarity statements, whose direction coincides with the relative prominence of the stimuli.

To test for asymmetry in direct judgments of similarity, we presented two groups of 77 subjects each with the same list of 21 pairs of countries and asked subjects to rate their similarity on a 20-point scale. The only difference between the two groups was the order of the countries within each pair. For example, one group was asked to assess "the degree to which the USSR is similar to Poland," whereas the second group was asked to assess "the degree to which Poland is similar to the USSR." The lists were constructed so that the more prominent country appeared about an equal number of times in the first and second positions.

For any pair (p,q) of stimuli, let p denote the more prominent element, and let q denote the less prominent element. The average $s(q,p)$ was significantly higher than the average $s(p,q)$ across all subjects and pairs: t test for correlated samples yielded $t(20) = 2.92$, $p < .01$. To obtain a statistical test based on individual data, we computed for each subject a directional asymmetry score defined as the average similarity for comparisons with a prominent referent, that is, $s(q,p)$, minus the average similarity for comparisons with a prominent subject, $s(p,q)$. The average difference was significantly positive: $t(153) = 2.99$, $p < .01$.

The above study was repeated using judgments of difference instead of judgments of similarity. Two groups of 23 subjects each participated in this study. They received the same list of 21 pairs except that one group was asked to judge the degree to which country a differed from country b, denoted $d(a,b)$, whereas the second group was asked to judge the degree to which country b was different from country a, denoted $d(b,a)$. If judgments of difference follow the contrast model, and $\alpha > \beta$, then we expect the prominent stimulus p to differ from the less prominent stimulus q more than q differs from p; that is, $d(p,q) > d(q,p)$. This hypothesis was tested using the same set of 21 pairs of countries and the prominence ordering established earlier. The average $d(p,q)$, across all subjects and pairs, was significantly higher than the average $d(q,p)$: t test for correlated samples yielded $t(20) = 2.72$, $p < .01$. Furthermore, the average asymmetry score, computed as above for each subject, was significantly positive, $t(45) = 2.24$, $p < .05$.

Similarity of Figures

A major determinant of the salience of geometric figures is goodness of form. Thus, a "good figure" is likely to be more salient than a "bad figure," although the latter is generally more complex. However, when two figures are roughly equivalent with respect to goodness of form, the more complex figure is likely to be more salient. To investigate these hypotheses and to test the asymmetry prediction, two sets of eight pairs of geometric figures were constructed. In the first set, one figure in each pair (denoted p) had better form than the other (denoted q). In the second set, the two figures in each pair were roughly matched in goodness of form, but one figure (denoted p) was richer or more complex than the other (denoted q). Examples of pairs of figures from each set are presented in Figure 3.

A group of 69 subjects was presented with the entire list of 16 pairs of figures, where the two elements of each pair were displayed side by side. For each pair, the subjects were asked to indicate which of the following two statements they preferred to use: "The left figure is similar to the right figure," or "The right figure is similar to the left figure." The positions of the stimuli were randomized so that p and q appeared an equal number of times on the

---

[1] The subjects in all our experiments were Israeli college students, ages 18–28. The material was presented in booklets and administered in a group setting.

left and on the right. The results showed that in each one of the pairs, most of the subjects selected the form "q is similar to p." Thus, the more salient stimulus was generally chosen as the referent rather than the subject of similarity statements.

To test for asymmetry in judgments of similarity, we presented two groups of 67 subjects each with the same 16 pairs of figures and asked the subjects to rate (on a 20-point scale) the degree to which the figure on the left was similar to the figure on the right. The two groups received identical booklets, except that the left and right positions of the figures in each pair were reversed. The results showed that the average $s(q,p)$ across all subjects and pairs was significantly higher than the average $s(p,q)$. A t test for correlated samples yielded $t(15) = 2.94$, $p < .01$. Furthermore, in both sets the average asymmetry scores, computed as above for each subject, were significantly positive: In the first set $t(131) = 2.96$, $p < .01$, and in the second set $t(131) = 2.79$, $p < .01$.

Similarity of Letters

A common measure of similarity between stimuli is the probability of confusing them in a recognition or an identification task: The more similar the stimuli, the more likely they are to be confused. While confusion probabilities are often asymmetric (i.e., the probability of confusing a with b is different from the probability of confusing b with a), this effect is typically attributed to a response bias. To eliminate this interpretation of asymmetry, one could employ an experimental task where the subject merely indicates whether the two stimuli presented to him (sequentially or simultaneously) are identical or not. This procedure was employed by Yoav Cohen and the present author in a study of confusion among block letters.

The following eight block letters served as stimuli: Γ, C, Π, □, F, E, F, B. All pairs of letters were displayed on a cathode-ray tube, side by side, on a noisy background. The letters were presented sequentially, each for approximately 1 msec. The right letter always followed the left letter with an interval of 630 msec. in between. After each presentation the subject pressed one of two keys to indicate whether the two letters were identical or not.

Figure 3. Examples of pairs of figures used to test the prediction of asymmetry. The top two figures are examples of a pair (from the first set) that differs in goodness of form. The bottom two are examples of a pair (from the second set) that differs in complexity.

A total of 32 subjects participated in the experiment. Each subject was tested individually. On each trial, one letter (known in advance) served as the standard. For one half of the subjects the standard stimulus always appeared on the left, and for the other half of the subjects the standard always appeared on the right. Each one of the eight letters served as a standard. The trials were blocked into groups of 10 pairs in which the standard was paired once with each of the other letters and three times with itself. Since each letter served as a standard in one block, the entire design consisted of eight blocks of 10 trials each. Every subject was presented with three replications of the entire design (i.e., 240 trials). The order of the blocks in each design and the order of the letters within each block were randomized.

According to the present analysis, people compare the variable stimulus, which serves the role of the subject, to the standard, which serves the referent. The choice of standard, therefore, determines the directionality of the comparison. A natural partial ordering of the letters with respect to prominence is induced by the relation of inclusion among letters. Thus, one letter is assumed to have a larger measure than another if the former includes the latter. For example, E includes F and Γ but not □. For all 19 pairs in which one letter includes the other, let p denote the more prominent letter and q denote the less promi-

nent letter. Furthermore, let $s(a,b)$ denote the percentage of times that the subject judged the variable stimulus a to be the same as the standard b.

It follows from the contrast model, with $\alpha > \beta$, that the proportion of "same" responses should be larger when the variable is included in the standard than when the standard is included in the variable, that is, $s(q,p) > s(p,q)$. This prediction was borne out by the data. The average $s(q,p)$ across all subjects and trials was 17.1%, whereas the average $s(p,q)$ across all subjects and trials was 12.4%. To obtain a statistical test, we computed for each subject the difference between $s(q,p)$ and $s(p,q)$ across all trials. The difference was significantly positive, $t(31) = 4.41$, $p < .001$. These results demonstrate that the prediction of directional asymmetry derived from the contrast model applies to confusion data and not merely to rated similarity.

Similarity of Signals

Rothkopf (1957) presented 598 subjects with all ordered pairs of the 36 Morse Code signals and asked them to indicate whether the two signals in each pair were the same or not. The pairs were presented in a randomized order without a fixed standard. Each subject judged about one fourth of all pairs.

Let $s(a,b)$ denote the percentage of "same" responses to the ordered pair (a,b), i.e., the percentage of subjects that judged the first signal a to be the same as the second signal b. Note that a and b refer here to the first and second signal, and not to the variable and the standard as in the previous section. Obviously, Morse Code signals are partially ordered according to temporal length. For any pair of signals that differ in temporal length, let p and q denote, respectively, the longer and shorter element of the pair.

From the total of 555 comparisons between signals of different length, reported in Rothkopf (1957), $s(q,p)$ exceeds $s(p,q)$ in 336 cases, $s(p,q)$ exceeds $s(q,p)$ in 181 cases, and $s(q,p)$ equals $s(p,q)$ in 38 cases, by sign test. The average difference between $s(q,p)$ and $s(p,q)$ across all pairs is 3.3%, which is also highly significant. A t test for correlated samples yields $t(554) = 9.17$, $p < .001$.

The asymmetry effect is enhanced when we consider only those comparisons in which one signal is a proper subsequence of the other. (For example, ·· is a subsequence of ··· as well as of ---). From a total of 195 comparisons of this type, $s(q,p)$ exceeds $s(p,q)$ in 128 cases, $s(p,q)$ exceeds $s(q,p)$ in 55 cases, and $s(q,p)$ equals $s(p,q)$ in 12 cases, $p < .001$ by sign test. The average difference between $s(q,p)$ and $s(p,q)$ in this case is 4.7%, $t(194) = 7.58$, $p < .001$.

A later study following the same experimental paradigm with somewhat different signals was conducted by Wish (1967). His signals consisted of three tones separated by two silent intervals, where each component (i.e., a tone or a silence) was either short or long. Subjects were presented with all pairs of 32 signals generated in this fashion and judged whether the two members of each pair were the same or not.

The above analysis is readily applicable to Wish's (1967) data. From a total of 386 comparisons between signals of different length, $s(q,p)$ exceeds $s(p,q)$ in 241 cases, $s(p,q)$ exceeds $s(q,p)$ in 117 cases, and $s(q,p)$ equals $s(p,q)$ in 28 cases. These data are clearly asymmetric, $p < .001$ by sign test. The average difference between $s(q,p)$ and $s(p,q)$ is 5.9%, which is also highly significant, $t(385) = 9.23$, $p < .001$.

In the studies of Rothkopf and Wish there is no a priori way to determine the directionality of the comparison, or equivalently to identify the subject and the referent. However, if we accept the focusing hypothesis ($\alpha > \beta$) and the assumption that longer signals are more prominent than shorter ones, then the direction of the observed asymmetry indicates that the first signal serves as the subject that is compared with the second signal that serves the role of the referent. Hence, the directionality of the comparison is determined, according to the present analysis, from the prominence ordering of the stimuli and the observed direction of asymmetry.

Rosch's Data

Rosch (1973, 1975) has articulated and supported the view that perceptual and semantic categories are naturally formed and defined in terms of focal points, or prototypes. Because of the special role of prototypes in the formation of categories, she hypothesized that (i) in sentence frames involving hedges such as "a is essentially b," focal stimuli (i.e., prototypes) appear in the second position; and (ii) the perceived distance from the prototype to the variant is greater than the perceived distance from the variant to the prototype. To test these hypotheses, Rosch (1975) used three stimulus domains: color, line orientation, and number. Prototypical colors were focal (e.g., pure red), while the variants were either nonfocal (e.g., off-red) or less saturated. Vertical, horizontal, and diagonal lines served as prototypes for line orientation, and lines of other angles served as variants. Multiples of 10 (e.g., 10, 50, 100) were taken as prototypical numbers, and other numbers (e.g., 11, 52, 103) were treated as variants.

Hypothesis (i) was strongly confirmed in all three domains. When presented with sentence frames such as "— is virtually —," subjects generally placed the prototype in the second blank and the variant in the first. For instance, subjects preferred the sentence "103 is virtually 100" to the sentence "100 is virtually 103." To test hypothesis (ii), one stimulus (the standard) was placed at the origin of a semicircular board, and the subject was instructed to place the second (variable) stimulus on the board so as "to represent his feeling of the distance between that stimulus and the one fixed at the origin." As hypothesized, the measured distance between stimuli was significantly smaller when the prototype, rather than the variant, was fixed at the origin, in each of the three domains.

If focal stimuli are more salient than nonfocal stimuli, then Rosch's findings support the present analysis. The hedging sentences (e.g., "a is roughly b") can be regarded as a particular type of similarity statements. Indeed, the hedges data are in perfect agreement with the choice of similarity statements. Furthermore, the observed asymmetry in distance placement follows from the present analysis of asymmetry and the natural assumptions that the standard and the variable serve, respectively, as referent and subject in the distance-placement task. Thus, the placement of b at distance t from a is interpreted as saying that the (perceived) distance from b to a equals t. Rosch (1975) attributed the observed asymmetry to the special role of distinct prototypes (e.g., a perfect square or a pure red) in the processing of information. In the present theory, on the other hand, asymmetry is explained by the relative salience of the stimuli. Consequently, it implies asymmetry for pairs that do not include the prototype (e.g., two levels of distortion of the same form). If the concept of prototypicality, however, is interpreted in a relative sense (i.e., a is more prototypical than b) rather than in an absolute sense, then the two interpretations of asymmetry practically coincide.

Discussion

The conjunction of the contrast model and the focusing hypothesis implies the presence of asymmetric similarities. This prediction was confirmed in several experiments of perceptual and conceptual similarity using both judgmental and behavioral methods (e.g., rating) and behavioral methods (e.g., choice).

The asymmetries discussed in the previous section were observed in *comparative* tasks in which the subject compares two given stimuli to determine their similarity. Asymmetries were also observed in *production* tasks in which the subject is given a single stimulus and asked to produce the most similar response. Studies of pattern recognition, stimulus identification, and word association are all examples of production tasks. A common pattern observed in such studies is that the more salient object occurs more often as a response to the less salient object than vice versa. For example, "tiger" is a more likely associate to "leopard" than "leopard" is to "tiger." Similarly, Garner (1974) instructed subjects to select from a given set of dot patterns one that is similar—but not identical—to a given pattern. His results show that "good" patterns are usually chosen as responses to "bad" patterns and not conversely.

This asymmetry in production tasks has commonly been attributed to the differential availability of responses. Thus, "tiger" is a more likely associate to "leopard" than vice versa, because "tiger" is more common and hence a more available response than "leopard." This account is probably more applicable to situations where the subject must actually produce the response (as in word association or pattern recognition) than to situations where the subject merely selects a response from some specified set (as in Garner's task).

Without questioning the importance of response availability, the present theory suggests another reason for the asymmetry observed in production tasks. Consider the following translation of a production task to a question-and-answer scheme. Question: What is a like? Answer: a is like b. If this interpretation is valid and the given object a serves as a subject rather than as a referent, then the observed asymmetry of production follows from the present theoretical analysis, since $s(a,b) > s(b,a)$ whenever $f(B) > f(A)$.

In summary, it appears that proximity data from both comparative and production tasks reveal significant and systematic asymmetries whose direction is determined by the relative salience of the stimuli. Nevertheless, the symmetry assumption should not be rejected altogether. It seems to hold in many contexts, and it serves as a useful approximation in many others. It cannot be accepted, however, as a universal principle of psychological similarity.

Common and Distinctive Features

In the present theory, the similarity of objects is expressed as a linear combination, or a contrast, of the measures of their common and distinctive features. This section investigates the relative impact of these components and their effect on the relation between the assessments of similarity and difference. The discussion concerns only symmetric tasks, where $\alpha = \beta$, and hence $s(a,b) = s(b,a)$.

Elicitation of Features

The first study employs the contrast model to predict the similarity between objects from features that were produced by the subjects. The following 12 vehicles served as stimuli: bus, car, truck, motorcycle, train, airplane, bicycle, boat, elevator, cart, raft, sled. One group of 48 subjects rated the similarity between all 66 pairs of vehicles on a scale from 1 (no similarity) to 20 (maximal similarity). Following Rosch and Mervis (1975), we instructed a second group of 40 subjects to list the characteristic features of each one of the vehicles. Subjects were given 70 sec to list the features that characterized each vehicle. Different orders of presentation were used for different subjects.

The number of features per vehicle ranged from 71 for airplane to 21 for sled. Altogether, 324 features were listed by the subjects, of which 224 were unique and 100 were shared by two or more vehicles. For every pair of vehicles we counted the number of features that were attributed to both (by at least one subject), and the number of features that were attributed to one vehicle but not to the other. The frequency of subjects that listed each common or distinctive feature was computed.

In order to predict the similarity between vehicles from the listed features, the measures of their common and distinctive features must be defined. The simplest measure is obtained by counting the number of common and distinctive features produced by the subjects. The product-moment correlation between the (average) similarity of objects and the number of their common features was .68. The correlation between the similarity of objects and the number of their distinctive features was −.36. The multiple correlation between similarity and the numbers of common and distinctive features (i.e., the correlation between similarity and the contrast model) was .72.

The counting measure assigns equal weight to all features regardless of their frequency of mention. To take this factor into account, let X_a denote the proportion of subjects who attributed feature X to object a, and let N_X denote the number of objects that share feature X. For any a,b, define the measure of their common features by $f(A \cap B) = \Sigma X_a X_b / N_X$, where the summation is over all X in $A \cap B$, and the measure of their distinctive features by

$$f(A - B) + f(B - A) = \Sigma Y_a + \Sigma Z_b$$

where the summations range over all $Y \epsilon A - B$ and $Z \epsilon B - A$, that is, the distinctive features of a and b, respectively. The correlation between similarity and the above measure of the common features was .84; the correlation between similarity and the above measure of the distinctive features was −.64. The multiple correlation between similarity and the measures of the common and the distinctive features was .87.

Note that the above methods for defining the measure f were based solely on the elicited features and did not utilize the similarity data at all. Under these conditions, a perfect correlation between the two should not be expected because the weights associated with the features are not optimal for the prediction of similarity. A given feature may be frequently mentioned because it is easily labeled or recalled, although it does not have a great impact on similarity, and vice versa. Indeed, when the features were scaled using the additive tree procedure (Sattath & Tversky, in press) in which the measure of the features is derived from the similarities between the objects, the correlation between the data and the model reached .94.

The results of this study indicate that (i) it is possible to elicit from subjects detailed features of semantic stimuli such as vehicles (see Rosch & Mervis, 1975); (ii) the listed features can be used to predict similarity according to the contrast model with a reasonable degree of success; and (iii) the prediction of similarity is improved when frequency of mention and not merely the number of features is taken into account.

Similarity versus Difference

It has been generally assumed that judgments of similarity and difference are complementary; that is, judged difference is a linear function of judged similarity with a slope of −1. This hypothesis has been confirmed in several studies. For example, Hosman and Kuennapas (1972) obtained independent judgments of similarity and difference for all pairs of lowercase letters on a scale from 0 to 100. The product-moment correlation between the judgments was −.98, and the slope of the regression line was −.91. We also collected judgments of similarity and difference for 21 pairs of countries using a 20-point rating scale. The sum of the two judgments for each pair was quite close to 20 in all cases. The product-

moment correlation between the ratings was again −.98. This inverse relation between similarity and difference, however, does not always hold.

Naturally, an increase in the measure of the common features increases similarity and decreases difference, whereas an increase in the measure of the distinctive features decreases similarity and increases difference. However, the relative weight assigned to the common and the distinctive features may differ in the two tasks. In the assessment of similarity between objects the subject may attend more to their common features, whereas in the assessment of difference between objects the subject may attend more to their distinctive features. Thus, the relative weight of the common features will be greater in the former task than in the latter task.

Let d(a,b) denote the perceived difference between a and b. Suppose d satisfies the axioms of the present theory with the reverse inequality in the monotonicity axiom, that is, $d(a,b) \leq d(a,c)$ whenever $A \cap B \supset A \cap C$, $A - B \subset A - C$, and $B - A \subset C - A$. Furthermore, suppose s also satisfies the present theory and assume (for simplicity) that both d and s are symmetric. According to the representation theorem, therefore, there exist a nonnegative scale f and nonnegative constants θ and λ such that for all a,b,c,e,

$$s(a,b) > s(c,e) \text{ iff}$$
$$\theta f(A \cap B) - f(A - B) - f(B - A) >$$
$$\theta f(C \cap E) - f(C - E) - f(E - C),$$

and

$$d(a,b) > d(c,e) \text{ iff}$$
$$f(A - B) + f(B - A) - \lambda f(A \cap B) >$$
$$f(C - E) + f(E - C) - \lambda f(C \cap E).$$

The weights associated with the distinctive features can be set equal to 1 in the symmetric case with no loss of generality. Hence, θ and λ reflect the relative weight of the common features in the assessment of similarity and difference, respectively.

Note that if θ is very large then the similarity ordering is essentially determined by the common features. On the other hand, if λ is very small, then the difference ordering is determined primarily by the distinctive fea-

tures. Consequently, both $s(a,b) > s(c,e)$ and $d(a,b) > d(c,e)$ may be obtained whenever

$$f(A \cap B) > f(C \cap E)$$
and
$$f(A - B) + f(B - A) >$$
$$f(C - E) + f(E - C).$$

That is, if the common features are weighed more heavily in judgments of similarity than in judgments of difference, then a pair of objects with many common and many distinctive features may be perceived as both more similar and more different than another pair of objects with fewer common and fewer distinctive features.

To test this hypothesis, 20 sets of four countries were constructed on the basis of a pilot test. Each set included two pairs of countries: a prominent pair and a nonprominent pair. The prominent pairs consisted of countries that were well known to our subjects (e.g., USA–USSR, Red China–Japan). The nonprominent pairs consisted of countries that were known to the subjects, but not as well as the prominent ones (e.g., Tunis–Morocco, Paraguay–Ecuador). All subjects were presented with the same 20 sets. One group of 30 subjects selected between the two pairs in each set the pair of countries that were more *similar*. Another group of 30 subjects selected between the two pairs in each set the pair of countries that were more *different*.

Let Π_s and Π_d denote, respectively, the percentage of choices where the prominent pair of countries was selected as more similar or as more different. If similarity and difference are complementary (i.e., $\theta = \lambda$), then $\Pi_s + \Pi_d$ should equal 100 for all pairs. On the other hand, if $\theta > \lambda$, then $\Pi_s + \Pi_d$ should exceed 100. The average value of $\Pi_s + \Pi_d$, across all sets, was 113.5, which is significantly greater than 100, $t(59) = 3.27$, $p < .01$.

Moreover, on the average, the prominent pairs were selected more frequently than the nonprominent pairs in both the similarity and the difference tasks. For example, 67% of the subjects in the similarity group selected West Germany and East Germany as more similar to each other than Ceylon and Nepal, while 70% of the subjects in the difference group selected West Germany and East Germany as

more different from each other than Ceylon and Nepal. These data demonstrate how the relative weight of the common and the distinctive features varies with the task and support the hypothesis that people attend more to the common features in judgments of similarity than in judgments of difference.

Similarity in Context

Like other judgments, similarity depends on context and frame of reference. Sometimes the relevant frame of reference is specified explicitly, as in the questions, "How similar are English and French with respect to sound?" "What is the similarity of a pear and an apple with respect to taste?" In general, however, the relevant feature space is not specified explicitly but rather inferred from the general context.

When subjects are asked to assess the similarity between the USA and the USSR, for instance, they usually assume that the relevant context is the set of countries and that the relevant frame of reference includes all political, geographical, and cultural features. The relative weights assigned to these features, of course, may differ for different people. With natural, integral stimuli such as countries, people, colors, and sounds, there is relatively little ambiguity regarding the relevant feature space. However, with artificial, separable stimuli, such as figures varying in color and shape, or lines varying in length and orientation, subjects sometimes experience difficulty in evaluating overall similarity and occasionally tend to evaluate similarity with respect to one factor or the other (Shepard, 1964) or change the relative weights of attributes with a change in context (Torgerson, 1965).

In the present theory, changes in context or frame of reference correspond to changes in the measure of the feature space. When asked to assess the political similarity between countries, for example, the subject presumably attends to the political aspects of the countries and ignores, or assigns a weight of zero to, all other features. In addition to such restrictions of the feature space induced by explicit or implicit instructions, the salience of features and hence the similarity of objects are also influenced by the effective context (i.e., the set of objects under consideration). To understand this process, let us examine the factors that determine the salience of a feature and its contribution to the similarity of objects.

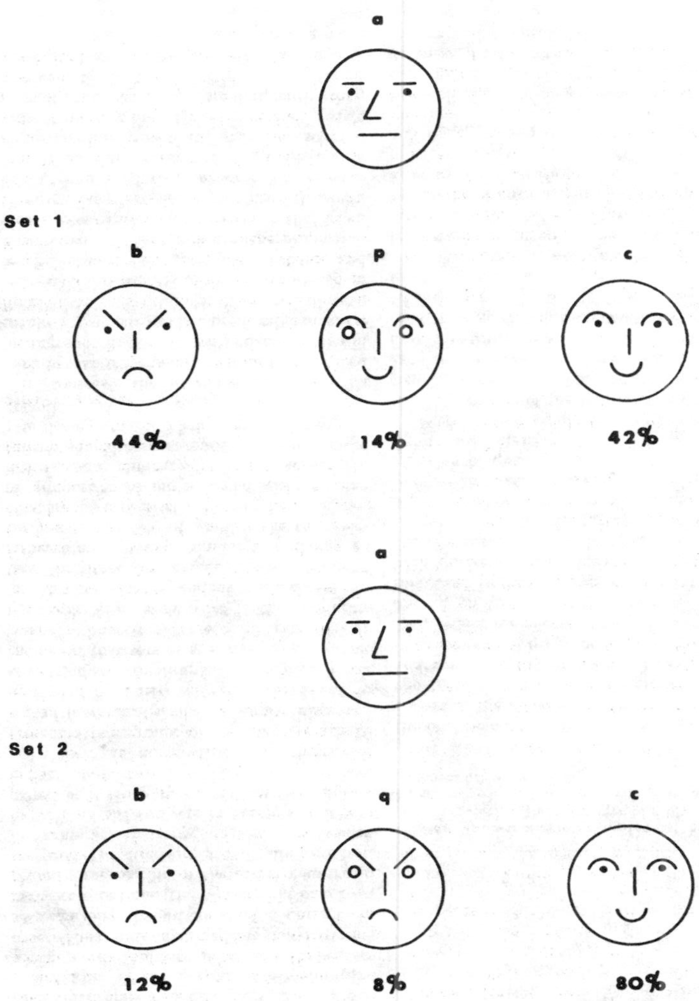

The Diagnosticity Principle

The salience (or the measure) of a feature is determined by two types of factors: intensive and diagnostic. The former refers to factors that increase intensity or signal-to-noise ratio, such as the brightness of a light, the loudness of a tone, the saturation of a color, the size of a letter, the frequency of an item, the clarity of a picture, or the vividness of an image. The diagnostic factors refer to the classificatory significance of features, that is, the importance or prevalence of the classifications that are based on these features. Unlike the intensive factors, the diagnostic factors are highly sensitive to the particular object set under study. For example, the feature "real" has no diagnostic value in the set of actual animals since it is shared by all actual animals and hence cannot be used to classify them. This feature, however, acquires considerable diagnostic value if the object set is extended to include legendary animals, such as a centaur, a mermaid, or a phoenix.

When faced with a set of objects, people often sort them into clusters to reduce information load and facilitate further processing. Clusters are typically selected so as to maximize the similarity of objects within a cluster and the dissimilarity of objects from different clusters. Hence, the addition and/or deletion of objects can alter the clustering of the remaining objects. A change of clusters, in turn, is expected to increase the diagnostic value of features on which the new clusters are based, and therefore, the similarity of objects that share these features. This relation between similarity and grouping—called the diagnosticity hypothesis—is best explained in terms of a concrete example. Consider the two sets of four schematic faces (displayed in Figure 4), which differ in only one of their elements (p and q).

The four faces of each set were displayed in a row and presented to a different group of 25 subjects who were instructed to partition them into two pairs. The most frequent partition of

Set 1 was c and p (smiling faces) versus a and b (nonsmiling faces). The most common partition of Set 2 was b and q (frowning faces) versus a and c (nonfrowning faces). Thus, the replacement of p by q changed the grouping of a: In Set 1 a was paired with b, while in Set 2 a was paired with c.

According to the above analysis, smiling has a greater diagnostic value in Set 1 than in Set 2, whereas frowning has a greater diagnostic value in Set 2 than in Set 1. By the diagnosticity hypothesis, therefore, similarity should follow the grouping. That is, the similarity of a (which has a neutral expression) to b (which is frowning) should be greater in Set 1, where they are grouped together, than in Set 2, where they are grouped separately. Likewise, the similarity of a to c (which is smiling) should be greater in Set 2, where they are grouped together, than in Set 1, where they are not.

To test this prediction, two different groups of 50 subjects were presented with Sets 1 and 2 (in the form displayed in Figure 4) and asked to select one of the three faces below (called the choice set) that was most similar to the face on the top (called the target). The percentage of subjects who selected each of the three elements of the choice set is presented below the face. The results confirmed the diagnosticity hypothesis: b was chosen more frequently in Set 1 than in Set 2, whereas c was chosen more frequently in Set 2 than in Set 1. Both differences are statistically significant, $p < .01$. Moreover, the replacement of p by q actually reversed the similarity ordering: In Set 1, b is more similar to a than c, whereas in Set 2, c is more similar to a than b.

A more extensive test of the diagnosticity hypothesis was conducted using semantic rather than visual stimuli. The experimental design was essentially the same, except that countries served as stimuli instead of faces. Twenty pairs of matched sets of four countries of the form {a,b,c,p} and {a,b,c,q} were constructed. An example of two matched sets is presented in Figure 5.

Note that the two matched sets (1 and 2) differ only by one element (p and q). The sets were constructed so that a (in this case Austria) is likely to be grouped with b (e.g.,

Figure 4. Two sets of schematic faces used to test the diagnosticity hypothesis. The percentage of subjects who selected each face (as most similar to the target) is presented below the face.

Sweden) in Set 1, and with c (e.g., Hungary) in Set 2. To validate this assumption, we presented two groups of 25 subjects with all sets of four countries and asked them to partition each quadruple into two pairs. Each group received one of the two matched quadruples, which were displayed in a row in random order. The results confirmed our prior hypothesis regarding the grouping of countries. In every case but one, the replacement of p by q changed the pairing of the target country in the predicted direction, $p < .01$ by sign test. For example, Austria was paired with Sweden by 60% of the subjects in Set 1, and it was paired with Hungary by 96% of the subjects in Set 2.

To test the diagnosticity hypothesis, we presented two groups of 35 subjects with 20 sets of four countries in the format displayed in Figure 5. These subjects were asked to select, for each quadruple, the country in the choice set that was most similar to the target country. Each group received exactly one quadruple from each pair. If the similarity of b to a, say, is independent of the choice set, then the proportion of subjects who chose b rather than c as most similar to a should be the same regardless of whether the third element in the choice set is p or q. For example, the proportion of subjects who select Sweden rather than Hungary as most similar to Austria should be independent of whether the odd element in the choice set is Norway or Poland.

In contrast, the diagnosticity hypothesis implies that the change in grouping, induced by the substitution of the odd element, will change the similarities in a predictable manner. Recall that in Set 1 Poland was paired with Hungary, and Austria with Sweden, while in Set 2 Norway was paired with Sweden, and Austria with Hungary. Hence, the proportion of subjects who select Sweden rather than Hungary (as most similar to Austria) should be higher in Set 1 than in Set 2. This prediction is strongly supported by the data in Figure 5, which show that Sweden was selected more frequently than Hungary in Set 1, while Hungary was selected more frequently than Sweden in Set 2.

Let $b(p)$ denote the percentage of subjects who chose country b as most similar to a when

the odd element in the choice set is p, and so on. As in the above examples, the notation is chosen so that b is generally grouped with q, and c is generally grouped with p. The differences $b(p) - b(q)$ and $c(q) - c(p)$, therefore, reflect the effects of the odd elements, p and q, on the similarity of b and c to the target a. In the absence of context effects, both differences should equal 0, while under the diagnosticity hypothesis both differences should be positive. In Figure 5, for example, $b(p) - b(q) = 49 - 14 = 35$, and $c(q) - c(p) = 60 - 36 = 24$. The average difference, across all pairs of quadruples, equals 9%, which is significantly positive, $t(19) = 3.65$, $p < .01$.

Several variations of the experiment did not alter the nature of the results. The diagnosticity hypothesis was also confirmed when (i) each choice set contained four elements, rather than three, (ii) the subjects were instructed to rank the elements of each choice set according to their similarity to the target, rather than to select the most similar element, and (iii) the target consisted of two elements, and the subjects were instructed to select one element of the choice set that was most similar to the two target elements. For further details, see Tversky and Gati (in press).

The Extension Effect

Recall that the diagnosticity of features is determined by the classifications that are based on them. Features that are shared by all the objects under consideration cannot be used to

classify these objects and are, therefore, devoid of diagnostic value. When the context is extended by the enlargement of the object set, some features that had been shared by all objects in the original context may not be shared by all objects in the broader context. These features then acquire diagnostic value and increase the similarity of the objects that share them. Thus, the similarity of a pair of objects in the original context will usually be smaller than their similarity in the extended context.

Essentially the same account was proposed and supported by Sjöberg (Note 1) in studies of similarity between animals, and between musical instruments. For example, Sjöberg showed that the similarities between string instruments (banjo, violin, harp, electric guitar) were increased when a wind instrument (clarinet) was added to this set. Since the string instruments are more similar to each other than to the clarinet, however, the above result may be attributed, in part at least, to subjects' tendency to standardize the response scale, that is, to produce the same average similarity for any set of comparisons.

This effect can be eliminated by the use of a somewhat different design, employed in the following study. Subjects were presented with pairs of countries having a common border and assessed their similarity on a 20-point scale. Four sets of eight pairs were constructed. Set 1 contained eight pairs of European countries (e.g., Italy–Switzerland). Set 2 contained eight pairs of American countries (e.g., Brazil–Uruguay). Set 3 contained four pairs from Set 1 and four pairs from Set 2, while Set 4 contained the remaining pairs from Sets 1 and 2. Each one of the four sets was presented to a different group of 30–36 subjects.

According to the diagnosticity hypothesis, the features "European" and "American", have no diagnostic value in Sets 1 and 2, although they both have a diagnostic value in Sets 3 and 4. Consequently, the overall average similarity in the heterogeneous sets (3 and 4) is expected to be higher than the overall average similarity in the homogeneous sets (1 and 2). This prediction was confirmed by the data, $t(15) = 2.11$, $p < .05$.

In the present study all similarity assessments involve only homogeneous pairs (i.e.,

pairs of countries from the same continent sharing a common border). Unlike Sjöberg's (Note 1) study, which extended the context by introducing nonhomogeneous pairs, our experiment extended the context by constructing heterogeneous sets composed of homogeneous pairs. Hence, the increase of similarity with the enlargement of context, observed in the present study, cannot be explained by subjects' tendency to equate the average similarity for any set of assessments.

The Two Faces of Similarity

According to the present analysis, the salience of a feature has two components: intensity and diagnosticity. The intensity of a feature is determined by perceptual and cognitive factors that are relatively stable across contexts. The diagnostic value of a feature is determined by the prevalence of the classifications that are based on it, which change with the context. The effects of context on similarity, therefore, are treated as changes in the diagnostic value of features induced by the respective changes in the grouping of the objects.

This account was supported by the experimental finding that changes in grouping (produced by the replacement or addition of objects) lead to corresponding changes in the similarity of the objects. These results shed light on the dynamic interplay between similarity and classification. It is generally assumed that classifications are determined by similarities among the objects. The preceding discussion supports the converse hypothesis: that the similarity of objects is modified by the manner in which they are classified. Thus, similarity has two faces: causal and derivative. It serves as a basis for the classification of objects, but it is also influenced by the adopted classification. The diagnosticity principle which underlies this process may provide a key to the analysis of the effects of context on similarity.

Discussion

In this section we relate the present development to the representation of objects in terms of clusters and trees, discuss the con-

		a Austria	
	b	p	c
Set 1	Sweden	Poland	Hungary
	49%	15%	36%
		a Austria	
	b	q	c
Set 2	Sweden	Norway	Hungary
	14%	26%	60%

Figure 5. Two sets of countries used to test the diagnosticity hypothesis. The percentage of subjects who selected each country (as most similar to Austria) is presented below the country.

Table 1
ADCLUS Analysis of the Similarities Among the Integers 0 Through 9 (from Shepard & Arabie, Note 2)

Rank	Weight	Elements of subset	Interpretation of subset
1st	.305	2 4 8	powers of two
2nd	.288	6 7 8 9	large numbers
3rd	.279	3 6 9	multiples of three
4th	.202	0 1 2	very small numbers
5th	.202	1 3 5 7 9	odd numbers
6th	.175	1 2 3	small nonzero numbers
7th	.163	5 6 7	middle numbers (largish)
8th	.160	0 1	additive and multiplicative identities
9th	.146	0 1 2 3 4	smallish numbers

cepts of prototypicality and family resemblance, and comment on the relation between similarity and metaphor.

Features, Clusters, and Trees

There is a well-known correspondence between features or properties of objects and the classes to which the objects belong. A red flower, for example, can be characterized as having the feature "red," or as being a member of the class of red objects. In this manner we associate with every feature in Φ the class of objects in Δ which possesses that feature. This correspondence between features and classes provides a direct link between the present theory and the clustering approach to the representation of proximity data.

In the contrast model, the similarity between objects is expressed as a function of their common and distinctive features. Relations among overlapping sets are often represented in a Venn diagram (see Figure 1). However, this representation becomes cumbersome when the number of objects exceeds four or five. To obtain useful graphic representations of the contrast model, two alternative simplifications are entertained.

First, suppose the objects under study are all equal in prominence, that is, $f(A) = f(B)$ for all a,b in Δ. Although this assumption is not strictly valid in general, it may serve as a reasonable approximation in certain contexts. Assuming feature additivity and symmetry,

we obtain

$$S(a,b) = \theta f(A \cap B) - f(A - B) - f(B - A)$$
$$= \theta f(A \cap B) + 2f(A \cap B) - f(A - B)$$
$$\quad - f(B - A) - 2f(A \cap B)$$
$$= (\theta + 2)f(A \cap B) - f(A) - f(B)$$
$$= \lambda f(A \cap B) + \mu,$$

since $f(A) = f(B)$ for all a,b in Δ. Under the present assumptions, therefore, similarity between objects is a linear function of the measure of their common features.

Since f is an additive measure, $f(A \cap B)$ is expressible as the sum of the measures of all the features that belong to both a and b. For each subset A of Δ, let $\Phi(A)$ denote the set of features that are shared by all objects in A, and are not shared by any object that does not belong to A. Hence,

$$S(a,b) = \lambda f(A \cap B) + \mu$$
$$= \lambda(\Sigma f(X)) + \mu$$
$$\qquad X \epsilon A \cap B$$
$$= \lambda(\Sigma f(\Phi(\Lambda))) + \mu$$
$$\qquad A \supset \{a,b\}.$$

Since the summation ranges over all subsets of A that include both a and b, the similarity between objects can be expressed as the sum of the weights associated with all the sets that include both objects.

This form is essentially identical to the additive clustering model proposed by Shepard and Arabie (Note 2). These investigators have developed a computer program, ADCLUS, which selects a relatively small collection of subsets

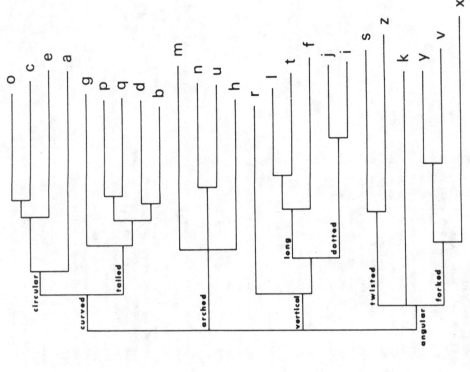

Figure 6. The representation of letter similarity as an additive (feature) tree. From Sattath and Tversky (in press).

and assigns weight to each subset so as to maximize the proportion of (similarity) variance accounted for by the model. Shepard and Arabie (Note 2) applied ADCLUS to several studies including Shepard, Kilpatric, and Cunningham's (1975) on judgments of similarity between the integers 0 through 9 with respect to their abstract numerical character.

A solution with 19 subsets accounted for 95% of the variance. The nine major subsets (with the largest weights) are displayed in Table 1 along with a suggested interpretation. Note that all the major subsets are readily interpretable, and they are overlapping rather than hierarchical.

The above model expresses similarity in terms of common features only. Alternatively, similarity may be expressed exclusively in terms of distinctive features. It has been shown by Sattath (Note 3) that for any symmetric contrast model with an additive measure f, there exists a measure g defined on the same feature space such that

$$S(a,b) = \theta f(A \cap B) - f(A - B) - f(B - A)$$
$$= \lambda - g(A - B) - g(B - A)$$

for some $\lambda > 0$.

This result allows a simple representation of dissimilarity whenever the feature space Φ is a tree (i.e., whenever any three objects in Δ can be labeled so that $A \cap B = A \cap C \subset B \cap C$). Figure 6 presents an example of a feature tree, constructed by Sattath and Tversky (in press) from judged similarities between lowercase letters, obtained by Kuennapas and Janson (1969). The major branches are labeled to facilitate the interpretation of the tree.

Each (horizontal) arc in the graph represents the set of features shared by all the objects (i.e., letters) that follow from that arc, and the arc length corresponds to the measure of that set. The features of an object are the features of all the arcs which lead to that object, and its measure is its (horizontal) distance to the root. The tree distance between objects a and b is the (horizontal) length of the path joining them, that is, $f(A - B) + f(B - A)$. Hence, if the contrast model holds, $\alpha = \beta$, and Φ is a tree, then dissimilarity (i.e., $-S$) is expressible as tree distance.

A feature tree can also be interpreted as a hierarchical clustering scheme where each arc length represents the weight of the cluster consisting of all the objects that follow from that arc. Note that the tree in Figure 6 differs from the common hierarchical clustering tree in that the branches differ in length. Sattath and Tversky (in press) describe a computer program, ADDTREE, for the construction of additive feature trees from similarity data and discuss its relation to other scaling methods.

It follows readily from the above discussion that if we assume both that the feature set Φ is a tree, and that $f(A) = f(B)$ for all a,b in Δ, then the contrast model reduces to the well-known hierarchical clustering scheme. Hence, the additive clustering model (Shepard & Arabie, Note 2), the additive similarity tree (Sattath & Tversky, in press), and the hierarchical clustering scheme (Johnson, 1967) are all special cases of the contrast model. These scaling models can thus be used to discover the common and distinctive features of the objects under study. The present development, in turn, provides theoretical foundations for the analysis of set-theoretical methods for the representation of proximities.

Similarity, Prototypicality, and Family Resemblance

Similarity is a relation of proximity that holds between two objects. There exist other proximity relations such as prototypicality and representativeness that hold between an object and a class. Intuitively, an object is prototypical if it exemplifies the category to which it belongs. Note that the prototype is not necessarily the most typical or frequent member of its class. Recent research has demonstrated the importance of prototypicality or representativeness in perceptual learning (Posner & Keele, 1968; Reed, 1972), inductive inference (Kahneman & Tversky, 1973), semantic memory (Smith, Rips, & Shoben, 1974), and the formation of categories (Rosch & Mervis, 1975). The following discussion analyzes the relations of prototypicality and family resemblance in terms of the present theory of similarity.

Let $P(a,A)$ denote the (degree of) prototypicality of object a with respect to class A, with cardinality n, defined by

$$P(a,A) = p_n(\lambda \Sigma f(A \cap B) - \Sigma(f(A - B) + f(B - A))),$$

where the summations are over all b in A. Thus, $P(a,A)$ is defined as a linear combination (i.e., a contrast) of the measures of the features of a that are shared with the elements of A and the features of a that are not shared with the elements of A. An element a of A is a prototype if it maximizes $P(a,A)$. Note that a class may have more than one prototype.

The factor p_n reflects the effect of category size on prototypicality, and the constant λ determines the relative weights of the common and the distinctive features. If $p_n = 1/n$, $\lambda = \theta$, and $\alpha = \beta = 1$, then $P(a,A) = 1/n\Sigma S(a,b)$ (i.e., the prototypicality of a with respect to A equals the average similarity of a to all members of A). However, in line with the focusing hypotheses discussed earlier, it appears likely that the common features are weighted more heavily in judgments of prototypicality than in judgments of similarity.

Some evidence concerning the validity of the proposed measure was reported by Rosch and Mervis (1975). They selected 20 objects from each one of six categories (furniture, vehicle, fruit, weapon, vegetable, clothing) and instructed subjects to list the attributes associated with each one of the objects. The prototypicality of an object was defined by the number of attributes or features it shared with each member of the category. Hence, the prototypicality of a with respect to A was defined by $\Sigma N(a,b)$, where $N(a,b)$ denotes the number of attributes shared by a and b, and the summation ranges over all b in A. Clearly, the measure of prototypicality employed by Rosch and Mervis (1975) is a special case of the proposed measure, where λ is large and $f(A \cap B) = N(a,b)$.

These investigators also obtained direct measures of prototypicality by instructing subjects to rate each object on a 7-point scale according to the extent to which it fits the "idea or image of the meaning of the category." The rank correlations between these ratings and the above measure were quite high in all categories: furniture, .88; vehicle, .92; weapon, .94; fruit, .85; vegetable, .84; clothing, .91. The rated prototypicality of an object in a category, therefore, is predictable by the number of features it shares with other members of that category.

In contrast to the view that natural categories are definable by a conjunction of critical features, Wittgenstein (1953) argued that several natural categories (e.g., a game) do not have any attribute that is shared by all their members, and by them alone. Wittgenstein proposed that natural categories and concepts are commonly characterized and understood in terms of family resemblance, that is, a network of similarity relations that link the various members of the class. The importance of family resemblance in the formation and processing of categories has been effectively underscored by the work of Rosch and her collaborators (Rosch, 1973; Rosch & Mervis, 1975; Rosch, Mervis, Gray, Johnson, & Boyes-Braem, 1976). This research demonstrated that both natural and artificial categories are commonly perceived and organized in terms of prototypes, or focal elements, and some measure of proximity from the prototypes. Furthermore, it lent substantial support to the claim that people structure their world in terms of basic semantic categories that represent an optimal level of abstraction. Chair, for example, is a basic category; furniture is too general and kitchen chair is too specific. Similarly, car is a basic category; vehicle is too general and sedan is too specific. Rosch argued that the basic categories are selected so as to maximize family resemblance—defined in terms of cue validity.

The present development suggests the following measure for family resemblance, or category resemblance. Let A be some subset of Δ with cardinality n. The category resemblance of A denoted $R(A)$ is defined by

$$R(A) = r_n(\lambda \Sigma f(A \cap B) - \Sigma(f(A - B) + f(B - A))),$$

the summations being over all a,b in A. Hence, category resemblance is a linear combination of the measures of the common and the distinctive features of all pairs of objects in that category. The factor r_n reflects the effect of category size on category resemblance, and the constant λ determines the relative weight of the common and the distinctive features. If $\lambda = \theta$, $\alpha = \beta = 1$, and $r_n = 2/n(n - 1)$, then

$$R(A) = \frac{\Sigma S(a,b)}{\binom{n}{2}},$$

the summation being over all a,b in A; that is, category resemblance equals average similarity between all members of A. Although the proposed measure of family resemblance differs from Rosch's, it nevertheless captures her basic notion that family resemblance is highest for those categories which "have the most attributes common to members of the category and the least attributes shared with members of other categories" (Rosch et al., 1976, p. 435).

The maximization of category resemblance could be used to explain the formation of categories. Thus, the set A rather than Γ is selected as a natural category whenever R(A) > R(Γ). Equivalently, an object a is added to a category A whenever R((A ∪ a)) > R(A). The fact that the preferred (basic) categories are neither the most inclusive nor the most specific imposes certain constraints on r_n.

If $r_n = 2/n(n-1)$ then R(A) equals the average similarity between all members of A. This index leads to the selection of minimal categories because average similarity can generally be increased by deleting elements. The average similarity between sedans, for example, is surely greater than the average similarity between cars; nevertheless, car rather than sedan serves as a basic category. If $r_n = 1$ then R(A) equals the sum of the similarities between all members of A. This index leads to the selection of maximal categories because the addition of objects increases total similarity, provided S is nonnegative.

In order to explain the formation of intermediate-level categories, therefore, category resemblance must be a compromise between an average and a sum. That is, r_n must be a decreasing function of n that exceeds $2/n(n-1)$. In this case, R(A) increases with category size whenever average similarity is held constant, and vice versa. Thus, a considerable increase in the extension of a category could outweigh a small reduction in average similarity.

Although the concepts of similarity, prototypicality, and family resemblance are intimately connected, they have not been previously related in a formal explicit manner. The present development offers explications of similarity, prototypicality, and family resemblance within a unified framework, in which they are viewed as contrasts, or linear combinations, of the measures of the appropriate sets of common and distinctive features.

Similes and Metaphors

Similes and metaphors are essential ingredients of creative verbal expression. Perhaps the most interesting property of metaphoric expressions is that despite their novelty and nonliteral nature, they are usually understandable and often informative. For example, the statement that Mr. X resembles a bulldozer is readily understood as saying that Mr. X is a gross, powerful person who overcomes all obstacles in getting a job done. An adequate analysis of connotative meaning should account for man's ability to interpret metaphors without specific prior learning. Since the message conveyed by such expressions is often pointed and specific, they cannot be explained in terms of a few generalized dimensions of connotative meaning, such as evaluation or potency (Osgood, 1962). It appears that people interpret similes by scanning the feature space and selecting the features of the referent that are applicable to the subject (e.g., by selecting features of the bulldozer that are applicable to the person). The nature of this process is left to be explained.

There is a close tie between the assessment of similarity and the interpretation of metaphors. In judgments of similarity one assumes a particular feature space, or a frame of reference, and assesses the quality of the match between the subject and the referent. In the interpretation of similes, one assumes a resemblance between the subject and the referent and searches for an interpretation of the space that would maximize the quality of the match. The same pair of objects, therefore, can be viewed as similar or different depending on the choice of a frame of reference.

One characteristic of good metaphors is the contrast between the prior, literal interpretation, and the posterior, metaphoric interpretation. Metaphors that are too transparent are uninteresting; obscure metaphors are uninterpretable. A good metaphor is like a good detective story. The solution should not be apparent in advance to maintain the reader's interest, yet it should seem plausible after the fact to maintain coherence of the story. Consider the simile "An essay is like a fish." At first, the statement is puzzling. An essay is not expected to be fishy, slippery, or wet. The puzzle is resolved when we recall that (like a fish) an essay has a head and a body, and it occasionally ends with a flip of the tail.

Reference Notes

1. Sjöberg, L. A cognitive theory of similarity. *Psychological Reports* (No. 10), 1972.
2. Shepard, R. N., & Arabie, P. Additive cluster analysis of similarity data. *Proceedings of the U.S.–Japan Seminar on Theory, Methods, and Applications of Multidimensional Scaling and Related Techniques.* San Diego, August 1975.
3. Sattath, S. *An equivalence theorem.* Unpublished note, Hebrew University, 1976.

References

Beals, R., Krantz, D. H., & Tversky, A. Foundations of multidimensional scaling. *Psychological Review,* 1968, 75, 127–142.

Bush, R. R., & Mosteller, F. A model for stimulus generalization and discrimination. *Psychological Review,* 1951, 58, 413–423.

Carroll, J. D., & Wish, M. Multidimensional perceptual models and measurement methods. In E. C. Carterette & M. P. Friedman (Eds.), *Handbook of perception.* New York: Academic Press, 1974.

Eisler, H., & Ekman, G. A mechanism of subjective similarity. *Acta Psychologica,* 1959, 16, 1–10.

Garner, W. R. *The processing of information and structure.* New York: Halsted Press, 1974.

Gibson, E. *Principles of perceptual learning and development.* New York: Appleton-Century-Crofts, 1969.

Goldmeier, E. Similarity in visually perceived forms. *Psychological Issues,* 1972, 8, 1–136.

Gregson, R. A. M. *Psychometrics of similarity.* New York: Academic Press, 1975.

Hosman, J., & Kuennapas, T. *On the relation between similarity and dissimilarity estimates* (Report No. 354). University of Stockholm, Psychological Laboratories, 1972.

Jakobson, R., Fant, G. G. M., & Halle, M. *Preliminaries to speech analysis: The distinctive features and their correlates.* Cambridge, Mass.: MIT Press, 1961.

Johnson, S. C. Hierarchical clustering schemes. *Psychometrika,* 1967, 32, 241–254.

Kahneman, D., & Tversky, A. On the psychology of prediction. *Psychological Review,* 1973, 80, 237–251.

Krantz, D. H., Luce, R. D., Suppes, P., & Tversky, A. *Foundations of measurement* (Vol. 1). New York: Academic Press, 1971.

Krantz, D. H., & Tversky, A. Similarity of rectangles: An analysis of subjective dimensions. *Journal of Mathematical Psychology,* 1975, 12, 4–34.

Kuennapas, T., & Janson, A. J. Multidimensional similarity of letters. *Perceptual and Motor Skills,* 1969, 28, 3–12.

Neisser, U. *Cognitive psychology.* New York: Appleton-Century-Crofts, 1967.

Osgood, C. E. Studies on the generality of affective meaning systems. *American Psychologist,* 1962, 17, 10–28.

Posner, M. I., & Keele, S. W. On the genesis of abstract ideas. *Journal of Experimental Psychology,* 1968, 77, 353–363.

Reed, S. K. Pattern recognition and categorization. *Cognitive Psychology,* 1972, 3, 382–407.

Restle, F. A metric and an ordering on sets. *Psychometrika,* 1959, 24, 207–220.

Restle, F. *Psychology of judgment and choice.* New York: Wiley, 1961.

Rosch, E. On the internal structure of perceptual and semantic categories. In T. E. Moore (Ed.), *Cognitive development and the acquisition of language.* New York: Academic Press, 1973.

Rosch, E. Cognitive reference points. *Cognitive Psychology,* 1975, 7, 532–547.

Rosch, E., & Mervis, C. B. Family resemblances: Studies in the internal structure of categories. *Cognitive Psychology,* 1975, 7, 573–603.

Rosch, E., Mervis, C. B., Gray, W., Johnson, D., & Boyes-Braem, P. Basic objects in natural categories. *Cognitive Psychology,* 1976, 8, 382–439.

Rothkopf, E. Z. A measure of stimulus similarity and errors in some paired-associate learning tasks. *Journal of Experimental Psychology,* 1957, 53, 94–101.

Sattath, S., & Tversky, A. Additive similarity trees. *Psychometrika,* in press.

Shepard, R. N. Attention and the metric structure of the stimulus space. *Journal of Mathematical Psychology,* 1964, 1, 54–87.

Shepard, R. N. Representation of structure in similarity data: Problems and prospects. *Psychometrika,* 1974, 39, 373–421.

Shepard, R. N., Kilpatric, D. W., & Cunningham, J. P. The internal representation of numbers. *Cognitive Psychology,* 1975, 7, 82–138.

Smith, E. E., Rips, L. J., & Shoben, E. J. Semantic memory and psychological semantics. In G. H. Bower (Ed.), *The psychology of learning and motivation* (Vol. 8). New York: Academic Press, 1974.

Smith, E. E., Shoben, E. J., & Rips, L. J. Structure and process in semantic memory: A featural model for semantic decisions. *Psychological Review,* 1974, 81, 214–241.

Torgerson, W. S. Multidimensional scaling of similarity. *Psychometrika,* 1965, 30, 379–393.

Tversky, A. Elimination by aspects: A theory of choice. *Psychological Review,* 1972, 79, 281–299.

Tversky, A., & Gati, I. Studies of similarity. In E. Rosch & B. Lloyd (Eds.), *On the nature and principle of formation of categories.* Hillsdale, N. J.: Erlbaum, in press.

Tversky, A., & Krantz, D. H. The dimensional representation and the metric structure of similarity data. *Journal of Mathematical Psychology,* 1970, 7, 572–597.

von Neumann, J., & Morgenstern, O. *Theory of games and economic behavior.* Princeton, N. J.: Princeton University Press, 1947.

Wish, M. A model for the perception of Morse Code-like signals. *Human Factors,* 1967, 9, 529–540.

Wittgenstein, L. *Philosophical investigations.* New York: Macmillan, 1953.

Appendix

An Axiomatic Theory of Similarity

Let $\Delta = \{a,b,c,\dots\}$ be a collection of objects characterized as sets of features, and let $A,B,C,$ denote the sets of features associated with $a,b,c,$ respectively. Let $s(a,b)$ be an ordinal measure of the similarity of a to b, defined for all distinct a,b in Δ. The present theory is based on the following five axioms. Since the first three axioms are discussed in the paper, they are merely restated here; the remaining axioms are briefly discussed.

1. *Matching*: $s(a,b) = F(A \cap B, A - B, B - A)$ where F is some real-valued function in three arguments.

2. *Monotonicity*: $s(a,b) \geq s(a,c)$ whenever $A \cap B \supset A \cap C$, $A - B \subset A - C$, and $B - A \subset C - A$. Moreover, if either inclusion is proper then the inequality is strict.

Let Φ be the set of all features associated with the objects of Δ, and let $X,Y,Z,$ etc. denote finite subsets of Φ. The expression $F(X,Y,Z)$ is defined whenever there exist a,b in Δ such that $A \cap B = X$, $A - B = Y$, and $B - A = Z$, whence $s(a,b) = F(X,Y,Z)$. Define $V \simeq W$ if one or more of the following hold for some X,Y,Z: $F(V,Y,Z) = F(W,Y,Z)$, $F(X,V,Z) = F(X,W,Z)$, $F(X,Y,V) = F(X,Y,W)$. The pairs (a,b) and (c,d) *agree* on one, two, or three components, respectively, whenever one, two, or three of the following hold: $(A \cap B) \simeq (C \cap D)$, $(A - B) \simeq (C - D)$, $(B - A) \simeq (D - C)$.

3. *Independence*: Suppose the pairs (a,b) and (c,d), as well as the pairs (a',b') and (c', d'), agree on the same two components, while the pairs (a,b) and (a',b'), as well as the pairs (c,d) and (c',d'), agree on the remaining (third) component. Then

$$s(a,b) \geq s(a',b') \text{ iff } s(c,d) \geq s(c',d').$$

4. *Solvability*:
(i). For all pairs (a,b), (c,d), (e,f), of objects in Δ there exists a pair (p,q) which agrees with them, respectively, on the first, second, and third component, that is, $P \cap Q \simeq A \cap B$, $P - Q \simeq C - D$, and $Q - P \simeq F - E$.
(ii). Suppose $s(a,b) > t > s(c,d)$. Then there exist e,f with $s(e,f) = t$, such that if (a,b) and (c,d) agree on one or two components, then (e,f) agrees with them on these components.
(iii). There exist pairs (a,b) and (c,d) of objects in Δ that do not agree on any component.

Unlike the other axioms, solvability does not impose constraints on the similarity order; it merely asserts that the structure under study is sufficiently rich so that certain equations can be solved. The first part of Axiom 4 is analogous to the existence of a factorial structure. The second part of the axiom implies that the range of s is a real interval: There exist objects in Δ whose similarity matches any real value that is bounded by two similarities. The third part of Axiom 4 ensures that all arguments of F are essential.

Let Φ_1, Φ_2, and Φ_3 be the sets of features that appear, respectively, as first, second, or third arguments of F. (Note that $\Phi_1 = \Phi_3$.) Suppose X and X' belong to Φ_1, while Y and Y' belong to Φ_2. Define $(X,X')_1 \simeq (Y,Y')_2$ whenever the two intervals are matched, that is, whenever there exist pairs (a,b) and (a',b') of equally similar objects in Δ which agree on the third factor. Thus, $(X,X')_1 \simeq (Y,Y')_2$ whenever

$$s(a,b) = F(X',Y,Z) = F(X',Y,Z) = s(a',b').$$

This definition is readily extended to any other pair of factors. Next, define $(V,V')_i \simeq (W, W')_i$, $i = 1,2,3$ whenever $(V,V')_i \simeq (X,X')_j \simeq (W,W')_i$, for some $(X,X')_j$, $j \neq i$. Thus, two intervals on the same factor are equivalent if both match the same interval on another factor. The following invariance axiom asserts that if two intervals are equivalent on one factor, they are also equivalent on another factor.

5. *Invariance*: Suppose V,V', W,W' belong to both Φ_i and Φ_j, $i,j = 1,2,3$. Then

$$(V,V')_i \simeq (W,W')_i \text{ iff } (V,V')_j \simeq (W,W')_j.$$

Representation Theorem

Suppose Axioms 1–5 hold. Then there exist a similarity scale S and a nonnegative scale f such that for all a,b,c,d in Δ

(i). $S(a,b) \geq S(c,d)$ iff $s(a,b) \geq s(c,d)$.
(ii). $S(a,b) = \theta f(A \cap B) - \alpha f(A - B) - \beta f(B - A)$, for some $\theta, \alpha, \beta \geq 0$.
(iii). f and S are interval scales.

While a self-contained proof of the representation theorem is quite long, the theorem can be readily reduced to previous results.

Recall that Φ_i is the ith argument of F, and let $\Psi_i = \Phi_i / \simeq$, $i = 1,2,3$. Thus, Ψ_i is the set of equivalence classes of Φ_i with respect to $\simeq$. It follows from Axioms 1 and 3 that each Ψ_i is well defined, and it follows from Axiom 4 that $\Psi = \Psi_1 \times \Psi_2 \times \Psi_3$ is equivalent to the domain of F. We wish to show that Ψ, ordered by F, is a three-component, additive conjoint structure, in the sense of Krantz, Luce, Suppes, and Tversky (1971, Section 6.11.1).

This result, however, follows from the analysis of decomposable similarity structures, developed by Tversky and Krantz (1970). In particular, the proof of part (c) of Theorem 1 in that paper implies that, under Axioms 1,3, and 4, there exist nonnegative functions f_i defined on Ψ_i, $i = 1,2,3$, so that for all a,b,c,d in Δ

$$s(a,b) \geq s(c,d) \text{ iff } S(a,b) \geq S(c,d)$$

where $S(a,b) = f_1(A \cap B) + f_2(A - B) + f_3(B - A)$

and f_1, f_2, f_3 are interval scales with a common unit.

According to Axiom 5, the equivalence of intervals is preserved across factors. That is, for all V,V', W,W' in $\Phi_i \cap \Phi_j$, $i,j, = 1,2,3$.

$$f_i(V) - f_i(V') = f_i(W) - f_i(W') \text{ iff } f_j(V) - f_j(V') = f_j(W) - f_j(W')$$

Hence by part (i) of Theorem 6.15 of Krantz et al. (1971), there exist a scale f and constants θ_i, such that $f_i(X) = \theta_i f(X)$, $i = 1,2,3$. Finally, by Axiom 2, S increases in f_1 and decreases in f_2 and f_3. Hence, it is expressible as

$$S(a,b) = \theta f(A \cap B) - \alpha f(A - B) - \beta f(B - A),$$

for some nonnegative constants θ, α, β.

Received November 17, 1976 ∎

Structure-Mapping:
A Theoretical Framework for Analogy*

DEDRE GENTNER
Bolt Beranek and Newman Inc.

A theory of analogy must describe how the meaning of an analogy is derived from the meanings of its parts. In the *structure-mapping theory*, the interpretation rules are characterized as implicit rules for mapping knowledge about a base domain into a target domain. Two important features of the theory are (a) the rules depend only on syntactic properties of the knowledge representation, and not on the specific content of the domains; and (b) the theoretical framework allows analogies to be distinguished cleanly from literal similarity statements, applications of abstractions, and other kinds of comparisons.

Two mapping principles are described: (a) Relations between objects, rather than attributes of objects, are mapped from base to target; and (b) The particular relations mapped are determined by systematicity, as defined by the existence of higher-order relations.

When people hear an analogy such as "An electric battery is like a reservoir" how do they derive its meaning? We might suppose that they simply apply their knowledge about reservoirs to batteries, and that the greater the match, the better the analogy. Such a "degree of overlap" approach seems reasonably correct for literal similarity comparisons. In Tversky's (1977) contrast model, the similarity between A and B is greater the greater size of the intersection (A∩B) of their feature sets and the less the size of the two complement sets (A − B) and (B − A).[1] However, although the degree-of-overlap model appears to work well for literal similarity comparisons, it does not provide a good account of analogy. The strength of an analogical match does not seem to depend on the overall degree of featural overlap; not all features are equally relevant to the interpretation. Only certain kinds of mismatches count for or against analogies. For example, we could not support the battery-reservoir analogy by remarking (even if true) that batteries and reservoirs both tend to be cylindrical; nor does it weaken the analogy to show that their shapes are different. The essence of the analogy between batteries and reservoirs is that both store potential energy, release that energy to provide power for systems, etc. We can be quite satisfied with the analogy in spite of the fact that the average battery differs from the average reservoir in size, shape, color, and substance.

As another example of the selectiveness of analogical mapping, consider the simple arithmetic analogy 3:6::2:4. We do not care how many features 3 has in common with 2, nor 6 with 4. It is not the overall number of shared versus nonshared features that counts here, but only the relationship "twice as great as" that holds between 3 and 6 and also between 2 and 4. To underscore the implicit selectiveness of the feature match, note that we do not consider the analogy 3:6::2:4 better or more apt than the analogy 3:6::200:400, even though by most accounts 3 has more features in common with 2 than with 200.

A theory based on the mere relative numbers of shared and non-shared predicates cannot provide an adequate account of analogy, nor, therefore, a sufficient basis for a general account of relatedness. In the structure-mapping theory, a simple but powerful distinction is made among predicate types that allows us to state which ones will be mapped. The central idea is that an analogy is an assertion that a relational structure that normally applies in one domain can be applied in another domain. Before laying out the theory, a few preliminaries are necessary.

PRELIMINARY ASSUMPTIONS

1. Domains and situations are psychologically viewed as systems of objects, object-attributes and relations between objects.[3]

*This research was supported by the Department of the Navy, Office of Naval Research under Contract No. N00014-79-C-0338, and by the National Institute of Education under Contracts No. NIE-400-80-0030 and NIE-400-80-0031. I thank my colleagues Allan Collins, Ken Forbus, Don Gentner, Ed Smith, and Al Stevens, who collaborated on the development of these ideas; and Susan Carey, John Clement, Andy diSessa, Georges Rey, David Rumelhart, Patrick Winston, and Marianne Wiser for insightful discussions of this approach. I also thank Judith Block, Phillip Kohn, Mary McManamon, Patricia Stuart, Edna Sullivan and Ben Teitelbaum for their help with the research on which this paper is based, and Cindy Hunt for preparing the manuscript. Correspondence and requests for reprints should be sent to Dedre Gentner, Bolt Beranek and Newman Inc., Cambridge, MA 02238.

[1] According to Tversky (1977), the negative effects of the two complement sets are not equal; for example, if we are asked "How similar is A to B", the set (B − A)—features of B not shared by A—counts much more than the set (A − B).

[3] These "objects" may be clear entities (e.g., "rabbit"), component parts of a larger object (e.g., "rabbit's ear"), or even coherent combinations of smaller units (e.g., "herd of rabbits"); the important point is that they function as wholes at a given level of organization.

2. Knowledge is represented here as propositional networks of nodes and predicates (cf. Miller & Johnson-Laird, 1976; Norman, Rumelhart, & the LNR Group, 1975; Rumelhart & Ortony, 1977; Schank & Abelson, 1977). The nodes represent concepts treated as wholes; the predicates applied to the nodes express propositions about the concepts.

3. Two essentially syntactic distinctions among predicate types will be important. The first distinction is between object attributes and relationships. This distinction can be made explicit in the predicate structure: *Attributes* are predicates taking one argument, and *relations* are predicates taking two or more arguments. For example, COLLIDE (x,y) is a relation, while LARGE (x) is an attribute.[3]

   The second important syntactic distinction is between first-order predicates (taking objects as arguments) and second- and higher-order predicates (taking propositions as arguments). For example, if COLLIDE (x,y) and STRIKE (y,z) are first-order predicates, CAUSE [COLLIDE (x,y), STRIKE (y,z)] is a second-order predicate.

4. These representations, including the distinctions between different kinds of predicates, are intended to reflect the way people construe a situation, rather than what is logically possible.[4]

STRUCTURE-MAPPING:
INTERPRETATION RULES FOR ANALOGY

The analogy "A T is (like) a B" defines a mapping from B to T. T will be called the *target*, since it is the domain being explicated. B will be called the *base*, since it is the domain that serves as a source of knowledge. Suppose that the representation of the base domain B can be stated in terms of object nodes $b_1, b_2, \ldots, b_n$ and predicates such as A, R, R', and that the *target* domain has object nodes $t_1, t_2, \ldots, t_m$.[5] The analogy maps the object nodes of B onto the object nodes of T:

$$M: b_i \dashrightarrow t_i$$

These object correspondences are used to generate the candidate set of inferences in the target domain. Predicates from B are carried across[6] to T, using the node substitutions dictated by the object correspondences. The mapping rules are

1. Discard attributes of objects:

$$A(b_j)] \;-\!+\!\to\; [A(t_j)]$$

2. Try to preserve relations between objects:

$$R(b_i, b_j)] \;-\!\to\; [R(t_i, t_j),$$

3. (The Systematicity Principle) To decide *which* relations are preserved, choose systems of relations:

$$R'(R_1(b_i, b_j), R_2(b_k, b_l)] \;-\!-\!\to$$
$$[R'(R_1(t_i, t_j), R_2(t_k, t_l)$$

Higher-order relations play an important role in analogy, as is discussed below.

Notice that this discussion has been purely structural; the distinctions invoked rely only on the syntax of the knowledge representation, not on the content. The *content* of the relations may be static spatial information, as in UNDER(x,y), or FULL(CONTAINER, WATER); or constraint information, as in PROPORTIONAL [(PRESSURE[(liquid, source, goal), FLOW-RATE (liquid, source, goal)]; or dynamic causal information, as in CAUSE {AND [PUNCTURE (CONTAINER), FULL(CONTAINER, WATER)], FLOW-FROM (WATER, CONTAINER)}.

---

[5] Most explanatory analogies are 1-1 mappings, in which m = n. However, there are exceptions (Gentner, 1982).

[6] The assumption that predicates are brought across as *identical* matches is crucial to the clarity of this discussion. The position that predicates need only be similar between the base and the domain (e.g., Hesse, 1966; Ortony, 1979) leads to a problem of infinite regress, with similarity of surface concepts defined in terms of similarity of components, etc. I will assume instead that similarity can be restated as identity among some number of component predicates.

[3] One clarification is important here. Many attributive predicates implicitly invoke comparisons between the value of their object and some standard value on the dimension. LARGE (x) implicitly means "X is large for its class." For example, a large star is of a different size than a large mouse. But if LARGE (x) is implicitly interpreted as LARGER THAN $(X$, prototype-x), this might suggest that many surface attributes are implicitly two-place predicates. The theory assumes that only relations that apply *within* the domain of discourse are psychologically stored and processed as true relations. Thus, in the domain of the solar system, a relation such as LARGER THAN (sun, planet), that applies between two objects in the domain, is processed as a relation; whereas an external attributive comparison, such as LARGER THAN (sun, prototype-star), is processed as an attribute.

[4] Logically, a relation R(a,b,c) can perfectly well be represented as Q(x), where Q(x) is true just in case R(a,b,c) is true. Psychologically, the representation must be chosen to model the way people think about the domain.

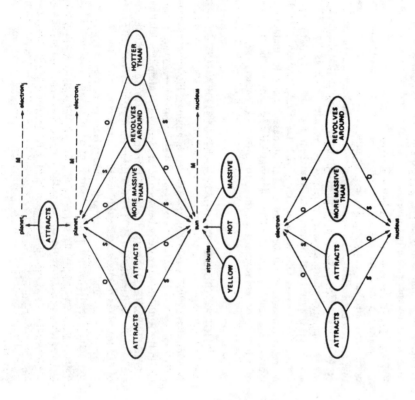

Figure 1. Structure-mapping for the Rutherford analogy: "The atom is like the solar system."

KINDS OF DOMAIN COMPARISONS

In the structure-mapping framework, the interpretation rules for analogy can be distinguished from those for other kinds of domain comparisons. The syntactic type of the shared versus nonshared predicates determines whether a given comparison is thought of as analogy, as literal similarity, or as the application of an abstraction.

In this section, different kinds of domain comparisons are described, using the solar system as a common theme. The top half of Figure 1 shows a partial representation of what might be a person's knowledge of our solar system. Both object-attributes, such as YELLOW (sun), and relations between objects, such as REVOLVE AROUND (planet, sun) are shown. Assuming that the hearer has the correct object correspondences, the question is which predicates will be mapped for each type of comparison.

(1) A *literal similarity* statement is a comparison in which a large number of predicates is mapped from base to target, relative to the number of nonmapped predicates (e.g., Tversky, 1977). The mapped predicates include *both* object-attributes and relational predicates.

EXAMPLE 1. The X12 star system in the Andromeda galaxy is like our solar system.
INTERPRETATION: Intended inferences include both object characteristics—e.g., "The X12 star is YELLOW, MEDIUM-SIZED, etc., like our sun," and relational characteristics, such as "The X12 planets REVOLVE AROUND the X12 star, as in our system."
In a literal similarity comparison, all or most of the predicates shown would be mapped.

(2) An *analogy* is a comparison in which relational predicates, but few or no object attributes, can be mapped from base to target.

EXAMPLE 2. The hydrogen atom is like our solar system.
INTERPRETATION: Intended inferences concern chiefly the relational structure: e.g., "The electron REVOLVES AROUND the nucleus, just as the planets REVOLVE AROUND the sun," but not "The nucleus is YELLOW, MASSIVE, etc., like the sun." The bottom half of Figure 1 shows these mapped relations. If higher-order relations are present in the base, they can be mapped as well: e.g., The hearer might map "The fact that the nucleus ATTRACTS the electron *CAUSES* the electron to REVOLVE around the nucleus" from "The fact that the sun ATTRACTS the planets *CAUSES* the planets to REVOLVE AROUND the sun." (This relation is not shown in Figure 1.)

(3) An *abstraction* is a comparison in which the base domain is an abstract relational structure. Such a structure would resemble Figure 1, except that the object nodes would be generalized physical enti-

ties, rather than particular objects like "sun" and "planet". Predicates from the abstract base domain are mapped into the target domain; there are no nonmapped predicates.

EXAMPLE 3. The hydrogen atom is a central force system.
INTERPRETATION: Intended inferences include "The nucleus ATTRACTS the electron;" "The electron REVOLVES AROUND the nucleus." These are mapped from base propositions such as "The central object ATTRACTS the peripheral object;" or "The less massive object REVOLVES AROUND the more massive object." These intended inferences resemble those for the analogy (Example 2). The difference is that in the

Metaphor

A number of different kinds of comparisons go under the term "metaphor." Many (perhaps most) metaphors are predominantly relational comparisons, and are thus essentially analogies. For example, in A. E. Housman's comparison, "I could no more define poetry than a terrier can define a rat," the object correspondences are terrier–poet and rat–poetry. Clearly, the intended inference is not that the poet is like a terrier, nor certainly that poetry is like a rat, but rather, that the relation between poet and poetry is like the relation between terrier and rat. Again, in Shakespeare's "... What light from yonder window breaks?/ It is the east, and Juliet is the sun!..." Romeo does not mean that Juliet is yellow, hot or gaseous. Rather, he means that she appears above him, bringing him hope and gladness, etc. Though some attributes may be mapped from sun to Juliet (perhaps "beautiful"), the metaphor chiefly conveys a set of spatial and affective relationships.

Although most metaphors are relationally focused, some are predominantly attribute matches. These generally involve shared attributes that are few but striking, and often more salient in the base than in the target ([Ortony, 1979]: e.g., "She's a giraffe," used to convey that she is tall. Many such metaphors involve conventional dimensional matches, such as "a deep/shallow idea". [Glucksberg, Gildea, & Bookin, 1982; Lakoff & Johnson, 1980]). Moreover, metaphors can be mixtures of all of these. Finally, for metaphors that are analyzable as analogies or combinations of analogies, the mapping rules tend to be less regular than those for analogy (Gentner, 1982).

HIGHER-ORDER PREDICATES AND SYSTEMATICITY

Relations have priority over object-attributes in analogy. However, as mentioned earlier, not all relations are equally likely to be preserved. For example, in the Rutherford analogy between solar system and atom, the relation MORE MASSIVE THAN (sun, planet) is mapped across to the atom, but the formally similar relation HOTTER THAN (sun, planet) is not. The goal of this section is to characterize this analogical relevance explicitly.

Part of our understanding about analogy is that it conveys a system of connected knowledge, not a mere assortment of independent facts. Such a system can be represented by an interconnected predicate structure in which higher-order predicates enforce connections among lower-order predicates.[']

[']The *Order* of a relation is determined by the order of its arguments. A first-order relation takes objects as its arguments. A second-order relation has at least one first-order relation among its arguments; and in general an nth order relation has at least one (n-1)th order argument.

---

analogy there are other base predicates that are not mapped, such as "The sun is YELLOW."

All three kinds of comparison involve substantial overlap in relations, but, except for literal similarity, not in object-attributes. What happens if there is strong overlap in object-attributes but not in relations; e.g., "A sunflower looks like the sun." or "The symbol for infinity is a sideways 8." Such a match is considered a mere appearance match. Unlike the comparisons considered so far, these matches do not involve relational mappings. Although they can be appealing and locally useful, their explanatory power is sharply limited. Mere appearance matches will not concern us further.

Table 1 summarizes these distinctions. Overlap in relations is necessary for any strong perception of similarity between two domains. Overlap in both object-attributes and inter-object relationships is seen as literal similarity, and overlap in relationships but not objects is seen as analogical relatedness. Overlap in object-attributes but not relationships is seen as a mere appearance match. Finally, a comparison with neither attribute nor relational overlap is simply an anomaly.

TABLE 1
Kinds of Predicates Mapped in Different Types of Domain Comparison

	No. of attributes mapped to target	No. of relations mapped to target	Example
Literal Similarity	Many	Many	The K5 solar system is like our solar system.
Analogy	Few	Many	The atom is like our solar system.
Abstraction	Few[a]	Many	The atom is a central force system.
Anomaly	Few	Few	Coffee is like the solar system.

[a]Abstraction differs from analogy and the other comparisons in having few object-attributes in the base domain as well as few object-attributes in the target domain.

According to this analysis, the contrast between analogy and literal similarity is a continuum, not a dichotomy. Given that two domains overlap in relationships, they are more literally similar to the extent that their object-attributes also overlap. A different sort of continuum applies between analogies and general laws: In both cases, a relational structure is mapped from base to target. If the base representation includes concrete objects whose individual attributes must be left behind in the mapping, the comparison is an analogy. As the object nodes of the base domain becomes more abstract and variable-like, the comparison is seen as an abstraction.

To reflect this tacit preference for coherence in analogy, I propose the *systematicity principle*: A predicate that belongs to a mappable system of mutually interconnecting relationships is more likely to be imported into the target than is an isolated predicate.

In the Rutherford model, the set of predicates that forms a mappable system includes the following lower-order relations:

(1) DISTANCE (sun, planet)
(2) ATTRACTIVE FORCE (sun, planet)
(3) REVOLVES AROUND (planet, sun)
(4) MORE MASSIVE THAN (sun, planet)

One symptom of this systematicity is that changing one of these relations affects the others. For example, suppose we decrease the attraction between sun and planet; then the distance between them will increase, all else being equal. Thus relations (1) and (2) are interrelated. Again, suppose we reverse relation (4) to state that the planet is more massive than the sun; then we must also reverse relation (3), for the sun would then revolve around the planet.[8] One way of expressing these dependencies among the lower-order relations is as a set of simultaneous constraint equations:

$$F_{grav} = \frac{Gm_p m_s}{R^2} = m_p a_p = m_s a_s$$

where F_{grav} is the gravitational force, m_p is the mass of the planet; a_p is the radial acceleration of the planet (and similarly m_s and a_s for the sun); R is the distance between planet and sun; and G is the gravitational constant.

The same interdependencies hold for the atom, if we make the appropriate node substitutions:

(5) DISTANCE (nucleus, electron)
(6) ATTRACTIVE FORCE (nucleus, electron)
(7) REVOLVES AROUND (electron, nucleus)
(8) MORE MASSIVE THAN (nucleus, electron)

The corresponding equations for the atom are

$$F_{elec} = \frac{-q_e q_n}{R^2} = m_e a_e = m_n a_n$$

where F_{elec} is the electromagnetic force, q_e is the charge on the electron; m_e is the mass of the electron; a_e is the radial acceleration of the electron (and similarly for the nucleus); R_e is the distance between electron and nucleus and -1 is the electromagnetic constant.

[8] This follows from the simultaneous equations below. The radial acceleration of either object is given by the force divided by its own mass; thus the lighter object has the greater radial acceleration. To maintain separation, it must also have a tangential velocity sufficient to keep it from falling into the larger object.

These equations embody higher-order relations that connect the lower-order relations (1) through (4) into a mutually constraining structure. By the systematicity principle, to the extent that people recognize (however vaguely) that the system of predicates connected with central forces is the deepest, most interconnected mappable system for this analogy, they will favor relations that belong to that system in their interpretations.[9] This is why MORE MASSIVE THAN is preserved while HOTTER THAN is not: Only MORE MASSIVE THAN participates in the central-force system of predicates.

As another demonstration of the operation of the systematicity principle, consider the analogy ''Heat is like water,'' used to explain heat transfer from a warm house in cold weather. Suppose the hearer's knowledge about water includes two scenarios:

1. AND[CONTAIN(vessel, water), ON-TOP-OF (lid, vessel)]
2. CAUSE {AND [PUNCTURE(vessel), CONTAIN(vessel, water)], FLOW-FROM (water, vessel)}.

These can be paraphrased roughly as follows: (1) The vessel contains water and has a lid; (2) if a vessel that contains water is punctured, water will flow out. Assuming that the hearer has made the obvious object correspondences (water --> heat, vessel --> house, and lid --> roof),[10] which will be mapped?

Intuitively, the second scenario is more interesting than the first: (1) conveys merely a static spatial description, while (2) conveys a dynamic causal description. We would like chain (2) to be favored over chain (1), so that dynamic causal knowledge is likely to be present in the candidate set of attempted predications (to use Ortony's [1979] term). We could accomplish this by postulating that analogies select for dynamic causal knowledge, or more generally, for appropriate abstractions. Either of these would be a mistake: The former course limits the scope of analogy unreasonably, and the latter course is both vague, in that ''appropriateness'' is difficult to define explicitly, and incorrect, in that analogies can also convey inappro-

[9] I make the assumption here that partial knowledge of the system is often sufficient to allow a person to gauge its interconnectedness. In the present example, a person may recognize that force, mass, and motion are highly interrelated without having full knowledge of the governing equations.

[10] In this discussion I have made the simplifying assumption that, in comprehension of analogy, the hearer starts with the object correspondences and then maps across the relations. The actual order of processing is clearly variable. If the object assignment is left unspecified, the hearer can use knowledge about matching relations to decide on the object correspondences. Therefore, it is more accurate to replace the statement that the object correspondences are decided before the relational mappings *begin* with the weaker statement that the object correspondences are decided before the relational mappings are *finished*. This is largely because in a complex analogy, the number of mappable relations is largely compared to the number of object correspondences; indeed the number of mappable relations may have no clear upper bound.

priate abstractions.'' We want our rules for analogical interpretation to choose chain (2) over chain (1), but we want them to operate, at least initially, without appeal to specific content or appropriateness. The systematicity principle offers a way to satisfy both requirements. Dynamic causal information [e.g., (2)] will usually be represented in a more deeply embedded structure than simple stative information [e.g., (1)]. Thus, by promoting deeply nested relational chains, the systematicity principle operates to promote predicates that participate in causal chains and in other constraint relations. It is a purely syntactic mechanism that guarantees that the set of candidate mappings will be as interesting—in the sense that a mutually interconnected system of predicates is interesting—as the knowledge base allows.

In the next section, empirical support for the structure-mapping theory is briefly discussed. First, however, let us review the performance of the theory against a set of a priori theoretical criteria. The structure-mapping theory satisfies the first requirement of a theory of analogy, that it describe the rules by which the interpretation of an analogy is derived from the meanings of its parts. Further, the rules are such as to distinguish analogy from other kinds of domain comparisons, such as abstraction or literal similarity. Finally, a third feature of the structure-mapping theory is that the interpretation rules are characterizable purely syntactically. That is, the processing mechanism that selects the initial candidate set of predicates to map attends only to the *structure* of the knowledge representations for the two analogs, and not to the content.

EMPIRICAL SUPPORT

There is research supporting the structure-mapping approach. In one set of studies, subjects wrote out interpretations of analogical comparisons such as "A cigarette is like a time bomb." These interpretations were read to naive judges, who rated each assertion as to whether it was an attribute or a relation. (For a fuller description, see Gentner, 1980b). The results indicated a strong focus on relational information in interpreting analogies. Relational information predominates over attributional information in analogy interpretations, but not in object descriptions generated by the same sub-

''Unless we distinguish the structural rules for generating the candidate set from other conceptual criteria (such as appropriateness, insightfulness, or correctness) that can be applied to the candidate set, we rob analogy of its power to convey new information. Just as we can perform a syntactic analysis of what a sentence conveys, even when the information it conveys is semantically novel or implausible (e.g., "Man bites dog."), so we must be able to derive a structural analysis of an analogy that does not depend on a priori conceptual plausibility. Of course, our ultimate acceptance of the analogy will depend on whether its candidate set of predicates is plausible; but this is a separate matter.

jects. Further, a correlation of aptness ratings and relationality ratings revealed that subjects rated as most apt those analogies for which they wrote the greatest amount of relational information.

Other experimental evidence for structure-mapping as part of the psychological process of interpreting complex analogies has included developmental studies (Gentner, 1977a,b; 1980b) and studies of how people use analogies in learning science (Collins & Gentner, in preparation; Gentner, 1980a, 1981; Gentner & Gentner, 1983).

RELATED RESEARCH

Complex explanatory analogies have until recently received little attention in psychology, perhaps because such analogies require fairly elaborate representations of meaning. Studies of analogy in scientific learning and in reasoning have emphasized the importance of shared complex representational structures (Clement, 1981, 1982; Collins & Gentner, in preparation; Darden, 1980; Gentner, 1980a; Gentner & Gentner, 1983; Hesse, 1966; Hobbs, 1979; Hoffman, 1980, Moore & Newell, 1973; Oppenheimer, 1955; Polya, 1973; Riley, 1981; Rumelhart & Norman, 1981; Steels, 1982; Stevens, Collins & Goldin, 1979; VanLehn & Brown, 1980). Although some of this work has been empirically tested, most of it remains in the area of interesting but unvalidated theory. In contrast, much of the psychological experimentation on analogy and metaphor has been either theory-neutral (e.g., Schustack & Anderson, 1979; Verbrugge & McCarrell, 1977) or based on rather simple representations of meaning: e.g., feature-list representations (e.g., Ortony, 1979) or multidimensional space representations (e.g., Rumelhart & Abrahamson, 1973; Tourangeau & Sternberg, 1981). These kinds of representations can deal well with object attributes, but are extremely limited in their ability to express relations between objects, and especially higher-order relations.

Recent work in cognitive science has begun to explore more powerful representational schemes. The Merlin system (Moore & Newell, 1973) featured a mechanism for "viewing x as y" (see also Steels, 1982) which involved explicit comparisons of the shared and nonshared predicates of two situations. Winston (1980, 1981), using a propositional representation system, has simulated the process of matching a current situation with a previously stored precedent and using the similarity match to justify importing inferences from the precedent to the current situation. Further, in recent work he has investigated importance-dominated matching; here the match between old and new situations is performed by counting only those predicates that occur in causal chains. This requirement is somewhat more restrictive than the structure-mapping principle that participation in *any* higher-order chain results in preferential mapping. However, it has the similar effect of focusing the matcher on systematic relational structures rather than on haphazard resemblances between situation. One valuable aspect of Winston's work is his modelling of the process of abstracting general rules from the analogical matches. Gick and Holyoak have also emphasized the relationship between analogical matching and the formation of general schemas in an interesting series of studies of transfer in problem-solving (Gick & Holyoak, 1980, 1983; Holyoak, in press).

Other researchers have explored specific instances of relational mapping. VanLehn and Brown (1980) have analyzed analogical learning of procedural rules in arithmetic, postulating mapping rules compatible with the rules proposed here. Clement (1981, 1982) has proposed four-stage series of processes of generating analogical comparisons during problem-solving. Rumelhart and Norman (1981) have used a schema-based representational system to discuss analogical transfer. Burstein (1983) and Carbonell (1981) have characterized the comprehension of analogy, emphasizing common goals and subgoals as organizing principles. In the main, these accounts are compatible with that given by the structure-mapping theory in each of the problem domains. Relations tend to be preserved across domains with dissimilar object-attributes: e.g., the matching of like procedures that apply to unlike sets of objects (VanLehn & Brown, 1980).

THE ANALOGICAL SHIFT CONJECTURE

Some of the distinctions made here may appear rather academic. To illustrate their potential relevance, let us apply these distinctions to the spontaneous comparisons that people make in the course of learning a domain. An informal observation is that the earliest comparisons are chiefly literal-similarity matches, followed by analogies, followed by general laws. For example, Ken Forbus and I have observed a subject trying to understand the behavior of water flowing through a constricted pipe. His first comparisons were similarity matches, e.g., water coming through a constricted hose. Later, he produced analogies such as a train speeding up or slowing down, and balls banging into the walls and transferring momentum. Finally, he arrived at a general statement of the Bernoulli principle, that velocity increases and pressure decreases in a constriction.

This sequence can be understood in terms of the kinds of differences in predicate overlap discussed in this paper. In the structure-mapping framework, we can suggest reasons that the accessibility and the explanatory usefulness of a match may be negatively related. Literal similarity matches are highly accessible, since they can be indexed by object descriptions, by relational structures, or by both. But they are not very useful in deriving causal principles, precisely because there is too much overlap to know what is crucial. Potential analogies are less likely to be noticed, since they require accessing the data base via relational matches; object matches are of no use. However, once found, an analogy should be more useful in deriving the key principles, since the shared data structure is sparse enough to permit analysis. Moreover, if we assume the systematicity principle, then the set of overlapping predicates is likely to include higher-order relations such as CAUSE and IMPLIES. To state a general law requires another step beyond creating a temporary correspondence between unlike domains: The person must create a new relational structure whose objects are so lacking in specific attributes that the structure can be applied across widely different domains. (Forbus & Gentner, 1983; Gick & Holyoak, 1980; 1983).

SUMMARY

The *structure-mapping theory* describes the implicit interpretation rules of analogy. The central claims of the theory are that analogy is characterized by the mapping of relations between objects, rather than attributes of objects, from base to target; and, further, that the particular relations mapped are those that are dominated by higher-order relations that belong to the mapping (the *systematicity* claim). These rules have the desirable property that they depend only on syntactic properties of the knowledge representation, and not on the specific content of the domain. Further, this theoretical framework allows us to state the differences between analogies and literal similarity statements, abstractions and other kinds of comparisons.

REFERENCES

Burstein, M. H. Concept formation by incremental analogical reasoning and debugging. *Proceedings of the 1983 International Machine Learning Workshop*. Monticello, IL, June 1983.

Carbonell, J. G. Towards a computational model of problem solving and learning by analogy. Unpublished manuscript, Carnegie-Mellon University, February 1981.

Clement, J. Analogy generation in scientific problem solving. *Proceedings of the Third Annual Meeting of the Cognitive Science Society*, 1981.

Clement, J. Spontaneous analogies in problem solving: The progressive construction of mental models. Paper presented at the meeting of the American Education Research Association, New York, 1982.

Collins, A. M., & Gentner, D. Constructing runnable mental models, in preparation.

Darden, L. Theory construction in genetics. In T. Nickles (Ed.) *Scientific discovery: Case studies*. D. Reidel Publishing Co., 1980.

Forbus, K. D. & Gentner, D. Learning physical domains: Towards a theoretical framework. *Proceedings of the 1983 International Machine Learning Workshop*, Monticello, IL, June 1983.

Gentner, D. Children's performance on a spatial analogies ask. *Child Development*, 1977, *48*, 1034–1039. (a)

Gentner, D. If a tree had a knee, where would it be? Children's performance on simple spatial metaphors. *Papers and Reports on Child Language Development*, 1977, *13*, 157–164. (b).

Gentner, D. The structure of analogical models in science (BBN Rrt No. 4451). Cambridge, MA: Bolt Beranek and Newman Inc., 1980. (a)

Gentner, D. Metaphor as structure-mapping. Paper presented at the meeting of the American Psychological Association, Montreal, September 1980. (b)

Gentner, D. Generative analogies as mental models. *Proceedings of the Third Annual Cognitive Science Society*, Berkeley, California, August 1981.

Gentner, D. Are scientific analogies metaphors? In D.Miall (Ed.), *Metaphor: Problems and perspectives*. Brighton, England: Harvester Press Ltd., 1982.

Gentner, D., & Gentner, D. R. Flowing waters or teeming crowds: Mental models of electricity. In D. Gentner & A. L. Stevens (Eds.), *Mental models*. Hillsdale, NJ: Lawrence Erlbaum Associates, 1983.

Gentner, D., & Grudin, J. Ninety years of mental metaphors. *Proceedings of the Fifth Annual Cognitive Science Society*, Rochester, NY, April 1983.

Gick, M. L., & Holyoak, K. J. Analogical problem solving. *Cognitive Psychology*, 1980, *12*, 306–355.

Gick, M. L., & Holyoak, K. J. Schema induction and analogical transfer. *Cognitive Psychology*, 1983, *15*, 1–38.

Glucksberg, S., Gildea, P., & Bookin, H. B. On understanding nonliteral speech: Can people ignore metaphors? *Journal of Verbal Learning and Verbal Behavior*, 1982, *21*, 85–98.

Hesse, M. B. *Models and analogies in science*. Notre Dame, IN: University of Notre Dame Press, 1966.

Hobbs, J. R. *Metaphor, metaphor schemata, and selective inferencing* (SRI Technical Note 204). Menlo Park, CA: SRI International, Artificial Intelligence Center, December 1979.

Hoffman, R. R. Metaphor in science. In R. P. Honeck & R. R. Hoffman (Eds.), *The psycholinguistics of figurative language*. Hillsdale, NJ: Lawrence Erlbaum Associates, 1980.

Holyoak, K. J. Analogical thinking and human intelligence. In R. J. Sternberg (Ed.), *Advances in the psychology of human intelligence* (Vol. 2). Hillsdale, NJ: Lawrence Erlbaum Associates, in press.

Lakoff, G., & Johnson, M. *Metaphors we live by*. Chicago, IL: University of Chicago Press, 1980.

Miller, G. A. Images and models, similes and metaphors. In A. Ortony (Ed.), *Metaphor and thought*. Cambridge: Cambridge University Press, 1979.

Miller, G. A., & Johnson-Laird, P. N. *Language and perception*. Cambridge, MA: Harvard University Press, 1976.

Moore, J., & Newell, A. How can Merlin understand? In L. Gregg (Ed.), *Knowledge and cognition*. Potomac, MA: Lawrence Erlbaum Associates, 1973.

Norman, D. A., Rumelhart, D. E., & the LNR Research Group. *Explorations in cognition*. San Francisco, CA: W. H. Freeman & Co., 1975.

Oppenheimer, R. Analogy in science. Paper presented at the 63rd Annual Meeting of the American Psychological Association, San Francisco, September 1955.

Ortony, A. Beyond literal similarity. *Psychological Review*, 1979, *87*, 161–180.

Polya, G. *Mathematics and plausible reasoning* (Volume 1). Princeton, NJ: Princeton University Press, 1973.

Riley, M. S. Representation and the acquisition of problem-solving skill in basic electricity/electronics. Paper presented at the Computer-based Instructional Systems and Simulation meeting, Carnegie-Mellon University, January 1981.

Rumelhart, D. E., & Abrahamson, A. A. A model for analogical reasoning. *Cognitive Psychology*, 1973, *5*, 1–28.

Rumelhart, D. E., & Ortony, A. Representation of knowledge. In R. C. Anderson, R. J. Spiro, & W. E. Montague (Eds.), *Schooling and the acquisition of knowledge*. Hillsdale, NJ: Lawrence Erlbaum Associates, 1977.

Rumelhart, D. E., & Norman, D. A. Analogical processes in learning. In J. R. Anderson (Ed.), *Cognitive skills and their acquisition*. Hillsdale, NJ: Lawrence Erlbaum Associates, 1981.

Schank, R., & Abelson, R. *Scripts, plans, goals, and understanding*. Hillsdale, NJ: Lawrence Erlbaum Associates, 1977.

Schustack, M. W., & Anderson, J. R. Effects of analogy to prior knowledge on memory for new information. *Journal of Verbal Learning and Verbal Behavior*, 1979, *18*, 565–583.

Steels, L. *An applicative view of object oriented programming* (MIT A.I. Memo No. 15). Cambridge, MA: Massachusetts Institute of Technology, March 1982.

Stevens, A., Collins, A., & Goldin, S. E. Misconceptions in student's understanding. *Journal of Man-Machine Studies*, 1979, *11*, 145–156.

Tourangeau, R., & Sternberg, R. J. Aptness in metaphor. *Cognitive Psychology*, 1981, *13*, 27–55.

Tversky, A. Features of similarity. *Psychological Review*, 1977, *84*, 327–352.

VanLehn, K., & Brown, J. S. Planning nets: A representation for formalizing analogies and semantic models of procedural skills. In R. E. Snow, P. A. Federico, & W. E. Montague (Eds.), *Aptitude, learning and instruction: Cognitive process analyses*. Hillsdale, NJ: Lawrence Erlbaum Associates, 1980.

Verbrugge, R. R., & McCarrell, N. S. Metaphoric comprehension: Studies in reminding and resembling. *Cognitive Psychology*, 1977, *9*, 494–533.

Winston, P. H. Learning and reasoning by analogy. *CACM*, 1980, *23*, No. 12.

Winston, P. H. *Learning new principles from precedents and exercises*. (MIT Artificial Intelligence Memo No. 632). Cambridge, MA: Massachusetts Institute of Technology, May 1981.

Prototypes

The term *prototype* has been used to refer to either (1) a description of a category that is more appropriate to some members than it is to others, or (2) a best example of a category. Under either meaning, prototypes are critical for understanding categorization, in part because categorization is often a matter of determining an object's similarity to a prototype, and in part because when people think in terms of categories, they usually are thinking in terms of prototypes.

Rosch has been particularly important in developing the notion of a prototype. Her paper summarizes two aspects of her work. The first aspect concerns prototypes, and the fact that the instances of any category vary with respect to how prototypical they are. The second aspect concerns levels of categories, and the fact that there is a preferred or basic level of categorization (e.g., the object on which you are sitting is likely to be categorized first as a *chair*, rather than as a *desk chair* or a *piece of furniture*).

The paper by Smith and Osherson deals with the problem of how prototypes for simple categories, such as *apple* and *chair*, can be combined into prototypes for complex categories, such as *brown apple* and *comfortable chair*. This kind of *compositionality* is important inasmuch as it provides a fundamental means for increasing our stock of categories. In tackling the compositionality problem, Smith and Osherson combine frame representations for categories with Tversky's similarity rule.

Principles of Categorization

Eleanor Rosch
University of California, Berkeley

The following is a taxonomy of the animal kingdom. It has been attributed to an ancient Chinese encyclopedia entitled the *Celestial Emporium of Benevolent Knowledge*:

On those remote pages it is written that animals are divided into (a) those that belong to the Emperor, (b) embalmed ones, (c) those that are trained, (d) suckling pigs, (e) mermaids, (f) fabulous ones, (g) stray dogs, (h) those that are included in this classification, (i) those that tremble as if they were mad, (j) innumerable ones, (k) those drawn with a very fine camel's hair brush, (l) others, (m) those that have just broken a flower vase, (n) those that resemble flies from a distance (Borges, 1966, p. 108).

Conceptually, the most interesting aspect of this classification system is that it does not exist. Certain types of categorizations may appear in the imagination of poets, but they are never found in the practical or linguistic classes of organisms or of man-made objects used by any of the cultures of the world. For some years, I have argued that human categorization should not be considered the arbitrary product of historical accident or of whimsy but rather the result of psychological principles of categorization, which are subject to investigation. This chapter is a summary and discussion of those principles.

The chapter is divided into five parts. The first part presents the two general principles that are proposed to underlie categorization systems. The second part shows the way in which these principles appear to result in a basic and primary level of categorization in the levels of abstraction in a taxonomy. It is essentially a summary of the research already reported on basic level objects (Rosch et al., 1976). Thus the second section may be omitted by the reader already sufficiently familiar with that material. The third part relates the principles of categorization to the formation of prototypes in those categories that are at the same level of abstraction in a taxonomy. In particular, this section attempts to clarify the operational concept of prototypicality and to separate that concept from claims concerning the role of prototypes in cognitive processing, representation, and learning for which there is little evidence. The fourth part presents two issues that are problematical for the abstract principles of categorization stated in Part I: (1) the relation of context to basic level objects and prototypes; and (2) assumptions about the nature of the attributes of real-world objects that underlie the claim that there is structure in the world. The fifth part is a report of initial attempts to base an analysis of the attributes, functions, and contexts of objects on a consideration of objects as props in culturally defined events.

It should be noted that the issues in categorization with which we are primarily concerned have to do with explaining the categories found in a culture and coded by the language of that culture at a particular point in time. When we speak of the formation of categories, we mean their formation in the culture. This point is often misunderstood. The principles of categorization proposed are not as such intended to constitute a theory of the development of categories in children born into a culture nor to constitute a model of how categories are processed (how categorizations are made) in the minds of adult speakers of a language.

THE PRINCIPLES

Two general and basic principles are proposed for the formation of categories: The first has to do with the function of category systems and asserts that the task of category systems is to provide maximum information with the least cognitive effort; the second has to do with the structure of the information so provided and asserts that the perceived world comes as structured information rather than as arbitrary or unpredictable attributes. Thus maximum information with least cognitive effort is achieved if categories map the perceived world structure as closely as possible. This condition can be achieved either by the mapping of categories to given attribute structures or by the definition or redefinition of attributes to render a given set of categories appropriately structured. These principles are elaborated in the following.

Cognitive Economy. The first principle contains the almost common-sense notion that, as an organism, what one wishes to gain from one's categories is a great deal of information about the environment while conserving finite resources as much as possible. To categorize a stimulus means to consider it, for purposes of that categorization, not only equivalent to other stimuli in the same category but also different from stimuli not in that category. On the one hand, it would appear to the organism's advantage to have as many properties as possible predictable from knowing any one property, a principle that would lead to formation of large numbers of categories with as fine discriminations between categories as possible. On the other hand, one purpose of categorization is to reduce the infinite differences among stimuli to behaviorally and cognitively usable proportions. It is to the organism's advantage not to differentiate one stimulus from others when that differentiation is irrelevant to the purposes at hand.

Perceived World Structure. The second principle of categorization asserts that unlike the sets of stimuli used in traditional laboratory-concept attainment tasks, the perceived world is not an unstructured total set of equiprobable co-occurring attributes. Rather, the material objects of the world are perceived to possess (in Garner's, 1974, sense) high correlational structure. That is, given a knower who perceives the complex attributes of feathers, fur, and wings, it is an empirical fact provided by the perceived world that wings co-occur with feathers more than with fur. And given an actor with the motor programs for sitting, it is a fact of the perceived world that objects with the perceptual attributes of chairs are more likely to have functional sit-on-able-ness than objects with the appearance of cats. In short, combinations of what we perceive as the attributes of real objects do not occur uniformly. Some pairs, triples, etc., are quite probable, appearing in combination sometimes with one, sometimes another attribute; others are rare; others logically cannot or empirically do not occur.

It should be emphasized that we are talking about the perceived world and not a metaphysical world without a knower. What kinds of attributes *can be* perceived are, of course, species-specific. A dog's sense of smell is more highly differentiated than a human's, and the structure of the world for a dog must surely include attributes of smell that we, as a species, are incapable of perceiving. Furthermore, because a dog's body is constructed differently from a human's, its motor interactions with objects are necessarily differently structured. The "out there" of a bat, a frog, or a bee is surely more different still from that of a human. What attributes *will* be perceived given the ability to perceive them is undoubtedly determined by many factors having to do with the functional needs of the knower interacting with the physical and social environment. One influence on how attributes will be defined by humans is clearly the category system already existent in the culture at a given time. Thus, our segmentation of a bird's body such that there is an attribute called "wings" may be influenced not only by perceptual factors such as the gestalt laws of form (Palmer, in press) but also by the fact that at present we already have a cultural and linguistic category called "birds." Viewing attributes as, at least in part, constructs of the perceiver does not negate the higher-order structural fact about attributes at issue, namely that the attributes of wings and that of feathers do co-occur in the perceived world.

These two basic principles of categorization, a drive toward cognitive economy combined with structure in the perceived world, have implications both for the level of abstraction of categories formed in a culture and for the internal structure of those categories once formed.

For purposes of explication, we may conceive of category systems as having both a vertical and horizontal dimension. The vertical dimension concerns the level of inclusiveness of the category – the dimension along which the terms collie, dog, mammal, animal, and living thing vary. The horizontal dimension concerns the segmentation of categories at the same level of inclusiveness – the dimension on which dog, cat, car, bus, chair, and sofa vary. The implication of the two principles of categorization for the vertical dimension is that not all possible levels of categorization are equally good or useful; rather, the most basic level of categorization will be the most inclusive (abstract) level at which the categories can mirror the structure of attributes perceived in the world. The implication of the principles of categorization for the horizontal dimension is that to increase the distinctiveness and flexibility of categories, categories tend to become defined in terms of prototypes or prototypical instances that contain the attributes most representative of items inside and least representative of items outside the category.

THE VERTICAL DIMENSION OF CATEGORIES: BASIC-LEVEL OBJECTS

In a programmatic series of experiments, we have attempted to argue that categories within taxonomies of concrete objects are structured such that there is generally one level of abstraction at which the most basic category cuts can be made (Rosch et al., 1976a). By *category* is meant a number of objects that are considered equivalent. Categories are generally designated by names (e.g., *dog, animal*). A *taxonomy* is a system by which categories are related to one another by means of class inclusion. The greater the inclusiveness of a category within a taxonomy, the higher the level of abstraction. Each category within a taxonomy is entirely included within one other category (unless it is the highest level category) but is not exhaustive of that more inclusive category (see Kay, 1971). Thus the term *level of abstraction* within a taxonomy refers to a particular level of inclusiveness. A familiar taxonomy is the Linnean system for the classification of animals.

Our claims concerning a basic level of abstraction can be formalized in terms of cue validity (Rosch et al., 1976a) or in terms of the set theoretic representation of similarity provided by Tversky (1977, and Chapter 4 in this volume). Cue validity is a probabilistic concept; the validity of a given cue *x* as a predictor of a given category *y* (the conditional probability of *y/x*) increases as the frequency with which cue *x* is associated with category *y* increases and decreases as the frequency with which cue *x* is associated with categories other than *y* increases (Beach, 1964a, 1964b; Reed, 1972). The cue validity of an entire category may be defined as the summation of the cue validities for that category of each of the attributes of the category. A category with high cue validity is, by definition, more differentiated from other categories than one of lower cue validity. The elegant formulization that Tversky provides in Chapter 4 is in terms of the variable "category resemblance," which is defined as the weighted sum of the measures of all of the common features within a category minus the sum of the measures of all of the distinctive features. Distinctive features include those that belong to only some members of a given category as well as those belonging to contrasting categories. Thus Tversky's formulization does not weight the effect of contrast categories as much as does the cue validity formulation. Tversky suggests that two disjoint classes tend to be combined whenever the weight of the added common features exceeds the weight of the distinctive features.

A working assumption of the research on basic objects is that (1) in the perceived world, information-rich bundles of perceptual and functional attributes occur that form natural discontinuities, and that (2) basic cuts in categorization are made at these discontinuities. Suppose that basic objects (e.g., chair, car) are at the most inclusive level at which there are attributes common to all or most members of the category. Then both total cue validities and category resemblance are maximized at that level of abstraction at which basic objects are categorized. This is, categories one level more abstract will be superordinate categories (e.g., furniture, vehicle) whose members share only a few attributes among each other. Categories below the basic level will be bundles of common attributes, predictable attributes and functions but contain many attributes that overlap with other categories (for example, kitchen chair shares most of its attributes with other kinds of chairs).

Superordinate categories have lower total cue validity and lower category resemblance than do basic-level categories, because they have fewer common attributes; in fact, the category resemblance measure of items within the superordinate can even be negative due to the high ratio of distinctive to common features. Subordinate categories have lower total cue validity than do basic categories, because they also share most attributes with contrasting subordinate categories; in Tversky's terms, they tend to be combined because the weight of the added common features tends to exceed the weight of the distinctive features. That basic objects are categories at the level of abstraction that maximizes cue validity and maximizes category resemblance is another way of asserting that basic objects are the categories that best mirror the correlational structure of the environment.

We chose to look at concrete objects because they appeared to be a domain that was at once an indisputable aspect of complex natural language classifications yet at the same time were amenable to methods of empirical analysis. In our investigations of basic categories, the correlational structure of concrete objects was considered to consist of a number of inseparable aspects of form and function, any one of which could serve as the starting point for analysis. Four investigations provided converging operational definitions of the basic level of abstraction: attributes in common, motor movements in common, objective similarity in shape, and identifiability of averaged shapes.

Common Attributes. Ethnobiologists had suggested on the basis of linguistic criteria and field observation that the folk genus was the level of classification at which organisms had bundles of attributes in common and maximum discontinuity between classes (see Chapter 1). The purpose of our research was to provide a systematic empirical study of the co-occurrence of attributes in the most common taxonomies of biological and man-made objects in our own culture.

The hypothesis that basic level objects are the most inclusive level of classification at which objects have numbers of attributes in common was tested for categories at three levels of abstraction for nine taxonomies: tree, bird, fish, fruit, musical instruments, tool, clothing, furniture, and vehicle. Examples of the three levels for one biological and one nonbiological taxonomy are shown in Table 2.1. Criteria for choice of these specific items were that the taxonomies contain the most common (defined by word frequency) categories of concrete nouns in English, that the levels of abstraction bear simple class-inclusion relations to each other, and that those class-inclusion relations be generally known to our subjects (be agreed upon by a sample of native English speakers). The middle level of abstraction was the hypothesized basic level: For nonbiological taxonomies, this corresponded to the intuition of the experimenters (which also turned out to be consistent with Berlin's linguistic criteria); for biological categories, we assumed that the basic level would be the level of the folk generic.

Subjects received sets of words taken from these nine taxonomies; the subject's task was to list all of the attributes he could think of that were true of the items included in the class of things designated by each object name. Thus, for purposes of this study, attributes were defined operationally as whatever subjects agreed them to be with no implications for whether such analysis of an object could or could not be perceptually considered prior to knowledge of the object itself. Results of the study were as predicted: Very few attributes were listed for the superordinate categories, a significantly greater number listed for the supposed

TABLE 2.1

Examples of Taxonomies Used in Basic Object Research

Superordinate	Basic Level	Subordinate
Furniture	Chair	Kitchen chair
		Living-room chair
	Table	Kitchen table
		Dining-room table
	Lamp	Floor lamp
		Desk lamp
tree	Oak	White oak
		Red oak
	Maple	Silver maple
		Sugar maple
	Birch	River birch
		White birch

basic-level objects, and not significantly more attributes listed for subordinate-level objects than for basic-level. An additional study showed essentially the same attributes listed for visually present objects as for the object names. The single unpredicted result was that for the three biological taxonomies, the basic level, as defined by numbers of attributes in common, did not occur at the level of the folk generic but appeared at the level we had originally expected to be superordinate (e.g., *tree* rather than *oak*).

Motor Movements. Inseparable from the perceived attributes of objects are the ways in which humans habitually use or interact with those objects. For concrete objects, such interactions take the form of motor movements. For example, when performing the action of sitting down on a chair, a sequence of body and muscle movements are typically made that are inseparable from the nature of the attributes of chairs – legs, seat, back, etc. This aspect of objects is particularly important in light of the role that sensory–motor interaction with the world appears to play in the development of thought (Bruner, Olver, & Greenfield, 1966; Nelson, 1974; Piaget, 1952).

In our study of motor movements, each of the sets of words used in the previous experiment was administered to new subjects. A subject was asked to describe, in as much finely analyzed detail as possible, the sequences of motor movements he made when using or interacting with the object. Tallies of agreed upon listings of the same movements of the same body part in the same part of the movement sequence formed the unit of analysis. Results were identical to those of the attribute listings; basic objects were the most general classes to have motor sequences in common. For example, there are few motor programs we carry out to items of furniture in general and several specific motor programs carried out in regard to sitting down on chairs, but we sit on kitchen and living-room chairs using essentially the same motor programs.

Similarity in Shapes. Another aspect of the meaning of a class of objects is the appearance of the objects in the class. In order to be able to analyze correlational structures by different but converging methods, it was necessary to find a method of analyzing similarity in the visual aspects of the objects that was not dependent on subjects' descriptions, that was free from effects of the object's name (which would not have been the case for subjects' ratings of similarity), and that went beyond similarity of analyzable, listable attributes that had already been used in the first study described. For this purpose, outlines of the shape of two-dimensional representations of objects were used, an integral aspect of natural forms. Similarity in shape was measured by the amount of overlap of the two outlines when the outlines (normalized for size and orientation) were juxtaposed.

Results showed that the ratio of overlapped to nonoverlapped area when two objects from the same basic-level category (e.g., two cars) were superimposed was far greater than when two objects from the same superordinate category

were superimposed (e.g., a car and a motorcycle). Although some gain in ratio of overlap to nonoverlap also occurred for subordinate category objects (e.g., two sports cars), the gain obtained by shifting from basic-level to subordinate objects was significantly less than the gain obtained by shifting from superordinate to basic-level objects.

Identifiability of Averaged Shapes. If the basic level is the most inclusive level at which shapes of objects of a class are similar, a possible result of such similarity may be that the basic level is also the most inclusive level at which an averaged shape of an object can be recognized. To test this hypothesis, the same normalized superimposed shapes used in the previous experiment were used to draw an average outline of the overlapped figures. Subjects were then asked to identify both the superordinate category and the specific object depicted. Results showed that basic objects were the most general and inclusive categories at which the objects depicted could be identified. Furthermore, overlaps of subordinate objects were no more identifiable than objects at the basic level.

In summary, our four converging operational definitions of basic objects all indicated the same level of abstraction to be basic in our taxonomies. Admittedly, the basic level for biological objects was not that predicted by the folk genus; however, this fact appeared to be simply accounted for by our subjects' lack of knowledge of the additional depth of real-world attribute structure available at the level of the folk generic (see Rosch et al., 1976a).

Implications for Other Fields

The foregoing theory of categorization and basic objects has implications for several traditional areas of study in psychology; some of these have been tested.

Imagery. The fact that basic-level objects were the most inclusive categories at which an averaged member of the category could be identified suggested that basic objects might be the most inclusive categories for which it was possible to form a mental image isomorphic to the appearance of members of the class as a whole. Experiments using a signal-detection paradigm and a priming paradigm, both of which have been previously argued to be measures of imagery (Peterson & Graham, 1974; Rosch, 1975c), verified that, in so far as it was meaningful to use the term *imagery*, basic objects appeared to be the most abstract categories for which an image could be reasonably representative of the class as a whole.

Perception. From all that has been said of the nature of basic classifications, it would hardly be reasonable to suppose that in perception of the world, objects were first categorized either at the most abstract or at the most concrete level possible. Two separate studies of picture verification (Rosch et al., 1976a; Smith, Balzano, & Walker, 1978) indicate that, in fact, objects may be first **seen** or recognized as members of their basic category, and that only with the said of additional processing can they be identified as members of their superordinate or subordinate category.

Development. We have argued that classification into categories at the basic level is overdetermined because perception, motor movements, functions, and iconic images would all lead to the same level of categorization. Thus basic objects should be the first categorizations of concrete objects made by children. In fact, for our nine taxonomies, the basic level was the first named. And even when naming was controlled, pictures of several basic-level objects were sorted into groups "because they were the same type of thing" long before such a technique of sorting has become general in children.

Language. From all that has been said, we would expect the most useful and, thus, most used name for an item to be the basic-level name. In fact, we found that adults almost invariably named pictures of the subordinate items of the nine taxonomies at the basic level, although they knew the correct superordinate and subordinate names for the objects. On a more speculative level, in the evolution of languages, one would expect names to evolve first for basic-level objects, spreading both upward and downward as taxonomies increased in depth. Of great relevance for this hypothesis are Berlin's (1972) claims for such a pattern for the evolution of plant names, and our own (Rosch et al., 1976a) and Newport and Bellugi's (Chapter 3, this volume) finding for American Sign Language of the Deaf, that it was the basic-level categories that were most often coded by single signs and super- and subordinate categories that were likely to be missing. Thus a wide range of converging operations verify as basic the same levels of abstraction.

THE HORIZONTAL DIMENSION:
INTERNAL STRUCTURE OF CATEGORIES: PROTOTYPES

Most, if not all, categories do not have clear-cut boundaries. To argue that basic object categories follow clusters of perceived attributes is not to say that such attribute clusters are necessarily discontinuous.

In terms of the principles of categorization proposed earlier, cognitive economy dictates that categories tend to be viewed as being as separate from each other and as clear-cut as possible. One way to achieve this is by means of formal, necessary and sufficient criteria for category membership. The attempt to impose such criteria on categories marks virtually all definitions in the tradition of Western reason. The psychological treatment of categories in the standard concept-identification paradigm lies within this tradition. Another way to achieve separateness and clarity of actually continuous categories is by conceiv-

ing of each category in terms of its clear cases rather than its boundaries. As Wittgenstein (1953) has pointed out, categorical judgments become a problem only if one is concerned with boundaries — in the normal course of life, two neighbors know on whose property they are standing without exact demarcation of the boundary line. Categories can be viewed in terms of their clear cases if the perceiver places emphasis on the correlational structure of perceived attributes such that the categories are represented by their most structured portions.

By prototypes of categories we have generally meant the clearest cases of category membership defined operationally by people's judgments of goodness of membership in the category. A great deal of confusion in the discussion of prototypes has arisen from two sources. First, the notion of prototypes has tended to become reified as though it meant a specific category member or mental structure. Questions are then asked in an either—or fashion about whether something is or is not the prototype or part of the prototype in exactly the same way in which the question would previously have been asked about the category boundary. Such thinking precisely violates the Wittgensteinian insight that we can judge how clear a case something is and deal with categories on the basis of clear cases in the total absence of information about boundaries. Second, the empirical findings about prototypicality have been confused with theories of processing — that is, there has been a failure to distinguish the structure of categories from theories concerning the use of that structure in processing. Therefore, let us first attempt to look at prototypes in as purely structural a fashion as possible. We will focus on what may be said about prototypes based on operational definitions and empirical findings alone without the addition of processing assumptions.

Perception of typicality differences is, in the first place, an empirical fact of people's judgments about category membership. It is by now a well-documented finding that subjects overwhelmingly agree in their judgments of how good an example or clear a case members are of a category, even for categories about whose boundaries they disagree (Rosch, 1974, 1975b). Such judgments are reliable even under changes of instructions and items (Rips, Shoben, & Smith, 1973; Rosch, 1975b, 1975c; Rosch & Mervis, 1975). Were such agreement and reliability in judgment not to have been obtained, there would be no further point in discussion or investigation of the issue. However, given the empirical verification of degree of prototypicality, we can proceed to ask what principles determine which items will be judged the more prototypical and what other variables might be affected by prototypicality.

In terms of the basic principles of category formation, the formation of category prototypes should, like basic levels of abstraction, be determinate and be closely related to the initial formation of categories. For categories of concrete objects (which do not have a physiological basis, as categories such as colors and forms apparently do — Rosch, 1974), a reasonable hypothesis is that prototypes develop through the same principles such as maximization of cue validity and maximization of category resemblance[1] as those principles governing the formation of the categories themselves.

In support of such a hypothesis, Rosch and Mervis (1975) have shown that the more prototypical of a category a member is rated, the more attributes it has in common with other members of the category and the fewer attributes in common with members of the contrasting categories. This finding was demonstrated for natural language superordinate categories, for natural language basic-level categories, and for artificial categories in which the definition of attributes and the amount of experience with items was completely specified and controlled. The same basic principles can be represented in ways other than through attributes in common. Because the present theory is a structural theory, one aspect of it is that centrality shares the mathematical notions inherent in measures like the mean and mode. Prototypical category members have been found to represent the means of attributes that have a metric, such as size (Reed, 1972; Rosch, Simpson, & Miller, 1976).

In short, prototypes appear to be just those members of a category that most reflect the redundancy structure of the category as a whole. That is, if categories form to maximize the information-rich cluster of attributes in the environment and, thus, the cue validity or category resemblance of the attributes of categories, prototypes of categories appear to form in such a manner as to maximize such clusters and such cue validity still further within categories.

It is important to note that for natural language categories both at the superordinate and basic levels, the extent to which items have attributes common to the category was highly negatively correlated with the extent to which they have attributes belonging to contrast categories. This appears to be part of the structure of real-world categories. It may be that such structure is given by the correlated clusters of attributes of the real world. Or such structure, may be a result of the human tendency once a contrast exists to define attributes for contrasting categories so that the categories will be maximally distinctive. In either case, it is a fact that both representativeness within a category and distinctiveness from contrast categories are correlated with prototypicality in real categories. For artificial categories, either principle alone will produce prototype effects (Rosch et al., 1976b; Smith & Balzano, personal communication) depending on the structure of the stimulus set. Thus to perform experiments to try to distinguish which principle is the one that determines prototype formation and category processing appears to be an artificial exercise.

[1]Tversky formalizes prototypicality as the member or members of the category with the highest summed similarity to all members of the category. This measure, although formally more tractable than that of cue validity, does not take account, as cue validity does, of an item's dissimilarity to contrast categories. This issue is discussed further later.

Effects of Prototypicality on Psychological Dependent Variables

The fact that prototypicality is reliably rated and is correlated with category structure does not have clear implications for particular processing models nor for a theory of cognitive representations of categories (see the introduction to Part III and Chapter 9). What is very clear from the extant research is that the prototypicality of items within a category can be shown to affect virtually all of the major dependent variables used as measures in psychological research.

Speed of Processing: Reaction Time. The speed with which subjects can judge statements about category membership is one of the most widely used measures of processing in semantic memory research within the human information-processing framework. Subjects typically are required to respond true or false to statements of the form: X item is a member of Y category, where the dependent variable of interest is reaction time. In such tasks, for natural language categories, responses of true are invariably faster for the items that have been rated more prototypical. Furthermore, Rosch et al. (1976b) had subjects learn artificial categories where prototypicality was defined structurally for some subjects in terms of distance of a gestalt configuration from a prototype, for others in terms of means of attributes, and for still others in terms of family resemblance between attributes. Factors other than the structure of the category, such as frequency, were controlled. After learning was completed, reaction time in a category membership verification task proved to be a function of structural prototypicality.

Speed of Learning of Artificial Categories (Errors) and Order of Development in Children. Rate of learning of new material and the naturally obtainable measure of learning (combined with maturation) reflected in developmental order are two of the most pervasive dependent variables in psychological research. In the artificial categories used by Rosch et al. (1976b), prototypicality for all three types of stimulus material predicted speed of learning of the categories. Developmentally, Anglin (1976) obtained evidence that young children learn category membership of good examples of categories before that of poor examples. Using a category-membership verification technique, Rosch (1973) found that the differences in reaction time to verify good and poor members were far more extreme for 10-year-old children than for adults, indicating that the children had learned the category membership of the prototypical members earlier than that of other members.

Order and Probability of Item Output. Item output is normally taken to reflect some aspect of storage, retrieval, or category search. Battig and Montague (1969) provided a normative study of the probability with which college students listed instances of superordinate semantic categories. The order is correlated with prototypicality ratings (Rosch, 1975b). Furthermore, using the artificial categories in which frequency of experience with all items was controlled, Rosch et al. (1976b) demonstrated that the most prototypical items were the first and most frequently produced items when subjects were asked to list the members of the category.

Effects of Advance Information on Performance: Set, Priming. For colors (Rosch, 1975c), for natural superordinate semantic categories (Rosch, 1975b), and for artificial categories (Rosch et al., 1976b), it has been shown that degree of prototypicality determines whether advance information about the category or name facilitates or inhibits responses in a matching task.

The Logic of Natural Language Use of Category Terms: Hedges, Substitutability into Sentences, Superordination in ASL. Although logic may treat categories as though membership is all or none, natural languages themselves possess linguistic mechanisms for coding and coping with gradients of category membership.

1. *Hedges.* In English there are qualifying terms such as "almost" and "virtually," which Lakoff (1972) calls "hedges." Even those who insist that statements such as "A robin is a bird" and "A penguin is a bird" are equally true, have to admit different hedges applicable to statements of category membership. Thus it is correct to say that a penguin is technically a bird but not that a robin is technically a bird, because a robin is more than just technically a bird; it is a real bird, a bird par excellence. Rosch (1975a) showed that when subjects were given sentence frames such as "X is virtually Y," they reliably placed the more prototypical member of a pair of items into the referent slot, a finding which is isomorphic to Tversky's work on asymmetry of similarity relations (Chapter 4).

2. *Substitutability into sentences.* The meaning of words is intimately tied to their use in sentences. Rosch (1977) has shown that prototypicality ratings for members of superordinate categories predicts the extent to which the member term is substitutable for the superordinate word in sentences. Thus, in the sentence "Twenty or so birds often perch on the telephone wires outside my window and twitter in the morning," the term "sparrow" may readily be substituted for "bird" but the result turns ludicrous by substitution of "turkey," an effect which is not simply a matter of frequency (Rosch, 1975d).

3. *Productive superordinates in ASL.* Newport and Bellugi (Chapter 3) demonstrate that when superordinates in ASL are generated by means of a partial fixed list of category members, those members are the more prototypical items in the category.

In summary, evidence has been presented that prototypes of categories are related to the major dependent variables with which psychological processes are

typically measured. What the work summarized does not tell us, however, is considerably more than it tells us. The pervasiveness of prototypes in real-world categories and of prototypicality as a variable indicates that prototypes must have some place in psychological theories of representation, processing, and learning. However, prototypes themselves do not constitute any particular model of processes, representations, or learning. This point is so often misunderstood that it requires discussion:

1. To speak of *a prototype* at all is simply a convenient grammatical fiction; what is really referred to are judgments of degree of prototypicality. Only in some artificial categories is there by definition a literal single prototype (for example, Posner, Goldsmith, & Welton, 1967; Reed, 1972; Rosch et al., 1976b). For natural-language categories, to speak of a single entity that is the prototype is either a gross misunderstanding of the empirical data or a covert theory of mental representation.

2. Prototypes do not constitute any particular processing model for categories. For example, in pattern recognition, as Palmer (Chapter 9) points out, a prototype can be described as well by feature lists or structural descriptions as by templates. And many different types of matching operations can be conceived for matching to a prototype given any of these three modes of representation of the prototype. Other cognitive processes performed on categories such as verifying the membership of an instance in a category, searching the exemplars of a category for the member with a particular attribute, or understanding the meaning of a paragraph containing the category name are not bound to any single process model by the fact that we may acknowledge prototypes. What the facts about prototypicality do contribute to processing notions is a constraint — process models should not be inconsistent with the known facts about prototypes. For example, a model should not be such as to predict equal verification times for good and bad examples of categories nor predict completely random search through a category.

3. Prototypes do not constitute a theory of representation of categories. Although we have suggested elsewhere that it would be reasonable in light of the basic principles of categorization, if categories were represented by prototypes that were most representative of the items in the category and least representative of items outside the category (Rosch & Mervis, 1975; Rosch, 1977), such a statement remains an unspecified formula until it is made concrete by inclusion in some specific theory of representation. For example, different theories of semantic memory can contain the notion of prototypes in different fashions (Smith, 1978). Prototypes can be represented either by propositional or image systems (see Chapters 8 and 9). As with processing models, the facts about prototypes can only constrain, but do not determine, models of representation. A representation of categories in terms of conjoined necessary and sufficient attributes alone would probably be incapable of handling all of the presently

known facts, but there are many representations other than necessary and sufficient attributes that are possible.

4. Although prototypes must be learned, they do not constitute any particular theory of category learning. For example, learning of prototypicality in the types of categories examined in Rosch and Mervis (1975) could be represented in terms of counting attribute frequency (as in Neuman, 1974), in terms of storage of a set of exemplars to which one later matched the input (see Chapter 6 and the introduction to Part II), or in terms of explicit teaching of the prototypes once prototypicality within a category is established in a culture (e.g., "Now that's a *real* coat.")

In short, prototypes only constrain but do not specify representation and process models. In addition, such models further constrain each other. For example, one could not argue for a frequency count of attributes in children's learning of prototypes of categories if one had reason to believe that children's representation of attributes did not allow for separability and selective attention to each attribute (see Chapter 5 and the introduction to Part II).

TWO PROBLEMATICAL ISSUES

The Nature of Perceived Attributes. The derivations of basic objects and of prototypes from the basic principles of categorization have depended on the notion of a structure in the perceived world – bundles of perceived world attributes that formed natural discontinuities. When the research on basic objects and their prototypes was initially conceived (Rosch et al., 1976a), I thought of such attributes as inherent in the real world. Thus, given an organism that had sensory equipment capable of perceiving attributes such as wings and feathers, it was a fact in the real world that wings and feathers co-occurred. The state of knowledge of a person might be ignorant of (or indifferent or inattentive to) the attributes or might know of the attributes but be ignorant concerning their correlation. Conversely, a person might know of the attributes and their correlational structure but exaggerate that structure, turning partial into complete correlations (as when attributes true only of many members of a category are thought of as true of all members). However, the environment was thought to constrain categorizations in that human knowledge could not provide correlational structure where there was none at all. For purposes of the basic object experiments, perceived attributes were operationally defined as those attributes listed by our subjects. Shape was defined as measured by our computer programs. We thus seemed to have our system grounded comfortably in the real world.

On contemplation of the nature of many of the attributes listed by our subjects, however, it appeared that three types of attributes presented a problem

for such a realistic view: (1) some attributes, such as "seat" for the object "chair," appeared to have names that showed them not to be meaningful prior to knowledge of the object as chair; (2) some attributes such as "large" for the object "piano" seemed to have meaning only in relation to categorization of the object in terms of a superordinate category – piano is large for furniture but small for other kinds of objects such as buildings; (3) some attributes such as "you eat on it" for the object "table" were functional attributes that seemed to require knowledge about humans, their activities, and the real world in order to be understood (see Chapter 10). That is, it appeared that the analysis of objects into attributes was a rather sophisticated activity that our subjects (and indeed a system of cultural knowledge) might well be considered to be able to impose only *after* the development of the category system.

In fact, the same laws of cognitive economy leading to the push toward basic-level categories and prototypes might also lead to the definition of attributes of categories such that the categories once given would appear maximally distinctive from one another and such that the more prototypical items would appear even more representative of their own and less representative of contrastive categories. Actually, in the evolution of the meaning of terms in languages, probably both the constraint of real-world factors and the construction and reconstruction of attributes are continually present. Thus, given a particular category system, attributes are defined such as to make the system appear as logical and economical as possible. However, if such a system becomes markedly out of phase with real-world constraints, it will probably tend to evolve to be more in line with those constraints – with redefinition of attributes ensuing if necessary. Unfortunately, to state the matter in such a way is to provide no clear place at which we can enter the system as analytical scientists. What is the unit with which to start our analysis? Partly in order to find a more basic real-world unit for analysis than attributes, we have turned our attention to the contexts in which objects occur – that is, to the culturally defined events in which objects serve as props.

The Role of Context in Basic-Level Objects and Prototypes. It is obvious, even in the absence of controlled experimentation, that a man about to buy a chair who is standing in a furniture store surrounded by different chairs among which he must choose will think and speak about chairs at other than the basic level of "chair." Similarly, in regard to prototypes, it is obvious that if asked for the most typical African animal, people of any age will not name the same animal as when asked for the most typical American pet animal. Because interest in context is only beginning, it is not yet clear just what experimentally defined contexts will affect what dependent variables for what categories. But it is predetermined that there will be context effects for both the level of abstraction at which an object is considered and for which items are named, learned, listed, or expected in a category. Does this mean that our findings in regard to basic levels and prototypes are relevant only to the artificial situation of the laboratory in which a context is not specified?

Actually, both basic levels and prototypes are, in a sense, theories about context itself. The basic level of abstraction is that level of abstraction that is appropriate for using, thinking about, or naming an object in most situations in which the object occurs (Rosch et al., 1976a). And when a context is not specified in an experiment, people must contribute their own context. Presumably, they do not do so randomly. Indeed, it seems likely that, in the absence of a specified context, subjects assume what they consider the normal context or situation for occurrence of that object. To make such claims about categories appears to demand an analysis of the actual events in daily life in which objects occur.

THE ROLE OF OBJECTS IN EVENTS

The attempt we have made to answer the issues of the origin of attributes and the role of context has been in terms of the use of objects in the events of daily human life. The study of events grew out of an interest in categorizations of the flow of experience. That is, our initial interest was in the question of whether any of the principles of categorization we had found useful for understanding concrete objects appeared to apply to the cutting up of the continuity of experience into the discrete bounded temporal units that we call *events*.

Previously, events have been studied primarily from two perspectives in psychology. Within ecological and social psychology, an observer records and attempts to segment the stream of another person's behavior into event sequences (for example, Barker & Wright, 1955; Newtson, 1976). And within the artificial intelligence tradition, Story Understanders are being constructed that can "comprehend," by means of event scripts, statements about simple, culturally predictable sequences such as going to a restaurant (Shank, 1975).

The unit of the event would appear to be a particularly important unit for analysis. Events stand at the interface between an analysis of social structure and culture and an analysis of individual psychology. It may be useful to think of scripts for events as the level of theory at which we can specify how culture and social structure enter the individual mind. Could we use events as the basic unit from which to derive an understanding of objects? Could we view objects as props for the carrying out of events and have the functions, perceptual attributes, and levels of abstraction of objects fall out of their role in such events?

Our research to date has been a study rather than an experiment and more like a pilot study at that. Events were defined neither by observation of others nor by a priori units for scripts but introspectively in the following fashion. Students in a seminar on events were asked to choose a particular evening on which to list the events that they remembered of that day – e.g., to answer the question what did I do? (or what happened to me?) that day by means of a list of the names of the events. They were to begin in the morning. The students were aware of the nature of the inquiry and that the focus of interest was on the units that they would perceive as the appropriate units into which to chunk the days' happenings. After completing the list for that day, they were to do the same sort of lists for events remembered from the previous day, and thus to continue backwards to preceding days until they could remember no more day's events. They also listed events for units smaller and larger than a day: for example, the hour immediately preceding writing and the previous school quarter.

The results were somewhat encouraging concerning the tractability of such a means of study. There was considerable agreement on the kinds of units into which a day should be broken – units such as making coffee, taking a shower, and going to statistics class. No one used much smaller units: That is, units such as picking up the toothpaste tube, squeezing toothpaste onto the brush, etc., never occurred. Nor did people use larger units such as "got myself out of the house in the morning" or "went to all my afternoon classes." Furthermore, the units that were listed did not change in size or type with their recency or remoteness in time to the writing. Thus, for the time unit of the hour preceding writing, components of events were not listed. Nor were larger units of time given for a day a week past than for the day on which the list was composed. Indeed, it was dramatic how, as days further and further in the past appeared, fewer and fewer events were remembered although the type of unit for those that were remembered remained the same. That is, for a day a week past, a student would not say that he now only remembered getting himself out of the house in the morning (though such "summarizing" events could be inferred); rather he either did or did not remember feeding the cat that day (an occurrence that could also be inferred but for which inference and memory were introspectively clearly distinguishable). Indeed, it appeared that events such as "all the morning chores" as a whole do not have a memory representation separate from memory of doing the individual chores – perhaps in the way that superordinate categories, such as furniture, do not appear to be imageable per se apart from imaging individual items in the category. It should be noted that event boundaries appeared to be marked in a reasonable way by factors such as changes of the actors participating with ego, changes in the objects ego interacts with, changes in place, and changes in the type or rate of activity with an object, and by notable gaps in time between two reported events.

A good candidate for the basic level of abstraction for events is the type of unit into which the students broke their days. The events they listed were just those kinds of events for which Shank (1975) has provided scripts. Scripts of events analyze the event into individual units of action; these typically occur in a predictable order. For example, the script for going to a restaurant contains script elements such as entering, going to a table, ordering, eating, and paying. Some recent research has provided evidence for the psychological reality of scripts and their elements (Bower, 1976).

Our present concern is with the role of concrete objects in events. What categories of objects are required to serve as props for events at the level of abstraction of those listed by the students? In general, we found that the event name itself combined most readily with superordinate noun categories; thus, one gets dressed with clothes and needs various kitchen utensils to make breakfast. When such activities were analyzed into their script elements, the basic level appeared as the level of abstraction of objects necessary to script the events; e.g., in getting dressed, one puts on pants, sweater, and shoes, and in making breakfast, one cooks eggs in a frying pan.

With respect to prototypes, it appears to be those category members judged the more prototypical that have attributes that enable them to fit into the typical and agreed upon script elements. We are presently collecting normative data on the intersection of common events, the objects associated with those events and the other sets of events associated with those objects.[2] In addition, object names for eliciting events are varied in level of abstraction and in known prototypicality in given categories. Initial results show a similar pattern to that obtained in the earlier research in which it was found that the more typical members of superordinate categories could replace the superordinate in sentence frames generated by subjects told to "make up a sentence" that used the superordinate (Rosch, 1977). That is, the task of using a given concrete noun in a sentence appears to be an indirect method of eliciting a statement about the events in which objects play a part; that indirect method showed clearly that prototypical category members are those that can play the role in events expected of members of that category.

The use of deviant forms of object names in narratives accounts for several recently explored effects in the psychological literature. Substituting object names at other than the basic level within scripts results in obviously deviant descriptions. Substitution of superordinates produces just those types of narrative descriptions that Bransford and Johnson (1973) have claimed are not comprehended; for example, "The procedure is actually quite simple. First you arrange things into different groups. Of course, one pile may be sufficient [p. 400]." It should be noted in the present context that what Bransford and Johnson call context cues are actually names of basic-level events (e.g., washing clothes) and that one function of hearing the event name is to enable the reader to translate the superordinate terms into basic-level objects and actions. Such a translation appears to be a necessary aspect of our ability to match linguistic descriptions to world knowledge in a way that produces the "click of comprehension."

On the other hand, substitution of subordinate terms for basic-level object names in scripts gives the effect of satire or snobbery. For example, a review (Garis, 1975) of a pretentious novel accused of actually being about nothing more than brand-name snobbery concludes, "And so, after putting away my 10-year-old Royal 470 manual and lining up my Mongol number 3 pencils on my Goldsmith Brothers Formica imitation-wood desk, I slide into my oversize squirrel-skin L. L. Bean slippers and shuffle off to the kitchen. There, holding *Decades* in my trembling right hand, I drop it, *plunk*, into my new Sears 20-gallon, celadon-green Permanex trash can [p. 48]."

Analysis of events is still in its initial stages. It is hoped that further understanding of the functions and attributes of objects can be derived from such an analysis.

SUMMARY

The first part of this chapter showed how the same principles of categorization could account for the taxonomic structure of a category system organized around a basic level and also for the formation of the categories that occur within this basic level. Thus the principles described accounted for both the vertical and horizontal structure of category systems. Four converging operations were employed to establish the claim that the basic level provides the cornerstone of a taxonomy. The section on prototypes distinguished the empirical evidence for prototypes as structural facts about categories from the possible role of prototypes in cognitive processing, representation, and learning. Then we considered assumptions about the nature of the attributes of real-world objects and assumptions about context — insofar as attributes and contexts underlie the claim that there is structure in the world. Finally, a highly tentative pilot study of attributes and functions of objects as props in culturally defined events was presented.

REFERENCES

Anglin, J. Les premiers termes de référence de l'enfant. In S. Ehrlich & E. Tulving (Eds.), *La memoire sémantique*. Paris: Bulletin de Psychologie, 1976.

Barker, R.., & Wright, H. *Midwest and its children*. Evanston, Ill.: Row-Peterson, 1955.

Battig, W. F., & Montague, W. E. Category norms for verbal items in 56 categories: A replication and extension of the Connecticut category norms. *Journal of Experimental Psychology Monograph*. 1969, 80(3, Pt. 2).

Beach, L. R. Cue probabilism and inference behavior. *Psychological Monographs*. 1964, 78, (Whole No. 582). (a)

Beach, L. R. Recognition, assimilation, and identification of objects. *Psychological Monographs*, 1964, 78(Whole No. 583). (b)

Berlin, B. Speculations on the growth of ethnobotanical nomenclature. *Language in Society*, 1972, 1, 51–86.

Borges, J. L. *Other inquisitions 1937–1952*. New York: Washington Square Press, 1966.

Bower, G. *Comprehending and recalling stories*. Paper presented as Division 3 presidential address to the American Psychological Association, Washington, D.C., September 1976.

---

[2]This work is being done by Elizabeth Kreusi.

Shank, R. C. The structure of episodes in memory. In D. G. Bobrow & A. Collins (Eds.), *Representation and understanding: Studies in cognitive science.* New York: Academic Press, 1975.

Smith, E. E. Theories of semantic memory. In W. K. Estes (Ed.), *Handbook of learning and cognitive processes* (Vol. 5). Hillsdale, N.J.: Lawrence Erlbaum Associates, 1978.

Smith, E. E., & Balzano, G. J. Personal communication, April 1977.

Smith, E. E., Balzano, G. J., & Walker, J. H. Nominal, perceptual, and semantic codes in picture categorization. In J. Cotton & R. Klatzky (Eds.), *Semantic factors in cognition.* Hillsdale, N.J.: Lawrence Erlbaum Associates, 1978.

Tversky, S. Features of similarity. *Psychological Review,* 1977, *84,* 327–352.

Wittgenstein, L. *Philosophical investigations.* New York: Macmillan, 1953.

Bransford, J. D., & Johnson, M. K. Considerations of some problems of comprehension. In W. Chase (Ed.), *Visual information processing.* New York: Academic Press, 1973.

Bruner, J. S., Olver, R. R., & Greenfield, P. M. *Studies in cognitive growth.* New York: Wiley, 1966.

Garis, L. The Margaret Mead of Madison Avenue. *Ms.,* March 1975, pp. 47–48.

Garner, W. R. *The processing of information and structure.* New York: Wiley, 1974.

Kay, P. Taxonomy and semantic contrast. *Language,* 1971, *47,* 866–887.

Lakoff, G. Hedges: A study in meaning criteria and the logic of fuzzy concepts. *Papers from the eighth regional meeting, Chicago Linguistics Society.* Chicago: University of Chicago Linguistics Department, 1972.

Nelson, K. Concept, word and sentence: Interrelations in acquisition and development. *Psychological Review,* 1974, *81,* 267–285.

Neuman, P. G. An attribute frequency model for the abstraction of prototypes. *Memory and Cognition,* 1974, *2,* 241–248.

Newton, D. Foundations of attribution: The perception of ongoing behavior. In J. Harvey, W. Ickes, & R. Kidd (Eds.), *New directions in attribution research.* Hillsdale, N.J.: Lawrence Erlbaum Associates, 1976.

Palmer, S. Hierarchical structure in perceptual representation. *Cognitive Psychology,* in press.

Peterson, M. J., & Graham, S. E. Visual detection and visual imagery. *Journal of Experimental Psychology,* 1974, *103,* 509–514.

Piaget, J. *The origins of intelligence in children.* New York: International Universities Press, 1952.

Posner, M. I., Goldsmith, R., & Welton, K. E. Perceived distance and the classification of distorted patterns. *Journal of Experimental Psychology,* 1967, *73,* 28–38.

Reed, S. K. Pattern recognition and categorization. *Cognitive Psychology,* 1972, *3,* 382–407.

Rips, L. J., Shoben, E. J., & Smith, E. E. Semantic distance and the verification of semantic relations. *Journal of Verbal Learning and Verbal Behavior,* 1973, *12,* 1–20.

Rosch, E. On the internal structure of perceptual and semantic categories. In T. E. Moore (Ed.), *Cognitive development and the acquisition of language.* New York: Academic Press, 1973.

Rosch, E. Linguistic relativity. In A. Silverstein (Ed.), *Human communication: Theoretical perspectives.* New York: Halsted Press, 1974.

Rosch, E. Cognitive reference points. *Cognitive Psychology,* 1975, *7,* 532–547. (a)

Rosch, E. Cognitive representations of semantic categories. *Journal of Experimental Psychology: General.,* 1975, *104,* 192–233. (b)

Rosch, E. The nature of mental codes for color categories. *Journal of Experimental Psychology: Human Perception and Performance,* 1975, *1,* 303–322. (c)

Rosch, E. Universals and cultural specifics in human categorization. In R. Brislin, S. Bochner, & W. Lonner (Eds.), *Cross-cultural perspectives on learning.* New York: Halsted Press, 1975. (d)

Rosch, E. Human categorization. In N. Warren (Ed.), *Advances in cross-cultural psychology* (Vol. 1). London: Academic Press, 1977.

Rosch, E., & Mervis, C. B. Family resemblances: Studies in the internal structure of categories. *Cognitive Psychology,* 1975, *7,* 573–605.

Rosch, E., Mervis, C. B., Gray, W. D., Johnson, D. M., & Boyes-Braem, P. Basic objects in natural categories. *Cognitive Psychology,* 1976, *8,* 382–439. (a)

Rosch, E., Simpson, C., & Miller, R. S. Structural bases of typicality effects. *Journal of Experimental Psychology: Human Perception and Performance.* 1976, *2,* 491–502. (b)

Conceptual Combination with Prototype Concepts*

EDWARD E. SMITH
Bolt Beranek and Newman, Inc.

DANIEL N. OSHERSON
Massachusetts Institute of Technology

This paper deals with how people combine simple, prototype concepts into complex ones; e.g., how people combine the prototypes for *brown* and *apple* so they can determine the typicality of objects in the conjunction *brown apple*. We first consider a proposal from fuzzy-set theory (Zadeh, 1965), namely, that the typicality of an object in a conjunction is equal to the minimum of that object's typicality in the constituents (e.g., an object's typicality as a *brown apple* cannot exceed its typicality as a *brown* or as an *apple*). We evaluated this "min rule" against the typicality ratings of naive subjects in two experiments. For each of numerous pictured objects, one group of subjects rated its typicality with respect to an adjective concept, a second group rated its typicality vis-à-vis a noun concept, and a third group rated its typicality with respect to the adjective-noun conjunction. In both studies, most objects were rated as more typical of the conjunction than of the noun. These findings violate not only the min rule but also other simple rules for relating typicality in a conjunction to typicalities in the constituents. As an alternative to seeking such rules, we argue for an approach to conceptual combination that starts with the prototype representations themselves. We illustrate one version of this approach in some detail, and show how it accounts for the major findings of the present experiments.

CONCEPTUAL COMBINATION WITH PROTOTYPE CONCEPTS

Recent work on natural concepts like *apple, fish, hammer,* and *shirt* has led many researchers to a prototype view of the mental representations of such classes. While proponents of this view have yet to phrase a precise theory, they generally agree upon certain critical issues. Most proponents of the view deny that the mental representation of a natural class specifies necessary and sufficient conditions for membership; it is claimed, instead, that the representation specifies properties that are merely characteristic of the class, or perhaps of only some exemplars of the class (see discussion in Smith & Medin, 1981). Prototype theorists usually also assert that entities fall neither sharply in or sharply out of a concept's extension, the boundary between membership and nonmembership being inherently fuzzy (see discussion in Osherson & Smith, 1981; 1982).[1]

Until recently, all empirical work on concepts-as-prototypes dealt with "simple" concepts, roughly, concepts denoted by single words such as "fish" and "apple." Issues about the combination of these simple concepts into complex ones, and the use of these composites in categorization and other mental activities, have been largely ignored. As a consequence there are few explicit proposals relevant to the combination problem within prototype theory, and none of these proposals appears to be consistent with strong intuitions about combinatorial phenomena involving adjective-noun conjunctions, disjunctions, logically-empty and logically-universal concepts, and truth conditions for inclusion. The matter is reviewed in Jones (1982), Osherson and Smith (1981; 1982), Smith and Osherson (1982), and Zadeh (1982).

The present paper continues our analysis of prototypes and conceptual combination but differs from our earlier work in three ways. First, in the present paper we deal with a more restricted set of phenomena: we consider only adjective-noun conjunctions, such as *pet fish* and *brown apple,* and deal only with their use in categorization. The latter restriction is motivated by the following hypotheses: (a) concepts have a dual structure, with the "identification procedure" being chiefly responsible for categorizing instances of the concept and the "core" of a concept playing a central role in certain reasoning situations; and (b) only the identification procedure conforms to the prototype view (for a defense of these hypotheses, see, e.g., Armstrong, Gleitman, & Gleitman, 1983, and Osherson & Smith,

---

[1] What we are calling the "prototype view corresponds to what Smith and Medin (1981) called the "Probabilistic" and "Exemplar" views.

[2] We use quotes to indicate words, while reversing italics for the concepts that these words denote.

---

* We thank Helene Chaikin, Deborah Pease, and Maggie Kean for their invaluable assistance in all phases of the research reported here. We are also greatly indebted to the following people for their many, many, critical comments, which have helped foster and shape this research: Ken Albert, Susan Carey, Allan Collins, Dedre Gentner, David Israel, Michael Lipton, Mary Potter, and Lance Rips. The research was supported by U.S. Public Health Service Grant MH37208 and by the National Institute of Education under Contract No. US-HEW-C-400-82-0030.

Requests for reprints should be sent to Edward E. Smith, Bolt Beranek and Newman, Inc., 10 Moulton Street, Cambridge, MA 02238.

1981; 1982). A second difference from our previous work is that rather than rely exclusively on just our own intuitions about a few instance-concept pairs, we consider experimental data derived from numerous instance-concept pairs. The third difference from our previous papers pertains to the kinds of theories we entertain. Though initially we focus once again on fuzzy-set theory, eventually we consider in detail a representational approach to conceptual combination.

In more detail, our exposition is organized as follows. In the next section we briefly summarize the fuzzy-set theory approach to conceptual combination and its attendant problems. Section 3 develops a taxonomy of adjective-noun conjunctions and presents two experimental tests of fuzzy-set theory's ability to explain certain phenomena associated with various of the taxa. In the final section we consider an alternative to fuzzy-set theory, one that emphasizes representations.

FUZZY-SET THEORY AND CONCEPTUAL COMBINATION

Characteristic Functions

Fuzzy-set theory (e.g., Zadeh, 1965) is of interest to cognitive scientists because it offers a calculus for combining prototype concepts. A key notion in the application of the theory is that of a characteristic function, c_A: D—[0, 1]. This function maps entities in domain D (the domain of discourse) into the real numbers 0 through 1 in a way that indicates the degree to which the entity is a member of concept A. To illustrate, consider the characteristic function, c_F, which measures degree of membership in the concept *fish* (F). When applied to any relevant creature, x, c_F (x) yields a number that reflects the degree to which x is member of *fish*, where the larger c_F (x) is the more x belongs to *fish*. Since our pet guppy is not very typical of *fish*, it gets a characteristic-function value of .80; our pet dog will get an even lower value, say .05. If we consider the concept *pet* (P), and its characteristic function, c_P, then our guppy and dog might be assigned the values of .70 and .90.

The question of interest concerns the relation between the characteristic function of a conjunction and those of its constituents. How, for example, do we specify $c_{P\&F}$ (the characteristic function of *pet fish*) in terms of c_P and c_F? The answer from Zadeh's 1965 version of fuzzy-set theory is that the conjunction's characteristic-function value is the minimum of the constituents' values; i.e., $c_{P\&F}$ (x) is the minimum of c_P (x) and c_F (x). Applying this min rule to our pet guppie, g, yields,

$$(1)\, c_{P\&F} (g) = \min [c_P(g), c_F(g)]$$
$$= \min (.70, .80) = .70.$$

Assuming that characteristic-function values can be estimated by judgements of typicality, (1) provides a testable claim about the relation between an object's typicality in a conjunction and its typicalities in the constituents.'

Counterexamples to the Min Rule

The min rule is wrong. For (1) says that our guppy is no more typical of *pet fish* than it is of *fish*, and as Osherson and Smith (1981) point out, intuition suggests that a guppy will be more typical of the conjunction *pet fish* than of either constituent, *pet* or *fish*. Osherson and Smith further argue that this *pet fish* example is just one of many counterexamples to the min rule (e.g., a perfectly brown apple seems to be more typical of the conjunction *brown apple* than of either *brown* or *apple*).

However, there are two problems with the foregoing counterexamples. First, they rest only on our own intuitions; such claims need to be tested against typicality ratings of naive subjects. Second, there is no indication of the generality of the failure of fuzzy-set theory; perhaps, the cited counterexamples are of a few types in some underlying taxonomy of conjunctions, where other types might conform to the theory. To deal with these questions, we first present a taxonomy of adjective-noun conjunctions and then describe some relevant experimental work.

TAXONOMY AND EXPERIMENTAL TESTS

A Taxonomy of Adjective-Noun Conjunctions

All counterexamples of the type *pet fish* and *brown apple* share the following characteristic: the adjective concept (i.e., the property denoted by the adjective) is negatively diagnostic of the noun; for example, being brown counts against an object being an apple. More precisely, an adjective is "negatively diagnostic" of a noun to the extent that the applicably of the adjective to a given object decreases the probability that the noun is a true description of that object, and the inapplicability of the adjective to the object increases the probability that the noun is true of that object. An adjective is "positively diagnostic" of a noun to the extent that the adjective being

' Note that there are two interpretations of this min rule: people's judgements may simply *conform* to the rule or they may *follow* it. In the former case, the min rule expresses an abstract constraint between typicalities. In the latter case, the rule offers a processing account of typicality judgements; i.e., people decide on membership in a conjunction by determining membership for each constituent separately, and then combine these two separate determinations.

a true (false) description of a given object increases the probability that the noun is a true (false) description of that object. And an adjective is "nondiagnostic" of a noun to the extent that the applicability of the adjective to a given object has no bearing on whether the noun is true or false of that object. As examples: in *unsliced apple* the adjective is positively diagnostic; in *red apple* the adjective is negatively diagnostic; and, in *brown apple* the adjective is negatively diagnostic. We thus have three distinct cases in our taxonomy.

In addition to the relation between the constituents, we also need to consider the degree to which the conjunction provides a true description of an object that is to be categorized. To keep things simple, we consider only whether the to-be-categorized object manifests the property denoted by the adjective in the conjunction, and we let the object either obviously manifest this property (e.g., an apple that is red coupled with the conjunction *red apple*), or obviously fail to manifest this property (e.g., an apple that is brown coupled with *red apple*). We will refer to these two possibilities as a "good match" and a "poor match," respectively. When these two possibilities are combined with the previously described variations in diagnosticity, we have a total of six cases, and the resulting taxonomy is presented in Table I.

For each case in Table I, consider the relation between typicality judgments for the conjunction and for the constituent concepts. In Case 1, the constituents are relatively independent of one another; accordingly, people may judge separately the degree to which an object is an instance of the adjective and of the noun concepts, and then use some rule to combine the outcomes of these judgments into an overall typicality rating. The min rule (1) is a plausible candidate for this rule since it uniquely meets certain natural conditions on conjunctive operators (see Dubois & Prade, 1980, pp.

TABLE I
Taxonomy of Adjective-Noun Conjunctions

Relation of Adjective Concept to Noun Concept	Degree to Which Object Manifests Property	
	Good Match	Poor Match
Nondiagnostic	(1) unsliced apple object is unsliced	(2) unsliced apple object is sliced
Positively Diagnostic	(3) red apple object is red	(4) red apple object is brown
Negatively Diagnostic	(5) brown apple object is brown	(6) brown apple object is red

11-12.) This line of reasoning suggests that some variant of fuzzy-set theory may be adequate for Case 1. The same intuitive prediction holds for Case 2. In Case 3, since the adjective and noun concepts are not independent, there is no obvious reason to expect the judgment for the conjunction to be a simple function of the judgments for the constituents. Nor is there reason to expect a violation of fuzzy-set theory. We simply lack firm intuitions for this case (as well as for Case 4). Case 5, where the adjective is negatively diagnostic of the noun, captures the counterexamples used in Osherson and Smith (1981). Here intuition strongly suggests that an object that is a good match (e.g., an apple that is indeed brown) will be rated more typical of the conjunction *brown apple* than of either constituent, *brown* or *apple*. This intuition does not hold when the object is a poor match, as in Case 6 (e.g., an apple that is red makes a better *apple* than a *brown apple*).

To summarize our intuitive predictions: For Cases 1 and 2, the only ones where the adjective and noun concepts are largely independent, the min rule of fuzzy-set theory might work, while for Case 5, which includes the Osherson and Smith counterexamples, the min rule should unequivocally fail. The outcomes for the remaining Cases (3, 4, and 6) may fall somewhere in between.

Experiment 1

Overview. The purpose of Experiment 1 was to determine the relation between typicality ratings for conjunctions and their constituents for each case in our taxonomy. For each of 48 pictured objects, one group of 20 subjects rated the object's typicality with respect to an adjective concept, a second group of 20 rated its typicality vis-à-vis a noun concept, and a third group of 20 rated its typicality with respect to the adjective-noun conjunction. The adjective-noun conjunctions were such that all six cases of our taxonomy were tested.

Materials. Table 2 specifies the concepts used. The first column gives the 12 noun concepts (6 natural kinds and 6 artifacts). Column 2-5 give the 48 adjective concepts. Those adjectives in Column 2 are presumed to be positively diagnostic of their corresponding noun concepts, those in Column 3 are presumed to be negatively diagnostic, and those in Columns 4 and 5 are presumed to be largely nondiagnostic. (Later, we will present data that support these presumptions). Each adjective was combined with its corresponding noun to form a conjunctive concept, yielding a total of 48 conjunctions. In addition to designating a conjunction, each intersection of an adjective and noun in a row of Table 2 specifies a pictured object; i.e., 48 pictures were constructed, where one was of a red apple, a second was of a brown apple, a third was of a sliced apple, a fourth was of an unsliced apple, etc. All pictures were hand drawn, photographed, and made into slides.

Procedure. We will consider the procedure for each of the three rating groups in turn. In the "Noun" group, on each trial the experimenter spoke the name of a noun concept, then 1½ s later a pictured object appeared and subjects rated how good an example it was of the concept. Each picture was presented once. Since there were four different pictures for each noun (e.g., four pictures contained apples), each noun occurred four times. This yielded a total of 48 trials. Two quasi-random orders of the trials were created. Each order minimized repetitions of the same concepts on successive trials, and each was used with 10 subjects.

In the "Adjective" group, on every trial the experimenter spoke the name of an adjective concept, then 1½ s later a pictured object appeared and subjects rated how good an example the pictured property was of the concept (e.g., how good an example a particular red apple was of the concept *red*). Now each picture was presented twice, once with an adjective denoting a property for which the pictured object was a good match, and once with an adjective denoting a property for which the pictured object was a poor match. As examples, the picture of the red apple and that of a brown apple were each presented once with "red" and once with "brown." Each adjective thus occurred twice, for a total of 96 trials. Again, two different quasi-random orders of the trials were used, with 10 subjects per order.

The third group is the "Adj-Noun" group. On each trial the experimenter spoke the name of an adjective-noun conjunction, then 1½ s later a picture was presented and subjects rated how good an example it was of the concept. Each picture was presented twice, once with a conjunction for which it was a good match, and once with a conjunction for which it was a poor match. For example, the picture of a red apple was presented once with "red apple" and once with "brown apple." Each conjunction occurred twice, with 24 of the conjunctions being positively diagnostic, 24 being negatively diagnostic, and the remaining 48 being nondiagnostic. There was thus a total of 96 trials, and as usual two quasi-random orders were used with ten subjects receiving each order.

All subjects had 10 s to make a judgment, the judgments being made on a 11-point scale where "0" indicated the object was not an instance of the concept and "10" indicated it was a perfect example. The subjects, 60 Harvard undergraduates who participated for pay, were given 16 practice trials before rating the test items. The concepts and pictures in the practice trials were different from those employed in the test trials.

Results. The top half of Table III contains the data for the three cases of the taxonomy where the object was a good match, while the bottom half has the results for the three cases where the object was a poor match. For each case, the second, third, and fourth columns give the average typicality ratings for the adjective concept, the noun concept, and the conjunction, respectively. (The huge differences between the entries in the top and bottom halves of the table attest to the effectiveness of our variation in degree-of-match.) The final column in Table III specifies the signed difference between the typicality rating of the conjunction and the minimum value of its constituents, providing a measure of how well the min rule of fuzzy-set theory fits the data. As an aid to understanding we have included, in parentheses, indications of sample pictures and concepts for each case. (The results are averaged over natural-kinds and artifacts since there were no interesting differences between the two types of concepts, nor did this variation in type of concept interact with other factors of interest.)

Let us start with the top half of Table III, with those cases where the pictured objects were good matches. For the nondiagnostic conjunctions,

TABLE II
Materials Used in Experiment 1

Noun Concepts	Adjective Concepts			
	Positively Diagnostic	Negatively Diagnostic	Nondiagnostic	Nondiagnostic
apple	red	brown	sliced	unsliced
cantaloupe	round	square	split	whole
corn	straight	bent	husked	unhusked
peas	green	yellow	shelled	unshelled
canary	yellow	red	caged	uncaged
ostrich	feathered	unfeathered	standing	running
chair	symmetric	asymmetric	overturned	upright
table	level	tilted	round	square
car	four-wheeled	three-wheeled	convertible	sedan
bicycle	metal	wooden	red	brown
jacket	sleeved	sleeveless	yellow	red
shoes	leather	wool	laced	unlaced

1 Inspection of the adjectives in Columns 4 and 5 of Table II suggests that some of them may not be nondiagnostic in the intended sense of independent probabilities. We had intended that the probability of a noun being true of an object be independent of whether a nondiagnostic adjective was true of that object, but such independence seems not to apply when the noun denotes, say, *car* and the adjective denotes *convertible* or *sedan*. In cases like these, what nondiagnosticity seems to amount to is that the probability of the noun being true is roughly the same regardless of which adjective it is conditionalized on. For other adjectives in Table II, however, nondiagnosticity in the intended sense does seem to hold; e.g., the probability of an object being a *jacket* is independent of it being *red*. Since our experiments failed to reveal any marked difference in results between cases like *convertible car* and *red jacket*, we will have little more to say about this problem.

we expected the min rule to work because the adjective is largely irrelevant to the noun (though see Footnote 4). The results are otherwise: the conjunction's typicality clearly exceeded the minimum of its constituents. When we look at the trios of concepts contributing to the averages in this case (where a sample trio consists of *unsliced, apple,* and *unsliced apple*), we find that the conjunction's typicality exceeded the minimum in 18 of 24 trios ($p < .05$ by sign test). There is a comparable deviation from the min rule for the positively-diagnostic conjunctions. For the concept trios contributing to the averages in this case, the min rule was violated 10 of 12 times ($p < .05$ by sign test). For the negatively-diagnostic conjunctions, where we had expected the largest violations of the min rule, the conjunctions' typicality exceeded the minimum value of the constituents by virtually half the scale. Inspection of the concept trios contributing to the average indicated the min rule was violated in 11 of 12 trios ($p < .05$ by sign test).

An analysis of variance on the good-match data indicated that the more salient differences in Table III can be taken seriously. Rating groups differed, $F(2, 162) = 19.90$, $p < .01$, and so did the three cases of our taxonomy, $F(2, 162) = 84.12$, $p < .01$. More informatively, rating groups and taxonomic cases interacted, $F(4, 162) = 20.94$, $p < .01$. The bulk of this interaction was due to the noun ratings being much lower in the negatively-diagnostic case, 3.54, than in the other two cases, an average of 7.53. This result attests to the effectiveness of our diagnosticity variation. Adjective ratings were also somewhat lower in the negatively-diagnostic case, 6.93, than in the other two cases, an average of 8.60. This result may reflect a diagnosticity effect—e.g., "it's less of a brown if it's an apple"—or an effect of the pictures themselves—e.g., our brown apple may not have been as good a brown as our red apple was a red.

The most important result, then, is that the min rule was violated in all cases where the object was a best match. Nor is there a simple alternative to the min rule within fuzzy-set theory that seems to do a better job. Perhaps the most plausible alternative is that the conjunction's typicality be the average of its constituents, but this is violated by all three good-match cases (see Table III). The best-fitting post hoc rule is that the conjunction's typicality is the maximum of its constituents (or equivalently, that the conjunction's typicality is the same as that of the adjective constituent). The "max" rule works reasonably well for the nondiagnostic and positively-diagnostic cases, but fails for the negatively-diagnostic case (see Table III). And it is not really a serious possibility in fuzzy-set theory, for if conjunctive concepts are represented by a maximum then there is no obvious way to represent disjunctive concepts.

The bottom half of Table III contains the results for cases where the pictured objects were poor matches. For all three cases the min rule works well, but only because subjects in the Adjective and Adj-Noun groups rated

TABLE III

Mean Typicality Ratings for Adjective Concepts, Noun Concepts and Conjunctions, Separately for Each Case of the Taxonomy (Experiment 1).

Cases (Sample Picture)	Adjective (Sample Concept)	Noun (Sample Concept)	Adj-Noun (Sample Concept)	Adj-Noun Minus Minimum
a. Good Matches:				
Nondiagnostic (unsliced apple)	8.71 (unsliced)	7.25 (apple)	8.65 (unsliced apple)	1.40
Positively diagnostic (red apple)	8.50 (red)	7.81 (apple)	8.87 (red apple)	1.06
Negatively diagnostic (brown apple)	6.93 (brown)	3.54 (apple)	8.52 (brown apple)	4.98
b. Poor Matches:				
Nondiagnostic (sliced apple)	0.45 (unsliced)	7.25ª (apple)	0.52 (unsliced apple)	0.07
Positively Diagnostic (brown apple)	0.02 (red)	3.54ª (apple)	0.10 (red apple)	0.08
Negatively Diagnostic (red apple)	0.81 (brown)	7.81ª (apple)	0.39 (brown apple)	-0.42

ªSince the variation between good and poor matches does not apply to noun ratings, the means here are simply the repeats of the means listed directly above, i.e., these three means are not new data. Note, however, that the assignment of means to positively- and negatively-diagnostic cases must be reversed in moving from the top to the bottom of the table, e.g., a picture of a red apple paired with apple corresponds to the positively-diagnostic case in the top of the table but to the negatively-diagnostic case in the bottom of the table.

TABLE IV
Materials Used in Experiment 2

Noun Concepts	Adjective Concepts			
	Positively Diagnostic	Negatively Diagnostic	Nondiagnostic	Nondiagnostic
apple	red	brown	peeled	unpeeled
cantaloupe	round	square	sliced	unsliced
corn	straight	bent	husked	unhusked
peas	green	yellow	shelled	unshelled
ostrich	feathered	unfeathered	standing	walking
canary	yellow	red	caged	uncaged

form a conjunction, yielding a total of 24 conjunctions. Like Experiment 1, each intersection of an adjective and noun in a row of the table also specified a picture. Unlike Experiment 1, the cells in the table do not exhaust the pictures used. Specifically, "between" a pair of pictures that corresponded to related adjectives—e.g., the pictures of red and brown apples—we introduced a picture that had an intermediate value on the adjective—e.g., a picture of a reddish-brown apple. There were 12 such intermediate pictures, yielding a total of 36 pictures in all.

Procedure. Separate groups of subjects (16 Harvard undergraduates per group) gave typicality ratings in the Noun, Adjective, and Adj-Noun groups. The procedure was the same as in Experiment 1 save the following exceptions: (a) On each trial, 1½ s after the experimenter spoke the name of a concept, all the pictures were presented. Subjects had 20 s to rate all the pictures for typicality. (b) Prior to each trial, subjects were presented for 2 s each the three pictures they would have to rate.

Results. The average typicality ratings are in Table V. The top third of the table contains the data for good matches, the middle third for intermediate matches, and the bottom third for poor matches. The substantial differences between the entries in the top, middle, and bottom of the table attest to the effectiveness of our variation in degree-of-match. As an aid to understanding, we have included in parentheses sample pictures and concepts for each case.

Let us start with the good-match cases. These data replicate the major findings in Experiment 1, and if anything provide an even stronger refutation of fuzzy-set theory. For all three cases, the typicality ratings for the conjunction substantially exceeded the conjunction's typicality and the minimum typicality of its constituents. The difference between the conjunction's typicality and the minimum typicality of its constituents is significant at the .05 level for all three cases by sign tests. In addition, an analysis of variance yielded results similar to those obtained in Experiment 1. There were significant effects due

the pictured objects to be unequivocal *nonmembers* of the relevant concepts. When presented a picture of a brown apple, for example, and asked to judge its typicality for *red or red apple*, most subjects gave it zero ratings. This finding reflects an uninteresting conformity to fuzzy-set theory; at best it indicates that in tasks such as ours subjects adopt a threshold, below which all objects are rated as nonmembers; at worst the finding suggests that there is something wrong with the prototype view that lies behind fuzzy-set theory.

We suspect that the zero ratings reflect a poor choice on our part of how to experimentally implement our degree-of-match variable, and consequently that the data in the bottom of Table III can not be taken as a sensitive test of the min rule. (For this reason, we will not bother to provide statistical analyses.) Thus, had we used pictures of red apples and reddish-brown apples, it is likely that we would not have obtained so many zero ratings for the concepts *red* and *red apple*. This change was made in Experiment 2.

Summary. For the three cases of our taxonomy where the objects are clearcut members of conjunctive concepts, fuzzy-set theory unequivocally failed to account for the relation between an object's typicality in the conjunction and its typicalities in the constituents. What remains an open question is whether the theory fares better for items that are poorer matches to concepts.

Experiment 2

Overview. To provide a more sensitive test of how well fuzzy-set theory accounts for conceptual combination when the objects are poor matches, we made two changes from the previous study. First we added pictures that had intermediate values on the properties denoted by the adjectives, e.g., in addition to pictures of a red apple and a brown apple, we included a picture of a reddish-brown apple. We expected that ratings for such intermediate matches would be substantially greater than zero. Second, we had subjects rate the three related pictures—e.g., the red apple, the reddish-brown apple, and the brown apple—on a single trial. This move should also foster nonzero ratings.

Materials. Table IV specifies the concepts used. The first column gives the six noun concepts, all of which are natural kinds. Columns 2–5 give the 24 adjective concepts: those in Column 2 are positively diagnostic, those in Column 3 are negatively diagnostic, and those in Columns 4 and 5 are relatively nondiagnostic of their corresponding noun concepts (though, see Footnote 4). Each adjective was combined with its corresponding noun to to taxonomic cases, $F(2, 135) = 58.73$, $p < .01$ and to rating groups, $F(2, 135) = 87.24$, $p < .01$. (This time rating for conjunctions significantly exceeded those for both nouns and adjectives; for the planned comparison between conjunctions and nouns, $F(1, 141) = 66.27$, $p < .01$; for the comparison between conjunctions and adjectives, $F(1, 141) = 12.64$, $p < .01$). And again, rating groups interacted with taxonomic cases, $F(4, 135) = 30.57$, $p < .01$, reflecting the fact that both adjective and noun ratings were lower in the negatively-diagnostic case than in the other two cases.

Let us move on to the middle of Table V, and the data for intermediate matches. Our use of intermediate pictures eliminated the all-or-none responding of Experiment 1, as all ratings in the middle of Table V are substantially greater than zero. A glance at the last column indicates that, for all three cases, the conjunction's typicality exceeded the minimum of its constituents. These deviations from the min rule, however, are less pronounced than those observed with good matches. An analysis of variance yielded a main effect of rating groups, $F(2,135) = 29.42$, $p < .01$, and planned comparisons indicated that ratings for the conjunction exceeded those for the adjective, $F(2, 135) = 5.64$, $p < .01$, which is sufficient to reject the min rule. There was also an effect of taxonomic cases, $F(2, 135) = 12.75$, $p < .01$, and an interaction between taxonomic case and rating group, $F(4, 135) = 12.85$, $p < .01$. Both of these effects are explicable in terms of our diagnosticity variation.

The bottom of Table V contains the data for the poor matches. Our variations in materials and procedure seemed to have induced the subjects to treat our variation in degree-of-match as a continuum, i.e., they no longer responded to the poor matches as out-and-out nonmembers. Still, a couple of the numbers at the bottom of Table V are perilously close to zero. With this caution in mind, inspection of the last column of these data indicates that the min rule of fuzzy-set theory works rather well here. An analysis of variance supports this conclusion. While there was a main effect of rating groups, $F(2, 135) = 313.71$, $p < .01$, it reflected only higher ratings for nouns, as ratings for conjunctions were clearly close to those for adjectives (the minimum constituent). There was also an effect of taxonomic cases, $F(2, 135) = 37.78$, $p < .01$, and an interaction between case and rating group, $F(4, 135) = 51.95$, $p < .01$. As usual these two effects are explicable in terms of our diagnosticity variation.

Summary. We have replicated the good-match results of Experiment 1: when the objects were clear-cut members of conjunctions, the min rule of fuzzy-set theory unequivocally failed. Fuzzy-set theory also failed when the objects were intermediate matches to the relevant concepts. Indeed, the only cases where the min rule correctly described the relation between typicality in a conjunction and typicality in its constituents was when the objects were

TABLE V
Mean Typicality Ratings for Adjective Concepts, Noun Concepts and Conjunctions, Separately for Each Case of the Taxonomy (Experiment 2)

Cases (Sample Pictures)	Adjective (Sample Concept)	Noun (Sample Concept)	Adj-Noun (Sample Concept)	Adj-Noun Minus Minimum
a. Good Matches:				
Nondiagnostic (most peeled apple)	7.04 (peeled)	6.58 (apple)	7.75 (peeled apple)	1.17
Positively diagnostic (red apple)	8.25 (red)	7.08 (apple)	8.75 (red apple)	1.67
Negatively diagnostic (brown apple)	6.50 (brown)	2.17 (apple)	8.42 (brown apple)	6.25
b. Intermediate Matches:				
Nondiagnostic (medium-peeled apple)	4.13 (peeled)	7.33 (apple)	4.29 (peeled apple)	0.16
Positively diagnostic (reddish-brown apple)	4.50 (red)	4.92 (apple)	5.08 (red apple)	0.58
Negatively diagnostic (reddish-brown apple)	2.92 (brown)	4.92 (apple)	4.42 (brown apple)	1.50
c. Poor Matches:				
Nondiagnostic (least peeled apple)	1.25 (peeled)	7.25 (apple)	1.25 (peeled apple)	0
Positively diagnostic (brown apple)	1.33 (red)	2.17[a] (apple)	1.17 (red apple)	−0.16
Negatively diagnostic (red apple)	0.25 (brown)	7.08[a] (apple)	0.50 (brown apple)	0.25

[a] The means here are repeats of the means listed in the top of the table, with the assignment of means to positively- and negatively-diagnostic cases being reversed in moving from the top to the bottom of the table.

judged to be very poor members of the relevant concepts. This seems, at best, a minor victory. A theory that can predict membership ratings only for objects that are close to nonmembers is clearly missing much of what is going on. One should be able to construct theories that capture more of the data, and in what follows we attempt to do so.[3]

A REPRESENTATIONAL APPROACH TO CONCEPTUAL COMBINATION

Rationale for a Representational Approach

The min rule does not account for typicality judgments in conjunctive concepts. This is the burden of the two experiments just reported. We now wish to argue that the difficulty for fuzzy-set theory lies not in the min function itself, but in the use of characteristic functions to the exclusion of the mental representations that they summarize.

Let us briefly sketch the case against such exclusive dependence on characteristic functions. Our experimental data are inconsistent with the use of min, average, and maximum rules to explain judgments of typicality in conjunctive concepts on the basis of judgments of typicality in their constituents. What about other simple rules or functions? In a previous paper (Osherson & Smith, 1982), we presented a formal argument against there being any simple function that relates the typicality properties of conjunctive concepts to those of its constituents. (See Tversky and Kahneman, 1983, for a comparable argument regarding the similarity properties of conjunctive concepts.) If our argument is correct, proponents of fuzzy-set approaches will have to revert to "complex" functions (that is, functions that consider more than just the typicality of constituent concepts).

Zadeh (1982) and Jones (1982) have done precisely this, although the uses made of characteristic functions by these two researchers are very different. Unfortunately, both approaches appear to be fraught with problems

as severe as those besetting the original fuzzy-set theory. The matter is discussed in Osherson & Smith (1982). These negative findings suggest that it is time to explore an approach to conceptual combination that starts with the prototype representations themselves. Such a shift of emphasis has previously been argued for by Cohen and Murphy (1984), Hampton (1973), and Thagard (1983).

The following representation-based analyses are primarily suggestive (a more formal account is presented in Smith, Osherson, Rips, Albert, & Keane, forthcoming). In developing these analyses, we have focused on two critical findings from the foregoing experiments (re-presented in Table VI): (a) when an object matched the adjective in a conjunctive concept, the object was judged more typical of that conjunctive concept than of the noun constituent; (b) in contrast, if an object did not match the adjective in a conjunctive concept it was judged less typical of that conjunctive concept than of the noun. Thus, red apples were more typical of red apple than of apple, while brown apples were less typical of red apple than of apple—and similarly for the concepts brown apple and peeled apple (see Table VI).

TABLE VI

Mean Typicality Ratings for Noun Concepts and Conjunctions, Separately for Objects that Match or Mismatched the Adjective in the Conjunction

Cases	Experiment 1		Experiment 2	
	Noun	Adj-Noun	Noun	Adj-Noun
a. Object Matched Adjective:				
Nondiagnostic	7.25	8.65	6.58	7.75
Positively Diagnostic	7.81	8.87	7.08	8.75
Negatively Diagnostic	3.54	8.52	2.17	8.42
Average	6.20	8.68	5.28	8.31
b. Object Mismatched Adjective:				
Nondiagnostic	7.25	0.52	7.25	1.25
Positively Diagnostic	3.54	0.10	2.17	1.17
Negatively Diagnostic	7.81	0.39	7.08	0.50
Average	6.20	0.34	5.28	0.97

Prototype Representations of Noun Concepts

In constructing a representational account of typicality judgements for conjunctive concepts, a useful starting point is to consider the comparable account for simple noun concepts. According to recent work: (a) both a simple concept and an object can be represented by a set of attributes and their associated values or "features," (e.g., Smith & Medin, 1981); and (b) the typicality of an object in a concept is a direct function of the object's similarity to the concept, where similarity is assessed in terms of a contrast between common and distinctive features (Tversky, 1977). Figure 1 illustrates the key assumptions.

[3] One might, however, question the definitiveness of our data on the following grounds. In both our experiments type of rating was varied between subjects, which leaves open the possibility that different groups used the rating scale differentially. Subjects in the Adj-Noun group, for example, might have considered different domains of objects when making their ratings than did subjects in the Noun group, and this might have affected how the subjects divided up the rating scale (L. Rips, personal communication, June, 1983). This possibility suggests the need for a study similar to Experiments 1 and 2 but with rating-type as a within-subject variable. We performed a pilot study along these lines and found that the min rule still failed to account for the typicality ratings for best matches, which argues against the above-mentioned scaling problem. Our pilot results also suggested that the within-subject variation in rating-type led to the use of task specific strategies (e.g., "always order the three ratings in the same way"), which suggests that our original between-subjects design is preferable.

$$\text{(2)} \quad \text{Sim} (A, O) = af (A \cap O) - bf (A - O) - cf (O - A).$$

Here, $A \cap O$ designates the set of features common to the concept and object, $A - O$ designates the set of features distinct to the concept, and $O - A$ designates the set of features distinct to the object. In addition, f is a function that measures the salience or prominence of each feature, and a, b and c are parameters that determine the relative contribution of the three feature sets. The basic idea is that similarity is an increasing function of the features common to the concept and object, and a decreasing function of the features distinct to the concept and of those distinct to the object. In making the computations in Figure 1 (as well as in subsequent figures), we have assumed that a, b, and c are equal to one. We have further assumed that f is the weighted sum of all features that are common to the object and concept, and similarly for $F (A - O)$ and $F (O - A)$ (where the weight of a feature is given by the weight of the corresponding attribute in the concept.) For the examples provided in Figure 1, application of the contrast model correctly predicts that the red apple should be judged to be more typical of *apple* than is the brown apple.[6]

Prototype Representations for Conjunctions

We now want to extend this kind of account to adjective-noun conjunctions. The first order of business is to specify how the adjective will interact with the noun concept. There are two obvious possibilities. One is that the adjective is represented in a similar way to the noun and that the two representations are *intersected*. Alternatively, the adjective may play a different role than that of the noun, in that it is used to *modify* the noun. There are a number of reasons for favoring the modification approach over that of intersection (see Cohen & Murphy, 1984, for a discussion of some of these issues), and modification is the track that we will take.[7]

Figure 2 illustrates our assumptions about adjective modification (to keep things simple, we consider only adjectives that presumably contain a single feature, e.g., *red* and *brown*). In essence, the adjective does three things: (1) it picks out the relevant attribute in the noun (e.g., color); (2) it dictates where the asterisk for the relevant attribute should be positioned (e.g., *red*); and (3) it increases the diagnosticity weight associated with the relevant attribute. In the example at the top of Figure 2, the critical asterisk

[6] Technically, we are using a generalized version of the contrast model where the weight assigned to a feature depends on the concept as well as the feature. For example, the weight for *red* may differ for *apple* and *brick*. Tversky's formalism, given in [2], is a stronger theory in that it assigns the same weight to a feature regardless of what concept that feature is part of.

[7] We are indebted to Amos Tversky for highlighting the intersection-modification distinction to us.

	Apple (A)	a red apple (O_1)	a brown apple (O_2)
3 color	red* / white / brown	red* / white / brown	red / white / brown*
1 shape	round* / square	round* / square	round* / square
2 texture	smooth* / rough	smooth* / rough	smooth* / rough

$$\text{Sim. } (O_1, A) = 6 - 0 - 0 = 6$$

$$\text{Sim} (O_2, A) = 3 - 3 - 3 = -3$$

Figure 1. Illustration of attribute-value representations of noun concept (*apple*) and relevant objects (a red apple and a brown apple): beneath each object representation is the similarity between the object and the concept.

The left-most panel of the figure contains a sample representation for the concept *apple*. The representation specifies: (a) a set of relevant attributes (color, shape, texture, etc.), and (b) for each attribute, a set of possible values, or features, that instances of the concept can assume on that attribute (e.g., for color, the features include red, white, and brown). In addition, the representation also specifies (c) the most likely feature for each attribute, as indicated by the position of an asterisk, as well as (d) the diagnosticity of each attribute for the concept, as indicated by the number to the left of each attribute. This kind of representation is essentially a frame (e.g., Minsky, 1975; Winston & Horn, 1981), with *attributes* being *slot-names*, *features* being *values*, and *most-likely features* being *default values*.

In the remaining panels of Figure 1, we have given sample representations for two specific objects, one a typical red apple and the other a brown apple. Note that an object representation is simpler than a concept representation, as the former specifies only a set of relevant attributes, and the actual value of each attribute for that object. Beneath each object representation we have calculated its similarity to the concept *apple* using Tversky's (1977) "contrast" model. In terms of this model, the similarity between the most-likely features of *apple* (labelled "A") and the actual features of the object (labelled "O") is given by:

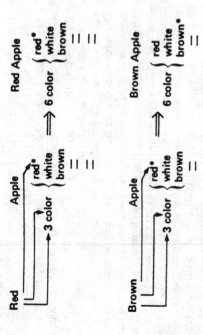

Red ⟶ Apple ⟶ 3 color $\left\{\begin{array}{l}\text{red*}\\\text{white}\\\text{brown}\end{array}\right.$ == ==

Red Apple ⟹ 6 color $\left\{\begin{array}{l}\text{red*}\\\text{white}\\\text{brown}\end{array}\right.$ == ==

Brown ⟶ Apple ⟶ 3 color $\left\{\begin{array}{l}\text{red*}\\\text{white}\\\text{brown}\end{array}\right.$ ==

Brown Apple ⟹ 6 color $\left\{\begin{array}{l}\text{red}\\\text{white}\\\text{brown*}\end{array}\right.$ ==

Figure 2. Illustration of three aspects of adjective modification.

The Positively - Diagnostic Case

Red Apple (RA)

6 color $\left\{\begin{array}{l}\text{red*}\\\text{white}\\\text{brown}\end{array}\right.$ ==

1 shape $\left\{\begin{array}{l}\text{round*}\\\text{square}\end{array}\right.$ ==

2 texture $\left\{\begin{array}{l}\text{smooth*}\\\text{rough}\end{array}\right.$ ==

a red apple (O$_1$)

color $\left\{\begin{array}{l}\text{red*}\\\text{white}\\\text{brown}\end{array}\right.$ ==

shape $\left\{\begin{array}{l}\text{round*}\\\text{square}\end{array}\right.$ ==

texture $\left\{\begin{array}{l}\text{smooth*}\\\text{rough}\end{array}\right.$ ==

a brown apple (O$_2$)

color $\left\{\begin{array}{l}\text{red}\\\text{white}\\\text{brown*}\end{array}\right.$ ==

shape $\left\{\begin{array}{l}\text{round*}\\\text{square}\end{array}\right.$ ==

texture $\left\{\begin{array}{l}\text{smooth*}\\\text{rough}\end{array}\right.$ ==

Sim. (O$_1$, RA) = 9-0-0 = 9

Sim. (O$_2$, RA) = 3 -6 -6 = -9

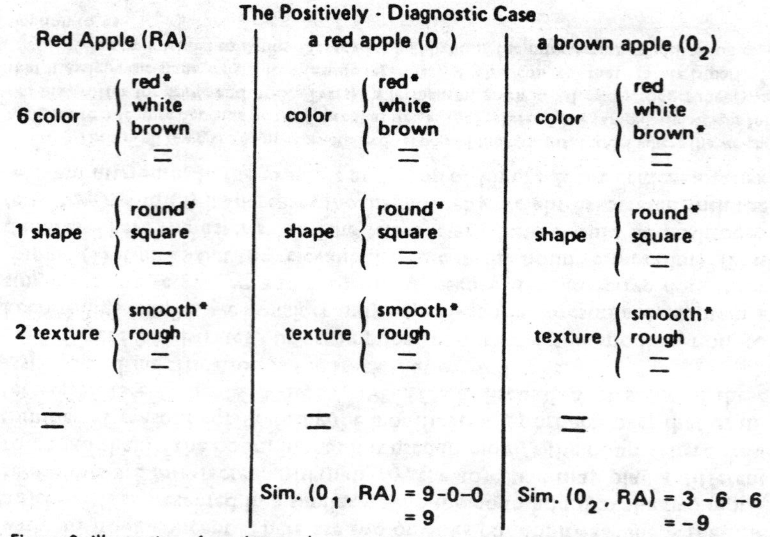

Figure 3. Illustration of attribute-value representations of *red apple* and relevant objects; beneath each object representation is the similarity between the object and the conjunction.

The Negatively - Diagnostic Case

Brown Apple (BA)

6 color $\left\{\begin{array}{l}\text{red}\\\text{white}\\\text{brown*}\end{array}\right.$ ==

1 shape $\left\{\begin{array}{l}\text{round*}\\\text{square}\end{array}\right.$ ==

2 texture $\left\{\begin{array}{l}\text{smooth*}\\\text{rough}\end{array}\right.$ ==

a red apple (O$_1$)

color $\left\{\begin{array}{l}\text{red*}\\\text{white}\\\text{brown}\end{array}\right.$ ==

shape $\left\{\begin{array}{l}\text{round*}\\\text{square}\end{array}\right.$ ==

texture $\left\{\begin{array}{l}\text{smooth*}\\\text{rough}\end{array}\right.$ ==

a brown apple (O$_2$)

color $\left\{\begin{array}{l}\text{red}\\\text{white}\\\text{brown*}\end{array}\right.$ ==

shape $\left\{\begin{array}{l}\text{round*}\\\text{square}\end{array}\right.$ ==

texture $\left\{\begin{array}{l}\text{smooth*}\\\text{rough}\end{array}\right.$ ==

Sim. (O$_1$, BA) = 3-6-6 = -9

Sim. (O$_2$, BA) = 9 -0 -0 = 9

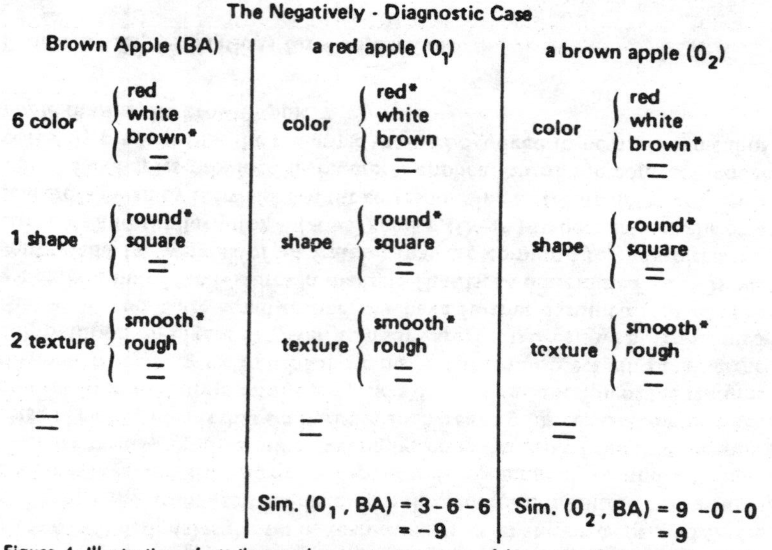

Figure 4. Illustration of attribute-value representations of *brown apple* and relevant objects; beneath each object representation is the similarity between the object and the conjunction.

---

was already on the feature specified by the adjective, *red*, and hence no change in the asterisk's position is needed. This situation is the hallmark of positively-diagnostic conjunctions like *red apple*. There is, however, a change in the weights, as the diagnosticity of the attribute color has doubled. In the example at the bottom of Figure 2, the critical asterisk has to be moved from the default feature, *red*, to an atypical value, *brown*. This situation is the hallmark of negatively-diagnostic conjunctions like *brown apple*. In addition, there is again a doubling of the diagnosticity of color.

Figure 3 illustrates the implications of the above changes for typicality ratings with positively-diagnostic conjunctions. The left-most panel of the figure contains the representation for the conjunction *red apple*. In keeping with our assumptions about modification, the only difference between this representation and that of *apple* is in the diagnostic importance of being *red*. The effects of this difference on typicality are illustrated in the remaining panels of Figure 3. There we have repeated the object representations for our red and brown apples, and computed the similarity for each of these objects in the conjunction. When these similarity scores are compared to those in the Figure 1, the result is that the red apple is more similar to *red apple* than it is to *apple*, while the brown apple is less similar to *red apple* than it is to *apple*. We have therefore reconstructed our major findings for the positively-diagnostic case, that an object that matches the adjective in a conjunctive concept is more typical of the conjunction than of its noun constituent, while an object that does not match the adjective in a conjunction is more typical of the noun constituent.

Figure 4 illustrates a comparable analysis for negatively-diagnostic conjunctions. The left-most panel of the figure contains the representation for *brown apple*. In keeping with our modification proposal, this representation differs from that of *apple* in two ways: (1) color is more diagnostic, and (2) the value of color is now *brown* rather than *red*. The effects of these changes on typicality are shown in the remaining panels of Figure 4. Again, we have reproduced our object representations for the red and brown apples, and computed the similarity for each object in the conjunction. Now, in comparison to our original computations in Figure 1, we find that the red apple is less similar to *brown apple* than it is to *apple*, while the brown apple is more similar to *brown apple* than it is to *apple*. Again, we have reconstructed our major findings. Note, however, that in this case the results reflect changes in both (a) diagnosticity weights and (b) the number of common and distinctive features (e.g., the brown apple shares more features with *brown apple* that with *apple*).

The last case to be considered is the nondiagnostic one, and it is illustrated in Figure 5. The left-most panel of the figure contains the representation for *peeled apple*. This representation differs from that of *apple* in three ways: (1) peeledness, and attribute that presumably was only implicit

in *apple*, is now represented explicitly;[2] (2) peeledness has become quite diagnostic; and (3) the value of peeledness is now *peeled*. (Presumably, there was no asterisk in the relevant attribute of the noun before modification: this situation is the hallmark of nondiagnostic conjunctions.) The consequences of these changes are displayed in the remaining panels of Figure 5. There, we have given object representations for our peeled and unpeeled apples and have computed the similarity for each object in the conjunction. To see how well these results fit with our major findings, we need to know the similarity of peeled and unpeeled apple to the concept of *apple*. These similarities turn out to be identical to those of a red apple, namely 6, (see Figure 1).[3] Thus, the peeled apple is found to be more similar to *peeled apple* than to *apple*, while the unpeeled apple is found to be less similar to *peeled apple* than to *apple*. Once more we have captured our major findings.

The results of these illustrative analyses are summarized in Table VII. These results make it clear that when we combine proposals about attribute-value representations for nouns and adjectives with our specific proposals about modification, the resulting package captures the major qualitative findings of our experiments.

TABLE VII
Resulting Similarity Scores in Illustrative Analysis

Concepts	Objects			
	red apple	brown apple	peeled apple	unpeeled apple
Apple	6	−3		
Red Apple	9	−9		
Apple	6	−3		
Brown Apple	−9	9		
Apple			6	6
Peeled Apple			9	0

Some Extensions

The preceding analyses considered only good and poor matches. We can extend these analyses to intermediate matches by enriching our representation of default features. The asterisk approach we have been employing assumes

[2] To assume that peeledness was implicit in *apple* is to assume that though possibly relevant to being an apple, the attribute had no default feature nor weight, and consequently played no role in judgments of typicality for *apple*. These assumptions go beyond the specifics of our modification proposal. An alternative assumption is the peeledness is added to the representation of *apple* during modification.

[3] The only representational difference between, say, our peeled apple and our red apple is that the former is implicitly marked for peeledness, but since this attribute presumably has no weight in *apple* it has no effect on the similarity computations.

The Nondiagnostic Case

	Peeled Apple (PA)	a peeled apple (O_3)	an unpeeled apple (O_4)
3 color	$\left\{\begin{array}{l}\text{red*}\\\text{white}\\\text{brown}\end{array}\right.=$	color $\left\{\begin{array}{l}\text{red*}\\\text{white}\\\text{brown}\end{array}\right.=$	color $\left\{\begin{array}{l}\text{red*}\\\text{white}\\\text{brown}\end{array}\right.=$
1 shape	$\left\{\begin{array}{l}\text{round*}\\\text{square}\end{array}\right.=$	shape $\left\{\begin{array}{l}\text{round*}\\\text{square}\end{array}\right.=$	shape $\left\{\begin{array}{l}\text{round*}\\\text{square}\end{array}\right.=$
2 texture	$\left\{\begin{array}{l}\text{smooth*}\\\text{rough}\end{array}\right.=$	texture $\left\{\begin{array}{l}\text{smooth*}\\\text{rough}\end{array}\right.=$	texture $\left\{\begin{array}{l}\text{smooth*}\\\text{rough}\end{array}\right.=$
3 peeledness	$\left\{\begin{array}{l}\text{peeled*}\\\text{unpeeled}\end{array}\right.=$	peeledness $\left\{\begin{array}{l}\text{peeled*}\\\text{unpeeled}\end{array}\right.=$	peeledness $\left\{\begin{array}{l}\text{peeled}\\\text{unpeeled*}\end{array}\right.=$
		Sim. $(O_3, PA) = 9 - 0 - 0$ $= 9$	Sim. $(O_4, PA) = 6 - 3 - 3$ $= 0$

Figure 5. Illustration of attribute-value representations of *peeled apple* and relevant objects; beneath each object representation is the similarity between the object and the conjunction

Apple	Red Apple	a red apple (O_1)	a red - brown apple (O_5)
3 color $\left\{\begin{array}{l}\text{red 8}\\\text{white 1}\\\text{brown 1}\end{array}\right.$ =	6 color $\left\{\begin{array}{l}\text{red 10}\\\text{white}\\\text{brown}\end{array}\right.$ =	color $\left\{\begin{array}{l}\text{red 9}\\\text{white 1}\\\text{brown}\end{array}\right.$	color $\left\{\begin{array}{l}\text{red 5}\\\text{white}\\\text{brown 5}\end{array}\right.$
1 shape $\left\{\begin{array}{l}\text{round 9}\\\text{square 1}\end{array}\right.$ =	1 shape $\left\{\begin{array}{l}\text{round 9}\\\text{square 1}\end{array}\right.$ =	shape $\left\{\begin{array}{l}\text{round 9}\\\text{square 1}\end{array}\right.$	shape $\left\{\begin{array}{l}\text{round 9}\\\text{square 1}\end{array}\right.$
2 texture $\left\{\begin{array}{l}\text{smooth 9}\\\text{rough 1}\end{array}\right.$ =	2 texture $\left\{\begin{array}{l}\text{smooth 9}\\\text{rough 1}\end{array}\right.$ =	texture $\left\{\begin{array}{l}\text{smooth 9}\\\text{rough 1}\end{array}\right.$	texture $\left\{\begin{array}{l}\text{smooth 9}\\\text{rough 1}\end{array}\right.$
=	=	=	=

Figure 6. Illustration of attribute-value representations of *apple*, *red apple*, and relevant objects, with feature weights rather than asterisks.

that each attribute has a single default, and that the default for any one attribute is as important as that for any other attribute. Suppose, instead, that we assume the representation is like that in Figure 6. The first two panels contain representations for the concepts *apple* and *red apple*. For every attribute, instead of an asterisk we have a distribution of numbers, or weights, over features, where these weights indicate the "default mixture" of the relevant features. For example, with regard to color, the prototypical *apple* is mainly red but has some white and brown in it, while the prototypical *red apple* is weighted only for red. In the last two panels of the figure we have object representations for our red apple and our reddish-brown apple (the latter being an intermediate match). We have assumed that the red apple is weighted heavily for red while the reddish-brown apple is half red and half brown. Taking these feature weights into account, it is apparent that regardless of the specifics of the similarity computations, the reddish-brown apple is less similar to either *apple* or *red apple* than is the red apple; this accounts for why, in comparison to good matches, intermediates were judged less typical of both *apple* and *red apple*. In essence, intermediate matches do not match closely either of the above concepts because each concept requires a different weighting of colors than the object in fact manifests. In Smith, Osherson, Rips, Albert, & Kean, 1984, we provide a thorough treatment of such feature weights and their consequences for similarity.

Another restriction of the present paper is that it dealt only with adjective-noun conjunctions. Our representational approach, however, can readily be extended to other kinds of combinations. One relatively straightforward extension involves adverbs like *very* and *slightly*. Such adverbs can be represented as "scalars" (e.g., Cliff, 1959), which multiply feature weights. Thus, in *very red apple*, essentially *very* multiplies the weight of *red* in *red apple*. In Smith et al. (forthcoming), we provide an extensive treatment of such adverbs.

Other possible extensions could be mentioned, but it seems best to close on a cautionary note. We doubt that any approach based only on prototype representations can provide a complete account of conceptual combination. In particular, it seems unlikely (at least to us) that the approach illustrated here can illuminate the nature of logically-empty concepts (e.g., *apple and non apple*) and logically-universal concepts (e.g., *apple or not an apple*), or inclusion relations between concepts, (e.g., *all coconuts are fruits*). There is more to a concept than its prototype. As we mentioned at the outset, a concept may contain an identification procedure, which has a prototype structure, as well as a core, which does not, and it may be the core that is critical in representing logically-empty and logically-universal concepts and in accounting for inclusion relations. We expressed these same reservations when we examined fuzzy-set theory as a calculus for prototype representations (Osherson & Smith, 1981; 1982), and we do not think that the calculus we have proposed here obviates these fundamental problems.

REFERENCES

Armstrong, S. L., Gleitman, L. R., & Gleitman, H. (1983). What some concepts might not be. *Cognition, 13*, 263–308.

Cliff, N. (1959). Adverbs as multipliers. *Psychological Review, 66*, 27–44.

Cohen, B., & Murphy, G. L. (1984). Models of concepts. *Cognitive Science, 8*, 27–60.

Dubois, D., & Padre, H. (1980). *Fuzzy sets and systems: Theory and applications*. New York: Academic Press.

Hampton, J. A. (1983). A composite prototype model of conceptual conjunction. Unpublished manuscript, The City University, London.

Jones, G. V. (1982). Stacks not fuzzy sets: An ordinal basis for prototype theory of concepts. *Cognition, 12*, 281–290.

Minsky, M. A. (1975). A framework for representing knowledge. In P. H. Winston (Ed.), *The Psychology of Computer Vision*. New York: McGraw-Hill.

Osherson, D. N., & Smith, E. E. (1981). On the adequacy of prototype theory as a theory of concepts. *Cognition, 9*, 35–58.

Osherson, D. N., & Smith, E. E. (1982). Gradedness and conceptual combination. *Cognition, 12*, 299–318.

Smith, E. E., & Medin, D. L. (1981). *Categories and concepts*. Cambridge, MA: Harvard University Press.

Smith, E. E., & Osherson, D. N. (1982). Conceptual combination and fuzzy set theory. *Proceedings of the Fourth Annual Conference of the Cognitive Science Society*, Ann Arbor, MI.

Smith, E. E., Osherson, D. N., Rips, L. J., Albert, K., and Kean, M. (1984). A theory of conceptual combination for prototype concepts. (Manuscript in preparation). Cambridge, MA: Bolt Beranek and Newman, Inc.

Thagard, P. (1983). Conceptual combination: A frame-based theory. Paper presented at the Society for Philosophy and Psychology. Wellesley, MA.

Tversky, A. (1977). Features of similarity. *Psychological Review, 84*, 327–352.

Tversky, A., & Kahneman, D. (1983). Extensional versus intuitive reasoning: The conjunction fallacy in probability judgment. *Psychological Review, 90, 4*, 293–315.

Winston, P. & Horn, B. (1981). *Lisp*. Reading, MA: Addison-Wesley.

Zadeh, L. A. (1965). Fuzzy sets. *Information and Control, 8*, 338–353.

Zadeh, L. A. (1982). A note on prototype theory and fuzzy sets. *Cognition, 12*, 291–297.

Chapter 4

Learning

Human Learning

Most of the research in cognitive science on human learning has focused on learning of procedures. Both of the articles in this section center on learning mathematical procedures, although both are concerned more generally with all procedural learning.

Brown and VanLehn offer a theory of human procedural learning that postulates that learning occurs at *impasses*. This notion is related to Schank's idea of failure-driven learning (see Schank, R. C. (1982). *Dynamic Memory: A Theory of Learning in Computers and People*. Cambridge, MA: Cambridge University Press). Brown and VanLehn have looked extensively at human errors in subtraction and their hypothesis is that, when students are doing a problem that their subtraction procedure cannot handle, they encounter an impasse. At that point, the students invoke one of their repair procedures to deal with the impasse. This repair may lead to constructing a correct procedure, but more often it leads to constructing "buggy" or incorrect procedures.

Anderson presents a three-stage model of procedural learning within his ACT theory of human cognition. In the first stage, the *interpretive stage*, people use declarative knowledge to solve problems, much like a computer program is used as data by a computer-language interpreter. The second stage is called the *knowledge compilation* stage, where productions that occur repeatedly in the interpretive stage are *composed* by the joining together of pairs of productions, and are *proceduralized* by instantiation of variables. The third stage, *tuning*, involves refinement of this procedural knowledge by generalization, discrimination, and strengthening of different productions. Anderson's ACT theory is an attempt to build a very general architecture for human cognition, using semantic networks to represent declarative knowledge and production systems to represent procedural knowledge.

Repair Theory: A Generative Theory of Bugs in Procedural Skills

JOHN SEELY BROWN
KURT VANLEHN

Xerox Palo Alto Research Center

This paper describes a generative theory of bugs. It claims that all bugs of a procedural skill can be derived by a highly constrained form of problem solving acting on incomplete procedures. These procedures are characterized by formal deletion operations that model incomplete learning and forgetting. The problem solver and the deletion operator have been constrained to make it impossible to derive "star-bugs"—algorithms that are so absurd that expert diagnosticians agree that the alogorithm will never be observed as a bug. Hence, the theory not only generates the observed bugs, it fails to generate star-bugs.

The theory has been tested on an extensive data base of bugs for multidigit subtraction that was collected with the aid of the diagnostic systems BUGGY and DEBUGGY. In addition to predicting bug occurrence, by adoption of additional hypotheses, the theory also makes predictions about the frequency and stability of bugs, as well as the occurrence of certain latencies in processing time during testing. Arguments are given that the theory can be applied to domains other than subtraction and that it can be extended to provide a theory of procedural learning that accounts for bug acquisition. Lastly, particular care has been taken to make the theory principled so that it can not be tailored to fit any possible data.

1. INTRODUCTION

This paper presents our current efforts to form a generative theory of bugs in procedural skills. Given a procedural skill, it predicts which systematic errors or bugs will occur in the behavior of students learning the skill.

1.1 Background: Bugs and "Bug Stories"

Over the past few years our group has been engaged in the task of fusing computer science tools with modelling techniques from cognitive science in order to construct systems for diagnosing systematic student errors. These diagnostic systems, BUGGY and more recently DEBUGGY, have been used to analyze thousands of students' work (Brown & Burton, 1978; Burton, 1981; VanLehn & Friend, 1980) and have enabled us to construct an extensive catalogue of precisely defined systematic errors or bugs for place-value subtraction. Several other investigations of errors in arithmetic have uncovered the same "bug" phenomenon (Buswell, 1926; Brownell, 1941; Roberts, 1968; Lankford, 1972; Cox, 1975; Ashlock, 1976; Young & O'Shea, forthcoming).

A child's errors are said to be systematic if there exists a procedure that produces his erroneous answers. In nearly all cases, we have found that systematic errors are minor peturbations from the correct procedure for that skill. Precisely defined erroneous variations of a procedure are known as bugs. To say that a subject "has" a certain bug is to predict not only which problems he will answer incorrectly on a test, but also to predict the digits of those answers as well. Because an entire test's answers must be generated by a bug before we are willing to say the bug exists, there is very little chance that bugs are just "random" errors. Indeed, bugs seem to be complex, intentional actions reflecting mistaken beliefs about the skill. This is not to say that random, unsystematic errors do not occur. They do. But such errors have the appearance of "slips," where the subject did something which they did not intend to do. (Norman, 1979, argues for the widespread existence of slips in adult performance.) The subtleties of the slip/bug distinction and the data analysis techniques that were used to determine the difference are discussed in VanLehn (forthcoming). For this paper, we will assume the viability of the bug concept. Appendix 2 lists the subtraction bugs that we have observed.

BUGGY and DEBUGGY provided both a notation for precisely describing bugs and a powerful diagnostic tool which we used to sieve large amounts of student data in search of still unaccounted for errors, which could then be analyzed by hand to determine if they stemmed from a new, previously undiscovered bug. Now that several thousand student tests have been analyzed, we have reached a stage where our data base of bugs is converging. We are able to account for a substantial number of student errors and only a small number of new bugs are being discovered.

This rather extensive data base of bugs now enables a much deeper question to be investigated, namely, what is the cause of these bugs and why do just they occur and not others? Whereas our earlier effort explained a student's errors as symptoms manifested by bugs in a correct procedure, our current effort is to explain these known bugs in terms of a set of formal principles that transform a procedural skill into all of its possible buggy variants. We shall call the set of principles and the process that interprets them a *generative theory* of bugs. Using "→" to mean "explains," this can be graphically stated:

generative theory of bugs → bugs → systematic errors

The challenge of a generative theory of bugs is twofold. It must generate all the known or expected bugs for a particular skill and it must generate no others.

Many bugs appear to have a rational basis. That is, it is often easy to construct a plausible "bug story" about how a certain bug could have been acquired. We are not alone in this belief in rational genesis. Young and O'Shea (forthcoming) show that models of bugs can be constructed by editing a model of the correct skill in such a way that most of the edits have plausible, albeit informal explanations. For example, a model of a certain, observed bug is created by replacing the rule that normally decides when to borrow by a rule that says to borrow always. By similar replacements, deletions and additions, models for many common bugs can be created. However, it is not the case that every possible edit creates a model for a bug—the theorists must carefully select the edit. Hence, the fact that editing can produce models for bugs is just a tribute to the expressive power and modularity of their representation language. What is important are the bug stories that accompany and presumably constrain most of the edits they describe. For example, in describing the edit mentioned above, they say "Such a rule could result from a student's believing that borrowing is an essential part of subtraction, perhaps as a consequence of being given a series of examples in which borrowing was always necessary." Such bug stories are insightful but informal. A generative theory can be viewed as formalizing such bug stories. Indeed, before we constructed our generative theory, we constructed multiple bug stories for each of our bugs in order to discover possible patterns that would enable us to decide which of each bug's stories to choose in order to build a unified theory.

1.2 The Key Idea is Repairing Impasses

In this paper we describe our current efforts to form a generative theory of bugs, one that is capable of explaining why we found the bugs that we did and not other ones, one that is capable of explaining how bugs are caused, and most importantly, one that is capable of predicting what bugs will exist for procedural skills we have not yet analyzed.

The theory is motivated by the belief that when a student has unsuccessfully applied a procedure to a given problem, he will attempt a *repair*. Let us suppose that he is missing a fragment of some correct procedural skill, either because he never learned the fragment or maybe he forgot it. Attempting to rigorously follow the impoverished procedure will often lead to an *impasse*. That is a situation in which some current step of the procedure dictates a primitive action which the student believes cannot be carried out. For example, an impasse would follow from an attempt to decrement a zero, provided the student knows (or discovers) that the decrement primitive has as a precondition that its input can't be a zero. When a constraint or precondition gets violated the student, unlike a typical computer program, is not apt to just quit. Instead he will often be *inventive*, invoking his problem solving skills in an attempt to repair the impasse so that he can continue to execute the procedure, albeit in a potentially erroneous way. We believe that many bugs can best be explained as "patches"

derived from repairing a procedure that has encountered an impasse while solving a particular problem.

The key idea of the generative theory is the notion of *repair*. Hence, we refer to the theory as Repair Theory. A bug's derivation in the theory has two parts. The first is a series of operations that generate an incomplete procedure, namely, a procedure that may reach an *impasse* on certain problems. The second part is a series of operations that represent the repair of the procedure so that it can proceed. It is an important assertion of the theory that these two parts are independent. That is, the kind of repair attempted depends only on the procedure and its current impasse, not on how the incomplete procedure was derived.

This paper reports on work in progress. Although a precise theory will be presented, it is not as empirically adequate as we would like. The first part of the theory, namely that which generates incomplete procedures, has known inadequacies. However, the repair generation part appears adequate. The theory is worth presenting now, in its naive form, because it raises many new distinctions that have allowed us to frame several interesting theoretical and empirical questions in a sharp, clear fashion. In particular, several predictions concerning phenomena such as processing time, bug stability and bug frequency, fall naturally out of what was originally conceived of as a theory of bug occurrence.

The paper first presents the theory and gives examples of bug derivations. The second half of the paper is a discussion of the methodology of our research along with a careful statement of its claims and their empirical support. We have tried to be very clear about what the core support is, and how it is extended through adoption of hypotheses that project the claims of the theory to become claims about other phenomena. We think such an examination of methodology is important for understanding how complex theories of complex cognitive phenomena can be evaluated and extended.

2. THE FORM OF THE GENERATIVE THEORY

As mentioned above, the generation of a bug has two parts: generation of an incomplete procedure and generation of a repair to any impasse that that procedure may encounter. Repair Theory defines the set of incomplete procedures by applying a set of *deletion principles* to a formal representation of the correct procedure. The set of repairs is defined by a set of *repair heuristics* and a set of *critics* in the following manner. When an incomplete procedure is applied to a problem and reaches an impasse, a set of repairs is performed by a *generate and test* problem solver. The set of all observable repairs is characterized by the set of repair heuristics in conjunction with a "tester" or filter which can reject certain proposed repairs based on a set of critics. That is, the heuristics suggest repairs and the critics veto some of them. Given this form, there are four major components that must be designed:

2.1 The Method of Investigation

Since our primary concern is to provide a *principled* account of a set of buts and to use these principles to predict bugs for skills yet to be analyzed, we invoke as little problem solving machinery as possible to account for the data. We fully recognize that there exists much more powerful problem solving models that may, in fact, better capture what a student is actually thinking while inventing a patch. We will also utilize as little of an actual process model as is possible and instead proceed under the assumption that if a rule is applicable it will be used. The trouble with invoking a process model is that it is hard to get a crisp boundary on precisely what bugs will be generated by the model since, for example, it is never certain what scheduling strategies a student might be using to select his rules or what specialization strategies he might possess for transforming a weak heuristic into a specific repair rule. We will sidestep such issues and see just how far we can get with specific repair rules that apply universally.

It is particularly important not to interpret the deletion principles in process model terms. *We are not claiming that a student knew the correct procedure, then forgot part of it. The deletion principles are a formal characterization of the set of incomplete procedures, and hence impasses, that are used and possibly repaired.* One of us (VanLehn) is constructing a learning theory which can generate that same set by simulating a student's miscomprehension of examples in the teaching sequence. We use a set of deletion principles operating on the correct skill as a precise way to characterize the set of procedures that are subject to repair while realizing that a deeper explanation for this set may be found in theories of forgetting or mislearning.

The evaluation of a generative theory rests on its ability to generate all the known bugs but to avoid predicting wild, improbable bugs. To expedite the evaluation of such theories on our data base, a "workbench" has been implemented on a computer. The workbench allows the construction of a representation language and its deletion principles, then systematically applies a deletion operator to every part of a correct procedure's representation. This generates a set of incomplete procedures, which after being repaired, are run on a highly diagnostic screening test. Their answers are analyzed by the workbench, and the set of known bugs, if any, that match each procedure's behavior are reported. Thus the workbench allows rapid comparison of representation languages, as well as help in settling fine points in the structuring of a correct procedure's representation. Our experience has been that comparison of representations has proven to be a powerful tool for zeroing in on the right skill decomposition. This topic is treated in detail in (VanLehn, 1980).

We have adopted the principle that each piece of information in the representation of a procedure must be used in the correct solution of at least one problem. This principle rules out the representation of bugs as "dead code," or information that is accessed only in the case of a deletion. With no principles governing the presence of dead code, allowing it would mean that the explana-

1. *A representation of the given procedural skill.* In determining this, several issues must be addressed. One concerns the representation language and its associated interpreter. Another is the representation of the physical page which bears the test problems. A very important issue concerns the structural decomposition of the skill that is to be embedded in the chosen representation language. The same procedural skill or method can often be decomposed in more than one way, which can have subtle theoretical ramifications.

2. *A set of principles for deleting fragments of the correct procedure.* These principles will determine what parts of the original skill can be deleted, thereby reflecting what parts of the procedure might become inaccessible in long term memory or may never have been learned (given the circumstances of our testing, it is often the case that students are given problems requiring subprocedures that they have not been taught yet). For example, the simplest principle might assert that any step of a procedure can be deleted; other principles might restrict the deletions to reflect a possible learning sequence of the procedure.

The next two constituents concern the elements of the generate-and-test problem solver charged with carrying out the requisite repairs.

3. *A set of repair heuristics to propose repairs.* The generator can examine the preconditions that have been violated on a primitive and propose explicit repairs based on a set of repair heuristics. Our later discussion of this component will circumvent control issues of how one repair heuristic might be initially chosen over another. Instead, we will focus on what the actual repair heuristics are and claim that *any* heuristic whose repair is not rejected by the tester must generate a bug.

4. *A set of critics to filter out some repairs.* Closely allied to the generator is the tester, which filters out those repairs that it considers to be unreasonable based on the form of the solution stemming from the proposed patch. Again, our interest here will be on the precise set of filtering conditions or "critics" and not so much on the process of invoking the critics and performing the necessary backtracking.

There are several noteworthy points to the form of this theory. The most important concerns its *composite* nature. We could have tried to account for all the known bugs in a skill by searching for a set of transformations that operate on the skill and directly produce all and only those bugs. Our theory, on the other hand, involves two parts. The first part edits the skill as dictated by a set of deletion principles which in themselves are not intended to explain all the sought after bugs. Instead, each possible edit or deleted portion generates a procedural variant which when followed (or executed) will often lead to an impasse that sets the stage for part two, the repair process. This second part uses a set of repairs to fix the procedure and allow it to continue.

It is the set of all valid repairs (i.e. those not filtered out by critics) to all possible impasses that is meant to predict the set of all possible bugs.

And/Or graphs (except that the "try special cases first" conflict resolution strategy is not used—a minor difference). The nodes and links of AO graphs correspond, respectively, to the goals and rules of this language. However, this language provides a generalization of the And and Or types of AO graphs. The generalization of these two types is to allow a goal to exit when a given *condition* is true. This exit condition is named the "satisfaction condition" of the goal. Rules of a goal are executed in sequence until either the goal's satisfaction condition becomes true, or all the applicable rules have been tried. Note that this is not an iteration construct—an "until" loop—since a rule can only be executed once. The AND types become satisfaction conditions consisting of the constant FALSE. Since rules are executed until the satisfaction condition becomes true (which it never does for the AND) or all the rules have been tried, giving the AND goal FALSE as the satisfaction condition means that it always executes all its rules. Conversely, OR's become the constant TRUE—the goal exists after just one rule is executed. The language is named Generalized And/Or graphs (GAO graphs).

An important concept in the representation is "focus of attention." By this term, we mean where the procedure is in the problem, that is, its "current location" on the test page. Focus is strongly associated with subgoals. Focus can only be shifted by calling a subgoal—there is no assignment statement for focus. Similarly, when control returns to a goal after a subgoal that it called is finished, focus is restored as well. (In computer science terms, focus is bound locally. In fact, focus is represented syntactically by giving arguments to goals just like the arguments of procedures. For example, the SubCol goal which processes a column has three arguments named TC, BC and AC which are bound by the caller to the top, bottom and answer cells of the current column.) Thus, there are no calls to a focus shifting function to move focus back to the initiating column after a borrow is completed. Instead, focus is restored automatically when the goal stack pops. In short, the procedure's control location and its external location are maintained in exactly the same manner.

Figure 1 shows the GAO graph for a standard version of subtraction taught in the United States. Since it will be used for examples throughout this paper, it is worth a moment to explain it. The Sub goal simply initializes the column traversal to start with the units column. ColSequence is the loop across columns, expressed recursively of course since there are no loop constructions in the language. SubCol processes a column. If the bottom cell is blank, it writes the contents of the top cell in the answer (L4). If the top digit is less than the bottom digit, it calls the Borrow subgoal (L5). Otherwise, it calls the primitive Diff which writes the difference on the top and bottom digits in the answer (L6).

The Borrow goal is a conjunction of borrowing into the column originating the borrow (L8—Add10 is a primitive), and borrowing from the column (L7). By convention, borrowing-from occurs before borrowing-into. Borrowing from the next column is easy if its top digit is non-zero; the digit is decremented by the

tion for a bug that involved the dead code would not be completely contained within the theory, a situation we would like to avoid.

2.2 The Representation of the Procedure

The representation of procedures has an impact on all parts of the theory. Some of the issues involved are the decomposition of the skill, the level of primitives, and the language for expressing the procedure. A great deal of effort has been spent comparing various choices along these dimensions in order to find ones that maximize the expected empirical fit of the theory. The method used in this part of the investigation involved extensive use of the workbench to assess the ramifications of a simplified version of the theory on the representation. The results of this investigation are presented in a technical paper (VanLehn, 1980).

The language that was finally chosen to express procedures is a descendent of production systems (i.e. a collection of condition-action rules, c.f. Newell & Simon, 1972). There are several syntactic restrictions on the rules. Each rule's conditions must mention exactly one internal symbol (= goal). The other conditions, if any, test some features of the external world (i.e. the test problem being worked on). Each rule has exactly one action, which is either a primitive action or a subgoal. Rules are labeled for ease of reference, but the labels play no role in their interpretation.

Like production systems, rules are eligible to be run when their conditions are true. When more than one rule is eligible, the following conflict resolution strategies are applied in order until the choice is unambiguous:

Only try once: If this rule has been executed before, and the goal it matches this time is the same instantiation (token) as the goal it matched last time, then eliminate this rule from consideration.

Try special case rules first: If the conditions of this rule are a subset of the conditions of some other eligible rule (i.e. the other rule is a special case of this rule), then eliminate this rule from consideration.

Stipulated order: If there is still more than one eligible rule, then take the one that occurs first in the list of rules.

These conflict resolution strategies are found in many production system languages (McDermott & Forgy 1978).

Unlike most production systems, rules are interpreted with a stack. When the action of a rule is a goal, execution of that action pushes the current internal state onto the stack, and the new goal becomes current. Only rules matching the current goal are eligible to run. Goals have a type-like construction that controls when they are exited (i.e. when the stack pops). Two types are AND and OR. What the AND type means is to "exit only when all my rules have been executed." The OR type means to "exit as soon as one of my rules has been executed."

The control structure described thus far is isomorphic to that found in satisfaction condition is not true yet, L6 runs and Diff takes the column difference.

Although there are many other versions of subtraction, and several other ways to express this version in the GAO language, the decomposition of figure 1 has been found to optimize the empirical predictions of the theory.

This concludes the discussion of the representation. As mentioned earlier, there are arguments for each of the architectural features of GAO graphs. These arguments are long and subtle enough to deserve a paper of their own (VanLehn, 1980).

2.3 Deletion

Concomitant with the development of the representation, a variety of deletion principles were tried. The one that performed the best was deletion of rules.

When a rule is deleted, its sister rules will often be executed in its place, which frequently leads to an impasse. For example, when L4 of Figure 1 has been deleted, and the procedure is run on the problem

$$27$$
$$\underline{-4}$$

an impasse is reached in the tens column because the interpreter choses L6, the only rule that applies given that L4 is gone. Running L6 results in calling the primitive action Diff. Diff takes a column difference by taking the difference of its first two arguments' contents and writing the result in the cell pointed to by the third argument. But Diff has a precondition that neither of its arguments be blank. Since this precondition is violated when Diff is called on the tens column, the procedure is at an impasse. This impasse can be repaired in a variety of ways. For example, the procedure could simply do nothing instead of take the column difference (the "no-op" repair heuristic). Control would return from Diff, and ultimately the procedure would terminate normally leaving 3 as the answer. This way of repairing the impasse generates the bug Quit-When-Bottom-Blank. (The bug names were published (Brown and Burton, 1978) before Repair Theory was developed, so some of the names are a little inappropriate.)

Not all deletions lead to impasses. For example, when L12 is deleted, the only action that is executed during a borrow across zero is the action Write9, which scratches out a zero and writes a 9 over it. No preconditions are violated, so no repairs are needed. The resulting procedure is the bug Borrow-From-Zero. A test item answered by this procedure would look like

$$207$$
$$\underline{128}$$
$$179$$

Unconstrained deletion overgenerates. That is, deleting certain links leads to

---

The syntax is:

Goal (goal's arguments) Satisfaction Condition: *goal's satisfaction condition*
   label: {*rule's conditions*} --->   *rule's action*
          other rules for achieving the goal...

The rules for the version of subtraction used in this paper are:

```
Sub () Satisfaction Condition: TRUE
   L1: {} --->          (ColSequence RightmostTopCell
                          RightmostBottomCell RightmostAnswerCell)

ColSequence (TC BC AC) Satisfaction Condition: (Blank? (Next TC))
   L2: {} --->          (SubCol TC BC AC)
   L3: {} --->          (ColSequence (Next TC) (Next BC) (Next AC))

SubCol (TC BC AC) Satisfaction Condition: (NOT (Blank? AC))
   L4: {(Blank? BC)} --->     (WriteAns TC AC)
   L5: {(Less? TC BC)} --->   (Borrow TC)
   L6: {} --->          (Diff TC BC AC)

Borrow (TC) Satisfaction Condition: FALSE
   L7: {} --->          (BorrowFrom (Next TC))
   L8: {} --->          (Add10 TC)

BorrowFrom (TC) Satisfaction Condition: TRUE
   L9:  {(Zero? TC)} --->     (BorrowFromZero TC)
   L10: {} --->          (Decr TC)

BorrowFromZero (TC) Satisfaction Condition: FALSE
   L11: {} --->          (Write9 TC)
   L12: {} --->          (BorrowFrom (Next TC) )
```

TC, BC and AC are variables. Their names are mnemonic for their contents, which happen to be the top, bottom and answer cells of a column.

The primitive actions and their associated preconditions are listed below. All of their arguments are cells. The actions expecting digits in certain arguments have precondition that those cells not be blank.

Diff -- Subtracts the digit contained in its second argument from the digit contained in its first argument and writes the result in the third argument. The second argument can not be larger than the first argument.

Decr -- Subtracts one from the digit contained in its first argument and writes the result back in the same cell. The input digit must be larger than zero.

WriteAns -- Writes the digit contained in its first argument in its second argument.

Add10 -- Adds ten to the digit contained in its argument and writes the result back in the same cell. The cell can not be blank.

Write9 -- Writes a nine in its argument. The cell can not be blank originally.

Figure 1. A GAO graph for a standard version of subtraction

primitive Decr (L10). If the digit is zero, it is changed to a nine (L11) and BorrowFrom is called recursively (L12) to try to decrement the next column. When borrowing is completed, control returns to SubCol. Because SubCol's procedures that we have never observed, and moreover, the procedures are so counter-intuitive that we strongly believe they will be observed. Such procedures are called "star-bugs" after the linguistic convention of putting a star before sentences judged to be unacceptable. Deleting L10 would generate a star-bug. The procedure resulting from the deletion never violates a precondition and hence is not repaired. It has the strange property that it only borrows correctly when the borrow is from zero—regular, "simple" borrows are not done. A test item solved by this star-bug would be

$$\begin{array}{r} 3075 \\ 1298 \\ \hline 2787 \end{array}$$

Intuitively, it seems implausible to delete the ordinary case while leaving the special case intact since presumably the ordinary case had been mastered some time before the special case had been taught. Indeed, in VanLehn's learning theory (forthcoming), learning the rule that is a special case of another rule, in that its conditions are a super-set of the other rule's conditions, requires the prior existence of the ordinary-case rule. Hence, a deletion blocking principle can be derived from a somewhat more plausible principle, namely, that a new rule is forgotten more readily than an old one (or, recalling that the testee's are often in the middle of the subtraction curriculum, that rules are taught in the order that they can be learned). In short, there is a basis in learning for the following principle:

A Deletion Blocking Principle

If two rules have the same goal and one is a special case of the other rule (i.e. its conditions are a superset of the more general rule's conditions), then the general rule can not be deleted unless the special case rule is deleted as well.

Since L9 is a special case of L10, the latter can not be deleted in isolation, and hence the star-bug mentioned earlier is not generated. It may seem that incorporating a special-case predicate into the theory is ad hoc and unmotivated, but this is not the case. Special case checking is needed anyway by the interpreter to sequence rules (c.f. the preceding discussion of conflict resolution).

The deletion blocking principle is in fact just the tip of the learning theory iceberg. We now believe that a better way to generate incomplete procedures would involve a complicated derivation that mimics in part the learning sequence of the subject prior to the point of testing. In this light deleting when constrained by the deletion blocking principle can be seen as an elegant, simple way to derive the incomplete procedures of subjects who never mis-learn anything, but have only learned (or remembered) part of the total algorithm. Further comments on this view will be made after discussion of the problem solver that generates repairs.

2.4 Examples of Repair Generation

We believe that a student following a procedure that specifies that a particular primitive is now to be executed but which can't be, for whatever reason, is apt to invent some repair to circumvent his current dilemma. For example, suppose he is trying to perform a column subtract with a larger number from a smaller number and he can't because there is no appropriate entry in his facts table (or because he knows he can't). What might he do? One obvious repair might be to *skip* trying to execute that primitive action and move on to the next step of the procedure. Another repair might be to *swap the focus vertically* before calling Diff—that is, if it doesn't work taking the bottom digit from the top one, try swapping them around. And a last example might involve his being very clever and resorting to invoking the counting-based subtraction procedure that he originally used to generate or understand the facts table. For example, he might reason that if he had five apples and Tommy took seven away, then he certainly wouldn't have any apples left. Or he might count backwards from five in synchrony with counting up from seven, ending as the former becomes zero. Either way, the overall effect of reverting to the "semantics" of the facts table is to arrive at zero as the column's answer.

Examples of simple repairs. In a moment, the details of how repairs are created will be presented. But first, we will go through some examples to see how repair-generated bugs produce erroneous answers.

Suppose that rule L5 (see Figure 1) is deleted. This is the rule that says to borrow when the top digit is too small. If L5 is deleted, then L6, the rule for processing ordinary columns, will be executed on every column, including larger from smaller (LFS) columns where one ought to borrow. LFS columns violate a precondition of Diff (the action called by L6), namely that the first input number be larger than the second input number. This precondition violation is an impasse, and the problem solver is called in to repair it.

Several bugs can be generated by repairing this impasse in different ways. A natural repair is to skip the primitive whose precondition is violated. In this example, the so-called "No-op" repair heuristic (because it replaces the primitive with a null operation) generates a bug named Blank-Instead-of-Borrow. Since Diff is simply skipped when its precondition is violated, the bug does not write an answer in an LFS column.

Other repairs to the same impasse generate other bugs. If the "Quit" repair heuristic is used, then the bug is Doesn't-Borrow, because the problem is given up as soon as a LFS column is encountered. A more complicated repair heuristic is to swap cells when they are in the same column (as they are in this case). When this "Swap Vertically" repair heuristic is used, the bug Smaller-From-Larger results. This bug takes the absolute difference of each column's digits.

An even more complicated repair heuristic is used to generate the Zero-

Instead-of-Borrow bug. This bug answers all LFS columns with zero. It is generated by forgetting about the facts table and reverting to the counting procedure that underlies it. As mentioned above, there are several procedural "semantics." We call for the facts table that return zero when invoked with such arguments. We call the repair "Dememoize" because it is the inverse of the computer programing technique of "memorizing," a function by replacing it with a table that pairs its inputs with the outputs it would generate if it had been run.

In short, four procedures are generated by repairing the same impasse four different ways. We can summarize these procedures as:

Repairs	Bugs
Skip	Blank-Instead-of-Borrow
Quit	Doesn't-Borrow
Swap Vertically	Smaller-From-Larger
Dememoize	Zero-Instead-of-Borrow

These four heuristics can be used in conjunction with the deletion of L8 to generate four more procedures. L8 is the rule that adds ten to to the top of the column being borrowed into. When L8 is deleted, the procedure does the decrement part of borrow correctly but fails to add ten to the top digit of the column which caused the borrow. Hence, after borrowing is done, and rule L6 is run, Diff is entered with the column in its original LFS state. Hence, the precondition that was mentioned above is violated, and an impasse occurs. Repairing this impasse with the same four repair heuristics generate four new procedures:

Repairs	Bugs
Skip	*Blank-With-Borrow
Quit	Doesn't-Borrow
Swap Vertically	Smaller-From-Larger-With-Borrow
Dememoize	Zero-After-Borrow

The first procedure, *Blank-With-Borrow, is a star-bug. By convention, star-bugs' names are preceded with astericks. Star-bugs have not occurred and are judged by experts to be so absurd that they will never occur. They should not be generated by the theory. In this case, the generation of *Blank-With-Borrow is blocked by a critic which filters out repairs that leave blanks in the interior of the answer. This critic also filters out the observed bug Blank-Instead-of-Borrow, which is generated by deleting L5, as illustrated just above. In order to avoid generating the star-bug, it was necessary to forgo generation of a good bug. Critics, and this tradeoff in particular, will be discussed shortly.

Examples of compound repairs. Sometimes the repair to one impasse creates a procedure that has a second impasse. Repairing the second impasse can result in bug, but on occasion the resulting procedure reaches a third impasse.

Although such a derivation could in principle go on forever, we have yet to see a bug that required more than three repairs in its derivation.

To illustrate such compound repairs, suppose that rule L9 is deleted. L9 is the rule that tells the procedure how to borrow from zero. When it is deleted, and the procedure is given a problem that requires borrowing across zero, L10 will run instead of the missing L9. Since L10 is the ordinary borrow rule, Decrement will be called with zero as its input. This violates one of its preconditions. Although many repairs lead immediately to bugs, a compound derivation can be illustrated by supposing that this impasse is repaired by the heuristic "Backup." Backup is a well known strategy in problem solving: one backs up control to the last point where a choice was made. In this case, control moves up through Borrow, which is an AND goal, and settles on SubCol. The effect of this shifting of attention is to skip the Decrement operation and the Add10 operation. In other words, instead of trying to decrement a zero, the procedure forgets about borrowing entirely and returns to examining the LFS column, which is still in its original form. Since the borrowing rule L5 has already once for this instantiation of SubCol, it can not be run again, so the ordinary column processing rule L6 is run, and Diff's precondition is violated. The four repair heuristics mentioned above now generate these procedures:

Repairs	Bugs
Skip	?Blank-Instead-of-Borrow-From-Zero
Quit	Borrow-Won't-Recurse
Swap Vertically	Smaller-From-Larger-Instead-of-Borrow-From-Zero
Dememoize	Zero-Instead-of-Borrow-From-Zero

Due to the critic that objects to blanks inside answers, the procedure ?Blank-Instead-of-Borrow-From-Zero is filtered out. In this case, no harm nor good is done, since it is neither an observed bug nor a star-bug. Procedures that are possible bugs (i.e. the experts do not consider them absurd enough to be star-bugs) but have not been observed are preceded by "?".

In short, with just three deletions and four repair heuristics, we have generated eleven different procedures (Doesn't-Borrow is generated two different ways), eight of which are observed bugs. An important point to notice is that repair is not always a simple process because the repair of the original impasse can create secondary impasses.

Another important point is that there is not a one-to-one correspondence between deletions and impasses: some deletions leave procedures that do not violate any preconditions. For example, if rule L7 is deleted, the resulting procedure never does the decrementing half of borrowing, but only the add-ten half. This procedure does not violate and preconditions, and hence no repairs are generated. This is the bug Borrow-No-Decrement. This repair-less generation of bugs is not common. Only two of the nine possible deletions of rules in Figure 1 lead to impasse-free procedures. Hence, of all the bugs generated from this GAO graph, the derivations of all but two involve some repair.

2.5 The Problem Solver Is Local

The architecture of the problem solver is very simple. First, a repair heuristic proposes that a certain action be done instead of the primitive action that is stuck. Second, the preconditions of the new action are checked. If a precondition is violated, the repair is unusable. Also, each critic checks to see if its condition would be violated by executing the action. If a critic is violated, the repair is rejected as well (in the discussion section, we consider what the impact of relaxing this last restriction would be on the empirical coverage of the theory). If neither a precondition nor a critic is violated, the repair occurs and the procedure derived from this repair is predicted to occur as a bug.

There are several ways that this architecture makes the problem solver weak. First, there is no ability to "look ahead" and see what the effects of a proposed repair might be some number of steps further in the problem. If there were such an ability, then the problem solver could avoid having to do secondary repairs by looking ahead far enough to see the secondary impasses such as the ones involved in the compound repair mentioned above. However, bugs involving compound repairs have occurred, so it seems the problem solver should have no ability to look ahead. In other words, the "vision" of the problem solver is local—it can only see the current state of the interpreter and the subtraction problem.

A second restriction is that the problem solver can propose only a single action. That is, the solver can't generate a repair that is a new goal, complete with new rules for satisfying it. It can propose a primitive action (see VanLehn 1980 for a discussion of the "grain size" of the primitive actions) or a "known" goal, such as Borrow. In other words, its repairs are small. Because of the local "vision" of the problem solver and the restriction that its repairs be small, the problem solver is called a *local* problem solver.

2.6 A Set of Repair Heuristics

The following set of repair heuristics seems fairly optimal. The empirical adequacy of the theory given this set will be discussed in the discussion section of the paper. We introduce the heuristics here, grouped under some suggestive headings, in order to discuss some theoretical points:

Four Weak Methods or General Purpose Heuristics

I. Escape and Flee
   a) Skip
   b) Quit
   c) Backup to last choice

II. Relocate/refocus the operation
   a) Swap Vertically
   b) Refocus Left
   c) Refocus Right

III. Use an operation that worked in an analogous situation/focus
   a) Use Increment (from carrying) for Decrement
   b) Use a top-row operation (i.e. Add10, Write9 or Decrement) to replace another top-row operation.
   c) Use a column operation (i.e. SubBlank, Diff) to replace another column operation.

IV. Dememoize

The headings are meant to suggest that the repair heuristics are really just instances of more general purpose heuristics. Take the third category for example. The repair heuristic Increment for Decrement is just an instance of a general heuristic: if incrementing worked in an analogous situation, namely the "left half" of the regrouping operation of addition, then it ought to work here, in the "left half" of the regrouping operation of subtraction.

In one sense, it is quite heartening that the repair heuristics that fit best empirically can be viewed as instances of more general problem solving heuristics. It is a little easier to believe that students bring a few powerful heuristics, perhaps developed elsewhere, to subtraction than that they bring a diverse set of special purpose subtraction repair heuristics. Indeed, we propose to constrain the power of the theory by stipulating that all repair heuristics be *domain independent* in that they could plausibly be derived from general purpose problem solving strategies. Although this is not very constraining, it allows us to hope that equivalent repair heuristics will be found when the theory is applied to a new domain. There will be more discussion of this point later.

There is a tradeoff in designing a set of repair heuristics. Too few heuristics means an inability to generate some known bugs. But too many heuristics means predicting nonbugs. For example, there is a bug called Stutter-Subtract where the student reacts to nonrectangular problems by subtracting the last digit in the bottom row from top digits that are over blanks. Here is an example of Stutter-Subtract's solution to a problem:

$$\begin{array}{r} 7654 \\ 31 \\ \hline 4323 \end{array}$$

The Repair Theory analysis of this bug involves deleting the rule L4. Since this is the rule that handles blanks in the bottom row, deleting it causes Diff to be entered with a blank as its second argument, which causes a precondition violation. To generate Stutter-Subtract, we need a repair heuristic, Refocus Right. (This heuristic searches horizontally, moving rightward from the place where Diff expected to find its second argument. It stops at the first cell which is nonblank, and gives the digit to Diff as the second argument.) In short, Refocus

Right seems necessary for generating Stutter-Subtract. However Refocus Right can now be used to repair other precondition violations as well. Suppose, for example, that it is used to repair the zero precondition of Decrement. This would generate a procedure that instead of borrowing across zero would decrement the column borrowed *into*. This bug has never been observed, and seems rather implausible. In short, one has a choice of failing to generate Stutter-Subtract, or generating bugs that have not been observed.

We have chosen to accept the intuitively more plausible position that repair heuristics are just special cases of general purpose problem solving heuristics, and therefore we accept Refocus Right as a legitimate repair. To deal with the overgeneration, we propose to use a set of *critics* that test and filter out proposed repairs.

2.7 Critics

In the generate-and-test architecture of the problem solver that creates repairs, the ''test'' or filter component is driven by a collection of critics. A critic signals that something about the current state is unusual. For example, decrementing a digit that is the result of a previous decrement triggers a certain critic.

Critics, most likely, are tacitly acquired by the student's observing and abstracting the patterns that all computations appear to satisfy—especially those that were produced by the teacher working through example subtraction problems. These abstractions fall naturally into several categories. The most obvious of these concern the form of what gets written (the answer and the scratch marks). Some examples of critics in this category are:

I. Form-of-the-Writing Critics (or Constraints)

1. Don't leave a blank in the middle of the answer.
2. Don't have more than one digit per column in the answer.
3. Don't decrement a digit that is the result of a decrement.

Another category of critics has to do with the information flow. They could also be induced from examples, or they may perhaps have been deduced from more general beliefs about procedures. Some examples are:

II. Information Theoretic Critics

1. Don't change a column after its answer is written (or more generally, each operation must make a difference to the answer).
2. Don't borrow twice for the same LFS column (or more generally, avoid infinite loops).

Originally, critics were included in the theory in order to prevent overgeneration. When a procedure has been modified by repair, it may violate some critics. Such procedures can not, by hypothesis, become bugs. Thus, for example, the No-op repairs which lead to the unobserved procedures *Blank-With-Borrow and ?Blank-Instead-of-Borrow-From-Zero would be rejected because they leave a

blank in the answer, thus violating the ''No blanks inside the answer'' critic. Critics explain why such procedures have not been observed.

After critics were incorporated in the theory, it was noted that the function of filtering repairs was also being performed by the preconditions of the primitives. That is, a repair heuristic sometimes generates an action that violates a precondition, in which case it can not be used. For example, when L4 is deleted, an attempt is made to execute Diff when the bottom cell in the column is blank. This violates the precondition that Diff's inputs must be digits. Repairing this impasse with Swap Vertically produces an attempt to execute Diff with the other input blank. Since this violates a precondition (in fact, the same precondition), the Swap Vertically repair is reject. In short, preconditions also filter repairs, just as critics do.

Since both critics and preconditions filter repairs, symmetry suggested that violating a critic ought to create an impasse just as violating a preconditions does. We tested this hypothesis, and found that indeed some bugs could be generated from impasses triggered by critics. It had escaped our attention earlier since such bugs are much less common than precondition-triggered bugs.

An example of a critic-triggered impasse involves the bug Don't-Decrement-Zero. This bug does borrowing across zero by changing the zero to a ten instead of a nine. It cannot be generated from the version of subtraction of Figure 1, but is generated instead from another common version. Whereas the version of Figure 1 does borrowing across zero by changes the zeros to nines as it moves to the left, the version needed here changes the zeros to tens as it moves left, then decrements them to nine as it moves right. (This version is in fact the one most often taught in school, and the version of Figure 1 is an optimization of it.) To generate Don't-Decrement-Zero, one deletes the rule that decrements the newly written ten to nine as the procedure moves rightward. Hence, the net effect is a procedure that changes zeros to tens as it borrows across them.

This deletion creates a procedure that does not violate any preconditions. But it does violate a critic on certain problems. When the procedure must borrow across a zero that is over another zero, such as

$$\begin{array}{r} 504 \\ \underline{108} \end{array}$$

it first changes the upper zero to ten. When it later comes to processing the tens column, it subtracts zero from ten and attempts to write ten in the answer. Since ten is two digits long, there is a critic violation.

Most of the repair heuristics are inapplicable, but two succeed in generating bugs. The first is to form an analogy to addition: the units digit of ten is written in the answer and the tens digit is carried to the next column. This generates the bug Don't-Decrement-Zero-Carrying-Answer-Overflow. The bug Don't-Decrement-Zero is generated by a hitherto unmentioned repair heuristic, namely simply ignoring the critic violation. In this case, the action generated is just to write ten as the column's answer. The "Ignore" repair heuristic can only be applied to critic-triggered impasses, which is why it wasn't mentioned earlier. Preconditions of primitives, almost by definition, can not be ignored.

The symmetry between preconditions and critics is to be built into the theory as a principle:

The filter/trigger symmetry
    Any condition which can trigger impasses can filter repairs, and vice-versa.

This principle serves to constraint the class of critics. A new critic can not be added to the class unless it can function both as a repair filter and as a trigger for impasses. That is, adding a critic to block a certain star-bug may cause a different star-bug to be generated via an impasse triggered by the new critic.

2.8 Filtering Repairs versus Triggering Secondary Impasses

(This subsection discusses some technical details of the theory and can be skipped by the general reader.) Suppose a repair has just generated an action, and the action violates a critic. Since a critic can both filter repairs and trigger impasses, which will it do?

A convention is needed. The convention captures the intuition that the student will not use a repair if he can tell there is something wrong with using it *at the time he is considering whether to use it*. However, if he can successfully apply it before running into trouble, he will not backup and reject the repair but instead will repair the impasse at hand. This is an intuition about the performance of repair, but it can be captured with a locality constraint on the theory:

Definition of "filtering out" a repair
    Given a repair and a procedure that has an impasse generated by running it on a certain problem, if application of the repair heuristic to the impasse generates an action whose execution would *immediately violate* a critic or a precondition, then that repair is *filtered out* as a repair of that impasse.

This definition is essentially a formal expression of the locality of the problem solver. It says that the problem solver can not look ahead to see future violations of critics and preconditions. Filtering occurs only when a violation is detected concerning the proposed action in the context of the current state. For example, the Backup repair to the "Don't decrement zero" impasse, which was discussed in section 2.4, generates an action that pops the goal stack. This popping action does not violate any critics or preconditions, so the repair is not filtered. Of course, when the stack is reset, the interpreter choses a rule that executes Diff on the original LFS column, which violates a precondition as mentioned in section 2.4. But this violation can not be "seen" by the local problem solver at the time it is considering whether to use the Backup repair. The problem solver can not, by definition, predict what the interpreter will do after the popping action is executed so it can not tell that Diff will be chosen to run.

A contrasting example is the application of Refocus Right to the same decrement-zero impasse. On certain problems, such as

(a)   5061
      1278

the repair immediately violates a critic. On problem (a), the impasse occurs when an attempt is made to decrement the zero in the hundreds column. Refocusing right generates an action that would decrement the tens column. However, the six has been decremented by a previous borrow, so this action would violate the critic "don't decrement twice." The problem sets up a situation where the use of Refocus Right causes an immediate critic violation. By definition, Refocus Right is filtered out as a repair to the decrement-zero impasse.

This example with Refocus Right illustrates a new difficulty with the distinction between filtering and triggering. On some problem, such as that displayed above, Refocus Right is filtered out as a repair for the given impasse. However, on other problems, such as

(b)   5069
      1278

it is not filtered out. The procedure generated by applying Refocus Right to the impasse created by problem (b) is not the end-product of the derivation since it will reach an impasse if it is run on problems (a). That is, we do not consider the derivation of a procedure to have ended until the procedure can be applied to any problem without reaching an impasse.

One solution to this problem is simply to let this second impasse be repaired. That is, we could allow a derivation to span more than one problem. But this entails that all possible sequences of problems be investigated because different problem sequences can generate different procedures. The sequence [b, a] generates procedures that the sequence [a, b] does not.

There is no way to avoid examining the behavior of a procedure on all possible problems since we need to determine whether it is completely derived. However, we can avoid examining all possible *sequences* of problems by adopting the following constraint:

Definition of "valid" repairs
    A repair is a valid repair to an impasse only if it is not filtered out on any problem.

That is, a repair is valid only if it is universally unfiltered. To invalidate a repair, it is only necessary that *some* problem exist where the repair violates a critic.

This definition seems to entail a search through an infinite number of problems, thus raising the issue of decidability. In practice, however, the search for problems to filter the repair is not really infinite. The crucial simplification depends on the fact that preconditions and critics are local: their conditions test only the arguments of the action they filter, or in some cases the other cells in the column referred to by the arguments. Because of this locality, one can apply the repair, then examine just the column effected by the action the repair generates. Since only a few hundred combinations of digits and blanks are possible for a column, it is quite feasible to determine if there exists a column such that the action violates a critic or precondition. Provided the preconditions and critics are local, this suffices for checking all possible problems for filtering. This heuristic argument is only meant to show that the definition is usable. It is not meant to describe actual application of critics by a subject during a test situation—that would require a performance theory.

This definition of validity is not without its penalties. It causes us to reject a repair which would otherwise have generated an observed bug, Borrow-From-Bottom-Instead-of-Zero. Applying the Swap Vertically repair to the decrement-zero impasse mentioned above generates an action that attempts to decrement the bottom digit of the column. This succeeds on common problems, such as (a) below, but violates the decrement-zero precondition on rare problems such as (b), where both digits in the column borrowed from are zero.

$$
\text{(a)} \quad
\begin{array}{r} 506 \\ \underline{139} \end{array}
\qquad
\text{(b)} \quad
\begin{array}{r} 506 \\ \underline{109} \end{array}
$$

In a performance theory, one could regain the generation of Borrow-From-Bottom-Instead-of-Zero by replacing the universal quantifier of the definition with an assertion that the problems causing critic violation are rare enough that the student will have practiced the use of the repair on many problems before encountering a problem that causes a critic violation. The practice would "install" the repair so that the eventual critic violation would not cause its rejection, but rather would trigger a secondary impasse. However, this not a performance theory. Notions of "sufficient practice" and "installed repairs" are beyond its scope, although they play a role in work to reported in (VanLehn, forthcoming). The definition above is the best we have been able to devise within the generative framework.

2.9 Summary

This completes the description of Repair Theory. In form, it is a process that generates bugs using two mechanisms: a constrained rule deletion mechanism acting on a representation of the correct procedure for the given skill, and a local problem solver with a generate-and-test architecture that repairs the impasses that arise during execution of the impoverished procedures created by deletion. There are four main "classes" or choices that determine the theory's predictions: (1) the representation used for the procedure that undergoes deletion, (2) the constraints on the deletion operator, (3) the heuristics used to generate repairs, and (4) the critics that are used for filtering repairs and triggering impasses. The most remarkable feature of the theory is perhaps its attention to principles, such as the independence of repairs and impasses. These are the topic of the next section and will be summarized at its end.

The remainder of the paper considers the empirical adequacy of the theory, and suggests some extensions. Appendix 1 details the derivations of all the procedures that are generated from the version of subtraction presented in Figure 1. Each deletion is followed by the impasses, if any, that it entails. Impasses are followed by the results of apply each of the repair heuristics. The predictions stemming from this derivation are discussed in the next section.

3. RESULTS AND DISCUSSION

It is often thought that empirical adequacy is the only measure of a theory's worth. However, it is not very difficult to get empirical adequacy if that is the only goal. We propose five criteria for evaluating this theory, and by extension other information processing theories of cognition.

3.1 Five Criteria for Theories

The first criterion is of course empirical. In the case of this theory, empirical adequacy means generating all the observed bugs and none of the star-bugs. (A star-bug is a procedure that can never occur as a bug.) Star-bugs are a necessity. Unless some bugs are labeled a priori as being unable to occur, then something which could generate all procedures (e.g. an exhaustive generator of GAO graphs) would be empirically adequate since it would generate all the bugs. It is unfortunate that we can not assume our data base is complete in that it contains all possible bugs. Many of the bugs that have shown us the most about how to structure the theory also turn out to be rather rare. To fix the current data base as an approximation of the set of all possible bugs would be to make the theory virtually immune to major revisions instigated by the data. The bug that triggers the crucial insight might be a rare one. Consequently, we must leave the door open for new bugs, and that necessitates taking the judgment of experts as an approximation of star-bugs.

The second criterion is the "tailorability" or degrees of freedom of the theory. A theory that can be tailored to fit any data base is not saying much of interest (Pylyshyn, 1980; forthcoming). For example, the ways that Repair Theory can be tailored are by adding new repair heuristics, adding new critics, or restructuring the GAO graph to get slightly different impasses. One way to limit tailorability is to make the theorist pay a heavy price for such changes. That is, any change to increase empirical adequacy must make other predictions that may or may not be correct. In short, changes have *entailments*. For example, because it is an axiom of the theory that repairs are independent of impasses, adding a new repair heuristic in order to generate a certain bug will cause the theory to predict many new procedures, namely all procedures that are derived by applying the new heuristic to all the other impasses. Some of these predicted bugs may exist, in which case the addition is good. But more often, the procedures are not bugs and in fact may be star-bugs. So, adding a repair heuristic may entail making many dubious if not incorrect predictions. By strict adherence to the principles of the theory, such as impasse-repair independence, tailorability can be limited.

Most theories of cognition are initially stated in a certain domain, in this case subtraction. This is not surprising: to study thinking, the subjects must be thinking about something. The natural question to ask at the completion of such a domain-bounded study is to what extent does the theory depend on the domain. Thus, the third criterion is the degree of domain independence of the theory. In the case of Repair Theory, this means finding out what kinds of procedural skills are such that (a) students' misunderstandings as they learn the skill are stable enough that they make systematic errors, (b) the systematic errors can be analyzed as bugs, and (c) the bugs are predicted by Repair Theory.

The fourth criterion for the theory is its ability to elucidate phenomena other than the one studied. One need not go outside the domain for such phenomena. For example, Repair Theory could perhaps explain some of the mysteries of "bug migration." Bug migration is a phenomenon wherein a subject has a different bug on two tests given only a few days apart. This phenomenon appears to have a pattern to it, in that only certain bugs "migrate" into each other, and moreover, this migration appears to define an equivalence relation on the set of all bugs. For example, Stops-Borrow-At-Zero has been observed to migrate into Borrow-Across-Zero, and vice-versa. Now it just so happens that these two bugs can be derived from the same deletion via different repair heuristics. To explain the pattern, a "projection hypothesis" is adopted. In this case, the hypothesis is that bugs will migrate into each other if they are derived by different repairs to the same impasse. Note that without this hypothesis, Repair Theory has nothing to say about bug migration. Moreover, the hypothesis might not be quite right. One must have a projection hypothesis, but it could be wrong. Hence, the empirical success of the projection supports the theory, but the lack of empirical success does not refute it since the projection hypothesis could be wrong.

The fifth criterion stems from a desire to replace Repair Theory with one that is even deeper and has a strong sense of explanation to it. In that arithmetic is certainly learned rather than innate, a learning theory seems essential to a complete understanding of the cognition involved. Repair Theory is a theory of what bugs exist. Its model is a process, which gives the derivation a chronology. However, we have never asserted that this chronology has anything to do with the chronology of a subject's acquisition of a bug. The job of explaining acquisitional chronology (or perhaps difficulty) belongs to a theory of learning. Much of Repair Theory can be seen as groundwork for that learning theory. A number of principles, such as the independence of impasses and repairs, could be taken as constraints on the learning theory. In this light, Repair Theory succeeds to the extent that such principles can be abstracted from it and made available to its successor.

Having introduced the five criteria that Repair Theory will be measured by, the tradeoffs in its evaluation can be discussed in detail.

3.2 Empirical Adequacy

Repair Theory using the GAO graph, the heuristics and the critics described above generates 33 different subtraction procedures. GAO graphs for several other versions of correct subtraction have been tried, including one that does subtraction without using scratch marks, but their predictions differed only slightly from the predictions of the given GAO graph. Of the 33 procedures, 21 are well documented bugs, one is a star-bug, one is a correct procedure, and the other 10 have not been observed and hence are the theory's predictions for future bug discoveries. To give a sense of context, it is worth pointing out that when Repair Theory was first tested in September 1979, only 16 of its 33 procedures were known bugs. The current figures are from December 1979. So, in the intervening three months, 6 of the predicted bugs were actually found. We fully expect to find the other 10 predicted bugs eventually. The derivation of the 33 procedures, as well as the derivations of the procedures that are filtered out by critics, are summarized in Appendix 1.

The star-bug that is generated could be blocked, but only by adding an ad hoc deletion blocking principle. The star-bug results from deleting the tail-recursive call to ColSequence (L3) so that the procedure will only process the units column. That in itself is not unusual, but since no other links are deleted, the star-bug will borrow perfectly, even when it must borrow from zero. That a student would have mastered borrowing and yet be unable to traverse the columns is utterly unlikely. Blocking this star-bug requires a new deletion blocking principle. Unfortunately, the new principle would have to end up mentioning links from different nodes, namely L3 and L5. Since the other deletion blocking principles mention only links from the same node, this means dropping a constraint on deletion blocking principles, a move that would lead us one step closer to infinite tailorability.

In this case, such a move can be justified since the deletion mechanism is a prime candidate for replacement by a learning-based mechanism. In other words, we don't think the constraint on locality of deletion blocking principles holds universally, and since this leaves the principles virtually unconstrained (and thus infinitely tailorable), there must be something wrong with the deletion mechanism itself. We believe that it should be viewed as an instance of a much more complicated sub-theory that takes into account the fact that many of our subjects are in the middle of the subtraction curriculum. In short, the theory overgenerates by one bug, but it can be easily blocked. However, blocking the star-bug would leave the theory too unconstrained. Actually, the star-bug reveals that deletion is a fundamental inadequacy in the theory.

The theory only generates 21 of the observed 89 bugs. This is a rather severe undergeneration problem. Several extensions to the theory are possible. Their pros and cons will now be discussed.

One extension is to give the problem solver more power by equiping it with more powerful heuristics. For example, one of the bugs that can not currently be derived is Diff-0-N=N. To generate this bug, which borrows normally except when the top digit is zero, the problem solver would have to be called before borrowing occurs. This means that rule L5 would have to be deleted, so the problem solver can't borrow at all. No other deletion would do. Hence, the problem solver must be powerful enough to synthesize the whole borrow procedure so that Diff-0-N=N will borrow correctly when the top digit is not 0. However, allowing such powerful heuristics abandons one of the major principles of the theory: the repair generator is a *local* problem solver. Dropping this principle allows the theory to be too easily tailored to the data. Also, this locality principle could turn out to be a very important one in a theory of learning. So, let us leave the problem solver weak, and search for another solution to undergeneration.

3.3 Interrupt Conditions and the "Periodic Table"

On considering Diff-0-N=N, the undergeneration problem isn't that the heuristics aren't powerful enough, but the opportunities to perform repairs are too infrequent. For Diff-0-N=N, the Swap repair will suffice, but the place where this repair should be triggered does not involve a precondition violation. Indeed, the needed impasse occurs just when Borrow has been entered and T = 0 is true (T stands for the top digit in the current column, and B stands for the bottom digit). What is needed is a way to interrupt the execution of the procedure just when the goal Borrow is set and T = 0 is true.

What follows is an ad hoc extension to Repair Theory. We have not incorporated it in the theory even though it doubles the empirical coverage. To do so would make the theory too easily tailored. However, it is described here as a target for explanation. If principles can be found that generate or constrain this extension, the increased coverage of this extension could be had by incorporating them in the theory.

Suppose the deletion operator is replaced with a new operator that simply affixes a condition to a goal in such a way that when the goal is entered (i.e. is called by some rule's right hand side), an impasse is generated. In other words, the operator attaches an *interrupt condition* to the goal. The interrupt condition installation operator will produce procedures that will trigger repair in hopefully just the right places.

As an attempt to avoid infinite tailorability, we will stipulate that if a condition can be an interrupt for one goal, it *must* be an interrupt for any goal. Hence, T = 0 must generate bugs when attached to any of the four non-terminal nodes of the GAO graph of Figure 1 (we are cheating a little here by ignoring the top two nodes, which do the main column traversal). This constraint is analogous

to the stipulation that the deletion operator can delete any rule (almost—the deletion blocking principles define the exceptions); the interrupt condition installation operator can install an interrupt condition on any goal (almost).

Naturally, a list of predictions will have to be provided for use as interruption conditions. T = 0 will be one. The following set of nine conditions has been tailored, through experimentation on the workbench, to optimize the empirical coverage of the extended theory:

Interrupt Conditions for Triggering Repairs

T = 0	T = B	B = 0
T < B	T = 1	TRUE
B = #	(DoubleZero? T)	(EverDecremented?)

The only ones whose meaning might be obscure are those in the last row. B = # tests whether the bottom digit is a blank. (DoubleZero? T) is true if the top digit and the digit immediately to its left are both zero. (EverDecremented?) is true whenever at least one Decr action has happened in the current problem. To reiterate, these predicates have been chosen to fit the data; in a sense, they are just as ad hoc as a list of the bugs themselves.

Using these nine conditions as interrupts, the number of bugs generated increases to 43 from the 22 of Repair Theory. Since there are currently 89 bugs in the data base, there is still an undergeneration problem, but it is drastically reduced by the replacement of deletion with interrupt conditions. Unfortunately, we do not know how many of the procedures generated by the extended theory are star bugs, due to the way the extension was implemented on the workbench.

Figure 2 contains a "periodic table" of the procedures generated by the extended theory. (It is so named because it displays a pattern but doesn't explain it, just as the periodic table of elements does.) It demonstrates the independence of impasses and repair heuristics in a particularly graphic manner. The impasses are displayed along the vertical axis, and the repair heuristics (some of them) along the horizontal axis. Each cell of the matrix represents the procedure formed by putting the given interrupt condition on the given goal, thus establishing an impasse, and applying the given repair heuristic to that impasse. In the matrix, a cell has a "B" in it if the procedure is a known bug or "OK" if it is the correct procedure. If the procedure violates a critic, "C" appears in the cell. The empty cells of the table are procedures that no critic triggers on and yet have not been observed. The point of the periodic table is that each row has more than one entry, and each column has more than one entry. This illustrates the independence of impasses and repairs.

One problem with extending the theory with interrupt conditions is that there are no constraints on the set of interrupt condition predicates, and thus the extended theory is too easily tailored to fit the data. A second problem is that the extension degrades the theory's domain independence. The predicates of the interrupt conditions are specific to subtraction (e.g. EverDecrement? mentions

L9—the subject hasn't learned about borrowing across zero. Suppose further that he doesn't realize that T = 0 is a precondition of decrementing. When he encounters a decrement-zero impasse, he will attempt to subtract one from zero, perhaps by counting backwards, and discovers that he can not do so. That is, he discovers the precondition. Now he not only has the opportunity to abstract and remember his repair, but also to abstract and store the newly discovered precondition. Suppose that he abstracts the precondition, but in the process, he over-generalizes and thinks T = 0 is an exception not only to the "left half" of borrowing, but to the "right half" as well. That is, he generalizes from "you can't borrow *from* zero" to "you can't borrow *into* zero." The next time he processes a column of the form 0-N, he believes he has a precondition violation, and hence does a repair. If he applied Swap Vertically, for example, the bug Diff-0-N=N would be generated. Applying the Dememoize repair heuristic generates the bug Diff-0-N=0. So, this approach—overgeneralizing preconditions—can generate interrupt conditions.

This approach to generating interrupt conditions is being explored and will be reported in (VanLehn, forthcoming). If it is successful, the effects of the ad hoc extension discussed above can be had by making a principled extension to Repair Theory.

3.4 Acquisition of Critics

Another approach to solving the undergeneration problem that is independent of the interrupt condition extension involves the critics. The proposal is to drop the stipulation that critics *always* filter out repairs. This amounts to saying that not all subjects have all critics. The approach seems at first sight an admirable one since at least one bug, Blank-Instead-of-Borrow, is generated only to be blocked by a critic, namely "don't leave blanks in the middle of the answer." Since this critic depends only on the form of the answer, it would veto the bug no matter how the bug is generated. The only way to let this bug exist is to turn off the critic. However, making critics optional increases tailorability drastically. To block a certain star-bug, *Blank-With-Borrow, one invokes the critic. To allow the observed bug, Blank-Instead-of-Borrow, one ignores it.

The only way out of the dilemma is to try to say which subjects have which critics. This could probably be done in the context of a learning theory. The basic intuition is that since borrowing is taught early in the curriculum, it is plausible that the subject will not have abstracted the critic and hence Blank-Instead-of-Borrow can be safely generated. However, if one had gotten as far as learning how to borrow across zero, then such naivete would be extremely unlikely. Since the star-bug *Blank-With-Borrow knows how to borrow across zero, a subject who could generate it would also have the critic, and hence would filter it out. In short, it looks like a learning theory is once again necessary to increase the empirical adequacy of the theory.

Impasses		Repairs					
when	what	Noop	Quit	Swap	Left	FAdd	FSelf
T<B	SC	B+C	B	B	B+C		
T<B	BF	B	B	B	C		
T<B	BFZ		B	C	C		
B=#	SC	B		OK	B	OK	OK
B=#	B	B		B	B	NA	B
B=#	BFZ	B		C	C	B	B
T=0	SC	C		B+C	C	B	B
T=0	BF	B	B		B+C	B	B+C
T=0	BFZ	C			C		B
T=1	SC	C		C	C	NA	C
T=1	BF	B		OK	OK	OK	OK
T=1	BFZ	OK	OK	OK	B	OK	OK
T=B	SC	OK	OK	OK	OK	NA	OK
T=B	BF				B		C
T=B	BFZ	B	B	C	B		C
EvD	SC	B		B+C	C	NA	B
EvD	B	C			C		C
EvD	BF	B		C	C		C
EvD	BFZ						

B = bug
C = critic
OK = correct procedure
NA = not applicable

SC = SubCol
B = Borrow
BF = BorrowFrom
BFZ = BorrowFromZero

Figure 2. The "Periodic Table"

decrementing). Hence, they are not as domain independent as the repair heuristics and the critics.

A solution to both these problems is to *generate* the interrupt predicates instead of just postulating their existence. Since there are only nine predicates in the class, and the whole GAO graph is available as a potential source, it isn't very difficult to devise some operators to generate the class. In fact, *it is so easy that we can't tell which of several alternative schemes is right*, in the sense that it will produce accurate predictions when the theory is applied in a new domain. Our strategy is to look outside the theory for constraints on the choice of a scheme to generate the interrupt conditions. Hopefully, the generation of interrupt conditions will fall out of the learning mechanisms. To show how this might come about, consider the following story for how the interrupt condition T = 0 might be acquired.

Suppose that a subject (actually our model of the subject) is missing

3.5 Domain Independence

In the case of Repair Theory, domain independence can be tested quite clearly. One picks a new domain, say multidigit multiplication or addition of fractions. The theorist devises a collection of GAO graphs that decompose the multiplication procedure in slightly different ways. If necessary, the repair heuristics are adapted to the new domain, but they remain specializations of the same weak methods. Those critics that are domain independent, notably the information graph is run through the deletion/repair program and produces a collection of predicted bugs. These bugs are used to initialize DEBUGGY's data base. DEBUGGY is then run over the test results of a large number of subjects. Any subjects possessing predicted bugs will be found and their work checked by hand. After a sufficiently large number of bugs are verified, the procedures that did not occur are examined by expert (multiplication) diagnosticians to see if any star-bugs were generated. Carrying out this programme and *verifying its predictions* without major overhaul of the theory would demonstrate domain independence.

The theory has been designed to be relatively domain independent, but it has not yet been put to the test. We expect it to be able to predict the bugs that occur during the learning of mathematical skills, such as arithmetic, algebra or calculus. Representation problems in other branches of mathematics involving spatial reasoning may prove too difficult. Other procedural skills, such as operating reactors or computer systems, or controlling air traffic, are not out of the question.

There is a pretheoretic constraint on the choice of the domain, namely that it be possible to observe bugs during the skill's acquisition. Pragmatically, this means that the procedure has to be short enough that a student can solve enough test problems in a testing session to exhibit any systematic errors that may exist. Spreading the diagnosis across several testing sessions is not advisable since bugs can be highly unstable (see the discussion of bug migration below), making systematicity difficult to observe across sessions. A second problem is that devising a highly diagnostic set of test problems is extremely difficult, even for expert teachers. Some technical aids for developing diagnostic tests are discussed in (Burton, 1981).

3.6 A Projection to Bug Frequency

Repair Theory is a theory of which bugs occur. Two closely related kinds of data involve how often a bug occurs in the population (bug frequency), and how long a subject keeps a bug (bug stability). It turns out that some interesting aspects of these phenomena are qualitative ones. Hence, we can begin to speculate on how Repair Theory projects to these phenomena without getting involved in statistical calculation.

As menioned above, it is necessary to adopt a projection hypothesis to make the theory applicable to a phenomenon other than the one it was designed for. In the case of the frequency of occurrence of bugs, the obvious hypothesis to adopt is to assign each impasse and each repair heuristic a probability of occurrence. The independence assumption of Repair Theory, when mapped over to the frequency domain by the projection hypothesis, predicts that the frequency of a bug should be the product of the probabilities of its impasse and its repair.

However, complexities arise due to bugs derived without repair (i.e. there was no impasse) or by using multiple repairs. Adjustments would also have to be made for filtering of repairs by preconditions and critics. Also, only a dozen bugs occur frequently enough that their relative frequencies can be reliably compared. Given these difficulties, we don't expect to be able to verify the predictions in any rigorous way. Nonetheless, we have observed that the No-op, Swap and Refocus Left repairs are by far the most common, and that their relative frequency appears to be consistently higher than the other repairs across a variety of impasses. If this observation is correct, then support for the independence of impasses and repairs has been found in the frequency data. At the conclusion of the current testing program, we may be able to present some data that support this informal observation.

There is a very interesting pattern in the frequency data that has defied explanation until just recently. It involves the so-called "compound bugs" (Brown & Burton, 1978. The frequency data used below is contained in an appendix to a technical report superseded by that article. Copies of the appendix are available from the present authors. More comprehensive frequency data will be published in VanLehn & Friend, 1980). Some subjects are diagnosed as having two or more bugs at the same time. One such compound bug, for example, is Diff-0-N=N co-occurring with Borrow-Across-Zero. Compound bugs are quite common.

However, bugs do not compound independently. That is, a successful model could not be constructed wherein primitive bugs are assigned a probability of occurrence such that the probability of a compound bug's occurrence is the product of its constituents' probabilities. For example, Borrow-From-Zero is much more common in isolation than Borrow-Across-Zero. However, the compound [Borrow-From-Zero, Diff-0-N=N] is much *less* common than the compound [Borrow-Across-Zero, Diff-0-N=N]. This could not be predicted by a simple linear model of bug compounding.

Repair Theory provides such a variety of structure that it is not difficult to devise explanations for examples of nonlinear compounding. The particular example cited above, however, has defied explanation until just recently, when the search for a way to generate interrupt conditions led to the following tentative explanation.

Suppose that the story given previously for the generation of Diff-0-N=N from preconditions is correct. That is, the discovery that one can't decrement a zero is overgeneralized to become a $T=0$ interrupt on borrowing *into* as zero as well as borrowing *from* a zero. Hence, Diff-0-N=N is derived from a decrement-zero impasse. But the decrement-zero impass would itself have to be repaired as well. Hence, Diff-0-N=N is derived at the same time as some decrement zero bug.

This story predicts that Diff-0-N=N will occur more commonly with decrement-zero bugs than in isolation or with other bugs. From the limited frequency data on hand now, this appears to be the case. In particular, since Borrow-Across-Zero is a decrement-zero bug, but Borrow-From-Zero is not (its most common derivation is probably deletion of L12, which creates no impasses), we have an explanation for the nonlinear compounding example mentioned above. The story also predicts that decrement-zero bugs will occur much more commonly with 0-N bugs than they do in isolation—another apparently true prediction.

In short, we believe the structure of Repair Theory is sufficiently rich so that successful projections into the frequency data can be developed. The problem in such a study would be, of course, to find some way to avoid infinite tailorability. A formal projection of the theory would be a major theoretical endeavor.

3.7 A Projection to Bug Stability

The study of bug stability is essentially a study of memory. To make Repair Theory contact this new topic, we once again need a projection hypothesis. One projection hypothesis involves the concept of *a patch retention strategy*. A patch is the instantiation of a repair heuristic for a given impasse. A patch retention strategy determines when to commit repairs to memory. Let us assume that in addition to long term memory, there is some kind of memory which is sufficient to store a patch for the duration of a test (call it "intermediate term memory"). Given these two kinds of memory, a subject could have basically three strategies for the creation and storage of patches:

Patch Retention Strategies:

1. At the first occurance of a certain impasse on a test, create a patch and use it throughout the test by sorting it in intermediate term memory (ITM). However, don't bother to put the patch in long term memory (LTM).

2. Same as the above, but put the patch in LTM.

3. At some or all of the occurances of the impasse, don't use the patch that was (perhaps) stored in ITM, but instead create a new patch, use it and perhaps store it in ITM.

If a subject always follows the first patch retention strategy, wherein he remembers a bug only for the length of the test, then we would expect to see a phenomenon we call "bug migration." When the subject is given two tests a couple of days apart (long enough to wipe out ITM but short enough that very little learning intervenes), we would observe a consistent bug on the first test and a consistent *but different* bug on the second test. The first bug has "migrated" into the second bug. Repair Theory predicts that bugs which migrate into each other will be related in that they are different repairs to the same impasse. For example, Borrow-Across-Zero would migrate into Stops-Borrow-At-Zero, but not into Borrow-From-Zero. We have anecdotal evidence for this phenomenon, and are currently conducting a pilot experiment to verify bug migration.

If a subject follows the second strategy of memorizing patches, then we would expect to find subjects with the same bug several months apart. Such subjects have been found.

If a subject follows the third patch retention strategy of changing patches in the middle of a test, we would expect to find a phenomenon called "tinkering". This means we would see a certain bug for part of a test, then a related bug for another part of the test, and so on. However, *all the bugs would have to be derivable as different repairs to the same impasse.* It is this constraint that all the bugs on the test be derived from the same impasse that separates tinkering from pure noise. Tinkering is difficult to spot because such subjects are not assigned a diagnosis by DEBUGGY since they are not consistently following a bug. However, by intensive hand examination of a small fraction of the data base, a few examples of tinkering have been found. We are in the process of designing analytic tools to help us find more.

In summary, there is some informal evidence that all three patch retention strategies exist. Their existance would be strong evidence of the veracity of Repair Theory, but the fact that the theory can already make such precise predictions confirms its worth.

New Distinctions for Bugs. The notion of a patch retention strategy suggests that the empirical phenomenon of bugs is *not* necessarily just like the computer science notion of a bug. Since bugs in computer programs are just as stable as the rest of the program, it was assumed that the rules that encode bugs in procedural skills are just as stable as the correct parts of the skill. That is, we had been blinded by our metaphor. Indeed, bug stability was such an inherent part of our computational viewpoint that our first reaction to data suggesting bug migration was shock and disbelief. We now see that a subtraction bug may be systematic and yet not stable. So, the patch retention strategy concept extends the original notion of bug that was used to describe systematic, stable behavior (strategy one, bug migration) to include systematic but unstable behavior (strategy two, bug migration).

3.8 A Projection to Latency

There is a third phenomenon that could help us understand Repair Theory better. Children sometimes stop in the middle of a problem and appear to think very hard about something. Often, they are just doing the mental equivalent of counting on their fingers in order to reconstruct a subtraction fact. However, it is possible that some of the thoughtful pauses might be due to problem solving. These pauses could provide support for a strong equivalence between the interpretation/repair coroutine and the cognitive mechanisms used by students to work problems.

We propose the projection hypothesis that running the local problem solver takes more resources than running the GAO interpreter. Hence, a repair event will be signalled by a significant pause between two steps in a subject's performance. This pause will occur the first time the impasse occurs on the test (and perhaps on subsequent occurrences if the subject is tinkering), and moreover the step following the pause must be generable by some repair to that impasse. Although a timed protocol of a third grader's activity is guaranteed to have many superfluous pauses, the stringent conditions surrounding the pauses we are looking for may enable us to find them.

Apparatus has been constructed to automatically collect such protocols. If it turns out to be impossible to find such pauses, the theory would not be overturned. Instead, it is likely that the projection hypothesis is wrong, namely, the local problem solver runs just as fast as the interpreter.

3.9 Toward a Theory of Bug Acquisition

There is no doubt that learning should play an active role in a theory of bugs since bugs develop during a period when the subjects are learning the skill. However, learning is a very difficult phenonemon to study due to the longitudinal nature of the data, questions of motivation, and the variability of the subjects' prior knowledge. And yet choices must be made about representation, primitives, process architecture and so on. It is very difficult to make these choices on an empirical basis especially given only the difficult data that a direct study of learning provides. A major service that a generative theory of bugs, which is based on comparatively clean data, could perform would be to give credibility to a set of principles that constrain a theory of skill acquisition. We believe the principles of Repair Theory do just that.

Some of these principles serve to constrain the architecture of the learning model. For example, the locality constraint on Repair Theory's problem solver could be adopted. The prohibitions against multi-step lookahead and creation of non-primitive nodes when adopted by the learning model could perhaps explain why skills are best taught incrementally, one step at a time. That is, the locality constraint provides a precise hypothesis about how to make the learning model incremental.

The overall architecture of Repair Theory—deletions, repairs and critics—serves to break the problem of forming a learning theory into several subproblems and to define constraints that tentative models for each must satisfy. In particular, a learning theory would need to

1. Replicate the effects of the deletion operator and the deletion blocking principles with a method for generating incomplete procedures that is based on the teaching sequence of the skill. More importantly, *this would make the method of generating incomplete procedures more general in the sense that it would not have to be revised (as the deletion blocking principles would) to be consistent with new teaching sequences.*

2. Provide a mechanism to generate interrupt conditions, or at least the bugs that interrupt conditions can generate.

3. Provide an explanation for how critics are abstracted from examples or specialized from domain independent heuristics in such a way that some of the critics can be missing early in the teaching sequence.

These subproblems have been mentioned before as critical for improving the adequacy of Repair Theory. Solving them in the context of a theory of bug acquisition will hopefully allow a unified account wherein their solutions share qualitative if not structural properties with each other and with Repair Theory's local problem solver. The attempt to unify these structures while preserving the principles of Repair Theory will lead to a learning theory that has limited tailorability and excellent support from the bug occurance data while making interesting, precise predictions about learning that can hopefully be verified without enormous longitudinal studies.

Lastly, we expect a learning theory to provide an account for most of the bugs that Repair Theory has not been able to generate. There are several bugs which have cogent, albeit informal, explanations as cases of mis-abstraction. As an example, consider the bug Always-Borrow-Left. This bug always decrements the leftmost, top digit of a problem regardless of where the column that caused the borrow is. Suppose that the subject who has this bug was tested at a point in his schooling where he had only practiced borrowing on two column problems. In such problems, the correct digit to decrement is exactly the leftmost, top digit. The subject has not yet had problems of the proper form to descriminate between the "leftmost" abstraction and the "left-adjacent" abstraction. A learning theory that learns procedures from examples could perhaps predict that such mis-abstraction bugs will occur when the learning process is incomplete. In short, it appears that the solution to the undergeneration problem of Repair Theory could best be attacked by developing a learning theory for procedures.

3.10 Summary and Concluding Remarks

The major constraints on Repair Theory (presented in Section 2) are listed below:

1. Repairs are independent of impasses. Any repair heuristic can be run on any impasse. Unless a critic or precondition filters it out, the repair will lead to a bug.

2. Critics and preconditions can both filter repairs and cause impasses. If a critic is hypothesized for one purpose, it must be usable for the other as well.

3. The problem solver can not look ahead. A repair is filtered only if the action generated by it immediately violates a critic or a precondition.

4. The problem solver can generate only primitive actions or calls to extant subgoals.

5. The rules that represents the correct procedure can not have dead code. Each rule must be used during the correct solution of at least one subtraction problem.

6. Any rule can be deleted, unless deletion is blocked by a deletion blocking principle.

7. Deletion blocking principles must be motivated by the learning sequence of the skill.

8. The repair heuristics must be specializations of domain-independent weak methods. For example, they can not mention the primitives of subtraction explicitly.

The purpose of these principles is to constrain the tailorability of the theory. Without them, the theory would have so many degrees of freedom that it could be fit to any data, and consequently would lose predictive power.

Since the theory is not able to generate all the known bugs, two extensions have been suggested. One is to replace deletion with interrupt conditions, and the other is to make critics optional. Both of these extensions are ad hoc in that they drastically increase the tailorability of the theory. Hence, they have not been incorporated in the current theory but instead are being incorporated in a learning-based theory that is being built on top of Repair Theory. The empirical results of Repair Theory and the interrupt condition extension are:

	Repair Theory	Interrupt Conditions
bugs	21	43
star-bugs	1	unknown
correct procedures	1	10
predicted bugs	10	unknown
total	33	180 (apprx.)

The theory can be projected to make predictions about several kinds of performance data, namely the frequency and co-occurrence of bugs, their stability between tests and even during tests, and the temporal latencies in the performance of subjects working problems.

The theory has been designed to be relatively domain independent, but as yet it has not been applied to domains other than place-value subtraction. Investigating new domains is an important direction for further research.

Perhaps one of the most important functions of a theory is to create new distinctions, new ways to look at the world. The distinctions created by this theory are based on a particularly active form of misunderstanding by the child. Since students were clearly not being taught the bugs, they must have been performing some form of invention. Overgeneralization and similar forms of mislearning just do not seem powerful enough to explain the existence of many bugs. Repair Theory formalized this intuition by making a clear distinction between incomplete procedures which are generated by mislearning or forgetting, and the inventions that are necessary to account for certain bugs.

But formalization for its own sake leads nowhere. Crucially, the formalization of repairs vs. mislearning has spawned a host of new general distinctions such as "impass," "repair heuristic," "critic" and "patch retention strategy" which may be of service in theories of wholly unrelated phenomena. In particular, the notion of unstable but systematic errors may prove quite useful.

Lastly, the struggle for empirical adequacy has forced us into building a whole inventory of theory formation tools. The prime tool is DEBUGGY—the data analysis tool that enables the whole investigation. Using the bugs uncovered by DEBUGGY, the workbench plays the role of the naive informant in linguistics—in a matter of days, a new version of the theory could be subjected to testing. This fast turn around time allowed us to methodically test a variety of representations and other details whose effects are very subtle.

At this stage in our research, we are struck by how different the theory is from our initial intuitive approach of spinning hypothetical "stories" concerning how each bug might have been produced. We quickly discovered that there were numerous possible stories for each bug. Was there a consistent basis to all those stories? This theory is a partial answer to that question,

ACKNOWLEDGMENTS

This research would have been impossible without the support of Richard Burton and Jamesine Friend. We have benefitted from discussions with many people including Richard Young, Alan Collins, Tom Moran, and Tim O'Shea. The strong encouragement of Zenon Pylyshyn, James Greeno, and Lauren Resnick is greatly appreciated. VanLehn is supported by grant N0014-78-C-0022 from the Office of Naval Research to the Learning Research and Development Center, University of Pittsburgh.

REFERENCES

Ashlock, R. B. Error patterns in computation. Columbus, Ohio: Bell and Howell, 1976.
Brown, J. S. & Burton, R. B. Diagnostic models for procedural bugs in basic mathematical skills. Cognitive Science, 1978, 2, 155–192.

Appendix 1

Procedures Generated by the Current Version of Repair Theory

Deletions refer to the rules of the GAO graph of Figure 1. The names of repair heuristics are abbreviated. Although most of the abbreviations will be clear, two require some explanation. FAdd means to import an analogous action from addition. FSelf means to use an analogous action from subtraction. FSelf will not use an action from the subtree rooted by the deleted rule. This represents the constraint that one can not form an analogy to an action that has not yet been learned. For example, when L9 is deleted, Write9 can not be used by FSelf. Because L9 enters the subskill of borrowing across zero, which is the only part of the algorithm where Write9 is used, we can assume that Write9 has not yet been learned.

*indicates a "star-bug", a procedure that is so absurd that we doubt it will ever occur.
?indicates a bug that has not occurred.
Unmarked bugs have occurred.

Delete L1:
Impasse: None.
Can't-Subtract

Delete L2:
Deletion is blocked by the Stipulated Orders deletion blocking principle (see VanLehn 1980).

Delete L3:
Impasse: None.
*Only-Do-Units-Column

Delete L4:
Impasse: Diff called with blank cell as second argument.
Ignore: inapplicable
Noop: Quit-When-Bottom-Blank
Quit: Quit-When-Bottom-Blank
Backup: inapplicable
Swap: filtered out by "Can't subtract blanks"
Left: filtered out by "Can't subtract blanks"
Right: Shutter-Subtract
FAdd: the correct procedure is regenerated
Demamo: inapplicable
FSelf: inapplicable

Delete L5:
Impasse: Diff called with T<B.
Ignore: inapplicable
Noop: filtered out by "No blanks inside the answer"
Quit: Doesn't-Borrow
Backup: inapplicable
Swap: Smaller-From-Larger
Left: filtered out by "Can't subtract blanks" and "Don't subtract when T<B"

Brown, J. S. & VanLehn, K. Towards a generative theory of bugs. Proceedings of the Wingspread Conference. Madison: University of Wisconsin, Wisconsin Research and Development Center for Individualized Schooling, 1980.

Brownell, W. A. The evaluation of learning in arithmetic. In Arithmetic in General Education. 16th Yearbook of the National Council of Teachers of Mathematics. Washington, D.C.: N.C.T.M., 1941.

Burton, R. B. DEBUGGY: Diagnosis of errors in basic mathematical skills. In D. H. Sleeman & J. S. Brown (Eds.) Intelligent tutoring systems. London: Academic Press, 1981.

Buswell, G. T. Diagnostic studies in arithmetic. Chicago: University of Chicago Press, 1926.

Cox, L. S. Diagnosing and remediating systematic errors in addition and subtraction computations. The Arithmetic Teacher, February 1975.

Lankford, F. G. Some computational strategies of seventh grade pupils. ERIC reports. School of Education, Virginia University, 1972.

McDermott, J. & Forgy, C. L. Production system conflict resolution strategies. In D. A. Waterman & F. Hayes-Roth (Eds.), Pattern-directed inference systems. New York: Academic Press, 1978.

Newell, A. & Simon, H. A., Human problem solving, Englewood Cliffs, N. J.: Prentice-Hall, 1972.

Norman, D. A. Slips of the Mind and an Outline for a Theory of Action (CHIP report No. 88). La Jolla: University of California, Center for Human Information Processing, 1979.

Pylyshyn, Z. W. Computation and Cognition: Issues in the foundations of cognitive science. The Behavioral and Brain Sciences, 1980.

Pylyshyn, Z. W. Computation and Cognition. forthcoming.

Roberts, G. H. The failure strategies of third grade arithmetic pupils. The Arithmetic Teacher, May, 1968.

VanLehn, K. On the representation of procedures in Repair Theory. Pittsburgh: University of Pittsburgh, Learning Research and Development Laboratory technical report, 1980.

VanLehn, K. & Friend, J. Results from DEBUGGY: An analysis of systematic subtraction errors. Palo Alto California: Xerox Palo Alto Science Center technical report, 1980.

VanLehn, K. A theory of bug acquisition. Doctoral dissertation, Massachusetts Institute of Technology. forthcoming.

Young, R. M. & O'Shea, T. Errors in Children's Subtraction. Submitted for publication, forthcoming.

Right: filtered out by "Can't subtract blanks" and "Don't subtract when T<B"
FAdd: ?Add-Instead-of-Borrow
Dememo: Zero-Instead-of-Borrow
FSelf: (SubBlank): ?Write-Top-Instead-of-Borrow

Delete L6: Deletion blocked by Special Case deletion blocking principle.

Delete L7: Impasse: None.
Borrow-No-Decrement

Delete L8: Impasse: Diff called with T<B after borrow has been completed.
Ignore: inapplicable
Noop: filtered out by "No blanks inside the answer"
Quit: Doesn't-borrow
Backup: inapplicable
Swap: Smaller-From-Larger-With-Borrow
Left: filtered out by "Can't subtract blanks" and "Don't subtract when T<B"
Right: filtered out by "Can't subtract blanks" and "Don't subtract when T<B"
FAdd: ?Add-With-Borrow
Dememo: Zero-After-Borrow
FSelf: (SubBlank): ?Write-Top-With-Borrow

Delete L9: Impasse: Decr called with T=0.
Ignore: inapplicable
Noop: Stops-Borrow-At-Zero
Quit: Borrow-Won't-Recurse
Backup: inapplicable
Second impasse: called with T<B. Occurs on all problems.
Ignore: inapplicable
Noop: filtered out by "No blanks inside the answer"
Quit: Borrow-Won't-Recurse
Backup: inapplicable
Swap: Smaller-From-Larger-Instead-of-Borrow-From-Zero
Left: filtered out by "Don't subtract with T<B"
Right: filtered by "Can't subtract blanks" & "Don't subtract when T<B"
FAdd: ?Add-Instead-of-Borrow-From-Zero
Dememo: Zero-Instead-of-Borrow-From-Zero
FSelf: (SubBlank): ?Write-Top-Instead-of-Borrow-From-Zero

Swap: filtered out by "Don't decrement zero" generates the same impasses and procedures as deleting L11
Left: filtered out by "Don't decrement twice", "Don't decrement blanks," and "Don't change a column after its answer is written."
Right: Borrow-Add-Decrement-Instead-of-Zero
FAdd: Stops-Borrow-At-Zero
Dememo: (Add10): Second Impasse: On problems where the zero that was borrowed from is over a zero, Diff trys to write a two digit number (10) as the answer, violating the answer overflow critic. A similar impasse occurs with zeros over blanks.
Ignore: Borrow-From-Zero-Is-Ten
Noop: filtered by "No blanks inside the answer"
Quit: ?Borrow-From-Zero-Is-Ten-Quit-Answer-Overflow
Backup: inapplicable

Swap: inapplicable
Left: filtered out by "No answer overflows"
Right: filtered out by "No answer overflows"
FAdd: Borrow-From-Zero-Is-Ten-Carrying-Answer-Overflow
Dememo: inapplicable
FSelf: inapplicable

Delete L10: Deletion is blocked by Special Case deletion blocking principle.

Delete L11: Impasse: Deleting L11 creates a procedure that does not change zeros to nines when borrowing across zero. Consequently, a borrow is often needed in these "touched zero" columns. This borrow trys to decrement the same digit that was decremented on the first borrow, violating the "Don't decrement twice" critic.
Borrow-Across-Zero
Borrow-Across-Zero-Touched-Zero-Is-Ten
?Borrow-Across-Zero-Quit-On-Touched-Zero
Second Impasse: Diff called with T<B.
Ignore: inapplicable
Noop: filtered by "No blanks inside the answer"
Quit: ?Borrow-Across-Zero-Quit-On-Touched-Zero
Backup: inapplicable
Swap: Borrow-Across-Zero-Touched-0-N=N
Left: filtered out by "Don't subtract when T<B"
Right: filtered by "Can't subtract blanks" & "Don't subtract when T<B"
FAdd: Borrow-Across-Zero-Touched-0-N=N
Dememo: Borrow-Across-Zero-Touched-0-N=0
FSelf: (SubBlank): Borrow-Across-Zero-Touched-0-N='0
filtered out by "Don't decrement zero" and "Can't decrement a blank"
filtered out by "Can't decrement a blank"
filtered out by "Don't decrement zero"
?a subtle variant of Stops-Borrow-At-Zero
inapplicable
(Add10): ?Borrow-Across-Zero-Add10-For-Double-Decr

Delete L12: Impasse: None.
Borrow-From-Zero

Appendix 2
Description of Procedural Errors (Bugs)

0-N=0/AFTER/BORROW
When a column has a 1 that was changed to a 0 by a previous borrow, the student writes 0 as the answer to that column. (914 − 486 = 508)

0-N=N/AFTER/BORROW
When a column has a 1 that was changed to a 0 by a previous borrow, the student writes the bottom digit as the answer to that column. (512 − 136 = 436)

1-1=0/AFTER/BORROW
If a column starts with 1 in both top and bottom and is borrowed from, the student writes 0 as the answer to that column. (812 − 518 = 304)

1-1=1/AFTER/BORROW
If a column starts with 1 in both top and bottom and is borrowed from, the student writes 1 as the answer to that column. (812 − 518 = 314)

ADD/BORROW/CARRY/SUB
The student adds instead of subtracting but subtracts the carried digit instead of adding it. (54 − 38 = 72)

ADD/BORROW/DECREMENT
Instead of decrementing the student adds 1, carrying to the next column if necessary.

```
 863        893
−134       −104
 749        809
```

ADD/BORROW/DECREMENT/WITHOUT/CARRY
Instead of decrementing the student adds 1. If this addition results in 10 the student does not carry but simply writes both digits in the same space.

```
 863        8 93
−134       −1 04
 749        7109
```

ADD/INSTEAD/OF/SUB
The student adds instead of subtracting. (32 − 15 = 47)

ADD/NOCARRY/INSTEADOF/SUB
The student adds instead of subtracting. If carrying is required he does not add the carried digit. (47 − 25 = 62)

ALWAYS/BORROW
The student borrows in every column regardless of whether it is necessary. (488 − 299 = 1159)

ALWAYS/BORROW/LEFT
The student borrows from the leftmost digit instead of borrowing from the digit immediately to the left. (733 − 216 = 427)

BLANK/INSTEADOF/BORROW
When a borrow is needed the student simply skips the column and goes on to the next (425 − 283 = 22)

BORROW/ACROSS/TOP/SMALLER/DECREMENTING/TO
When decrementing a column in which the top is smaller than the bottom, the student adds 10 to the top digit, decrements the column being borrowed into and borrows from the next column to the left. Also the student skips any column which has a 0 over a 0 or a blank in the borrowing process.

```
 183        513
 −95       −268
  97        254
```

BORROW/ACROSS/ZERO
When borrowing across a 0, the student skips over the 0 to borrow from the next column. If this causes him to have to borrow twice he decrements the same number both times.

```
 904        904
  −7       −237
 807        577
```

BORROW/ACROSS/ZERO/OVER/BLANK
When borrowing across a 0 over a blank, the student skips to the next column to decrement. (402 − 6 = 306)

BORROW/ACROSS/ZERO/OVER/ZERO
Instead of borrowing across a 0 that is over a 0, the student does not change the 0 but decrements the next column to the left instead. (802 − 304 = 308)

BORROW/ACROSS/ZERO/TOUCHED/0-N=0
Instead of borrowing across a 0, the student does not change the 0 but decrements the next column on the left instead. Also, if borrowing is needed in a column headed by a zero that should have been changed, the student writes zero in the answer instead. (802 − 324 = 508)

BORROW/ACROSS/ZERO/TOUCHED/0-N=N
Instead of borrowing across a 0, the student does not change the 0 but decrements the next column to the left instead. Also, if borrowing is needed in a column headed by a zero that should have been changed, the student writes the bottom digit in the answer instead. (802 − 324 = 528)

BORROW/ACROSS/ZERO/TOUCHED/ZERO/IS/TEN
Instead of borrowing across a 0, the student does not change the 0 but decrements the next column to the left instead. Also, if borrowing is needed in a column headed by a zero that should have been changed, the student adds ten to the zero but does no decrementing. (802 − 324 = 588)

BORROW/ADD/DECREMENT/INSTEADOF/ZERO
Instead of borrowing across a 0, the student changes the 0 to 1 and doesn't decrement any column to the left. (307 − 108 = 219)

BORROW/ADD/IS/TEN
The student changes the number that causes the borrow into 10 instead of adding 10 to it. (83 − 29 = 51)

BORROW/DECREMENTING/TO/BY/EXTRAS
When there is a borrow across 0's, the student does not add 10 to the column he is doing but instead adds 10 minus the number of 0's borrowed across.

```
 308        3008
−139       −1359
 168        1647
```

BORROW/DIFF/0-N=N&SMALL-LARGE=0
The student doesn't borrow. For columns of the form 0 - N he writes N as the answer. Otherwise he writes 0. (304 - 179 = 270)

BORROW/DON'T/DECREMENT/TOP/SMALLER
The student will not decrement a column if the top number is smaller than the bottom number.

```
  732      732
 -484     -434
  258      298
 Wrong   Correct
```

BORROW/DON'T/DECREMENT/UNLESS/BOTTOM/SMALLER
The student will not decrement a column unless the bottom number is smaller than the top number.

```
  732      732
 -484     -434
  258      308
 Wrong
```

BORROW/FROM/ALL/ZERO
Instead of borrowing across 0's, the student changes all the 0's to 9's but does not continue borrowing from the column to the left. (3006 - 1807 = 2199)

BORROW/FROM/BOTTOM
The student borrows from the bottom row instead of the top one.

```
   87      827
  -28     -208
   79      839
```

BORROW/FROM/BOTTOM/INSTEAD/OF/ZERO
When borrowing from a column of the form 0 - N, the student decrements the bottom number instead of the 0.

```
  608      108
 -249      -49
  379       79
```

BORROW/FROM/LARGER
When borrowing, the student decrements the larger digit in the column regardless of whether it is on the top or the bottom. (872 - 294 = 598)

BORROW/FROM/ONE/IS/NINE
When borrowing from a 1, the student treats the 1 as if it were 10, decrementing it to a 9. (316 - 139 = 267)

BORROW/FROM/ONE/IS/TEN
When borrowing from a 1, the student changes the 1 to 10 instead of to 0. (414 - 277 = 237)

BORROW/FROM/ZERO
Instead of borrowing across a 0, the student changes the 0 to 9 but does not continue borrowing from the column to the left.

```
  306     3006      103
 -187    -1807      -45
  219     1299      158
```

BORROW/FROM/ZERO/IS/TEN
When borrowing across 0, the student changes the 0 to 10 and does not decrement any digit to the left. (604 - 235 = 479)

BORROW/FROM/ZERO/IS/TEN/CARRYING/ANSWER/OVERFLOW
When borrowing across 0, the student changes the 0 to 10 and does not decrement any digit to the left. However, if the newly created 10 is over zero, the student carries instead of trying to write ten in the answer. (604 - 205 = 509)

```
  306     3006      103      203
 -187    -1807      -45      -45
  219     1299       58      158
 Wrong    Wrong   Correct  Correct
```

BORROW/FROM/ZERO&LEFT/OK
Instead of borrowing across a 0, the student changes the 0 to 9 but does not continue borrowing from the column to the left. However if the digit to the left of the 0 is over a blank then the student does the correct thing.

```
  306     3006      103      203
 -187    -1807      -45      -45
  219     1299       58      258
 Wrong    Wrong   Correct   Wrong
```

BORROW/FROM/ZERO&LEFT/TEN/OK
Instead of borrowing across a 0, the student changes the 0 to 9 but does not continue borrowing from the column to the left. However if the digit to the left of the 0 is a 1 over a blank then the student does the correct thing.

```
  306      103      203
 -187      -45      -45
  219       58      258
 Wrong   Correct   Wrong
```

BORROW/IGNORE/ZERO/OVER/BLANK
When borrowing across a 0 over a blank, the student treats the column with the zero as if it weren't there.

```
  505      508
   -7       -7
  4 8      501
 Wrong   Correct
```

BORROW/INTO/ONE=TEN
When a borrow is caused by a 1, the student changes the 1 to a 10 instead of adding 10 to it. (71 - 38 = 32)

BORROW/NO/DECREMENT
When borrowing the student adds 10 correctly but doesn't change any column to the left. (62 - 44 = 28)

BORROW/ONCE/THEN/SMALLER/FROM/LARGER
The student will borrow only once per exercise. From then on he subtracts the smaller from the larger digit in each column regardless of their positions. (7127 - 2389 = 4278)

BORROW/ONCE/WITHOUT/RECURSE
The student will borrow only once per problem. After that, if another borrow is required the student adds the 10 correctly but does not decrement. If there is a borrow across a 0 the student changes the 0 to 9 but does not decrement the digit to the left of the 0.

```
  535      408
 -278     -239
  357      269
```

BORROW/ONLY/FROM/TOP/SMALLER
When borrowing, the student tries to find a column in which the top number is smaller than the bottom. If there is one he decrements that, otherwise he borrows correctly. (9283 - 3566 = 5627)

BORROW/ONLY/ONCE
When there are several borrowers, the student decrements only with the first borrower. (535 – 278 = 357).

BORROW/SKIP/EQUAL
When decrementing, the student skips over columns in which the top digit and the bottom digit are the same. (923 – 427 = 406)

BORROW/TEN/PLUS/NEXT/DIGIT/INTO/ZERO
When a borrow is caused by a 0 the student does not add 10 correctly. What he does instead is add 10 plus the digit in the next column to the left. He will give answers like this: (50 – 38 = 17)

BORROW/TREAT/ONE/AS/ZERO
When borrowing from 1, the student treats the 1 as if it were 0; that is, he changes the 1 to 9 and decrements the number to the left of the 1. (313 – 159 = 144)

BORROW/UNIT/DIFF
The student borrows the difference between the top digit and the bottom digit of the current column. In other words, he borrows just enough to do the subtraction, which then always results in 0. (86 – 29 = 30)

BORROW/WON'T/RECURSE
Instead of borrowing across a 0, the student stops doing the exercise. (8035 – 2662 = 3)

BORROWED/FROM/DON'T/BORROW
When there are two borrows in a row the student does the first borrow correctly but with the second borrow he does not decrement (he does add 10 correctly). (143 – 88 = 155)

CAN'T/SUBTRACT
The student skips the entire problem. (8 – 3 =)

DECREMENT/ALL/ON/MULTIPLE/ZERO
When borrowing across a 0 and the borrow is caused by 0, the student changes the right 0 to 9 instead of 10. (600 – 142 = 457)

DECREMENT/BY/TWO/OVER/TWO
When borrowing from a column of form N – 2, the student decrements the N by 2 instead of 1. (83 – 29 = 44)

DECREMENT/LEFT/MOST/ZERO/ONLY
When borrowing across two or more 0's the student changes the leftmost of the row of 0's to 9 but changes the other 0's to 10's. He will give answers like: (1003 – 958 = 1055)

DECREMENT/MULTIPLE/ZEROS/BY/NUMBER/TO/RIGHT
When borrowing across 0's the student changes the rightmost 0 to a 9, changes the next 0 to 8, etc. (8002 – 1714 = 6188)

DECREMENT/ON/FIRST/BORROW
The first column that requires a borrow is decremented before the column subtract is done. (832 – 265 = 566)

DECREMENT/ONE/TO/ELEVEN
Instead of decrementing a 1, the student changes the 1 to an 11. (314 – 6 = 2118)

DIFF/0–N=0
When the student encounters a column of the form 0 – N he doesn't borrow; instead he writes 0 as the column answer. (40 – 21 = 20)

DIFF/0–N=N
When the student encounters a column of the form 0 – N, he doesn't borrow. Instead he writes N as the answer. (80 – 27 = 67)

DIFF/0–N=N/WHEN/BORROW/FROM/ZERO
When borrowing across a 0 and the borrow is caused by a 0, the student doesn't borrow. Instead he writes the bottom number as the column answer. He will borrow correctly in the next column or in other circumstances.

$$\begin{array}{r} 100 \\ -\ 32 \\ \hline 72 \end{array} \qquad \begin{array}{r} 400 \\ -248 \\ \hline 168 \end{array}$$

DIFF/1–N=1
When a column has the form 1 – N the student writes 1 as the column answer. (51 – 27 = 31)

DIFF/N–0=0
The student thinks that N – 0 is 0. (57 – 20 = 30)

DIFF/N–N=N
Whenever there is a column that has the same number on the top and the bottom, the student writes that number as the answer. (83 – 13 = 73)

DOESN'T/BORROW
The student stops doing the exercise when a borrow is required. (833 – 262 = 1)

DON'T/DECREMENT/SECOND/ZERO
When borrowing across a 0 and the borrow is caused by a 0, the student changes the 0 he is borrowing across into a 10 instead of a 9. (700 – 258 = 452)

DON'T/DECREMENT/ZERO
When borrowing across a 0, the student changes the 0 to 10 instead of 9. (506 – 318 = 198)

DON'T/DECREMENT/ZERO/CARRYING/ANSWER/OVERFLOW
When borrowing across a 0, the student changes the 0 to 10 instead of 9. However, if the newly created to is over a zero, the student carries instead of writing a ten as the answer for that column. (506 – 308 = 208)

DON'T/DECREMENT/ZERO/OVER/BLANK
When borrowing across a 0 that is over a blank, the student skips over the 0 and decrements the next digit to the left. (305 – 9 = 106)

DON'T/DECREMENT/ZERO/OVER/ZERO
When borrowing across a 0 that is over another 0, the student skips over the 0 and decrements the next digit to the left. (305 – 107 = 208)

DON'T/DECREMENT/ZERO/UNTIL/BOTTOM/BLANK
When borrowing across a 0, the student changes the 0 to a 10 instead of a 9 unless the 0 is over a blank, in which case he does the correct thing.

$$\begin{array}{r} 506 \\ -318 \\ \hline 198 \\ \text{Wrong} \end{array} \qquad \begin{array}{r} 304 \\ -\ \ 9 \\ \hline 295 \\ \text{Correct} \end{array}$$

DOUBLE/DECREMENT/ONE
When borrowing from a 1, the student treats the 1 as a 0 (changes the 1 to 9 and continues borrowing to the left. (813 – 515 = 288)

SMALLER/FROM/LARGER/WITH/BORROW
When borrowing the student decrements correctly, then subtracts the smaller digit from the larger as if he had not borrowed at all. (73 − 24 = 411)

STOPS/BORROW/AT/MULTIPLE/ZERO
Instead of borrowing across several 0's, the student adds 10 to the column he's doing but doesn't change any column to the left. (4004 − 9 = 4005)

STOPS/BORROW/AT/ZERO
Instead of borrowing across a 0, the student adds 10 to the column he's doing but doesn't decrement from a column to the left. (404 − 187 = 227)

STUTTER/SUBTRACT
When there are blanks in the bottom number, the student subtracts the leftmost digit of the bottom number in every column that has a blank. (4369 − 22 = 2147)

SUB/BOTTOM/FROM/TOP
The student always subtracts the top digit from the bottom digit. If the bottom digit is smaller, he decrements the top digit and adds 10 to the bottom before subtracting. If the bottom digit is zero, however, he writes the top digit in the answer. If the top digit is 1 greater than the bottom he writes 9. He will give answers like this. (4723 − 3065 = 9742)

SUB/COPY/LEAST/BOTTOM/MOST/TOP
The student does not subtract. Instead he copies digits from the exercise to fill in the answer space. He copies the leftmost digit from the top number and the other digits from the bottom number. He will give answers like this: (648 − 231 = 631)

SUB/ONE/OVER/BLANKS
When there are blanks in the bottom number, the student subtracts 1 from the top digit. (548 − 2 = 436)

TREAT/TOP/ZERO/AS/NINE
When a borrow is caused by a 0, the student doesn't borrow. Instead he treats the 0 as if it were a 9. (30 − 4 = 39)

TREAT/TOP/ZERO/AS/TEN
When a borrow is caused by a 0, the student adds 10 to it correctly but doesn't change any column to the left. (40 − 27 = 23)

TREAT/ZERO/AS/NOTHING
The student ignores 0's. (407 − 5 = 42)

ZERO/AFTER/BORROW
When a column requires a borrow, the student decrements correctly but writes 0 as the answer. (65 − 48 = 10)

ZERO/INSTEAD/OF/BORROW/FROM/ZERO
The student won't borrow if he has to borrow across 0. Instead he will write 0 as the answer to the column requiring the borrow.

```
  702         702
 −  8        −348
  700         630
```

ZERO/INSTEAD/OF/BORROW
The student doesn't borrow; he writes 0 as the answer instead. (42 − 16 = 30)

FORGET/BORROW/OVER/BLANKS
The student doesn't decrement a number that is over a blank. (347 − 9 = 348)

IGNORE/LEFTMOST/ONE/OVER/BLANK
When the left column of the exercise has a 1 that is over a blank, the student ignores that column. (143 − 22 = 21)

IGNORE/ZERO/OVER/BLANK
Whenever there is column that has a 0 over a blank, the student ignores that column. (907 − 5 = 92)

INCREMENT/OVER/LARGER
When borrowing from a column in which the top is smaller than the bottom, the student increments instead of decrementing. (833 − 277 = 576)

INCREMENT/ZERO/OVER/BLANK
When borrowing across a 0 over a blank, the student increments the 0 instead of decrementing. (402 − 6 = 416)

N-9 = N-1/AFTER/BORROW
If a column is of the form N − 9 and has been borrowed from, when the student does that column he subtracts 1 instead of subtracting 9. (834 − 796 = 127)

N-N=1/AFTER/BORROW
If a column had the form N − N and was borrowed from, the student writes 1 as the answer to that column. (944 − 348 = 616)

N-N=9/PLUS/DECREMENT
When a column has the same number on the top and the bottom the student writes 9 as the answer and decrements the next column to the left even though borrowing is not necessary. (94 − 34 = 59)

ONCE/BORROW/ALWAYS/BORROW
Once a student has borrowed he continues to borrow in every remaining column in the exercise. (488 − 229 = 1159)

QUIT/WHEN/BOTTOM/BLANK
When the bottom number has fewer digits than the top number, the student quits as soon as the bottom number runs out. (439 − 4 = 5)

SIMPLE/PROBLEM/STUTTER/SUBTRACT
When the bottom number is a single digit and the top number has two or more digits, the student repeatedly subtracts the single bottom digit from each digit in the top number. (348 − 2 = 126)

SMALLER/FROM/LARGER
The student doesn't borrow; in each column he subtracts the smaller digit from the larger one. (81 − 38 = 57)

SMALLER/FROM/LARGER/INSTEAD/OF/BORROW/FROM/ZERO
The student does not borrow across 0. Instead he will subtract the smaller from the larger digit.

```
  306         306
 −  8        −148
  302         162
```

SMALLER/FROM/LARGER/WHEN/BORROWED/FROM
When there are two borrows in a row the student does the first one correctly but for the second one he does not borrow; instead he subtracts the smaller from the larger digit regardless of order. (824 − 157 = 747)

Acquisition of Cognitive Skill

John R. Anderson
Carnegie-Mellon University

A framework for skill acquisition is proposed that includes two major stages in the development of a cognitive skill: a declarative stage in which facts about the skill domain are interpreted and a procedural stage in which the domain knowledge is directly embodied in procedures for performing the skill. This general framework has been instantiated in the ACT system in which facts are encoded in a propositional network and procedures are encoded as productions. Knowledge compilation is the process by which the skill transits from the declarative stage to the procedural stage. It consists of the subprocesses of composition, which collapses sequences of productions into single productions, and proceduralization, which embeds factual knowledge into productions. Once proceduralized, further learning processes operate on the skill to make the productions more selective in their range of applications. These processes include generalization, discrimination, and strengthening of productions. Comparisons are made to similar concepts from past learning theories. How these learning mechanisms apply to produce the power law speedup in processing time with practice is discussed.

It requires at least 100 hours of learning and practice to acquire any significant cognitive skill to a reasonable degree of proficiency. For instance, after 100 hours a student learning to program a computer has achieved only a very modest facility in the skill. Learning one's primary language takes tens of thousands of hours. The psychology of human learning has been very thin in ideas about what happens to skills under the impact of this amount of learning—and for obvious reasons. This article presents a theory about the changes in the nature of a skill over such large time scales and about the basic learning processes that are responsible.

This research was sponsored by the Personnel and Training Research Programs, Psychological Sciences Division, Office of Naval Research, under Contract N00014-81-C-0335, Contract Authority Identification Number, NR 157-465, and Grant IST-80-15357 from the National Science Foundation. My ability to put together this theory has depended critically on input from colleagues I have worked with over the past few years: Charles Beasley, Jim Greeno, Paul Kline, Pat Langley, and David Neves. This is not to suggest that any of the above would endorse all of the ideas in this paper. I would like to thank those who have provided me with valuable advice and feedback on the paper: Renee Elio, Jim Greeno, Paul Kline, Jill Larkin, Clayton Lewis, Miriam Schustack, and especially Lynne Reder.

Requests for reprints should be sent to John Anderson, Department of Psychology, Carnegie-Mellon University, Schenley Park, Pittsburgh, Pennsylvania 15213.

Fitts (1964) considered the process of skill acquisition to fall into three stages of development. The first stage, called the *cognitive stage*, involves an initial encoding of the skill into a form sufficient to permit the learner to generate the desired behavior to at least some crude approximation. In this stage it is common to observe verbal mediation in which the learner rehearses information required for the execution of the skill. The second stage, called the *associative stage*, involves the "smoothing out" of the skill performance. Errors in the initial understanding of the skill are gradually detected and eliminated. Concomitantly, there is a dropout of verbal mediation. The third stage, the *autonomous stage*, is one of gradual continued improvement in the performance of the skill. The improvements in this stage often continue indefinitely. Although these general observations about the course of skill development seem true for a wide range of skills, they have defied systematic theoretical analysis.

The theory to be presented in this article is in keeping with these general observations of Fitts (1964) and provides an explanation of the phenomena associated with his three stages. In fact, the three major sections of this article correspond to the three stages. In the first stage the learner receives instruc-

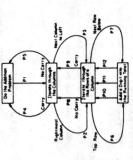

Figure 1. A representation of the flow of control in Table 1 between various goals. (The boxes correspond to goal states, and the arrows to productions that can change these states. Control starts with the top goal.)

tion and information about a skill. The instruction is encoded as a set of facts about the skill. These facts can be used by general interpretive procedures to generate behavior. This initial stage of skill corresponds to Fitts's cognitive stage. In this article it will be referred to as the *declarative stage*. Verbal mediation is frequently observed because the facts have to be rehearsed in working memory to keep them available for the interpretive procedures.

According to the theory to be presented here, Fitts's second stage is really a transition between the declarative stage and a later stage. With practice the knowledge is converted into a procedural form in which it is directly applied without the intercession of other interpretive procedures. The gradual process by which the knowledge is converted from declarative to procedural form is called *knowledge compilation*. Fitts's associative stage corresponds to the period over which knowledge compilation applies.

According to the theory, Fitts's autonomous stage involves further learning that occurs after the knowledge achieves procedural form. In particular, there is further tuning of the knowledge so that it will apply more appropriately, and there is a gradual process of speedup. This will be called the *procedural stage* in this article.

This article presents a detailed theory about the use and development of knowledge in both the declarative and procedural form

and about the transition between these two forms. The theory is based on the ACT production system (Anderson, 1976) in which the distinction between procedural and declarative knowledge is fundamental. Procedural knowledge is represented as productions, whereas declarative knowledge is represented as a propositional network. Before describing the theory of skill acquisition, it will be necessary to specify some of the basic operating principles of the ACT production system.

The ACT Production System

The ACT production system consists of a set of productions that can operate on facts in the declarative data base. Each production has the form of a primitive rule that specifies a cognitive contingency, that is, a production specifies when a cognitive act should take place. The production has a condition that specifies the circumstances under which the production can apply and an action that specifies what should be done when the production applies. The sequence of productions that apply in a task correspond to the cognitive steps taken in performing the task. In the actual computer simulations, these production rules have often quite technical syntax, but in this article I will usually give the rules quite English-like renditions. For current purposes application of a production can be thought of as a step of cognition. Much of the ACT performance theory is concerned with specifying how productions are selected to apply, and much of the ACT learning theory is concerned with how these production rules are acquired.

An Example

To explain some of the basic concepts of the ACT production system, it is useful to have an illustrative set of productions that performs some simple task. Such a set of productions for performing addition is given in Table 1. Figure 1 illustrates the flow of control in that production set among goals. It is easiest to understand such a production system by tracing its application to a problem such as adding a column of numbers:

Table 1
A Production System for Performing Addition

P1. IF   the goal is to do an addition problem.
     THEN the subgoal is to iterate through the columns of the problem.

P2. IF   the goal is to iterate through the columns of an addition problem and the rightmost column has not been processed.
     THEN the subgoal is to iterate through the rows of that rightmost column and set the running total to zero.

P3. IF   the goal is to iterate through the columns of an addition problem and a column has just been processed and another column is to the left of this column.
     THEN the subgoal is to iterate through the rows of this column to the left and set the running total to the carry.

P4. IF   the goal is to iterate through the columns of an addition problem and the last column has been processed and there is a carry.
     THEN write out the carry and POP the goal.

P5. IF   the goal is to iterate through the columns of an addition problem and the last column has been processed and there is no carry.
     THEN POP the goal.

P6. IF   the goal is to iterate through the rows of a column and the top row has not been processed.
     THEN the subgoal is to add the digit of the top row into the running total.

P7. IF   the goal is to iterate through the rows of a column and a row has just been processed and another row is below it.
     THEN the subgoal is to add the digit of the lower row to the running total.

P8. IF   the goal is to iterate through the rows of a column and the last row has been processed and the running total is a digit.
     THEN write the digit and delete the carry and mark the column as processed and POP the goal.

P9. IF   the goal is to iterate through the rows of a column and the last row has been processed and the running total is of the form "string + digit".
     THEN write the digit and set carry to the string and mark the column as processed and POP the goal.

P10. IF   the goal is to add a digit to a number and the number is a digit and a sum is the sum of the two digits.
     THEN the result is the sum and mark the digit as processed and POP the goal.

P11. IF   the goal is to add a digit to a number and the number is of the form "string + digit" and a sum is the sum of the two digits and the sum is less than 10.
     THEN the result is "string + sum" and mark the digit as processed and POP the goal.

P12. IF   the goal is to add a digit to a number and the number is of the form "string + digit" and a sum is the sum of the two digits and the sum is of the form "1 + digit*" and another number sum* is the sum of 1 plus string.
     THEN the result is "sum* + digit*" and mark the digit as processed and POP the goal.

```
 614
 438
 683
```

Production P1 is the first to apply and would set as a subgoal to iterate through the columns. Then Production P2 applies and changes the subgoal to adding the digits of the rightmost column. It also sets the running total to 0. Then Production P6 applies to set the new subgoal to adding the top digit of the column (4) to the running total. In terms of Figure 1, this sequence of three productions has moved the system down from the top goal of performing a basic addition operation. The system has the four goals in Figure 1 stacked with attention focused on the bottom goal.

At this point Production P10 applies, which calculates 4 as the new value of the running total and POPs the goal of adding the digit to the running total. This amounts to removing this goal from the stack and returning attention to the goal of iterating through the rows of the column. Then P7 applies, which sets the new subgoal of adding 8 into the running total. P10 applies again to change the running total to 12; then P7 applies to create the subgoal of adding 3 into the running total; then P11 calculates the new running total as 15. At this point the system is back at the goal of iterating through the rows and has processed the bottom row of the column. Then Production P9 applies, which writes out the 5 in 15, sets the carry to the 1, and POPs back to the goal of iterating through the columns. At this point the production system has processed one column of the problem.

I will not trace out any further the application of this production set to the problem, but the reader is invited to carry out the hand simulation. Note that Productions P2–P5 form a subroutine for iterating through the columns, Productions P6–P9 an embedded subroutine for processing a column, and Productions P10–P12 an embedded subroutine for adding a digit to the running total. In Figure 1 all the productions correspond to a subroutine emanate from the same goal box.

Significant Features of the Performance System

A number of features of the production system are important for the learning theory to be presented. The productions themselves are the system's procedural component. For a production to apply, the clauses specified in its condition must be matched against information active in working memory. This information is part of the system's declarative component. Elsewhere (Anderson, 1976, 1980) I have discussed the network encoding of that declarative knowledge and the process of spreading activation defined on that network.

Goal structure. As noted above, the productions in Table 1 are organized into subroutines, where each subroutine is associated with a goal state and all the productions in the subroutine are trying to achieve. Because the system can have only one goal at any moment in time, productions from only one of these subroutines can apply at any one time. This forces a considerable seriality into the behavior of the system. These goal-seeking productions are hierarchically organized. The idea that hierarchical structure is fundamental to human cognition has been emphasized by Miller, Galanter, and Pribram (1960) and many others. Greeno (1976) used the idea of goal structuring for production systems. Brown and Van Lehn (1980) have recently introduced a similar goal structuring for production systems.

In the original ACT system (Anderson, 1976), there was a scheme for achieving the effect of subroutines by the setting of control variables. There are several important differences between the current scheme and that older one. First, as noted, the current scheme forces a strong degree of seriality into the system. Second, because the goals are not arbitrary nodes but rather meaningful assertions, it is much easier for ACT's learning system to acquire new productions that make reference to goals. Evidence for this last assertion will be given as the various ACT learning mechanisms are discussed.

In achieving a hierarchical subroutine structure by means of a goal-subgoal structure, I am accepting the claim that the hierarchical control of behavior derives from the structure of problem solving. This amounts to making the assertion that problem solving, and the goal structure it produces, is a fundamental category of cognition. This assertion has been advanced by others (e.g., Newell, 1980). Thus, this learning discussion contains a rather strong presupposition about the architecture of cognition. I think the presupposition is too abstract to be defended directly; rather, evidence for it will come from the fruitfulness of the systems that we can build based on the architectural assumption.

Conflict resolution. Every production system requires some rules of conflict resolution, that is, principles for deciding which of those productions that match will be executed. ACT has a set of conflict-resolution principles that can be seen as variants of the 1976 ACT (Anderson, 1976) or the OPS system (Forgy & McDermott, 1977). One powerful principle is refractoriness: that the same production cannot apply to the same data in working memory twice in the same way. This prevents the same production from repeating over and over again and was implicit in the preceding hand simulation of Table 1.

The two other principles of conflict resolution in ACT are specificity and strength. Neither was illustrated in Table 1 but both are important to understanding the learning discussion. If two productions can apply and the condition of one is more specific than the other, then the more specific production takes precedence. Condition A is more specific than Condition B if the set of situations in which Condition A can match is a proper subset of the set of situations where Condition B can match. The specificity rule allows exceptions to general rules to have more specific conditions. For instance, suppose we had the following pair of productions:

PA.   IF the goal is to generate the plural of man.
      THEN say "MEN."

PB.   IF the goal is to generate the plural of a noun,
      THEN say "noun + s."

The condition of Production PA is more specific than the condition of Production PB and so will apply over the general pluralization rule.

Each production has a strength that reflects the frequency with which that production has been successfully applied. I will describe the rules that determine strength accumulation later in this article; here I describe the role of production strength in conflict resolution. Elsewhere (e.g., Anderson, 1976; Anderson, Kline, & Beasley, 1979) I have given a version of this role of strength that assumes discrete time intervals. Here I give a continuous version. Productions are indexed by the constants in their conditions. For instance, the Production PA above would be indexed by *plural* and *man*. If these concepts are active in working memory, the production will be selected for consideration. In this way ACT can focus its attention on just the subset of productions that may be potentially relevant. Only if a production is selected is a test made to see if its condition is satisfied. (For future reference if a production is selected, it is said to be on the

APPLYLIST.) A production takes a time T_1 to be selected and another time T_2 to be tested and to apply. The selection time T_1 varies with the production's strength, whereas the application time is a constant over productions. It is further assumed that the time T_1 for the production to be selected will randomly vary from selection to selection. The expected time is a/s where s is the production strength and a is a constant. Although there are no compelling reasons for making any assumption about the distribution, we have assumed that T_1 has an exponential distribution, and this is its form in all our simulations.

A production will actually apply if it is selected and it has completed application before a more specific production is selected. This provides the relationship between strength and specificity in the theory. A more specific production will take precedence over a more general production only if its selection time is less than the selection plus application times of the more general production. Because strength reflects frequency of practice, only exceptions that have some criterion frequency will be able to reliably take precedence over general rules. This corresponds, for instance, to the fact that words with irregular inflections tend to be of relatively high frequency. It is possible for an exception to be of borderline strength so that it sometimes is selected in time to beat out the general rule but sometimes not. This corresponds, for instance, to the stage in language development when an irregular inflection is being used with only partial reliability (R. Brown, 1973).

Variables. Productions contain variable slots that can take on different values in different situations. The use of these variables is often implicit, as in Table 1, but sometimes it is important to acknowledge the variables that are being assumed. As an illustration let us consider a variabilized form of a production from Table 1. If Production P9 from that table were to be written in a way to expose its variable structure, it would have the form below, where the terms prefixed by LV are local variables:

IF the goal is to iterate through the rows of LVcolumn
    and LVrow is the last row of LVcolumn

and LVrow has been processed
and the running total is of the form "LVstring + LVdigit."
THEN write LVdigit
    and set carry to LVstring
    and mark LVcolumn as processed
    and POP the goal.

Local variables can be reassigned to new values each time the production applies. Thus, for instance, the terms *LVcolumn, LVrow, LVstring,* and *LVdigit* will match to whatever elements lead to a complete match of the condition to working memory. Suppose, for instance, that the following elements were in working memory:

The goal is to iterate through the rows of Column 2.
Row x is the last row of Column 2.
Running total is of the form 2 + 4.

The production would match this working memory information with the following variable bindings:

LVcolumn = Column 2.
LVrow = Row x.
LVstring = 2.
LVdigit = 4.

Local variables assume values within a production for the purposes of matching the condition and executing the action. After application of the production, variables lose their values.

Learning in ACT

This article is concerned with the processes underlying the acquisition of cognitive skill. As is clear from examples like Table 1, there is a closer connection in ACT between productions and skill performance than between declarative knowledge and skill performance. This is because the control over cognition and behavior lies directly in the productions. Facts are used by the productions. So in a real sense facts are instruments of the productions, which are the agents. For instance, we saw that Production P10 used the addition fact that $4 + 8 = 12$. Although productions are closer to performance than facts, I will be claiming that when a person initially learns about a skill, he or she learns only facts about the skill and does not directly acquire productions. These facts are used interpretively by general-purpose productions. The first major

section of this article, on the declarative stage, will illustrate how general-purpose productions can interpret these facts to generate performance of the skill.

The next major section of the article will discuss the evidence for and nature of the knowledge compilation process that results in the translation from a declarative base for a skill to a procedural base for the skill. (For instance, the production set in Table 1 is a procedural base for the addition skill.) After this section the remainder of the article will discuss two aspects of the continued improvement of a skill after it has achieved a procedural embodiment: one is the tuning of the skill so that it is applied more appropriately; the second is the very lawful way in which application of the skill speeds up.

The Declarative Stage: Interpretive Procedures

One of the things that becomes apparent in studying the initial stages of skill acquisition in areas of mathematics like geometry or algebra (e.g., Neves, 1981) is that the instruction seldom if ever directly specifies

---

1-7 Proofs in Two-Column Form

You prove a statement in geometry by using deductive reasoning to show that the statement follows from the accepted types 'Given Steps,' and other accepted material. Often the assertions made in a proof are listed in one column, and reasons which support the assertions are listed in an adjacent column.

EXAMPLE A proof in two column form

Given   AED AD = AB
Prove   AK + KD = AB
Proof

STATEMENTS		REASONS
1 AED		1 Given
2 AK + KD = AD		2 Definition of between
3 AD = AB		3 Given
4 AK + KD = AB		4 Transitive property of equality

Some people prefer to support Statement 4 above with the reason "The Substitution Principle." Both reasons are correct. The reasons used in the example are of three types 'Given,' 'Steps,' and 'Definition.' Step, and 'Postulate.' Step ... just one other ... end of reason. Theorem, can be used in a mathematical proof. Postulates and theorems from both algebra and geometry can be used.

Reasons Used in Proofs

Given (Facts provided for a particular problem)
Definitions
Postulates
Theorems that have already been proved

Figure 2. The text instruction for a two-column proof. (From *Geometry* by R. C. Jurgensen, A. J. Donnelly, J. E. Maier, and G. R. Rising. Boston: Houghton Mifflin 1975, p. 25. Copyright 1975 by Houghton Mifflin Co. Reprinted by permission.)

Table 2
Interpretive Productions Evoked in Performing the Reason-Giving Task

P1. IF   the goal is to do a list of problems,
THEN set as a subgoal to do the first problem in the list.

P2. IF   the goal is to do a list of problems and a problem has just been finished,
THEN set as a subgoal to do the next problem.

P3. IF   the goal is to do a list of problems and there are no unfinished problems on the list,
THEN POP the goal with success.

P4. IF   the goal is to write the name of a relation for an argument,
THEN set as a subgoal to find what the relation is for the argument.

P5. IF   the goal is to write the name of a relation for an argument and a name has been found,
THEN write the name and POP the goal with success.

P6. IF   the goal is to write the name of a relation for an argument and no name has been found,
THEN POP the goal with failure.

P7. IF   the goal is to find a relation and there is a list of methods for achieving the relation,
THEN set as a subgoal to try the first method.

P8. IF   the goal is to find a relation and there is a list of methods for achieving the relation and a method has just been unsuccessfully tried,
THEN set as a subgoal to try the next method.

P9. IF   the goal is to find a relation and there is a list of methods for achieving the relation and a method has been successfully tried,
THEN POP the goal with success.

P10. IF   the goal is to find a relation and there is a list of methods for achieving the relation and they have all proven unsuccessful,
THEN POP the goal with failure.

P11. IF   the goal is to try a method and that method involves establishing a relationship.
THEN set as a subgoal to establish the relationship.

P12. IF   the goal is to try a method and the subgoal was a success,
THEN POP the goal with success.

P13. IF   the goal is to try a method and the subgoal was a failure,
THEN POP the goal with failure.

P14. IF   the goal is to establish that a statement is among a list and the list contains the statement,
THEN POP the goal with success.

P15. IF   the goal is to establish that a statement is among a list and the list does not contain the statement,
THEN POP the goal with failure.

P16. IF   the goal is to establish that a line is implied by a rule in a set and the set contains a rule of the form "consequent if antecedents" and the consequent matches the line,
THEN set as a subgoal to determine if the antecedents correspond to established statements and tag the rule as tried.

P17. IF   the goal is to establish that a line is implied by a rule in a set and the set contains a rule of the form "consequent if antecedents" and the consequent matches the line and the antecedents have been established,
THEN POP the goal with success.

P18. IF   the goal is to establish that a line is implied by a rule in a set and there is no untried rule in the set that matches the line,
THEN POP the goal with failure.

P19. IF   the goal is to determine if antecedents correspond to established statements and there is an unestablished antecedent clause and the clause matches an established statement,
THEN tag the clause as established.

P20. IF   the goal is to determine if antecedents correspond to established statements and there are no unestablished antecedent clauses,
THEN POP the goal with success.

P21. IF   the goal is to determine if antecedents correspond to established statements and there is an unestablished antecedent clause and it matches no established statement,
THEN POP the goal with failure.

---

a procedure to be applied. Still, the student is able to emerge from this type of instruction with an ability to generate behavior that reflects knowledge contained in the instruction. Figures 2, 3, and 4 from my work on geometry illustrate this point. Figure 2 is taken from the text of Jurgensen, Donnelly, Maier, & Rising (1975) and represents the total of that text's instruction on two-column proofs. Immediately after studying this, three of our students attempted to give reasons for two-column proof problems. The first such proof problem is the one illustrated in Figure 3. All three of the students were able to deal with this problem with some success. Behavior on these reason-giving problems is rather constant across subjects, at least at a global level. Figure 4 is a representation at the global level of these constancies. Clearly, nowhere in Figure 2 is there a specification of the flow of control that is in Figure 4. However, before reading the instruction of Figure 2, subjects were not capable of the flow of control in Figure 4, and after reading the instruction they were. So somehow the instruction in Figure 2 makes the procedure in Figure 4 possible.

Given that the instructions do not specify flow of control, the learners must call on existing procedures to direct their behavior in this task. These procedures must use the information specified in the instructions to guide their behavior. The instructional information is being used by these procedures in the same way Production P10 in Table 1

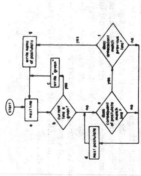

Figure 4. A flowchart showing the general flow of control in a reason-giving task.

Written Copy everything shown. Complete the proof by writing reasons.
Exercises

Figure 3. A reason-giving task is that that is the first problem that the student encounters requiring use of the knowledge about two-column proofs. (This figure is taken from the instructors' copy of the text and shows the correct reasons. These reasons are not given in the students' text. From Geometry by R. C. Jurgensen, A. J. Donnelly, J. E. Maier, and G. R. Rising. Boston: Houghton Mifflin, 1975, p. 26. Copyright 1975 by Houghton Mifflin Co. Reprinted by permission.)

used the addition facts to guide its behavior. For this reason, I say that the knowledge about the skill is being used *interpretatively*. The term reflects the fact that the knowledge is data for other procedures in just the way a computer program is data for an interpreter.

The basic claim is that general interpretative procedures with no domain-specific knowledge can be applied to some facts about the domain and produce coherent and domain-appropriate behavior. On first consideration it was not obvious to many people, including myself, how it was possible to model novice behavior in a task like Figure 3 by a purely interpretive system. However, it is absolutely critical to the theory presented here that there be an interpretive system in ACT that accurately describes the behavior of a novice in a new domain. It is essential because the theory claims that knowledge in a new domain always starts out in declarative form and is used interpretively. Therefore, I took it as a critical test case to develop a detailed example of how a student, extracting only declarative information from Figure 2, could generate task-appropriate behavior in Figure 3. The example, described below, assumes some general-purpose working-backwards problem-solving techniques. It captures important aspects of the behavior of my three high school students on this problem.

I want to emphasize that I am not claiming that such general problem-solving procedures are the only way that learners can bridge the gap between instruction and behavior. There are probably many different types of interpretive procedures. From my work on geometry, it is clear, for instance, that procedures for making analogies between worked-out examples and new tasks serve as an additional, important means for bridging the gap.

Application of General Problem-Solving Methods

Even though students coming upon the instruction in Figure 2 have no procedures specific to doing two-column proof problems, they have procedures for solving problems in general, for doing mathematics like exercises, and perhaps even for certain types of deductive reasoning. These general problem-solving procedures can use the instruction such as that in Figure 2 as data for generating task-appropriate behavior when faced with a problem like that in Figure 3. They serve as the procedures for interpreting the task-specific example. Table 2 provides a list of the set of productions that embody the needed problem-solving procedures, and Figure 5 illustrates their flow of control when applied to problems like the one in Figure 2.

I will trace the application of this production set to the first two lines in Figure 5. It is assumed that the student encodes (declaratively) the exercise in Figure 3 as a list of subproblems, where each subproblem is to write a reason for a line of the proof. Production P1 from Table 2 matches to this list encoding of the problems. Therefore, P1 applies first and focuses attention on the first subproblem, that is, it sets as the subgoal to write a reason for $RO \cong NY$. Next, Production P4 applies. P4's condition, "the goal is to write the name of a relation for an argument," matches the current subgoal "to write the name of the reason for $\overline{RO} \cong \overline{NY}$." P4 creates the subgoal of finding a reason for the line. P4 is quite general and reflects the existence of a prior procedure for writing statements that satisfy a constraint.

The student presumably has encoded the boxed information in Figure 2 as indicating a list of methods for providing a reason for a line. If so, Production P7 applies next and

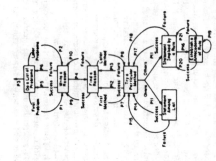

sets as a subgoal to try givens (the first rule on the reason list) as a justification for the current line. Note this is one point where a fragment of the instruction is used by a general problem-solving procedure (in this case for searching a list of methods) to determine the course of behavior. Two of the students in fact went back and reviewed the methods when they started this problem.

The students I studied had extracted from the instruction in Figure 2 that the "given" reason is used when the line to be justified is among the givens of the problem. Note that this fact is not explicitly stated in the instruction but is strongly implied. Thus, it is assumed that the student has encoded the fact that "the givens method involves establishing that the statement is among the givens." Production P11 will match this fact in its condition and so will set as a subgoal to establish that $RO \cong NY$ is among the givens of the problem. Production P14 models the successful recognition that $RO \cong NY$ is among the givens and returns a success from the subgoal. That is, its action "POP the goal with success" tags the goal "to find $\overline{RO} \cong \overline{NY}$ among the givens" with success and sets as the current goal the higher goal of trying

Figure 5. A representation of the flow of control in Table 2 between the various goals. (Control starts with the top goal.)

the givens method. Then P12 and P9 POP success back up to the next-to-top-level goal of writing a reason for the line. Then Production P5 applies to write *given* as a reason and POPs back to the top-level goal. In fact, all of the students likewise scanned the given list and had no difficulty with the first line of this proof.

At this point Production P2 applies to set the subgoal of writing a reason for the second line, RO = NY. Then Productions P4, P7, and P11 apply in that order, setting the subgoal of seeing whether RO = NY was among the givens of the problem. Production P15 recognizes this as a failed given and then Production P13 returns control back to the level of choosing methods to establish a reason. Production P8 selects the definition reason to try next. Thus, the production set first unsuccessfully tries the given method before trying other methods. One of the students explicitly verbalized trying givens and failed. There was no indication in the protocol of our other students that givens was considered first, although it may have been implicitly.

Clearly, the instruction in Figure 2 contains no explanation of how a definition should be applied. However, the assumption of the text is that the student knows that a definition should imply the statement. There were some earlier exercises on conditional and biconditional statements that makes this assumption at least conceivable. All three subjects knew that some inferencelike activity was required, but they had a faulty understanding of the nature of the application of inference to this task. In any case, assuming that the student knows as a fact (in contrast to a procedure) that use of definitions involves inferential reasoning, Production P11 will match in its condition the fact that "definitions involve establishing the fact that statement is implied by a definition," and P11 will set the subgoal of proving that RO = NY was implied by a definition.

At this point I have to leave these students behind momentarily and describe the ideal student. The textbook assumes that the student already has a functioning procedure for finding a rule that implies a statement by means of a set of established rules. Productions P16–P21 constitute such a procedure.

None of my students had this procedure in its entirety. These productions work as a general inference-testing procedure and apply equally well to postulates and theorems as well as definitions. Production P16 selects a conditional rule that matches the current line (the exact details of the match are not unpacked in Table 2). It is assumed that a biconditional definition is encoded as two implications each of the form "consequent if antecedent." The definition relevant to the current Line 2 is that two line segments are congruent if and only if they are of equal measure, which is encoded as

$$XZ = UV \text{ if } \overline{XZ} \cong \overline{UV}$$
$$\text{and } \overline{XZ} \cong \overline{UV} \text{ if } XZ = UV.$$

The first implication is the one that is selected, and the subgoal is set to establish the antecedent $\overline{XZ} \cong \overline{UV}$ (or $RO \cong NY$, in the current instantiation). The production set P19–P21 describes a procedure for matching zero or more clauses in the antecedent of a rule. In this case P19 finds a match to the one condition, $XZ \cong UV$, with $RO \cong NY$ in the first line. Then P20 POPs with success followed by successful POPping of P17, then P12, and then P9, which returns the system to the goal of writing out a reason for the line.

Significant features of the example. I will not further trace the application of the production set to the example. I would like to identify, however, the essential aspects of how this production set allows the student to bridge the gap between instruction and the problem demands. Figure 5 illustrates the flow of control with each box being a level in the goal structure and serving as a subroutine. Although it is not transparent, the subgoal organization in Figure 5 results in the same flow of control as the flowchart organization of Figure 4. However, as the production rendition of Figure 5 establishes, the flow of control in Figure 5 is not something fixed ahead of time but rather emerges in response to the instruction and the problem statement.

The top level goal in Figure 5 of iterating through a list of problems is provided by the problem statement and, given the problem statement, it is unpacked into a set of subgoals to write statements indicating the reasons for each line. This top level procedure reflects a general strategy the student has for decomposing problems into linearly ordered subproblems. Then another prior problem-solving procedure is invoked. At this point the instruction about the list of acceptable relationships is called into play (through yet another problem-solving procedure) and is used to set a series of subgoals to try out the various possible reasons for a statement. So the unpacking of subgoals in Figure 5 from "do a list of problems" to "find a reason" is in response to the problem statement; the further unpacking into the methods of givens, postulates, definitions, and theorems is in response to the instruction. The instruction is the source of information identifying that the method of givens involves searching the given list, and the other methods involve application of inferential reasoning. The ability to search a list for a match is assumed by the text, reasonably enough, as a prior procedure on the part of the student. The ability to apply inferential reasoning is also assumed as a prior procedure, but in this case the assumption is mistaken.

In summary, then, we see in Figure 5 a set of separate problem-solving procedures that are joined together in a novel combination by the declarative information in the problem statement and instruction. In this sense the student's general problem-solving procedures are interpreting the problem statement and instruction. Note that the problem statement and the instruction are brought into play by being matched as data in the conditions of the productions of Table 2.

Student understanding of implication. All three students that were studied had serious misunderstandings about how one determines whether a statement is implied by a rule, and some time was spent correcting each student's misconceptions. However, their misunderstandings did not become clear on Line 2. Their faulty understanding was sufficient for that line but the problems showed up on later lines. Thus, rather than a correct subroutine for inference application like the one embodied by Productions P16–P21, these students had subroutines that only sometimes produced the correct answer.

Two of the students thought that it was insufficient to determine that the consequent of the rule matched the to-be-justified statement and did not bother to test the antecedent. For them the subroutine call (subgoal setting) of Production P16 did not exist. One student argued, for instance, that Line 4 could be justified by the substitution principle of equality because that principle gave an equality as its consequent.

The third student had more exotic misunderstandings. This is also best illustrated in his efforts to justify Line 4 (RO + ON = ON + NY) in Figure 3. The student thought the transitive property of equality was the right justification for Line 4. The transitive property of equality is stated as "a = b, b = c, implies a = c." The student physically drew out the following correspondence between the antecedents of this postulate and the to-be-justified statement:

```
a = b,    b = c
|   |     |   |
RO + ON = ON + NY
```

That is, he found that he could put the variables of the antecedent in order with the terms of the statement. He noted that he also needed to match to a = c in the consequent of the transitive postulate but noted that a previous line had RO = NY, which given the earlier variable matches satisfied his need.

This student had at least two misunderstandings. First, he seemed unable to appreciate the tight constraints on pattern matching (e.g., one cannot match "=" against "+"). Second, he failed to appreciate that the consequent of the postulate should be matched to the statement, and the antecedent to earlier statements. Either he had it the other way around or, more likely, he did not think it mattered which way it was used. However, given the instruction he had to date, this is not surprising because none of this was specified.

All students required remedial instruction. Thus, these errors created the opportunity for new learning. Although I have not analyzed this in detail, I believe that remedial instruction amounted to providing additional declarative information. This information could be used by other general procedures to provide interpretive behavior in place of the compiled procedures that Table 2 is assuming in Productions P16–P21. This is a simple form of debugging: When the instruction assumes precompiled procedures that do not exist, remedial instruction can correct the situation by providing the data for interpretive procedures.

The Need for an Initial Declarative Encoding

This section has been concerned with showing how students can generate behavior in a new domain when they do not have specific procedures for acting in that domain. Their knowledge of the domain is declarative and is interpreted by general procedures. One can argue that it is adaptive for a learning system to start out this way. New productions have to be integrated with the general flow of control in the system. Clearly, we are not in possession of an adequate understanding of our flow of control to form such productions directly. One of the reasons why instruction is often so inadequate is that the teacher likewise has a poor conception of the flow of control in the student. Attempts to directly encode new procedures, as in the Instructible Production System (Rychener & Newell, 1978; Rychener, Note 1), have run into trouble because of this problem of integrating new elements into a complex existing flow of control.

As an example of the problem with creating new procedures out of whole cloth, consider the use of the definition of congruence by the production set in Table 2 to provide a reason for the second line in Figure 3. One could build a production that would directly recognize the application of the definition of this situation rather than go through the interpretive rigmarole of Figure 5 (Table 2). This production would have the form

IF the goal is to give a reason for $\overline{XY} = \overline{UV}$
    and a previous line has $\overline{XY} \cong \overline{UV}$,
THEN POP with success,
    and the reason is definition of segment congruence.

However, it is very implausible that the subject could know that this knowledge was needed in this procedural form before he or she stumbled on its use to solve Line 2 in Figure 3. Thus, ACT should not be expected to encode its knowledge into procedures until it has seen examples of how the knowledge is to be used.

Although new productions have to be created sometimes, forming new productions is potentially dangerous. Because productions have direct control over behavior, there is the ever-present danger that a new production may wreak great havoc in a system. Anyone who incrementally augments computer programs will be aware of this problem. A single erroneous statement can destroy the behavior of a previously fine program. In computer programming the cost is slight—one simply has to edit out the bugs the new procedure brought in. For an evolving creature the cost of such a failure might well be death. In the next section I will describe a highly conservative and adaptive way of entering new procedures.

As the examples reviewed in this section illustrate, declarative knowledge can have impact on behavior, but that impact is filtered through an interpretive system that is well oiled in achieving the goals of the system. This does not guarantee that new learning will not result in disaster, but it does significantly lower the probability. If a new piece of knowledge proves to be faulty, it can be tagged as such and so disregarded. It is much more difficult to correct a faulty procedure.

As a gross example suppose I told a gullible child, "If you want something, then you can assume it has happened." Translated into a production it would take on the following form:

IF the goal is to achieve X,
THEN POP with X achieved.

This would lead to a perhaps blissful but deluded child who never bothered to try to achieve anything because he or she believed it was already achieved. As a useful cognitive system he or she would come to an immediate halt. However, even if the child were gullible enough to encode this in declarative form at face value and perhaps even act upon it, he or she would quickly identify it as a lie (by contradiction procedures he or she has), tag it as such, and so prevent it from having further impact on behavior and continue on a normal life of goal achievement. New information should enter in declarative form because one can encode information declaratively without committing control to it and because one can be circumspect about the behavioral implications of declarative knowledge.

In earlier publications (e.g., Anderson et al., 1979, 1980) we proposed a designation process that allowed productions to be directly created. Basically, we could build an arbitrary knowledge structure in working memory and, by the action of a single designating production, convert that knowledge structure into a production. This was rightfully criticized (e.g., Norman, 1980) as too powerful computationally to be human. It meant, for instance, that one could directly commit to memory production rules for applying a novel procedure. For instance, a subject given a target set in the Sternberg (1969) task could designate specific productions to recognize each member of the set and so avoid any effect of set size. We were always aware of such problems with designation. For instance, in my discussion of induction in the 1976 ACT book (Anderson, 1976, Section 12.3), I was stubbornly avoiding such a process. However, a few years ago there seemed no way to construct a learning theory without such a mechanism. Now, thanks to the development of ideas about knowledge compilation, the designation mechanism is no longer necessary.

Knowledge Compilation

Interpreting knowledge in declarative form has the advantage of flexibility, but it also has serious costs in terms of time and working memory space. The process is slow because interpretation requires retrievals of declarative information from long-term memory and because the individual production steps of an interpreter are small in order to achieve generality. (For instance, the steps of problem refinement in Table 2 and Figure 5 were painfully small.) The interpretive productions require that the declarative information be represented in working memory and this can place a heavy burden on working memory capacity. Many of the subjects' errors and much of their slowness seem attributable to working memory errors. Students can be seen to repeat themselves over and over again as they lose critical intermediate results and have to recompute them. This section of the paper is devoted to describing the compilation processes by which the system goes from this interpretive application of declarative knowledge to procedures (productions) that directly apply that knowledge. By building up procedures to perform specific tasks like reason giving in geometry, a great deal of efficiency is achieved both in terms of time and working memory demands.

The Phenomenon of Compilation

One of the processes in geometry that I have focused on is how students match postulates against problem statements. Consider the side-angle-side (SAS) postulate whose presentation in the text is given in Figure 6. I followed a student through the exercises in the text that followed the section that contained this postulate and the side-side-side (SSS) postulate. The first problem that required use of SAS is illustrated in Figure 7. The following is the portion of his protocol where he actually called up this postulate and managed to put it in correspondence to the problem:

If you looked at the side-angle-side postulate [long pause] RK and RJ could almost be [long pause] what the missing [long pause] the missing side. I think

POSTULATE 14 — SAS POSTULATE: If two sides and the included angle of one triangle are congruent to the corresponding parts of another triangle the triangles are congruent

According to Postulate 14
If $\overline{AB} \cong \overline{DE}$, $\overline{AC} \cong \overline{DF}$, and $\angle A \cong \angle D$ then $\triangle ABC \cong \triangle DEF$

Figure 6. Statement in the text of the side-angle-side (SAS) postulate. (From *Geometry* by R. C. Jurgensen, A. J. Donnelly, J. E. Maier, and G. R. Rising. Boston: Houghton Mifflin, 1975, p. 122. Copyright 1975 by Houghton Mifflin Co. Reprinted by permission.)

Given: $\angle 1$ and $\angle 2$ are right angles
JS = KS
Prove: $\triangle RSJ \cong \triangle RSK$

Figure 7. The first proof-generation problem that a student encounters that requires application of the side-angle-side postulate.

somehow the side-angle-side postulate works its way into here [long pause]. Let's see what it says: "two sides and the included angle." What would I have to have to use two sides. JS and KS are one of them. Then you could go back to RS = RS. So that would bring up the side-angle-side postulate [long pause]. But where would $\angle 1$ and $\angle 2$ are right angles fit in [long pause] wait I see how they work [long pause] JS is congruent to KS [long pause] and with Angle 1 and Angle 2 are right angles that's a little problem [long pause]. OK, what does it say—check it one more time: "If two sides and the included angle of one triangle are congruent to the corresponding parts." So I have got to find the two sides and the included angle. With the included angle you get Angle 1 and Angle 2. I suppose [long pause] they are both right angles, which means they are congruent to each other. My first side is JS to KS. And the next one is RS to RS. So these are the two sides. Yes, I think it is the side-angle-side postulate.

After reaching this point there was still a long process by which the student actually went through writing out the proof, but this is the relevant portion in terms of assessing what goes into recognizing the relevance of SAS.

After a series of four more problems (two were solved by SAS and two by SSS), I came to the student's application of the SAS postulate for the problem illustrated in Figure 8. The method recognition portion of the protocol follows:

Right off the top of my head I am going to take a guess at what I am supposed to do: $\angle DCK \cong \angle ABK$. There is only one or two and the side-angle-side postulate is what they are getting to.

A number of things seem striking about the contrast between these two protocols. One is that there has been a clear speedup in the application of the postulate. A second is that there is no verbal rehearsal of the statement of the postulate in the second case. I take this as evidence that the student is no longer calling a declarative representation of the problem into working memory. Note also in the first protocol that there are a number of failures of working memory—points where the student recomputed forgotten information. The third feature of difference is that in the first protocol there is a clear piecemeal application of the postulate by which the student is separately identifying every element of the postulate. This is absent in the second protocol. It gives the appearance of the postulate being matched in a single step. These three features—speedup, dropout of verbal rehearsal, and elimination of piecemeal application—are among the features that I want to associate with the processes of knowledge compilation.

The Mechanisms of Compilation

The knowledge compilation processes in ACT can be divided into two subprocesses. One, which is called *composition*, takes sequences of productions that follow each other in solving a particular problem and

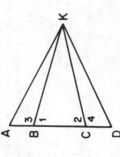
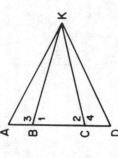

Given: $\angle 1 \cong \angle 2$
$\overline{AB} \cong \overline{DC}$
$\overline{BK} \cong \overline{CK}$

Prove: $\triangle ABK \cong \triangle DCK$

Figure 8. The fourth proof-generation problem that a student encounters that requires application of the side-angle-side postulate.

collapses them into a single production that has the effect of the sequence. The idea of composition was first developed by Lewis (1978). This produces considerable speedup by creating new operators that embody the sequences of steps that are used in a particular problem domain. The second process, *proceduralization*, builds versions of the productions that no longer require the domain-specific declarative information to be retrieved into working memory. Rather, the essential products of these retrieval operations are built into the new productions.

The technical details about how knowledge compilation is implemented are given in Neves and Anderson (1981). Here I will simply present the basic ideas and then focus on assessing some of the relevant literature. I will explain the basic processes with respect to an interesting example of telephone numbers. It has been noted (Anderson, 1976) that people develop special procedures for dialing frequently used telephone numbers. Sometimes declarative access to the number is lost and the only access one has to the number is through the procedure for dialing it.

Consider the following two productions that might serve to dial a telephone number:

P1. IF the goal is to dial LVtelephone-number
        and LVdigit1 is the first digit of LVtele-
        phone-number,
     THEN dial LVdigit1.

P2. IF the goal is to dial LVtelephone-number
        and LVdigit1 has just been dialed
        and LVdigit2 is after LVdigit1 in LV-
        telephone-number,
     THEN dial LVdigit2.

Composition creates "macroproductions," which do the operation of a pair of productions that occurred in sequence. Applied to the sequence of Production P1 above followed by P2, composition would create

P1&P2. IF the goal is to dial LVtelephone-number
            and LVdigit1 is the first digit of LV-
            telephone-number
            and LVdigit2 is after LVdigit1,
        THEN dial LVdigit1 and then LVdigit2.

Compositions like this reduce the number of production applications to perform the task.

A composed production like P1&P2 still requires that the information (in this case, the phone number) be held in working mem-ory. This information must be retrieved from long-term memory and matched to the second and third clauses in P1&P2. Proceduralization eliminates clauses in the condition of a production that require information to be retrieved from long-term memory and held in working memory. In the above production, P1&P2, the second and third condition clauses would be eliminated. The local variables that would have been bound in matching these clauses are replaced by the values they are bound to in the special case. So suppose this production is repeatedly applied in the dialing of Mary's telephone number, which is 432-2815. The local variables in P1&P2 would be bound as follows:

LVtelephone-number = Mary's number.
    LVdigit1 = 4.
    LVdigit2 = 3.

Producing the substitution of these values for the variables and eliminating the second and third condition clauses we get

P1&P2*. IF the goal is to dial Mary's telephone
             number,
         THEN dial 4 and then 3.

By continued composition and proceduralization, a production can be built that dials the full number.

P*. IF the goal is to dial Mary's number,
     THEN dial 432-2815.

It should be emphasized that forming this production does not imply the necessary loss of the declarative representation of the knowledge. The few instances reported of loss of declarative access to a telephone number probably reflect cases where the declarative knowledge ceases to be used and is simply forgotten.

An important consequence of proceduralization is that it reduces the load on working memory in that the long-term information need no longer be held in working memory. This makes it more likely that the system can simultaneously perform a second task that does make working memory demands. Of course, this is achieved by creating a procedure that is knowledge specific. The original Productions P1 and P2 could dial any telephone number. P* can only dial Mary's number.

It should be clear from this example how knowledge compilation produces the three phenomena noted in the protocols at the introduction of this section. The composition of multiple steps into one produces the speedup and leads to unitary rather than piecemeal application. The dropout of verbal rehearsal is a result of the fact that proceduralization eliminates the need to hold long-term memory information in working memory.

An important issue concerns the limits on the composition process. How many small productions can be combined to form a large one? The limit comes from the capacity of working memory. All the information in the production's condition must be active in working memory for the production to apply. If a composed production is created with a condition too large to be matched by working memory, that production will never apply and so will not be able to enter into further compositions. It should be noted that proceduralization serves to reduce the demands made by a production on working memory. Hence, proceduralized versions of productions may be able to enter into more compositions than nonproceduralized forms. However, even when proceduralized, the conditions of productions will grow with further compositions and hence there will be a limit on the amount of composition. I will discuss later the potential for practice to increase the capacity of working memory and so permit productions, which had been too large to match, to match and be composed.

Remarks About the Composition Mechanism

In the above discussion and in the computer implementation, the assumption has been that a pair of productions will be composed if they follow each other. This means that on repeated applications of the same problem, the number of productions should be halved each time. More generally, however, one might assume that the number of productions in each application is reduced to a proportion a of the previous application that involved composition. If $a > 1/2$, this might reflect the fact that compositions are formed with probability less than 1. If $a < 1/2$, this might reflect the fact that composition involved more than a pair of productions. Thus, after n compositions the expected number of productions would be Na^n, where N was the initial number. As will be argued later, the rate of composition (n) may not be linear in number of applications of the production set to problems.

There is the opportunity for spurious pairs of productions to accidently follow each other and so be composed together. If spurious pairs of productions were allowed to be composed together, there would not be disastrous consequences but it would be quite wasteful. Also, spurious productions might intervene between the application of productions that really belong together. So, for instance, suppose the following three productions had happened to apply in sequence:

P1. IF the subgoal is to add in a digit,
     THEN set as a subgoal to add the digit and the
          running total.

P2. IF I hear footsteps in the aisle,
     THEN the teacher is coming my way.

P3. IF the goal is to add two digits
        and a sum is the sum of the two digits,
     THEN the result is the sum
          and POP.

This sequence of productions might apply, for instance, as a child is performing arithmetic exercises in a class. The first and third are set to process subgoals in solving the problem. The first sets up the subgoal that is met by the third. The second production is not related to the other two and is merely an inference production that interprets sounds of the teacher approaching. It just happens to intervene between the other two. Composition as described would produce the following pairs:

P1&P2. IF the subgoal is to add in a digit
            and I hear footsteps in the aisle,
        THEN set as a subgoal to add the digit and
             the running total
             and the teacher is coming my way.

P2&P3. IF I hear footsteps in the aisle
            and the goal is to add two digits
            and a sum is the sum of the two digits,
        THEN the teacher is coming my way
             and the result is the sum
             and POP.

These productions are harmless but basically useless. They have also prevented formation of the following useful composition:

P1&P3. IF the subgoal is to add in a digit
and the sum is the sum of the digit
and the running total,
THEN the result is the sum.

Therefore, it seems reasonable to advance a sophistication over the composition mechanism proposed in Neves and Anderson (1981). In this new scheme productions are composed only if they are linked by goal setting (as in the case of P1&P3), and productions that are linked by goal setting will be composed even if there are intervening productions that make no goal reference (as in the case of P2). This is an example where the learning mechanisms can profitably exploit the goal structuring of production systems.

Phenomena Explained by Knowledge Compilation

In addition to the three qualitative features of skill development (speedup, unitary application, elimination of verbal rehearsal), knowledge compilation can help explain some of the more provocative results in the experimental literature. In this section, I would like to focus on three such results: disappearance of set size effects in the Sternberg (1969) paradigm, disappearance of set size and display size effects in the scan task, (Shiffrin & Schneider, 1977), and the Einstellung effect (Luchins, 1942) in problem solving.

Before we get into the specifics of ACT's explanation of these three phenomena, it should be acknowledged that there already exist other explanations of these phenomena in the literature. However, ACT's explanation relies on mechanisms that were not fashioned to address these phenomena. Rather, they were fashioned by Neves and Anderson (1981) to address various phenomena associated with the speedup of postulate application in geometry. Thus, the fact that the compilation mechanisms extend to these other phenomena is an important demonstration of the generality of the theory.

The Sternberg paradigm. In the Sternberg paradigm (e.g., Sternberg, 1969) subjects are asked to indicate if a probe comes from a small set of items. The classic result is that decision time increases with set size. It has been shown that effects of size of memory set can diminish with repeated practice (Briggs & Blaha, 1969). A sufficient condition for this to occur is that the same memory set be used repeatedly. The following are two productions that a subject might use for performing the scan task at the beginning of the experiment:

PA. IF the goal is to recognize LVprobe
and LVprobe is an LVtype
and the memory set contains an LVitem of LVtype,
THEN say "yes"
and POP the goal.

PB. IF the goal is to recognize LVprobe
and LVprobe is an LVtype
and the memory set does not contain an LVitem of LVtype,
THEN say "no"
and POP the goal.

In the above, LVprobe and LVitem will match tokens of letters and LVtype will match a particular letter type (e.g., the letter A). This production set is basically the same as the production system for the Sternberg task given in Anderson (1976) except that it is in a somewhat more readable form that will expose the essential character of the processing. These productions require that the contents of the memory set be held active in working memory. As discussed in Anderson (1976), the more items required to be held active in working memory, the lower the activation of each and the slower the recognition judgment, which produces the typical set-size effect.

Repeated practice of those productions on the same memory set will produce an eventual elimination of set-size effects. Consider, to be concrete, a situation where these productions are repeatedly applied on the same list—say a list consisting of A, J, and N with foils coming from a list of L, B, and K—then through proceduralization we would get the following productions from PA:

P1. IF the goal is to recognize LVprobe
and LVprobe is an A,
THEN say "yes"
and POP the goal.

P2. IF the goal is to recognize LVprobe
and LVprobe is a J,
THEN say "yes"
and POP the goal.

P3. IF the goal is to recognize LVprobe
and LVprobe is an N,
THEN say "yes"
and POP the goal.

The preceding are productions for recognizing the positive set. Specific productions would also be produced by proceduralization from PB to reject the foils:

P4. IF the goal is to recognize LVprobe
and LVprobe is an L,
THEN say "no"
and POP the goal.

P5. IF the goal is to recognize LVprobe
and LVprobe is a B,
THEN say "no"
and POP the goal.

P6. IF the goal is to recognize LVprobe
and LV probe is a K,
THEN say "no"
and POP the goal.

It is interesting to note here that Shiffrin and Dumais (1981) report that the automatization effect they observe in such tasks is as much due to subjects' ability to reject specific foils as it is their ability to accept specific targets. These productions no longer require the memory set to be held in working memory and will apply in a time independent of memory set size. However, there still may be some effect of set size in the subject's behavior. These productions do not replace PA and PB; rather, they coexist and it is possible for a classification to proceed by the original PA and PB. Thus, we have two parallel bases for classification racing, with the judgment being determined by the fastest one. This will produce a set-size effect that will diminish as P1-P6 become strengthened.

The scan task. Shiffrin and Schneider (1977) report an experiment in which they gave subjects a set of items to remember. Then subjects were shown a series of displays in rapid succession, each display containing a set of items. The subjects' task was to decide if any of the displays contained an item in the memory set. When Shiffrin and Schneider kept both the members of the study set and the distractors constant, they found considerable improvement with practice in subjects' performance on the task. They interpreted their results as indicating diminishing effects of both memory set size and the number of alternatives in the display.

Again ACT's knowledge compilation mechanisms can be shown to predict the result. Consider what a production set might be like that scanned an array to see if any member of the array matched a memory set item:

PC*. IF the goal is to see if LVarray contains a memory item
and LVprobe is in POSITION*,
THEN the subgoal is to recognize LVprobe.

PD. IF the goal is to recognize LVprobe
and LVprobe is an LVtype
and the memory set contains LVitem of LVtype,
THEN tag the goal as successful
and POP the goal.

PE. IF the goal is to recognize LVprobe
and LVprobe is an LVtype
and the memory set does not contain an LVitem of LVtype,
THEN tag the goal as failed
and POP the goal.

PF. IF the goal is to see if LVarray contains a memory item
and there is a successful subgoal.
THEN say "yes"
and POP the goal.

PG. IF the goal is to see if LVarray contains a memory item,
THEN say "no"
and POP the goal.

Production PC* is a schema for a set of productions such that each one would recognize an item in a particular position. An example might be

IF the goal is to see if LVarray contains a memory item
and LVprobe is in the upper right corner.
THEN set as a subgoal to recognize LVprobe.

PD and PE are similar to PA and PB given earlier—they check whether each position focused by PC* contains a match. PF will apply if one of the probes lead to a successful match, and the default production PG will apply if none of the positions leads to success. The behavior of this production set is one in which individual versions of PC* apply serially, focusing attention on individual positions. PD and PE are responsible for the judgment of individual probes. This continues until a positive probe is hit and PF applies or until there are no more probe positions and PG applies. (PG will only be selected when there are no more positions because specificity will prefer PC* and PF over it.) Because of the need to keep the memory set active, an effect of set size is expected. The serial examination of positions produces an effect of display size. These two factors should be multiplicative, which is what Schneider and Shiffrin (1977) report.

Consider what will happen with knowledge compilation. Composing a PC* production with PD and with PF and proceduralizing, we will get positive productions of the form

P7.   IF the goal is to see if LVarray contains a memory item
and the upper right-hand position contains an LVprobe
and the LVprobe is an A.
THEN say "yes"
and POP the goal.

The negative production would be formed by composing together a sequence of PC* productions paired with PE and a final application of PG. All the subgoal and POP-ping would be composed out. The strict composition of this sequence would be productions like

P8.   IF the goal is to see if LVarray contains a memory item
and the upper left-hand position contains an LVprobe1
and LVprobe1 is a K
and the upper right-hand position contains an LVprobe2
and LVprobe2 is a B
and the lower left-hand position contains an LVprobe3
and LVprobe3 is an L
and the lower right-hand position contains an LVprobe4
and LVprobe4 is a K,
THEN say "no"
and POP the goal.

where a separate such production would have to be formed for each possible foil combination. These productions would not be affected by set size or probe size. This is consistent with the Schneider and Shiffrin (1977) findings.

The Einstellung phenomenon. Another phenomenon that is predictable from knowledge compilation processes is the Einstellung effect (Luchins, 1942; Luchins & Luchins, 1959) in problem solving. One of the examples used by Luchins to demonstrate this phenomenon is illustrated in Figure 9 (a).

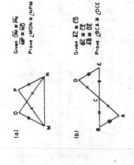

(a)   Given $\overline{OM} \cong \overline{PM}$, $\overline{MP} \cong \overline{NO}$
Prove $\angle MON \cong \angle NPM$

(b)   Given $\overline{RC} \cong \overline{EO}$
$\overline{RC} \cong \overline{CE}$
$\overline{AB} \cong \overline{DE}$
Prove $\angle BCA \cong \angle DCE$

Figure 9. After solving a series of problems like (a), students are more likely to choose the nonoptimal solution for (b).

Luchins presented his subjects with a sequence of geometry problems like the one in Figure 9 (a). For each problem in the sequence, the student had to prove that two triangles were congruent in order to prove that two angles were congruent. Then subjects were given a problem like the one in Figure 9 (b). Subjects proved this by means of congruent triangles even though it has a much simpler proof by means of vertical angles. Subjects not given the initial experience with problems like the one in Figure 9 (a) show a much greater tendency to use the vertical angle proof. Their experimental experience caused subjects to solve the problem in a nonoptimal way.

Lewis (1978) has examined the Einstellung effect and its relation to the composition process. He defines as perfect composites compositions that do not change the behavior of the system but just speed it up. Such compositions cannot produce Einstellung effects, of course. However, he notes that there are a number of natural ways to produce nonperfect composites that produce Einstellung effects. The ACT theory provides an example of such a nonperfect composition process. Composites are nonperfect in ACT because of its conflict-resolution principles.

Productions P1 through P4 provide a model of part of the initial state of the student's production system.

P1.   IF the goal is to prove $\angle XYZ \cong \angle UVW$
and the points are ordered X, Y, and W on a line
and the points are ordered Z, Y, and U on a line,

THEN this can be achieved by vertical angles
and POP the goal.

P2.   IF the goal is to prove $\angle XYZ \cong \angle UVW$,
THEN set as subgoals:
1. To find a triangle that contains $\angle XYZ$,
2. To find a triangle that contains $\angle UVW$,
3. To prove the two triangles congruent, and
4. To use corresponding parts of congruent triangles.

P3.   IF the goal is to find a figure that has a relation to the object to an object
and Figure X has the relation to the object,
THEN the result is Figure X
and POP the goal.

P4.   IF the goal is to prove $\Delta XYZ \cong \Delta UVW$
and $\overline{XY} \cong \overline{UV}$
and $\overline{YZ} \cong \overline{VW}$
and $\overline{ZX} \cong \overline{WU}$.
THEN this can be achieved by SSS
and POP the goal.

Production P1 is responsible for immediately recognizing the applicability of the vertical angle postulate. Productions P2-P4 are part of the production set that is responsible for proof through the route of corresponding parts of congruent triangles. Production P2 decomposes the main goal into the subgoals of finding the containing triangles, of proving they are congruent, and then of using the corresponding-parts principle. P3 finds the containing triangles, and P4 encodes one production that would recognize triangle congruence. This production set, applied to a problem like that in Figure 9 (b), would lead to a solution by vertical angles. This is because Production P1, for vertical angles, is more specific in its condition than is Production P2, which starts off the corresponding-angles proof. As explained earlier, ACT's conflict resolution prefers specific productions.

Consider, however, what would happen after Productions P2-P4 had been exercised on a number of problems and composition had taken place. Production P2&P3&P4 represents a composition of the sequence P2, then P3, and then P4. Its condition is not less specific than that of P1 and, in fact, contains more clauses. However, because these clauses are not a superset of P1's clauses, it is not the case that either production is technically more specific than the other. They are both in potential conflict and, because both change the goal state,

application of one will block the application of the other. In this case strength serves as the basis for resolving the conflict. Production P2&P3&P4, because of its recent practice, may be stronger and therefore might be selected.

P2&P3&P4.   IF the goal is to prove $\angle XYZ \cong \angle UVW$
and $\angle XYZ$ is part of ΔXYZ
and $\angle UVW$ is part of ΔUVW
and $\overline{XY} \cong \overline{UV}$
and $\overline{YZ} \cong \overline{VW}$
and $\overline{ZX} \cong \overline{WU}$.
THEN set $\Delta XYZ \cong \Delta UVW$
and set as a subgoal to use corresponding parts of congruent triangles.

This example illustrates how practice can change the specificity ordering of productions through composition and how it can directly change the strength. These two factors—change of specificity and change of strength—can cause ACT's conflict-resolution mechanism to change the behavior of the system, producing Einstellung effects. Under this analysis it can be seen that the Einstellung effect is an aberrant phenomenon reflecting what is basically an adaptive adjustment on the system's part. Through strength and composition ACT is utilizing and favoring sequences of problem-solving behaviors that have been recently successful. It is a good bet that such sequences will prove useful again. It is to the credit of the cleverness of Luchins's design (1942, Luchins & Luchins, 1959) that it exposed the potential cost of these usually beneficial adaptations.

It has been suggested that one could produce the Einstellung effect by simply strengthening particular productions. So one might suppose that Production P2 is strengthened over P1. The problem with this explanation is that subjects can be shown to have a preference for a particular sequence of productions not merely single productions in isolation. Thus, in the water jug problems, described by Luchins (1942), subjects will fixate on a specific sequence of operators implementing a subtraction method and will not notice other simpler subtraction methods. The composition mechanism explains how the subject encodes this operator sequence.

It is interesting to compare the time scale for producing Einstellung effects with the time scale for producing the automatization effects in the Sternberg paradigm and the scan paradigm. Strong Einstellung effects can be produced after a half-dozen trials, whereas the automatization results require hundreds of trials. This suggests that composition that underlies the Einstellung effect can proceed more rapidly than the proceduralization that underlies the automatization effects. Proceduralization is really more responsible for creating domain-specific procedures than is composition. Composition creates productions that encode the sequence of general productions for a task, but the composed productions are still general. In contrast, by replacing variables with domain constants, proceduralization creates productions that are committed to a particular task. Apparently, the learning system is reluctant to create this degree of specialization unless there is ample evidence that the task will be repeated frequently.

The Adaptive Value of Knowledge Compilation

In the previous section on initial encoding, it was argued that it is dangerous for a system to directly create productions to embody knowledge. For this reason and for a number of others, it was argued that knowledge should first be encoded declaratively and then interpreted. This declarative knowledge could affect behavior, but only indirectly, via the intercession of existing procedures for correctly interpreting that knowledge. We have in the process of composition and proceduralization a means of converting declarative facts into production form.

It is important to note that productions created from compilation really do not change the behavior of the system, except in terms of possible reorderings of specificity relations as noted in our discussion of the Einstellung effect. Thus, knowledge compiled in this way has much of the same safeguards built into it that interpretive application of the knowledge does. The safety in interpretive applications is that a particular piece of knowledge does not impact on behavior until it has undergone the scru-tiny of all the system's procedures (which can, for instance, detect contradiction of facts or of goals). Because compilation only operates on successful sequences of productions that pass this scrutiny, it tends to produce only production embodiments of knowledge that pass that scrutiny. This is the advantage of learning from doing. Another advantage with interpretive application is that the use of the knowledge is forced to be consistent with existing conventions for passing control among goals. By compiling from actual use of this knowledge, the compiled productions are guaranteed to be likewise consistent with the system's goal structure.

We can understand why human compilation is gradual (in contrast to computer compilation) and occurs as a result of practice if we consider the difference between the human situation and the typical computer situation. For one thing the human does not know what is going to be procedural in an instruction until he or she tries to use the knowledge in the instruction. In contrast, the computer has built in the difference between program and data. Another reason for gradual compilation is to provide some protection against the errors that enter into a compiled procedure because of the omission of conditional tests. For instance, if the system is interpreting a series of steps that include pulling a lever, it can first reflect on the lever-pulling step to see if it involves any unwanted consequences in the current situation. These tests will be in the form of productions checking for error conditions. (These error-checking productions can be made more specific so that they would take precedence over the normal course of action.) When that procedure is totally compiled, the lever pulling will be part of a prepackaged sequence of actions with many conditional tests eliminated (see the discussion of the Einstellung effect). If the procedure transits gradually between the interpretive and compiled stages, it is possible to detect the erroneous compiling out of a test at a stage where the behavior is still being partially monitored interpretively and can be corrected. It is interesting to note here the folk wisdom that most errors in acquisition of a skill, like airplane flying, occur neither with the novices nor with experts. Rather, they occur at intermediate stages of learning. This is presumably where the conversion from procedural to declarative is occurring and the point where unmonitored mistakes might slip into the performance. So by making compilation gradual, one does not eliminate the possibility of error, but one does reduce the probability.

Procedural Learning: Tuning

Much learning goes on after a skill has been compiled into a task-specific procedure, and this learning cannot just be attributed to further speedup due to more composition. One type of learning involves an improvement in the choice of method by which the task is performed. All tasks can be characterized as having a search associated with them, although in some cases the search is trivial. By search I mean that there are alternate paths of steps by which the problem can be tackled, and the subject must choose among them. Some of these paths lead to no solution and some lead to more complex solutions than necessary. A clear implication of much of the novice-expert research (e.g., Larkin, McDermott, Simon, & Simon, 1980) is that with high levels of expertise in a task domain, the problem solver becomes much more judicious in his choice of paths and may fundamentally alter his method of search. In terms of the traditional learning terminology, the issue is similar to, though by no means identical to, the issue of trial and error versus insight in problem solving. A novice's search of a problem space is largely a matter of trial-and-error exploration. With experience the search becomes more selective and more likely to lead to rapid success. I refer to the learning underlying this selectivity as *tuning*. My use of the term is quite close to that of Rumelhart and Norman (1978).

In 1977 we proposed a set of three learning mechanisms that still serves as the basis for much of our work on the tuning of search (Anderson, Kline, & Beasley, Note 2). There was a generalization process by which production rules become broader in their range of applicability, a discrimination process by which the rules become narrower, and a strengthening process by which better rules are strengthened and poorer rules weakened. These ideas have nonaccidental relations to concepts in the traditional learning literature, but as we will see they have been somewhat modified to be computationally more adequate. One can think of production rules as implementing a search, where individual rules correspond to individual operators for expanding the search space. Generalization and discrimination serve to produce a "metasearch" over the production rules, looking for the right features to constrain the application of these productions. Strength serves as an evaluation for the various constraints produced by the other two processes.

In this section I will illustrate how these three central learning constructs operate in the ACT system with examples from language acquisition. It is a major claim of the theory that these learning mechanisms will apply equally well to domains as diverse as language processing and geometry proof generation. Elsewhere we have discussed how these processes apply to schema abstraction or prototype formation (Anderson et al., 1979) and to proof generation (Anderson, Greeno, Kline, & Neves, 1981). That they apply in such diverse circumstances is important evidence for the generality of these learning mechanisms.

In Anderson (1981a) I focused on the issue of language acquisition per se and that article should be consulted for a fuller discussion of these issues. Language acquisition is being used here to illustrate the basic learning mechanisms. The examples here will concern how production rules are acquired to generate the correct syntactic structures. Unlike some of the other domains (e.g., proof generation), productions for language generation seldom result in one path for generation being tried and then a second path being tried after the first fails. Rather, in the language generation case, if the wrong generation path is followed, a faulty syntactic structure will be generated. Thus, errors of choice or search in language generation result in incorrect generations. In proof generation they would more likely result in longer times to reach a solution.

Generalization

The ability to perform successfully in novel situations is the hallmark of human cognition. For example, productivity has often been identified as the most important feature of natural languages, where this refers to the speaker's ability to generate and comprehend utterances never before encountered. Traditional learning theories have been criticized because of their inability to account for this productivity (e.g., McNeill, 1968), and it was one of our goals in designing ACT to avoid this sort of criticism.

An example. ACT's generalization algorithm looks for similarities between a pair of productions and creates a new production rule that captures what these individual productions have in common. Consider the following pair of rules for language generation that might arise as the consequence of compiling individual special productions do not apply. Thus, the claim for the ACT gen-

P1. IF the goal is to indicate that a coat belongs to me,
    THEN say "My coat."

P2. IF the goal is to indicate that a ball belongs to me,
    THEN say "My ball."

From these two production rules, ACT can form the following generalization:

P3. IF the goal is to indicate that LVobject belongs to me,
    THEN say "My LVobject."

in which the variable LVobject has replaced the particular object. The rule now formed is productive in the sense that it will fill in the LVobject slot with any object. Of course, it is just this productivity in child speech that has been commented on, at least since Braine (1963). It is important to note that the general production does not replace the original two and that the original two will continue to apply in their special circumstances.

The basic function of the ACT generalization process is to extract from different special productions what they have in common. These common aspects are embodied in a production that will apply in new situations where original special productions do not apply. Thus, the claim for the ACT gen-

eralization mechanism is that transfer is facilitated if the same components are taught in two procedures so generalization can occur. So, for instance, transfer to a new text editor will be more facilitated if one has studied two other text editors than if one has studied only one.

Another example. The example above does not illustrate the full complexity at issue in forming generalizations. The following is a fuller illustration of the complexity:

P4. IF the goal is to indicate the relation in (LVobject1 chase LVobject2)
    and LVobject1 is dog
    and LVobject1 is singular
    and LVobject2 is cat
    and LVobject2 is plural,
    THEN say "CHASES."

P5. IF the goal is to indicate the relation in (LVobject3 scratch LVobject4)
    and LVobject3 is cat
    and LVobject3 is singular
    and LVobject4 is dog
    and LVobject4 is plural,
    THEN say "SCRATCHES."

P6. IF the goal is to indicate the relation in (LVobject1 LVrelation LVobject2)
    and LVobject1 is singular
    and LVobject2 is plural,
    THEN say "LVrelation + s."

P6 is the generalization that would be formed from P4 and P5. It illustrates that clauses can be deleted in a generalization as well as variables introduced (in this case LVrelation). In this example, the generalization has been made that the verb inflection does not depend on the category of the subject or of the object and does not depend on the verb. This generalization remains overly specific in that the rule still tests whether the object is plural—this is something the two examples have in common. Further generalization would be required to delete this unnecessary test. On the other hand, the generalized rule does not test for present tense and so is overly general. This is because this information was not represented in the original productions. The discrimination process (to be described later) can bring in this missing information.

The technical work defining generalization in ACT is given in Anderson et al. (1980) and similar definitions are to be found in Hayes-Roth and McDermott (1976)

and Vere (1978). I will skip these technical definitions here for brevity's sake. The basic generalization process is clear without them.

Comparisons to earlier conceptions of generalization. The process of production generalization clearly has similarities to the process of stimulus generalization in earlier learning theories (for a review see Heinemann & Chase, 1975), but there are also clear differences. Past theories frequently proposed that a response conditioned to one stimulus would generalize to stimuli similar on various dimensions. So, for instance, a bar press conditioned to one tone would tend to be evoked by other tones of similar pitch and loudness. An important feature of this earlier conception is that generalization was an automatic outcome of a single learned connection and did not require any further learning. Learning in these theories was all a matter of discrimination—restricting the range of the learned response. In contrast, in the ACT theory generalization is an outcome of comparing two or more learned rules and extracting what they have in common. Thus, it requires additional learning over and above the learning of the initial rules, and it depends critically on the relation between the rules learned. There is evidence (Elio & Anderson, 1981) for ACT's stronger assumption that generalization depends on the interitem similarity among the learning experiences as well as the similarity of the test situation to the learning experiences.

Another clear difference between generalization as presented here and many earlier generalization theories is that the current generalization proposed is structural and involves clause deletion and variable creation rather than the creation of ranges on continuous dimensions. We have focused on structural generalizations because of the symbolic domains that have been our concern. However, these generalization mechanisms can be extended to apply to generalization over intervals on continuous dimensions (Brown, 1977; Larson & Michalski, 1977). ACT's generalization ideas are much closer to what happens in stimulus-sampling theory (Burke & Estes, 1957; Estes, 1950), where responses conditioned to one set of stimulus elements can generalize to overlapping sets. This is the same

as the notion in ACT of generalization on the basis of clause overlap. However, there is nothing in stimulus-sampling theory that corresponds to ACT's generalization by replacing constants in clauses with variables. This is because stimulus-sampling theory does not have the representational construct of propositions with arguments.

Discrimination

Just as it is necessary to generalize overly specific procedures, so it is necessary to restrict the range of application of overly general procedures. It is possible for productions to become overly general either because of the generalization process or because the critical information was not attended to in the first place. It is for this reason that the discrimination process plays a critical role in the ACT theory. This discrimination process tries to restrict the range of application of productions to just the appropriate circumstances. The discrimination process requires that ACT have examples both of correct and incorrect application of the production. The discrimination algorithm remembers and compares the values of the variables in the correct and incorrect applications. It randomly chooses a variable for discrimination from among those that have different values in the two applications. Having selected a variable, it looks for some attribute that the variable has in only one of the situations. A test is added to the condition of the production for the presence of this attribute.

An example. Suppose ACT starts out with the following production:

P1. IF the goal is to indicate the relation in (LVsubject LVrelation LVobject),
    THEN say "LVrelation + s."

This rule for generating the present tense singular of a verb is, of course, overly general in the above form. For instance, this rule would apply when the sentence subject was plural, generating "LVrelation + s." when what is wanted is "LVrelation." By comparing circumstances where the above rule applied correctly with the current incorrect situation, ACT could notice that the variable LVsubject was bound to different values and that the value in the correct situation had singular number but the value in the incorrect situation had plural number. ACT can formulate a rule for the current situation that recommends the correct action:

P2.   IF the goal is to indicate the relation in
          (LVsubject LVrelation LVobject)
          and LVsubject is plural.
       THEN say "LVrelation."

ACT can also form a modification of the previous rule for the past situation:

P3.   IF the goal is to indicate the relation in
          (LVsubject LVrelation LVobject)
          and LVsubject is singular,
       THEN say "LVrelation + s."

The first discrimination, P2, is called an *action discrimination* because it involves learning a new action, whereas the second discrimination, P3, is called a *condition discrimination* because it involves restricting the condition for the old action. Because of specificity ordering, the action discrimination will block misapplication of the overly general P1. The condition discrimination, P3, is an attempt to reformulate P1 to make it more restrictive. It is important to note that these discriminations do not replace the original production; rather, they coexist with it.

ACT does not always form both action and condition discriminations. ACT can only form an action discrimination when feedback is obtained about the correct action for the situation. If ACT only receives feedback that the old action is incorrect, it can only form a condition discrimination. However, ACT will only form a condition discrimination if the old rule (i.e., P1 in the above example) has achieved a level of strength to indicate that it has some history of success. The reason for this restriction on condition discriminations is that a rule can be formulated that is simply wrong and we do not want to have it perseverate by a process of endlessly proposing new discriminations.

Note that Productions P2 and P3 are improvements over P1 but are still not sufficiently refined. The discrimination algorithm can apply to these, however, comparing where they applied successfully and unsuccessfully. If discriminations of these tense and

if both response and condition discriminations were formed, we would have the following set of productions:

P4.   IF the goal is to indicate the relation in
          (LVsubject LVrelation LVobject)
          and LVsubject is plural
          and LVrelation has past tense,
       THEN say "LVrelation + ed."

P5.   IF the goal is to indicate the relation in
          (LVsubject LVrelation LVobject)
          and LVsubject is plural
          and LVrelation has present tense,
       THEN say "LVrelation."

P6.   IF the goal is to indicate the relation in
          (LVsubject LVrelation LVobject)
          and LVsubject is singular
          and LVrelation has past tense,
       THEN say "LVrelation + ed."

P7.   IF the goal is to indicate the relation in
          (LVsubject LVrelation LVobject)
          and LVsubject is singular
          and LVrelation has present tense,
       THEN say "LVrelation + s."

A more thorough consideration of how these mechanisms would apply to acquisition of the verb auxiliary system of English is given in Anderson (1981a). The current example is only an illustration of the basic discrimination mechanism.

Recall that the feature selected for discrimination is determined by comparing the variable bindings in the successful and unsuccessful production applications. A variation on which they differ is selected, and features are selected to restrict the bindings. It is possible for this discrimination mechanism to choose the wrong variables or wrong features on which to discriminate. So, for instance, it may turn out that LVobject has a different number in two circumstances, and the system may set out to produce a discrimination on that basis, rather than discriminating on the correct variable, LVsubject. In the case of condition discriminations, such mistakes have no negative impact on the behavior of the system. The discriminated production produces the same behavior as the original in the restricted situation, so it cannot lead to worse behavior. (Recall that the original production still exists to produce the same behavior in other situations.) If an incorrect discrimination is produced, it may block by specificity the correct application of the original production

in other situations. However, even here the system can recover by producing the correct discrimination and then giving the correct discrimination a specificity or strength advantage over the incorrect discrimination.

The current discrimination mechanism also attempts to speed up the process of finding useful discriminations by its method of selecting propositions from the data base. Though a random process is used to guarantee that any appropriate propositions in the data will eventually be found, this random choice is biased in certain ways to increase the likelihood of a correct discrimination. The discrimination mechanism chooses propositions with probabilities that vary with their activation levels. The greater the amount of activation that has spread to a proposition, the more likely it is that the proposition will be relevant to the current situation.

The previous example illustrated a critical prerequisite for discrimination to work. The system must receive feedback indicating that a particular production has misapplied, and in the case of an action discrimination, it must receive feedback as to what the correct action should have been.

In principle, a production application could be characterized as being in one of three states: known to be incorrect, known to be correct, or correctness unknown. However, the mechanisms we have implemented for ACT do not use the distinction between the second and third states. If a production applies and there is no comment on its success, it is treated as if it were a successful application. So the real issue is how ACT identifies that a production application is in error. A production is considered to be in error if it puts into working memory a fact that is later tagged as incorrect. There are two basic ways for this error tagging to occur: one is through external feedback and the other is through internal computation. In the external-feedback situation, learners may be directly told that their behavior is in error or they may infer this by comparing their behavior to an external referent (e.g., the behavior of a model or a textbook answer). In the internal-computation case, the learner must identify that a fact is contradictory, that a goal has failed, or that there is some other failure to meet internal norms. As dis-

cussed in Anderson (1981b), the goal structure of ACT productions is very helpful in correctly identifying successful and failed productions.

Strengthening

The generalization and discrimination mechanisms are the inductive components of the learning system in that they are trying to extract from examples of success and failure the features that characterize when a particular production rule is applicable. The generalization and discrimination processes produce multiple variants on the conditions controlling the same action. It is important to realize that at any time the system is entertaining as its hypothesis a set of different productions with different conditions to control the action—not just a single production (condition-action rule). There are advantages to be gained in expressive power by means of multiple productions for the same action, differing in their conditions. Because the features in a production condition are treated conjunctively but separate productions are treated disjunctively, one can express the condition for an action as a disjunction of conjunctions of conditions. Many real-world categories have the need for this rather powerful expressive logic. Also, because of specificity ordering, productions can enter into more complex logical relations, as we noted.

However, because they are inductive processes, sometimes generalization and discrimination will err and produce incorrect productions. There are possibilities for overgeneralizations and useless discriminations. The phenomenon of overgeneralization is well documented in the language acquisition literature, occurring both in the learning of syntactic rules and in the learning of natural language concepts. The phenomena of pseudodiscriminations are less well documented in language because a pseudodiscrimination does not lead to incorrect behavior, just unnecessarily restrictive behavior. However, there are some documented cases in the careful analyses of language development (e.g., Maratsos & Chalkley, 1981). One reason that a strength mechanism is needed is because of these inductive failures. It is also the case that the system may simply create productions that are incorrect—either because of misinformation or because of mistakes in its computations. ACT uses its strength mechanism to eliminate wrong productions, whatever their source.

The strength of a production affects the probability that it will be placed on the APPLYLIST and is also used in resolving ties among competing productions of equal specificity on the APPLYLIST. These factors were discussed earlier with respect to the full set of conflict-resolution principles in ACT (see section on conflict resolution). ACT has a number of ways of adjusting the strength of a production in order to improve performance. Productions have a strength of .1 when first created. Each time it applies, a production's strength increases by an additive factor of .025. However, when a production applies and receives negative feedback, its strength is reduced by a multiplicative factor of .25. Because a multiplicative adjustment produces a greater change in strength than does an additive adjustment, this "punishment" has much more impact than a reinforcement does.

Although these two mechanisms are sufficient to adjust the behavior of any fixed set of productions, additional strengthening mechanisms are required to integrate new productions into the behavior of the system. Because these new productions are introduced with low strength, they would seem to be victims of a vicious cycle: They cannot apply unless they are strong, and they are not strong unless they have applied. What is required to break out of this cycle is a means of strengthening productions that does not rely on their actual application. This is achieved by taking all of the strength adjustments made to a production that applies and making these adjustments to all of its generalizations as well. Because a general production will be strengthened every time any one of its possibly numerous specializations applies, new generalizations can amass enough strength to extend the range of situations in which ACT performs successfully. Also, because a general production applies more widely, a successful general production will come to gather more strength than its specific variants.

For purposes of strengthening, re-creation of a production that is already in the system, whether by proceduralization, composition, generalization, or discrimination, is treated as equivalent to a successful application. That is, the re-created production receives a .025 strength increment and so do all of its generalizations.

The exact strengthening values encoded into the ACT system are somewhat arbitrary. The general relations among the values are certainly important, but the exact relations probably are not. If all the strength values were multiplied by some scaling factor, one would get the same performance from the system. They were selected to give satisfactory performance in a set of language-learning examples described by Anderson et al. (1980).

Comparison to Other Discrimination Theories

As in the case of generalization, ACT's mechanisms for discrimination have clear similarities to earlier ideas about discrimination. ACT's discrimination mechanisms, like its generalization mechanisms, focus on structural relations, whereas traditional efforts were more focused on continuous dimensions. Brown (1977) has sketched out ways for extending ACT-like discrimination mechanisms to continuous dimensions, although we have not developed them in ACT. Also, it is the case that ACT discrimination mechanisms are really specified for an operant-conditioning paradigm (in that the action of productions are evaluated according to whether they achieve desired behavior and goals) and do not really address the classical-conditioning paradigm in which a good deal of research has been done on discrimination. However, despite these major differences in character, a number of interesting connections can be drawn between ACT and the older conceptions of discrimination. In making these comparisons I will be drawing on strengthening and other conflict-resolution principles in ACT as well as the discrimination mechanism.

Shift experiments. One of the supposedly critical issues in choosing between the discontinuity and continuity theories of discrimination was the shift experiment (Spence, 1940). In that paradigm, subjects who were still responding at a chance level with respect to some discrimination (e.g., white-black) had the reinforcement contingencies changed so that a different response was appropriate. According to the discontinuity theory, the subject's chance performance indicated control by an incorrect hypothesis, so the shift should not hurt, but according to the continuity theory, the subject could still be building up "habit strength" for the correct response and a shift would hurt. Continuity theory tended to be supported on this issue for infrahuman subjects (e.g., see Kendler & Kendler, 1975). ACT is like the discontinuity theory in that its various productions represent alternative hypotheses about how to solve a problem; however, its predictions are in accord with the continuity theory because it can be accruing strength for a hypothesis before the production is strong enough to apply and produce behavior. Of course, ACT's discrimination mechanisms cannot account for the shift data with adults (e.g., Trabasso & Bower, 1968), but we have argued elsewhere (Anderson et al., 1979) that such data should be ascribed to a conscious hypothesis-testing process that produces declarative learning rather than an automatic procedural learning process.

Stimulus generalization and eventual discrimination. As noted earlier, the clauses in a production condition are like the elements of stimulus-sampling theory. A problem for stimulus-sampling theory (see Medin, 1976, for a recent discussion) is how to accommodate both the fact of stimulus generalization and the fact of eventual perfect discrimination. The fact of stimulus generalization can easily be explained in stimulus-sampling theory by assuming that two stimulus conditions overlap in their elements. However, if so, the problem becomes how perfect discrimination behavior can be achieved when the common elements can be associated to the wrong response.

In the ACT theory one can think of the original productions for behavior as basically testing for the null set of elements:

P1.   IF the goal is X,
       THEN do Y.

With discrimination, elements can be brought in to discriminate between successful and unsuccessful situations, for example,

P2.   IF the goal is X
         and B is present,
       THEN do Y.

P3.   IF the goal is X
         and B is present
         and C is present,
       THEN do Z.

P4.   IF the goal is X
         and D is present,
       THEN do Y.

and so forth. This is like the conditioning of features to responses in stimulus-sampling theory.

If some features occur sometimes in situations for Response Y and sometimes in situations for Response Z, discrimination can cause them to become parts of productions recommending one of the actions. For instance, suppose B is such a feature that really does not discriminate between the actions. Suppose B is present in the current situation where response Z is executed, but the system receives feedback indicating that Y is correct. Further, suppose B was not present (or not attended) in the past prior situation where response Z had proved successful. Production P2 would be formed as an action discrimination. The B test is useless because B is just as likely to occur in a Z situation. This corresponds to the conditioning of common elements. However, in ACT the strengthening, discrimination, and specificity processes can eventually repress productions that are responding just to common elements. For instance, further discriminative features can be added (as in P3) that will serve to block out the incorrect application of P2. Also, it is possible to simply weaken P2 and add a new production like P4, which perhaps contains the correct discrimination.

Patterning effects. The ACT discrimination theory also explains how subjects can learn to give a response in the presence of Stimuli A and B together but neither A nor B alone. This simply requires that two discriminative clauses be added to the production, one for A and one for B. Responding to such configural cues was a problem for some of the earlier discrimination theories (see Rudy & Wagner, 1975, for a review). The power of the ACT theory over these early theories is that productions can respond to patterns of elements rather than to each element separately.

ACT also explains the fact that in the presence of correlated stimuli, one stimulus may partially or completely overshadow a second one (see MacKintosh, 1975, for a review). Thus, if both A and B are trained as a correlated pair to response R, one may find that A has less ability to evoke R alone than if it were the only cue associated with R. Sometimes if B is much more salient, A may have no control over R at all. In ACT the discrimination mechanism will choose among the available features (A, B, and other irrelevant stimuli) with probabilities reflecting their salience. Thus, it is possible that a satisfactory discrimination involving B will be found and that this production will be strengthened to where it is dominating behavior and producing satisfactory results so that the A discrimination will never be made. It is also possible that even after a production is formed with the B discrimination, it is too weak to apply, an error occurs, and an A discrimination occurs. In that case both A and B might develop as alternate and equally strong bases for responding. Thus, the ACT theory does not predict that overshadowing will always occur but allows it to occur and predicts it to be related to the differential salience of the competing stimuli.

Evidence for the ACT Tuning Mechanisms

We have spent and are spending some considerable effort in gathering evidence relevant to evaluation of the tuning mechanisms described here. One issue concerns sufficiency: Are the learning mechanisms described here adequate to produce intelligent, adaptive, and stable performance as an end product? Anderson et al. (1981) describe our efforts to establish sufficiency for the domain of geometry theorem proving. We were able to show adaptive behavior on the small scale, but size limitations on our simulation program prevented us from assessing what the eventual behavior of the program would be if it were to work through a course of study like that of a high school student.

Because of various technical optimizations, I was able to assess this issue of sufficiency more adequately in the case of language acquisition (Anderson, 1981a). Although not able to achieve anything so grand as a language, I was able to show that the learning mechanisms did converge to produce correct syntactic behavior on various subsets of a number of different languages.

It is difficult to assess the psychological accuracy of the programs in these areas. Because of the scale of the phenomena, there are no careful empirical characterizations of the variety with which an experimental psychologist likes to work. For the same reason it is not possible to get reliable statistics about the performance of the simulation programs. In addition, the simulations require rather major simplifying assumptions. So, to check the empirical accuracy of the tuning mechanisms, we have looked at behavior of the program on various schema-abstraction or prototype-formation tasks (e.g., Franks & Bransford, 1971; Hayes-Roth & Hayes-Roth, 1977; and Medin & Schaffer, 1978). These are relatively tractable empirical phenomena on which it is possible to do careful analytic experiments. In Anderson et al. (1979), we were able to show our mechanisms capable of simulating many of the established phenomena. In Elio and Anderson (1981), we were able to confirm predictions from ACT's generalization mechanism that served to discriminate it from other theories.

Procedural Learning: The Power Law

One aspect of skill acquisition is distinguished both by its ubiquity and by its surface contradiction to ACT's multiple stage, multiple mechanism view of skill development. This is the log-linear or power law for practice: A plot of the logarithm of time to perform a task against the logarithm of amount of practice approximates a straight line. It has been widely discussed with respect to human performance (Fitts & Posner, 1967; Welford, 1968) and has been the subject of a number of recent theoretical analyses (Newell & Rosenbloom, 1981; Lewis, Note 3). It is found in phenomena as

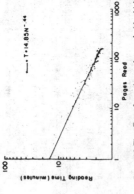

$$T = 14.85N^{-.44}$$

Figure 10. The effect of practice on the speed with which subjects can read inverted text. (From Kolers, 1975.)

diverse as motor skills (Snoddy, 1926), pattern recognition (Neisser, Novick, & Lazar, 1963), problem solving (Neves & Anderson, 1981), memory retrieval (Anderson, in press), and, suspiciously, in machine building by industrial plants (an example of institutional learning rather than human learning; Hirsch, 1952). Figure 10 illustrates one example: the effect of practice on the speed with which inverted text can be read (Kolers, 1975). This ubiquitous phenomenon would seem to contradict the ACT theory of skill acquisition because at first it seems that a theory that proposes changing mechanisms of skill acquisition would not predict the apparent uniformity of the speedup. Also, it is not immediately clear why ACT would predict a power function rather than, say, an exponential function. Because of the ubiquity of the power law, it is important to show that the ACT learning theory is consistent with this phenomenon.

The general form of the equation relating time (T) to perform a task to amount of practice (P) is

$$T = X + AP^{-b}, \tag{1}$$

where X is the asymptotic speed, X + A is the speed on Trial 1, and b is the slope of the function on a log–log plot—where time is plotted as log(T − X). The value of b is almost always in the interval 0 to 1. The asymptotic X is usually very small relative to X + A, and the rate of approach to asymptote is slow in a power function. This means that it is often possible to get very good fits in plots like Figure 10, assuming a zero

asymptote. However, careful analysis of data with enough practice does indicate evidence for nonzero asymptotes.

These facts about skill speedup have appeared contradictory to ACT-like learning mechanisms because ACT mechanisms would seem to imply speedup that is faster than one would obtain with a power law. Composition, as developed earlier, collapsed pairs of productions into single productions. It was noted (p. 384) that composition seems to predict a speedup on the order of Ba^P—which is to say an exponential function of practice, P (a is less than 1). An exponential law, as noted by Newell and Rosenbloom (1981), is in some sense the natural prediction about speedup. It implies that with each practice trial the subject can improve a constant fraction (a) of his current time (or has a constant probability of improving by a constant amount). When we look at ACT's tuning mechanisms of discrimination and generalization, it is harder to make general claims about the speedup they will produce because their speedup will depend on the characteristics of the problem space. However, it is at least plausible to propose that each discrimination or generalization has a constant expected factor of improvement. Composition, generalization, and discrimination improve performance by reducing the expected number of productions applied in performing a task. I will refer to improvement due to reduction in number of productions as *algorithmic improvement*.

In contrast to algorithmic improvement, strengthening reduces the time for individual productions of the procedure to apply. I will show that the strengthening process in ACT does result in a power law. However, even if strengthening obeys a power law, it is not immediately obvious why the total processing, which is a product of both algorithmic improvement and strengthening, should obey a power law. Nonetheless, I will set forth a set of assumptions under which this is just what is predicted by ACT and in so doing will resolve the problem.

Strengthening

Although complex processes like editing or proof generation appear to obey a power law, it is also the case that simple processes like simple choice reaction time (Mowbray & Rhoades, 1959) or memory retrieval (Anderson, in press) may do the same. In these cases the speedup cannot be modeled as an algorithmic improvement in number of production steps. There cannot be more than a small number of productions (e.g., 10) applying in the less than 500 msec required for these tasks. A process of reducing that number would not produce the continuous improvements observed. Moreover, subjects may well start out with optimal or near optimal procedures in terms of minimum number of productions, so there often is little or no room for algorithmic improvement. Here we have to assume that the speedup observed is due to a basic increase in the rate of production application, as would be produced by ACT's strengthening process.

Recall from the earlier discussions (see the section on conflict resolution) that time to apply a production is $c + (a/s)$ where s is the production strength, c reflects processes in production application, and a is the time for a unit-strength production to be selected. Strength increases by one unit (a unit in our theory) with each trial of practice. Therefore, we can simply replace s in the expression above by P, the number of trials of practice. Then, the form of the practice function for production execution in ACT takes the form

$$T = c + aP^{-1}, \qquad (2)$$

which is a hyperbolic function, one form of the power law. This assumes that on the first measured trial ($P = 1$), the production already has 1 unit of strength from an earlier encoding opportunity. The time for N such productions to apply would be

$$T = cN + aNP^{-1} \qquad (3)$$

$$\text{or } T = C + AP^{-1}. \qquad (4)$$

where $C = cN$ and $A = aN$. This is a power law where the exponent is equal to 1 and the asymptote is C. The problem is that unless prior practice (see Newell & Rosenbloom, 1981), the exponent obtained is typically much less than 1 (usually in the range .1 to .6).

However, the smaller exponents are to be predicted when one takes into account that there is forgetting or loss of strength from prior practice. Thus, a better form of Equation 4 would be

$$T = C + [A / \sum_{i=0}^{P-1} s(i, P)], \qquad (5)$$

where $s(i, P)$ denotes the strength remaining from the ith strengthening when the Pth trial comes about. In the above $s(0, P)$ denotes the strength on Trial P of the initial encoding trial. To understand the behavior of this function we have to understand the behavior of the critical sum:

$$S = \sum_{i=0}^{P-1} s(i, P). \qquad (6)$$

Wickelgren (1976) has shown that the strength of the memory trace decays as a power law. Assuming that time is linear in number of practice trials we have

$$s(i, P) = D(P - i)^{-d}, \qquad (7)$$

where D is the initial strength and $d < 1$. Combining Equations 6 and 7 we get

$$S = \sum_{i=1}^{P} Di^{-d}. \qquad (8)$$

This function is bounded below and above as follows:

$$\frac{D}{1-d}[(P+1)^{1-d} - 1]$$

$$< S < \frac{D}{1-d}(P^{1-d} - d); \qquad (9)$$

S can be approximated by the average of these upper and lower bounds and because the difference between $(P + 1)^{1-d}$ and P^{1-d} becomes increasingly small with large P we may write

$$S \approx \frac{D}{1-d}(P^{1-d} - X),$$

where $X = (1 + d)/2$. This factor X will become increasingly insignificant as P gets large. So, the important observation is that to a close approximation, total strength will grow as a power law. Substituting back into Equation 5 we get

$$T = C(P) + A'P^{-g}, \qquad (10)$$

where $A' = A(1 - d)/D$; $g = 1 - d$; and $C(P)$ obeys the equation

$$C(P) = C + \frac{A(1 - d)X}{DP^{1-d} - (P^{1-d} - X)}, \qquad (11)$$

which converges to C as P gets large. So for large P, Equation 10 will give a good approximation to a power law. Equation 10 has also proven to provide a good approximation for small P in my hand-calculated examples. Thus, the ACT model predicts that time for a fixed sequence of productions should decrease as a power law with the exponent deviating from 1 (and a hyperbolic function) to the degree that there is forgetting. The basic prediction of a power function is confirmed in simple tasks; the further prediction relating the exponent to forgetting is a difficult issue requiring further research. However, it is known that forgetting does reduce the effect of practice (e.g., Kolers, 1975). Given that forgetting must be an important factor in the long-term development of a skill, the ACT analysis of the power law is at a distinct advantage over other analyses that do not accommodate forgetting effects.

Algorithmic Improvement

There is an interesting relation between this power law for simple tasks, based just on strength accumulation, and the power law for complex tasks where there is also the potential for reduction in number of production steps. We noted in the case of composition that a limit on this process is that all the information to be matched by the composed production must be active in working memory. Because the size of production conditions (despite the optimization produced by proceduralization) tends to increase exponentially with compositions, the requirements on working memory for the next composition tend to increase exponentially with the number of compositions. It is also the case that as successful discriminations and generalizations proceed, there will be an increase in the amount of information that needs to be held in working memory so that another useful feature can be identified. In this case it is not possible to make precise statements concerning the factor of increase, but it is not unreasonable to suppose that this increase is also exponential with number of improvements. It is then implied that the following relation should define the size (W) of working memory needed for the ith algorithmic improvement:

$$W = GH^i, \qquad (12)$$

where G and H are the parameters of the exponential function.

The ACT theory predicts that a power law should describe the amount of activation of a knowledge structure as a function of practice (in the concepts or links that define that structure). By the same analysis as the one just given for production strength, ACT predicts that the strength of memory structures should increase as a power function of practice. The strength of a memory structure directly determines the amount of activation it will receive. Thus, we have the following equation describing total memory activation (A) as a function of practice:

$$A = QP^r, \qquad (13)$$

where Q and r are the parameters of the power function. (Note that P is raised to a positive exponent, r, less than one.) This equation is more than just theoretical speculation; work in our laboratory on effects of practice on memory retrieval has supported this relation. A small proportion of this work is discussed in Anderson (in press).

There is a strong relationship in the ACT theory between the working memory requirements described by Equation 12 and the total activation described by Equation 13. For an amount, W, of information to be available in working memory, the information must reach a threshold level of activation L, which means that the total amount of activation of the information structure will be described by

$$A = WL. \qquad (14)$$

Equations 12, 13, and 14 may be combined to derive a relation between the number of improvements (i) and amount of practice:

$$i = r\frac{\log(P)}{\log(H)} + \frac{\log(Q)}{\log(H)}$$

$$- \frac{\log(L)}{\log(H)} - \frac{\log(G)}{\log(H)} \qquad (15)$$

or, more simply,

$$j = a + b \log(P). \qquad (16)$$

Thus, because of working memory limitations, the rate of algorithmic improvement is a logarithmic rather than a linear function of practice. Continuing with the assumption that the number of steps (N) should be reduced by a constant fraction, f, with each improvement, we get

$$N = N_0 f^j \qquad (17)$$

or

$$N = N_0' P^{-r}. \qquad (18)$$

where

$$f' = -b \log(f) \quad \text{and} \quad N_0' = N_0 f^a. \qquad (19)$$

Thus, the number of productions applied should decrease as a power function of practice. Equation 18 assumes that in the limit, 0 steps are required to perform the task, but there must be some minimum N^* that is the optimal procedure. Clearly, N^* has at least the value 1. Exactly, how to introduce this minimum into Equation 18 will depend on one's analysis of the improvements. If we simply add it, we get the standard power function for improvement to an asymptote:

$$N = N^* + N_0' P^{-r}. \qquad (20)$$

Let us review the analysis of the power law to date. We started with the observation that, assuming that the rate of algorithmic improvement is linear with practice and that each improvement has a proportional decrease in number of productions, an exponential practice function is predicted, not a power practice function. We noted that the mechanisms of strength accumulation predict that individual productions should speed up as a power function. Similar strength dynamics governing the growth of working memory size imply that the rate of algorithmic improvement is actually logarithmic and therefore the decrease in number of productions would be a power function.

It should be noted that the relation between working memory capacity and improvements in the production algorithm corresponds to a common subject experience on complex tasks. Initially, subjects report feel-ing swamped, trying just to keep up with the task, and have no sense of the overall organization of the task. With practice, subjects report beginning to perceive the structure of the task and claim to be able to see how to make improvements. It is certainly the case that we observe subjects to be better able to maintain current state and goal and better able to retrieve past goals and states of the task. Thus, it seems that their working memory for the problem improves with practice and subjects claim that being able to apprehend at once a substantial portion of the problem is what is critical to making improvements.

Algorithmic Improvement and Strengthening Combined

The total time to perform a task is determined by the number of productions and the time per production. Therefore, the simplest prediction about total time (TT) would be to combine multiplicatively Equation 10, describing time per production, and Equation 20, describing number of productions:

$$TT = (N^* + N_0' P^{-r})(C + A P^{-s}). \qquad (21)$$

Because of the asymptotic components, N^* and C, the above will not be a pure power law but it will look like a power function to a good approximation (as good an approximation as is typically observed empirically). If N^* and C were 0, then we would have a pure power law of the form

$$TT = N_0' A P^{-(r+s)}, \qquad (22)$$

which has a zero asymptote. Because the initial time is so large relative to final time, most data are fit very well assuming a zero asymptote. This is the form of the equation we will use for further discussion.

One complication ignored in the foregoing discussion is that algorithmic improvements in the number of productions typically mean creation of new productions. According to the theory new productions start off with low strength. Thus, productions at later points in the experiment will not have been practiced since the beginning of the experiment and will have lower strength than assumed in Equations 21 and 22. Another complication on top of this is that a completely new

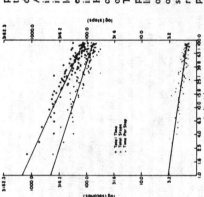

Figure 11. The effect of practice on a reason-giving task. (Plotted separately are the effects on number of steps, time per step, and total time. From Neves and Anderson, 1981.)

set of productions will not be instituted with each improvement; only a subset will change. Suppose that at any time the productions in use were introduced an average of j improvements ago. This means (by Equation 15) that after the ith improvement the average production has been practiced from Trial KL^{i-1} to Trial KL^i and therefore has had $KL^i(1 - L^{-1})$ trials of practice, where $K = H^{-s/r}$ and $L = H^{1/r}$ from Equations 15 and 16. Thus, the number of trials of practice (P^*) for a production is expected to be a constant fraction of the total number of trials (P) on the task:

$$P^* = qP, \qquad (23)$$

where $q = (1 - L)$. This implies that the correct form of Equation 20 is

$$TT = N_0 A q^{-s} P^{-(r+s)}. \qquad (24)$$

Thus, this argument does not at all affect the expectation of a power function.

An Experimental Test

The basic prediction of this analysis is that both number of productions and time per production should decrease as a power function of practice. As a result, total time will decrease as a power function. Neves and Anderson (1981) have tested this prediction in an experiment that studied subjects' ability to give reasons for the lines of an abstract logic proof. This reason-giving task is modeled after a frequent kind of exercise found in high school geometry texts (see Figure 3). However, we wanted to use the task with college students and wanted to see the effects of practice, starting from the beginning. Therefore, we invented a novel artificial proof system. Each proof consisted of 10 lines. Each line could be justified as a given or derived from earlier lines by application of one of nine postulates. Subjects could only see the current line of the proof and had to request of a computer to display particular prior lines, givens, or postulates. The method of requesting this information was very easy, and so we hoped to be able to trace, by subjects' request behavior, the steps of the algorithm they were following. The relation between requests and production application is almost certainly one to many, but we believe that we can use these requests as an index of the number of productions that are applying. The basic assumption is that the ratio of productions to requests will not change over time. This assumption certainly could be challenged, but I think it is plausible and is strongly supported by the orderliness of the results. Under this assumption if we plot number of requests as a function of practice, we are looking at the reduction in the number of productions or algorithmic improvement. If we plot time per request, we are looking at the improvement in the speed of individual productions.

Figure 11 presents the analysis of these data averaged over three subjects (individual subjects show the same pattern). Subjects took about 25 minutes to do the first problem. After 90 problems they were often taking under 2 minutes to do the proofs. This reflects the impact of approximately 10 hours of practice. As can be seen from Figure 11, both number of steps (information requests) and time per step (interval between requests) go down as power functions of practice. Hence, total time also obeys a power function. The exponent for the number of steps is −.346 (ranging from −.315 to −.373 for individual subjects), whereas the exponent for the time per step is −.198 (ranging from −.144 to −.226).

The Neves and Anderson (1981) experiment does provide evidence that underlying a power law in complex tasks are power laws both in number of steps applied and in time per step. I have shown how a power law in strength accumulation may underlie both of these phenomena. Although it is true that algorithmic improvement would tend to produce exponential speedup, the underlying strength dynamics determine working memory capacity and produce a power function in algorithmic improvement. It is tempting to think of these strength dynamics as describing a process at the neural level of the system. Therefore, it is interesting to note Eccles's (1972) review of the evidence that individual neurons increase with practice and decrease with disuse in their rate of transmitter release and pickup across synapses.

Summary

We have now reviewed the basic progression of skill acquisition according to the ACT learning theory. It starts out as the interpretive application of declarative knowledge; this becomes compiled into a procedural form, and this procedural form undergoes a process of continual refinement of conditions and raw increase in speed. In a sense this is a stage analysis of human learning. Much as other stage analyses of human behavior, this stage analysis of ACT is being offered as an approximation to characterize a rather complex system of interactions. Any interesting behavior is produced by a set of elementary components, and different components can be at different stages. For instance, part of a task can be performed interpretively, whereas another part is performed as compiled.

The claim is that the configuration of learning mechanisms described is involved in the full range of skill acquisition from language acquisition to problem solving to schema abstraction. Another strong claim is that the basic control architecture across these situations is hierarchical, goal struc-tured, and basically organized for problem solving. This echoes the claim made elsewhere (Newell, 1980) that problem solving is the basic mode of cognition. The claim is that the mechanisms of skill acquisition basically function within the mold provided by the basic problem-solving character of skills. As skills evolve they become more tuned and compiled, and the original search of the problem space may drop out as a significant aspect. I have presented a variety of theoretical analyses and experimental analyses that provide positive evidence for this broad view of skill acquisition. Clearly, many more analyses and experimental tests can be done. However, the available evidence at least conveys a modest degree of credibility to the theory presented.

In conclusion, I would like to point out that the learning theory proposed here has achieved a unique accomplishment. Unlike past learning theories it has cogently addressed the issue of how symbolic or cognitive skills are acquired. (Indeed, I have been so focused on this, I have ignored some of the phenomena that traditional learning addressed, such as classical conditioning.) The inadequacies of past learning theories to account for symbolic behavior have been a major source of criticism. On the other hand, unlike many of the current cognitive theories, ACT not only provides an analysis of the performance of a cognitive skill but also an analysis of its acquisition. Many researchers (e.g., Estes, 1975; Langley & Simon, 1981; Rumelhart & Norman, 1978) have lamented how the strides in task analysis within cognitive psychology have not been accompanied by strides in development of learning theory.

If I were to select the conceptual developments most essential to this theory of the acquisition of cognitive skills, I would point to two. First, there is the clear separation made in ACT between declarative knowledge (propositional network of facts) and procedural knowledge (production system). The declarative system has the capacity to represent abstract facts. The production system through its use of variables can process the propositional character of this data base. Also, productions through their reference to goal structures have the capacity to shift attention and control in a symbolic way. These basic symbolic capacities are essential to the success of the learning mechanisms. Knowledge is integrated into the system by first being encoded declaratively and then being interpreted. We argued that the successful integration of knowledge into behavior requires that it first go through such an interpretive stage. The various learning mechanisms all are structured around variable use and reference to goal structures. Moreover, the learning processes impact on the course of the symbolic processing, making it both faster and more judicious in choice. In ACT we see how learning and symbolic processing could be synergetic. These two aspects of cognition surely are synergetic in man, and this fact commends the theory for consideration at least as much as any specific issue that was considered.

Second is the ACT production system architecture itself. Productions are relatively simple and well-defined objects, and this is essential if one is to produce general learning mechanisms. The general learning mechanisms must be constituted so that they will correctly operate on the full range of structures (productions) that they might encounter. It is possible to construct such learning mechanisms for ACT productions; it would not be possible if the procedural formalism were as diverse and unconstrained as are LISP functions. ACT productions have the virtue of stimulus–response bonds with respect to their simplicity but also have considerable computational power. A problem with many production system formalisms with respect to learning is that it is hard for the learning mechanism to appreciate the function of the production in the overall flow of control. This is why the use of goal structures is such a significant augmentation to the ACT architecture. By inspecting the goal structure in which a production application participates, it is possible to understand the role of the production. This is essential to a system that learns by doing.

Reference Notes

1. Rychener, M. D. Approaches to knowledge acquisition: The instructable production system project. Unpublished manuscript, Carnegie-Mellon University, 1981.

2. Anderson, J. R., Kline, P. J., & Beasley, C. M. A theory of the acquisition of cognitive skills (ONR Tech. Rep. 77-1). New Haven, Conn.: Yale University, Department of Psychology, 1977.
3. Lewis, C. H. Speed and practice. Unpublished manuscript, 1979. (Available from C. H. Lewis, IBM Research Center, Yorktown Heights, New York 10598.)

References

Anderson, J. R. Language, memory, and thought. Hillsdale, N.J.: Erlbaum, 1976.
Anderson, J. R. Cognitive psychology and its implications. San Francisco, Calif.: Freeman, 1980.
Anderson, J. R. A theory of language acquisition based on general learning mechanisms. Proceedings of the Seventh International Joint Conference on Artificial Intelligence, 1981, 97–103. (a)
Anderson, J. R. Tuning of search of the problem space for geometry proofs. Proceedings of the Seventh International Joint Conference on Artificial Intelligence, 1981, 165–170. (b)
Anderson, J. R. Retrieval of information from long-term memory. Science, in press.
Anderson, J. R., Greeno, J. G., Kline, P. J., & Neves, D. M. Acquisition of problem-solving skill. In J. R. Anderson (Ed.), Cognitive skills and their acquisition. Hillsdale, N.J.: Erlbaum, 1981.
Anderson, J. R., Kline, P. J., & Beasley, C. M. A general learning theory and its application to schema abstraction. In G. H. Bower (Ed.), The psychology of learning and motivation (Vol. 13). New York: Academic Press, 1979, 277–318.
Anderson, J. R., Kline, P. J., & Beasley, C. M. Complex learning processes. In R. E. Snow, P. A. Federico, & W. E. Montague (Eds.), Aptitude, learning, and instruction (Vol. 2). Hillsdale, N.J.: Erlbaum, 1980.
Braine, M. D. S. On learning grammatical order of words. Psychological Review, 1963, 70, 323–348.
Briggs, G. E., & Blaha, J. Memory retrieval and central comparison times in information processing. Journal of Experimental Psychology, 1969, 79, 395–402.
Brown, D. J. H. Concept learning by feature value interval abstraction. Proceedings of the Workshop on Pattern-Directed Inference Systems, 1977, 55–60.
Brown, J. S., & Van Lehn, K. Repair theory: A generative theory of bugs in procedural skills. Cognitive Science, 1980, 4, 379–426.
Brown, R. A first language. Cambridge, Mass.: Harvard University Press, 1973.
Burke, C. J., & Estes, W. K. A component model for stimulus variables in discrimination learning. Psychometrika, 1957, 22, 133–145.
Eccles, J. C. Possible synaptic mechanisms subserving learning. In A. G. Karyman & J. C. Eccles (Eds.), Brain and human behavior. New York: Springer-Verlag, 1972.
Elio, R., & Anderson, J. R. Effects of category generalizations and instance similarity on schema abstraction. Journal of Experimental Psychology: Human Learning and Memory, 1981, 7, 397–417.
Estes, W. K. Toward a statistical theory of learning. Psychological Review, 1950, 57, 94–107.

Estes, W. K. The state of the field: General problems and issues of theory and metatheory. In W. K. Estes (Ed.), *Handbook of learning and cognitive processes* (Vol. 1). Hillsdale, N.J.: Erlbaum, 1975.

Fitts, P. M. Perceptual-motor skill learning. In A. W. Melton (Ed.), *Categories of human learning*. New York: Academic Press, 1964.

Fitts, P. M., & Posner, M. I. *Human performance*. Monterey, Calif.: Brooks/Cole, 1967.

Forgy, C., & McDermott, J. OPS, a domain-independent production system. *Proceedings of the Fifth International Joint Conference on Artificial Intelligence*, 1977, 933-939.

Franks, J. J., & Bransford, J. D. Abstraction of visual patterns. *Journal of Experimental Psychology*, 1971, 90, 65-74.

Greeno, J. G. Indefinite goals in well-structured problems. *Psychological Review*, 1976, 83, 479-491.

Hayes-Roth, B., & Hayes-Roth, F. Concept learning and the recognition and classification of exemplars. *Journal of Verbal Learning and Verbal Behavior*, 1977, 16, 321-338.

Hayes-Roth, F., & McDermott, J. Learning structured patterns from examples. *Proceedings of the Third International Joint Conference on Pattern Recognition*, 1976, 419-423.

Heinemann, E. C., & Chase, S. Stimulus generalization. In W. K. Estes (Ed.), *Handbook of learning and cognitive processes* (Vol. 2). Hillsdale, N.J.: Erlbaum, 1975.

Hirsh, W. Z. Manufacturing progress functions. *Review of Economics and Statistics*, 1952, 34, 143-155.

Jurgensen, R. C., Donnelly, A. J., Maier, J. E., & Rising, G. R. *Geometry*. Boston, Mass.: Houghton Mifflin, 1975.

Kendler, H. H., & Kendler, T. S. From discrimination learning to cognitive development: A neobehavioristic odyssey. In W. K. Estes (Ed.), *Handbook of learning and cognitive processes* (Vol. 1). Hillsdale, N.J.: Erlbaum, 1975.

Kolers, P. A. Memorial consequences of automatized encoding. *Journal of Experimental Psychology: Human Learning and Memory*, 1975, 1, 689-701.

Langley, P., & Simon, H. A. The central role of learning in cognition. In J. R. Anderson (Ed.), *Cognitive skills and their acquisition*. Hillsdale, N.J.: Erlbaum, 1981.

Larkin, J. H., McDermott, J., Simon, D. P., & Simon, H. A. Expert and novice performance in solving physics problems. *Science*, 1980, 208, 1335-1342.

Larson, J., & Michalski, R. S. Inductive inference of VL decision rules. *Proceedings of the Workshop on Pattern-Directed Inference Systems*, 1977, 38-44.

Lewis, C. H. Production system models of practice effects. Unpublished doctoral dissertation, University of Michigan, 1978.

Luchins, A. S. Mechanization in problem solving. *Psychological Monograph*, 1942, 54(6, Whole No. 248).

Luchins, A. S., & Luchins, E. H. *Rigidity of behavior: a variational approach to the effect of Einstellung*. Eugene: University of Oregon Books, 1959.

MacKintosh, N. J. From classical conditioning to discrimination learning. In W. K. Estes (Ed.), *Handbook of learning and cognitive processes* (Vol. 1). Hillsdale, N.J.: Erlbaum, 1975.

Maratsos, M. P., & Chalkley, M. A. The internal language of children's syntax: The ontogenesis and representation of syntactic categories. In K. Nelson (Ed.), *Children's language* (Vol. 1). New York: Gardner Press, 1981.

McNeill, D. On theories of language acquisition. In T. R. Dixon & D. L. Horton (Eds.), *Verbal behavior and general behavior theory*. Englewood Cliffs, N.J.: Prentice-Hall, 1968.

Medin, D. L. Theories of discrimination learning and learning set. In W. K. Estes (Ed.), *Handbook of learning and cognitive processes* (Vol. 3). Hillsdale, N.J.: Erlbaum, 1976.

Medin, D. L., & Schaffer, M. M. A context theory of classification learning. *Psychological Review*, 1978, 85, 207-238.

Miller, G. A., Galanter, E., & Pribram, K. H. *Plans and the structure of behavior*. New York: Holt, Rinehart & Winston, 1960.

Mowbray, G. H., & Rhoades, M. V. On the reduction of choice reaction times with practice. *Quarterly Journal of Experimental Psychology*, 1959, 11, 16-23.

Neisser, U., Novick, R., & Lazar, R. Searching for ten targets simultaneously. *Perceptual and Motor Skills*, 1963, 17, 955-961.

Neves, D. M. *Learning procedures from examples*. Unpublished doctoral dissertation, Carnegie-Mellon University, 1981.

Neves, D. M., & Anderson, J. R. Knowledge compilation: Mechanisms for the automatization of cognitive skills. In J. R. Anderson (Ed.), *Cognitive skills and their acquisition*. Hillsdale, N.J.: Erlbaum, 1981.

Newell, A. Reasoning, problem-solving, and decision processes: The problem space as a fundamental category. In R. Nickerson (Ed.), *Attention and performance VIII*. Hillsdale, N.J.: Erlbaum, 1980.

Newell, A., & Rosenbloom, P. Mechanisms of skill acquisition and the law of practice. In J. R. Anderson (Ed.), *Cognitive skills and their acquisition*. Hillsdale, N.J.: Erlbaum, 1981.

Norman, D. A. Discussion: Teaching, learning, and the representation of knowledge. In R. E. Snow, P. A. Federico, & W. E. Montague (Eds.), *Aptitude, learning, and instruction* (Vol. 2). Hillsdale, N.J.: Erlbaum, 1980.

Rudy, J. W., & Wagner, A. R. Stimulus selection in associative learning. In W. K. Estes (Ed.), *Handbook of learning and cognitive processes* (Vol. 2). Hillsdale, N.J.: Erlbaum, 1975.

Rychener, M. D., & Newell, A. An instructible production system: Basic design issues. In D. A. Waterman & F. Hayes-Roth (Eds.), *Pattern-directed inference systems*. New York: Academic Press, 1978.

Schneider, W., & Shiffrin, R. M. Controlled and automatic human information processing: I. Detection, search, and attention. *Psychological Review*, 1977, 84, 1-66.

Shiffrin, R. M., & Dumais, S. T. The development of automatism. In J. R. Anderson (Ed.), *Cognitive skills and their acquisition*. Hillsdale, N.J.: Erlbaum, 1981.

Shiffrin, R. M., & Schneider, W. Controlled and automatic human information processing: II. Perceptual learning, automatic attending, and a general theory. *Psychological Review*, 1977, 84, 127-190.

Snoddy, G. S. Learning and stability. *Journal of Applied Psychology*, 1926, 10, 1-36.

Spence, K. W. Continuous versus noncontinuous interpretations of discrimination learning. *Psychological Review*, 1940, 47, 271-288.

Sternberg, S. Memory scanning: Mental processes revealed by reaction time experiments. *American Scientist*, 1969, 57, 421-457.

Trabasso, T. R., & Bower, G. H. *Attention in learning*. New York: Wiley, 1968.

Vere, S. A. Inductive learning of relational productions. In D. A. Waterman & F. Hayes-Roth (Eds.), *Pattern-directed inference systems*. New York: Academic Press, 1978.

Welford, A. T. *Fundamentals of skill*. London: Methuen, 1968.

Wicklegren, W. A. Memory storage dynamics. In W. K. Estes (Ed.), *Handbook of learning and cognitive processes* (Vol. 4). Hillsdale, N.J.: Erlbaum, 1976.

Received July 16, 1981
Revision received December 18, 1981 ■

Machine Learning

There are two traditions in machine learning—what Mitchell, Keller, and Kedar-Cabelli refer to as *similarity-based learning* and *explanation-based learning*. Similarity-based learning considers multiple exemplars of a concept and induces a rule that distinguishes exemplars from nonexemplars (e.g., widgets are blue rectangles with wheels). Explanation-based learning induces a general rule based on a single exemplar using knowledge about the domain to construct the generalization. Although similarity-based learning is related to the concept-attainment literature in psychology, it has not been a focus of research in cognitive science. Explanation-based learning is related to the problems of knowledge representation and language understanding, which are more central to research in cognitive science. The paper by Mitchell, Keller, and Kedar-Cabelli provides a nice integration of the research on explanation-based learning to date, including an account of the seminal work by DeJong (DeJong, G. (1981). Generalization based on explanation, in *Proceedings of the Seventh International Joint Conference on Artificial Intelligence*. Los Altos, CA: Morgan Kaufmann).

The Rumelhart, Hinton, and Williams paper is outside the mainstream of research in machine learning, because it uses a connectionist model.

This research extends the delta rule developed much earlier for learning in perceptron systems. The delta rule applies to two layer perceptron systems, where there is a layer of input nodes and a layer of output nodes. It assumes there is training or feedback with respect to what the output should be from each node. If the expected output for any node is greater than is the actual output, then the rule increases the weight of any inputs to the node that were acting to increase the output of the node (and to decrease the weight of those acting to decrease the output). Similarly, if the expected output is less than is the actual output, the rule decreases the weight of any input to the node that acts to increase the output of the node. The generalized delta rule developed by Rumelhart, Hinton, and Williams extends the delta rule to multiple-layer networks by backward propagation from the output nodes to each preceding layer. Multiple-layer networks are necessary to handle learning of certain kinds of input–output mappings, and Rumelhart, Hinton, and Williams show that these systems can learn such mappings without being trapped in local minima. Their research answers a major challenge put to perceptron systems by Minsky and Papert (Minsky, M. & Papert, S. (1969). *Perceptrons*. Cambridge, MA: MIT Press) some years earlier.

Explanation-Based Generalization: A Unifying View

TOM M. MITCHELL   (MITCHELL @ RED.RUTGERS.EDU)
RICHARD M. KELLER   (KELLER @ RED.RUTGERS.EDU)
SMADAR T. KEDAR-CABELLI   (SMADAR-CABELLI @ RED.RUTGERS.EDU)
Computer Science Department, Rur~   NJ 08901, U.S.A.

(Received August 1, 1985)

Abstract. The problem of formulating general concepts from specific training examples has long been a major focus of machine learning research. While most previous research has focused on empirical methods for generalizing from a large number of training examples using no domain-specific knowledge, in the past few years new methods have been developed for applying domain-specific knowledge to formulate valid generalizations from single training examples. The characteristic common to these methods is that their ability to *generalize* from a single example follows from their ability to *explain* why the training example is a member of the concept being learned. This paper proposes a general, domain-independent mechanism, called EBG, that unifies previous approaches to explanation-based generalization. The EBG method is illustrated in the context of several example problems, and used to contrast several existing systems for explanation-based generalization. The perspective on explanation-based generalization afforded by this general method is also used to identify open research problems in this area.

Key words: explanation-based learning, explanation-based generalization, goal regression, constraint back-propagation, operationalization, similarity-based generalization.

1. Introduction and motivation

The ability to generalize from examples is widely recognized as an essential capability of any learning system. Generalization involves observing a set of training examples of some general concept, identifying the essential features common to these examples, then formulating a concept definition based on these common features. The generalization process can thus be viewed as a search through a vast space of possible concept definitions, in search of a correct definition of the concept to be learned. Because this space of possible concept definitions is vast, the heart of the generalization problem lies in utilizing whatever training data, assumptions and knowledge are available to constrain this search.

Most research on the generalization problem has focused on empirical, data-intensive methods that rely on large numbers of training examples to constrain the search for the correct generalization (see Mitchell, 1982; Michalski, 1983; Dieterich,

1982 for overviews of these methods). These methods all employ some kind of *inductive bias* to guide the inductive leap that they must make in order to define a concept from only a subset of its examples (Mitchell, 1980). This bias is typically built into the generalizer by providing it with knowledge only of those example features that are presumed relevant to describing the concept to be learned. Through various algorithms it is then possible to search through the restricted space of concepts definable in terms of these allowed features, to determine concept definitions consistent with the training examples. Because these methods are based on searching for features that are common to the training examples, we shall refer to them as *similarity-based* generalization methods.[1]

In recent years, a number of researchers have proposed generalization methods that contrast sharply with these data-intensive, similarity-based methods (e.g., Borgida et al., 1985; DeJong, 1983; Kedar-Cabelli, 1985; Keller, 1983; Lebowitz, 1985; Mahadevan, 1985; Minton, 1984; Mitchell, 1983; Mitchell et al., 1985; O'Rorke, 1984; Salzberg & Atkinson, 1984; Schank, 1982; Silver, 1983; Utgoff, 1983; Winston et al., 1983). Rather than relying on many training examples and an inductive bias to constrain the search for a correct generalization, these more recent methods constrain the search by relying on knowledge of the task domain and of the concept under study. After analyzing a single training example in terms of this knowledge, these methods are able to produce a valid generalization of the example *along with a deductive justification of the generalization in terms of the system's knowledge*. More precisely, these *explanation-based* methods[2] analyze the training example by first constructing an explanation of how the example satisfies the definition of the concept under study. The features of the example identified by this explanation are then used as the basis for formulating the general concept definition. The justification for this concept definition follows from the explanation constructed for the training example.

Thus, by relying on knowledge of the domain and of the concept under study, explanation-based methods overcome the fundamental difficulty associated with inductive, similarity-based methods: their inability to justify the generalizations that they produce. The basic difference between the two classes of methods is that similarity-based methods must rely on some form of inductive bias to guide generalization, whereas explanation-based methods rely instead on their domain knowledge. While explanation-based methods provide a more reliable means of

---

[1] The term *similarity-based generalization* was suggested by Lebowitz (1985). We use this term to cover both methods that search for similarities among positive examples, and for differences between positive and negative examples.

[2] The term *explanation-based generalization* was first introduced by DeJong (1981) to describe his particular generalization method. The authors have previously used the term *goal-directed generalization* (Mitchell, 1983) to refer to their own explanation-based generalization method. In this paper, we use the term explanation-based generalization to refer to the entire class of methods that formulate generalizations by constructing explanations.

generalization, and are able to extract more information from individual training examples, they also require that the learner possess knowledge of the domain and of the concept under study. It seems clear that for a large number of generalization problems encountered by intelligent agents, this required knowledge is available to the learner. In this paper we present and analyze a number of such generalization problems.

The purpose of this paper is to consider in detail the capabilities and requirements of explanation-based approaches to generalization, and to introduce a single mechanism that unifies previously described approaches. In particular, we present a domain-independent method (called EBG) for utilizing domain-specific knowledge to guide generalization, and illustrate its use in a number of generalization tasks that have previously been approached using differing explanation-based methods. EBG constitutes a more general mechanism for explanation-based generalization than these previous approaches. Because it requires a larger number of explicit inputs (i.e., the training example, a domain theory, a definition of the concept under study, and a description of the form in which the learned concept must be expressed) EBG can be instantiated for a wider variety of learning tasks. Finally, EBG provides a perspective for identifying the present limitations of explanation-based generalization, and for identifying open research problems in this area.

The remainder of this paper is organized as follows. Section 2 introduces the general EBG method for explanation-based generalization, and illustrates the method with an example. Section 3 then illustrates the EBG method in the context of two additional examples: (1) learning a structural definition of a cup from a training example plus knowledge about the function of a cup (based on Winston et al.'s (1983) work), and (2) learning a search heuristic from an example search tree plus knowledge about search and the search space (based on Mitchell et al.'s (1983) work on the LEX system). Section 4 concludes with a general perspective on explanation-based generalization and a discussion of significant open research issues in this area. The appendix relates DeJong's (1981, 1983) research on explanation-based generalization and explanatory schema acquisition to the other work discussed here.

2. Explanation-based generalization: discussion and an example

The key insight behind explanation-based generalization is that it is possible to form a justified generalization of a single positive training example provided the learning system is endowed with some explanatory capabilities. In particular, the system must be able to explain to itself *why* the training example is an example of the concept under study. Thus, the generalizer is presumed to possess a definition of the concept under study as well as domain knowledge for constructing the required explanation. In this section, we define more precisely the class of generalization problems covered by explanation-based methods, define the general EBG method, and illustrate it in terms of a specific example problem.

2.1 The explanation-based generalization problem

In order to define the generalization problem considered here, we first introduce some terminology. A *concept* is defined as a predicate over some universe of instances, and thus characterizes some subset of the instances. Each *instance* in this universe is described by a collection of ground literals that represent its features and their values. A *concept definition* describes the necessary and sufficient conditions for being an example of the concept, while a *sufficient concept definition* describes sufficient conditions for being an example of the concept. An instance that satisfies the concept definition is called an *example*, or *positive example* of that concept, whereas an instance that does not satisfy the concept definition is called a *negative example* of that concept. A *generalization* of an example is a concept definition which describes a set containing that example.[3] An *explanation* of how an instance is an example of a concept is a proof that the example satisfies the concept definition. An *explanation structure* is the proof tree, modified by replacing each instantiated rule by the associated general rule.

The generic problem definition shown in Table 1 summarizes the class of generalization problems considered in this paper. Table 2 illustrates a particular instance of an explanation-based generalization problem from this class. As indicated by these tables, defining an explanation-based learning problem involves specifying four kinds of information:

- The *goal concept* defines the concept to be acquired. For instance, in the problem defined in Table 2 the task is to learn to recognize pairs of objects <x,y> such that it is safe to stack x on top of y. Notice that the goal concept

Table 1. The explanation-based generalization problem

Given:

- *Goal Concept*: A concept definition describing the concept to be learned. (It is assumed that this concept definition fails to satisfy the Operationality Criterion.)
- *Training Example*: An example of the goal concept.
- *Domain Theory*: A set of rules and facts to be used in explaining how the training example is an example of the goal concept.
- *Operationality Criterion*: A predicate over concept definitions, specifying the form in which the learned concept definition must be expressed.

Determine:

- A generalization of the training example that is a sufficient concept definition for the goal concept and that satisfies the operationality criterion.

---

[3] In fact, we use the term *generalization* in this paper both as a noun (to refer to a general concept definition), and as a verb (to refer to the process of deriving this generalization).

that agent and task. For this problem, the operationality criterion requires that the final concept definition be described in terms of the predicates used to describe the training example (e.g., COLOR, VOLUME, DENSITY) or in terms of a selected set of easily evaluated predicates from the domain theory (e.g., LESS). Reexpressing the goal concept in these terms will make it operational with respect to the task of *efficiently recognizing examples of the concept*.

Given these four inputs, the task is to determine a generalization of the *training example* that is a sufficient concept definition for the *goal concept* and that satisfies the *operationality criterion*. Note that the notion of operationality is crucial for explanation-based generalization: if the operationality criterion were not specified, the input goal concept definition could always be a correct output concept definition and there would be nothing to learn! The operationality criterion imposes a requirement that learned concept definitions must be not only correct, but also *in a usable form* before learning is complete. This additional requirement is based on the viewpoint that concept definitions are not learned as theoretical entities, but rather as practical entities to be used by a particular agent for a particular task.

2.2 The EBG method

The EBG method, which is designed to address the above class of problems, is defined as follows:

The EBG method

1. *Explain:* Construct an explanation in terms of the *domain theory* that proves how the *training example* satisfies the *goal concept* definition.

   • This explanation must be constructed so that each branch of the explanation structure terminates in an expression that satisfies the *operationality criterion*.

2. *Generalize:* Determine a set of sufficient conditions under which the explanation structure holds, stated in terms that satisfy the *operationality criterion*.

   • This is accomplished by regressing the *goal concept* through the explanation structure. The conjunction of the resulting regressed expressions constitutes the desired concept definition.

To see more concretely how the EBG method works, consider again the problem of learning the concept SAFE-TO-STACK (x, y). The bottom of Figure 1 shows a training example for this problem, described in terms of a semantic network of objects and relations. In particular, the example consists of two physical objects, OBJ1

Table 2. The SAFE-TO-STACK generalization problem after Borgida et al. (1985)

Given:

• *Goal Concept:* Pairs of objects < x, y > such that SAFE-TO-STACK (x, y), where SAFE-TO-STACK (x, y) ⟺ NOT (FRAGILE (y)) ∨ LIGHTER (x, y).

• *Training Example:*
ON (OBJ1, OBJ2)
ISA (OBJ1, BOX)
ISA (OBJ2, ENDTABLE)
COLOR (OBJ1, RED)
COLOR (OBJ2, BLUE)
VOLUME (OBJ1, 1)
DENSITY (OBJ1, .1)

• *Domain Theory:*
VOLUME (p1, v1) ∧ DENSITY (p1, d1) → WEIGHT (p1, v1*d1)
WEIGHT (p1, w1) ∧ WEIGHT (p2, w2) ∧ LESS (w1, w2) → LIGHTER (p1, p2)
ISA (p1, ENDTABLE) → WEIGHT (p1, 5) (default)
LESS (.1, 5)

• *Operationality Criterion:* The concept definition must be expressed in terms of the predicates used to describe examples (e.g., VOLUME, COLOR, DENSITY) or other selected, easily evaluated, predicates from the domain theory (e.g., LESS).

Determine:

• A generalization of training example that is a sufficient concept definition for the goal concept and that satisfies the operationality criterion.

here, SAFE-TO-STACK, is defined in terms of the predicates FRAGILE and LIGHTER, whereas the training example is defined in terms of other predicates (i.e., COLOR, DENSITY, VOLUME, etc.).

• The *training example* is a positive example of the goal concept. For instance, the training example of Table 2 describes a pair of objects, a box and an endtable, where one is safely stacked on the other.

• The *domain theory* includes a set of rules and facts that allow explaining how training examples are members of the goal concept. For instance, the domain theory for this problem includes definitions of FRAGILE and LIGHTER, rules for inferring features like the WEIGHT of an object from its DENSITY and VOLUME, rules that suggest default values such as the WEIGHT of an ENDTABLE, and facts such as '.1 is LESS than 5'.

• The *operationality criterion* defines the terms in which the output concept definition must be expressed. Our use of this term is based on Mostow's (1981) definition that a procedure is *operational* relative to a given agent and task, provided that the procedure can be applied by the agent to solve the task. Similarly, we assume that the learned concept definition will be used by some agent to perform some task, and must be defined in terms operational for portion of Figure 1 is given in the top portion of the figure. As shown there, the pair of objects <OBJ1, OBJ2> satisfies the goal concept SAFE-TO-STACK because OBJ1 is LIGHTER than OBJ2. Furthermore, this is known because the WEIGHTs of OBJ1 and OBJ2 can be inferred. For OBJ1, the WEIGHT is inferred from its DENSITY and VOLUME, whereas for OBJ2 the WEIGHT is inferred based on a rule that specifies the default weight of ENDTABLEs in general.

Through this chain of inferences, the explanation structure demonstrates how OBJ1 and OBJ2 satisfy the goal concept definition. Note that the explanation structure has been constructed so that each of its branches terminates in an expression that satisfies the operationality criterion (e.g., VOLUME (OBJ1, 1), LESS (.1, 5)). In this way, the explanation structure singles out those features of the training example that are relevant to satisfying the goal concept, and that provide the basis for constructing a justified generalization of the training example. For the current example, these relevant training example features are shown shaded over in the figure, and correspond to the conjunction VOLUME (OBJ1, 1) ∧ DENSITY (OBJ1, 0.1) ∧ ISA (OBJ2, ENDTABLE).

Whereas the first step of the EBG method isolates the relevant features of the training example, it does not determine the desired generalized constraints on feature values. For instance, while the feature VOLUME (OBJ1, 1) is relevant to explaining how the present training example satisfies the goal concept, the general constraint on acceptable values for VOLUME is yet to be determined. The second step of the EBG method therefore generalizes on those feature values selected by the first step, by determining sufficient conditions on these feature values that allow each step in the explanation structure to carry through.

In order to determine general sufficient conditions under which the explanation holds, the second step of the EBG method involves regressing (back propagating) the goal concept step by step back through the explanation structure. In general, *regressing* a given formula F through a rule R is a mechanism for determining the necessary and sufficient (weakest) conditions under which that rule R can be used to infer F. We employ a slightly modified version of the goal-regression algorithm described by Waldinger (1977) and Nilsson (1980).[4] Our modified goal regression algorithm computes an expression that represents only a sufficient condition (rather than necessary and sufficient conditions) under which rule R can be used to infer formula F, but that corresponds closely to the training example under consideration. In particular, whereas the general goal regression algorithm considers all possible variable bindings (unifications) under which R can infer F, our modified algorithm considers only the specific variable bindings used in the explanation of the training example. Furthermore, if the rule R contains a disjunctive antecedent (left-hand side), then our

---

[4] Dijkstra (1976) introduces the related notion of *weakest preconditions* in the context of proving program correctness. The *weakest preconditions* of a program characterize the set of all initial states of that program such that activation guarantees a final state satisfying some postcondition.

EXPLANATION STRUCTURE:

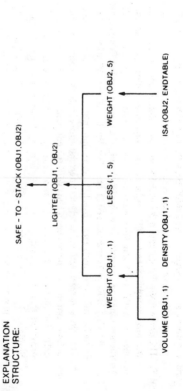

TRAINING EXAMPLE:

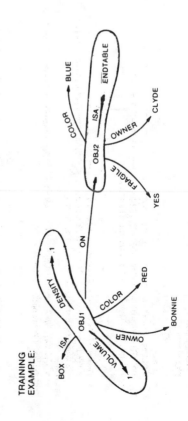

Figure 1. Explanation of SAFE-TO-STACK (OBJ1, OBJ2).

and OBJ2, in which OBJ1 is ON OBJ2, and for which several features of the objects are described (e.g., their OWNERs, COLORs).

Given this training example, the task is to determine which of its features are relevant to characterizing the goal concept, and which are irrelevant. To this end, the first step of the EBG method is to construct an explanation of how the training example satisfies the goal concept. Notice that the explanation constitutes a proof, and constructing such an explanation therefore may involve in general the complexities of theorem proving. The explanation for the training example depicted in the lower the rule to yield some set of substitutions (particular variable bindings). The substitution consistent with the example is then applied to the antecedent (left-hand side) of the rule to yield the resulting regressed expression.[6] Any conjuncts of the original expression which cannot be unified with the consequent of any rule are simply added to the resulting regressed expression (with the substitutions applied to them). As illustrated in the figure, regressing the conjunct WEIGHT (x, w1) through the rule VOLUME (p1, v1) ∧ DENSITY (p1, d1) → WEIGHT (p1, v1*d1) therefore yields VOLUME (x, v1) ∧ DENSITY (x, d1). Regressing the conjunct WEIGHT (y, w2) through the rule ISA (p2, ENDTABLE) → WEIGHT (p2, 5) yields ISA (y, END-TABLE). Finally, since no rule consequent can be unified with the conjunct LESS (w1, w2), this conjunct is simply added to the resulting regressed expression after applying the substitutions produced by regressing the other conjuncts. In this case these substitutions are {x/p1, v1*d1/w1, y/p2, 5/w2}, which yield the third conjunct LESS (v1*d1, 5). The final, operational definition for SAFE-TO-STACK (x, y) is therefore:

$$
\begin{aligned}
&\text{VOLUME (x, v1)}\\
&\wedge\ \text{DENSITY (x, d1)}\\
&\wedge\ \text{LESS (v1*d1, 5)}\\
&\wedge\ \text{ISA (y, ENDTABLE)} \qquad \rightarrow\ \text{SAFE-TO-STACK (x, y)}
\end{aligned}
$$

This expression characterizes in operational terms the features of the training example that are sufficient for the explanation structure to carry through in general. As such, it represents a justified generalization of the training example, for which the explanation structure serves as a justification.

2.3 Discussion

Several general points regarding the EBG method are illustrated in the above example. The main point of the above example is that the EBG method produces a justified generalization from a single training example in a two-step process. The first step creates an explanation that separates the relevant feature values in the examples from the irrelevant ones. The second step analyzes this explanation to determine the particular constraints on these feature values that are sufficient for the explanation structure to apply in general. Thus, explanation-based methods such as EBG overcome the main limitation of similarity-based methods: their inability to produce justified generalizations. This is accomplished by assuming that the learner has available knowledge of the domain, the goal concept, and the operationality

[6] It is correctly observed in DeJong (1986) that the substitution list used to regress expressions through previous steps in the explanation must be applied to the current expression before the next regression step.

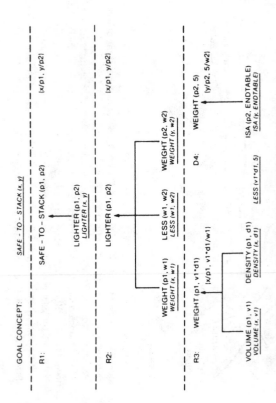

Figure 2. Generalizing from the explanation of SAFE-TO-STACK (OBJ1, OBJ2). (Underlined expressions are the results of regressing the goal concept.)

algorithm considers only the particular disjuncts satisfied by the training example.

Figure 2 illustrates the second step of the EBG method in the context of the SAFE-TO-STACK example. In the first (topmost) step of this figure, the goal concept expression SAFE-TO-STACK (x, y) is regressed through the rule LIGHTER (p1, p2) → SAFE-TO-STACK (p1, p2),[5] to determine that LIGHTER (x, y) is a sufficient condition for inferring SAFE-TO-STACK (x, y). Similarly, regressing LIGHTER (x, y) through the next step in the explanation structure yields the expression WEIGHT (x, w1) ∧ WEIGHT (y, w2) ∧ LESS (w1, w2). This expression is in turn regressed through the final steps of the explanation structure to yield the operational definition for SAFE-TO-STACK (x, y).

To illustrate the goal regression process in greater detail, consider the final step of Figure 2 in which the expression WEIGHT (x, w1) ∧ WEIGHT (y, w2) ∧ LESS (w1, w2) is regressed through the final steps of the explanation structure. Each conjunct of the expression is regressed separately through the appropriate rule, in the following way. The conjunct is unified (matched) with the consequent (right-hand side) of

[5] Notice that the definition of SAFE-TO-STACK given in Table 2 is a disjunctive definition. As noted above, the procedure considers only the disjunct that is satisfied by the current training example (e.g., the disjunct involving the LIGHTER predicate).

criterion, whereas similarity-based generalization does not rely on any of these inputs.

A second point illustrated by the above example is that the language in which the final concept definition is stated can be quite rich. Notice in the above example that the final generalization includes a constraint that the product of the DENSITY and VOLUME of x must be less than 5. There are very many such relations among the parts of the training example that might be considered during generalization (e.g., why not consider the fact that the OWNERs of the two objects are of different SEX?). The interesting point here is that the appropriate constraint was derived directly by analyzing the explanation, without considering the universe of possible relations among parts of the training example. This is in marked contrast with similarity-based generalization methods (e.g. Michalski, 1983; Quinlan, 1985). Such methods are typically based on a heuristic focusing criterion, such as the heuristic that 'less complex features are preferred over more complex features for character-izing concepts'. Therefore, before such methods will consider the feature LESS $(v1*d1, 5)$ as a plausible basis for generalization, they must first consider vast numbers of syntactically simpler, irrelevant features.

A final point illustrated by this example is that the final concept definition pro-duced by EBG is typically a specialization of the goal concept rather than a direct reexpression of the concept. This is largely due to the fact that the explanation struc-ture is created for the given training example, and does not explain every possible example of the goal concept. Thus, the generalization produced from analyzing this explanation will only cover examples for which the explanation holds. Furthermore, because the modified goal regression algorithm computes only sufficient (not necessary and sufficient) conditions under which the explanation holds, it leads to a further specialization of the concept. This limitation of explanation-based generalization suggests an interesting problem for further research: developing explanation-based methods that can utilize multiple training examples (see the discus-sion in Section 4).

3. Other examples and variations

This section discusses two additional examples of explanation-based generalization that have previously been reported in the literature. The first is Winston, Binford, Katz, and Lowry's (1983) research on learning structural definitions of concepts such as 'cup' from their functional definitions. The second is Mitchell, Keller, and Utgoff's (1983) research on learning search heuristics from examples (see also Utgoff, 1984; Keller, 1983). A common perspective on these two systems is provided by instantiating the EBG method for both problems. Differences among the two original approaches and the EBG method are also considered, in order to underscore some subtleties of the EBG method, and to suggest some possible variations.

3.1 An example: learning the concept CUP

In this subsection we first summarize the application of the EBG method to a second example of an explanation-based generalization problem: the CUP generalization problem, patterned after the work of Winston et al. (1983). We then discuss the rela-tionship between the EBG method and the ANALOGY program of Winston et al., which addresses this same problem.

The CUP generalization problem, defined in Table 3, involves learning a structural definition of a cup from its functional definition. In particular, the goal concept here is the concept CUP, defined as the class of objects that are OPEN-VESSEL, LIFT-ABLE, and STABLE. The domain theory includes rules that relate these properties to the more primitive structural properties of physical objects, such as FLAT, HAN-DLE, etc. The operationality criterion requires that the output concept definition be useful for the task of visually recognizing examples of CUPs. It thus requires that the output concept definition be expressed in terms of its structural features.

Figure 3 illustrates a training example describing a particular cup, OBJ1, along with the explanation that shows how OBJ1 satisfies the goal concept CUP. In par-ticular, the explanation indicates how OBJ1 is LIFTABLE, STABLE, and an OPEN-VESSEL. As in the SAFE-TO-STACK example, this explanation distinguishes the relevant features of the training example (e.g., its LIGHTness) from irrelevant features (e.g., its COLOR). The second step of the EBG method, regressing the goal concept through the explanation structure, results in the following general definition of the CUP concept:

$$(\text{PART-OF }(x, xc) \wedge \text{ISA }(xc, \text{CONCAVITY}) \wedge \text{IS }(xc, \text{UPWARD-POINTING})$$
$$\wedge \text{PART-OF }(x, xb) \wedge \text{ISA }(xb, \text{BOTTOM}) \wedge \text{IS }(xb, \text{FLAT})$$
$$\wedge \text{PART-OF }(x, xh) \wedge \text{ISA }(xh, \text{HANDLE}) \wedge \text{IS }(x, \text{LIGHT})) \rightarrow \text{CUP }(x)$$

Table 3. The CUP generalization problem after Winston et al. (1983)

Given:

- Goal Concept: Class of objects, x, such that CUP(x), where
  CUP(x) ⟺ LIFTABLE(x) ∧ STABLE(x) ∧ OPEN-VESSEL(x)
- Training Example:
  OWNER(OBJ1, EDGAR)
  PART-OF(OBJ1, CONCAVITY-1)
  IS(OBJ1, LIGHT)
  ...
- Domain Theory:
  IS(x, LIGHT) ∧ PART-OF(x, y) ∧ ISA(y, HANDLE) → LIFTABLE(x)
  PART-OF(x, y) ∧ ISA(y, BOTTOM) ∧ IS(y, FLAT) → STABLE(x)
  PART-OF(x, y) ∧ ISA(y, CONCAVITY) ∧ IS(y, UPWARD-POINTING) → OPEN-VESSEL(x)
  ...
- Operationality Criterion: Concept definition must be expressed in terms of structural features used in describing examples (e.g., LIGHT, HANDLE, FLAT, etc.).

Determine:

- A generalization of training example that is a sufficient concept definition for the goal concept and that satisfies the operationality criterion.

3.1.1 Discussion

As in the first example, the EBG method is able to produce a valid generalization from a single training example, by explaining and analyzing how the training example satisfies the definition of the goal concept. Notice that the regression step in this example is quite straightforward, and leads to generalizing the training example features effectively by replacing constants with variables (i.e., replacing OBJ1 by x). It is interesting that several earlier attempts at explanation-based generalization (e.g., Mitchell, 1983) involved the assumption that the explanation could always be generalized simply by replacing constants by variables in the explanation, without the need to regress the goal concept through the explanation structure.[7] As the earlier SAFE-TO-STACK example illustrates, this is not the case. In general, one must regress the goal concept through the explanation structure to ensure a valid generalization of the training example (which may involve composing terms from different parts of the explanation, requiring constants where no generalization is possible, and so on).

Several interesting features of this example come to light when the EBG method is compared to the method used in Winston et al.'s (1983) ANALOGY program, upon which this example problem is based. The most striking difference between the two methods is that although ANALOGY does construct an explanation, and also uses this explanation to generalize from a single example, the system has no domain theory of the kind used in the above example. Instead, Winston's program constructs its explanations by drawing analogies between the training example and a library of precedent cases (e.g., annotated descriptions of example suitcases, bricks, bowls, etc.). For example, ANALOGY explains that the FLAT BOTTOM of OBJ1 allows OBJ1 to be STABLE, by drawing an analogy to a stored description of a brick which has been annotated with the assertion that its FLAT BOTTOM 'causes' it to be STABLE. Similarly, it relies on an annotated example of a suitcase to explain by analogy why a handle allows OBJ1 to be LIFTABLE.

In general, the precedents used by ANALOGY are assumed to be annotated by links that indicate which features of the precedent account for which of its properties. Thus, for the ANALOGY program, the causal links distributed over the library of precedents constitute its domain theory. However, this theory is qualitatively different than the domain theory used in the CUP example above: it is described by extension rather than intention (i.e., by examples rather than by general rules), and is therefore a weaker domain theory. Because ANALOGY's knowledge about causality is summarized by a collection of instances of causal relations rather than by general rules of causality, its theory cannot lead *deductively* to assertions about new causal links.

---

[7] This observation is due in part to Sridhar Mahadevan.

EXPLANATION
STRUCTURE:

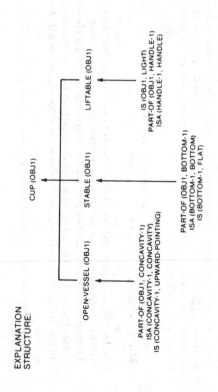

TRAINING
EXAMPLE:

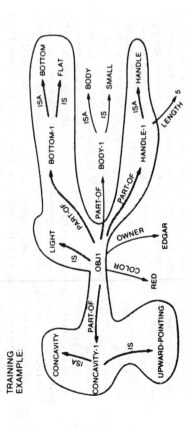

Figure 3. Explanation of CUP (OBJ1).

Table 4. The search heuristic generalization problem after Mitchell et al. (1983)

Given:

- *Goal Concept:* The class of integral expressions that can be solved by first applying operator OP3 (removing a constant from the integrand); that is, the class of integrals, x, such that USEFUL-OP3(x), where

$$\text{USEFUL-OP3}(x) \Leftrightarrow \text{NOT(SOLVED}(x)) \wedge \text{SOLVABLE(OP3}(x))$$

and

- *Training Example:* $\int 7x^2\, dx$.

$$\text{OP3: } \int r \cdot <any\text{-}fn> dx \rightarrow r \int <any\text{-}fn> dx.$$

- *Domain Theory:*

$$\text{SOLVABLE}(x) \Leftrightarrow (\exists op)\ (\text{SOLVED}(op(x)) \vee \text{SOLVABLE}(op(x)))$$
$$\text{MATCHES}(x, \text{`}[\ <any\text{-}fn> dx\text{'}] \rightarrow \text{NOT (SOLVED}(x))$$
$$\text{MATCHES}(x, \ <any\text{-}fn>\text{'}) \rightarrow \text{SOLVED}(x)$$
$$\text{MATCHES}(op(x), y) \Leftrightarrow \text{MATCHES}(x, \text{REGRESS}(y, op))$$

- *Operationality Criterion:* Concept definition must be expressed in a form that uses *easily-computable* features of the problem state, x, (e.g., features such as $<polynomial\text{-}fn>$, $<transcendental\text{-}fn>$, $<any\text{-}fn>$, r, k).

Determine:

- A generalization of training example that is a sufficient concept definition of the goal concept and that satisfies the operationality criterion.

---

be useful. This is defined to be the class of problem states that are NOT already SOLVED (i.e., algebraic expressions that contain an integral sign), and for which applying OP3 leads to a SOLVABLE problem state. The domain theory in this case contains rules that relate SOLVED and SOLVABLE to observable features of problem states (e.g., one rule states that if problem state x MATCHES the expression $\int <any\text{-}fn> dx$, then x is NOT a SOLVED state.). Notice that some of the domain theory rules constitute knowledge about search and problem solving in general (e.g., the definition of SOLVABLE), while other rules represent knowledge specific to integral calculus (e.g., that the absence of an integral sign denotes a SOLVED state). The operationality condition in this problem requires that the final concept definition be stated in terms of *easily-computable* features of the given problem state. This requirement assures that the final concept definition will be in a form that permits its effective use as a search control heuristic.[9] For the LEX program, the set of *easily-computable* features is described by a well-defined generalization language over problem states that includes features (e.g., $<trigonometric\text{-}fn>$, $<real\text{-}constant>$) which LEX can efficiently recognize using its MATCHES predicate.

[9] If the concept definition were permitted to include features that are difficult to compute (e.g., SOLVABLE), then the resulting heuristic would be so expensive to evaluate that its use would degrade, rather than improve, the problem solver's performance.

Because its domain theory is weak, the ANALOGY system raises some interesting questions about explanation-based generalization. Whereas the SAFE-TO-STACK and CUP examples above show how a sufficient set of domain theory rules can provide powerful guidance for generalization, ANALOGY suggests how a weaker, extensional theory might be used to focus the generalization process in a weaker fashion. In particular, the causal links are used by ANALOGY to construct a plausible explanation, but not a proof, that the training example satisfies the goal concept definition. As discussed above, such plausible explanations can guide generalization by focusing on plausibly relevant features of the training example. But since ANALOGY lacks general inference rules to characterize the links in this explanation, it cannot perform the second (goal regression) step in the EBG method, and therefore has no valid basis for generalizing the explanation. In fact, the ANALOGY program generalizes anyway, implicitly, assuming that each causal link of the form (feature (OBJ1) → property (OBJ1)) is supported by a general rule of the form (($\forall x$) feature (x) → property (x)).[8] Thus, ANALOGY represents an important step in considering the use of a weak domain theory to guide generalization, and helps to illuminate a number of open research issues (see the discussion in Section 4).

3.2 An example: learning a search heuristic

This section presents a third example of an explanation-based generalization problem – this one involving the learning of search heuristics. This example is based on the problem addressed by the LEX program (Mitchell et al., 1983) which learns search control heuristics for solving problems in the integral calculus. In particular, LEX begins with a set of legal operators (transformations) for solving integrals (e.g., integration by parts, moving constants outside the integrand). For each such operator, the system learns a heuristic that summarizes the class of integrals (problem states) for which it is useful to apply that operator. For example, one typical heuristic learned by the LEX system is:

IF the integral is of the form $\int <polynomial\text{-}fn> \cdot <trigonometric\text{-}fn> dx$,
THEN apply Integration-by-Parts

Thus, for each of its given operators, LEX faces a generalization problem: learning the class of integrals for which that operator is useful in reaching a solution.

Table 4 defines the generalization problem that corresponds to learning when it is useful to apply OP3 (moving constants outside the integrand). Here the goal concept USEFUL-OP3 (x) describes the class of problem states (integrals) for which OP3 will

[8] Winston's (1985) own work on building rule censors can be viewed as an attempt to address difficulties that arise from this implicit assumption.

This is in turn explained by indicating that applying OP9[10] to the resulting state produces a SOLVED problem, as evidenced by the fact that the resulting state MATCHES the expression '$<any-fn>$' (i.e., that it contains no integral sign). Thus, up to this point (marked as (a) in the figure), each step in the right-hand branch of the explanation structure corresponds to some step along the solution path of the training example.

By point (a), the explanation has indicated that one relevant feature of the training example state is that the result of applying OP3 followed by OP9, is a state that MATCHES '$<any-fn>$'. The operationality criterion requires, however, that the explanation be in terms of features of the single given training example state, rather than features of its resulting solution state. Thus, the remainder of the explanation consists of reexpressing this constraint in terms of the training example state. This is accomplished by applying the last rule in the domain theory of Table 4. This rule[11] allows back propagating the expression '$<any-fn>$' through the general definitions of OP9 and OP3, to determine the equivalent constraint on the training example state. The resulting constraint is that the training example state must MATCH the expression '$<any-fn> \int r_1 \cdot x\, r_2 \neq -1\, dx$' (Here r_1 and r_2 stand for two distinct real numbers, where r_2 must not be equal to -1.). This together with the left-hand branch of the explanation structure, explains which features of $\int 7x^2\, dx$ guarantee that it satisfies the goal concept USEFUL-OP3.

Given this explanation structure, the second step of the EBG method is straightforward. As in the CUP example, regressing the goal concept expression USEFUL-OP3 (x) through the explanation structure effectively results in replacing the training example state by a variable, so that the resulting generalization (taken from the leaves of the explanation tree) is:

$$\text{MATCHES } (x, \text{'} \int <any-fn> dx\text{'}) \wedge$$
$$\text{MATCHES } (x, \text{'}<any-fn> \int r_1 \cdot x\, r_2 \neq -1\, dx\text{'}) \rightarrow \text{USEFUL-OP3}$$

which simplifies to:

$$\text{MATCHES } (x, \text{'}<any-fn> \int r_1 \cdot x\, r_2 \neq -1\, dx\text{'}) \rightarrow \text{USEFUL-OP3 } (x)$$

[10] OP9: $\int x^{r \neq -1}\, dx \rightarrow x^{r+1}/(r+1)$.

[11] The domain theory rule MATCHES (op (x), y) ⇒ MATCHES (x, REGRESS (y, op)) indicates that if the result of applying operator *op* to state *x* MATCHES some expression *y*, then the state *x* MATCHES some expression which can be computed by REGRESSing the expression *y* through operator *op*. Notice that the regression here involves propagating constraints on problem states through problem solving operators. This is a different regression step from the second step of the EBG process, in which the goal concept is regressed through the domain theory rules used in the explanation structure.

EXPLANATION STRUCTURE:

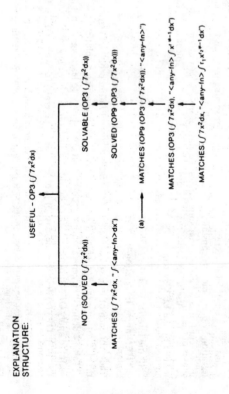

TRAINING EXAMPLE:

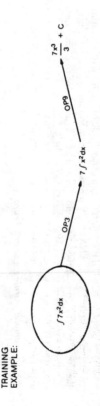

Figure 4. Explanation of USEFUL-OP3 ($\int 7x^2 dx$).

A training example for the goal concept USEFUL-OP3 is shown in the bottom portion of Figure 4. In particular, the problem state $\int 7x^2\, dx$ constitutes a training example of a problem state for which application of OP3 is useful. The training example described in the figure is shown along with the other problem states involved in its solution.

The explanation of USEFUL-OP3 ($\int 7x^2 dx$) is shown in the top portion of Figure 4. The left-hand branch of this explanation structure leads to a node which asserts that USEFUL-OP3 is satisfied in part because the training example state is not already a SOLVED state. The right-hand branch of the explanation structure explains that applying OP3 to the example state leads to a SOLVABLE problem state.

3.2.1 Discussion

To summarize, this example demonstrates again the general EBG method of constructing an explanation in terms that satisfy the operationality condition, then regressing the goal concept through the explanation structure to determine a justified generalization of the training example. As in the previous examples, this process results in a generalization of the training example which is a sufficient condition for satisfying the goal concept, and which is justified in terms of the goal concept, domain theory, and operationality criterion.

In the above example, the goal concept corresponds to the precondition for a search heuristic that is to be learned. The domain theory therefore involves both domain-independent knowledge about search (e.g., the definition of SOLVABLE) and domain-dependent knowledge (e.g., how to recognize a SOLVED integral). To use this method to learn heuristics in a new domain, one would have to replace only the domain-dependent portion of the theory. To learn a different type of heuristic in the same domain, one could leave the domain theory intact, changing only the definition of the USEFUL-OP3 goal concept accordingly. For example, as suggested in Mitchell (1984), the system could be modified to learn heuristics that suggest only steps along the *minimum cost* solution path, by changing the goal concept to

USEFUL-OP3 (s) ⇔ NOT(SOLVED (s)) ∧
MIN-COST-SOLN (SOLUTION-PATH (OP3, s))

Note that the explanation structure in this example, like the domain theory, separates into a domain-independent and a domain-dependent portion. Domain-independent knowledge about search is applied above point (a) in Figure 4, and domain-dependent knowledge about calculus problem solving operators is applied below point (a). In the implementation of the LEX2 program (Mitchell, 1983), these two phases of the explanation were considered to be two unrelated subprocesses and were implemented as separate procedures. From the perspective afforded by the EBG method, however, these two subprocesses are better seen as different portions of the same explanation-generation step.

One final point regarding the current example has to do with the ability of explanation-based methods to augment their description language of concepts. In LEX2, as in the SAFE-TO-STACK problem, this method is able to isolate fairly complex features of the training example that are directly related to the explanation of how it satisfies the goal concept. In the context of the LEX project, Utgoff (1985) studied this issue and developed the STABB subsystem. STABB is able to extend the initial vocabulary of terms used by LEX, by naming and assimilating terms that correspond to the constraints derived during the regression step. For example, in one instance STABB derived the definition of odd integers through this regression step, defining it as 'the set of real numbers, x, such that subtracting 1 then dividing by 2 produces an integer'.

3.2.2 Related methods for strategy learning

There are a number of additional systems that learn problem solving strategies by analyzing single examples of successful solutions.[12] These systems (e.g. Fikes et al., 1972; Utgoff, 1984; Minton, 1984; Mahadevan, 1985), which we might call STRIPS-like systems, can all be viewed as systems that learn a goal concept of the following form: 'the set of problem states such that applying a given operator sequence, OS, yields a final state matching a given solution property, P.' Since these systems are tuned to this single goal concept, and are not intended to learn other forms of concepts, they typically do not represent the goal concept and explanation declaratively. However, they do represent the solution property, P, explicitly, and regress this property through the operator sequence OS to determine an operational definition of the (implicit) goal concept. From the perspective of the above LEX example, the steps that they perform correspond to constructing the portion of the explanation below point (a) in Figure 4. It is in constructing these steps of the explanation that LEX regresses its solution property 'MATCHES (x, $<any-fn>$)' through the operator sequence $<OP3, OP9>$ to determine the equivalent constraint on the initial problem state. These STRIPS-like systems do not construct the portion of the explanation corresponding to the section above point (a) in Figure 4. Because they are tuned to a fixed goal concept, they do not need to generate this portion of the explanation explicitly for each training example.

To illustrate this point, consider Minton's (1984) program for learning search heuristics in two-person games such as Go-Moku, Tic-Tac-Toe, and Chess. This program analyzes one positive instance of a sequence of moves that leads to a winning board position, in order to determine an operational definition of the goal concept 'the class of board positions for which the given sequence of moves leads to a forced win'. But Minton's system has no explicit definition of this goal concept. It has only a definition of the solution property P that characterizes a winning position. For example, in the game of Go-Moku, (a variant of Tic-Tac-Toe) this solution property characterizes a winning board position as 'a board position with five X's in a row'. This solution property is regressed by Minton's program through the operator sequence for the given training example. In this way, the program determines that an effective definition of its implicit goal concept is 'board positions that contain three X's, with a blank space on one side, and two blank spaces on the other'.

[12] See Kibler and Porter (1985) for a thoughtful critique of analytic goal regression methods for learning search control heuristics. They discuss certain requirements for regression to succeed: that the operators be invertible, and that the representation language be able to express goal regression products.

4. Perspective and research issues

The previous sections presented a general method for explanation-based generalization, and illustrated its application to several generalization tasks. This section summarizes some general points regarding explanation-based generalization, and considers a number of outstanding research issues.

To summarize, explanation-based generalization utilizes a domain theory and knowledge of the goal concept to guide the generalization process. By doing so, the method is able to produce a valid generalization of the training example, along with an explanation that serves as a justification for the generalization. The EBG method introduced here unifies mechanisms for explanation-based generalization that have been previously reported for a variety of task domains. The generality of the EBG method stems from the fact that the goal concept, domain theory, and operationality criterion are made explicit inputs to the method, rather than instantiated implicitly within the method.

4.1 Perspectives on explanation-based generalization

Several perspectives on explanation-based generalization, and on the EBG method in particular, are useful in understanding their strengths and weaknesses:

EBG as theory-guided generalization of training examples. EBG can be seen as the process of interpreting or perceiving a given training example as a member of the goal concept, based on a theory of the domain. Soloway's (1978) early work on learning action sequences in the game of baseball shares this viewpoint on generalization. This is the perspective stressed in the above sections, and it highlights the centrality of the goal concept and domain theory. It also highlights an important feature of EBG: that learning depends strongly on what the learner already knows. One consequence of this is that the degree of generalization produced for a particular training example will depend strongly on the generality with which the rules in the domain theory are expressed. A second consequence is that the learning system can improve its *learning* performance to the degree that it can learn new rules for its domain theory.

EBG as example-guided operationalization of the goal concept. One can also view EBG as the process of reformulating the goal concept in terms that satisfy the operationality criterion, with the domain theory providing the means for reexpressing the goal concept. Given this perspective, one wonders why training examples are required at all. In principle, they are not. Mostow's (1983) FOO system operationalizes general advice about how to play the card game of Hearts, without considering specific examples that apply that advice. Similarly, Keller (1983) describes a process of *concept operationalization*, by which a sequence of transformations is applied to

the goal concept in search of a reformulation that satisfies the operationality criterion, without the guidance of specific training examples.

However, training examples can be critical in guiding the learner to consider relevant transformations of the goal concept. For instance, consider the CUP learning task as described in Section 3.1, where a functional definition of CUP is expressed in structural terms for use by a vision system recognizing cups. A system that reformulates the functional definition of CUP in structural terms, without the guidance of training examples, amounts to a system for producing all possible structural definitions for classes of cups (i.e., for *designing* all possible classes of cups). Since there are so many possible designs for cups, and since so few of these are actually encountered in the world, the learning system could easily waste its effort learning structural definitions corresponding to cups that will never be seen by the vision system![13] Training examples thus provide a means of focusing the learner on formulating only concept descriptions that are relevant to the environment in which it operates.

EBG as Reformulating/Operationalizing/Deducing from what is already known. The above paragraph suggests that explanation-based generalization does not lead to acquiring truly 'new' knowledge, but only enables the learner to reformulate/ operationalize/deduce what the learner already knows implicitly. While this statement is true, it is somewhat misleading. Consider, for example, the task of learning to play chess. Once one is told the rules of the game (e.g., the legal moves, and how to recognize a checkmate), one knows *in principle* everything there is to know about chess – even the optimal strategy for playing chess follows deductively from the rules of the game. Thus, although the EBG method is restricted to compiling the deductive consequences of its existing domain theory, this kind of learning is often nontrivial (as is the case for learning chess strategies). Nevertheless, it is a significant limitation that EBG is highly dependent upon its domain theory. As discussed below, further research is needed to extend the method to generalization tasks in which the domain theory is not sufficient to deductively infer the desired concept.

4.2 Research issues

4.2.1 Imperfect theory problems

As the above discussion points out, one important assumption of EBG is that the

---

[13] Of course information about what types of cups are to be encountered by the vision system also could be presented in the *operationality criterion*, since this information relates to the *use* of the concept definition for the recognition task. This information, however, may not be easily described in the declarative form required by the *operationality criterion*.

domain theory is sufficient to *prove* that the training example is a member of the goal concept; that is, that the inferred generalizations follow deductively (even if remotely) from what the learner already knows. Although this assumption is satisfied in each of the example problems presented above, and although there are interesting domains in which this assumption is satisfied (e.g., chess, circuit design (Mitchell et al., 1985), for the majority of real-world learning tasks it is unrealistic to assume that the learner begins with such a strong theory. For both the SAFE-TO-STACK domain and the CUP domain, it is easy to imagine more realistic examples for which the required domain theory is extremely complex, difficult to describe, or simply unknown. For generalization problems such as inferring general rules for predicting the stock market or the weather, it is clear that available theories of economics and meteorology are insufficient to produce absolutely predictive rules. Thus, a major research issue for explanation-based generalization is to develop methods that utilize imperfect domain theories to guide generalization, as well as methods for improving imperfect theories as learning proceeds. The problem of dealing with imperfect theories can be broken down into several classes of problems:

The Incomplete Theory Problem. The stock market and weather prediction examples above both illustrate the incomplete theory problem. The issue here is that such theories are not complete enough to *prove* that the training example is a member of the goal concept (e.g., to prove why a particular training example stock has doubled over a twelve month period). However, even an incomplete theory might allow constructing *plausible explanations* summarizing likely links between features of the training example and the goal concept. For example, even a weak theory of economics allows one to suggest that the 'cash on hand' of the company may be relevant to the goal concept 'stocks that double over a twelve month period', whereas the 'middle initial of the company president' is probably an irrelevant feature. Thus, incomplete theories that contain only information about plausible cause-effect relations, with only qualitative rather than quantitative associations, can still provide important guidance in generalizing. Methods for utilizing and refining such incomplete theories would constitute a major step forward in understanding explanation-based generalization.

The Intractable Theory Problem. A second class of imperfect theories includes those which are complete, but for which it is computationally prohibitive to construct explanations in terms of the theory. For instance, quantum physics constitutes a fairly complete theory that would be inappropriate for generating explanations in the SAFE-TO-STACK problem – generating the necessary explanations in terms of quantum physics is clearly intractable. Similarly, although the rules of chess constitute a domain theory sufficient to explain why any given move is good or bad, one would never use this theory to explain why the opening move 'pawn to king four' is a member of the goal concept 'moves that lead to a win or draw for white'. In fact,

this theory of chess is intractable for explaining why nearly any move is good or bad. Humans tend to respond to this problem by constructing more abstract, tractable theories that are approximations to the underlying intractable theory. In chess, for example, the learner might formulate a more abstract theory that includes approximate assertions such as 'there is no threat to the king if it is surrounded by many friendly pieces' (Tadepalli, 1985). Such approximate, abstracted theories can be tractable enough and accurate enough to serve as a useful basis for creating and learning from explanations. Developing computer methods that can construct such abstracted theories, and that can judge when they can safely be applied, is a problem for further research.

The Inconsistent Theory Problem. A third difficulty arises in theories from which inconsistent statements can be derived. The domain theory in the SAFE-TO-STACK problem provides one example of such a theory. While this theory has a default rule for inferring the weight of an end table, it also has a rule for computing weights from the known density and volume. Thus, the theory will conclude two different weights for a given end table provided that its density and volume are known, and provided that these are inconsistent with the default assumption about its weight. In such cases, it is possible to construct inconsistent explanations for a single training example. Furthermore, if two different training examples of the same concept are explained in inconsistent terms (e.g., by utilizing one default assumption for one example, and some other assumptions for the second example), difficulties will certainly arise in merging the resulting generalizations. Because of this, and because default assumptions are commonplace in theories of many domains, the problem of dealing with inconsistent theories and inconsistent explanations is also an important one for future research.

4.2.2 Combining explanation-based and similarity-based methods

While EBG infers concept definitions deductively from a single example, similarity-based methods infer concept definitions inductively from a number of training examples. It seems clearly desirable to develop combined methods that would utilize both a domain theory and multiple training examples to infer concept definitions. This kind of combined approach to generalization will probably be essential in domains where only imperfect theories are available.

Although few results have been achieved in combining explanation-based and similarity-based methods, a number of researchers have begun to consider this issue. Lebowitz (Lebowitz, 1985) is exploring methods for combining similarity-based methods and explanation-based methods in his UNIMEM system. UNIMEM examines a database of the voting records of congresspersons, searching for empirical, similarity-based generalizations (e.g., midwestern congresspersons vote in favor of farm subsidies). The system then attempts to verify these empirical generalizations by explaining them in terms of a domain theory (e.g. explaining how midwestern congresspersons satisfy the goal concept 'people who favor farm subsidies'). This approach has the advantage that the similarity-based techniques can be used to generate a candidate set of possible generalizations from a large number of potentially noisy training examples. Once such empirical generalizations are formulated, explanation-based methods can help prune and refine them by using other knowledge in the system.

Whereas Lebowitz's approach involves applying similarity-based generalization followed by explanation-based methods, an alternative approach is to first apply explanation-based methods to each training example, then to combine the resulting generalized examples using a similarity-based generalization technique. Consider, for example, using the version space method[14] to combine the results of explanation-based generalizations of a number of training examples (Mitchell, 1984). Since the explanation-based generalization of a positive training example constitutes a sufficient condition for the goal concept, this can be used as a generalized positive example to refine (generalize) the specific boundary set of the version space. Similarly, one could imagine generalizing negative training examples using explanation-based generalization, by explaining why they are not members of the goal concept. The resulting generalized negative example could then be used to refine (specialize) the general boundary set of the version space. Thus, while this combined method still suffers the main disadvantage of similarity-based methods (i.e., it makes inductive leaps based on its generalization language, which it cannot justify), it converges more rapidly on a final concept definition because it employs EBG to generalize each training example.

Kedar-Cabelli (1984, 1985) proposes an alternative method for combining the results of explanation-based generalizations from multiple training examples. This method, Purpose-Directed Analogy, involves constructing an explanation of one example by analogy with an explanation of a familiar example, then combining the two explanations to produce a general concept definition based on both. Given explanations for two different examples, the proposed system combines the explanations as follows: Common portions of the two explanations remain unaltered in the combined explanation. Differing portions either become disjunctive subexpressions in the combined explanation, or are generalized to the next more specific common subexpression in the explanation. For example, given an explanation that a blue, ceramic mug is a CUP, and a second example of a white styrofoam cup, the explanation of the first example is used to construct by analogy an explanation for the

second example. The two resulting explanations may differ in how they explain that the two example cups are GRASPABLE (assume the second is GRASPABLE because it has a handle, whereas the first example cup is GRASPABLE because it is conical). In this case, a generalization of the two explanations would include a disjunction, that either the conical shape, or a handle, makes it graspable. That, along with the common features of the two objects in the combined explanation structure leads to the generalization that cups include objects which are concave upward, have a flat bottom, are light, and have either a conical shape or a handle. Alternatively, the combined explanation would retain only the next most-specific common subexpression, GRASPABLE, which would lead to a slightly more general, yet less operational, definition of a cup. Thus, this method of combining explanations of multiple examples provides a principled method for introducing disjunctions where needed into the common generalization of the two examples.

The three methods discussed above for combining similarity-based and explanation-based generalization offer differing advantages. The first method uses similarity-based generalization to determine empirical generalizations which may then be validated and refined by explanation-based methods. The second method involves employing a similarity-based method to combine the results of explanation-based generalizations from multiple examples. It suffers the disadvantage that this combination of methods still produces unjustified generalizations. The third method merges the explanations of multiple examples in order to produce a combined generalization that is justified in terms of the merged explanations. More research is required on these and other possible methods for employing explanation-based methods when multiple training examples are available.

4.2.3 Formulating generalization tasks

The above discussion focuses on research issues within the framework of explanation-based generalization. An equally important set of research issues has to do with how such methods for generalization will be used as subcomponents of larger systems that improve their performance at some given task. As our understanding of generalization methods advances, questions about how to construct performance systems that incorporate generalization mechanisms will become increasingly important.

One key issue to consider in this regard is how generalization tasks are initially formulated. In other words, where do the inputs to the EBG method (the goal concept, the domain theory, the operationality criterion) come from? Is it possible to build a system that automatically formulates its own generalization tasks and these inputs? Is it possible to build learning systems that automatically shift their focus of attention from one learning problem to the next as required? What kind of knowledge must be transmitted between the performance system and the learning system to enable the automatic formulation of generalization tasks?

---

[14] The version space method (Mitchell, 1978) is a similarity-based generalization method based on summarizing the alternative plausible concept definitions by maintaining two sets: the 'specific' set contains the set of most specific concept definitions consistent with the observed data, and the 'general' set contains the most general concept definitions consistent with the data. All other plausible concept definitions lie between these two sets in the general-to-specific ordering over concept definitions.

4.2.4 Using contextual knowledge to solve the generalization task

Above we have discussed some approaches to automatically formulating learning tasks, given knowledge of the performance task for which the learning takes place. In cases where the learner formulates its own learning task, information about how and why the task was formulated can provide important guidance in solving the learning task. Keller's (1986) METALEX system provides an example of how such information can be used in guiding learning. Like LEX2, METALEX addresses the learning task of operationalizing the goal concept USEFUL-OP3. It takes as input a procedural representation of the *performance task* to be improved (the calculus problem solver), a specification of the *performance objectives* to be achieved ('minimize problem solving time') and knowledge of the *performance improvement plan* (search space pruning via filtering), which is a record of how the operationalization task was originally formulated. METALEX uses this additional knowledge about the context in which its learning task was formulated to guide its search for an operational transformation of the goal concept. Specifically, it executes the calculus problem solver using the initial (and subsequent intermediary) definitions of the goal concept to collect diagnostic information which aids in operationalizing the goal concept if performance objectives are not satisfied.

In effect, the performance task and performance objective inputs required by METALEX elaborate on the operationality criterion required by the EBG method. Instead of evaluating operationality in terms of a binary-valued predicate over concept definitions (as in EBG), METALEX evaluates the *degree* of operationality of the concept definition in relation to the performance task and objective. This ability to make a more sophisticated analysis of operationality enables METALEX to make important distinctions among alternative concept definitions. For example, because METALEX uses approximating (non truth-preserving) transforms to modify the goal concept, it can generate concept definitions that only approximate the goal concept. In such cases, METALEX is able to determine whether such an approximate concept definition is desirable based on the degree to which it helps improve the performance objectives.

As the first sections of this paper demonstrate, explanation-based generalization methods offer significant promise in attempts to build computer models of learning systems. Significant progress has been made in understanding explanation-based generalization, especially for problems in which the learner possesses a complete and correct theory. As the final section illustrates, much more remains to be discovered about how a learner can use what it already knows to guide the acquisition of new knowledge.

Again, little work has been devoted to these issues. The SOAR system (Laird et al., 1984, Laird et al., 1986) is one example of a learning system that formulates its own generalization tasks. Each time that SOAR encounters and solves a subgoal, it formulates the generalization problem of inferring the general conditions under which it can reuse the solution to this subgoal. SOAR then utilizes a technique closely related to explanation-based generalization, called *implicit generalization* (Laird et al., 1986), to infer these subgoal preconditions.

A second research effort which confronts the problem of formulating learning tasks is Keller's research on *contextual learning* (Keller, 1983, 1985, 1986). In this work, Keller suggests how a problem solving system could itself formulate generalization problems such as those addressed by the LEX2 system. In particular, he shows how the task of learning the goal concept USEFUL-OP3 arises as a subgoal in the process of planning to improve performance at solving calculus problems. By reasoning from a top-level goal of improving the efficiency of the problem solver, the method derives the subgoal of introducing a filter to prune the search moves that it considers. The definition of this filter includes the specification that it is to allow only problem solving steps that are 'useful' (i.e., that lead toward solutions). The subgoal of introducing this filter leads, in turn, to the problem of operationalizing the definition of 'useful' (i.e., to the subgoal corresponding to the LEX2 generalization task).

Recent work by Kedar-Cabelli (1985) also addresses the problem of formulating learning tasks. In this work, Kedar-Cabelli proposes a system to automatically formulate definitions of goal concepts in the domain of artifacts. In particular, the proposed system derives functional definitions of artifacts (e.g., CUP) from information about the purpose for which agents use them (e.g., to satisfy their thirst). Given two different purposes for which an agent might use a cup (e.g., as an ornament, versus to satisfy thirst), two different functional definitions can be derived.[15] To derive the functional definition of the artifact, the proposed system first computes a plan of actions that leads to satisfying the agent's goal. For example, if the agent's goal is to satisfy thirst, then this plan might be to POUR the liquids into the cup, GRASP the cup with the liquid in order to LIFT, and finally DRINK the liquids. In order to be used as part of this plan, the artifact must satisfy the preconditions of those plan actions in which it is involved. These preconditions form the functional definition of a cup: an open-vessel, which is stable, graspable, liftable. Thus, formulating functional definitions of artifacts is accomplished by analyzing the role that the artifact plays in facilitating the goal of some agent.

[15] This extends Winston's work (see Section 3.1), in that it can derive its own goal concept from a given purpose.

It then produces as output a generalized schema for KIDNAPPING. The KIDNAPPING schema contains only the relevant details of the kidnapping (e.g., that three people are involved: Person A who wants money, Person B who has money and Person C who is valued by Person B), but none of the irrelevant details (e.g., that Person C wears blue jeans).

DeJong's system uses a generalization method that closely parallels the EBG method. Although there is no direct counterpart to the goal concept in DeJong's system, the goal concept can be thought of as 'the class of action sequences that achieve personal goal X for actor Y.' For the kidnapping story, the actor's personal goal is 'attainment of wealth.' The system constructs an explanation for how the actions in the story lead to the kidnapper's 'attainment of wealth' as a by-product of the story-understanding process. During the story parse, *data dependency links* are created to connect actions in the story with the inference rules that are used by the parser in interpreting the actions. The set of inference rules constitutes a domain theory for DeJong's system, and includes knowledge about the goals and plans of human actors, as well as causal knowledge used to set up and verify expectations for future actions. The network of all the data dependency links created during the story parse is called an *inference justification network*, and corresponds to an explanation for the action sequence.

Generalization of the inference justification network is carried out by replacing general entities for the specific objects and events referenced in the network. As with the EBG method, the entities in the inference justification network are generalized as far as possible while maintaining the correctness of the data dependency links.[16] Then a new schema is constructed from the network. The issue of operationality enters into the process of determining an appropriate level of generalization for the schema constructed from the network. Should, for example, a generalized schema be created to describe the KIDNAPPING action sequence or the more general action sequences representing BARGAINING-FOR-MONEY or BARGAINING-FOR-WEALTH? All of these schemata explain the actions in the example story. DeJong cites several criteria to use in determining the level of generalization at which to represent the new schema (DeJong, 1983). The criteria include such considerations as: 1) Will the generalized schema be useful in processing stories in the future, or does the schema summarize an event that is unlikely to recur? 2) Are the preconditions for schema activation commonly achievable? 3) Will the new schema represent a more efficient method of achieving personal goals than existing schemata? Note that these schema generalization criteria roughly correspond to the operationalization criteria used in the EBG method. Because the generalized schemata are subsequently used for a story-understanding task, the operationality criteria pertain to that task.

[16] It is unclear whether the system regresses its equivalent of the goal concept through the inference justification network.

Acknowledgments

The perspective on Explanation-Based Generalization reported here has arisen from discussions over a period of time with a number of people in the Machine Learning Group at Rutgers and elsewhere. Discussions with the following people have been particularly useful in formulating the ideas presented here: Alex Borgida, Gerry DeJong, Thomas Dietterich, Thorne McCarty, Sridhar Mahadevan, Jack Mostow, Michael Sims, Prasad Tadepalli, Paul Utgoff, and Keith Williamson. We also thank the following people for providing useful comments on an earlier draft of this paper: Pat Langley, Sridhar Mahadevan, Jack Mostow, Louis Steinberg, Prasad Tadepalli, and Keith Williamson.

This material is based on work supported by the Defense Advanced Research Projects Agency under Research Contract N00014-81-K-0394, by the National Science Foundation under grants DCS83-51523 and MCS80-08889, by the National Institutes of Health under grant RR-64309, by GTE under grant GTE840917, and by a Rutgers University Graduate Fellowship. The views and conclusions contained in this document are those of the authors and should not be interpreted as necessarily representing the official views or policies of these sponsors.

Appendix

The appendix describes DeJong's research on explanation-based generalization. In particular, it casts the work on learning schemata for story understanding in terms of the EBG method. In addition to this project, there has been a great deal of recent research on explanation-based generalization, including (DeJong, 1985; Ellman, 1985; Mooney, 1985; O'Rorke, 1985; Rajamoney, 1985; Schooley, 1985; Segre, 1985; Shavlik, 1985; Sims, 1985; Watanabe, 1985; Williamson, 1985). DeJong (1981, 1983) developed one of the earliest successful explanation-based generalization systems as part of his research on *explanatory schema acquisition*. DeJong is interested in the problem of learning schemata for use in natural language story understanding. DeJong's system takes as input an example story and produces as output a generalized schema representing the stereotypical action sequence that is instantiated in the story. For example, the system can process the following story (adapted from G. DeJong, personal communication, November 16, 1984):

Fred is Mary's father. Fred is rich. Mary wears blue jeans. John approached Mary. He pointed a gun at her. He told her to get into his car. John drove Mary to the hotel. He locked her in his room. John called Fred. He told Fred he had Mary. He promised not to harm her if Fred gave him $250,000 at Treno's Restaurant. Fred delivered the money. Mary arrived home in a taxi.

Table 5. The wealth acquisition schema generalization problem: Learning about ways to achieve wealth (DeJong, 1983)

Given:

• *Goal Concept:* The class of action sequences (i.e., a general schema) by which actor x can achieve wealth:

WEALTH-ACQUISITION-ACTION-SEQUENCE (<a1, a2, ..., an>, x) ⇒
NOT (WEALTHY (x, s0)) ∧ WEALTHY (x, EXECUTE (x, <a1, a2, ..., an>, s0))

where

<a1, a2, ..., an> is an action sequence; x is the actor; s0 is the actor's current state; and EXE-
CUTE (a, b, c) returns the state resulting from the execution of action sequence b by actor a in state
c.

• *Training Example:* The kidnapping story:
FATHER-OF (FRED, MARY) ∧ WEALTHY (FRED)
∧ DESPERATE (JOHN) ∧ WEARS (MARY, BLUE-JEANS)
∧ APPROACHES (JOHN, MARY, s0) ∧ POINTS-GUN-AT (JOHN, MARY, s1)
...
∧ EXCHANGES (FRED, JOHN, $250000, MARY, s12)

• *Domain Theory:* Rules about human interaction, and knowledge about human goals, intentions,
desires, etc.:
FATHER-OF (person1, person2) → LOVES (person1, person2)
∧ VALUES (person1, person2)

WEALTHY (person) → HAS (person, $250000)
EXCHANGES (person 1, person2, object1, object2) ⇒
NOT (HAS (person1, object1)) ∧ VALUES (person1, object1)
∧ NOT (HAS (person2, object2)) ∧ VALUES (person2, object2)
∧ HAS (person1, object2) ∧ HAS (person2, object1)

• *Operationality Criterion:* Acquired generalization (i.e., the generalized schema) must satisfy the requirements for future usefulness in story-understanding (see text).

Determine:

• A generalization of training example (i.e., a generalized schema) that is a sufficient concept definition for the goal concept (i.e., that is a specialization of the wealth acquisition schema) and that
satisfies the operationality criterion.

Table 5 summarizes the explanation-based generalization problem addressed by
the explanatory schema acquisition research.

References

Borgida, A., Mitchell, T. & Williamson, K.E. (1985). Learning improved integrity constraints and schemas from exceptions in data and knowledge bases. In M.L. Brodie & J. Mylopoulos (Eds.), *On knowledge base management systems.* New York, NY: Springer Verlag.

DeJong, G. (1981). Generalizations based on explanations. *Proceedings of the Seventh International Joint Conference on Artificial Intelligence* (pp. 67–69). Vancouver, B.C., Canada: Morgan Kaufmann.

DeJong, G. (1983). Acquiring schemata through understanding and generalizing plans. *Proceedings of the Eighth International Joint Conference on Artificial Intelligence* (pp. 462–464). Karlsruhe, West Germany: Morgan Kaufmann.

DeJong, G. (1985). A brief overview of explanatory schema acquisition. *Proceedings of the Third International Machine Learning Workshop.* Skytop, PA, June.

DeJong, G., & Mooney, R. (in press). Explanation-based learning: An alternative view. *Machine learning.*

Dietterich, T.G., London, B., Clarkson, K., & Dromey, G. (1982). Learning and Inductive Inference. In P.R. Cohen, & E.A. Feigenbaum (Eds.), *The handbook of artificial intelligence.* Los Altos, CA: William Kaufmann, Inc.

Dijkstra, E.W. (1976). *A discipline of programming.* Englewood Cliffs, NJ: Prentice Hall.

Ellman, T. (1985). Explanation-based learning in logic circuit design. *Proceedings of the Third International Machine Learning Workshop.* Skytop, PA, June.

Fikes, R., Hart, P., & Nilsson, N.J. (1972). Learning and executing generalized robot plans. *Artificial intelligence, 3,* 251–288. Also in B.L. Webber & N.J. Nilsson (Eds.), *Readings in artificial intelligence.*

Kedar-Cabelli, S.T. (1984). *Analogy with purpose in legal reasoning from precedents.* (Technical Report LRP-TR-17). Laboratory for Computer Science Research, Rutgers University, New Brunswick, NJ.

Kedar-Cabelli, S.T. (1985). Purpose-directed analogy. *Proceedings of the Cognitive Science Society Conference.* Irvine, CA: Morgan Kaufmann.

Keller, R.M. (1983). Learning by re-expressing concepts for efficient recognition. *Proceedings of the National Conference on Artificial Intelligence* (pp 182–186). Washington, D.C.: Morgan Kaufmann.

Keller, R.M. (1985). Development of a framework for contextual concept learning. *Proceedings of the Third International Machine Learning Workshop.* Skytop, PA, June.

Keller, R.M. (1986). Contextual learning: A performance-based model of concept acquisition. Unpublished doctoral dissertation, Rutgers University.

Kibler, D., & Porter, B. (1985). A comparison of analytic and experimental goal regression for machine learning. *Proceedings of the Ninth International Joint Conference on Artificial Intelligence.* Los Angeles, CA: Morgan Kaufmann.

Laird, J.E., Rosenbloom, P.S., Newell, A. (1984). Toward chunking as a general learning mechanism. (pp 188–192). *Proceedings of the National Conference on Artificial Intelligence.* Austin, TX: Morgan Kaufmann.

Laird, J.E., Rosenbloom, P.S., & Newell, A. (1986). SOAR: The architecture of a general learning mechanism. *Machine learning, 1,* 11–46.

Lebowitz, M. (1985). Concept learning in a rich input domain: Generalization-based memory. In R.S. Michalski, J.G. Carbonell & T.M. Mitchell (Eds.), *Machine learning: An artificial intelligence approach,* Vol. 2. Los Altos, CA: Morgan Kaufmann.

Mahadevan, S. (1985). Verification-based learning: A generalization strategy for inferring problem-decomposition methods. *Proceedings of the Ninth International Joint Conference on Artificial Intelligence.* Los Angeles, CA: Morgan Kaufmann.

Michalski, R.S. (1983). A theory and methodology of inductive learning. *Artificial intelligence, 20,* 111–161. Also in R.S. Michalski, J.G. Carbonell & T.M. Mitchell (Eds.), *Machine learning: An artificial intelligence approach.*

Minton, S. (1984). Constraint-based generalization: Learning game-playing plans from single examples. (pp 251–254). *Proceedings of the National Conference on Artificial Intelligence.* Austin, TX: Morgan Kaufmann.

Mitchell, T.M. (1978). *Version spaces: An approach to concept learning.* PhD thesis, Department of Electrical Engineering. Stanford University. Also Stanford CS reports STAN-CS-78-711, HPP-79-2.

Mitchell, T.M. (1980). *The need for biases in learning generalizations* (Technical Report CBM-TR-117). Rutgers University, New Brunswick, NJ.

Mitchell, T.M. (1982). Generalization as search. *Artificial intelligence*, March, *18*(2), 203–226.

Mitchell, T.M. (1983). Learning and Problem Solving. *Proceedings of the Eighth International Joint Conference on Artificial Intelligence* (pp 1139–1151). Karlsruhe, West Germany: Morgan Kaufmann.

Mitchell, T.M. (1984). Toward combining empirical and analytic methods for learning heuristics. In A. Elithorn & R. Banerji (Eds.), *Human and artificial intelligence*. Amsterdam: North-Holland Publishing Co. Also Rutgers Computer Science Department Technical Report LCSR-TR-27, 1981.

Mitchell, T.M., Utgoff, P.E., & Banerji, R.B. (1983). Learning by experimentation: Acquiring and refining problem-solving heuristics. In R.S. Michalski, J.G. Carbonell & T.M. Mitchell (Eds.), *Machine learning*. Palo Alto, CA: Tioga.

Mitchell, T.M., Mahadevan, S., & Steinberg, L. (1985). *LEAP*: A learning apprentice for VLSI design. *Proceedings of the Ninth International Joint Conference on Artificial Intelligence* (pp. 573–580). Los Angeles, CA: Morgan Kaufmann.

Mooney, R. (1985). Generalizing explanations of narratives into schemata. *Proceedings of the Third International Machine Learning Workshop*. Skytop, PA.

Mostow, D.J. (1981). *Mechanical transformation of task heuristics into operational procedures*. PhD thesis, Department of Computer Science, Carnegie-Mellon University, Pittsburgh, PA.

Mostow, D.J. (1983). Machine transformation of advice into a heuristic search procedure. In R.S. Michalski, J.G. Carbonell, & T.M. Mitchell (Eds.), *Machine learning*. Palo Alto, CA: Tioga.

Nilsson, N.J. (1980). *Principles of artificial intelligence*. Palo Alto, CA: Tioga.

O'Rorke, P. (1984). Generalization for explanation-based schema acquisition. *Proceedings of the National Conference on Artificial Intelligence* (pp 260–263). Austin, TX: Morgan Kaufmann.

O'Rorke, P. (1985). Recent progress on the 'mathematician's apprentice' project. *Proceedings of the Third International Machine Learning Workshop*. Skytop, PA.

Quinlan, J.R. (1985). The effect of noise on concept learning. In R.S. Michalski, J.G. Carbonell & T.M. Mitchell (Eds.), *Machine learning: An artificial intelligence approach*, Vol. 2. Los Altos, CA: Morgan Kaufmann. Modified, also in *Proceedings of the Second International Machine Learning Workshop*.

Rajamoney, S. (1985). Conceptual knowledge acquisition through directed experimentation. *Proceedings of the Third International Machine Learning Workshop*. Skytop, PA.

Salzberg, S., & Atkinson, D.J. (1984). Learning by building causal explanations. *Proceedings of the Sixth European Conference on Artificial Intelligence* (pp 497–500). Pisa, Italy.

Schank, R.C. (1982). Looking at learning. *Proceedings of the Fifth European Conference on Artificial Intelligence* (pp 11–18). Paris, France.

Schooley, P. (1985). Learning state evaluation functions. *Proceedings of the Third International Machine Learning Workshop*. Skytop, PA.

Segre, A.M. (1985). Explanation-based manipulator learning. *Proceedings of the Third International Machine Learning Workshop*. Skytop, PA.

Shavlik, J.W. (1985). Learning classical physics. *Proceedings of the Third International Machine Learning Workshop*. Skytop, PA.

Sims, M. (1985). An investigation of the nature of mathematical discovery. *Proceedings of the Third International Machine Learning Workshop*. Skytop, PA.

Silver, B. (1983). Learning equation solving methods from worked examples. *Proceedings of the Second International Machine Learning Workshop* (pp. 99–104). Urbana, IL.

Soloway, E.M. (1978). *Learning = interpretation + generalization: A case study in knowledge-directed learning*. PhD thesis, Department of Computer and Information Science, University of Massachusetts, Amherst. Computer and Information Science Report COINS TR-78-13.

Tadepalli, P.V. (1985). Learning in intractable domains. *Proceedings of the Third International Machine Learning Workshop*. Skytop, PA.

Utgoff, P.E. (1983). Adjusting bias in concept learning. *Proceedings of the Eighth International Conference on Artificial Intelligence* (pp. 447–449). Karlsruhe, West Germany: Morgan Kaufmann.

Utgoff, P.E. (1984). *Shift of bias for inductive concept learning*. PhD thesis, Department of Computer Science, Rutgers University, New Brunswick, NJ

Utgoff, P.E. (1985). Shift of bias for inductive concept learning. In R.S. Michalski, J.G. Carbonell & T.M. Mitchell (Eds.), *Machine learning: An artificial intelligence approach*, Vol. 2. Los Altos, CA: Morgan Kaufmann. Modified, also in *Proceedings of the Second International Machine Learning Workshop*.

Waldinger, R. (1977). Achieving several goals simultaneously. In E. Elcock & D. Michie, D. (Eds.), *Machine intelligence 8*, London: Ellis Horwood, Limited. Also in B.L. Webber & N.J. Nilsson (Eds.), *Readings in artificial intelligence*.

Watanabe, M. (1985). Learning implementation rules in operating-conditions depending on states in VLSI design. *Proceedings of the Third International Machine Learning Workshop*. Skytop, PA.

Williamson, K. (1985). Learning from exceptions to constraints in databases. *Proceedings of the Third International Machine Learning Workshop*. Skytop, PA.

Winston, P.H. (1985). Learning by augmenting rules and accumulating censors. In R.S. Michalski, J.G. Carbonell & T.M. Mitchell (Eds.), *Machine learning: An artificial intelligence approach*, Vol. 2. Los Altos, CA: Morgan Kaufmann.

Winston, P.H. Binford, T.O., Katz, B., & Lowry, M. (1983). Learning physical descriptions from functional definitions, examples, and precedents. *National Conference on Artificial Intelligence* (pp. 433–439). Washington, D.C.: Morgan Kaufmann.

Learning Internal Representations by Error Propagation

D. E. RUMELHART, G. E. HINTON, and R. J. WILLIAMS

THE PROBLEM

We now have a rather good understanding of simple two-layer associative networks in which a set of input patterns arriving at an input layer are mapped directly to a set of output patterns at an output layer. Such networks have no *hidden* units. They involve only *input* and *output* units. In these cases there is no *internal representation*. The coding provided by the external world must suffice. These networks have proved useful in a wide variety of applications (cf. Chapters 2, 17, and 18). Perhaps the essential character of such networks is that they map similar input patterns to similar output patterns. This is what allows these networks to make reasonable generalizations and perform reasonably on patterns that have never before been presented. The similarity of patterns in a PDP system is determined by their overlap. The overlap in such networks is determined outside the learning system itself—by whatever produces the patterns.

The constraint that similar input patterns lead to similar outputs can lead to an inability of the system to learn certain mappings from input to output. Whenever the representation provided by the outside world is such that the similarity structure of the input and output patterns is very different, a network without internal representations (i.e., a network without hidden units) will be unable to perform the necessary mappings. A classic example of this case is the *exclusive-or* (XOR) problem illustrated in Table 1. Here we see that those patterns which overlap least are supposed to generate identical output values. This problem and many others like it cannot be performed by networks without hidden units with which to create their own internal representations of the input patterns. It is interesting to note that had the input patterns contained a third input taking the value 1 whenever the first two have value 1 as shown in Table 2, a two-layer system would be able to solve the problem.

Minsky and Papert (1969) have provided a very careful analysis of conditions under which such systems are capable of carrying out the required mappings. They show that in a large number of interesting cases, networks of this kind are incapable of solving the problems. On the other hand, as Minsky and Papert also pointed out, if there is a layer of simple perceptron-like hidden units, as shown in Figure 1, with which the original input pattern can be augmented, there is always a recoding (i.e., an internal representation) of the input patterns in the hidden units in which the similarity of the patterns among the hidden units can support any required mapping from the input to the output units. Thus, if we have the right connections from the input units to a large enough set of hidden units, we can always find a representation that will perform any mapping from input to output through these hidden units. In the case of the XOR problem, the addition of a feature that detects the conjunction of the input units changes the similarity

TABLE 1

Input Patterns		Output Patterns
00	→	0
01	→	1
10	→	1
11	→	0

TABLE 2

Input Patterns		Output Patterns
000	→	0
010	→	1
100	→	1
111	→	0

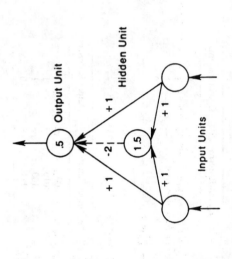

FIGURE 2. A simple XOR network with one hidden unit. See text for explanation.

The existence of networks such as this illustrates the potential power of hidden units and internal representations. The problem, as noted by Minsky and Papert, is that whereas there is a very simple guaranteed learning rule for all problems that can be solved without hidden units, namely, the perceptron convergence procedure (or the variation due originally to Widrow and Hoff, 1960, which we call the delta rule; see Chapter 11), there is no equally powerful rule for learning in networks with hidden units. There have been three basic responses to this lack. One response is represented by competitive learning (Chapter 5) in which simple *unsupervised* learning rules are employed so that useful hidden units develop. Although these approaches are promising, there is no external force to *insure* that hidden units appropriate for the required mapping are developed. The second response is to simply *assume* an internal representation that, on some a priori grounds, seems reasonable. This is the tack taken in the chapter on verb learning (Chapter 18) and in the interactive activation model of word perception (McClelland & Rumelhart, 1981; Rumelhart & McClelland, 1982). The third approach is to attempt to *develop* a learning procedure capable of learning an internal representation adequate for performing the task at hand. One such development is presented in the discussion of Boltzmann machines in Chapter 7. As we have seen, this procedure involves the use of stochastic units, requires the network to reach equilibrium in two different phases, and is limited to symmetric networks. Another recent approach, also employing stochastic units, has been developed by Barto (1985) and various of his colleagues (cf. Barto

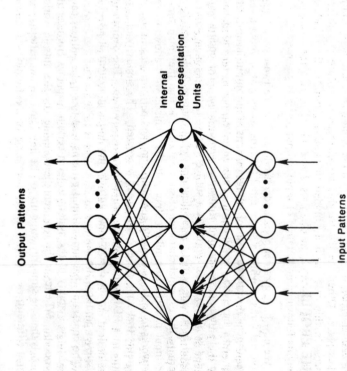

FIGURE 1. A multilayer network. In this case the information coming to the input units is *recoded* into an internal representation and the outputs are generated by the internal representation rather than by the original pattern. Input patterns can always be encoded, if there are enough hidden units, in a form so that the appropriate output pattern can be generated from any input pattern.

structure of the patterns sufficiently to allow the solution to be learned. As illustrated in Figure 2, this can be done with a single hidden unit. The numbers on the arrows represent the strengths of the connections among the units. The numbers written in the circles represent the thresholds of the units. The value of +1.5 for the threshold of the hidden unit insures that it will be turned on only when both input units are on. The value 0.5 for the output unit insures that it will turn on only when it receives a net positive input greater than 0.5. The weight of −2 from the hidden unit to the output unit insures that the output unit will not come on when both input units are on. Note that from the point of view of the output unit, the hidden unit is treated as simply another input unit. It is as if the input patterns consisted of three rather than two units.

& Anandan, 1985). In this chapter we present another alternative that works with deterministic units, that involves only local computations, and that is a clear generalization of the delta rule. We call this the *generalized delta rule*. From other considerations, Parker (1985) has independently derived a similar generalization, which he calls *learning-logic*. Le Cun (1985) has also studied a roughly similar learning scheme. In the remainder of this chapter we first derive the generalized delta rule, then we illustrate its use by providing some results of our simulations, and finally we indicate some further generalizations of the basic idea.

THE GENERALIZED DELTA RULE

The learning procedure we propose involves the presentation of a set of pairs of input and output patterns. The system first uses the input vector to produce its own output vector and then compares this with the *desired output*, or *target* vector. If there is no difference, no learning takes place. Otherwise the weights are changed to reduce the difference. In this case, with no hidden units, this generates the standard delta rule as described in Chapters 2 and 11. The rule for changing weights following presentation of input/output pair p is given by

$$\Delta_p w_{ji} = \eta (t_{pj} - o_{pj}) i_{pi} = \eta \delta_{pj} i_{pi} \qquad (1)$$

where t_{pj} is the target input for jth component of the output pattern for pattern p, o_{pj} is the jth element of the actual output pattern produced by the presentation of input pattern p, i_{pi} is the value of the ith element of the input pattern. $\delta_{pj} = t_{pj} - o_{pj}$, and $\Delta_p w_{ji}$ is the change to be made to the weight from the ith to the jth unit following presentation of pattern p.

The delta rule and gradient descent. There are many ways of deriving this rule. For present purposes, it is useful to see that for linear units it minimizes the squares of the differences between the actual and the desired output values summed over the output units and all pairs of input/output vectors. One way to show this is to show that the derivative of the error measure with respect to each weight is proportional to the weight change dictated by the delta rule, with negative constant of proportionality. This corresponds to performing steepest descent on a surface in weight space whose height at any point in weight space is equal to the error measure. (Note that some of the following sections

are written in italics. These sections constitute informal derivations of the claims made in the surrounding text and can be omitted by the reader who finds such derivations tedious.)

To be more specific, then, let

$$E_p = \frac{1}{2} \sum_j (t_{pj} - o_{pj})^2 \qquad (2)$$

be our measure of the error on input/output pattern p and let $E = \sum_p E_p$ be our overall measure of the error. We wish to show that the delta rule implements a gradient descent in E when the units are linear. We will proceed by simply showing that

$$-\frac{\partial E_p}{\partial w_{ji}} = \delta_{pj} i_{pi},$$

which is proportional to $\Delta_p w_{ji}$ as prescribed by the delta rule. When there are no hidden units it is straightforward to compute the relevant derivative. For this purpose we use the chain rule to write the derivative as the product of two parts: the derivative of the error with respect to the output of the unit times the derivative of the output with respect to the weight.

$$\frac{\partial E_p}{\partial w_{ji}} = \frac{\partial E_p}{\partial o_{pj}} \frac{\partial o_{pj}}{\partial w_{ji}}. \qquad (3)$$

The first part tells how the error changes with the output of the jth unit and the second part tells how much changing w_{ji} changes that output. Now, the derivatives are easy to compute. First, from Equation 2

$$\frac{\partial E_p}{\partial o_{pj}} = -(t_{pj} - o_{pj}) = -\delta_{pj}. \qquad (4)$$

Not surprisingly, the contribution of unit u_i to the error is simply proportional to δ_{pj}. Moreover, since we have linear units,

$$o_{pj} = \sum_i w_{ji} i_{pi}, \qquad (5)$$

from which we conclude that

$$\frac{\partial o_{pj}}{\partial w_{ji}} = i_{pi},$$

Thus, substituting back into Equation 3, we see that

$$-\frac{\partial E_p}{\partial w_{ji}} = \delta_{pj} i_{pi} \qquad (6)$$

$$net_{pj} = \sum_i w_{ji} o_{pi}$$
(7)

where $o_i = i_i$ if unit i is an input unit. Thus, a semilinear activation function is one in which

$$o_{pj} = f_j(net_{pj})$$
(8)

and f is differentiable and nondecreasing. The generalized delta rule works if the network consists of units having semilinear activation functions. Notice that linear threshold units do not satisfy the requirement because their derivative is infinite at the threshold and zero elsewhere.

To get the correct generalization of the delta rule, we must set

$$\Delta_p w_{ji} \propto -\frac{\partial E_p}{\partial w_{ji}},$$
(9)

where E is the same sum-squared error function defined earlier. As in the standard delta rule it is again useful to see this derivative as resulting from the product of two parts: one part reflecting the change in error as a function of the change in the net input to the unit and one part representing the effect of changing a particular weight on the net input. Thus we can write

$$\frac{\partial E_p}{\partial w_{ji}} = \frac{\partial E_p}{\partial net_{pj}} \frac{\partial net_{pj}}{\partial w_{ji}}.$$

By Equation 7 we see that the second factor is

$$\frac{\partial net_{pj}}{\partial w_{ji}} = \frac{\partial}{\partial w_{ji}} \sum_k w_{jk} o_{pk} = o_{pi}.$$
(10)

Now let us define

$$\delta_{pj} = -\frac{\partial E_p}{\partial net_{pj}}.$$

(By comparing this to Equation 4, note that this is consistent with the definition of δ_{pj} used in the original delta rule for linear units since $o_{pj} = net_{pj}$ when unit u_i is linear.) Equation 9 thus has the equivalent form

$$-\frac{\partial E_p}{\partial w_{ji}} = \delta_{pj} o_{pi}.$$

This says that to implement gradient descent in E we should make our weight changes according to

$$\Delta_p w_{ji} = \eta \delta_{pj} o_{pi},$$
(11)

---

as desired. Now, combining this with the observation that

$$\frac{\partial E}{\partial w_{ji}} = \sum_p \frac{\partial E_p}{\partial w_{ji}}$$

should lead us to conclude that the net change in w_{ji} after one complete cycle of pattern presentations is proportional to this derivative and hence that the delta rule implements a gradient descent in E. In fact, this is strictly true only if the values of the weights are not changed during this cycle. By changing the weights after each pattern is presented we depart to some extent from a true gradient descent in E. Nevertheless, provided the learning rate (i.e., the constant of proportionality) is sufficiently small, this departure will be negligible and the delta rule will implement a very close approximation to gradient descent in sum-squared error. In particular, with small enough learning rate, the delta rule will find a set of weights minimizing this error function.

The delta rule for semilinear activation functions in feedforward networks. We have shown how the standard delta rule essentially implements gradient descent in sum-squared error for linear activation functions. In this case, without hidden units, the error surface is shaped like a bowl with only one minimum, so gradient descent is guaranteed to find the best set of weights. With hidden units, however, it is not so obvious how to compute the derivatives, and the error surface is not concave upwards, so there is the danger of getting stuck in local minima. The main theoretical contribution of this chapter is to show that there is an efficient way of computing the derivatives. The main empirical contribution is to show that the apparently fatal problem of local minima is irrelevant in a wide variety of learning tasks.

At the end of the chapter we show how the generalized delta rule can be applied to arbitrary networks, but, to begin with, we confine ourselves to *layered feedforward* networks. In these networks, the input units are the bottom layer and the output units are the top layer. There can be many layers of hidden units in between, but every unit must send its output to higher layers than its own and must receive its input from lower layers than its own. Given an input vector, the output vector is computed by a forward pass which computes the activity levels of each layer in turn using the already computed activity levels in the earlier layers.

Since we are primarily interested in extending this result to the case with hidden units and since, for reasons outlined in Chapter 2, hidden units with linear activation functions provide no advantage, we begin by generalizing our analysis to the set of nonlinear activation functions which we call *semilinear* (see Chapter 2). A semilinear activation function is one in which the output of a unit is a nondecreasing and differentiable function of the net total output, the unit receiving input along that line and the output of the unit sending activation along that line. In symbols,

$$\Delta_p w_{ji} = \eta \delta_{pj} o_{pi}.$$

The other two equations specify the error signal. Essentially, the determination of the error signal is a recursive process which starts with the output units. If a unit is an output unit, its error signal is very similar to the standard delta rule. It is given by

$$\delta_{pj} = (t_{pj} - o_{pj}) f'_j(net_{pj})$$

where $f'_j(net_{pj})$ is the derivative of the semilinear activation function which maps the total input to the unit to an output value. Finally, the error signal for hidden units for which there is no specified target is determined recursively in terms of the error signals of the units to which it directly connects and the weights of those connections. That is,

$$\delta_{pj} = f'_j(net_{pj}) \sum_k \delta_{pk} w_{kj}$$

whenever the unit is not an output unit.

The application of the generalized delta rule, thus, involves two phases: During the first phase the input is presented and propagated forward through the network to compute the output value o_{pj} for each unit. This output is then compared with the targets, resulting in an error signal δ_{pj} for each output unit. The second phase involves a backward pass through the network (analogous to the initial forward pass) during which the error signal is passed to each unit in the network and the appropriate weight changes are made. This second, backward pass allows the recursive computation of δ as indicated above. The first step is to compute δ for each of the output units. This is simply the difference between the actual and desired output values times the derivative of the squashing function. We can then compute weight changes for all connections that feed into the final layer. After this is done, then compute δ's for all units in the penultimate layer. This propagates the errors back one layer, and the same process can be repeated for every layer. The backward pass has the same computational complexity as the forward pass, and so it is not unduly expensive.

We have now generated a gradient descent method for finding weights in any feedforward network with semilinear units. Before reporting our results with these networks, it is useful to note some further observations. It is interesting that not all weights need be variable. Any number of weights in the network can be fixed. In this case, error is still propagated as before; the fixed weights are simply not

just as in the standard delta rule. The trick is to figure out what δ_{pj} should be for each unit u_j in the network. The interesting result, which we now derive, is that there is a simple recursive computation of these δ's which can be implemented by propagating error signals backward through the network.

To compute $\delta_{pj} = -\frac{\partial E_p}{\partial net_{pj}}$, we apply the chain rule to write this partial derivative as the product of two factors, one factor reflecting the change in error as a function of the output of the unit and one reflecting the change in the output as a function of changes in the input. Thus, we have

$$\delta_{pj} = -\frac{\partial E_p}{\partial net_{pj}} = -\frac{\partial E_p}{\partial o_{pj}} \frac{\partial o_{pj}}{\partial net_{pj}}.$$ (12)

Let us compute the second factor. By Equation 8 we see that

$$\frac{\partial o_{pj}}{\partial net_{pj}} = f'_j(net_{pj}),$$

which is simply the derivative of the squashing function f_j for the jth unit, evaluated at the net input net_{pj} to that unit. To compute the first factor, we consider two cases. First, assume that unit u_j is an output unit of the network. In this case, it follows from the definition of E_p that

$$\frac{\partial E_p}{\partial o_{pj}} = -(t_{pj} - o_{pj}),$$

which is the same result as we obtained with the standard delta rule. Substituting for the two factors in Equation 12, we get

$$\delta_{pj} = (t_{pj} - o_{pj}) f'_j(net_{pj})$$ (13)

for any output unit u_j. If u_j is not an output unit we use the chain rule to write

$$\sum_k \frac{\partial E_p}{\partial net_{pk}} \frac{\partial net_{pk}}{\partial o_{pj}} = \sum_k \frac{\partial E_p}{\partial net_{pk}} \frac{\partial}{\partial o_{pj}} \sum_i w_{ki} o_{pi} = \sum_k \frac{\partial E_p}{\partial net_{pk}} w_{kj} = -\sum_k \delta_{pk} w_{kj}.$$

In this case, substituting for the two factors in Equation 12 yields

$$\delta_{pj} = f'_j(net_{pj}) \sum_k \delta_{pk} w_{kj}$$ (14)

whenever u_j is not an output unit. Equations 13 and 14 give a recursive procedure for computing the δ's for all units in the network, which are then used to compute the weight changes in the network according to Equation 11. This procedure constitutes the generalized delta rule for a feedforward network of semilinear units.

These results can be summarized in three equations. First, the generalized delta rule has exactly the same form as the standard delta rule of Equation 1. The weight on each line should be changed by an amount proportional to the product of an error signal, δ, available to

$$o_{pj} = \frac{1}{1 + e^{-(\sum_i w_{ji}o_{pi} + \theta_j)}} \qquad (15)$$

where θ_j is a bias similar in function to a threshold.[1] In order to apply our learning rule, we need to know the derivative of this function with respect to its total input, net_{pj}, where $net_{pj} = \sum_i w_{ji}o_{pi} + \theta_j$. It is easy to show that this derivative is given by

$$\frac{\partial o_{pj}}{\partial net_{pj}} = o_{pj}(1 - o_{pj}).$$

Thus, for the logistic activation function, the error signal, δ_{pj}, for an output unit is given by

$$\delta_{pj} = (t_{pj} - o_{pj})o_{pj}(1 - o_{pj}),$$

and the error for an arbitrary hidden u_i is given by

$$\delta_{pj} = o_{pj}(1 - o_{pj})\sum_k \delta_{pk}w_{kj}.$$

It should be noted that the derivative, $o_{pj}(1 - o_{pj})$, reaches its maximum for $o_{pj} = 0.5$ and, since $0 \leq o_{pj} \leq 1$, approaches its minimum as o_{pj} approaches zero or one. Since the amount of change in a given weight is proportional to this derivative, weights will be changed most for those units that are near their midrange and, in some sense, not yet committed to being either on or off. This feature, we believe, contributes to the stability of the learning of the system.

One other feature of this activation function should be noted. The system can not actually reach its extreme values of 1 or 0 without infinitely large weights. Therefore, in a practical learning situation in which the desired outputs are binary {0,1}, the system can never actually achieve these values. Therefore, we typically use the values of 0.1 and 0.9 as the targets, even though we will talk as if values of {0,1} are sought.

The learning rate. Our learning procedure requires only that the change in weight be proportional to $\partial E_p/\partial w$. True gradient descent requires that infinitesimal steps be taken. The constant of proportionality is the learning rate in our procedure. The larger this constant, the larger the changes in the weights. For practical purposes we choose a

---

[1] Note that the values of the bias, θ_j, can be learned just like any other weights. We simply imagine that θ_j is the weight from a unit that is always on.

modified. It should also be noted that there is no reason why some output units might not receive inputs from other output units in earlier layers. In this case, those units receive two different kinds of error: that from the direct comparison with the target and that passed through the other output units whose activation it affects. In this case, the correct procedure is to simply add the weight changes dictated by the direct comparison to that propagated back from the other output units.

SIMULATION RESULTS

We now have a learning procedure which could, in principle, evolve a set of weights to produce an arbitrary mapping from input to output. However, the procedure we have produced is a gradient descent procedure and, as such, is bound by all of the problems of any hill climbing procedure—namely, the problem of local maxima or (in our case) minima. Moreover, there is a question of how long it might take a system to learn. Even if we could guarantee that it would eventually find a solution, there is the question of whether our procedure could learn in a reasonable period of time. It is interesting to ask what hidden units the system actually develops in the solution of particular problems. This is the question of what kinds of internal representations the system actually creates. We do not yet have definitive answers to these questions. However, we have carried out many simulations which lead us to be optimistic about the local minima and time questions and to be surprised by the kinds of representations our learning mechanism discovers. Before proceeding with our results, we must describe our simulation system in more detail. In particular, we must specify an activation function and show how the system can compute the derivative of this function.

A useful activation function. In our above derivations the derivative of the activation function of unit u_i, $f'_j(net_j)$, always played a role. This implies that we need an activation function for which a derivative exists. It is interesting to note that the linear threshold function, on which the perceptron is based, is discontinuous and hence will not suffice for the generalized delta rule. Similarly, since a linear system achieves no advantage from hidden units, a linear activation function will not suffice either. Thus, we need a continuous, nonlinear activation function. In most of our experiments we have used the *logistic* activation function in which learning rate that is as large as possible without leading to oscillation. This offers the most rapid learning. One way to increase the learning rate without leading to oscillation is to modify the generalized delta rule to include a *momentum* term. This can be accomplished by the following rule:

$$\Delta w_{ji}(n+1) = \eta(\delta_{pj}o_{pi}) + \alpha\Delta w_{ji}(n) \qquad (16)$$

where the subscript n indexes the presentation number, η is the learning rate, and α is a constant which determines the effect of past weight changes on the current direction of movement in weight space. This provides a kind of momentum in weight space that effectively filters out high-frequency variations of the error-surface in the weight space. This is useful in spaces containing long ravines that are characterized by sharp curvature across the ravine and a gently sloping floor. The sharp curvature tends to cause divergent oscillations across the ravine. To prevent these it is necessary to take very small steps, but this causes very slow progress along the ravine. The momentum filters out the high curvature and thus allows the effective weight steps to be bigger. In most of our simulations α was about 0.9. Our experience has been that we get the same solutions by setting $\alpha = 0$ and reducing the size of η, but the system learns much faster overall with larger values of α and η.

Symmetry breaking. Our learning procedure has one more problem that can be readily overcome and this is the problem of symmetry breaking. If all weights start out with equal values and if the solution requires that unequal weights be developed, the system can never learn. This is because error is propagated back through the weights in proportion to the values of the weights. This means that all hidden units connected directly to the output inputs will get identical error signals, and, since the weight changes depend on the error signals, the weights from those units to the output units must always be the same. The system is starting out at a kind of *local maximum*, which keeps the weights equal, but it is a maximum of the error function, so once it escapes it will never return. We counteract this problem by starting the system with small random weights. Under these conditions symmetry problems of this kind do not arise.

The XOR Problem

It is useful to begin with the exclusive-or problem since it is the classic problem requiring hidden units and since many other difficult problems involve an XOR as a subproblem. We have run the XOR problem many times and with a couple of exceptions discussed below, the system has always solved the problem. Figure 3 shows one of the solutions to the problem. This solution was reached after 558 sweeps through the four stimulus patterns with a learning rate of $\eta = 0.5$. In this case, both the hidden unit and the output unit have *positive biases* so they are on unless turned off. The hidden unit turns on if neither input unit is on. When it is on, it turns off the output unit. The connections from input to output units arranged themselves so that they turn off the output unit whenever both inputs are on. In this case, the network has settled to a solution which is a sort of mirror image of the one illustrated in Figure 2.

We have taught the system to solve the XOR problem hundreds of times. Sometimes we have used a single hidden unit and direct connections to the output unit as illustrated here, and other times we have allowed two hidden units and set the connections from the input units to the outputs to be zero, as shown in Figure 4. In only two cases has the system encountered a *local minimum* and thus been unable to solve the problem. Both cases involved the two hidden units version of the

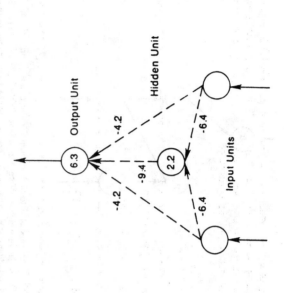

FIGURE 3. Observed XOR network. The connection weights are written on the arrows and the biases are written in the circles. Note a positive bias means that the unit is on unless turned off.

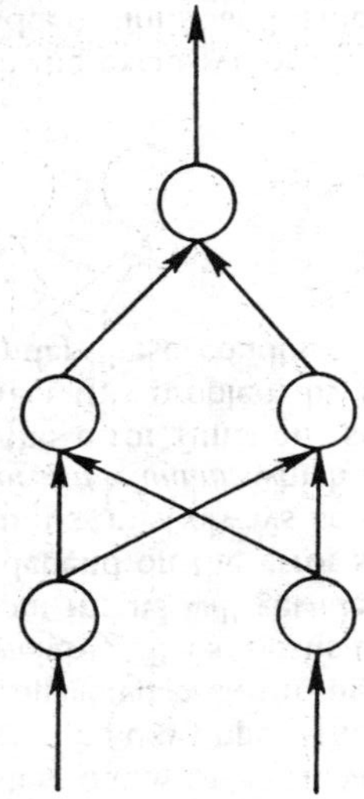

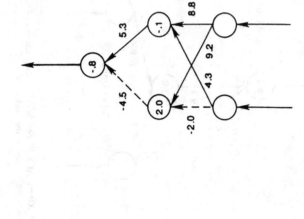

FIGURE 4. A simple architecture for solving XOR with two hidden units and no direct connections from input to output.

FIGURE 5. A network at a local minimum for the exclusive-or problem. The dotted lines indicate negative weights. Note that whenever the right most input unit is on it turns on *both* hidden units. The weights connecting the hidden units to the output are arranged so that when both hidden units are on, the output unit gets a net input of *zero*. This leads to an output value of 0.5. In the other cases the network provides the correct answer.

problem and both ended up in the same local minimum. Figure 5 shows the weights for the local minimum. In this case, the system correctly responds to two of the patterns—namely, the patterns 00 and 10. In the cases of the other two patterns 11 and 01, the output unit gets a net input of zero. This leads to an output value of 0.5 for both of these patterns. This state was reached after 6,587 presentations of each pattern with η=0.25.[2] Although many problems require more presentations for learning to occur, further trials on this problem merely increase the magnitude of the weights but do not lead to any improvement in performance. We do not know the frequency of such local minima, but our experience with this and other problems is that they are quite rare. We have found only one other situation in which a local minimum has occurred in many hundreds of problems of various sorts. We will discuss this case below.

The XOR problem has proved a useful test case for a number of other studies. Using the architecture illustrated in Figure 4, a student in our laboratory, Yves Chauvin, has studied the effect of varying the

number of hidden units and varying the learning rate on time to solve the problem. Using as a learning criterion an error of 0.01 per pattern, Yves found that the average number of presentations to solve the problem with η = 0.25 varied from about 245 for the case with two hidden units to about 120 presentations for 32 hidden units. The results can be summarized by $P = 280 - 33\log_2 H$, where P is the required number of presentations and H is the number of hidden units employed. Thus, the time to solve XOR is reduced linearly with the logarithm of the number of hidden units. This result holds for values of H up to about 40 in the case of XOR. The general result that the time to solution is reduced by increasing the number of hidden units has been observed in virtually all of our simulations. Yves also studied the time to solution as a function of learning rate for the case of eight hidden units. He found an average of about 450 presentations with η = 0.1 to about 68 presentations with η = 0.75. He also found that

[2] If we set η = 0.5 or above, the system escapes this minimum. In general, however, the best way to avoid local minima is probably to use very small values of η.

learning rates larger than this led to unstable behavior. However, within this range larger learning rates speeded the learning substantially. In most of our problems we have employed learning rates of $\eta = 0.25$ or smaller and have had no difficulty.

Parity

One of the problems given a good deal of discussion by Minsky and Papert (1969) is the parity problem, in which the output required is 1 if the input pattern contains an odd number of 1s and 0 otherwise. This is a very difficult problem because the most similar patterns (those which differ by a single bit) require different answers. The XOR problem is a parity problem with input patterns of size two. We have tried a number of parity problems with patterns ranging from size two to eight. Generally we have employed layered networks in which direct connections from the input to the output units are not allowed, but must be mediated through a set of hidden units. In this architecture, it requires at least N hidden units to solve parity with patterns of length N. Figure 6 illustrates the basic paradigm for the solutions discovered by the system. The solid lines in the figure indicate weights of +1 and the dotted lines indicate weights of -1. The numbers in the circles represent the biases of the units. Basically, the hidden units arranged themselves so that they count the number of inputs. In the diagram, the one at the far left comes on if one or more input units are on, the next comes on if two or more are on, etc. All of the hidden units come on if all of the input lines are on. The first m hidden units come on whenever m bits are on in the input pattern. The hidden units then connect with alternately positive and negative weights. In this way the net input from the hidden units is zero for even numbers and +1 for odd numbers. Table 3 shows the actual solution attained for one of our simulations with four input lines and four hidden units. This solution was reached after 2,825 presentations of each of the sixteen patterns with $\eta = 0.5$. Note that the solution is roughly a mirror image of that shown in Figure 6 in that the number of hidden units turned on is equal to the number of zero input values rather than the number of ones. Beyond that the principle is that shown above. It should be noted that the internal representation created by the learning rule is to arrange that the number of hidden units that come on is equal to the number of zeros in the input and that the particular hidden units that come on depend *only* on the number, not on which input units are on. This is exactly the sort of recoding *required* by parity. It is not the kind of representation readily discovered by unsupervised learning schemes such as competitive learning.

The Encoding Problem

Ackley, Hinton, and Sejnowski (1985) have posed a problem in which a set of orthogonal input patterns are mapped to a set of orthogonal output patterns through a small set of hidden units. In such cases the internal representations of the patterns on the hidden units must be rather efficient. Suppose that we attempt to map N input patterns onto N output patterns. Suppose further that $\log_2 N$ hidden units are provided. In this case, we expect that the system will learn to use the

TABLE 3

Number of *On* Input Units	Hidden Unit Patterns	Output Value
0	1111	0
1	1011	1
2	1010	0
3	0010	0
4	0000	0

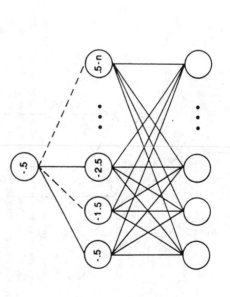

FIGURE 6. A paradigm for the solutions to the parity problem discovered by the learning system. See text for explanation.

output as in the input. Table 5 shows the mapping generated by our learning system on this example. It is of some interest that the system employed its ability to use intermediate values in solving this problem. It could, of course, have found a solution in which the hidden units took on only the values of zero and one. Often it does just that, but in this instance, and many others, there are solutions that use the intermediate values, and the learning system finds them even though it has a bias toward extreme values. It is possible to set up problems that *require* the system to make use of intermediate values in order to solve a problem. We now turn to such a case.

Table 6 shows a very simple problem in which we have to convert from a *distributed representation* over two units into a *local representation* over four units. The similarity structure of the distributed input patterns is simply not preserved in the local output representation.

We presented this problem to our learning system with a number of constraints which made it especially difficult. The two input units were only allowed to connect to a single hidden unit which, in turn, was allowed to connect to four more hidden units. Only these four hidden units were allowed to connect to the four output units. To solve this problem, then, the system must first convert the distributed

TABLE 5

Input Patterns	Hidden Unit Patterns			Output Patterns
10000000	.5	0	0	10000000
01000000	0	1	0	01000000
00100000	1	1	0	00100000
00010000	1	1	1	00010000
00001000	0	1	1	00001000
00000100	.5	0	1	00000100
00000010	0	0	.5	00000010
00000001	1	0	0	00000001

TABLE 6

Input Patterns	Output Patterns
00	1000
01	0100
10	0010
11	0001

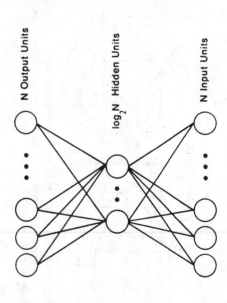

FIGURE 7. A network for solving the encoder problem. In this problem there are N orthogonal input patterns each paired with one of N orthogonal output patterns. There are only $\log_2 N$ hidden units. Thus, if the hidden units take on binary values, the hidden units must form a binary number to encode each of the input patterns. This is exactly what the system learns to do.

N Output Units

$\log_2 N$ Hidden Units

N Input Units

hidden units to form a binary code with a distinct binary pattern for each of the N input patterns. Figure 7 illustrates the basic architecture for the encoder problem. Essentially, the problem is to learn an encoding of an N bit pattern into a $\log_2 N$ bit pattern and then learn to decode this representation into the output pattern. We have presented the system with a number of these problems. Here we present a problem with eight input patterns, eight output patterns, and three hidden units. In this case the required mapping is the identity mapping illustrated in Table 4. The problem is simply to turn on the same bit in the

TABLE 4

Input Patterns	Output Patterns
10000000	10000000
01000000	01000000
00100000	00100000
00010000	00010000
00001000	00001000
00000100	00000100
00000010	00000010
00000001	00000001

representation of the input patterns into various intermediate values of the singleton hidden unit in which different activation values correspond to the different input patterns. These continuous values must then be converted back through the next layer of hidden units— first to another distributed representation and then, finally, to a local representation. This problem was presented to the system and it reached a solution after 5,226 presentations with $\eta = 0.05$.[3] Table 7 shows the sequence of representations the system actually developed in order to transform the patterns and solve the problem. Note each of the four input patterns was mapped onto a particular activation value of the singleton hidden unit. These values were then mapped onto distributed patterns at the next layer of hidden units which were finally mapped into the required local representation at the output level. In principle, this trick of mapping patterns into activation values and then converting those activation values back into patterns could be done for any number of patterns, but it becomes increasingly difficult for the system to make the necessary distinctions as ever smaller differences among activation values must be distinguished. Figure 8 shows the network the system developed to do this job. The connection weights from the hidden units to the output units have been suppressed for clarity. (The sign of the connection, however, is indicated by the form of the connection—e.g., dashed lines mean inhibitory connections). The four different activation values were generated by having relatively large weights of opposite sign. One input line turns the hidden unit full on, one turns it full off. The two differ by a relatively small amount so that when both turn on, the unit attains a value intermediate between 0 and 0.5. When neither turns on, the near zero bias causes the unit to attain a value slightly over 0.5. The connections to the second layer of hidden units is likewise interesting. When the hidden unit is full on,

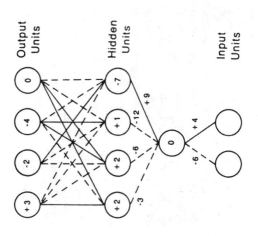

FIGURE 8 The network illustrating the use of intermediate values in solving a problem. See text for explanation.

the right-most of these hidden units is turned on and all others turned off. When the hidden unit is turned off, the other three of these hidden units are on and the left-most unit off. The other connections from the singleton hidden unit to the other hidden units are graded so that a distinct pattern is turned on for its other two values. Here we have an example of the flexibility of the learning system.

Our experience is that there is a propensity for the hidden units to take on extreme values, but, whenever the learning problem calls for it, they can learn to take on graded values. It is likely that the propensity to take on extreme values follows from the fact that the logistic is a sigmoid so that increasing magnitudes of its inputs push it toward zero or one. This means that in a problem in which intermediate values are required, the incoming weights must remain of moderate size. It is interesting that the derivation of the generalized delta rule does not depend on all of the units having identical activation functions. Thus, it would be possible for some units, those required to encode information in a graded fashion, to be linear while others might be logistic. The linear unit would have a much wider dynamic range and could encode more different values. This would be a useful role for a linear unit in a network with hidden units.

TABLE 7

Input Patterns		Singleton Hidden Unit		Remaining Hidden Units					Output Patterns
10	→	0	→	1	1	1	0	→	0010
11	→	.2	→	1	1	0	0	→	0001
00	→	.6	→	.5	0	0	.3	→	1000
01	→	1	→	0	0	0	1	→	0100

[3] Relatively small learning rates make units employing intermediate values easier to obtain.

will be on. The next most important thing to note about the solution is that the weights on each side of the midpoint of the string are in the ratio of 1:2:4. This insures that each of the eight patterns that can occur on each side of the midpoint sends a unique activation sum to the hidden unit. This assures that there is no pattern on the left that will exactly balance a non-mirror-image pattern on the right. Finally, the two hidden units have identical patterns of weights from the input units except for sign. This insures that for every nonsymmetric pattern, at least one of the two hidden units will come on and turn on the output unit. To summarize, the network is arranged so that both hidden units will receive exactly zero activation from the input units when the pattern is symmetric, and at least one of them will receive positive input for every nonsymmetric pattern.

This problem was interesting to us because the learning system developed a much more elegant solution to the problem than we had previously considered. This problem was not the only one in which this happened. The parity solution discovered by the learning procedure was also one that we had not discovered prior to testing the problem with our learning procedure. Indeed, we frequently discover these more elegant solutions by giving the system more hidden units than it needs and observing that it does not make use of some of those provided. Some analysis of the actual solutions discovered often leads us to the discovery of a better solution involving fewer hidden units.

Addition

Another interesting problem on which we have tested our learning algorithm is the simple binary addition problem. This problem is interesting because there is a very elegant solution to it, because it is the one problem we have found where we can reliably find local minima and because the way of avoiding these local minima gives us some insight into the conditions under which local minima may be found and avoided. Figure 10 illustrates the basic problem and a minimal solution to it. There are four input units, three output units, and two hidden units. The output patterns can be viewed as the binary representation of the sum of two two-bit binary numbers represented by the input patterns. The second and fourth input units in the diagram correspond to the low-order bits of the two binary numbers and the first and third units correspond to the two higher order bits. The hidden units correspond to the *carry bits* in the summation. Thus the hidden unit on the far right comes on when both of the lower order bits in the input pattern are turned on, and the one on the left comes

Symmetry

Another interesting problem we studied is that of classifying input strings as to whether or not they are symmetric about their center. We used patterns of various lengths with various numbers of hidden units. To our surprise, we discovered that the problem can always be solved with only two hidden units. To understand the derived representation, consider one of the solutions generated by our system for strings of length six. This solution was arrived at after 1,208 presentations of each six-bit pattern with $\eta = 0.1$. The final network is shown in Figure 9. For simplicity we have shown the six input units in the center of the diagram with one hidden unit above and one below. The output unit, which signals whether or not the string is symmetric about its center, is shown at the far right. The key point to see about this solution is that for a given hidden unit, weights that are symmetric about the middle are equal in magnitude and opposite in sign. That means that if a symmetric pattern is on, both hidden units will receive a net input of zero from the input units, and, since the hidden units have a negative bias, both will be off. In this case, the output unit, having a positive bias,

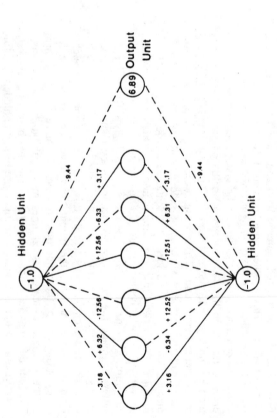

FIGURE 9. Network for solving the symmetry problem. The six open circles represent the input units. There are two hidden units, one shown above and one below the input units. The output unit is shown to the far right. See text for explanation.

difficult. Note that the middle bit should come on whenever an odd number of the set containing the two higher order input bits and the lower order carry bit is turned on. Observation will confirm that the network shown performs that task. The left-most hidden unit receives inputs from the two higher order bits and from the carry bit. Its bias is such that it will come on whenever two or more of its inputs are turned on. The middle output unit receives positive inputs from the same three units and a negative input of −2 from the second hidden unit. This insures that whenever just one of the three are turned on, the second hidden unit will remain off and the output bit will come on. Whenever exactly two of the three are on, the hidden unit will turn on and counteract the two units exciting the output bit, so it will stay off. Finally, when all three are turned on, the output bit will receive −2 from its carry bit and +3 from its other three inputs. The net is positive, so the middle unit will be on. Finally, the third output bit should turn on whenever the second hidden unit is on—that is, whenever there is a carry from the second bit. Here then we have a minimal network to carry out the job at hand. Moreover, it should be noted that the concept behind this network is generalizable to an arbitrary number of input and output bits. In general, for adding two m bit binary numbers we will require $2m$ input units, m hidden units, and $m+1$ output units.

Unfortunately, this is the one problem we have found that reliably leads the system into local minima. At the start in our learning trials on this problem we allow any input unit to connect to any output unit and to any hidden unit. We allow any hidden unit to connect to any output unit, and we allow one of the hidden units to connect to the other hidden unit, but, since we can have no loops, the connection in the opposite direction is disallowed. Sometimes the system will discover essentially the same network shown in the figure.[4] Often, however, the system ends up in a local minimum. The problem arises when the XOR problem on the low-order bits is not solved in the way shown in the diagram. One way it can fail is when the "higher" of the two hidden units is "selected" to solve the XOR problem. This is a problem because then the other hidden unit cannot "see" the carry bit and therefore cannot finally solve the problem. This problem seems to stem from the fact that the learning of the second output bit is always dependent on learning the first (because information about the carry is necessary to learn the second bit) and therefore lags behind the learning of the first bit and has no influence on the selection of a hidden unit to

---

[4] The network is the same except for the highest order bit. The highest order bit is always on whenever three or more of the input units are on. This is always learned first and always learned with direct connections to the input units.

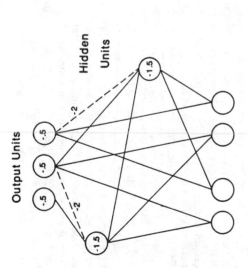

Output Units

Hidden Units

Input Units

FIGURE 10. Minimal network for adding two two-bit binary numbers. There are four input units, three output units, and two hidden units. The output patterns can be viewed as the binary representation of the sum of two two-bit binary numbers represented by the input patterns. The second and fourth input units in the diagram correspond to the low-order bits of the two binary numbers, and the first and third units correspond to the two higher order bits. The hidden units correspond to the carry bits in the summation. The hidden unit on the far right comes on when both of the lower order bits in the input pattern are turned on, and the one on the left comes on when both higher order bits are turned on or when one of the higher order bits and the other hidden unit is turned on. The weights on all lines are assumed to be +1 except where noted. Negative connections are indicated by dashed lines. As usual, the biases are indicated by the numbers in the circles.

on when both higher order bits are turned on or when one of the higher order bits and the other hidden unit is turned on. In the diagram, the weights on all lines are assumed to be +1 except where noted. Inhibitory connections are indicated by dashed lines. As usual, the biases are indicated by the numbers in the circles. To understand how this network works, it is useful to note that the lowest order output bit is determined by an exclusive-or among the two low-order input bits. One way to solve this XOR problem is to have a hidden unit come on when both low-order input bits are on and then have it inhibit the output unit. Otherwise either of the low-order input units can turn on the low-order output bit. The middle bit is somewhat more solve the first XOR problem. Thus, about half of the time (in this problem) the wrong unit is chosen and the problem cannot be solved. In this case, the system finds a solution for all of the sums except the $11+11 \rightarrow 110$ ($3+3 = 6$) case in which it misses the carry into the middle bit and gets $11+11 \rightarrow 100$ instead. This problem differs from others we have solved in as much as the hidden units are not "equipotential" here. In most of our other problems the hidden units have been equipotential, and this problem has not arisen.

It should be noted, however, that there is a relatively simple way out of the problem—namely, add some extra hidden units. In this case we can afford to make a mistake on one or more selections and the system can still solve the problems. For the problem of adding two-bit numbers we have found that the system always solves the problem with one extra hidden unit. With larger numbers it may require two or three more. For purposes of illustration, we show the results of one of our runs with three rather than the minimum two hidden units. Figure 11 shows the state reached by the network after 3,020 presentations of each input pattern and with a learning rate of $\eta = 0.5$. For convenience, we show the network in four parts. In Figure 11A we show the connections to and among the hidden units. This figure shows the internal representation generated for this problem. The "lowest" hidden unit turns off whenever either of the low-order bits are on. In other words it detects the case in which no low-order bit is turn on. The "highest" hidden unit is arranged so that it comes on whenever the sum is less than two. The conditions under which the middle hidden unit comes on are more complex. Table 8 shows the patterns of hidden units which occur to each of the sixteen input patterns. Figure 11B shows the connections to the lowest order output unit. Noting that the relevant hidden unit comes on when neither low-order input unit is on, it is clear how the system computes XOR. When both low-order inputs are off, the output unit is turned off by the hidden unit. When both low-order input units are on, the output is turned off directly by the two input units. If just one is on, the positive bias on the output unit keeps it on. Figure 11C gives the connections to the middle output unit, and in Figure 11D we show those connections to the left-most, highest order output unit. It is somewhat difficult to see how these connections always lead to the correct output answer, but, as can be verified from the figures, the network is balanced so that this works.

It should be pointed out that most of the problems described thus far have involved hidden units with quite simple interpretations. It is much more often the case, especially when the number of hidden units exceeds the minimum number required for the task, that the hidden units are not readily interpreted. This follows from the fact that there is very little tendency for *localist* representations to develop. Typically

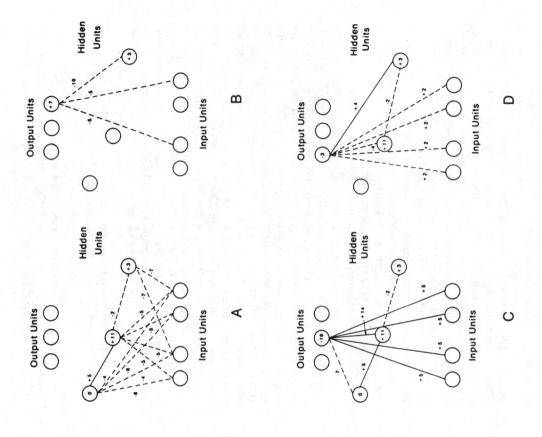

FIGURE 11. Network found for the summation problem. *A:* The connections from the input units to the three hidden units and the connections among the hidden units. *B:* The connections from the input and hidden units to the lowest order output unit. *C:* The connections from the input and hidden units to the middle output unit. *D:* The connections from the input and hidden units to the highest order output unit.

TABLE 8

Input Patterns		Hidden Unit Patterns		Output Patterns
00 + 00	→	111	→	000
00 + 01	→	110	→	001
00 + 10	→	011	→	010
00 + 11	→	010	→	011
01 + 00	→	110	→	001
01 + 01	→	010	→	010
01 + 10	→	010	→	011
01 + 11	→	000	→	100
10 + 00	→	011	→	010
10 + 01	→	010	→	011
10 + 10	→	001	→	100
10 + 11	→	000	→	101
11 + 00	→	010	→	011
11 + 01	→	000	→	100
11 + 10	→	000	→	101
11 + 11	→	000	→	110

the internal representations are distributed and it is the *pattern* of activity over the hidden units, not the meaning of any particular hidden unit that is important.

The Negation Problem

Consider a situation in which the input to a system consists of patterns of $n+1$ binary values and an output of n values. Suppose further that the general rule is that n of the input units should be mapped directly to the output patterns. One of the input bits, however, is special. It is a negation bit. When that bit is off, the rest of the pattern is supposed to map straight through, but when it is on, the complement of the pattern is to be mapped to the output. Table 9 shows the appropriate mapping. In this case the left element of the input pattern is the negation bit, but the system has no way of knowing this and must learn which bit is the negation bit. In this case, weights were allowed from any input unit to any hidden or output unit and from any hidden unit to any output unit. The system learned to set all of the weights to zero except those shown in Figure 12. The basic structure of the problem and of the solution is evident in the figure. Clearly the problem was reduced to a set of three XORs between the negation bit

TABLE 9

Input Patterns		Output Patterns
0000	→	000
0001	→	001
0010	→	010
0011	→	011
0100	→	100
0101	→	101
0110	→	110
0111	→	111
1000	→	111
1001	→	110
1010	→	101
1011	→	100
1100	→	011
1101	→	010
1110	→	001
1111	→	000

and each input. In the case of the two right-most input units, the XOR problems were solved by recruiting a hidden unit to detect the case in which *neither* the negation unit *nor* the corresponding input unit was on. In the third case, the hidden unit detects the case in which *both* the negation unit *and* relevant input were on. In this case the problem was solved in less than 5,000 passes through the stimulus set with $\eta = 0.25$.

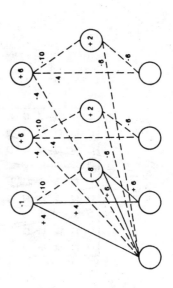

FIGURE 12. The solution discovered for the negation problem. The left-most unit is the negation unit. The problem has been reduced and solved as three exclusive-ors between the negation unit and each of the other three units.

The T-C Problem

Most of the problems discussed so far (except the symmetry problem) are rather abstract mathematical problems. We now turn to a more geometric problem—that of discriminating between a *T* and a *C*—independent of translation and rotation. Figure 13 shows the stimulus patterns used in these experiments. Note, these patterns are each made of five squares and differ from one another by a single square. Moreover, as Minsky and Papert (1969) point out, when considering the set of patterns over all possible translations and rotations (of 90°, 180°, and 270°), the patterns do not differ in the set of distances among their pairs of squares. To see a difference between the sets of patterns one must look, at least, at configurations of triplets of squares. Thus Minsky and Papert call this a problem of *order three*.[5] In order to facilitate the learning, a rather different architecture was employed for this problem. Figure 14 shows the basic structure of the network we employed. Input patterns were now conceptualized as two-dimensional patterns superimposed on a rectangular grid. Rather than allowing each input unit to connect to each hidden unit, the hidden units themselves were organized into a two-dimensional grid with each unit receiving input from a square 3×3 region of the input space. In this sense, the overlapping square regions constitute the predefined *receptive field* of the hidden units. Each of the hidden units, over the entire input field, feeds into a single output unit which is to take on the value

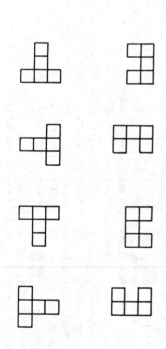

FIGURE 13. The stimulus set for the T-C problem. The set consists of a block *T* and a block *C* in each of four orientations. One of the eight patterns is presented on each trial.

[5] Terry Sejnowski pointed out to us that the T-C problem was difficult for models of this sort to learn and therefore worthy of study.

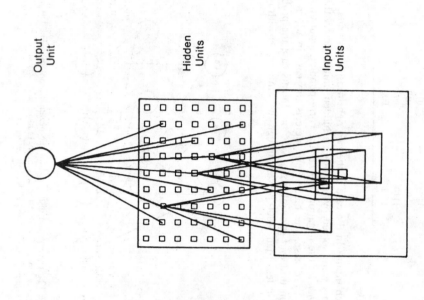

FIGURE 14. The network for solving the T-C problem. See text for explanation.

1 if the input is a *T* (at any location or orientation) and 0 if the input is a *C*. Further, in order that the learning that occurred be independent of where on the field the pattern appeared, we constrained all of the units to learn exactly the same pattern of weights. In this way each unit was constrained to compute exactly the same function over its receptive field—the receptive fields were constrained to all have the same shape. This guarantees translation independence and avoids any possible "edge effects" in the learning. The learning can readily be extended to arbitrarily large fields of input units. This constraint was accomplished by simply adding together the weight changes dictated by the delta rule for each unit and then changing all weights exactly the same amount. In

this way, the whole field of hidden units consists simply of replications of a single feature detector centered on different regions of the input space, and the learning that occurs in one part of the field is automatically generalized to the rest of the field.[6]

We have run this problem in this way a number of times. As a result, we have found a number of solutions. Perhaps the simplest way to understand the system is by looking at the form of the receptive field for the hidden units. Figure 15 shows several of the receptive fields we have seen.[7] Figure 15A shows the most local representation developed. This *on-center-off-surround* detector turns out to be an excellent *T* detector. Since, as illustrated, a *T* can extend into the on-center and achieve a net input of +1, this detector will be turned on for a *T* at any orientation. On the other hand, any *C* extending into the center must cover at least *two* inhibitory cells. With this detector the bias can be set so that only one of the whole field of inhibitory units will come on whenever a *T* is presented and none of the hidden units will be turned on by any *C*. This is a kind of *protrusion* detector which differentiates between a *T* and *C* by detecting the protrusion of the *T*.

The receptive field shown in Figure 15B is again a kind of *T* detector. Every *T* activates one of the hidden units by an amount +2 and none of the *C*'s. As shown in the figure, *T*'s at 90° and 270° send a total of +2 to the hidden units on which the crossbar lines up. The *T*'s at the other two orientations receive +2 from the way it detects the vertical protrusions of those two characters. Figure 15C shows a more distributed representation. As illustrated in the figure, each *T* activates five different hidden units whereas each *C* excites only three hidden units. In this case the system again is differentiating between the characters on the basis of the protruding end of the *T* which is not shared by the *C*.

Finally, the receptive field shown in Figure 15D is even more interesting. In this case every hidden unit has a positive bias so that it is on unless turned off. The strength of the inhibitory weights are such that if a character overlaps the receptive field of a hidden unit, that unit turns off. The system works because a *C* is more compact than a *T* and therefore the *T* turns off more units that the *C*. The *T* turns off 21 hidden units, and the *C* turns off only 20. This is a truly distributed

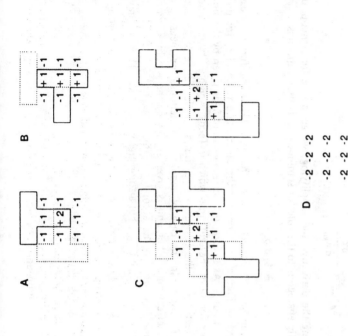

A

B

C

D

FIGURE 15. Receptive fields found in different runs of the T-C problem. *A:* An on-center-off-surround receptive field for detecting *T*'s. *B:* A vertical bar detector which responds to *T*'s more strongly than *C*'s. *C:* A diagonal bar detector. A *T* activates five such detectors whereas a *C* activates only three such detectors. *D:* A compactness detector. This inhibitory receptive field turns off whenever an input covers any region of its receptive field. Since the *C* is more compact than the *T* it turns off 20 such detectors whereas the *T* turns off 21 of them.

representation. In each case, the solution was reached in from about 5,000 to 10,000 presentations of the set of eight patterns.[8]

It is interesting that the inhibitory type of receptive field shown in Figure 15D was the most common and that there is a predominance of inhibitory connections in this and indeed all of our simulations. This can be understood by considering the trajectory through which the learning typically moves. At first, when the system is presented with a

[6] A similar procedure has been employed by Fukushima (1980) in his *neocognitron* and by Kienker, Sejnowski, Hinton, and Schumacher (1985).

[7] The ratios of the weights are about right. The actual values can be larger or smaller than the values given in the figure.

[8] Since translation independence was built into the learning procedure, it makes no difference *where* the input occurs; the same thing will be learned wherever the pattern is presented. Thus, there are only eight distinct patterns to be presented to the system.

difficult problem, the initial random connections are as likely to mislead as to give the correct answer. In this case, it is best for the output units to take on a value of 0.5 than to take on a more extreme value. This follows from the form of the error function given in Equation 2. The output unit can achieve a constant output of 0.5 by turning off those units feeding into it. Thus, the first thing that happens in virtually every difficult problem is that the hidden units are turned off. One way to achieve this is to have the input units inhibit the hidden units. As the system begins to sort things out and to learn the appropriate function some of the connections will typically go positive, but the majority of the connections will remain negative. This *bias* for solutions involving inhibitory inputs can often lead to nonintuitive results in which hidden units are often on unless turned off by the input.

More Simulation Results

We have offered a sample of our results in this section. In addition to having studied our learning system on the problems discussed here, we have employed back propagation for learning to multiply binary digits, to play tic-tac-toe, to distinguish between vertical and horizontal lines, to perform sequences of actions, to recognize characters, to associate random vectors, and a host of other applications. In all of these applications we have found that the generalized delta rule was capable of generating the kinds of internal representations required for the problems in question. We have found local minima to be very rare and that the system learns in a reasonable period of time. Still more studies of this type will be required to understand precisely the conditions under which the system will be plagued by local minima. Suffice it to say that the problem has not been serious to date. We now turn to a pointer to some future developments.

SOME FURTHER GENERALIZATIONS

We have intensively studied the learning characteristics of the generalized delta rule on feedforward networks and semilinear activations functions. Interestingly these are not the most general cases to which the learning procedure is applicable. As yet we have only studied a few examples of the more fully generalized system, but it is relatively easy to apply the same learning rule to sigma-pi units and to recurrent networks. We will simply sketch the basic ideas here.

The Generalized Delta Rule and Sigma-Pi Units

It will be recalled from Chapter 2 that in the case of sigma-pi units we have

$$o_j = f_j\left(\sum_i w_{ji} \prod_k o_k\right) \tag{17}$$

where i varies over the set of conjuncts feeding into unit j and k varies over the elements of the conjuncts. For simplicity of exposition, we restrict ourselves to the case in which no conjuncts involve more than two elements. In this case we can notate the weight from the conjunction of units i and j to unit k by w_{kij}. The weight on the direct connection from unit i to unit j would, thus, be w_{jii}, and since the relation is multiplicative, $w_{kij} = w_{kji}$. We can now rewrite Equation 17 as

$$o_j = f_j\left(\sum_{i,h} w_{jih} o_h o_i\right).$$

We now set

$$\Delta_p w_{kij} \propto -\frac{\partial E_p}{\partial w_{kij}}.$$

Taking the derivative and simplifying, we get a rule for sigma-pi units strictly analogous to the rule for semilinear activation functions:

$$\Delta_p w_{kij} = \delta_k o_i o_j.$$

We can see the correct form of the error signal, δ, for this case by inspecting Figure 16. Consider the appropriate value of δ_i for unit u_i in the figure. As before, the correct value of δ_i is given by the sum of the δ's for all of the units into which u_i feeds, weighted by the amount of effect due to the activation of u_i times the derivative of the activation function. In the case of semilinear functions, the measure of a unit's effect on another unit is given simply by the weight w connecting the first unit to the second. In this case, the u_i's effect on u_k depends not only on w_{kij} but also on the value of u_j. Thus, we have

$$\delta_i = f'_i(net_i)\sum_{j,k}\delta_k w_{kij} o_j$$

if u_i is not an output unit and, as before,

$$\delta_i = f'_i(net_i)(t_i - o_i)$$

if it is an output unit.

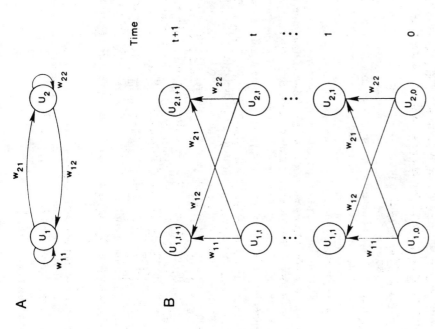

Time

FIGURE 17. A comparison of a recurrent network and a feedforward network with identical behavior. *A*: A completely connected recurrent network with two units. *B*: A feedforward network which behaves the same as the recurrent network. In this case, we have a separate unit for each time step and we require that the weights connecting each layer of units to the next be the same for all layers. Moreover, they must be the same as the analogous weights in the recurrent case.

The appropriate method for maintaining the constraint that all weights be equal is simply to keep track of the changes dictated for each weight at each level and then change each of the weights according to the *sum* of these individually prescribed changes. Now, the general rule for determining the change prescribed for a weight in the system for a particular time is simply to take the product of an appropriate error

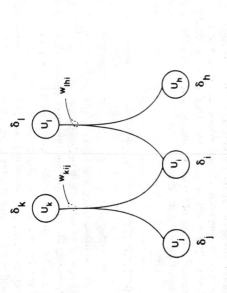

FIGURE 16. The generalized delta rule for sigma-pi units. The products of activation values of individual units activate output units. See text for explanation of how the δ values are computed in this case.

Recurrent Nets

We have thus far restricted ourselves to *feedforward* nets. This may seem like a substantial restriction, but as Minsky and Papert point out, there is, for every recurrent network, a feedforward network with identical behavior (over a finite period of time). We will now indicate how this construction can proceed and thereby show the correct form of the learning rule for the recurrent network. Consider the simple recurrent network shown in Figure 17A. The same network in a feedforward architecture is shown in Figure 17B. The behavior of a recurrent network can be achieved in a feedforward network at the cost of duplicating the hardware many times over for the feedforward version of the network.[9] We have distinct units and distinct weights for each point in time. For naming convenience, we subscript each unit with its unit number in the corresponding recurrent network and the time it represents. As long as we constrain the weights at each level of the feedforward network to be the same, we have a feedforward network which performs identically with the recurrent network of Figure 17A.

---

[9] Note that in this discussion, and indeed in our entire development here, we have assumed a discrete time system with synchronous update and with each connection involving a unit delay.

experiments. We turn first to a very simple problem in which the system is induced to invent a shift register to solve the problem.

Learning to be a shift register. Perhaps the simplest class of recurrent problems we have studied is one in which the input and output units are one and the same and there are no hidden units. We simply present a pattern and let the system process it for a period of time. The state of the system is then compared to some target state. If it hasn't reached the target state at the designated time, error is injected into the system and it modifies its weights. Then it is shown a new input pattern and restarted. In these cases, there is no constraint on the connections in the system. Any unit can connect to any other unit. The simplest such problem we have studied is what we call the *shift register* problem. In this problem, the units are conceptualized as a circular shift register. An arbitrary bit pattern is first established on the units. They are then allowed to process for two time-steps. The target state, after those two time-steps, is the original pattern shifted two spaces to the left. The interesting question here concerns the state of the units between the presentation of the start state and the time at which the target state is presented. One solution to the problem is for the system to become a shift register and shift the pattern exactly one unit to the left during each time period. If the system did this then it would surely be shifted two places to the left after two time units. We have tried this problem with groups of three or five units and, if we constrain the biases on all of the units to be negative (so the units are off unless turned on), the system always learns to be a shift register of this sort.[10] Thus, even though in principle any unit can connect to any other unit, the system actually learns to set all weights to zero except the ones connecting a unit to its left neighbor. The left-most unit developed a strong connection to the right-most unit. The system learns this relatively quickly. With $\eta = 0.25$ it learns perfectly in fewer than 200 sweeps through the set of possible patterns with either three- or five-unit systems.

The tasks we have described so far are exceptionally simple, but they do illustrate how the algorithm works with unrestricted networks. We have attempted a few more difficult problems with recurrent networks.

---

[10] If the constraint that biases be negative is not imposed, other solutions are possible. These solutions can involve the units passing through the complements of the shifted pattern or even through more complicated intermediate states. These trajectories are interesting in that they match a simple shift register on all even numbers of shifts, but do not match following an odd number of shifts.

measure δ and the input along the relevant line both for the appropriate times. Thus, the problem of specifying the correct learning rule for recurrent networks is simply one of determining the appropriate value of δ for each time. In a feedforward network we determine δ by multiplying the derivative of the activation function by the sum of the δ's for those units it feeds into weighted by the connection strengths. The same process works for the recurrent network—except in this case, the value of δ associated with a particular unit changes in time as a unit passes error back, sometimes to itself. After each iteration, as error is being passed back through the network, the change in weight for that iteration must be added to the weight changes specified by the preceding iterations and the sum stored. This process of passing error through the network should continue for a number of iterations equal to the number of iterations through which the activation was originally passed. At this point, the appropriate changes to all of the weights can be made.

In general, the procedure for a recurrent network is that an input (generally a sequence) is presented to the system while it runs for some number of iterations. At certain specified times during the operation of the system, the output of certain units are compared to the target for that unit at that time and error signals are generated. Each such error signal is then passed back through the network for a number of iterations equal to the number of iterations used in the forward pass. Weight changes are computed at each iteration and a sum of all the weight changes dictated for a particular weight is saved. Finally, after all such error signals have been propagated through the system, the weights are changed. The major problem with this procedure is the memory required. Not only does the system have to hold its summed weight changes while the error is being propagated, but each unit must somehow record the sequence of activation values through which it was driven during the original processing. This follows from the fact that during each iteration while the error is passed back through the system, the current δ is relevant to a point earlier in time and the required weight changes depend on the activation levels of the units at that time. It is not entirely clear how such a mechanism could be implemented in the brain. Nevertheless, it is tantalizing to realize that such a procedure is potentially very powerful, since the problem it is attempting to solve amounts to that of finding a sequential program (like that for a digital computer) that produces specified input-sequence/output-sequence pairs. Furthermore, the interaction of the teacher with the system can be quite flexible, so that, for example, should the system get stuck in a local minimum, the teacher could introduce "hints" in the form of desired output values for intermediate stages of processing. Our experience with recurrent networks is limited, but we have carried out some and every output unit was also connected to every other output unit and to itself. All the connections started with small random weights uniformly distributed between −0.3 and +0.3. All the hidden and output units started with an activity level of 0.2 at the beginning of each sequence.

We used a version of the learning procedure in which the gradient of the error with respect to each weight is computed for a whole set of examples before the weights are changed. This means that each connection must accumulate the sum of the gradients for all the examples and for all the time steps involved in each example. During training, we used a particular set of 20 examples, and after these were learned almost perfectly we tested the network on the remaining examples to see if it had picked up on the obvious regularity that relates the first two items of a sequence to the subsequent four. The results are shown in Table 11. For four out of the five test sequences, the output units all have the correct values at all times (assuming we treat values above 0.5 as 1 and values below 0.5 as 0). The network has clearly captured the rule that the first item of a sequence determines the third and fourth, and the second determines the fifth and sixth. We repeated the simulation with a different set of random initial weights, and it got all five test sequences correct.

The learning required 260 sweeps through all 20 training sequences. The errors in the output units were computed as follows: For a unit that should be on, there was no error if its activity level was above 0.8, otherwise the derivative of the error was the amount below 0.8. Similarly, for output units that should be off, the derivative of the error was the amount above 0.2. After each sweep, each weight was decremented by .02 times the total gradient accumulated on that sweep plus 0.9 times the previous weight change.

We have shown that the learning procedure can be used to create a network with interesting sequential behavior, but the particular problem we used can be solved by simply using the hidden units to create "delay lines" which hold information for a fixed length of time before allowing it to influence the output. A harder problem that cannot be solved with delay lines of fixed duration is shown in Table 12. The output is the same as before, but the two input items can arrive at variable times so that the item arriving at time 2, for example, could be either the first or the second item and could therefore determine the states of the output units at either the fifth and sixth or the seventh and eighth times. The new task is equivalent to requiring a buffer that receives two input "words" at variable times and outputs their "phonemic realizations" one after the other. This problem was solved successfully by a network similar to the one above except that it had 60 hidden units and half of their possible interconnections were omitted at random. The

One of the more interesting involves learning to complete sequences of patterns. Our final example comes from this domain.

Learning to complete sequences. Table 10 shows a set of 25 sequences which were chosen so that the first two items of a sequence uniquely determine the remaining four. We used this set of sequences to test out the learning abilities of a recurrent network. The network consisted of five input units (A, B, C, D, E), 30 hidden units, and three output units (1, 2, 3). At Time 1, the input unit corresponding to the first item of the sequence is turned on and the other input units are turned off. At Time 2, the input unit for the second item in the sequence is turned on and the others are all turned off. Then all the input units are turned off and kept off for the remaining four steps of the forward iteration. The network must learn to make the output units adopt states that represent the rest of the sequence. Unlike simple feedforward networks (or their iterative equivalents), the errors are not only assessed at the final layer or time. The output units must adopt the appropriate states *during* the forward iteration, and so during the back-propagation phase, errors are injected at each time-step by comparing the remembered actual states of the output units with their desired states.

The learning procedure for recurrent nets places no constraints on the allowable connectivity structure.[11] For the sequence completion problem, we used one-way connections from the input units to the hidden units and from the hidden units to the output units. Every hidden unit had a one-way connection to every other hidden unit and to itself,

TABLE 10

25 SEQUENCES TO BE LEARNED

AA1212	AB1223	AC1231	AD1221	AE1213
BA2312	BB2323	BC2331	BD2321	BE2313
CA3112	CB3123	CC3131	CD3121	CE3113
DA2112	DB2123	DC2131	DD2121	DE2113
EA1312	EB1323	EC1331	ED1321	EE1313

11 The constraint in feedforward networks is that it must be possible to arrange the units into layers such that units do not influence units in the same or lower layers. In recurrent networks this amounts to the constraint that during the forward iteration, future states must not affect past ones.

TABLE 12

SIX VARIATIONS OF THE SEQUENCE EA1312 PRODUCED BY PRESENTING THE FIRST TWO ITEMS AT VARIABLE TIMES

EA――1312	E―A―1312	E――A1312
―EA―1312	―E―A1312	――EA1312

Note: With these temporal variations, the 25 sequences shown in Table 10 can be used to generate 150 different sequences.

CONCLUSION

In their pessimistic discussion of perceptrons, Minsky and Papert (1969) finally discuss multilayer machines near the end of their book. They state:

> The perceptron has shown itself worthy of study despite (and even because of!) its severe limitations. It has many features that attract attention: its linearity; its intriguing learning theorem; its clear paradigmatic simplicity as a kind of parallel computation. There is no reason to suppose that any of these virtues carry over to the many-layered version. Nevertheless, we consider it to be an important research problem to elucidate (or reject) our intuitive judgement that the extension is sterile. Perhaps some powerful convergence theorem will be discovered, or some profound reason for the failure to produce an interesting "learning theorem" for the multilayered machine will be found. (pp. 231-232)

Although our learning results do not *guarantee* that we can find a solution for all solvable problems, our analyses and results have shown that as a practical matter, the error propagation scheme leads to solutions in virtually every case. In short, we believe that we have answered Minsky and Papert's challenge and *have* found a learning result sufficiently powerful to demonstrate that their pessimism about learning in multilayer machines was misplaced.

One way to view the procedure we have been describing is as a parallel computer that, having been shown the appropriate input/output exemplars specifying some function, programs itself to compute that function in general. Parallel computers are notoriously difficult to program. Here we have a mechanism whereby we do not actually have to know how to write the program in order to get the system to do it. Parker (1985) has emphasized this point.

TABLE 11

PERFORMANCE OF THE NETWORK ON FIVE NOVEL TEST SEQUENCES

Input Sequence	A	D	—	—	—	—
Desired Outputs	—	—	1	2	2	1
Actual States of:						
Output Unit 1	0.2	0.12	0.90	0.22	0.11	0.83
Output Unit 2	0.2	0.16	0.13	0.82	0.88	0.03
Output Unit 3	0.2	0.07	0.08	0.03	0.01	0.22
Input Sequence	B	E	—	—	—	—
Desired Outputs	—	—	2	3	1	3
Actual States of:						
Output Unit 1	0.2	0.12	0.20	0.25	0.48	0.26
Output Unit 2	0.2	0.16	0.80	0.05	0.04	0.09
Output Unit 3	0.2	0.07	0.02	0.79	0.48	0.53
Input Sequence	C	A	—	—	—	—
Desired Outputs	—	—	3	1	1	2
Actual States of:						
Output Unit 1	0.2	0.12	0.19	0.80	0.87	0.11
Output Unit 2	0.2	0.16	0.19	0.00	0.13	0.70
Output Unit 3	0.2	0.07	0.80	0.13	0.01	0.25
Input Sequence	D	B	—	—	—	—
Desired Outputs	—	—	2	1	2	3
Actual States of:						
Output Unit 1	0.2	0.12	0.16	0.79	0.07	0.11
Output Unit 2	0.2	0.16	0.80	0.15	0.87	0.05
Output Unit 3	0.2	0.07	0.20	0.01	0.13	0.96
Input Sequence	E	C	—	—	—	—
Desired Outputs	—	—	1	3	3	1
Actual States of:						
Output Unit 1	0.2	0.12	0.80	0.09	0.27	0.78
Output Unit 2	0.2	0.16	0.20	0.13	0.01	0.02
Output Unit 3	0.2	0.07	0.07	0.94	0.76	0.13

learning was much slower, requiring thousands of sweeps through all 136 training examples. There were also a few more errors on the 14 test examples, but the generalization was still good with most of the test sequences being completed perfectly.

On many occasions we have been surprised to learn of new methods of computing interesting functions by observing the behavior of our learning algorithm. This also raised the question of generalization. In most of the cases presented above, we have presented the system with the entire set of exemplars. It is interesting to ask what would happen if we presented only a subset of the exemplars at training time and then watched the system generalize to remaining exemplars. In small problems such as those presented here, the system sometimes finds solutions to the problems which do not properly generalize. However, preliminary results on larger problems are very encouraging in this regard. This research is still in progress and cannot be reported here. This is currently a very active interest of ours.

Finally, we should say that this work is not yet in a finished form. We have only begun our study of recurrent networks and sigma-pi units. We have not yet applied our learning procedure to many very complex problems. However, the results to date are encouraging and we are continuing our work.

Chapter 5

Thinking

Reasoning

Reasoning typically involves considering evidence relative to a hypothesis or conclusion. Roughly, to reason is to generate or evaluate an argument. Formal logic distinguishes two types of arguments: (1) *deductive* arguments, where it is *necessary* that the conclusion be true given that the premises (evidence) are true; and (2) *inductive* arguments, where it is only *probable* that the conclusion be true given that the premises are true. The first selection in this section deals with deductive reasoning, the second with inductive reasoning.

Johnson-Laird presents a novel proposal concerning how people reason about deductive problems (syllogisms in this case). The standard proposal has been that people try to solve deductive problems by applying rules like those in propositional logic (see Rips, L. J. (1983). Cognitive processes in propositional reasoning. *Psychological Review*, *90*, 38–71). In contrast, Johnson-Laird argues that people solve deductive problems by constructing a mental model of a situation described by the premises, then checking to see what conclusion follows in that model. The term *mental model* is used here in a somewhat different sense than that used earlier in Part 2, *Representation*. Here a mental model is basically a concrete representation of the premises. Johnson-Laird shows that mental models can explain many aspects of reasoning.

Tversky and Kahneman also offer a somewhat new approach to an old problem. Prior to their work, it was commonly thought that people's natural inductive reasoning resembled that of an intuitive statistician. The evidence reviewed by Tversky and Kahneman argues persuasively against this idea, because people consistently violate fundamental principles of probability and statistics. Rather than using intuitive statistics, people rely on a few general heuristics in drawing inductions, such as that the conclusion resemble the evidence. This line of research has had profound effects in all disciplines concerned with judgment and decision making.

Mental Models
P.N. Johnson-Laird
(Chapter 5)

How to reason syllogistically

In this chapter, I am going to describe a theory of syllogistic inference that my colleagues and I have gradually developed over the last seven years (see Johnson-Laird, 1975a; Johnson-Laird and Steedman, 1978; Johnson-Laird and Bara, 1982). It may seem surprising that it has taken so long to explain how people derive conclusions from what are, formally speaking, only sixty-four different pairs of premises. But the theory is, I believe, essentially correct; it is both descriptively and explanatorily adequate according to the criteria introduced in the previous chapter. Its various versions have been modelled in computer programs, and it has been corroborated by independent experimental results. It is in fact a special case of a more general theory of reasoning, but it is worth concentrating first on syllogisms because they straddle the boundary of human logical competence – some are literally child's play while others are beyond the ability of all but the most expert reasoners.

The externalization of syllogistic inference

Let us begin by considering an imaginary method of externalizing the process of deduction. Suppose you want to draw a conclusion from the premises:

    All the artists are beekeepers
    All the beekeepers are chemists

without relying on Euler circles or Venn diagrams. One way in which to proceed is to employ a group of actors to construct a 'tableau' in which some of them act as artists, some as beekeepers, and some as chemists. To represent the first premise, every person acting as an artist is also instructed to play the part of a beekeeper, and, since the first premise is consistent with there being beekeepers who are not artists, that role is assigned to other actors, who are told that it is uncertain whether or not they exist. In short, a tableau of the following sort is set up:

    artist = beekeeper
    artist = beekeeper
    artist = beekeeper
              (beekeeper)
              (beekeeper)

There are three actors playing the joint roles, and two actors taking the part of the beekeepers who are not artists – the parentheses designate a directorial device establishing that the latter may or may not exist. Obviously, the numbers of actors playing the different roles is entirely arbitrary. The tableau is easily extended to accommodate the second premise:

    All the beekeepers are chemists.

Those actors playing beekeepers are instructed to take on the role of chemists, and an arbitrary number of new actors are introduced to play the role of chemists who are not beekeepers – a type which, once again, may or may not exist:

    artist = beekeeper = chemist
    artist = beekeeper = chemist
    artist = beekeeper = chemist
              (beekeeper) = (chemist)
              (beekeeper) = (chemist)
                            (chemist)

At this point, if you were asked whether it followed that *All the artists are chemists*, you could readily inspect the tableau and determine that this conclusion is indeed true. All that you have done is to externalize and to combine the information in two premises. Deductive inference, however, requires more than just the construction of an integrated representation of the premises: it calls for a search for counter-examples. A more complicated example will illustrate this point.

Consider how a troupe of actors could represent the premises:

    None of the authors are burglars.
    Some of the chefs are burglars.

The first premise is represented by two distinct groups acting as the authors and the burglars, and they are instructed that they are never allowed to possibility. There could be several chefs who are not burglars, and each author could be identical to such a chef:

```
author    =    chef
author    =    chef
author    =    chef
------------   burglar = chef
               burglar = chef
                (burglar)
```

The tableau is still consistent with the premises, but what it shows is that the conclusion that *Some of the authors are not chefs* is invalid. There is no other assignment of roles that is compatible with the premises, and you might therefore suppose that there is no valid conclusion (as did six subjects in the experiment). But in all three of the tableaux it is the case that at least *Some of the chefs are not authors.* This conclusion is accordingly valid. (It was drawn by seven subjects.)

An effective procedure for syllogistic inference

The idea of employing actors to take on different parts suggests, of course, a hypothesis about how people might actually make inferences. Instead of arranging an external tableau, they could construct a mental model – an internal tableau containing elements that stand for the members of sets in just the same way that the actors did. A general procedure for making inferences in this way requires three main steps.

1. *Construct a mental model of the first premise.* The representation of a universal affirmative assertion has the following structure:

$$\text{All of the X are Y}: . \quad x = y$$
$$x = y$$
$$(y)$$
$$(y)$$

where the number of tokens corresponding to x's and y's is arbitrary, and the items in parentheses represent the possible existence of y's that are not x's. The representations of the other forms of syllogistic premise are

take on each other's role. The two groups are, as it were, fenced off from each other:

```
author
author
author
-----------
burglar
burglar
burglar
```

The tableau indicates that no author is identical to any burglar. The information in the second premise, *Some of the chefs are burglars*, is added by extending the tableau in a straightforward way, where *some* is taken to mean *at least some*:

```
author
author
author
-----------
burglar  =  chef
burglar  =  chef
(burglar)  (chef)
```

It is tempting, at this point, to conclude that *None of the authors are chefs*, or conversely, that *None of the chefs are authors.* (Six subjects out of twenty drew conclusions of this form in an experiment reported by Johnson-Laird and Steedman, 1978.) Both conclusions are certainly consistent with the tableau. But neither is warranted, because there is another way of representing the premises:

```
author
author
author     =     chef
----------- burglar = chef
            burglar = chef
            (burglar)
```

You can check for yourself that this interpretation is wholly consistent with the premises (*None of the authors are burglars*, and *Some of the chefs are burglars*), yet it invalidates the previous conclusions and suggests instead that *Some of the authors are not chefs.* However, there is still another straightforward:

Some of the X are Y: x = y
                            x = y
                           (x) (y)

None of the X are Y: x
                            x
                          - - - -
                          (x) = y
                                y

Some of the X are not Y: x
                            x
                          - - - -
                          (x) = y
                                y

It should be noted that each premise requires only a single mental model.

A crucial point about mental models is that the system for constructing and interpreting them must embody the knowledge that the number of entities depicted is irrelevant to any syllogistic inference that is drawn. In the case of numerical or proportional inferences, however, the numbers or proportions will matter. The procedure must accordingly have an independent way of keeping track of which particular proposition is being modelled. Human reasoners appear to retain a superficial representation of the propositions expressed by the premises – one that is close to their linguistic form – but from the errors they make, they appear to make inferences by manipulating mental models rather than by deploying rules of inference on these superficial representations.

2. *Add the information in the second premise to the mental model of the first premise, taking into account the different ways in which this can be done.* In addition to the purely interpretative skills required to construct mental models, reasoners must appreciate the fundamental semantic principle underlying valid deduction: an inference is valid if and only if there is no way of interpreting the premises that is consistent with a denial of the conclusion. This principle motivates the search for alternative ways of adding the information from the second premise.

For some syllogisms, there is only one possible integrated model. For example, a premise of the form *Some of the A are B* yields the model:

a = b
a = b
(a) (b)

and a second premise of the form *All of the B are C* can be integrated only by forming the model:

a = b = c
a = b = c
(a) (b) = c
          (c)

from which it follows that *Some of the A are C*. There is no alternative model of the premises that violates this conclusion.

For other syllogisms, it is necessary to construct and evaluate two models. For example, premises of the form:

Some of the A are not B
All the C are B

can be represented by the model:

```
        a
        a
  - - - - - - -
(a) = b = c
      b = c
      (b)
```

In this model, the conclusion *Some of the A are not C* is true because the A's above the broken line are not C's, and the converse conclusion *Some of the C are not A* is also true because there is at least one C that is not linked to an A. The search for an alternative model to falsify these putative conclusions yields a second model:

```
      a
      a
 - - - - - -
(a) = b = c
(a) = b = c
      (b)
```

This model rules out the second conclusion because all the C's are A's, but there is no way to destroy the first conclusion, *Some of the A are not C*, which is accordingly valid.

Still other premises yield three different models. For example, the premises:

All of the B are A
None of the B are C

yield the model:

```
c
c
- - - - -
b = a
b = a
   (a)
```

which suggests the conclusion *None of the C are A*, or its converse *None of A are C*. The search for a counter-example yields the model:

```
c
c   =  a
-_-__-
b = a
b = a
   (a)
```

which falsifies both of these conclusions and suggests instead that *Some of the C are not A* or conversely that *Some of the A are not C*. The search for a counter-example to these conclusions yields:

```
c      =  a
c   =  a
-_-__-
b = a
b = a
   (a)
```

which shows that only the conclusion *Some of the A are not C* is valid. The last model by itself, of course, suggests the invalid conclusion that *All of the C are A*, but that conclusion is ruled out by the previous models. Although these premises have three models, they do not all have to be constructed *ab initio*: an entirely feasible strategy, as illustrated here, is to construct one model and then to try out various modifications of it that are consistent with the premises.

Since the procedure is based on the assumption that each of the four forms of syllogistic premise is represented by just one mental model, it avoids the explosion of combinatorial possibilities that so embarrasses the theories based on Euler circles. The assumption is feasible provided that optional entities are directly represented within a model, as in the representation of *All A are B* as:

```
a = b
a = b
   (b)
```

Is it logically possible to extend this notion so that instead of the three models required by the last example just one model suffices? Such a model might have the following form:

```
c    (= a)
c    (= a)
-_-__-
b = a
b = a
   (a)
```

However, its correct interpretation requires a new notational principle to be introduced in order to make plain that both, one, or neither of the identities above the broken line may apply. Such a device is merely a notational variation on the present theory: it is still necessary to consider three logically distinct possibilities corresponding to all, some, or none of the c's being identical to a's.

Syllogisms never require more than three different mental models to be constructed, and Table 5.1 presents the number of models that are required for each of the twenty seven pairs of premises that yield a non-trivial valid conclusion. The table indicates when such a conclusion is contrary to the figural effect, and should therefore be harder to draw. It also presents the percentages of correct responses made by subjects in an experiment designed to test the theory (see Johnson-Laird and Bara, 1982). Every subject was presented with each of the sixty-four possible premises with a different sensible content and asked to state what conclusion, if any, followed from the premises. The results will be analysed later in the chapter together with those from other experiments.

3. *Frame a conclusion to express the relation, if any, between the 'end' terms that holds in all the models of the premises.* An 'end' term is one which occurs in only a single premise, unlike the 'middle' term which occurs in both premises. If there is no such relation between the end terms, the only valid conclusions that can be drawn are trivial ones, such as a conjunction or disjunction of the premises, and subjects generally respond that there is no valid conclusion.

The difficulty of syllogistic inference depends on the number of mental models of the premises

If every step of the procedure is carried out correctly, then as a computer implementation of it (in POP-10) shows, the result is a completely rational

Table 5.1 *The number of mental models required for the twenty-seven pairs of premises yielding valid conclusions, and the number of subjects out of twenty drawing the correct conclusions in an experiment reported by Johnson-Laird and Bara (1982). The entries show where premises have a valid conclusion that runs contrary to the figural effect*

FIRST PREMISE

SECOND PREMISE	All the A are B	Some of the A are B	None of the A are B	Some of the A are not B
All the B are C	1 model All the A are C: 19	1 model Some of the A are C: 18 Some of the C are A: 0	3 models (contrary to figure) Some of the C are not A: 0	
Some of the B are C			3 models (contrary to figure) Some of the C are not A: 1	
None of the B are C	1 model None of the A are C: 14 None of the C are A: 3	3 models Some of the A are not C: 4		
Some of the B are not C				
All the C are B			1 model None of the A are C: 8 None of the C are A: 5	2 models Some of the A are not C: 7
Some of the C are B			3 models Some of the C are not A: 1	
None of the C are B	1 model None of the C are A: 8 None of the A are C: 4	3 models Some of the A are not C: 0		
Some of the C are not B	2 models Some of the C are not A: 4			

FIRST PREMISE

SECOND PREMISE	All the B are A	Some of the B are A	None of the B are A	Some of the B are not A
All the B are C	2 models Some of the A are C: 0 Some of the C are A: 0	1 model Some of the C are A: 10 Some of the A are C: 3	3 models Some of the C are not A: 0	2 models Some of the C are not A: 0
Some of the B are C	1 model Some of the A are C: 9 Some of the C are A: 4		3 models Some of the C are not A: 2	
None of the B are C	3 models Some of the A are not C: 0	3 models Some of the A are not C: 3		
Some of the B are not C	2 models Some of the A are not C: 9			
All the C are B	1 model All the C are A: 15		1 model None of the C are A: 12 None of the A are C: 2	
Some of the C are B	1 model Some of the C are A: 19 Some of the A are C: 1		3 models Some of the C are not A: 6	
None of the C are B	3 models (contrary to figure) Some of the A are not C: 0	3 models (contrary to figure) Some of the A are not C: 0		
Some of the C are not B				

and error-free performance. A mistake in any step may, or may not, vitiate the conclusion. Since the first and third steps are common to the comprehension and production of much discourse, they are likely to be relatively free of error. The task of drawing a valid conclusion should be relatively easy when there is only one possible integrated model: even an individual who does not appreciate the need to search for counter-examples should make the correct response. The major source of difficulty should be the construction and evaluation of alternative models. This process places an additional load on working memory – the memory system that is used for holding the mental models while they are manipulated. The greater the number of models to be considered, the harder it should be to construct and to evaluate them. Hence, the task should be harder when it is necessary to construct two models, and harder still when it is necessary to construct three models.

Working with various colleagues – principally Janellen Huttenlocher, Kate Ehrlich, and Bruno Bara – I have carried out a number of experiments on inference in which subjects have been asked to state what, if anything, follows from a series of syllogistic premises. We have used premises with sensible contents, but which do not predispose the subjects to any particular conclusions on a factual basis. Table 5.2 summarizes the results of three of our experiments. In experiment 1, twenty students at Teachers College, Columbia University were given all sixty-four possible pairs of premises. In experiment 2, twenty students at Milan University were also given the sixty-four pairs of premises. And in experiment 3, a further twenty Milanese students were given the same problems but had only ten seconds to respond to each of them. The table shows the percentages of correctly drawn valid conclusions as a function of the number of mental models that have to be constructed to make the right response for the right reason. Despite the variety of conditions and subjects in the experiments, there was a highly reliable trend in each of them: the greater the number of models to be considered, the harder the task of drawing a valid conclusion.

Subjects do indeed attempt to assess alternative models of the premises, but often the task exceeds the capacity of their working memories. It is difficult to hold in mind one model whilst attempting to construct and to evaluate an alternative model. This conclusion is corroborated by the nature of the errors that the subjects make. They almost invariably (i.e. 90% or more) respond with a conclusion that is congruent with only *some* of the possible models of the premises.

The figural effects

There is one other major factor that affects syllogistic inference: the figure of the premises. The figural effects consist in a bias towards certain forms of conclusion, and an increase in the difficulty and latency of drawing correct conclusions over the four figures. These phenomena are important because they cannot be readily explained in terms of atmosphere, illicit conversion, or the theories based on Euler circles and Venn diagrams. But they can be accounted for in terms of the processes that occur in forming an integrated mental model of premises. If the two occurrences of the middle term are in a figure that readily permits the two premises to be integrated, the task is relatively easy; if they are in a figure that does not permit an immediate integration, then additional operations have to be carried out to make it possible, and the premises that require these additional operations are harder to integrate. These additional operations have been modelled in the computer program too. The fundamental assumption on which they are based is that working memory operates on a 'first in, first out' basis. For example, it is easier to recall a list of digits in the order in which they were presented – the first digit recalled first, the second digit recalled second, and so on – than in the opposite order (see Broadbent, 1958, p. 236). The same principle applies to syllogisms, and the natural order in which to state a conclusion is the order in which the terms were used to construct a mental model of the premises.

Table 5.2 *The percentages of correct valid conclusions that were drawn in three different experiments on syllogistic reasoning. The percentages are shown as a function of the number of different models that have to be constructed to yield the correct conclusion*

	Premises requiring one model	Premises requiring two models	Premises requiring three models
Experiment 1	92	46	27
Experiment 2	80	20	9
Experiment 3	62	20	3

Note. Experiment 1 is reported in Johnson-Laird and Steedman (1978); Experiments 2 and 3 are reported in Johnson-Laird and Bara (1982). The data from Experiment 2 on individual valid problems were presented in Table 5.1. In Experiment 1, twenty American subjects were given all sixty-four possible pairs of premises; and, in Experiment 2, twenty Italian subjects were also given the sixty-four pairs of premises. In Experiment 3, a further twenty Italian subjects were given only ten seconds to respond to each problem.

With premises in the A – B, B – C figure, the two instances of the middle term, B, occur one after the other, and it is easy to construct a mental model of the first premise and then immediately to integrate the information from the second premise. For example, with premises of the form:

Some of the A are B
All of the B are C

a reasoner can form a model of the first premise:

$$a = b$$
$$a = b$$
$$(a)\ (b)$$

and then immediately integrate the content of the second premise by substituting c's for b's:

$$a = c$$
$$a = c$$
$$(a)\ (c)$$

This procedure of substituting one type of token for another was deliberately omitted in the account of the theory earlier in the chapter, but it is an essential part of the explanation of the figural effects, because the substitution requires an appropriate ordering of the terms within the premises: there has to be temporal contiguity between the original items (b's) and the ones that replace them (c's). Since the a's preceded the c's into working memory in the example, the 'first in, first out' principle leads to a conclusion of the form *Some of the A are C* rather than its equally valid converse. The same principle applies to any premises in the A – B, B – C figure, and thus favours conclusions of the form A – C rather than C – A (cf. Table 5.3).

With premises in the B – A, C – B figure, the two instances of the middle term do not occur one after the other. They are separated and therefore the process of substitution cannot occur. A natural way to proceed, however, is to construct a model of the second premise, C – B, renew the interpretation of the first premise, B – A, and then substitute the information it contains in the model of the second premise. The reordering of the premises brings together the two occurrences of the middle term. For example, with premises of the form:

All of the B are A
Some of the C are B

reasoners are unable to make an immediate substitution, because of the separation of the two occurrences of the middle term. They accordingly construct a model of the second premise:

$$c = b$$
$$c = b$$
$$(c)\ (b)$$

make a renewed interpretation of the first premise, and substitute its information in the model:

$$c = a$$
$$c = a$$
$$(c)\ (a)$$
$$(a)$$

On the 'first in, first out' principle of working memory, the resulting mental model will yield a conclusion of the form *Some of the C are A*. In general, premises in this figure should produce a bias towards C – A conclusions (cf. Table 5.3).

The two remaining figures are still more complicated. There are two possible routes by which to integrate premises in the A – B, C – B figure. Reasoners can construct a model of the first premise, A – B, and then switch round the order of the terms in their interpretation of the second premise to B – C so that the two instances of the middle term occur one after the other. Alternatively, they can construct a model of the second premise, C – B, renew their interpretation of the first premise, then switch it round to B – A so as to make the substitution possible. Switching round an interpretation must not be confused with the operation of converting a premise, though the two notions are similar. The converse of *Some A are B* is *Some B are A* and they are equivalent in that when one is true the other is true; the converse of *All A are B* is *All B are A*, and they are not equivalent. If reasoners simply formed the converse of an expression, they would often fall into error. Although various theorists have argued that illicit conversions are a source of error (see Chapter 4), the idea of switching round an interpretation concerns only the order of information in working memory. The interpretation of *All the A are B* takes the form:

$$a = b$$
$$a = b$$
$$(b)$$
$$(b)$$

Table 5.3 *The operations required to form an integrated model of premises in the four figures, together with the predicted and obtained response bias*

Operations	Figure of premises					
	A – B B – C	B – A C – B	A – B C – B		B – A B – C	
Switch round	—	—	—	—	Premise 1	Premise 2
Build model	Premise 1	Premise 2	Premise 1	Premise 2	Premise 1	Premise 2
Renew	—	Premise 1	—	Premise 1	—	Premise 1
Switch round	—	—	Premise 2	Premise 1	—	—
Integrate	Premise 2	Premise 1	Premise 2	Premise 1	Premise 2	Premise 1
Predicted reponse bias:	A – C	C – A	A – C	C – A	A – C	C – A
Obtained response bias:						
Experiment 1	89%	91%	50%	50%	64%	36%
Experiment 2	93%	86%	55%	45%	62%	38%
Experiment 3	94%	66%	56%	44%	73%	27%

If this interpretation is switched round, it takes the form:

$$b = a$$
$$b = a$$
$$(b)$$
$$(b)$$

This revision is logically accurate: an illicit conversion would only occur if the tokens representing the possibility of b's that were not a's were dropped in the process. The purpose of the operation is to ensure that the two instances of the middle term occur one after the other.

In the remaining figure, B – A, B – C, there are again two alternative procedures. Reasoners may switch round a model of the first premise to A – B, form a model of it, and then substitute the information from the second premise, B – C, in the model. Alternatively, they may switch round a model of the second premise to C – B, renew their interpretation of the first premise, B – A, and substitute its information in the model.

The operations that are required to form a mental model from premises in the four figures are summarized in Table 5.3. The bias they create towards one particular form of conclusion for the asymmetric figures, A – B B – C and B – A C – B, is highly reliable. The slight bias towards A – C conclusions for the symmetric figures, A – B C – B and B – A B – C, probably reflects a preference both for constructing an initial model from the first premise and for a process that requires fewer operations.

Two basic operations are required to construct a model of the premises in the A – B B – C figure: building an initial model and integrating the information from the second premise. A third operation of renewing the interpretation of a premise is required for premises in the B – A B – C figure. A more complex operation is required by both procedures for premises in the C – B figure: switching round the interpretation of a premise so that information about its end term can be substituted in the model. Finally, a still more complex operation is required by both procedures for premises in the B – A B – C figure:

switching round the interpretation of a premise as a whole as a prerequisite for constructing an initial model.

Since the complexity of the operations required to form a mental model increases over the four figures, there should be a corresponding increase in the difficulty of drawing a valid conclusion, and in the latency of responses. An experiment carried out by Johnson-Laird and Bara (1982) was specifically designed to test these predictions (see Experiment 2 of Table 5.2). There was a reliable decline in the percentages of correct conclusions over the four figures: 51%, 48%, 35%, and 22% respectively. As Table 5.2 shows, the percentages of correct responses where three models had to be constructed were too small to allow us to obtain reliable estimates of latency, while premises requiring two models only occur in the two symmetric figures and hence their data did not enable us to test the latency prediction. However, the trend in latencies for the premises requiring one model reliably confirmed the prediction; over the four figures, the means were 11·6, 12·9, 18·7, and 22·1 seconds respectively.

An alternative explanation of the figural effects

In principle, there are many other possible explanations for the effects of figure on the form of conclusions, their accuracy, and their latency. I believe, however, that the present theory is correct in its essentials, and to substantiate this claim I shall consider an alternative account and some further experimental results.

Many psychologists confronted with the figural effects assume that they somehow reflect the order of the premises and their 'given – new' structure, that is, the position of the given information and the new information in the premises. In fact, this superficially appealing hypothesis fails to account for the phenomena. It is certainly true that the optimal ordering of given and new information corresponds to the figure:

A – B
B – C

with the given information in the second premise, B, referring back to the most recent new information in the first premise. The hypothesis predicts that the other figures, which violate this optimal ordering, should be harder to understand, but it does not explain the trend in difficulty over the remaining figures. Likewise, it does not account for the bias in the form of the conclusions.

A further difficulty for the 'given – new' explanation of the figural effects derives from a series of experiments reported by Ehrlich and Johnson-Laird (1982). In one condition of these experiments, the subjects had to remember premises of the form:

A is on the right of B
B is in front of C
C is on the left of D

in order to draw a corresponding diagram. These experiments, which will be reported in Chapter 14, were primarily concerned with quite a different matter, but one of the independent variables was the figural arrangement of the terms, A, B, C, D, which in fact designated common objects. Figure had no consistent effects on reading times or on memory for the premises, as reflected in the accuracy of the diagrams. It therefore seems that figural effects occur primarily when an inference has to be made, and in particular when a direct link has to be established between the end terms – with the middle term dropping out of the final representation of the conclusion.

If figural effects are a consequence of the operations required to make inferences, then they should occur in all forms of deduction. There should be figural effects, for example, in simple three-term series problems of the form:

Alice is taller than Bertha.
Bertha is taller than Carol.

Indeed, in his classic paper, Ian Hunter (1957) proposed that the difficulty of such problems exactly reflected their figural arrangement. Yet, despite the many studies of three-term problems, there had been no investigation of the conclusions that subjects spontaneously state in their own words until Bruno Bara, Patrizia Tabossi and I carried out two experiments using this procedure in order to test whether there was a figural bias on such conclusions.

One factor that affects the difficulty of three-term series problems is that there is, as Herb Clark has established, a difference in the ease of understanding such pairs of expressions as *taller than* and *shorter than* (see Clark and Clark, 1977). *Taller than* is a neutral expression that implies nothing about the absolute heights of the entities it relates, whereas *shorter than* suggests that these entities are short rather than tall. This contrast between the neutral or 'unmarked' term and its 'marked' antonym is clearest in the difference between such questions as 'Which of the two is the taller?' and 'Which of the two is the shorter?', and in the fact that *tallness* rather than *shortness* is the name of the dimension as a whole. In general, unmarked terms are easier to grasp than marked terms. Hence, in order to obviate this factor in our experiments, we used problems in which the relational term is its own converse:

> Alice is related to Bertha
> Bertha is related to Carol

where it was clear to the subjects that the premises were about blood-relationships. The experiments showed that there was a general bias towards A – C conclusions, and that, as predicted, premises in the A – B, B – C figure enhanced this bias (77% A – C conclusions), whereas those in the B – A, C – B figure eliminated it (only 47% A – C conclusions).

Evidently, the figural effect is not peculiar to syllogisms, but truly mirrors the task of combining premises in working memory. The present theory seems to give a comprehensive account of it.

Syllogisms that yield no valid conclusions interrelating end terms

There are thirty-seven out of the sixty-four pairs of syllogistic premises for which there are no valid conclusions interrelating end terms. In principle, their correct evaluation requires a reasoner to discover that the alternative models of the premises have nothing in common, but the right response may sometimes be made for the wrong reason.

If both premises are particular, i.e., contain the quantifier *some*, then they can be interpreted by alternative models that support contradictory conclusions. For example, the premises:

> Some of the A are B
> Some of the B are C

are readily interpretable both where identities are maximized:

```
        a = b = c
        a = b = c
       (a) (b) (c)
```

and where they are not:

```
        a = b     (c)
        a = b (c)
       (a)  b = c
             b = c
```

Hence, it is readily apparent that such premises do not support a valid conclusion interrelating the end terms. When both premises are negative, they likewise support blatantly inconsistent models. For example, the premises:

> None of the A are B
> None of the B are C

yield both the model:

```
  a
  a  - - - -
          - - - b
          - - - c
                  c
```

and the model:

```
        a = c
        a = c
         - - - b
               b
```

in which there is no relation between the end items common to both interpretations.

The remaining premise pairs require three models to be constructed if the correct response of 'No valid conclusion' is to be guaranteed. For example, the premises:

> All of the A are B
> Some of the B are not C

yield a model:

```
  a
  a
      - - - (c)
             c
```

which suggests that *None of the A are C*, or its converse. They also yield another model:

```
  a
      - - - -
        a = c
             c
```

which rules out the previous conclusions and suggests instead that *Some* of the A are not C or its converse. These conclusions are only falsified by constructing a third model of the premises:

```
          b
       - - - -
       a = c
       a = c
```

The second and third models taken together suggest that at least *Some of the A are C*, or its converse; these conclusions are eliminated only by bearing in mind the first model.

In summary, the theory establishes three main categories of problem for which there is no valid conclusion interrelating the end terms. There are no grounds for supposing that it should be easier to construct two inconsistent models from two particular premises than from two negative premises, or vice versa. The two sorts of problem require independent skills. What can be predicted, however, is that both should be easier than problems that definitely require three models to be constructed to refute putative conclusions. As Table 5.4 indicates, the results of the experiments reliably confirmed this prediction.

Table 5.4 *The percentages of correct responses to premises with no valid conclusions in three experiments. The percentages are shown as a function of the number of models that have to be constructed in order to guarantee the correctness of the response*

	Premises requiring two models	Premises requiring three models
Experiment 1	68	40
Experiment 2	46	18
Experiment 3	71	40

Inference and working memory

The theory of mental models implies that two principal factors affect the difficulty of making an inference: the number of models to be constructed, and the figural arrangement of terms within the premises. As the results of our experiments show, both factors affect performance highly significantly, but they do not interact. Their effects do add up, however, to produce a peculiarly difficult variety of syllogism. Four pairs of premises out of the sixty-four require three models to be constructed that have in common only a conclusion that runs counter to the 'first in, first out'

---

principle underlying the figural effect. Here is an example of such a problem, which the reader may recall from the previous chapter:

All of the bankers are athletes.
None of the councillors are bankers.

There are three ways of integrating the premises in a mental model:

```
    a       a        a
    a       a        a
            (a)
  - - - -  - - - -  - - - -
    c      c = a    c = a
    c      c        c = a
```

The first model suggests the conclusion:

None of the councillors are athletes

which was drawn by twelve subjects in Experiment 1 – the experiment that yielded the best overall performance. Two subjects drew the converse conclusion. The second model shows that both these conclusions are invalid and suggests instead:

Some of the councillors are not athletes

which was drawn by a further two subjects. The third model shows that this conclusion is invalid, too. Four subjects may have succeeded in constructing this model, since they responded that there was no valid conclusion. Not a single subject, however, appreciated that there is a conclusion that covers all three models, though it runs counter to the figure of the premises:

Some of the athletes are not councillors.

These results are characteristic for the four most difficult syllogisms of all – those that run counter to figure and require three models to be evaluated.

The effects of both number of models and figure arise from an inevitable bottleneck in the inferential machinery: the processing capacity of working memory, which must hold one representation in a store, while at the same time the relevant information from the current premise is substituted in it. This problem is not obviated by allowing subjects to have the written premises in front of them throughout the task: the integration of premises has to occur in working memory, unless the subjects are allowed to use paper and pencil so as to externalize the process.

The effect of number of models on inferential performance, so amply confirmed by the studies of syllogisms, is also detectable in other sorts of inference. In an experiment carried out by Johnson-Laird and Wason (1970) the task was to check whether a *description* of the contents of an envelope was correct. The subjects selected diagrams one at a time from a set laid out in front of them, and they were told by the experimenter whether or not each such diagram was in the envelope. The subjects could use this information to determine whether the description was true or false. The logically prudent strategy in this task is to concentrate on diagrams that do *not* fit the description on the envelope: if such a diagram is in the envelope, plainly the description is false. Some subjects, however, choose diagrams that fit the description. That choice is uninformative once it is known that the envelope contains something, because there is no reason why a diagram that fits the description should not also be outside the envelope. What the experiment showed was that a complex disjunctive description:

There is a dot which is not connected to any dot or every dot is connected to every dot

had a striking effect on the subjects' insight into the task. A subject would perform perfectly with other descriptions, only to lose that insight on the very next trial when the disjunctive description occurred. The effect did not seem to be merely a function of the presence of a negation or of several quantifiers, because the subjects were able to cope with such descriptions as:

There is a dot connected to a dot to which no other dot is connected.

The crucial factor seemed to be that this description could be represented in a single mental model of a prototypical relation:

where the required dot, A, is connected to another dot, B, that has no other connections. The disjunctive description, however, contains two mutually exclusive states of affairs:

There is a dot which is not connected to any dot

or:

Every dot is connected to every dot.

Hence, it can be represented only by keeping in mind a disjunction of two alternative prototypical relations:

which satisfies the first disjunct, and:

which satisfies the second. As Wason and I wrote:

it is possible that this [disjunctive description] occupies a greater amount of short-term memory than a single complex rule, and thus leaves a smaller amount of 'computing space' available for handling the selection of the diagrams. (Johnson-Laird and Wason, 1970, p. 58)

More recently, Baddeley and his colleagues have made a comprehensive examination of the role of working memory in simple verbal inferences. They have found that when subjects are asked to hold in mind a string of digits, their performance in reasoning tasks is adversely affected in comparison with a control group that had no such load on memory (see Baddeley and Hitch, 1974; Hitch and Baddeley, 1976). It is therefore plausible to suppose that the effect of having to construct a greater number of models has its *locus* in working memory.

Individual differences in reasoning ability

What causes people to differ in their ability to make inferences? That they do differ is, of course, evident from the longstanding use of syllogisms in tests of intelligence. Yet no one knows for certain what aspects of mental processing make one person a good reasoner and another a poor reasoner. Whatever the general merit of investigating 'individual differences' by way of mental tests, their use is unfortunately of little value in the study of reasoning. The data they yield are, as I argued in Chapter 4, too gross to elucidate differences in mental processes from one individual to another.

The theory of mental models offers an explanatory framework that helps both to make sense of differences in reasoning ability and to go beyond a merely 'actuarial' account of mental processes. It specifies the separate components underlying inferences and places constraints on the possible differences between individuals. The theory assumes that inferences depend on three component skills: (1) the ability to form an integrated model of the premises; (2) the appreciation that an inference is sound only if there are no counter-examples to it, together with the capacity to put this principle into practice, and (3) the ability to put into words the common characteristics of a set of mental models. Bruno Bara and I have explored the differences in the protocols of subjects carrying out syllogistic inferences, and I shall summarize the outcome of our research.

The only way to convey the 'feel' of the results is to present data from individual subjects. Table 5.5 gives the percentages of valid conclusions drawn by twenty American students, and Table 5.6 gives the percentages for twenty Italian students (the results are from Experiments 1 and 2 reported earlier). Both tables show the percentages as a function of the number of mental models that have to be constructed to draw a valid conclusion. Fortuitously, the two samples of subjects differed in their inferential ability. The most striking overall pattern in the two samples of data is the decline in performance as the number of models to be constructed increases: thirty-three out of the forty subjects conform precisely to this predicted trend, and of the remainder only two showed competence

contrary to the predictions – subjects 1 and 2 in the Italian sample were able to cope with three-model problems, but not two-model problems. I will now examine the individual data in the light of the three main components of the theory.

The process of forming an integrated mental model of premises is nothing more than the proper comprehension of discourse: it is required in order to grasp the full impact of what a speaker has to say. The ability to carry it out should be common to all native speakers of a language, and, since it and its complementary skill of putting models into words suffice for competency with syllogisms requiring only one model, it is hardly surprising that the subjects were almost universally able to cope with these syllogisms. Every single subject performed more accurately with them than with any other sort (for those who relish significance levels, the chance probability of such a result is less than one in a billion). The main difficulty in constructing an integrated model is that a representation of one premise

Table 5.6 The percentages of correct conclusions drawn by twenty Italian subjects in an experiment on syllogistic reasoning. The percentages are shown as a function of the number of models to be constructed in order to draw a valid conclusion (Johnson-Laird and Bara, 1982)

Subjects	One model (n=10)	Two models (n=5)	Three models (n=12)	Overall percentages (n=27)
1	100	20	33	56
2	80	20	42	52
3	100	20	17	48
4	90	40	8	44
5	90	40	8	44
6	70	40	17	41
7	70	20	25	41
8	90	20	8	41
9	100	20	0	41
10	90	40	0	41
11	80	20	8	37
12	80	40	0	37
13	90	20	0	37
14	90	0	8	37
15	70	20	0	30
16	80	0	0	30
17	60	20	0	26
18	70	0	0	26
19	50	0	0	19
20	40	0	0	15
Overall %	80	20	9	37

Table 5.5 The percentages of correct conclusions drawn by twenty American subjects in an experiment on syllogistic reasoning. The percentages are shown as a function of the number of models to be constructed in order to draw a valid conclusion (Johnson-Laird and Steedman, 1978)

Subjects	One model (n=10)	Two models (n=5)	Three models (n=12)	Overall percentages (n=27)
1	100	80	75	85
2	100	60	75	74
3	90	60	42	63
4	90	80	33	63
5	90	80	33	63
6	100	80	25	63
7	100	60	33	63
8	100	40	33	59
9	90	80	17	56
10	100	60	17	56
11	100	40	25	56
12	80	60	25	52
13	100	60	8	52
14	100	0	25	48
15	100	20	17	48
16	90	20	17	44
17	80	20	17	41
18	80	0	17	37
19	70	0	25	37
20	80	20	0	33
Overall %	92	46	27	55

must be held in working memory while information from a representation of the other premise is combined with it. The two subjects (19 and 20) in the Italian experiment who failed to do better than chance with one model were quite unable to cope, as one would expect, when the premises required more than one model to be constructed. Likewise, the figural arrangement of terms had a striking effect on their performance: they could only form a model for premises of the A – B, B – C and B – A, C – B figures. With premises in the other figures, which require interpretations to be switched round, they either declared erroneously that there was no valid conclusion or else forgot one of the end terms and mistakenly replaced it with a middle term so as to form a conclusion that was blatantly inconsistent with one of the premises. Their tendency to assert that there was no valid conclusion if (and only if) the figures required interpretations to be switched round gave rise to a spuriously good performance with syllogisms that have no interesting conclusions in these figures.

Only where a valid inference depends on constructing alternative models of the premises are genuine differences in *inferential* ability to be observed. A reasoner must appreciate the need to construct and to evaluate alternative models, and must be able to carry out this procedure within the processing limitations of working memory. An important general point is that the subjects' performance with valid syllogisms and their performance with invalid syllogisms is not reliably correlated ($\tau = 0.11$, $p > 0.2$, for the American subjects; $\tau = -0.13$, $p > 0.2$, for the Italian subjects). The lack of a correlation arises from the responses to those premises for which more than one model can be constructed, which include, of course, all the problems for which there is no valid conclusion. A few subjects seem not to appreciate the need to consider alternatives. The hallmark of their performance is a string of erroneous conclusions and a reluctance to respond that there is no valid conclusion. None of the Americans fell into this category: even subject 20 got 32% of the problems with no valid conclusion correct. There were, however, three Italian subjects (13, 14 and 15) who performed poorly with premises requiring more than one model and who responded correctly to the problems lacking a valid conclusion on less than 20% of occasions. Subject 15, in particular, got only two of these thirty-seven problems correct, otherwise drawing a conclusion based on a single model of them. Other subjects perceive the need to construct alternatives, and are able to do so, but are wholly incapable of assessing them. The hallmark of their performance is a tendency to respond 'No valid conclusion', whether or not it is justified. They accordingly perform spuriously well with premises that do not yield a conclusion, but fall down badly with premises that require assessing more than one model to yield a valid conclusion. Any subject who performs better with invalid syllogisms than with valid syllogisms is showing symptoms of this syndrome. Among the Americans, four subjects (11, 14, 17 and 18) showed marked signs of it: e.g. subject 17 got 89% of the invalid problems correct, but also tended to respond 'No valid conclusion' to valid problems which required more than one model to be constructed. The two most striking instances of the syndrome among the Italians were subject 16 (81% of the invalid syllogisms correct) and subject 17 (62% of the invalid syllogisms correct).

Most subjects are able to construct some alternative models, but from time to time they fall down in assessing what, if anything, they have in common. They are particularly prone to error in those figures that require interpretations to be switched round, failing to detect either that a putative conclusion is violated by one alternative model or else that there is a conclusion common to all the alternatives. It is noteworthy that only one out of the forty subjects in the two experiments showed any competence in dealing with the most difficult syllogisms of all, namely, those with three models where the conclusion runs counter to figure.

There are several other differences in performance between the subjects, including their susceptibility to figural effects, which I shall not analyse here. My point has been to establish that the theory of mental models at least provides a framework suitable for describing individual differences, and even suggests some explanations for them. Indeed, Jane Oakhill and I have recently confirmed in an unpublished study that there is a reliable correlation ($\rho = 0.7$) between a simple measure of the processing capacity of working memory – the number of pairs of letters (e.g. IB) that can be converted in a fixed interval of time into those that are two places later in the alphabet (KD) – and accuracy in syllogistic reasoning. Of course, there are other general personal characteristics, such as impulsivity, that are likely to affect reasoning ability just as they affect the performance of any other intellectual task.

Children's ability to reason syllogistically

Such is Piaget's influence on the study of intellectual development that the majority of psychologists, whether or not they subscribe to his theories, probably believe that children learn to reason formally by the age of 11 to 12 years – the age of Piaget's putative stage of 'formal operations'. There have been many studies which establish that children are able to make deductions at a much earlier age than is dreamt of in Piagetian lore (see, for example, Mehler and Bever, 1967; Bryant and Trabasso, 1971; Donaldson, 1978). But what is equally important is that there are varieties of deduction that are mastered only after the age of twelve. The best evidence comes from the study of syllogisms.

Debbie Bull and I designed an experiment to investigate the ability of two groups of intelligent children (nineteen 9- to 10-year-olds and nineteen 11- to 12-year-olds) to draw their own conclusions from syllogistic premises. It was not possible to use all sixty-four pairs of premises – the task would have been too gruelling – but we carefully selected twenty pairs (of which sixteen yielded valid conclusions) in order to examine the children's general competence. The experiment showed that there was only a slight difference between the abilities of the two groups, that the children were just as susceptible to the effects of figure as adults, but that, unlike most adults, they could only draw valid conclusions that depended on constructing one mental model. The older group responded correctly on 58% of the one-model problems – there were eight such problems and a child had to get four of them right to perform reliably better than chance. Not one of these older subjects drew a correct conclusion to the two-model problem or to the six three-model problems. The younger group responded correctly to 41% of the one-model problems, three subjects (16%) responded correctly to the two-model problem, and not a single subject responded correctly to the three-model problems. In short, some of the children were competent with one-model problems, three of them might have been competent with the two-model problem, but none of them was competent with three-model problems. The syllogism that elicited the best performance from both groups was of the form:

All the A are B
All the B are C
∴ All the A are C.

Doubtless, Aristotle would have predicted this result, because the syllogism is in the form that he considered to be perfect.

Granted that the children taking part in the experiment are intelligent – and the teachers selected the brightest of their children – then they should at a later stage develop a logical ability on a par with the adults that we have tested: they should improve significantly in their ability to reason syllogistically.

Educational applications: how to improve reasoning ability

Educationalists have developed a variety of methods designed to improve the ability to reason. They include the pedagogical use of stories illustrating logical principles (Lipman and Sharp, 1978), the deployment of special reasoning problems (Feuerstein, Hoffman, and Miller, 1980), and various courses on thinking and problem solving (e.g., Whimbey and Lochhead, 1980). Psychologists have become increasingly involved in such matters, especially since the start of the project to raise the intelligence of the entire population of Venezuela (the international newsletter *Human Intelligence* has published several reports on this project, which includes work carried out by researchers at Harvard University, Bolt Beranek and Newman, Inc., and many other research organizations). Applied psychologists need to devise an economical technique for assessing the strengths and weaknesses of an individual's inferential skills, and they need to implement effective remedial procedures that will overcome the various deficiencies underlying poor performance. The work that my colleagues and I have carried out has two main implications. First, it is important to diagnose and to distinguish between weaknesses in reasoning ability that result from the following factors:

1. Cultural or personal characteristics that underlie apparently poor performance, but that have nothing whatsoever to do with basic intellectual ability (cf. Luria, 1977; Scribner, 1977).

2. Linguistic impairments that make it difficult to understand and to remember verbal premises, or to put into words conclusions that have been drawn.

3. Failures to appreciate the fundamental principle of valid inference, or to understand that a reasoning test calls for conclusions that follow of necessity.

4. An inability to construct integrated representations of the premises, or to evaluate alternative representations, as a result of a limited working memory.

Such deficiencies are readily detectable if subjects are asked to state what conclusions follow of necessity from the sixty-four different pairs of syllogistic premises. The premises should each be presented with a sensible everyday content that does not predispose subjects to any particular conclusion on the basis of general knowledge. If the test is followed up by a 'debriefing' session in which the subjects are asked to explain the reasons for their fallacious conclusions, it is relatively easy to identify the causes of their particular problems.

Second, our work suggests that the most common cause of difficulty in reasoning for individuals living in a literate society is the limited processing capabilities of working memory. Its effects have been apparent in every subject that we have tested (see, e.g., Tables 5.5 and 5.6). It must be emphasized, however, that there is a spontaneous improvement in reasoning ability simply as a consequence of practice (with no feedback). The subjects whose data are reported in Table 5.5 were tested again one week later. They were given no forewarning that they would be retested, but their overall performance increased by 10%, and nineteen out of the twenty subjects returned an improved score. One striking differential effect of practice occurred with the valid conclusions drawn from premises in the most difficult figure, B – A, B – C. Here, there was an overall improvement of 20%, and half of it was due to a decline in erroneous responses to the effect that there was no valid conclusion. The result of practice must in part be to increase the efficiency of the encoding operations of working memory, enabling subjects to switch round the interpretation of a premise. The B – A, B – C figure is difficult according to the mental model theory, precisely because it is always necessary to switch round the interpretation of at least one premise. Subjects who earlier were unable either to form alternative integrated models, or to assess their implications, improved with practice. Experience with the task may also produce a growing awareness of general principles governing the logical properties of the problems. Some subjects may notice, for example, that two negative conclusions never yield a valid conclusion and in this way they may begin to perform like logicians and no longer need to construct mental models.

Some commentators on our work have suggested that diagrams of mental models might serve a useful pedagogical function in teaching people the principles of deduction. Although the prospect is appealing, it may be dangerous. Whenever I have presented a reasoning problem informally, I have noticed the difficulties that people get themselves into if they use Euler circles. The problem is that there is no simple algorithm for using them that one can learn as one learns, say, the algorithm for long multiplication. Merely drawing circles does not guarantee that all their possible combinations will be considered exhaustively. The same problem applies to the notation of mental models – if there were a simple algorithm that guaranteed an exhaustive search, doubtless most of us would have mastered it when we first learnt to reason. Educators are probably better advised to ensure that their students understand the fundamental principle of inference and get plenty of opportunities to put it into practice – at least until someone should chance upon an effective way of increasing the processing capacity of working memory.

Conclusions

This chapter has outlined a theory of syllogistic inference based on the assumption that reasoners construct integrated mental models of the premises. These models have an important structural property deriving from a constraint on the set of possible mental models: a *natural* mental model of discourse has a structure that corresponds directly to the structure of the state of affairs that the discourse describes. The sophisticated notations of Euler circles and Venn diagrams lack this property, and consequently they are not natural mental models. For example, a premise such as:

All the artists are beekeepers

describes a state of affairs in which one finite set of individuals is mapped into another. A natural mental model likewise contains one finite set of individual tokens mapped into another. Neither Euler circles nor Venn diagrams, however, contain finite sets of individual tokens: they map finite sets of individuals into infinities of points. Because any syllogistic premise can be represented in a single mental model of the present sort, the theory avoids the combinatorial problems that bedevil Euler circles, and similarly the maximal load on working memory (three different models) is considerably less than would be required for Venn diagrams (eight different contingencies). The theory has been corroborated experimentally and the results that have been presented establish its descriptive adequacy according to the criteria introduced in Chapter 4: it accounts for the relative difficulty of different syllogisms and for the systematic errors and biases in performance (criterion 1); it describes the characteristic patterns of individual differences (criterion 2); and it also has some implications for pedagogy (criterion 7). The theory extends to other sorts of deductive inference, and I propose to evaluate the explanatory adequacy of the general theory rather than the specific instance of it presented here.

Psychological Review

VOLUME 90   NUMBER 4   OCTOBER 1983

Extensional Versus Intuitive Reasoning:
The Conjunction Fallacy in Probability Judgment

Amos Tversky   Daniel Kahneman
Stanford University   University of British Columbia, Vancouver,
                                      British Columbia, Canada

Perhaps the simplest and the most basic qualitative law of probability is the conjunction rule: The probability of a conjunction, $P(A\&B)$, cannot exceed the probabilities of its constituents, $P(A)$ and $P(B)$, because the extension (or the possibility set) of the conjunction is included in the extension of its constituents. Judgments under uncertainty, however, are often mediated by intuitive heuristics that are not bound by the conjunction rule. A conjunction can be more representative than one of its constituents, and instances of a specific category can be easier to imagine or to retrieve than instances of a more inclusive category. The representativeness and availability heuristics therefore can make a conjunction appear more probable than one of its constituents. This phenomenon is demonstrated in a variety of contexts including estimation of word frequency, suspicion of criminal acts, medical prognosis, decision under risk, suspicion of criminal acts, and political forecasting. Systematic violations of the conjunction rule are observed in judgments of lay people and of experts in both between-subjects and within-subjects comparisons. Alternative interpretations of the conjunction fallacy are discussed and attempts to combat it are explored.

Uncertainty is an unavoidable aspect of the human condition. Many significant choices must be based on beliefs about the likelihood of such uncertain events as the guilt of a defendant, the result of an election, the future value of the dollar, the outcome of a medical operation, or the response of a friend. Because we normally do not have adequate formal models for computing the probabilities of such events, intuitive judgment is often the only practical method for assessing uncertainty.

The question of how lay people and experts evaluate the probabilities of uncertain events has attracted considerable research interest in

This research was supported by Grant NR 197-058 from the U.S. Office of Naval Research. We are grateful to friends and colleagues, too numerous to list by name, for their useful comments and suggestions on an earlier draft of this article.

Requests for reprints should be sent to Amos Tversky, Department of Psychology, Jordan Hall, Building 420, Stanford University, Stanford, California 94305.

the last decade (see, e.g., Einhorn & Hogarth, 1981; Kahneman, Slovic, & Tversky, 1982; Nisbett & Ross, 1980). Much of this research has compared intuitive inferences and probability judgments to the rules of statistics and the laws of probability. The student of judgment uses the probability calculus as a standard of comparison much as a student of perception might compare the perceived sizes of objects to their physical sizes. Unlike the correct size of objects, however, the "correct" probability of events is not easily defined. Because individuals who hold different knowledge or who hold different beliefs must be allowed to assign different probabilities to the same event, no single value can be correct for all people. Furthermore, a correct probability cannot always be determined even for a single person. Outside the domain of random sampling, probability theory does not determine the probabilities of uncertain events—it merely imposes constraints on the relations among

them. For example, if A is more probable than B, then the complement of A must be less probable than the complement of B.

The laws of probability derive from extensional considerations. A probability measure is defined on a family of events and each event is construed as a set of possibilities, such as the three ways of getting a 10 on a throw of a pair of dice. The probability of an event equals the sum of the probabilities of its disjoint outcomes. Probability theory has traditionally been used to analyze repetitive chance processes, but the theory has also been applied to essentially unique events where probability is not reducible to the relative frequency of "favorable" outcomes. The probability that the man who sits next to you on the plane is un-married equals the probability that he is a bachelor plus the probability that he is either divorced or widowed. Additivity applies even when probability does not have a frequentistic interpretation and when the elementary events are not equiprobable.

The simplest and most fundamental qualitative law of probability is the extension rule: If the extension of A includes the extension of B (i.e., $A \supset B$) then $P(A) \geq P(B)$. Because the set of possibilities associated with a conjunction A&B is included in the set of possibilities associated with B, the same principle can also be expressed by the conjunction rule $P(A\&B) \leq P(B)$. A conjunction cannot be more probable than one of its constituents. This rule holds regardless of whether A and B are independent and is valid for any probability assignment on the same sample space. Furthermore, it applies not only to the standard probability calculus but also to nonstandard models such as upper and lower probability (Dempster, 1967; Suppes, 1975), belief function (Shafer, 1976), Baconian probability (Cohen, 1977), rational belief (Kyburg, in press), and possibility theory (Zadeh, 1978).

In contrast to formal theories of belief, intuitive judgments of probability are generally not extensional. People do not normally analyze daily events into exhaustive lists of possibilities or evaluate compound probabilities by aggregating elementary ones. Instead, they commonly use a limited number of heuristics, such as representativeness and availability (Kahneman et al., 1982). Our conception of natural as-

sessments that are routinely carried out as part of the perception of events and the comprehension of messages. Such natural assessments include computations of similarity and representativeness, attributions of causality, and evaluations of the availability of associations and exemplars. These assessments, we propose, are performed even in the absence of a specific task set, although their results are used to meet task demands as they arise. For example, the mere mention of "horror movies" activates instances of horror movies and evokes an assessment of their availability. Similarly, the statement that Woody Allen's aunt had hoped that he would be a dentist elicits a comparison of the character to the stereotype and an assessment of representativeness. It is presumably the mismatch between Woody Allen's personality and our stereotype of a dentist that makes the thought mildly amusing. Although these assessments are not tied to the estimation of frequency or probability, they are likely to play a dominant role when such judgments are required. The availability of horror movies may be used to answer the question, "What proportion of the movies produced last year were horror movies?", and representativeness may control the judgment that a particular boy is more likely to be an actor than a dentist.

The term *judgmental heuristic* refers to a strategy—whether deliberate or not—that relies on a natural assessment to produce an estimation or a prediction. One of the manifestations of a heuristic is the relative neglect of other considerations. For example, the resemblance of a child to various professional stereotypes may be given too much weight in predicting future vocational choice, at the expense of other pertinent data such as the base-rate frequencies of occupations. Hence, the use of judgmental heuristics gives rise to predictable biases. Natural assessments can affect judgments in other ways, for which the term *heuristic* is less apt. First, people sometimes misinterpret their task and fail to distinguish the required judgment from the natural assessment that the problem evokes. Second, the natural assessment may act as an anchor to which the required judgment is assimilated, even when the judge does not intend to use the one to estimate the other.

Previous discussions of errors of judgment have focused on deliberate strategies and on misinterpretations of tasks. The present treatment calls special attention to the processes of anchoring and assimilation, which are often neither deliberate nor conscious. An example from perception may be instructive: If two objects in a picture of a three-dimensional scene have the same picture size, the one that appears more distant is not only seen as "really" larger but also as larger in the picture. The natural computation of real size evidently influences the (less natural) judgment of picture size, although observers are unlikely to confuse the two values or to use the former to estimate the latter.

The natural assessments of representativeness and availability do not conform to the extensional logic of probability theory. In particular, a conjunction can be more representative than one of its constituents, and instances of a specific category can be easier to retrieve than instances of a more inclusive category. The following demonstration illustrates the point. When they were given 60 sec to list seven-letter words of a specified form, students at the University of British Columbia (UBC) produced many more words of the form _ _ _ _ i n g than of the form _ _ _ _ _ n _, although the latter class includes the former. The average numbers of words produced in the two conditions were 6.4 and 2.9, respectively, $t(44) = 4.70$, $p < .01$. In this test of availability, the increased efficacy of memory search suffices to offset the reduced extension of the target class.

Our treatment of the availability heuristic (Tversky & Kahneman, 1973) suggests that the differential availability of *ing* words and of *n _* words should be reflected in judgments of frequency. The following questions test this prediction.

In four pages of a novel (about 2,000 words), how many words would you expect to find that have the form _ _ _ _ i n g (seven-letter words that end with "ing")? Indicate your best estimate by circling one of the values below:

0 1-2 3-4 5-7 8-10 11-15 16+.

A second version of the question requested estimates for words of the form _ _ _ _ _ n _. The median estimates were 13.4 for *ing* words ($n = 52$), and 4.7 for *_ n _* words ($n = 53$, $p < .01$, by median test), contrary to the extension rule. Similar results were obtained for the comparison of words of the form _ _ _ _ l y with words of the form _ _ _ _ _ l _; the median estimates were 8.8 and 4.4, respectively.

This example illustrates the structure of the studies reported in this article. We constructed problems in which a reduction of extension was associated with an increase in availability or representativeness, and we tested the conjunction rule in judgments of frequency or probability. In the next section we discuss the representativeness heuristic and contrast it with the conjunction rule in the context of person perception. The third section describes conjunction fallacies in medical prognoses, sports forecasting, and choice among bets. In the fourth section we investigate probability judgments for conjunctions of causes and effects and describe conjunction errors in scenarios of future events. Manipulations that enable respondents to resist the conjunction fallacy are explored in the fifth section, and the implications of the results are discussed in the last section.

Representative Conjunctions

Modern research on categorization of objects and events (Mervis & Rosch, 1981; Rosch, 1978; Smith & Medin, 1981) has shown that information is commonly stored and processed in relation to mental models, such as prototypes and schemata. It is therefore natural and economical for the probability of an event to be evaluated by the degree to which that event is representative of an appropriate mental model (Kahneman & Tversky, 1972, 1973; Tversky & Kahneman, 1971, 1982). Because many of the results reported here are attributed to this heuristic, we first briefly analyze the concept of representativeness and illustrate its role in probability judgment.

Representativeness is an assessment of the degree of correspondence between a sample and a population, an instance and a category, an act and an actor, or, more generally, between an outcome and a model. The model may refer to a person, a coin, or the world economy, and the respective outcomes could be marital status, a sequence of heads and tails, or the current price of gold. Representativeness can be investigated empirically by asking people, for example, which of two sequences of heads and tails is more representative of a fair coin or which of two professions is more representative of a given personality. This relation differs from other notions of proximity in that it is distinctly directional. It is natural to describe a sample as more or less representative of its parent population or a species (e.g., robin, penguin) as more or less representative of a superordinate category (e.g., bird). It is awkward to describe a population as representative of a sample or a category as representative of an instance.

When the model and the outcomes are described in the same terms, representativeness is reducible to similarity. Because a sample and a population, for example, can be described by the same attributes (e.g., central tendency and variability), the sample appears representative if its salient statistics match the corresponding parameters of the population. In the same manner, a person seems representative of a social group if his or her personality resembles the stereotypical member of that group. Representativeness, however, is not always reducible to similarity (see, e.g. Chapman & Chapman, 1967; Jennings, Amabile, & Ross, 1982; Nisbett & Ross, 1980). A particular act (e.g., suicide) is representative of a person because we attribute to the actor a disposition to commit the act, not because the act resembles the person. Thus, an outcome is representative of a model if the salient features match or if the model has a propensity to produce the outcome.

Representativeness tends to covary with frequency: Common instances and frequent events are generally more representative than unusual instances and rare events. The representative summer day is warm and sunny, the representative American family has two children, and the representative height of an adult male is about 5 feet 10 inches. However, there are notable circumstances where representativeness is at variance with both actual and perceived frequency. First, a highly specific outcome can be representative but infrequent. Consider a numerical variable, such as weight, that has a unimodal frequency distribution in a given population. A narrow interval near the mode of the distribution is generally more representative of the population than a wider interval near the tail. For example, 68% of a group of Stanford University undergraduates ($N = 105$) stated that it is more representative for a female Stanford student "to weigh between 124 and 125 pounds" than "to weigh more than 135 pounds". On the other hand, 78% of a different group ($N = 102$) stated that among female Stanford students there are more "women who weigh more than 135 pounds" than "women who weigh between 124 and 125 pounds." Thus, the narrow modal interval (124-125 pounds) was judged to be more representative but less frequent than the broad tail interval (above 135 pounds).

Second, an attribute is representative of a class if it is very diagnostic, that is, if the relative frequency of this attribute is much higher in that class than in a relevant reference class. For example, 65% of the subjects ($N = 105$) stated that it is more representative for a Hollywood actress "to be divorced more than 4 times" than "to vote Democratic." Multiple divorce is diagnostic of Hollywood actresses because it is part of the stereotype that the incidence of divorce is higher among Hollywood actresses than among other women. However, 83% of a different group ($N = 102$) stated that, among Hollywood actresses, there are more "women who vote Democratic" than "women who are divorced more than 4 times." Thus, the more diagnostic attribute was judged to be more representative but less frequent than an attribute (voting Democratic) of lower diagnosticity. Third, an unrepresentative instance of a category can be fairly representative of a superordinate category. For example, chicken is a worse exemplar of a bird than of an animal, and rice is an unrepresentative vegetable, although it is a representative food.

The preceding observations indicate that representativeness is nonextensional: It is not determined by frequency, and it is not bound by class inclusion. Consequently, the test of the conjunction rule in probability judgments offers the sharpest contrast between the extensional logic of probability theory and the psychological principles of representativeness. Our first set of studies of the conjunction rule were conducted in 1974, using occupation and political affiliation as target attributes to be predicted singly or in conjunction from brief personality sketches (see Tversky & Kahneman, 1982, for a brief summary). The studies described in the present section replicate and extend our earlier work. We used the following personality sketches of two fictitious individuals, Bill and Linda, followed by a set of occupations and avocations associated with each of them.

Bill is 34 years old. He is intelligent, but unimaginative, compulsive, and generally lifeless. In school, he was strong in mathematics but weak in social studies and humanities.

Bill is a physician who plays poker for a hobby.
Bill is an architect.
Bill is an accountant. (A)
Bill plays jazz for a hobby. (J)
Bill surfs for a hobby.
Bill is a reporter.
Bill is an accountant who plays jazz for a hobby. (A&J)
Bill climbs mountains for a hobby.

Linda is 31 years old, single, outspoken and very bright. She majored in philosophy. As a student, she was deeply concerned with issues of discrimination and social justice, and also participated in anti-nuclear demonstrations.

Linda is a teacher in elementary school.
Linda works in a bookstore and takes Yoga classes.
Linda is active in the feminist movement. (F)
Linda is a psychiatric social worker.
Linda is a member of the League of Women Voters.
Linda is a bank teller. (T)
Linda is an insurance salesperson.
Linda is a bank teller and is active in the feminist movement. (T&F)

As the reader has probably guessed, the description of Bill was constructed to be representative of an accountant (A) and unrepresentative of a person who plays jazz for a hobby (J). The description of Linda was constructed to be representative of an active feminist (F) and unrepresentative of a bank teller (T). We also expected the ratings of representativeness to be higher for the classes defined by a conjunction of attributes (A&J for Bill, T&F for Linda) than for the less representative constituent of each conjunction (J and T, respectively).

A group of 88 undergraduates at UBC ranked the eight statements associated with each description by "the degree to which Bill (Linda) resembles the typical member of that class." The results confirmed our expectations. The percentages of respondents who displayed the predicted order (A > A&J > J for Bill; F > T&F > T for Linda) were 87% and 85%, respectively. This finding is neither surprising nor objectionable. If, like similarity and prototypicality, representativeness depends on both common and distinctive features (Tver-sky, 1977), it should be enhanced by the addition of shared features. Adding eyebrows to a schematic face makes it more similar to another schematic face with eyebrows (Gati & Tversky, 1982). Analogously, the addition of feminism to the profession of bank teller improves the match of Linda's current activities to her personality. More surprising and less acceptable is the finding that the great majority of subjects also rank the conjunctions (A&J and T&F) as more *probable* than their less representative constituents (J and T). The following sections describe and analyze this phenomenon.

Indirect and Subtle Tests

Experimental tests of the conjunction rule can be divided into three types: *indirect tests*, *direct-subtle tests* and *direct-transparent tests*. In the indirect tests, one group of subjects evaluates the probability of the conjunction, and another group of subjects evaluates the probability of its constituents. No subject is required to compare a conjunction (e.g., "Linda is a bank teller and a feminist") to its constituents. In the direct-subtle tests, subjects compare the conjunction to its less representative constituent, but the inclusion relation between the events is not emphasized. In the direct-transparent tests, the subjects evaluate or compare the probabilities of the conjunction and its constituent in a format that highlights the relation between them.

The three experimental procedures investigate different hypotheses. The indirect procedure tests whether probability judgments conform to the conjunction rule; the direct-subtle procedure tests whether people will take advantage of an opportunity to compare the critical events; the direct-transparent procedure tests whether people will obey the conjunction rule when they are compelled to compare the critical events. This sequence of tests also describes the course of our investigation, which began with the observation of violations of the conjunction rule in indirect tests and proceeded—to our increasing surprise—to the finding of stubborn failures of that rule in several direct-transparent tests.

Three groups of respondents took part in the main study. The statistically *naive* group consisted of undergraduate students at Stanford University and UBC who had no background in probability or statistics. The *informed* group consisted of first-year graduate students in psychology and in education and of medical students at Stanford who were all familiar with the basic concepts of probability after one or more courses in statistics. The *sophisticated* group consisted of doctoral students in the decision science program of the Stanford Business School who had taken several advanced courses in probability, statistics, and decision theory.

Subjects in the main study received one problem (either Bill or Linda) first in the format of a direct test. They were asked to rank all eight statements associated with that problem (including the conjunction, its separate constituents, and five filler items) according to their probability, using 1 for the most probable and 8 for the least probable. The subjects then received the remaining problem in the format of an indirect test in which the list of alternatives included either the conjunction or its separate constituents. The same five filler items were used in both the direct and the indirect versions of each problem.

Table 1 presents the average ranks (R) of the conjunction R(A&B) and of its less representative constituents R(B), relative to the set of five filler items. The percentage of violations of the conjunction rule in the direct test is denoted by V. The results can be summarized as follows: (a) the conjunction is ranked higher than its less likely constituents in all 12 comparisons, (b) there is no consistent difference between the ranks of the alternatives in the direct and indirect tests, (c) the overall incidence of violations of the conjunction rule in direct tests is 88%, which virtually coincides with the incidence of the corresponding pattern in judgments of representativeness, and (d) there is no effect of statistical sophistication in either indirect or direct tests.

The violation of the conjunction rule in a direct comparison of B to A&B is called the *conjunction fallacy*. Violations inferred from between-subjects comparisons are called *conjunction errors*. Perhaps the most surprising aspect of Table 1 is the lack of any difference between indirect and direct tests. We had expected the conjunction to be judged more probable than the less likely of its constituents in an indirect test, in accord with the pattern observed in judgments of representativeness. However, we also expected that even naive respondents would notice the repetition of some attributes, alone and in conjunction with others, and that they would then apply the conjunction rule and rank the conjunction below its constituents. This expectation was violated, not only by statistically naive undergraduates but even by highly sophisticated respondents. In both direct and indirect tests, the subjects apparently ranked the outcomes by the degree to which Bill (or Linda) matched the respective stereotypes. The correlation between the mean ranks of probability and representativeness was .96 for Bill and .98 for Linda. Does the conjunction rule hold when the relation of inclusion is made highly transparent? The studies described in the next section abandon all subtlety in an effort to compel the subjects to

Table 1
Tests of the Conjunction Rule in Likelihood Rankings

Subjects	Problem	Direct test				Indirect test		
		V	R (A & B)	R (B)	N	R (A & B)	R (B)	Total N
Naive	Bill	92	2.5	4.5	94	2.3	4.5	88
	Linda	89	3.3	4.4	88	3.3	4.4	86
Informed	Bill	86	2.6	4.5	56	2.4	4.2	56
	Linda	90	3.0	4.3	53	2.9	3.9	55
Sophisticated	Bill	83	2.6	4.7	32	2.5	4.6	32
	Linda	85	3.2	4.3	32	3.1	4.3	32

Note. V = percentage of violations of the conjunction rule; R (A & B) and R (B) = mean rank assigned to A & B and to B, respectively; N = number of subjects in the direct test; Total N = total number of subjects in the indirect test, who were about equally divided between the two groups.

detect and appreciate the inclusion relation between the target events.

Transparent Tests

This section describes a series of increasingly desperate manipulations designed to induce subjects to obey the conjunction rule. We first presented the description of Linda to a group of 142 undergraduates at UBC and asked them to check which of two alternatives was more probable:

Linda is a bank teller. (T)

Linda is a bank teller and is active in the feminist movement. (T&F)

The order of alternatives was inverted for one half of the subjects, but this manipulation had no effect. Overall, 85% of respondents indicated that T&F was more probable than T, in a flagrant violation of the conjunction rule.

Surprised by the finding, we searched for alternative interpretations of the subjects' responses. Perhaps the subjects found the question too trivial to be taken literally and consequently interpreted the inclusive statement T as T&not-F; that is, "Linda is a bank teller and is *not* a feminist." In such a reading, of course, the observed judgments would not violate the conjunction rule. To test this interpretation, we asked a new group of subjects ($N = 119$) to assess the probability of T and of T&F on a 9-point scale ranging from 1 (extremely unlikely) to 9 (extremely likely). Because it is sensible to rate probabilities even when one of the events includes the other, there was no reason for respondents to interpret T as T&not-F. The pattern of responses obtained with the new version was the same as before. The mean ratings of probability were 3.5 for T and 5.6 for T&F, and 82% of subjects assigned a higher rating to T&F than they did to T.

Although subjects do not spontaneously apply the conjunction rule, perhaps they can recognize its validity. We presented another group of UBC undergraduates with the description of Linda followed by the two statements, T and T&F, and asked them to indicate which of the following two arguments they found more convincing.

Argument 1. Linda is more likely to be a bank teller than she is to be a feminist bank teller, because every feminist

bank teller is a bank teller, but some women bank tellers are not feminists, and Linda could be one of them.

Argument 2. Linda is more likely to be a feminist bank teller than she is likely to be a bank teller, because she resembles an active feminist more than she resembles a bank teller.

The majority of subjects (65%, $n = 58$) chose the invalid resemblance argument (Argument 2) over the valid extensional argument (Argument 1). Thus, a deliberate attempt to induce a reflective attitude did not eliminate the appeal of the representativeness heuristic.

We made a further effort to clarify the inclusive nature of the event T by representing it as a disjunction. (Note that the conjunction rule can also be expressed as a disjunction rule $P(A$ or $B) \geq P(B)$). The description of Linda was used again, with a 9-point rating scale for judgments of probability, but the statement T was replaced by

Linda is a bank teller whether or not she is active in the feminist movement. (T*)

This formulation emphasizes the inclusion of T&F in T. Despite the transparent relation between the statements, the mean ratings of likelihood were 5.1 for T&F and 3.8 for T* ($p < .01$, by t test). Furthermore, 57% of the subjects ($n = 75$) committed the conjunction fallacy by rating T&F higher than T*, and only 16% gave a lower rating to T&F than to T*.

The violations of the conjunction rule in direct comparisons of T&F to T* are remarkable because the extension of "Linda is a bank teller whether or not she is active in the feminist movement" clearly includes the extension of "Linda is a bank teller and is active in the feminist movement." Many subjects evidently failed to draw extensional inferences from the phrase "whether or not," which may have been taken to indicate a weak disposition. This interpretation was supported by a between-subjects comparison, in which different subjects evaluated T, T*, and T&F on a 9-point scale after evaluating the common filler statement, "Linda is a psychiatric social worker." The average ratings were 3.3 for T, 3.9 for T*, and 4.5 for T&F, with each mean significantly different from both others. The statements T and T* are of course extensionally equivalent, but they are assigned different probabilities. Because feminism fits Linda, the

mere mention of this attribute makes T* more likely than T, and a definite commitment to it makes the probability of T&F even higher!

Modest success in loosening the grip of the conjunction fallacy was achieved by asking subjects to choose whether to bet on T or on T&F. The subjects were given Linda's description, with the following instruction:

If you could win \$10 by betting on an event, which of the following would you choose to bet on? (Check one)

The percentage of violations of the conjunction rule in this task was "only" 56% ($n = 60$), much too high for comfort but substantially lower than the typical value for comparisons of the two events in terms of probability. We conjecture that the betting context draws attention to the conditions in which one bet pays off whereas the other does not, allowing some subjects to discover that a bet on T dominates a bet on T&F.

The respondents in the studies described in this section were statistically naive undergraduates at UBC. Does statistical education eradicate the fallacy? To answer this question, 64 graduate students of social sciences at the University of California, Berkeley and at Stanford University, all with credit for several statistics courses, were given the rating-scale version of the direct test of the conjunction rule for the Linda problem. For the first time in this series of studies, the mean rating for T&F (3.5) was lower than the rating assigned to T (3.8), and only 36% of respondents committed the fallacy. Thus, statistical sophistication produced a markable difference in the expected direction in this group of intelligent and sophisticated respondents.

Elsewhere (Kahneman & Tversky, 1982a), we distinguished between positive and negative accounts of judgments and preferences that violate normative rules. A positive account focuses on the factors that produce a particular response; a negative account seeks to explain why the correct response was not made. The positive analysis of the Bill and Linda problems invokes the representativeness heuristic. The stubborn persistence of the conjunction fallacy in highly transparent problems, however, lends special interest to the characteristic question of a negative analysis: Why do intelligent and

reasonably well-educated people fail to recognize the applicability of the conjunction rule in transparent problems? Postexperimental interviews and class discussions with many subjects shed some light on this question. Naive as well as sophisticated subjects generally noticed the nesting of the target events in the direct-transparent test, but the naive, unlike the sophisticated, did not appreciate its significance for probability assessment. On the other hand, most naive subjects did not attempt to defend their responses. As one subject said after acknowledging the validity of the conjunction rule, "I thought you only asked for my opinion."

The interviews and the results of the direct transparent tests indicate that naive subjects do not spontaneously treat the conjunction rule as decisive. Their attitude is reminiscent of children's responses in a Piagetian experiment. The child in the preconservation stage is not altogether blind to arguments based on conservation of volume and typically expects quantity to be conserved (Bruner, 1966). What the child fails to see is that the conservation argument is decisive and should overrule the perceptual impression that the tall container holds more water than the short one. Similarly, naive subjects generally endorse the conjunction rule in the abstract, but their application of this rule to the Linda problem is blocked by the compelling impression that T&F is more representative of her than T is. In this context, the adult subjects reason as if they had not reached the stage of formal operations. A full understanding of a principle of physics, logic, or statistics requires knowledge of the conditions under which it prevails, over conflicting arguments, such as the height of the liquid in a container or the representativeness of an outcome. The recognition of the decisive nature of rules distinguishes different developmental stages in studies of conservation; it also distinguishes different levels of statistical sophistication in the present series of studies.

More Representative Conjunctions

The preceding studies revealed massive violations of the conjunction rule in the domain of person perception and social stereotypes. Does the conjunction rule fare better in other areas of judgment? Does it hold when the uncertainty regarding the target events is attributed to chance rather than to partial ignorance? Does expertise in the relevant subject matter protect against the conjunction fallacy? Do financial incentives help respondents see the light? The following studies were designed to answer these questions.

Medical Judgment

In this study we asked practicing physicians to make intuitive predictions on the basis of clinical evidence.[1] We chose to study expert judgment because physicians possess expert knowledge and because intuitive judgments often play an important role in medical decision making. Two groups of physicians took part in the study. The first group consisted of 37 internists from the greater Boston area who were taking a postgraduate course at Harvard University. The second group consisted of 66 internists with admitting privileges in the New England Medical Center. They were given problems of the following type:

A 55-year-old woman had pulmonary embolism documented angiographically 10 days after a cholecystectomy.

Please rank order the following in terms of the probability that they will be among the conditions experienced by the patient (use 1 for the most likely and 6 for the least likely). Naturally, the patient could experience more than one of these conditions.

dyspnea and hemiparesis (A&B)	syncope and tachycardia hemiparesis (B)
calf pain	hemoptysis
pleuritic chest pain	

The symptoms listed for each problem included one, denoted B, which was judged by our consulting physicians to be nonrepresentative of the patient's condition, and the conjunction of B with another highly representative symptom denoted A. In the above example of pulmonary embolism (blood clots in the lung), dyspnea (shortness of breath) is a typical symptom, whereas hemiparesis (partial paralysis) is very atypical. Each participant first received three (or two) problems in the indirect format, where the list included either B or the conjunction A&B, but not both, followed by two (or three) problems in the direct format illustrated above. The design was balanced so that each problem appeared about an equal number of times in each format. An independent group of 32 physicians from Stanford University were asked to rank each list of symptoms "by the degree to which they are representative of the clinical condition of the patient."

The design was essentially the same as in the Bill and Linda study. The results of the two experiments were also very similar. The correlation between mean ratings by probability and by representativeness exceeded .95 in all five problems. For every one of the five problems, the conjunction of an unlikely symptom with a likely one was judged more probable than the less likely constituent. The ranking of symptoms was the same in direct and indirect tests: The overall mean ranks of A&B and of B, respectively, were 2.7 and 4.6 in the direct tests and 2.8 and 4.3 in the indirect tests. The incidence of violations of the conjunction rule in direct tests ranged from 73% to 100%, with an average of 91%. Evidently, substantive expertise does not displace representativeness and does not prevent conjunction errors.

Can the results be interpreted without imputing to these experts a consistent violation of the conjunction rule? The instructions used in the present study were especially designed to eliminate the interpretation of Symptom B as an exhaustive description of the relevant facts, which would imply the absence of Symptom A. Participants were instructed to rank symptoms in terms of the probability "that they will be among the conditions experienced by the patient." They were also reminded that "the patient could experience more than one of these conditions." To test the effect of these instructions, the following question was included at the end of the questionnaire:

In assessing the probability that the patient described has a particular symptom X, did you assume that (check one)

X is the only symptom experienced by the patient?

X is among the symptoms experienced by the patient?

Sixty of the 62 physicians who were asked this question checked the second answer, rejecting an interpretation of events that could have justified an apparent violation of the conjunction rule.

An additional group of 24 physicians, mostly residents at Stanford Hospital, participated in a group discussion in which they were confronted with their conjunction fallacies in the same questionnaire. The respondents did not defend their answers, although some references were made to "the nature of clinical experience." Most participants appeared surprised and dismayed to have made an elementary error of reasoning. Because the conjunction fallacy is easy to expose, people who committed it are left with the feeling that they should have known better.

Predicting Wimbledon

The uncertainty encountered in the previous studies regarding the prognosis of a patient or the occupation of a person is normally attributed to incomplete knowledge rather than to the operation of a chance process. Recent studies of inductive reasoning about daily events, conducted by Nisbett, Krantz, Jepson, and Kunda (1983), indicated that statistical principles (e.g., the law of large numbers) are commonly applied in domains such as sports and gambling, which include a random element. The next two studies test the conjunction rule in predictions of the outcomes of a sports event and of a game of chance, where the random aspect of the process is particularly salient.

A group of 93 subjects, recruited through an advertisement in the University of Oregon newspaper, were presented with the following problem in October 1980:

Suppose Bjorn Borg reaches the Wimbledon finals in 1981. Please rank order the following outcomes from most to least likely.

A. Borg will win the match (1.7)
B. Borg will lose the first set (2.7)
C. Borg will lose the first set but win the match (2.2)
D. Borg will win the first set but lose the match (3.5)

The average rank of each outcome (1 = most probable, 2 = second most probable, etc.) is given in parentheses. The outcomes were chosen to represent different levels of strength for the player, Borg, with A indicating the highest strength; C, a rather lower level because it indicates a weakness in the first set; B, lower still because it only mentions this weakness; and D, lowest of all.

After winning his fifth Wimbledon title in 1980, Borg seemed extremely strong. Consequently, we hypothesized that Outcome C would be judged more probable than Outcome B, contrary to the conjunction rule, because C represents a better performance for Borg than does B. The mean rankings indicate that this hypothesis was confirmed; 72% of the respondents assigned a higher rank to C than to B, violating the conjunction rule in a direct test.

Is it possible that the subjects interpreted the target events in a nonextensional manner that could justify or explain the observed ranking? It is well-known that connectives (e.g., and, or, if) are often used in ordinary language in ways that depart from their logical definitions. Perhaps the respondents interpreted the conjunction (A and B) as a disjunction (A or B), an implication, (A implies B), or a conditional statement (A if B). Alternatively, the event B could be interpreted in the presence of the conjunction as B and not-A. To investigate these possibilities, we presented to another group of 56 naive subjects at Stanford University the hypothetical results of the relevant tennis match, coded as sequences of wins and losses. For example, the sequence LWWLW denotes a five-set match in which Borg lost (L) the first and the third sets but won (W) the other sets and the match. For each sequence the subjects were asked to examine the four target events of the original Borg problem and to indicate, by marking + or −, whether the given sequence was consistent or inconsistent with each of the events.

With very few exceptions, all of the subjects marked the sequences according to the standard (extensional) interpretation of the target events. A sequence was judged consistent with the conjunction "Borg will lose the first set but win the match" when both constituents were satisfied (e.g., LWWLW) but not when either one or both constituents failed. Evidently, these subjects did not interpret the conjunction as an implication, a conditional statement, or a disjunction. Furthermore, both LWWLW and LWLWL were judged consistent with the inclusive event "Borg will lose the first set," contrary to the hypothesis that the inclusive event B is

[1] We are grateful to Barbara J. McNeil, Harvard Medical School, Stephen G. Pauker, Tufts University School of Medicine, and Edward Baer, Stanford Medical School, for their help in the construction of the clinical problems and in the collection of the data.

understood in the context of the other events as "Borg will lose the first set and the match." The classification of sequences therefore indicated little or no ambiguity regarding the extension of the target events. In particular, all sequences that were classified as instances of B, but some sequences that were classified as instances of B&A, in accord with the standard interpretation in which the conjunction rule should be satisfied.

Another possible interpretation of the conjunction error maintains that instead of assessing the probability $P(B/E)$ of Hypothesis B (e.g., that Linda is a bank teller) in light of evidence E (Linda's personality), subjects assess the inverse probability $P(E/B)$ of the evidence given to the hypothesis in question. Because $P(E/A\&B)$ may well exceed $P(E/B)$, the subjects' responses could be justified under this interpretation. Whatever plausibility this account may have in the case of Linda, it is surely inapplicable to the present study where it makes no sense to assess the conditional probability that Borg will reach the finals given the outcome of the final match.

Risky Choice

If the conjunction fallacy cannot be justified by a reinterpretation of the target events, can it be rationalized by a nonstandard conception of probability? On this hypothesis, representativeness is treated as a legitimate nonextensional interpretation of probability rather than as a fallible heuristic. The conjunction fallacy, then, may be viewed as a misunderstanding regarding the meaning of the word *probability*. To investigate this hypothesis we tested the conjunction rule in the following decision problem, which provides an incentive to choose the most probable event, although the word *probability* is not mentioned.

Consider a regular six-sided die with four green faces and two red faces. The die will be rolled 20 times and the sequence of greens (G) and reds (R) will be recorded. You are asked to select one sequence, from a set of three, and you will win $25 if the sequence you chose appears on successive rolls of the die. Please check the sequence of greens and reds on which you prefer to bet.

1. RGRRR
2. GRGRRR
3. GRRRRR

Note that Sequence 1 can be obtained from Sequence 2 by deleting the first G. By the conjunction rule, therefore, Sequence 1 must be more probable than Sequence 2. Note also that all three sequences are rather unrepresentative of the die because they contain more Rs than Gs. However, Sequence 2 appears to be an improvement over Sequence 1 because it contains a higher proportion of the more likely color. A group of 50 respondents were asked to rank the events by the degree to which they are representative of the die; 88% ranked Sequence 2 highest and Sequence 3 lowest. Thus, Sequence 2 is favored by representativeness, although it is dominated by Sequence 1.

A total of 260 students at UBC and Stanford University were given the choice version of the problem. There were no significant differences between the populations, and their results were pooled. The subjects were run in groups of 30 to 50 in a classroom setting. About one half of the subjects ($N = 125$) actually played the gamble with real payoffs. The choice was hypothetical for the other subjects. The percentages of subjects who chose the dominated option of Sequence 2 were 65% with real payoffs and 62% in the hypothetical format. Only 2% of the subjects in both groups chose Sequence 3.

To facilitate the discovery of the relation between the two critical sequences, we presented a new group of 59 subjects with a (hypothetical) choice problem in which Sequence 2 was replaced by RGRRRG. This new sequence was preferred over Sequence 1, RGRRR, by 63% of the respondents, although the first five elements of the two sequences were identical. These results suggest that subjects coded each sequence in terms of the proportion of Gs and Rs and ranked the sequences by the discrepancy between the proportions in the two sequences (1/5 and 1/3) and the expected value of 2/3.

It is apparent from these results that conjunction errors are not restricted to misunderstandings of the word *probability*. Our subjects followed the representativeness heuristic even when the word was not mentioned and even in choices involving substantial payoffs. The results further show that the conjunction fallacy is not restricted to esoteric interpretations of the connective *and*, because that

connective was also absent from the problem. The present test of the conjunction rule was direct, in the sense defined earlier, because the subjects were required to compare two events, one of which included the other. However, informal interviews with some of the respondents suggest that the test was subtle: The relation of inclusion between Sequences 1 and 2 was apparently noted by only a few of the subjects. Evidently, people are not attuned to the detection of nesting among events, even when these relations are clearly displayed.

Suppose that the relation of dominance between Sequences 1 and 2 is called to the subjects' attention. Do they immediately appreciate its force and treat it as a decisive argument for Sequence 1? The original choice problem (without Sequence 3) was presented to a new group of 88 subjects at Stanford University. These subjects, however, were not asked to select the sequence on which they preferred to bet but only to indicate which of the following two arguments, if any, they found correct.

Argument 1: The first sequence (RGRRR) is more probable than the second (GRGRRR) because the second sequence is the same as the first with an additional G at the beginning. Hence, every time the second sequence occurs, the first sequence must also occur. Consequently, you can win on the first and lose on the second, but you can never win on the second and lose on the first.

Argument 2: The second sequence (GRGRRR) is more probable than the first (RGRRR) because the proportions of R and G in the second sequence are closer than those of the first sequence to the expected proportions of R and G for a die with four green and two red faces.

Most of the subjects (76%) chose the valid extensional argument over an argument that formulates the intuition of representativeness. Recall that a similar argument in the case of Linda was much less effective in combating the conjunction fallacy. The success of the present manipulation can be attributed to the combination of a chance setup and a gambling task, which promotes extensional reasoning by emphasizing the conditions under which the bets will pay off.

Fallacies and Misunderstandings

We have described violations of the conjunction rule in direct tests as a fallacy. The term *fallacy* is used here as a psychological hypothesis, not as an evaluative epithet. A

judgment is appropriately labeled a fallacy when most of the people who make it are disposed, after suitable explanation, to accept the following propositions: (a) They made a nontrivial error, which they would probably have repeated in similar problems, (b) the error was conceptual, not merely verbal or technical, and (c) they *should* have known the correct answer or a procedure to find it. Alternatively, the same judgment could be described as a failure of communication if the subject misunderstands the question or if the experimenter misinterprets the answer. Subjects who have erred because of a misunderstanding are likely to reject the propositions listed above and to claim (as students often do after an examination) that they knew the correct answer all along, and that their error, if any, was verbal or technical rather than conceptual.

A psychological analysis should apply interpretive charity and should avoid treating genuine misunderstandings as if they were fallacies. It should also avoid the temptation to rationalize any error of judgment by ad hoc interpretations that the respondents themselves would not endorse. The dividing line between fallacies and misunderstandings, however, is not always clear. In one of our earlier studies, for example, most respondents stated that a particular description is more likely to belong to a physical education teacher than to a teacher. Strictly speaking, the latter category includes the former, but it could be argued that *teacher* was understood in this problem in a sense that excludes physical education teacher, much as *animal* is often used in a sense that excludes insects. Hence, it was unclear whether the apparent violation of the extension rule in this problem should be described as a fallacy or as a misunderstanding. A special effort was made in the present studies to avoid ambiguity by defining the critical event as an intersection of well-defined classes, such as bank tellers and feminists. The comments of the respondents in postexperimental discussions supported the conclusion that the observed violations of the conjunction rule in direct tests are genuine fallacies, not just misunderstandings.

Causal Conjunctions

The problems discussed in previous sections included three elements: a causal model M

(Linda's personality); a basic target event B, which is unrepresentative of M (she is a bank teller); and an added event A, which is highly representative of the model M (she is a feminist). In these problems, the model M is positively associated with A and is negatively associated with B. This structure, called the M → A paradigm, is depicted on the left-hand side of Figure 1. We found that when the sketch of Linda's personality was omitted and she was identified merely as a "31-year-old woman," almost all respondents obeyed the conjunction rule and ranked the conjunction (bank teller and active feminist) as less probable than its constituents. The conjunction error in the original problem is therefore attributable to the relation between M and A, not to the relation between A and B.

The conjunction fallacy was common in the Linda problem despite the fact that the stereotypes of bank teller and feminist are mildly incompatible. When the constituents of a conjunction are highly incompatible, the incidence of conjunction errors is greatly reduced. For example, the conjunction "Bill is bored by music and plays jazz for a hobby" was judged as less probable (and less representative) than its constituents, although "bored by music" was perceived as a probable (and representative) attribute of Bill. Quite reasonably, the incompatibility of the two attributes reduced the judged probability of their conjunction.

The effect of compatibility on the evaluation of conjunctions is not limited to near contradictions. For instance, it is more representative (as well as more probable) for a student to be in the upper half of the class in both mathematics and physics or to be in the lower half of the class in both fields than to be in the upper half in one field and in the lower half in the other. Such observations imply that the judged probability (or representativeness) of a conjunction cannot be computed as a function (e.g., product, sum, minimum, weighted average) of the scale values of its constituents. This conclusion excludes a large class of formal models that ignore the relation between the constituents of a conjunction. The viability of such models of conjunctive concepts has generated a spirited debate (Jones, 1982; Osherson & Smith, 1981, 1982; Zadeh, 1982; Lakoff, Note 1).

The preceding discussion suggests a new formal structure, called the A → B paradigm,

THE M → A PARADIGM   THE A → B PARADIGM

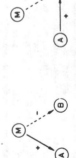

Figure 1. Schematic representation of two experimental paradigms used to test the conjunction rule. (Solid and broken arrows denote strong positive and negative association, respectively, between the model M, the basic target B, and the added target A.)

which is depicted on the right-hand side of Figure 1. Conjunction errors occur in the A → B paradigm because of the direct connection between A and B, although the added event, A, is not particularly representative of the model, M. In this section of the article we investigate problems in which the added event, A, provides a plausible cause or motive for the occurrence of B. Our hypothesis is that the strength of the causal link, which has been shown in previous work to bias judgments of conditional probability (Tversky & Kahneman, 1980), will also bias judgments of the probability of conjunctions (see Beyth-Marom, Note 2). Just as the thought of a personality evokes an assessment of their similarity, the thought of an effect and a possible cause evokes an assessment of causal impact (Ajzen, 1977). The natural assessment of propensity is expected to bias the evaluation of probability.

To illustrate this bias in the A → B paradigm consider the following problem, which was presented to 115 undergraduates at Stanford University and UBC:

A health survey was conducted in a representative sample of adult males in British Columbia of all ages and occupations.

Mr. F. was included in the sample. He was selected by chance from the list of participants.

Which of the following statements is more probable? (check one)

Mr. F. has had one or more heart attacks.

Mr. F. has had one or more heart attacks and he is over 55 years old.

This seemingly transparent problem elicited a substantial proportion (58%) of conjunction errors among statistically naive respondents. To test the hypothesis that these errors are produced by the causal (or correlational) link between advanced age and heart attacks, rather than by a weighted average of the component probabilities, we removed this link by uncoupling the target events without changing their marginal probabilities.

A health survey was conducted in a representative sample of adult males in British Columbia of all ages and occupations.

Mr. F. and Mr. G. were both included in the sample. They were unrelated and were selected by chance from the list of participants.

Which of the following statements is more probable? (check one)

Mr. F. has had one or more heart attacks.

Mr. F. has had one or more heart attacks and Mr. G. is over 55 years old.

Assigning the critical attributes to two independent individuals eliminates in effect the A → B connection by making the events (conditionally) independent. Accordingly, the incidence of conjunction errors dropped to 29% (N = 90).

The A → B paradigm can give rise to dual conjunction errors where A&B is perceived as more probable than each of its constituents, as illustrated in the next problem.

Peter is a junior in college who is training to run the mile in a regional meet. In his best race, earlier this season, Peter ran the mile in 4:06 min. Please rank the following outcomes from most to least probable.

Peter will run the mile under 4:06 min.

Peter will run the mile under 4 min.

Peter will run the second half-mile under 1:55 min.

Peter will run the second half-mile under 1:55 min. and will complete the mile under 4 min.

Peter will run the first half-mile under 2:05 min.

The critical event (a sub-1:55 minute second half and a sub-4 minute mile) is clearly defined as a conjunction and not as a conditional. Nevertheless, 76% of a group of undergraduate students from Stanford University (N = 96) ranked it above one of its constituents, and 48% of the subjects ranked it above both constituents. The natural assessment of the relation between the constituents apparently contaminated the evaluation of their con-

junction. In contrast, no one violated the extension rule by ranking the second outcome (a sub-4 minute mile) above the first (a sub-4:06 minute mile). The preceding results indicate that the judged probability of a conjunction cannot be explained by an averaging model because in such a model P(A&B) lies between P(A) and P(B). An averaging process, however, may be responsible for some conjunction errors, particularly when the constituent probabilities are given in a numerical form.

Motives and Crimes

A conjunction error in a motive-action schema is illustrated by the following problem—one of several of the same general type administered to a group of 171 students at UBC:

John P. is a meek man, 42 years old, married with two children. His neighbors describe him as mild-mannered, but somewhat secretive. He owns an import-export company based in New York City, and he travels frequently to Europe and the Far East. Mr. P. was convicted once for smuggling precious stones and metals (including uranium) and received a suspended sentence of 6 months in jail and a large fine.

Mr. P. is currently under police investigation.

Please rank the following statements by the probability that they will be among the conclusions of the investigation. Remember that other possibilities exist and that more than one statement may be true. Use 1 for the most probable statement, 2 for the second, etc.

Mr. P. is a child molester.

Mr. P. is involved in espionage and the sale of secret documents.

Mr. P. is a drug addict.

Mr. P. killed one of his employees.

One half of the subjects (n = 86) ranked the events above. Other subjects (n = 85) ranked a modified list of possibilities in which the last event was replaced by

Mr. P. killed one of his employees to prevent him from talking to the police.

Although the addition of a possible motive clearly reduces the extension of the event (Mr. P. might have killed his employee for other reasons, such as revenge or self-defense), we hypothesized that the mention of a plausible but nonobvious motive would increase the perceived likelihood of the event. The data confirmed this expectation. The mean rank of the conjunction was 2.90, whereas the mean rank of the inclusive statement was 3.17 ($p < .05$, by t test). Furthermore, 50% of the respondents ranked the conjunction as more likely than the outcome that Mr. P. was a drug addict, but only 23% ranked the more inclusive target event as more likely than drug addiction. We have found in other problems of the same type that the mention of a cause or motive tends to increase the judged probability of an action when the suggested motive (a) offers a reasonable explanation of the target event, (b) appears fairly likely on its own, (c) is nonobvious, in the sense that it does not immediately come to mind when the outcome is mentioned.

We have observed conjunction errors in other judgments involving criminal acts in both the A → B and the M → A paradigms. For example, the hypothesis that a policeman described as violence prone was involved in the heroin trade was ranked less likely (relative to a standard comparison set) than a conjunction of allegations—that he is involved in the heroin trade and that he recently assaulted a suspect. In that example, the assault was not causally linked to the involvement in drugs, but it made the combined allegation more representative of the suspect's disposition. The implications of the psychology of judgment to the evaluation of legal evidence deserve careful study because the outcomes of many trials depend on the ability of a judge or a jury to make intuitive judgments on the basis of partial and fallible data (see Rubinstein, 1979; Saks & Kidd, 1981).

Forecasts and Scenarios

The construction and evaluation of scenarios of future events are not only a favorite pastime of reporters, analysts, and news watchers. Scenarios are often used in the context of planning, and their plausibility influences significant decisions. Scenarios for the past are also important in many contexts, including criminal law and the writing of history. It is of interest, then, to evaluate whether the forecasting or reconstruction of real-life events is subject to conjunction errors. Our analysis suggests that a scenario that includes a possible cause and an outcome could appear more probable than the outcome on its own. We tested this hypothesis in two populations: statistically naive students and professional forecasters.

A sample of 245 UBC undergraduates were requested in April 1982 to evaluate the probability of occurrence of several events in 1983. A 9-point scale was used, defined by the following categories: less than .01%, .1%, .5%, 1%, 2%, 5%, 10%, 25%, and 50% or more. Each problem was presented to different subjects in two versions: one that included only the basic outcome and another that included a more detailed scenario leading to the same outcome. For example, one half of the subjects evaluated the probability of

a massive flood somewhere in North America in 1983, in which more than 1000 people drown.

The other half of the subjects evaluated the probability of

an earthquake in California sometime in 1983, causing a flood in which more than 1000 people drown.

The estimates of the conjunction (earthquake and flood) were significantly higher than the estimates of the flood ($p < .01$, by a Mann-Whitney test). The respective geometric means were 3.1% and 2.2%. Thus, a reminder that a devastating flood could be caused by the anticipated California earthquake made the conjunction of an earthquake and a flood appear more probable than a flood. The same pattern was observed in other problems.

The subjects in the second part of the study were 115 participants in the Second International Congress on Forecasting held in Istanbul, Turkey in July 1982. Most of the subjects were professional analysts, employed by industry, universities, or research institutes. They were professionally involved in forecasting and planning, and many had used scenarios in their work. The research design and the response scales were the same as before. One group of forecasters evaluated the probability of

a complete suspension of diplomatic relations between the USA and the Soviet Union, sometime in 1983.

The other respondents evaluated the probability of the same outcome embedded in the following scenario:

a Russian invasion of Poland, and a complete suspension of diplomatic relations between the USA and the Soviet Union, sometime in 1983.

Although *suspension* is necessarily more probable than *invasion and suspension*, a Russian invasion of Poland offered a plausible scenario leading to the breakdown of diplomatic relations between the superpowers. As expected, the estimates of probability were low for both problems but significantly higher for the conjunction *invasion and suspension* than for *suspension* ($p < .01$, by a Mann-Whitney test). The geometric means of estimates were .47% and .14%, respectively. A similar effect was observed in the comparison of the following outcomes:

a 30% drop in the consumption of oil in the US in 1983.

a dramatic increase in oil prices and a 30% drop in the consumption of oil in the US in 1983.

The geometric means of the estimated probability of the first and the second outcomes, respectively, were .22% and .36%. We speculate that the effect is smaller in this problem (although still statistically significant) because the basic target event (a large drop in oil consumption) makes the added event (a dramatic increase in oil prices) highly available, even when the latter is not mentioned.

Conjunctions involving hypothetical causes are particularly prone to error because it is more natural to assess the probability of the effect given the cause than the joint probability of the effect and the cause. We do not suggest that subjects deliberately adopt this interpretation; rather we propose that the higher conditional estimate serves as an anchor that makes the conjunction appear more probable.

Attempts to forecast events such as a major nuclear accident in the United States or an Islamic revolution in Saudi Arabia typically involve the construction and evaluation of scenarios. Similarly, a plausible story of how the victim might have been killed by someone other than the defendant may convince a jury of the existence of reasonable doubt. Scenarios can usefully serve to stimulate the imagination, to establish the feasibility of outcomes, or to set bounds on judged probabilities (Kirkwood & Pollock, 1982; Zentner, 1982). However, the use of scenarios as a prime instrument for the assessment of probabilities can be highly misleading. First, this procedure favors a conjunctive outcome produced by a sequence of likely steps (e.g., the successful execution of a plan) over an equally probable disjunctive outcome (e.g., the failure of a careful plan), which can occur in many unlikely ways (Bar-Hillel, 1973; Tversky & Kahneman, 1973). Second, the use of scenarios to assess probability is especially vulnerable to conjunction errors. A detailed scenario consisting of causally linked and representative events may appear more probable than a subset of these events (Slovic, Fischhoff, & Lichtenstein, 1976). This effect contributes to the appeal of scenarios and to the illusory insight that they often provide. The attorney who fills in guesses regarding unknown facts, such as motive or mode of operation, may strengthen a case by improving its coherence, although such additions can only lower probability. Similarly, a political analyst can improve scenarios by adding plausible causes and representative consequences. As Pooh-Bah in the *Mikado* explains, such additions provide "corroborative details intended to give artistic verisimilitude to an otherwise bald and unconvincing narrative."

Extensional Cues

The numerous conjunction errors reported in this article illustrate people's affinity for nonextensional reasoning. It is nonetheless obvious that people can understand and apply the extension rule. What cues elicit extensional considerations and what factors promote conformity to the conjunction rule? In this section we focus on a single estimation problem and report several manipulations that induce extensional reasoning and reduce the incidence of the conjunction fallacy. The participants in the studies described in this section were statistically naive students at UBC. Mean estimates are given in parentheses.

A health survey was conducted in a sample of adult males in British Columbia, of all ages and occupations.

Please give your best estimate of the following values:

What percentage of the men surveyed have had one or more heart attacks? (18%)

What percentage of the men surveyed both are over 55 years old and have had one or more heart attacks? (30%)

This version of the health-survey problem produced a substantial number of conjunction errors among statistically naive respondents: 65% of the respondents ($N = 147$) assigned a strictly higher estimate to the second question than to the first.[2] Reversing the order of the constituents did not significantly affect the results.

The observed violations of the conjunction rule in estimates of relative frequency are attributed to the A → B paradigm. We propose that the probability of the conjunction is biased toward the natural assessment of the strength of the causal or statistical link between age and heart attacks. Although the statement of the question appears unambiguous, we considered the hypothesis that the respondents who committed the fallacy had actually interpreted the second question as a request to assess a conditional probability. A new group of UBC undergraduates received the same problem, with the second question amended as follows:

Among the men surveyed who are over 55 years old, what percentage have had one or more heart attacks?

The mean estimate was 59% ($N = 55$). This value is significantly higher than the mean of the estimates of the conjunction (45%) given by those subjects who had committed the fallacy in the original problem. Subjects who viewed the conjunction rule therefore do not simply substitute the conditional $P(B/A)$ for the conjunction $P(A\&B)$.

A seemingly inconsequential change in the problem helps many respondents avoid the conjunction fallacy. A new group of subjects ($N = 159$) were given the original questions but were also asked to assess the "percentage of the men surveyed who are over 55 years old" prior to assessing the conjunction. This manipulation reduced the incidence of conjunction error from 65% to 31%. It appears that many subjects were appropriately cued by the requirement to assess the relative frequency of both classes before assessing the relative frequency of their intersection.

The following formulation also facilitates extensional reasoning:

A health survey was conducted in a sample of 100 adult males in British Columbia, of all ages and occupations.

Please give your best estimate of the following values:

How many of the 100 participants have had one or more heart attacks?

How many of the 100 participants both are over 55 years old and have had one or more heart attacks?

The incidence of the conjunction fallacy was

only 25% in this version ($N = 117$). Evidently, an explicit reference to the number of individual cases encourages subjects to set up a representation of the problems in which class inclusion is readily perceived and appreciated. We have replicated this effect in several other problems of the same general type. The rate of errors was further reduced to a record 11% for a group ($N = 360$) who also estimated the number of participants over 55 years of age prior to the estimation of the conjunctive category. The present findings agree with the results of Beyth-Marom (Note 2), who observed higher estimates for conjunctions in judgments of probability than in assessments of frequency.

The results of this section show that nonextensional reasoning sometimes prevails even in simple estimates of relative frequency in which the extension of the target event and the meaning of the scale are completely unambiguous. On the other hand, we found that the replacement of percentages by frequencies markedly reduced the incidence of the conjunction fallacy. It appears that extensional considerations are readily brought to mind by seemingly inconsequential cues. A contrast worthy of note exists between the effectiveness of extensional cues in the health-survey problem and the relative inefficacy of the methods used to combat the conjunction fallacy in the Linda problem (argument, betting, "whether or not"). The force of the conjunction rule is more readily appreciated when the conjunctions are defined by the intersection of concrete classes than by a combination of properties. Although classes and properties are equivalent from a logical standpoint, they give rise to different mental representations in which different relations and rules are transparent. The formal equivalence of properties to classes is apparently not programmed into the lay mind.

Discussion

In the course of this project we studied the extension rule in a variety of domains; we tested more than 3,000 subjects on dozens of

---

[2] The incidence of the conjunction fallacy was considerably lower (28%) for a group of advanced undergraduates at Stanford University ($N = 62$) who had completed one or more courses in statistics.

problems, and we examined numerous variations of these problems. The results reported in this article constitute a representative though not exhaustive summary of this work.

The data revealed widespread violations of the extension rule by naive and sophisticated subjects in both indirect and direct tests. These results were interpreted within the framework of judgmental heuristics. We proposed that a judgment of probability or frequency is commonly biased toward the natural assessment that the problem evokes. Thus, the request to estimate the frequency of a class elicits a search for exemplars, the task of predicting vocational choice from a personality sketch evokes a comparison of features, and a question about the co-occurrence of events induces an assessment of their causal connection. These assessments are not constrained by the extension rule. Although an arbitrary reduction in the extension of an event typically reduces its availability, representativeness, or causal coherence, there are numerous occasions in which these assessments are higher for the restricted than for the inclusive event. Natural assessments can bias probability judgment in three ways: The respondents (a) may use a natural assessment deliberately as a strategy of estimation, (b) may be primed or anchored by it, or (c) may fail to appreciate the difference between the natural and the required assessments.

Logic Versus Intuition

The conjunction error demonstrates with exceptional clarity the contrast between the extensional logic that underlies most formal conceptions of probability and the natural assessments that govern many judgments and beliefs. However, probability judgments are not always dominated by nonextensional heuristics. Rudiments of probability theory have become part of the culture, and even statistically naive adults can enumerate possibilities and calculate odds in simple games of chance (Edwards, 1975). Furthermore, some real-life contexts encourage the decomposition of events. The chances of a team to reach the playoffs, for example, may be evaluated as follows: "Our team will make it if we beat team B, which we should be able to do since we have a better defense, or if team B loses to

both C and D, which is unlikely since neither one has a strong offense." In this example, the target event (reaching the playoffs) is decomposed into more elementary possibilities that are evaluated in an intuitive manner.

Judgments of probability vary in the degree to which they follow a decompositional or a holistic approach and in the degree to which the assessment and the aggregation of probabilities are analytic or intuitive (see, e.g., Hammond & Brehmer, 1973). At one extreme there are questions (e.g., What are the chances of beating a given hand in poker?) that can be answered by calculating the relative frequency of "favorable" outcomes. Such an analysis possesses all the features associated with an extensional approach: It is decompositional, frequentistic, and algorithmic. At the other extreme, there are questions (e.g., What is the probability that the witness is telling the truth?) that are normally evaluated in a holistic, singular, and intuitive manner (Kahneman & Tversky, 1982b). Decomposition and calculation provide some protection against conjunction errors and other biases, but the intuitive element cannot be entirely eliminated from probability judgments outside the domain of random sampling.

A direct test of the conjunction rule pits an intuitive impression against a basic law of probability. The outcome of the conflict is determined by the nature of the evidence, the formulation of the question, the transparency of the event structure, the appeal of the heuristic, and the sophistication of the respondents. Whether people obey the conjunction rule in any particular direct test depends on the balance of these factors. For example, we found it difficult to induce naive subjects to apply the conjunction rule in the Linda problem, but minor variations in the health-survey question had a marked effect on conjunction errors. This conclusion is consistent with the results of Nisbett et al. (1983), who showed that lay people can apply certain statistical principles (e.g., the law of large numbers) to everyday problems and that the accessibility of these principles varied with the content of the problem and increased significantly with the sophistication of the respondents. We found, however, that sophisticated and naive respondents answered the Linda problem similarly in indirect tests and only parted company in the most transparent versions of the problem. These observations suggest that statistical sophistication did not alter intuitions of representativeness, although it enabled the respondents to recognize in direct tests the decisive force of the extension rule.

Judgment problems in real life do not usually present themselves in the format of a within-subjects design or of a direct test of the laws of probability. Consequently, subjects' performance in a between-subjects test may offer a more realistic view of everyday reasoning. In the indirect test it is very difficult even for a sophisticated judge to ensure that an event has no subset that would appear more probable than it does and no superset that would appear less probable. The satisfaction of the extension rule could be ensured, without direct comparisons of A&B to B, if all events in the relevant ensemble were represented as disjoint unions of elementary possibilities. In many practical contexts, however, such analysis is not feasible. The physician, judge, political analyst, or entrepreneur typically focuses on a critical target event and is rarely prompted to discover potential violations of the extension rule.

Studies of reasoning and problem solving have shown that people often fail to understand or apply an abstract logical principle even when they can use it properly in concrete familiar contexts. Johnson-Laird and Wason (1977), for example, showed that people who err in the verification of *if then* statements in an abstract format often succeed when the problem evokes a familiar schema. The present results exhibit the opposite pattern: People generally accept the conjunction rule in its abstract form (B is more probable than A&B) but defy it in concrete examples, such as the Linda and Bill problems, where the rule conflicts with an intuitive impression.

The violations of the conjunction rule were not only prevalent in our research, they were also sizable. For example, subjects' estimates of the frequency of seven-letter words ending with *ing* were three times as high as their estimates of the frequency of seven letter words ending with *n*_. A correction by a factor of three is the smallest change that would eliminate the inconsistency between the two estimates. However, the subjects surely know that there are many _n_ words that are not *ing*

words (e.g., *present*, *content*). If they believe, for example, that only one half of the _n_ words end with *ing*, then a 6:1 adjustment would be required to make the entire system coherent. The ordinal nature of most of our experiments did not permit an estimate of the adjustment factor required for coherence. Nevertheless, the size of the effect was often considerable. In the rating-scale version of the Linda problem, for example, there was little overlap between the distributions of ratings for T&F and for T. Our problems, of course, were constructed to elicit conjunction errors, and they do not provide an unbiased estimate of the prevalence of these errors. Note, however, that the conjunction error is only a symptom of a more general phenomenon: People tend to overestimate the probabilities of representative (or available) events and/or underestimate the probabilities of less representative events. The violation of the conjunction rule demonstrates this tendency even when the "true" probabilities are unknown or unknowable. The basic phenomenon may be considerably more common than the extreme symptom by which it was illustrated.

Previous studies of the subjective probability of conjunctions (e.g., Bar-Hillel, 1973; Cohen & Hansel, 1957; Goldsmith, 1978; Wyer, 1976; Beyth-Marom, Note 2) focused primarily on testing the multiplicative rule $P(A\&B) = P(B)P(A/B)$. This rule is strictly stronger than the conjunction rule; it also requires cardinal rather than ordinal assessments of probability. The results showed that people generally overestimate the probability of conjunctions in the sense that $P(A\&B) > P(B)P(A/B)$. Some investigators, notably Wyer and Beyth-Marom, also reported data that are inconsistent with the conjunction rule.

Conversing Under Uncertainty

The representativeness heuristic generally favors outcomes that make good stories or good hypotheses. The conjunction *feminist bank teller* is a better hypothesis about Linda than *bank teller*, and the scenario of a Russian invasion of Poland followed by a diplomatic crisis makes a better story than simply *diplomatic crisis*. The notion of a good story can be illuminated by extending the Gricean concept of cooperativeness (Grice, 1975) to con-

versations under uncertainty. The standard analysis of conversation rules assumes that the speaker knows the truth. The maxim of quality enjoins him or her to say only the truth. The maxim of quantity enjoins the speaker to say all of it, subject to the maxim of relevance, which restricts the message to what the listener needs to know. What rules of cooperativeness apply to an uncertain speaker, that is, one who is uncertain of the truth? Such a speaker can guarantee absolute quality only for tautological statements (e.g., "Inflation will continue so long as prices rise"), which are unlikely to earn high marks as contributions to the conversation. A useful contribution must convey the speaker's relevant beliefs even if they are not certain. The rules of cooperativeness for an uncertain speaker must therefore allow for a trade-off of quality and quantity in the evaluation of messages. The expected value of a message can be defined by its information value if it is true, weighted by the probability that it is true. An uncertain speaker may wish to follow the maxim of value: Select the message that has the highest expected value.

The expected value of a message can sometimes be improved by increasing its content, although its probability is thereby reduced. The statement "Inflation will be in the range of 6% to 9% by the end of the year" may be a more valuable forecast than "Inflation will be in the range of 3% to 12%," although the latter is more likely to be confirmed. A good forecast is a compromise between a point estimate, which is sure to be wrong, and a 99.9% credible interval, which is often too broad. The selection of hypotheses in science is subject to the same trade-off: A hypothesis must risk refutation to be valuable, but its value declines if refutation is nearly certain. Good hypotheses balance informativeness against probable truth (Good, 1971). A similar compromise obtains in the structure of natural categories. The basic level category *dog* is much more informative than the more inclusive category *animal* and only slightly less informative than the narrower category *beagle*. Basic level categories have a privileged position in language and thought, presumably because they offer an optimal combination of scope and content (Rosch, 1978). Categorization under uncertainty is a case in point. A moving object dimly seen in the dark may be appropriately labeled *dog*,

where the subordinate *beagle* would be rash and the superordinate *animal* far too conservative.

Consider the task of ranking possible answers to the question, "What do you think Linda is up to these days?" The maxim of value could justify a preference for T&F over T in this task, because the added attribute *feminist* considerably enriches the description of Linda's current activities, at an acceptable cost in probable truth. Thus, the analysis of conversation under uncertainty identifies a pertinent question that is legitimately answered by ranking the conjunction above its constituent. We do not believe, however, that the maxim of value provides a fully satisfactory account of the conjunction fallacy. First, it is unlikely that our respondents interpret the request to rank statements by their probability as a request to rank them by their expected (informational) value. Second, conjunction fallacies have been observed in numerical estimates and in choices of bets, to which the conversational analysis simply does not apply. Nevertheless, the preference for statements of high expected (informational) value could hinder the appreciation of the extension rule. As we suggested in the discussion of the interaction of picture size and real size, the answer to a question can be biased by the availability of an answer to a cognate question—even when the respondent is well aware of the distinction between them.

The same analysis applies to other conceptual neighbors of probability. The concept of surprise is a case in point. Although surprise is closely tied to expectations, it does not follow the laws of probability (Kahneman & Tversky, 1982b). For example, the message that a tennis champion lost the first set of a match is more surprising than the message that she lost the first set but won the match, and a sequence of four consecutive heads in a coin toss is more surprising than four heads followed by two tails. It would be patently absurd, however, to bet on the less surprising event in each of these pairs. Our discussions with subjects provided no indication that they interpreted the instruction to judge probability as an instruction to evaluate surprise. Furthermore, the surprise interpretation does not apply to the conjunction fallacy observed in judgments of frequency. We conclude that surprise and informational value do not properly explain the conjunction fallacy, although they may well contribute to the ease with which it is induced and to the difficulty of eliminating it.

Cognitive Illusions

Our studies of inductive reasoning have focused on systematic errors because they are diagnostic of the heuristics that generally govern judgment and inference. In the words of Helmholtz (1881/1903), "It is just those cases that are not in accordance with reality which are particularly instructive for discovering the laws of the processes by which normal perception originates." The focus on bias and illusion is a research strategy that exploits human error, although it neither assumes nor entails that people are perceptually or cognitively inept. Helmholtz's position implies that perception is not usefully analyzed into a normal process that produces accurate percepts and a distorting process that produces errors and illusions. In cognition, as in perception, the same mechanisms produce both valid and invalid judgments. Indeed, the evidence does not seem to support a "truth plus error" model, which assumes a coherent system of beliefs that is perturbed by various sources of distortion and error. Hence, we do not share Dennis Lindley's optimistic opinion that "inside every incoherent person there is a coherent one trying to get out," (Lindley, Note 3) and we suspect that incoherence is more than skin deep (Tversky & Kahneman, 1981).

It is instructive to compare a structure of beliefs about a domain, (e.g., the political future of Central America) to the perception of a scene (e.g., the view of Yosemite Valley from Glacier Point). We have argued that intuitive judgments of all relevant marginal, conjunctive, and conditional probabilities are not likely to be coherent, that is, to satisfy the constraints of probability theory. Similarly, estimates of distances and angles in the scene are unlikely to satisfy the laws of geometry. For example, there may be pairs of political events for which $P(A)$ is judged greater than $P(B)$ but $P(A/B)$ is judged less than $P(B/A)$—see Tversky and Kahneman (1980). Analogously, the scene may contain a triangle ABC for which the A angle appears greater than the B angle, although the BC distance appears to be smaller than the AC distance.

The violations of the qualitative laws of geometry and probability in judgments of distance and likelihood have significant implications for the interpretation and use of these judgments. Incoherence sharply restricts the inferences that can be drawn from subjective estimates. The judged ordering of the sides of a triangle cannot be inferred from the judged ordering of its angles, and the ordering of marginal probabilities cannot be deduced from the ordering of the respective conditionals. The results of the present study show that it is even unsafe to assume that $P(B)$ is bounded by $P(A\&B)$. Furthermore, a system of judgments that does not obey the conjunction rule cannot be expected to obey more complicated principles that presuppose this rule, such as Bayesian updating, external calibration, and the maximization of expected utility. The presence of bias and incoherence does not diminish the normative force of these principles, but it reduces their usefulness as descriptions of behavior and hinders their prescriptive applications. Indeed, the reconciliation of incoherent judgments and the reconciliation of incoherent assessments pose serious problems that presently have no satisfactory solution (Lindley, Tversky & Brown, 1979; Shafer & Tversky, Note 4).

The issue of coherence has loomed larger in the study of preference and belief than in the study of perception. Judgments of distance and angle can readily be compared to objective reality and can be replaced by objective measurements when accuracy matters. In contrast, objective measurements of probability are often unavailable, and most significant choices under risk require an intuitive evaluation of probability. In the absence of an objective criterion of validity, the normative theory of judgment under uncertainty has treated the coherence of belief as the touchstone of human rationality. Coherence has also been assumed in many descriptive analyses in psychology, economics, and other social sciences. This assumption is attractive because the strong normative appeal of the laws of probability makes violations appear implausible. Our studies of the conjunction rule show that normatively inspired theories that assume coherence are descriptively inadequate, whereas psychological analyses that ignore the appeal of normative rules are, at best, incomplete. A comprehensive account of human judgment must reflect the tension between compelling logical rules and seductive nonextensional intuitions.

Reference Notes

1. Lakoff, G. Categories and cognitive models (Cognitive Science Report No. 2). Berkeley: University of California, 1982.
2. Beyth-Marom, R. The subjective probability of conjunctions (Decision Research Report No. 81-12). Eugene, Oregon: Decision Research, 1981.
3. Lindley, Dennis. Personal communication, 1980.
4. Shafer, G., & Tversky, A. Weighing evidence: The design and comparisons of probability thought experiments. Unpublished manuscript, Stanford University, 1983.

References

Ajzen, I. Intuitive theories of events and the effects of base-rate information on prediction. Journal of Personality and Social Psychology, 1977, 35, 303-314.

Bar-Hillel, M. On the subjective probability of compound events. Organizational Behavior and Human Performance, 1973, 9, 396-406.

Bruner, J. S. On the conservation of liquids. In J. S. Bruner, R. R. Olver, & P. M. Greenfield, et al. (Eds.), Studies in cognitive growth. New York: Wiley, 1966.

Chapman, L. J., & Chapman, J. P. Genesis of popular but erroneous psychodiagnostic observations. Journal of Abnormal Psychology, 1967, 73, 193-204.

Cohen, J., & Hansel, C. M. The nature of decision in gambling: Equivalence of single and compound subjective probabilities. Acta Psychologica, 1957, 13, 357-370.

Cohen, L. J. The probable and the provable. Oxford, England: Clarendon Press, 1977.

Dempster, A. P. Upper and lower probabilities induced by a multivalued mapping. Annals of Mathematical Statistics, 1967, 38, 325-339.

Edwards, W. Comment. Journal of the American Statistical Association, 1975, 70, 291-293.

Einhorn, H. J., & Hogarth, R. M. Behavioral decision theory: Processes of judgment and choice. Annual Review of Psychology, 1981, 32, 53-88.

Gati, I., & Tversky, A. Representations of qualitative and quantitative dimensions. Journal of Experimental Psychology: Human Perception and Performance, 1982, 8, 325-340.

Goldsmith, R. W. Assessing probabilities of compound events in a judicial context. Scandinavian Journal of Psychology, 1978, 19, 103-110.

Good, I. J. The probabilistic explication of information, evidence, surprise, causality, explanation, and utility. In V. P. Godambe & D. A. Sprott (Eds.), Foundations of statistical inference. Toronto, Ontario, Canada: Holt, Rinehart & Winston, 1971.

Grice, H. P. Logic and conversation. In G. Harman & D. Davidson (Eds.), The logic of grammar. Encino, Calif.: Dickinson, 1975.

Hammond, K. R., & Brehmer, B. Quasi-rationality and distrust: Implications for international conflict. In L. Rappoport & D. A. Summers (Eds.), Human judgment and social interaction. New York: Holt, Rinehart & Winston, 1973.

Helmholtz, H. von. Popular lectures on scientific subjects (E. Atkinson, trans.). New York: Green, 1903. (Originally published, 1881.)

Jennings, D., Amabile, T., & Ross, L. Informal covariation assessment. In D. Kahneman, P. Slovic, & A. Tversky (Eds.), Judgment under uncertainty: Heuristics and biases. New York: Cambridge University Press, 1982.

Johnson-Laird, P. N., & Wason, P. C. A theoretical analysis of insight into a reasoning task. In P. N. Johnson-Laird & P. C. Wason (Eds.), Thinking. Cambridge, England: Cambridge University Press, 1977.

Jones, G. V. Stacks not fuzzy sets: An ordinal basis for prototype theory of concepts. Cognition, 1982, 12, 281-290.

Kahneman, D., Slovic, P., & Tversky, A. (Eds.) Judgment under uncertainty: Heuristics and biases. New York: Cambridge University Press, 1982.

Kahneman, D., & Tversky, A. Subjective probability: A judgment of representativeness. Cognitive Psychology, 1972, 3, 430-454.

Kahneman, D., & Tversky, A. On the psychology of prediction. Psychological Review, 1973, 80, 237-251.

Kahneman, D., & Tversky, A. On the study of statistical intuitions. Cognition, 1982, 11, 123-141. (a)

Kahneman, D., & Tversky, A. Variants of uncertainty. Cognition, 1982, 11, 143-157. (b)

Kirkwood, C. W., & Pollock, S. M. Multiple attribute scenarios, bounded probabilities, and threats of nuclear theft. Futures, 1982, 14, 545-553.

Kyburg, H. E. Rational belief. The Behavioral and Brain Sciences, in press.

Lindley, D. V., Tversky, A., & Brown, R. V. On the reconciliation of probability assessments. Journal of the Royal Statistical Society, 1979, 142, 146-180.

Mervis, C. B., & Rosch, E. Categorization of natural objects. Annual Review of Psychology, 1981, 32, 89-115.

Nisbett, R. E., Krantz, D. H., Jepson, C., & Kunda, Z. The use of statistical heuristics in everyday inductive reasoning. Psychological Review, 1983, 90, 339-363.

Nisbett, R., & Ross, L. Human inference: Strategies and shortcomings of social judgment. Englewood Cliffs, N.J.: Prentice-Hall, 1980.

Osberson, D. N., & Smith, E. E. On the adequacy of prototype theory as a theory of concepts. Cognition, 1981, 9, 35-58.

Osberson, D. N., & Smith, E. E. Gradedness and conceptual combination. Cognition, 1982, 12, 299-318.

Rosch, E. Principles of categorization. In E. Rosch & B. B. Lloyd (Eds.), Cognition and categorization. Hillsdale, N.J.: Erlbaum, 1978.

Rubinstein, A. False probabilistic arguments vs. faulty intuition. Israel Law Review, 1979, 14, 247-254.

Saks, M. J., & Kidd, R. F. Human information processing and adjudication: Trials by heuristics. Law & Society Review, 1981, 15, 123-160.

Shafer, G. A mathematical theory of evidence. Princeton, N.J.: Princeton University Press, 1976.

Slovic, P., Fischhoff, B., & Lichtenstein, S. Cognitive processes and societal risk taking. In J. S. Carroll & J. W. Payne (Eds.), *Cognition and social behavior*. Potomac, Md.: Erlbaum, 1976.

Smith, E. E. & Medin, D. L. *Categories and concepts*. Cambridge. Mass.: Harvard University Press, 1981.

Suppes, P. Approximate probability and expectation of gambles. *Erkenntnis*, 1975, *9*, 153–161.

Tversky, A. Features of similarity. *Psychological Review*, 1977, *84*, 327–352.

Tversky, A., & Kahneman, D. Belief in the law of small numbers. *Psychological Bulletin*, 1971, *76*, 105–110.

Tversky, A., & Kahneman, D. Availability: A heuristic for judging frequency and probability. *Cognitive Psychology*, 1973, *5*, 207–232.

Tversky, A., & Kahneman, D. Causal schemas in judgments under uncertainty. In M. Fishbein (Ed.), *Progress in social psychology*. Hillsdale, N.J.: Erlbaum, 1980.

Tversky, A., & Kahneman, D. The framing of decisions and the psychology of choice. *Science*, 1981, *211*, 453–458.

Tversky, A., & Kahneman, D. Judgments of and by representativeness. In D. Kahneman, P. Slovic, & A. Tversky (Eds.), *Judgment under uncertainty: Heuristics and biases*. New York: Cambridge University Press, 1982.

Wyer, R. S., Jr. An investigation of the relations among probability estimates. *Organizational Behavior and Human Performance*, 1976, *15*, 1–18.

Zadeh, L. A. Fuzzy sets as a basis for a theory of possibility. *Fuzzy Sets and Systems*, 1978, *1*, 3–28.

Zadeh, L. A. A note on prototype theory and fuzzy sets. *Cognition*, 1982, *12*, 291–297.

Zentner, R. D. Scenarios, past, present and future. *Long Range Planning*, 1982, *15*, 12–20.

Received July 7, 1982
Revision received May 2, 1983 ∎

Third Edition of the *Publication Manual*

APA has just published the third edition of the *Publication Manual*. This new edition replaces the 1974 second edition of the *Manual*. The new *Manual* updates APA policies and procedures and incorporates changes in editorial style and practice since 1974. It amplifies and refines some parts of the second edition, reorganizes other parts, and presents new material. (See the March issue of the *American Psychologist* for more on the third edition.)

All manuscripts to be published in the 1984 volumes of APA's journals will be copy edited according to the third edition of the *Manual*. Therefore, manuscripts being prepared now should be prepared according to the third edition. Beginning in 1984, submitted manuscripts that depart significantly from third edition style will be returned to authors for correction.

The third edition of the *Publication Manual* is available for $12 for members of APA and $15 for nonmembers. Orders of $25 or less must be prepaid. A charge of $1.50 per order is required for shipping and handling. To order the third edition, write to the Order Department, APA, 1400 N. Uhle Street, Arlington, VA 22201.

Problem Solving

Almost any cognitive activity can be construed as an instance of problem solving, but the kinds of situations labeled *problem solving* typically require that a person put together a novel sequence of processes and behaviors to achieve some goal. Such situations include solving mathematical puzzles, playing complex games such as chess, and thinking about scientific problems.

Newell and Simon have dominated the study of problem solving since the late 1950s. The first paper in this section presents some of their earlier work, which emphasized general heuristics, in particular *means–ends analysis*. Means–ends analysis operates roughly as follows. If there is a method to reach a goal directly, then that method is applied; if there is no such method, then a subgoal is generated that reduces the difference between the present state and the goal. If there is a method to reach the subgoal directly, then this method is applied; otherwise, a subsubgoal is generated; and so on. Means–ends analysis has been widely used to characterize human problem solving.

Because general heuristics can be used in any domain, they are the main tools that a novice has at his or her disposal. But as a person gains expertise in a domain, the methods of problem solving change. This difference is strikingly illustrated in the paper by Chase and Simon, which analyzes differences between novice and expert chess players. Experts differ from the novices primarily in that they have stored representations of a huge number of possible board configurations, and presumably use these configurations to trigger specific moves. Thus, whereas a novice uses heuristics such as means–ends analysis to *reason* about a possible move, experts use domain-specific knowledge virtually to *see* a possible move.

GPS, A PROGRAM THAT SIMULATES HUMAN THOUGHT

by Allen Newell & H. A. Simon

This article is concerned with the psychology of human thinking. It sets forth a theory to explain how some humans try to solve some simple formal problems. The research from which the theory emerged is intimately related to the field of information processing and the construction of intelligent automata, and the theory is expressed in the form of a computer program. The rapid technical advances in the art of programming digital computers to do sophisticated tasks have made such a theory feasible.

It is often argued that a careful line must be drawn between the attempt to *accomplish* with machines the same tasks that humans perform, and the attempt to *simulate* the processes humans actually use to accomplish these tasks. The program discussed in the report, GPS (General Problem Solver), maximally confuses the two approaches—with mutual benefit. GPS has previously been described as an attempt to build a problem-solving program (Newell, Shaw, and Simon, 1959a, 1960a), and in our own research it remains a major vehicle for exploring the area of artificial intelligence. Simultaneously, variants of GPS provide simulations of human behavior (Newell and Simon, 1961a). It is this latter aspect—the use of GPS as a theory of human problem-solving—that we want to focus on exclusively here, with special attention to the relation between the theory and the data.

As a context for the discussion that is to follow, let us make some brief comments on some history of psychology. At the beginning of this century the prevailing thesis in psychology was Associationism. It was an atomistic doctrine, which postulated a theory of hard little elements, either sensations or ideas, that became hooked or associated together without modifica-

tion. It was a mechanistic doctrine, with simple fixed laws of contiguity in time and space to account for the formation of new associations. Those were its assumptions. Behavior proceeded by the stream of associations: Each association produced its successors, and acquired new attachments with the sensations arriving from the environment.

In the first decade of the century a reaction developed to this doctrine through the work of the Wurzburg school. Rejecting the notion of a completely self-determining stream of associations, it introduced the task (*Aufgabe*) as a necessary factor in describing the process of thinking. The task gave direction to thought. A noteworthy innovation of the Wurzburg school was the use of systematic introspection to shed light on the thinking process and the contents of consciousness. The result was a blend of mechanics and phenomenalism, which gave rise in turn to two divergent antitheses, Behaviorism and the Gestalt movement.

The behavioristic reaction insisted that introspection was a highly unstable, subjective procedure, whose futility was amply demonstrated in the controversy on imageless thought. Behaviorism reformulated the task of psychology as one of explaining the response of organisms as a function of the stimuli impinging upon them and measuring both objectively. However, Behaviorism accepted, and indeed reinforced, the mechanistic assumption that the connections between stimulus and response were formed and maintained as simple, determinate functions of the environment.

The Gestalt reaction took an opposite turn. It rejected the mechanistic nature of the associationist doctrine but maintained the value of phenomenal observation. In many ways it continued the Wurzburg school's insistence that thinking was more than association—thinking has direction given to it by the task or by the set of the subject. Gestalt psychology elaborated this doctrine in genuinely new ways in terms of holistic principles of organization.

Today psychology lives in a state of relatively stable tension between the poles of Behaviorism and Gestalt psychology. All of us have internalized the major lessons of both: We treat skeptically the subjective elements in our experiments and agree that all notions must eventually be made operational by means of behavioral measures. We also recognize that a human being is a tremendously complex, organized system, and that the simple schemes of modern behavioristic psychology seem hardly to reflect this at all.

An Experimental Situation

In this context, then, consider the following situation. A human subject, a student in engineering in an American college, sits in front of a blackboard on which are written the following expressions:

$$(R \supset \sim P) \cdot (\sim R \supset Q) \mid \sim (\sim Q \cdot P)$$

This is a problem in elementary symbolic logic, but the student does not know it. He does know that he has twelve rules for manipulating expressions containing letters connected by "dots" ($\cdot$), "wedges" ($\vee$), "horseshoes" ($\supset$), and "tildes" ($\sim$), which stand respectively for "and," "or," "implies," and "not." These rules, given in Fig. 1, show that expressions of certain forms (at the tails of the arrows) can be transformed into expressions of somewhat different form (at the heads of the arrows). (Double arrows indicate transformations can take place in either direc-

Objects are formed by building up expressions from letters (P, Q, R, ...) and connectives $\cdot$ (dot), $\vee$ (wedge), $\supset$ (horseshoe), and $\sim$ (tilde). Examples are P, $\sim Q$, $P \vee Q$, $\sim (R \supset S) \cdot \sim P$; $\sim\sim P$ is equivalent to P throughout. Twelve rules exist for transforming expressions (where A, B, and C may be any expressions or subexpressions):

R1. $A \cdot B \rightarrow B \cdot A$ $A \vee B \rightarrow B \vee A$ — Applies to main expression only.

R2. $A \supset B \rightarrow \sim B \supset \sim A$

R3. $A \cdot A \leftrightarrow A$ $A \vee A \leftrightarrow A$

R4. $A \cdot (B \cdot C) \leftrightarrow (A \cdot B) \cdot C$ $A \vee (B \vee C) \leftrightarrow (A \vee B) \vee C$

R5. $A \vee B \leftrightarrow \sim(\sim A \cdot \sim B)$

R6. $A \supset B \leftrightarrow \sim A \vee B$

R7. $A \cdot (B \vee C) \leftrightarrow (A \cdot B) \vee (A \cdot C)$ $A \vee (B \cdot C) \leftrightarrow (A \vee B) \cdot (A \vee C)$

R8. $A \cdot B \rightarrow A$ $A \cdot B \rightarrow B$ — Applies to main expression only.

R9. $A \rightarrow A \vee X$ — Applies to main expression only.

R10. $\left.\begin{array}{l}A\\B\end{array}\right\} \rightarrow A \cdot B$ — A and B are two main expressions.

R11. $\left.\begin{array}{l}A\\A \supset B\end{array}\right\} \rightarrow B$ — A and $A \supset B$ are two main expressions.

R12. $\left.\begin{array}{l}A \supset B\\B \supset C\end{array}\right\} \rightarrow A \supset C$ — $A \supset B$ and $B \supset C$ are two main expressions.

Example, showing subject's entire course of solution on problem:

$(R \supset \sim P) \cdot (\sim R \supset Q) \mid \sim (Q \cdot P)$

1.	$(R \supset \sim P) \cdot (\sim R \supset Q)$	
2.	$(\sim R \vee \sim P) \cdot (\sim R \supset Q)$	Rule 6 applied to left and right of 1.
3.	$(\sim R \vee \sim P) \cdot (\sim R \supset Q)$	Rule 6 applied to left of 1.
4.	$R \supset \sim P$	Rule 8 applied to 1.
5.	$\sim R \vee \sim P$	Rule 6 applied to 4.
6.	$\sim R \supset Q$	Rule 8 applied to 1.
7.	$R \vee Q$	Rule 6 applied to 6.
8.	$(\sim R \vee \sim P) \cdot (R \vee Q)$	Rule 10 applied to 5. and 7.
9.	$P \supset \sim R$	Rule 2 applied to 4.
10.	$\sim Q \supset R$	Rule 2 applied to 6.
11.	$P \supset Q$	Rule 12 applied to 6. and 9.
12.	$\sim P \vee Q$	Rule 6 applied to 11.
13.	$\sim(P \cdot \sim Q)$	Rule 5 applied to 12.
14.	$\sim(\sim Q \cdot P)$	Rule 1 applied to 13. QED.

Figure 1. The task of symbolic logic.

tion.) The subject has practiced applying the rules, but he has previously done only one other problem like this. The experimenter has instructed him that his problem is to obtain the expression in the upper right corner from the expression in the upper left corner using the twelve rules. At any time the subject can request the experimenter to apply one of the rules to an expression that is already on the blackboard. If the transformation is legal, the experimenter writes down the new expression in the left-hand column, with the name of the rule in the right-hand column beside it. The subject's actual course of solution is shown beneath the rules in Fig. 1.

The subject was also asked to talk aloud as he worked; his comments were recorded and then transcribed into a "protocol,"—*i.e.*, a verbatim record of all that he or the experimenter said during the experiment. The initial section of this subject's protocol is reproduced in Fig. 2.

Well, looking at the left hand side of the equation, first we want to eliminate one of the sides by using rule 8. It appears too complicated to work with first. Now – no, – no, I can't do that because I will be eliminating either the Q or the P in that total expression. I won't do that at first. Now I'm looking for a way to get rid of the horseshoe inside the two brackets that appear on the left and right sides of the equation. And I don't see it. Yeh, if you apply rule 6 to both sides of the equation, from there I'm going to see if I can apply rule 7.

Experimenter writes: 2. $(\sim R \vee \sim P) \cdot (R \vee Q)$

I can almost apply rule 7, but one R needs a tilde. So I'll have to look for another rule. I'm going to see if I can change that R to a tilde R. As a matter of fact, I should have used rule 6 on only the left hand side of the equation. So use rule 6, but only on the left hand side.

Experimenter writes: 3. $(\sim R \vee \sim P) \cdot (\sim R \supset Q)$

Now I'll apply rule 7 as it is expressed. Both – excuse me, excuse me, it can't be done because of the horseshoe. So – now I'm looking – scanning the rules here for a second, and seeing if I can change the R to a $\sim$R in the second equation, but I don't see any way of doing it. (Sigh.) I'm just sort of lost for a second.

Figure 2. Subject's protocol on first part of problem.

The Problem of Explanation

It is now proposed that the protocol of Fig. 2 constitutes data about human behavior that are to be explained by a psychological theory. But what are we to make of this? Are we back to the introspections of the Wurzburgers? And how are we to extract information from the behavior of a single subject when we have not defined the operational measures we wish to consider?

There is little difficulty in viewing this situation through behavioristic eyes. The verbal utterances of the subject are as much behavior as would be his arm movements or galvanic skin responses. The subject was not introspecting; he was simply emitting a continuous stream of verbal behavior while solving the problem. Our task is to find a model of the human problem-solver that explains the salient features of this stream of behavior. This stream contains not only the subject's extemporaneous comments, but also his commands to the experimenter, which determine whether he solves the problem or not.

Although this way of viewing the behavior answers the questions stated above, it raises some of its own. How is one to deal with such variable behavior? Isn't language behavior considered among the most complex human behavior? How does one make reliable inferences from a single sample of data on a single subject?

The answers to these questions rest upon the recent, striking advances that have been made in computers, computer programming and artificial intelligence. We have learned that a computer is a general manipulator of symbols—not just a manipulator of numbers. Basically, a computer is a transformer of patterns. By suitable devices, most notably its addressing logic, these patterns can be given all the essential characteristics of linguistic symbols. They can be copied and formed into expressions. We have known this abstractly since Turing's work in the mid-thirties, but it is only recently that computers have become powerful enough to let us actually explore the capabilities of complex symbol manipulating systems.

For our purpose here, the most important branch of these explorations is the attempt to construct programs that solve tasks requiring intelligence. Considerable success has already been attained (Gelernter, 1959b; Kilburn et al, 1959; Minsky, 1961a; Newell, Shaw, and Simon, 1957a, 1958b; Samuel, 1959a; Tonge, 1960). These accomplishments form a body of psychological theories. (Much of the work on artificial intelligence, especially our own, has been partly motivated by concern for psychology; hence, the resulting rapprochement is not entirely coincidental.)

We may then conceive of an intelligent program that manipulates symbols in the same way that our subject does—by taking as inputs the symbolic logic expressions, and producing as ouputs a sequence of rule applications that coincides with the subject's. If we observed this program in operation, it would be considering various rules and evaluating various expressions, the same sorts of things we see expressed in the protocol of the subject. If the fit of such a program were close enough to the overt behavior of our human subject—i.e., to the protocol—then it would constitute a good theory of the subject's problem-solving.

Conceptually the matter is perfectly straightforward. A program prescribes in abstract terms (expressed in some programming language) how

a set of symbols in a memory is to be transformed through time. It is completely analogous to a set of difference equations that prescribes the transformation of a set of numbers through time. Given enough information about an individual, a program could be written that would describe the symbolic behavior of that individual. Each individual would be described by a different program, and those aspects of human problem-solving that are not idiosyncratic would emerge as the common structure and content of the programs of many individuals.

But is it possible to write programs that do the kinds of manipulation that humans do? Given a specific protocol, such as the one of Fig. 2, is it possible to induct the program of the subject? How well does a program fit the data? The remainder of the report will be devoted to answering some of these questions by means of the single example already presented. We will consider only how GPS behaves on the first part of the problem, and we will compare it in detail with the subject's behavior as revealed in the protocol. This will shed considerable light on how far we can consider programs as theories of human problem-solving.

The GPS Program

We will only briefly recapitulate the GPS program, since our description will add little to what has already been published (Newell, Shaw, and Simon, 1959a, 1960a). GPS deals with a task environment consisting of *objects* which can be transformed by various *operators*; it detects *differences* between objects; and it organizes the information about the task environment into *goals*. Each goal is a collection of information that defines what constitutes goal attainment, makes available the various kinds of information relevant to attaining the goal, and relates the information to other goals. There are three types of goals:

Transform object A into object B,
Reduce difference D between object A and object B,
Apply operator Q to object A.

For the task of symbolic logic, the objects are logic expressions; the operators are the twelve rules (actually the specific variants of them); and the differences are expressions like "change connective" or "add a term." Thus the objects and operators are given by the task; whereas the differences are something GPS brings to the problem. They represent the ways of relating operators to their respective effects upon objects.

Basically, the GPS program is a way of achieving a goal by setting up subgoals whose attainment leads to the attainment of the initial goal. GPS has various schemes, called methods, for doing this. Three crucial methods are presented in Fig. 3, one method associated with each goal type.

Thus, to transform an object A into an object B, the objects are first matched—put into correspondence and compared element by element. If the match reveals a difference, D, between the two objects, then a subgoal is set up to reduce this difference. If this subgoal is attained, a new object, A', is produced which (hopefully) no longer has the difference D when compared with object B. Then a new subgoal is created to transform A' into B. If the transformation succeeds, the entire goal has been attained in two steps: from A to A' and from A' to B.

If the goal is to reduce the difference between two objects, the first step is to find an operator that is relevant to this difference. Relevance here means that the operator affects objects with respect to the difference. Operationally, relevance can be determined by applying the matching process already used to the input and output forms of the operators, due account being taken of variables. The results can be summarized in a table of connections, as shown in Fig. 3, which lists for each difference the operators that are relevant to it. This table also lists the differences that GPS recognizes. [This set is somewhat different from the one given in Newell, Shaw, and Simon (1959a); it corresponds to the program we will deal with in this report.] If a relevant operator, Q, is found, it is subjected to a preliminary test of feasibility, one version of which is given in Fig. 3. If the operator passes this test, a subgoal is set up to apply the operator to the object. If the operator is successfully applied, a new object, A', is produced which is a modification of the original one in the direction of reducing the difference. (Of course, other modifications may also have occurred which nullify the usefulness of the new object.)

If the goal is to apply an operator, the first step is to see if the conditions of the operator are satisfied. The preliminary test above by no means guarantees this. If the conditions are satisfied, then the output, A, can be generated. If the conditions are not satisfied, then some difference, D, has been detected and a subgoal is created to reduce this difference, just as with the transform goal. Similarly, if a modified object, A', is obtained, a new subgoal is formed to try to apply the operator to this new object.

These methods form a recursive system that generates a tree of subgoals in attempting to attain a given goal. For every new difficulty that is encountered a new subgoal is created to overcome this difficulty. GPS has a number of tests it applies to keep the expansion of this goal tree from proceeding in unprofitable directions. The most important of these is a test which is applied to new subgoals for reducing differences. GPS contains an ordering of the differences, so that some differences are considered easier than others. This ordering is given by the table of connections in Fig. 3, which lists the most difficult differences first. GPS will not try a subgoal if it is harder than one of its supergoals. It will also not try a goal if it follows an easier goal. That is, GPS insists on working on the hard differences first and expects to find easier ones as it goes along. The other tests that GPS applies involve external limits (e.g., a limit on the total depth of a goal tree it will tolerate) and whether new objects or goals are identical to ones already generated.

GPS on the Problem

The description we have just given is adequate to verify the reasonableness, although not the detail, of a trace of GPS's behavior on a specific problem. (In particular we have not described how the two-line rules, R10

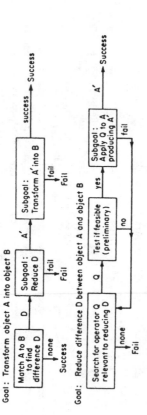

Goal: Transform object A into object B

Goal: Reduce difference D between object A and object B

Goal: Apply operator Q to object A

For the logic task of the text:

Feasibility test (preliminary):
Is the mean connective the same? (e.g., A·B → B fails against P∨Q)
Is the operator too big? (e.g., (A∨B)·(A∨C) → A∨(B·C) fails against P·Q)
Is the operator too easy? (e.g., A → A·A applies to anything)
Are the side conditions satisfied? (e.g., R8 applies only to main expressions)

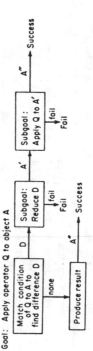

Table of connections

	R1	R2	R3	R4	R5	R6	R7	R8	R9	R10	R11	R12
Add terms									x		x	x
Delete terms	x								x	x	x	
Change connective		x						x		x		
Change sign				x	x							
Change lower sign					x	x						
Change grouping			x	x								
Change position			x									

x means some variant of the rule is relevant. GPS will pick the appropriate variant.

Figure 3. Methods for GPS.

through R12, are handled, since they do not enter into the protocol we are examining.) In Fig. 4, we give the trace on the initial part of problem D1. Indentation is used to indicate the relation of a subgoal to a goal. Although the methods are not shown, they can clearly be inferred from the goals that occur.

The initial problem is to transform L1 into L0. Matching L1 to L0 reveals that there are R's in L1 and no R's in L0. This difference leads to the formulation of a reduce goal, which for readability has been given its functional name, *Delete*. The attempt to reach this goal leads to a search for rules which finds rule 8. Since there are two forms of rule 8, both of which are admissible, GPS chooses the first. (Variants of rules are not indicated, but can be inferred easily from the trace.) Since rule 8 is

applicable, a new object, L2, is produced. Following the method for transform goals, at the next step a new goal has been generated: to transform L2 into L0. This in turn leads to another reduce goal: to restore a Q to L2. But this goal is rejected by the evaluation, since adding a term is more difficult than deleting a term. GPS then returns to goal 2 and seeks another rule which will delete terms. This time it finds the other form of rule 8 and goes through a similar excursion, ending with the rejection of goal 8.

Returning again to goal 2 to find another rule for deleting terms, GPS obtains rule 7. It selects the variant $(A \vee B) \cdot (A \vee C) \rightarrow A \vee (B \cdot C)$, since only this one both decreases terms and has a dot as its main connective. Rule 7 is not immediately applicable; GPS first discovers that there is a difference of connective in the left subexpression, and then that there is one in the right subexpression. In both cases it finds and applies rule 6 to change the connective from horseshoe to wedge, obtaining successively L4 and L5. But the new expression reveals a difference in sign, which leads again to rule 6—that is, to the same rule as before, but perceived as accomplishing a different function. Rule 6 produces L6, which happens to be identical with L4 although GPS does not notice the identity here. This leads, in goal 19, to the difference in connective being redetected; whereupon the goal is finally rejected as representing no progress over goal 13. Further attempts to find alternative ways to change signs or connectives fail to yield anything. This ends the episode.

Comparison of the GPS Trace with the Protocol

We now have a highly detailed trace of what GPS did. What can we find in the subject's protocol that either confirms or refutes the assertion that this program is a detailed model of the symbol manipulations the subject is carrying out? What sort of correspondence can we expect? The program does not provide us with an English language output that can be put into one-one correspondence with the words of the subject. We have not even given GPS a goal to "do the task and talk at the same time," which would be a necessary reformulation if we were to attempt a correspondence in such detail. On the other hand, the trace, backed up by our knowledge of how it was generated, does provide a complete record of all the task content that was considered by GPS, and the order in which it was taken up. Hence, we should expect to find every feature of the protocol that concerns the task mirrored in an essential way in the program trace. The converse is not true, since many things concerning the task surely occurred without the subject's commenting on them (or even being aware of them). Thus, our test of correspondence is one-sided but exacting.

```
L0  ~(~Q·P)
L1  (R⊃~P)·(~R⊃Q)

GOAL 1 TRANSFORM L1 INTO L0
  GOAL 2 DELETE R FROM L1
    GOAL 3 APPLY R8 TO L1
      PRODUCES L2 R⊃~P

      GOAL 4 TRANSFORM L2 INTO L0
        GOAL 5 ADD Q TO L2
          REJECT

      GOAL 2
        GOAL 6 APPLY R8 TO L1
          PRODUCES L3 ~R⊃Q

      GOAL 7 TRANSFORM L3 INTO L0
        GOAL 8 ADD P TO L3
          REJECT

  GOAL 2
    GOAL 9 APPLY R7 TO L1
      GOAL 10 CHANGE CONNECTIVE TO V IN LEFT L1
        GOAL 11 APPLY R6 TO LEFT L1
          PRODUCES L4 (~R∨~P)·(~R⊃Q)

      GOAL 12 APPLY R7 TO L4
        GOAL 13 CHANGE CONNECTIVE TO V IN RIGHT L4
          GOAL 14 APPLY R6 TO RIGHT L4
            PRODUCES L5 (~R∨~P)·(R∨Q)

        GOAL 15 APPLY R7 TO L5
          GOAL 16 CHANGE SIGN OF LEFT RIGHT L5
            GOAL 17 APPLY R6 TO RIGHT L5
              PRODUCES L6 (~R∨~P)·(~R⊃Q)

          GOAL 18 APPLY R7 TO L6
            GOAL 19 CHANGE CONNECTIVE TO V
              IN RIGHT L6
              REJECT

          GOAL 16
            NOTHING MORE

        GOAL 13
          NOTHING MORE

      GOAL 10
        NOTHING MORE
```

Figure 4. Trace of GPS on first part of problem.

Let us start with the first sentence of the subject's protocol (Fig. 2):

Well, looking at the left-hand side of the equation, first we want to eliminate one of the sides by using rule 8.

We see here a desire to decrease L1 or eliminate something from it, and the selection of rule 8 as the means to do this. This stands in direct correspondence with goals 1, 2, and 3 of the trace. Let us skip to the third and fourth sentences:

Now—no,—no, I can't do that because I will be eliminating either the Q or the P in that total expression. I won't do that at first.

We see here a direct expression of the covert application of rule 8, the subsequent comparison of the resulting expression with L0, and the rejection of this course of action because it deletes a letter that is required in the final expression. It would be hard to find a set of words that expressed these ideas more clearly. Conversely, if the mechanism of the program (or something essentially similar to it) were not operating, it would be hard to explain why the subject uttered the remarks that he did.

One discrepancy is quite clear. The subject handled both forms of rule 8 together, at least as far as his comment is concerned. GPS, on the other hand, took a separate cycle of consideration for each form. Possibly the subject followed the program covertly and simply reported the two results together. However, we would feel that the fit was better if GPS had proceeded something as follows:

```
GOAL 2 DELETE R FROM L1
  GOAL 3 APPLY R8 TO L1
    PRODUCES L2  R⊃~P OR ~R⊃Q

GOAL 4 TRANSFORM L2 INTO L0
  GOAL 5 ADD Q TO R⊃~P OR ADD P TO ~R⊃Q
    REJECT
```

We will consider further evidence on this point later. Let us return to the second sentence, which we skipped over:

It appears too complicated to work with first.

Nothing in the program is in simple correspondence with this statement, though it is easy to imagine some possible explanations. For example, this could merely be an expression of the matching—of the fact that L1 is such a big expression that the subject cannot absorb all its detail. There is not enough data locally to determine what part of the trace should correspond to this statement, so the sentence must stand as an unexplained element of the subject's behavior.

Now let us consider the next few sentences of the protocol:

Now I'm looking for a way to get rid of the horseshoe inside the two brackets that appear on the left and right side of the equation. And I don't see it. Yeh, if you apply rule 6 to both sides of the equation, from there I'm going to see if I can apply rule 7.

This is in direct correspondence with goals 9 through 14 of the trace. The comment at the end makes it clear that applying rule 7 is the main concern and that changing connectives is required in order to accomplish this. Further, the protocol shows clearly that rule 6 was selected as the means. All three rule selections provide some confirmation that a preliminary test for feasibility was made by the subject—as by GPS—in the reduce goal method. If there was not selection on the main connective, why wasn't rule 5 selected instead of rule 6? Or why wasn't the $(A \cdot B) \vee (A \cdot C) \rightarrow A \cdot (B \vee C)$ form of rule 7 selected?

However, there is a discrepancy between trace and protocol, for the subject handles both applications of rule 6 simultaneously, (and apparently was also handling the two differences simultaneously); whereas GPS handles them sequentially. This is similar to the discrepancy noted earlier in handling rule 8. Since we now have two examples of parallel processing, it is likely that there is a real difference on this score. Again, we would feel better if GPS proceeded somewhat as follows:

```
GOAL 9 APPLY R7 TO L1
GOAL 10 CHANGE CONNECTIVE TO∨IN LEFT L1 AND RIGHT L1
  GOAL 11 APPLY R6 TO LEFT L1 AND RIGHT L1
    PRODUCES L5 (~R∨~P)·(R∨Q)
```

A common feature of both these discrepancies is that forming the compound expressions does not complicate the methods in any essential way. Thus, in the case involving rule 8, the two results stem from the same input form, and require only the single match. In the case involving rule 7, a single search was made for a rule and the rule applied to both parts simultaneously, just as if only a single unit was involved.

There are two aspects in which the protocol provides information that the program is not equipped to explain. First, the subject handled the application of rule 8 covertly but commanded the experimenter to make the applications of rule 6 on the board. The version of GPS used here did not make any distinction between internal and external actions. To this extent it fails to be an adequate model. The overt-covert distinction has consequences that run throughout a problem, since expressions on the blackboard have very different memory characteristics from expressions generated only in the head. Second, this version of GPS does not simulate the search process sufficiently well to provide a correspondent to "And I don't see it. Yeh, . . .". This requires providing a facsimile of the rule sheet, and distinguishing search on the sheet from searches in the memory.

The next few sentences read:

I can almost apply rule 7, but one R needs a tilde. So I'll have to look for another rule. I'm going to see if I can change that R to a tilde R.

Again the trace and the protocol agree on the difference that is seen. They also agree that this difference was not attended to earlier, even though it was present. Some fine structure of the data also agrees with the trace. The right-hand R is taken as having the difference (R to $\sim$ R) rather than the left-hand one, although either is possible. This preference arises in the program (and presumably in the subject) from the language habit of working from left to right. It is not without consequences, however, since it determines whether the subject goes to work on the left side or the right side of the expression; hence, it can affect the entire course of events for quite a while. Similarly, in the rule 8 episode the subject apparently worked from left to right and from top to bottom in order to arrive at "Q or P" rather than "P or Q." This may seem like concern with excessively detailed features of the protocol, yet those details support the contention that what is going on inside the human system is quite akin to the symbol manipulations going on inside GPS.

The next portion of the protocol is:

As a matter of fact, I should have used rule 6 on only the left-hand side of the equation. So use 6, but only on the left-hand side.

Here we have a strong departure from the GPS trace, although, curiously enough, the trace and the protocol end up at the same spot, $(\sim R \lor \sim P) \cdot (\sim R \supset Q)$. Both the subject and GPS found rule 6 as the appropriate one to change signs. At this point GPS simply applied the rule to the current expression; whereas the subject went back and corrected the previous application. Nothing exists in the program that corresponds to this. The most direct explanation is that the application of rule 6 in the inverse direction is perceived by the subject as undoing the previous application of rule 6. After following out this line of reasoning, he then takes the simpler (and less foolish-appearing) alternative, which is to correct the original action.

The final segment of the protocol reads:

Now I'll apply rule 7 as it is expressed. Both—excuse me, excuse me, it can't be done because of the horseshoe. So—now I'm looking— scanning the rules here for a second, and seeing if I can change the R to $\sim$R in the second equation, but I don't see any way of doing it. (Sigh). I'm just sort of lost for a second.

The trace and the protocol are again in good agreement. This is one of the few self-correcting errors we have encountered. The protocol records the futile search for additional operators to affect the differences of sign and connective, always with negative results. The final comment of mild despair can be interpreted as reflecting the impact of several successive failures.

Summary of the Fit of the Trace to the Protocol

Let us take stock of the agreements and disagreements between the trace and the protocol. The program provides a complete explanation of the subject's task behavior with five exceptions of varying degrees of seriousness.

There are two aspects in which GPS is unprepared to simulate the subject's behavior: in distinguishing between the internal and external worlds, and in an adequate representation of the spaces in which the search for rules takes place. Both of these are generalized deficiencies that can be remedied. It will remain to be seen how well GPS can then explain data about these aspects of behavior.

The subject handles certain sets of items in parallel by using compound expressions; whereas GPS handles all items one at a time. In the example examined here, no striking differences in problem solving occur as a result, but larger discrepancies could arise under other conditions. It is fairly clear how GPS could be extended to incorporate this feature.

There are two cases in which nothing corresponds in the program to some clear task-oriented behavior in the protocol. One of these, the early comment about "complication," seems to be mostly a case of insufficient information. The program is making numerous comparisons and evaluations which could give rise to comments of the type in question. Thus this error does not seem too serious. The other case, involving the "should have . . ." passage, does seem serious. It clearly implies a mechanism (maybe a whole set of them) that is not in GPS. Adding the mechanism required to handle this one passage could significantly increase the total capabilities of the program. For example, there might be no reasonable way to accomplish this except to provide GPS with a little continuous hindsight about its past actions.

An additional general caution must be suggested. The quantity of data is not large considering the size and complexity of the program. This implies that there are many degrees of freedom available to fit the program to the data. More important, we have no good way to assess how many relevant degrees of freedom a program possesses, and thus to know how easy it is to fit alternative programs. All we do know is that numerous minor modifications could certainly be made, but that no one has proposed any major alternative theories that provide anything like a comparably detailed explanation of human problem-solving data.

It would help if we knew something of how idiosyncratic the program was. We have discussed it here only in relation to one sample of data for one subject. We know enough about subjects on logic problems to assert that the same mechanisms show up repeatedly, but we cannot discuss these data here in detail. In addition, several recent investigations more generally support the concept of information processing theories of human thinking (Bruner et al., 1956; Feigenbaum, 1961a; Feldman, 1961a; Hovland and Hunt, 1960; Miller et al., 1960).

Conclusion

We have been concerned in this report with showing that the techniques that have emerged for constructing sophisticated problem-solving programs also provide us with new, strong tools for constructing theories of human thinking. They allow us to merge the rigor and objectivity associated with Behaviorism with the wealth of data and complex behavior associated with the Gestalt movement. To this end their key feature is not that they provide a general framework for understanding problem-solving behavior (although they do that, too), but that they finally reveal with great clarity that the free behavior of a reasonably intelligent human can be understood as the product of a complex but finite and determinate set of laws. Although we know this only for small fragments of behavior, the depth of the explanation is striking.

THE MIND'S EYE IN CHESS

William G. Chase and Herbert A. Simon
Carnegie-Mellon University

In this paper, we would like to describe the progress we have made toward understanding chess skill. In the first section of the paper we will summarize our earlier work on perception in chess, adding some new analyses of the data. Next, we will give a simple theoretical formulation that we think begins to characterize how expert chess players perceive the chess board. Then we will describe some new tasks that also correlate well with chess skill, and finally we will give a more complete account of our current thinking about the cognitive processes of skilled chess players.

Experiments on Chess Perception

Chess is interesting to us because it is a very complicated thinking task that involves a great deal of visual-perceptual processing. Our earlier work (Chase & Simon, 1973), in conjunction with the pioneering work of de Groot, has led us to conclude that the most important processes underlying chess mastery are these immediate visual-perceptual processes rather than the subsequent logical-deductive thinking processes. The evidence for this conjecture is incomplete, but nevertheless quite compelling.

The early work on chess skill was done over 30 years ago by de Groot (cf. de Groot, 1965). He asked what it is that differentiates Master chess players from weaker players, and he studied some of the best chess players in the world at that time. What de Groot did was to show chess players an interesting position, ask them to find the best move, and ask them to talk aloud while thinking. From an analysis of the verbal protocols, de Groot concluded that there was nothing in the gross thought processes and the search through possible moves that distinguished Masters from weaker players. Masters search about as deep as weaker players; if anything, Masters consider fewer alternatives than weaker players before choosing a move. In a difficult position, a Master might typically consider 30 to 50 moves, and search to a depth of 2 or 3 moves.[1] It is quite unusual for a Master to consider a continuation tree of more than 100 moves or to search deeper than 5 moves, and this is true of weaker players also. One result of de Groot's analysis, then, was to dispel the idea that Masters typically "see" further ahead than weaker players.[2]

In short, de Groot found that Masters and weaker players have a great deal in common in the gross structure of their thought processes, but he was unable to discover any quantitative differences that might underlie chess skill. And nothing has been discovered in the past 30 years to change this basic finding. Nevertheless, Masters invariably explore strong moves, whereas weaker players spend considerable time analyzing the consequences of bad moves.

[1] A "move" sometimes refers to the move of a single piece, and sometimes to the moves of White and Black pieces in succession. We will use the term "ply" to refer to the move of a single piece, and "move" to refer to a pair of successive plies.

[2] There are occasional documented reports of Masters seeing as far ahead as 10 or 15 moves (e.g., Alekhine, 1927, Game 43), but this is very rare, and generally occurs under very special circumstances when the branching of the search tree is very sparse --as when a series of "forcing" moves is explored.

The best move, or at least a very good one, just seems to come to the top of the Master's list of plausible moves for analysis.

de Groot did, however, find an intriguing difference between Masters and weaker players in their ability to perform a task involving perceptual and short-term memory processes. Masters were able to reconstruct a chess position almost perfectly after viewing it for only 5 seconds or so. There was a sharp drop-off in this ability for players below the Master level. This result could not be attributed to a generally superior visual short-term memory capability of the Masters because, when the pieces were placed randomly on the board, recall was equally poor for Masters and weaker players. Masters are subject to the same limitations on short-term memory as everyone else.

To understand this feat of memory, therefore, we must ask what it is that the Master is perceiving during the brief exposure of a coherent position. It appears that the Master is perceiving familiar or meaningful constellations of pieces that are already structured for him in memory, so that all he has to do is store the label or internal name of each such structure in short-term memory. At recall, then, the Master simply uses the label to retrieve the structure from long-term memory. With a normal memory span of about 5 to 7 chunks (Miller, 1956), the Master must be perceiving about 4 or 5 pieces per chunk in order to recall about 25 pieces.

We believe that this interesting demonstration of de Groot's, far from being an incidental side effect of chess skill, actually reveals one of the most important processes that underlie chess skill: the ability to perceive familiar patterns of pieces. To understand the skilled process more fully, we must isolate and characterize these perceptual structures that the Master holds in memory. Our earlier work was aimed at developing a technique for isolating these structures; the basic idea was to use pauses in the recall to define their temporal boundaries.

Isolating and Characterizing the Structures

In our first experiment we used two tasks. The *Memory* task was very similar to de Groot's task: chess players saw a position for 5 seconds and then attempted to recall it. Unlike de Groot, we used multiple trials--5 seconds of viewing followed by recall--until the position was recalled perfectly. For our purposes, however, we will mostly be interested in performance on the first trial. The second task, which we will call the *Perception* task for simplicity, involved showing chess players a position in plain view. Adjacent to this position was an empty board and some pieces, and the task was to reproduce the position on the empty board as quickly and accurately as possible. In both tasks, the behavior of the subjects was recorded on video tape.[3]

We used the pauses in the recall phase of the Memory task to segment the output into chunks, on the assumption that a pause will be associated with the retrieval of a new chunk from memory. And in the Perception task, we used the player's head movements, as he looked back at the position, to segment the output into chunks, on the assumption that when the player looks back at the position he will encode only a single chunk and place those pieces on the adjacent board before looking back again. We hoped that with these two tasks we could identify the perceptual structures.

We studied three chess players of varying strength in these experiments: a Master, a Class A player, and a beginner. The Master is currently one of the top 25 players in the country, and he has also won the World Correspondence Chess Championship. The

---

[3] For further descriptions of these experiments and their results, see Chase & Simon (1973).

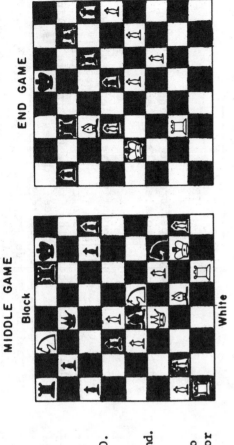

MIDDLE GAME
Black

White

END GAME

RANDOM END GAME

RANDOM MIDDLE GAME

Fig. 1. Examples of a middle game, an end game, and their randomized counterparts.

Class A player ranks at about the eighty-fifth percentile of players rated by the United States Chess Federation. The beginner has never competed in any tournaments, and has played very little chess. The three players are otherwise roughly equated for intelligence: the Class A player has a Ph.D. and the Master and beginner are both candidates for the Ph.D. The probability that the Class A player could beat the Master, or the beginner could beat the Class A player, is extremely small--perhaps one in a thousand. By a rough estimate, the amount of time each player has spent playing chess, studying chess, and otherwise staring at chess positions is perhaps 10,000 to 50,000 hours for the Master; 1,000 to 5,000 hours for the Class A player; and less than 100 hours for the beginner.

In both tasks, players saw five middle game positions, five end game positions from games between advanced players and published in chess books and magazines, and four randomized positions--a total of 28 positions in all. Figure 1 shows examples of a middle game, an end game, and the corresponding randomized positions.

Figure 2 shows the accuracy data from the middle games, with results that verify de Groot's basic findings. The top part of the figure shows that the Master was placing about 16 pieces correctly on the first trial, the Class A player about 8 pieces, and the beginner about 4 pieces. On subsequent trials, the Master very quickly learned the positions, while the beginner typically took many more trials to learn and the Class A player was intermediate between the others. The bottom part of Figure 2 shows that, unlike the coherent positions, recall of the randomized positions was the same for everyone, and uniformly poor. Everyone placed only 2 or 3 pieces correctly on the first trial, which is even poorer than the beginner's first trial performance with coherent positions.

Figure 3 shows pretty much the same story for end games, although here there wasn't as big a difference between levels of chess skill as for the middle games, presumably because there is less familiar structure in the end games.

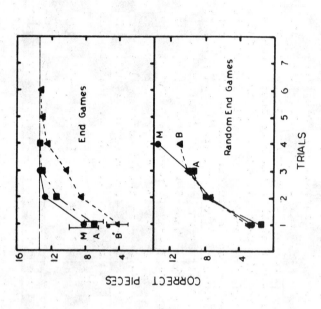

Fig. 3, Recall performance for end games (top) and their randomized counterparts (bottom).

There were some quantitative differences between our results and de Groot's. Our Master was only recalling about 16 pieces out of 24 or 25 pieces in the middle games, whereas de Groot's Masters were getting 23 and 24 out of 25 pieces. The reason for this difference seems to lie in the differences between our positions and de Groot's. de Groot very carefully chose his positions so that they were quiet,

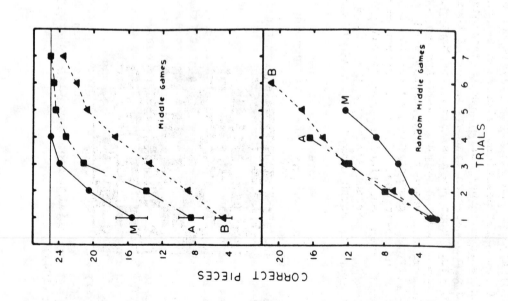

Fig. 2. Number of pieces correctly recalled for the Master (M), the Class A player (A), and beginner (B) over trials for the middle games (top) and their randomized counterparts (bottom). The brackets on Trial 1 represent one standard error, based on five positions.

whereas our positions were chosen at some arbitrary point in the game. Several of our positions caught the game at a point where an exchange was in progress. The middle game shown in Figure 1 is a good example of this kind of position. In this case, there are both black and white pieces in the middle of an exchange. Our Master complained that he had trouble "getting the sense" of these positions.

Accordingly, we ran all three players for one trial on 9 new quiet positions taken from a book of chess puzzles from actual Master games (Reinfeld, 1945). Figure 4 shows an example of one of these positions. For these new positions, the Master, the Class A player, and the beginner averaged 81, 49, and 33 percent correct, respectively, as compared to 62, 34, and 19 percent, respectively, on the first trial of the previous positions. Taking these new results into account, then, our findings unequivocally replicate de Groot's important findings. One unexpected result we found is worth commenting on at this point.

The Master recognized 4 of these 9 new positions--he was, for example, able to name the people who played the game--and always within the first second of exposure, yet his performance was virtually identical for recognized vs. unrecognized positions: 83 vs. 79 per cent, respectively. Also, for one of the previous middle games, the Master suddenly recognized the game after he had placed the pieces on Trial 1, but his discovery did not help him learn the position on subsequent trials.

We explored one further difference between our procedure and de Groot's. We asked for immediate recall from our players, whereas de Groot encouraged his players to "concentrate for some time (with eyes closed)... to 'integrate' his data. The usual result of such delays, if anything, is to weaken the memory for material that has been most recently attended to (the recency portion of the serial position curve), presumably because this material is less well organized and therefore susceptible to retroactive interference. To investigate this possibility, the Class A player was shown 20 diagrams from Reinfeld's (1945) book for 5 seconds each; half the positions were recalled immediately and half were recalled after a 30-second delay. There was no significant difference in recall between these two procedures: 60% correct for immediate recall and 58% correct for delayed recall. We can therefore discount this minor difference in procedures.

One clue to the underlying representation is found in the kinds of errors that occur. Most errors are errors of omission, but there are some interesting aspects to the errors of commission. Given that a piece is incorrectly recalled, what kind of information is still present? We classified the misplaced pieces into four categories: (1) Translation errors: the right piece is misplaced by a square or two. (2) Wrong piece: a piece is placed on a square that requires a different piece of the same color. (3) Wrong color: the correct piece is placed on the correct

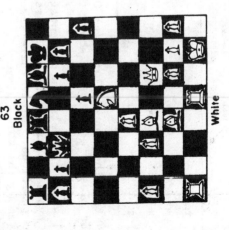

63
Black

White

Fig. 4. An example of a quiet position from Reinfeld (1945).

look at the distribution of times between the placement of two pieces in the Memory task and infer two
underlying processes--slow times associated with retrieving a new chunk from memory, and fast times
associated with placing pieces from the same chunk.
We used the distribution of times from the Perception
task to help identify these two processes, specifically, the times associated with placing successive
pieces without looking back at the displayed position.

Table 1. Percentage of Various Types of Placement
Errors for Real and Random Positions

Errors	Real Positions	Random Positions
Translation	76.7	74.7
Wrong Piece	6.6	8.2
Wrong Color	1.6	3.5
Other	15.1	13.5

square, but it is the wrong color. (4) Other: errors
that can't be classified into the above three categories.

Table 1 shows the relative percentages of each
of the four types of errors for the 19 real positions
and 4 random positions. Since there weren't any
differences among the three players, the errors were
summed over the three levels of chess skill. These
percentages are based on 305 errors in the real positions and 170 errors in the random positions.

At least 85% of the placement errors still preserve some information about the location, identity,
and color of the pieces. Almost all the information-
preserving errors were translation errors, and there
were very few wrong-piece and wrong-color errors.
These translation errors often occurred as units (e.g.,
Pawn chains), so that several pieces were displaced
one or more squares, but the correct configuration of
pieces still remained intact. Another type of translation error occurred when pieces were displaced along
paths that they control, such as Bishops along diagonals or Rooks along ranks or files. This kind of
error still preserves an important function: the
control of squares within the scope of a piece. These
errors suggest that the absolute location of pieces
is not as important as their relative location--rela-
tive to other pieces in a configuration and relative
to squares under their control.

We asked next whether the pauses in recall would
segment the chunks for us. It is not an easy task to

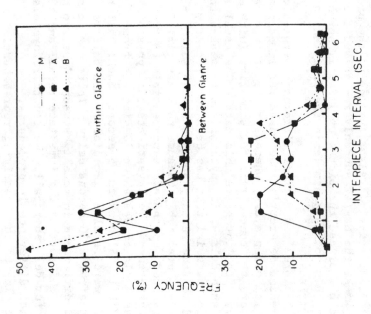

Fig. 5. The distribution of interpiece latencies within a single glance (top) and between glances
(bottom), for the Master (M), the Class A player (A),
and the beginner (B).

The top part of Figure 5 shows that almost all of these times are less than 2 seconds, and the distributions look pretty much the same for everyone.[4] We decided to use this 2-second time as the criterion cutoff point in the Memory experiment. We hypothesized that a pause longer than 2 seconds is associated with the retrieval of a new structure from short-term memory, whereas a pause less than 2 seconds is associated with a succession of pieces drawn from the same perceptual structure. This 2-second criterion is admittedly somewhat arbitrary, but our results would not be seriously altered by lengthening or shortening the interval a bit.

An interesting aspect of the between-glance latencies, shown in the bottom of Figure 5, is that the Master generally took only a second or two to gather new information by looking back in the Perception experiment whereas the beginner's modal "look-back" time was about 4 seconds. The Class A player's times were generally intermediate between the Master and the beginner. The speed with which players can perceive information on the chess board depends, then, upon their chess skill.

One fairly strong prediction of our chunking hypothesis is that a chunk, defined by our 2-second criterion, should have a tendency to remain a chunk on subsequent trials. The tendency to recall pieces in the same order from trial to trial did increase over trials, but it is difficult to define chunks on subsequent trials because as the position gets learned, the interpiece latencies become shorter and more uniform. Also, chunk boundaries probably disappear as new relations are learned.

[4] The second mode at around one second is an artifact due to the extra time needed to find and pick up additional pieces at the side of the Board. The control for this artifact is described later in the paper.

Since we have developed an objective criterion for chunk boundaries only for the first trial, we analyzed the first two trials of the middle and end games to see if the pieces within a chunk on the first trial, defined by the 2-second criterion, tended to be recalled together on the second trial. Since there were so few chunks involving two or more pieces for the beginner, we present data only for the Master and the Class A player.

As expected, there was a considerable tendency for chunks to remain intact on the second trial. A chunk was defined as intact on the second trial if at least two thirds of its pieces were recalled together. Some 65% of the Master's chunks and 96% of the Class A player's chunks remained intact on the second trial. It is interesting, however, that pieces were recalled in the same order for only about half of the intact chunks. A common example of this phenomenon is when a player recalls a Pawn chain in reverse order from the previous trial. We conclude from these data, therefore, that chunks, as we have defined them, show the necessary stability over trials, but that there is no stereotyped order of recall of pieces within a chunk.

We asked next whether the time between two successive pieces depends upon the chess relations between the two pieces. We expected that the shorter the time between two pieces, the more likely that the two pieces are closely related in some way. And if two pieces with short times are closely related, what is the relation?

We scored five relations between the two pieces: Do they attack each other (A); do they defend each other (D); are the pieces proximate, that is, is one of the pieces within one of the eight adjoining squares of the other (P); are they the same color (C); and are they the same type, for example, both Pawns (S). There are sixteen possible combinations of these five relations containing from 0 to 4 relations each. For example, a King and a Queen of the same color placed next to each other on the board have three relations between them (DPC), while two adjacent Pawns in a Pawn chain have four relations between them (DPCS).

Figure 6 shows quite conclusively that the shorter the latency between the placing of two pieces, the more likely they are to have many relations between them. These data are for recall on the first trial only, and the function looks the same for all three levels of chess skill.

On the basis of this evidence, taking the data from the Memory experiment, we separated successively placed pieces on the first trial into those that were separated by at least 2 seconds and those separated by less than 2 seconds, and then analyzed the structural relations between pieces placed within 2 seconds of each other. We then compared these relations with the relations one would expect if the two pieces were simply picked at random.

Table 2 shows the statistics (for all three players combined) for the sixteen possible combinations of chess relations. The statistics of most interest are the mean latencies, the observed probabilities (P_o), and the probabilities one would expect if the two pieces were randomly chosen (P_e). If there is no structure in the recall, then we would expect P_o and P_e to be the same. However, if there is structure in the output, then the important structural relations should occur with frequencies that are much greater than chance. These probabilities are compared in Table 2 with the aid of the z-distribution.

It can be seen from Table 2 that there is a great deal of non-randomness or structure between pieces placed within 2 seconds of each other, but the data are virtually random for successive pieces separated by at least 2 seconds.

We asked next whether these relations correspond to those noticed in the Perception experiment. If our assumption that the Perception and Memory tasks converge on the underlying perceptual structures—i.e., that the within-glance latencies reveal the

Table 2. Chess Relations for the Memory Data for Long and Short Interpiece Latencies

Relations	Less Than 2 Sec.						Greater Than 2 Sec.					
	N	$\overline{RT}$	$SE_{\overline{RT}}$	P_o	P_e	z	N	$\overline{RT}$	$SE_{\overline{RT}}$	P_o	P_e	z
--	15	1.75	.062	.031	.320	-36.4	99	6.42	.612	.258	.320	-2.8
A	5	1.50	.188	.010	.0201	-2.1	7	5.53	1.452	.018	.0201	-.3
P	2	1.75	.177	.004	.0057	-.5	4	4.45	1.073	.010	.0057	.9
C	43	1.48	.052	.089	.255	-12.7	86	5.54	.586	.224	.255	-1.5
S	14	1.23	.121	.029	.148	-15.5	27	5.43	.994	.070	.148	-6.0
AP	7	1.39	.168	.015	.0077	1.3	9	4.58	.670	.023	.0077	2.0
AS	5	1.44	.100	.010	.0025	1.7	3	3.00	.245	.008	.0025	1.2
DC	26	1.22	.082	.054	.0423	1.1	24	6.17	1.079	.063	.0423	1.6
PC	13	1.48	.114	.027	.0159	1.5	12	6.20	1.444	.031	.0159	1.7
PS	4	1.00	.300	.008	.0075	.2	1	7.20	--	.003	.0075	-1.9
CS	22	1.18	.120	.046	.0939	-5.1	18	5.10	1.096	.047	.0939	-4.4
APS	2	.50	.91	.004	.0022	-.7	0	--	--	0	.0022	--
DPC	95	1.28	.045	.198	.0469	8.3	73	4.28	.392	.190	.0469	7.2
DCS	38	.91	.071	.079	.0057	6.0	6	2.97	.259	.016	.0057	1.6
PCS	104	.57	.044	.216	.0105	11.0	5	4.58	1.564	.013	.0105	.4
DPCS	86	.68	.046	.179	.0162	9.3	10	3.34	.583	.026	.0162	1.2
		1.02						5.40				

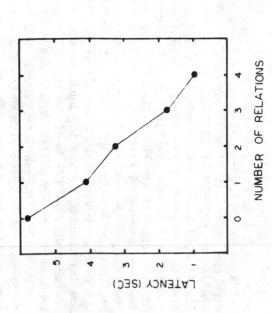

Fig. 6. Average latency between two pieces as a function of the number of relations between them.

within-chunk retrieval distribution and that when the players look back at the board they are encoding a new perceptual chunk--then there must be considerable correspondence between the two tasks.

Table 3 shows that there is indeed a close similarity between the two tasks. This table shows the correlations that exist between various conditions across the sixteen observed probabilities. (We don't include the data from the randomized boards in the Memory experiment because there simply weren't enough data from the first trial.) There are two clusters of correlations in this table. First, the within-glance relations for games from the Perception experiment correlate .89 with the short pauses (less than 2 seconds) from the Memory experiment. In other words, the same structure exists for the short pauses in the Memory experiment and the within-glance data from the Perception experiment. Second, the probabilities estimated on the assumption of randomness, the long pauses from the Memory experiment (greater than 2 seconds), and the between-glance relations from both structured and random games all correlate about .90. In other words, pieces separated by long pauses in the Memory experiment and pieces separated by a glance back at the board in the Perception

Table 3. Intercorrelation Matrix for the Perceptual, Memory, and Random Chess Relation Probabilities

Task	1	2	3	4	5	6	7
1 Within-Glance (Random)		.49	.59	.06	.02	.09	-.19
2 Within-Glance (Games)			.89	.06	.12	.18	-.04
3 Less Than 2 Sec.				.08	.10	.23	-.03
4 Between-Glance (Random)					.92	.93	.91
5 Between-Glance (Games)						.91	.81
6 Greater Than 2 Sec.							.87
7 Random							

experiment both look virtually random. Third, there was even a moderate correlation between pairs of pieces placed within a single glance from random boards in the Perception experiment and the highly structured pairs (the short pauses in the Memory experiment and the within-glance pairs from real games of the Perception experiment). It would seem that even in the randomized boards, players are noticing the same kinds of structures as those they perceive in the coherent positions, even though these structures occur rarely in the randomized boards.

Apparently, our technique really does segment the output in terms of the perceptual structures. What kind of structures are they? They are things like Pawn chains, and clusters of pieces of the same color that lie close together and usually also defend each other; the players see local clusters of pieces on the board. It is interesting to note that in addition to the chess relations such as defense and same piece (which is important for Pawn chains, and for Rook and Knight pairs), visual properties, such as color and spatial proximity, seem also to be important. Even the same-piece relation may represent visual properties because of the physical identity of the pieces.

We were a little surprised at the importance of these visual properties and, related to this, we were surprised that the players made so little use of the attack relation. Granted that in real game positions attacking relations are relatively rare, they are of great importance when they do occur and we would expect them to be noticed. However, the data clearly indicate that the attack relation was not often noticed. Finally, we were a little surprised that there were no differences in the kinds of relations noticed by different players. For example, we expected the Master to notice more attacks, but that was not the case. The only difference was that the structures were bigger for the better players.

When we took a more detailed look at the Master's chunks, we were able to classify 75% of them as highly stereotyped. Of the 77 chunks that he gave us on the first trial of the Memory experiment, 47 were Pawn chains, sometimes with a nearby supporting or block-ading piece. Ten chunks were castled King positions --a very common defensive structure. Twenty-seven chunks were clusters of pieces of the same color (exclusive of castled King positions), and 19 of these were of familiar types: 9 chunks consisted of pieces on the back rank, often in their original undeveloped positions; and 9 chunks consisted of connected Rooks, or the Queen connected with one or two Rooks--a very powerful attacking structure. These categories are not mutually exclusive, but they give the flavor of the kind of chunks that the Master was recalling.

Table 4 gives an example of the recall protocol of the Master for one of the positions in the Memory experiment and Figure 7 illustrates the chunk-by-chunk recall of the position. In this position, the Master made only a single mistake, placing White's Pawn at Queen's Rook 3 rather than Queen's Rook 2. The notation in the first column of Table 4 refers to the placed piece (K=King, Q=Queen, R=Rook, P=Pawn), its color (w=White, b=Black), and the square where it was placed (e.g., KN1=King's Knight 1). The second and third columns give the inter-piece latencies and chess relations, respectively. This position contains instances of Pawn chains, Rook- and Queen-Rook connections, and some degenerate remnants of castled King positions. The recall protocol here is fairly typical of the kind of data we got from the Master, and many of the stereotyped structures appear as chunks in the recall. So it does appear that these perceptual structures are very stereotyped, and are seen every day when the Master looks at the chess board.

We carried out one further analysis of the Master's protocols to see if we could determine whether he was attending to attacks. Taking the five middle game and nine puzzle positions in the Memory experiment, we identified the pieces taking part in the strongest attacks. Of the 18 strong attacks we were able to identify, 11 were chunked in the Master's protocols in the sense that at least two of the attacking pieces appeared within the same chunk. Rarely did the attacked pieces also appear in the same chunk as the attackers. Of these 11 attacks, 6 consisted of Rook and Queen-Rook combinations--one chunk also contained a Pawn in combination with the Queen and Rook--and the other 5 chunks consisted of a Knight in combination with a Queen or Rook. In these chunks, no direct attack relation is scored.

We conclude from this analysis that two kinds of attacks are perceived. The first kind is a fortuitous attack characterized by an attack relation between two adjacent pieces (the AP relation was greater than chance). The second kind of attack is more abstract and involves combinations of pieces of the

Table 4. A Sample of the Master's Recall of Pieces, Interpiece Latencies, and Chess Relations

Piece and Square	Time (sec.)	Relations
Kw at KR3	1.3	S
Kb at KN1	2.7	--
Rw at K5	2.7	DPC
Pw at KB4	.3	DPCS
Pw at KN3	3.4	S
Pb at KB4	.2	DPCS
Pb at KN3	1.3	DPCS
Pb at KR4	.4	PS
Pw at KR4	2.1	CS
*Pw at QR3	1.5	S
Pb at QR2	.2	DPCS
Pb at QN3	2.2	C
Rb at Q4	1.2	DCS
Rb at Q1	1.6	DPC
Qb at Q2	2.1	--
Rw at K2	1.6	DPC
Qw at Q1		

*Incorrect

same color converging, usually, on the opponent's King position—classic maneuvers against a stereotyped defensive position.

To sum up our progress so far, we have shown that the amount of information extracted from a briefly exposed chess position varies with playing strength, thus confirming earlier experiments of de Groot. With the aid of the Perception and Memory tasks, we have analyzed the perceptual structures that chess players see when they look briefly at chess positions. By measuring the time intervals between placements of successive pieces when the players attempted to reconstruct the positions, we were able to identify the boundaries of perceptual chunks. And on the basis of this technique, we characterized these structures as local clusters of pieces of the same color that usually defend each other. The evidence seems to suggest that these structures are built around visual features, such as color and spatial proximity, as well as chess functions, such as defense and identity of type of piece.

Memory Span for Chunks

Having segmented the recall protocols into chunks, we need to address the question of how large the memory span is for these chunks. This question is important to us because we will later talk about a theoretical account of the cognitive processes underlying chess and these chess-like tasks which relies fairly heavily upon a short-term memory of limited capacity for chunks. We consider the hypotheses (1) that everyone has about the same memory span for chunks, (2) that this limit is about the same as the traditional limit of short-term memory, 7 ± 2 chunks, and (3) that the superior recall of skilled players is associated with larger chunks.

Table 5 shows that two of the three hypotheses are supported, and a third is not. First, for both middle and end games, the average number of chunks recalled is in the right range for the traditional short-term memory capacity. Second, chunk size is

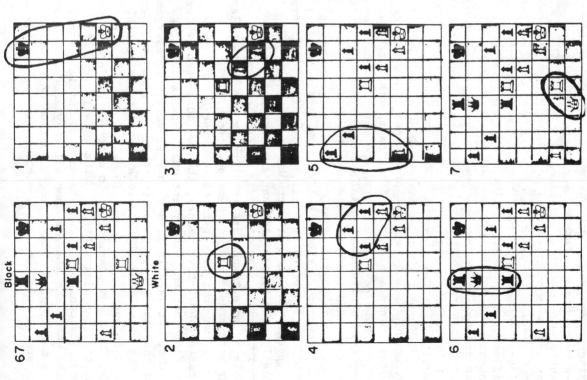

Fig. 7. The chunk-by-chunk recall of Position 67 from Reinfeld (1945). Each new chunk is circled.

Table 5. Average Sizes of Successive Chunks on the First Trial of the Middle Game and End Game Positions of the Memory Experiments for the Master (M), Class A player (A), and Beginner (B)

		Successive Chunks								Average Chunk Per Trial
		1	2	3	4	5	6	7	8	
Middle Games	M	3.8	3.0	2.5	2.3	1.9	1.5	2.2	2.0	7.7
	A	2.6	2.5	1.8	1.6	1.7	1.7	2.1	2.5	5.7
	B	2.4	2.1	2.0	1.6	1.4	1.5	1.0	2.0	5.3
End Games	M	2.6	1.6	1.4	1.8	1.8	1.2	2.3	1.0	7.6
	A	2.4	1.4	2.0	2.0	1.0	1.0	1.0	1.0	6.4
	B	2.2	2.4	2.2	1.0	1.0	1.0	1.0	0	4.2

larger for better players. For example, the size of the first chunk recalled for the middle game positions averaged 3.8, 2.6, and 2.4 pieces per chunk for the Master, Class A player, and beginner, respectively. For the more skilled players, the size of these chunks then gets progressively smaller for subsequent chunks in recall and the difference in chunk size between the players disappears. Also, for the end games, which are less structured, there is less of a difference in size as a function of chess skill, and again, the difference disappears for the later chunks in the protocol. Finally, the hypothesis that everyone has the same memory span is disconfirmed. As can be seen from Table 5, more chunks are recalled by the better players for both middle and end game positions.

If we want to retain the concept of a limited capacity short-term memory, then we must account for the fact that the Master not only recalls larger chunks, but recalls more chunks as well. If everyone has the same memory capacity, then where do these extra chunks come from? There are at least three possible explanations.

The first possibility is that the difference is due to a guessing artifact. The recall protocols generally consist of two phases: an initial recall phase where the players dump all they know from short-term memory, and then a reconstruction phase where players tend to guess or "problem-solve" where the res-

of the pieces ought to be. During the first phase, recall is fast and the chunks tend to be large and error-free, but during the second phase recall is piece-by-piece with long pauses and many errors. This second phase was more prominent in the Master's protocols than in the others. We tried to remove this reconstruction phase from the data by eliminating the portion of the protocol following a long pause (10 seconds or more) followed mostly by errors, or the portion having a series of long pauses (5 seconds or more) with errors. However, we may have been unsuccessful in eliminating the reconstruction phase entirely, particularly if the Master is very good at guessing. de Groot (1966), for example, has shown that players can average better than 44% pieces correct simply by putting down the most typical, or prototype, position derived from Master games. And the Master can undoubtedly reconstruct far better than 44% accuracy when partial information is already available.[5]

A second possibility is that the Master's long-term memory is structured so that information associated with particular chunks serves as a cue to retrieve other chunks from memory. Thus, whenever the first member of such a pair of chunks is retrieved, the retrieval of the second member is thereby cued. In this way a single chunk in short-term memory could permit the recall of several chunks from long-term memory.

[5]The Pennies-Guessing Task is an interesting demonstration of how easy it is to reconstruct a position from partial information. This task involves selecting a quiet position from a Master game and replacing all the pieces with pennies. The player's task is then to replace all the pennies with the correct pieces. The Master is virtually perfect at this task, and the Class A player also scores well over 90% correct.

regardless of whether the chunk is stored in long-term memory as a single unit or assembled hierarchically in short-term memory out of several chunks from long-term memory.[6] A chunk, according to this view, is a collection of pieces related in some way, regardless of whether or not the relations are overlearned in long-term memory.

All of these possibilities are quite plausible, they represent interesting processes in and of themselves, and there may be some truth to all three. However, the evidence is fairly strong in support of some kind of limited-capacity short-term memory where these structures or the internal names of familiar structures are stored.

Effect of Changing the Stimulus Notation

The first round of experiments supports the hypothesis that much of the skilled processing in chess occurs at the perceptual front end. We have conducted some experiments to test this perceptual hypothesis against one possible artifact, and we were further interested in seeing how robust the perceptual processing is when the stimuli are subjected to a degrading transformation.

One possible alternative to our perceptual hypothesis is that the structures we are isolating actually

[6]There are probably subtle differences in the speed of recall for these different chunks. For example, Pawn chains, double rooks, etc., are usually recalled very fast (less than 1/2 second per piece), so that chunks containing these sub-structures would probably be recalled with a slight pause (but still less than 2 seconds) between these sub-structures. Although there are some indications of this hierarchical organization in our data (e.g., in Castled King positions), we haven't studied this problem in any systematic way as yet.

For example, a Pawn at KR2 defending a Pawn at KN3 (a chunk) might later evolve the overlapping pattern: a Pawn at KN3 defending a Pawn at KB4. Or, in Fig. 7, the long-term memory representation of the Rook-Queen-Rook configuration (the sixth chunk) might have contained the information that there was a target piece on Q1, leading to the retrieval of the next Queen-Rook chunk (the seventh chunk).

We have no direct evidence to support this explanation, but the Master did appear to find, in pieces already placed on the board, cues to additional chunks. Until we have additional data, the possibility remains speculative.

A third possibility, on which we will comment further below, is that a "chunk" is not a unit of quite uniform size. A highly overlearned structure of information may occupy only a little short-term memory (only its "name" need be held), while to hold a less well-learned structure of equal complexity may require several pieces of descriptive or relational information to be retained. For example, the Rook-Queen-Rook configuration in Fig. 7 (the sixth chunk) might be represented in long-term memory as a single chunk and only its name held in short-term memory. Or it might be a composite of two chunks from long-term memory (e.g., Rook-Queen and Queen-Rook) and the chunk might be structured in short-term memory as a proposition involving the names of the two chunks plus the relation that holds them together. In the limit, the poorer player might have to represent this configuration in terms of even more elementary propositions about the two defense relations, the location of pieces relative to each other, and the location of the total configuration on the board. Thus, the efficiency of the code for a chunk in short-term memory would depend upon how much structure is available in long-term memory to build upon. Then, in short-term memory of given size, more overlearned chunks could be held than chunks that required partial descriptions.

The additional assumption we need to make is that the speed of recall of pieces within a chunk is fast, arise from the organization of the output at recall rather than from the perceptual process, and the pauses really represent an artifact because players need to pause in order to pick up a new set of pieces before continuing their recall. This hypothesis has trouble explaining why pieces recalled together in time are also functionally related, but it is possible that this organization is somehow imposed at recall rather than at the time of perception.

We reasoned that if our perceptual hypothesis were true, then we ought to be able to disrupt these perceptual processes by perturbing the stimuli in some way. However, if the response organization hypothesis is true, then the way to disrupt performance is by changing the response mode.

We presented the Class A player with 32 new positions taken from Reinfeld (1945), but half the positions were presented as schematic diagrams in which a piece is represented by the first letter of its name, and black pieces are circled. Figure 8 shows an example of such a letter diagram position. The other 16 positions were shown normally, as pieces on an actual board.

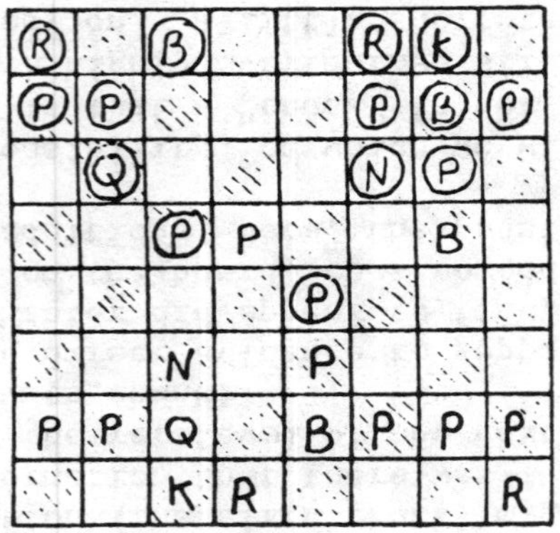

Also, half the positions were recalled normally by placing pieces on a board, and the other half were recalled by writing letter diagrams like Fig. 8. Thus, we have a 2 x 2 design with boards vs. letter diagrams as stimuli, and boards vs. letter diagrams as responses.

The results, shown in Table 6, are straightforward. Looking at the data on the first 16 trials, it didn't make any difference, in response, whether pieces were placed on a board or a schematic diagram was drawn. On the stimulus side, however, it made a big difference whether real boards or letter diagrams were presented. The Class A player was getting almost twice as many pieces correct when real boards were presented as when diagram stimuli were shown. This result was highly significant statistically ($p < 10^{-6}$), and neither the response mode nor the stimulus–response interaction was significant.

The advantage of boards over letter diagrams was due to more chunks being recalled for boards than for diagrams (7.5 vs. 4.0, respectively); the number of pieces per chunk was relatively constant for the different stimulus conditions (2.3 vs. 3.0, respectively).

Table 6. Percent Correct Recall
for Boards vs Diagrams as Stimuli and as Responses

Trials	Response	Stimulus		
		Written Diagram	Board	Average
1-16	Written Diagram	37	58	48
	Board	33	67	49
	Average	35	62	49
17-32	Written Diagram	50	46	48
	Board	48	55	51
	Average	49	50	50

Fig. 8. Example of a letter diagram.

It appears, therefore, that the schematic diagrams slow down the perceptual process, so that fewer perceptual structures are seen in the 5-second exposure.

However, this effect washes out very quickly with practice, so that after about an hour or so the Class A player was seeing these schematic diagrams about as well as real board positions. Neither the main effects nor the interaction was significant for the second block of 16 trials.

This experiment shows, first, that regardless of whether the player writes a letter diagram of the position or whether he picks up pieces at the side of the board and places them on the board, his performance is the same. This result eliminates the possibility that the pauses are artifacts due to picking up the pieces. Second, the fact that stimuli in the form of letter diagrams are initially disruptive suggests that performance in this task really depends upon perceptual rather than recall processes. The Class A player rapidly overcomes the difficulties of viewing the letter diagrams. Apparently some easy perceptual learning takes place so that the non-essential surface characteristics of the diagrams are ignored and the underlying invariant relations are perceived.

In a second experiment, we were interested in seeing how chess players of various strengths are affected by diagrams. In this experiment, we gave two Class A players and a beginner the same 5-second task, but this time we compared real board positions with printed (pictorial) diagrams from chess books. Figure 9 shows an example of these pictorial diagrams, selected from Reinfeld (1945), and in both cases real pieces were placed on a board at recall. Performance on pictorial diagrams is interesting because chess players spend a lot of time looking at diagrams like these when they read chess books and magazines.

Table 7 shows the basic results. Both Class A players did equally well for real boards and pictorial diagrams, but the beginner recalled real boards better than diagrams ($p < .001$). These limited data provide no evidence of a practice effect. These results

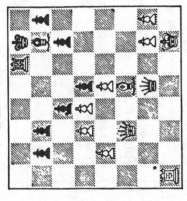

169

BLACK

WHITE
Black moves

Fig. 9. Example of a pictorial diagram (No. 169) taken from Reinfeld (1945).

presumably reflect the fact that the Class A players have had considerable experience with pictorial diagrams (but not with letter diagrams), whereas the beginner has had little or none.

An Information Processing Theory

In this section, we discuss a concrete theoretical formulation that we believe begins to characterize the perceptual processes we have described. The theory, developed by Simon & Gilmartin (1973), tries to capture the pattern recognition processes that underlie performance in de Groot's immediate memory task by postulating a few simple processes.[7] The basic idea is that

[7] For details of the theory, see Simon & Gilmartin (1973).

Table 7. Percent Correct Recall of Boards and Diagrams for two Class A Players and a Beginner

Player	Stimuli	
	Boards	Diagrams
1. Class A	61	60
2. Class A	56	58
3. Beginner	35	24

a large repertoire of patterns is stored in long-term memory and there is some mechanism that accesses these patterns: a discrimination net (EPAM net). In addition, a short-term memory of limited capacity stores the labels (names) of the patterns.

Another important component of the system is a process that makes a preliminary scan of the board to detect salient pieces. It is assumed that the same relations among pieces that account for chunking will cause a piece having many such relations to be perceptually salient. This idea is derived from PERCEIVER, an earlier simulation of the elementary processes that determine eye movements over a chess board. Simon & Barenfeld (1969) showed that PERCEIVER could produce a good simulation of the initial (5 seconds) eye movements of a skilled chess player scanning a chess position. The saliency score of a piece depends not only on the relations it has with other pieces, but also on its intrinsic importance, which, in turn, is correlated with its physical size (Kings and Queens largest, Pawns smallest).

The EPAM discrimination net itself is organized as a tree structure, with each node of the net representing a test for a piece on a certain square. Suppose, for example, that the King on KN1 were the salient piece. The next test then might ask for the piece in front of the King—on KN2. At this node the tree might have, say, three branches corresponding to a Pawn, a Bishop, or an empty square. The next node on the branch containing the Bishop might ask for the piece on KR2, and so on. The net, then, amounts to a set of instructions to the perceptual system for scanning the board systematically for prescribed patterns of pieces. Each path through the tree represents a different pattern of pieces on the board. Finally, at the end of each path is stored the internal name or label representing the pattern that was discovered or perceived by following that path. It is this label that is stored in short-term memory for later use at recall.

The theory, then, is very simple. The salient piece detector first derives a list of salient pieces rank-ordered from highest down.[8] Each salient piece is sorted in turn through the EPAM net and the label of the pattern that is recognized is stored in short-term memory. This label can be thought of as representing both (internally) a path through the EPAM net and (externally) a cluster of pieces about the salient piece. This recognition process continues until attention has been directed to all the salient pieces or short-term memory is filled with labels.[9] Finally, in recall, the labels from short-term memory are used

[8]In the present program all salient pieces are detected before the patterns surrounding them are recognized. A more plausible, detailed simulation would interleaf the processes of detecting salient pieces and recognizing patterns.

[9]The control processes of short-term memory are greatly oversimplified--there is no rehearsal, organization or forgetting in the present version of the theory. But it is probably true that short-term memory fills very quickly in this task and there is some rehearsal and organization and a lot of retroactive interference. The weaker players report that there is a tremendous amount of forgetting, and all players report that they tend to recall the most recently attended pieces first.

to derive from the EPAM net the information about the location of pieces in the chunk, and the result is the reproduction of each pattern that has been recognized.

To test their theory, Simon and Gilmartin first grew EPAM nets of various sizes—the largest containing about 4,000 nodes of which about 1,000 were terminal nodes. Their largest net was therefore able to recognize about 1,000 different patterns. The authors selected their patterns in an informal way—simply choosing chess positions from books and magazines and then breaking these positions down into patterns that seemed intuitively reasonable to the second author (KG). The selection of patterns was largely independent of the patterns that we obtained from our human players, since the selector (KG) had only a passing familiarity with those patterns. Standard EPAM learning techniques, of little interest here, were used for the actual mechanis of the net-growing process (see Feigenbaum, 1961).

The first question Simon and Gilmartin asked was how well the program recognizes patterns. Table 8 shows these data for the five middle game positions and the nine quiet positions that we used in our earlier research (Chase & Simon, 1973). The simulation, with a repertoire of about 1,000 patterns, does about as well as the Class A player, but significantly poorer than the Master. Notice also that the theory shows nearly the same proportionate improvement in performance as the humans on the nine quiet positions as compared with the five middle game positions.

A comparison of which pieces are remembered and which pieces are not remembered by human chess players and by the theory, revealed a considerable overlap. For example, the simulation recalled 51% of pieces placed by the Master in the five middle game positions and 60% in the nine quiet positions, but only about 30% of the pieces that the Master missed in these positions.

Finally, Simon and Gilmartin demonstrated the similarity between the humans' chunks and the chunks derived by the simulation in a third way. The within-chunk and between-chunk boundaries can be defined objectively from the output of the simulation since the chunks in the internal net from which the output is derived can be examined directly. The statistics on the chess relations—attack, defense, proximity, same color, same piece—between successively placed pieces were partitioned into within-chunk and between-chunk placements, and then compared with the corresponding statistics obtained from human chess players (Chase & Simon, 1973). Comparing the data from the five middle game positions, the results are fairly clear: the same kinds of correlations occurred for the within-chunk placements as for the short-latency and within-glance data of the human players, and the between-chunk placements were pretty much random, as were the long latency and between-glance data of the human players.

In sum, the simulation shows a good correspondence with the human data in terms of the percentage of pieces recalled correctly, in terms of which particular pieces are remembered and which are forgotten, and even in terms of the fine-grained detail of the order in which pieces are placed on the board.

Simon and Gilmartin also estimated how many patterns a Master would need in long-term memory in order to perform well on the 5-second recall task. For the quiet positions, the simulation recognizes about 50% of each position with about 1,000 patterns in memory, whereas the Master averages over 80%. How many more patterns would the simulation need in order to perform as well as the Master?

Simon and Gilmartin assumed that the frequency distribution of these patterns was similar to the distribution of frequency of words in natural language

Table 8. Percentage of Pieces Placed Correctly by Master, Class A Player, and the Theory in two Sets of Positions

Positions	Master	Class A	Theory
Five Middle Game	62	34	43
Nine Quiet Puzzle	81	49	54
Row 2 / Row 1 Ratio	1.305	1.438	1.255

prose, which is usually well approximated by the harmonic distribution--the most frequent pattern occurring with frequency f, the next most frequent pattern with frequency $1/2\,f$, the third most frequent pattern with frequency $1/3\,f$, and so on. If we start with a net containing the 1,000 most frequent patterns, and if these account for 50% of all pattern occurrences, how many more patterns would have to be added in order to include about 80% of all occurrences? The answer is about 30,000.

Using this and other ways of estimating the size of the Master's repertoire of patterns, Simon and Gilmartin concluded that the size of his vocabulary lies between 10,000 and 100,000 patterns. Similar estimates have been obtained from quite different considerations (Simon & Barenfeld, 1969). The estimate also seems reasonable because it is about as large as a good reader's recognition vocabulary, which is consistent with the fact that chess Masters spend as much time viewing chess positions as good readers do reading

Taken in perspective, then, what does the theory suggest about skilled chess performance? First, there is a very large repertoire of patterns in long-term memory--patterns that are held together by a small set of chess relations something like those we found in our earlier research. Second, there is a mechanism that scans the board, that recognizes pieces and the functional relations between pieces, and that finds the important pieces to build these little patterns around. And third, there are severe limits on the capacity of short-term memory, where the internal names of the patterns are stored.

There is one important mechanism, however, that is missing in the Simon-Gilmartin theory, as it is presently formulated. The simulation (unlike the earlier Simon-Barenfeld program) makes no provision for the perception of meaningful but unfamiliar patterns; only familiar patterns stored in long-term memory are recognized. As we mentioned earlier, there is a real possibility that if a player notices a relation between one or more pieces, this structural information may be

stored in short-term memory. Such a structure is not a chunk, in the sense in which that term is now generally used, because in order to remember it, some details of the structure, and not just its internal name, must be retained in short-term memory.

The issue we are raising is that there must be some mechanism for perceiving meaningful structures—meaningful in the sense that the pieces comprising the structure are functionally related in some way—even though the structure is unfamiliar. This mechanism would be needed in order for such structures to become familiar in the first place. And the basic functions are undoubtedly the geometric and chess functions we have been studying.

One way of thinking about this mechanism is in terms of a set of production rules that create new structures, given certain inputs. For example, *if A attacks B and A attacks C, then A forks B and C.* The production in this case would consist of a condition side (*A attacks B, and A attacks C*) which needs to be fulfilled before any action is taken. The action in this case is to construct a new structure containing the pieces A, B, and C. This structure is meaningful because it is organized around the concept of a fork, but this particular fork need not be familiar. The structure would contain information about the relative locations of the three pieces, as well as the more abstract relation, *A forks B and C.* This relation might enter into a still more complicated production that takes a fork as a condition. And there must, of course, be more elementary productions that take pieces and the squares they control as input and construct relations like *A attacks B.*[10] A collection of rules of this form is called a production system (Newell & Simon, 1972).

Regardless of the organization of these rules, the perception of meaningful structures must be more rule-bound (generative) than is necessary for the

---

[10]We point out, again, that the structure contains the relative locations of the pieces as well as the underlying functional relationship.

While this theory is simply a rough first approximation, it does offer a concrete application of cognitive principles to the task of playing skilled chess, and these principles are not derived or applied *ad hoc*: the basic elements of the theory--the EPAM organization of long-term memory, the elementary perceptual processes of PERCEIVER, and the limited capacity of short-term memory--are derived from an already existing body of theory about cognitive psychology that stands on a considerable data base of its own.

Further Experiments on Chess Skill

We have presented an empirical and theoretical treatment of the immediate perceptual processing of a chess position which specifies cognitive processes to account for the remarkable ability of chess Masters to remember so much from a brief exposure of a position. Other kinds of chess-like tasks show an equally dramatic effect of chess skill. In this section of the paper, we present our experiments on these other tasks along with our speculations about the underlying processes.

Long-Term Memory for Positions

In this experiment, we asked chess players to memorize a game until it was well learned, and then to reconstruct the position at a certain point in the game. The cue for recall was simply a move of the game, such as "White's twenty-third move: Bishop takes Knight." The player's task was then to reconstruct the position at that point.

We wanted to know if recall of these positions showed as large an effect of chess skill as the immediate recall of positions. We were further interested in the kind of chunks that would be revealed in this task. We conjectured that in order to recall these positions, the players would have to rely in part on their memory for the dynamic move sequences, and we were therefore expecting a different kind of chunk in

familiar structures. In the latter case, the recognition relies heavily on a simple mechanism with a few rules--the interpreter for the EPAM net--to sort through a large set of familiar patterns. Since familiar patterns are also meaningful, a familiar pattern might be recognized in two ways, although the recognition mechanism for familiar patterns is probably much faster.[11] The system for perceiving meaningful patterns is surely more elaborate for skilled players than for beginners.[12]

These processes are not necessarily organized as a production system or an EPAM net. That is a matter for further research. We merely wish to make the distinction between meaningful and familiar perceptual structures, and to point out that the Simon-Gilmartin simulation has only a mechanism for perceiving the familiar patterns.

---

[11] It is quite possible that this dual process is responsible for the results of the experiment on lette[r] diagrams, as follows. Letter diagrams are initially unfamiliar, so the player has to notice pieces and relations individually as they are decoded, and he the[n] uses this information to construct unfamiliar chunks. With a little learning, however, the player is able to modify his recognition mechanism to substitute letters for pieces, and the familiar patterns in long-term memory then become accessible.

[12] If it is true that some of the patterns are recalled because they are meaningful, and that the Master is better at perceiving meaningful but unfamiliar patterns, then Simon & Gilmartin have over-estim[at]ed the size of the Master's repertoire of familiar patterns. Also, in the present version of the program, patterns are associated with particular squares. However, it is probably the case that most patterns need not be tied to exact squares (cf. the data on placement errors in recall). If this restriction is relaxed, Simon & Gilmartin's estimate could be substantially lowered.

the recall of these positions than we found in the immediate recall experiments. We were expecting, for example, less reliance on spatial properties, such as proximity, and more reliance on the chess functions, such as attack.

For this experiment, our three chess players--the Master, the Class A player, and the beginner--learned the moves of a 25-move game (50 plies) until they could reproduce the same perfectly twice in a row. The game was learned by the study-test method where each move (ply) was read out at the rate of 5 seconds per move, and the player then executed the move for himself on a chess board. During the test phase, the player tried to recall each move for himself by playing it on a chess board, and he was told the correct move if he made a wrong move or if 10 seconds had elapsed since the previous move. When the player had reproduced the whole sequence of moves perfectly, each move (ply) being made in less than 10 seconds, a second test trial was administered immediately. Upon successful completion of the second test trial, the player was then asked to reproduce the position after a specified move (e.g., after White's tenth move: Knight to Bishop Three). On five subsequent days following this learning session, the players returned for a single test trial on the same game, and then another reproduction of a different position from the game. We thus have six reproductions of positions taken from the same game, but widely spaced at different points throughout the game. All of this behavior was videotaped and analyzed by the same methods as were used in the earlier experiments.

Table 9 shows the simple statistics on recall of positions after a game had been learned. First of all, the Master just doesn't make many errors (99% correct) but the beginner does extremely well also (90% correct). The beginner, in fact, reproduces more of these positions than the Master did after the 5-second exposure (81%). With respect to chunk size, defined by the same 2-second pause as previously, it turns out that the Master recalls about 4 pieces per chunk, and the Class A player about 2 or 3 pieces per chunk. Thus, these

Table 9. Recall of Positions from Long-Term Memory

Player	Percent Correct	Pieces per Chunk	Chunks per Position
Master	99	4.0	7.7
Class A	95	2.5	10.5
Beginner	90	1.2	22.8

chunks are about the same size as the first chunk recalled after the 5-second exposures of the middle game positions. However, chunk size is relatively constant here; it does not fall off with successively recalled chunks as it did for the 5-second exposures. Also, the number of chunks per position varies inversely with the chunk size since all players were able to recall most of the positions from long-term memory. (Clearly, number of chunks recalled in this experiment should be independent of short-term memory limits.)

Looking at the beginner's data, we see something very interesting. His chunk size is smaller than before; in fact, his average chunk size is hardly more than one piece. Some 82% of his chunks contained only a single piece, whereas this percentage was much smaller for the Master and Class A player (26 and 37 percent, respectively). Apparently, the beginner doesn't have access to many patterns in long-term memory. He virtually has to reconstruct the position piece by piece from the moves of the game.

The next thing we looked at was the relationship between the interpiece latencies and the chess relations. Figure 10 shows that there is a strong (negative) correlation between the number of relations between two pieces and their interpiece latency. But unlike the case of the 5-second recall data, there is an interaction with chess skill. When two pieces, placed sequentially in the output, are highly related, then both the Master and the Class A player place them in rapid succession. However, with the pieces having few relations (0, 1, and possibly 2), the Master's interpiece intervals are about half as long as the Class A player's intervals. The average intervals for the beginner are longer than the skilled players, even for the highly related pieces. This reflects the fact that the beginner had only a few intervals less than 2 seconds (18%), and these were for the highly related pieces (2, 3, and 4 relations).

Thus, the recall of positions from a game is accelerated by recalling them in chunks of related pieces. Although there is also a difference in the amount of material recalled as a function of chess skill, this difference isn't nearly as impressive as in the 5-second recall task; but there is a striking difference in the speed of recall.

We interpret these data in the following way. Once a chunk has been retrieved from long-term memory, recall of the pieces is equally fast for all levels of chess skill (probably a second or less per piece). However, the differences in chess skill manifest themselves in the speed with which successive new chunks

are retrieved from long-term memory: 3 or 4 seconds for the Master, 6 or 8 seconds for the Class A player, and about 12 seconds for the beginner. This is a tremendous range of times when it is considered that most simple mental operations take place in only a few tenths of a second!

Finally, when we ask what kinds of chunks are being recalled, we find that they look just like the chunks in the 5-second recall task. For short pauses (less than 2 seconds) there is a lot of structure, and the structure is the same: a preponderance of Pawn chains and local clusters of pieces of the same color that mutually defend each other. The expected more frequent appearance of the attack' relation failed to occur. These data for the short pauses apply mostly to the Master and the Class A player, since the beginner had few latencies under 2 seconds.

For the longer interpiece latencies (greater than 2 seconds), the relations again looked almost as if the two pieces were chosen randomly. Table 10 compares the frequencies of the 16 possible interpiece relations by examining the correlations between the various conditions involving long and short interpiece latencies for short-term and long-term recall tasks. There are two clusters of high correlations in this table: (1) between interpiece relations for short pauses in both long-term and short-term recall, and (2) between interpiece relations for long pauses in both long-term and

Table 10. Intercorrelation Matrix for Short-Term Memory, Long-Term Memory, and Random Chess Relation Probabilities

Task	1	2	3	4	5
1 STM Less Than 2 Sec.		.86	.23	.26	-.03
2 LTM Less Than 2 Sec.			.26	.37	.03
3 STM Greater Than 2 Sec.				.92	.87
4 LTM Greater Than 2 Sec.					.81
5 Random					

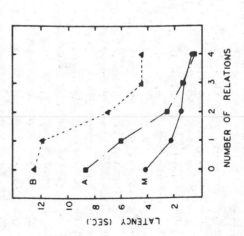

Fig. 10. Average interpiece latencies for the Master (M), Class A player (A), and beginner (B) as a function of the number of relations between the two pieces.

short-term recall and the *a priori* random relations. In short, these data show that for skilled chess players (but perhaps not for the beginner), the same kinds of perceptual structures are recalled in short-term recall of briefly viewed positions and in recall of positions from the long-term memory of a game.

Another interesting finding that we haven't documented very well yet is worth mentioning at this point. From the verbal protocols it appears that the first piece in a chunk is recalled dynamically--in terms of the moves of the game--and then its neighbors are filled in by reference to the local features with strong spatial components that are characteristic of the perceptual structures we have been studying. The most common reasons given by players for remembering these initial pieces are in terms of a move made earlier in the game, together with the purpose of the move.

The fact that skilled chess players recall these positions from long-term memory by means of perceptual structures suggests that they are organizing the moves of the game in terms of these structures and their alternations as the game goes along. Of course, there is more to remembering a game than this: the moves themselves must be remembered, and these are undoubtedly organized according to the semantics of the game (we will say more about this later). But part of the remembered organization of a game involves the perceptual structures.

The beginner, however, doesn't seem to make use of these structures, which suggests that he doesn't have a very large repertoire of chunks in long-term memory. When it comes to recalling a position from the game, the beginner is reduced to generating the positions of the pieces from his rote memory of the moves. This doesn't say that the beginner makes no use of perceptual structures. It means that he has to build such structures from pieces and relations that he notices on the board, since he doesn't have them familiarized for easy recognition in long-term memory. In the 5-second recall task, the beginner needs visual access to the board in order to build these structures, and, we have hypothesized, he has a smaller memory span than the skilled

players for these structures because they are not simple chunks. He has to store considerable information about the relations of pieces in short-term memory. In the long-term recall of positions, however, the beginner doesn't have visual access to the position, so he can't build any structures, and he has long since lost from short-term memory any structures that he had originally assembled from the position.

Long-Term Memory for Games

In this experiment, we asked how chess players organize a game in memory. When a player recalls the moves of a game, we suspect that here, too, he organizes his sequences of moves in bursts which are held together closely by chess relations, and which are segmented by longer pauses. We further hypothesized that forgetting ought to be very selective. That is, with forgetting, the game ought to come apart at the seams, so to speak, with long pauses and errors at those points in the game where new chunks begin.

The data we consider here are the learning and recall of moves for the 25-move game mentioned in the previous section. We recorded the recall of moves, as well as positions, on video tape, including the trials to criterion on Day 1 and the recall trials on the 5 subsequent days.

The results show conclusively that rates of learning and forgetting the moves of a game strongly depend upon chess skill. In terms of trials to criterion, errors to criterion, and total learning time, the Master learned very rapidly (as rapidly as the moves were given to him), whereas the beginner spent considerable time and effort memorizing the game, and the Class A player was intermediate between these two. Table 11 shows the actual data. So here is another task, like memory for positions, that shows a very strong effect of chess skill.

Further, if we categorize each move in terms of its chess function, the latencies are very different for moves with different functions. We categorized moves into six simple categories: (1) Opening: these moves are in the beginning of the game that develop the pieces. These moves usually follow fairly stereo-typed patterns that are well known to skilled chess players. (2) Exchange: the exchange of one piece for another. (3) Defense: a move which defends an attacked piece or square. (4) Attack: a move that threatens to win material or gain a favorable position. (5) Counter-attack: a move that counters an attacking move with a threat of its own. (6) Quiet: a move that is none of the above. In a game between skilled players, these latter moves generally represent the maneuvering for a favorable position according to some strategic plan (e.g., to gain control of the dark squares on the King side). Against weaker opponents, the "quiet" and attacking moves are the ones that Masters make which usually lead to wins.

The latency data, shown in Table 12, indicate that latencies are generally longer for quiet moves and attacking moves than for the others. This seems to be true both for the test trials during learning and the recall trials over the 5 days following learning, although there are occasional deviations from this generalization. For example, the Class A player had repeated trouble recalling one move in the opening, and this single instance was enough to increase signi-ficantly his average opening-move latencies relative to the average latencies for exchange, defense, and counter-attack moves.

Too much significance should not be attached to these data since they are based on a single game. The standard errors, for example, vary widely because the number of observations vary for different conditions. (For example, in the learning trials there were only two trials for the Master and twelve trials for the beginner.) Also, there weren't many errors, particu-larly in the recall phase: .4, 1.7, and 2.1 percent for the Master, Class A player, and beginner, respec-tively. The memory for this game was highly tenacious over a period of a week. Thus, with this one game, we were unable to see if forgetting would occur at the chunk boundaries.

However, one result seems fairly robust in these data: the relatively long pauses associated with the quiet and attacking moves. We take this to mean that chunks (sometimes involving only a single move) are organized around the ideas (semantics) behind the quiet and attacking moves. Recall of these moves is slow because the underlying idea must be retrieved from long-term memory. Associated with this idea may be a series of more or less stereotyped moves--exchanges, and defensive or counterattacking moves--which are chunked together by virtue of their relation (hierarchical) to the underlying idea. These chunks are generally only a few plies deep (say 2-4), whereas the openings usually run at least 10 plies. Although there are underlying semantics associated with the opening moves, these moves are overlearned by exper-ienced players and usually are played by rote.

Table 11. Long-Term Memory for Games

Player	Trials to Criterion	Errors to Criterion	Learning Time (Minutes)
Master	2	4	10
Class A	5	13	29
Beginner	12	94	81

Table 12. Move Latencies (Sec.) and their Standard Errors (in Parentheses) for Long-Term Recall of Moves

Move	Learning			Recall		
	Master	Class A	Beginner	Master	Class A	Beginner
Opening	1.0 (.08)	1.7 (.18)	2.1 (.13)	1.3 (.11)	1.9 (.31)	1.5 (.08)
Exchange	1.8 (.51)	1.6 (.19)	2.5 (.19)	1.1 (.05)	1.2 (.08)	1.5 (.10)
Defense	2.0 (.56)	2.2 (.37)	3.4 (.34)	1.2 (.07)	1.6 (.15)	1.4 (.12)
Attack	3.0 (.92)	2.5 (.25)	3.9 (.26)	1.6 (.10)	2.1 (.21)	2.4 (.20)
Counterattack	1.6 (.11)	2.5 (.60)	3.3 (.50)	1.0 (.11)	1.1 (.10)	1.6 (.21)
Quiet	4.4 (.81)	3.0 (.33)	3.7 (.23)	1.6 (.10)	2.5 (.21)	2.5 (.25)

This leads us to consider how memory for games is organized. Skilled chess players have hundreds and perhaps thousands of sequences of moves stored away in long-term memory. The top players have thousands of opening variations—some running over 40 plies deep—committed to memory. There are also hundreds, perhaps thousands, of traps and winning combinations of moves that every Master knows. The question is whether most chunks comprising a game beyond the opening—simple exchanges, defensive moves, etc.—are also represented somewhere in this vast repertoire of move sequences, or whether these moves can be executed with a minimum of information because of the redundancy associated with the underlying idea behind the chunk. This is a question we can't resolve at the moment. It is clear, however, that the skilled player's recall of a game involves recognition memory for perceptual structures as well as sequences of moves, both of which must somehow be accessed in long-term memory.

Immediate Recall of Moves

In this experiment, we were interested in seeing if immediate recall of moves from a game yielded analogous results to those for immediate recall of a briefly exposed position. Specifically, we expected that immediate recall of a coherent sequence of moves from a real game would depend upon the level of chess skill, whereas memory for a random sequence of moves would be uniformly poor for all levels of chess skill. And we further expected that longer pauses and errors ought to occur on the same type of moves as in the previous section.

The Master, Class A player, and beginner were each given twenty 10-move sequences (20 plies) for immediate recall.[13] Half the move sequences were taken from Master games and half were random sequences. The initial positions were all taken from a book of Dr. Lasker's games (Lasker, 1935), with the restrictions that the sequence begin around Move 20, that it begin with a move by White, that there be at least 10 more moves in the game, and that there be at least 18 pieces on the board. The real sequences of 10 moves were taken from the game from that point, and the random sequences were generated from that point by randomly selecting a piece of the correct color, and then randomly selecting a move from the set of legal moves for that piece.

To familiarize the players with each initial position, they were required to set up the position on a board in front of them by viewing a diagram of the position. The players were then allowed 30 seconds to study the position before the sequence of moves was presented. Following this initial familiarization, the next 10 moves (20 plies) were read to the player at the rate of 5 seconds per ply, and the player executed each move (ply) on the board as he heard it. Five seconds after the last move was executed, the board was removed, the video tape was turned on, and a new board containing the initial position was placed in front of the player. There was about a 10-second delay between removal of the final position and presentation of the initial position. The player then immediately began to recall the sequence of moves by executing the moves on the board. The correct move was given to the player only if he made a wrong move, or if 10 seconds had elapsed since the previous move.

The first important result, shown in Table 13, is that the Master was virtually perfect at recalling the real game moves. The Class A player was also good at recalling the real move sequences, but the beginner made over 40% errors. This result confirms our expectation that immediate recall of moves is a function of chess skill. Contrary to our expectation, however, was the finding that even for the random sequences of moves, accuracy of recall depended upon the level of chess skill. Apparently, the skilled players were able to find some meaning in the randomly generated moves.

---

[13] We lost half the beginner's data due to a defective tape recorder, but the data we did obtain are enough for comparisons with the Master and Class A player's data.

Table 13. Percent Errors for Short-Term Recall of Moves

Move	Real Moves			Random Moves		
	Master	Class A	Beginner	Master	Class A	Beginner
Exchange	0	0	29	10	23	73
Defense	4	0	25	25	13	50
Attack	3	11	39	25	28	67
Quiet	0	8	57	25	36	85
Average	1	6	43	22	31	85

Table 14. Move Latencies (Sec.) and their Standard Errors (In Parentheses) for Short-Term Recall of Moves

Move	Real Moves			Random Moves		
	Master	Class A	Beginner	Master	Class A	Beginner
Exchange	2.2 (.22)	2.2 (.34)	4.2 (.86)	4.3 (.47)	3.6 (.58)	6.9 (1.21)
Defense	2.1 (.29)	2.0 (.32)	4.4 (.71)	2.8 (.52)	4.5 (.83)	4.8 (1.50)
Attack	2.5 (.28)	3.4 (.47)	6.4 (.80)	4.0 (.45)	4.2 (.58)	7.1 (1.06)
Quiet	3.5 (.23)	3.8 (.27)	6.5 (.58)	5.1 (.33)	4.4 (.35)	8.3 (.56)
Average	2.8	3.1	5.7	4.6	4.3	7.3

Second, there was some indication that errors were more likely to occur on the attacking and quiet moves than on the exchange and defensive moves. This is true only for the real moves, and only for those players who made errors--the Master made only 2 errors on the real moves. (We have eliminated the counter-attacking moves from this analysis since they were so rare.)

The latency data, shown in Table 14, reveal that for all levels of chess skill, the attacking and quiet moves from real games were recalled relatively more slowly, on the average, than the exchange and defensive moves. Not surprisingly, there were few systematic latency differences among the different moves when they were randomly generated. Also, the latency differences were not systematically related to chess skill; the only consistent difference was that between the beginner and the two skilled players. Finally, for all levels of chess skill, average latencies were longer for the random moves than for the real moves.

The results of this experiment parallel those of the 5-second recall task in that recall of a coherent sequence of moves from a game is far superior to that of a random sequence of moves, and further, performance depends upon the level of chess skill, with the Master showing virtually perfect recall. However, unlike the 5-second recall task, performance on the random sequence also depends on chess skill.

We should point out that there is less reliance on short-term memory for immediate recall of moves than for recall of positions because total presentation time of moves is almost 2 minutes before recall. In this amount of time, a great deal of organization and more permanent storage almost certainly occurs.

Finally, these results, taken in conjunction with those in the previous section on long-term memory for moves, suggest that pauses and errors in recalling the moves of a game give a clue as to how this memory is structured. Memory for moves is probably segmented into little episodes, each organized around some goal. These episodes begin with a high information move which may represent a direct threat (attack), or some more subtle plan. These latter moves are categorized as "quiet" since the purpose or plan that motivates them is not always readily apparent. Sometimes, episodes are only a single ply deep--such is the nature of chess that the game can change completely with a single move-- and sometimes these episodes continue with more predictable moves involving exchanges, defenses, counter- attacks, and probably more attacks. It is probably true that the moves are organized hierarchically, with higher level plans involving episodes within episodes; our research represents only a modest beginning in understanding how these memories are structured.

The Knight's Tour

There is another task, described in a recent chess magazine (Radojcic, 1971), which purports to measure chess talent, i.e., the *potential* to play-skilled chess. Figure 11 shows the task, which is to move the Knight from its initial position at Queen's Rook One to each successive square until it finally ends up on the Queen's Rook Eight square. The Knight can make only legal moves, and it must progress by touching successive squares in a rank. That is, it must go next to the QN1 square, which it can do via the route QB2-QR3-QN1. Then the next target square is QB1, and so on, until it reaches the KR1 square at the end of the First Rank. Then the Knight must traverse the Second Rank, starting with the KR2 square, which it can reach via KB2 and KN4. The Knight proceeds thus, rank by rank, until it ends up on the QR8 square. An additional requirement makes the task interesting: the Knight cannot go to a square where it can be taken by one of the black Pawns, nor can it capture a black Pawn. The strategically placed Pawns thus break up any stereotyped pattern of moves by the Knight, and they force the player to search for the right sequence of moves. The idea is to see how fast the player can do this.

This task was calibrated several years ago on a large sample of chess-playing school children in Czechoslovakia. Four children were far faster than all the others in their age group, and the boy who performed best on this test is currently one of the strongest players in the world, and was a candidate for the World's Championship this year. The other three children who solved the problem rapidly all turned out to be Grand-masters or International Masters. Radojcic also reports that the times on this task are correlated with the playing strengths of various Masters. Masters usually complete the task in 2 to 5 minutes.

We have confirmed the fact that this task measures chess skill. Our Master performed the task in 3 minutes, the Class A player in 7 minutes, and the beginner in 25 minutes. Perhaps the task also measures talent, the potential for chess skill, but we don't have the right data to answer that question. Our main concern here is with understanding the cognition of already existing chess skill, and we will leave open the question of chess talent.

One additional interesting phenomenon was the manner in which players executed the Knight moves. The skilled players (Master and Class A) invariably paused after reaching each successive target square. During the pause, they would search for the next series of Knight moves that would get the Knight to the next target square, and then execute these moves very rapidly (usually less than 1/2 second per move). It was at the pauses, when the players searched for the series of moves to the next target square, where chess skill had its effect. The Master averaged about 3 seconds per pause whereas the Class A player averaged over 7 seconds per pause. These times are similar to the chunk retrieval times in the long-term memory task, but perhaps this is a coincidence. Further, the length of the pause was strongly correlated with the number of moves

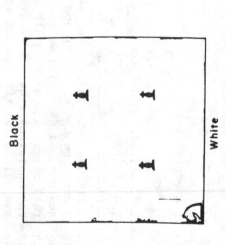

Fig. 11. Starting position for the Knight's tour.

necessary to reach the next target square, and this time interacted with chess skill (Table 15). For the short sequences, both players were about equally fast, but for the two longer sequences, the Master showed increasing superiority over the Class A player. Also, the Class A player executed three sequences that were longer than necessary.

For the beginner, there was no such neat division of the latencies, although his latencies did appear to consist of pauses followed by a series of more or less rapid moves. It seems fairly clear from the beginner's verbal report that he too was pausing to search for the correct path, but he often got lost. He sometimes executed partial solutions, and sometimes, after failing to discover a path, he would simply try to find a solution by trial and error.

We think the ability that underlies this task is very similar to that underlying the 5-second recall task: the ability to perceive a familiar pattern--in this case, the pattern of squares representing the Knight's path to the next target square. Here, too, the Master's perceptual processes appear to be all-important.

Cognitive Processes in Chess

All of our studies point to the perceptual processing--the ability to perceive familiar patterns quickly--as the basic ability underlying chess skill. We have surveyed several tasks that measure chess skill, and we believe that in each case we were measuring similar perceptual abilities. We think that is true for the Knight's Tour, and true even for the memory of the moves

of a game; we will outline our ideas on these tasks later in more detail. We first summarize our current thinking about the cognitive processes underlying chess skill.

The Contents of Thought

The slow, partly conscious, inferential processes that are available from verbal protocols just won't tell us very much about chess skill. Chess protocols are filled with statements like, "If I take him, then he takes that piece, then I go there . . ." and so on. de Groot showed that the structure of a player's thought processes while he is doing this are the same for all levels of chess skill. It is the *contents* of thought, not the structure of thought, that really makes the difference in quality of outcome. And we suggest that the contents of thought are mainly these perceptual structures that skilled chess players retrieve, for the most part, from long-term memory.[14]

Finding Good Moves

We believe we are in a position now to answer-- albeit speculatively--the following question: Why, as has often been observed, does the Master so frequently hit upon good moves before he has even analyzed the consequences of various alternatives? Because, we conjecture, when he stares at the chess board, the familiar perceptual structures that are evoked from long-term memory by the patterns on the board act as move generators. In the Master's long-term memory-- at the end of his EPAM net, or wherever that information is stored--there is associated with the internal name,

[14]Probably the moves derived from these structures, sequences of moves retrieved from long-term memory, and perhaps some strategic plans (e.g., center control) are also important.

Table 15. Pause Time (Sec.) Before a Move Sequence

Player	Sequence Length			Average
	2	3	5	
Master	1.5	2.6	10.5	2.9
Class A	2.1	5.6	28.6	7.4

structural information about the pattern that he can use to build an internal representation (a simulacrum in the mind's eye), and information about plausible good moves for some of the patterns. It is this organization of stored information that permits the Master to come up with good moves almost instantaneously, seemingly by instinct and intuition.

We can conceive this part of long-term memory to be organized as a production system (see Newell & Simon, 1972, pp. 728-735). Each familiar pattern serves as the *condition* part of a production. When this condition is satisfied by recognition of the pattern, the resulting *action* is to evoke a move associated with this pattern and to bring the move into short-term memory for consideration.

Forward Search in Chess

When the Master is staring at a chess board trying to choose his next move, he is engaged in a forward search through some kind of problem space. The problem space has generally been characterized as a branching tree where the initial node is the current board position, the branches represent moves, and the next nodes off these branches represent the new board positions reached by those moves (Newell & Simon, 1972, p. 665). But the Master's problem space is certainly more complicated than this, because he doesn't have the board position organized in short-term memory as a single unitary structure. As we have shown, the board is organized into smaller units representing more local clusters of pieces. Since some of these patterns have plausible moves associated with them in long-term memory, the Master will start his search by taking one of these moves and analyzing its consequences.

Since some of the recognizable patterns will be relevant, and some irrelevant, to his analysis, we hypothesize that he constructs a more concrete internal representation of the relevant patterns in the mind's eye, and then modifies these patterns to reflect the consequences of making the evoked move. The information

processing operations needed to perform this perturbation, whatever they are, are akin to the mental rotation processes studied by Shepard (cf. Cooper & Shepard's chapter in this volume) and the mental processes for solving cube-painting and cube-cutting puzzles studied by Baylor (1971). When the move is made in the mind's eye—that is, when the internal representation of the position is updated—the result is then passed back through the pattern perception system and new patterns are perceived. These patterns in turn will suggest new moves, and the search continues.

External memory (Sperling, 1960), eye movements, and peripheral vision are also important for the search. When the player executes a move in the mind's eye, he generally looks at the location on the actual, external board where the piece would be, imagines the piece at that location, and somehow forms a composite image of the generated piece together with pieces on the board. Peripheral vision is important because the fovea can resolve only a very few squares (perhaps 4), so that verification of the location of the pieces within the image requires detection of cues in the periphery. Thus, forward search involves coordinating information available externally on the visible chess board with updating information held in the mind's eye. (For eye-movement studies of the coordination of external with internally stored information in a different problem-solving task, see Winikoff, 1967.)

If the Master wants to reconstruct his path of moves through the problem space, all he needs to store in short-term memory are the internal names of the relevant quiet patterns along the path, since the rest of the information can be retrieved, as we have seen, from long-term memory. This provides a tremendous saving of space in short-term memory for other operations, and time for the subsequent progressive deepening that is so often seen in the protocols.

We thus conceive of search through the problem space as involving an iteration of the pattern system's processes, and repeated updating of information in the mind's eye. Only the barest outline of this complex process is explicit in the verbal protocols. Given the known time constants for the mind's eye and for long-term memory retrieval (cf. Cavanagh, 1972; Cooper & Shepard's chapter; Sternberg, 1969), each iteration takes perhaps half a second.

The Properties of the Mind's Eye

What goes on in the mind's eye, then, would seem to be of central importance for the search process, and we should spell out in more detail the properties of this system, as they are revealed by human performance in tasks calling for visualization.

We conceive of the mind's eye as a system that stores perceptual structures and permits them to be subjected to certain mental operations. The perceptual system then has access to these new structures in order to perceive the consequences of these changes. Although the repertoire of operations that can be performed in the mind's eye is yet to be determined, they are often analogous to external operations that cause visual-structural changes of objects in the real world. "Painting," "cutting," and rotating objects spatially are operations that have been shown experimentally to be performable.

Perhaps the most important (and "eye-like") property of the mind's eye is that spatial relations can be readily derived from the image. This property is illustrated as follows. Suppose an image is a structure describable in the two propositions: *A is to the left of B* and *B is above C*. Then people know directly from their image that *A is above and to the left of C*. By directly, we mean that people can use the perceptual system to abstract quickly from the mind's eye a new spatial proposition, something like *A is northwest of C*. Although people could also "problem-solve" such a proposition inferentially, this information is more quickly derived by taking advantage of the spatial operators of the mind's eye.

This property of the mind's eye probably also underlies much simple problem-solving behavior. For example, DeSoto, London, and Hendel (1965) were the

first to point out that people seem to solve problems of the form *If A is better than B, and C is worse than B, then who is best?* by placing A, B, and C in a mental image and replacing *better* by the spatial relation *above*. Then to find *best or worst*, people find the top or bottom item, respectively, in the image. People seem to solve these problems faster by this "spatial paralogic" than by the use of deductive reasoning.[15]

There appear to be severe constraints on how much detail can be held at any moment in the mind's eye. It is not clear whether the source of this limitation is in the mind's eye itself or in short-term memory, which presumably contains the perceptual structure (the input), the instructions needed to generate and transform the image (the control structures), and the new structures which are abstracted from the transformed image (the output). Because of this limited capacity, the mind's eye may image only part of a perceptual structure at a time.

Although an exact characterization of the mind's eye has yet to be worked out, we emphasize four properties of this system: (1) it is the meeting point where current visual information is coordinated and combined with remembered visual information stored in long-term and short-term memory; (2) it can be operated on by processes isomorphic to those that cause visual-structural changes of objects in the external world; (3) it can be operated on by the perceptual processes that abstract new information; and (4) it contains relational structures, hence the unstructured images and the feature-extractors of the visual system lie between it and the retina.

[15]We should point out that the relative difficulty of solving these syllogisms has been shown by Clark (1969) to be due primarily to the linguistic processes needed to comprehend the sentences in the first place.

Characteristics of Perceptual Structures

Although the precise manner in which perceptual structures are represented internally is not known, some of their abstract properties have been determined by experiment. The psycholinguist tends to conceive of them as somehow analogous to "kernel sentences." "Propositions" would be a better term, provided we interpret it abstractly and provided we do not attribute specifically verbal or linguistic characteristics to the structures.

In artificial intelligence studies (e.g., Baylor, 1971; Baylor & Simon, 1966; Coles, 1972; Quillian, 1966; T. Williams, 1972), perceptual structures are represented as assemblages of description lists, the elementary components of which are propositions asserting that certain relations hold among elements (e.g., *A is to the right of B*). We will here refer to perceptual structures as relational structures whose components are propositions. It should be understood that they are generally web-like or network-like, rather than tree-like in overall topology.

If this interpretation be accepted, then the "deep structures" postulated by psycholinguists, the "schemas" postulated by psychologists of perception, and the "internal representations" postulated by information processing psychologists are not to be regarded as separate entities, but simply as different ways of naming a single system of representations and processes for acting on those representations. Images in the mind's eye can be generated from such structures derived from visual inputs, from verbal inputs (as in the experiments of Baylor), or from structures stored in long-term memory, by the processes we have just described.

For the representation of abstract information, most investigators have concluded that a propositional or relational format is necessary (see Baylor, 1971; Clark & Chase, 1972; Kintsch, 1972; Newell & Simon, 1972, pp. 23-28, for examples). We hypothesize that perceptual structures are organizations of propositions about the three-dimensional world we live in (e.g., *X is blue, X is above, X attacks Y*, etc.) where the relations (*blue, above*, . . .) and their arguments (*X, Y*, . . .) should be thought of as abstract symbols representing the meaning of objects, actions, spatial relations, and the like.

Relations and arguments in turn can sometimes be represented in terms of more elementary relational structures (Kintsch, 1972). *Above*, for example, might in turn be represented (+ *Polar*, + *Vertical*), semantic features for markedness and verticality (Clark & Chase, 1972). Objects can also have multiple representations. The symbol +, for example, might be represented as the single symbol representing "plus" or as a proposition with vertical and horizontal lines as arguments and their proper juxtaposition in space as the relation. Chess pieces (e.g., Queen) and chess relations (e.g., attack) can be represented in terms of more primitive features. Thus, there is no *a priori* reason why a sensory feature, such as a contour of a certain orientation, can't also appear as an argument in a perceptual structure. This hierarchical organization has certain practical advantages, since one would want to hold only the relevant propositions in short-term memory; other information in the hierarchy can be retrieved from long-term memory or generated from redundancy rules upon demand.

The most important question about these perceptual structures is how each is organized. Although this is an empirical question, we think of these structures, for chess at least, as description list structures or directed graphs comprised of object-relation-object triples. In chess, the directed graph of a chunk would usually involve pieces or squares at the nodes and chess relations as pointers to new pieces or squares. The size of such a structure, the number of redundant relations, and the detail of information at the nodes depend upon how much learning (or forgetting) has taken place.

These perceptual structures contain the "meaning" of a position in both senses of the word: to the extent that the representations contain structure, they have

The Mind's Eye in the Knight's Tour

Performance in the Knight's Tour also depends upon basic processes involving perceptual structures and the mind's eye. The scope of the Knight--the eight squares of opposite color situated in a circle about the square containing the Knight--is stored as a perceptual structure in long-term memory. Perhaps the advantage of skilled players lies in the speed with which this structure can be retrieved from long-term memory, an image built in the mind's eye, and a new structure generated for the path of the Knight to its next location. As the search branches out, the skilled player holds an advantage in his ability to retrieve a sequence of moves as a chunk--in this case as a sequence of stereotyped moves to get the Knight to an adjoining square. The pattern of squares is generated in the mind's eye to see if the path works--that is, reaches the desired square without illegal intermediate moves.

Another principle illustrated by the Knight's Tour is the ability to superimpose a representation from memory onto the external representation. When the player is searching for the next series of Knight moves, he might imagine the Knight on successive squares and then construct the sequence of squares representing the potential next moves (phenomenally, these squares stand out as a pattern). From this pattern, he chooses the next move to be executed in the mind's eye, and the search continues.

This process is not unique to the Knight's Tour, but must also underlie the general ability to search ahead for a good move. In order to perceive chess relations, players must be able to visualize the path of a piece in order to see what lies in the path. This process is probably the same as that described by Hayes (this volume), when people generate, as a mnemonic device, images of partial solutions imposed on visually presented arithmetic problems. This capacity to construct an image combining perceptual structures from internal memory with sensory features from external memory is probably one of the very basic cognitive processes.

---

meaning in the Gestalt sense; and to the extent that there are internal labels that stand for familiar configurations in long-term memory, they have meaning in the sense of designation (cf. Garner, 1962; Newell & Simon, 1972, p. 24). These representations are abstract in the sense that they are built out of functional chess relations (e.g., defense), but they also have strong geometric components.

The Mind's Eye in Recalling a Game

We have already discussed the presumptive role of the mind's eye in the search process when a skilled player is trying to find a good move. We hypothesize that these perceptual structures and the mind's eye play a similar role in recall of moves from a game. In this view, a player's memory for a game involves both perceptual structures and their changes during the course of a game. Players store the game as a series of quiet positions along with information, mostly in chunks in long-term memory, that allows the player to get from one quiet position to the next. There is no need to remember the intermediate positions if they can be regenerated from more general information, from the redundancy of the position, or from plausible moves stored with these positions.

Thus, the perceptual structures relevant to the next move can be used to generate an image in the mind's eye, some transformation can be applied to the structure, and the next few moves can be abstracted from the mind's eye. A series of forced exchanges, for example, would be particularly suited to this process. The tendency of players to recall positions from a game in terms of chunks is evidence that these structures have been stored in memory as the game was memorized; and the inability of players to recall non-quiet positions is evidence that these positions are usually remembered only as transformations of quiet positions.

Organization of the Perceptual Processor

The processes and representational structures we have outlined here are frankly speculative and sketchy. We have speculated in some detail about the nature of the representations that hold perceptual information, but we have been deliberately vague about the system of memories that holds this information, and about the relation of the mind's eye to other memory structures. Our excuse for this vagueness is that the available empirical evidence does not choose among several alternative possibilities nor make one of them much more plausible than others.

The mind's eye is the meeting point where visual information from the external world is combined and coordinated with visual representations stored in short-term and long-term memory. Let us call the whole complex collection of visual processes and storage points for visual information that lie between the retina and this meeting point the "visual vestibule." The vestibular representation is by no means an unprocessed pictorial replica of the external world: contours are enhanced, the fovea is disproportionately represented, and there is a loss of resolution in the periphery. Within this vestibular passage there take place, for example, the processes of feature extraction--colors, contours, and shapes that serve to identify pieces and squares on the chess board--and probably also the short-term storage of visual information revealed by Sperling's (1960, 1963) experiments. Although we have not placed much emphasis on this vestibular memory in our research, evidence for such a memory in chess is provided, for example, by the difficulty an average player experiences in trying to play blindfold chess. The point we make here is that the mind's eye is located at the interface between this visual vestibule and the organized memories.

With this description of the visual system, imaging can be described as involving the interaction of three components, or memories: (1) An abstract representation in short-term or long-term memory where structural information about clusters of pieces is stored. (2) The "vestibule" memory, described above, where a fairly concrete representation of the board is maintained. (3) An image in the mind's eye that combines, in a common format, information from both short-term memory and vestibule. Unlike the vestibular memory, the image has structure based on meaning and familiarity, and unlike the representations in long-term and short-term memory, the image contains features in specific spatial locations.

The proposed theory has the attractive property that it explains why we should expect eye movements to accompany mental imaging. If the eyes normally extract information about the same part of the visual scene which short-term memory is structuring, and if these two sources of information are to be combined in the mind's eye, then it is essential that the imaging processes control eye movements to bring about this coordination.

Before we take our hypothesized memory systems too seriously, we will need to examine them in relation to many known perceptual phenomena. In particular, it is not obvious that the system, which postulates that the mind's eye contains relational structures similar to those in short-term and long-term memory, can accommodate the mental rotation experiments of Shepard (and perhaps the interference experiments of Brooks, 1968, and Segal & Fusella, 1970) which have sometimes been interpreted as implying an analog system (cf. Cooper & Shepard's chapter), rather than relational symbol structures, as the heart of visual memory. But further evaluation of these and other possibilities will have to be left to later studies.

Conclusion

Our specific aim in the experiments described in this paper has been to explain why it has been impossible to find non-chess tasks (such as general memory span) that measure chess skill, and to give some account of where that skill lies. Our answer is that chess skill depends in large part upon a vast, organized long-term memory of specific information about chessboard patterns. Only chess-related tasks that tap this organization (such as the 5-second recall task) are sensitive to chess skill. Although there clearly must be a set of specific aptitudes (e.g., aptitudes for handling spatial relations) that together comprise a talent for chess, individual differences in such aptitudes are largely overshadowed by immense individual differences in chess experience. Hence, the overriding factor in chess skill is practice. The organization of the Master's elaborate repertoire of information takes thousands of hours to build up, and the same is true of any skilled task (e.g., football, music). That is why *practice* is the major independent variable in the acquisition of skill.

References

Alekhine, A. *My best games of chess 1908-1923*. New York: McKay, 1927.

Baylor, G. W., Jr. A treatise on the mind's eye: an empirical investigation of visual mental imagery. Unpublished doctoral dissertation, Carnegie-Mellon University, 1971.

Baylor, G. W., Jr. & Simon, H. A. A chess mating combinations program. *AFIPS Conference Proceedings, 1966 Spring Joint Computer Conference*, 1966, 28, 431-447.

Brooks, L. R. Spatial and verbal components of the act of recall. *Canadian Journal of Psychology*, 1968, 72, 349-368.

Cavanaugh, J. P. Relation between the immediate memory span and the memory search rate. *Psychological Review*, 1972, In press.

Chase, W. G., & Simon, H. A. Perception in chess. *Cognitive Psychology*, 1973, In press.

Clark, H. H. Linguistic processes in deductive reasoning. *Psychological Review*, 1969, 76, 387-404.

Clark, H. H., & Chase, W. G. On the process of comparing sentences against pictures. *Cognitive Psychology*, 1972, 3, 472-517.

Coles, L. S. Syntax directed interpretation of natural language. In H. A. Simon & L. Siklóssy (Eds.), *Representation and meaning*. Englewood Cliffs, N.J.: Prentice-Hall, 1972.

de Groot, A. *Thought and choice in chess*. The Hague: Mouton, 1965.

de Groot, A. Perception and memory versus thought: some old ideas and recent findings. In B. Kleinmuntz (Ed.), *Problem solving*. New York: Wiley, 1966.

DeSoto, C., London, M., & Handel, S. Social reasoning and spatial paralogic. *Journal of Personality and Social Psychology*, 1965, 2, 513-521.

Feigenbaum, E. A. The simulation of verbal learning behavior. *Proceedings of the 1961 Western Joint Computer Conference*, 1961, 121-132.

Garner, W. R. *Uncertainty and structure as psychological concepts*. New York: Wiley, 1962.

Kintsch, W. Notes on the structure of semantic memory. In E. Tulving & W. Donaldson (Eds.), *Organization of memory*. New York: Academic Press, 1972.

Lasker, E. *Lasker's greatest chess games*. New York: Dover, 1935.

Miller, G. A. The magical number seven, plus or minus two: some limits on our capacity for processing information. *Psychological Review*, 1956, 63, 81-97.

Newell, A., & Simon, H. A. *Human problem solving*. Englewood Cliffs, N.J.: Prentice-Hall, 1972.

Quillian, M. R. *Semantic memory*. Cambridge, Mass.: Bolt, Beranek and Newman Scientific Report No. 2, 1966.

Radojcic, M. What is your chess IQ? *Chess Life and Review*, December 1971, 709-710.

Reinfeld, F. *Win at chess*. New York: Dover, 1945.

Segal, S. J., & Fusella, V. Influence of imagined pictures and sounds on detection of auditory and visual signals. *Journal of Experimental Psychology*, 1970, 81, 458-464.

Simon, H. A., & Barenfeld, M. Information processing analysis of perceptual processes in problem solving. *Psychological Review*, 1969, 76, 473–483.

Simon, H. A., & Gilmartin, K. A simulation of memory for chess positions. *Cognitive Psychology*, 1973, In press.

Sperling, G. The information available in brief visual presentations. *Psychological Monographs*, 1960, 74, [11, Whole No. 498].

Sperling, G. A model for visual memory tasks. *Human Factors*, 1963, 5, 19–31.

Sternberg, S. Memory scanning: mental processes revealed by reaction-time experiments. *American Scientist*, 1969, 57, 421–457.

Williams, T. G. Some studies in game playing with a digital computer. In H. A. Simon & L. Siklóssy (Eds.), *Representation and meaning*. Englewood Cliffs, N.J.: Prentice-Hall, 1972.

Winikoff, A. Eye movements as an aid to protocol analysis of problem solving behavior. Unpublished doctoral dissertation, Carnegie-Mellon University, 1967.

Acknowledgments

This research was supported by a grant from the National Institutes of Mental Health (MH-07722), from the Department of Health, Education and Welfare.

We wish to thank Larry Macupa for his help in running subjects, analyzing data, and drawing graphs. We are especially indebted to Hans Berliner for serving as our Master subject and for his many conversations about, and insights into, the mental life of a chess Master. We thank Michelene Chi for her patience as the beginner subject, and for her helpful comments concerning the perspective of a novice chess player. We owe a special debt of gratitude to Neil Charness, who performed a major portion of the work in setting up and conducting the experiments, analyzing data, and who greatly contributed conceptually to all phases of the research program.

Planning

Historically, the planning literature grew out of attempts to build robots that could move objects around rooms or stack blocks on a table. Thus, planning was closely tied to problem solving. The Hayes-Roths developed a theory of planning that is clearly in the problem-solving tradition, but their theory is much more grounded in psychological data than was earlier work in planning. The Hayes-Roths studied how people carried out an errand-planning task, and found that people are "opportunistic" in the planning process, unlike most artificial-intelligence planning systems. To account for this opportunism, they used what is called a "blackboard" architecture that was developed for the Hearsay speech understanding system at Carnegie-Mellon University. In a blackboard architecture, various processes operate independently and communicate with one another by writing messages in a common space called the blackboard. The Hayes-Roths characterize human planning as operating in five different conceptual planes: These planes range from the highest level of executive decision making, where the general strategy is chosen, down to the actual planning level, where errands are selected in a particular order. They also describe their computer simulation of human planning in the errand task.

Wilensky approached planning from the direction of understanding plans, not of constructing plans. Working initially with Schank and Abelson (see the section on Frames, Scripts, and Schemas in Part 2, *Representation*), he built a story-understanding system that recognized the plans of characters in stories. Later, he extended his work to the construction of new plans, which requires some of the same planning knowledge, but used in different ways. These different uses of planning knowledge made it evident that there were two types of planning knowledge: (1) knowledge about people's goals and methods for achieving those goals, and (2) metaknowledge about the planning process itself, such as different ways to resolve goal conflicts. In this paper, Wilensky proposes to represent both kinds of knowledge in a common declarative format, so that it can be used both in plan understanding and in plan construction.

A Cognitive Model of Planning*

BARBARA HAYES-ROTH
AND
FREDERICK HAYES-ROTH

The Rand Corporation, Santa Monica, California

This paper presents a cognitive model of the planning process. The model generalizes the theoretical architecture of the Hearsay-II system. Thus, it assumes that planning comprises the activities of a variety of cognitive "specialists." Each specialist can suggest certain kinds of decisions for incorporation into the plan in progress. These include decisions about: (a) how to approach the planning problem; (b) what knowledge bears on the problem; (c) what specific actions to try to plan; (d) what specific actions to plan; and (e) how to allocate cognitive resources during planning. Within each of these categories, different specialists suggest decisions at different levels of abstraction. The activities of the various specialists are not coordinated in any systematic way. Instead, the specialists operate opportunistically, suggesting decisions whenever promising opportunities arise. The paper presents a detailed account of the model and illustrates its assumptions with a "thinking aloud" protocol. It also describes the performance of a computer simulation of the model. The paper contrasts the proposed model with successive refinement models and attempts to resolve apparent differences between the two points of view.

1. INTRODUCTION

Planning is a familiar cognitive activity. We all have many opportunities to decide how we will behave in future situations. For example, we plan how to get to work in the morning, where and with whom to eat lunch, and how to spend our evenings. We also make longer-term plans, such as what to do on our vacations, how to celebrate Christmas, and what career path to follow. Thus, planning influences many activities, from the most mundane to the most consequential, in everyday life.

We define planning as the predetermination of a course of action aimed at achieving some goal. It is the first stage of a two-stage problem-solving process. The second stage entails monitoring and guiding the execution of the plan to a successful conclusion. We refer to these two stages as *planning and control*. This paper focuses on the planning stage of planning and control. We have two main objectives: to characterize the planning process and to propose a theoretical account of it.

Sacerdoti's (1975) work is probably the best-known previous research on planning. His computer program, NOAH, implements a successive refinement approach to planning. NOAH formulates problems in terms of high-level goals that specify sequences of actions (for example, the monkey should get the bananas and then eat them). NOAH expands each constituent subgoal into additional subgoals, maintaining any indeterminate sequential orderings as long as possible. In this manner, NOAH eventually generates correct plans specifying sequences of elementary actions. When executed, these actions transform initial conditions into a series of intermediate conditions, culminating in the goal state. (See also: Ernst & Newell, 1969; Fahlman, 1974; Fikes, 1977; Fikes & Nilsson, 1971; Sacerdoti, 1974; Sussman, 1973).

While not incompatible with successive-refinement models, our view of planning is somewhat different. We share the assumption that planning processes operate in a two-dimensional planning space defined on time and abstraction dimensions. However, we assume that people's planning activity is largely *opportunistic*. That is, at each point in the process, the planner's current decisions and observations suggest various opportunities for plan development. The planner's subsequent decisions follow up on selected opportunities. Sometimes, these decision-sequences follow an orderly path and produce a neat top-down expansion as described above. However, some decisions and observations might also suggest less orderly opportunities for plan development. For example, a decision about how to conduct initial planned activities might illuminate certain constraints on the planning of later activities and cause the planner to refocus attention on that phase of the plan. Similarly, certain low-level refinements of a previous, abstract plan might suggest an alternative abstract plan to replace the original one.

In general, the assumption that people plan opportunistically implies that interim decisions can lead to subsequent decisions at arbitrary points in the planning space. Thus, a decision at a given level of abstraction, specifying an action to be taken at a particular point in time, may influence subsequent decisions at higher or lower levels of abstraction, specifying actions to be taken at earlier or later points in time.

This view of the planning process suggests that planners will produce many coherent decision sequences, but some less coherent sequences as well. In extreme cases, the overall process might appear chaotic. The relative orderliness of particular planning processes presumably reflects individual differences among planners as well as different task demands.

We have tried to develop a theoretical framework that can accommodate both systematic approaches to planning, like successive refinement, and the more

*ONR Contract N00014-78-C-0039, NR 157-411 supported this research. We thank Bob Anderson, Ed Feigenbaum, Penny Nii, Perry Thorndyke and members of the Rand Cognitive Sciences Brownbag for many valuable discussions of this research. Bob Anderson, Bill Faught, Phil Klahr, Stan Rosenschein, and Bob Wesson provided useful comments on an earlier version of this manuscript. We thank Allan Collins for outstanding editorial assistance. Send reprint requests to: Barbara Hayes-Roth, The Rand Corporation, 1700 Main Street, Santa Monica, California, 90406.

generally opportunistic process described above. The next section of the paper presents a "thinking-aloud" protocol that illustrates the kind of behavior the model must explain. Section 3 describes the proposed planning model. Section 4 shows how the model could produce the thinking-aloud protocol. Section 5 describes a computer implementation of the model and compares its performance to the performance of the human subject. Section 6 addresses questions of theoretical complexity. Section 7 attempts to resolve apparent differences between the proposed model and successive refinement models. Section 8 summarizes our conclusions.

2. PLANNING A DAY'S ERRANDS

The thinking aloud protocol in Figure 1 illustrates the kind of behavior a comprehensive planning model must explain. A college graduate produced it while planning a hypothetical day's errands. We have collected a total of thirty protocols from five different subjects performing six different versions of such errand-planning tasks. The protocol shown in Figure 1 is representative of this set.

The subject began with the following problem description:

You have just finished working out at the health club. It is 11:00 and you can plan the rest of your day as you like. However, you must pick up your car from the Maple Street parking garage by 5:30 and then head home. You'd also like to see a movie today, if possible. Show times at both movie theaters are 1:00, 3:00, and 5:00. Both movies are on your "must see" list, but go to whichever one most conveniently fits into your plan. Your other errands are as follows:

> pick up medicine for your dog at the vet;
> buy a fan belt for your refrigerator at the appliance store;
> check out two of the three luxury apartments;
> meet a friend for lunch at one of the restaurants;
> buy a toy for your dog at the pet store;
> pick up your watch at the watch repair;
> special order a book at the bookstore;
> buy fresh vegetables at the grocery;
> buy a gardening magazine at the newsstand;
> go to the florist to send flowers to a friend in the hospital

Note that the problem description specifies more errands than the subject could reasonably expect to accomplish in the time available. The subject's task was to formulate a realistic plan indicating which errands he would do, when he would do them, and how he would travel among them.

Figure 2 shows the hypothetical town in which the subject planned his errands. Each of the pictures on the map symbolizes a particular store or other destination. The subject was quite familiar with both the symbology and the layout of the town. In addition, the map was available during planning.

We have numbered small sections of the protocol in Figure 1 to facilitate the discussion. Also, for convenience, we refer to specific errands by the names of the associated stores or other destinations.

---

1 Let's go back down the errand list. Pick up medicine for the dog at veterinary supplies. That's definitely a primary, anything taking care of health. Fan belt for refrigerator. Definitely a primary because you need to keep the refrigerator. Checking out two out of three luxury apartments. It's got to be a secondary, another browser. Meet the friend at one of the restaurants for lunch. All right. Now, that's going to be able to be varied I hope. That's a primary though because it is an appointment, something you have to do. Buy a toy for the dog at the pet store. It is not, the dog can play with something else. Movie in one of the movie theaters. Better write that down, those movie times, 1, 3, or 5. Write that down on my sheet just to remember. And that's a primary because it's something I have to do. Pick up the watch at the watch repair. That's one of those borderline ones. Do you need your watch or not? Give it a primary. Special order a book at the bookstore.

2 We're having an awful lot of primaries in this one. It's going to be a busy day.

3 Fresh vegetables at the grocery. That's another primary. You need the food. Gardening magazine at the newsstand. Definitely secondary. All the many obligations of life.

4 Geez, can you believe all these primaries?

5 All right. We are now at the health club.

6 What is going to be the closest one?

7 The appliance store is a few blocks away. The medicine for the dog at the vet's office isn't too far away. Movie theaters—let's hold off on that for a little while. Pick up the watch. That's all the way across town. Special order a book at the bookstore.

8 Probably it would be best if we headed in a southeasterly direction. Start heading this way. I can see later on there are a million things I want to do in that part of town.

9 No we're not. We could end up with a movie just before we get the car. I had thought at first that I might head in a southeasterly direction because there's a grocery store, a watch repair, a movie theater all in that general area. Also a luxury apartment. However, near my parking lot also is a movie, which would make it convenient to get out of the movie and go to the car. But I think we can still end up that way.

10 All right. Apparently the closest one to the health club is going to be the vet's shop. So I might as well get that out of the way. It's a primary and it's the closest. We'll start ...

[The experimenter mentions that he has overlooked the nearby restaurant and flower shop.]

11 Oh, how foolish of me. You're right. I can still do that and still head in the general direction.

12 But, then again, that puts a whole new light on things. We do have a bookstore. We do have ... OK. Break up town into sections. We'll call them northwest and southeast. See how many primaries are in that section. Down here in the southeast section, we have the grocery store, the watch repair and the movie theater. In the northwest section we have the grocery store, the bookstore, the flower shop, the vet's shop, and the restaurant.

13 And since we are leaving at 11:00, we might be able to get those chores done so that some time when I'm in the area, hit that restaurant. Let's try for that. Get as many of those out of the way as possible. We really could have a nice day here.

14 OK. First choose number one. At 11:00 we leave the health club. Easily, no doubt about it, we can be right across the street in 5 minutes to the flower shop. Here we go. Flower shop at 11:05. Let's give ourselves 10 minutes to browse through some bouquets and different floral arrangements.

Figure 1. Thinking aloud protocol from the errand-planning task.

You know, you want to take care in sending the right type of flowers. That's something to deal with personal relationships.

15. At 11:10 we go north on Belmont Avenue to the Chestnut Street intersection with Belmont and on the northwest corner is a grocery.

16. Oh, real bad. Don't want to buy the groceries now because groceries rot. You're going to be taking them with you all day long. Going to have to put the groceries way towards the end.

17. And that could change it again. This is not one of my days. I have those every now and again. Let's go with our original plan. Head to the southeast corner.

18. Still leaving the flower shop at 11:10. And we are going to go to the vet's shop next for medicine for the dog. We'll be there at 11:15, be out by 11:20. The vet's shop.

19. Proceeding down Oak Street. I think it would be. let's give ourselves a little short-cut.

20. Maybe we'll knock off a secondary task too.

21. Proceed down Oak Street to Belmont. Belmont south to the card and gift shop, or rather, to the department store. Cut through the department store to Johnson Street to the newsstand. Pick up our gardening magazine at the newsstand.

22. We're heading this way. We're going to make a definite southeast arrow.

23. Third item will be the newsstand since we are heading in that direction. Often I like to do that. I know buying a gardening magazine is hardly a primary thing to do, but since I'm heading that way, it's only going to take a second. Let's do it. Get it out of the way. Sometimes you'll find at the end of the day you've done all your primary stuff, but you still have all those little nuisance secondary items that you wish you would have gotten done. So, 11:20 we left the vet's office. We should arrive 11:25 at the newsstand. 11:30 we've left the newsstand.

24. Now let's start over here. We're going to be in trouble a little bit because of that appliance store hanging way up north. So we could: appliance store is a primary. It's got to be done.

25. All right, let's do this. This could work out. Market Square, we leave the Market Square exit of the newsstand up to Washington, arrive at the pet store, buy a toy for the dog at the pet store. We're there at 11:35, out at 11:40. Pretty good. 11:40. Proceeding east just slightly, up north Dunbar Street to the appliance store, we arrive there at 11:45, and we leave there, fan belt, leave at 11:50.

26. We're looking good. We've knocked off a couple of secondaries that really we hadn't planned on, but because of the locations of some stores that are in the way that could be convenient.

27. Now it's 11:50, right near noontime.

28. And I think one of the next things to do, checking our primaries, what we have left to do, would be to go to the restaurant. And we can be at the restaurant at 5 minutes to noon. We're going to go down Dunbar Street, south on Dunbar Street to Washington east, to the restaurant which is located on the very eastern edge of the map. Meeting our friend there for lunch at 11:55, allowing a nice leisurely lunch. No, oh yeah. An hour. 12:55.

29. Now we've got to start being concerned about a few other things. We can pick up the car from the Maple Street garage by 5:30.

30. It's 12:55, done with lunch. Primary left to do, see a movie, pick up a watch, special order a book, and get fresh vegetables.

31. I would like to plan it so I can see the movie, pick up the vegetables, pick up my car, and then go home. Vegetables would rot.

32. So then with what we have left now to do is special order a book at a bookstore and pick up the watch at the watch repair.

33. So, I think we can make this a very nice trip. We're at the restaurant on Washington Avenue. Let's proceed west one block to Madison, south to Cedar Street. Cedar Street west right there at the intersection of Cedar and Madison is the watch repair. Pick up the watch at the watch repair. We should be at the watch repair by 1:05. Give us a good 10 minutes. 1:05 at the watch repair. Pick up a watch. We're out of there by 1:10.

34. Now I'm going to go just a slight back down Madison to one of the luxury apartments. I arrive at one of the luxury apartments at 1:15. I allow myself 15 minutes to browse. Two bathroom apartment. 1:30. Now I'm leaving that.

35. Next, I'm going to go west on Lakeshore, north on Dunbar, west on Cedar to the bookstore. And I will arrive at the bookstore at 1:35. Special order my book. 1:40.

36. From the bookstore I can go west on Cedar Street just a hair, down Kingsway, to a second luxury apartment. Find out what's happening at that luxury apartment. And I'm there at 1:45, allowing myself another 15 minutes there, 2:00 we're out.

37. We're taken care of checking out 2 out of 3 luxury apartments. We ordered our book.

38. Now we do have a problem. It's 2:00 and all we have left to do is see a movie and get the vegetables. And that's where I think I've blown this plan. I've got an hour left there before the movie.

39. So the best way to eliminate as much time as possible since we are now located at the Cedar Lakeshore apartments. That's not going to be . . .

40. If I go get the groceries now, it's not really going to be consistent with the plans throughout the day because I've been holding off on the groceries for rotting. If I take them to a movie . . . Vegetables don't really perish like ice cream.

41. We leave the luxury apartment on Lakeshore, proceed due east to Dunbar, and we're at the grocery store at 2:05. 2:05 at the grocery store. Hunt around for fresh vegetables, and we can give ourselves 20 minutes there. So we leave there at 2:25.

42. We leave there and we proceed up Dunbar, north to Cedar, Cedar west to the movie theater.

43. We probably arrive at the movie theater at 2:35. 2:35 we arrive at the movie theater which still gives us 25 minutes to kill before the next showing. But that's that. We're going to have to simply do it. I'm going to have to go with it for right now.

44. The plan seems to have worked well enough up until then. We made better time than we had thought. That happens in life sometimes. How did I get here so fast?

45. 2:25. We catch the 3:00 showing. We leave there at 5:00. Proceed immediately down Johnson, up Belmont to the parking structure, and we're there at 5:05 at the parking structure. We had to pick it up by 5:30.

46. Got everything done, the only problem being having a little bit of time to kill in that one period.

47. You could have stretched out, to make things fair, you could have said, well, okay, I'll give myself an hour and 15 minutes at lunch, but as I did plan it, I did come up 30 minutes over. 25 minutes there. And that's a little bit of, when that happens you feel bad. You remember the old Ben Franklin saying about don't kill time because it's time that kills us. And I hate to have time to waste. I've got to have things work very nicely.

In sections 1–4, the subject defines his goal and characterizes his task. Thus, in 1 and 3, he uses world knowledge to categorize the errands on his list as either primary errands, which he feels he must do, or secondary errands. In 2 and 4, he infers that, given the time constraints, his goal will be difficult to achieve.

In sections 5–7, the subject begins planning how to go about doing his errands. Notice that he begins planning at a fairly detailed level of abstraction. He has made only one kind of prior high-level decision—defining his goal. He has not considered what might be an efficient way to organize his plan. He has not made any effort to group his errands. Instead he immediately begins sequencing individual errands, working forward in time from his initial location. Thus, he ascertains his initial location, the health club, indicates that he wants to sequence the closest errand next, and begins locating the primary errands on his list, looking for the closest one.

In section 8, the subject changes his level of abstraction. In the course of looking for the closest errand to his current location, he apparently discovers a cluster of errands in the southeast corner of town. This observation leads him to make a decision at a "higher" or more abstract level than he had previously. Thus, he decides to treat the errands in the southeast corner as a cluster. He plans to go to the southeast corner and do those errands at about the same time.

In section 9, the subject modifies his high-level cluster. He discovers that one of the errands in the cluster, the movie, can also be done on the west side of town, near his final destination, the Maple Street parking structure. He changes back to the more detailed level of abstraction. Planning backward in time from his final location, he decides to end his day by going to the movie and then picking up his car. In so doing, he removes the movie from the high-level cluster.

In section 10, the subject begins to instantiate his high-level plan to go to the southeast corner at the lower, errand-sequencing level. Again, he is looking for the closest errand on his way, and he chooses the vet.

At that point, the experimenter interrupts to point out to the subject that he has overlooked several closer errands.

In sections 11 and 12, the subject incorporates the new information into his planning. His first reaction, in 11, is to continue working at the errand-sequencing level, simply considering the newly identified errands among those he might do next. However, additional observation at this level leads him to make a decision at the more abstract level. Again, he decides to treat a group of errands, those in the northwest corner of town, as a cluster. This leads him to revise his high-level plan to include two clusters of errands, the northwest cluster and the southeast cluster.

In section 13, the subject begins instantiating his new high-level plan. He notes the initial time, 11:00, and the presence of a restaurant, another errand in the northwest cluster. These observations lead him to formulate an intermediate level plan regarding how to sequence errands within the northwest cluster. He

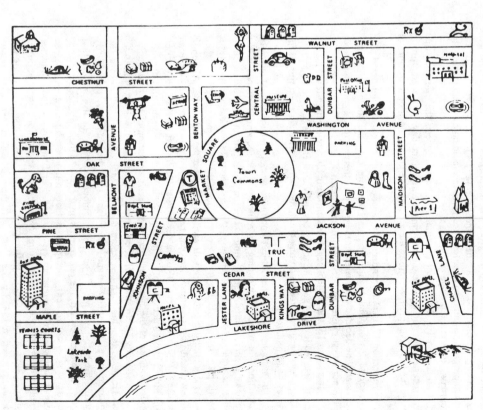

Figure 2 Town map for the errand-planning task.

decides to sequence the errands in that cluster to permit him to arrive at the restaurant in time for lunch.

In sections 14–15, the subject works on instantiating his revised high-level plan at a very detailed level of abstraction. Here, he not only sequences individual errands (the florist and the grocery), he specifies the exact routes he will take among them. In addition, the subject mentally simulates execution of his plan in progress, estimating how long each errand should take and computing the "current" time at each stage of the plan.

In section 16, the subject's mental simulation suggests the inference that his groceries will perish if he picks them up early in the day. This leads him to revise his low-level plan, assigning the grocery a sequential position at the end of the plan.

In section 17, the subject decides to abandon his two cluster high-level plan in favor of his original high-level plan including only the southeast cluster. Presumably he decided that, without the grocery, there were not enough errands in the northwest cluster to occupy him until lunch.

In section 18, the subject begins instantiating his original high-level plan at a more detailed level. Again, he sequences individual errands (the florist and the vet) and specifies exact routes among them, mentally simulating execution of his plan as he formulates it.

In sections 19–23, the subject continues working at the lowest level of abstraction. He works on planning his route from the sequenced errands to the southeast corner, mentally simulating execution of his plan in the process. In so doing, he notices a "short-cut" through the card and gift shop and incorporates it into his plan, later replacing it with one through the department store. He then notices that taking the short-cut will put him very near the newsstand. Although the newsstand is a secondary errand, he decides to incorporate it in his plan because it is so convenient. Thus, a decision at the lowest level of abstraction leads him to make a decision at the next higher level. Note also that this decision implies addition of the newsstand to the subject's definition of his goal.

In sections 24–26, the subject continues working at a low level of abstraction. He notes that his high-level plan does not include any provision for the appliance store, a primary errand. He plans to go there directly, temporarily ignoring his high-level plan to go to the southeast corner. He also notices that another secondary errand, the pet store, is on the way to the appliance store and, because it is so convenient, incorporates that errand into his plan. Again, he plans at the level of sequencing errands and specifying routes and simulates execution of the plan as he goes along. Note that these decisions imply addition of the pet store to the subject's definition of the goal. (Note also that, while the short-cut planned in 19–23 was a short-cut to the southeast corner, it is a detour in the planned route to the appliance store.)

The remainder of the protocol (sections 27–45) documents the completion of the subject's plan. In the interests of brevity, we simply summarize this part of the protocol. Basically, the subject decides to incorporate the appliance store and the restaurant before finally arriving at the southeast corner. Then he plans all of the remaining errands, including all remaining secondary errands. Figure 9 below shows the subject's final plan.

This protocol illustrates a number of the points made above. First, the subject's plan develops incrementally at various points in the planning space we described. He plans actions at various points in the plan's temporal sequence, and he also plans at different levels of abstraction. Second, the subject appears to plan opportunistically, "jumping about" in the planning space to develop promising aspects of the plan in progress. For example, the planner does not plan strictly forward in time. Instead, he plans temporally-anchored sub-plans at arbitrary points on the time dimension and eventually concatenates the sub-plans. Similarly, the planner does not plan in a systematic top-down fashion across the different levels of abstraction. He frequently plans low-level sequences of errands or routes in the absence, and sometimes in violation, of a prescriptive high-level plan. Finally, decisions at a given point in the planning space appear to influence subsequent decisions at both later and earlier points in the temporal sequence and at both higher and lower levels of abstraction. The protocol contains examples of each of these kinds of influence.

The protocol illustrates another important component of the planning process—the ability to simulate execution of a plan mentally and to use the results of the simulation to guide subsequent planning. Mental simulation can answer a variety of questions for the subject: At what time will I arrive at (or leave) a particular destination? How long will I take to perform a certain action? What sequence of operations will I perform to satisfy a particular sub-goal? How long will it take to execute a plan or partial plan? What effects will my actions produce? What have I accomplished so far? The subject can use this information to evaluate and revise prior planning and to constrain subsequent planning.

The subject performs two kinds of mental simulation corresponding to *time-driven* and *event-driven* processes. Sometimes he simulates his plan by mentally stepping through a sequence of time units for each planned action (e.g., walking, carrying a package, performing an errand). With each successive step, he extrapolates the results of each planned action, updating his understanding of the "current state" accordingly. At other times, the subject performs "event-driven" simulation. In this case, he mentally moves directly from one planned situation to another, ignoring any actions in the intervening temporal interval. He then computes certain consequences arising from the transition.

More importantly, in the present context, the subject simulates execution of plans at different levels of abstraction. Thus, in sections 14–15, he simulates execution of a detailed plan. By stepping through his plan, the subject computes expected times for performing individual errands and traveling specific routes. In sections 24–26, the subject simulates execution of his high-level plan for performing errands in the northwest and then those in the southeast. Here, he performs event-driven simulation, inferring that if he executes his high-level plan, proceeding directly to the southeast corner of town, he will neglect a primary errand.

In the next section, we describe the proposed planning model in detail. The model postulates specific levels of abstraction and a structural organization for the planning space. In addition, it postulates decision-making mechanisms that permit theoretical interpretation of subjects' apparently chaotic progress through the planning space.

3. AN OPPORTUNISTIC MODEL OF PLANNING

Overview

The proposed model assumes that the planning process comprises the independent actions of many distinct cognitive *specialists* (akin to demons in Selfridge's (1959) Pandemonium model). Each specialist makes tentative *decisions* for incorporation into a tentative *plan*. Further, different specialists influence different aspects of the plan. For example, some specialists suggest high-level, abstract additions to the plan, while others suggest detailed sequences of specific actions.

All specialists record their decisions in a common data structure, called the *blackboard*. The blackboard enables the specialists to interact and communicate. Each specialist can retrieve prior decisions of interest from the blackboard, regardless of which specialists recorded them. The specialist combines these earlier decisions with its own decision-making heuristics to generate new decisions.

The model partitions the blackboard into several *planes* containing conceptually different categories of decisions. For example, one plane contains decisions about explicitly planned activities, while another contains decisions about data that might be useful in generating planned activities. The model further partitions each plane into several *levels* of abstraction. These partitionings serve two functions. First, they provide a conceptual taxonomy of the decisions made during planning. Second, they restrict the number of prior decisions each individual specialist must consider in generating its own decisions (see also Englemore & Nii, 1977). Thus, most specialists deal with information that occurs at only a few levels of particular planes of the blackboard.

The proposed model generalizes the theoretical architecture developed by Reddy and his associates (Cf. CMU Computer Science Research Group, 1977; Lesser, Fennell, Erman, & Reddy, 1975; Erman & Lesser, 1975; Lesser & Erman, 1977; Hayes-Roth & Lesser, 1977) for the Hearsay-II speech-understanding system. Others have since applied it to image understanding (Prager, Nagin, Kohler, Hanson, & Riseman, 1977), reading comprehension (Rumelhart, 1976), protein-crystallographic analysis (Nii & Feigenbaum, 1977),

and inductive inference (Soloway & Riseman, 1977). The proposed model is, to our knowledge, the first attempt to adapt the Hearsay-II architecture to a "generation" problem. We describe it in detail below.

Specialists

As mentioned above, independent cognitive specialists generate decisions during the planning process. The model operationalizes specialists as condition-action rules.

The condition component describes circumstances under which the specialist can contribute to the plan. Ordinarily, the condition requires the planner to have made certain prior decisions. However, it may also require satisfaction of other, arbitrarily complex criteria. For example, one specialist's condition might require a prior decision to organize the plan by spatial clusters of errands and prior identification of useful clusters.

The action component defines the specialist's behavior. The action may include an arbitrary amount of computation, but always results in the generation of a new decision or modification of a prior decision. For example, one specialist might detect and identify spatial clusters of errands on the map. Another might generate an abstract organizational design for the plan as a whole.

Thus, specialists generalize the symbol-manipulation capabilities of production rules (Newell & Simon, 1972) to more complex, pattern-directed activity (see also: CMU Computer Science Research Group, 1977; Hayes-Roth, Waterman, & Lenat, 1978; Lenat, 1975).

The Blackboard

As discussed above, specialists record their decisions in a common data structure called the blackboard. The blackboard contains five conceptual planes: *plan, plan-abstractions, knowledge-base, executive* and *meta-plan*. We characterize each of these below.

We have already characterized the plan plane in our discussion of the thinking-aloud protocol. Decisions on this plane represent actions the planner intends to take in the world. For example, the planner might decide to travel in a circle around town, performing errands along the way, or to travel from the florist to the vet along Belmont Avenue and Oak Street. Both of these decisions describe explicit actions the planner intends to carry out.

Decisions on the plan-abstractions plane characterize desired attributes of potential plan decisions. Thus, these decisions indicate the kinds of actions the planner would like to take without specifying the actions themselves. For example, the planner might decide to go to the closest errand next. This decision characterizes a desired sequence of errands, but does not identify a particular

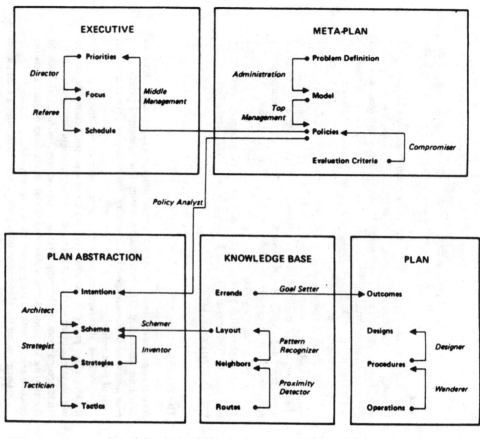

Figure 3. The planning blackboard and the actions of illustrative specialists.

sequence. Similarly, the planner might decide to organize the plan around spatial clusters of errands. Again, this decision characterizes a desired abstract plan, but does not instantiate it (i.e. does not specify particular spatial clusters).

The knowledge-base contains observations and computations regarding relationships in the world that might bear on the planning process. These computations are useful in suggesting plan-abstractions and instantiating them in the plan. For example, the planner might ascertain that the florist is the closest errand to the health club. That information would permit instantiation of a prior plan-abstraction decision to go to the closest errand next. As a second example, the planner might observe that several errand–sites cluster in close proximity on the map. That observation might suggest a subsequent plan-abstraction decision to organize the plan around several such spatially arrayed clusters.

Plan, plan-abstractions, and knowledge-base decisions determine features of the developing plan. Executive decisions, by contrast, determine features of the planning process. Thus, the executive plane contains decisions about the allocation of cognitive resources during the planning process. These decisions determine which aspect of the plan the planner will develop and which specialist the planner will bring to bear at each point in the process. For example, the planner might decide to determine which errands to include in the plan before working out the details of the plan. As a second example, the planner might decide to focus on working out routes among previously sequenced errands.

The meta-plan plane contains decisions about how to approach the planning problem. These decisions reflect the planner's understanding of the problem, the methods she or he intends to apply to it, and the criteria she or he will use to evaluate prospective solutions.

As mentioned above, the model further partitions each plane of the blackboard into several levels of abstraction. In the following sections, we describe the postulated levels of abstraction for each of the five planes (see Figure 3).

Levels of the Plan Plane. The plan plane has four levels of abstraction. Decisions at the four levels form a potential hierarchy, with decisions at each level specifying a more refined plan than those at the next higher level. Beginning at the most abstract level, *outcomes* indicate what the planner intends to accomplish by executing the finished plan. For the errand-planning task, outcomes indicate what errands the planner intends to accomplish by executing the plan. For example, the planner might decide to accomplish the desired errands at the florist, the vet, and the grocery store. At the next lower level, *designs* characterize the general behavioral approach by which the planner intends to achieve the outcomes. For the errand-planning task, designs characterize the general order in which the planner intends to perform errands. For example, the planner might decide to head toward the southeast cluster. Next, *procedures* specify specific sequences of gross actions. For the errand-planning task, procedures specify sequences of errands. For example, the planner might decide to go to the vet after the florist. Finally, *operations* specify sequences of more minute actions. For the errand-planning task, operations specify the details of performing individual errands and the routes by which the planner will proceed from each errand to the next. For example, the planner might decide to travel from the vet to the florist via Belmont Avenue and Oak Street.[1]

Levels of the Plan-Abstractions Plane. The plan-abstractions plane contains four levels. Each level characterizes types of decisions suggested for incorporation into the corresponding level of the plan plane. For example, the planner might indicate an *intention* to establish all of the "critical" errands as the outcome of the plan. At the next lower level, the planner might generate a *scheme* that suggests generating a design featuring spatial clusters of errands. At the next level, the planner might develop a *strategy* to go to the closest errand next, characterizing a desirable procedure level decision. Finally, the planner might adopt a *tactic* to search for a short-cut between one errand and the next, characterizing a desirable operation level decision.

Levels of the Knowledge Base Plane. The knowledge base also has four levels of abstraction. Each level contains observations and computations useful in suggesting decisions at the corresponding level of the plan-abstractions plane or instantiating them at the corresponding level of the plan plane. Because the lower levels of the knowledge base contain problem-specific information, we have given them problem-specific names. At the *errand* level, for example, the planner might determine the relative importance of each desired errand. At the *layout* level, the planner might observe that several errands form a convenient spatial cluster. At the *neighbor* level, the planner might observe that two planned errands are near one another. At the *route* level, the planner might detect a short-cut.

Levels of the Executive Plane. The executive plane has three levels of abstraction. Decisions made at the three levels on this plane form a hierarchy, with decisions at each level potentially refining ones at the level above. Beginning at the top, *priority* decisions establish principles for allocating cognitive resources during the entire planning process. These decisions generally indicate preferences for allocating processing activity to certain areas of the planning blackboard before others. For example, by approaching the errand-planning task as a resource-limited scheduling problem, the planner might decide to determine which errands to do before working out the details of the plan. At the next lower level, *focus* decisions indicate what kind of decision to make at a specific point in time. For example, the planner might decide to focus attention on generating an operation-level refinement of a previously generated procedure. Finally, *schedule* decisions resolve any remaining conflicts among competing specialists. If, given current priorities and focus decisions, more than one specialist can make a contribution to the plan, the planner must make schedule decisions to decide among them. Schedule decisions select specialists on the basis of relative efficiency, reliability, etc. (Hayes-Roth & Lesser, 1977).

Levels of the Meta-Plan Plane. The meta-plan plane has four levels: *problem definition, problem-solving model, policies,* and *evaluation criteria.* Unlike the levels on the other four planes, these levels do not produce a neat hierarchy of decisions. However, they emphasize different aspects of the subject's approach to the planning problem and relate in systematic ways to the other planes of the blackboard.

Beginning at the top, problem definition decisions characterize the planner's own formulation of the task. These include descriptions of goals, available resources, possible actions, and constraints. For the errand-planning task, the problem definition would reflect the subject's understanding of the list of errands, contextual information, and associated instructions.

The chosen problem-solving model indicates how the planner intends to represent the problem and generate potential solutions. For example, the planner might view the errand-planning task as an instance of the familiar "traveling salesman" problem (Christophides, 1975) and approach the problem accordingly. Problem-solving models can also consist of general problem-solving strategies, such as "divide and conquer," "define and successively refine" (Aho, Hopcroft, & Ullman, 1974), etc. The planner presumably chooses a particular problem-solving model from known alternatives in response to specific problem characteristics. The problem-solving model, in turn, bears directly on subsequent executive decisions. For example, adoption of the traveling salesman model should lead to basically "bottom-up" executive decisions. That is, the planner should focus attention on the procedures and operations levels of the plan plane and on corresponding levels of the plan-abstractions and knowledge-base planes.

The planner's policies specify global constraints and desirable features for the developing plan. For example, the planner might decide that the plan must be efficient or that it should minimize certain risks. Some policy decisions derive implicitly from particular problem-solving models. For example, the traveling salesman model naturally implies a route-efficiency policy. Other policies are model-independent. In either case, policy decisions bear directly on subsequent plan-abstractions decisions. Particular policy decisions make particular plan-abstractions more or less desirable. For example, the route efficiency policy favors a strategy to go to the closest errand next. By contrast, it inhibits an intention to achieve only the most important errands.

---

[1] Obviously, partitioning plan decisions into four discrete categories is arbitrary and probably over-simplified. However, we find these categories intuitively appealing and they provide a convenient terminology for discussion. In addition, Hayes-Roth and Thorndyke (1979) have shown that theoretically naive subjects group statements drawn from planning protocols in exactly these four categories.

Finally, solution-evaluation criteria specify how the planner intends to evaluate prospective plans. For example, the planner might decide to speculate on what could go wrong during execution and insure that the plan is robust over those contingencies. Again, some of these decisions derive implicitly from particular problem-solving models, while others are independent. Obviously, the planner brings these criteria to bear on the developing plan and uses them to determine which plan decisions to preserve and which to change.

Control of the Planning Process

Under the control of the executive, the planning process proceeds through a series of "cycles" during which various specialists execute their actions. At the beginning of each cycle, some number of specialists have been invoked—that is, their conditions have been satisfied. The executive selects one of the invoked specialists to execute its action—that is, to generate a new decision and record it on the blackboard. The new decision invokes additional specialists and the next cycle begins. This process ordinarily continues until: (a) the planner has integrated mutually consistent decisions into a complete plan; and (b) the planner has decided that the existing plan satisfies important evaluation criteria. Under certain circumstances, the process might also terminate in failure.

4. ANALYSIS OF THE PLANNING PROTOCOL UNDER THE OPPORTUNISTIC MODEL

In this section, we use the proposed model to "parse" sections 1–10 of the protocol. We intend this exercise to demonstrate the descriptive power of the model. Of course, the psychological validity of the model rests on more than this informal sufficiency test. In subsequent sections of the paper, we discuss a more formal sufficiency test based on a computer simulation and summarize several empirical tests of the model's assumptions.

Figures 4–8 show blackboard representations of sections 1-10 of the protocol as individual decisions. They also show how individual specialists respond to the presence of particular decisions on the blackboard by generating other decisions and recording them at appropriate locations on the blackboard. Each arrow represents the invocation and execution of a specialist. Thus, an arrow from one decision to another indicates that the former decision invoked a specialist that recorded the latter decision. In order to clarify the flow of activity, we have numbered decisions in Figures 4–8 according to their presumed order of occurrence. Note, however, that arrows need not connect consecutively numbered decisions. Occasionally, an early decision invokes a specialist that is not scheduled until after one or more other specialists have been scheduled and added their decisions to the blackboard.

We have omitted only one kind of decision from these illustrations—schedule decisions. As discussed above, at each point in the sequence of recorded decisions, a schedule decision selects one of the currently invoked specialists to execute its action. We have omitted these decisions from Figures 4–8 for simplicity. However, it is appropriate to assume that a schedule decision selected each of the indicated specialist actions (noted by arrows).

Figure 4 shows the blackboard representation of sections 1–4 of the protocol. In sections 1 and 3, the subject works through the list of errands, assigning binary importance values (primary versus secondary) to each one. In sections 2 and 4, the subject remarks that the large number of primary errands implies that he will have a busy day. According to our assumptions, a specialist calculates importance values for individual errands and records these at the errands level of the knowledge base. However, we assume that a considerable amount of activity, unstated in the protocol, preceded and motivated this action. Figure 4 shows the blackboard representation of this implicit activity.

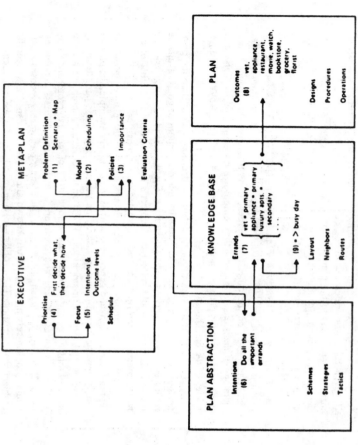

Figure 4. Blackboard representation of sections 1–4 of the protocol.

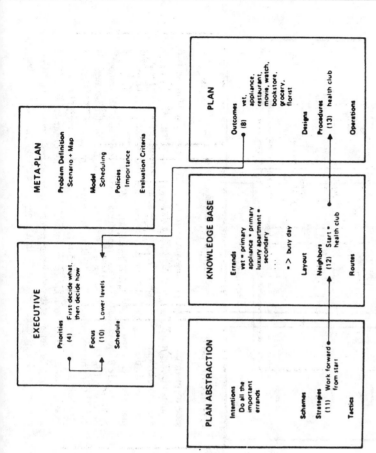

Figure 5. Blackboard representation of section 5 of the protocol.

The subject begins the task with a problem definition (1), including the scenario and map provided by the experimenter. The protocol suggests that the subject categorizes the problem as a resource-limited scheduling problem (2). In other words, the subject apparently views the task as one in which he cannot do all of the things he wants to do and, therefore, must decide which things to do and then how to do them. The appearance of this problem-solving model on the blackboard presumably invokes two other specialists, One generates and records a useful policy (3), emphasizing the importance of individual errands. The other generates and records an appropriate set of priorities (4). The priorities, in turn, motivate a decision to focus on the intentions and outcomes levels of the plan-abstraction and plan planes (5). Given this focus and the errand-importance policy, a specialist records an intention to do all the important errands (6). This intention presumably invokes the specialist described above that calculates the errand-importance values actually stated in the protocol (7). This activity implies another unstated decision, that the intended outcomes should include the designated primary errands (8). Finally, the statements in sections 2 and 4 of the protocol imply that the errand-importance calculations invoke another specialist that infers: "It's going to be a busy day" (9).

Figure 5 shows the blackboard representation of section 5 of the protocol. In section 5, the subject states: "All right. We are now at the health club." This statement conveys a procedure-level specification of the initial location (13). Figure 5 shows the implicit sequence of activity that produced this statement, given the prior state of the blackboard shown in Figure 4. First, having decided what to do (8), the subject proceeds to his second priority, deciding how to do it. Accordingly, he changes focus to the lower levels of the blackboard (10). Given this focus, a strategy-generating specialist records its decision to plan forward from the initial location (11). This decision motivates another specialist to identify the initial location (12) which, in turn, motivates a specialist to record the initial location at the procedure level of the blackboard (13).

Figure 6 shows the blackboard representation of sections 6–8 of the protocol. In section 6, the subject asks, "What is going to be the closest one?" This question indicates a strategic decision to plan to perform the closest errand next in the procedure sequence (14). The appearance of this strategy on the blackboard invokes a specialist that evaluates the relative proximities of other primary errands to the initial location, the health club (15). Section 7 of the protocol describes these evaluations.

Section 8 of the protocol reflects a discontinuity in the planning process. The preceding statements aim toward recording the second errand in the procedural sequence. Instead, however, the subject states in section 8: "Probably it would be best if we headed in a southeasterly direction. Start heading this way. I can see later on there are a million things I want to do in that part of town." This statement expresses a higher-level design, recorded on the blackboard as a decision to perform the errands in the southeast cluster, performing whatever other

errands occur along the route from the initial location to the southeast cluster (18).

Let us consider how the subject might have arrived at this design. The subject's immediately-preceding overt activity, evaluation of proximities, requires him to locate each errand in the list. In doing so, the subject locates (at least) three consecutive errands, the movie, the watch repair, and the bookstore, in the southeast corner of town. Apparently, this sequence of visual observations invokes a specialist that identifies clusters of errands and records the identity of the detected cluster at the layout level of the knowledge base (16). The appearance of the cluster on the blackboard invokes another specialist that generates schemes. It suggests exploiting the spatial cluster of errands by organizing a design around it (17). Another specialist responds to the new scheme and the identified cluster by recording the appropriate design on the blackboard (18).

Figure 7 shows the blackboard representation of section 9 of the protocol. In section 9, the subject indicates a procedure decision to sequence the movie

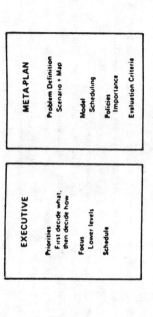

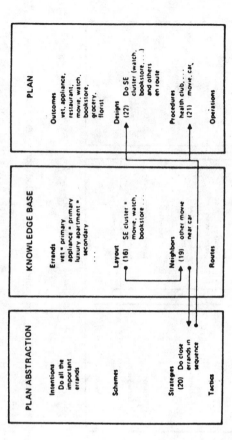

Figure 7. Blackboard representation of section 9 of the protocol.

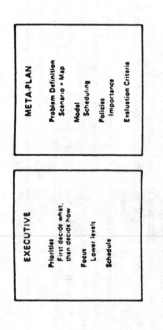

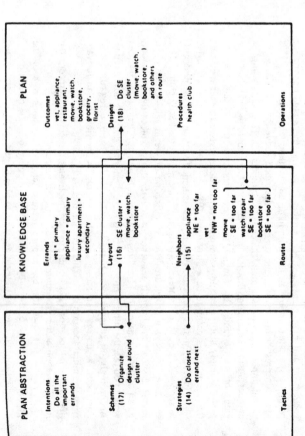

Figure 6. Blackboard representation of sections 6—8 of the protocol.

side of town close to the parking structure (19). The proximity of these two errands invokes a specialist that suggests a more general strategy to perform two proximate errands in sequence (20). This new strategy invokes another specialist that records the suggested sequence, movie–car, at the procedure level of the plan plane (21) and amends the prior design accordingly (22).

Figure 8 shows the blackboard representation of section 10 of the protocol. In section 10, the subject decides to go to the vet after the health club because it is the closest primary errand. Thus, section 10 conveys a procedure-level decision (26) and the strategy that motivated it (24). We assume that the presence of a modified design on the blackboard motivates a narrowing of the focus to aim at instantiating the design at the procedure level (23). In accordance with this focus, the design also invokes a specialist that generates a strategy to do the closest

right before picking up his car at the end of the day (21). He tells us explicitly that, in so doing, he is removing the movie from the previously-defined southeast cluster (22). He also tells us why he has made this decision: because it would be "convenient to get out of the movie and go to the car'' (20).

Figure 7 models these decisions, beginning with the subject's prior definition of the southeast cluster (16). Presumably, attention to one of the errands in the cluster, the movie, invokes a specialist that notices another movie on the west errand in the right direction (24). This strategy invokes a specialist that evaluates the proximities of individual errands at the neighbors level of the knowledge base (25). Finally, the observation that the vet is the closest errand to the initial location, the health club, invokes a specialist that records the vet as the next errand in the procedural sequence (26).

We can analyze the remainder of the protocol in much the same fashion. However, we conclude the analysis at this stage for brevity.

The analysis reinforces the main points made in section 2. The subject plans at different points in the planning space along both temporal and abstractness dimensions. In particular, the subject appears to make decisions at each of the postulated levels on all five planes of the blackboard. Further, the subject makes decisions opportunistically. Rather than working systematically through the levels along either of the two dimensions, he enters the planning space at various points and moves about freely within it. The subject's observations and computations on the available data (the map and the scenario) exert a powerful influence on the point in the planning space at which he makes each successive decision. This produces a strong "bottom-up" component to the planning process. However, prior decisions at both higher and lower levels influence the subject's decisions, as assumed by the model.

5. COMPUTER SIMULATION

We have implemented a computer simulation of the planning model described above. The simulation is written in INTERLISP. It contains an internal representation of the map shown in Figure 1, a blackboard structure to organize planning decisions, and about forty specialists. (See Hayes-Roth, Hayes-Roth, Rosenschein, & Cammarata (1979) for a detailed description of the simulation.)

We designed the specialists to model some of the knowledge in our subject's protocol. Following the reasoning used in section 4, we postulated condition-action rules for producing many of the decisions in the protocol, as well as rules for producing the necessary intermediate decisions. The specialists generalize these rules. For example, in section 8 of the protocol, the subject notices that certain errands appear in close proximity in the southeast part of town. Based on this section of the protocol, we designed a specialist whose condition requires that at least three errands have been located on the map and that they appear in the same region (northwest, northeast, southwest, or southeast). Its action is to identify as a cluster any set of errands that satisfies its condition. Thus, this specialist can identify not only the particular cluster the subject noticed, but other clusters as well.

The simulation includes specialists for most of the condition-action rules inferred from the protocol. However, we did not attempt to capture all of the subject's idiosyncracies. For example, although the subject used several slightly different navigation rules, the simulation has only one. Thus, the simulation represents an approximate model of the subject's knowledge.

We can evaluate two aspects of the simulation's performance: the plans it produces and the process by which it produces them. We discuss each of these below.

Figure 9 shows the plan the subject produced for the problem discussed above. Figure 10 shows the plan produced by the simulation. The two plans are quite similar. Both plans include all primary errands and at least some of the secondary errands. While the subject included all secondary errands, the simulation included only one very convenient secondary errand. While the simulation and the subject planned different routes, both routes are fairly efficient, though clearly sub-optimal. Both the simulation and the subject planned to arrive at

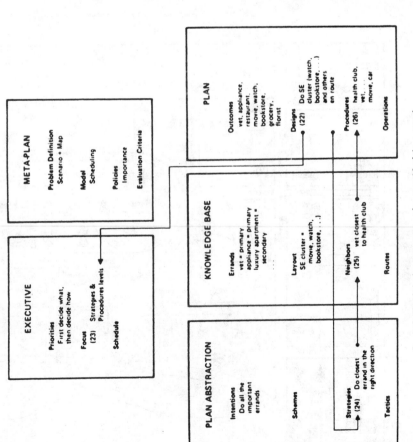

Figure 8. Blackboard representation of section 10 of the protocol.

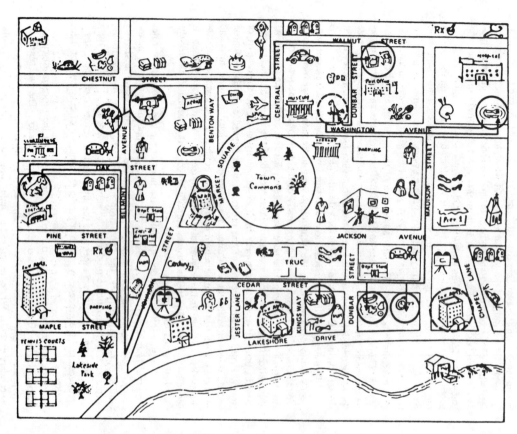

Figure 10. Plan produced by the computer simulation.

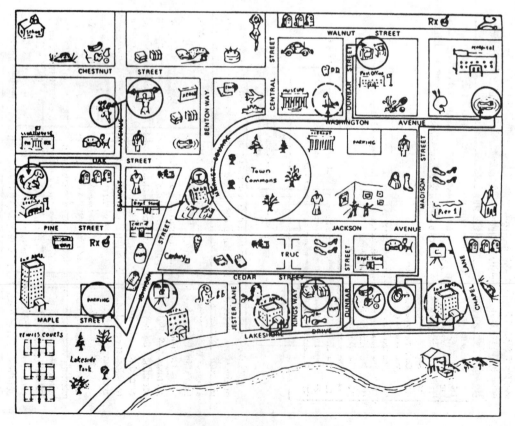

Figure 9 Plan produced by the human subject.

subject's protocol. Common decisions are preceded by "*" in Fig. 11. Of course, the remainder of the simulation's protocol does not always mirror the subject's protocol as closely as the section in Figure 11. Two factors produce the divergences.

First, as mentioned above, the simulation does not contain the entire set of specialists used by the subject. Thus, the simulation occasionally uses a specialist that is slightly different from the one the subject uses. This produces differences in both the protocols and the resulting plans. For example, in section 18 of the protocol, the subject decides to go from the health club to the vet on the way to the southeast part of town. At the same point in its protocol, the simulation decided to go from the health club to the appliance store. Both were trying to find the closest errand along the way, but they used slightly different specialists, and, as a consequence, chose different errands.

Second, the simulation's executive is incomplete. On some cycles, two or more invoked specialists are equally attractive and the simulation chooses randomly among them. Frequently, this random choice fails to select the specialist the subject used at that point. In such cases, the protocols also diverge.

In our opinion, it would be unproductive to model the subject's performance at a level of detail sufficient to counteract the effects of these two factors. Therefore, we look for the same general features in the two protocols, rather than exact replication. Such commonalities are readily apparent. Both the simulation and the subject made decisions at various levels of abstraction on each of the five planes of the planning blackboard. Both exhibited many coherent decision sequences in which each decision appeared to build on its predecessors. However, both also frequently "jumped about" the planning blackboard, rather than working systematically along any particular dimension. In particular, both the simulation and the subject occasionally redirected or dramatically changed their own activity in response to fortuitous observations or computations on the available data (e.g., the map).

6. THEORETICAL COMPLEXITY

The opportunistic model seems, at first glance, fairly complex. It postulates five different conceptual "planes" of decisions and several levels of abstraction within each of those planes. It postulates numerous planning specialists whose simultaneous efforts to participate in the planning process require the supervision of a fairly sophisticated executive. Although a number of complex models have proved fruitful in the last few years (Cf., Anderson, 1976; Anderson & Bower, 1973; Rumelhart, Lindsay, & Norman, 1972; Winograd, 1972), most of us still adhere to the law of parsimony, preferring simpler models to complex models.

In fact, the proposed model is computationally quite simple. It postulates a uniform decision mechanism, the specialist, to perform all of the varied decision-making functions planners perform. By modeling executive decisions

time-constrained destinations (e.g. the restaurant and the movie) at reasonable times. The major difference between the two plans lies in their relative "realism." The subject's plan is quite unrealistic—one could not execute the complete plan in the time available for doing so. The simulation's plan is somewhat more realistic, primarily because it omits many of the secondary errands.

```
1-9   [Omitted]
*10   Work forward for the starting location.
*11   The starting location is the Health Club which is on Belmont Avenue.
*12   Begin at the Health Club.
*13   Go to the closest errand next.
*14   The vet is on Oak Street.
*15   The appliance store is on Walnut Street.
16    The restaurant is on Washington Avenue.
*17   The watch repair is on Cedar Street.
*18   The bookstore is on Cedar Street.
19    The grocery is on Cedar Street.
*20   The watch repair, the bookstore, and the grocery are all in a cluster in the southeast part of town.
21    Organize the plan around spatial clusters.
*22   Proceed from the Health Club toward the southeast cluster.
```

Figure 11. Excerpt from the simulation's protocol.

Like the subject, the simulation produced a planning protocol—the series of decisions underlying the final plan. Figure 11 shows an excerpt from this protocol—decisions 10–22. (The protocol actually produced by the simulation is a series of decision "nodes" in list notation. Figure 11 translates the protocol into standard English for clarity.)

Decisions 10–22 of the simulation's protocol correspond quite closely to sections 5–8 of the subject's protocol. Recall that, in those sections, the subject identified the health club as the starting location, decided to schedule the closest errand to the health club next, located several errands on the map in his search for the closest errand, detected a cluster of errands in the southeast part of town and, accordingly, decided to head in that general direction.

Now consider the simulation's protocol. Decision 10 establishes a strategy to work forward from the starting location. Decisions 11 and 12 identify the starting location as the health club and establish it as the first errand in the procedure. Decision 13 establishes a strategy to go to the closest errand next. Decisions 14–19 locate individual errands on the map in a search for the closest errand to the health club. Decision 20 detects the cluster of errands in the southeast part of town. Decision 21 suggests organizing an overall design for the plan around the spatial cluster and decision 22 does so.

In addition to performing essentially the same functions the subject performed, the simulation made many of the decisions explicitly declared in the with the same mechanism, it can account for a wide range of distinct planning styles without additional assumptions. (See Hayes-Roth (1979) for a discussion of executive "flexibility.")

Most of the apparent complexity in the model derives from the details of the blackboard structure. However, the blackboard partitions provide another important computational efficiency. Each specialist gets invoked whenever a new decision on the blackboard satisfies its condition. If the blackboard were simply an unstructured collection of decisions, each specialist would have to examine every new decision to determine whether the decision satisfied its condition. This would require an enormous amount of computation, much of it unnecessary. The blackboard partitions reduce the amount of computation required by permitting each specialist to restrict its "attention" to only those new decisions that occur at particular levels.

The blackboard structure also permits the model to capture an important psychological feature—interruptability. People have the power to interrupt their own cognitive processing at arbitrary points. After performing some more or less related processing, they may or may not continue the interrupted task. This interruptability appears throughout our protocols and we believe it is a salient feature of cognitive processing in general. In the proposed model, interruption can occur only between individual decisions. Thus, the blackboard structure embodies our view of possible loci for interruption.

7. COMPARISON WITH SUCCESSIVE REFINEMENT MODELS

As discussed in the introduction to this paper, our view of planning differs somewhat from earlier views of planning as a process of successive refinement. This section explores several differences between the two views and attempts to resolve the differences.

Top-Down versus Multi-Directional Processing

While earlier work has assumed that planning is a top-down process, the proposed model treats planning as a multi-directional process. The diverse observations people make while planning often guide subsequent planning. Some of these observations arise from planning at an abstract level and guide subsequent planning at a more detailed level. The errand-planning protocol illustrates this kind of top-down processing in section 10, where the subject begins to instantiate a previously planned design at the lower procedure level. However, observations also arise from planning at a low level and guide subsequent planning at a more abstract level. The protocol illustrates this kind of bottom-up processing in section 8 where the subject formulates a design based on observations related to previous decisions at the lower procedure level. Many other examples of both top-down and bottom-up processing appear throughout this protocol and the others we have collected.

The sample protocol confirms the more general assumption of multi-directionality in another way. If the subject were operating in a top-down fashion, he would begin planning at the highest (most abstract) level of the planning space. He could plan at a lower level only if he had already planned that particular subtask at all higher levels. The errand-planning protocol disconfirms this presumption repeatedly. The subject begins forming his actual plan at a relatively low level, the procedure level. Thus, he plans at this level in the absence of any corresponding high-level plans. Similar instances of planning a subtask at a low level without having previously planned it at higher levels appear throughout this protocol and our others. These findings follow directly from the multi-directional assumption. (See Hayes-Roth and Thorndyke, 1979, for additional evidence on this point.)

Complete versus Incremental Planning

A second difference between the earlier view of planning and the proposed model concerns the relative completeness attributed to abstract plans. The earlier work assumes that, while initial plans may be abstract, they will be complete and fully integrated. Under a breadth-first processing assumption, this requires that complete plans at each level must precede any planning at the next lower level. Under a depth-first processing assumption, it requires only that the highest-level plan must be complete before planning activity can proceed at lower levels. Under either assumption, the earlier view presupposes that complete plans will eventually exist at all levels of abstraction.

By contrast, we assume that planning is incremental and, therefore, will rarely produce complete plans in the systematic fashion described above. We assume that people make tentative decisions without the requirement that each one fit into a current, completely integrated plan. As the planner relates each new decision to some subset of his previous decisions, the plan grows by incremental accretion. Further, the developing plan need not grow as a coherent integrated plan. Alternative subplans can develop independently either within or between levels of abstraction. The planner can incorporate these sub-plans into the final plan as she or he wishes.

The sample protocol provides evidence for these assumptions. For example, in section 9, having established only his initial location at the procedure level, the subject plans a sequence of two errands with which to conclude. In the following several sections of the protocol, he intermittently plans alternative designs (none of which covers the planned concluding sequence) and initial sequences of errands (none of which he concatenates with the planned concluding sequence). Similar partial plans appear throughout the protocol as well as in the other protocols we collected. These findings confirm our assumption that specialists record tentative decisions in various locations on the blackboard in response to relevant prior decisions.

Hierarchical versus Heterarchical Plan Structures

Earlier conceptions of plans as hierarchical structures responded to the appealing simplicity of hierarchically structured programs and the successive refinement method. None of our observations denies the putative merits of these hierarchical approaches. Of course, one can always interpret a sequence of actions as a hierarchy with some number of levels. Therefore, one must perform some more informative analysis to contrast hypothesized hierarchical plans with more complex plan structures. More importantly, a satisfactory theory of planning must describe all decisions made during the planning process as well as those that appear in completed plans.

Our efforts to model the planning process suggest that people make many decisions that do not fit a simple hierarchical structure. Under the proposed model, one might attempt to construe the final set of decisions on the plan plane as a hierarchical structure, but our protocols do not provide strong evidence for such a structure. For example, the design maintained throughout most of the sample protocol dictates that errands on the way to the southeast cluster should be performed first followed by those errands within the cluster itself. However, much of the subject's planning at lower levels concerns errands not covered by this design (e.g., the newsstand, the pet store, the appliance store, and the restaurant).

The assumption of hierarchical plan structure becomes more tenuous if we consider the many other kinds of decisions our subject made while planning. We have observed four categories of decisions that do not describe what the subject actually plans to do at all. These correspond to the four remaining planes of the planning blackboard. Thus, the subject makes decisions about data—how long errands should take, how important individual errands are, what the consequences of a particular action might be. etc. He makes decisions about abstract features of plans—what *kinds* of plan decisions might be useful. He makes meta-planning decisions—how to approach the problem and how to constrain and evaluate his plan. Finally, the subject makes executive decisions about how to allocate his cognitive resources during planning. While all of these decisions contribute to the planning process, they do not exhibit a single hierarchical planning structure. For these reasons, we prefer to think in terms of heterarchical plan structures.

Relative Advantages of Hierarchical versus Opportunistic Planning

We might also speculate on the relative merits of hierarchical versus opportunistic planning. The orderly, systematic nature of the top-down process and the simplicity of its hierarchical structure argue in its favor. The recent emphasis on structured programming, a top-down approach to software engineering, reflects these merits (Cf., Dahl, Dykstra, & Hoare, 1972). One might also argue that top-down processes would minimize memory load (Cf., Thorndyke, 1978). The planner could restrict attention to a single area of the hierarchy, rather than attending intermittently to several different areas of the planning space.

On the other hand, planning in tasks fraught with complexity and uncertainty might benefit from less of the discipline imposed by a top-down process. In such complex tasks, general, a priori solutions or problem-solving methods may not exist or may be computationally intractable. Even if some general approach were available, opportunistic planning would free the planner of the burden of maintaining a structurally integrated plan at each decision point. Instead, the planner could formulate and pursue promising partial plans as opportunity suggested.

More importantly, a multi-directional process might produce better plans. It certainly permits more varied plans than a strictly top-down process does. If the planner always began with a fixed high-level plan, she or he could refine it in only a limited number ways. The bottom-up component in multi-directional processing provides a potentially important source of innovation in planning. Low-level decisions and related observations can inspire novel higher-level plans. We observed this in the errand-planning protocol, for example, when the subject generated a high-level design based on observations and decisions made at the lower procedure level. Similarly, Feitelson and Stefik (1977) observed that their expert geneticist deliberately exploited the potential for innovation in bottom-up processing:

> Thus, not only is the planning process largely event driven but sometimes steps are taken somewhat outside the plan of the experiment to make a possibly interesting observation. This kind of behavior reflects the convenience of making certain interesting observations while the equipment is set up. Often this is done to verify the successful completion of an experimental step, but sometimes the observations seem to correspond more to fishing for interesting possibilities. (p. 31)

Resolving the Two Points of View

Although the preceding discussion argues for the proposed opportunistic model in favor of successive refinement models, we would not "reject" either model in favor of the other. Obviously, both models have merit and can best explain different situations. We can suggest three variables which might influence a planner's approach to a particular problem: problem characteristics, individual differences, and expertise.

Problem characteristics could have a major impact on the approach a planner takes. For example, planners might usefully exploit a top-down approach to planning whenever the problem at hand exhibited an inherent hierarchical structure. A study by Byrne (1977) supports this conjecture. His subjects planned dinner menus. As one might expect, subjects appeared to plan menus by deciding on type of dinner (e.g., Chinese dinner, Christmas dinner), main course (e.g., roast beef, turkey), and accompaniments (e.g., cranberry sauce, mashed potatoes). This is a nice example of a hierarchical planning structure. In addition, Byrne's subjects appeared to make decisions within this structure in a top-down fashion.

By contrast, the errand-planning problems discussed in this paper did not exhibit any obvious hierarchical structure. In such circumstances, planners might reasonably resort to more opportunistic methods. Apparently, this is what our subjects did.

A study by Hayes-Roth (1979) provides more direct evidence for the influence of problem characteristics. She successfully induced alternative planning approaches by manipulating the amount of time available for plan execution. For problems that imposed severe time constraints, most subjects adopted a top-down approach. For problems that imposed minimal time constraints, most subjects adopted a bottom-up approach.

The Hayes-Roth (1979) study also provides evidence for the impact of individual differences on planning methods. Many of her subjects exhibited a strong proclivity to adopt a bottom-up approach regardless of problem characteristics. Even with explicit instruction, some subjects persisted in using the bottom-up approach. Other subjects were more flexible, adopting an appropriate approach in response to problem characteristics or instruction.

Finally, planning expertise might influence which planning model a planner brings to bear on particular problems. A practiced planner working on a familiar, constrained problem may possess well-learned, reliable abstract plans for dealing with the problem. This extensive experience may support the application of standard methods for systematically refining abstract plans. On the other hand, a practiced planner working on an unconstrained problem can also exploit opportunistic methods to advantage. Feitelson's and Stefik's (1977) study of the experiment-planning of an expert molecular geneticist provides a nice illustration:

> The experiments described here reflect a combination of goal driven behavior and event driven behavior. . . If there were no goals, behavior might seem very erratic and follow no general course. If there is no event driven component to the planning process, then the experimental procedure must admit no feedback or changes of plans as a result of observations. Thus, no advantage will be made of fortunate observations. What is being suggested here is that the planning in this experiment involved far more exploitation of events and changes of plan according to the events than the authors had anticipated. (p. 30)

One resolution of the apparent conflict between the two models would simply incorporate the top-down model as a special case of the opportunistic model. We have discussed the importance of the problem-solving method a planner brings to bear on a task. This decision can have a major impact on subsequent executive decisions and, consequently, on the planner's progress through the remaining levels of the blackboard. For example, a planner might adopt a "define and successively refine" problem-solving method. Given strict adherence to this method, the planner's formulation of decisions on the plan plane would indeed proceed in a systematic top-down fashion. These are exactly the decisions modeled in the earlier work on top-down planning.

Note that "define and refine" is only one of many problem-solving methods adoptable in the framework of the opportunistic model. Thus, the question is no longer which model is correct, but rather, under what circumstances do planners bring alternative problem-solving methods to bear? We have suggested problem characteristics, individual differences, and expertise as important factors. We should also ask which problem-solving methods work best for different kinds of problems.

8. CONCLUSIONS

The opportunistic model draws on earlier theoretical work in cognitive psychology and artificial intelligence. It incorporates the strongest points of these models with its own assumptions regarding multi-directionality, opportunism, and incrementation in a heterarchical plan structure. We believe that the model is flexible enough to handle the complexity and variability of people's planning behavior. Yet, it is vulnerable to data. We hope the opportunistic model will provide a useful framework for future investigations of the planning process.

REFERENCES

Aho, A. V., Hopcroft, J. E., & Ullman, J. D. *The design and analysis of computer algorithms.* Reading, Mass.: Addison-Wesley, 1974.

Anderson, J. R. *Language, memory, and thought.* Hillsdale, N.J.: Lawrence Erlbaum Associates, 1976.

Anderson, J. R., & Bower, G. H. *Human associative memory.* Washington, D.C.: V. H. Winston, 1973.

Byrne, R. Planning meals: Problem-solving on a real data-base. *Cognition,* 1977, *5,* 287-332.

CMU Computer Science Research Group. Summary of the CMU five-year ARPA effort in speech understanding research. Technical Report, Carnegie-Mellon University, 1977.

Christophides, N. *Graph theory: An algorithmic approach.* New York: Academic Press, 1975.

Dahl, O. J., Dykstra, E. W., & Hoare, C. A. R. *Structured programming.* New York: Academic Press, 1972.

Engelmore, R. S., & Nii, H. P. A knowledge-based system for the interpretation of protein x-ray crystallographic data. Report No. STAN-CS-77-589, Stanford University, 1977.

Erman, L. D., & Lesser, V. R. A multi-level organization for problem solving using many diverse cooperating sources of knowledge. *Proceedings of the Fourth International Joint Conference on Artificial Intelligence.* Tbilisi, USSR, 1975, 483-490.

Ernst, G. W., & Newell, A. *GPS: A case study in generality and problem solving*. New York: Academic Press, 1969.

Fahlman, S. E. A planning system for robot construction tasks. *Artificial Intelligence*, 1974, 5, 1–49.

Feitelson, J., & Stefik, M. A case study of the reasoning in a genetics experiment. Heuristic Programming Project, Working Paper 77–18, Department of Computer Science, Stanford University, April 1977.

Fikes, R. E. Knowledge representation in automatic planning systems. In A. K. Jones (ed.), *Perspectives on computer science*. New York: Academic Press, 1977.

Fikes, R. E., & Nilsson, N.J. STRIPS: A new approach to the application of theorem proving to problem solving. *Artificial Intelligence*, 1971, 2, 189–203.

Hayes-Roth, B. Flexibility in executive strategies. N:1170, The Rand Corporation, Santa Monica, California, 1979.

Hayes-Roth, B., Hayes-Roth, F., Rosenschein, S., & Cammarata, S. Modeling planning as an incremental, opportunistic process. *Proceedings of the Sixth International Joint Conference on Artificial Intelligence*. Tokyo, Japan, 1979.

Hayes-Roth, B., and Thorndyke, P. Decision-making during the planning process. N:1213, The Rand Corporation, Santa Monica, California, 1979.

Hayes-Roth, F., & Lesser, V. R. Focus of attention in the Hearsay-II speech understanding system. *Proceedings of the Fifth International Joint Conference on Artificial Intelligence*, Boston, Mass., 1977, 27–35.

Hayes-Roth, F., Waterman, D. A., & Lenat, D. E. Principles of pattern-directed inference systems. In Waterman D. A. & Hayes-Roth F. (eds.), *Pattern-directed inference systems*. New York: Academic Press, 1978.

Lesser, V. R., Fennell, R. D., Erman, L. D., & Reddy, D. R. Organization of the Hearsay-II speech understanding system. *IEEE Transactions on Acoustics, Speech and Signal Processing*, ASSP-23, 1975, 11–23.

Lesser, V. R., & Erman, L. D. A retrospective view of the Hearsay-II architecture. *Proceedings of the Fifth International Joint Conference on Artificial Intelligence*, Boston, Mass., 1977, 790–800.

Newell, A., & Simon, H. A. *Human problem solving*. Englewood Cliffs, N.J.: Prentice-Hall, 1972.

Nii, H. P., & Feigenbaum, E. A. Rule-based understanding of signals. In D. A. Waterman & F. Hayes-Roth (eds.), *Pattern-directed inference systems*. New York: Academic Press, 1978.

Prager, J., Nagin, P., Kohler, R., Hanson, A., & Riseman, E. Segmentation processes in the VISIONS system. *Proceedings of the Fifth International Joint Conference on Artificial Intelligence*. Boston, Mass., 1977.

Rumelhart, D. E. Toward an interactive model of reading. Technical Report 56, Center for Human Information Processing, University of California at San Diego, La Jolla, Ca., 1976.

Rumelhart, D., Lindsay, P. H., & Norman, D. A. A process model for long-term memory. In E. Tulving & W. Donaldson (eds.), *Organization of memory*. New York: Academic Press, 1972.

Sacerdoti, E. D. Planning in a hierarchy of abstraction spaces. *Artificial Intelligence*, 1974, 5, 115–135.

Sacerdoti, E. D. A structure for plans and behavior. Technical Note 109, Standford Research Institute, Menlo Park, California, August, 1975.

Selfridge, O. Pandemonium: A paradigm for learning. *Symposium on the mechanization of thought*. London: HM Stationery Office, 1959.

Soloway, E. M., & Riseman, E. M. Knowledge-directed learning. *Proceedings of the Workshop on Pattern-Directed Inference Systems*, special edition of the *SIGART Newsletter*. New York: Association for Computing Machinery, June, 1977.

Sussman, G. J. A computational model of skill acquisition. AI TR-297, Artificial Intelligence Laboratory, Massachusetts Institute of Technology, Cambridge, Mass., 1973.

Thorndyke, P. W. Pattern-directed processing of knowledge from text. In D. A. Waterman & F. Hayes-Roth (eds.), *Pattern-directed inference systems*. New York: Academic Press, 1978.

Winograd, T. A program for understanding natural language. *Cognitive Psychology*, 1972, 3.

Meta-Planning: Representing and Using Knowledge About Planning in Problem Solving and Natural Language Understanding*

ROBERT WILENSKY

Computer Science Division
Department of EECS
University of California, Berkeley

This paper is concerned with those elements of planning knowledge that are common to both understanding someone else's plan and creating a plan for one's own use. This planning knowledge can be divided into two bodies: Knowledge about the world, and knowledge about the planning process itself. Our interest here is primarily with the latter corpus. The central thesis is that much of the planning process itself can be formulated in terms of higher-level goals and plans called meta-goals and meta-plans. These entities can then be used by the same understanding and planning mechanisms that process ordinary goals and plans. However, the meta-planning knowledge now enables these mechanisms to handle much more complicated situations in a uniform manner.

Systems based on meta-planning would have a number of advantages over existing problem solving and understanding systems. The same knowledge could be shared by both a planner and understander, and both would be able to handle complex situations elegantly. In addition, in planning, the use of meta-planning has several advantages over more traditional methods involving constraints or critics. Meta-planning allows the full power of a problem solver to be applied to situations that are generally amenable only to special purpose processing. In addition, meta-planning facilitates the representation of some situations that are difficult to express otherwise. We have begun to introduce meta-planning knowledge into two systems: PAM, a story understanding program, and PANDORA, a problem solving and planning system.

*Research sponsored in part by the National Science Foundation under grant MCS79-06543.

1.0 INTRODUCTION

This paper is concerned with the problems of problem solving and understanding. These problems are related because both problem solvers and understanders make use of planning knowledge to perform their respective tasks: A problem solver may generate a plan as the solution to some problem, while a natural language understander must apply knowledge about people's goals and plans in order to make the inferences necessary to explain the behavior of a character in a story (Wilensky, 1978). While a story understander is quite different from a planner, both must embody a theory of planning knowledge.

I have been developing such a theory in the construction of PAM (Plan Applier Mechanism), a story understanding program. This paper is concerned not with the understanding mechanism itself, but with that part of its planning knowledge which is independent of whether that knowledge is used to explain someone's behavior or to generate a plan for one's own use. We are currently attempting to use the same theory of planning knowledge upon which PAM is based to construct a problem solving system called PANDORA (Plan ANalysis with Dynamic Organization, Revision, and Application).

This planning knowledge can be divided into two bodies: Knowledge about the world, and knowledge about the planning process itself. Our interest here is primarily with the latter corpus. The central thesis is that much of the knowledge about the planning process itself can be formulated in terms of higher-level goals and plans (meta-plans). These entities can then be used by the same sort of mechanisms that are needed for processing ordinary goals and plans. However, the meta-planning knowledge now enables these mechanisms to handle much more complicated situations involving multiplicities of goals in a quite uniform manner.

1.1 A Comparison of Problem Solving with Understanding

Before we develop the idea of meta-planning, it is useful to compare problem solving and understanding in some detail. Problem solving programs often have the construction of a plan whose execution will bring about a desired state as their goal. The domain over which plan construction is performed varies considerably, involving, for example, robots finding their way through rooms (Fikes & Nilsson, 1971; Sacerdoti, 1974), "missionary and cannibals" type problems (Newell & Simon, 1972), electronic circuit design (McDermott, 1977) and program construction (Rich & Shrobe, 1976; Barstow, 1977). The domain over which problem solving can be performed may happen to involve natural language. For example, participating in a conversation and producing an utterance have been viewed as problems in plan construction, where the problem is to create an utterance that would satisfy goals involving the transmission of certain contents or intentions (Bruce, 1975; Perrault, Allen, & Cohen, 1978).

This characterization of the two processes is actually somewhat flawed. In particular, I intend to show below that a good problem solver should have incorporated in it some of the capabilities that were just attributed to understanding mechanisms. For example, a good planning system should be able to infer its own goals and to infer the goals of others. Most planning programs simply do not have this property. However, the fact that comprehensive understanding and planning systems may embody components of both understanding and planning mechanisms does not defeat the central tenet of the argument above. Such systems are decomposable into separate understanding and planning components, neither of which is more fundamental than the other.

In the previous discussion, and in most of what follows, I sometimes use the term understanding to mean "understanding the plans and goal of characters in written texts". This is not meant to imply that the two are equivalent. Certainly, much more goes on in understanding than following people's plans and goals. However, here we are concerned only with this aspect of understanding. More importantly, understanding may also refer to understanding utterances, or to understanding actions in real life. I emphasize story understanding here only because it is the one area of understanding with which I have had the most experience, and where some of the ideas in this paper have had at least tentative testing. If in fact these ideas are useful for text understanding, then it seems reasonable to believe that they will apply to understanding in general. Indeed, our work on building PANDORA seems to bear this out. However, these other aspects of understanding have not as yet been explored sufficiently to know whether they entail additional problems to those with which we are already familiar.

1.2 Knowledge in Common Between the Planner and the Understander

Thus, understanding and problem solving are quite different, possibly inverse processes. While each requires different programs and functions, it would be a mistake to ignore the important commonalities that these processes do have. In particular, it would seem that they should have a great deal in common in terms of the knowledge about planning that they each require. One part of this planning knowledge is essentially world knowledge. This includes a classification of intentional structures into elements like plans, goals, and themes (Schank & Abelson, 1975), a description of the structure of these elements (e.g., plans have preconditions and actions that instantiate them, plans are used to achieve goals, etc.), and an actual body of knowledge about particular elements (e.g., asking for something is a way of getting something from someone). This point is developed at some length (Rieger, 1975).

As an example, consider the fact that having possession of a book is a precondition for reading it. In problem solving, this fact would be useful if the planner had already decided that it wanted to read some particular book. Check-

Thus, while problem solving may involve plan construction over quite different domains, including some linguistic ones, the essential nature of the task is the same: Given a goal, create a plan to satisfy it. In contrast, in understanding, quite a different application of plans is found. Here, the understander needs to follow the goals and plans of actors in a situation in order to make inferences (Wilensky, 1978). Rather than actually create a plan, an understander must be able to use knowledge about plans to understand the plan under which someone else is operating.

While problem solving and understanding both heavily involve the use of plans, it is important to emphasize how different these processes are. Problem solving has often been abstractly characterized as searching through a solution space for an answer to some problem. That is, given a goal, a set of operators, and an initial state of the world, the task is to construct a sequence of operators that transforms the initial state into the goal state. Understanding generally involves just the opposite in terms of what is known and what must be computed. For example, stories often state that a character took some action, from which the reader must infer why he did so and what things must have been the case for the action to have been taken. That is, the reader is given the "solution", in problem solving terminology, and must reconstruct the goal and state of the world from it. Rather than searching through solution space for an answer, an understander searches through "explanation space" to find a set of circumstances that would explain a character's behavior.

This characterization of planning and of understanding demonstrates that while explanation-finding is a relative of problem solving, it is not entailed by it or dependent upon it. That is, having a good story understander does not require it to be a problem solver, nor does the existence of a problem solver fulfill the requirements of an explanation mechanism. The tasks that arise in understanding impose different requirements than do any involved in problem solving. Some simply have no correlate.

For example, the understanding task may require that a goal be inferred from the occurrence of an action, and that the existence of a goal be explained. If an understander were told that John proposed to Mary, the understander would need to infer that John probably has the goal of marrying Mary, and that this goal might have come into existence because John loved her. Problem solvers do not have the facility to infer goals, nor the need to explain where goals come from. Their purpose is simply to act on goals given them from on high. A problem solver told that John wants to marry Mary might deduce that he should try proposing to her. But it could not explain where this goal came from nor could it infer that John has the goal from some action he undertook. Furthermore, the plan that a character chose to use might be an unusual one that the reader must therefore be able to comprehend a character's behavior in terms of a plan that it would never produce itself.

ing to see if the preconditions of this plan were fulfilled, the planner would need to consult the fact above. Learning that possessing the book is a precondition for its intended action, the planner would check to see if that condition held, and if not, would attempt to make it so. That is, the planner would establish the subgoal of achieving this precondition and then try to construct a plan to fulfill it.

An understander might use the same fact in the following manner: Given that it learned that someone had the goal of possessing a book, the understander would try to explain why this person had this goal. One kind of explanation for having a goal is that the state it is directed at is a precondition for a plan for some higher-level goal. The understander would, therefore, check to see if it knew of any plans for which possessing a book is a precondition. Finding the fact stated above, the understander could infer that reading the book is such a plan. The understander could then hypothesize reading a book as an explanation for wanting to possess one.

Thus both planning and understanding make use of the identical fact, although they need to index it in different ways: in planning, one needs to get from an operator to its preconditions; and, in understanding, one needs to get from a precondition to that for which it is a precondition. The point here is that it is a bad idea to bury away such facts within the bowels of an understander or a planner so that they each require separate copies and possibly even separate representations of the same information. Not only is this inelegant and bad economy, it misses the point that such facts are not really "understanding" knowledge or "problem solving" knowledge. They are merely facts about the world that these processes (and possibly lots of others) happen to find useful for their particular tasks.

In actuality, many problem solvers and understanders do represent such facts declaratively. This, at least potentially, allows these facts to be shared by another process, although the representations used may be biased one way or another to facilitate the particular task for which the knowledge base was designed. One exception to this was a previous version of my own program, PAM, which had most of its knowledge procedurally encoded. The current version encodes its knowledge declaratively in an associative knowledge base for the reasons being developed here, as well as for other knowledge engineering advantages.

There is a second body of knowledge related to planning. This is knowledge about the planning process itself. This body is also required by both problem solvers and understanders, and should be shared by them. However, existing systems do not encode this knowledge explicitly, or in a declarative and sharable form. My claim is that it is just as natural and important to have an explicit and sharable representation of this knowledge as it is for world knowledge. Moreover, such a formulation of this knowledge suggests improvements in the design of both understanders and planners.

The exact nature and need for the declarative meta-knowledge I refer to

becomes apparent when one considers planning and understanding in situations involving multiple goals. By multiple goals, I refer to cases in which a planner or story character is simultaneously trying to satisfy a number of goals at once, or in which there are a number of planners present, each with their own plans and goals. It is the interactions between these intentional elements that cause much of the complexity in both understanding and planning.

For example, consider the following stories:

(1) John was in a hurry to get to Las Vegas, but he noticed that there were a lot of cops around so he stuck to the speed limit.
(2) John was eating dinner when he noticed that a thief was trying to break into his house. After he finished his dessert, John called the police.

In (1), a plausible plan to achieve John's goal is to speed, but John chose to abandon this goal instead. What's needed to understand this story is not just knowledge about cops and speeding tickets, but knowledge that a person might abandon one goal if it conflicts with another goal he considers to be more significant.

Likewise (2) strikes most people as strange since John should have reacted to the intruder more strongly. The unusualness of this story is due not to knowledge of the plans and goals involved, but the apparent unproductive scheduling of these plans. A more intelligent planner would have dealt with the threat immediately, and then perhaps returned to his meal when that situation had been disposed of.

Thus, to understand the behavior of a character, or to generate an intelligent plan, it is necessary to take into account the interactions between goals. The previous version of PAM handled understanding such situations through the use of special mechanisms and knowledge to detect various kinds of goal interactions. Thus, PAM had a packet of knowledge whose sole function was to spot conflicts between a character's goals, a mechanism to detect adverse interactions across the goals of different characters (goal competition), etc. The possible actions a character might take in such a situation were handled similarly.

There are a number of ways in which this solution is unsatisfactory. For one, these mechanisms for goal conflict detection, etc., were pretty much unrelated to the general explanation-finding behavior of the program when it tried to generate explanations involving just a simple goal structure. That is, PAM's normal processing was driven by the need to find an explanation for an event. It would, therefore, hypothesize plans that might underlie an action, or hypothesize goals that might have spawned a plan, etc., until it had found a possible explanation for the input. However, detection of goal conflicts, etc., did not fit into this model at all. It was simply a mechanism off to the side that performed a function PAM would later need, but which was not at all integrated into the basic explanation function.

While this objection may appear to be primarily aesthetic, recall that the try to resolve the goal conflict. That is, a planner must know that if it has a goal conflict, then it should have the goal of resolving it. An understander must know that if a character has a goal conflict, then that character may have the goal of resolving it. This is not so much knowledge about the world (as "state X is a precondition for action Y" would be), but knowledge about planning itself. Such knowledge is now usually procedurally encoded in critics or special conflict detection mechanisms. But to obtain the advantage of shared knowledge and general reasoning capabilities mentioned above, this knowledge must be explicitly and declaratively formulated.

Note also that if we formulate this knowledge explicitly, it is possible to do away with the aesthetic problem of PAM's separate mechanism for dealing with goal interactions. If PAM explicitly knew that people had the goal of resolving conflicts, then detecting a conflict would be part of the more general problem of determining that a character had a goal. PAM must have such a mechanism anyway, so that it can infer that someone who is hungry is likely to have the goal of satisfying that hunger, or that someone who loves someone else may have the goal of preventing them from harm. Explaining a character's attempt at resolving a goal conflict would simply be an instance of interpreting the action as the execution of a plan aimed at the goal of resolving a goal conflict. This is exactly PAM's ordinary explanation algorithm. It now applies to the complex situation because resolving a goal conflict is now viewed as just another goal to be achieved.

In sum, we have taken the following position:

1. We have given a number of reasons that knowledge involved in planning and understanding should be declaratively represented whenever possible. In addition to all the standard knowledge engineering arguments for declarative representations, in the particular case of planning knowledge, an important advantage of declarative representations is that they allow the sharing of knowledge between a planner and an understander. This is desirable since shared knowledge avoids duplication, eliminates problems of multiple representational forms, and simplifies extending both systems. Moreover, it pays homage to the fact that human problem solvers and understanders are not separate beings. A person probably does not learn most facts just for the purpose of understanding a story or solving some problem; rather, knowledge is accumulated through diverse kinds of experience and only later applied to problem solving or story understanding.

2. While knowledge about the world is kept declaratively in many systems, knowledge about the planning process itself is usually procedurally encoded.

3. However, all the reasons for expressing ordinary world knowledge declaratively also apply to planning meta-knowledge: It is used both in understanding and in problem solving, and thus it should be sharable by the two processes for all the advantages given above. Expressing this knowledge declaratively allows a system to use this knowledge in general reasoning processes, rather than restricting its use to the particular functions embedded in a specific program or critic. In addition, when this knowledge is cast declaratively, certain uniformities emerge. For example, in understanding,

ultimate function of detecting a goal conflict in PAM is to state an explanation for a subsequent action. For example, if in a version of story (1) we learned that John had purchased a radar detection device, the proper explanation would be that John intended to speed but didn't want to get caught. This explanation is coherent only as a plan to resolve the goal conflict between getting to a place quickly and not getting a ticket. That is, a plan to get somewhere quickly is to speed, and a way not to get a ticket is to avoid speeding. Buying a radar detection device is a plan not directed at either goal *per se*, but at addressing the conflict between the goals. The problem here is that determining that an action is a way of resolving a goal conflict is a form of explanation. Yet, it has no structural or procedural similarity to simple PAM explanations.

Another problem that this formulation poses for PAM is shared by planning programs as well. Various planning programs (e.g., Sussman, 1975; Sacerdoti, 1977) deal with some forms of goal interactions by providing specific programmed mechanisms that are germane to particular situations. For example, Sussman's HACKER has a celebrated critic that knows about goals clobbering "brother goals", and detects this bug in plans suggested by the plan synthesizer. Planning programs deal almost exclusively with conflicting subgoals and constraint violations and are not concerned with the more general cases of goal conflict, nor do they address the problems of goal interactions in cases where they must contend with other competitive planners. Other such limitations will be examined more fully below.

The difficulty with this type of solution is that it once again buries knowledge about how to plan in a procedure. This assures that such knowledge cannot be shared by a program that wishes to use this knowledge to understand someone else's behavior in a complicated situation. For example, if a planning program were given the goal of getting somewhere fast, it might use a critic to determine that this plan violated a "don't get ticketed" constraint, and possibly even to suggest that a radar detection device be acquired. However, as this knowledge would be procedurally embedded in the critic, it could not be used by an understander to explain why someone else was behaving in accordance with this same reasoning.

In addition, there are drawbacks for this approach within the problem solving world itself. When knowledge is embedded inside a critic, it becomes difficult to reason about this knowledge in a very general way. For example, if the resources of the critic to resolve a conflict are exhausted, it may still be possible to come up with a novel solution if the goal conflict itself were stated as a formal problem and handed to the general problem solver. But building all knowledge into a critic precludes reasoning about that knowledge in a very general manner.

The knowledge involved in the previous examples is of a somewhat different character than more mundane world knowledge. For example, it involves facts like the following: If a person has conflicting goals, then that person may detecting a goal conflict, and explaining an attempt at its resolution becomes a specific instance of the general problem of determining that a character has a goal and that an action is part of a plan to achieve a goal. No special mechanisms are required, and one theory of explanation applies both to the simple and more complicated cases.

4. Meta-knowledge about the planning process takes the form of higher-level goals, particularly those expressing the goals of the planning process itself in situations involving multiple goals and plans. We will develop this point in detail below.

2.0 META-PLANNING

This body of knowledge about the planning process is called *meta-planning* knowledge. This means that knowledge about how to plan should itself be expressed in terms of a set of goals for the planning process (*meta-goals*), and a set of plans to achieve them (*meta-plans*). The idea is that by expressing this knowledge in terms of goals and plans, the same planning mechanism (plan understander) that is used to produce a plan (explanation) for simple situations can operate in the more complex domain of goal interactions.

For example, consider the following situation, either from the point of view of plan understanding or plan generation:

(3) John's wife called him and told him they were all out of milk. He decided to pick some up on his way home from work.

An intelligent planner could come up with John's plan, assuming it knew that it passes by a grocery store on the route home. In order to produce this plan, it is necessary to go through the following processes:

1. Realizing that the goal of getting home and getting some milk are *overlapping*, and they should be pursued together rather than independently.
2. Adjusting one's plans accordingly. In this case, the plan is modified so as to:
   a) Produce a route that takes the planner near the grocery store.
   b) The "go home" plan is suspended at the point at which the grocery store is reached.
   c) The "get milk" plan is executed.
   d) The "go home" plan is resumed.

Two facts of the meta-knowledge variety are involved in this example. First, one needs to know that it is generally desirable to do no more than is necessary to achieve a goal. This fact is needed in realizing that the two goals in the situation should be pursued together, and is a piece of meta-knowledge because it is not a fact about how to achieve a particular goal. Rather, it is based on a very general fact about the goals of the planning process, namely, that executing unnecessary steps should be avoided.

The second place in which meta-knowledge is needed is in splicing together the plans for the two goals to create a single plan. The fact used here is that it is possible to make some saving, if two plans involving similar actions are executed together. This is a general fact about how to manipulate plans, not a particular fact about a specific plan or goal.

In terms of meta-planning, this situation has the following analysis: The goal of avoiding unnecessary steps comes from the meta-theme "Don't Waste Resources". A theme is defined as something that gives rise to a goal, usually in a given situation. A meta-theme is a theme that gives rise to a meta-goal. One can think of themes (and meta-themes) as "being around" all the time, while goals (and meta-goals) come into existence only as specific entities. In this case, the situation of goal overlap causes the "Don't Waste Resources" meta-theme to bring into existence the meta-goal "Combine Plans". This is a goal like any other, and the planner now proceeds to find a plan for it. A plan that is applicable here is the meta-plan "Integrate Plans", that is, merging two existing plans to take advantage of their common subcomponents. The application of this meta-plan achieves the "Combine Plans" meta-goal.

2.1 Meta-planning, Constraints, and Critics

One advantage of the meta-planning approach is that the problem of how to deal with complex goal interactions can be stated as a problem to be solved by the same planning mechanism one applies to "ordinary" goals. For example, one may first try out a number of canned solutions, then some standard planning procedures, and if all else fails, try to construct a novel solution.

In addition, since declarative meta-goals motivate the creation of the plan above, they can also be used to explain the behavior of a character whom a reader observed functioning in the manner described. That is, a reader of story (3) could explain John's behavior as part of a plan to achieve two specific goals, and, at the same time, avoided wasting any resources unnecessarily.

Note that there are a number of important differences between meta-planning and planning using constraints or critics. As was just pointed out, meta-planning involves the use of declarative knowledge that can be used for both understanding and planning, whereas knowledge in the form of a critic is usually procedural and planning, therefore unsharable. Another difference is that constraints and plan generators are asymmetric, in that constraints reject plans, but they don't themselves propose new ones. Generally, if a constraint is violated, a plan is rejected and it is left to the plan generator to propose a new plan. In contrast, meta-goals accomplish what constraints are intended for by formulating a problem that the current plan entails. Unlike a constraint, the existence of a meta-goal causes the planner to try to solve a particular problem, rather than just return control to the plan generator.

Unlike constraints, critics can change the existing planning structures to eliminate a problem. However, such changes are limited to particular types of transformations known to the critic. The meta-planning approach separates the voltage gets above .57meV, then this causes our circuit to melt. We would also have to specify that melting ruins parts and ruining things is undesirable. Then, the Preservation theme, which roughly states that undesirable anticipated states should be avoided, would cause the planner to have the goal of preventing this from happening if it anticipates the occurrence of a situation that might bring about such a state of affairs.

McDermott's notion of a *policy*, or a secondary task comes closest to the notion of meta-planning I propose here. A policy is essentially an explicitly represented constraint (McDermott, 1978). Like meta-goals, policies have the advantage that they may easily enter into general deductions. The primary differences between a policy and a meta-goal are that meta-goals include goals that are not necessarily constraints *per se*. Meta-goals refer only to facts about planning as their domain, whereas policies may include domain specific information. Policies often entail the creation of pseudo-tasks, whereas meta-goals have meta-plans that deviate less from the structure of normal plans.

Another idea similar to the notion of meta-planning proposed here is due to Stefik (1980). Stefik uses meta-planning to address control issues that arise in the design of problem solving systems. For the design of the MOLGEN expert system, he proposed a multiple-layered system in which each layer is essentially another problem solver dedicated to the meta-problems that arise on the previous layer. This control structure is used to replace the complex interpreter one would use in a single-layered agenda based system.

Thus Stefik's notion of meta-planning addresses the same issues as I address here. However, our solutions are formulated in quite different ways. In particular, Stefik does not formulate his meta-level problem solvers in terms of explicit meta-goals; instead, specific strategies are employed on each level. MOLGEN represents its problem level goals and constraints explicitly, but does not have explicit representations of meta-level goals or of meta-constraints (i.e., constraints involved in the reasoning process itself).

While MOLGEN does not embody explicit meta-goals, they would seem to be compatible with the nature of that system. However, the division of MOLGEN into a multiple-level problem solver is an approach explicitly resisted in my analysis. The multiple-level approach presumes that there is nothing in common about the problem solving on each layer, and that, therefore, a separate problem solving system is required for each level. The approach taken here makes exactly the opposite presumption. Namely, that the planning and meta-planning are essentially the same sort of activity. Only different goals and plans are specified in each case. Both goal and meta-goals are to be handled exactly alike and by the same planning mechanism.

This notion of a homogeneous planner based on meta-planning will be developed in more detail below. While I believe the homogeneous solution is the most elegant and versatile, it is not without drawbacks. The relative efficiency and psychological accuracy that might be attributed in principle to either design will probably take considerable time and experimental effort to discern.

formulation of the problem from its detection and solution. Activating a meta-goal corresponds to detecting a violation, the meta-goal itself to the formulation of the problem, and finding an appropriate meta-plan to creating a solution. The advantage of this approach is that it does not require the critic to embody this advantage of this approach is that it does not require the critic to embody the planning process. Meta-planning allows all the benefits of having a general problem solver to be available to the task of resolving a constraint violation. Since the implicit assumption is that having a general problem solver is a good idea to begin with, then we are better off having a general problem solver at hand to handle constraint violations and the like rather than relegating this responsibility to an expert critic. Of course, this does not prevent us from having such expert knowledge as a critic possesses available. We are simply allowing this knowledge to interact with all other knowledge as it can now take part in general deductions.

In addition to increasing the chances of finding an answer, the meta-planning formulation also provides more flexibility when no answer is available. In general, when a critic finds fault in a plan, it tries to put a fix into effect right away. If it cannot apply one, the plan must be rejected. However, since a meta-goal represents the formulation of a problem, the existence of the problem may be dealt with beyond its being resolved. For example, the problem solver may simply decide to accept the flawed plan if the violation is viewed as not being too important. In fact, it may be the case that changing the existing plan to resolve the problem may result in other problems that are deemed even more serious. In this case, the best choice is to accept the original flawed plan. By separating solving the problem from its formulation, the problem may be accessed as opposed to treated, an option that critics do not usually leave open.

Meta-planning is also meant to cover a somewhat different scope than that covered by critics and constraints. To begin with, meta-planning knowledge is not always critical in nature. For example, it might be possible to suggest a plan for combining the normal plans for two goals as in the case of example (3) without first proposing a flawed planning structure. That is, the knowledge may productively affect the planning process without there necessarily being a bad plan around for a critic to react to. In general, meta-planning advises the planner about goal interactions and the like, and only some of this knowledge specifies situations to be avoided.

Furthermore, meta-goal are an independent domain, encoding only knowledge about planning in general. In most planning systems, constraints and critics embody knowledge that is domain dependent as well as that which is not. For example, a specific critic may exist that encodes knowledge about the types of situations to avoid in a particular task domain, such as "don't allow the voltage on an amplifier to ever get above .57meV". With meta-goals, task-specific constraints are enforced by specifying that some particular situation would activate some more general principle. For example, we might specify that if the

Hayes-Roth and Hayes-Roth (1978) uses the term meta-planning to refer to decisions about the planning process. While my use of the term is similar to theirs, they include all types of planning decisions under this name, and their meta-planning is not formulated in terms of explicit meta-goals and meta-plans. I use the term to refer only to a subset of this knowledge, and only when that knowledge is expressed in terms of explicit meta-goals and meta-plans.

2.2 Kinds of Meta-goals

The following is a brief description of the more important meta-goals so far encountered, along with the meta-themes and situations in which they arise, and some of the meta-plans applicable to them. This list is not meant to be complete. It merely reflects the current state of our analysis. As our experimentation with actually using meta-planning in our artificial intelligence systems is still being carried out, we expect that the following analysis will be subject to revision.

Situations, Meta-themes, Meta-goals, and Meta-plans:

1. Meta-theme — Don't Waste Resources
   Situations to detect
   A) Goal Overlap
      Meta-goals initiated:
      1. Combine-Plans
         Associated meta-plans:
         a) Schedule Common Subgoals First
         b) Plan Integration
         c) Plan Piggybacking (Find a new plan that simultaneously fulfills both goals)
   B) Goal Concord
      Meta-goals initiated:
      1. Ally-Plans
         Associated meta-plans:
         a) Divide Task
         b) Piggyback Goal (Try to capitalize on the plan of another planner to fulfill one's own goal)
   C) Multiple Planning Options (More than one plan is applicable to a known goal)
      Meta-goals initiated:
      1. Choose-Least-Costly-Scenario
         Associated meta-plans:
         a) Simulate-and-Select (Determine the cost of the various options and pick the least costly one)
   D) Recurring Goals (A goal that arises repeatedly)
      Meta-goals initiated:
      1. Establish-Subsumption-State (Establish a state that fulfills a precondition for a plan for the goal and which endures over a period of time (see Wilensky, 1978b))
         Associated meta-plans:
         a) Plans are a function of the subsumption state to be achieved

2. Meta-theme — Achieve As Many Goals As Possible
   Situations to detect
   A) Goal Conflict
      Meta-goals initiated:
      1. Resolve-Goal-Conflict
         Associated meta-plans:
         a) Use-Normal-Plans (See if there are any plans available for the specific kind of goal conflict at hand)
         b) Try-Alternate-Plan (Try other possible plans for the goals to find a non-conflicting set)
         c) Change-Circumstances (Try changing the circumstances in which the plans are being used to enable their use without causing a conflict, e.g., obtain more resources if the conflict is based on a resource shortage)

3. Meta-theme—Maximize the Value of the Goals Achieved
   Situations to detect
   A) Unresolvable Goal Conflict
      Meta-goals initiated:
      1. Choose-Most-Valuable-Scenario
         Associated meta-plans:
         a) Simulate-and-Select (Includes sub-plan of Goal-Modification as a way of producing alternatives to consider)

4. Meta-theme—Avoid Impossible Goals
   Situations to detect
   A) Circular Subgoals (A subgoal generated in a plan is the same as some goal to which it is instrumental)
      Meta-goals initiated:
      1. Resolve-Circularity
         Associated meta-plans:
         a) Goal substitution
         b) Plan modification
   B) Too-Difficult-Goal
      Meta-goals initiated:
      1. Form-Alliance (Look for an ally with concordant goals)
      2. Resolve-Need
         Associated meta-plans:
         a) Goal substitution
         b) Plan modification

In addition to these meta-themes, the following theme is prominently involved in meta-planning, although it does not produce meta-goals per se:

Theme — Don't Violate Desirable States
Situations to detect:

1. Danger
   Goals initiated:
   A) Preserve-Endangered-State

This is strictly a preservation goal, although its presence often invokes meta-planning actions.

Associated meta-plans:

1. Prevent-Endangering-Event
2. Change-Circumstances (Modify circumstances so that the plan will not have anticipated negative effect)

2. Maintenance Time

Goals initiated:

A) Perform-Maintenance

2.3 Example

The following example is a sketch of how meta-goals are used in the planning process. Suppose a planner were given the task of fetching a newspaper from outside, and it's raining. We will assume that the planner will first consider the "normal" plan for a task if one is known. The normal plan for getting the newspaper is walking outside and carrying it back in, which in this case would cause the planner to get its clothes wet. This situation would cause the "Don't Violate Desirable States" theme to create the goal, that being the Preserve-Endangered-State (Clothes be dry). For the time being, we will ignore the problem of just exactly how the planner finds the themes relevant to a given situation, thereby creating an appropriate goal.

Since this preservation goal came into existence as the result of some intended action by the planner itself, a goal conflict must exist between this goal and the goal from which the other action originated. Since a goal conflict threatens the fulfillment of a goal, the meta-theme "Achieve As Many Goals As Possible" causes the meta-goal Resolve-Goal-Conflict (GI,PI) to come into existence, where GI is the goal of having the newspaper and PI the goal of preserving the dryness of the planner's clothing. The state of the planning at this point is diagrammed in the figure below:

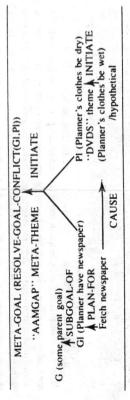

META-GOAL (RESOLVE-GOAL-CONFLICT(GI,PI))

"AAMGAP" META-THEME INITIATE

PI (Planner's clothes be dry)

"DVDS" theme INITIATE (Planner's clothes be wet) /hypothetical

G (some parent goal) SUBGOAL-OF GI (Planner have newspaper) PLAN-FOR Fetch newspaper CAUSE

Now a plan for this meta-goal is sought. Since the meta-goal is treated just like an ordinary goal by the planner, normal plans for resolving the conflict are sought first. That is, we apply the Use-Normal-Plan meta-plan, which looks for a plan specifically designed to resolve these particular kind of goal conflicts. One specific stored plan for this situation is to wear a raincoat while performing the plan for goal GI. Suppose the planner proposed this plan, which spawns the sub-goal of acquiring a raincoat. If a raincoat were readily available, then the plan for resolving the goal conflict succeeds and the plan for GI can be executed.

On the other hand, the subgoal of obtaining a raincoat might spawn a plan that involves going outside. As this is a circular subgoal, the "Avoid Impossible Goals" initiates a Resolve-Circular-Goals (GI,SI) meta-goal, where SI is the subgoal just created that is identical to GI. A meta-plan applicable here is Modify-Plan, which tries to choose another plan that does not spawn subgoal SI. Suppose that this fails, and no other canned plan for achieving the Resolve-Goal-Conflict (GI,PI) can be found. Since this is treated just like any ordinary goal, the planner might try to create a more novel plan here. The more novel plans for goal conflict resolution are Try-Alternative-Plan and Change-Circumstances. For example, the planner might try the alternative plan of getting his dog to fetch the paper, as this plan does not involve the planner getting wet. Or the planner might try to alter the circumstances that enable an intended action to have its undesirable effect. For example, the planner might try interposing some object in between himself and the rain, like an old newspaper, or simply wait for the rain to stop. Both waiting and actively changing a circumstance are general strategies applied to this particular situation.

Suppose that such plans are not generated or are rejected for other reasons. Then, the planner has failed to fulfill its Resolve-Goal-Conflict goal. The existence of an unresolvable goal conflict indicates that some goal is about to fail, and the "Maximize the Value of the Goals Achieved" meta-theme activates the Achieve-the-Most-Valuable-Scenario (GI, PI) meta-goal. The plan for this goal is Simulate-and-Select. That is, invoke the subgoal Create-Alternative-Scenario (GI,PI), evaluate each one, and then abandon the goals deemed least important. The situation at this point is as follows:

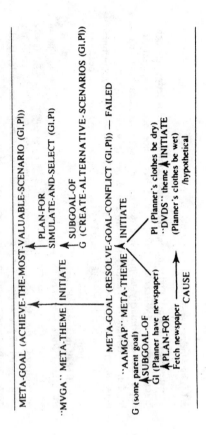

META-GOAL (ACHIEVE-THE-MOST-VALUABLE-SCENARIO (GI,PI))

PLAN-FOR

"MVGA" META-THEME INITIATE SIMULATE-AND-SELECT (GI,PI)

SUBGOAL-OF G (CREATE-ALTERNATIVE-SCENARIOS (GI,PI))

META-GOAL (RESOLVE-GOAL-CONFLICT (GI,PI)) — FAILED

"AAMGAP" META-THEME INITIATE

PI (Planner's clothes be dry)

"DVDS" theme INITIATE (Planner's clothes be wet) /hypothetical

G (some parent goal) SUBGOAL-OF GI (Planner have newspaper) PLAN-FOR Fetch newspaper CAUSE

In this case, Create-Alternative-Scenarios has a relatively straightforward task, as there are only two scenarios: Abandoning G1, or abandoning P1. Actually, Create-Alternative-Scenarios is more complex, as it also has the possibility of proposing "partial goal achievement" scenarios. For example, it might suggest only partially achieving P1. That is, achieving "Keep clothes as dry as possible", is a case in which a suitable plan might be to *run* out to get the paper. While the creation of these scenarios is somewhat more complex, we assume that they are evaluated in the manner we now describe for simpler scenarios. Now the planner has to make a judgment on the relative value of the goals involved. To make this evaluation, we assume that the planner is able to attach some sort of a value on each of its goals, say, for example, a value between 0 (don't care) and 10 (life or death). The value of each scenario is defined as the sum of the value of its individual goals. If "not getting my best suit wet" is a 5 and "having the paper" a 3, the two scenarios have a relative value of 5 and 3, so P1 is selected over G1. In this case, the planner stays inside and does without his paper.

Scenarios involving goal modification are handled the same way. For example, if getting one's clothes just a trifle wet is a 2, then that scenario is valued as a 7 (since one ends up with the paper as well), and would be chosen over either of the two more polarized versions. It is important to stress that true goal abandonment is a strategy of last resort. A planner is much more likely to try to re-plan away the problem, or to use partial goal achievement as a strategy. For example, a planner is much more likely to listen to the news on the radio, wait for the rain to stop, try to get someone else to bring in the paper, change to less valuable clothing, use something instead of a raincoat, etc., instead of abandoning his goal altogether.

In the example above, meta-planning allows the problems faced by the planner to be formulated as goals and then given to the planner to solve in a general fashion. Similarly, suppose we were trying to understand a story about someone who wanted to bring in the paper in the rain. After reading this much, a reader could infer that that person has the preservation goal of not getting his clothing wet. If the reader then learns that he decided not to go out, for example, the reader can infer the following explanation for this behavior: The person must have had a failed Resolve-Goal-Conflict between the two goals, and was now trying to fulfill the Achieve-the-Most-Valuable-Scenario meta-goal. Since the planner chose to stay dry and abandoned getting the paper, the former must have been the goal the planner valued most. While the processing is quite different than in the planning example above, the same declarative meta-knowledge is used in both cases.

3.0 THE STRUCTURE OF A PLANNER AND AN UNDERSTANDER BASED ON META-PLANNING

The example above illustrates the use of meta-planning in both planning and understanding. In this section, a more detailed description of my view of these processes is given.

3.1 The Understander

The design of a story understander that uses intentional knowledge has been given elsewhere (Wilensky, 1978). PAM has since been completely re-implemented, primarily to give it a declarative associative data base and to handle some higher-level story structures described in Wilensky (1980). A detailed description of this implementation will appear in a forthcoming technical report. Thus only the changes implied by the meta-planning approach need to be discussed here.

Recall that one of the understander's tasks is to interpret the actions of a character in a text as part of some reasonable plan. This involves inferring that an action is part of a plan for some goal, inferring that a character has a goal, and accounting for the effects of goal interactions. These processes are driven by the need to find an explanation for a character's behavior. Thus, if an understander learns that someone picked up a phone book, it might hypothesize that the person was going to use it to find someone's phone number to call that person up and to have a conversation, etc.

To make these inferences, the understander needs to know when goals arise. For example, if an understander learned that John wanted to eat, it might infer that he was hungry. If it learned he wanted to marry Mary, it might infer that he loved her or was after her money. In general, the understander must be able to detect situations that give rise to goals in order to interpret a character's behavior.

Given that the understander has the ability to hypothesize a character's goals, the introduction of meta-planning knowledge gives a rather straightforward way of dealing with more complicated goal interactions. The problem here is to interpret a character's behavior when faced with a number of interacting goals at the same time. For example, if we were told that John wanted to go out with his secretary but was afraid his wife would find out, we could explain his calling to tell her he had to work late that night as a way of getting around this conflict. As was mentioned above, this previously required a separate process to monitor goal interactions and attempts at dealing with these effects.

Using meta-planning, however, we simply supply the understander with the description of the situations in which meta-themes cause meta-goals to arise, and with knowledge about the meta-plans associated with each meta-goal. If a goal conflict arises in a story, the understander will spot it and infer that the character has the meta-goal of resolving it just as it will infer that a character has the goal of eating if it learns that that character is hungry. For example, going out with one's secretary gives rise to the preservation goal of preventing one's spouse from knowing. The meta-theme "Achieve As Many Goals As Possible" recognizes this situation as one leading to the Resolve-Goal-Conflict meta-goal. Thus, this goal can be inferred, and subsequent actions interpreted as plans to fulfill it. In this case, telling one's wife that he has to work late might be interpreted as a normal plan for this goal.

3. The Executor

The executor simply carries out the plan steps as proposed by the plan generator. It is responsible for the detection of errors, although not with their correction. In general, this might entail establishing a new goal and creating a plan to set things right.

The only part that is really new here is the goal detector. As we mentioned above, most planners do not worry about where their goals come from. High-level goals are generally handed to the planner in the form of a problem to be solved. However, it is desirable for a robot problem solver to worry about goal detection for a number of reasons:

1. For the problem solver to be autonomous, it will need to know when it should go into action. For example, before it solves the monkeys and bananas problem, the robot would need to recognize that it was hungry and that it should try to feed itself. If it were given a set of tasks that included "keep the nuclear reactor from melting down", it would need to know that it should have the goal of shutting the reactor down when the dial on the control panel indicates a cooling failure.

2. An autonomous planner would also need to deal with its own preservation. It would therefore need to react to changes in its environment. For example, it would need to know it should have the goal of getting out of the way of an avalanche. It should also be capable of knowing when it needs maintenance or when it should replenish its power supply. Moreover, a real planner may have to deal with adversity. For example, a robot operating a nuclear power plant might need to fend off a terrorist attempting to sabotage its activities. Other planners may interfere with its goals in a number of ways. The point is that the robot planner trying to solve the monkeys and bananas problem may have to contend with another robot also trying to get the bananas for itself.

3. Even a non-autonomous planner would need to know when it should help. For example, a system designed for man-machine interaction would need to know when it should take over control from its human operator and when it should relinquish it. It would need to know which aspects of the problem being worked on were its responsibility so that it could assist the human in the appropriate situations without the human explicitly engaging it.

4. The planner needs to know about internally generated goals. For example, virtually all problem solvers detect that they have a subgoal. In addition, they must also know when they should be trying to resolve a goal conflict, when they should try to combine their own plans to produce a more efficient one, and when they should evaluate the relative importance of their goals. For example, the robot in charge of the nuclear reactor might have an unresolvable goal conflict between "output as much electricity as possible", "keep the floors clean" and "prevent a meltdown". It must therefore determine which of these is the most important to achieve.

The goal detector operates through the use of a mechanism called the *Noticer*. The Noticer is a general facility in charge of recognizing that something has occurred that is of interest to some part of the system. The Noticer monitors changes in the external environment and in the internal states of the system. When it detects the presence of something that it was previously instructed to

---

Again, the advantage of the meta-planning approach is that nothing special is done for these more complicated situations other than to supply the understander with meta-knowledge in the form of themes, goals and plans. Recognizing a complicated situation and inferring what a character might do is reduced to the problem of knowing that a theme is active and what goals it may give rise to. Since a mechanism that does this is needed to find ordinary explanations, no additional mechanisms are warranted here.

Note that this is true even for some basic control-related issues. For example, one problem that often arises in story understanding is whether to make a "backwards" or a "forwards" inference. For example, an understander often needs to infer that John loves Mary upon learning that he wants to marry her. Sometimes, it needs to hypothesize that he wants to marry her upon learning that he loves her. In one case, a goal is hypothesized from a theme; in the other, a theme is inferred from the presence of a goal. In general, it is difficult to know which strategy to employ for any given situation. Exactly what will happen is often a function of the number of different things that can be predicted from a known fact, the specificity of the knowledge available to the system, etc.

The same exact situation arises in the use of meta-planning for the detection of goal conflicts and other goal interactions. Sometimes the presence of a goal conflict might only be inferable from the action a character takes to resolve it. It might also be predictable from the presence of two goals. The point here is that we need not commit ourselves to a particular control strategy for these cases, any more than we did for making simpler inferences. Since detecting goal interactions is now done in terms of higher-level meta-goals, the same criteria that influence the inference process for simpler cases is applicable here.

3.2 The Planner

The design of a planner based on meta-planning is now given. This planner is composed of the following major components.

1. The Goal Detector

This mechanism is responsible for determining that the planner has a goal. The goal detector has access to the planner's likes and dislikes, to the state of the world and any changes that may befall it, and to the planner's own internal planning structures and other internal states. The goal detector may therefore establish a new goal because of some change in the environment because such a goal is instrumental to another goal, or in resolving a problem in a planning structure it is creating.

2. The Plan Generator

The plan generator proposes plans for the goals already detected. It may dredge up stereotyped solutions, it may edit previously known plans to fit the current situation, or it may create fairly novel solutions. The plans may be applicable to a single goal, or to several of the goals present at once. The plan generator is also responsible for expanding high-level plans into their primitive components to allow execution.

monitor, it reports this occurrence to the source that originally told it to look for that thing.

The Noticer can be thought of as a collection of IF-ADDED demons whose only action is to report some occurrence to some other mechanism. In addition, demons usually monitor only insertions into the data base of a system, while the Noticer may have to monitor external changes, or the state of a systems process as well.

Goals are detected by having themes and meta-themes asserted into the Noticer with orders to report to the goal detector. When an event matching the desired specifications occurs, the goal detector can then assert the existence of some particular goal. For example, suppose the planner knew that a person is aware of some undesirable circumstance occurring and has the goal of preventing that circumstance from happening. This knowledge could be represented as follows:

```
(INITIATE
  (AND
    (AWARE ?ACTOR ?X/HYPOTHETICAL)
    (UNDESIRABLE ?X ?ACTOR))
  (GOAL ?ACTOR (PREVENT ?X)))
```

That is, the existence of conditions described in the first clause causes the condition described in the second to come about. As usual, question marks indicate variables. The slash notation is used to express a qualification and it may be thought of as a shorthand for an additional ISA conjunct. McDermott (1978) and others have pointed out that the semantics of terms like "hypothetical" are highly problematic. Here I use it simply to mean that the planner has reasoned that some circumstance will occur in the future. Similarly, the predicate "undesirable" should simply be read as "positive". This is a primitive evaluative judgment.

The first argument in this predication would be handed to the Noticer. If it were the case that "(UNDESIRABLE (DEAD ?ACTOR) ?ACTOR)" were in the planner's data base (i.e., that the planner knew that being dead was considered undesirable for oneself), and the planner later learned that (DEAD *EGO*) were imminent, the Noticer would notice that a condition it was told to watch for had been matched, and would report this occurrence back to the goal detector. The goal detector then uses the formula this condition originated from to infer the goal ("PREVENT (DEAD *EGO*)),;;, or prevent itself from dying.

Note that this formulation would cause the Noticer and goal detector to infer that someone else would have the goal of preventing their own death if that person became aware of some danger. This is a valid inference, but of course, not a goal of the planner making it. There are several ways of handling this. One is to restrict the predications by replacing the appropriate references to ?ACTOR

with *EGO* so that the Noticer doesn't "false alarm" to other people's goals. Another solution is to let the system make these inferences, and then have the goal detector examine them to see if it has deduced one of its own goals. The second solution has the advantage that inferring the goals of other planners is something that usually needs to be done anyway for other purposes, and allows the same piece of knowledge to be used for both cases. Probably a mixture of both strategies would be valid, as it is plausible that people possess some knowledge that is used to infer one's own goals but not the goals of others.

When a new goal is detected, it is moved to the front of the "goal queue". This is the storage structure for currently active goals. If it was inappropriate to put this goal here, say, because some other goal is clearly more important or urgent, this will cause a meta-theme to create a re-scheduling meta-goal. This will be first on the queue, with an urgency at least as high as that of any of the goals it is to reschedule. It will therefore be executed immediately, and demote the unimportant goal.

As was just indicated, the goal at the front of the queue is worked on first. That is, it is given to the planner, which tries to reduce that goal to a "task network" of plans and subgoals that eventually bottoms out in a set of primitively executable actions. Our planner consists of three components:

1. The Prosper, that suggests plausible plans to try
2. The Projector, which tests plans by trying to compute what it would be like to execute them
3. The Revisor, which can edit and remove certain parts of a task network upon

The Proposer begins by suggesting the most specific plan it knows of that is applicable to the goal. If this plan is rejected or fails the Proposer will propose successively more general and "creative" solutions. We will have little to say about this process here, as we place most of our emphasis on dealing with the interactions between fairly standard plans rather than upon the creation of strikingly original ones.

Once the Proposer has suggested a plan, the Projector starts computing what will happen to the world as the plan is executed. The difficult problems in conducting a simulation involves reasoning about "possible world" type situations which are not amenable to standard temporal logic (McCarthy & Hayes, 1969). However, we previously finessed this issue by defining hypothetical states in terms of what the planner thinks of in the course of plan construction. In other words, our solution is to let the system assert the changes that would be made into a hypothetical data base, in the meantime letting the goal detector have access to these states. Thus if the plan being simulated would result in the planner dying, say, this would constitute a hypothetical undesirable state, which might trigger further goals, etc.

As the Projector hypothetically carries out the plan, and other goals and planner is trying to fulfill? It is not properly a subgoal, as none of these goals require the knowledge requested: Flying on a plane does not require one to know how much it costs—only that one has enough money. So what is the relation of this task to the original problem?

If the planning process itself is highly-taskified, this problem is elegantly resolved. Projection is itself a task, and part of this task requires knowing facts such as the one mentioned above. Thus finding out this answer is properly a subgoal of the meta-task of conducting the simulation, and can be handled by the standard planner goal-subgoal mechanisms.*

*I would like to thank James Allen for bringing this problem to my attention.

The question still remains as to how far one should go in the direction of taskification. Such formulations are elegant but they may be costly. An ultimately taskified system reduces many problems to the problem of juggling dozens of tiny tasks at any given time. Whether this reduction is fortuitous or not remains to be seen.

4.0 SOME DETAILS OF META-GOALS AND META-PLANS

In this section some of the more important meta-themes, goals and plans are described in somewhat more detail. Many of these items deal with interactions between goals. In particular, the following goal relationships seem to play a significant role:

1. Goal Conflict—An adverse interaction between the goals of a planner.
2. Goal Competition—An adverse interaction between the goals of different planners.
3. Goal Overlap—A positive interaction between the goals of a planner.
4. Goal Concord—A positive interaction between the goals of different planners.
5. Goal Subsumption—Establishing a state that makes it easier to fulfill a recurring goal.

Most of these relationships have been described in Wilensky (1978). The only new one is goal overlap. This relationship is discussed in detail in the following section.

4.1 The Value and Cost of Goals and Meta-Goals

In the discussion of meta-goals that follows, it is necessary to refer to the cost of achieving a goal and the value of that goal to the planner. These issues arise, for example, in trying to decide which of two conflicting goals should be pursued, or whether a plan for a goal is worth the resources it consumes. The theory of planning presented here does not specify values for particular goals, or a particular "goal calculus" of goal value manipulation. However, it does require that the value of a goal and the cost of a plan have the following properties:

meta-goals are detected by the goal detector, the original plan may have to be modified. This is done by explicit calls to the Revisor, which knows the plan structure and can make edits or deletions upon request. The modified plan structure is simulated again until it is either found satisfactory or the entire plan is given up and a new one suggested by the Proposer.

Actually, the function of the Projector is somewhat more pervasive than has so far been described. The Projector must be capable of projecting current events into future possibilities based both on the intentions of the planner and on its analysis of those events themselves. For example, if the planner sees a boulder rolling down the mountain, it is the job of the Projector to infer the future path that the boulder will traverse. If the projected path crosses that of the planner, for example, a preservation goal should be detected. Thus the Projector is a quite powerful and general device that is used to make hypothetical projections.

The Projector is probably influenced by the level of the representation used in a plan. For example, when a plan is first conceived, it is formulated at a relatively high level of abstraction, but by the time it is executed, the representation should be much more detailed. Presumably, simulation will go on all levels. This would explain why details can be overlooked by an initial simulation, but are caught easily right before execution time. Just before the execution of a task, its most detailed structure must become manifest, and the simulation that goes on at that point show errors in detail that are not apparent at a grosser level.

For example, a plan to get one's mail might specify leaving one's office, but probably not opening one's door. As one executes each piece of this plan, the need to specify the detailed level arises. The simulation might now include turning the doorknob, etc. If a precondition for such a plan were not true, this would only be discovered during a simulation when such details become explicit in the plan's representation.

3.2.1 How Far Taskification? Meta-planning is a move in the direction of ultimate "taskification". The decisions of the planner, for example, are themselves formulated as tasks to be worked on. The planner itself is really just the shell of a program, as almost all of the system's knowledge about planning is contained in meta-plans rather than in the planner per se.

It seems as if it may be useful to take this notion of taskification even further. For example, the formulation just given views simulation as an activity of the planner itself. A reasonable alternative to this is for simulations to be spun off as subtasks of the planning process. Aside from the aesthetic advantages of making simulation a subtask, it may resolve some other interesting issues.

For example, suppose a planner needs to know some fact in order to decide what plan it should choose. It might want to know, for example, the price of a plane ticket to a given location. A reasonable strategy is to set up a goal of finding out this fact. But what is the relation of this goal to the other goal the

1. All goals and costs are in principle comparable, although the result of the comparison need not be definitive. That is, the planner may have to judge whether slighting a friend is worth a certain amount of money, or whether two apples is worth three oranges. One way to make such comparisons is to assign to every goal a point or a range on a numerical scale. Goals with overlapping ranges would constitute difficult decisions, whereas goals with disjoint ranges should constitute clear preferences.

2. The cost of using a resource is equivalent to the value of the preservation goal of keeping that resource. Thus, what we say about evaluating costs below will generally apply to evaluating goals, and vice versa, as a cost is just a negative value.

3. The value of a set of goals is computable from the values of its members. For example, linear summation seems to work for independent goals. That is, the value of two goals is the sum of their values, and the value of a goal given a plan with a certain cost is that value minus the cost. By independent, I mean that the goals cannot be merged into a single bigger goal, although they may interact with each other. For example, the values of having a car and eating an ice cream cone is the sum of the value of each goal. But the value of eating five ice cream cones may be somewhat less than five times the value of eating one.

Resulting values can be compared as well. That is, the degree to which one set of goals is better than another is the difference between the sums of the values of the two sets. Of course, we do not need to commit ourselves to a particular theory of how to combine the values of goals here. We need only assume that it is possible to do so.

4. The value of high-level goals can be evaluated separately and independent of context. We must assume that we can assign a value to a goal (or more precisely, to the state the goal is aimed at bringing about) just by considering that goal. This is done without regard to any costs incurred by a plan for the goal or to any added benefits one gets from executing such a plan. We can then assess the net value of a task network by adding together all the benefits it brings about and subtracting all its costs.

Of course, assigning a value to a goal at times will be difficult, and sometimes only a vague indication of value is possible. For example, the value people usually attach to human life is "very high". However, this assessment is not much help in comparing the value with other goals in the high value range. Difficulties of assigning values is one of the factors that creates difficulty for goal comparison.

5. On the other hand, the value of a subgoal is computable from the value of the goals to which it is instrumental. In general, the value is equivalent to the sum of the values of the dependent goals. These values are not inherent, of course, as the value of a subgoal may change if a plan involving that goal is altered.

6. The value of a meta-goal is strictly inherited from the values of the goals it refers to. For example, the meta-goal Resolve-Goal-Conflict is worth the value of the goals that would be abandoned if the conflict were not resolved.

One consequence of these assumptions is that meta-goals can be compared with ordinary goals for planning purposes. If the meta-goal Resolve-Goal-Conflict ends up conflicting with some other goal, then another Resolve-Goal-Conflict meta-goal may be created whose value is the minimum of the value of the first Resolve-Goal-Conflict meta-goal and the other goal.

This situation is actually fairly common and works out rather nicely. For example, time-based goal conflicts can often be resolved by giving up a "background goal" like eating or sleeping. However, this leads to a second conflict between resolving the first conflict and satisfying hunger or tiredness. If this conflict cannot be resolved, the planner may have to either abandon resolving its first goal conflict, or abandon a background goal. He makes this decision simply by comparing the value of the first Resolve-Goal-Conflict goal, which is the minimum of the value of its two goals, with the value of the background goal.

It might at first seem like a problem would arise here with scheduling, as by definition, the value of a Resolve-Goal-Conflict goal will usually be less than the value of the most valuable of the conflicting goals. All other things being equal, Resolve-Goal-Conflict goals would receive less attention than the more important goal in the conflict, which would subsequently be attempted before the conflict were resolved. However, a number of things prevent this from happening. In general, "Achieve As Many Goals As Possible" motivates the scheduling of goals, so conflict resolution goals will initially get precedence over those goals whose conflicts they are trying to resolve. Only when it appears that some goal is failing will "Maximize the Value of the Goals Achieved" be useful. In other words, Resolve-Conflict goals are treated like subgoals, in that they are worked on before their parent goals are looked at again.

4.2 Meta-goal Details

4.2.1 Combine-Plans.
Most of the meta-knowledge concerning goal overlap falls under the "Don't Waste Resources" meta-theme. The meta-goal given rise to here is Combine-Plans, which is satisfied when part of the task networks for the overlapping goals come to be joined together. Several plans for doing this were referred to in the preceding section, including Schedule Common Subgoals First, Plan Integration, and Plan Piggybacking. The details of goal overlap are discussed in the next section.

4.2.2 Choose-Least-Costly-Scenario.
This meta-goal arises in situations involving multiple planning options under the meta-theme of "Don't Waste Resources". Given a set of plans for a goal, this meta-goal is achieved when the scenario with the cheapest cost is computed. The Simulate-and-Select meta-plan is useful here. This works by first computing a number of plausible scenarios, and then calling the Projector to determine the state of the world that would exist for each one. The cost of each scenario can then be measured from the values of the resources consumed and the states that exist before and after the plan is executed. The least costly scenario can then be selected. In the case of Choose-Least-Costly-Scenario, the scenarios are generated simply by considering alternative plans.

4.2.5 Resolve-Goal-Conflict.

Resolve-Goal-Conflict is invoked by the "Achieve As Many Goals As Possible" meta-theme, and occurs whenever a goal conflict is present. Note that by goal conflict, we mean to include situations in which goals are in conflict through the plans chosen for them, as well as those cases in which the goals themselves are inimicable. I distinguish between three cases of goal conflict: Those based on a shortage of resources, those based on mutually exclusive states, and those based on invoking a preservation goal in the course of planning for another goal.

Since there are different causes of goal conflict, different plans are applicable in different situations. In fact, one general strategy for Resolve-Goal-Conflict is called Use-Normal-Plan, and consists of finding a canned plan that is specific to conflict between a particular pair of goals. For example, as was mentioned above, a canned plan for going outside in the rain and not getting one's clothes wet is to wear a raincoat. A standard plan for leaving one's home but not allowing anyone to enter in one's absence is to lock the door. The number of such plans is quite large, and, in fact, seems to account for a substantial portion of one's total planning knowledge.

On a more general level, there are two courses of action available if no normal plan can be found:

1. Try-Alternate-Plan is a strategy to avoid a goal conflict by changing the plans that originally lead to it. This is a generalized form of Use-Normal-Plan, and both may be considered parts of a more encompassing Re-plan meta-plan. Of course, either strategy may only be used if it is the plans rather than the goal states themselves that are to blame.

   Try-Alternate-Plan may be used in two ways: intelligently and exhaustively. In the intelligent use of this meta-plan, the Make-Attribution sub-plan is used to propose problems with the existing set of plans. Then a new plan for one of the goals will be sought that does not contain the objectionable condition. If this fails, then random combinations of plans may be tried until a workable combination is found. The advantage of intelligent use of Try-Alternative-Plan is that fewer combinations are likely to be tested. Of course, the price paid for this is to have a rather sophisticated Make-Attribution sub-plan, and a memory mechanism capable of retrieving plans very selectively. The cost is probably not as great as it may seem, as we need to have both these mechanisms for many other purposes anyway.

2. The most general conflict resolution strategy is the Change-Circumstance meta-plan. The idea is to use Make-Attribution to propose what circumstances, other than one's own plans, are causing the goals to conflict, and to set up a goal of changing those circumstances, so that a problem is not encountered in executing the original set of plans. For example, in the case of going out into the rain, interposing an object between the rain and oneself will change the circumstances so that being in the rain no longer causes one's clothing to get wet. One particular variant here is *waiting*, in which case the planner does no action in hopes that the circumstances will change themselves.

4.2.3 Choose-Most-Valuable-Scenario.

The Choose-Most-Valuable-Scenario is a similar meta-goal that arises when the "Maximize the Value of the Goals Achieved" meta-theme is activated by the existence of an unresolvable goal conflict. Given a set of goals in unresolvable conflict, the meta-goal is to choose the subset of them to work on which maximizes the gain to the planner. The Simulate-and-Select meta-plan is applicable here as well. In this case, the plan can suggest various goals to abandon, and measures the value of the remaining goals.

In addition, Simulate-and-Select can attempt to partially fulfill goals as a way of generating plausible scenarios. To do this, this meta-plan suggests that one or more of the goals involved be achieved only to the greatest degree possible. The value of these partial goal fulfillment scenarios are compared along with the ordinary abandonment scenarios to obtain a reasonable choice of action.

As was noted above, partial goal fulfillment seems to be the case rather than the exception. Giving up a goal altogether is unusual. For example, if there is a conflict between one's career and one's personal life, the general solution is to sacrifice the degree to which one is achieved in order to partially fulfill the other, rather than to give one up entirely.

An alternative way of dealing with partial goal fulfillment is to say that the semantics of achieving a goal is really to achieve it to a degree. The difference between this formulation and the one presented so far is that it suggests that plans that partially fulfill a goal would be proposed right along with plans for complete fulfillment. In the current formulation, these are only suggested by the planner after other plans fail. For example, in this formulation, the goal of not getting wet would be interpreted as getting as little wet as possible, whereas in the formulation given above, a modified goal has to be created to allow this possibility. In addition, this alternative formulation would suggest that in general, goals are only partially rather than totally fulfilled, which is probably the case.

The problem with this formulation is that it makes it difficult to specify goals that must be achieved exactly. For example, if it is raining deadly acid rain whose slightest touch is death, then partially fulfilling "don't get wet" just won't do. Thus, the correct solution seems to be to consider partial fulfillment as a separate strategy, rather than fudge the semantics of goal fulfillment in general.

4.2.4 Establish-Subsumption-State.

This goal arises when the planner has a recurring goal that is either not subsumed, or whose current subsumption state is inadequate for some reason. For example, if John finds himself needing some tool repeatedly he might decide to buy one so that achieving this goal will be easier next time the need arises. Establishing a subsumption state first requires determining what a subsumption state is for the recurring goal involved, and then embarking on a plan to achieve this state. This latter plan is of course totally dependent on the nature of the subsumption state one must achieve.

several goals simultaneously is easier than the combined fulfillment of each goal individually. For example, consider the following stories:

(4) John needed some wood finisher. While he was at the hardware store, he picked up some sandpaper.

(5) John wanted to get rid of his old car. Then he heard that Bill was in the market for a '57 Chevy, and would pay considerably more than the car was worth.

(6) John thought he could use some exercise. He also felt like he needed some fresh air, so he decided to go jogging in the park.

In each of these stories, a character has two goals that stand in a favorable relationship to one another. In story (4), John's two goals are to get some wood finisher and to get some sandpaper. Both goals are amenable to the same plan, namely, buying the items. This plan requires the planner to be at a place that sells the desired item. Since this precondition is the same in both cases, the planner can fulfill the precondition once and then execute both plans simultaneously.

Story (5) also refers to two goals. Getting rid of an old car and wanting to possess money. The second goal must be inferred by the reader. Once it has been inferred, a single plan can be seen to have the effect of fulfilling both of John's goals. Likewise, in story (6), John's goals of getting some exercise and of getting some fresh air are both addressed at no additional cost to one another by virtue of a common plan.

The goals in each of the stories above have the following property: It is easier to fulfill the goals when they are considered together than when each goal is attended to independently from the other. Thus in story (4), pursuing both goals independently may lead to two trips to the hardware store, but together, only one trip is required. John might only get rid of his vehicle and not profit from it if he refrains from considering his goal of having money at the same time in story (5). In story (6), John may have to make two trips, and certainly spend more time, if he doesn't realize that a single plan is applicable to both his goals.

A situation in which the pursuit of several goals simultaneously is more advantageous than their independent pursuit is called *goal overlap*. In story understanding, it is important to recognize overlapping goals because this situation strongly influences the plans a character will choose. For example, suppose John had the goals mentioned in story (4), but that he made two trips to the hardware store. Since these goals overlap so as to eliminate the need for two separate trips, a reader would need to infer an explanation for John's behavior. For example, the reader might conjecture that John is simple minded, or that he isn't getting along with his wife and is looking for excuses to get out of the house, that he is procrastinating because he is intimidated by the task he has to perform, or that he had a lapse of memory. Ignoring the goal overlap gives evidence to these theories, and together with other indications may cause the reader to infer one of them.

Since goal overlap influences the process of plan selection, a planning

Change-Circumstances generally requires a detailed knowledge of the type of goal conflict at hand. For example, if the conflict is based on a scarcity of resources, then a Change-Circumstance should propose obtaining more of the resource in order to resolve the conflict. How to obtain more of a resource is very much a function of the particular resources involved. For example, if the resource is time, then one may try to remove a deadline in order to obtain more time. If the scarce resource is money, a different set of plans is applicable.

4.2.6 Resolve-Circularity. Resolve-Circularity means dealing with a subgoal that is identical to some ancestral goal. This meta-goal originates from the "Avoid Impossible Goals" meta-theme, as circular subgoals are ordinarily either unachievable, or the plan for the subgoal should be directly applicable to the parent goal. The meta-plans that are applicable here are goal modification and plan modification. With either change, try a new plan that does not involve the circular subgoal, or modify the goal so that it is no longer identical to a goal for which it is instrumental.

The latter plan is generally useful when the circular subgoals stem from the normal plans for their respective goals. For example, suppose one's goal were to be a flasher, for which the normal plan involves having a raincoat. Suppose further that the normal plan doesn't own one, and that it's raining outside. If the normal plan proposed involves having a raincoat, it need not be abandoned altogether because of the circularity. Rather, it can be modified to "have umbrella," or "have old newspaper," neither of which would be appropriate for the superior goal. The point here is that the two goals serve quite different functions. It may therefore be possible to satisfy one by a modification that is not applicable to the other.

4.2.7 Resolve-Need. Resolve-Need occurs when a goal that is too difficult arises. It is almost the same situation as Resolve-Circularity, as the only meta-plans applicable are plan and goal modification. Here, their function is to ascertain why the goal is needed, and if possible, to come up with a modified plan that does not involve it or with a modified goal that does not cause the same problem.

4.2.8 Form-Alliance. Another tactic that can be tried if a goal is deemed too difficult is to try to couple up with another planner and use the combined resources to execute a plan that neither could effectively do alone. The plans applicable here are all the ways of encouraging someone to join in an alliance.

5.0 GOAL OVERLAP

In this section, we discuss the goal relationship of goal overlap in some detail. Goal overlap refers to those internal goal interactions in which the fulfillment of mechanism must be able to detect overlapping goals in order to plan effectively in multigoal situations. For example, we would be unwilling to accept a plan of going to a store twice when only one trip is necessary, or of giving away an unwanted item when it could be sold, or of wasting time performing two activities when only one is required. This would violate the "Don't Waste Resources" meta-theme. A powerful planning mechanism must be able to detect overlapping goals when they are present, and of taking this information into account in choosing a plan of action.

5.1 Kinds of Goal Overlap

Goal overlap may be categorized further into a number of cases. Each case is characterized by a different kind of structural relationship between the goals or their plans, and is associated with its own way of reducing the total expenditure of resources and effort. First, there is a primary division into two main classes, which reflect whether the overlap is due to the nature of the goals themselves or to the plans one might use to achieve these goals.

Kinds of Goal Overlap
1. Mutual Inclusion—The goals overlap by virtue of inherent relationships between the states constituting their realization.
2. Piggybacking—The goals themselves have no inherent overlap, but some plan is applicable to more than one goal at once.

Each category is now further refined:

5.2 Mutual Inclusion

Mutual inclusion means that a planner has the same goal for more than one reason. Actually, the goals need not be literally identical, but may be in one of a number of relationships. Consider the following examples:

(7) John thought killing animals was morally wrong. He also thought that eating vegetables made one healthy.
(8) John had to stay home because he expected a visitor. He also had to stay in his study because he was trying to write a paper.

These examples contain two different kinds of goal relatedness, which are identity and entailment. For example, in story (7), John has the goal of eating vegetables for two independent reasons. Thus the identical goal arises twice independently, producing a goal overlap situation. Alternatively, one goal may be a specific instance of a more general goal. Story (8) is an instance of this case, as being in one's study is a special case of being in one's home via logical entailment.

To determine if two goals are identical, they merely need to be matched against one another. However, determining if one goal state implies the other requires some specific knowledge. For example, the fact that ''A is inside B implies that A is inside C if B is part of C'' is needed to determine the relatedness of the goals in (8) above. Obviously, logical entailments could get arbitrarily complex. However, the everyday situations dealt with here seem to require only the straightforward application of heuristics such as the one just mentioned.

Each type of relatedness also has its own particular consequences for a planner or understander:

1. Identity—If the goals are in fact identical, then one simply follows a plan for the goal.
2. Entailment—If one goal is implied by the other, then the implying goal is pursued. That is, if John needs to stay home and stay in his study, he should pursue the goal of staying in his study.

These heuristics are meant to be useful both to a story understander to interpret the behavior of a character, and to a planner to determine its own behavior. For example, an understander that inferred the presence of mutually inclusive goals would expect the character with such goals to act in accordance with the heuristic above, and if he did not, would try to find some additional factor to explain the character's behavior. Alternatively, a planner who found itself with such goals would use this heuristic to generate reasonably efficient behavior.

The further refinements in the category of mutually inclusive goal overlap come from the way in which the overlapping goals may come about. Recall that a goal may arise either because it is generated by a theme, or because it is instrumental to another goal. Of particular interest is the case in which the overlapping goals are instrumental to other goals. This situation is called *limited subsumption* to emphasize its relation to goal subsumption.

5.2.1 Limited Subsumption. It is often the case that the establishment of a single state is required for a multiplicity of goals. In the case where these goals are recurring instances of a single goal, the situation is termed goal subsumption, and is discussed in length in the last section.

However, it may be that the establishment of a single state is instrumental to a set of goals that is of a definite number, unlike the unlimited recurrences involved in goal subsumption. In these situations, the kind of reasoning that is required of a planner or of a natural language understander is of a very different character. For example, since the goals themselves may be different and require different plans, the situations tend to be more dynamic than goal subsumption, and therefore require somewhat more elaborate reasoning. Thus while this form of goal overlap is behaviorally distinct from subsumption, we stress the structural similarities by terming it *limited subsumption.*

For example, consider the following stories:

(9) John was going to go camping for a week. He went to the supermarket and bought a week's worth of groceries.

(10) Johnny wanted a toy and a candy bar. He asked his father for some money.

(11) John had to go to a conference in Pittsburgh. While he was there, he decided to call up an old girlfriend.

Example (9) is closest to a true case of goal subsumption. Here John anticipates a number of recurring hunger goals to satisfy. Since he is required to buy food, and this requires that he be at a store, he fulfills this common precondition for all of them at once. This example is somewhat different from goal subsumption in that a goal subsumption state usually satisfies an indefinite number of repetitions of the same goal, whereas in limited subsumption the actual state brought about is a function of the number of goals anticipated. In this example, John buys enough groceries to cover one week's worth of hunger goals.

Johnny's goals in example (10) are a yet more limited form of subsumption. Here there are only two overlapping goals, both of which the planner is attempting to achieve by asking his father for money. The reader of this story uses this knowledge to infer that Johnny probably asked his father for enough money for both of his goals.

Story (11) is even further removed from a case of goal subsumption because different plans are involved in each goal, and their interaction seems accidental, not principled. That is, John had to be in Pittsburgh in order to attend a conference, and being in Pittsburgh is also instrumental to seeing someone who lives there. The two goals overlap on this precondition, although the plans of attending a conference and seeing an old girlfriend are themselves not similar. Rather, the overlap appears fortuitous, and possibly even novel to some readers. Limited subsumption occurs, then, in situations in which a character has several (but a definite number of) goals, or the normal plans for these goals require related preconditions. When limited subsumption occurs, a planner's strategy is apt to be the following:

1. Fulfill the common precondition,
2. Execute one of the plans, and
3. Execute the remaining plans before taking some action that undoes the common precondition.

In the case in which one precondition makes it easier to fulfill another, then the same strategy is followed except that one of the plans may be suspended momentarily while another is executed, and continued after the other plan is completed.

These heuristics are actually somewhat more general than has been claimed, since they are applicable to cases in which some, but not all of the

overlapping goal states are instrumental to other goals. That is, a goal stemming directly from a theme may overlap with a goal that is instrumental to another goal. The same heuristics still apply. The general principle embodied here is that a state should be maintained until it is no longer instrumental to any unfulfilled goal.

5.3 Piggybacking

Occasionally, a fortuitous situation arises in which the execution of a single action simultaneously fulfills a number of distinct goals. The usual form this situation takes is that a single action achieves one of the goals directly, and the other by what is normally considered a side effect. For example, consider the following stories:

(12) John had a crack on his wall. He decided to cover it with his favorite poster.

(13) John decided he should be more physically fit. He was also something of a masochist, so he decided to take up jogging.

(14) John wanted to go see the new disaster movie. He also wanted to see Mary, so he called her up and asked her if she'd go see the movie with him.

In story (12), John's goals are to put up a poster that he like to look at, and to hide a crack on his wall. Since a side effect of putting up a poster is to cover the area behind it, one plan can be executed that accomplishes both goals simultaneously. The goals in story (13) are to get in shape, and to experience a little discomfort. Again, both can be accomplished through the execution of a single plan. In story (14), one plan also accomplishes two goals. Here the goals are a little more equal, however. The plan of going on a date is normally associated with several goals, including enjoying someone's company and enjoying some activity. Thus the selection of this plan is a fairly stereotyped procedure for satisfying several goals at once.

Since a plan that simultaneously fulfills a number of goals is generally a normal plan for one of these goals and just happens to fulfill another goal in a particular set of circumstances, we refer to these relationships as *goal piggybacking*. These situations are said to occur when one character has several goals, or the normal plan for one goal has a consequence that fulfills the other goals. We include in this definition those cases in which the normal plan for one goal also happens to be the normal plan for the others. This is the case in example (14) above.

When a goal piggybacking situation arises, it is expected that the planner execute the single plan that fulfills both goals. This may require the planner to execute this plan in a particular manner. For example, in story (12), the plan piggybacks both goals only if the poster is put on the wall over the crack. This requires that the understander or planner realize that the goal of covering the crack is a specific instance of the state that results as a side effect of putting up the poster. This relationship is discussed further in the next section.

Goal piggybacking is related to goal subsumption in that many subsumption states address a number of goals at once. For example, social relationships like marriage usually subsume social, emotional, pragmatic and financial goals simultaneously. Thus establishing such a subsumption state is a plan that piggybacks the goals of subsuming all these needs. A person might marry primarily for love, for example, but also hope to serve secondary goals involving beauty and wealth as well.

5.3.1 Closeness. One special case of piggybacking occurs when the execution of a plan for one goal makes it easier to fulfill another goal, rather than accomplishing that goal outright. For example, consider the following stories:

(15) John needed some instant pudding. He decided to pick some up at the supermarket he passed on the way home from work.
(16) John was shopping for a watch for himself. Then he noticed that the store was having a fabulous one cent sale, so he bought a watch as a present for Mary as well.

Both stories (15) and (16) contain pairs of goals that are related to one another only in how the plans for the goals interact. In story (15) for example, John has the goal of possessing some instant pudding, and the goal of being at home. Being at a supermarket is a precondition for a plan for the first goal, and executing a plan for the second reduces the distance John must travel to achieve this state. Thus, John plans to execute his shopping plan in the middle of his plan of driving home as a way to minimize his effort.

In story (16), John's goals are to have a watch, and to get a gift for Mary. Since the purchase of one watch vastly reduces the price of another, John decides to execute a plan to get Mary's gift at this point, minimizing the cost of that plan.

A state in which the amount of a resource needed to fulfill a goal is trivial is said to be "close" to the goal. Thus in stories (15) and (16), the execution of one plan brings about a state that is close to a state involved in the fulfillment of another goal. Being near the supermarket reduces the cost required to be at the supermarket, and buying one watch reduces the price of the second watch.

Determining whether one state makes it easier to achieve another requires heuristic planning knowledge specific to the particular states involved. For example, a heuristic about location states that the nearer you are to a place, the easier it is to get there. This heuristic is needed in (15) to understand why stopping off at a store is a good idea.

Once it has been determined that a goal overlap situation based on closeness exists, the following plan scheduling heuristic applies. The planner should pursue the first plan until it effects the "close" state, then suspend that plan, then pursue the other plan to completion, and then resume the suspended plan. For example, in story (15), John pursues his plan to get home until he is near the store, then goes to the store and makes his purchase, and finally, resumes his plan of driving home. In story (16), the plan for buying the second object needs to be executed at the point where the plan for the first object is to be executed.

The idea of closeness is important in a number of other planning contexts. For example, in dealing with a number of goals at the same time, one often has to suspend execution of one plan and pursue the execution of another. Usually, it is undesirable to undo a state that is a precondition for an active plan while pursuing another plan. However, it is usually allowable to undo such a state if the resulting state is close to the one undone. Thus a planner who is waiting at a location to meet someone might cross the street to buy a paper, say, even though this violates a previously established condition, since the cost of restoring this state is normally considered to be small.

6.0 APPLICATIONS

We are currently attempting to use meta-planning in two programs. PAM, a story understanding system, uses knowledge about goal interactions to understand stories involving multiple goals. That is, PAM can detect situations like goal conflict and goal competition; and, realizing that these threaten certain meta-goals, PAM will interpret a character's subsequent behavior as a meta-plan to address the negative consequences of these interactions. As PAM has been discussed at length elsewhere, and its relation to meta-goals discussed above, we will not discuss it further here.

Meta-planning is also being used in the development of a planning program called PANDORA (Plan ANalyzer with Dynamic Organization, Revision and Application). PANDORA is a planning system developed along the lines described toward the beginning of this paper. PANDORA is given a description of a situation and determines if it has any goals it should act upon. It then creates plans for these goals. PANDORA is dynamically told about new developments, and changes its plans accordingly. PANDORA's ultimate objective is to act both as an independent planner and as a planning assistant that suggests plausible plans to try in complicated situations.

The following is typical of the kind of situational planning PANDORA is capable of working on. PANDORA is presented with a situation in which it believes it is cooking dinner for itself. PANDORA then receives a call from an old friend, who's only in town for a short while. PANDORA infers that it has the goal of meeting with this old friend, and that this goal is in conflict with the original goal of preparing dinner as they both occupy the same time slot. Realizing that the "Achieve As Many Goals As Possible" meta-theme is activated by this situation, PANDORA infers that it has a Resolve-Conflict goal. It now looks for a meta-plan for this goal. One such plan currently available to PANDORA is

Plan Integration. That is, PANDORA generates a new plan that modifies the old one by inviting the friend to join it for dinner.

REFERENCES

Barstow, David R. Automatic construction of algorithms and data structures using a knowledge base of programming rules. Stanford AI Memo AIM-308, 1977.

Bruce, B. Generation as a Social Action. Proceedings of the Conference on Theoretical Issues in Natural Language Processing. Cambridge, Mass., 1975.

Fikes, R. & Nilsson, N. J. STRIPS: A new approach to the application of theorem proving to problem solving. *Artificial Intelligence*, 1971, 2, 189–208.

Hayes-Roth, B., & Hayes-Roth, F. Cognitive Processes in Planning. RAND Report R-2366-ONR, 1978.

McCarthy, J., & Hayes, P. J. Some philosophical problems from the standpoint of artificial intelligence. Edited by Meltzer and D. Michie. *Machine intelligence*, vol. 4. New York: American Elsevier, 1969, 463–502.

McDermott, Drew. Flexibility and efficiency in a computer program for designing circuits. Cambridge: MIT AI Laboratory Technical Report 402, 1977.

McDermott, Drew. Planning and Acting. *Cognitive Science*, vol. 2, no. 2, 1978.

Newell, A., & Simon, H. A. *Human Problem Solving*. Englewood Cliffs, N.J.: Prentice-Hall, 1972.

Perrault, C. R., Allen, J. F., & Cohen, P. R. Speech acts as a basis for understanding dialogue coherence. Proceedings of the second conference on theoretical issues in natural language processing. Champaigne-Urbana, Illinois, 1978.

Rich, C., & Shrobe, H. Initial report on a LISP programmer's apprentice. MIT AI Lab Technical Report 354, 1976.

Rieger, C. One System for Two Tasks: A Commonsense Algorithm Memory that Solves Problems and Comprehends Language. MIT AI Lab working paper 114, 1975.

Sacerdoti, E. D. Planning in a hierarchy of abstraction spaces. *Artificial Intelligence*, vol. 5, no. 2, 1974, 115–135.

Sacerdoti, E. D. *A Structure for Plans and Behavior*. North-Holland, Amsterdam: Elsevier, 1977.

Schank, R. C., & Abelson, R. P. *Scripts, Plans, Goals, and Understanding*. Hillsdale, N.J.: Lawrence Erlbaum Press, 1977.

Stefik, Mark J. Planning and Meta-Planning-MOLGEN: Part 2. Stanford Heuristic Programming Project HPP-80-13 (working paper), Computer Science Department, Stanford University, 1980.

Stefik, Mark J., & Martin, Nancy. A Review of Knowledge Based Problem Solving as a Basis For a Genetics Experiment Designing System. Stanford Heuristic Programming Project Memo HPP-77-5. Computer Science Department Report No. STAN-CS-77-596. Stanford University, 1977.

Sussman, G. J. *A Computer Model of Skill Acquisition*. New York: American Elsevier, 1975.

Wilensky, R. Understanding goal-based stories. Yale University Research Report 140, 1978.

Wilensky, R. Points: A theory of story content. Berkeley Electronic Research Laboratory Memorandum No. UCB/ERL/M80/17, 1980.

Chapter 6

Perception

Vision

Vision can be divided into stages, with earlier stages using retinal information to construct two- and then three-dimensional descriptions of input objects, and later stages matching these descriptions to stored representations. The first two selections in this section deal with the earlier stages of vision; the last paper focuses on the matching stage.

Marr championed a computational approach to the study of vision, illustrated in the selection by Marr and Poggio. The paper provides a model of human perception of stereograms, utilizing a connectionist architecture. The stereograms consist of two random-dot patterns; one pattern is an exact copy of the other except that the pattern of dots in a region of one of the patterns is shifted horizontally with respect to the rest of the pattern. When one of these dot patterns is projected to the left eye and the other to the right eye, an observer sees the shifted region hovering in front of or behind the plane. The goal of Marr and Poggio's model is to find those correspondences between the two patterns that represent real correspondences in depth and to suppress those that represent spurious correspondences.

Ullman's paper deals with processes carried out on object descriptions during the earlier stages of perception (i.e., processes carried out prior to matching). The processes of interest are simple visual routines, such as tracing along a boundary, filling in a region, marking a part, and sequentially processing different locations. The outputs of these processes characterize basic properties of prominent objects in the scene, such as the objects' rough shapes and spatial relationships. This characterization, in turn, may trigger matching processes that are specific to particular classes of objects. Thus, the general-purpose routines set the stage for domain-specific matching processes.

The paper by McClelland and Rumelhart deals with the recognition of simple patterns—namely, letters and words—and provides a precise model of the matching process. Matching is implemented via a connectionist network using top-down and bottom-up activation and inhibition processes, operating over separate levels for features (i.e., line segments at different orientations), letters, and words. The model explains in detail a host of empirical findings, and remains the best account of letter and word perception. The success of this particular model has fostered the development of connectionist models in general.

A computational theory of human stereo vision†

By D. Marr‡ and T. Poggio§

‡ M.I.T. Psychology Department, 79 Amherst Street,
Cambridge Ma 02139, U.S.A.

§ Max-Planck-Institut für Biologische Kybernetik,
7400 Tübingen, Spemannstrasse 38, Germany

(Communicated by S. Brenner, F.R.S. – Received 26 January 1978)

An algorithm is proposed for solving the stereoscopic matching problem. The algorithm consists of five steps: (1) Each image is filtered at different orientations with bar masks of four sizes that increase with eccentricity; the equivalent filters are one or two octaves wide. (2) Zero-crossings in the filtered images, which roughly correspond to edges, are localized. Positions of the ends of lines and edges are also found. (3) For each mask orientation and size, matching takes place between pairs of zero-crossings or terminations of the same sign in the two images, for a range of disparities up to about the width of the mask's central region. (4) Wide masks can control vergence movements, thus causing small masks to come into correspondence. (5) When a correspondence is achieved, it is stored in a dynamic buffer, called the 2½-D sketch.

It is shown that this proposal provides a theoretical framework for most existing psychophysical and neurophysiological data about stereopsis. Several critical experimental predictions are also made, for instance about the size of Panum's area under various conditions. The results of such experiments would tell us whether, for example, co-operativity is necessary for the matching process.

COMPUTATIONAL STRUCTURE OF THE STEREO-DISPARITY PROBLEM

Because of the way our eyes are positioned and controlled, our brains usually receive similar images of a scene taken from two nearby points at the same horizontal level. If two objects are separated in depth from the viewer, the relative positions of their images will differ in the two eyes. Our brains are capable of measuring this disparity and of using it to estimate depth.

Three steps (S) are involved in measuring stereo disparity: (S1) a particular location on a surface in the scene must be selected from one image; (S2) that same location must be identified in the other image; and (S3) the disparity in the two corresponding image points must be measured.

If one could identify a location beyond doubt in the two images, for example by illuminating it with a spot of light, steps S1 and S2 could be avoided and the

† A preliminary and lengthier version of this theory is available from the M.I.T. A.I. Laboratory as Memo 451 (1977).

problem would be easy. In practice one cannot do this (figure 1), and the difficult part of the computation is solving the correspondence problem. Julesz (1960) found that we are able to interpret random dot stereograms, which are stereo pairs that consist of random dots when viewed monocularly but fuse when viewed stereoscopically to yield patterns separated in depth. This might be thought surprising, because when one tries to set up a correspondence between two arrays of random dots, false targets arise in profusion (figure 1). Even so and in the absence of any monocular or high level cues, we are able to determine the correct correspondence.

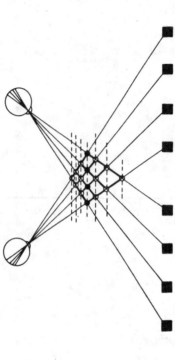

FIGURE 1. Ambiguity in the correspondence between the two retinal projections. In this figure, each of the four points in one eye's view could match any of the four projections in the other eye's view. Of the 16 possible matchings only four are correct (filled circles), while the remaining 12 are 'false targets' (open circles). It is assumed here that the targets (filled squares) correspond to 'matchable' descriptive elements obtained from the left and right images. Without further constraints based on global considerations, such ambiguities cannot be resolved. Redrawn from Julesz (1971. fig. 4.5-1).

In order to formulate the correspondence computation precisely, we have to examine its basis in the physical world. Two constraints (C) of importance may be identified (Marr 1974): (C1) a given point on a physical surface has a unique position in space at any one time; and (C2) matter is cohesive, it is separated into objects, and the surfaces of objects are generally smooth compared with their distance from the viewer.

These constraints apply to locations on a physical surface. Therefore, when we translate them into conditions on a computation we must ensure that the items to which they apply in the image are in one-to-one correspondence with well-defined locations on a physical surface. To do this, one must use image predicates that correspond to surface markings, discontinuities in the visible surfaces, shadows, and so forth, which in turn means using predicates that correspond to changes in intensity. One solution is to obtain a primitive description of the intensity changes present in each image, like the primal sketch (Marr 1976), and then to match these descriptions. Line and edge segments, blobs, termination

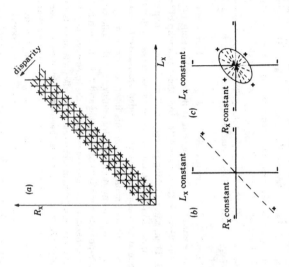

FIGURE 2. The explicit structure of the two rules R1 and R2 for the case of a one dimensional image is represented in (a). L_x and R_x represent the positions of descriptive elements in the left and right images. The continuous vertical and horizontal lines represent lines of sight from the left and the right eyes. Their intersection points correspond to possible disparity values. R1 states that only one match is allowed along any given horizontal or vertical line; R2 states that solution planes tend to spread along the dotted diagonal lines, which are lines of constant disparity.

In a network implementation of these rules, one can place a 'cell' at each node; then solid lines represent 'inhibitory' interactions, and dotted lines represent 'excitatory' ones. The local structure at each node of the network in (a) is given in (b). This algorithm may be extended to two dimensional images, in which case each node in the corresponding network has the local structure shown in (c). The ovals in this figure represent circular two dimensional disks rising out of the plane of the page. Formally, the algorithm represented by this network may be written as the iterative algorithm

$$C_{x,y;d}^{t+1} = \sigma\left\{ \sum_{x',y',d' \in S(x,y,d)} C_{x',y';d'}^t - \epsilon \sum_{x',y',d' \in O(x,y,d)} C_{x',y';d'}^t + C_{x,y;d}^0 \right\}$$

where $C_{x,y;d}^t$ denotes the state of the cell (0 for inactive, 1 for active) corresponding to position (x, y), disparity d and time t in the network of (a); $S(x, y, d)$ is a local excitatory neighbourhood confined to the same disparity layer, and (x, y, d) the inhibitory neighbourhood, consists of cells lying on the two lines of sight (c). ϵ is an inhibition constant, and σ is a threshold function. The initial state C^0 contains all possible matches, including false targets, within the prescribed disparity range. The rules R1 and R2 are implemented through the geometry of the inhibitory and excitatory neighbourhoods O and S (c). (From Marr & Poggio 1976, fig. 2; copyright by the American Association for the Advancement of Science.)

points, and tokens, obtained from these by grouping, usually correspond to items that have a physical existence on a surface.

The stereo problem may thus be reduced to that of matching two primitive symbolic descriptions, one from each eye. One can think of the elements of these descriptions as carrying only position information, like the black dots in a random dot stereogram, although for a full image there will exist rules that specify which matches between descriptive elements are possible and which are not. The two physical constraints C1 and C2 can now be translated into two rules (R) for how the left and right descriptions are combined:

(R1) *Uniqueness.* Each item from each image may be assigned at most one disparity value. This condition relies on the assumption that an item corresponds to something that has unique physical position.

(R2) *Continuity.* Disparity varies smoothly almost everywhere. This condition is a consequence of the cohesiveness of matter, and it states that only a small fraction of the area of an image is composed of boundaries that are discontinuous in depth.

In practice, R1 cannot be applied simply to grey level points in an image, because a grey level point is in only implicit correspondence with a physical location. It is in fact impossible to ensure that a grey level point in one image corresponds to exactly the same physical position as a grey level point in the other. A sharp change in intensity, however, usually corresponds to a surface marking, and therefore defines a single physical position precisely. The positions of such changes may be detected by finding peaks in the first derivative of intensity, or zero-crossings in the second derivative.

In a recent article, Marr & Poggio (1976) derived a cooperative algorithm which implements these rules (see figure 2), showing that it successfully solves the false targets problem and extracts disparity information from random dot stereograms (see also Marr, Palm & Poggio 1978).

THE BIOLOGICAL EVIDENCE

Apart from AUTOMAP (Julesz 1963) and Sperling (1970), all of the current stereo algorithms proposed as models for human stereopsis are based on Julesz's (1971) proposal that stereo matching is a cooperative process (Julesz 1971, p. 203 ff.; Julesz & Chang 1976; Nelson 1975; Dev 1975; Hirai & Fukushima 1976; Sugie & Suwa 1977; Marr & Poggio 1976). None of them has been shown to work on natural images.

An essential feature of these algorithms is that they are designed to select correct matches in a situation where false targets occur in profusion. They require many 'disparity detecting' neurons, whose peak sensitivities cover a range of disparity values that is much wider than the tuning curves of the individual neurons. That is, apart possibly from early versions of Julesz's dipole model, they do not critically rely on eye movements, since in principle, they have the ability to interpret a random dot stereogram without them.

by successively finer filtering, are used during fusion, providing increasing and, in the limit, very fine disparity resolution at the cost of decreasing disparity range.

A notable feature of a system organized along these lines is its reliance on eye movements for building up a comprehensive and accurate disparity map from two viewpoints. The reason for this is that the most precise disparity values are obtainable from the high resolution channels, and eye movements are therefore essential so that each part of a scene can ultimately be brought into the small disparity range within which high resolution channels operate. The importance of vergence eye movements is also attractive in view of the extremely high degree of precision with which they may be controlled (Riggs & Niehl 1960; Rashbass & Westheimer 1961a).

These observations suggest a scheme for solving the fusion problem in the following way (Marr & Poggio 1977a, b): (1) Each image is analysed through channels of various coarsenesses, and matching takes place between corresponding channels from the two eyes for disparity values of the order of the channel resolution. (2) Coarse channels control vergence movements, thus causing finer channels to come into correspondence.

This scheme contains no hysteresis, and therefore does not account for the hysteresis observed by Fender & Julesz (1967). Recent work in the theory of intermediate visual information processing argues on computational grounds that a key goal of early visual processing is the construction of something like an 'orientation and depth map' of the visible surfaces round a viewer (Marr & Nishihara 1978, fig. 2; Marr 1977, § 3). In this map, information is combined from a number of different and probably independent processes that interpret disparity, motion, shading, texture, and contour information. These ideas are illustrated by the representation shown in figure 3, which Marr & Nishihara called the 2½-D sketch.

Suppose now that the hysteresis Fender & Julesz observed is not due to a co-operative process during matching, but is in fact the result of using a memory buffer, like the 2½-D sketch, in which to store the depth map of the image as it is discovered. Then, the matching process itself need not be cooperative (even if it still could be), and in fact it would not even be necessary for the whole image ever to be matched simultaneously, provided that a depth map of the viewed surface were built and maintained in this intermediate memory.

Our scheme can now be completed by adding to it the following two steps: (3) when a correspondence is achieved, it is held and written down in the 2½-D sketch; (4) there is a backwards relation between the memory and the masks, acting through the control of eye movements, that allows one to fuse any piece of a surface easily once its depth map has been established in the memory.

Eye movements seem, however, to be important for human stereo vision (Richards 1977; Frisby & Clatworthy 1975; Saye & Frisby 1975). Other findings these algorithms fail to explain include (a) the ability of some subjects to tolerate a 15% expansion of one image (Julesz 1971, fig. 2.8-8), (b) the findings about independent spatial-frequency-tuned channels in binocular fusion, of which our tolerance to severe defocusing of one image is a striking demonstration (Julesz 1971, fig. 3.10-3), (c) the physiological, clinical, and psychophysical evidence about Richards' two pools hypothesis (Richards 1970, 1971; Richards & Regan 1973); and (d) the size of Panum's fusional area (6-18', Fender & Julesz 1967; Julesz & Chang 1976) which seems surprisingly small to have to resort to cooperative mechanisms for the elimination of false targets.

Taken together, these findings indicate that a rather different approach is necessary. In this article, we formulate an algorithm designed specifically as a theory of the matching process in human stereopsis, and present a theoretical framework for the overall computational problem of stereopsis. We show that our theory accounts for most of the available evidence and formulate the predictions to which it leads.

For a more comprehensive review of the relevant psychophysics and neuro-physiology see Marr & Poggio (1977a).

AN OUTLINE OF THE THEORY

The basic computational problem in binocular fusion is the elimination of false targets, and for any given monocular features the difficulty of this problem is in direct proportion to the range and resolution of the disparities that are considered. The problem can therefore be simplified by reducing either the range, or the resolution, or both, of the disparity measurements that are taken from two images. An extreme example of the first strategy would lead to a diagram like figure 2 in which only three adjacent disparity planes were present (e.g. +1, 0, -1) each specifying their degree of disparity rather precisely. The second strategy, on the other hand, would amount to maintaining the range of disparities shown in figure 2, but reducing the resolution with which they are represented. In the extreme case, only three disparity values would be represented, crossed, roughly zero, and uncrossed.

These schemes, based on just three pools of disparity values, substantially eliminate the false targets problem at the cost on the one hand of a very small disparity range, and on the other, of poor disparity resolution. Thus the price of computational simplicity is a trade-off between range and resolution.

One would, however, expect the human visual system to possess both range and resolution in its disparity processing. In this connection, the existence of independent spatial frequency tuned channels in binocular fusion (Kaufman 1964; Julesz 1971, §§ 3.9 and 3.10; Julesz & Miller 1975; Mayhew & Frisby 1976) is of especial interest, because it suggests that several copies of the image, obtained receptive field sizes; and (b) the correlation of these two components with anatomical and physiological data about the scatter of receptive field sizes and their dependence on eccentricity.

On the basis of detection studies, they formulated an initial model embodying the following conclusions: (1) at each position in the visual field, there exist 'bar-like' masks (see figure 4a), whose tuning curves have the form of figure 4b, and which have a half power bandwidth of between one and two octaves. (2) The half power bandwidth of the local sensitivity function at each eccentricity

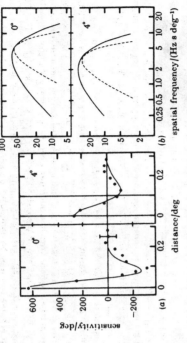

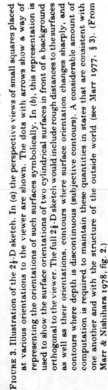

FIGURE 4. (a) Line spread functions measured psychophysically at threshold at two different eccentricities. The points are fitted using the difference of two Gaussian functions with space constants in the ratio 1.5 : 1.0. The inhibitory surround exactly balances the excitatory centre so that the area under the curve is zero. (b) Predictions of local spatial frequency sensitivity from frequency gradient data and from line spread function data. The local frequency sensitivity functions are plotted as solid lines. The dashed lines are the local frequency response predicted by Fourier transforming the line spread functions in (a), which were measured at the appropriate eccentricities. (Redrawn from Wilson & Giese 1977. figs. 9 and 10.)

is about three octaves. Hence the range of receptive field sizes present at each eccentricity is about 4 : 1. In other words, at least three and probably four receptive field sizes are required at each point of the visual field. (3) Average receptive field size increases linearly with eccentricity. In humans at 0° the mean width w of the central excitatory region of the mask is about 6′ (range 3′–12′); and at 4° eccentricity, $w = 12′$ (range 6′–24′) (Wilson & Giese 1977, fig. 9; Hines 1976, figs 2 and 3). If one assumes that this receptive field is described by the difference of two Gaussian functions with space constants in the ratio 1 : 1.5, the corresponding peak frequency sensitivity of the channel is given by $1/f = \lambda = 2.2w$. These figures agree quite well with physiological studies in the Macaque. Hubel & Wiesel (1974, fig. 6a) reported that the mean width of the receptive field (s) increases linearly with eccentricity e (approximately), $s = 0.05e + 0.25°$, so that at

THE NATURE OF THE CHANNELS

The articles by Julesz & Miller (1975) and Mayhew & Frisby (1976) establish that spatial-frequency-tuned channels are used in stereopsis and are independent. Julesz & Miller's findings imply that two octaves is an upper bound for the bandwidth of these channels, and suggest that they are the same channels as those previously found in monocular studies (Campbell & Robson 1968; Blakemore & Campbell 1969). Although strictly speaking it has not been demonstrated that these two kinds of channel are the same, we shall make the assumption that they are. This will allow us to use the numerical information available from monocular studies to derive quantitative estimates of some of the parameters involved in our theory.

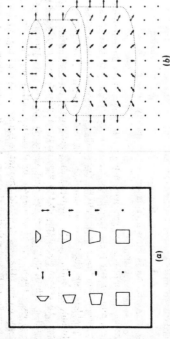

FIGURE 3. Illustration of the 2½-D sketch. In (a) the perspective views of small squares placed at various orientations to the viewer are shown. The dots with arrows show a way of representing the orientations of such surfaces symbolically. In (b), this representation is used to show the surface orientations of two cylindrical surfaces in front of a background orthogonal to the viewer. The full 2½-D sketch would include rough distances to the surfaces as well as their orientations, contours where surface orientation changes sharply, and contours where depth is discontinuous (subjective contours). A considerable amount of computation is required to maintain these quantities in states that are consistent with one another and with the structure of the outside world (see Marr 1977. § 3). (From Marr & Nishihara 1978. fig. 2.)

The idea that there may be a range of different sized or spatial-frequency-tuned mechanisms was originally introduced on the basis of psychophysical evidence by Campbell & Robson (1968). This led to a virtual explosion of papers dealing with spatial frequency analysis in the visual system. Recently, Wilson & Giese (1977) and Cowan (1977) integrated these and other anatomical and physiological data into a coherent logical framework. The key to their framework is (a) the partitioning of the range of sizes associated with the channels into two components, one due to spatial inhomogeneity of the retina, and one due to local scatter of

$\ell = 4°$, $s = 27'$ which gives a value for $w = \frac{1}{3}s$ of about 9' as opposed to the figure of 12' assumed here for humans). The data of Schiller, Finlay & Volman (1977, p. 1347, figs. 12 and 14) are in rough agreement with Hubel & Wiesel's.

(4) Essentially all of the psychophysical data on the detection of spatial patterns at contrast threshold can be explained by (1), (2) and (3) together with the hypothesis that the detection process is based on a form of spatial probability summation in the channels.

With the characteristic perverseness of the natural world, this happy and concise state of affairs does not provide a precise account of suprathreshold conditions. The known discrepancies can however be explained by introducing two extra hypotheses: (5) contrast sensitivities of the various channels are adjusted appropriately to the stimulus contrast (Georgeson & Sullivan 1975). The point of this is merely to ensure that bars of the same contrast but different widths actually appear to have the same contrast; (6) receptive field properties change slightly with contrast, the inhibition being somewhat decreased when contrast is low (Cowan 1977, p. 511).

In a more recent article, Wilson & Bergen (1979) have found that the situation at threshold may also be more complicated. They proposed a model consisting of four size-tuned mechanisms centred at each point, the smaller two showing relatively sustained temporal responses, and the larger two being relatively transient. As far as is known, this model accurately accounts for all published threshold sensitivity studies.

The two sustained channels, which Wilson & Bergen call N and S, have w values 3.1' and 6.2'; the transient channels, called T and U, have w equal to 11.7' and 21'. The sizes of these channels increase with eccentricity in the same way as described above.

The S channel is the most sensitive under both transient and sustained stimulation, and the U channel is the least, having only $\frac{1}{4}$ to $\frac{1}{3}$ the sensitivity of the S channel. The extent to which the U channel, for example, plays a role in stereopsis is of course unknown.

In what follows, we shall assume that the figures given by Wilson & Giese for the numbers and dimensions of receptive field centres and their scatter hold roughly for suprathreshold conditions. If future experiments confirm that Wilson & Bergen's more recent numbers are relevant for stereopsis, some modification of our quantitative estimates may be necessary.

Wilson & Giese's figures allow us to estimate the minimum sampling density required by each channel, i.e. the minimum spatial density of the corresponding receptive fields. From fig. 10 of Wilson & Giese (1977), a channel with peak sensitivity at wavelength λ is band-limited on the high frequency side by wavelengths of about $\frac{3}{2}\lambda$, and $\lambda = 2.2w$. This figure is for a threshold criterion of 15–30%, but is rather insensitive to the exact value chosen. Hence by the sampling theorem (Papoulis 1968, p. 119), the minimum distance between samples (i.e. receptive fields), in a direction perpendicular to their preferred orientation, is at

TABLE 1. SPATIAL FILTERING: SUMMARY OF PSYCHOPHYSICAL EVIDENCE

(a) At each point in the visual field the image is filtered through receptive fields having these characteristics (the half-power bandwidth B is about 1 octave):

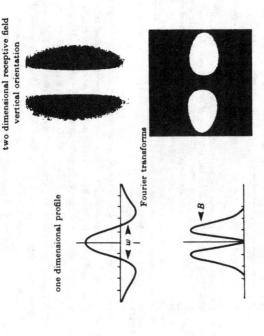

two dimensional receptive field
vertical orientation

one dimensional profile

Fourier transforms

(b) For each position and orientation there are four receptive field sizes, the smallest being $\frac{1}{4}$ of the largest. The profile $R(x)$ and Fourier transform $\hat{R}(\omega)$ of each receptive field are given by:

$$R(x) = (2\pi)^{-1}\{\sigma_e^{-1}\exp[-x^2/2\sigma_e^2] - \sigma_i^{-1}\exp[-x^2/2\sigma_i^2]\},$$
$$\hat{R}(\omega) = \exp[-\tfrac{1}{2}\omega^2\sigma_e^2] - \exp[-\tfrac{1}{2}\omega^2\sigma_i^2],$$

where σ_e, σ_i are the excitatory and inhibitory space constants, and are in the ratio $1:1.5$. The half-power bandwidth spanned by the four receptive field cells at each point is two octaves.

(c) w increases with eccentricity: $w = 3'-12'$ (possibly 20') at 0° and $w = 6'-34'$ at 4°. Note. receptive field sizes and corresponding spectral sensitivity curves in the suprathreshold condition may be different from the values given here, which were measured at threshold.

(d) Formally the output of step 1 is given by the convolution $F_{w,\theta}(x,y) = I \cdot B_{w,\theta}$, where $I(x, y)$ denotes the light intensity at the image point (x, y), and $B_{w,\theta}(x, y)$ describes the receptive field of a bar-shaped mask at orientation θ, with central region of width w. θ covers the range 0–180° with 12 values about 15° apart and w takes four values in the range defined by (c) above.

(e) In practice, cells with on-centre receptive fields will signal positive values of the filtered signal, and cells with off-centre receptive fields will signal negative values.

most $\frac{3}{4}\lambda$. Assuming the overall width of the receptive field is about $\frac{3}{4}\lambda$, the minimum number of samples per receptive field width is about 4.5.

An estimate of the minimum longitudinal sampling distance may be obtained as follows. Assume that the receptive field's longitudinal weighting function (see table 1) is Gaussian with space-constant σ, thus extending over an effective distance of say 4σ–6σ. (A value of $\sigma = w'$ will give an approximately square receptive field.) Its Fourier transform is also Gaussian with space constant in the frequency domain (ω) of $1/\sigma$, and for practical purposes can be assumed to be band-limited with $f_{max} = 3/(2\pi\sigma)$ to $2/(2\pi\sigma)$. By the sampling theorem, the corresponding minimum sampling intervals are σ to 1.5σ, that is about four samples per longitudinal receptive field distance. Hence the minimum number of measurements (i.e. cells or receptive fields) per receptive field area is about 18. It follows that the number of multiplications required to process the image through a given channel is roughly independent of the receptive field size associated with that channel. Not too much weight should be attached to the estimate of 18, although we feel that the sampling density cannot be significantly lower. In the biological situation, total sampling density will decrease as eccentricity increases.

This model of the preliminary processing of the image is summarized in table 1. There are in fact more efficient ways of implementing it (see Marr & Hildreth 1979).

THE DOMAIN OF THE MATCHING FUNCTION

In view of this information, the first step in our theory can be thought of as filtering the left and right spatial images through bar masks of four sizes and about twelve orientations at each point in the images. We assume that this operation is roughly linear, for a given intensity and contrast. When matching the left and right images, one cannot simply use the raw values measured by this first stage, because they do not correspond directly to physical features on visible surfaces on which matching may be based. One first has to obtain from these measurements some symbol that corresponds with high probability to a physical item with a well defined spatial position. This observation, which has been verified through computer experiments in the case of stereo vision (Grimson & Marr 1979) formed the starting point for a recent approach to the early processing of visual information (Marr 1974, 1976).

Perhaps the simplest way of obtaining suitable symbols from an image is to find signed peaks in the first (directional) derivative of the intensity array, or alternatively, zero-crossings in the second derivative. The bar masks of table 1 measure an approximation to the second directional derivative at roughly the resolution of the mask size, provided that the image does not vary locally along the orientation of the mask (Marr & Hildreth 1979). If this is so, clear signed zero-crossings in the convolution values obtained along a line lying perpendicular to the receptive field's longitudinal axis (cf. Marr 1976, fig. 2) would specify

accurately the position of an edge in the image.† Edges whose orientations lie near the vertical will of course play a dominant role in stereopsis.

In practice, however, it is not enough to use just oriented edges to obtain horizontal disparity information. Julesz (1971, p. 80) showed that minute breaks in horizontal lines can lead to fusion of two stereograms even when the breaks lie close to the limit of visual acuity, and such breaks cannot be obtained by simple operations on the measurements from even the smallest vertical masks. These breaks probably have to be localized by a specialized process for finding terminations by examining the values and positions of rows of zero-crossings (cf. Marr 1976, p. 496).

Thus zero-crossings and (less importantly) terminations have both to be made explicit (cf. Marr 1976, p. 485). The matching process will then operate on descriptions, of the left and right images, that are built of these two kinds of symbolic primitives, and which specify their precise positions, the mask size and orientation from which they were obtained, and their signs.

MATCHING

At the heart of the matching problem lies the problem of false targets. If each channel were very narrowly tuned to a wavelength λ, the minimum distance between zero-crossings of the same sign in each image would be about λ. In this case, matching would be unambiguous in a disparity range up to λ. The same argument holds qualitatively for the actual channels, but because they are not so narrowly tuned, the disparity range for unambiguous matching will be smaller and must be estimated. We have done this only for zero-crossings, since terminations are sparser and pose less of a false-target problem.

Let us consider a two dimensional image filtered through a vertically oriented mask. Matching will take place between zero-crossings of the same sign along corresponding horizontal lines in the two images. If two such zero-crossings lie very close together in one image, the danger of false targets will arise. Hence a critical parameter in our analysis will be the distance between adjacent zero-crossings of the same sign along each of these lines.

This problem is now one dimensional, and we approach it by estimating the probability distribution of the interval between adjacent zero-crossings of the same sign. This depends on (a) the image characteristics, and (b) the filter (or mask) characteristics. For (a) we take the worst case, that in which the power spectrum of the input to the filter is white (within the filter's spectral range). We also assume, for computational convenience, that the filtered output is a

† It is perhaps worth noting that this rather direct way of locating sharp intensity changes in the image is not the only nor necessarily the best method from the point of view of an actual implementation. It is shown elsewhere (Marr & Hildreth 1979) that under certain conditions, the zeroes in an image filtered through a Laplacian operator (like an X-type retinal ganglion cell) provide an equivalent way of locating edges, whose orientation must then be determined.

Our problem is now transformed into one that many authors have considered, dating from the pioneering work of Rice (1945), and the appendix sets out the formulae in detail. The results we need are all contained in figure 5. P_0 is the probability distribution of the interval between adjacent zero-crossings (which perforce have opposite signs), and P_1 the distribution of the interval to the second zero-crossing. Since alternate zero-crossings have the same sign, P_1 is the quantity of interest, and its integral $\int P_1$ is also given in figure 5.

$\int P_1$ can be understood in the following way. Suppose a positive zero-crossing occurs at the point O. Then $\int P_1$ represents the probability that at least one other positive zero-crossing will occur within a distance ξ of O. (In figure 5b(iii), the width w of the central part of the receptive field associated with the filter is equal to 2.8 on the ξ scale.)

From the graphs in figure 5, we see for example that the 0.05 probability level for $\int P_1$ occurs at $\xi = 4.1$ (approximately $\lambda/1.52$) for the ideal band pass filter one octave wide, centred on wavelength λ (figure 5a(i)), and at $\xi = 3.1$ for the receptive field of fig. 5b(i). In the second case, ξ is approximately $\frac{1}{2}\lambda$, where w is the principal wavelength associated with the channel, and $\lambda = 2.2w$, where w is the measured width of the central excitatory area of the receptive field. Thus in this case, the 95 % confidence limit occurs at approximately w ($\xi = 3.1$, $w = 2.8$).

At the 0.001 probability level, the ideal bandpass filter is 50 % better (the corresponding ξ is 50 % larger) than the receptive field filter with the same centre frequency: at the 0.05 probability level it is 30 % better; and at the 0.5 probability level, it is 13 % better. The legend to figure 5 provides more details about these results.

We have made a similar comparison between the sustained and transient channels of Wilson (1978a) and of Wilson & Bergen (1979). If the sustained channels correspond to the case of figure 5b, the transient channels have a larger ratio of the space constants for inhibition and excitation, a somewhat larger excitatory space constant, and an excitatory area larger than the inhibitory. Even under these conditions, the values change only slightly.

The matching process

We now apply the results of these calculations to the matching process. Our analysis applies directly to channels with vertical orientation, and is roughly valid for channels with orientation near the vertical.

Within a channel of given size, there are in practice two possible ways of dealing with false targets. If one wishes essentially to avoid them altogether, the disparity range over which a match is sought must be restricted to $\pm\frac{1}{2}w$ (see figure 6a). For suppose zero-crossing L in the left image matches zero-crossing R in the right image. The above calculations assure us that the probability of another zero-crossing of the same sign within w of R in the right image is less than 0.05. Hence if the disparity between the images is less than $\frac{1}{2}w$, a search for matches in the range $\pm\frac{1}{2}w$ will yield only the correct match R (with probability

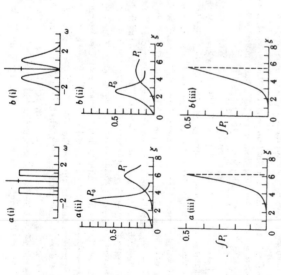

FIGURE 5. Interval distributions for zero-crossings. A 'white' Gaussian random process is passed through a filter with the frequency characteristic (transfer function) shown in (i). The approximate interval distribution for the first (P_0) and second (P_1) zero-crossings of the resulting zero-mean Gaussian process is shown in (ii). Given a positive zero-crossing at the origin, the probability of having another within a distance ξ is approximated by the integral of P_1 and shown in (iii). In (a), these quantities are given for an ideal band pass filter one octave wide and with centre frequency $\omega = 2\pi/\lambda$; (b) represents the case of the receptive field described by Cowan (1977) and Wilson & Giese (1977). The corresponding spatial distribution of excitation and inhibition, i.e. the inverse Fourier transform of (bi) appears, in the same units, in table 1. The ratio of space constants for excitation and inhibition is 1:1.5. The width w of the central excitatory portion of the receptive field is 2.8 in the units in which ξ is plotted.

For case (a) a probability level of $\int P_1 = 0.001$ occurs at $\xi = 2.3$, and a probability level of 0.5 occurs at $\xi = 6.1$. The corresponding figures for case (b) are $\xi = 1.5$ and $\xi = 5.4$. If the space constant ratio is 1:1.75 (Wilson 1978b) the values of $\int P_1$ change by not more than 5 %.

Gaussian (zero-mean) process. This hypothesis is quite realistic (E. Hildreth, personal communication).

For (b), we examine two cases. Since the actual filters have a half-power bandwidth of around one octave, the first case we consider is that of an ideal linear bandpass filter of width one octave, as illustrated in figure 5a(i). The second case (figure 5b(ii)) is the receptive field suggested by the threshold experiments of Wilson & Giese (1977), consisting of excitatory and inhibitory Gaussian distributions, with space constants in the ratio 1 : 1.5 (see figure 4).

0.95). Such a low error rate can be accommodated without resorting to sophisticated algorithms. For example, two reasonable ways of increasing the matching reliability are (a) to demand rough agreement between the slopes of the matched zero-crossings, and (b) to fail to accept an isolated match all of whose neighbours give different disparity values. Of course if the disparity between the images exceeds $\frac{1}{2}w$, this procedure will fail, a circumstance that we discuss later.

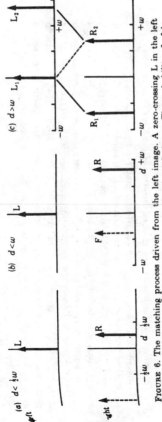

FIGURE 6. The matching process driven from the left image. A zero-crossing L in the left image matches one R displaced by disparity d in the right image. The probability of a false target within w of R is small, so provided that $d < \frac{1}{2}w$ (case a), almost no false targets will arise in the disparity range $\pm\frac{1}{2}w$. This gives the first possible algorithm. Alternatively (case b), all matches within the range $\pm w$ may be considered. Here, false targets (F) can arise in about 50% of the cases, but the correct solution is also present. If the correct match is convergent, the false target will with high probability be divergent. Therefore in the second algorithm, unique matches from either image are accepted as correct, and the remainder as ambiguous and subject to the 'pulling effect', illustrated in case (c). Here, L_1 could match R_1 or R_2, but L_2 can match only R_2. Because of this, and because the two matches have the same disparity. L_1 is assigned to R_1.

There is, however, an alternative strategy, that allows one to deal with the possible matching problem over a larger disparity range. Let us consider the possible situations if the disparity between the images is d, where $|d| < w$ (figure 6b). Observe firstly that if $d > 0$, the correct match is almost certainly ($p < 0.05$) the only convergent candidate in the range $(0, w)$. Secondly, the probability of a (divergent) false target is at most 0.5. Therefore, 50% of all possible matches will be unambiguous and correct, and the remainder will be ambiguous, mostly consisting of two alternatives, one convergent and one divergent, one of which is always the correct one. In the ambiguous cases, selection of the correct alternative can be based simply on the sign of neighbouring unambiguous matches. This algorithm will fail for image disparities that significantly exceed $\pm w$, since the percentage of unambiguous matches will be too low (roughly 0.2 for $\pm 1.5w$). Notice that if there is a match near zero disparity, it is likely ($p > 0.9$) to be the only candidate.

Sparse images like an isolated line or bar, that yield few or no false targets, pose a different problem. They often give rise to unique matches, and may there-

fore be relied upon over quite a large disparity range. Hence if the above strategy fails to disclose candidate matches in its disparity range, the search for possible matches may proceed outwards, ceasing as soon as one is found.

In summary then there are two immediate candidates for matching algorithms. The simpler is restricted to a disparity range of $\pm\frac{1}{2}w$ and in its most straightforward form will fail to assign 5% of the matches. The second involves some straightforward comparisons between neighbouring matches, but even before these comparisons, the 50% unambiguous matches could be used to drive eye movements, and provide a rough sensation of depth.

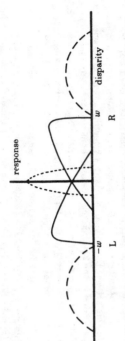

FIGURE 7. An implementation of the second matching algorithm. For each mask size of central width w, there are two pools of disparity detectors, signalling crossed or uncrossed disparities and spanning a range of $\pm w$. There may be additional detectors finely tuned to near-zero disparities. Additional diplopic disparities probably exist beyond this range. They are vetoed by detectors of smaller absolute disparity.

The implementation of the first of these algorithms is straightforward. The second one can be implemented most economically using two 'pools', one sensitive in a graded way to convergent and the other to divergent disparities (see figure 7). (In this sense, the first algorithm requires only one 'pool', that is, a single unit sensitive in a graded way to the disparity range $\pm\frac{1}{2}w$.) Candidate matches near zero disparity are likely to be correct, and this fact can be used to improve performance. One way is to add, to the two basic pools, high resolution units tuned to near-zero disparities.

In the second algorithm, matches that are unambiguous or already assigned can 'pull' neighbouring ambiguous matches to whichever alternative has the same sign. This is a form of cooperativity, and may be related to the 'pulling effect' described in psychophysical experiments by Julesz & Chang (1976). Notice however that this algorithm requires the existence of pulling only across pools and not within pools (in the terminology of Julesz & Chang 1976, p. 119).

Disparities larger than w can be examined in very sparse images. If, for example, both primary pools (covering a disparity range of $\pm w$) are silent, detectors operating outside this range, possibly with a broad tuning curve, may be consulted. In a biologically plausible implementation, these detectors should be inhibited by activity in the primary pools (see figure 7). It is tempting to suggest that detectors for these outlying disparities (i.e. exceeding about $\pm w$) may give rise to depth sensations and eye movement control in diplopic conditions.

If the image is not sparse, and the disparity exceeds the operating range, both algorithms will fail. Can the failure be recognized simply at this low level?

For the first algorithm, no correct match will be possible in the range $\pm \frac{1}{2}w$. The probability of a random match in this range is less than 1.0. When the disparity between the two images lies in the range $\pm \frac{1}{2}w$, there will *always* be at least one match. It is therefore relatively easy to discriminate between these two situations.

For the second algorithm, an analogous argument applies; in this case the probability of no candidate match is about 0.3 for image disparities lying outside the range $\pm w$, and zero for disparities lying within it. Again, it is relatively easy to discriminate between the situations.

Finally, W. E. L. Grimson (personal communication) has pointed out that matching can be carried out from either image or from both. Observe for example in figure 6c, that if matching is initiated from the left image, the match for L_1 is ambiguous, but for L_2 it is unambiguous. Similarly from the right image.

It seems most sensible to initiate matching simultaneously from both images. Then, before any 'pulling', there are three possible outcomes. (1) The matching of an element starting from both images is unambiguous, in which case the two must agree. (2) Matching from one image is ambiguous, but from the other it is not. In this case, the unambiguous match should be chosen. (3) Matching from both images is ambiguous, in which case they must be resolved by pulling from unambiguous neighbours.

Implications for psychophysical measurements of Panum's fusional area

Using the second of the above algorithms, matches may be assigned correctly for a disparity range $\pm w$. The precision of the disparity values thus obtained should be quite high, and a roughly constant proportion of w (which one can estimate from stereoacuity results at about $\frac{1}{20}w$). For foveal channels, this means $\pm 3'$ disparity with resolution 10" for the smallest, and $\pm 12'$ (perhaps up to $\pm 20'$ if Wilson & Bergen (1979) holds for stereopsis) with resolution 40' for the largest ones. At 4° eccentricity, the range is $\pm 5.3'$ to about $\pm 34'$. We assume that this range corresponds to stereoscopic fusion, and that outside it one enters diplopic conditions, in which disparity can be estimated only for relatively sparse images.

Under these assumptions, our predicted values apparently correspond quite well to available measures of the fusional limits without eye movements (see Mitchell 1966; Fender & Julesz 1967; Julesz & Chang 1976; and predictions 3–6 below).

DYNAMIC MEMORY STORAGE: THE 2½-D SKETCH

According to our theory, once matches have been obtained using masks of a given size, they are represented in a temporary buffer. These matches also control vergence movements of the two eyes, thus allowing information from large masks to bring small masks into their range of correspondence.

The reasons for postulating the existence of a memory are of two kinds, those arising from general considerations about early visual processing, and those concerning the specific problem of stereopsis. A memory like the 2½-D sketch (see figure 3) is computationally desirable on general grounds, because it provides a representation in which information obtained from several early visual processes can be combined (Marr 1977; §3.6 and table 1). The more particular reason associated specifically with stereopsis is the computational simplicity of the matching process, which requires a buffer in which to preserve its results as (1) disjunctive eye movements change the plane of fixation, and (2) objects move in the visual field. In this way, the 2½-D sketch becomes the place where 'global' stereopsis is actually achieved, combining the matches provided independently by the different channels and making the resulting disparity map available to other visual processes.

The nature of the memory

The 2½-D sketch is a dynamic memory with considerable intrinsic computing power. It belongs to early visual processing, and cannot be influenced directly from higher levels, for example via verbal instructions, a priori knowledge or even previous visual experience.

One would however expect a number of constraints derived from the physical world to be embedded in its internal structure. For example, the rule R2 stated early in this article, that disparity changes smoothly almost everywhere, might be implemented in the 2½-D sketch by connections similar to those that implement it in Marr & Poggio's (1976) cooperative algorithm (figure 2c). This active rule in the memory would be responsible for the sensation of a continuous surface to which even a sparse stereogram can give rise (Julesz 1971; fig. 4.4–5).

Another constraint is, for example, the continuity of discontinuities in the visible surfaces, which we believe underlies the phenomenon of subjective contours (Marr 1977, §3.6). It is possible that even more complicated consistency relations, concerning the possible arrangements of surfaces in three dimensional space, are realized by computations in the memory (e.g. constraints in the spirit of those made explicit by Waltz 1975). Such constraints may eventually form the basis for an understanding of phenomena like the Necker-cube reversal.

From this point of view, it is natural that many illusions concerning the interpretation of three dimensional structure (the Necker cube, subjective contours, the Muller-Lyer figure, the Poggendorff figure, etc., Julesz 1971, Blomfield 1973) should take place after stereoscopic fusion.

According to this theory, the memory roughly preserves depth (or disparity) information during the scanning of a scene with disjunctive eye movements, and during movement of viewed objects. Information management will have limitations both in depth and in time, and the main questions here are over what range of disparities can the 2½-D sketch maintain a record of a match in the presence of incoming information, and how long can it do this in its absence? The temporal question is less interesting because the purpose of the buffer is to organize incoming perceptual information, not to preserve it when there is none.

The spatial aspects of the 2½-D sketch raise a number of interesting questions. First, are the maximal disparities that are preserved by the memory in stabilized image conditions the same as the maximum range of disparities that are simultaneously visible in a random dot stereogram under normal viewing conditions? Secondly, does the distribution of the disparities that are present in a scene affect the range that the memory can store? For example, is the range greater for a stereogram of a spiral, in which disparity changes smoothly, than in a simple square-and-surround stereogram of similar overall disparity?

For the first question, the available evidence seems to indicate that the range is the same in the two cases. According to Fender & Julesz (1967), the range is about 2° for a random dot stereogram. When the complex stereograms given by Julesz (1971; e.g. 4.5-3) are viewed from about 20 cm, they give rise to disparities of about the same order. If this were true, it would imply that the maximal range of simultaneously perceivable disparities is a property of the 2½-D sketch alone, and is independent of eye movements.

With regard to the second question, it seems at present unlikely that the maximum range of simultaneously perceivable disparities is much affected by their distribution. It can be shown that the figure of about 2°, which holds for stabilized image conditions and for freely viewed stereograms with continuously varying disparities, also applies to stereograms with a single disparity.

Perception times do however depend on the distribution of disparities in a scene (Frisby & Clatworthy 1975; Saye & Frisby 1975). A stereogram of a spiral staircase ascending towards the viewer did not produce the long perception times associated with a two planar stereogram of similar disparity range. This is to be expected, within the framework of our theory, because of the way in which we propose vergence movements are controlled. We now turn to this topic.

VERGENCE MOVEMENTS

Disjunctive eye movements, which change the plane of fixation of the two eyes, are independent of conjunctive eye movements (Rashbass & Westheimer 1961b), are smooth rather than saccadic, have a reaction time of about 160 ms, and follow a rather simple control strategy. The (asymptotic) velocity of eye vergence depends linearly on the amplitude of the disparity, the constant of proportionality being about 8°/s per degree of disparity (Rashbass & Westheimer 1961a). Vergence movements are accurate to within about 2' (Riggs & Niehl 1960), and voluntary binocular saccades preserve vergence nearly exactly (Williams & Fender 1977). Furthermore, Westheimer & Mitchell (1969) found that tachistoscopic presentation of disparate images led to the initiation of an appropriate vergence movement, but not to its completion. These data strongly suggest that the control of vergence movements is continuous rather than ballistic.

Our hypothesis is, that vergence movements are accurately controlled by matches obtained through the various channels, acting either directly or indirectly through the 2½-D sketch. This hypothesis is consistent with the observed strategy and precision of vergence control, and also accounts for the findings of Saye & Frisby (1975). Scenes like the spiral staircase, in which disparity changes smoothly, allow vergence movements to scan a large disparity range under the continuous control of the outputs of even the smallest masks. On the other hand, two-planar stereograms with the same disparity range require a large vergence shift, but provide no accurate information for its continuous control. The long perception times for such stereograms may therefore be explained in terms of a random-walk-like search strategy by the vergence control system. In other words, guidance of vergence movements is a simple continuous closed loop process (cf. Richards 1975) which is usually inaccessible from higher levels.

There may exist some simple learning ability in the vergence control system. There is some evidence that an observer can learn to make an efficient series of vergence movements (Frisby & Clatworthy 1975). This learning effect seems however to be confined to the type of information used by the closed loop vergence control system. A priori, verbal or high level cues about the stereogram are ineffective.

EXPERIMENTS

In this section, we summarize the experiments that are important for the theory. We separate psychophysical experiments from neurophysiological ones, and divide the experiments themselves into two categories according to whether their results are critical and are already available (A), or are critical and not available and therefore amount to predictions (P). In the case of experimental predictions, we make explicit their importance to the theory by a system of stars; three stars indicates a prediction which, if falsified, would disprove the theory. One star indicates a prediction whose disproof remnants of the theory could survive.

Computation

The algorithm we have described has been implemented, and is apparently reliable at solving the matching problem for stereo pairs of natural images (Grimson & Mar 1979). It depends on the uniqueness and continuity conditions formulated at the beginning of this article, and it is perhaps of some interest to see exactly how.

The continuity assumption is used in two ways. First, vergence movements driven by the larger masks are assumed to bring the smaller masks into register over a *neighbourhood* of the match obtained through the larger masks. Secondly, local matching ambiguities are resolved by consulting the sign of *nearby* unambiguous matches.

The uniqueness assumption is used in quite a strong way. If a match found from one image is unique, it is assigned without further checking. This is permissible only because the uniqueness assumption is based on true properties of the physical world. If the algorithm is presented with a stereo pair in which the uniqueness assumption is violated, as it is in Panum's limiting case, the algorithm will assign a match that is unique from one image but not from the other (O. J. Braddick, in preparation).

Psychophysics

1 (A, P**). Independent spatial-frequency-tuned channels are known to exist in binocular fusion and rivalry. The theory identifies these with the channels described from monocular experiments (Julesz & Miller 1975; Mayhew & Frisby 1976; Frisby & Mayhew 1979; Wilson & Giese 1977; Cowan 1977; Wilson 1978a, b; Wilson, Phillips, Rentschler & Hilz 1979; Wilson & Bergen 1979; and Felton, Richards & Smith 1972).

2 (P***). Terminations, and signed, roughly oriented zero-crossings in the filtered image are used as the input to the matching process.

3 (P**). In the absence of eye movements, discrimination between two disparities in a random dot stereogram is only possible within the range $\pm w$, where w is the width associated with the largest active channel. Stereo acuity should scale with the width w of the smallest active matched channels (i.e. about 10" for the smallest and 40" for the largest foveal channels).

4 (P***). In the absence of eye movements, the magnitude of perceived depth in non-diplopic conditions is limited by the lowest spatial-frequency channel stimulated.

5 (P***). In the absence of eye movements, the minimum fusable disparity range (Panum's fusional area) is $\pm 3.1'$ in the fovea, and $\pm 5.3'$ at 4° eccentricity. This requires that only the smallest channels be active.

6 (P***). In the absence of eye movements, the maximum fusable disparity range is $\pm 12'$ (possibly up to $\pm 20'$) in the fovea, and about $\pm 34'$ at 4° eccentricity. This requires that the largest channels be active, for example by using bars or other large bandwidth stimuli.

Comments. (1) Mitchell (1966) used small flashed line targets and found, in keeping with earlier studies, that the maximum amount of convergent or divergent disparity without diplopia is 10–14' in the fovea, and about 30' at 5° eccentricity. The extent of the so-called Panum fusional area is therefore twice this.

Under stabilized image conditions, Fender & Julesz (1967) found that fusion occurred between line targets (13' by 1° high) at a maximum

disparity of 40'. This value probably represents the whole extent of Panum's fusional area. Using the same technique on a random dot stereogram, Fender & Julesz arrived at a figure of 14' (6' displacement and 8' disparity within the stereogram). Since the dot size was only 2', one may expect more energy in the high frequency channels than in the low, which would tend to reduce the fusional area. Julesz & Chang (1976), using a 6' dot size over a visual angle of 5°, routinely achieved fusion up to $\pm 18'$ disparity. Taking all factors into account, these figures seem to be consistent with our expectations.

(2) Prediction 6 should hold for dynamic stereograms with the following caveats. First, motion cues must be eliminated. Secondly nonlinear temporal summation between frames at the receptor level may introduce unwanted low spatial-frequency components in the two images.

7 (P**). In the absence of eye movements, the perception of rivalrous random dot stereograms is subject to certain limitations. For example, for images of sufficiently high quality, fig. 2b of Mayhew & Frisby (1976) should give rise to depth sensations, but fig. 2c should not. In the presence of eye movements, fig. 2c gives a sensation of depth. This could be explained if vergence eye movements can be driven by the relative imbalance between the numbers of unambiguous matches in the crossed and uncrossed pools over a small neighbourhood of the fixation point.

8 (A). As measured by disparity specific adaptation effects, the optimum stimulus for a small disparity is a high spatial frequency grating, whereas for large disparities, the most effective stimulus is a low spatial frequency grating. Furthermore, the adaptation effect specific to disparity is greatest for gratings whose periods are twice the disparity (Felton, Richards & Smith 1972). (In our terms, in fact, λ is approximately $2.2w$ where λ is the centre frequency of the channel.)

9 (A). Evidence for the two pools hypothesis (Richards 1970, 1971; Richards & Regan 1973) is consistent with the minimal requirement for the second of the matching algorithms we described (figures 6 and 7).

10 (P***). In the absence of eye movements, the perception of tilt in stereoscopically viewed grating pairs of different spatial frequencies is limited by 4, 5, and 6 above.

11 (A). Individuals impaired in one of the two disparity pools show corresponding reductions in depth sensations accompanied by a loss of vergence movements in the corresponding direction (Jones 1972).

12 (P**). Outside Panum's area, the dependence of depth sensation on disparity should be roughly proportional to the initial vergence velocity under the same conditions.

13 (P***). For a novel two planar stereogram, vergence movements should exhibit a random-search-like structure. The three star status holds when the disparity range exceeds the size of the largest masks activated by the pattern.

14 (P***). The range of vergence movements made during the successful and precise interpretation of complex, high frequency, multi layer, random dot stereograms should span the range of disparities.

15 (P*). Perception times for a random dot stereogram portraying two small planar targets separated laterally and in depth, against an uncorrelated background, should be longer than the two planar case (13). Once found, their representation in the memory should be labile if an important aspect of the representation there consists of local disparity differences.

Neurophysiology

16 (partly A). At each point in the visual field, the scatter of bar mask receptive field sizes is about 4 : 1 (Hubel & Wiesel 1974, figs. 1 and 4; Wilson & Gieze 1977, p. 27). More data are however needed on this point. This range is spanned by four populations of receptive field size.

17 (P**). There exist binocularly driven cells sensitive to disparity. A given cell signals a match between either a zero-crossing pair or a termination pair, both items in its pair having the same sign, size and rough orientation.

18 (P**). Each of the populations defined by (17) is divided into at least two main disparity pools, tuned to crossed and uncrossed disparities respectively, with sensitivity curves extending outwards to a disparity of about the width of its corresponding receptive field centre (see figure 7). Being sensitive to pure disparity, these cells are sensitive to changes in disparity induced by vergence movements. In addition, there may be units quite sharply tuned to near-zero disparities.

19 (P*). In addition to the basic disparity pools of (18), there may exist cells tuned to more outlying (diplopic) disparities (compare figure 7). These cells should be inhibited by any activity in the basic pools (cf. Foley, Applebaum & Richards 1975).

20 (P**). There exists a neural representation of the 2½-D sketch. This includes cells that are highly specific for some monotonic function of depth and disparity, and which span a depth range corresponding to about 2° of disparity. Within a certain range, these cells may not be sensitive to disjunctive eye movements. This corresponds to the notion that the plane of fixation currently being represented in the 2½-D sketch.

21 (P*). The diplopic disparity cells of (20) are especially concerned with the control of disjunctive eye movements.

Comments. Because of the computational nature of this approach, we have been able to be quite precise about the nature of the processes that are involved in this theory. Since a process may in general be implemented in several different ways, our physiological predictions are more speculative than our psychophysical ones. They should perhaps be regarded as guidelines for investigation rather than as necessary consequences of the theory.

Unfortunately, the technical problems associated with the neuro-physiology of stereopsis are considerable, and rather little quantitative data is currently available. Since Barlow, Blakemore & Pettigrew's (1967) original paper, relatively few examples of disparity tuning curve have been published (see for example, Pettigrew, Nikara & Bishop 1968; Bishop, Henry & Smith 1971; Nelson, Kato & Bishop 1977). Recently however, Poggio & Fischer (1978, in the monkey), and von der Heydt, Adorjani, Hanny & Baumgartner (1978, in the cat) have published properly controlled disparity tuning curves. On the whole, these studies (see also Clarke, Donaldson & Whitteridge 1976) favour the pools idea (see prediction 18).

Discussion

Perhaps one of the most striking features of our theory is the way it returns to Fender & Julesz's (1967) original suggestion, of a cortical memory that accounts for the hysteresis and which is distinct from the matching process. Consequently fusion does not need to be cooperative, and our theory and its implementation (Grimson & Marr 1979) demonstrate that the computational problem of stereoscopic matching can be solved without cooperativity. These arguments do not however forbid its presence. Critical for this question are the predictions about the exact extent of Panum's fusional area for each channel. If the empirical data indicate a fusable disparity range significantly larger than $\pm w$, false targets will pose a problem not easily overcome using straightforward matching techniques like algorithm (2) of figure 6. In these circumstances, the matching problem could be solved by an algorithm like Marr & Poggio's (1976) operating within each channel, to eliminate possible false targets arising as a result of an extended disparity sensitivity range.

As it stands, there are a number of points on which the theory is indefinite, especially concerning the 2½-D sketch. For example:

(1) What is its exact structure, and how are the various constraints implemented there?

(2) What is the relationship between the spatial structure of the information written in the memory and the scanning strategy of disjunctive and conjunctive eye movements?

(3) Is information moved around in the 2½-D sketch during disjunctive or conjunctive eye movements, and if so, how? For example, does the current fixation point always correspond to the same point in the 2½-D sketch?

Finally, we feel that an important feature of this theory is that it grew from an analysis of the computational problems that underlie stereopsis, and is devoted to a characterization of the processes capable of solving it without specific reference to the machinery in which they run. The elucidation of the precise neural mechanisms that implement these processes, obfuscated as they must inevitably be by the vagaries of natural evolution, poses a fascinating challenge to classical techniques in the brain sciences.

We are deeply indebted to Whitman Richards for many remarks that we understand only in retrospect. We are especially grateful to Jack Cowan, John Frisby, Eric Grimson, David Hubel, Bela Julesz, John Mayhew and Hugh Wilson, and to Werner Reichardt and the Max Planck Society for their kind hospitality in Tübingen. Karen Prendergast prepared the illustrations. The Royal Society kindly gave permission for reproduction of figure 3, and Science and the American Association for the Advancement of Science for figure 2. This work was conducted at the Max-Planck-Institut für Biologische Kybernetik in Tübingen, and at the Artificial Intelligence Laboratory, a Massachusetts Institute of Technology research program supported in part by the Advanced Research Projects Agency of the Department of Defense, and monitored by the Office of Naval Research under contract number N00014-75-C-0643. D.M. was partly supported by NSF contract number 77-07569-MCS.

REFERENCES

Barlow, H. B., Blakemore, C. & Pettigrew, J. D. 1967 The neural mechanism of binocular depth discrimination. J. Physiol., Lond. 193, 327–342.

Bishop, P. O., Henry, G. H. & Smith, C. J. 1971 Binocular interaction fields of single units in the cat striate cortex. J. Physiol., Lond. 216, 39–68.

Blakemore, C. & Campbell, F. W. 1969 On the existence of neurons in the human visual system selectively sensitive to the orientation and size of retinal images. J. Physiol., Lond. 203, 237–260.

Blomfield, S. 1973 Implicit features and stereoscopy. Nature, new Biol. 245, 256.

Campbell, F. W. & Robson, J. 1968 Application of Fourier analysis to the visibility of gratings. J. Physiol., Lond. 197, 551–566.

Clarke, P. G. H., Donaldson, I. M. L. & Whitteridge, D. 1976 Binocular visual mechanisms in cortical areas I and II of the sheep. J. Physiol., Lond. 256, 509–526.

Cowan, J. D. 1977 Some remarks on channel bandwidths for visual contrast detection. Neurosci. Res. Progr. Bull. 15, 492–517.

Dev, P. 1975 Perception of depth surfaces in random-dot stereograms: a neural model. Int. J. Man-Machine Stud. 7, 511–528.

Felton, T. B., Richards, W. & Smith, R. A. Jr. 1972 Disparity processing of spatial frequencies in man. J. Physiol., Lond. 225, 349–362.

Fender, D. & Julesz, B. 1967 Extension of Panum's fusional area in binocularly stabilized vision. J. opt. Soc. Am. 57, 819–830.

Foley, J. M., Applebaum, T. H. & Richards, W. A. 1975 Stereopsis with large disparities: discrimination and depth magnitude. Vision Res. 15, 417–422.

Frisby, J. P. & Clatworthy, J. L. 1975 Learning to see complex random-dot stereograms. Perception 4, 173–178.

Frisby, J. P. & Mayhew, J. E. W. 1979 Spatial frequency selective masking and stereopsis. (In preparation.)

Georgeson, M. A. & Sullivan, G. D. 1975 Contrast constancy: deblurring in human vision by spatial frequency channels. J. Physiol., Lond. 252, 627–656.

Grimson, W. E. L. & Marr, D. 1979 A computer implementation of a theory of human stereo vision. (In preparation.)

Hines, M. 1976 Line spread function variation near the fovea. Vision Res. 16, 567–572.

Hirai, Y. & Fukushima, K. 1976 An inference upon the neural network finding binocular correspondence. Trans. IECE J59-D, 133–140.

Hubel, D. H. & Wiesel, T. N. 1974 Sequence regularity and geometry of orientation columns in monkey striate cortex. J. comp. Neurol. 158, 267–294.

Jones, R. 1972 Psychophysical and oculomotor responses of manual and stereoanomalous observers to disparate retinal stimulation. Doctoral dissertation, Ohio State University. Dissertation Abstract N. 72-20970.

Julesz, B. 1960 Binocular depth perception of computer-generated patterns. Bell System Tech. J. 39, 1125–1162.

Julesz, B. 1963 Towards the automation of binocular depth perception (AUTOMAP-1). Proceedings of the IFIPS Congress, Munich 1962 (ed. C. M. Popplewell). Amsterdam: North Holland.

Julesz, B. 1971 Foundations of cyclopean perception. The University of Chicago Press.

Julesz, B. & Chang, J. J. 1976 Interaction between pools of binocular disparity detectors tuned to different disparities. Biol. Cybernetics 22, 107–120.

Julesz, B. & Miller, J. E. 1975 Independent spatial-frequency-tuned channels in binocular fusion and rivalry. Perception 4, 125–143.

Kaufman, L. 1964 On the nature of binocular disparity. Am. J. Psychol. 77, 393–402.

Leadbetter, M. R. 1969 On the distributions of times between events in a stationary stream of events. J. R. statist. Soc. B 31, 295–302.

Longuet-Higgins, M. S. 1962 The distribution of intervals between zeros of a stationary random function. Phil. Trans. R. Soc. Lond. A 254, 557–599.

Marr, D. 1974 A note on the computation of binocular disparity in a symbolic, low-level visual processor. M.I.T. A.I. Lab. Memo 327.

Marr, D. 1976 Early processing of visual information. Phil. Trans. R. Soc. Lond. B 275, 483–524.

Marr, D. 1977 Representing visual information. AAAS 143rd Annual Meeting. Symposium on Some Mathematical Questions in Biology, February. Published in Lectures on mathematics in the life sciences 10, 101–180 (1978). Also available as M.I.T. A.I. Lab. Memo 415.

Marr, D. & Hildreth, E. 1979 Theory of edge detection. (In preparation.)

Marr, D. & Nishihara, H. K. 1978 Representation and recognition of the spatial organization of three-dimensional shapes. Proc. R. Soc. Lond. B 200, 269–294.

Marr, D., Palm, G. & Poggio, T. 1978 Analysis of a cooperative stereo algorithm. Biol. Cybernetics 28, 223–229.

Marr, D. & Poggio, T. 1976 Cooperative computation of stereo disparity. Science, N.Y. 194, 283–287.

Marr, D. & Poggio, T. 1977a A theory of human stereo vision. M.I.T. A.I. Lab. Memo 451.

Marr, D. & Poggio, T. 1977b Theory of human stereopsis. J. opt. Soc. Am. 67, 1400.

Mayhew, J. E. W. & Frisby, J. P. 1976 Rivalrous texture stereograms. Nature, Lond. 264, 53–56.

Mitchell, D. E. 1966 Retinal disparity and diplopia. Vision Res. 6, 441–451.

Nelson, J. I. 1975 Globality and stereoscopic fusion in binocular vision. J. theor. Biol. 49, 1–88.

Nelson, J. I., Kato, H. & Bishop, P. O. 1977 Discrimination of orientation and position disparities by binocularly activated neurons in cat striate cortex. J. Neurophysiol. 40, 260–283.

Papoulis, A. 1968 Systems and transforms with applications in optics. New York: McGraw Hill.

Pettigrew, J. D., Nikara, T. & Bishop, P. O. 1968 Binocular interaction on single units in cat striate cortex: simultaneous stimulation by single moving slit with receptive fields in correspondence. Exp. Brain Res. 6, 311–410.

Poggio, G. F. & Fischer, B. 1978 Binocular interaction and depth sensitivity of striate and prestriate cortical neurons of the behaving rhesus monkey. J. Neurophysiol. 40, 1392–1405.

von der Heydt, R., Adorjani, Cs., Hanny, P. & Baumgartner, G. 1978 Disparity sensitivity and receptive field incongruity of units in the cat striate cortex. Exp. Brain Res. 31, 523–545.

Rashbass, C. & Westheimer, G. 1961a Disjunctive eye movements. J. Physiol., Lond. 159, 339–360.

$$P_0(\xi) = \frac{1}{2\pi} \left[\frac{\psi(0)}{-\psi''(0)} \right]^{\frac{1}{2}} \frac{M_{23}(\xi)}{H(\xi)} \, (\psi^2(0) - \psi^2(\xi))[1 + H(\xi)\operatorname{arccot}(-H(\xi))],$$

$$P_1(\xi) = \frac{1}{2\pi} \left[\frac{\psi(0)}{-\psi''(0)} \right]^{\frac{1}{2}} \frac{M_{23}(\xi)}{H(\xi)} \, (\psi^2(0) - \psi^2(\xi))[1 - H(\xi)\operatorname{arccot}(H(\xi))],$$

where $\psi(\xi)$ is the autocorrelation of the underlying stochastic process, a prime denotes differentiation with respect to ξ, and also

$$H(\xi) = M_{23}(\xi)[M_{22}(\xi) - M_{23}(\xi)]^{-\frac{1}{2}},$$

$$M_{22}(\xi) = -\psi''(0)(\psi^2(0) - \psi^2(\xi)) - \psi(0)\,\psi'^2(\xi),$$

$$M_{23}(\xi) = \psi''(\xi)(\psi^2(0) - \psi^2(\xi)) + \psi(\xi)\,\psi'^2(\xi).$$

These approximations cease to be accurate for large values of ξ (i.e. of order λ, where $2\pi/\lambda$ is the centre frequency of the channel; see Longuet-Higgins (1962) for a discussion of various approximations), where they overestimate P_0 and P_1. The autocorrelation $\psi(\xi)$ can be easily computed analytically for the two filters of figure 5.

Rashbass, C. & Westheimer, G. 1961b Independence of conjunctive and disjunctive eye movements. *J. Physiol., Lond.* **159**, 361-364.

Rice, S. O. 1945 Mathematical analysis of random noise. *Bell Syst. Tech. J.* **24**, 46-156.

Richards, W. 1970 Stereopsis and steroblindness. *Exp. Brain Res.* **10**, 380-388.

Richards, W. 1971 Anomalous stereoscopic depth perception. *J. opt. Soc. Am.* **61**, 410-414.

Richards, W. 1975 Visual space perception. In *Handbook of Perception*, vol. 5, *Seeing*, ch. 10, pp. 351-386 (ed E. C. Carterete & M. D. Freidman). New York: Academic Press.

Richards, W. A. 1977 Stereopsis with and without monocular cues. *Vision Res.* **17**, 967-969.

Richards, W. A. & Regan, D. 1973 A stereo field map with implications for disparity processing. *Invest. Ophthal.* **12**, 904-909.

Riggs, L. A. & Niehl, E. W. 1960 Eye movements recorded during convergence and divergence. *J. opt. Soc. Am.* **50**, 913-920.

Saye, A. & Frisby, J. P. 1975 The role of monocularly conspicuous features in facilitating stereopsis from random-dot stereograms. *Perception* **4**, 159-171.

Schiller, P. H., Finlay, B. L. & Volman, S. F. 1977 Quantitative studies of single-cell properties in monkey striate cortex. III. Spatial frequency. *J. Neurophysiol.* **39**, 1334-1351.

Sperling, G. 1970 Binocular vision: a physical and a neural theory. *Am. J. Psychol.* **83**, 461-534.

Sugie, N. & Suwa, M. 1977 A scheme for binocular depth perception suggested by neurophysiological evidence. *Biol. Cybernetics* **26**, 1-15.

Waltz, D. 1975 Understanding line drawings of scenes with shadows. In *The psychology of computer vision* (ed. P. H. Winston), pp. 19-91. New York: McGraw-Hill.

Westheimer, G. & Mitchell, D. E. 1969 The sensory stimulus for disjunctive eye movements. *Vision Res.* **9**, 749-755.

Williams, R. H. & Fender, D. H. 1977 The synchrony of binocular saccadic eye movements. *Vision Res.* **17**, 303-306.

Wilson, H. R. 1978a Quantitative characterization of two types of line spread function near the fovea. *Vision Res.* **18**, 971-981.

Wilson, H. R. 1978b Quantitative prediction of line spread function measurements: implications for channel bandwidths. *Vision Res.* **18**, 493-496.

Wilson, H. R. & Bergen, J. R. 1979 A four mechanism model for spatial vision. *Vision Res.* (in the press).

Wilson, H. R. & Giese, S. C. 1977 Threshold visibility of frequency gradient patterns. *Vision Res.* **17**, 1177-1190.

Wilson, H. R., Phillips, G., Rentschler, I. & Hilz, R. 1979 Spatial probability summation and disinhibition in psychophysically measured line spread functions. *Vision Res.* (in the press).

APPENDIX. STATISTICAL ANALYSIS OF ZERO-CROSSINGS

We assume that $f(x) = \int I(x,y) h(y) \, dy$, where $I(x,y)$ is the image intensity and $h(y)$ represents the longitudinal weighting function of the mask, is a white Gaussian process. Our problem is that of finding the distribution of the intervals between alternate zero-crossings by the stationary normal process obtained by filtering $f(x)$ through a linear (bandpass) filter.

Assume that there is a zero-crossing at the origin, and let $P_0(\xi)$, $P_1(\xi)$ be the probability densities of the distances to the first and second zero-crossings. P_0 and P_1 are approximated by the following formulae (Rice 1945, eqns 1.2.1 and 1.2.3; Leadbetter 1969):

Visual routines*

SHIMON ULLMAN

Massachusetts Institute of Technology

Abstract

This paper examines the processing of visual information beyond the creation of the early representations. A fundamental requirement at this level is the capacity to establish visually abstract shape properties and spatial relations. This capacity plays a major role in object recognition, visually guided manipulation, and more abstract visual thinking.

For the human visual system, the perception of spatial properties and relations that are complex from a computational standpoint nevertheless often appears deceivingly immediate and effortless. The proficiency of the human system in analyzing spatial information far surpasses the capacities of current artificial systems. The study of the computations that underlie this competence may therefore lead to the development of new more efficient methods for the spatial analysis of visual information.

The perception of abstract shape properties and spatial relations raises fundamental difficulties with major implications for the overall processing of visual information. It will be argued that the computation of spatial relations divides the analysis of visual information into two main stages. The first is the bottom-up creation of certain representations of the visible environment. The second stage involves the application of processes called 'visual routines' to the representations constructed in the first stage. These routines can establish properties and relations that cannot be represented explicitly in the initial representations.

Visual routines are composed of sequences of elemental operations. Routines for different properties and relations share elemental operations. Using a fixed set of basic operations, the visual system can assemble different routines to extract an unbounded variety of shape properties and spatial relations.

At a more detailed level, a number of plausible basic operations are suggested, based primarily on their potential usefulness, and supported in part by empirical evidence. The operations discussed include shifting of the processing focus, indexing to an odd-man-out location, bounded activation, boundary tracing, and marking. The problem of assembling such elemental operations into meaningful visual routines is discussed briefly.

1. The perception of spatial relations

1.1. Introduction

Visual perception requires the capacity to extract shape properties and spatial relations among objects and objects' parts. This capacity is fundamental to visual recognition, since objects are often defined visually by abstract shape properties and spatial relations among their components.

A simple example is illustrated in Fig. 1a, which is readily perceived as representing a face. The shapes of the individual constituents, the eyes, nose, and mouth, in this drawing are highly schematized; it is primarily the spatial arrangement of the constituents that defines the face. In Fig. 1b, the same components are rearranged, and the figure is no longer interpreted as a face. Clearly, the recognition of objects depends not only on the presence of certain features, but also on their spatial arrangement.

The role of establishing properties and relations visually is not confined to the task of visual recognition. In the course of manipulating objects we often rely on our visual perception to obtain answers to such questions as "is *A* longer than *B*", "does *A* fit inside *B*", etc. Problems of this type can be solved without necessarily implicating object recognition. They do require, however,

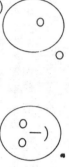

Figure 1.   *Schematic drawings of normally-arranged (a) and scrambled (b) faces. Figure 1a is readily recognized as representing a face although the individual features are meaningless. In 1b, the same constituents are rearranged, and the figure is no longer perceived as a face.*

*This report describes research done at the Artificial Intelligence Laboratory of the Massachusetts Institute of Technology. Support for the laboratory's artificial intelligence research is provided in part by the Advanced Research Projects Agency of the Department of Defense under Office of Naval Research contract N00014-80-C-0505 and in part by National Science Foundation Grant 79-23110MCS. Reprint requests should be sent to Shimon Ullman Department of Psychology and Artificial Intelligence Laboratory, M.I.T., Cambridge, MA 02139, U.S.A.

the visual analysis of shape and spatial relations among parts.[1] Spatial relations in three-dimensional space therefore play an important role in visual perception.

In view of the fundamental importance of the task, it is not surprising that our visual system is indeed remarkably adept at establishing a variety of spatial relations among items in the visual input. This proficiency is evidenced by the fact that the perception of spatial properties and relations that are complex from a computational standpoint, nevertheless often appears immediate and effortless. It also appears that some of the capacity to establish spatial relations is manifested by the visual system from a very early age. For example, infants of 1–15 weeks of age are reported to respond preferentially to schematic face-like figures, and to prefer normally arranged face figures over 'scrambled' face patterns (Fantz, 1961).

The apparent immediateness and ease of perceiving spatial relations is deceiving. As we shall see, it conceals in fact a complex array of processes that have evolved to establish certain spatial relations with considerable efficiency. The processes underlying the perception of spatial relations are still unknown even in the case of simple elementary relations. Consider, for instance, the task of comparing the lengths of two line segments. Faced with this simple task, a draftsman may measure the length of the first line, record the result, measure the second line, and compare the resulting measurements. When the two lines are present simultaneously in the field of view, it is often possible to compare their lengths by 'merely looking'. This capacity raises the problem of how the 'draftsman in our head' operates, without the benefit of a ruler and a scratchpad. More generally, a theory of the perception of spatial relations should aim at unraveling the processes that take place within our visual system when we establish shape properties of objects and their spatial relations by 'merely looking' at them.

The perception of abstract shape properties and spatial relations raises fundamental difficulties with major implications for the overall processing of visual information. The purpose of this paper is to examine these problems and implications. Briefly, it will be argued that the computation of spatial relations divides the analysis of visual information into two main stages. The first is the bottom up creation of certain representations of the visible environment. Examples of such representations are the primal sketch (Marr, 1976) and the 2½-D sketch (Marr and Nishihara, 1978). The second stage involves the top–down application of visual routines to the representations constructed

in the first stage. These routines can establish properties and relations that cannot be represented explicitly in the initial base representations. Underlying the visual routines there exists a fixed set of elemental operations that constitute the basic 'instruction set' for more complicated processes. The perception of a large variety of properties and relations is obtained by assembling appropriate routines based on this set of elemental operations.

The paper is divided into three parts. The first introduces the notion of visual routines. The second examines the role of visual routines within the overall scheme of processing visual information. The third (Sections 3 and 4) examines the elemental operations out of which visual routines are constructed.

1.2. An example: The perception of inside/outside relations

The perception of inside/outside relationships is performed by the human perceptual system with intriguing efficiency. To take a concrete example, suppose that the visual input consists of a single closed curve, and a small 'X' figure (see Fig. 2), and one is required to determine visually whether the X lies inside or outside the closed curve. The correct answers in Fig. 2a and 2b appear to be immediate and effortless, and the response would be fast and accurate.[2]

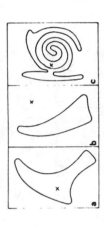

Figure 2. Perceiving inside and outside. In 2a and 2b, the perception is immediate and effortless; in 2c, it is not.

---

[1]Shape properties (such as overall orientation, area, etc.) refer to a single item, while spatial relations (such as above, inside, longer-than, etc.) involve two or more items. For brevity, the term spatial relations used in the discussion would refer to both shape properties and spatial relations.

[2]For simple figures such as 2a, viewing time of less than 50 msec with moderate intensity, followed by effective masking is sufficient. This is well within the limit of what is considered immediate, effortless perception (e.g., Julesz, 1975). Reaction time of about 500 msec can be obtained in two-choice experiments with simple figures (Varanese, 1981). The response time may vary with the presentation conditions, but the main point is that in/out judgments are fast and reliable and require only a brief presentation.

One possible reason for our proficiency in establishing inside/outside relations is their potential value in visual recognition based on their stability with respect to the viewing position. That is, inside/outside relations tend to remain invariant over considerable variations in viewing position. When viewing a face, for instance, the eyes remain within the head boundary as long as they are visible, regardless of the viewing position (see also Sutherland (1968) on inside/outside relations in perception).

The immediate perception of the inside/outside relation is subject to some limitations (Fig. 2c). These limitations are not very restrictive, however, and the computations performed by the visual system in distinguishing 'inside' from 'outside' exhibit considerable flexibility: the curve can have a variety of shapes, and the positions of the X and the curve do not have to be known in advance.

The processes underlying the perception of insde/outside relations are entirely unknown. In the following section I shall examine two methods for computing 'insideness' and compare them with human perception. The comparison will then serve to introduce the general discussion concerning the notion of visual routines and their role in visual perception.

1.2.1. Computing inside and outside

The ray-intersection method. Shape perception and recognition is often described in terms of a hierarchy of 'feature detectors' (Barlow, 1972; Milner, 1974). According to these hierarchical models, simple feature detecting units such as edge detectors are combined to produce higher order units such as, say, triangle detectors, leading eventually to the detection and recognition of objects. It does not seem possible, however, to construct an 'inside/outside detector' from a combination of elementary feature detectors. Approaches that are more procedural in nature have therefore been suggested instead. A simple procedure that can establish whether a given point lies inside or outside a closed curve is the method of ray-intersections. To use this method, a ray is drawn, emanating from the point in question, and extending to 'infinity'. For practical purposes, 'infinity' is a region that is guaranteed somehow to lie outside the curve. The number of intersections made by the ray with the curve is recorded. (The ray may also happen to be tangential to the curve without crossing it at one or more points. In this case, each tangent point is counted as two intersection points.) If the resulting intersection number is odd, the origin point of the ray lies inside the closed curve. If it is even (including zero), then it must be outside (see Fig. 3a, b).

This procedure has been implemented in computer programs (Evans, 1968; Winston, 1977, Ch. 2), and it may appear rather simple and straightforward. The success of the ray-intersection method is guaranteed, however, only if

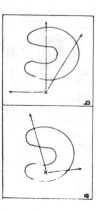

Figure 3. *The ray intersection method for establishing inside/outside relations. When the point lies inside the closed curve, the number of intersections is odd (a); when it lies outside, the number of intersections is even (b).*

rather restrictive constraints are met. First, it must be assumed that the curve is closed, otherwise an odd number of intersections would not be indicative of an 'inside' relation (see Fig. 4a). Second, it must be assumed that the curve is isolated: in Figs. 4b and 4c, point p lies within the region bounded by the closed curve c, but the number of intersections is even.[3]

These limitations on the ray-intersection method are not shared by the human visual system: in all of the above examples the correct relation is easily established. In addition, some variations of the inside/outside problem pose almost insurmountable difficulties to the ray-intersection procedure, but not to human vision. Suppose that in Fig. 4d the problem is to determine whether any of the points lies inside the curve C. Using the ray-intersection procedure, rays must be constructed from all the points, adding significantly to the complexity of the solution. In Figs. 4e and 4f the problem is to determine whether the two points marked by dots lie inside the same curve. The number of intersections of the connecting line is not helpful in this case in establishing the desired relation. In Fig. 4g the task is to find an innermost point—a point that lies inside all of the three curves. The task is again straightforward, but it poses serious difficulties to the ray-intersection method.

It can be concluded from such considerations that the computations employed by our perceptual system are different from, and often superior to the ray-intersection method.

---

[3] In Fig. 4c region p can also be interpreted as lying inside a hole cut in a planar figure. Under this interpretation the result of the ray-intersection method can be accepted as correct. For the original task, however, which is to determine whether p lies within the region bounded by c, the answer provided by the ray-intersection method is incorrect.

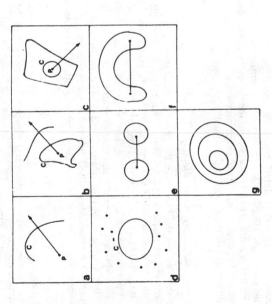

Figure 4. *Limitations of the ray-intersection method. a, An open curve. The number of intersections is odd, but p does not lie inside C. b—c, Additional curves may change the number of intersections, leading to errors. d—g, Variations of the inside/outside problem that render the ray-intersection method in-effective. In d the task is to determine visually whether any of the dots lie inside C, in (—f). whether the two dots lie inside the same curve; in g the task is to find a point that lies inside all three curves.*

The 'coloring' method. An alternative procedure that avoids some of the limitations inherent in the ray-intersection method uses the operation of activating, or 'coloring' an area. Starting from a given point, the area around it in the internal representation is somehow activated. This activation spreads outward until a boundary is reached, but it is not allowed to cross the boundary. Depending on the starting point, either the inside or the outside of the curve, but not both, will be activated. This can provide a basis for separating inside from outside. An additional stage is still required, however, to complete the procedure, and this additional stage will depend on the specific problem at hand. One can test, for example, whether the region surrounding a 'point at infinity' has been activated. Since this point lies outside the curve in question,

it will thereby be established whether the activated area constitutes the curve's inside or the outside. In this manner a point can sometimes be determined to lie outside the curve without requiring a detailed analysis of the curve itself. In Fig. 5, most of the curve can be ignored, since activation that starts at the X will soon 'leak out' of the enclosing corridor and spread to 'infinity'. It will thus be determined that the X cannot lie inside the curve, without analyzing the curve and without attempting to separate its inside from the outside.[4]

Alternatively, one may start at an infinity point, using for instance the following procedure: (1) move towards the curve until a boundary is met; (2) mark this meeting point; (3) start to track the boundary, in a clockwise direction, activating the area on the right; (4) stop when the marked position is reached. If a termination of the curve is encountered before the marked position is reached, the curve is open and has no inside or outside. Otherwise, when the marked position is reached again and the activation spread stops, the inside of the curve will be activated. Both routines are possible, but, depending on the shape of the curve and the location of the X, one or the other may become more efficient.

The coloring method avoids some of the main difficulties with the ray-intersection method, but it also falls short of accounting for the performance of human perception in similar tasks. It seems, for example, that for human perception the computation time is to a large extent scale independent. That

Figure 5. *That the x does not lie inside the curve C can be established without a detailed analysis of the curve.*

[4]In practical applications 'infinity points' can be located if the curve is known in advance not to extend beyond a limited region. In human vision it is not clear what may constitute an 'infinity point', but it seems that we have little difficulty in finding such points. Even for a complex shape, that may not have a well-defined inside and outside, it is easy to determine visually a location that clearly lies outside the region occupied by the shape.

is, the size of the figures can be increased considerably with only a small effect on the computation time.[5] In contrast, in the activation scheme outlined above computation time should increase with the size of the figures.

The basic coloring scheme can be modified to increase its efficiency and endow it with scale independence, for example by performing the computation simultaneously at a number of resolution scales. Even the modified scheme will have difficulties, however, competing with the performance of the human perceptual system. Evidently, elaborate computations will be required to match the efficiency and flexibility exhibited by the human perceptual system in establishing inside/outside relationships.

The goal of the above discussion was not to examine the perception of inside/outside relations in detail, but to introduce the problems associated with the seemingly effortless and immediate perception of spatial relations. I next turn to a more general discussion of the difficulties associated with the perception of spatial relations and shape properties, and the implications of these difficulties to the processing of visual information.

1.3. Spatial analysis by visual routines

In this section, we shall examine the general requirements imposed by the visual analysis of shape properties and spatial relations. The difficulties involved in the analysis of spatial properties and relations are summarized below in terms of three requirements that must be faced by the 'visual processor' that performs such analysis. The three requirements are (i) the capacity to establish abstract properties and relations (abstractness), (ii) the capacity to establish a large variety of relations and properties, including newly defined ones (open-endedness), and (iii) the requirement to cope efficiently with the complexity involved in the computation of spatial relations (complexity).

1.3.1. Abstractness

The perception of inside/outside relations provides an example of the visual system's capacity to analyze abstract spatial relations. In this section the notion of abstract properties and relations and the difficulties raised by their perception will be briefly discussed.

Formally, a shape property P defines a set S of shapes that share this property. The property of closure, for example, divides the set of all curves

into the set of closed curves that share this property, and the complementary set of open curves. (Similarly, a relation such as 'inside' defines a set of configurations that satisfy this relation.)

Clearly, in many cases the set of shapes S that satisfy a property P can be large and unwieldy. It therefore becomes impossible to test a shape for property P by comparing it against all the members of S stored in memory. The problem lies in fact not simply in the size of the set S, but in what may be called the size of the *support* of S. To illustrate this distinction, suppose that given a plane with one special point X marked on it we wish to identify the black figures containing X. This set of figures is large, but, given an isolated figure, it is simple to test whether it is a member of the set: only a single point, X, need be inspected. In this case the relevant part of the figure, or its support, consists of a single point. In contrast, the set of supports for the property of closure, or the inside/outside relation, is unmanageably large.

When the set of supports is small, the recognition of even a large set of objects can be accomplished by simple template matching. This means that a small number of patterns is stored, and matched against the figure in question.[6] When the set of supports is prohibitively large, a template matching decision scheme will become impossible. The classification task may nevertheless be feasible if the set contains certain regularities. This roughly means that the recognition of a property P can be broken down into a set of operations in such a manner that the overall computation required for establishing P is substantially less demanding than the storing of all the shapes in S. The set of all closed curves, for example, is not just a random collection of shapes, and there are obviously more efficient methods for establishing closure than simple template matching. For a completely random set of shapes containing no regularities, simplified recognition procedures will not be possible. The minimal program required for the recognition of the set would be in this case essentially as large as the set itself (cf. Kolmogorov, 1968).

The above discussion can now serve to define what is meant here by 'abstract' shape properties and spatial relations. This notion refers to properties and relations with a prohibitively large set of supports that can nevertheless be established efficiently by a computation that captures the regularities in the set. Our visual system can clearly establish abstract properties and

---

[5] The dependency of inside/outside judgments on the size of the figure is currently under empirical investigation. There seems to be a slight increase in reaction time as a function of the figure size.

[6] For the present discussion, template-matching between plane figures can be defined as their cross-correlation. The definition can be extended to symbolic descriptions in the plane. In this case at each location in a plane a number of symbols can be activated, and a pattern is then a subset of activated symbols. Given a pattern P and a template T, their degree of match m is a function that is increasing in $P \cap T$ and decreasing in $P \cup T - P \cap T$ (when P is 'positioned over' T so as to maximize m).

relations. The implication is that it should employ sets of processes for establishing shape properties and spatial relations. The perception of abstract properties such as insideness or closure would then be explained in terms of the computations employed by the visual system to capture the regularities underlying different properties and relations. These computations would be described in terms of their constituent operations and how they are combined to establish different properties and relations.

We have seen in Section 1.2 examples of possible computations for the analysis of inside/outside relations. It is suggested that processes of this general type are performed by the human visual system in perceiving inside/outside relations. The operations employed by the visual system may prove, however, to be different from those considered in Section 1.2. To explain the perception of inside/outside relations it would be necessary, therefore, to unravel the constituent operations employed by the visual system, and how they are used in different judgments.

1.3.2. Open-endedness

As we have seen, the perception of an abstract relation is quite a remarkable feat even for a single relation, such as insideness. Additional complications arise from the requirement to recognize not only one, but a large number of different properties and relations. A reasonable approach to the problem would be to assume that the computations that establish different properties and relations share their underlying elemental operations. In this manner a large variety of abstract shape properties and spatial relations can be established by different processes assembled from a fixed set of elemental operations. The term 'visual routines' will be used to refer to the processes composed out of the set of elemental operations to establish shape properties and spatial relations.

A further implication of the open-endedness requirement is that a mechanism is required by which new combinations of basic operations can be assembled to meet new computational goals. One can impose goals for visual analysis, such as "determine whether the green and red elements lie on the same side of the vertical line". That the visual system can cope effectively with such goals suggests that it has the capacity to create new processes out of the basic set of elemental operations.

1.3.3. Complexity

The open-endedness requirement implied that different processes should share elemental operations. The same conclusion is also suggested by complexity considerations. The complexity of basic operations such as the bounded activation (discussed in more detail in Section 3.4) implies that differ-

ent routines that establish different properties and relations and use the same mechanism rather than have their own separate mechanisms.

A special case of the complexity consideration arises from the need to perform a given computation at different spatial locations. The ability to apply the same computation at different spatial locations can be obtained by having an independent processing module at each location. For example, the orientation of a line segment at a given location seems to be performed in the primary visual cortex largely independent of other locations. In contrast, the computations of more complex relations such as inside/outside independent of location cannot be explained by assuming a large number of independent 'inside/outside modules', one for each location. Routines that establish a given property or relation at different positions are likely to share some of their machinery, similar to the sharing of elemental operations by different routines.

Certain constraints will be imposed upon the computation of spatial relations by the sharing of elemental operations. For example, the sharing of operations by different routines will restrict the simultaneous perception of different spatial relations. The application of a given routine to different spatial locations will be similarly restricted. In applying visual routines the need will consequently arise for the sequencing of elemental operations, and for selecting the location at which a given operation is applied.

In summary, the three requirements discussed above suggest the following implications.

(1) Spatial properties and relations are established by the application of visual routines to a set of early visual representations.
(2) Visual routines are assembled from a fixed set of elemental operations.
(3) New routines can be assembled to meet newly specified processing goals.
(4) Different routines share elemental operations.
(5) A routine can be applied to different spatial locations. The processes that perform the same routine at different locations are not independent.
(6) In applying visual routines mechanisms are required for sequencing elemental operations and for selecting the locations at which they are applied.

1.4. Conclusions and open problems

The discussion so far suggests that the immediate perception of seemingly simple spatial relations requires in fact complex computations that are difficult to unravel, and difficult to imitate. These computations were termed above 'visual routines'. The general proposal is that using a fixed set of basic operations, the visual system can assemble routines that are applied to the visual representations to extract abstract shape properties and spatial relations.

The use of visual routines to establish shape properties and spatial relations raises fundamental problems at the levels of computational theory, algorithms, and the underlying mechanisms. A general problem on the computational level is which spatial properties and relations are important for object recognition and manipulation. On the algorithmic level, the problem is how these relations are computed. This is a challenging problem, since the processing of spatial relations and properties by the visual system is remarkably flexible and efficient. On the mechanism level, the problem is how visual routines are implemented in neural networks within the visual system.

In concluding this section, major problems raised by the notion of visual routines are listed below under four main categories.

(1) *The elemental operations.* In the examples discussed above the computation of inside/outside relations employed operations such as drawing a ray, counting intersections, boundary tracking, and area activation. The same basic operations can also be used in establishing other properties and relations. In this manner a variety of spatial relations can be computed using a fixed and powerful set of basic operations, together with means for combining them into different routines that are then applied to the base representation. The first problem that arises therefore is the identification of the elemental operations that constitute the basic 'instruction set' in the composition of visual routines.

(2) *Integration.* The second problem that arises is how the elemental operations are integrated into meaningful routines. This problem has two aspects. First, the general principles of the integration process, for example, whether different elemental operations can be applied simultaneously. Second, there is the question of how specific routines are composed in terms of the elemental operations. An account of our perception of a given shape property or relation such as elongation, above, next-to, inside/outside, taller-than etc. should include a description of the routines that are employed in the task in question, and the composition of each of these routines in terms of the elemental operations.

(3) *Control.* The questions in this category are how visual routines are selected and controlled, for example, what triggers the execution of different routines during visual recognition and other visual tasks, and how the order of their execution is determined.

(4) *Compilation.* How new routines are generated to meet specific needs, and how they are stored and modified with practice.

The remainder of this paper is organized as follows. In Section 2 I shall discuss the role of visual routines within the overall processing of visual information. Section 3 will then examine the first of the problems listed above, the elemental operations problem. Section 4 will conclude with a few brief comments pertaining to the other problems.

2. Visual routines and their role in the processing of visual information

The purpose of this section is to examine how the application of visual routines fits within the overall processing of visual information. The main goal is to elaborate the relations between the initial creation of the early visual representations and the subsequent application of visual routines. The discussion is structured along the following lines.

The first half of this section examines the relation between visual routines and the creation of two types of visual representations: the bare representation (Section 2.1) that precedes the application of visual routines, and the incremental representations that are produced by them (Section 2.2). The second half examines two general problems raised in the first half. These problems are: the initial selection of routines (Section 2.3) and the parallel processing of visual information (Section 2.4).

2.1. Visual routines and the base representations

In the scheme suggested above, the processing of visual information can be divided into two main stages. The first is the 'bottom-up' creation of some base representations by the early visual processes (Marr, 1980). The second stage is the application of visual routines. At this stage, procedures are applied to the base representations to define distinct entities within these representations, establish their shape properties, and extract spatial relations among them. In this section we shall examine more closely the distinction between these two stages.

2.1.1. The base representations

The first stage in the analysis of visual information can usefully be described as the creation of certain representations to be used by subsequent visual processes. Marr (1976) and Marr and Nishihara (1978) have suggested a division of these early representations into two types: the primal sketch, which is a representation of the incoming image, and the 2½-D sketch, which is a representation of the visible surfaces in three-dimensional space. The early visual representations share a number of fundamental characteristics: they are unarticulated, viewer-centered, uniform, and bottom-up driven. By 'unarticulated' I mean that they are essentially local descriptions that represent properties such as depth, orientation, color, and direction of motion at a point. The definition of larger more complicated units, and the extraction and description of spatial relationships among their parts, is not achieved at this level.

The base representations are spatially uniform in the sense that, with the exception of a scaling factor, the same properties are extracted and represented across the visual field (or throughout large parts of it). The descriptions of different points (e.g., the depth at a point) in the early representations are all with respect to the viewer, not with respect to one another. Finally, the construction of the base representations proceeds in a bottom-up fashion. This means that the base representations depend on the visual input alone.[7] If the same image is viewed twice, at two different times, the base representations associated with it will be identical.

2.1.2. Applying visual routines to the base representations

Beyond the construction of the base representations, the processing of visual information requires the definition of objects and parts in the scene, and the analysis of spatial properties and relations. The discussion in Section 1.3 concluded that for these tasks the uniform bottom-up computation is no longer possible, and suggested instead the application of visual routines. In contrast with the construction of the base representations, the properties and relations to be extracted are not determined by the input alone: for the same visual input different aspects will be made explicit at different times, depend-

ing on the goals of the computation. Unlike the base representations, the computations by visual routines are not applied uniformly over the visual field (e.g., not all of the possible inside/outside relations in the scene are computed), but only to selected objects. The objects and parts to which these computations apply are also not determined uniquely by the input alone; that is, there does not seem to be a universal set of primitive elements and relations that can be used for all possible perceptual tasks. The definition of objects and distinct parts in the input, and the relations to be computed among them may change with the situation. I may recognize a particular cat, for instance, using the shape of the white patch on its forehead. This does not imply, however, that the shapes of all the white patches participate are universally made explicit in some internal representation. More generally, the definition of what constitutes a distinct part, and the relations to be established often depends on the particular object to be recognized. It is therefore unlikely that a fixed set of operations applied uniformly over the base representations would be sufficient to capture all of the properties and relations that may be relevant for subsequent visual analysis. A final distinction between the two stages is that the construction of the base representations is fixed and unchanging, while visual routines are open-ended and permit the extraction of newly defined properties and relations.

In conclusion, it is suggested that the analysis of visual information divides naturally into two distinct successive stages: the creation of the base representations, followed by the application of visual routines to these representations. The application of visual routines can define objects within the base representations and establish properties and spatial relations that cannot be established within the base representations.[8]

It should be noted that many of the relations that are established at this stage are defined not in the image but in three-dimensional space. Since the base representations already contain three-dimensional information, the visual routines applied to them can also establish properties and relations in three-dimensional space.[9]

---

[7] Although 'bottom-up' and 'top-down' processing are useful and frequently used terms, they lack a precise, well-accepted definition. As mentioned in the text, the definition I adopt is that bottom-up processing is determined entirely by the input. Top-down processing depends on additional factors, such as the goal of the computation (but not necessarily on object-specific knowledge).
Physiologically, various mechanisms that are likely to be involved in the creation of the base representation appear to be bottom-up: their responses can be predicted from the parameters of the stimulus alone. They also show strong similarity in their responses in the awake, anesthetized, and naturally sleeping animal (e.g., Livingstone and Hubel, 1981).

[8] The argument does not preclude the possibility that some grouping processes that help to define distinct parts and some local shape descriptions take place within the base representations.

[9] Many spatial judgments we make depend primarily on three dimensional relations rather than on projected, two-dimensional ones (see e.g., Joynson and Kirk, 1960; Kappin and Fuqua, 1983). The implication is that various visual routines such as those used in comparing distances, operate upon a three-dimensional representation, rather than a representation that resembles the two-dimensional image.

while the incremental representations would vary.

Various other perceptual phenomena can be interpreted in a similar manner in light of the distinction between the base and the incremental representations. I shall mention here only one recent example from a study by Rock and Gutman (1981). Their subjects were presented with pairs of overlapping red and green figures. When they were instructed to attend selectively to the green or red member of the pair, they were later able to recognize the 'attended' but not the 'unattended' figure. This result can be interpreted in terms of the distinction between the base and the incremental representations. The creation of the base representations is assumed to be a bottom-up process, unaffected by the goal of the computation. Consequently, the two figures would not be treated differently within these representations. Attempts to attend selectively to one sub-figure resulted in visual routines being applied preferentially to it. A detailed description of this sub-figure is consequently created in the incremental representations. This detailed description can then be used by subsequent routines subserving comparison and recognition tasks.

The creation and use of incremental representations imply that visual routines should not be thought of merely as predicates, or decision processes that supply 'yes' or 'no' answers. For example, an inside/outside routine does not merely signal 'yes' if an inside relation is established, and 'no' otherwise. In addition to the decision process, certain structures are being created during the execution of the routine. These structures are maintained in the incremental representation, and can be used in subsequent visual tasks. The study of a given routine is therefore not confined to the problem of how a certain decision is reached, but also includes the structures constructed by the routine in question in the incremental representations.

In summary, the use of visual routines introduces a distinction between two different types of visual representations: the base representations and incremental representations. The base representations provide the initial data structures on which the routines operate, and the incremental representations maintain results obtained by the application of visual routines.

The second half of Section 2 examines two general issues raised by the nature of visual routines as introduced so far. Visual routines were described above as sequences of elementary operations that are assembled to meet specific computational goals. A major problem that arises is the initial selection of routines to be applied. This problem is examined briefly in Section 2.3. Finally, sequential application of elementary operations seems to stand in contrast with the notion of parallel processing in visual perception. (Biederman et al., 1973; Donderi and Zelnicker, 1969; Egeth et al., 1972; Jonides and Gleitman, 1972; Neisser et al., 1963). Section 2.4 examines the distinction

2.2. The incremental representations

The creation of visual representations does not stop at the base representations. It is reasonable to expect that results established by visual routines are retained temporarily for further use. This means that in addition to the base representations to which routines are applied initially representations are also being created and modified in the course of executing visual routines. I shall refer to these additional structures as 'incremental representations'. Unlike the base representations, the incremental representations are not created in a uniform and unguided manner: the same input can give rise to different incremental representations, depending on the routines that have been applied.

The role of the incremental representations can be illustrated using the inside/outside judgments considered in Section 1. Suppose that following the response to an inside/outside display using a fairly complex figure, an additional point is lit up. The task is now to determine whether this second point lies inside or outside the closed figure. If the results of previous computations are already summarized in the incremental representation of the figure in question, the judgment in the second task would be expected to be considerably faster than the first, and the effects of the figure's complexity might be reduced.[10] Such facilitation effects would provide evidence for the creation of some internal structure in the course of reaching a decision in the first task that is subsequently used to reach a faster decision in the second task. For example, if area activation or 'coloring' is used to separate inside from outside, then following the first task the inside of the figure may be already 'colored'. If, in addition, this coloring is preserved in the incremental representation, then subsequent inside/outside judgments with respect to the same figure would require considerably less processing, and may depend less on the complexity of the figure.

This example also serves to illustrate the distinction between the base representations and the incremental representations. The 'coloring' of the curve in question will depend on the particular routines that happened to be employed. Given the same visual input but a different visual task, or the same task but applied to a different part of the input, the same curve will not be 'colored' and a similar saving in computation time will not be obtained. The general point illustrated by this example is that for a given visual stimulus but different computational goals the base representations remain the same,

[10]This example is due to Steve Kosslyn. It is currently under empirical investigations.

between sequential and parallel processing, its significance to the processing of visual information, and its relation to visual routines.

2.3. Universal routines and the initial access problem

The act of perception requires more than the passive existence of a set of representations. Beyond the creation of the base representations, the perceptual process depends upon the current computational goal. At the level of applying visual routines, the perceptual activity is required to provide answers to queries, generated either externally or internally, such as: "is this my cat?" or, at a lower level, "is A longer than B?" Such queries arise naturally in the course of using visual information in recognition, manipulation, and more abstract visual thinking. In response to these queries routines are executed to provide the answers. The process of applying the appropriate routines is apparently efficient and smooth, thereby contributing to the impression that we perceive the entire image at a glance, when in fact we process only limited aspects of it at any given time. We may not be aware of the restricted processing since whenever we wish to establish new facts about the scene, that is, whenever an internal query is posed, an answer is provided by the execution of an appropriate routine.

Such application of visual routines raises the problem of guiding the perceptual activity and selecting the appropriate routines at any given instant. In dealing with this problem, several theories of perception have used the notion of schemata (Bartlett, 1932; Biederman et al., 1973; Neisser, 1967) or frames (Minsky, 1975) to emphasize the role of expectations in guiding perceptual activity. According to these theories, at any given instant we maintain detailed expectations regarding the objects in view. Our perceptual activity can be viewed according to such theories as hypothesizing a specific object and then using detailed prior knowledge about this object in an attempt to confirm or refute the current hypothesis.

The emphasis on detailed expectations does not seem to me to provide a satisfactory answer to the problem of guiding perceptual activity and selecting the appropriate routines. Consider for example the 'slide show' situation in which an observer is presented with a sequence of unrelated pictures flashed briefly on a screen. The sequence may contain arbitrary ordinary objects, say, a horse, a beachball, a printed letter, etc. Although the observer can have no expectations regarding the next picture in the sequence, he will experience little difficulty identifying the viewed objects. Furthermore, suppose that an observer does have some clear expectations, e.g., he opens a door expecting to find his familiar office, but finds an ocean beach instead. The contradiction to the expected scene will surely cause a surprise, but no

major perceptual difficulties. Although expectations can under some conditions facilitate perceptual processes significantly (e.g. Potter, 1975), their role is not indispensable. Perception can usually proceed in the absence of prior specific expectations and even when expectations are contradicted.

The selection of appropriate routines therefore raises a difficult problem. On the one hand, routines that establish properties and relations are situation-dependent. For example, the white patch on the cat's forehead is analyzed in the course of recognizing the cat, but white patches are not analyzed invariably in every scene. On the other hand, the recognition process should not depend entirely on prior knowledge or detailed expectations about the scene being viewed. How then are the appropriate routines selected?

It seems to me that this problem can be best approached by dividing the process of routine selection into two stages. The first stage is the application of what may be called universal routines. These are routines that can be usefully applied to any scene to provide some initial analysis. They may be able, for instance, to isolate some prominent parts in the scene and describe, perhaps crudely, some general aspects of their shape, motion, color, the spatial relations among them etc. These universal routines will provide sufficient information to allow initial indexing to a recognition memory, which then serves to guide the application of more specialized routines.

To make the motion of universal routines more concrete, I shall cite one example in which universal routines probably play a role. Studying the comparison of shapes presented sequentially, Rock et al. (1972) found that some parts of the presented shapes can be compared reliably while others cannot. When a shape was composed, for example, of a bounding contour and internal lines, in the absence of any specific instructions only the bounding contour was used reliably in the successive comparison task, even if the first figure was viewed for a long period (5 sec). This result would be surprising if only the base representations were used in the comparison task, since there is no reason to assume that in these representations the bounding contours of such line drawings enjoy a special status. It seems reasonable, however, that the bounding contour is special from the point of view of the universal routines, and is therefore analyzed first. If successive comparisons use the incremental representation as suggested above, then performance would be superior on those parts that have been already analyzed by visual routines. It is suggested, therefore, that in the absence of specific instructions, universal routines were applied first to the bounding contour. Furthermore, it appears that in the absence of specific goals, no detailed descriptions of the entire figure are generated even under long viewing periods. Only those aspects analyzed by the universal routines are summarized in the incremental representation. As a result, a description of the outside boundary alone has been created in the incremental representation. This description could then be compared against the second figure. It is of interest to note that the description generated in this task appears to be not just a coarse structural description of the figure, but has template-like quality that enable fine judgments of shape similarity.

These results can be contrasted with the study mentioned earlier by Rock and Gutman (1981) using pairs of overlapping and green figures. When subjects were instructed to "attend" selectively to one of the subfigures, they were subsequently able to make reliable shape comparisons to this, but not the other, subfigure. Specific requirements can therefore bias the selection and application of visual routines. Universal routines are meant to fill the void when no specific requirements are set. They are intended to acquire sufficient information to then determine the application of more specific routines.

For such a scheme to be of value in visual recognition, two interrelated requirements must be met. The first is that with universal routines alone it should be possible to gather sufficiently useful information to allow initial classification. The second requirement has to do with the organization of the memory used in visual recognition. It should contain intermediate constructs of categories that are accessible using the information gathered by the universal routines, and the access to such a category should provide the means for selecting specialized routines for refining the recognition process. The first requirement raises the question of whether universal routines, unaided by specific knowledge regarding the viewed objects, can reasonably be expected to supply sufficiently useful information about any viewed scene. The question is difficult to address in detail, since it is intimately related to problems regarding the structure of the memory used in visual recognition. It nonetheless seems plausible that universal routines may be sufficient to analyze the scene in enough detail to allow the application of specialized routines.

The potential usefulness of universal routines in the initial phases of the recognition process is supported in part by Marr and Nishihara's (1978) study of shape recognition. This work has demonstrated that at least for certain classes of shapes crude overall shape descriptions, which can be obtained by universal routines without prior knowledge regarding the viewed objects, can provide a powerful initial categorization. Similarly, the "perceptual 20 question game" of W. Richards (1982) suggests that a small fixed set of visual attributes (such as direction and type of motion, color, etc.) is often sufficient to form a good idea of what the object is (e.g., a walking person) although identifying a specific object (e.g., who the person is) may be considerably more difficult [cf. Milner, 1974]. These examples serve to illustrate the dis-

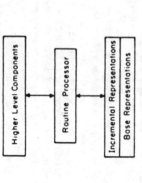

Figure 6. *The routine processor acts as an intermediary between the visual representations and higher level components of the system.*

tinction in visual recognition between universal and specific stages. In the first, universal routines can supply sufficient information for accessing a useful general category. In the second, specific routines associated with this category can be applied.

The relations between the different representations and routines can now be summarized as follows. The first stage in the analysis of the incoming visual input is the creation of the base representations. Next, visual routines are applied to the base representations. In the absence of specific expectations or prior knowledge universal routines are applied first, followed by the selective application of specific routines. Intermediate results obtained by visual routines are summarized in the incremental representation and can be used by subsequent routines.

2.3.1. Routines as intermediary between the base representations and higher-level components

The general role of visual routines in the overall processing of visual information as discussed so far is illustrated schematically in Fig. 6. The processes that assemble and execute visual routines (the 'routines processor' module in the figure) serve as an intermediary between the visual representations and higher level components of the system, such as recognition memory. Communication required between the higher level components and the visual representations for the analysis of shape and spatial relations are channeled via the routine processor.[11]

[11]Responses to certain visual stimuli that do not require abstract spatial analysis could bypass the routine processor. For example, a looming object may initiate an immediate avoidance response (Regan and Beverly, 1978). Such 'visual reflexes' do not require the application of visual routines. The visual system of lower animals such as insects or the frog, although remarkably sophisticated, probably lack routine mechanisms, and can perhaps be described as collections of 'visual reflexes'.

Visual routines operate in the middle ground that, unlike the bottom-up creation of the base representations, is a part of the top-down processing and yet is independent of object-specific knowledge. Their study therefore has the advantage of going beyond the base representations while avoiding many of the additional complications associated with higher level components of the system. The recognition of familiar objects. for example, often requires the use of knowledge specific to these objects. What we know about telephones or elephants can enter into the recognition process of these objects. In contrast, the extraction of spatial relations, while important for object recognition. is independent of object-specific knowledge. Such knowledge can determine the routine to be applied: the recognition of a particular object may require, for instance, the application of inside/outside routines. When a routine is applied, however, the processing is no longer dependent on object-specific knowledge.

It is suggested, therefore, that in studying the processing of visual information beyond the creation of the early representations, a useful distinction can be drawn between two problem areas. One can approach first the study of visual routines almost independently of the higher level components of the system. A full understanding of problems such as visually guided manipulation and object recognition would require. in addition, the study of higher level components, how they determine the application of visual routines, and how they are affected by the results of applying visual routines.

2.4. Routines and the parallel processing of visual information

A popular controversy in theories of visual perception is whether the processing of visual information proceeds in parallel or sequentially. Since visual routines are composed of sequences of elementary operations, they may seem to side strongly with the point of view of sequential processing in perception. In this section I shall examine two related questions that bear on this issue. First, whether the application of visual routines implies sequential processing. Second, what is the significance of the distinction between the parallel and sequential processing of visual information.

2.4.1. Three types of parallelism

The notion of processing visual information 'in parallel' does not have a unique, well-defined meaning. At least three types of parallelism can be distinguished in this processing: spatial, functional, and temporal. Spatial parallelism means that the same or similar operations are applied simultaneously to different spatial locations. The operations performed by the retina and the primary visual cortex, for example, fall under this category. Functional parallelism means that different computations are applied simultane-

ously to the same location. Current views of the visual cortex (e.g., Zeki 1978a. b) suggest that different visual areas in the extra-striate cortex process different aspects of the input (such as color, motion, and stereoscopic disparity) at the same location simultaneously, thereby achieving functional parallelism.[12] Temporal parallelism is the simultaneous application of different processing stages to different inputs (this type of parallelism is also called 'pipelining'.[13]

Visual routines can in principle employ all three types of parallelism. Suppose that a given routine is composed of a sequence of operations $O_1, O_2, \ldots O_n$. Spatial parallelism can be obtained if a given operation O_i is applied simultaneously to various locations. Temporal parallelism can be obtained by applying different operations O_i simultaneously to successive inputs. Finally, functional parallelism can be obtained by the concurrent application of different routines.

The application of visual routines is thus compatible in principle with all three notions of parallelism. It seems, however, that in visual routines the use of spatial parallelism is more restricted than in the construction of the base representations.[14] At least some of the basic operations do not employ extensive spatial parallelism. The internal tracking of a discontinuity boundary in the base representation, for instance, is sequential in nature and does not apply to all locations simultaneously. Possible reasons for the limited spatial parallelism in visual routines are discussed in the next section.

2.4.2. Essential and non-essential sequential processing

When considering sequential *versus* spatially parallel processing, it is useful to distinguish between essential and non-essential sequentially. Suppose, for example, that O_1 and O_2 are two independent operations that can, in principle, be applied simultaneously. It is nevertheless still possible to apply them in sequence, but such sequentiality would be non-essential. The total computation required in this case will be the same regardless of whether the operations are performed in parallel or sequentially. Essential sequentiality, on the other hand, arises when the nature of the task makes parallel processing impossible or highly wasteful in terms of the overall computation required.

[12]Disagreements exist regarding this view, in particular. the role of area V4 in the rhesus monkey i processing color (Schein et al. 1982). Although the notion o "one cortical area for each function" is too simplistic, the physiological data support in general the notion of functional parallelism.

[13]Suppose that a sequence of operations $O_1, O_2, \ldots O_n$ is applied to each input in a temporal sequence $I_1, I_2, I_3 \ldots$. First, O_1 is applied to I_1. Next, as O_2 is applied to I_1, O_1 can be applied to I_2. In general $O_j, 1 < i < k$ can be applied simultaneously to I_{i-}. Such a simultaneous application constitute temporal parallelism.

[14]The general notion of an extensively parallel stage followed by a more sequential one is in agreement with various findings and theories of visual perception (e.g., Estes, 1972; Neisser, 1967; Shiffrin et al., 1976).

Problems pertaining to the use of spatial parallelism in the computation of spatial properties and relations were studied extensively by Minsky and Papert (1969) within the perceptrons model.[15] Minsky and Paper have established that certain relations, including the inside/outside relation, cannot be computed at all in parallel by any diamater-limited or order-limited perceptrons. This limitation does not seem to depend critically upon the perceptron-like decision scheme. It may be conjectured, therefore, that certain relations are inherently sequential in the sense that it is impossible or highly wasteful to employ extensive spatial parallelism in their computation. In this case sequentiality is essential, as it is imposed by the nature of the task, not by particular properties of the underlying mechanisms. Essential sequentiality is theoretically more interesting, and has more significant ramifications, than non-essential sequential ordering. In non-essential sequential processing the ordering has no particular importance, and no fundamentally new problems are introduced. Essential sequentiality, on the other hand, requires mechanisms for controlling the appropriate sequencing of the computation.

It has been suggested by various theories of perception that sequential ordering in perception is non-essential, arising primarily from a capacity limitation of the system (see, e.g., Holtzman and Gazzaniga, 1982; Kahneman, 1973; Rumelhart, 1970). In this view only a limited region of the visual scene (1 degree, Eriksen and Hoffman, 1972; see also Humphreys, 1981; Mackworth, 1965) is processed at any given time because the system is capacity-limited and would be overloaded by excessive information unless a spatial restriction is employed. The discussion above suggests, in contrast, that sequential ordering may in fact be essential, imposed by the inherently sequential nature of various visual tasks. This sequential ordering has substantial implications since it requires perceptual mechanisms for directing the processing and for concatenating and controlling sequences of basic operations.

Although the elemental operations are sequenced, some of them, such as the bounded activation, employ spatial parallelism and are not confined to a limited region. This spatial parallelism plays an important role in the inside/outside region. To appreciate the difficulties in computing inside/outside relations without the benefit of spatial parallelism, consider solving a tactile

[15]In the perceptron scheme the computation is performed in parallel by a large number of units ϕ. Each unit examine a restricted part of the 'retina' R. In a diamater-limited perceptron, for instance, the region examined by each unit is restricted to lie within a circle whose diameter is small compared to the size of R. The computation performed by each unit is a predicate of its inputs (i.e., $\phi_i = 0$ or $\phi_i = 1$). For example, a unit may be a 'corner detector' at a particular location, signalling 1 in the presence of a corner and 0 otherwise. All the local units then feed a final decision stage, assumed to be a linear threshold device. That is, it tests whether the weighted sum of the inputs $\Sigma_i \, \omega_i \, \phi_i$ exceeds a predetermined threshold θ.

version of the same problem by moving a cane or a fingertip over a relief surface. Clearly, when the processing is always limited to a small region of space, the task becomes considerably more difficult. Spatial parallelism must therefore play an important role in visual routines.

In summary, visual routines are compatible in principle with spatial, temporal, and functional parallelism. The degree of spatial parallelism employed by the basic operations seems nevertheless limited. It is conjectured that this reflects primarily essential sequentiality, imposed by the nature of the computations.

3. The elemental operations

3.1. Methodological considerations

In this section, we examine the set of basic operations that may be used in the construction of visual routines. In trying to explore this set of internal operations, at least two types of approaches can be followed. The first is the use of empirical psychological and physiological evidence. The second is computational: one can examine, for instance, the types of basic operations that would be useful in principle for establishing a large variety of relevant properties and relations. In particular, it would be useful to examine complex tasks in which we exhibit a high degree of proficiency. For such tasks, processes that match in performance the human system are difficult to devise. Consequently, their examination is likely to provide useful constraints on the nature of the underlying computations.

In exploring such tasks, the examples I shall use will employ schematic drawings rather than natural scenes. The reason is that simplified artificial stimuli allow more flexibility in adapting the stimulus to the operation under investigation. It seems to me that insofar as we examine visual tasks for which our proficiency is difficult to account for, we are likely to be exploring useful basic operations even if the stimuli employed are artificially constructed. In fact, this ability to cope efficiently with artificially imposed visual tasks underscores two essential capacities in the computation of spatial relations. First, that the computation of spatial relations is flexible and open-ended: new relations can be defined and computed efficiently. Second, it demonstrates our capacity to accept non-visual specification of a task and immediately produce a visual routine to meet these specifications.

The empirical and computational studies can then be combined. For example, the complexity of various visual tasks can be compared. That is, the theoretical studies can be used to predict how different tasks should vary in role in visual information processing, starting from early processing stages. The main directions of studies that have been pursued are reviewed briefly in the next two sections.

3.2.1. Psychological evidence

A number of psychological studies have suggested that the focus of visual processing can be directed, either voluntarily or by manipulating the visual stimulus, to different spatial location in the visual input. They are listed below under three main categories.

The first line of evidence comes from reaction time studies suggesting that it takes some measurable time to shift the processing focus from one location to another. In a study by Eriksen and Schultz (1977), for instance, it was found that the time required to identify a letter increased linearly with the eccentricity of the target letter, the difference being on the order of 100 msec at 3° from the fovea center. Such a result may reflect the effect of shift time, but, as pointed out by Eriksen and Schultz, alternative explanations are possible.

More direct evidence comes from a study by Posner et al. (1978). In this study a target was presented seven degrees to the left or right of fixation. It was shown that if the subjects correctly anticipated the location at which the target will appear using prior cueing (an arrow at fixation), then their reaction time to the target in both detection and identification tasks were consistently lower (without eye movements). For simple detection tasks, the gain in detection time for a target at 70 eccentricity was on the order of 30 msec.

A related study by Tsal (1983) employed peripheral rather than central cueing. In his study a target letter could appear at different eccentricities, preceded by a brief presentation of a dot at the same location. The results were consistent with the assumption that the dot initiated a shift towards the cued location. If a shift to the location of the letter is required for its identification, the cue should reduce the time between the letter presentation and its identification. If the cue precedes the target letter by k msec, then by the time the letter appears the shift operation is already k msec under way, and the response time should decrease by this amount. The facilitation should therefore increase linearly with the temporal delay between the cue and target until the delay equals the total shift time. Further increase of the delay should have no additional effect. This is exactly what the experimental results indicated. It was further found that the delay at which facilitation saturates (presumably the total shift time) increases with eccentricity, by about 8 msec on the average per 1° of visual angle.

A second line of evidence comes from experiments suggesting that visual sensitivity at different locations can be somewhat modified with a fixed eye

complexity, and the predicted complexity measure can be gauged against human performance. We have seen in Section 1.2 an example along this line, in the discussion of the inside/outside computation. Predictions regarding relative complexity, success, and failure, based upon the ray-intersection method prove largely incompatible with the human performance, and consequently the employment of this method by the human perceptual system can be ruled out. In this case, the refutation is also supported by theoretical considerations exposing the inherent limitations of the ray-intersection method.

In this section, only some initial steps towards examining the basic operations problem will be taken. I shall examine a number of plausible candidates for basic operations, discuss the available evidence, and raise problems for further study. Only a few operations will be examined; they are not intended to form a comprehensive list. Since the available empirical evidence is scant, the emphasis will be on computational considerations of usefulness. Finally, some of the problems associated with the assembly of basic operations into visual routines will be briefly discussed.

3.2. Shifting the processing focus

A fundamental requirement for the execution of visual routines is the capacity to control the location at which certain operations take place. For example, the operation of area activation suggested in Section 1.2 will be of little use if the activation starts simultaneously everywhere. To be of use, it must start at a selected location, or along a selected contour. More generally, in applying visual routines it would be useful to have a 'directing mechanism' that will allow the application of the same operation at different spatial locations. It is natural, therefore, to start the discussion of the elemental operations by examining the processes that control the locations at which these operations are applied.

Directing the processing focus (that is, the location to which an operation is applied) may be achieved in part by moving the eyes (Noton and Stark, 1971). But this is clearly insufficient: many relations, including, for instance, the inside/outside relation examined in Section 1.2, can be established without eye movements. A capacity to shift the processing focus internally is therefore required.

Problems related to the possible shift of internal operations have been studied empirically, both psychophysically and physiologically. These diverse studies still do not provide a complete picture of the shift operations and their use in the analysis of visual information. They do provide, however, strong support for the notion that shifts of the processing focus play an important position. Experiments by Shulman et al. (1979) can be interpreted as indicating that a region of somewhat increased sensitivity can be shifted across the visual field. A related experiment by Remington (1978, described in Posner, 1980), showed an increase in sensitivity at a distance of 8° from the fixation point 50–100 msec after the location has been cued.

A third line of evidence that may bear on the internal shift operations comes from experiments exploring the selective readout from some form of short term visual memory (e.g., Shiffrin et al., 1976; Sperling, 1960). These experiments suggest that some internal scanning can be directed to different locations a short time after the presentation of a visual stimulus.

The shift operation and selective visual attention. Many of the experiments mentioned above were aimed at exploring the concept of 'selective attention'. This concept has a variety of meanings and connotations (cf. Estes, 1972), many of which are not related directly to the proposed shift of processing focus in visual routines. The notion of selective visual attention often implies that the processing of visual information is restricted to small region of space, that to avoid 'overloading' the system with excessive information. Certain processing stages have, according to this description, a limited total 'capacity' to invest in the processing, and this capacity can be concentrated in a spatially restricted region. Attempts to process additional information would detract from this capacity, causing interference effects and deterioration of performance. Processes that do not draw upon this general capacity are, by definition, pre-attentive. In contrast, the notion of processing shift discussed above stems from the need for spatially-structured processes, and it does not necessarily imply such notions as general capacity or protection from overload. For example, the 'coloring' operation used in Section 1.2 for separating inside from outside started from a selected point or contour. Even with no capacity limitations such coloring would not start simultaneously everywhere, since a simultaneous activation will defy the purpose of the coloring operation. The main problem in this case is in coordinating the process, rather than excessive capacity demands. As a result, the process is spatially structured, but not in a simple manner as in the 'spotlight model' of selective attention. In the course of applying a visual routine, both the locations and the operations performed at the selected locations are controlled and coordinated according to the requirement of the routine in question.

Many of the results mentioned above are nevertheless in agreement with the possible existence of a directable processing focus. They suggest that the redirection of the processing focus to a new location may be achieved in two ways. The experiments of Posner and Shulman et al. suggest that it can be 'programmed' to move along a straight path using central cueing. In other experiments, such as Remmington's and Tsal's, the processing focus is shifted by being attracted to a peripheral cue.

3.2.2. Physiological evidence

Shift-related mechanisms have been explored physiologically in the monkey in a number of different visual areas: the superior colliculus, the posterior parietal lobe (area 7) the frontal eye fields, areas V1, V2, V4, MT, MST, and the inferior temporal lobe.

In the superficial layers of the superior colliculus of the monkey, many cells have been found to have an enhanced response to a stimulus when the monkey uses the stimulus as a target for a saccadic eye movement (Goldberg and Wurtz, 1972). This enhancement is not strictly sensory in the sense that it is not produced if the stimulus is not followed by a saccade. It also does not seem strictly associated with a motor response, since the temporal delay between the enhanced response and the saccade can vary considerably (Wurtz and Mohler, 1976a). The enhancement phenomenon was suggested as a neural correlate of "directing visual attention", since it modifies the visual input and enhances it at selective locations when the sensory input remains constant (Goldberg and Wurtz, op. cit.). The intimate relation of the enhancement to eye movements, and its absence when the saccade is replaced by other responses (Wurtz and Mohler, op. cit.; Wurtz et al., 1982) suggest, however, that this mechanism is specifically related to saccadic eye movements rather than to operations associated with the shifting of an internal processing focus. Similar enhancement that depends on saccade initiation to a visual target has also been described in the frontal eye fields (Wurtz and Mohler, 1976b) and in prestriate cortex, probably area V4 (Fischer and Boch, 1981).

Another area that exhibits similar enhancement phenomena, but not exclusively to saccades, is area 7 of the posterior parietal lobe of the monkey. Using recordings from behaving monkeys, Mountcastle and his collaborators (Mountcastle, 1976, Mountcastle et al., 1975) found three populations of cells in area 7 that respond selectively (i) when the monkey fixates an object of interest within its immediate surrounding (fixation neurons), (ii) when it tracks an object of interest (tracking neurons), and (iii) when it saccades to an object of interest (saccade neurons). (Tracking neurons were also described in area MST (Newsome and Wurtz, 1982).) Studies by Robinson et al. (1978) indicated that all of these neurons can also be driven by passive sensory stimulation, but their response is considerably enhanced when the stimulation is 'selected' by the monkey to initiate a response. On the basis of such findings it was suggested by Mountcastle (as well as by Posner, 1980; Robinson et al., 1978; Wurtz et al., 1982) that mechanisms in area 7 are responsible for "directing visual attention" to selected stimuli. These mechanisms may be primarily related, however, to tasks requiring hand-eye coordination for manipulation in the reachable space (Mountcastle, 1976), and there is at present no direct evidence to link them with visual routines and the shift of processing focus discussed above.[16]

In area TE of the inferotemporal cortex units were found whose responses depend strongly upon the visual task performed by the animal. Fuster and Jervey (1981) described units that responded strongly to the stimulus' color, but only when color was the relevant parameter in a matching task. Richmond and Sato (1982) found units whose responses to a given stimulus were enhanced when the stimulus was used in a pattern discrimination task, but not in other tasks (e.g., when the stimulus was monitored to detect its dimming).

In a number of visual areas, including V1, V2, and MT, enhanced responses associated with performing specific visual tasks were not found (Newsome and Wurtz, 1982; Wurtz et al., 1982). It remains possible, however, that task-specific modulation would be observed when employing different visual tasks. Finally, responses in the pulvinar (Gattas et al., 1979) were shown to be strongly modulated by attentional and situational variables. It remains unclear, however, whether these modulations are localized (i.e., if they are restricted to a particular location in the visual field) and whether they are task-specific.

Physiological evidence of a different kind comes from visual evoked potential (VEP) studies. With fixed visual input and in the absence of eye movements, changes in VEP can be induced, for example, by instructing the subject to "attend" to different spatial locations (e.g., van Voorhis and Hillyard, 1977). This evidence may not be of direct relevance to visual routines, since it is not clear whether there is a relation between the voluntary 'direction of visual attention' used in these experiments and the shift of processing focus in visual routines. VEP studies may nonetheless provide at least some evidence regarding the possibility of internal shift operations.

In assessing the relevance of these physiological findings to the shifting of the processing focus it would be useful to distinguish three types of interactions between the physiological responses and the visual task performed by the experimental animal. The three types are task-dependent, task-location dependent, and location-dependent responses.

A response is task-dependent if, for a given visual stimulus, it depends upon the visual task being performed. Some of the units described in area TE, for instance, are clearly task-dependent in this sense. In contrast, units in area V1 for example, appear to be task-independent. Task-dependent responses suggest that the units do not belong to the bottom-up generation of the early visual representations, and that they may participate in the application of visual routines. Task-dependence by itself does not necessarily imply, however, the existence of shift operations. Of more direct relevance to shift operations are responses that are both task- and location-dependent. A task-location dependent unit would respond preferentially to a stimulus when a given task is performed at a given location. Unlike task-dependent units, it would show a different response to the same stimulus when an identical task is applied to a different location. Unlike the spotlight metaphor of visual attention, it would show different responses when different tasks are performed at the same locations.

There is at least some evidence for the existence of such task-location dependent responses. The response of a saccade neuron in the superior colliculus, for example, is enhanced only when a saccade is initiated in the general direction of the unit's receptive field. A saccade towards a different location would not produce the same enhancement. The response is thus enhanced only when a specific location is selected for a specific task.

Unfortunately, many of the other task-dependent responses have not been tested for location specificity. It would be of interest to examine similar task-location dependence in tasks other than eye movement, and in the visual cortex rather than the superior colliculus. For example, the units described by Fuster and Jervey (1981) showed task-dependent response (responded strongly during a color matching task, but not during a form matching task). It would be interesting to know whether the enhanced response is also location specific. For example, if during a color matching task, when several stimuli are presented simultaneously, the response would be enhanced only at the location used for the matching task.

Finally, of particular interest would be units referred to above as location-dependent (but task-independent). Such a unit would respond preferentially to a stimulus when it is used not in a single task but in a variety of different visual tasks. Such units may be a part of a general 'shift controller' that selects a location for processing independent of the specific operation to be applied. Of the areas discussed above, the responses in area 7, the superior colliculus, and TE, do not seem appropriate for such a 'shift controller'. The pulvinar remains a possibility worthy of further exploration in view of its rich pattern of reciprocal and orderly connections with a variety of visual areas (Beneveneto and Davis, 1977; Rezak and Beneveneto, 1979).

---

[16]A possible exception is some preliminary evidence by Robinson et al. (1978) suggesting that, unlike the superior colliculus, enhancement effects in the parietal cortex may be dissociated from movement. That is, a response of a cell may be facilitated when the animal is required to attend to a stimulus even when the stimulus is not used as a target for hand or eye movement.

3.3. Indexing

Computational considerations strongly suggest the use of internal shifts of the processing focus. This notion is supported by psychological evidence, and to some degree by physiological data.

The next issue to be considered is the selection problem: how specific locations are selected for further processing. There are various manners in which such a selection process could be realized. On a digital computer, for instance, the selection can take place by providing the coordinates of the next location to be processed. The content of the specified address can then be inspected and processed. This is probably not how locations are being selected for processing in the human visual system. What determines, then, the next location to be processed, and how is the processing focus moved from one location to the next?

In this section we shall consider one operation which seems to be used by the visual system in shifting the processing focus. This operation is called 'indexing'. It can be described as a shift of the processing focus to special 'odd-man-out' locations. These locations are detected in parallel across the base representations, and can serve as 'anchor points' for the application of visual routines.

As an example of indexing, suppose that a page of printed text is to be inspected for the occurrence of the letter 'A'. In a background of similar letters, the 'A' will not stand out, and considerable scanning will be required for its detection (Nickerson, 1966). If, however, all the letters remain stationary with the exception of one which is jiggled, or if all the letters are red with the exception of one green letter, the odd-man-out will be immediately identified.

The identification of the odd-man-out items proceeds in this case in several stages.[17] First the odd-man-out location is detected on the basis of its unique motion or color properties. Next, the processing focus is shifted to this odd-man-out location. This is the indexing stage. As a result of this stage, visual routines can be applied to the figure. By applying the appropriate routines, the figure is identified.

Indexing also played a role in the inside/outside example examined in Section 1.2. It was noted that one plausible strategy is to start the processing at the location marked by the X figure. This raises a problem, since the location of the X and of the closed curve were not known in advance. If the X can define an indexable location, that is, if it can serve to attract the processing focus, then the execution of the routine can start at that location. More generally, indexable locations can serve as starting points or 'anchors' for visual routines. In a novel scene, it would be possible to direct the processing focus immediately to a salient indexable item, and start the processing at that location. This will be particularly valuable in the execution of universal routines that are to be applied prior to any analysis of the viewed objects.

The indexing operation can be further subdivided into three successive stages. First, properties used for indexing, such as motion, orientation, and color, must be computed across the base representations. Second, an 'odd-man-out operation' is required to define locations that are sufficiently different from their surroundings. The third and final stage is the shift of the processing focus to the indexed location. These three stages are examined in turn in the next three subsections.

3.3.1. Indexable properties

Certain odd-man-out items can serve for immediate indexing, while others cannot. For example, orientation and direction of motion are indexable, while a single occurrence of the letter 'A' among similar letters does not define an indexable location. This is to be expected, since the recognition of letters requires the application of visual routines while indexing must precede their application. The first question that arises, therefore, is what the set of elemental properties is that can be computed everywhere across the base representations prior to the application of visual routines.

One method of exploring indexable properties empirically is by employing an odd-man-out test. If an item is singled out in the visual field by an indexable property, then its detection is expected to be immediate. The ability to index an item by its color, for instance, implies that a red item in a field of green items should be detected in roughly constant time, independent of the number of green distractors.

Using this and other techniques, A. Treisman and her collaborators (Treisman, 1977; Treisman and Gelade, 1980; see also Beck and Ambler, 1972, 1973; Pomerantz et al., 1977) have shown that color and simple shape parameters can serve for immediate indexing. For example, the time to detect a target blue X in a field of brown T's and green X's does not change significantly as the number of distractors is increased (up to 30 in these experiments). The target is immediately indexable by its unique color. Similarly, a target green S letter is detectable in a field of brown T's and green X's in constant time. In this case it is probably indexable by certain shape parameters, although it cannot be determined from the experiments what the relevant parameters include (i) curvature, (ii) orientation, since the S contains some orientations that are missing in the X and

[17]The reasons for assuming several stages are both theoretical and empirical. On the empirical side, the experiments by Posner, Treisman, and Tsal provide support for this view.

sistent with a serial self-terminating search in which the items are examined sequentially until the target is reached.

The difference between single and double indexing supports the view that the computations performed in parallel by the distributed local units are severely limited. In particular, these units cannot combine two indexable properties to define a new indexable property. In a scheme where most of the computation is performed by a directable central processor, these results also place constraints on the communication between the local units and the central processor. The central processor is assumed to be computationally powerful, and consequently it can also be assumed that if the signals relayed to it from the local units contained sufficient information for double indexing, this information could have been put to use by the central processor. Since it is not, the information relayed to the central processor must be limited.

The results regarding single and double indexing can be explained by assuming that the local computation that precedes indexing is limited to simple local comparisons. For example, the color in a small neighborhood may be compared with the color in a surrounding area, employing, perhaps, lateral inhibition between similar detectors (Estes, 1972; Andriessen and Bouma, 1976; Pomerantz et al., 1977). If the item differs significantly from its surround, the difference signal can be used in shifting the processing focus to that location. If an item is distinguishable from its surround by the conjunction of two properties such as color and orientation, then no difference signal will be generated by either the color or the orientation comparisons, and direct indexing will not be possible. Such a local comparison will also allow the indexing of a local, rather than a global, odd-man-out. Suppose, for example, that the visual field contains green and red elements in equal numbers, but one and only one of the green elements is completely surrounded by a large region of red elements. If the local elements signaled not their colors but the results of local color comparisons, then the odd-man-out alone would produce a difference signal and would therefore be indexable. To explore the computations performed at the distributed stage it would be of interest, therefore, to examine the indexability of local odd-men-out. Various properties can be tested, while manipulating the size and shape of the surrounding region.

3.3.3. Shifting the processing focus to an indexable location

The discussion so far suggests the following indexing scheme. A number of elementary properties are computed in parallel across the visual field. For each property, local comparisons are performed everywhere. The resulting difference signals are combined somehow to produce a final odd-man-out signal at each location. The processing focus then shifts to the location of the strongest signal. This final shift operation will be examined next.

T, and (iii) the number of terminators, which is two for the S, but higher for the X and T. It would be of interest to explore the indexability of these and other properties in an attempt to discover the complete set of indexable properties.

The notion of a severely limited set of properties that can be processed 'pre-attentively' agrees well with Julesz' studies of texture perception (see Julesz (1981) for a review). In detailed studies, Julesz and his collaborators have found that only a limited set of features, which he termed 'textons', can mediate immediate texture discrimination. These textons include color, elongated blobs of specific sizes, orientations, and aspect ratios, and the terminations of these elongated blobs.

These psychological studies are also in general agreement with physiological evidence. Properties such as motion, orientation, and color, were found to be extracted in parallel by units that cover the visual field. On physiological grounds these properties are suitable, therefore, for immediate indexing.

The emerging picture is, in conclusion, that a small number of properties are computed in parallel over the base representations prior to the application of visual routines. Several of these properties are known, but a complete list is yet to be established. The results are then used in a number of visual tasks including, probably, texture discrimination, motion correspondence, stereo, and indexing.

3.3.2. Defining an indexable location

Following the initial computation of the elementary properties, the next stage in the indexing operation requires comparisons among properties computed at different locations to define the odd-man-out indexable locations.

Psychological evidence suggests that only simple comparisons are used at this stage. Several studies by Treisman and her collaborators examined the problem of whether different properties measured at a given location can be combined prior to the indexing operation.[18] They have tested, for instance, whether a green T could be detected in a field of brown T's and Green X's. The target in this case matches half the distractors in color, and the other half in shape. It is the combination of shape and color that makes it distinct. Earlier experiments have established that such a target is indexable if it has a unique color or shape. The question now was whether the conjunction of two indexable properties is also immediately indexable. The empirical evidence indicates that items cannot be indexed by a conjunction of properties: the time to detect the target increases linearly in the conjunction task with the number of distractors. The results obtained by Treisman et al. were con-

[18]Treisman's own approach to the problem was somewhat different from the one discussed here.

Several studies of selective visual attention likened the internal shift operation to the directing of a spotlight. A directable spotlight is used to 'illuminate' a restricted region of the visual field, and only the information within the region can be inspected. This is, of course, only a metaphor that still requires an agent to direct the spotlight and observe the illuminated region. The goal of this section is to give a more concrete notion of the shift in processing focus, and, using a simple example, to show what it means and how it may be implemented.

The example we shall examine is a version of the property-conjunction problem mentioned in the previous section. Suppose that small colored bars are scattered over the visual field. One of them is red, all the others are green. The task is to report the orientation of the red bar. We would like therefore to 'shift' the processing focus to the red bar and 'read out' its orientation.

A simplified scheme for handling this task is illustrated schematically in Fig. 7. This scheme incorporates the first two stages in the indexing operation discussed above. In the first stage ($S1$ in the figure) a number of different properties (denoted by P_1, P_2, P_3 in the figure) are being detected at each location. The existence of a horizontal green bar, for example, at a given location, will be reflected by the activity of the color- and orientation-detecting units at that location. In addition to these local units there is also a central common representation of the various properties, denoted by CP_1, CP_2, CP_3.

in the figure. For simplicity, we shall assume that all of the local detectors are connected to the corresponding unit in the central representation. There is, for instance, a common central unit to which all of the local units that signal vertical orientation are connected.

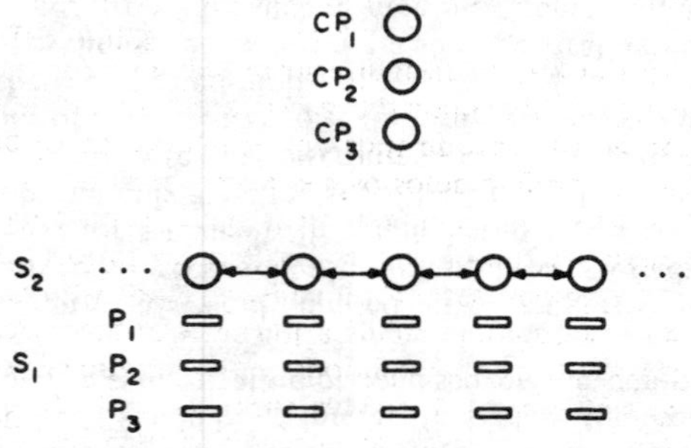

It is suggested that to perform the task defined above and determine the orientation of the red bar, this orientation must be represented in the central common representation. Subsequent processing stages have access to this common representation, but not to all of the local detectors. To answer the question, "what is the orientation of the red element", this orientation alone must therefore be mapped somehow into the common representation.

In section 3.3.2, it was suggested that the initial detection of the various local properties is followed by local comparisons that generate difference signals. These comparisons take place in stage $S2$ in Fig. 7, where the odd-man-out item will end up with the strongest signal. Following these two initial stages, it is not too difficult to conceive of mechanisms by which the most active unit in $S2$ would inhibit all the others, and as a result the properties of all but the odd-man-out location would be inhibited from reaching the central representation.[19] The central representations would then represent faithfully the properties of the odd-man-out item, the red bar in our example. At this stage the processing is focused on the red element and its properties are consequently represented explicitly in the central representation, accessible to subsequent processing stages. The initial question is thereby answered, without the use of a specialized vertical red line detector.

In this scheme, only the properties of the odd-man-out item can be detected immediately. Other items will have to await additional processing stages. The above scheme can be easily extended to generate successive 'shifts of the processing focus' from one element to another, in an order that depends on the strength of their signals in $S2$. These successive shifts mean that the properties of different elements will be mapped successively onto the common representations.

Possible mechanisms for performing indexing and processing focus shifts would not be considered here beyond the simple scheme discussed so far. But even this simplified scheme illustrates a number of points regarding shift and indexing. First, it provides an example for what it means to shift the processing focus to a given location. In this case, the shift entailed a selective

[19]Models for this stage are being tested by C. Koch at the M.I.T. A.I. Lab. One interesting result from this modeling is that a realization of the inhibition among units leads naturally to the processing focus being shifted continuously from item to item rather than 'leaping', disappearing at one location and reappearing at another. The models also account for the phenomenon that being an odd-man-out is not a simple all or none property (Engel, 1974). With increased dissimilarity, a target item can be detected immediately over a larger area.

Figure 7. *A simplified scheme that can serve as a basis for the indexing operation. In the first stage (S_1), a number of properties (P_1, P_2, P_3 in figure) are detected everywhere. In the subsequent stage (S_2), local comparisons generate difference signals. The element generating the strongest signal is mapped onto the central common representations (CP_1, CP_2, CP_3).*

readout to the central common representations. Second, it illustrates that shift of the processing focus can be achieved in a simple manner without physical shifts or an internal 'spotlight'. Third, it raises the point that the shift of the processing focus is not a single elementary operation but a family of operations, only some of which were discussed above. There is, for example, some evidence for the use of 'similarity enhancement': when the processing focus is centered on a given item, similar items nearby become more likely to be processed next. There is also some degree of 'central control' over the processing focus. Although the shift appears to be determined primarily by the visual input, there is also a possibility of directing the processing focus voluntarily, for example to the right or to the left of fixation (van Voorhis and Hillyard, 1977).

Finally, it suggests that psychophysical experiments of the type used by Julesz, Treisman and others, combined with physiological studies of the kind described in Section 3.2, can provide guidance for developing detailed testable models for the shift operations and their implementation in the visual system.

In summary, the execution of visual routines requires a capacity to control the locations at which elemental operations are applied. Psychological evidence, and to some degree physiological evidence, are in agreement with the general notion of an internal shift of the processing focus. This shift is obtained by a family of related processes. One of them is the indexing operation, which directs the processing focus towards certain odd-man-out locations. Indexing requires three successive stages. First, a set of properties that can be used for indexing, such as orientation, motion, and color, are computed in parallel across the base representation. Second, a location that differs significantly from its surroundings in one of these properties (but not their combinations) can be singled out as an indexed location. Finally, the processing focus is redirected towards the indexed location. This redirection can be achieved by simple schemes of interactions among the initial detecting units and central common representations that lead to a selective mapping from the initial detectors to the common representations.

3.4. Bounded activation (coloring)

The bounded activation, or 'coloring' operation, was suggested in Section 1.2. in examining the inside/outside relation. It consisted of the spread of activation over a surface in the base representation emanating from a given location or contour, and stopping at discontinuity boundaries.

The results of the coloring operation may be retained in the incremental representation for further use by additional routines. Coloring provides in

this manner one method for defining larger units in the unarticulated base representations: the 'colored' region becomes a unit to which routines can be applied selectively. A simple example of this possible role of the coloring operation was mentioned in Section 2.2: the initial 'coloring' could facilitate subsequent inside/outside judgments.

A more complicated example along the same line is illustrated in Fig. 8. The visual task here is to identify the sub-figure marked by the black dot. One may have the subjective feeling of being able to concentrate on this sub-figure, and 'pull it out' from its complicated background. This capacity to 'pull out' the figure of interest can also be tested objectively, for example, by testing how well the sub-figure can be identified. It is easily seen in Fig. 8 that the marked sub-figure has the shape of the letter G. The area surrounding the sub-figure in close proximity contains a myriad of irrelevant features, and therefore identification would be difficult, unless processing can be directed to this sub-figure.

The sub-figure of interest in Fig. 8 is the region inside which the black dot resides. This region could be defined and separated from its surroundings by using the area activation operation. Recognition routines could then concentrate on the activated region, ignoring the irrelevant contours. This examples uses an artificial stimulus, but the ability to identify a region and process it selectively seems equally useful for the recognition of objects in natural scenes.

3.4.1. Discontinuity boundaries for the coloring operation

The activation operation is supposed to spread until a discontinuity bounded.

Figure 8. *The visual task here is to identify the subfigure containing the black dot. This figure (the letter 'C') can be recognized despite the presence of confounding features in close proximity to its contours, the capacity to 'pull out' the figure from the irrelevant background may involve the bounded activation operation.*

ary is reached. This raises the question of what constitutes a discontinuity boundary for the activation operation. In Fig. 8, lines in the two-dimensional drawing served for this task. If activation is applied to the base representations discussed in Section 2, it is expected that discontinuities in depth, surface orientation, and texture, will all serve a similar role. The use of boundaries to check the activation spread is not straightforward. It appears that in certain situations the boundaries do not have to be entirely continuous in order to block the coloring spread. In Fig. 9, a curve is defined by a fragmented line, but it is still immediately clear that the X lies inside and the black dot outside this curve.[20] If activation is to be used in this situation as well, then incomplete boundaries should have the capacity to block the activation spread. Finally, the activation is sometimes required to spread across certain boundaries. For example, in Fig. 10, which is similar to Fig. 8, the letter G is still recognizable, in spite of the internal bounding contours. To allow the coloring of the entire sub-figure in this case, the activation must spread across internal boundaries.

In conclusion, the bounded activation, and in particular, its interactions with different contours, is a complicated process. It is possible that as far as the activation operation is concerned, boundaries are not defined universally, but may be defined somewhat differently in different routines.

3.4.2. A mechanism for bounded activation and its implications

The 'coloring' spread can be realized by using only simple, local operations. The activation can spread in a network in which each element excites all of its neighbors.

Figure 9. *Fragmented boundaries. The curve is defined by a dashed line, but inside/ outside judgments are still immediate.*

Figure 10. *Additional internal lines are introduced into the G-shaped subfigure. If bounded activation is used to 'color' this figure, it must spread across the internal contours.*

A second network containing a map of the discontinuity boundaries will be used to check the activation spread. An element in the activation network will be activated if any of its neighbors is turned on, provided that the corresponding location in the second, control network, does not contain a boundary. The turning on of a single element in the activation network will thus initiate an activation spread from the selected point outwards, that will fill the area bounded by the surrounding contours. (Each element may also have neighborhoods of different sizes, to allow a more efficient, multi-resolution implementation.)

In this scheme, an 'activity layer' serves for the execution of the basic operation, subject to the constraints in a second 'control layer'. The control layer may receive its content (the discontinuity boundaries) from a variety of sources, which thereby affect the execution of the operation.

An interesting question to consider is whether the visual system incorporates mechanisms of this general sort. If this were the case, the interconnected network of cells in cortical visual areas may contain distinct subnetworks for carrying out the different elementary operations. Some layers of cells within the retinotopically organized visual areas would then be best understood as serving for the execution of basic operations. Other layers receiving their inputs from different visual areas may serve in this scheme for the control of these operations.

If such networks for executing and controlling basic operations are incorporated in the visual system, they will have important implications for the interpretation of physiological data. In exploring such networks, physiological studies that attempt to characterize units in terms of their optimal stimuli would run into difficulties. The activity of units in such networks would be

---

[20] Empirical results show that inside/outside judgments using dashed curves require somewhat longer times compared with continuous curves, suggesting that fragmented boundaries may require additional processing. The extra cost associated with fragmental boundaries is small. In a series of experiments performed by J. Varanese at Harvard University this cost averaged about 20 msec. The mean response time was about 540 msec (Varanese, 1983).

tracing operation. Each display in this study contained two separate curves. In all trials there was an X at the fixation point, intersecting one of the curves. A second X could lie either on the same or on the second curve, and the observer's task was to decide as quickly as possible whether the two X's lay on the same or different curves. The physical distance separating the two X's was always 1.8° of visual angle. When the two X's lay on the same curve, their distance along the curve could be changed, however, in increments of 2.2° of visual angle (measured along the curve).

The main result from a number of related experiments was that the time to detect that the two X's lay on the same curve increased monotonically, and roughly linearly, with their separation along the curve. This result suggests the use of a tracing operation, at an average speed of about 24 msec per degree of visual angle. The short presentation time (250 msec) precluded the tracing of the curve using eye movements, hence the tracing operation must be performed internally.

Although the task in this experiment apparently employed a rather elaborate visual routine, it nevertheless appeared immediate and effortless. Response times were relatively short, about 750 msec for the fastest condition. When subjects were asked to describe how they performed the task, the main response was that the two X's were "simply seen" to lie on either the same curve or on different curves. No subject reported any scanning along a curve before making a decision.

The example above employed the tracking of a single contour. In other cases, it would be advantageous to activate a number of contours simultaneously. In Fig. 12a, for instance, the task is to establish visually whether there is a path connecting the center of the figure to the surrounding contour. The solution can be obtained effortlessly by looking at the figure, but again, it must involve in fact a complicated chain of processing. To cope with this

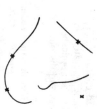

Figure 11. *The task here is to determine visually whether the two X's lie on the same curve. This simple task requires in fact complex processing that probably includes the use of a contour tracing operation.*

better understood not in terms of high-order features extracted by the units, but in terms of the basic operations performed by the networks. Elucidating the basic operations would therefore provide clues for understanding the activity in such networks and their patterns of interconnections.

3.5. Boundary tracing and activation

Since contours and boundaries of different types are fundamental entities in visual perception, a basic operation that could serve a useful role in visual routines is the tracking of contours in the base representation. This section examines the tracing operation in two parts. The first shows examples of boundary tracing and activation and their use in visual routines. The second examines the requirements imposed by the goal of having a useful, flexible, tracing operation.

3.5.1. Examples of tracing and activation

A simple example that will benefit from the operation of contour tracing is the problem of determining whether a contour is open or closed. If the contour is isolated in the visual field, an answer can be obtained by detecting the presence or absence of contour terminators. This strategy would not apply, however, in the presence of additional contours. This is an example of the 'figure in a context' problem (Minsky and Papert, 1969): figural properties are often substantially more difficult to establish in the presence of additional context. In the case of open and closed curves, it becomes necessary to relate the terminations to the contour in question. The problem can be solved by tracing the contour and testing for the presence of termination points on that contour.

Another simple example which illustrates the role of boundary tracing is shown in Fig. 11. The question here is whether there are two X's lying on a common curve. The answer seems immediate and effortless, but how is it achieved? Unlike the detection of single indexable items, it cannot be mediated by a fixed array of two-X's-on-a-curve detectors. Instead, I suggest that this simple perception conceals, in fact, an elaborate chain of events. In response to the question, a routine has been compiled and executed. An appropriate routine can be constructed if the repertoire of basic operations included the indexing of the X's and the tracking of curves. The tracking provides in this task a useful 'identity', or 'sameness' operator: it serves to verify that the two X figures are marked on the same curve, and not on two disconnected curves.

This task has been investigated recently by Jolicoeur et al. (1984, Reference note 1) and the results strongly supported the use of an internal contour

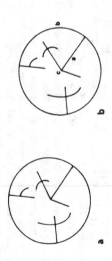

Figure 12. *The task in a is to determine visually whether there is a path connecting the center of the figure to the surrounding circle. In b the solution is labeled. The interpretation of such labels relys upon a set of common natural visual routines.*

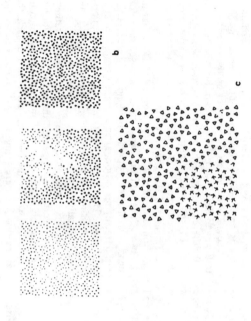

Tracking boundaries in the base representations. The examples mentioned above used contours in schematic line drawings. If boundary tracking is indeed a basic operation in establishing properties and spatial relations, it is expected to be applicable not only to such lines, but also to the different types of contours and discontinuity boundaries in the base representations. Exper-

Figure 13. *Certain texture boundaries can delineate effectively shape for recognition (a), while others cannot (b). Micropatterns that are ineffective for delineating shape boundaries can nevertheless give rise to discriminable textures (c). (From Riley, 1981).*

seemingly simple problem, visual routine must (i) identify the location referred to as "the center of the figure", (ii) identify the outside contour, and (iii) determine whether there is a path connecting the two. (It is also possible to proceed from the outside inwards.) By analogy with the area activation, the solution can be found by activating contours at the center point and examining the activation spread to the periphery. In Fig. 12b, the solution is labeled: the center is marked by the letter c, the surrounding boundary by b, and the connecting path by a. Labeling of this kind is common in describing graphs and figures. A point worth noting is that to be unambiguous, such notations must reply upon the use of common, natural visual routines. The label b, for example, is detached from the figure and does not identify explicitly a complete contour. The labeling notation implicitly assumes that there is a common procedure for identifying a distinct contour associated with the label.[21]

In searching for a connecting contour in Fig. 12, the contours could be activated in parallel, in a manner analogous to area coloring. It seems likely that at least in certain situations, the search for a connecting path is not just an unguided sequential tracking and exploration of all possible paths. A definite answer would require, however, an empirical investigation, for example, by manipulating the number of distracting cul-de-sac paths connected to the center and to the surrounding contour. In a sequential search, detection of the connecting path should be strongly affected by the addition of distracting paths. If, on the other hand, activation can spread along many paths simultaneously, detection will be little affected by the additional paths.

[21]It is also of interest to consider how we locate the center of figures. In Noton and Stark's (1971) study of eye movements, there are some indications of an ability to start the scanning of a figure approximately at its center.

(b) Tracking across intersections and branches. In tracing a boundary crossings and branching points can be encountered. It will then become necessary to decide which branch is the natural continuation of the curve. Similarity of color, contrast, motion, etc. may affect this decision. For similar contours, collinearity, or minimal change in direction (and perhaps curvature) seem to be the main criteria for preferring one branch over another.

Tracking a contour through an intersection can often be useful in obtaining a stable description of the contour for recognition purposes. Consider, for example, the two different instances of the numeral '2' in Fig. 14a. There are considerable differences between these two shapes. For example, one contains a hole, while the other does not. Suppose, however, that the contours are traced, and decomposed at places of maxima in curvature. This will lead to the decomposition shown in Fig. 14b. In the resulting descriptions, the

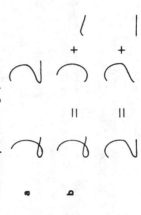

Figure 14. The tracking of a contour through an intersection is used here in generating a stable description of the contour. a, Two instances of the numeral '2'. b, In spite of the marked difference in their shape, their eventual decomposition and description are highly similar.

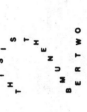

Figure 15. Tracing a skeleton. The overall figure can be traced and recognized without recognizing first all of the individual components.

iments with textures, for instance, have demonstrated that texture boundaries can be effective for defining shapes in visual recognition. Figure 13a (reproduced from Riley (1981)) illustrates an easily recognizable Z shape defined by texture boundaries. Not all types of discontinuity can be used for rapid recognition. In Fig. 13b, for example, recognition is difficult. The boundaries defined for instance by a transition between small k-like figures and triangles cannot be used in immediate recognition, although the texture generated by these micropatterns is easily discriminable (Fig. 13c)).

What makes some discontinuities considerably more efficient than others in facilitating recognition? Recognition requires the establishment of spatial properties and relations. It can therefore be expected that recognition is facilitated if the defining boundaries are already represented in the base representations, so that operations such as activation and tracking may be applied to them. Other discontinuities that are not represented in the base representations can be detected by applying appropriate visual routines, but recognition based on these contours will be considerably slower.[22]

3.5.2. Requirements on boundary tracing

The tracing of a contour is a simple operation when the contour is continuous, isolated, and well defined. When these conditions are not met, the tracing operation must cope with a number of challenging requirements. These requirements, and their implications for the tracing operation, are examined in this section.

(a) Tracing incomplete boundaries. The incompleteness of boundaries and contours is a well-known difficulty in image processing systems. Edges and contours produced by such systems often suffer from gaps due to such problems as noise and insufficient contrast. This difficulty is probably not confined to man-made systems alone; boundaries detected by the early processes in the human visual system are also unlikely to be perfect. The boundary tracing operation should not be limited, therefore, to continuous boundaries only. As noted above with respect to inside/outside routines for human perception, fragmented contours can indeed often replace continuous ones.

[22]M. Riley (1981) has found a close agreement between texture boundaries that can be used in immediate recognition and boundaries that can be used in long-range apparent motion (cf. Ullman, 1979). Boundaries participating in motion correspondence must be made explicit within the base representations, so that they can be matched over discrete frames. The implication is that the boundaries involved in immediate recognition also preexist in the base representations.

decomposition into strokes, and the shapes of the underlying strokes, are highly similar.

(c) *Tracking at different resolutions.* Tracking can proceed along the main skeleton of a contour without tracing its individual components. An example is illustrated in Fig. 15, where a figure is constructed from a collection of individual tokens. The overall figure can be traced and recognized without tracing and identifying its components.

Examples similar to Fig. 15 have been used to argue that 'global' or 'holistic' perception precedes the extraction of local features. According to the visual routines scheme, the constituent line elements are in fact extracted by the earliest visual process and represented in the base representations. The constituents are not recognized, since their recognition requires the application of visual routines. The 'forest before the trees' phenomenon (Johnston and McLelland, 1973; Navon, 1977; Pomerantz et al., 1977) is the result of applying appropriate routines that can trace and analyze aggregates without analyzing their individual components, thereby leading to the recognition of the overall figure prior to the recognition of its constituents.

The ability to trace collections of tokens and extract properties of their arrangement raises a question regarding the role of grouping processes in early vision. Our ability to perceive the collinear arrangement of different tokens, as illustrated in Fig. 16, has been used to argue for the existence of sophisticated grouping processes within the early visual representations that detect such arrangements and make them explicit (Marr, 1976). In this view, these grouping processes participate in the construction of the base representations, and consequently collinear arrangements of tokens are detected and represented throughout the base representation prior to the application of visual routines. An alternative possibility is that such arrangements are identified in fact as a result of applying the appropriate routine. This is not to deny the existence of certain grouping processes within the base representations. There is, in fact, strong evidence in support of the existence of such processes.[23] The more complicated and abstract grouping phenomena such as in Fig. 16 may, nevertheless, be the result of applying the appropriate routines, rather than being explicitly represented in the base representations.

Finally, from the point of view of the underlying mechanism, one obvious possibility is that the operation of tracing an overall skeleton is the result of applying tracing routines to a low resolution copy of the image, mediated by low frequency channels within the visual system. This is not the only possibil-

[23]For evidence supporting the existence of grouping processes within the early creation of the base representations using dot-interference patterns see Glass (1969), Glass and Perez (1973), Marroquin (1976), Stevens (1978). See also a discussion of grouping in early visual processing in Barlow (1981).

ity, however, and in attempting to investigate this operation further, alternative methods for tracing the overall skeleton of figures should also be considered.

In summary, the tracing and activation of boundaries are useful operations in the analysis of shape and the establishment of spatial relations. This is a complicated operation since flexible, reliable, tracing should be able to cope with breaks, crossings, and branching, and with different resolution requirements.

3.6. Marking

In the course of applying a visual routine, the processing shifts across the base representations from one location to another. To control and coordinate the routine, it would be useful to have the capability to keep at least a partial track of the locations already processed.

A simple operation of this type is the marking of a single location for future reference. This operation can be used, for instance, in establishing the closure of a contour. As noted in the preceding section, closure cannot be tested in general by the presence or absence of terminators, but can be established using a combination of tracing and marking. The starting point of the tracing operation is marked, and if the marked location is reached again the tracing is completed, and the contour is known to be closed.

Figure 17 shows a similar problem, which is a version of a problem examined in the previous section. The task here is to determine visually whether there are two X's on the same curve. Once again, the correct answer is perceived immediately. To establish that only a single X lies on the closed curve c, one can use the above strategy of marking the X and tracking the

Figure 16. *The collinearity of tokens (items and endpoints) can easily be perceived. This perception may be related to a routine that traces collinear arrangements, rather than to sophisticated grouping processes within the base representations.*

curve. It is suggested that the perceptual system has marking and tracing in its repertoire of basic operations, and that the simple perception of the X on the curve involved the application of visual routines that employ such operations.

Other tasks may benefit from the marking of more than a single location. A simple example is visual counting, that is, the problem of determining as fast as possible the number of distinct items in view (Atkinson et al., 1969; Kowler and Steinman, 1979).

For a small number of items visual counting is fast and reliable. When the number of items is four or less, the perception of their number is so immediate, that it gave rise to conjecture regarding special *Gestalt* mechanisms that can somehow respond directly to the number of items in view, provided that this number does not exceed four (Atkinson et al., 1969).

In the following section, we shall see that although such mechanisms are possible in principle, they are unlikely to be incorporated in the human visual system. It will be suggested instead that even the perception of a small number of items involves in fact the execution of visual routines in which marking plays an important role.

3.6.1. Comparing schemes for visual counting

Perception-like counting networks. In their book *Perceptrons*, Minsky and Papert (1969, Ch. 1) describe parallel networks that can count the number of elements in their input (see also Milner, 1974). Counting is based on computing the predicates "the input has exactly M points" and "the input has between M and N points" for different values of M and N. For any given

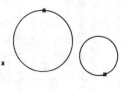

Figure 17. *The task here is to determine visually whether there are two X's on a common curve. The task could be accomplished by employing marking and tracing operations.*

value of M, it is thereby possible to construct a special network that will respond only when the number of items in view is exactly M. Unlike visual routines which are composed of elementary operations, such a network can adequately be described as an elementary mechanism responding directly to the presence of M items in view. Unlike the shifting and marking operations, the computation is performed by these networks uniformly and in parallel over the entire field.

Counting by visual routines. Counting can also be performed by simple visual routines that employ elementary operations such as shifting and marking. For example, the indexing operation described in Section 3.3 can be used to perform the counting task provided that it is extended somewhat to include marking operations. Section 3.3 illustrated how a simple shifting scheme can be used to move the processing focus to an indexable item. In the counting problem, there is more than a single indexable item to be considered. To use the same scheme for counting, the processing focus is required to travel among all of the indexable items, without visiting an item more than once.

A straightforward extension that will allow the shifting scheme in Section 3.3 to travel among different items is to allow it to mark the elements already visited. Simple marking can be obtained in this case by 'switching off' the element at the current location of the processing focus. The shifting scheme described above is always attracted to the location producing the strongest signal. If this signal is turned off, the shift would automatically continue to the new strongest signal. The processing focus can now continue its tour, until all the items have been visited, and their number counted.

A simple example of this counting routine is the 'single point detection' task. In this problem, it is assumed that one or more points can be lit up in the visual field. The task is to say 'yes' if a single point is lit up, and 'no' otherwise. Following the counting procedure outlined above, the first point will soon be reached and masked. If there are no remaining signals, the point was unique and the correct answer is 'yes'; otherwise, it is 'no'.

In the above scheme, counting is achieved by shifting the processing focus among the items of interest without scanning the entire image systematically. Alternatively, shifting and marking can also be used for visual counting by scanning the entire scene in a fixed predetermined pattern. As the number of items increases, programmed scanning may become the more efficient strategy. The two alternative schemes will behave differently for different numbers of items. The fixed scanning scheme is largely independent of the number of items, whereas in the traveling scheme, the computation time will depend on the number of items, as well as on their spatial configuration.

There are two main differences between counting by visual routines of one type or another on the one hand, and by specialized counting networks on the other. First, unlike the perception-like networks, the process of determining the number of items by visual routines can be decomposed into a sequence of elementary operations. This decomposition holds true for the perception of a small number of items and even for the single item detection. Second, in contrast with a counting network that is specially constructed for the task of detecting a prescribed number of items, the same elementary operations employed in the counting routine also participate in other visual routines.

This difference makes counting by visual routines more attractive than the counting networks. It does not seem plausible to assume that visual counting is essential enough to justify specialized networks dedicated to this task alone. In other words, visual counting is simply unlikely to be an elementary operation. It is more plausible in my view that visual counting can be performed efficiently as a result of our general capacity to generate and execute visual routines, and the availability of the appropriate elementary operations that can be harnessed for the task.

3.6.2. Reference frames in marking

The marking of a location for later reference requires a coordinate system, or a frame of reference, with respect to which the location is defined. One general question regarding marking is, therefore, what is the referencing scheme in which locations are defined and remembered for subsequent use by visual routines. One possibility is to maintain an internal 'egocentric' spatial map that can then be used in directing the processing focus. The use of one or more objects can be remembered, so that they can be reached (approximately) in the dark without external reference cues. It is also possible to use an internal map in combination with external referencing. For example, the

Figure 18. *The use of an external reference. The position of point q can be defined and retained relative to the predominant X nearby.*

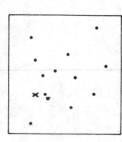

position of point q in Fig. 18 can be defined and remembered using the prominent X figure nearby. In such a scheme it becomes possible to maintain a crude map with which prominent features can be located, and a more detailed local map in which the position of the marked item is defined with respect to the prominent feature.

The referencing problem can be approached empirically, for example by making a point in figures such as Fig. 18 disappear, then reappear (possibly in a slightly displaced location), and testing the accuracy at which the two locations can be compared. (Care must be taken to avoid apparent motion.) One can test the effect of potential reference markers on the accuracy, and test marking accuracy across eye movements.

3.6.3. Marking and the integration of information in a scene

To be useful in the natural analysis of visual scenes, the marking map should be preserved across eye motions. This means that if a certain location in space is marked prior to an eye movement, the marking should point to the same spatial location following the eye movement. Such a marking operation, combined with the incremental representation, can play a valuable role in integrating the information across eye movements and from different regions in the course of viewing a complete scene.[24]

Suppose, for example, that a scene contains several objects, such as a man at one location, and a dog at another, and that following the visual analysis of the man figure we shift our gaze and processing focus to the dog. The visual analysis of the man figure has been summarized in the incremental representation, and this information is still available at least in part as the gaze is shifted to the dog. In addition to this information we keep a spatial map, a set of spatial pointers, which tell us that the dog is at one direction, and the man at another. Although we no longer see the man clearly, we have a clear notion of what exists where. The 'what' is supplied by the marking map.

representations, and the 'where' by the marking map.

In such a scheme, we do not maintain a full panoramic representation of the scene. After looking at various parts of the scene, our representation of it will have the following structure. There would be a retinotopic representation of the scene in the current viewing direction. To this representation we can apply visual routines to analyze the properties of, and relations among, the items in view. In addition, we would have markers to the spatial locations of items in the scene already analyzed. These markers can point to peripheral

[24]The problem considered here is not limited to the integration of views across saccadic eye motions, for which an 'integrative visual buffer' has been proposed by Rayner (1978).

objects, and perhaps even to locations outside the field of view (Attneave and Pierce, 1978). If we are currently looking at the dog, we would see it in detail, and will be able to apply visual routines and extract information regarding the dog's shape. At the same time we know the locations of the other objects in the scene (from the marking map) and what they are (from the incremental representation). We know, for example, the location of the man in the scene. We also know various aspects of his shape, although it may now appear only as a blurred blob, since they are summarized in the incremental representation. To obtain new information, however, we would have to shift our gaze back to the man figure, and apply additional visual routines.

3.6.4. On the spatial resolution of marking and other basic operations

In the visual routines scheme, accuracy in visual counting will depend on the accuracy and spatial resolution of the marking operation. This conclusion is consistent with empirical results obtained in the study of visual counting.[25] Additional perceptual limitations may arise from limitations on the spatial resolution of other basic operations. For example, it is known that spatial relations are difficult to establish in peripheral vision in the presence of distracting figures. An example, due to J. Lettvin (see also Andriessen and Bouma, 1976; Townsend et al., 1971), is shown in Fig. 19. When fixating on the central point from a normal reading distance, the N on the left is recognizable, while the N within the string TNT on the right is not. The flanking letters exert some 'lateral masking' even when their distance from the central letter is well above the two-point resolution at this eccentricity (Riggs, 1965).

Interaction effects of this type may be related to limitations on the spatial resolution of various basic operations, such as indexing, marking, and boundary tracking. The tracking of a line contour, for example, may be distracted by the presence of another contour nearby. As a result, contours may inter-

fere with the application of visual routines to other contours, and consequently with the establishment of spatial relations. Experiments involving the establishment of spatial relations in the presence of distractors would be useful in investigating the spatial resolution of the basic operations, and its dependence on eccentricity.

The hidden complexities in perceiving spatial relationships. We have examined above a number of plausible elemental operations including shift, indexing, bounded activation, boundary tracing and activation, and marking. These operations would be valuable in establishing abstract shape properties and spatial relations, and some of them are partially supported by empirical data. (They certainly do not constitute, however, a comprehensive set.)

The examination of the basic operations and their use reveals that in perceiving spatial relations the visual system accomplishes with intriguing efficiency highly complicated tasks. There are two main sources for these complexities. First, as was illustrated above, from a computational standpoint, the efficient and reliable implementation of each of the elemental operations poses challenging problems. It is evident, for instance, that a sophisticated specialized processor would be required for an efficient and flexible bounded activation operation, or for the tracing of contours and collinear arrangements of tokens.

In addition to the complications involved in the realization of the different elemental operations, new complications are introduced when the elemental operations are assembled into meaningful visual routines. As illustrated by the inside/outside example, in perceiving a given spatial relation different strategies may be employed, depending on various parameters of the stimuli (such as the complexity of the boundary, or the distance of the X from the bounding contour). The immediate perception of seemingly simple relations often requires, therefore, selection among possible routines, followed by the coordinated application of the elemental operations comprising the visual routines. Some of the problems involved in the assembly of the elemental operations into visual routines are discussed briefly in the next section.

4. The assembly, compilation, and storage of visual routines

The use of visual routines allows a variety of properties and relations to be established using a fixed set of basic operations. According to this view, the establishment of relations requires the application of a coordinated sequence of basic operations. We have discussed above a number of plausible basic operations. In this section I shall raise some of the general problems as-

Figure 19. *Spatial limitations of the elemental operations. When the central mark is fixated, the N on the left is recognizable, while the one on the right is not. This effect may reflect limitations on the spatial resolution of basic operations such as indexing, marking, and boundary tracing.*

N   TNT

[25]For example, Kowler and Steinman (1979) report a puzzling result regarding counting accuracy. It was found that eye movements increase counting accuracy for large (2°) displays, but were not helpful, and sometimes detrimental, with small displays. This result could be explained under the plausible assumptions that marking accuracy is better near fixation, and that it deteriorates across eye movements. As a result, eye movements will improve marking accuracy for large, but not for small, displays.

sociated with the construction of useful routines from combinations of basic operations.

The appropriate routine to be applied in a given situation depends on the goal of the computation, and on various parameters of the configuration to be analyzed. We have seen, for example, that the routine for establishing inside/outside relations may depend on various properties of the configuration: in some cases it would be efficient to start at the location of the X figure, in other situations it may be more efficient to start at some distant locations.

Similarly, in Treisman's (1977, 1980) experiments on indexing by two properties (e.g., a vertical red item in a field of vertical green and horizontal red distractors) there are at least two alternative strategies for detecting the target. Since direct indexing by two properties is impossible, one may either scan the red items, testing for orientation, or scan the vertical items, testing for color.[26] The distribution of distractors in the field determines the relative efficiency of these alternative strategies. In such cases it may prove useful, therefore, to precede the application of a particular routine with a stage where certain relevant properties of the configuration to be analyzed are sampled and inspected. It would be of interest to examine whether in the double indexing task, for example, the human visual system tends to employ the more efficient search strategy.

The above discussion introduces what may be called the 'assembly problem'; that is, the problem of how routines are constructed in response to specific goals, and how this generation is controlled by aspects of the configuration to be analyzed. In the above examples, a goal for the computation is set up externally, and an appropriate routine is applied in response. In the course of recognizing and manipulating objects, routines are usually invoked in response to internally generated queries. Some of these routines may be stored in memory rather than assembled anew each time they are needed.

The recognition of a specific object may then use pre-assembled routines for inspecting relevant features and relations among them. Since routines can also be generated efficiently by the assembly mechanism in response to specific goals, it would probably be sufficient to store routines in memory in a skeletonized form only. The assembly mechanism will then fill in details and generate intermediate routines when necessary. In such a scheme, the perceptual activity during recognition will be guided by setting pre-stored goals that the assembly process will then expand into detailed visual routines.

[26]There is also a possibility that all the items must be scanned one by one without any selection by color or orientation. This question is relevant for the shift operation discussed in Section 3.2. Recent results by J. Rubin and N. Kanwisher at M.I.T. suggest that it is possible to scan only the items of relevant color and ignore the others.

The application of pre-stored routines rather then assembling them again each time they are required can lead to improvements in performance and the speed-up of performing familiar perceptual tasks. These improvements can come from two different sources. First, assembly time will be saved if the routine is already 'compiled' in memory. The time saving can increase if stored routines for familiar tasks, which may be skeletonized at first, become more detailed, thereby requiring less assembly time. Second, stored routines may be improved with practice, for example, as a result of either external instruction, or by modifying routines when they fail to accomplish their tasks efficiently.

Summary

1. Visual perception requires the capacity to extract abstract shape properties and spatial relations. This requirement divides the overall processing of visual information into two distinct stages. The first is the creation of the base representations (such as the primal sketch and the 2½-D sketch). The second is the application of visual routines to the base representations.

2. The creation of the base representations is a bottom-up and spatially uniform process. The representations it produces are unarticulated and viewer-centered.

3. The application of visual routines is no longer bottom-up, spatially uniform, and viewer-centered. It is at this stage that objects and parts are defined, and their shape properties and spatial relations are established.

4. The perception of abstract shape properties and spatial relations raises two major difficulties. First, the perception of even seemingly simple, immediate properties and relations requires in fact complex computation. Second, visual perception requires the capacity to establish a large variety of different properties and relations.

5. It is suggested that the perception of spatial relation is achieved by the application to the base representations of visual routines that are composed of sequences of elemental operations. Routines for different properties and relations share elemental operations. Using a fixed set of basic operations, the visual system can assemble different routines to extract an unbounded variety of shape properties and spatial relations.

6. Unlike the construction of the base representation, the application of visual routines is not determined by the visual input alone. They are selected or created to meet specific computational goals.

7. Results obtained by the application of visual routines are retained in the incremental representation and can be used by subsequent processes.

8. Some of the elemental operations employed by visual routines are applied to restricted locations in the visual field, rather than to the entire field in parallel. It is suggested that this apparent limitation on spatial parallelism reflects in part essential limitations, inherent to the nature of the computation, rather than non-essential capacity limitations.

9. At a more detailed level, a number of plausible basic operations were suggested, based primarily on their potential usefulness, and supported in part by empirical evidence. These operations include:

9.1. *Shift of the processing focus.* This is a family of operations that allow the application of the same basic operation to different locations across the base representations.

9.2. *Indexing.* This is a shift operation towards special odd-man-out locations. A location can be indexed if it is sufficiently different from its surroundings in an indexable property. Indexable properties, which are computed in parallel by the early visual processes, include contrast, orientation, color, motion, and perhaps also size, binocular disparity, curvature, and the existence of terminators, corners, and intersections.

9.3. *Bounded activation.* This operation consists of the spread of activation over a surface in the base representation, emanating from a given location or contour, and stopping at discontinuity boundaries. This is not a simple operation, since it must cope with difficult problems that arise from the existence of internal contours and fragmented boundaries. A discussion of the mechanisms that may be implicated in this operation suggests that specialized networks may exist within the visual system, for executing and controlling the application of visual routines.

9.4. *Boundary tracing.* This operation consists of either the tracing of a single contour, or the simultaneous activation of a number of contours. This operation must be able to cope with the difficulties raised by the tracing of incomplete boundaries, tracing across intersections and branching points, and tracing contours defined at different resolution scales.

9.5. *Marking.* The operation of marking a location means that this location is remembered, and processing can return to it whenever necessary. Such an operation would be useful in the integration of information in the processing of different parts of a complete scene.

10. It is suggested that the seemingly simple and immediate perception of spatial relations conceals in fact a complex array of processes involved in the selection, assembly, and execution of visual routines.

References

Andriessen, J.J. and Bouma. H. (1976) Eccentric vision: adverse interactions between line segments. *Vis. Res.*, 16. 71–78.

Atkinson, J., Campbell, F. W. and Francis, M.R. (1969) The magic number 4 ± 0: A new look at visual numerosity judgments. *Perception*, 5, 327–334.

Attneave. F. and Pierce. C.R. (1978) The accuracy of extrapolating a pointer into perceived and imagined space. *Am. J. Psychol.* 91(3), 371–387.

Barlow. H.H. (1972) Single units and sensation: A neuron doctrine for perceptual psychology? *Perception. I*, 371–394.

Barlow. H.B. (1981) Critical limiting factors in the design of the eye and the visual cortex. The Ferrier Lecture 1980. *Proc. Roy. Soc. Lond. B*, 212. 1–34.

Bartlett. F.C. (1932) *Remembering*. Cambridge. Cambridge University Press.

Beck, J. and Ambler. B. (1972) Discriminability of differences in line slope and in line arrangement as a function of mask delay. *Percep. Psychophys.* 12(1A), 33–38.

Beck, J. and Ambler. B. (1973) The effects of concentrated and distributed attention on peripheral acuity. *Percept. Psychophys.*, 14(2), 225–230.

Beneveneto. L.A. and Davis. B. (1977) Topographical projections of the prestriate cortex to the pulvinar nuclei in the macaque monkey: an autoradiographic study. *Exp. Brain Res.* 30. 405–424.

Biederman. I. Glass. A.L. and Stacy, E.W. (1973) Searching for objects in real-world scenes. *J. exp. Psychol.* 97(1), 22–27.

Donders. D.C. and Zelnicker. D. (1969) Parallel processing in visual same–different decisions. *Percep. Psychophys.* 5(4). 197–200.

Egeth. H., Jonides. J. and Wall. S. (1972) Parallel processing of multi-element displays. *Cog. Psychol.* 3. 674–698.

Engel. F.L. (1971) Visual conspicuity, directed attention and retinal locus. *Vis. Res.*, 11. 563–576.

Eriksen. C.W. and Hoffman. J.E. (1972) Temporal and spatial characteristics of selective encoding from visual displays. *Percep. Psychophys.*, 12(2B), 201–204.

Eriksen. C.W. and Schultz. D.W. (1977) Retinal locus and acuity in visual information processing. *Bull. Psychon. Soc.* 9(2). 81–84.

Estes, W.K. (1972) Interactions of signal and background variables in visual processing. *Percep. Psychophys.*, 12(3), 278–286.

Evans. T.G. (1968) A heuristic program to solve geometric analogy problems. In M. Minsky (ed.), *Semantic Information Processing*. Cambridge. MA. M.I.T. Press.

Fantz. R.L. (1961) The origin of form perception. *Scient. Am.*, 204(5), 66–72.

Fischer. B. and Boch. R. (1981) Enhanced activation of neurons in prelunate cortex before visually guided saccades of trained rhesus monkey. *Exp. Brain Res.*, 44, 129–137.

Fuster, J.M. and Jervey, J.P. (1981) Inferotemporal neurons distinguish and retain behaviorally relevant features of visual stimuli. *Science*, 212. 952–955.

Gattas, R., Oscaldo Cruz, E. and Sousa. A.P.B. (1979) Visual receptive fields of units in the pulvinar of cebus monkey. *Brain Res.*, 160. 413–430.

Glass. L. (1969) Moire effect from random dots. *Nature*, 243, 578–580.

Glass. L. and Perez. R. (1973) Perception of random dot interference patterns. *Nature*, 246. 360–362.

Goldberg. M.E. and Wurtz. R.H. (1972) Activity of superior colliculus in behaving monkey. II. Effect of attention of neural responses. *J. Neurophysiol*, 35, 560–574.

Holtzman. J.D. and Gazzaniga. M.S. (1982) Dual task interactions due exclusively to limits in processing resources. *Science*, 218, 1325–1327.

Humphreys. G.W. (1981) On varying the span of visual attention: evidence for two modes of spatial attention. *Q. J. exp. Psychol.*, 33A, 17–31.

Johnston, J.C. and McClelland, J.L. (1973) Visual factors in word perception. *Percep. Psychophys.*, *14(2)*, 365–370.

Jonides, J. and Gleitman, H. (1972) A conceptual category effect in visual search: O as a letter or as digit. *Percep. Psychophys.*, *12(6)*, 457–460.

Johnson, R.B. and Kirk, N.S. (1960) The perception of size: An experimental synthesis of the associationist and gestalt accounts of the perception of size. Part III. *Q. J. exp. Psychol.*, *12*, 221–230.

Julesz, B. (1975) Experiments in the visual perception of texture. *Scient. Am.*, *232(4)*, April 1975, 34–43.

Julesz, B. (1981) Textons, the elements of texture perception, and their interactions. *Nature*, *290*, 91–97.

Kahneman, D. (1973) *Attention and Effort.* Englewood Cliffs, NJ, Prentice-Hall.

Kolmogorov, A.N. (1968) Logical basis for information theory and probability theory. *IEEE Trans. Info. Theory*, *IT-14(5)*, 662–664.

Kowler, E. and Steinman, R.M. (1979) Miniature saccades: eye movements that do not count. *Vis. Res.*, *19*, 105–108.

Lappin, J.S. and Fuqua, M.A. (1983) Accurate visual measurement of three-dimensional moving patterns. *Science*, *221*, 480–482.

Livingstone, M.L. and Hubel, D.J. (1981) Effects of sleep and arousal on the processing of visual information in the cat. *Nature*, *291*, 554–561.

Mackworth, N.H. (1965) Visual noise causes tunnel vision. *Psychon. Sci.*, *3*, 67–68.

Marr, D. (1976) Early processing of visual information. *Phil. Trans. Roy. Soc. and B*, *275*, 483–524.

Marr, D. (1980) Visual information processing: the structure and creation of visual representations. *Phil. Trans. Roy. Soc. Lond. B*, *290*, 199–218.

Marr, D. and Nishihara, H.K. (1978) Representation and recognition of the spatial organization of three-dimensional shapes. *Proc. Roy. Soc. B*, *200*, 269–291.

Marroquin, J.L. (1976) Human visual perception of structure. MSc. Thesis, Department of Electrical Engineering and Computer Science, Massachusetts Institute of Technology.

Milner, P.M. (1974) A model for visual shape recognition. *Psychol. Rev.* *81(6)*, 521–535.

Minsky, M. and Papert, S. (1969) *Perceptrons.* Cambridge, MA and London: The M.I.T. Press.

Minsky, M. (1975) A framework for representing knowledge. In P.H. Winston (ed.), *The Psychology of Computer Vision.* New York, Prentice Hall.

Mountcastle, V.B. (1976) The world around us: neural command functions for selective attention. The F.O. Schmitt Lecture in Neuroscience 1975. *Neurosci. Res. Prog. Bull.*, *14*, Supplement 1–37.

Mountcastle, V.B., Lynch, J.C., Georgopoulos, A., Sakata, H. and Acuna, A. (1975) Posterior parietal association cortex of the monkey: command functions for operations within extrapersonal space. *J. Neurophys.*, *38*, 871–908.

Navon, D. (1977) Forest before trees: the precedence of global features in visual perception. *Cog. Psychol.*, *9*, 353–383.

Neisser, U. (1967) *Cognitive Psychology.* New York, Prentice-Hall.

Neisser, U., Novick, R. and Lazar, R. (1963) Searching for ten targets simultaneously. *Percep. Mot. Skills*, *17*, 955–961.

Newsome, W.T. and Wurtz, R.H. (1982) Identification of architectonic zones containing visual tracking cells in the superior temporal sulcus of macaque monkeys. *Invest. Ophthal. Vis. Sci.*, Suppl. 3, *22*, 238.

Nickerson, R.S. (1966) Response times with memory-dependent decision task. *J. exp. Psychol.*, *72(5)*, 761–769.

Noton, D. and Stark, L. (1971) Eye movements and visual perception. *Scient. Am.*, *224(6)*, 34–43.

Pomerantz, J.R., Sager, L.C. and Stoever, R.J. (1977) Perception of wholes and of their component parts: some configural superiority effects. *J. exp. Psychol., Hum. Percep. Perf.*, *3(3)*, 422–435.

Posner, M.I. (1980) Orienting of attention. *Q. J. exp. Psychol.*, *32*, 3–25.

Posner, M.I., Nissen, M.J. and Ogden, W.C. (1978) Attended and unattended processing modes: the role of set for spatial location. In Saltzman, I.J. and H.L. Pick (eds.), *Modes of Perceiving and Processing Information.* Hillsdale, NJ, Lawrence Erlbaum.

Potter, M.C. (1975) Meaning in visual search. *Science*, *187*, 965–966.

Rayner, K. (1948) Eye movements in reading and information processing. *Psychol. Bull.*, *85(3)*, 618–660.

Regan, D. and Beverley, K.I. (1978) Looming detectors in the human visual pathway. *Vis. Res.*, *18*, 209–212.

Rezak, M. and Beneveneto, A. (1979) A comparison of the organization of the projections of the dorsal lateral geniculate nucleus. the inferior pulvinar and adjacent lateral pulvinar to primary visual area (area 17) in the macaque monkey. *Brain Res.*, *167*, 19–40.

Richards, W. (1982) How to play twenty questions with nature and win. *M.I.T.A.I. Laboratory Memo 660.*

Richmond, B.J. and Sato, T. (1982) Visual responses of inferior temporal neurons are modified by attention to different stimulus dimensions. *Soc. Neurosci. Abst.*, *8*, 812.

Riggs, L.A. (1965) Visual acuity. In C.H. Graham (ed.) *Vision and Visual Perception.* New York, John Wiley.

Riley, M.D. (1981) The representation of image texture. M.Sc. Thesis. Department of Electrical Engineering and Computer Science, Massachusetts Institute of Technology.

Robinson, D.L., Goldberg, M.G. and Staton, G.B. (1978) Parietal association cortex in the primate: sensory mechanisms and behavioral modulations. *J. Neurophysiol.*, *41(4)*, 910–932.

Rock, I., Halper, F. and Clayton, T. (1972) The perception and recognition of complex figures. *Cog. Psychol.*, *3*, 655–673.

Rock, I. and Gutman, D. (1981) The effect of inattention of form perception. *J. exp. Psychol.: Hum. Percep. Perf.*, *7(2)*, 275–285.

Rumelhart, D.E. (1970) A multicomponent theory of the perception of briefly exposed visual displays. *J. Math. Psychol.*, *7*, 191–218.

Schein, S.J., Marrocco, R.T. and De Monasterio, F.M. (1982) Is there a high concentration of color-selective cells in area V4 of monkey visual cortex? *J. Neurophysiol.*, *47(2)*, 193–213.

Shiffrin, R.M., McKay, D.P. and Shaffer, W.O. (1976) Attending to forty-nine spatial positions at once. *J. exp. Psychol.: Human Percep. Perf.*, *2(1)*, 14–22.

Shulman, G.L., Remington, R.W. and McLean, J.P. (1979) Moving attention through visual space. *J. exp. Psychol.: Huma. Percep. Perf.*, *5*, 522–526.

Sperling, G. (1960) The information available in brief visual presentations. *Psychol. Mono.*, *74*, (11. Whole No. 498).

Stevens, K.A. (1978) Computation of locally parallel structure. *Biol. Cybernet.*, *29*, 19–28.

Sutherland, N.S. (1968) Outline of a theory of the visual pattern recognition in animal and man. *Proc. Roy. Soc. Lond. B*, *171*, 297–317.

Townsend, J.T., Taylor, S.G. and Brown, D.R. (1971) Latest masking for letters with unlimited viewing time. *Percep. Psycholphys.*, *10(5)*, 375–378.

Treisman, A. (1977) Focused attention in the perception and retrieval of multidimensional stimuli. *Percep. Psychophys.*, *22*, 1–11.

Treisman, A. and Celade, G. (1980) A feature integration theory of attention. *Cog. Psychol.*, *12*, 97–136.

Tsal, Y. (1983) Movements of attention across the visual field. *J. exp. Psychol.: Hum. Percep. Perf.* (In Press).

Ullman, S. (1979) *The Interpretation of Visual Motion.* Cambridge, MA, and London: The M.I.T. Press.

Varanese, J. (1983) Abstracting spatial relations from the visual world B.Sc. thesis in Neurobiology and Psychology. Harvard University.

van Voorhis, S. and Hillyard, S.A. (1977) Visual evoked potentials and selective attention to points in space. *Percep. Psychophys.*, *22(1)*, 54–62.

Winston, P.H. (1977) *Artificial Intelligence.* Reading, MA., Addison-Wesley.

Wurtz, R.H. and Mohler, C.W. (1976a) Organization of monkey superior colliculus: enhanced visual response of superficial layer cells. *J. Neurophysiol.*, *39(4)*, 745–765.

Wurtz, R.H. and Mohler, C.W. (1976b) Enhancement of visual response in monkey striate cortex and frontal eye fields. *J. Neurophysiol.*, *39*, 766–772.

Wurtz, R.H., Goldberg, M.E. and Robinson D.L. (1982) Brain mechanisms of visual attention. *Scient. Am..*, 246(6), 124-135.

Zeki, S.M. (1978a) Functional specialization in the visual cortex of the rhesus monkey. *Nature*, 274, 423-428.

Zeki, S.M. (1978b) Uniformity and diversity of structure and function in rhesus monkey prestriate visual cortex. *J. Physiol.*, 277, 273-290.

Reference Note

1. Joliceur, P., Ullman, S. and Mackay, M. (1984) Boundary Tracing: a possible elementary operation in the perception of spatial relations. Submitted for publication.

Résumé

Cet article porte sur le traitement de l'information visuelle après la création des premières représentations. La capacité de déterminer visuellement les propriétés formelles abstraites et les relations spatiales est un prérequis à ce niveau. Cette capacité joue un rôle majeur dans la reconnaissance d'objet, dans les manipulations guidées par la vision ainsi que dans la pensée visuelle plus abstraite.

Pour le système visuel humain, la perception des propriétés spatiales et des relations complexes au point de vue calcul apparaît trompeusement immédiate et facile. L'efficacité du système humain pour analyser l'information spatiale surpasse de loin les capacités des systèmes artificiels utilisés pour l'analyse spatiale de l'information visuelle.

La perception des propriétés de forme abstraite et des relations spatiales soulève des difficultés fondamentales avec des conséquences importantes pour le traitement général de l'information visuelle. Les auteurs défendent l'idée que le calcul des relations spatiales sépare l'analyse de l'information visuelle en deux stades principaux. Au cours du premier se créent. de bas en haut, certaines représentations de l'environnement visible. Au cours du second des processus dits 'routines visuelles' s'appliquent aux représentations issues du premier stade. Ces routines peuvent révéler des propriétés et des relations qui n'étaient pas représentées de façon explicite dans les représentations initiales.

Les routines visuelles sont composées de séquences d'opérations élémentaires conjointes pour les différentes propriétés et relations. En utilisant une suite illimitée de propriétés de forme et de relations spatiales. le système visuel peut assembler différentes routines pour extraire une série fixe d'opérations de base. en se fondant essentiellement sur leur utilité potentielle et. en partie. sur des preuves empiriques. Ces opérations incluent le changement du centre de traitement. l'indexation à une localisation d'un observateur extérieur. des' activations limitées, le tracage de frontières et des marquages. Les auteurs posent le problème de l'assemblage de ces opérations élémentaires en routines visuelles significantes.

Psychological Review

VOLUME 88   NUMBER 5   SEPTEMBER 1981

An Interactive Activation Model of Context Effects in Letter Perception: Part 1. An Account of Basic Findings

James L. McClelland and David E. Rumelhart
University of California, San Diego

A model of context effects in perception is applied to the perception of letters in various contexts. In the model, perception results from excitatory and inhibitory interactions of detectors for visual features, letters, and words. A visual input excites detectors for visual features in the display. These excite detectors for letters consistent with the active features. The letter detectors in turn excite detectors for consistent words. Active word detectors mutually inhibit each other and send feedback to the letter level, strengthening activation and hence perceptibility of their constituent letters. Computer simulation of the model exhibits the perceptual advantage for letters in words over unrelated contexts and is consistent with the basic facts about the word advantage. Most importantly, the model produces facilitation for letters in pronounceable pseudowords as well as words. Pseudowords activate detectors for words that are consistent with most of the active letters, and feedback from the activated words strengthens the activations of the letters in the pseudoword. The model thus accounts for apparently rule-governed performance without any actual rules.

As we perceive, we are continually extracting sensory information to guide our attempts to determine what is before us. In addition, we bring to perception a wealth of knowledge about the objects we might see or hear and the larger units in which these objects co-occur. As one of us has argued for the case of reading (Rumelhart, 1977), our knowledge of the objects we might be perceiving works together with the sensory information in the perceptual process. Exactly how does the knowledge that we have interact with the input? And how does this interaction facilitate perception?

In this two-part article we have attempted to take a few steps toward answering these questions. We consider one specific example of the interaction of knowledge and perception—the perception of letters in words and other contexts. In Part 1 we examine the main findings in the literature on perception of letters in context and develop a model called the interactive activation model to account for these effects. In Part 2 (Rumelhart & McClelland, in press) we extend the model in several ways. We present a set of studies introducing a new technique for studying the perception of letters in context, independently varying the duration and timing of the context and target letters. We show how the model fares in accounting for the results of these experiments and discuss how the model may be extended to account for a variety of phenomena. We also present an experiment that tests—and supports—a

Preparation of this article was supported by National Science Foundation Grants BNS-76-14830 and BNS-79-24062 to J. L. McClelland and Grant BNS-76-15024 to D. E. Rumelhart, and by the Office of Naval Research under contract N00014-79-C-0323. We would like to thank Don Norman, James Johnston, and members of the LNR research group for helpful discussions of much of the material covered in this article.

Requests for reprints may be sent to James L. McClelland or David E. Rumelhart at Department of Psychology, C-009, University of California, San Diego, La Jolla, California 92093.

counterintuitive prediction of the model. Finally, we consider how the mechanisms developed in the course of exploring our model of word perception might be extended to perception of other sorts of stimuli.

Basic Findings on the Role of Context in Perception of Letters

The notion that knowledge and familiarity play a role in perception has often been supported by experiments on the perception of letters in words (Bruner, 1957; Neisser, 1967). It has been known for nearly 100 years that it is possible to identify letters in words more accurately than letters in random letter sequences under tachistoscopic presentation conditions (Cattell, 1886; see Huey, 1908, and Neisser, 1967, for reviews). However, until recently such effects were obtained using whole reports of all of the letters presented. These reports are subject to guessing biases, so that it was possible to imagine that familiarity did not determine how much was seen but only how much could be inferred from a fragmentary percept. In addition, for longer stimuli, full reports are subject to forgetting. We may see more letters than we can actually report in the case of nonwords, but when the letters form a word, we may be able to retain as a single unit the item whose spelling may simply be read out from long-term memory. Thus, despite strong arguments to the contrary by proponents of the view that familiar context really does influence perception, it has been possible until recently to imagine that the context in which a letter was presented influences only the accuracy of postperceptual processes and not the process of perception itself.

The perceptual advantage of letters in words. The seminal experiment of Reicher (1969) suggests that context does actually influence perceptual processing. Reicher presented target letters in words, unpronounceable nonwords, and alone, following the presentation of the target display with a presentation of a patterned mask. The subject was then tested on a single letter in the display, using a forced choice between two alternative letters. Both alternatives fit the context to form an item of the type pre-

sented, so that, for example in the case of a word presentation, the alternative would also form a word in the context.

Forced-choice performance was more accurate for letters in words than for letters in nonwords or even for single letters. Since both alternatives made a word with the context, it is not possible to argue that the effect is due to postperceptual guessing based on equivalent information extracted about the target letter in the different conditions. It appears that subjects actually come away with more information relevant to a choice between the alternatives when the target letter is a part of a word. And, since one of the control conditions was a single letter, it is not reasonable to argue that the effect is due to forgetting letters that have been perceived. It is hard to see how a single letter, once perceived, could be subject to a greater forgetting than a letter in a word.

Reicher's (1969) finding seems to suggest that perception of a letter can be facilitated by presenting it in the context of a word. It appears, then, that our knowledge about words can influence the process of perception. Our model presents a way of bringing such knowledge to bear. The basic idea is that the presentation of a string of letters begins the process of activating detectors for letters that are consistent with the visual input. As these activations grow stronger, they begin to activate detectors for words that are consistent with the letters, if there are any. The active word detectors then produce feedback, which reinforces the activations of the detectors for the letters in the word. Letters in words are more perceptible, because they receive more activation than representations of either single letters or letters in an unrelated context.

Reicher's basic finding has been investigated and extended in a large number of studies, and there now appears to be a set of important related findings that must also be explained.

Irrelevance of word shape. The effect seems to be independent of the familiarity of the word as a visual configuration. The word advantage over nonwords is obtained for words in lowercase type, words in uppercase type, or words in a mixture of upper-

and lowercase (Adams, 1979; McClelland, 1976).

Role of patterned masking. The word advantage over single letters and nonwords appears to depend upon the visual masking conditions used (Johnston & McClelland, 1973; Massaro & Klitzke, 1979; see also Juola, Leavitt, & Choe, 1974; Taylor & Chabot, 1978). The word advantage is quite large when the target appears in a distinct, high-contrast display followed by a patterned mask of similar characteristics. However, the word advantage over single letters is actually reversed, and the word advantage over nonwords becomes quite small when the target is indistinct, low in contrast, and/or followed by a blank, nonpatterned field.

Extension to pronounceable pseudowords. The word advantage also applies to pronounceable nonwords, such as *REET* or *MAVE*. A large number of studies (e.g., Aderman & Smith, 1971; Baron & Thurston, 1973; Spoehr & Smith, 1975) have shown that letters in pronounceable nonwords (also called pseudowords) have a large advantage over letters in unpronounceable nonwords (also called unrelated letter strings), and three studies (Carr, Davidson, & Hawkins, 1978; Massaro & Klitzke, 1979; McClelland & Johnston, 1977) have obtained an advantage for letters in pseudowords over single letters.

Absence of effects of contextual constraint under patterned-mask conditions. One important finding, which rules out several of the models that have been proposed previously, is the finding that letters in highly constraining word contexts have little or no advantage over letters in weakly constraining word contexts under the distinct target/patterned-mask conditions that produce a word advantage (Johnston, 1978; see also Estes, 1975). For example, if the set of possible stimuli contains only words, the context _HIP constrains the first letter to be either an S, a C, or a W, whereas the context _INK is compatible with 12 to 14 letters (the exact number depends on what counts as a word). We might expect that the former, more strongly constraining context would produce superior detection of a target letter. But in a very carefully controlled and executed study, Johnston (1978) found no such effect. Although constraints do influence performance under other conditions (e.g., Broadbent & Gregory, 1968), they do not appear to make a difference under the distinct-target/patterned-mask conditions of the Johnston study.

To be successful, any model of word perception must provide an account not only for Reicher's (1969) basic effect but for these related findings as well. Our model accounts for all of these effects. We begin by presenting the model in abstract form. We then focus on the specific version of the model implemented in our simulation program and consider some of the details. Subsequently, we turn to detailed considerations of the findings we have discussed in this section.

The Interactive Activation Model

We approach the phenomena of word perception with a number of basic assumptions that we want to incorporate into the model. First, we assume that perceptual processing takes place within a system in which there are several levels of processing, each concerned with forming a representation of the input at a different level of abstraction. For visual word perception, we assume that there is a visual feature level, a letter level, and a word level, as well as higher levels of processing that provide "top-down" input to the word level.

Second, we assume that visual perception involves parallel processing. There are two different senses in which we view perception as parallel. We assume that visual perception is spatially parallel. That is, we assume that information covering a region in space at least large enough to contain a four-letter word is processed simultaneously. In addition, we assume that visual processing occurs at several levels at the same time. Thus, our model of word perception is spatially parallel (i.e., capable of processing several letters of a word at one time) and involves processes that operate simultaneously at several different levels. Thus, for example, processing at the letter level presumably occurs simultaneously with processing at the word level and with processing at the feature level. Third, we assume that perception is fundamentally an *interactive* process. That is, we assume that "top-down" or "conceptually driven" processing works simultaneously and in conjunction with "bottom-up" or "data driven" processing to provide a sort of multiplicity of constraints that jointly determine what we perceive. Thus, for example, we assume that knowledge about the words of the language interacts with the incoming featural information in codetermining the nature and time course of the perception of the letters in the word.

Finally, we wish to implement these assumptions by using a relatively simple method of interaction between sources of knowledge whose only "currency" is simple excitatory and inhibitory activations of a neural type.

Figure 1 shows the general conception of the model. Perceptual processing is assumed to occur in a set of interacting levels, each communicating with several others. Communication proceeds through a spreading activation mechanism in which activation at one level spreads to neighboring levels. The communication can consist of both excitatory and inhibitory messages. Excitatory messages increase the activation level of their recipients. Inhibitory messages decrease the activation level of their recipients. The arrows in the diagram represent excitatory connections, and the circular ends of the connections represent inhibitory connections. The intralevel inhibitory loop represents a kind of lateral inhibition in which incompatible units at the same level compete. For example, since a string of four letters can be interpreted as at most one four-letter word, the various possible words mutually inhibit one another and in that way compete as possible interpretations of the string.

It is clear that many levels are important in reading and perception in general, and the interactions among these levels are important for many phenomena. However, a theoretical analysis of all of these interactions introduces an order of complexity that obscures comprehension. For this reason, we have restricted the present analysis to an examination of the interaction between a single pair of levels, the word and letter levels. We have found that we can account for the phenomena reviewed above by considering only the interactions between letter level and word level elements. Therefore, for the present we have elaborated the model only on these two levels, as illustrated in Figure 2. We have delayed consideration of the effects of higher level processes and phonological processes, and we have ignored the reciprocity of activation that may occur between word and letter levels and any other levels of the system. We consider aspects of the fuller model including these influences in Part 2 (Rumelhart & McClelland, in press).

Specific Assumptions

Representation assumptions. For every relevant unit in the system we assume there is an entity called a *node*. We assume that there is a node for each word we know, and that there is a node for each letter in each letter position within a four-letter string.

The nodes are organized into levels. There are *word level* nodes and *letter level* nodes. Each node has connections to a number of

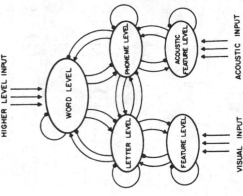

HIGHER LEVEL INPUT

WORD LEVEL — LETTER LEVEL — PHONEME LEVEL — FEATURE LEVEL — ACOUSTIC FEATURE LEVEL

VISUAL INPUT   ACOUSTIC INPUT

Figure 1. A sketch of some of the processing levels involved in visual and auditory word perception, with interconnections.

other nodes. The nodes to which a node connects are called its *neighbors*. Each connection is two-way. There are two kinds of connections: *excitatory* and *inhibitory*. If two nodes suggest each other's existence (in the way that the node for the word *the* suggests the node for an initial *t* and vice versa), then the connections are excitatory. If two nodes are inconsistent with one another (in the way that the node for the word *the* and the node for the word *boy* are inconsistent), then the relationship is inhibitory. Note that we iden-

tify nodes according to the units they detect, printing them in italics; stimuli presented to the system are in uppercase letters.

Connections may occur within levels or between adjacent levels. There are no connections between nonadjacent levels. Connections within the word level are mutually inhibitory, since only one word can occur at any one place at any one time. Connections between the word level and letter level may be either inhibitory or excitatory (depending on whether the letter is a part of the word in the appropriate letter position). We call the set of nodes with excitatory connections to a given node its *excitatory neighbors* and the set of nodes with inhibitory connections to a given node its *inhibitory neighbors*.

A subset of the neighbors of the letter *t* is illustrated in Figure 3. Again, excitatory connections are represented by the arrows ending with points, and inhibitory connections are represented by the arrows ending with dots. We emphasize that this is a small subset of the neighborhood of the initial *t*. The picture of the whole neighborhood, including all the connections among neighbors and their connections to their neighbors, is much too complicated to present in a two-dimensional figure.

Activation assumptions. There is associated with each node a momentary activation value. This value is a real number, and for node *i* we will represent it by $a_i(t)$. Any node with a positive activation value is said to be *active*. In the absence of inputs from its neighbors, all nodes are assumed to decay back to an inactive state, that is, to an activation value at or below zero. This resting level may differ from node to node and corresponds to a kind of a priori bias (Broadbent, 1967) determined by frequency of activation of the node over the long term. Thus, for example, the nodes for high-frequency words have resting levels higher than those for low-frequency words. In any case, the resting level for node *i* is represented by r_i. For units not at rest, decay back to the resting level occurs at some rate Θ_i.

When the neighbors of a node are active, they influence the activation of the node by either excitation or inhibition, depending on their relation to the node. These excitatory and inhibitory influences combine by a sim-

ple weighted average to yield a net input to the unit, which may be either excitatory (greater than zero) or inhibitory. In mathematical notation, if we let $n_i(t)$ represent the net input to the unit, we can write the equation for its value as

$$n_i(t) = \sum_j \alpha_{ij} e_j(t) - \sum_k \gamma_{ik} i_k(t), \quad (1)$$

where $e_j(t)$ is the activation of an active excitatory neighbor of the node, each $i_k(t)$ is the activation of an active inhibitory neighbor of the node, and α_{ij} and γ_{ik} are associated weight constants. Inactive nodes have no influence on their neighbors. Only nodes in an active state have any effects, either excitatory or inhibitory.

The net input to a node drives the activation of the node up or down, depending on whether it is positive or negative. The degree of the effect of the input on the node is modulated by the node's current activity level to keep the input to the node from driving it beyond some maximum and minimum values (Grossberg, 1978). When the net input is excitatory, $n_i(t) > 0$, the effect on the node, $\epsilon_i(t)$, is given by

$$\epsilon_i(t) = n_i(t)(M - a_i(t)), \quad (2)$$

where M is the maximum activation level of the unit. The modulation has the desired effect, because as the activation of the unit approaches the maximum, the effect of the input is reduced to zero. M can be thought

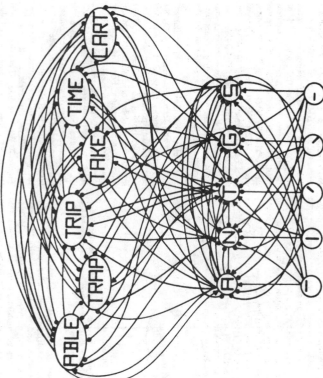

Figure 3. A few of the neighbors of the node for the letter T in the first position in a word, and their interconnections.

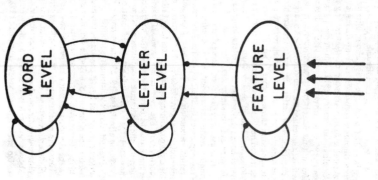

VISUAL INPUT

Figure 2. The simplified processing system.

of as a basic scale factor of the model, and we have set its value to 1.0.

In the case where the input is inhibitory, $n_i(t) < 0$, the effect of the input on the node is given by

$$\epsilon_i(t) = n_i(t)(a_i(t) - m),$$ (3)

where m is the minimum activation of the node.

The new value of the activation of a node at time $t + \Delta t$ is equal to the value at time t, minus the decay, plus the influence of its neighbors at time t:

$$a_i(t + \Delta t)$$
$$= a_i(t) - \Theta_i(a_i(t) - r_i) + \epsilon_i(t).$$ (4)

Input assumptions. Upon presentation of a stimulus, a set of featural inputs is made available to the system. Each feature in the display will be detected with some probability p. For simplicity it is assumed that feature detection occurs, if it is to occur at all, immediately after onset of the stimulus. The probability that any given feature will be detected is assumed to vary with the visual quality of the display. Features that are detected begin sending activation to all letter nodes that contain that feature. All letter-level nodes that do not contain the extracted feature are inhibited.

It is assumed that features are binary and that we can extract either the presence or absence of a particular feature. So, for example, when viewing the letter *R* we can extract, among other features, the presence of a diagonal line segment in the lower right corner and the absence of a horizontal line across the bottom. In this way the model honors the conceptual distinction between knowing that a feature is absent and not knowing whether a feature is present.

Presentation of a new display following an old one results in the probabilistic extraction of the set of features present in the new display. These features, when extracted, replace the old ones in corresponding positions. Thus, the presentation of an *E* following the *R* described above would result in the replacement of the two features described above with their opposites.

On making responses. One of the more problematic aspects of a model such as this one is a specification of how these relatively complex patterns of activity might be related to the content of percepts and the sorts of response probabilities we observe in experiments. We assume that responses and perhaps the contents of perceptual experience may depend on the temporal integration of the pattern of activation over all of the nodes. The integration process is assumed to occur slowly enough that brief activations may come and go without necessarily becoming accessible for purposes of responding or entering perceptual experience. However, as the activation lasts longer and longer, the probability that it will be reportable increases. Specifically, we think of the integration process as taking a running average of the activation of the node over previous time:

$$\bar{a}_i(t) = \int_{-\infty}^{t} a_i(x)e^{-(t-x)\nu}dx.$$ (5)

In this equation, the variable x represents preceding time, varying between $-\infty$ and time t. The exponential portion of the expression weights the contribution of the activation of the node in previous time intervals. Essentially, its effect is to reduce the contribution of prior activations as they recede further back in time. The parameter r represents the relative weighting given to old and new information and determines how quickly the output values change in response to changes in the activations of the underlying nodes. The larger the value of r, the more quickly the output values change. *Response strength*, in the sense of Luce's choice model (Luce, 1959), is an exponential function of the running average activation:

$$s_i(t) = e^{\mu \bar{a}_i(t)}.$$ (6)

The parameter μ determines how rapidly response strength grows with increases in activation. Following Luce's formulation, we assume that the probability of making a response based on node i is given by

$$p(R_i,t) = \frac{s_i(t)}{\sum_{j \in L} s_j(t)},$$ (7)

where L represents the set of nodes competing at the same level with node i.

Most of the experiments we will be considering test subjects' performance on one of the letters in a word or other type of display. In accounting for these results, we have adopted the assumption that responding is always based on the output of the letter level, rather than the output of the word level or some combination of the two. The forced choice is assumed to be based only on this letter-level information. The subject compares the letter selected for the appropriate position against the forced-choice alternatives. If the letter selected is one of the alternatives, then that alternative is chosen in the forced choice. If it is not one of the alternatives, then the model assumes that one of the alternatives would simply be chosen at random.

One somewhat problematical issue involves deciding when to read out the results of processing and select response letters for each letter position. When a target display is simply turned on and left on until the subject responds, and when there is no pressure to respond quickly, we assume that the subject simply waits until the output strengths have reached their asymptotic values. However, when a target display is presented briefly followed by a patterned mask, the activations produced by the target are transient, as we shall see. Under these conditions, we assume that the subject learns through experience in the practice phase of the experiment to read out the results of processing at a time that allows the subject to optimize performance. For simplicity, we have assumed that readout occurs in parallel for all four letter positions.

The Operation of the Model

Now, consider what happens when an input reaches the system. Assume that at time t_0 all prior inputs have had an opportunity to decay, so that the entire system is in its quiescent state, and each node is at its resting level. The presentation of a stimulus initiates a process in which certain features are extracted and excitatory and inhibitory pressures begin to act upon the letter-level nodes. The activation levels of certain letter nodes are pushed above their resting levels. Others receive predominantly inhibitory inputs and are pushed below their resting levels. These letter nodes, in turn, begin to send activation to those word-level nodes they are consistent with and inhibit those word nodes they are not consistent with. In addition, within a given letter position channel, the various letter nodes attempt to suppress each other, with the strongest ones getting the upper hand. As word-level nodes become active, they in turn compete with one another and send feedback down to the letter-level nodes. If the input features were close to those for one particular set of letters and those letters were consistent with those forming a particular word, the positive feedback in the system will work to rapidly converge on the appropriate set of letters and the appropriate word. If not, they will compete with each other, and perhaps no single set of letters or single word will get enough activation to dominate the others. In this case the various active units might strangle each other through mutual inhibition.

At any point during processing, the results of perceptual processing may be read out from the pattern of activations at the letter level into a buffer, where they may be kept through rehearsal or used as the basis for overt reports. The accuracy of this process depends on a running average of the activations of the correct node and of other competing nodes.

Simulations

Although the model is in essence quite simple, the interactions among the various nodes can become complex, so that the model is not susceptible to a simple intuitive or even mathematical analysis. Instead, we have relied on computer simulations to study the behavior of the model and to see if it is consistent with the empirical data. A description of the actual computer program is given in the Appendix.

For purposes of these simulations, we have made a number of simplifying assumptions. These additional assumptions fall into three classes: (a) discrete rather than continuous time, (b) simplified feature analysis of the input font, and (c) a limited lexicon. The simulation operates in discrete time slices, or ticks, updating the activations of all of the nodes in the system once each cycle on the basis of the values on the previous cycle. Obviously, this is simply a matter of computational convenience and not a fundamental assumption. We have endeavored to keep the time slices "thin" enough so that the model's behavior is continuous for all intents and purposes.

Any simulation of the model involves making explicit assumptions about the appropriate featural analysis of the input font. We have, for simplicity, chosen the font and featural analysis employed by Rumelhart (1970) and by Rumelhart and Siple (1974), illustrated in Figure 4. Although the experiments we have simulated employed different type fonts, we assume that the basic results do not depend on the particular font used. The simplicity of the present analysis recommends it for the simulations, though it obviously skirts several fundamental issues about the lower levels of processing.

Finally, our simulations have been restricted to four-letter words. We have equipped our program with knowledge of 1,179 four-letter words occurring at least two times per million in the Kucera and Francis (1967) word count. Plurals, inflected forms, first names, proper names, acronyms, abbreviations, and occasional unfamiliar entries arising from apparent sampling flukes

ABCDEFGHI
JKLMNOPQR
STUVWXYZ

Figure 4. The features used to construct the letters in the font assumed by the simulation program, and the letters themselves. (From "Process of Recognizing Words" by David E. Rumelhart and Patricia Siple, *Psychological Review,* 1974, *81,* 99–118. Copyright 1974 by the American Psychological Association. Reprinted by permission.)

have been excluded. This sample appears to be sufficient to reflect the essential characteristics of the language and to show how the statistical properties of the language can affect the process of perceiving letters in words.

An Example

Let us now consider a sample run of our simulation model. The parameter values employed in the example are those used to simulate all the experiments discussed in the remainder of Part 1. These values are described in detail in the following section. For the purposes of this example, imagine that the word *WORK* has been presented to the subject and that the subject has extracted those features shown in Figure 5. In the first three letter positions, the features of the letters *W, O,* and *R* have been completely extracted. In the final position a set of features consistent with the letters *K* and *R* have been extracted, with the features that would disambiguate the letter unavailable. We wish now to chart the activity of the system resulting from this presentation. Figure 6 shows the time course of the activations for selected nodes at the word and letter levels, respectively.

At the word level, we have charted the activity levels of the nodes for the words *work, word, wear,* and *weak.* Note first that *work* is the only word in the lexicon consistent with all the presented information. As a result, its activation level is the highest and reaches a value of .8 through the first 40 time cycles. The word *word* is consistent with the bulk of the information presented and therefore first rises and later is pushed back

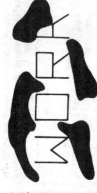

Figure 5. A hypothetical set of features that might be extracted on a trial in an experiment on word perception.

down below its resting level, as a result of competition with *work.* The words *wear* and *weak* are consistent with the only letter active in the first letter position, and one of the two active in the fourth letter position. They are also inconsistent with the letters active in Positions 2 and 3. Thus, the activation they receive from the letter level is quite

weak, and they are easily driven down well below zero, as a result of competition from the other word units. The activations of these units do not drop quite as low, of course, as the activation level of words such as *gill,* which contain nothing in common with the presented information. Although not shown in Figure 6, these words attain near-mini-

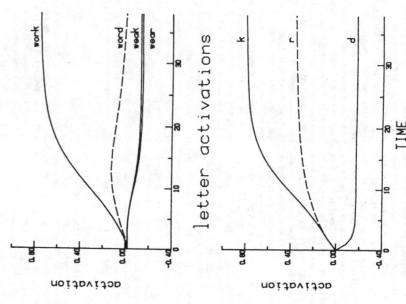

Figure 6. The time course of activations of selected nodes at the word and letter levels after extraction of the features shown in Figure 5.

mum activation levels of about –.20 and stay there as the stimulus stays on. Returning to *wear* and *weak*, we note that these words are equally consistent with the presented information and thus drop together for about the first 9 time units. At this point, however, the word *work* has clearly taken the upper hand at the word level, and produces feedback that reinforces the activation of the final *k* and not the final *r*. As a result, the word *weak* receives more activation from the letter level than the word *wear* and begins to gain a slight advantage over *wear*. The strengthened *k* continues to feed activation into the word level and strengthen consistent words. The words that contain an *R* continue to receive activation from the *r* node also, but they receive stronger inhibition from the words consistent with a *K* and are therefore ultimately weakened, as illustrated in the lower panel of Figure 6.

The strong feature–letter inhibition ensures that when a feature inconsistent with a particular letter is detected, that letter will receive relatively strong net bottom–up inhibition. Thus in our example, the information extracted clearly disconfirms the possibility that the letter *D* has been presented in the fourth position, and thus the activation level of the *d* node decreases quickly to near its minimum value. However, the bottom–up information from the feature level supports either a *K* or an *R* in the fourth position. Thus, the activation of each of these nodes rises slowly. These activations, along with those for *W*, *O*, and *R*, push the activation of *work* above zero, and it begins to feed back; by about Time Cycle 4, it is beginning to push the *k* above the *r* (because *WORR* is not a word). Note that this separation occurs just before the words *weak* and *wear* separate. It is the strengthening of *k* due to feedback from *work* that causes them to separate.

Ultimately, the *r* reaches a level well below that of *k* where it remains, and the *k* pushes toward a .8 activation level. As discussed below, the word-to-letter inhibition and the letter-to-letter inhibition have both been set to 0. Thus, *k* and *r* both co-exist at moderately high levels, the *r* fed only from the bottom up, and the *k* fed from both bottom up and top down.

Finally, consider the output values for the

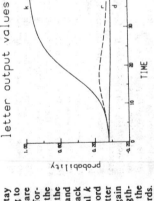

Figure 7. Output values for the letters *r*, *k*, and *d* after presentation of the display shown in Figure 5.

letter nodes *r*, *k*, and *d*. Figure 7 shows the output values for the simulation. The output value is the probability that if a response was selected at time *t*, the letter in question would be selected as the output or response from the system. As intended, these output values grow somewhat more slowly than the values of the letter activations themselves but eventually, as they reach and hold their asymptotic values, come to reflect the activations of the letter nodes. Since in the absence of masking subjects can afford to wait to read out a response until the output values have had a chance to stabilize, they would be highly likely to choose the letter *K* as the response.

Although this example is not very general in that we assumed that only partial information was available in the input for the fourth letter position, whereas full information was available at the other letter positions, it does illustrate many of the important characteristics of the model. It shows how ambiguous sensory information can be disambiguated by top–down processes. Here we have a very simple mechanism capable of applying knowledge of words in the perception of their component letters.

Parameter Selection

Once the basic simulation model was constructed, we began a lengthy process of attempting to simulate the results of several representative experiments in the literature.

Only two parameters of the model were allowed to vary from experiment to experiment: (a) the probability of feature extraction and (b) the timing of the presentation of the masking stimulus if one was used.

The probability of feature extraction is assumed to depend on the visual characteristics of the display. In most of the experiments we will consider, a bright, high-contrast target was used. Such a target would produce perfect performance if not followed by a patterned mask. In these cases probability of feature extraction was fixed at 1.0 and the timing of the target offset and coincident mask onset typically was adjusted to achieve 75% correct performance over the different experimental conditions of interest. In simulating the results of these experiments, we likewise varied the timing of the target offset/mask onset to achieve the right average correct performance from the model.

In some experiments no patterned mask was used, and performance was kept below perfect levels by using a dim or otherwise degraded target display. In these cases the probability of feature extraction was set to a value less than 1.0, which produces about the right overall performance level.

The process of exploring the behavior of the model amounted to an extended search for a set of values for all the other parameters that would permit the model to simulate, as closely as possible, the results of all of the experiments to be discussed later in Part 1, as well as those to be considered in Part 2 (Rumelhart & McClelland, in press). To constrain the search, we adopted various restrictive simplifications. First, we assumed that all nodes have the same maximum activation value. In fact, the maximum was set to 1.0, and served to scale all activations within the model. The minimum activation value for all nodes was set at –.20, a value that permits rapid reactivation of strongly inhibited nodes. The decay rate of all nodes was set to the value of .07. This parameter effectively serves as a scale factor that determines how quickly things are allowed to change in a single time slice. The .07 value was picked after some exploration, since it seemed to permit us to run our simulations with the minimum number of time slices per trial, at the same time as it minimized a kind

of reverberatory oscillation that sets in when things are allowed to change too much on any given time cycle. We also assigned the resting value of zero to all of the letter nodes. The resting value of nodes at the word level was set to a value between –.05 and 0, depending on word frequency.

We have assumed that the weight parameters, α_{ij} and γ_{ij} depend only on the processing levels of nodes *i* and *j* and on no other characteristics of their identity. This means, among other things, that the excitatory connections between all letter nodes and all of the relevant word nodes are equally strong, independent of the identity of the words. Thus, for example, the degree to which the node for the word *rock* excites the node for the word *this*, in spite of a substantial difference in frequency of usage. To further simplify matters, the word-to-letter inhibition was also set to zero. This means that feedback from the word level can strengthen activations at the letter level but cannot weaken them.

The output from the detector network has essentially two parameters. The value .05 was used for the parameter *r*, which determines how quickly the output values change in response to changes in the activations of the underlying nodes. This value is small enough that the output values change relatively slowly, so that transient activations can come and go without much effect on the output. The value 10 was given to the parameter μ in Equation 6 above. The parameter is essentially a scale factor relating activations in the model to response strengths in the Luce formulation.

The values of the remaining parameters were fixed at the values given in Table 1. It is worth noting the differences between the feature–letter influences and the letter–word influences. The feature–letter inhibition is 30 times as strong as the feature–letter excitation. This means that all of the features detected must be compatible with a particular letter before that letter will receive net excitation (since there are only 14 possible features, there can only be a maximum of 13 excitatory inputs whenever there is a single inhibitory input). The main reason for choosing this value was to permit the pre-

Table 1.
Parameter Values Used in the Simulations

Parameter	Value
Feature-letter excitation	.005
Feature-letter inhibition	.15
Letter-word excitation	.07
Letter-word inhibition	.04
Word-word inhibition	.21
Letter-letter inhibition	0
Word-letter excitation	.30

sentation of a mask to clear the previous pattern of activation. On the other hand, the letter–word inhibition is actually somewhat less than the letter–word excitation. When only one letter is active in each letter position, this means that the letter level will produce net excitation of all words that share two or more letters with the target word. Because of these multiple activations, strong word–word inhibition is necessary to "sharpen" the response of the word level, as we will see. In contrast, no such inhibition is necessary at the letter level. For these reasons, the letter-letter inhibition has been set to 0, whereas the word–word inhibition has been set to .21.

Comments on Related Formulations

Before turning to the application of the model to the experimental literature, some comments on the relationship of this model to other models extant in the literature is in order. We have tried to be synthetic. We have taken ideas from our own previous work and from the work of others in the literature. In what follows, we attempt to identify the sources of most of the assumptions of our model and to show in what ways our model differs from the models we have drawn on.

First of all, we have adopted the approach of formulating the model in terms similar to the way in which such a process might actually be carried out in a neural or neural-like system. We do not mean to imply that the nodes in our system are necessarily related to the behavior of individual neurons. We will, however, argue that we have kept well within the kinds of processing involved well within the bounds of capability for simple neural

circuits. The approach of modeling information processing in a neural-like system has recently been advocated by Szentagothai and Arbib (1975) and is represented in many of the articles presented in the volume by Hinton and Anderson (1981) as well as many of the specific models mentioned below.

One case in point is the work of Levin (1976). He proposed a parallel computational system capable of interactive processing that employs only excitation and inhibition as its currency. Although our model could not be implemented exactly in the format of their system (called Proteus), it is clearly in the spirit of their model and could readily be implemented within a variant of the Proteus system.

In a recent article McClelland (1979) has proposed a cascade model of perceptual processing in which activations on each level of the system drive those at the next higher level. This model has the properties that partial outputs are continuously available for processing and that every level of the system processes the input simultaneously. The present model certainly adopts these assumptions. It also generalizes them, permitting information to flow in both directions simultaneously.

Hinton (Note 1) has developed a *relaxation* model for visual perception in which multiple constraints interact by means of incrementing and decrementing real numbered strengths associated with various interpretations of a portion of the visual scene in an attempt to attain a maximally consistent interpretation of the scene. Our model can be considered a relaxation system in which activation levels are manipulated to get an optimal interpretation of an input word.

James Anderson and his colleagues (Anderson, 1977; Anderson, Silverstein, Ritz, & Jones, 1977) and Kohonen and his colleagues (Kohonen, 1977) have developed a pattern recognition system which they call an *associative memory* system. Their system shares a number of commonalities with ours. One feature the models share is the scheme of adding and subtracting weighted excitation values to generate output patterns that represent cleaned-up versions of the input

patterns. In particular, our α_{ij} and γ_{ij} correspond to the matrix elements of the associative memory models. Our model differs in that it has multiple levels and employs a nonlinear cumulation function similar to one suggested by Grossberg (1978), as mentioned above.

Our model also draws on earlier work in the area of word perception. There is, of course, a strong similarity between this model and the logogen model of Morton (1969). What we have implemented might be called a hierarchical, nonlinear, logogen model with feedback between levels and inhibitory interactions among logogens at the same level. We have also added dynamic assumptions that are lacking from the logogen model.

The notion that word perception takes place in a hierarchical information-processing system has, of course, been advocated by several researchers interested in word perception (Adams, 1979; Estes, 1975; Johnston & McClelland, 1980; LaBerge & Samuels, 1974; McClelland, 1976). Our model differs from those proposed in many of these papers in that processing at different levels is explicitly assumed to take place in parallel. Many of the models are not terribly explicit on this topic, although the notion that partial information could be passed along from one level to the next so that processing could go on at the higher level while it was continuing at the lower level had been suggested by McClelland (1976). Our model also differs from all of these others, except that of Adams (1979), in assuming that there is feedback from the word level to the letter level. The general formulation suggested by Adams (1979) is quite similar to our own, although she postulates a different sort of mechanism for handling pseudowords (excitatory connections among letter nodes) and does not present a detailed account.

Our mechanism for accounting for the perceptual facilitation of pseudowords involves, as we will see below, the integration of feedback from partial activation of a number of different words. The idea that pseudoword perception could be accounted for in this way was inspired by Glushko (1979), who suggested that partial activation and synthesis of word pronunciations could ac-

count for the process of constructing a pronunciation for a novel pseudoword.

The feature-extraction assumptions and the bottom-up portion of the word recognition model are nearly the same as those employed by Rumelhart (1970, Note 2) and Rumelhart and Siple (1974). The interactive feedback portion of the model is clearly one of the class of models discussed by Rumelhart (1977) and could be considered a simplified control structure for expressing the model proposed in that paper.

Application of the Simulation Model to Several Basic Findings

We are finally ready to see how well our model fares in accounting for the findings of several representative experiments in the literature. In discussing each account, we will try to explain not only how well the simulation works but why it behaves as it does. As we proceed through the discussion, we will have occasion to describe several interesting synergistic properties of the model that we did not anticipate but discovered as we explored the behavior of the system. As mentioned previously, the actual parameters used in all the examples that we will discuss and in the simulation results we will report are those summarized in Table 1. We will consider the robustness of the model, and the effects of changes in these parameters, in the discussion section at the end of Part 1.

The Word Advantage and the Effects of Visual Conditions

As we noted previously, word perception has been studied under a variety of different visual conditions, and it is apparent that different conditions produce different results. The advantage of words over nonwords appears to be greatest under conditions in which a bright, high-contrast target is followed by a patterned mask with similar characteristics. The word advantage appears to be considerably less when the target presentation is dimmer or otherwise degraded and is followed by a blank white field.

Typical data demonstrating these points (from Johnston & McClelland, 1973) are

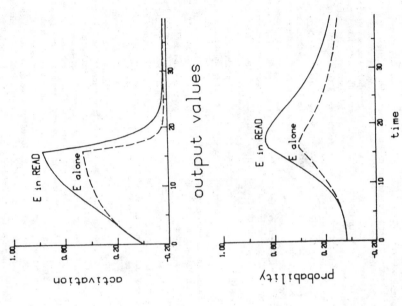

letter level activations

output values

Figure 8. Activation functions (top) and output values (bottom) for the letter E, in unrelated context and in the context of the word READ.

Table 2
Effect of Display Conditions on Proportion of Correct Forced Choices in Word and Letter Perception (From Johnston & McClelland 1973)

Visual condition	Display type	
	Word	Letter with number signs
Bright target/patterned mask	.80	.65
Dim target/blank mask	.78	.73

presented in Table 2. Forced-choice performance on letters in words is compared to performance on letters embedded in a row of number signs (e.g., READ vs. #E##). The number signs serve as a control for lateral facilitation or inhibition. This factor appears to be important under dim-target/blank-mask conditions.

Target durations were adjusted separately for each condition, so that it is only the pattern of differences within display conditions that is meaningful. The data show that a 15% word advantage was obtained in the bright-target/patterned-mask condition and only a 5% word advantage in the dim-target/blank-mask condition. Massaro and Klitzke (1979) obtained about the same size effects. Various aspects of these results have also been corroborated in two other studies (Juola et al., 1974; Taylor & Chabot, 1978).

To understand the difference between these two conditions it is important to note that in order to get about 75% correct performance in the no-mask condition, the stimulus must be highly degraded. Since there is no patterned mask, the iconic trace presumably persists considerably beyond the offset of the target. It is our assumption that the effect of the blank mask is simply to reduce the contrast of the icon by summing with it. Thus, the limit on performance is not so much the amount of time available in which to process the information as it is the quality of the information made available to the system. In contrast, when a patterned mask is employed, the mask produces spurious inputs, which can interfere with the processing of the target. Thus, in the bright-target/patterned-mask conditions, the pri-

mary limitation on performance is the amount of time that the information is available to the system in relatively legible form rather than the quality of the information presented. This distinction between the way in which blank masks and patterned masks interfere with performance has previously been made by a number of investigators, including Rumelhart (1970) and Turvey (1973). We now consider each of these sorts of conditions in turn.

Word perception under patterned-mask conditions. When a high-quality display is followed by a patterned mask, we assume that the bottleneck in performance does not come in the extraction of feature information from the target display. Thus, in our simulation of these conditions, we assume that all of the features presented can be extracted on every trial. The limitation on performance comes from the fact that the activations produced by the target are subject to disruption and replacement by the mask before they can be translated into a permanent form suitable for overt report. This general idea was suggested by Johnston and McClelland (1973) and considered by a number of other investigators, including Carr et al. (1978), Massaro and Klitzke (1979), and others. On the basis of this idea, a number of possible reasons for the advantage for letters in words have been suggested. One is that letters in words are for some reason translated more quickly into a nonmaskable form (Johnston & McClelland, 1973; Massaro & Klitzke, 1979). Another is that words activate representations removed from the direct effects of visual patterned masking (Carr et al., 1978; Johnston & McClelland, 1973, 1980; McClelland, 1976). In the interactive activation model, the reason letters in words fare better than the letters in nonwords is that they benefit from feedback that can drive them to higher activation levels. As a result, the probability that the activated letter representation will be correctly encoded is increased.

To understand in detail how this account works, consider the following example. Figure 8 shows the operation of our model for the letter E both in an unrelated (#) context and in the context of the word READ for a visual display of moderately high quality.

We assume that display conditions are sufficient for complete feature extraction, so that only the letters actually contained in the target receive net excitatory input on the basis of feature information. After some number of cycles have gone by, the mask is presented with the same parameters as the target. The mask simply replaces the target display at the feature level, resulting in a completely new input to the letter level. This input, because it contains features incompatible with the letter shown in all four positions, immediately begins to drive down the activations at the letter level. After only a few more cycles, these activations drop below resting level in both cases. Note that the correct letter was activated briefly, and no competing letter was activated. However, because of the sluggishness of the output process, these activations do not necessarily result in a high probability of correct report. As shown in the top half of Figure 8, the probability of correct report reaches a maximum after 16 cycles at a performance level far below the ceiling.

When the letter is part of the word (in this case, *READ*), the activation of the letters results in rapid activation of one or more words. These words, in turn, feed back to the letter level. This results in a higher net activation level for the letter embedded in the word.

Our simulation of the word advantage under patterned-mask conditions used the stimulus list that was used for simulating the blank-mask results. Since the internal workings of the model are completely deterministic as long as probability of feature extraction is 1.0, it was only necessary to run each item through the model once to obtain the expected probability that the critical letter would be encoded correctly for each item under each variation of parameters tried.

As described previously, we have assumed that readout of the results of processing occurs in parallel for all four letter positions and that the subject learns through practice to choose a time to read out in order to optimize performance. We have assumed that readout time may be set at a different point in different conditions, as long as they are blocked so that the subject knows in advance what type of material will be presented on each trial in the experiment. Thus, in simulating the Johnston and McClelland (1973) results, we allowed for different readout times for letters in words and letters in unrelated contexts, with the different times selected on the basis of practice to optimize performance on each type of material.

A final feature of the simulation is the duration of the target display. This was varied to produce an average performance on both letters embedded in number signs and letters in words that was as close as possible to the average performance on these two conditions in the 1973 experiment of John-

ston and McClelland. The value used for the run reported below was 15 cycles. As in the Johnston and McClelland study, the mask followed the target immediately.

The simulation replicated the experimental data shown in Table 2 quite closely. Accuracy on the forced choice was 81% correct for the letters embedded in words and 66% correct for letters in an unrelated (#) context.

It turns out that it is not necessary to allow for different readout times for different material types. A repetition of the simulation produced a 15% word advantage when the same readout time was chosen for both single letters and letters in words, based on optimal performance averaged over the two material types. Thus, the model is consistent with the fact that the word advantage does not depend on separating the different stimulus types into separate blocks (Massaro & Klitzke, 1979).

Perception of letters in words under conditions of degraded input. In conditions of degraded (but not abbreviated) input, the role of the word level is to selectively reinforce possible letters that are consistent with the visual information extracted and that are also consistent with the words in the subject's vocabulary. Recall that the task requires the subject to choose between two letters, both of which (on word trials) make a word with the rest of the context. There are two distinct cases to consider. Either the featural information extracted from the to-be-probed letter is sufficient to distinguish between the alternatives, or it is not. Whenever the featural information is consistent with both of the forced-choice alternatives, any feedback will selectively enhance both alternatives and will not permit the subject to distinguish between them. When the information extracted is inconsistent with one of the alternatives, the model produces a word advantage. The reason is that we assume forced-choice responses are based not on the feature information itself but on the subject's best guess about what letter was actually shown. Feedback from the word level increases the probability of correct choice in those cases where the subject extracts information that is inconsistent with the incorrect alternative but consistent with the correct alternative

and a number of others. Thus, feedback would have the effect of helping the subject select the actual letter shown from several possibilities consistent with the set of extracted features. Consider again, for example, the case of the presentation of *WORD* discussed above. In this case, the subject extracted incomplete information about the final letter consistent with both *R* and *K*. Assume that the forced choice the subject was to face on this trial was between a *D* and a *K*. The account supposes that the subject encodes a single letter for each letter position before facing the forced choice. Thus, if the features of the final letter had been extracted in the absence of any context, the subject would encode *R* or *K* equally often, since both are equally compatible with the features extracted. This would leave the subject with the correct response some of the time. But if *R* were chosen instead, the subject would enter the forced choice between *D* and *K* without knowing the correct answer directly. When the whole word display is shown, the feedback generated by the processing of all of the letters greatly strengthens the *K*, increasing the probability that it will be chosen over the *R* and thus increasing the probability that the subject will proceed to the forced choice with the correct response in mind.

Our interpretation of the small word advantage in blank-mask conditions is a specific version of the early accounts of the word advantage offered by Wheeler (1970) and Thompson and Massaro (1973) before it was known that the effect depends on masking. Johnston (1978) has argued that this type of account does not apply under patterned-mask conditions. We are suggesting that it does apply to the small word advantage obtained under blank-mask conditions like those of the Johnston and McClelland (1973) experiment. We will see below that the model offers a different account of performance under patterned-mask conditions.

We simulated our interpretation of the small word advantage obtained in blank-mask conditions in the following way. A set of 40 pairs of four-letter words that differed by a single letter was prepared. The differing letters occurred in each position equally often. From these words corresponding con-

trol pairs were generated in which the critical letters from the word pairs were presented in nonletter contexts (#s). Because they were presented in nonletter contexts, we assumed that these letters did not engage the word processing system at all.

Each member of each pair of items was presented to the model four times, yielding a total of 320 stimulus presentations of word stimuli and 320 presentations of single letters. On each presentation, the simulation sampled a random subset of the possible features to be detected by the system. The probability of detection of each feature was set at .45. As noted previously, these values are in a ratio of 1 to 30, so that if any one of the 14 features extracted is inconsistent with a particular letter, that letter receives net inhibition from the features and is rapidly driven into an inactive state.

For simplicity, the features were treated as a constant input, which remained on while letter and word activations (if any) were allowed to take place. At the end of 50 processing cycles, which is virtually asymptotic, output was sampled. Sampling results in the selection of one letter to fill each position; the selected letter is assumed to be all the subject takes away from the target display. As described previously, the forced choice is assumed to be based only on this letter identity information. The subject compares the letter selected for the appropriate position against the forced-choice alternatives. If the letter selected is one of the alternatives, then that alternative is selected. If it is not one of the alternatives, then one of the two alternatives is simply picked at random.

The simulation produced a 10% advantage for letters in words over letters embedded in number signs. Probability-correct forced choice for letters embedded in words was 78% correct, whereas for letters in number signs, performance was 68% correct.

The simulated results for the no-mask condition clearly show a smaller word advantage than for the patterned-mask case. However, the model produces a larger word advantage, which is observed in the experiment (Table 2). As Johnston (1978) has pointed out, there are a number of reasons why an account such as the one we have offered would overestimate the size of the word advantage. First, subjects may occasionally be able to retain an impression of the actual visual information they have been able to extract. On such occasions, feedback from the word level will be of no further benefit. Second, even if subjects only retain a letter identity code, they may tend to choose the forced-choice alternative that is most similar to the letter encoded—instead of simply guessing—when the letter encoded is not one of the two choices. This would tend to result in a greater probability of correct choices and less of a chance for feedback to increase accuracy of performance. It is hard to know exactly how much these factors should be expected to reduce the size of the word advantage under these conditions, but they would certainly bring it more closely in line with the results.

Perception of Letters in Regular Nonwords

One of the most important findings in the literature on word perception is that an item need not be a word in order to produce facilitation with respect to unrelated letter or single letter stimuli. The advantage for pseudowords over unrelated letters has been obtained in a very large number of studies (Aderman & Smith, 1971; Carr et al., 1978; Baron & Thurston, 1973; Spoehr & Smith, 1975; McClelland, 1976; Spoehr & Smith, 1975). The pseudoword advantage over single letters has been obtained in three studies (Carr et al., 1978; Massaro & Klitzke, 1979; McClelland & Johnston, 1977).

Our model produces the facilitation for pseudowords by allowing them to activate nodes for words that share more than one letter in common with the display. When they occur, these activations produce feedback which strengthens the letters that gave rise to them just as in the case of words. These activations occur in the model if the strength of letter-to-word inhibition is reasonably small compared to the strength of letter-to-word excitation.

To see how this takes place in detail, consider a brief presentation of the pseudoword MAVE followed by a patterned mask. (The pseudoword is one used by Glushko, 1979, in developing the idea that partial activa-

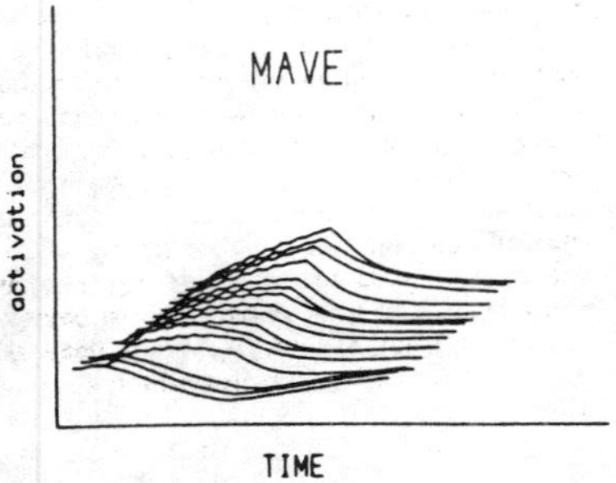

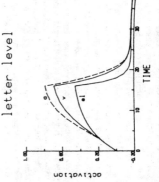

Figure 9. Activation at the word level upon presentation of the nonword *MAVE*.

tions of words are combined to derive pronunciations of pseudowords.) As illustrated in Figure 9, presentation of MAVE results in the initial activation of 16 different words. Most of these words, like *have* and *gave*, share three letters with MAVE. By and large, these words steadily gain in strength while the target is on and produce feedback to the letter level, sustaining the letters that supported them.

Some of the words are weakly activated for a brief period of time before they fall back below zero. These typically are words like *more* and *many*, which share only two letters with the target but are very high in frequency, so they need little excitation before they exceed threshold. But soon after they exceed threshold, the total activation at the word level becomes strong enough to overcome the weak excitatory input, causing them to drop down just after they begin to rise. Less frequent words sharing two letters with the word displayed have a worse fate still. Since they start out initially at a lower value, they generally fail to receive enough excitation to reach threshold. Thus, when there are several words that have three letters in common with the target, words that share only two letters with the target tend to exert little or no influence. In general then, with pronounceable pseudoword stimuli, the amount of feedback—and hence the amount of facilitation—depends primarily on the activation of nodes for words that share three letters with a displayed pseudoword. It is the

nodes for these words that primarily interact with the activations generated by the presentation of the actual target display. In what follows we will call the words that have three letters in common with the target letter string the neighbors of that string.

The amount of feedback a particular letter in a nonword receives depends, in the model, on two primary factors and two secondary factors. The two primary factors are the number of words in the neighborhood that contain the target letter and the number of words that do not. In the case of the M in MAVE, for example, there are seven words in the neighborhood of MAVE that begin with M, so the m node gets excitatory feedback from all of these. These words are called the "friends" of the m node in this case. Because of competition at the word level, the amount of activation that these words receive depends on the total number of words that have three letters in common with the target. Those that share three letters with the target but are inconsistent with the m node (e.g., *have*) produce inhibition that tends to limit the activation of the friends of the m node, and can thus be considered its "enemies." These words also produce feedback that tends to activate letters that were not actually presented. For example, activation from *have* produces excitatory input to the h node, thereby producing some competition with the m node. These activations, however, are usually not terribly strong. No one word gets very active, and so letters not in the actual display tend to get fairly weak excitatory feedback. This weak excitation is usually insufficient to overcome the bottom-up inhibition acting on nonpresented letters. Thus, in most cases, the harm done by top-down activation of letters that were not shown is minimal.

A part of the effect we have been describing is illustrated in Figure 10. Here, we compare the activations of the nodes for the letters in MAVE. Without feedback, the four curves would be identical to the one single-letter curve included for comparison. So although there is facilitation for all four letters, there are definitely differences in the amount, depending on the number of friends and enemies of each letter. Note that within a given pseudoword, the total number of friends and enemies (i.e., the total number

Figure 10. Activation functions for the letters a and v on presentation of *MAVE* (Activation function for e is indistinguishable from function for a, and that for m is similar to that for v. The activation function for a single letter (sl), or a letter in an unrelated context is included for comparison.)

of words with three letters in common) is the same for all the letters.

There are two other factors that affect the extent to which a particular word will become active at the word level when a particular pseudoword is shown. Although the effects of these factors are only weakly reflected in the activations at the letter level, they are nevertheless interesting to note, since they indicate some synergistic effects that emerge from the interplay of simple excitatory and inhibitory influences in the neighborhood. These are the *rich-get-richer effect* and the *gang effect*. The rich-get-richer effect is illustrated in Figure 11, which compares the activation curves for the nodes for *have*, *gave*, and *save* under presentation of *MAVE*. The words differ in frequency, which gives the words slight differences in baseline activation. What is interesting is that the difference gets magnified; so that at the point of peak activation, there is a much larger difference. The reason for the amplification can be seen by considering a system containing only two nodes, a and b, starting at different initial positive activation levels, a and b at time t. Let us suppose that a is stronger than b at t. Then at $t + 1$, a will exert more of an inhibitory influence on b, since inhibition of a given node is determined by the sum of the activations of all nodes other than itself. This

the "rich get richer" effect

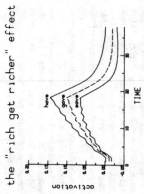

Figure 11. The rich-get-richer effect. (Activation functions for the nodes for have, gave, and save under presentation of MAVE.)

advantage for the initially more active nodes is compounded further in the case of the effect of word frequency by the fact that more frequent words creep above threshold first, thereby exerting an inhibitory effect on the lower frequency words when the latter are still too weak to fight back at all.

Even more interesting is the gang effect, which depends on the coordinated action of a related set of word nodes. This effect is depicted in Figure 12. Here, the activation curves for the move, male, and save nodes are compared. In the language, move and make are of approximately equal frequency, so their activations start out at about the same level. But they soon pull apart. Similarly, save starts out below move but soon reaches a higher activation. The reason for these effects is that male and save are both members of gangs with several members, whereas move is not. Consider first the difference between male and move. The reason for the difference is that there are several words that share the same three letters with MAVE as male does. In the list of words used in our simulations, there are six. These words all work together to reinforce the m, a, and a, and the e nodes, thereby producing much stronger reinforcement for themselves. Thus, these words make up a gang called the ma_e gang. In this example, there is also a _ave gang consisting of 6 other words, of which save is one. All of these work together to reinforce the a, v, and e. Thus, the a and e are reinforced by two gangs, whereas the

letters v and m are reinforced by only one each. Now consider the word move. This word is a loner; there are no other words in its gang, the m_ve gang. Although two of the letters in move receive support from one gang each, and one receives support from both other gangs, the letters of move are less strongly enhanced by feedback than the letters of the members of the other two gangs. Since continued activation of one word in the face of the competition generated by all of the other partially activated words depends on the activations of the component letter nodes, the words in the other two gangs eventually gain the upper hand and drive move back below the activation threshold.

As our study of the MAVE example illustrates, the pattern of activation produced by a particular pseudoword is complex and idiosyncratic. In addition to the basic friends and enemies effects, there are also the rich-get-richer and the gang effects. These effects are primarily reflected in the pattern of activation at the word level, but they also exert subtle influences on the activations at the letter level. In general though, the main result is that when the letter-to-word inhibition is low, all four letters in the pseudoword receive some feedback reinforcement. The result, of course, is greater accuracy of reporting letters in pseudowords compared to single letters.

Comparison of performance on words and pseudowords. Let us now consider the fact that the word advantage over pseudowords

the "gang" effect

Figure 12. The gang effect. (Activation functions for move, male, and save under presentation of MAVE.)

is generally rather small in experiments where the subject knows that the stimuli include pseudowords. Some fairly representative results, from the study of McClelland and Johnston (1977), are illustrated in Table 3. The visual conditions of the study were the same as those used in the patterned-mask condition in Johnston and McClelland (1973). Trials were blocked, so subjects could adopt the optimum strategy for each type of material. The slight word–pseudoword difference, though representative, is not actually statistically reliable in this study.

Table 3
Actual and Simulated Results of the McClelland & Johnston (1977) Experiments (Proportion of Correct Forced Choice)

Result class	Word	Pseudoword	Single letter
Actual data			
High BF	.81	.79	.67
Low BF	.78	.77	.64
Average	.80	.78	.66
Simulation			
High BF	.81	.79	.67
Low BF	.79	.77	.67
Average	.80	.78	.67

Note. BF = bigram frequency.

Words differ from pseudowords in that a word strongly activates one node at the word level, whereas a pseudoword does not. While we would tend to think of this as increasing the amount of feedback for words as opposed to pseudowords, there is the word-level inhibition that must be taken into account. This inhibition tends to equalize the total amount of activation at the word level between words and pseudowords. With words, the word shown tends to dominate the pattern of activity, thereby keeping all the words that have three letters in common with it from achieving the activation level they would reach in the absence of a node activated by all four letters. This situation is illustrated for the word CAVE in Figure 13. The result is that the sum of the activations of all the active units at the word level is not much different between the two cases. Thus, CAVE produces only slightly more facilitation for its constituent letters than MAVE, as illustrated in Figure 14.

In addition to the leveling effect of competition at the word level, it turned out that in our model, one of the common design features of studies comparing performance on words and pseudowords would operate to keep performance relatively good on pseudowords. In general, the stimulus materials used in most of these studies are designed by beginning with a list of pairs of words that differ by one letter (e.g., PEEL–PEEP). From each pair of words, a pair of nonwords is generated, differing from the orig-

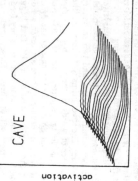

Figure 13. Activity at the word level upon presentation of CAVE, with weak letter-to-word inhibition.

a in different contexts

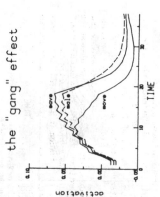

Figure 14. Activation functions for the letter a, under presentation of CAVE and MAVE and alone.

inal word pair by just one of the context letters and thereby keeping the actual target letters—and as much of the context as possible—the same between word and pseudoword items (e.g., *TEEL-TEEP*). A previously unnoticed side effect of this matching procedure is that it ensures that the critical letter in each pseudoword has at least one friend, namely the word from the matching pair that differs from it by one context letter. In fact, most of the critical letters in the pseudowords used by McClelland and Johnston (1977) tended to have relatively few enemies, compared to the number of friends. In general, a particular letter should be expected to have three times as many friends as enemies. In the McClelland and Johnston stimuli, the great majority of the stimuli had much larger differentials. Indeed, more than half of the critical letters had no enemies at all.

The puzzling absence of cluster frequency effects. In the account we have just described, facilitation of performance on letters in pseudowords was explained by the fact that pseudowords tend to activate a large number of words, and these words tend to work together to reinforce the activations of letters. This account might seem to suggest that pseudowords that have common letter clusters, and therefore have several letters in common with many words, would tend to produce the greatest facilitation. However, this factor has been manipulated in a number of studies, and little has been found in the way of an effect. The McClelland and Johnston (1977) study is one case in point. As Table 3 illustrates, there is only a slight tendency for superior performance on high cluster frequency words. This slight tendency is also observed in single letter control stimuli, suggesting that the difference may be due to differences in perceptibility of the target letters in the different positions, rather than cluster frequency per se. In any case, the effect is very small. Other studies have likewise failed to find any effect of cluster frequency (Spoehr & Smith, 1975; Manelis, 1974). The lack of an effect is most striking in the McClelland and Johnston study, since the high and low cluster frequency items differed widely in cluster frequency as measured in a number of ways.

In our model, the lack of a cluster frequency effect is due to the effect of mutual inhibition at the word level. As we have seen, this mutual inhibition tends to keep the total activity at the word level roughly constant over a variety of different input patterns, thereby greatly reducing the advantage for high cluster frequency items. Items containing infrequent clusters tend to activate few words, but there is less competition at the word level, so that the words that do become active reach higher activation levels.

The situation is illustrated for the nonwords *TEEL* and *HOET* in Figure 15. Although *TEEL* activates many more words, the total activation is not much different in the two cases.

The total activation is not, of course, the whole story. The ratio of friends to enemies is also important. And it turns out that this ratio is working against the high cluster items more than the low cluster items. In McClelland and Johnston's stimuli, only one of the low cluster frequency nonword pairs had critical letters with any enemies at all! For 23 out of 24 pairs, there was at least one friend (by virtue of the method of stimulus construction) and no enemies. In contrast, for the high cluster frequency pairs, there was a wide range, with some items having several more enemies than friends.

To simulate the McClelland and Johnston (1977) results, we had to select a subset of their stimuli, since some of the words they used were not in our word list. The stimuli had been constructed in sets containing a word pair, a pseudoword pair, and a single letter pair that differed by the same letters in the same position (e.g., *PEEL-PEEP*, *TEEL-TEEP*, __*L* __*P*). We simply selected all those sets in which both words in the pair appeared in our list. This resulted in a sample of 10 high cluster frequency sets and 10 low cluster frequency sets. The single letter stimuli derived from the high and low cluster frequency pairs were also run through the simulation. Both members of each pair were tested.

Since the stimuli were presented in the actual experiment blocked by material type, we separately selected an optimal time for readout for words, pseudowords, and single letters. Readout time was the same for high

and low cluster frequency items of the same type, since these were presented in a mixed list in the actual experiment. As in the simulation of the Johnston and McClelland (1973) results, the display was presented for a duration of 15 cycles.

The simulation results, shown in Table 3, reveal the same general pattern as the actual data. The magnitude of the pseudoword advantage over single letters is just slightly smaller than the word advantage, and the effect of cluster frequency is very slight.

We have yet to consider how the model deals with unrelated letter strings. This depends a little on the exact characteristics of the strings. First let us consider truly ran-

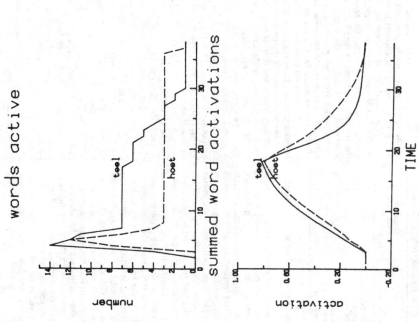

Figure 15. The number of words activated (top) and the total activation at the word level (bottom) upon presentation of the nonwords *TEEL* and *HOET*.

domly generated consonant strings. Such items typically produce some activation at the word level in our model, since they tend to share two letters with several words (one letter out of four is insufficient to activate a word, since three letters in common with any one word. Thus, they only tend to activate a few words very weakly, and because of the weakness of the bottom-up excitation, competition among partially activated words keep any one word from getting very active. So, little benefit results. When we ran our simulation on randomly generated consonant strings, there was only a 1% advantage over single letters.

Some items which have been used as unpronounceable nonwords or unrelated letter strings do produce a weak facilitation. We ran the nonwords used by McClelland and Johnston (1977) in their Experiment 2. These items contain a large number of vowels in positions that vowels typically occupy in words, and they therefore activate more words than, for example, random strings of consonants. The simulation was run under the same conditions as the one reported above for McClelland and Johnston's Experiment 1. The simulation produced a slight advantage for letters in these nonwords, compared to single letters, as did the experiment. In both the simulation and the actual experiment, forced-choice performance was 4% more accurate for letters in these unrelated letter strings than in single letter stimuli.

On the basis of this characteristic of our model, the results of one experiment on the importance of vowels in reading may be reinterpreted. Spoehr and Smith (1975) found that subjects were more accurate when reporting letters in unpronounceable nonwords that contained vowels than in those composed of all consonants. They interpreted the results as supporting the view that subjects parse letter strings into "vocalic center groups." However, an alternative possible account is that the strings containing vowels had more letters in common with actual words than the all consonant strings.

In summary, the model provides a good account of the perceptual advantage for let-

ters in pronounceable nonwords, and for the lack of such an advantage in unrelated letter strings. In addition, it accounts for the small difference between performance on words and pseudowords and for the absence of any really noticeable cluster frequency effect in the McClelland and Johnston (1977) experiment.

The Role of Lexical Constraints

The Johnston (1978) experiment. Several models that have been proposed to account for the word advantage rely on the idea that the context letters in a word facilitate performance by constraining the set of possible letters that might have been presented in the critical letter position. According to models of this class, contexts that strongly constrain what the target letter should be result in greater accuracy of perception than more weakly constraining contexts. For example, the context _HIP should facilitate the perception of an initial S more than the context _INK. The reason is that _HIP is more strongly constraining, since only three letters (S, C, and W) fit in the context to make a word, compared to _INK, where nine letters (D, F, K, L, M, P, R, S, and W) fit in the context to make a word. In a test of such models, Johnston (1978) compared accuracy of perception of letters occurring in high- and low-constraint contexts. The same target letters were tested in the same positions in both cases. For example, the letters S and W were tested in the high-constraint _INK context and the low-constraint _HIP context. Using bright-target/patterned-mask conditions, Johnston found no difference in accuracy of perception between letters in the high- and low-constraint contexts. The results of this experiment are shown in Table 4. Johnston measured letter perception in two ways. He not only asked the subjects to decide which of two letters had been presented (the forced-choice measure), but he also asked subjects to report the whole word and recorded how often they got the critical letter correct. No significant difference was observed in either case. In the forced choice there was a slight difference favoring low-constraint items,

but in the free report there was no difference at all.

Although our model does use contextual constraints (as they are embodied in specific lexical items), it turns out that it does not predict that highly constraining contexts will facilitate perception of letters much more than weakly constraining contexts under bright-target/patterned-mask conditions. Under such conditions, the role of the word level is not to help the subject select among alternatives left open by an incomplete feature analysis process, as most constraint-based models have assumed, but rather to help strengthen the activation of the nodes for the letters presented. Contextual constraints, at least as manipulated by Johnston, do not have much effect on the magnitude of this strengthening effect.

In detail, what happens in the model when a word is shown is that the presentation results in weak activation of the words that share three letters with the target. Some of these words are friends of the critical letter in that they contain the actual critical letter shown, as well as two of the letters from the context (e.g., shop is a friend of the initial S in SHIP). Some of the words, however, are enemies of the critical letter in that they contain the three context letters of the word but a different letter in the critical letter position (e.g., chip and whip are enemies of the S in SHIP). From our point of view, Johnston's (1978) constraint manipulation is essentially a manipulation of the number of enemies the critical letter has in the given context. Johnston's high- and low-constraint stimuli have equal numbers of friends, on the average, but (by design) the high-con-

Table 4
Actual and Simulated Results (Probability Correct) From Johnston (1978) Experiments

Result class	Constraint	
	High	Low
Actual data		
Forced choice	.77	.79
Free report	.54	.54
Simulation		
Forced choice	.77	.76
Free report	.56	.54

straint items have fewer enemies, as shown in Table 5.

In the simulation, the friends and enemies of the target word receive some activation. The greater number of enemies in the low-constraint condition is responsible for the small effect of constraint that the model produces. What happens is that the enemies of the critical letter tend to keep nodes for the presented word and for the friends of the critical letter from being quite as strongly activated as they would otherwise be. The effect is quite small for two reasons. First, the node for the word presented receives four excitatory inputs from the letter level, and all other words can only receive at most three excitatory inputs and at least one inhibitory input. As we saw in the case of the word CAVE, the node for the correct word dominates the activations at the word level and is predominantly responsible for any feedback to the letter level. Second, while the high-constraint items have fewer enemies, by more than a two-to-one margin, both high- and low-constraint items have, on the average, more friends than enemies. The friends of the target letter work with the actual word shown to keep the activations of the enemies in check, thereby reducing the extent of their inhibitory effect still further. The ratio of the number of friends over the total number of neighbors is not very different in the two conditions, except in the first serial position.

This discussion may give the impression that contextual constraint is not an important variable in our model. In fact, it is quite powerful. But its effects are obscured in the Johnston (1978) experiment because of the strong dominance of the target word when all the features are extracted and the fact that we are concerned with the likelihood of perceiving a particular letter rather than performance in identifying correctly what whole word was shown. We will now consider an experiment in which contextual constraints played a strong role, because the characteristics just mentioned were absent.

The Broadbent and Gregory (1968) experiment. Up to now we have found no evidence that either bigram frequency or lexical constraints have any effect on performance. However, in experiments using

Table 5
Friends and Enemies of the Critical Letters in the Stimuli Used by Johnston (1978)

Critical letter position	High constraint			Low constraint		
	Friends	Enemies	Ratio	Friends	Enemies	Ratio
1	3.33	2.22	.60	3.61	6.44	.36
2	9.17	1.00	.90	6.63	2.88	.70
3	6.30	1.70	.79	7.75	4.30	.64
4	4.96	1.67	.75	6.67	3.50	.66
Average	5.93	1.65		6.17	4.27	

Table 6
Actual and Simulated Results of the Broadbent and Gregory (1968) Experiment (Proportion of Correct Whole Report)

Result class	Word frequency	
	High	Low
Actual data		
High BF	.64	.43
Low BF	.64	.58
Simulation		
High BF	.41	.21
Low BF	.39	.37

Note. BF = bigram frequency.

the traditional whole report method, these variables have been shown to have substantial effects. Various studies have shown that recognition thresholds are lower, or recognition accuracy at threshold higher, when relatively unusual words are used (Bouwhuis, 1979; Havens & Foote, 1963; Newbigging, 1961). Such items tend to be low in bigram frequency and at the same time high in lexical constraint.

In one experiment, Broadbent and Gregory (1968) investigated the role of bigram frequency at two different levels of word frequency and found an interesting interaction. We now consider how our model can account for their results. To begin, it is important to note that the visual conditions discussed above, in that the target was shown briefly against an illuminated background, without being followed by any kind of mask. The dependent measure was the probability of correctly reporting the whole word. The results are indicated in Table 6. A slight advantage for high bigram frequency items over low bigram frequency was obtained for frequent words, although it was not consistent over different subsets of items tested. The main finding was that words of low bigram frequency had an advantage among infrequent words. For these stimuli, higher bigram frequency actually resulted in a lower percent correct.

Unfortunately, Broadbent and Gregory used five-letter words, so we were unable to run a simulation on their actual stimuli. However, we were able to select a subset of the stimuli used in the McClelland and Johnston (1977) experiment that fit the requirements of the Broadbent and Gregory design. We therefore presented these stimuli to our model, under the presentation parameters used in simulating the blank-mask condition of the Johnston and McClelland (1973) experiment above. The only difference was that the output was taken, not from the letter level, as in all of our other simulations, but directly from the word level. The results of the simulation, shown in Table 6, replicate the obtained pattern very nicely. The simulation produced a large advantage for the low bigram items, among the infrequent words, and produced a slight advantage for high bigram items among the frequent words.

In our model, low-frequency words of high bigram frequency are most poorly recognized, because these are the words that have the largest number of neighbors. Under conditions of incomplete feature extraction, which we expect to prevail under these visual conditions, the more neighbors a word has the more likely it is to be confused with some other word. This becomes particularly important for lower frequency words. As we have seen, if both a low-frequency word and a high-frequency word are equally compatible with the detected portion of the input, the higher frequency word will tend to dominate. When incomplete feature information is extracted, the relative activation of the target and the neighbors is much lower than when all the features have been seen. Indeed, some neighbors may turn out to be just as compatible with the features extracted as the target itself. Under these circumstances, the word of the highest frequency will tend to gain the upper hand. The probability of correctly reporting a low-frequency word will therefore be much more strongly influenced by the presence of a high-frequency neighbor compatible with the input than the other way around.

But why does the model actually produce a slight reversal with high-frequency words? Even here, it would seem that the presence of numerous neighbors would tend to hurt instead of facilitate performance. However, we have forgotten the fact that the activation of neighbors can be beneficial as well as harmful. The active neighbors produce feedback that strengthens most or all of the letters, and these in turn increase the activation of the node for the word shown. As it happens, there turns out to be a delicate balance for high-frequency words between the negative and positive effects of neighbors, which only slightly favors the words with more neighbors. Indeed, the effect only holds for some of these items. We have not yet had the opportunity to explore all the factors that determine whether the effect of neighbors in individual cases will on balance be positive or negative.

Different effects in different experiments. This discussion of the Broadbent and Gregory (1968) experiment indicates once again that our model is something of a chameleon. The model produces no effect of constraint or bigram frequency under the visual conditions and testing procedures used in the Johnston (1978) and McClelland and Johnston (1977) experiments but does produce such effects under the conditions of the Broadbent and Gregory (1968) experiment. This flexibility of the model, of course, is fully required by the data. While there are other models of word perception that can account for one or the other type of result, to our knowledge the model presented here is the only scheme that has been worked out to account for both.

Discussion

The interactive activation model does a good job of accounting for the results in the literature on the perception of letters in words and nonwords. The model provides a unified explanation of the results of a variety of experiments and provides a framework in which the effects of manipulations of the visual display characteristics used may be analyzed. In addition, as we shall see in Part 2 (Rumelhart & McClelland, in press), the model readily accounts for a variety of additional phenomena. Moreover, as we shall also show, it can be extended beyond its current domain of applicability with substantial success. In Part 2 we will report a number of experiments demonstrating what we call "context enhancement effects" and show how the model can explain the major findings in the experiments.

One issue that deserves some consideration is the robustness of the model. To what extent do the simulations depend upon particular parameter values? What are the effects of changes of the parameter values? These are extremely complex questions, and we do not have complete answers. However, we have made some observations. First, the basic Reicher (1969) effect can be obtained under a very wide range of different parameters, though of course its exact size will depend on the ensemble of parameter values. However, one thing that seems to be important is the overpowering effect of one incompatible feature in suppressing activations at the letter level. Without this strong bottom-up inhibition, the mask would not effectively drive out the activations previously established by the stimulus. Second, performance on pronounceable nonwords depends on the relative strength of letter–word excitation compared to inhibition and on the strength of the competition among word units. Parameter values can be found which produce no advantage for any multiletter strings except words, whereas other values can be found that produce large advantages for words, pseudowords, and even many nonword strings. The effects (or rather the lack of effects) of letter-cluster frequency and constraints likewise depend on these parameters.

It thus appears that relatively strong feature–letter inhibition is necessary, but at the same time, relatively weak letter–word inhibition is necessary. This discrepancy is a bit puzzling, since we would have thought that the same general principles of operation would have applied to both the letter and the word levels. A possible way to resolve the discrepancy might be to introduce a more sophisticated account of the way masking works. It is quite possible that new inputs act as position-specific "clear signals," disrupting activations created by previous patterns in corresponding locations. Some possible physiological mechanisms that would produce such effects at lower processing levels have been described by Weisstein, Ozog, and Szoc (1975) and by Breitmeyer and Ganz (1976), among others. If we used such a mechanism to account for the basic effect of masking, it might well be possible to lower the feature–letter inhibition considerably. Lowering feature–letter inhibition would then necessitate strong letter–letter inhibition, so that letters that exactly match the input would be able to dominate those with only partial matches. With these changes the letter and word levels would indeed operate by the same principles.

Perhaps it is a bit premature to discuss such issues as robustness, since there are a number of problems that we have not yet resolved. First, we have ignored the fact that there is a high degree of positional uncertainty in reports of letters—particularly letters in unrelated strings, but occasionally also in reports of letters in words and pseudowords (Estes, 1975; McClelland, 1976; McClelland & Johnston, 1977). Another thing that we have not considered very fully is the serial position curve. In general, it appears that performance is more accurate on the end letters in multiletter strings, particularly the first letter. In Part 2 we consider ways of extending the model to account for both of these aspects of perceptual performance.

Third, there are some effects of set on word perception that we have not considered. Johnston and McClelland (1974) found that perception of letters in words was actually hurt if subjects focused their attention on a single letter position in the word (see also Holender, 1979, and Johnston, 1974). In addition, Aderman and Smith (1971) found that the advantage for pseudowords over unrelated letters only occurs if the subject expects that pseudowords will be shown; and more recently, Carr et al. (1978) have replicated this finding, while at the same time showing that it is apparently not necessary to be prepared for presentations of actual words. Part 2 considers how our model is compatible with this effect also. We will also consider how our model might be extended to account for some recent findings demonstrating effects of letter and word masking on perception of letters in words and other contexts.

In all but one of the experiments we have simulated, the primary (if not the only) data for the experiments were obtained from forced choices between pairs of letters, or strings differing by a single letter. In these cases, it seemed to us most natural to rely on the output of the letter level as the basis for responding. However, it may well be that subjects often base their responses on the output of the word level. Indeed, we have assumed that they do in experiments like the Broadbent and Gregory (1968) study, in which subjects were told to report what word they thought they had seen. This may also have happened in the McClelland and Johnston (1977) and Johnston (1978) studies, in which subjects were instructed to report all four letters before the forced choice on some trials. Indeed, both studies found that the probability of reporting all four letters correctly for letters in words was greater than we would expect given independent processing of each letter position. It seems natural to account for these completely correct reports by assuming that they often occurred on occasions where the subject encoded the item as a word. Even in experiments where only a forced choice is obtained, on many occasions subjects may still come away with a word, rather than a sequence of letters.

In the early phases of the development of our model, we explicitly included the possibility of output from the word level as well as the letter level. We assumed that the subject would either encode a word, with some probability dependent on the activations at the word level or, failing that, would encode some letter for each letter position dependent on the activations at the letter level. However, we found that simply relying on the letter level permitted us to account equally well for the results. In essence, the reason is that the word-level information is incorporated into the activations at the letter level because of the feedback, so that the word level is largely redundant. In addition, of course, readout from the letter level is necessary to the model's account of performance with nonwords. Since it is adequate to account for all of the forced-choice data, and since it is difficult to know exactly how much of the details of free-report data should be attributed to perceptual processes and how much to such things as possible biases in the readout processes and so forth, we have stuck for the present with readout from the letter level.

Another decision that we adopted in order to keep the model within bounds was to exclude the possibility of processing interactions between the visual and phonological systems. However, in the model as sketched at the outset (Figure 1), activations at the letter level interacted with a phonological level as well as the word level. Perhaps the most interesting feature of our model is its ability to account for performance on letters in pronounceable nonwords without assuming any such interactions. We will also see in Part 2 (Rumelhart & McClelland, in press) that certain carefully selected unpronounceable consonant strings produce quite large contextual facilitation effects, compared to other sequences of consonants, which supports our basic position that pronounceability per se is not an important feature of the perceptual facilitation effects we have accounted for.

Another simplification we have adopted in Part 1 has been to consider only cases in which individual letters or strings of letters were presented in the absence of a linguistic context. In Part 2 we will consider the effects of introducing contextual inputs to the word level, and we will explore how the model might work in processing spoken words in context as well.

Reference Notes

1. Hinton, G. E. Relaxation and its role in vision. Unpublished doctoral dissertation, University of Edinburgh, Scotland, 1977.
2. Rumelhart, D. E. A multicomponent theory of confusion among briefly exposed alphabetic characters (Tech. Rep. 22). San Diego: University of California, San Diego, Center for Human Information Processing, 1971.

References

Adams, M. J. Models of word recognition. Cognitive Psychology, 1979, 11, 133-176.

Aderman, D., & Smith, E. E. Expectancy as a determinant of functional units in perceptual recognition. Cognitive Psychology, 1971, 2, 117-129.

Anderson, J. A. Neural models with cognitive implications. In D. LaBerge & S. J. Samuels (Eds.), Basic processes in reading: Perception and comprehension. Hillsdale, N.J.: Erlbaum, 1977.

Anderson, J. A., Silverstein, J. W., Ritz, S. A., & Jones, R. S. Distinctive features, categorical perception, and probability learning: Some applications of a neural model. Psychological Review, 1977, 84, 413-451.

Baron, J., & Thurston, I. An analysis of the word-superiority effect. Cognitive Psychology, 1973, 4, 207-228.

Bouwhuis, D. G. Visual recognition of words. Eindhoven, The Netherlands: Greve Offset B. V., 1979.

Breitmeyer, B. G., & Ganz, L. Implications of sustained and transient channels for theories of visual pattern masking, saccadic suppression, and information processing. Psychological Review, 1976, 83, 1-36.

Broadbent, D. E. Word-frequency effect and response bias. Psychological Review, 1967, 74, 1-15.

Broadbent, D. E., & Gregory, M. Visual perception of words differing in letter digram frequency. Journal of Verbal Learning and Verbal Behavior, 1968, 7, 569-571.

Bruner, J. S. On perceptual readiness. Psychological Review, 1957, 64, 123-152.

Carr, T. H., Davidson, B. J., & Hawkins, H. L. Perceptual flexibility in word recognition: Strategies affect orthographic computation but not lexical access. Journal of Experimental Psychology: Human Perception and Performance, 1978, 4, 674-690.

Cattell, J. M. The time taken up by cerebral operations. Mind, 1886, 11, 220-242.

Estes, W. K. The locus of inferential and perceptual processes in letter identification. Journal of Experimental Psychology: General, 1975, 1, 122-145.

Glushko, R. J. The organization and activation of orthographic knowledge in reading words aloud. Journal of Experimental Psychology: Human Perception and Performance, 1979, 5, 674-691.

UNIX on a VAX 11/780. When no other jobs are running on the VAX, a simulation of a single experimental trial takes approximately 15–30 sec.

Data Structures

The simulation relies on several arrays for each of the processing levels in the model. The input is held in an array that contains slots for each of the line segments in the Rumelhart-Siple font in each position. Segments can be present or absent, or their status can be indeterminate (as when the input is made deliberately incomplete). There is another array that holds the information the model has detected about the display. Each element of this array represents a detector for the presence or absence of a feature. When the corresponding feature is detected, the detector's value is set to 1 (remember that both absence and presence must be detected).

At the letter level, one array (the activation array) stores the current activation of each node. A second array (the excitatory buffer) is used to sum all of the excitatory influences reaching each node on a given tick of the clock, and a third array (the inhibitory buffer) is used to sum all of the inhibitory influences reaching each node. In addition there is an output array, containing the current output strength of each letter level node. At the word level, there is an activation array for the current activation of each node, as well as an excitatory buffer and an inhibitory buffer.

Knowledge of Letters and Words

The links among the nodes in the model are stored in a set of tables. There is a table in the program that lists which features are present in each letter and which are absent. Another table contains the spellings of each of the 1,179 words known to the program.

Input

Simulated visual input is entered from a computer terminal or from a text file. Several successive displays within a single "trial" may be specified. Each display is characterized by an onset time (tick number from the start of the trial—see below) and some array of visual information. Each lowercase letter stands for the array of features making up the corresponding letter. Other characters stand for particular mask characters, blanks, and so forth. As examples, "–" stands for a blank, and "O" stands for the ⊠ mask character. Thus the specification:

```
 0 mav-
12 mave
24 0000
```

instructs the program to present the visual array

consisting of the letters M, A, and V in the first, second, and third letter positions, respectively, at Cycle 0; to present the letter E in the fourth position at Cycle 12; and to present an ⊠ mask at Cycle 24. It is also possible to specify any arbitrary feature array to occur in any letter position.

Processing Occurring During Each Cycle

During each cycle, the values of all of the nodes are updated. The activations of letter and word nodes, which were determined on Cycle $t − 1$, are used to determine the activations of these nodes on Cycle t. Activations of feature nodes are updated first, so that they begin to influence letter nodes right away.

The first thing the program does on each cycle is update the input array to reflect any new changes in the display. On cycles when a new display is presented, detectors for features in letter positions in which there has been a change in the input are subject to resetting. A random number generator is used to determine whether each new feature is detected or not. When the new value of a particular feature (present or absent) is detected, the old value is erased. Probability of detection can be set to any probability (in many cases it is simply set to 1.0, so that all of the features are detected).

For each letter in each position, the program then checks the current activation value (i.e., the value computed on the previous cycle) in the activation array. If the node is active (i.e., if its activation is above threshold), its excitatory and inhibitory effects on each node at the word level are computed. To determine whether the letter in question excites or inhibits a particular word node, the program simply examines the spelling of each word to see if the letter is in the word in the appropriate position. If so, excitation is added to the word's excitatory buffer. If not, inhibition is added to the word's inhibitory buffer. The magnitudes of these effects are the product of the driving letter's activation and the appropriate rate parameters. Word-to-letter influences are computed in a similar fashion.

The next step is the computation of the word-word inhibition and the determination of the new word activation values. First, the activations of all the active word nodes are summed. The inhibitory buffer of each word node is incremented by an amount proportional to the summed activation of all other word nodes (i.e., by the product of the total word level activation minus its own activation, if it is active, times the word-word inhibition rate parameter). This completes the influences acting on the word nodes. The value in the inhibitory buffer is subtracted from the value in the excitatory buffer. The result is then subjected to floor and ceiling effects, as described in the article.

Grossberg, S. A theory of visual coding, memory, and development. In E. L. J. Leeuwenberg & H. F. J. M. Buffart (Eds.), *Formal theories of visual perception.* New York: Wiley, 1978.

Havens, L. L., & Foote, W. E. The effect of competition on visual duration threshold and its independence of stimulus frequency. *Journal of Experimental Psychology*, 1963, 65, 5–11.

Hinton, G. E., & Anderson, J. A. (Eds.), *Parallel models of associative memory.* Hillsdale, N.J.: Erlbaum, 1981.

Holender, D. Identification of letters in words and of single letters with pre- and postknowledge of the alternatives. *Perception & Psychophysics*, 1979, 25, 213–318.

Huey, E. B. *The psychology and pedagogy of reading.* New York: Macmillan, 1908.

Johnston, J. C. *The role of contextual constraint in the perception of letters in words.* Unpublished doctoral dissertation, University of Pennsylvania, 1974.

Johnston, J. C. A test of the sophisticated guessing theory of word perception. *Cognitive Psychology*, 1978, 10, 123–154.

Johnston, J. C., & McClelland, J. L. Visual factors in word perception. *Perception & Psychophysics*, 1973, 14, 365–370.

Johnston, J. C., & McClelland, J. L. Perception of letters in words: Seek not and ye shall find. *Science*, 1974, 184, 1192–1194.

Johnston, J. C., & McClelland, J. L. Experimental tests of a hierarchical model of word identification. *Journal of Verbal Learning and Verbal Behavior*, 1980, 19, 503–524.

Juola, J. F., Leavitt, D. D., & Choe, C. S. Letter identification in word, nonword, and single letter displays. *Bulletin of the Psychonomic Society*, 1974, 4, 278–280.

Kohonen, T. *Associative memory: A system-theoretic approach.* West Berlin: Springer-Verlag, 1977.

Kučera, H., & Francis, W. *Computational analysis of present-day American English.* Providence, R.I.: Brown University Press, 1967.

LaBerge, D., & Samuels, S. Toward a theory of automatic information processing in reading. *Cognitive Psychology*, 1974, 6, 293–323.

Levin, J. A. *Proteus: An activation framework for cognitive process models (ISI/WP-2).* Marina del Rey, Calif.: Information Sciences Institute, 1976.

Luce, R. D. *Individual choice behavior.* New York: Wiley, 1959.

Manelis, L. The effect of meaningfulness in tachistoscopic word perception. *Perception & Psychophysics*, 1974, 16, 182–192.

Massaro, D. W., & Klitzke, D. The role of lateral masking and orthographic structure in letter and word recognition. *Acta Psychologica*, 1979, 43, 413–426.

McClelland, J. L. Preliminary letter identification in the perception of words and nonwords. *Journal of Experimental Psychology: Human Perception and Performance*, 1976, 1, 80–91.

McClelland, J. L. On the time relations of mental processes: An examination of systems of processes in cascade. *Psychological Review*, 1979, 86, 287–330.

McClelland, J. L., & Johnston, J. C. The role of familiar units in perception of words and nonwords. *Perception & Psychophysics*, 1977, 22, 249–261.

Morton, J. Interaction of information in word recognition. *Psychological Review*, 1969, 76, 165–178.

Neisser, U. *Cognitive psychology.* New York: Appleton-Century-Crofts, 1967.

Newbigging, P. L. The perceptual reintegration of frequent and infrequent words. *Canadian Journal of Psychology*, 1961, 15, 123–132.

Reicher, G. M. Perceptual recognition as a function of meaningfulness of stimulus material. *Journal of Experimental Psychology*, 1969, 81, 274–280.

Rumelhart, D. E. A multicomponent theory of the perception of briefly exposed visual displays. *Journal of Mathematical Psychology*, 1970, 7, 191–218.

Rumelhart, D. E. Toward an interactive model of reading. In S. Dornic (Ed.), *Attention and performance IV.* Hillsdale, N.J.: Erlbaum, 1977.

Rumelhart, D. E., & McClelland, J. L. An interactive activation model of context effects in letter perception. Part 2. The contextual enhancement effect and some tests and extensions of the model. *Psychological Review*, in press.

Rumelhart, D. E., & Siple, P. The process of recognizing tachistoscopically presented words. *Psychological Review*, 1974, 81, 99–118.

Spoehr, K., & Smith, E. The role of orthographic and phonotactic rules in perceiving letter patterns. *Journal of Experimental Psychology: Human Perception and Performance*, 1975, 1, 21–34.

Szentagothai, J., & Arbib, M. A. *Conceptual models of neural organization.* Cambridge, Mass.: MIT Press, 1975.

Taylor, G. A., & Chabot, R. J. Differential backward masking of words and letters by masks of varying orthographic structure. *Memory & Cognition*, 1978, 6, 629–635.

Thompson, M. C., & Massaro, D. W. Visual information and redundancy in reading. *Journal of Experimental Psychology*, 1973, 98, 49–54.

Turvey, M. On peripheral and central processes in vision: Inferences from an information-processing analysis of masking with patterned stimuli. *Psychological Review*, 1973, 80, 1–52.

Weinstein, N., Ozog, G., & Szoc, R. A comparison and elaboration of two models of metacontrast. *Psychological Review*, 1975, 82, 325–343.

Wheeler, D. Processes in word recognition. *Cognitive Psychology*, 1970, 1, 59–85.

Appendix
Computer Simulation of the Model

The computer program for simulating the interactive activation model was written in the C programming language to run on a Digital PDP 11/45 computer under the UNIX (Trade Mark of Bell Laboratories) operating system. There is now a second version, also in C, which runs under to determine the net effect of the excitatory and inhibitory input. This net effect is then added to the current activation of the node, and the decay of the current value is subtracted to give a new current value, which is stored in the activation array. Finally, the excitatory and inhibitory buffers are cleared for new input on the next cycle.

Next is the computation of the feature-to-letter influences. For each feature in each letter position, if that feature has been detected, the program checks each letter to see if it contains the feature. If it does, the excitatory buffer for that letter in that position is incremented. If not, the corresponding inhibitory buffer is incremented. After this, the letter-letter inhibition is added into the inhibitory buffers following a similar procedure as was used in computing the word-word inhibitory effects. (Actually, this step is skipped in the reported simulations, since the value of letter-letter inhibition has been set to zero.)

Next is the computation of the new activation values at the letter level. These are computed in just the same way as the new activation values at the word level. Finally, the effect of the current activation is added into the letter's output strength, and the excitatory and inhibitory buffers are cleared for the next cycle.

The order of some of the preceding steps is arbitrary. What is important is that at the end of each cycle, the activations of all the word nodes have been updated to reflect letter activations of the previous cycle and vice versa. The fact that newly detected input influences the letter detectors immediately is not meaningful, since waiting until the next cycle would just add a fixed delay to all of the activations in the system.

Output

To simulate forced-choice performance, the program must be told when to read out the results of processing at the letter level, what position is being tested, and what the two alternatives are. In fact the user actually gives the program the full target display and the full alternative display (e.g., LEAD-LOAD), and the program compares them to figure out the critical letter position and the two choice alternatives. Various options are available for monitoring readout performance of the simulation. First, it is possible to have the program print out what the result of readout would be at each time cycle. Second, the user may specify a particular cycle for readout. Third, the user may tell the program to figure out the optimal time for readout and to print both the time and the resulting percent correct performance. This option is used in preliminary runs to determine

what readout time to use in the final simulation runs for each experiment.

On each cycle for which output is requested, the program computes the probability that the correct alternative is read out and the probability that the incorrect alternative is read out, based on their response strengths as described in the text. Probability-correct forced choice is then simply the probability that the correct alternative was read out, plus .5 times the probability that neither the correct nor the incorrect alternative was read out.

Observation and Manipulation

It is possible to examine the activation of any node at the end of each cycle. A few useful summaries are also available, such as the number of active word nodes and the sum of their activations, the number of active letter nodes in each position, and so on. It is also possible to alter any of the parameters of the model between cycles or to change a parameter and then start again at Time 0 in order to compare the response of the model under different parameter values.

Running a Simulation

When simulating an experiment with a number of different trials (i.e., a number of different stimulus items in each experimental condition), the information the computer needs about the input and the forced-choice alternatives can be specified in a file, with one line containing all of the necessary information for each trial of the simulation. Typically a few test runs are carried out to choose an optimal exposure duration and readout time. Then the simulation is run with a single specified readout time for each display condition (when different display types are mixed within the same block of trials in the experiment being simulated, a single readout time is used for all display conditions). Note that when the probability of feature detection is set to 1.0, the model is completely deterministic. That is, it computes readout and forced-choice probabilities on the basis of response strengths. These are determined completely by the knowledge stored in the system (e.g., what the system knows about the appearance of the letters and the spellings of the words), by the set of features extracted, and by the values of the various parameters.

Received March 11, 1981 ■

Imagery

The basic idea guiding imagery research is that *imagining is like perceiving*. The classic paper by Shepard and Metzler provides support for this idea. The time people need to decide that two forms are identical increases regularly with the rotational difference between the forms. This result suggests that people are "mentally rotating" one of the forms to "see" whether it coincides with the other. Mental rotation has become one of the most investigated phenomena in the study of imagery.

Recognition of phenomena such as mental rotation led to the development of specific models of imagery (most notably Kosslyn, S. M. (1980). *Image and Mind*. Cambridge, MA: Harvard University Press). The models have proved controversial, with their most forceful critic being Pylyshyn. In the current selection, Pylyshyn argues that imagery consists of the use of general thought processes to simulate physical or perceptual events, based on tacit knowledge of how physical events unfold. For example, mental rotation occurs because people are *thinking* (as opposed to *imagining*) in real time about the course of a physical rotation; they know implicitly the time needed to physically rotate an object, and they wait the corresponding amount of time before indicating their response.

The debate about imagery continues, and has led proponents of imagery to find new sources of evidence. In the final selection, Kosslyn turns to neuropsychology and the study of brain-damaged patients for evidence regarding a computational theory of imagery and of higher-level perception. Among other things, the theory accounts for brain-lateralization effects in both vision and imagery. This paper, and others like it, set the stage for a computational approach to neuropsychology.

SCIENCE – R.N. Shepard & J. Metzler

Mental Rotation of Three-Dimensional Objects

Abstract. The time required to recognize that two perspective drawings portray objects of the same three-dimensional shape is found to be (i) a linearly increasing function of the angular difference in the portrayed orientations of the two objects and (ii) no shorter for differences corresponding simply to a rigid rotation of one of the two-dimensional drawings in its own picture plane than for differences corresponding to a rotation of the three-dimensional object in depth.

Human subjects are often able to determine that two two-dimensional pictures portray objects of the same three-dimensional shape even though the objects are depicted in very different orientations. The experiment reported here was designed to measure the time that subjects require to determine such identity of shape as a function of the angular difference in the portrayed orientations of the two three-dimensional objects.

This angular difference was produced either by a rigid rotation of one of two identical pictures in its own picture plane or by a much more complex, nonrigid transformation, of one of the pictures, that corresponds to a (rigid) rotation of the three-dimensional object in depth.

This reaction time is found (i) to increase linearly with the angular difference in portrayed orientation and (ii) to be no longer for a rotation in 'depth than for a rotation merely in the picture plane. These findings appear to place rather severe constraints on possible explanations of how subjects go about determining identity of shape of differently oriented objects. They are, however, consistent with an explanation suggested by the subjects themselves. Although introspective reports must be interpreted with caution, all subjects claimed (i) that to make the required comparison they first had to imagine one object as rotated into the same orientation as the other and that they could carry out this "mental rotation" at no greater than a certain limiting rate; and (ii) that, since they perceived the two-dimensional pictures as objects in three-dimensional space, they could

imagine the rotation around whichever axis was required with equal ease.

In the experiment each of eight adult subjects was presented with 1600 pairs of perspective line drawings. For each pair the subject was asked to pull a right-hand lever as soon as he determined that the two drawings portrayed objects that were congruent with respect to three-dimensional shape and to pull a left-hand lever as soon as he determined that the two drawings depicted objects of different three-dimensional shapes. According to a random sequence, in half of the pairs (the "same" pairs) the two objects could be rotated into congruence with each other (as in Fig. 1, A and B), and in the other half (the "different" pairs) the two objects differed by a reflection as well as a rotation and could not be rotated into congruence (as in Fig. 1C).

The choice of objects that were mirror images or "isomers" of each other for the "different" pairs was intended to prevent subjects from discovering some distinctive feature possessed by only one of the two objects and thereby reaching a decision of noncongruence without actually having to carry out any mental rotation. As a further precaution, the ten different objects depicted in the various perspective drawings were chosen to be relatively unfamiliar and meaningless in overall three-dimensional shape.

Each object consisted of ten solid cubes attached face-to-face to form a rigid armlike structure with exactly three right-angled "elbows" (see Fig. 1). The set of all ten shapes included two subsets of five: within either subset, no shape could be transformed into itself

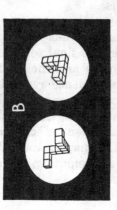 

Fig. 1. Examples of pairs of perspective line drawings presented to the subjects. (A) A "same" pair, which differs by an 80° rotation in the picture plane; (B) a "same" pair, which differs by an 80° rotation in depth; and (C) a "different" pair, which cannot be brought into congruence by *any* rotation.

or any other by any reflection or rotation (short of 360°). However, each shape in either subset was the mirror image of one shape in the other subset, as required for the construction of the "different" pairs.

For each of the ten objects, 18 different perspective projections—corresponding to one complete turn around the vertical axis by 20° steps—were generated by digital computer and associated graphical output (1). Seven of the 18 perspective views of each object were then selected so as (i) to avoid any views in which some part of the object

was wholly occluded by another part and yet (ii) to permit the construction of two pairs that differed in orientation by each possible angle, from 0° to 180°, in '20° steps, from 0° to 180°. These 70 line drawings were then reproduced by photooffset process and were attached to cards in pairs for presentation to the subjects.

Half of the "same" pairs (the "depth" pairs) represented two objects that differed by some multiple of a 20° rotation about a vertical axis (Fig. 1B). For each of these pairs, copies of two appropriately different perspective views were simply attached to the cards in the orientation in which they were originally generated. The other half of the "same" pairs (the "picture-plane" pairs) represented two objects that differed by some multiple of a 20° rotation in the plane of the drawings themselves (Fig. 1A). For each of these, one of the seven perspective views was selected for each object and two copies of this picture were attached to the card in appropriately different orientations. Altogether, the 1600 pairs presented to each subject included 800 "same" pairs, which consisted of 400 unique pairs (20 "depth" and 20 "picture-plane" pairs at each of the ten angular differences from 0° to 180°), each of which was presented twice. The remaining 800 pairs, randomly intermixed with these, consisted of 400 unique "different" pairs, each of which (again) was presented twice. Each of these "different" pairs corresponded to one "same" pair (of either the "depth" or "picture-plane" variety) in which, however, one of the three-dimensional objects had been reflected about some plane in three-dimensional space. Thus the two objects in each "different" pair differed, in general, by both a reflection and a rotation.

The 1600 pairs were grouped into blocks of not more than 200 and presented over eight to ten 1-hour sessions (depending upon the subject). Also, although it is only of incidental interest here, each such block of presentations was either "pure," in that all pairs involved rotations of the same type ("depth" or "picture-plane"), or "mixed," in that the two types of rotation were randomly intermixed within the same block.

Each trial began with a warning tone, which was followed half a second later by the presentation of a stimulus pair and the simultaneous onset of a timer. The lever-pulling response stopped the timer, recorded the subject's reaction time and terminated the visual display. The line drawings, which averaged between 4 and 5 cm in maximum linear extent, appeared at a viewing distance of about 60 cm. They were positioned, with a center-to-center spacing that subtended a visual angle of 9°, in two circular apertures in a vertical black surface (see Fig. 1, A to C).

The subjects were instructed to respond as quickly as possible while keeping errors to a minimum. On the average only 3.2 percent of the responses were incorrect (ranging from 0.6 to 5.7 percent for individual subjects). The reaction-time data presented below include only the 96.8 percent correct responses. However, the data for the incorrect responses exhibit a similar pattern.

In Fig. 2, the overall means of the reaction times as a function of angular difference in orientation for all correct (right-hand) responses to "same" pairs are plotted separately for the pairs differing by a rotation in the picture plane (Fig. 2A) and for the pairs differing by a rotation in depth (Fig. 2B). In both cases, reaction time is a strikingly linear function of the angular difference between the two three-dimensional objects portrayed. The mean reaction times for individual subjects increased from a value of about 1 second at 0° of rotation for all subjects to values ranging from 4 to 6 seconds at 180° of rotation, depending upon the particular individual. Moreover, despite such variations in slope, the linearity of the function is clearly evident when the data are plotted separately for individual three-dimensional objects or for individual subjects. Polynomial regression lines were computed separately for each subject under each type of rotation. In all 16 cases the functions were found to have a highly significant linear component ($P < .001$) when tested against deviations from linearity. No significant quadratic or higher-order effects were found ($P > .05$, in all cases).

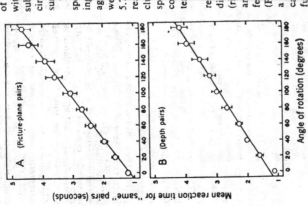

Fig. 2. Mean reaction times to two perspective line drawings portraying objects of the same three-dimensional shape. Times are plotted as a function of angular difference in portrayed orientation: (A) for pairs differing by a rotation in the picture plane only; and (B) for pairs differing by a rotation in depth. (The centers of the circles indicate the means and, when they extend far enough to show outside these circles, the vertical bars around each circle indicate a conservative estimate of the standard error of that mean based on the distribution of the eight component means contributed by the individual subjects.)

The angle through which different three-dimensional shapes must be rotated to achieve congruence is not, of course, defined. Therefore, a function like those plotted in Fig. 2 cannot be constructed in any straightforward manner for the "different" pairs. The overall mean reaction time for these pairs was found, however, to be 3.8 seconds—nearly a second longer than the corresponding overall means for the "same" pairs. (In the postexperimental interview, the subjects typically reported that they attempted to rotate one end of one object into congruence with the corresponding end of the other object; they discovered that the two objects were different when, after this "rotation," the two free ends still remained noncongruent.)

Not only are the two functions shown in Fig. 2 both linear but they are very similar to each other with respect to intercept and slope. Indeed, for the larger angular differences the reaction times were, if anything, somewhat shorter for rotation in depth than for rotation in the picture plane. However, since this small difference is either absent or reversed in four of the eight subjects, it is of doubtful significance. The determination of identity of shape may therefore be based, in both cases, upon a process of the same general kind. If we can describe this process as some sort of "mental rotation in three-dimensional space," then the slope of the obtained functions indicates that the average rate at which these particular objects can be thus "rotated" is roughly 60° per second.

Of course the plotted reaction times necessarily include any times taken by the subjects to decide how to process the pictures in each presented pair as well as the time taken actually to carry out the process, once it was chosen. However, even for these highly practiced subjects, the reaction times were still linear and were no more than 20 percent lower in the "pure" blocks of presentations (in which the subjects knew both the axis and the direction of the required rotation in advance of each presentation) than in the "mixed" blocks (in which the axis of rotation was unpredictable. Tentatively, this suggests that 80 percent of a typical one of these reaction times may represent some such process as "mental rotation" itself, rather than a preliminary process of preparation or search. Nevertheless, in further research now underway, we are seeking clarification of this point and others.

ROGER N. SHEPARD
JACQUELINE METZLER

Department of Psychology,
Stanford University,
Stanford, California 94305

References and Notes

1. Mrs. Jih-Jie Chang of the Bell Telephone Laboratories generated the 180 perspective projections for us by means of the Bell Laboratories' Stromberg-Carlson 4020 microfilm recorder and the computer program for constructing such projections developed there by A. M. Noll. See, for example, A. M. Noll, Computers and Automation 14, 20 (1965).
2. We thank Mrs. Chang [see (1)]; and we also thank Dr. J. D. Elashoff for her suggestions concerning the statistical analyses. Assistance in the computer graphics was provided by the Bell Telephone Laboratories. Supported by NSF grant GS-2283 to R.N.S.

9 March 1970; revised 8 September 1970

The Imagery Debate: Analogue Media Versus Tacit Knowledge

Zenon W. Pylyshyn

Center for Advanced Study in the Behavioral Sciences
Stanford, California

The debate over the nature of mental imagery, especially with respect to the interpretation of recent findings on the transformation of images, has failed to focus on the crucial differences between the so-called "analogue" and "propositional" approaches. In this paper I attempt to clarify the disagreements by focusing on the alleged spatial nature of images and on recent findings concerned with "rotation" and "scanning" of mental images. It is argued that the main point of disagreement concerns whether certain aspects of the way in which images are transformed should be attributed to intrinsic knowledge-independent properties of the medium in which images are instantiated or the mechanisms by which they are processed, or whether images are typically transformed in certain ways because subjects take their task to be the simulation of the act of witnessing certain real events taking place and therefore use their tacit knowledge of the imaged situation to cause the transformation to proceed as they believe it would have proceeded in reality. The fundamental difference between these two modes of processing is examined, and certain general difficulties inherent in the analogue account are discussed. It is argued that the tacit knowledge account is more plausible, at least in the cases examined, because it is a more general account and also because certain empirical results demonstrate that both "mental scanning" and "mental rotation" transformations can be critically influenced by varying the instructions given to subjects and the precise form of the task used and that the form of the influence is explainable in terms of the semantic content of subjects' beliefs and goals—that is, that these operations are cognitively penetrable by subjects' beliefs and goals. Functions that are cognitively penetrable in this sense, it is argued, must be explained, at least in part, by reference to computational cognitive processes whose behavior is governed by goals, beliefs, and tacit knowledge rather than by properties of analogue mechanisms.

This article was written while I was a fellow at the Center for Cognitive Science at MIT and at the Center for Advanced Study in the Behavioral Sciences at Stanford. The support of both these institutions is gratefully acknowledged, as well as the assistance provided by the Alfred P. Sloan Foundation and by a leave fellowship from the Social Science and Humanities Research Council of Canada. I would also like to thank Ned Block, Jerry Fodor, and Bob Moore for their helpful comments.

Requests for reprints should be sent to Zenon W. Pylyshyn, Department of Psychology, University of Western Ontario, London, Ontario, Canada N6A 5C2.

The study of mental imagery continues to be a major concern in cognitive psychology. Since regaining acceptance about 15 years ago, the study of processes underlying the sort of reasoning that is accompanied by perceptionlike experiences has become one of the focal points of the new mentalistic psychology. The purpose of this article is to comment on some of the recent theoretical work in this area in the light of the debate over the nature of mental imagery that has been recurring in the literature over the past 6 or 7 years. The various positions in this debate have been summarized in a number of places, including most recently in Shepard (1975, 1978), Kosslyn and Pomerantz (1977), Kosslyn, Pinker, Smith, and Shwartz (1979), Paivio (1977), Anderson (1978), and Pylyshyn (1973, 1978, 1979a, 1979b). What I shall do in this article is pick out what I consider to be the most substantive strand in this disagreement and discuss it in relation to some of the most persuasive recent empirical findings and the most widely accepted theoretical accounts of these findings. For this purpose I shall make extensive reference to the overview article by Kosslyn et al. (1979), since it represents the most explicit formulation of the "imagistic" (or "pictorial" or "analogical") position to date. In doing this I shall be highly selective in the questions I shall address. There is much in the imagery literature that can be (and has been) debated, not all of which is equally significant from a theoretical standpoint. Thus one could argue over whether images are continuous or discrete, concrete or abstract, holistic or articulated, pictorial or discursive (whether they depict, like pictures, or refer, like descriptions), and whether they constitute a fundamentally different form of cognition or are merely a species of a single form used in all cognitive processing (and at what level they are considered to be the same or different). There have even been arguments over whether images are epiphenomenal or whether they are functional in cognition; but questions such as the latter cannot even be addressed until one takes a theoretical stand concerning the properties of images. One cannot say of something that it is or is not epiphenomenal until one has a clear statement of what that something is. For example, to the extent that image refers to what I experience when I imagine a scene, then surely that exists in the same sense that any other sensation or conscious content does (e.g., pains, tickles, etc.). If, on the other hand, image refers to a certain theoretical construct that is claimed to have certain properties (e.g., to be spatially extended) and to play a specified role in certain cognitive processes, then the appropriate question to ask is not whether the construct is epiphenomenal but whether the theoretical claims are warranted, and indeed whether they are true.

In my view, however, the central theoretical question in this controversy is whether the explanation of certain imagery phenomena requires that we postulate special types of processes or mechanisms, such as ones commonly referred to by the term analogue. I shall discuss one plausible interpretation of this notion—one that does indeed represent a fundamental difference in approach from the one I have been advocating. In addition to this issue, several of the other distinctions mentioned above can also be touched upon if we focus as sharply as possible on one particular claim often made in the imagery literature, namely, the alleged spatiality of images, and on a set of prototypical experimental findings that have been taken as establishing this particular property of images, namely, those that demonstrate "mental rotation" and "mental scanning" of images. In this regard I shall argue that the only real issue that divides the proponents of what has unfortunately become known as the "images versus propositions" debate is the question of whether certain aspects of cognition, generally (though not exclusively) associated with imagery, ought to be viewed as governed by tacit knowledge—that is, whether they should be explained in terms of processes which operate upon symbolic encodings of rules and other representations (such as beliefs and goals) or whether they should be viewed as intrinsic properties of certain representational media or of certain mechanisms that are not alterable in nomologically arbitrary ways by tacit knowledge. I have elsewhere referred to such mechanisms as constituting the "functional architecture" of the mind (Pylyshyn, 1980a, 1980b). In this article I will present arguments and evidence in support of the view that most of the empirical phenomena involving transformations of images (such as the image scanning results of Kosslyn et al., 1979) are better explained according to the tacit knowledge theory.

The Appeal to Properties of an Analogue Medium

In discussing the question of whether images are epiphenomenal, Kosslyn et al. (1979) assert that "none of the models of imagery based on Artificial Intelligence research treat the images that people report experiencing as functional representations" (p. 536). This strange yet widely held view is based in part on a misconception concerning what in fact is reported in imagery. As Hebb (1968) has pointed out, what people report is not properties of their image but of the objects that they are imaging. Such properties as color, shape, size, and so on are clearly properties of the objects that are being imagined. This distinction is crucial. The seemingly innocent scope slip that takes *image of object X with property P* to mean *(image of object X) with property P* instead of the correct *image of (object X with property P)* is probably the most ubiquitous and damaging conceptual confusion in the whole imagery literature.

To see that this slip is not a mere way of speaking but carries considerable weight in explanations of imagery phenomena, consider the case of the generally accepted "spatial" character of images. Take, for example, the elegant experiments by Kosslyn (1973, 1975) and by Kosslyn, Ball, and Reiser (1978) involving "mental scanning" of images, which show that the further away an item is from the place on an image that is currently being focused on, the longer it takes to see or focus on and report that item in the image. I shall take up the question of the interpretation of these results in the Tacit Knowledge and Mental Scanning section below. For the present I simply wish to point out that the story that goes with Kosslyn's interpretation inherits its plausibility and compellingness from a systematic equivocation over which particular entity has the property *length* in precisely the manner suggested in the previous paragraph.

For example there can be no disputing the Kosslyn et al. (1979) claim that "these results seem to indicate that images do represent metrical distance." (p. 537). But in the very next sentence this format-neutral claim becomes transformed into the substantive assertion that "images have spatial extent"—that is, that the image itself has rather than represents length or size. This transformation, moreover, is essential to the particular account of the scanning experiments that Kosslyn et al. wish to promote. That is because the naturalness of the scanning notion comes from the lawfulness of

$$T = \frac{D}{S} \tag{1}$$

In this equation, of course, T, D, and S are to be interpreted as real time, real physical distance, and real mean speed, respec-

tively. If Equation 1 were literally applicable to the image, then this account of the scanning results would be a principled one, since the equation represents a universal principle or basic fact of nature. If, on the other hand, we were to keep with the first way Kosslyn et al. put their claim (viz., that images represent, rather than have distance), we would, instead, have to appeal to a different sort of regularity, one that might for instance be expressed roughly by

$$T = F(D', S'), \tag{2}$$

where $D' = R_1(D)$ is some representation of distance using encoding R_1, $S' = R_2(S)$ is some representation of mean speed using encoding R_2, and F is a function that maps pairs of representations D' and S' onto real time such that for all distances, d, and speeds, s, it will be the case that $F[R_1(d), R_2(s)] = d \div s$.

Now Equation 2 is clearly not a law of nature. There can be no general universal law governing the amount of time that it takes to transform some representations, since obviously that depends upon both the form of the representations and the available operations for transforming them. The equation $T = R_1(D) \div R_2(S)$ is far from expressing a nomological law. In fact, if F is to be realized computationally, we must view Equation 2 as asserting that there is some process, P, which, given the representations D' and S' as inputs (together with other specifications such as a beginning and ending state) takes T sec to complete, where T in this case has to equal $D \div S$. Obviously, unless the various representations and the process P are especially selected, Equation 2 will be false. For example, it is a nontrivial exercise to design an algorithm that always terminates after $D \div S$ sec when given two expressions representing the numerals for D and S (except for the degenerate case in which the algorithm calculates $D \div S$ and then simply waits idly for that amount of time to go by). Now by systematically leaving out the words *representation of* or by using ambiguous descriptions, such as saying that images "preserve relative metrical distances" (which can be interpreted as meaning either that they have or that they represent distances), it is possible to create the illusion of having the

explanatory power provided by Equation 1 while at the same time avoiding the ontological claim that goes with it (viz., that images are actually laid out in space somewhere in the brain).

Another way to put the point about the relative explanatory power of the literal account based on Equation 1, compared with the representation account based on Equation 1, is in terms of the degrees of freedom in these two explanatory principles. If we assume that it is literally the case that physical space is involved, then the form of the relation among distance, speed, and time would be fixed as in Equation 1. If, on the other hand, only a representation of space is involved, and thus the regularity is expressed by Equation 2, the form of the function F is actually a free empirical parameter that is obtained by observing instances of the very phenomena that require explaining. This means that an explanation based on Equation 2 has more degrees of freedom and hence less explanatory power than an explanation based on Equation 1. Even more seriously, however, if we take Equation 2 as the appropriate formulation, then we need a theoretical account of why the relation holds and by what mechanisms it is realized. Even if we maintain that the cognitive system has evolved that way for one reason or another we still want to know what cognitive mechanisms are responsible for that behavior. There have traditionally been two approaches to providing such an account.

1. The first is to say that a subject makes Equation 2 come out (perhaps voluntarily, though often unconsciously) because he or she has tacit knowledge of Equation 1. In other words, regardless of the form of his or her representation, the subject knows that Equation 1 holds in the world and therefore makes it be the case (using some form of symbolic analysis, the exact nature of which need not concern us here) that the amount of time spent imagining the scanning will conform to this relation. We shall discuss this possibility in greater detail in the Tacit Knowledge and Mental Scanning section below.

2. The second way is to say that Equation 2 is the case because of properties of the representational medium. This is just to say

that the observed function has that form as a consequence of the intrinsic lawful relations that hold among the particular physical properties that in fact represent distance and mean speed in the brain. For example, if distance were represented by the electrical potential between two points separated by a certain electrical capacitance, and mean speed were represented by current flow, then (within limits) the time taken would have the form given by Equation 2. This corresponds to what I would call the *analogue* view.

It should be appreciated that Alternatives 1 and 2 represent two fundamentally different ways of explaining the underlying process responsible for the observed behavioral regularities. Alternative 1 appeals to symbolically encoded facts about the world and to rules for transforming representations and drawing inferences. It is a "cognitivist" approach such as advocated by Fodor (1975, 1980), Chomsky (1980), Newell and Simon (1976), and others. On the other hand, Alternative 2 represents what I would call the *analogue* approach to mental representation and mental processing. The term *analogue* has been used to refer to a wide range of characteristics of models and representations covering everything from the mathematical continuity of representations to the simple requirement that the representation go through intermediate states representing the intermediate states that the actual system being represented would go through (e.g., Shepard, 1975). All of these capture something of what we intuitively mean by analogue. In my view, however, the only aspect of analogues that is relevant to the imagery debate (i.e. that differentiates among the major competing views) is the one raised by the distinction between Alternatives 1 and 2,—that is, an analogue process (represented by Alternative 2) is one whose behavior must be characterized in terms of intrinsic lawful relations among properties of a particular physical instantiation of a process, rather than in terms of rules and representations (or algorithms). Whenever people appeal to an "analogue representational medium" (e.g., Attneave, 1974) or to a "surface display" (e.g., Kosslyn, et al., 1979), they take it for granted that this medium incorporates a whole system of lawfully connected properties or intrinsic constraints (some of which have mathematical properties isomorphic to Equation 1 above) and that it is precisely this set of properties and relations that determines how objects behave. Such people specifically contrast these accounts with ones like our Alternative 1, which claims that how the representation will behave is a function of what the person knows about the actual behavior of the things represented, rather than of properties of the medium in which it is represented.

Although there are various conceptions of what analogue processing is (as I suggested above), I suspect that the other senses are actually derivative from the sense I am adopting. Thus, for instance, any process can be made to go through an appropriate sequence of intermediate states, and even to do so in very small (quasi-continuous) steps—even a purely verbal process. Yet we would not want to count such a model as analogue if the mechanism were not naturally constrained to go through such a sequence. Thus we would count the process as analogue if its going through particular intermediate states were a necessary consequence of intrinsic properties of the mechanism or medium, rather than simply being a stipulated restriction that we arbitrarily imposed on a mechanism that could carry out the task in a quite different way. Palmer (1978) has taken a similar position with regard to the distinction between analogical and nonanalogical processes. From this, however, Palmer draws the unwarranted conclusion that only biological evidence will distinguish between the two forms of processing. But, as I have argued at some length (Pylyshyn, 1979b, 1980b), if we contrast mechanisms with ones that operate on representations or tacit knowledge, the distinction can be seen to be a functional one that can be empirically decided by behavioral criteria. An example of one such criterion is discussed below. Other criteria are discussed in Pylyshyn (1979b, 1980b).

The Appeal to Tacit Knowledge

The distinction between analogue processes and rule-governed or cognitive processes (also referred to as computational or informational processes) is one that, in its most general form, needs to be drawn with some care, since after all, both are physically realized in the brain, although in quite different ways. The issue reduces to the question of when different forms of explanation of the behavior are appropriate. I have attempted to develop the general argument at length elsewhere (Pylyshyn, 1980a, 1980b). For the present purposes, however, a brief sketch of that discussion will do, since the only cases relevant to the imagery debate are unproblematic.

The operation of some processes can be explained perfectly well by giving an account of how various of their physical properties are causally connected, so that, for instance, altering some physical parameter here (e.g., by turning a knob) leads to specifiable changes in another parameter there because of some law connecting these two properties. Such a physical causal account will not do, however, to explain connections that are independent of the particular physical form the input takes yet that follow a single general principle that depends only on the semantic content of what might be called the input message. Thus, for example, if being told over the telephone that there is a fire in the building, seeing the word fire flash on a screen, hearing what you take to be a fire alarm, smelling smoke in the hallway, and so on without limit, all lead to the same building-evacuation behavior, the relevant generalization cannot be captured by a purely causal input-output story, since each such stimulus would involve a distinct causal chain and the set of such chains need have no physical laws in common. In that case, the generalization can only be stated by postulating internal belief and goal states (e.g., the belief that the building is on fire and knowledge about what one ought to do in such circumstances, as well as other tacit knowledge and the capacity to make inferences). Such processes are explainable only in terms of the mediation of rules and representations (since it is clear, for example, that neither a behavioral principle such as "Make sure you don't get too close to a fire" nor a logical principle such as modus ponens expresses a physical law and that they hold regardless of what kind of physical substance they are instantiated in).

A corollary of this explainability claim is that if a certain behavior pattern (or input-output function) can be altered in a way that is rationally connected with the meaning of certain inputs (i.e., what they refer to, as opposed to their physical properties alone) then the explanation of that function must appeal to operations upon symbolic representations such as beliefs and goals: It must, in other words, contain rule-governed cognitive or computational processes. A function that is alterable in this particular way is said to be *cognitively penetrable*. The criterion of cognitive penetrability (among other considerations) will be used in later discussions as a way of deciding whether particular empirically observed functions ought to be explained by Alternative 1 or by Alternative 2 above. Specifically, I shall maintain that if the form of certain image transformation functions reported in the literature can be altered in a particular sort of rationally explicable manner by changing what the subject believes the stimulus to be or by changing the subject's interpretation of the task (keeping all other conditions the same), then the explanation of the function must involve such constructs as beliefs, goals, or tacit knowledge, rather than the intrinsic properties of some medium—that is, some part of the explanation must take the form of Alternative 1.

The essence of the penetrability condition is this: Suppose subjects exhibit some behavior characterized by a function, f_1 (say, some relation between reaction time and distance or angle or perceived size of an imagined object), when they believe one thing, and some different function, f_2, when they believe another. Suppose further that which particular f they exhibit bears some logical or rational relation to the content of their belief: For example, they might believe that what they are imagining is very heavy and cannot accelerate rapidly under some particular applied force, and the observed f might then reflect slow movement of that object on their image. Such a logically coherent relation between the form of f and their belief (which we refer to as the "cognitive penetrability of f") must be explained somehow. Our claim is that to account for this sort of penetrability of the process, the explanation of f itself will have to contain processes that are rule governed or computational, such as processes of logical inference, and that make reference to semantically interpreted entities (i.e., symbols). The explanation cannot simply say that there are some causal (biological) laws which result in the observed function f (i.e., it cannot cite an analogue process), for exactly the same reason that an explanation of this kind would not be satisfactory in the building-evacuation example above: because the regularity in question depends on the semantic content (in this case of beliefs) and on logical relations that hold among these contents. Although in each particular case some physical process does cause the behavior, the general explanatory principle goes beyond the set of all observed cases (i.e., there may be token reduction but no type reduction of such principles to physical principles; (see Fodor, 1975). A process that is sensitive to the logical content of beliefs must itself contain at least some inferential (or other content-dependent) rule-governed process. It should be emphasized that cognitive penetrability refers not merely to any influence of cognitive factors on behavior but to a specific kind of semantically explicable (e.g., rational or logically coherent) relationship. The examples we shall encounter in connection with discussions of imagery will be clear cases of this sort of influence (for more on this particular point, see Pylyshyn, 1980a). It should also be noted that being cognitively penetrable does not prevent a process from having analogue components: It simply says that it should not be explained *solely* in terms of analogues with no reference to tacit knowledge, inference, or computational processes.

The concept of tacit knowledge—as a generalization and extension of the everyday notion of knowledge (much as the physicists' concept of energy is an extension of the everyday notion)—is one of the most powerful ideas to emerge from contemporary cognitive science (c.f. Fodor, 1968), although much remains to be worked out regarding the details of its form and function. It is already clear, however, that tacit knowledge cannot be freely accessed or updated by every cognitive process within the organism, nor can it enter freely into any logically valid inference. For example, much of it is not introspectable or verbally articulable (relevant examples of the latter would include our tacit knowledge of grammatical or logical rules, or even of most social conventions). A great deal needs to be learned about the control structures of the cognitive system that constrains our access to tacit knowledge in various elaborate ways. The existence of such constraints is no doubt what makes it possible for people to hold contradictory beliefs or to have beliefs that are only effective within certain relatively narrow classes of tasks. For example, it might well be that many people only have access to their tacit knowledge of physics when they are acting upon the world (e.g., playing baseball) or perhaps when they are engaged in something we call *visualizing* some physical process, but not when they have to reason verbally or answer certain kinds of questions in the abstract. Nonetheless, in all of these cases it would clearly be inappropriate to view such visualizing as being controlled by a medium or "surface display" that caused the laws of physics to hold in the image. A better way to view the cause of the regularities in the movement of objects in the visualized scene is in terms of subjects' tacit knowledge about the physical world and in terms of the inferences that they make from this knowledge. I shall consider other such examples in the next section when I argue that the appearance of autonomous unfolding of imagery sequences may be very misleading.

Incidentally, when one constructs a computer model using something called a matrix data structure rather than something called an analogue representational medium, one is not thereby relieved of the need to make a distinction between Alternatives 1 and 2. Because the existence of a computer model often carries the implication that there can no longer be any ambiguity or terminological confusions, it is worth examining one such model briefly.

In describing the Kosslyn and Shwartz (1977) computer model, Kosslyn et al. (1979) appear ready to admit that much of the model's explanatory and predictive capacity derives from what they refer to as the "cathode ray tube proto-model." In this proto-model there is no problem in seeing how a principled account of the scanning results can be derived. The CRT is a real physical device to which properties such as distance apply literally, and thus our earlier explanation of the observed scanning function applies in virtue of the applicability of Equation 1. But as we have already noted, such an explanation is a principled one only when it refers to a physical system whose intrinsic lawful behavior is described by Equation 1. Thus the explanatory power of the CRT proto-model only transfers to the human cognition case if there is something in the brain to which Equation 1 also applies. On the other hand, the version of the model that uses the matrix data structure, in which there is no actual physical CRT, lends itself equally to either one of the following two interpretations. In the first interpretation, the part of the model that contains the two-dimensional image (i.e., the 2-D matrix and its relevant access operations) is considered as merely a simulation of the physical screen, in which case the model really does assume the existence of a spatially laid out pattern in the brain. In the second interpretation, the matrix and the set of relevant accessing operations is viewed as a specific proposal for how the function F required by Equation 2 might be realized. In the latter case, however, when we give a theoretical interpretation of the claims associated with that part of the model, we still have a choice of the two basic views I have been calling Alternatives 1 and 2, exactly as we did when we were examining the informal account of the scanning results (e.g., Does the adjacency relation in the matrix represent subjects' knowledge that the elements referred to are next to one another, or is it an intrinsic constraint of that particular format?).

Appealing to a matrix in explaining certain imagery results is only useful if matrices constrain the representations or operations on representations in specified ways. If they do constrain the form of representations, then they function essentially as a simulation of an underlying analogue representational medium. (It might be noted in passing that if we were to take the matrix structure seriously, we would be stuck with the unavoidable conclusion that mentally represented space is necessarily nonisotropic. This is a formal consequence of the fact that a matrix is a tesselation of cells of some fixed shape and hence has certain essential nonisotropic properties. For example, if the cells are assumed to be square, then regardless of how fine we make them, scanning diagonally will be faster by a factor of the square root of two than scanning vertically or horizontally. Such an entailment cannot easily be glossed over, except by viewing the matrix as merely a metaphor for some unspecified spatial characteristics.)

The distinction between analogue and what I have sometimes referred to as propositional, but is perhaps better thought of as simply symbolic, is fundamental to a wide range of issues in the foundations of cognitive science (see Pylyshyn, 1980b). In the specific case of models of mental scanning, the distinction is important because Alternative 1 allows for the possibility that the results of mental scanning experiments may represent a discovery about what subjects believe and what they take the goal of the experiments to be, rather than a discovery about what the underlying mechanisms of image processing are. A consequence of the former alternative is that if subjects perceived the task differently or had different tacit beliefs about how the objects in question would move or about properties of space, then the experimental results could be quite different. On the other hand, if Alternative 2 were correct, then manipulation of such things as the form of the task and the instructions should not have a correspondingly, rationally explainable effect (provided, of course, that imagery was still being used). Otherwise we would have to say that the medium changes its properties to correspond to what subjects believe about the world, in which case appealing to the existence of an analogue medium would serve no function.

Before turning to a discussion of some specific theoretical proposals, let me summarize the picture I have presented. Figure 1 illustrates the structure of alternatives available in explaining a variety of imagery findings. We can, first, choose a literal spatially extended brain-projection model. Although there is no a priori reason for excluding this alternative, it does raise some special problems if we try to explain the full range of imagery phenomena this way, and as far as I can tell, no one since Wertheimer has taken it seriously (though some, for instance Arbib, 1972, have come close). In any case the literal approach can be viewed as a special case of the analogue approach I shall be discussing in detail later. Continuing down our tree of alternatives, if we take the functional, as opposed to the literal or structural, approach, our task becomes to explain how this function could be realized by some possible mechanism (e.g., how Equation 2 could be realized in the case of mental scanning). Here we come to what I take to be the fundamental bifurcation between the two camps in the imagery debate, between those who advocate the analogue (or intrinsic property of a medium) view and those who advocate the symbolic or tacit knowledge view. Much confusion arises in this debate because there is considerable equivocation regarding exactly what the referents of ambiguous phrases such as *spatial representation* or *preserves metric spatial information* are intended to be from the point of view of this tree of alternatives. However, once the problem has been formulated so as to factor away the misleading implications associated with the use of a physical vocabulary, or a vocabulary that is appropriate for describing the represented domain as opposed to the psychological processes or mechanisms (see the next section), we are left with a basic empirical question: Which aspects of an organism's function are attributable to intrinsic (analogue) processes, and which are attributable to transactions on a knowledge base? It is to this empirical question that I now turn.

The Autonomy of the Imagery Process

It seems to me that the single most intriguing property of imagery, and the property that appears, at least on first impression, to distinguish it from other forms of deliberate rational thought, is that it has a certain intrinsic autonomy—both in terms of requiring that certain properties of stimuli (e.g., shape, size) must always be represented in an image and with respect to the way in which dynamic imagery unfolds over time. Consider the second of these. The literature contains many anecdotes suggesting that in order to imagine a certain property, we first have to imagine something else (e.g., to imagine the color of someone's hair, we must first imagine the person's head or face; to imagine a certain door, we must first imagine entering it from a certain door; to imagine a figure in a certain orientation, we must first imagine it in a standard orientation and then imagine it rotating; to have a clear image of a tiny object, we must first imagine "zooming in" on it, and so on). Sometimes imagery even seems to resist our voluntary control. For example, in conducting a study of mental rotation of images, I instructed subjects to imagine moving around a figure, pictured as painted on the floor of a room. A number of subjects reported considerable difficulty in one of the conditions because the path of the imaginal movement was impeded by a wall visible in the photograph. They reported that they could not make themselves imagine moving around the figure because they kept bumping into the wall! Such responsiveness of the imagination to involuntary processes and unconcious control is one of the main reasons why imagery is associated with the creative process: It appears to have access to tacit knowledge and beliefs through other than deliberate intellectual routes.

Other examples involving imaginal move-

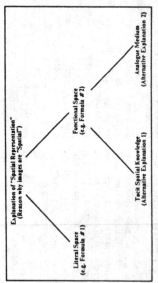

Figure 1. Theoretical positions on the nature of spatial representations.

Explanation of "Spatial Representation" (Reason why images are "Spatial")

Functional Space (e.g. Formula #2)

Analogue Medium (Alternative Explanation 2)

Literal Space (e.g. Formula #1)

Tacit Spatial Knowledge (Alternative Explanation 1)

ment may be even more compelling in this respect. Imagine dropping an object and watching it fall to the ground or throwing a ball and watching it bounce off a wall. Does it not naturally obey physical laws? Imagine rotating the letter C counterclockwise through 90°. Does it not suddenly appear to have the shape of a U without your having to deduce this? Imagine a square with a dot inside it. Now imagine the width of the square elongating until it becomes a wide rectangle. Is the dot not still inside the figure? Imagine the letters A through E written on a piece of paper in front of you. Can you not simply see by inspection that the letter D is to the right of the letter B? In none of these examples is there any awareness of what Haugeland (1978) calls "reasoning the problem through." The answer appears so directly and immediately available to inspection that it seems absurd to suggest, for example, that knowledge of topological properties of figures is relevant to the elongating square example or that tacit knowledge of the formal properties of the relation "to the right of" (that it is irreflexive, antisymmetric, transitive, connected, acyclic, etc.) is involved in the array of letters example. Such considerations have suggested to people that various intrinsic properties of imaginal representations are fixed by the underlying medium and that we exploit these fixed functional capacities when we reason imagistically. I believe that this intuition is the primary motivation for the widespread interest in analogue processes.

Now in general these are not implausible

views. One should, however, be cautious in what one assumes to be an intrinsic function that is *instantiated* by the underlying biological structure, as opposed to one that is *computed* from tacit knowledge by the application of rules to symbolically represented beliefs, goals, and so on. In the previous section (as well as in Pylyshyn, 1980b) I have attempted to provide some necessary (though not sufficient) conditions for a function's being instantiated in this sense. The condition that I have found to be particularly useful in clarifying this distinction, especially in the case of deciding how to interpret observations such as those sketched above, is the one I called the *cognitive impenetrability criterion.* Recall that a function was said to be cognitively impenetrable if it could not be altered in a way that exhibits a coherent relation to the meaning of its inputs. For example, although a function might still count as being cognitively impenetrable if it varied with such things as practice or arousal level or ingestion of drugs, it would not be viewed as cognitively impenetrable if it changed in rationally explainable ways as a function of such things as whether a subject believes that the visually presented stimulus depicts a heavy object (and hence visualizes it as moving very slowly) or whether the subject views it as consisting of one or two figures, or as depicting an old woman or a young lady (in the well-known illusion) and as a consequence behaves in a way appropriate to that reading of the stimulus. I argued that cognitively penetrable phenomena such as the latter would have to be explained in terms of a cognitive rule-governed process, acting upon semantically interpreted representations and involving such activity as logical inferences, problem solving, guessing, associative recall, and so on, rather than in terms of the sort of natural laws that explain the behavior of analogue process.

Now many functions that appear at first to be biologically instantiated, and therefore alterable only in certain highly constrained law-governed respects, could turn out on closer inspection to be arbitrarily alterable in logically coherent ways by changes in subjects' beliefs and goals (i.e., they could turn out to be cognitively penetrable) and therefore to require a cognitive process account

(based on appeal to tacit knowledge and rules). The tremendous flexibility of human cognition, especially in respect to the more central processes involved in thinking and commonsense reasoning, may very well not admit of many highly constrained (nonprogrammable) functions. It may illuminate the nature of the appeals to tacit knowledge if we consider some additional everyday examples. For instance, imagine holding in your two hands, and then simultaneously dropping, a large and a small object or two identically shaped objects of different weights. Which object in your image hits the ground first? Imagine turning a large heavy flywheel by hand. Now imagine applying the same torque to a small aluminum pulley. Which one completes one revolution in your image first? Imagine a transparent yellow filter and a transparent blue filter side by side. Now imagine slowly superimposing the two filters. What color do you see in your image through the superimposed filters? Form a clear and stable image of your favorite familiar scene. Can you now imagine it as a photographic negative, or as being out of focus, or in mirror image inversion, or upside down? Imagine a transparent plastic bag containing a colored fluid, being held open with four parallel rods at right angles to the mouth of the bag, and in such a way that the cross section of the bag is a square. Now imagine the four rods being moved apart so that, with the plastic bag still tight around them, the rods now give the bag a rectangular cross section. As you imagine this happening, does the fluid in the bag rise, fall, or stay at the same level (in other words, how does volume vary with changes of cross-sectional shape, perimeter remaining constant)? Imagine a glass half full of sugar and another nearly full of water. Imagine the sugar being poured into the glass with water in it. Examine your image to see the extent to which the resulting height of water rises (if at all).

These examples, it seems to me, are not in principle different from the ones in the first list I presented. For many people these imaginings also unfold naturally and effortlessly, without any need to reason through what would happen. Yet it seems clearer in these cases that whatever happens as the sequence unfolds under one's "mind's eye" is a function of what principles one believes govern the events in question. In fact, most people tend to get several of these examples wrong. Clearly the laws of dynamics or optics and the principles of geometry that determine the relation, say, between the perimeter and the area of a figure are not intrinsic (built in) to the representational media or to the functional mechanisms of the mind. Not only must one have tacit knowledge of them, but the way in which the imaginal events unfold naturally can usually be influenced with considerable freedom simply by informing the subject of the appropriate principle. Thus what seems to be a natural and autonomous unfolding process is cognitively penetrable—that is, it is under the control of an intellectual process, with all that this implies concerning the intervention of inferences and "reasoning through." As Harman (1973) has argued, our intuitions concerning when there are or are not inferences taking place must give way before the logical necessity to posit such processes. The mind, it seems, is faster than even the mind's eye.

Another particularly intriguing demonstration, by Ian Howard, shows that even in the case of a simple task involving the recognition of physically possible events, knowledge of physical principles is crucial—which suggests that in the case of imaging, such knowledge would be even more indispensable in explaining why images undergo transformations in certain systematic ways. Howard (1978) showed that over half the population of undergraduate subjects he tested could not correctly recognize trick photographs of tilted pitchers containing colored fluids whose surface orientations were artificially set at various anomalous angles relative to the horizontal. Using the method of random presentation and repeating the study with both stereoscopic photographs and motion pictures, Howard found that the subjects who failed the recognition task, for levels as much as 30° off horizontal, could nevertheless correctly report that the fluid surface was not parallel to shelves visible in the background, thus showing that it was not a failure of perceptual discrimination. What was particularly noteworthy, however, was that postexperimental interviews, scored blindly by two independent judges, revealed that every subject who scored perfect on the recognition test (i.e., no stimulus with orientation more than 5° off horizontal failed to be correctly classified as anomalous) could clearly articulate the principle of fluid level invariance, whereas no subject who made errors gave even a hint of understanding the relevant principle. In this case, unlike what typically happens in other areas such as phonology, evidence of the relevant knowledge was obtainable through direct interviews. Even when such direct evidence is not available, however, indirect behavioral evidence that tacit knowledge is involved can frequently be obtained—for example by demonstrating cognitive penetrability of the phenomenon to new knowledge.

Once examples of this kind are presented, no one finds the claim that tacit knowledge is required for some imaginings at all surprising. In fact, Kosslyn et al. (1979) admit that both image formation and image transformation can be cognitively penetrable and hence not explainable by appealing to properties of the imaginal medium. But given that these examples are not distinguishable from the earlier ones in terms of the apparent autonomy of their progression, why do we continue to find it so compelling to view mental scanning as providing evidence for an intrinsic property of the imaginal medium (or, as Kosslyn et al. put it, for the "spatial structure of the surface display")? Is it because processes such as mental scanning are more resistant to voluntary control? Is it really inconceivable that we could "search for" objects in a mental image without passing through intermediate points, or that we could compare two shapes in different orientations without necessarily first imagining one of them being at each of a large number of intermediate orientations?

I believe that what makes certain spatial operations resistant to a natural interpretation in terms of knowledge-governed reasoning through is primarily the "objective pull" I discussed in Pylyshyn (1978), which results in the tendency to view the cognitive process in terms of properties of the represented objects (i.e., the semantics of the representation) instead of the structure of the representation itself (i.e., the syntax of the representation). This tendency, however, leads to a way of stating the principles by which mental processes operate that deprives the principles of any explanatory value. This involves appealing to principles that are expressed in terms of properties of the represented object rather than in terms of the structure or form of the representation itself. But expressing a principle in terms of properties of the represented domain begs the question of why processing occurs this way. The mechanism has no access to the properties of the represented domain *except insofar as they are encoded in the form of the representation itself.* Consequently, a principle of mental processing must be stated in terms of the formal structural properties of its representations, not in terms of what they are taken to represent in the theory.

Consider the following example. In describing their model, Kosslyn et al. (1979) take care to abstract the general principles of operation of the model—a step that is essential if the model is to be explanatory. Such principles include, for example, "Mental images are transformed in small steps, so the images pass through intermediate stages of transformation" (p. 542), or "The degree of distortion will be proportional to the size of the transformational step" (p. 542). Shepard (1975) also cites such principles in discussing his image transformation results.

In each case these principles only make sense if terms such as *size* or *small steps* refer to the *represented* domain. In other words, the intended interpretation of the first of the above principles would have to be something like the following: Representations are transformed in such a way that successive representations correspond to small differences in the scene being depicted. However, what we need is a statement that refers only to the structure of the representation and its accessing process. We need to be able to say something like, "Representations are transformed in small structural steps or degrees," where *small* is relative to a metric defined over the formal structure of the representation and process. For example, relative to a binary representation of numbers and a machine with a bit-shifting operation, the formal (or syntactic) transformation from a representation of the number 137 to a representation of the number 274 is smaller than the transformation from a representation of 137 to a representation of 140 (since the former requires only one shift operation), even though it clearly corresponds to a larger (semantic) transformation in the represented domain of abstract numbers. It is thus important to distinguish between the intrinsic syntactic domain and the extrinsic semantic domain when speaking (typically ambiguously) about transformations of representations. Not only are the two domains logically distinct, but, as we have seen, they involve two quite different similarity metrics and their behavior is governed by quite different principles.

Cognitive principles such as those invoked by Kosslyn et al. (1979), Shepard (1975), and Anderson (1978) would only be theoretically substantive (i.e., explanatory) if they specified (a) how it was possible to have formal operations that had the desired semantic generalization as their consequence—that is, how one could arrange a formal representation and operations upon it so that small steps in the formal representations corresponded to small steps in the represented domain—and (b) why these particular operations, rather than some other ones that could also accomplish the task, should be used (this is the issue of making the underlying theory principled, or restricting its degrees of freedom by reducing the number of free parameters in it). Simply asserting that representations do, as a matter of fact, have this property (because, for example, they are said to "depict" rather than merely "represent"; c.f. Kosslyn et al., 1979) is not enough. One reason that it is not enough is that such a property is simply stipulated in order to conform to the data at hand: It is a free empirical parameter. Another reason is that, as with our earlier cases, there are two distinct options available to account for how this can happen. They correspond to our options 1 and 2: We can appeal either to tacit knowledge or to intrinsic properties of a representational medium. In other words, we can make the account principled by relating the process either to the rationality of the method adopted, given the organism's goals and tacit knowledge, or to the causal relations that hold among physical properties of the representational medium.

Before examining in greater detail the proposal that many imagery phenomena, including specifically those dealing with mental scanning, should be explained in terms of tacit knowledge, we need to touch on two additional points, since they frequently muddy the discussion. For this reason we shall make a brief digression.

Constraints of Habit and the Executive Retreat

The first point is that we must distinguish here, as we do in other areas of theory evaluation, between what typically or frequently or habitually happens and what must happen because of some lawful regularity. Insofar as the origin of visual imagery no doubt lies in visual experience, and insofar as we frequently see things happen in certain ways, this could easily influence the way in which we typically imagine certain kinds of events. For example, since our visual experiences are primarily with common, middle-sized objects, certain typical speeds of acceleration, deceleration, and trajectory shapes are much more common than others. If this sort of experience did influence our tendency to most frequently imagine movements in certain ways, it would clearly not be something attributable to the nature of the mechanism or to properties of the representational medium.

Examples of habitual modes of processing determined by the nature of our experience rather than by our fixed functional capacities are frequent in many areas of cognition. For example, when we learn to read, the teacher monitors our performance auditorily. Consequently, we first learn to read out loud and later to suppress the actual sound. As a result, many of us continue to read by converting written text into a phonetic form prior to further analysis. But there is good reason to believe that this stage of processing is not a necessary one (e.g., Forster, 1976). In fact, there is a plausible view that this habitual mode of processing is responsible for the slow reading speed that some of us suffer from and that we can be trained to abandon.

Although knowing the habitual modes of processing is useful if one is interested in describing the typical, or in accounting for variance, or in developing practical tools (say for education), providing an explanation of behavior requires that we understand the nature of the underlying mechanism (or medium). This, in turn, requires that we empirically establish how imaginal processing is constrained, or which of its functions are independent of particular beliefs or goals (i.e., we must discover the cognitively impenetrable properties of imaginal processing). Thus it becomes important to ask which particular characteristics (if any) the use of imagery forces on us, rather than to report the strategies that tend to go along with the use of imagery. For example, rather than asking whether, in using imagery, subjects *typically* take more time to locate (or otherwise focus their attention on) objects represented as more distant or to report the presence of features in an image that they describe as smaller, we should ask whether subjects *must* do so whenever the image mode of representation is being used. A variety of experimental findings (e.g., Kosslyn et al., 1979, Bannon, Note 1; Spoehr & Williams, Note 2) have demonstrated that, left to their own devices, people habitually solve certain kinds of problems (typically ones involving metrical or geometrical properties) by visualizing some physically possible event taking place (e.g., they imagine themselves witnessing the stimulus changing in certain characteristic ways). Yet no one, to my knowledge, has tried to set up an experimental situation in which subjects were discouraged from carrying out the task by this habitual means to determine whether they were constrained to do so by some cognitive mechanism or medium. Later in this paper I shall report several studies carried out with this goal in mind.

The second point that needs clearing up concerns the grain of truth in Anderson's (1978) claim that the form of representation cannot be determined unequivocally by appeal to behavioral data alone. Anderson's argument is that for any model using some particular form of representation, one can always conjure up another behaviorally indistinguishable model that uses a different form of representation simply by making compensatory changes in the accessing process. As I tried to show (Pylyshyn, 1979b), this cannot be done in general without considerable loss in explanatory power. One of the considerations that led Anderson to the indeterminism view is the apparent unsolvability of the so-called imaginal versus propositional representation debate. No sooner does one side produce what they take to be a damaging result than the other side finds a way to compensate for this by adjusting the process that accesses the representation while leaving fixed the assumed properties of the representation itself. In my view, the lesson to be learned from this observation is simply that in adjudicating such a debate, as in determining the correct interpretation of any empirical phenomenon, one should not appeal solely to data (for even adding neurophysiological and any other class of data does not solve the problem, since no finite amount of data alone can ever uniquely determine a theory), but one should also consider the explanatory power of the model—that is, how well it captures important generalizations, how constrained it is (i.e., how many free parameters it has), how general it is, and so on. Anderson's views on this criterion notwithstanding, the issue is not fraught with vagueness and subjectivity. Although it clearly is not simple to apply in practice, the notion of explanatory power is crucial to the conduct of scientific inquiry, inasmuch as we need to distinguish between such predictive devices as curve fitting or statistical extrapolations and genuine cases of law-like explanatory principles. I shall have more to say about the issue of predictive versus explanatory adequacy in the concluding section.

These remarks are intended as an introduction to the most common rejoinder made to arguments (such as those based on the informal examples considered above, as well as experimental observations of cognitive penetrability) that we should attribute the properties and behavior of images to tacit knowledge rather than to intrinsic properties of an imaginal medium. This rejoinder consists of the counterproposal that we retain the analogue medium but simply modify the processes that generate, transform, and interpret the representation and thus enable the analogical model to account for such findings. For example, my objections to certain particular analogue models of image processing, which are based on demonstrations that certain imaginal processes are cognitively penetrable, can often be sidestepped by merely adding an additional layer of executive process that varies the generation and transformation of images in response to cognitive factors. Sometimes this sort of executive overlay can be made to produce the desired behavior in an imagery model, but rarely can this be done without adding various ad hoc contrivances and consequently losing explanatory power.

Consider, for the sake of a concrete example, the case of the phenomenon called "mental rotation." I claimed (Pylyshyn, 1979a) that the operation of mentally rotating a whole image is not one of the functions that is instantiated by the knowledge-independent functional capacities of the brain and hence should not be explained by appealing to properties of some analogue medium. My conclusion in this case was based on the empirical finding that the slope of the relationship between the relative orientations of two figures and the time it takes to carry out certain comparisons between them (such as deciding whether they are identical)—which is generally taken as the behavioral measure of rate of mental rotation—depends on various cognitive factors such as figural complexity and the difficulty of the actual postrotation comparison task. In these studies the difficulty of the comparison task was varied by requiring subjects to decide whether one figure was embedded in the other and then varying the "goodness" or gestalt value of the embedding (see Pylyshyn, 1979a, for details). One counterargument to my conclusion suggested by Kosslyn et al. (1979)—and one, incidentally, that I considered in my original paper—is that these findings are compatible with a holistic analogue view because an executive process might have determined, on the basis of some property of the stimulus or probe figure, what rate of rotation to use and set this as the value of a parameter to the rotation function. A number of responses might be made to this suggestion.

First, although nothing in principle prevents one from making rotation rate a parameter of the analogue, such a proposal weakens the explanatory power of the model considerably, for any behavioral property, not just rate of rotation, could be made a parameter (including, for example, the form of the function relating reaction time to orientation). The more such parameters there are, the more the model becomes an exercise in curve fitting. Because these parameters are not constrained a priori, each contributes to the degrees of freedom available for fitting the observed data and hence detracts from the explanatory power of the model. This is another way of saying that unless we have some independent means of theoretically assigning a rotation rate to each stimulus, such a parametric feature of the model will be completely ad hoc. Thus there is considerable incentive to try to account for the comparison times in some principled way, either on the basis of some intrinsic property of the representational medium or else in terms of some aggregate characteristic of the cognitive process itself (such as, for example, the number of basic operations carried out in each condition).

It is this very consideration that leads me to agree with Kosslyn et al. (1979) when, in discussing the relative merits of the analogue view of mental rotation—as opposed to the alternative propositional account proposed by Anderson (1978), in which a parameter describing the orientation of a figure is incrementally recomputed—they state, "Thus the question now becomes: Is incremental transformation an equally motivated assumption in both theories, or is it integral to one and added on as an afterthought in the other?" (p. 545). From this point of view, the analogue proposal is clearly less ad hoc, since it posits a universal constraint that is associated with the medium itself (not with that phenomenon alone) and that is therefore not a free empirical parameter. However, it should be noted that this account is only principled when it refers to the intrinsic analogue medium model of rotation, not to the symbol-structure (or matrix) view I discussed earlier. In the latter case the princi-

ples (e.g., rotation proceeds by application of transformations that correspond to small distances) appeal to properties of the represented domain, rather than to intrinsic properties of the representation, precisely as does Anderson's ad hoc incremental parameter adjustment proposal. In both cases no principle based on some independently determined property of the representation or of the structure of the process is given for why this should be so. On the other hand, the trouble with the principled analogue view is that it appears to be false as it stands, as I argued in Pylyshyn (1979a).

Despite the fact that there is strong incentive to account for observed properties, such as rotation rate, in the principled ways suggested above, it could still turn out that the best we can do at the present time is to appeal to something like a rotation rate parameter. In fact, as I have argued (Pylyshyn, 1980b), there will necessarily be some primitive functions that are themselves not explainable in terms of symbol manipulation processes. These constitute what I called the "functional architecture" of the mind. There is no a priori reason why a one-argument version of the operator ROTATE(speed) cannot be such a process. In such a model, the speed parameter would be viewed as being adjusted by some physical means (e.g., a digital-to-analogue converter) on the basis of a cognitive analysis of the stimulus and the subject's beliefs and goals. The question of whether this is the correct story is ultimately an empirical one, just as was the original question of whether ROTATE is an instantiated analogue function (i.e., an intrinsic property of the medium, or what I have called Alternative 2). What has to be done in that case is to expose this new proposal to empirical tests such as those that assess cognitive penetrability. Of course, as I pointed out, each such retreat from the original holistic analogue hypothesis brings us closer to Alternative 1 (the tacit knowledge explanation), as more of the determinants of the phenomena are put into the class of logical analyses and inferences.

Finally it should be pointed out that the particular proposal for parametrizing rotation rate does not, in any case, apply to the experimental results I reported. In these

studies the slope of the reaction time versus angle curve was shown to be a function not merely of properties of the stimulus figure or the comparison figure but of the difficulty of the comparison task itself (i.e., the task of deciding whether the probe was an embedded subfigure of the stimulus). The holistic analogue model assumes that the comparison phase can only be carried out after the stimulus figure has been rotated into the appropriate (independently determined) orientation (indeed, that is the very phase of the process that is responsible for the linear relation between angle and time). In fact Kosslyn et al. (1979) appear to implicitly accept this particular order of events when they propose the alternative that "people may choose in advance slower rates for 'worse' probes" (p. 546). The trouble with this alternative, however, is that we found rotation rate to be not only a function of the nature of the stimulus and of the probe but also of the relation between them, specifically of how well the probe fits as an embedded part of the stimulus. Since this particular feature of the comparison phase cannot be known in advance of rotation, it could not possibly be used as a basis for setting a rate parameter.

Now I have no doubt that one could come up with some kind of executive process that utilized a holistic analogue and yet exhibited different rates of apparent rotation for the different conditions, as observed. However the fact that one could design such an executive would itself be of little interest. It would require some strong independent motivation for going to such lengths in order to retain the analogue rotation components. As I suggested earlier, the main attraction of the analogue model is that it is both principled (i.e., it posits a universal property of mind) and constrained. It is constrained because it permits only one way to transform an image of a figure in one orientation into an image of that figure in another orientation, in contrast with the unlimited number of ways in which an arbitrary symbol structure can in principle be transformed. This constraint would have constituted a powerful explanatory principle. But now as we locate more and more of the explanatory burden in the executive process, there remains less

and less reason to retain the ROTATE analogue operation, although as I stated above, we will always need to posit some knowledge-independent functional properties or capacities (i.e., *analogue* in my sense).

Having thus outlined two general methodological considerations that need to be kept in mind when interpreting empirical findings bearing on the contrast between the intrinsic property of the medium view and the tacit knowledge view, I am ready to consider the specific case of the mental scanning phenomena in some detail.

Tacit Knowledge and Mental Scanning

In examining what takes place in studies such as those discussed by Kosslyn et al. (1979), it is critical to note the difference between the following two tasks:

1a. Solve a particular problem by using a certain prescribed form of representation, or a certain medium or mechanism.

1b. Attempt to recreate as accurately as possible the sequence of perceptual events that would occur if you were actually observing a certain real event happening.

The reason this difference is critical is that quite different criteria of success apply in these two cases. For example, solving a problem by using a certain representational format does not entail that various incidental properties of a known situation even be considered, let alone simulated. On the other hand, this is precisely what is required of someone solving Task 1b. In this case failure to duplicate such conditions as the speed with which an event occurs would constitute a failure to carry out that task correctly. Take the case of imagining. The task of imagining that something is the case, or of considering an imagined situation in order to answer questions about it, does not entail (as part of the specification of the task itself) that it take any particular length of time. On the other hand, the task of imagining that an event is actually happening before your very eyes does entail, for a successful realization of this task, that you consider as many as possible of the characteristics of the event, even if they are irrelevant to the discrimination task itself, and that you attempt to place them into the correct time relationships.

For instance, in discussing how he imaged his music, Mozart claimed (see Ghiselin, 1952). "Nor do I hear in my imagination, the parts *successively*, but I hear them, as it were, all at once" (p. 45). He felt that he could hear a whole symphony in his imagination all at once and apprehend its structure and beauty. Clearly he had in mind a task that is best described in terms of 1a. Even the word *hear*, taken in the sense of having an auditorylike thing about the duration of that experience. We can be reasonably sure that Mozart did not intend the sense of *imagining* implied by 1b, simply because if what he claimed to be doing was imagining witnessing the real event of, say, sitting in the Odeon Conservatoire in Munich and hearing his Symphony Number 40 in G Minor being played with impeccable precision by the resident orchestra under the veteran Kapellmeister, and if he had been imagining that it was actually happening before him in real time and in complete detail—including the minutest flourishes of the horns and the trills of the flute and oboe, all in the correct temporal relations and durations—then he would have taken very close to 22 minutes for this task. If he had not taken that long to imagine it, this would only signify that he had not quite been doing what he had alleged, that is, he had not been imagining witnessing the actual real event in which every note was being played at its proper duration, or else we might conclude that what the had in fact been imagining was not a good performance of his symphony. In other words, if it takes *n* sec to witness a certain event, then an accurate mental simulation of the act of witnessing that same event should also take *n* sec, simply because how well the latter task is performed is by definition dependent on how accurately it mimics various properties of the former task. On the other hand, the same need not apply merely to the act of imagining that the *event has a* certain set of properties, that is, imagining a situation to be the case but without the added requirements as specified in the 1b version of the task. These are not empirical assertions

about how people imagine and think: They are simply claims about the existence of two distinct natural interpretations of the specification of a certain task.

Applying this to the particular case of mental scanning, one must be careful to distinguish between the following two tasks that subjects might set themselves:

2a. Using a mental image and focusing your attention on a certain object in that image, decide as quickly as possible whether a second named object is present elsewhere in that image.

2b. Imagine yourself in a certain real situation in which you are viewing a certain scene and are focusing directly on some particular object in that scene. Now imagine that you are looking for (or scanning toward, or glancing up at, or seeing a speck moving across the scene toward, etc.) a second named object in the scene. When you succeed in imagining yourself finding (and seeing) the object (or when you see the speck arrive at the object), press this button.

The relevant differences between Tasks 2a and 2b should be obvious. As in the previous examples, the criteria of successful completion of the task are different in the two cases. In particular, Task 2b includes, as part of its specification, such requirements as that subjects should attempt to imagine various intermediate states (corresponding to ones that they believe would be passed through in actually carrying out the corresponding real task) and that they spend more time visualizing those episodes that they believe (or infer) would take more time in the corresponding real task. The latter conditions are clearly not part of the specification of Task 2a, as there is nothing about Task 2a that requires that such incidental features of the visual task be considered in answering the question. In the words of Newell and Simon (1972), the two tasks have quite different "task demands."

To show that subjects are actually carrying out Task 2b in the various studies reported by Kosslyn (and therefore that the proper explanation of these findings should appeal to subjects' tacit knowledge of the depicted situation rather than to properties of their imaginal medium), I shall attempt to establish several independent points. First,

it is independently plausible that the methods used in experiments reported in the literature describe as inviting subjects to carry out Task 2b rather than Task 2a. Second, the arguments against experimental demand effects raised by Kosslyn et al. (1979) do not bear on the above proposal. Third, this alternative view has considerable generality and can account for a variety of imaginal phenomena. And fourth, there is independent experimental evidence showing that subjects can indeed be led to carry out Task 2a rather than Task 2b, and when they do, the increase in reaction time with increase in imagined distance disappears.

Task Demands of Scanning Experiments

With respect to the first point, all published studies that I am aware of in which larger image distances led to longer reaction times used instructions that quite explicitly required subjects to imagine witnessing the occurrence of a real physical event. In most scanning experiments subjects are asked to imagine a spot moving from one point to another, although in a few (e.g., in Kosslyn, 1973; Kosslyn, Ball, & Reiser, 1978, Experiment 4) they were asked to imagine shifting their attention or their glance from one imagined object to another in the same imagined scene. In each case, what subjects were required to imagine was a real physical event (since terms like *move* and *shift* refer to physical processes) about the duration of which they would clearly have some reasonable tacit knowledge. For example, they would know implicitly that it takes a moving object longer to move through a greater distance, that it takes longer to shift one's attention through greater distances (both transversely and in depth), and so on. Although subjects may or may not be able to state these regularities, they plainly do have that tacit knowledge, as evidenced by the critical precision necessary to make realistic motion pictures by splicing pan and zoom sequences. (The exact time relationships needed to make such sequences appear realistic, especially in the case of splicing together takes of slower and more deliberate movements of actors and of points of view, seem to depend on one's prior interpretation

of the actions. Hence the process involved in detecting poor film editing, like the process of imagining realistic scenarios, would seem to be knowledge dependent and therefore cognitively penetrable.)

The Arguments Against Demand Characteristics

Kosslyn et al. (1979) appear to recognize some of the force of the tacit knowledge position, but in responding to it they concern themselves only with the possibility that "experimental demand characteristics," or unintentional influences due to the experimental setting and subjects' expectations, might have been responsible for the outcome of the experiments. Although recent results by Richman, Mitchell, and Reznick (1979) and Mitchell and Richman (1980) indicate that phenomena such as those found in mental scanning experiments can be brought about by experimental demand factors, it has not yet been established that this is in fact the correct explanation for all such results. Kosslyn et al. have argued that it is unlikely that demand factors could explain all their results. On the other hand, neither have they provided any definitive control studies to rule out this alternative (the "pseudo-experiment" described by Kosslyn et al. is inadequate in this respect, inasmuch as simply asking subjects what they expect is the best way to invite acquiescence effects, as opposed to genuine expectations or other types of demand biases).

However, whether the case for experimental demand effects will stand up to empirical tests or whether the Kosslyn et al. counterarguments are correct is not relevant to the present proposal. There is a major difference between the contaminating effects of experimental demands, or subjects' expectations of the outcome or their desire to please, and the entirely legitimate task demands, or requirements placed on the solution process by the specifications of the task itself. In the latter case what is at issue is not a contamination of results but simply a case of subjects solving the task as they interpret it (or as they choose to interpret it, for one reason or another) by bringing to bear everything that they know about a class of physical events, which they take to be the ones that they are to imagine witnessing. If they take the task to be the one characterized in Task 2b, then they will naturally attempt to reproduce a temporal sequence of representations corresponding to the sequence they believe would arise from actually viewing the event of scanning across a scene (or seeing a spot move across the scene). Thus, beginning with the representation corresponding to "imagining seeing the initial point of focus," the process would continue until a representation was arrived at which corresponded to "imagining seeing the named point." Of course, according to this way of viewing what is going on, there is no need to assume that the process halts as a *result* of a certain imagined state's being reached, or when a certain visual predicate is satisfied. It could just as plausibly stop when some independent psychophysical mechanism had generated a time interval corresponding to an estimate of expected duration (we know such mechanisms exist, since subjects can generate time intervals with even greater reliability than they can estimate them; c.f. Fraisse, 1963). In other words, it could just as easily be independently estimated time intervals that drive the imagined state changes.

For the purpose of this account of the scanning results, we need assume little or nothing about intrinsic constraints on the process or even about the content of the sequence of representations that are generated. Such a sequence could, for example, simply consist of a sequence of beliefs such as that the spot is *now here* and *now it is there*—where the locative demonstratives are pointers into the symbolic representation being constructed and updated. Though the sequence is almost certainly more complex than this, there is no need to assume that it is constrained by any special property of the representational medium, as opposed to simply being governed by what subjects believe or infer about some likely intermediate stages of the event being imagined and about the relative times at which they would occur. Now such beliefs and inferences could obviously depend on anything that the subject might tacitly know or believe concerning

what usually happens in the corresponding perceptual situations. Thus the sequence could in one case depend on tacit knowledge of the dynamics of physical objects, in another on tacit knowledge of some aspects of eye movements or of what happens when one has to glance up or refocus on a more distant object, or even on tacit knowledge of how long it takes to notice or to recognize certain kinds of visual patterns (e.g., it might even take subjects longer to imagine trying to see something in dim light or against a camouflage background for this reason). Thus none of the examples and contrary evidence that Kosslyn et al. (1979) cite against one or another of the alternative "experimental demand" explanations is to the point here, since the exact domain of knowledge being appealed to can vary from case to case, as is to be expected if imagining is viewed as a species of commonsense reasoning, as opposed to a process that has access to a special sort of representational medium with extraordinary functional properties (e.g., being characterized by Euclidean axioms).

Sometimes experiments involving superimposing images on actual visual stimuli have been cited against the demand characteristics view (e.g., Kosslyn et al., 1979). However, such experiments differ from studies of imaginal thinking in several important respects that make them largely irrelevant to the present discussion. When a subject is instructed to view a display and then to imagine a stationary or a moving pattern superimposed on it (as in the studies by Hays, 1973; Finke, 1979; Shulman, Remington, & McLean, 1979; and those mentioned in Shepard, 1978), there is no need to posit an internal medium of representation to explain the stable, *geometrical* relationships that hold among features of the resulting construction. The perceived background itself is all we need in this case. For example, when a subject thinks of an imaginary spot as being *here* and then *there* (as in the discussion above), the locative terms can in this case be bound to places in a perceptual construction that are under direct stimulus control and that are generally veridical with respect to relative spatial locations. This is essentially equivalent to binding the internal symbols to the actual places

in the stimulus, which, being in the actual stimulus, will maintain their locations relative to one another regardless of subjects' beliefs about space or about what they are viewing (assuming only that perception is free from major time-varying distortions). In fact, Pylyshyn, Elcock, Marmor, and Sander (1978) have developed a model of how indexical binding of internal symbols to primitive perceptual features can be carried out within a limited-resource computational system and how such bindings can be used by the motor system to enable it to, say, point to the bound features.

Thus in such superposition cases if, for instance, the subject imagines a spot moving from perceived location A to perceived location B, then all that is required to ensure that the spot crosses some location C is (a) that the successive locations where the point is imagined to be actually correspond to a certain path on the stimulus (i.e., that the successive mental locatives in fact refer to a certain sequence of adjacent places on the stimulus) and (b) that place C actually be on that path, somewhere between A and B. In the pure imagery case, by contrast, the corresponding notions of *path, lying on,* and *between* are not available in the same literal sense (i.e., there are only representations of paths). In other words, subjects must not only imagine the spot to be moving with respect to an imagined background but they must have tacit knowledge of such things as that if C lies between A and B, then going from A to B requires passing through C. Another way to put this is to say that the geometrical properties of the layout that is being viewed (e.g., the relative locations of features in it) remain fixed because of the way the world being viewed is (in this case, rigid), and different geometrical characteristics of the layout can simply be "noticed" or "perceived" by the viewer, including the relative position of a place being attended to (i.e., a place that is bound to an internal locative indexical symbol). On the other hand, what remains fixed and what can be noticed in a purely constructed image depends either on intrinsic properties of some medium of representation or on subjects' tacit knowledge about the behavior of the sorts of things they are imagining and their

ability to draw inferences from such knowledge—exactly the dichotomy we are examining. This issue is closely connected with the general problem of reasoning about actions, which in artificial intelligence research raises a technical problem called the "frame problem." The relevance of such issues to the imagery controversy is discussed in Pylyshyn (1978, 1980b).

The Generality of the Tacit Knowledge View

With respect to the generality of explanations based on appeal to tacit knowledge, one could point to a variety of findings that fall nicely within this explanatory framework. For instance, the list of illustrative examples presented in the last section shows clearly that in order to imagine the episode of seeing certain physical events, one needs to have access to tacit knowledge about physical regularities. In some of these cases one might even say that one needed an implicit theory, since a variety of related generalizations must be brought to bear in order to correctly predict what some imagined process would do (e.g., the sugar solution or the color filter case). In other cases simply the knowledge (or recollection) that certain things typically happen in certain ways and that they take certain relative amounts of time will suffice.

Several of Kosslyn's findings, allegedly revealing properties of the "mind's eye," might also be explainable on this basis—including the finding (Kosslyn, 1975) that it takes longer to report properties of objects when the objects are imagined as being small. Consider that the usual way to inspect an object is to take up a viewing position at some convenient distance from the object which depends on its size (and in certain cases on other things as well; e.g., consider imagining a deadly snake or a raging fire). So long as we have a reasonably good idea of the object's true size we would imagine viewing it at the appropriate distance. Now if someone instructed me to imagine some object as especially small, I might perhaps think of myself as being further away or as seeing it through, say, the wrong end of a telescope. In any case if I were then asked to do something, such as report some of its properties, and if the instructions were to imagine that I could *actually see* the property I was reporting (which was the case in the experiments reported), or even if I simply chose to make that my task for some obscure reason, I would naturally try to imagine something that was in fact a plausible visual event, such as a zooming-in sequence (and indeed this is what many of Kosslyn's subjects reported). If that were the case then we would naturally expect the time relations to be as actually observed.

Although the above story may sound quite a bit like the one Kosslyn (1975) himself gives, there is one difference that is crucial from a theoretical standpoint. In this version of the account, no appeals need to be made to knowledge-independent functional properties of a medium, and especially to properties of a *geometrical* sort. The representational medium, although it no doubt has some relevant intrinsic properties that restrict how things can be represented, plays no role in accounting for any of the particular phenomena we have been examining. These phenomena are seen as arising from (a) subjects' tacit knowledge of how things typically happen in reality and (b) their ability to carry out such psychophysical tasks as to generate time intervals corresponding to inferred durations of certain possible physical events. This is not to deny the importance of different forms of representation, of the nature of such inferential capacities as alluded to above, or of the nature of the underlying mechanisms. It is simply to suggest that the particular findings we have been discussing do not necessarily tell us anything about such matters.

Although we intuitively feel that the visual image modality (or format, or medium) severely constrains both the form and the content of potential representations, it is no easy matter to say exactly what these constraints are (and the informal examples given earlier should cast at least some suspicions on the validity of such intuitions in general). It seems clear, for example, that we cannot image any arbitrary object whose properties we can describe, and this does give credence to the view that images are more constrained than descriptions. Although it is doubtlessly true that imagery is in some sense not as flexible as discursive symbol systems (such as language), it is crucial to know the nature of this constraint before we can say whether it is a constraint imposed by the medium or merely a habitual way of doing things or of interpreting the task demands, or whether it might even be a limitation attributable to the absence of certain knowledge or a failure to draw certain inferences. Once again I would argue that we cannot say a priori whether certain constraints implicated in the use of imagery ought to be attributed to the functional character of the biological medium of representation (the analogue view) or to the subject's possession and use (either voluntarily or habitually) of certain tacit knowledge.

Consider the following proposals made by Kosslyn et al. (1979) concerning the nature of the constraints on imagery. The authors clearly take such constraints to be given by the intrinsic nature of the representational medium. They suggest that something they call the "surface display" (a reference to their cathode ray tube proto-model) gives imagery certain fixed characteristics. For example, they state,

> We predict that this component will not allow cognitive penetration: that a person's knowledge, beliefs, intentions, and so on will not alter the spatial structure that we believe the display has. Thus we predict that a person cannot at will make his surface display four-dimensional, or non-Euclidean. (p. 549)

Now it does seem to be obviously true that one cannot image a four-dimensional or non-Euclidean space. Yet the very oddness of the supposition that we might be able to do so should make us suspicious as to the reason for this.

To see why little can be concluded from this fact, consider the following. Suppose a subject insisted that he or she could imagine a non-Euclidean space. Suppose further that mental scanning experiments were consistent with this claim (e.g., scan time conformed to, say, a city block metric). Would we believe this subject or would we conclude that what the subject really did was to

> *simulate* such properties in imagery by filling in the surface display with patterns of a certain sort in the same way that projections of non-Euclidean surfaces can be depicted on two-dimensional Euclidean paper? (Kosslyn et al., 1979 p. 547)

Of course we would conclude the latter. But the reason for doing so is exactly the reason we gave earlier for discounting one possible interpretation of what Mozart might have meant when he claimd to be able to imagine a whole symphony instantaneously. That reason, you will recall, had to do entirely with the implications of one particular sense of the phrase *imagine a symphony*—namely that the Task 2b sense demands that certain conditions be fulfilled. If we transpose this to the case of the spatial property of visual imagery, we can see that this is also the reason why the notion of imagining four-dimensional space in the sense of Task 2b is incoherent. The point is sufficiently central that it merits a brief elaboration.

Let us first distinguish, as I have been insisting we should, the sense of imagining (call it *imagine$_1$ X*) that means to *think of X* or to consider the hypothetical situation that X is the case (or mentally construct a symbolic model or a mental description of a possible world in which X is the case) from the sense of imagining (call this one *imagine$_2$ X*) that means to imagine that you are *seeing X* or to imagine yourself observing the actual event X happening. The reason for the inadmissibility of four-dimensional or non-Euclidean imaginal space becomes clear, as does its irrelevance to the question of what the properties of an imaginal medium are. The reason we cannot imagine$_2$ such spaces is that they are not the sorts of things that could be seen. Our inability to imagine$_2$ such things has nothing to do with intrinsic properties of a surface display, but with a lack of a certain sort of knowledge: We do not know what it would be like to see such a thing. We have no idea, for example, what kind of configuration of light and dark contours there would have to be, what sorts of visual features would need to appear, and so on. Presumably congenitally color-blind people cannot imagine$_2$ a colored scene for similar reasons. In this case it would hardly seem appropriate to attribute this failure to something's being wrong with their surface display. On the other hand, we do know, in nonvisual (i.e., nonoptical) terms, what a non-Euclidean space is like, and we can imagine$_1$ there being such a space in reality (certainly Einstein did) and thus solve problems about it. Perhaps, given sufficient familiarity with the facts of such spaces, we could even produce mental scanning results in conformity with non-Euclidean geometries. There have frequently been reports of people who claimed to have an intuitive grasp of four-dimensional space in the sense that they could do such things as mentally rotate a four-dimensional tesseract and imagine$_1$ its three-dimensional projection (for example, Hinton, 1906, has an interesting discussion of what is involved). If this were true, then they might be able to do a four-dimensional version of the Shepard mental rotation task.

Of course if we drop all this talk about the geometry of the display and consider the general point regarding the common conceptual constraints imposed on vision and imagery, there can be no argument: Something is responsible for the way we cognize the world. Whatever it is probably also explains both the way we see it and the way we image it. But that is as far as we can go. From this we can no more draw conclusions about the geometry, topology, or other structural property of a representational medium than we can draw conclusions about the structure of a language by considering the structure of things that can be described in that language. There is no reason to believe that the relation is anything but conventional—which is precisely what the formalist (or computational) version of functionalism claims (see Fodor, 1980).

Incidentally, the distinction discussed above also clarifies why various empirical findings involving imagery might tend to occur together. For example, there is a brief report in the authors' response section of Kosslyn, Jolicoeur, and Fliegel showing that when stimuli are sorted according to whether subjects tend to visualize them in reporting certain of their properties (i.e., whether subjects typically imagine, them in such tasks), then it is only those stimulus–property pairs that are classified as mental image evokers that yield the characteristic reaction time functions in mental scanning experiments. But that is hardly surprising, since anything that leads certain stimuli to be habitually processed in the imagine, mode will tend to exhibit all sorts of other characteristics associated with imagine, processing—including the scanning time results and such phenomena as the relation between latency and imagined size of objects (see the summary in Kosslyn et al., 1979). Of course nobody knows which features of a stimulus or task tend to elicit the imagine, habit or why some stimuli should do so more than others, but that is not a problem that distinguishes the analogue from the tacit knowledge views.

Some Empirical Evidence

Finally I shall consider some provisional evidence suggesting that subjects can be induced to use their visual image to carry out a task such as 2a that does not entail imagining oneself seeing a natural sequence of events happening. Recall that the question was whether mental scanning effects (i.e., the linear relation between time and distance) should be viewed as evidence for an intrinsic property of a representational medium or as evidence for such things as what tacit knowledge (of geometry and dynamics) people have and what they take the task to be. If the former were the correct interpretation, then it must not merely be the case that people usually take more time for retrieving information about more distant objects in an imagined scene. That could arise, as we have already noted, merely from some habitual or preferred way of imagining or a preferred interpretation of the task demands. If the phenomenon is due to an intrinsic property of the imaginal medium, then it must be a necessary consequence of using this medium; that is, the linear (or at least monotonic) relation between time and represented distance must hold whenever in-

formation is being accessed through the medium of imagery.

As it happens, there exists a strong preference for interpreting tasks involving doing something imaginally as tasks of type 1b—that is, as requiring one to imagine, an actual physically realizable event happening over time. In most of the mental scanning cases, it is the event of moving one's attention from place to place or of witnessing something moving between two points. It could also involve imagining such episodes as drawing or extrapolating a line and watching its progression (which may be what was involved, for example, in the Spoehr & Williams study, Note 2). But the question remains: Must a subject imagine such a physically realizable event in order to access information from an image, or more precisely, in order to produce an answer which the subject claims is based on examining the image?

A number of studies have been carried out in our laboratory which suggest that conditions can be set up so that a subject uses an image to access information, yet does so without having to imagine the occurrence of some particular real life temporal event (i.e., the subject can be induced to imagine, rather than imagine,). I will mention only two of these studies for purposes of illustration. The design of the experiments follows very closely that of experiments reported in Kosslyn, Ball, and Reiser (1978; see Bannon, Note 1, for more details). Subjects had to memorize a map containing approximately seven visually distinct places (e.g., a church, a castle, a beach) up to the criterion of being able to reproduce it with the relative location of places within 6 mm of the correct location. Then they were asked to image the map in front of them and to focus their attention on a particular named place, while keeping the rest of the map in view in their mind's eye. We then investigated various conditions in which they were given different instructions for what to do next, all of which (a) emphasized that the task was to be carried out exclusively by consulting their image and (b) required them to notice, on cue, a second named place on the map and to make some discriminatory response with respect to that place as quickly and as accurately as possible.

So far this description of the method is compatible with the Kosslyn et al. (1978) experiments. Indeed, when we instructed subjects to imagine a speck moving from the place of initial focus to the second named place, we obtained the same kind of strongly linear relation between distance and reaction time as did Kosslyn et al. When, however, the instructions specified merely that subjects should give the compass bearing of the second place—that is, to say whether the second place was N, NE, E, SE, and so forth of the first, there was no relation between distance and reaction time. (In this experiment subjects were first given practice in the use of the compass direction responses and were instructed to be as fast and accurate as possible within the resolution of the eight available categories. In postexperiment interviews, subjects reported that they carried out the task by consulting their image, as they had been instructed.)

This result suggests that it is possible to arrange a situation in which subjects use their images to retrieve information and yet do not feel compelled to imagine the occurrence of an event that would be described as scanning their attention between the two points (i.e., to imagine,). Although this result was suggestive, it lacked controls for a number of alternative explanations. In particular, since a subject must in any case know the bearing of a second place on the map before scanning to it (even in Kosslyn's experiments), one might wish to claim, for independent reasons, that in this experiment the relative bearing of pairs of points on the map was retrieved from a symbolic, as opposed to imaginal, representation, in spite of subjects' insistence that they did use their image in making their judgements. Although this tends to weaken the imagery story somewhat, since it allows a crucial spatial property to be represented off the display (and so raises the question, Why not represent other spatial properties this way?) and because it discounts subjects' reports of how they were carrying out the task in this case while accepting such reports in other comparable situations, it is nonetheless one possible avenue of retreat.

Consequently, a second instructional condition was investigated, aimed at making it

more plausible that subjects had to consult their image in order to make the response, and to make it more compelling that they must have been focused on the second place and mentally seeing both the original and the second place at the time of the response. The only change in the instructions that was made for this purpose was to explicitly require subjects to focus on the second place after they heard its name (e.g., *church*) and, using it as the origin, give the orientation of the first place (the place initially focused on) relative to the second. Thus the instructions strongly emphasized the necessity of focusing on the second place and of actually seeing both places before making the orientation judgment. Subjects were not told how to get to the second place from the first, but only to keep the image before their "mind's eye" and to use this image to read off the correct answer. In addition, for reasons to be mentioned shortly, the identical experiment was run (using a different group of subjects) entirely in the visual modality, so instead of having to image the map, subjects could actually examine the map in front of them. Eight subjects were run in the image condition and eight in the vision one. Each subject was given 84 trials, thus providing four times for each of the 21 interpoint distances.

What we found was that in the visual condition, there was a significant correlation between response time (measured from the presentation of the name of the second place) and the distance between places, whereas no such relation held in the imaginal condition. In doing the analysis, distances were grouped into small, medium, and large, and a linear regression was carried out on the grouped data. In the visual condition there was a significant correlation between distance and reaction time ($r = .50, p < .05$). In the imaginal condition there was no significant correlation ($r = -.03, ns$). The mean reaction time in the visual condition was 2.60 sec and in the imaginal condition was 2.90 sec. Such results indicate quite clearly that even though the linear relation between distance and time (the scanning phenomenon) is a frequent concomitant of imaging a transition between seeing two places on an image, it is not a necessary consequence of using the visual imagery modality and consequently that it is not due to an intrinsic (hence knowledge- and goal-independent) functional property of the representational medium for visual images.

Yet perhaps not surprisingly, results such as these can be accommodated without too much trouble by the Kosslyn et al. model. That model has been conveniently provided with the option of "blinking" its way to a second location—or of regenerating a new image from symbolic information. In that case it would clearly be able to respond in fixed time, regardless of the distance between places. Several remarks can be made concerning this alternative.

First, the existence of both scan and blink transforms can be used simply to ensure that no empirical data could falsify the assumption of an intrinsic medium of representation. Whether or not this is the case depends on what, if any, additional contraints are placed on the use of these transforms. Kosslyn et al. (1979) do suggest that people will use whichever transform is most efficient. Thus they ought to scan through short distances but blink over longer ones. This, however, presupposes that they know in advance how far away they will have to move over the image—and hence that distance information is available for arbitrary pairs of places without consulting the image and without requiring scanning. Clearly this assumption is inconsistent with the original assumption regarding how spatial information is accessed from images. We shall return to this point briefly in the concluding section, when we consider where the predictive power of such imagery models comes from.

Second, if the correct explanation for our results is that subjects used the blink transformation and hence generated new images instead of using their initial ones to locate the second place (as they were instructed to do, and as they reported having done), then we should be able to see the effect of this in the overall response times. Since it took our subjects 1 or 2 sec to generate the initial image, it is very unlikely that they were regenerating a completely new image and making the required orientation judgment in the 2.9 sec it took for them to respond. Perhaps they were only regenerating the two critical places within the existing outline in their image. But even that seems implausible for the following reason. The average reaction time to make orientation judgments in the visual condition, where no image had to be generated, was only 300 msec shorter than the average time to make the judgment in the imagery condition. This indicates that if an image had to be regenerated in the imagery condition, as assumed by the blink transformation explanation, it would have taken less than 300 msec to regenerate such an image. Since, according to Kosslyn, Reiser, Farrah, and Fliegel (Note 3), it usually takes several seconds to generate even simple images—and never less than 1 sec even for images containing only one simple part—there is insufficient time to both regenerate parts of an image and make an orientation judgment in the total 2.9 sec it took subjects to respond. Hence subjects could not have been using a blink transformation to regenerate their image in that case.

These experiments demonstrate that, at least in the one situation investigated, images can be examined without the putative constraints of the surface display postulated by Kosslyn and others. It is also reasonable to expect that other systematic relations between reaction time and image properties may disappear when appropriate instructions are given that are designed to encourage subjects to interpret the task as in 1a instead of 1b. For example, if subjects could be induced to generate what they considered small but highly detailed and clear images, then the effect of image size on time to report the presence of features (e.g. Kosslyn, 1975) might disappear as well. There is even some evidence that this might be the case from one of the studies reported in Kosslyn et al. (Note 3), the time to retrieve information from images was found to be independent of the size of the image. From the description of this experiment, it seems that a critical difference between it and the earlier ones (Kosslyn, 1975), in which an effect of image size was found, is that in this case subjects had time to study the actual objects, with instructions to practice generating equally clear images of each of them, and were also tested with these same instructions (which

I assume encouraged them to entertain equally detailed images at all sizes). Thus it seems that it is possible, when subjects are encouraged to have detailed information readily available, for subjects to put as fine a grain of detail as they wish into their imaginal constructions (though presumably the total amount of information in the image is still limited along some dimension, even if not the dimension of resolution). Unlike the case of real vision, however, such imaginal vision need not be limited by problems of grain or resolution or any other difficulty associated with making visual discriminations. Of course, as we have already noted, subjects can exhibit some of the behavioral characteristics associated with such limitations (e.g., taking longer to recall fine details), but that may very well be because they know what real vision is like and are simulating the relevant behavior as best they can, rather than because of the intrinsic nature of the imaginal medium.

Conclusions: What Is the Theoretical Claim?

It has often been said that imagery models (such as that of Kosslyn & Shwartz, 1977, or Shepard, 1975) contribute to scientific progress because they make correct predictions and because they motivate further research. Although I would not want to deny this claim, it is important to ask what it is about such imagery models that carries the predictive force. It is my view that there is only one empirical hypothesis responsible for the predictive success of the whole range of imagistic models and that nearly everything else about such models consists of free empirical parameters added ad hoc to accommodate particular experimental results. The one empirical hypothesis is just this: *When people imagine a scene or an event, what goes on in their minds is in many ways similar to what goes on when they observe the corresponding event actually happening.*

It is to the credit of both Shepard (1978) and Paivio (1977) that they recognize the central contribution of the perceptual metaphor. For example Shepard (1978) states,

> Most basically, what I am arguing for here is the notion that the internal process that represents the transformation of an external object, just as much as the internal process that represents the object itself, is in large part the same whether the transformation, or the object, is merely imagined or actually perceived. (p. 135)

Paivio (1977) has been even more direct in recognizing and approving of the metaphorical nature of this class of models when he asserts,

> The criteria for a psychological model should be what the mind can do, so why not begin with a psychological metaphor in which we try to extend our present knowledge about perception and behavior to the inner world of memory and thought. . . . The perceptual metaphor . . . holds the mirror up to nature and makes human competence itself the model of mind. (p. 71)

One difficulty with metaphorical explanation in general is that by leaving open the question of what the similarities are between the primary and secondary objects of the metaphor, it remains flexible enough to encompass most eventualities. Of course this open-endedness is also what gives metaphors their heuristic and motivational value and is what provides the feeling of having captured a system of regularities. But in the case of the perceptual metaphor for imagery, this sort of capturing of regularities is, to a large extent, illusory, because it is parasitic upon our informal commonsense knowledge of psychology and our tacit knowledge of the natural world. For example, I have argued that the reason I imagine things happening more or less the way that they actually do happen in the world is not because my brain or my cognitive endowments are structured to somehow correspond to nature but simply because I know how things generally happen—because I have been told, or have induced, what some of the general principles are. In other words I have a tacit physical theory which is good enough to predict most ordinary everyday natural events correctly most of the time. Now the claim that our imagery unfolds the same way as our perceptual process trades on this tacit knowledge in an even more insidious way, because it does so in the name of scientific explanation.

The story goes like this. The claim that imagery is (in some ways) like perception has predictive value because it enables us to predict that, say, it will take longer to mentally scan longer distances, to report the vi-

For example, if the facts supported the conclusion that size, shape, and orientation were naturally factored apart in one's mental representation (as I believe they do), or that grain size is nonhomogeneous and varies as a function of what the subject believes the referent situation to be like (e.g., how brightly lit, how detailed in its design, how important different features are to the task at hand), does anybody believe for one moment that this would undermine the claim that an array structure was being used? Clearly all that it would require is some minor adjustment in the system (e.g., making resolution depend on additional features of the image, allowing the cognitive process to access an orientation parameter in memory and so on). But if that is the case, then it is apparent that claiming an array structure places no constraints on the sorts of phenomena that can be accommodated—that is, that properties of this structure are *free empirical parameters*. Thus, although one may have the impression that there is a highly constraining core assumption that is crucial to the predictive success of the model, the way this impression is maintained is simply by giving the rest of the system enough degrees of freedom to overcome any effort to empirically reject that core assumption. So, whereas the intuitive view of the system continues to hang on the unsupported view that properties of imagery are determined by the intrinsic properties of an internal display medium, its predictive power may in fact come entirely from a single empirical hypothesis of imagery theory (viz., the perception metaphor).

The phenomenon of having the real appeal of a theoretical system come from a simplified (and strictly false) view of the system while its predictions come from more complex (and more ad hoc) aspects is commonplace in science. In fact, even the initial success of the Copernican world view might be attributable to such a characteristic. Copernicus published his epoch-making proposal, *de Revolutionibus*, in two volumes. The first volume showed how the solar-centered system could in principle elegantly handle certain aspects of stellar and planetary motions (involving reverse movements) without the necessity of such ad hoc devices as epicycles.

sual characteristics of smaller imagined objects, to rotate images through larger angles, to mentally compare more similar images, and so on. It does this because we know that these generalizations hold in the corresponding visual cases. But notice that the reason we can make such predictions is not that we have a corresponding theory of the visual cases. It is simply that our tacit commonsense knowledge is sufficiently accurate to provide us with the correct analogy would be to give, as a theory of Mary's behavior, the statement that Mary is a lot like Susan, whom we know very well. This would enable us to perhaps make very accurate predictions of Mary's behavior, but it would scarcely qualify as an adequate explanation of why she behaves as she does. Another parallel, even closer in spirit to the metaphorical explanation of imagery, would be if we gave as the explanation of why it takes longer to rotate a real object through a greater angle that this is the way we typically perceive it happen, or if we explained why it takes more time to visually compare two objects of very different sizes by saying that this is what happens in the mental comparison case. In both these cases we would be able to make the correct predictions as long as we were informally well enough acquainted with the second of each of these pairs of situations. Furthermore, in both cases there would be some nontrivial empirical claim involved. For instance, in these cases it would be the claim that perception is generally veridical or that what we see generally corresponds to what we know to be the case. Although these are real empirical claims, no one takes them to have the theoretical significance that is attributed to corresponding theories of imagery, even though both may in fact have the same underlying basis.

Of course some models of imagery appear to go beyond such mere metaphors. For example, Kosslyn and Shwartz (1977) actually have a computer model of imagery that accounts for a very wide range of experimental findings. However, as we suggested in referring to its use of the blink transformation, unless the model incorporated a greater number of principled constraints, it is much

too easy for it to accommodate any finding. It can do this because the model is, in fact, just a simulation of some largely commonsense ideas about what happens when we image. That is why the principles it appeals to are invariably stated in terms of properties of the represented domain (e.g., a principle such as *images must be transformed through small angles* clearly refers to what is being represented, since images themselves do not actually have orientations, as opposed to representing them). Yet this is how we often explain things in informal, everyday terms. We say that we imagine things in a certain way, because that is the way they really are. As I have already remarked, a theory of the underlying process should account for how imagery can come to have this character, not use this very property as an explanatory principle.

Another consequence of the model's being a simulation of commonsense views is that anything that could be stated informally as a description of what happens in the mind's eye can easily and naturally be accommodated in the model. For example, in arguing against the expectation or demand explanation of their scanning results, Kosslyn et al. (1979) cite one subject who said that he or she thought objects close together would take longer to image because it would be harder to see them or tell them apart. This is exactly the sort of process that could very easily be accommodated by the model. All that has to be done is to make the grain of the surface display whatever size is required to produce this effect. There is nothing to prevent this sort of tuning of the model to fit each situation. Such properties therefore have the status of free parameters, and unfortunately there is no limit to how many such parameters may be implicit in the model. Similarly, in our experiment (in which subjects judged the compass bearing of one place relative to a second) we found a negative correlation (for some of the subjects between reaction time and distance) jects between focal points on the imagined map. The computer model would have little difficulty accommodating that result if it turned out to be a general finding. In fact it is hard to think of any result which could not be naturally accommodated—including, as

Kosslyn et al. (1980) themselves suggest, the possibility of representing non-Euclidean space. What is crucial is not merely that such results could be accommodated, but that this could be done without violating any fundamental design criteria of the model and without threatening any basic principle of its operation—without, for example, violating any constraints imposed by the hypothesized surface display. What this amounts to is that the really crucial aspects of the model have the status of free parameters rather than structural constants.

Now to some extent Kosslyn appears to recognize this flexibility in his model. In the last section of Kosslyn et al. (1979), the authors insist that the model ought to be evaluated on the basis of its heuristic value. I agree with that proposal. The ad hoc quality characteristic of early stages of some scientific modeling may well be unavoidable. However we should make every effort to be realistic and rid ourselves of all the attending illusions. One of the illusions that goes with this way of thinking about imagery is that there is an essential core of the model that is not merely heuristic but is highly principled and highly constrained. That core is contained in the postulated properties of the surface display (or in the "cathode ray tube proto-model"). This immutable core involves the assumption that there is an internal display medium with intrinsic geometrical (or geometry-analogue) properties. For example, Pinker (1980) claims that the "array structure" captures a set of generalizations about images. But without knowing which properties of the array structure are doing the work, and whether such properties can be altered by changes in what the subject believes, this sort of capturing of generalizations may be no better than merely listing them. We need to know what it is about the intrinsic character of arrays that requires them to have the properties that Pinker suggests (e.g., "that they represent shape, size, and locations implicitly in an integral fashion, that they are bounded in size and grain, that they preserve interpoint distances" p. 148). If there is nothing apart from stipulation that requires arrays to have these properties, then each of these properties is precisely a free parameter.

In the second volume Copernicus worked out the details of his system for the more comprehensive case. That required reintroducing the ad hoc mechanisms of epicycles. In fact, Copernicus's system only did away with the five major Ptolomaic epicycles and retained all the complexity associated with the larger number of minor ones needed to make the theory fit the observations. Of course in time his system was vindicated because the discovery of the general principle of gravitation made it possible to subsume the otherwise ad hoc mechanisms under a universal law and hence to remove that degree of freedom from the theory.

The lesson for imagery is clear enough. In order for a theory of imagery to be principled it is necessary to locate the knowledge-independent functional properties correctly. We must be critical in laying a foundation of cognitively impenetrable functions to serve as the basic architecture of a formal model. The reason is not simply that in this way we can get to the most primitive level of explanation: It is rather that we can only get a principled and constrained (and therefore not ad hoc) model if we first fix those properties which are the basic functional capacities of the system. This does not mean, of course, that we must look to biology to provide us with a solution (though we can use help from all quarters), because the fixed functional capacities can be inferred behaviorally and specified functionally, as they are when the architecture of computers is specified. But it does mean that unless we set ourselves the goal of establishing the correct functional architecture or medium in order to properly constrain our models in the first place, we could well find ourselves in the position of having as many free parameters as we have independent observations.

Reference Notes

1. Bannon, L. *An investigation of image scanning.* Unpublished doctoral dissertation, Department of Psychology, University of Western Ontario, London, Canada, 1981.
2. Spoehr, K. T., & Williams, B. E. *Retrieving distance and location information from mental maps.* Paper presented at the 19th annual meeting of the Psychonomic Society, San Antonio, Texas, November 1978.
3. Kosslyn, S. M., Reiser, B. J., Farah, M., & Fliegel, S. L. *Generating visual images.* Unpublished manuscript (submitted for publication).

References

Anderson, J. R. Arguments concerning representations for mental imagery. *Psychological Review*, 1978, *85*, 249-277.

Arbib, M. *The metaphorical brain.* New York: Wiley, 1972.

Attneave, F. How do you know? *American Psychologist*, 1974, *29*, 493-499.

Chomsky, N. Rules and representations. *The Behavioral and Brain Sciences*, 1980, *3*(1), 1-62.

Finke, R. A. The functional equivalence of mental images and errors of movement. *Cognitive Psychology*, 1979, *11*, 235-264.

Fodor, J. A. The appeal to tacit knowledge in psychological explanation. *Journal of Philosophy*, 1968, *65*, 627-640.

Fodor, J. A. *The language of thought.* New York: Thomas Y. Crowell, 1975.

Fodor, J. A. Methodological solipsism considered as a research strategy for cognitive psychology. *The Behavioral and Brain Sciences*, 1980, *3*(1), 63-110.

Forster, K. I. Accessing the mental lexicon. In R. J. Wales & E. Walker (Eds.), *New approaches to language mechanisms.* Amsterdam: North-Holland, 1976.

Fraisse, P. *The psychology of time.* New York: Harper & Row, 1963.

Ghiselin, B. *The creative process.* New York: New American Library, 1952.

Hays, J. R. On the function of visual imagery in elementary mathematics. In W. G. Chase (Ed.), *Visual information processing.* New York: Academic Press, 1973.

Harman, G. *Thought.* Princeton, N.J.: Princeton University Press, 1973.

Haugeland, J. The nature and plausibility of cognitivism. *The Behavioral and Brain Sciences*, 1978, *2*, 215-260.

Hebb, D. O. Concerning imagery. *Psychological Review*, 1968, *75*, 466-477.

Hinton, C. H. *The fourth dimension.* London: George Allen & Unwin, 1906.

Howard, I. P. Recognition and knowledge of the water-level principle. *Perception*, 1978, *7*, 151-160.

Kosslyn, S. M. Scanning visual images: Some structural implications. *Perception & Psychophysics*, 1973, *14*, 90-94.

Kosslyn, S. M. The information represented in visual images. *Cognitive Psychology*, 1975, *7*, 341-370.

Kosslyn, S. M., Ball, T. M., & Reiser, B. J. Visual images preserve metric spatial information: Evidence from studies of image scanning. *Journal of Experimental Psychology: Human Perception and Performance*, 1978, *4*, 46-60.

Kosslyn, S. M., & Shwartz, S. P. A data driven simulation of visual imagery. *Cognitive Science*, 1977, *1*, 265-296.

Kosslyn, S. M., Pinter, S., Smith, G., & Shwartz, S. P. On the demystification of mental imagery. *The Behavioral and Brain Sciences*, 1979, *2*(3), 535-581.

Kosslyn, S. P., & Pomerantz, J. R. Imagery, propositions, and the form of internal representations. *Cognitive Psychology*, 1977, *9*, 52-76.

Mitchell, D. B., & Richman, C. L. Confirmed reservations: Mental travel. *Journal of Experimental Psychology: Human Perception and Performance*, 1980, *6*, 58-66.

Newell, A., & Simon, H. A. *Human problem solving.* Englewood Cliffs, N.J.: Prentice-Hall, 1972.

Newell, A., & Simon, H. A. Computer science as empirical inquiry. *Communications of the Association for Computing Machinery*, 1976, *19*, 113-126.

Paivio, A. U. Images, propositions and knowledge. In J. M. Nicholas (Ed.), *Images, perception, and knowledge.* Dordrech Holland: Reidel, 1977.

Palmer, S. F. Fundamental aspects of cognitive representation. In E. H. Rosch & B. B. Lloyd (Eds.), *Cognition and categorization.* Hillsdale, N.J.: Erlbaum, 1978.

Pinker, S. Explanations in theories of language and of imagery. *The Behavioral and Brain Sciences*, 1980, *3*(1), 147-148.

Pylyshyn, Z. W. What the mind's eye tells the mind's brain: A critique of mental imagery. *Psychological Bulletin*, 1973, *80*, 1-24.

Pylyshyn, Z. W. Imagery and artificial intelligence. In W. Savage (Ed.), *Perception and cognition: Issues in the foundations of psychology.* Minneapolis: University of Minnesota Press, 1978.

Pylyshyn, Z. W. The rate of "mental rotation" of images: A test of a holistic analogue hypothesis. *Memory & Cognition*, 1979, *7*, 19-28. (a)

Pylyshyn, Z. W. Validating computational models: A critique of Anderson's indeterminacy of representation claim. *Psychological Review*, 1979, *86*, 383-394. (b)

Pylyshyn, Z. W. Cognitive representation and the process-architecture distinction. *The Behavioral and Brain Sciences*, 1980, *3*(1), 154-169. (a)

Pylyshyn, Z. W. Computation and cognition: Issues in the foundations of cognitive science. *The Behavioral and Brain Sciences*, 1980, *3*(1), 111-132. (b)

Pylyshyn, Z. W., Elcock, E. W., Marmor, M., Sander, P. Explorations in perceptual-motor spaces. In *Proceedings of the second international conference of the Canadian Society for Computational Studies of Intelligence.* Toronto, Canada: University of Toronto, Department of Computer Science, 1978.

Richman, C. L., Mitchell, D. B., & Reznick, J. S. Mental travel: Some reservations. *Journal of Experimental Psychology: Human Perception and Performance*, 1979, *5*, 13-18.

Shepard, R. N. Form, formation, and transformation of internal representations. In R. L. Solso (Ed.), *Information processing in cognition: The Loyola Symposium.* Hillsdale, N.J.: Erlbaum, 1975.

Shepard, R. N. The mental image. *American Psychologist*, 1978, *33*, 125-137.

Shulman, G. L., Remington, R. W., & McLean, J. P. Moving attention through visual space. *Journal of Experimental Psychology: Human Perception and Performance*, 1979, *15*, 522-526.

Received October 11, 1979
Revision received January 20, 1980 ∎

Seeing and Imagining in the Cerebral Hemispheres: A Computational Approach

Stephen M. Kosslyn
Harvard University

Visual recognition, navigation, tracking, and imagery are posited to share certain high-level processing subsystems. In the first part of this article, a theory of some of these subsystems is formulated. This theory is developed in light of an analysis of problems that must be solved by the visual system and the constraints on the solutions to these problems; computational, neurological, and behavioral constraints are considered. In the second part, inferences about perceptual subsystems are used to develop a theory of how mental images are generated. Support for this theory is adduced from studies of split-brain patients and a review of relevant neuropsychological findings. In the third part, a computational mechanism is developed to account for how visual function becomes lateralized in the brain; this mechanism is used to predict how the hypothesized processing subsystems become lateralized. In the fourth part, some critical tests of the theory of lateralization of perceptual processing subsystems are reported, and in the fifth part the theory is extended to account for the lateralization of image-transformation subsystems. In the sixth part, the theory is used to account for the almost ubiquitous variability (both between subjects and within subjects) evident in the neuropsychological literature on lateralization. Finally, in the concluding part of the article, the computational-neuropsychological approach is discussed and evaluated.

There has been great interest in how the two cerebral hemispheres are specialized for visual processing since the time of John Hughlings Jackson, who in 1864 speculated that the right hemisphere is specialized for perception (Jackson, 1864; see also Jackson, 1874/1915). Theories of visual specialization, following the fashion in neuropsychology, have tended to focus on various dichotomies; for example, the right hemisphere has been said to be specialized for information about global shape and the left hemisphere specialized for information about details (see Bradshaw & Nettleton, 1981; Springer & Deutsch, 1981). This strategy, which attempts to discover a dimension that will capture differences in processing, has much to recommend it. Indeed, if there are general principles that distinguish types of processing systems, then those systems should be char-

acterizable in terms of sets of such dimensions. However, the dimensions that have been explored to date have not been closely related to theories of processing systems and generally have not been well motivated. Rather, the dimensions chosen typically are selected on the basis of intuition and apparent descriptive power.

In this article I present an alternative way of attempting to understand visual hemispheric specialization. This approach is based on the idea of "natural computation" (see Marr, 1982), in which we try to understand the brain in terms of processing subsystems that interpret and transform data in various ways. The theory developed here focuses on high-level visual processes. High-level visual processes operate on perceptual units that correspond to objects and parts thereof. Thus, high-level visual processing in perception occurs after bottom-up figure/ground segregation and parsing (which is done purely on the basis of stimulus properties). The present focus is on high-level processing in part because it is this sort of processing, as opposed to low-level, sensory visual processing, that is most obviously lateralized (e.g., see Kitterle, 1986; Moscovitch, 1979; Ratcliff, 1982; Sergent, 1982).

On this characterization, then, high-level visual processing is involved in visual recognition, navigation, tracking, and mental imagery. Of particular interest in this article are questions about how experience plays a role in the organization of such visual functions in the two cerebral hemispheres. In developing this theory I will make use of neurophysiological and neuroanatomical data from humans and nonhuman primates, computational constraints, and behavioral data from human subjects.

Visual Perception and Visual Imagery

Before starting to formulate a theory of how a function might be carried out by the brain, it is useful to begin by considering

This work was supported by Office of Naval Research Contract N00014-85-K-0291, National Institutes of Mental Health Grant MH39478-01, and a grant from the Sloan Foundation.

I wish to thank the following people for critical readings of earlier drafts of this paper (none of whom necessarily endorses any of these ideas): Jonathan Amsterdam, Carolyn Cave, Rex Flynn, Jerry Feldman, Jacob Feldman, John Gabrieli, Howard Gardner, Harold Hawkins, Jerry Kagan, Steve Kearns, Bill Milberg, David Mumford, Steve Pinker, Jim Roth, Anne Sereno, George Smith, Michael Van Kleeck, Eric Wanner, and Bob Wurtz. I also wish to thank Brenda Milner and Graham Ratcliff, who provided the initial inspiration for this project (through no fault of their own); Joyce Tang, who provided valuable editorial assistance; and Yadin Dudai, who brought my attention to Descartes' ideas about practice effects. Finally, this project profited from conversations with Mike Gazzaniga, Mortimer Mishkin, and Leslie Ungerleider.

Correspondence concerning this article should be addressed to Stephen M. Kosslyn, Department of Psychology, Harvard University, 33 Kirkland Street, Cambridge, Massachusetts 02138.

the purpose (or purposes) of that function. Vision has two primary purposes. First, we attempt to recognize objects and parts thereof. This function allows us to apply previously gained knowledge to newly encountered objects. For example, once one has recognized something as an apple, one knows that it is edible, has seeds inside, and so on. In order to carry out this function, visual input must be encoded in such a way that it makes contact with the appropriate previously stored information (e.g., see Marr, 1982). Second, we use vision to navigate through space and to track moving objects. In these cases, the goal is not to encode information in order to access relevant memory representations. Rather, the goal is to compute metric spatial relationships and to update them as a person and object or objects move relative to one another.

The purposes of imagery, in large part, parallel those of vision. Perhaps this is not surprising, given that virtually all definitions or characterizations of imagery hinge on its similarity to like-modality perception. For example, visual imagery is usually identified as producing "the experience of seeing in the absence of the appropriate sensory input" or the like. Having a visual mental image produces the conscious experience of "seeing," but with the "mind's eye" rather than with real ones.[1] One purpose of imagery apparently relies on the use of recognition processes to make explicit information stored implicitly in memory. That is, people encode patterns without classifying them in all possible ways; indeed, there may be an infinite number of ways to classify a shape (e.g., in terms of size relative to other objects). In order to make explicit a particular aspect of a remembered pattern, one may form an image and "internally recognize" that aspect of it. That is, one may "recognize" parts and properties of imaged objects that had not been previously considered. For example, consider how you answer the following questions: What shape are a beagle's ears? Which is darker green, a Christmas tree or a frozen pea? Which is bigger, a tennis ball or an orange? Most people claim to visualize the objects and "look" at them when trying to answer these questions, and the behavioral data support this introspection (see Kosslyn, 1980). Imagery is used in memory retrieval when the sought information is a subtle visual property that has not been explicitly considered previously and cannot be easily deduced from other facts (e.g., from information about the category in general; see Kosslyn & Jolicoeur, 1980).

A second purpose of visual imagery parallels the navigation and tracking functions of visual perception. Imagery is a way of anticipating what would happen if a person, or an object or objects, were to move in a particular way. That is, imagery can be used to perform mental simulations, in which one looks to "see" what would happen in the analogous physical situation. For example, one might imagine a jar and "see" whether there is room for it at a given spot on the refrigerator shelf, or one might mentally project an object's trajectory, "seeing" where it will hit. Imagery is apparently used here when one reasons about the appearance of objects as they are being transformed in some way, especially when subtle visual relations are important (cf. Shepard & Cooper, 1982).

Finally, imagery can be used more generally in the service of thinking and learning. Shepard and Cooper (1982) review numerous cases in which "imaged models" were aids to reasoning in scientific problem solving. For example, Albert Einstein claimed that he had his first insight into relativity theory when he considered what he "saw" when he imaged chasing after and matching the speed of a beam of light. Such imagery may be used more generally as an aid to comprehension and planning (cf. Denis, 1982). In addition, imagery can serve as an aid to memory (see Paivio, 1971). For example, the ancient Greeks discovered that imaging objects in a sequence of familiar locations greatly enhances memory for the objects. However, these kinds of uses of imagery seem to rely on the first two uses: In visual thinking, imagery is used as a way of retrieving tacit knowledge from memory and as a way of performing mental simulations. In learning, memory may be improved by having an imaged object simulate (stand in for) the actual object, allowing one to associate a perceptual representation of the object with the relevant context (e.g., that an object is on a list; see Paivio, 1971).

Given the apparent parallels between the purposes of imagery and vision, it is of interest that much empirical research has demonstrated that imagery and like-modality perception recruit some common processing mechanisms (for reviews, see Finke, 1980; Finke & Shepard, 1986; Kosslyn, 1980, 1983; Shepard & Cooper, 1982). For example, if one is holding in mind a visual image (e.g., of a flower), this will impair visual perception more than it impairs auditory perception, but the reverse is true if one is holding in mind an auditory image (e.g., the sound of a telephone ringing; see Segal, 1971; Segal & Fusella, 1970). Perhaps most interesting, manipulating objects in images reveals time-courses like those observed in the real world. For example, Shepard and Metzler (1971) asked subjects to decide whether two three-dimensional multiarm objects were the same or different shape, irrespective of their orientation. The objects were presented at different angular disparities, and decision time was measured. The time to make the decision increased linearly as the angular disparity between two objects increased, and this finding was interpreted as indicating that more "mental rotation" was required to bring the forms into congruence. This and other results (see Shepard & Cooper, 1982) provide strong evidence that subjects perform such tasks by forming a mental image of one object and rotating it until it is at the same orientation as the other. This result is impressive because images are not actual, rigid objects, and hence are not constrained by physics to have to pass through intermediate positions when the orientation of an imaged object is changed.

Similar results are obtained in studies of image scanning. For example, Kosslyn, Ball, and Reiser (1978) asked subjects to close their eyes and imagine a map of a fictional island; this map

---

[1] The term *image* is ambiguous, referring both to a phenomenological experience and to an internal representation (code) that gives rise to this perceptlike experience. In the present theory, "image" refers to the internal representation, not the experience itself. We assume that (for some unspecified reason) the conscious experience accompanies the brain state that functions as an image representation, and thus the experience of "having a mental image" can be taken as a hallmark that the underlying imagery brain state is present.

had seven locations, which were positioned so that there were 21 distinct interlocation distances between all possible pairs. The subjects began by mentally focusing on a given location on the imagined map (e.g., the tree) and then decided whether a second named location was on the map; they were asked to respond in the affirmative only after they had the second object clearly in focus in the mental image. More time was required to scan between pairs of locations that were farther apart on the map, with time increasing linearly with distance, indicating that an imaged map can stand in for the actual one. Kosslyn (1975) reports another finding that is especially suggestive: If an object is imagined at a small size, more time is required to "see" its parts than if the object is imagined at a larger size (see Kosslyn, 1980, 1983). This result is intriguing because it suggests that objects in images are subject to spatial summation (summing over a region of adjacent locations), a well-known property of neural mechanisms used in vision.

Processing Subsystems

Although the behavioral phenomena demonstrate that imagery and like-modality perception share underlying mechanisms, they do not reveal the nature of those mechanisms. However, such data become more illuminating when they are considered in combination with facts about the neural substrate and computational analyses. Indeed, behavioral and neuropsychological data are especially useful in guiding one to formulate what Marr (1982) called a *theory of the computation*. That is, a computation can be regarded as a "black box" that transforms input in a systematic, informationally interpretable way. A theory of a computation is a theory that specifies *what* must be computed and why. Such a theory justifies positing a given computation by an analysis of the problems that must be solved and the requirements for the solution to those problems. The goal of a computation is specified, as well as the nature of the input and constraints on the solution (such as the boundary conditions within which it will succeed). This sort of theory is to be distinguished from a *theory of the algorithm*, which specifies the specific steps actually used to carry out a computation. A theory of an algorithm fleshes out the details of *how* a computation is performed, not what the computation is.

The theory of the computation is of particular importance in formulating theories of *processing subsystems*. A processing subsystem is a functional unit; it is a set of neurons delineated on the basis of what the neurons do. A processing subsystem characterizes a group of neurons that carry out a computation or set of related computations to perform one component of a task. In this article I will focus on delineating subsystems of high-level vision, providing motivation for the hypothesized subsystems by developing theories of the computations they perform. I do not claim that the subsystems formulated here are primitive (the ultimate fundamental building blocks), but rather that they describe correct boundaries of separate subsystems. The strong claim is that although one of the present subsystems might be broken into a number of more specialized subsystems, further subdivision will not result in subsystems that cut across the boundaries of the subsystems posited here. I

adopt a coarse-to-fine strategy, attempting first to discover the rough lay of the land before doing the detailed cartography.

The observation that imagery shares mechanisms with perception implies a remarkable amount about the structure of the information-processing system underlying high-level vision. These implications become apparent when one considers some fundamental problems that must be solved by a visual system. The primate brain has apparently solved these problems in specific ways, and the outlines of these solutions are now apparent in the literature on the neurophysiology and neuroanatomy of visual perception; these solutions have direct implications for a theory of high-level visual processing.

Thus, in the following section I will begin to develop theories of some of the high-level subsystems of the visual system. These theories will be grounded in analyses of three problems that must be solved by any visual system and the apparent solutions to these problems adopted by primate brains.

Three Problems in Vision

The following problems have implications for both low- and high-level vision, but only the implications for high-level perceptual processing will be considered here. The ramifications of this reasoning for a theory of imagery will be explored in the following section.

The Problem of Position Variability

The same object is likely to occur at various positions in the visual field, and hence its image may fall on different parts of the retinae. Nevertheless, once we have seen an object, we can recognize it easily when it subsequently is in a different position in the field (provided, of course, that it is not too peripheral). Logically, there are two ways we could perform this feat. On the one hand, when an object is encoded initially, the visual system could associate a separate representation with each of the possible positions of the object. This seems to be the mechanism suggested by McClelland and Rumelhart (1981) in their theory of word perception. They associate a separate representation of each letter with each position in the field. (This was done so that the same letter could be detected in more than one position in a word.) On the other hand, when an object is encoded initially, it could be stored using representations that are associated with a set of positions in the field. In the limit, only one representation would be used for all positions. This is the solution Marr (1982) offered for the position variability problem. Marr suggested that the appearance of objects is stored in "object-centered" representations. In such representations, the locations of parts of objects are specified relative to other parts, not to positions in space. However, one need not encode an object-centered representation of shape (i.e., in which the parts are related to the object, independent of any particular point of view) to achieve this end; one can also encode a viewer-centered representation of shape (i.e., its appearance when seen at a given angle) but ignore where the shape was positioned in the field (see Jolicoeur & Kosslyn, 1983).

The solution adopted by primate visual systems to the problem of position variability now appears evident in the neurophysiological literature. In order to understand this mechanism, it is necessary first to review some basic findings about neurons that subserve high-level visual processing. It has been found in primates that there are cells in the inferior temporal lobe (area IT) that respond selectively to visual stimuli. Desimone, Albright, Gross, and Bruce (1984) found that about 43% of these cells selectively respond to variations in shape, color, or texture. (This number may be an underestimate, however, because it is possible that some additional, unexposed stimulus would have roused some of the 13% of the cells that were unresponsive, or some of the 14% that were only weakly responsive.) About 30% of the cells appeared to be nonselective, responding about as well to all of the stimuli tested (however, even within this group there was some tendency for stronger responses to complex objects than to slits or edges). Some of the selective cells (about 7%) respond only to hands or faces (see Desimone et al., 1984, p. 2053; Gross, Desimone, Albright, & Schwartz, 1984, p. 300). However, the cells in IT are not usually narrowly tuned for a specific object; most will respond to some degree to any complex visual stimulus. The representation of an object is probably a pattern of activity across these cells, not the activation of a specific detector cell (see Desimone et al., 1984, p. 2061). However, these cells are not arranged retinotopically, unlike those involved in low-level processing (e.g., in primary visual cortex; see Hubel & Weisel, 1977). Rather, the pattern of activation apparently reflects the presence or absence of rather high-level stimulus characteristics. Furthermore, if the inferior temporal lobe is removed, the animals have a severe and permanent impairment in learning to recognize patterns (see Mishkin, 1982). This impairment occurs even though acuity, extent of visual field, and various psychophysical thresholds all remain at normal levels (see Cowey & Weiskrantz, 1967; Gross, 1973; Gross et al., 1984).

It is of interest, then, that visual cells in area IT have very large receptive fields: They respond when a pattern is present over a wide range of positions. The receptive field sizes are often much larger than the median size of about 26 × 26° of visual angle. Furthermore, the most responsive area of the receptive fields of IT cells virtually always includes the fovea and extends 3–20° from the fovea (see Gross, Rocha-Miranda, & Bender, 1972). Thus, if stimuli fall near the center of gaze, differences in the relative responsiveness of different cells will not allow one to infer the location of the stimulus. Gross and Mishkin (1977; see also Gross, Bruce, Desimone, Fleming, & Gattass, 1981) review the relevant literature and conclude that the primate brain's solution to the position variability problem relies on not representing the position of a pattern in the high-level shape representation system. (Incidentally, this is a good example of how facts about the neurological underpinnings of behavior can have direct bearing on theories of cognition; this finding is a significant challenge to some aspects of the McClelland & Rumelhart [1981] model.)

However, primates do know where an object is when they see it. Thus, there must be a separate representation of an object's location, which implies two separate mechanisms: one to represent a shape independently of its position and one to represent its position. And in fact, it has long been thought that *what* and *where* are processed by different systems. For example, Schnei-

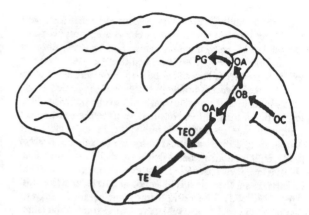

Figure 1. Ventral and dorsal visual systems in the primate brain. (Area IT is roughly equivalent to Areas TE and TEO illustrated here. From "Object Vision and Spatial Vision: Two Cortical Pathways" by M. Mishkin, L. G. Ungerleider, and K. A. Macko, 1983, *Trends in NeuroSciences, 6,* p. 414. Copyright 1983 by Elsevier Publications Cambridge. Adapted by permission.)

der (1967, 1969) found that the fibers running from the eye to the superior colliculus and then to the pulvinar (part of the thalamus) were involved in allowing an animal to orient in the direction of a stimulus, whereas the fibers running from the eye to the lateral geniculate body to striate cortex were involved in allowing an animal to perceive patterns (see also Ingle, 1967). More recently, Ungerleider and Mishkin (1982) summarize evidence for "two cortical visual systems," which are illustrated in Figure 1. Their claim is that the ventral system, running from area OC (primary visual cortex) through TEO down to the inferior temporal lobe, is concerned with analyzing what an object is, whereas the dorsal system, running almost directly from circumstriate area OB to OA and then to PG (in the parietal lobe) is concerned with analyzing where an object is. This parietal system is involved not just in orienting, but in actually forming representations of where objects are in space. The two cortical visual systems are putatively concerned with high-level visual processing and hence are of most interest in this article.

Two sorts of data are relevant to Ungerleider and Mishkin's claim. First, the neuroanatomy and neurophysiology support the proposed dichotomy. There are well-known neural connections running along both pathways, and the visual properties of these areas have been well documented (e.g., see Mishkin & Ungerleider, 1982; Van Essen, 1985). In addition, the visual areas of the parietal lobe appear to have different properties from those of the ventral visual system; for example, they rarely include the fovea in their receptive fields; are sensitive to direction of motion; are not particularly sensitive to size, shape, or color; and some cells in this region respond selectively to an object's location (as gated by eye position, see Andersen, Essick, & Siegel, 1985). Second, behavioral data provide dramatic evidence of the separability of what and where representations and of the critical role of the temporal and parietal lobes, respectively, in computing these representations. In a typical experiment (e.g., see Ungerleider & Mishkin, 1982a), monkeys are tested in an apparatus requiring them to lift up the lid covering one of two food wells placed before them; the task is to learn which of the lids conceals food. In one task, the two lids have different patterns on them, and the patterns are exchanged randomly from trial to trial; the food is always under a specific pattern. In another task, both lids are gray, and a small tower (a "landmark") is placed closer to one lid, with its position being varied from trial to trial; in this task, the food is always under the lid closest to the tower. If the temporal lobes are removed but the parietal lobes are left intact, animals are severely impaired in the first task (requiring them to learn to discriminate between patterns) but are not severely impaired in the second task (requiring them to learn locations). On the other hand, if the parietal lobes are removed and the temporal lobes are left intact, the reverse pattern occurs: The animals are severely impaired in their ability to discriminate on the basis of location but largely retain the ability to discriminate between patterns (see Mishkin & Ungerleider, 1982; Pohl, 1973; Ungerleider & Mishkin, 1982).[2]

The dissociation between what and where is also found in humans following damage to different parts of the cortex. For example, difficulty in localizing stimuli, without difficulty in recognition, is a hallmark of *Balint's syndrome*, which can result from bilateral damage to the parieto-occipital regions of the brain (see De Renzi, 1982, chap. 4). Holmes (1919), for example, reported patients who could recognize objects but could not localize them, as evident by their inability to reach, redirect gaze, estimate distance, or to navigate correctly (some patients kept bumping into things because they failed to realize the direction or distance of objects from themselves; see p. 231). And the reverse deficits also occur. For example, difficulty in visual learning and shape identification, without difficulty in localization, is a hallmark of the *Klüver–Bucy syndrome*, which can result from bilateral temporal lobe damage. In addition, it has been found that visual recognition abilities in humans are particularly sensitive to damage to the right temporal lobe (see Hecaen & Albert, 1978, chap. 4; Jones-Gotman & Milner, 1978; Milner, 1968). Finally, convergent evidence for distinct mechanisms for what and where in normal human subjects was produced by Sagi and Julesz (1985), who used psychophysical techniques to demonstrate distinct processing characteristics of the two systems.

Thus, we begin by hypothesizing a set of subsystems in the ventral system that encode shape. The initial subsystem accepts input from low-level visual mechanisms, and the final one produces a representation of the input shape. This encoding is then used to access stored representations that are associated with an individual part or with the overall shape envelope. In addition, we hypothesize a set of subsystems in the dorsal system that encodes location.

This separation of "what" and "where" leads to difficulties that must be overcome by the system, as is evident when we consider another problem of visual perception.

The Problem of Separate Encodings of Parts

Before one can recognize an object, "figure" must be segregated from "ground"; one must somehow pick out regions that are likely to correspond to distinct objects. The same processes that segregate figure from ground also result in our organizing a single object into its constituent parts (e.g., the arms, legs, and head of a person). There is good evidence that humans parse objects into parts and relationships among them (e.g., see Bower & Glass, 1976; Reed, 1974; Reed & Johnsen, 1975). For example, having seen a Star of David, one can later recognize a triangle as one of its constituent parts much more easily than one can recognize a parallelogram. When the star was first seen, it was organized into separate parts, which were encoded into memory. If a part seen later matches a stored one, recognition is easy; if it does not, recognition is difficult.

And herein lies a problem: If parts are encoded separately, the shape representation system will ignore their locations in the visual field. But the relative locations of parts is an important characteristic of many shapes. This problem will arise whenever one examines an object with multiple eye fixations, with different parts falling on the fovea over time. This problem will also arise even within a single eye fixation if one shifts attention; Moran and Desimone (1985) found that even when a stimulus fell within an IT cell's receptive field, the cell would not respond unless the animal was paying attention to the region where the stimulus appeared. (These animals were trained to fixate and then attend to one of two cued locations.) With either covert or overt (i.e., eye movements) attentional shifts, the representation of the shapes of the parts in the ventral system will not preserve their positions. But one *can* discern the arrangement of parts; the relations must be represented somehow.[3]

This problem can be solved if we allow a minor modification to the Ungerleider and Mishkin (1982) theory: The dorsal system may be used to represent not just locations of objects in a scene, but also spatial relations among parts of a single object. That is, the spatial relations among representations of parts that are encoded over multiple eye fixations may be represented the same way as are the spatial relations among separate objects in a scene. Consider Tyler's (1968) description of a patient with Balint's syndrome, who "could see only one object or part of one object at a time. . . . She reported seeing bits and fragments. For instance, when shown a picture of a U.S. flag, she said, 'I see a lot of lines. Now I see some stars'" (as cited in

---

[2] To my knowledge, a critical experiment addressing this claim has not been done. The question is whether the responses of these cells in IT change when the animal attends to the stimulus in different locations. The receptive fields of the shape-tuned neurons in IT virtually always include the fovea; does the output when a pattern is foveated depend on where the pattern is? If so, then the present conclusion is in jeopardy because shape and location information would be encoded together. But if this turns out to be true, then we must explain why ablation of the parietal lobe, while leaving IT intact, disrupts location learning so severely.

[3] Note that if the whole pattern can be apprehended in one fixation, multiple parts can be grouped into a single pattern and encoded into the ventral system. Evidence that this solution is used was presented by Desimone, Albright, Gross, and Bruce (1984), who found that the responses of "face cells" in IT are virtually eliminated if the features of a stimulus face are scrambled; the cells were responding to the pattern per se. However, if the object subtends too great a visual angle, it will fall on lower resolution parts of the retina and a blurred encoding will result. Thus, this way of encoding relations has only limited value.

Bauer & Rubens, 1985, p. 194). Apparently, this patient's representations of spatial relations were disrupted, resulting in disconnected perceptions of parts. In the experiments investigating pattern discrimination following parietal lesions, the animals have never been required to discriminate among patterns that differ only in the relations among parts; usually stimuli differ in terms of numerous characteristics, and the relations among the parts per se are not important (e.g., as is true for the square and plus signs used by Mishkin & Ungerleider, 1982, the difference between which may be discerned simply by looking in the center of the figure and seeing if there is a line).

One way in which information about shape and location could be coordinated during encoding is suggested by Moran and Desimone's (1985) finding that only stimuli at the location being attended to will drive cells in the inferior temporal lobe. This result can be taken to imply the existence of an "attention window" that selects a region at a lower level of processing (e.g., perhaps area V4, Moran and Desimone, 1985) for further processing (cf. Larsen & Bundesen, 1978; Treisman & Gelade, 1980). The contents of the window are passed down to the temporal lobe. The location of this window would be represented in the dorsal system while the contents of the window are being processed in the ventral system; the contents would be treated the same way in the ventral system, regardless of where the window is positioned. Thus, the attention window would serve to coordinate the dorsal and ventral systems during encoding, keeping a tight linkage between the two systems.

The dorsal system often may be used to represent spatial relations among parts even when the entire object could be encoded in a single fixation. To see why, we must consider other problems faced by the visual system and the requirements on the solutions to these problems. In so doing, we will be led to distinguish between two different processing subsystems in the dorsal system.

The Problem of Irrelevant Shape Variations

In order to recognize an object, one needs to pick out its characteristic properties and ignore irrelevant stimulus variations. In assigning an object to a category, the input must be represented in such a way that it makes contact with the appropriate stored representations. The kind of representation of shape that will best serve these ends depends in part on the nature of the object. Some objects are subject to a nearly infinite number of transformations (e.g., a human body) and so may not look the same from instance to instance, whereas other objects (e.g., a given face) vary little. For example, a human form can be configured in a huge number of different ways, crouching, arms raised, standing on one toe with the arms held out to the side, and so on. Similarly, letters of the alphabet can occur in numerous fonts, which are not simple transformations of each other. One cannot store a separate representation of all the possible configurations of most mutable objects, with the aim of being able to match input to a specific stored representation: There usually are simply too many possible configurations, and one often may encounter configurations not previously seen. Thus, for such objects it is useful to have a representation that will be stable across a wide range of transformations.

Two kinds of attributes remain constant under such transformations. First, the characteristic parts remain the same; although some may be hidden depending on the configuration, none are added or deleted from the object. Second, the topological relations among parts remain constant under all of these transformations. Topological relations are more abstract than the precise relative position of two parts as they appear in any given case (i.e., the topographic relations); they indicate which parts are connected to each other and which are contained within each other. For example, the topological relation between the arm and shoulder remains constant under all of the different positions the arm can take. However, literally topological relations are too weak; a teacup and a phonograph record are identical under a topological description. The relations of ears to the side of the head, or the thumb to a hand, are important and will remain constant under transformations. Thus, some general categories of relations, such as "top/bottom," "side of," "connected to at the end" and so on, must be used, not the actual topographic appearances (cf. Ullman, 1984).

Thus, this problem places requirements on what the dorsal system must do. This system must be able to derive a description of relations that will remain constant under a large number of ways of configuring an object; the dorsal system must be able to make use of more abstract, categorical representations. Such representations capture general properties of a relation without specifying the details (e.g., "next to" without specifying how much or exactly what angle). They are *categorical* in the sense of specifying that a relation is a member of a relatively broad equivalence class. These sorts of representations are particularly useful for specifying the relations among adjacent parts, with each relation being relative to a specific pair of parts. This kind of "local coordinate system" is useful for building up complex descriptive structures of flexible, multipart objects (cf. Marr, 1982). We can therefore posit a subsystem that computes a categorical spatial relation among perceptual units (parts or objects).

In contrast, there are other types of objects that would not be usefully represented for recognition using categorical relations. These objects do not vary much from instance to instance and have spatial relations among parts that differ only subtly from those of similar objects. For example, simply knowing that a person's eyes are next to each other, and are above the nose, which is above the mouth and so on, will not serve to allow one to recognize that particular face. Rather, one needs to know the actual metric spatial relations among the parts. For this sort of recognition problem, a metric coordinate representation of the locations of parts is very useful. This sort of representation specifies the coordinates of objects or parts relative to a single origin, which could be centered on an object or space (allocentric coordinates) or on one's body (egocentric coordinates); this is a "global coordinate system" because a single origin is used to coordinate multiple parts or objects. This representation provides information needed to compute second-order metric relations, such as ratios of distances among pairs of parts, which may be useful for recognizing faces and the like (e.g., see Diamond & Carey, 1986). In addition, a *coordinate* representation of this kind is especially useful for navigation, in which one needs to know where an obstacle is actually located, not just that it is against a wall or next to some object. In climbing a rocky path, one wants to know how far away two rocks are, and whether the gap between them is large enough to accommodate one's foot. We can therefore hypothesize a subsystem that computes coordinate spatial relations.

Thus, the present hypothesis is that distinct subsystems operate to compute categorical and coordinate representations of spatial relations. Both sorts of representations are presumably computed on the basis of spatiotopic "maps" of object and part locations that are available in both cerebral hemispheres (cf. Andersen et al., 1985; De Renzi, 1982; Ratcliff, 1982). That is, one needs to know where objects and parts are in actual space, not merely where their images fall on the retina. In order to generate such spatiotopic maps, one must combine information about the location of the attention window in the retinotopic maps of low-level vision with information about eye position, head position, and body position (cf. Andersen et al., 1985). This computation is sufficiently complex to warrant being carried out in a separate subsystem. This subsystem produces the representations that serve as input to the spatial relations subsystems, which in turn compute representations that make different information explicit as required for specific purposes in later processing.

Finally, given that we can recall where parts belong on objects, there must be an *associative memory* in which parts are associated with locations. The arrangement of parts is an important aspect of shape, and hence we expect the two sorts of information to come together at some stage in processing. A possible locus of this nexus is the association cortex near Wernicke's area (in the posterior, superior temporal lobe), which appears to be involved in semantic processing. However, this sort of arrangement is somewhat awkward in that the relations must be delivered in synchrony with the related perceptual units; if the inputs fall out of phase, one may make "illusory conjunctions." That is, one may conjoin units using the wrong relations. Interestingly enough, Treisman and Schmidt (1982) report just such illusory conjunctions when the system is pushed to perform well in a difficult task. These sorts of errors are rare, however; apparently, focusing one's attention on a stimulus will serve to link the units with the proper locations, thereby keeping the shape and location encoding processes coordinated (cf. Treisman & Gelade, 1980).

Components of Image Generation

One of the most obvious facts about mental images is that we do not experience them all of the time. When we need an image, it is generated on the basis of stored information. For example, if you are asked to describe the shape of Snoopy's ears, you probably form an image of the dog's head; but you probably did not have the image until you tried to answer the question. The image comes to mind, is generated, only when you need it. The image is a transient representation in short-term memory that is generated on the basis of information stored in long-term memory. It seems safe to assume that visual images are formed on the basis of representations that initially were encoded during perception; even an image of a novel shape must be composed of previously encountered components. If so, then we are

in a position to exploit the analyses presented in the previous section to formulate a theory of the processing subsystems used to generate images; we need not simply make up the theory out of whole cloth, but can build on our previous reasoning.

Subsystems Used in Image Generation

Our analyses of the solutions to problems in visual perception lead us to posit two subsystems that are used to generate mental images which rely on the perceptual subsystems. First, we can assume that information about shape is stored during perception. A processing subsystem must exist to activate this stored visual information, producing a pattern of activation in a structure Kosslyn (1980) called the *visual buffer;* this pattern of activation is an image representation. The pattern of activation in the visual buffer makes explicit the spatial properties of a shape, which is required to accomplish the purposes of imagery discussed earlier. The visual buffer is assumed to be a functionally defined storage medium that probably corresponds to the joint operation of at least some of the numerous topographically organized areas of cortex (see Van Essen, 1985; Van Essen & Maunsell, 1983). We hypothesize that these visual parts of cortex also can be activated from stored information, resulting in a mental image. This buffer is equivalent to the buffer that supports Marr's (1982) "2½ D sketch" in vision. Kosslyn (1980) called the image activation subsystem the PICTURE process.

When we see patterns, we actively organize and parse them into separate perceptual units, and these units are stored (e.g., see Reed, 1974; Reed & Johnsen, 1975). Multiple eye fixations are used when we inspect most objects, and hence the units will be stored as separate encodings (as was argued in the previous section). Thus, the processing subsystem that activates stored visual information will activate representations of individual previously encoded perceptual units. Activating a stored unit will result in an image of a single part or in a low-resolution image of the entire object, provided that such a unit was encoded. A single encoding of an entire object will be at a low resolution either because it was seen at such a large visual angle that some portions fell into the periphery or it was seen at such a small visual angle that not all of the parts were distinguishable.

If the relations among units are stored using categorical representations, then other subsystems must be used if a multipart or detailed object is to be imaged. One must access the descriptions of parts and their relations and use this information to juxtapose separate parts in the correct relative positions in an image. For example, in generating a detailed image of a car, one might access "front wheel" and discover the location description "under front wheelwell." (Such a categorical representation would be used because the precise locations of parts are not useful for recognition, given the variability in the appearances of cars.) According to Kosslyn's (1980) theory, one typically first activates a low-resolution image of the overall shape of the object (a "skeletal image"), which provides the reference points for details, should they be required to perform a given task. However, a sequence of images of individual segments can also be formed, each one being appropriately linked to the previous one.

Categorical representations specify relative positions. Thus, if such representations are stored, one must know the location of a reference point in order to add a part to a multipart image (e.g., the wheelwell for a car's wheel, or the shoulder for an arm); the reference point is a foundation part onto which another part is attached. Only after locating the foundation part will one be able to position another part correctly in an image. In order to locate a foundation part, a stored relation representation must be used to position the attention window in the correct location, so that the appropriate shape is sent to the shape-encoding subsystems for encoding into associative memory for recognition. We can therefore hypothesize a subsystem that accesses and interprets location-part descriptions and uses this information to position the attention window correctly. Kosslyn (1980) called this subsystem the PUT process.

Once the attention window is focused on the appropriate foundation part (e.g., the location of the wheelwell on the car's body, where the front wheel belongs), the description of the relation ("under") must be used to compute where a part should be positioned relative to the foundation part. This activity can be accomplished exactly the same way the attention window was positioned to find the foundation part, but now it is located where the to-be-imaged part belongs. Once the attention window is correctly positioned, the subsystem that activates visual memories can form an image of the new part at the attended location, in the correct relation to the foundation part. The image is formed by forcing a change of state in the visual buffer in the attended region, which can then be reprocessed as if it were perceptual input (e.g., the shape could be recategorized), thereby accomplishing the purposes of imagery that parallel those of perception (see this article's first section). This same mechanism could be used for priming in perception and could produce visual hallucinations if the input from memory was so strong that it overwhelmed perceptual input. Indeed, if the present approach is correct, the main difference between attentional priming, imagery, and hallucination may be the strength of the input to the visual buffer from memory (for evidence consistent with this notion, see Farah, 1985).

Neuropsychological Evidence for the Subsystems

If the theory of processing subsystems used in image generation is correct, we should be able to find a sort of brain damage that leaves some of the subsystems intact while disrupting the others. Farah (1984) analytically reviewed the clinical case studies of individuals who suffered brain damage and lost the ability to use mental images. She found that the ability to inspect objects perceptually could be intact even when patients apparently could not generate mental images. More recently, Farah, Levine, and Calvanio (in press) found a brain-damaged patient who had no difficulty recognizing objects but had great difficulty generating mental images. On the other hand, Jones-Gotman (1979) describes a patient who apparently could form images but could not encode them into memory. Thus, it would appear that the subsystems that encode and interpret patterns are in fact distinct from those that generate images. However, the available case studies are not sufficient to tell us about the underlying structure of the generation process itself.

One form of evidence that image generation is carried out by multiple subsystems would be a selective dissociation between the tasks that can be performed by the two hemispheres. For example, if both hemispheres can generate images of single-part objects, but only the left hemisphere can also generate images of nonrigid multipart objects, this would suggest that an additional subsystem or subsystems is used to generate images of these multipart objects. And in fact, a simple idea leads us to expect just this selective dissociation between the hemispheres: Language processing involves accessing and interpreting categorical representations, and so does the subsystem that accesses and interprets categorical representations to arrange parts in the appropriate locations in an image. Therefore, we can hypothesize that because language processing is typically better in the left cerebral hemisphere, perhaps the subsystem that accesses and interprets categorical relations to arrange parts would also be better in the left hemisphere. In contrast, we have no reason to expect lateralization of the subsystem that activates visual memories or of the subsystems that encode shape.

Thus, we began by investigating a prediction that was counterintuitive to many, namely that the left hemisphere should be better than the right at selected image-generation tasks (for details, see Kosslyn, Holtzman, Farah, & Gazzaniga, 1985). This prediction was especially interesting because, according to common wisdom, the right cerebral hemisphere is the seat of mental imagery (e.g., see Bradshaw & Nettleton, 1981; Ehrlichman & Barrett, 1983; Ley, 1979; Springer & Deutsch, 1981). Thus, if it can be shown that the left hemisphere is actually able to perform a wider range of imagery tasks, this will be particularly dramatic evidence of the usefulness of the computational approach. (The FIND process described by Kosslyn, 1980, and Kosslyn, Holtzman, Farah, & Gazzaniga, 1985, has now been replaced by the shape-encoding and location-encoding subsystems working in conjunction with the attention window and associative memory; the following discussion is recast slightly from that of Kosslyn, Holtzman, Farah, & Gazzaniga, 1985, in order to use these additional distinctions.)

Imagery Validation

We first showed that imagery was required to perform a task that should recruit all of the image-generation processing subsystems. The task was to decide from memory whether uppercase letters of the alphabet are composed of all straight lines (e.g., K, L) or have some curved lines (e.g., B, R). Our demonstration used the selective interference logic developed by Brooks (1968), Segal (1971), and others. These researchers showed that imaging and perceiving in the same modality interfere with each other more than do imaging in one modality (e.g., visualizing a flower) and perceiving in another (e.g., listening for a tone). We used a technique developed by Brooks: He asked subjects to visualize block letters and then to classify the corners (working clockwise around the letter) according to whether they were on the extreme top or bottom of the letter. For each corner, subjects were to respond by saying either yes or no aloud (as appropriate) or by pointing to Y or N on a page, working down crooked columns of the letters over the course of the task. Having to look for and point to the letters was much more difficult in this task than merely saying yes or no. In contrast, in another task subjects formed auditory images of spoken sentences and decided whether each word was a noun or not. Now saying the responses was harder than pointing to them. Thus visual perception interfered more with visualizing, and talking (and hearing) interfered more with auditory imaging.

We made use of Brooks' task to garner evidence that the straight/curved letter judgment requires imagery. College students read down a column of lowercase letters and made the straight/curved judgment about the corresponding uppercase versions. These subjects were asked to respond either by putting a check mark in the appropriate location on the page (which required looking for the place to respond) or by saying the response aloud. Looking and making check marks required more time, even though making check marks in isolation actually took less time than saying the response. These results in conjunction with Brooks' findings implicated imagery in this task (see Kosslyn, Holtzman, Farah, & Gazzaniga, 1984).

The next task was to demonstrate that images of uppercase letters are generated a segment at a time. This was important because the theory says that the PUT subsystem is only used when separate parts must be amalgamated into a composite image. We reasoned that people have seen so many uppercase letters that they typically do not image a particular one actually seen when asked to image a letter. When the reader images an uppercase *a*, it probably is not one actually seen (e.g., on the first page of yesterday's newspaper); rather, a prototypical *A* is probably imaged. We assume that the characteristic features of *A*s have been abstracted out, with the units being stored as prototypes and the relations as categorical representations. For example, for *A* two long lines and one short line might be stored as parts, and the categorical relations would specify something like "the two long lines meet at the top and are separated at the bottom; the short line connects the two long lines roughly half way down." (Although English is used to write the description here, I assume a more abstract code is used in the brain.) Such a description will represent the vast majority of exemplars of the category.

To test the claim that images of letters are created one segment at a time, Kosslyn, Backer, and Provost (1985; see also Kosslyn, Cave, Provost, & von Gierke, 1986) showed subjects two X marks in an otherwise empty 4 × 5 grid and asked them whether both Xs would fall on a given uppercase letter if it were present in the grid (as the letter appeared when it was actually presented previously). If the segments are imaged individually, then some will be present before others. If so, then the time it takes to affirm that the X marks would fall on the letter will depend on the location of the segments on which they fell. And indeed, the location of the X marks proved to be critical in the imagery condition, with more time being required for marks that fell on segments located toward the end of the sequence of strokes typically used to draw it.

A number of control conditions were devised to ensure that image generation, and not image inspection after the letter was formed, was responsible for the effects. In one, there were no effects of the position of segments in the hypothesized generation sequence (i.e., the typical drawing sequence) in a corresponding perceptual condition, when subjects actually saw the letters filling in the grid. In another, the ordinal position of segments in the hypothesized generation sequence predicted times better than did measures of the actual distance, which should have been correlated with times if images were scanned during inspection (see Kosslyn, 1980, chap. 3). (In fact, actual distance was correlated with times in a condition in which subjects were explicitly instructed to scan along their images.) In a third control experiment, subjects were asked to fixate their attention on the center of the grid. This manipulation was intended to impair scanning and did in fact succeed in eliminating all effects of distance per se; nevertheless, the effects of the position of segments in the hypothesized generation sequence were preserved.

The upshot of the preliminary work, then, was that images of uppercase letters are usually generated one part at a time, which presumably involves processing categorical relations among the parts, and that imagery is used to decide if named uppercase letters have any curved lines. The weak link here, of course, is the assumption that because letters are imaged a part at a time, they must be imaged on the basis of a stored categorical representation. There is a computational argument in support of this assumption, based on the large variability among instances of letters (as noted above), but it is enough simply to point out that if the experiments had not come out as predicted it may have been because this assumption was faulty.

An Image-Generation Deficit

Thus, we began by investigating whether both hemispheres of patient J. W. could perform the straight/curved imagery task. J. W. had his corpus callosum sectioned about 3 years prior to our testing because of severe intractable epilepsy; he has been extensively tested and his right hemisphere is capable of comprehending involved verbal instructions and of making simple deductions and classifications (see Sidtis, Volpe, Wilson, Rayport, & Gazzaniga, 1981, for further details).

In order to isolate performance to a single cerebral hemisphere, we asked J. W. to stare straight ahead at an asterisk on a screen and flashed lowercase letters 1.5° to the left or the right side of this fixation point. The construction of the retina and optic nerve ensures that such a lateralized stimulus is exposed to only one hemisphere, given that the corpus callosum is severed and hence interhemispheric communication is precluded. We asked J. W. to identify the lowercase letter and to decide whether the corresponding uppercase version had any curved lines. He pressed one button if he thought the uppercase letter had curves, and another if he thought it had only straight lines. He used his left arm for all responses (due to ipsilateral efferents, both hemispheres can control the major arm movements; fine motor movements are controlled only by the contralateral hemisphere).

The task, then, requires use of seven abilities (each of which is presumably carried out by a host of processes): First, the lowercase letter must be *encoded;* second, it must *access* the representation of the corresponding uppercase version in associative memory; third, the image of the uppercase version must be *generated;* fourth, the image must be *retained* long enough to be judged; fifth, the image must be *inspected;* sixth, a *judgment* must be made; and seventh, a *response* must be produced. Our first goal, then, was to demonstrate that the right hemisphere had a deficit in performing the task, and then to show that it was due to a problem in image generation per se. Following this, we sought to implicate a specific dissociation between the hypothesized subsystem that accesses and interprets categorical representations to arrange parts and the other hypothesized subsystems.

The results from the straight/curved imagery task were straightforward: In the first experiment, J. W.'s left hemisphere made straight/curved judgments perfectly, but his right hemisphere was accurate on only 70% of the trials; in the second experiment, the left hemisphere was perfect, and the right was accurate on only 65% of the trials. A number of control experiments were conducted to implicate a deficit in image generation per se. In one, we lateralized uppercase letters and asked J. W. to perform the judgment on the actual stimuli. Both hemispheres were virtually perfect (correct on at least 97.5% of the trials). Thus, both hemispheres could encode the letters, inspect them, make the judgment, and produce correct responses. In another control, we lateralized the lowercase versions and simply asked J. W. to select the corresponding uppercase version from the alphabet, which was displayed in free view. Both hemispheres were virtually perfect and thus the right could access the cross-case representation. Indeed, both hemispheres could even draw the uppercase letters (using contralateral hands) after seeing the lowercase cue, even when the hand was obscured from view (drawing under a table).

In another control, we lateralized three-letter words; the words were composed of uppercase letters (e.g., MUG). J. W. was then cued 2 s later as to which letter (first, second, or third) to classify as being straight or curved. Both hemispheres could do this task; in fact, the hemispheres performed as well as when the cue was given beforehand, and no imagery was required. Thus, the problem was not that the right hemisphere could not retain the image long enough to inspect it, nor was the problem that it could not inspect images.

Thus, we were able to demonstrate that the right hemisphere could perform all of the subtasks except image generation. However, additional possible accounts needed to be eliminated. Perhaps the right hemisphere could not combine subtasks. So, in another control, we showed pairs of letters, one uppercase and one lowercase (both drawn at the same size); on half the trials the uppercase was on the left side, and on half it was on the right side. The slides were lateralized so that only one hemisphere saw the pair. We asked J. W. to point to the uppercase version and to classify it. His right hemisphere clearly knew the differences between cases and could do a two-step task. The word-retention task described in the previous paragraph also required integrating multiple steps (encoding the stimulus, retaining an image, selecting the correct letter, inspecting the image, judging the shape, and responding). Thus, the right hemisphere did not suffer from an impairment in combining subtasks in general.

Alternatively, perhaps the lowercase stimulus somehow interfered with the uppercase task (e.g., it produced a kind of Stroop situation). In order to rule out this possibility we read the letters aloud to J. W. (and thus both hemispheres knew which letter was being queried). The pair "X O" or the pair "O X" was then presented to a single hemisphere. The task was to point to the

place on the screen where the X had been if the uppercase letter had only straight lines and to the location where the O had been if the uppercase letter had any curves. Again, the left hemisphere was virtually perfect (95% correct), whereas the right hemisphere was at chance (52%). Thus, the right hemisphere's poor performance was not due to a conflict between the visible lowercase version and the imaged uppercase version.

Both hemispheres could perform the judgment on visible stimuli, could perform it when the image was simply retained from external input, could make the association between upper- and lowercase, and could perform tasks of similar complexity involving selecting a case and making the judgment. And the right hemisphere's difficulty in performing the imagery task did not appear to lie in understanding the instructions; the other multistage tasks had comparably difficult instructions, and J. W.'s right hemisphere has been shown to understand complex instructions in other tasks (see Sidtis et al., 1981). Nor did its problem lie in combining subtasks or in having interference from the lowercase stimuli themselves. It appeared that J. W.'s right hemisphere simply could not generate images of the letters.

A Selective Image-Generation Deficit

The results described so far serve only to demonstrate an image-generation deficit in J. W.'s right hemisphere. They do rule out a deficit in the shape-encoding subsystems, given the good performance when images need not be generated, and previous work by Holtzman (1984) ruled out a deficit in the subsystems that actually shift attention; he found that J. W.'s right hemisphere is very effective at using cues to move his eyes to specific locations. However, we needed evidence that the deficit was in the subsystem that accesses and interprets categorical relations to arrange parts and not in the subsystem that activates visual memories, that the deficit was not simply in image generation in general. In order to implicate a deficit in using the subsystem that accesses and interprets categorical representations to arrange parts, we needed to show that both hemispheres can form images when this subsystem is not required. The subsystem that accesses and interprets categorical representations is only required when multipart images are generated; it is not required to generate images of the general shape of an object, if such a shape was encoded as a single low-resolution perceptual unit.

In fact, we discovered that both of J. W.'s hemispheres could perform tasks requiring the imaging of overall, general shapes: In one, we asked each of J. W.'s hemispheres to decide which of two similar-sized objects (e.g., goat vs. hog) was larger, a task previously shown to require imagery (see Kosslyn, 1980, chap. 9, for a detailed model of how this task is done). J. W. stared at a central fixation point, and a word was presented to one side or the other. If a goat was larger than the animal named by the word, he pushed one button; if the word named an animal larger than a goat, he pushed the other button. Both hemispheres performed this task virtually perfectly (only one error occurred during the entire session), with no significant difference in either the error rates or response times.

The ceiling effects observed in the size comparison experiment could conceal possible differences between the hemispheres. Thus, we conducted another experiment that required imaging single shapes. This task required the subject to decide whether named objects (e.g., book, nose, buckle) are taller than they are wide. The stimuli used here made this a rather difficult task. J. W. could perform this task equally well in both hemispheres, although neither hemisphere was near ceiling levels of performance. Both of the overall shape tasks require the subsystem that activates visual memories (to generate images of the overall shapes of the objects) and the shape-encoding and location-encoding subsystems (we assume that size is represented in the spatiotopic map and that the categorical relation "larger" can thereby be computed). Because no parts need to be added to the overall shape to perform either task, the subsystem that accesses and interprets categorical representations to arrange parts is not necessary, and the right hemisphere can accomplish the tasks by activating a single stored representation of an object's appearance. (Incidentally, these results are also important because they show that the right hemisphere's problem is not simply in processing letters, which are linguistic materials.)

We also conducted another task that we expected to require the subsystem that accesses and interprets categorical representations to arrange parts. This task made use of exactly the same stimulus materials used in the size-judgment task, which both hemispheres performed superbly. J. W. was asked to decide whether or not the named animals have ears that protrude above the top of the skull (e.g., an ape and a sheep do not, a cat and a mouse do). One response button was labeled with an inverted U (representing the top of the animal's head) with a triangle sticking above it; the other had the inverted U with a small u hanging down. The names of the animals were presented to the individual hemispheres, and they categorized the animals' ears. (J. W. lived on a farm and is quite familiar with animals.) The left hemisphere was correct on 87.5% of the trials, whereas the right hemisphere was correct on only 45% of the trials.

A second split-brain patient, V. P., was also tested. She too showed a right-hemisphere deficit in generating images of letters. In her case, however, she eventually was able to form such images—but only of the letters she had previously practiced imaging. This apparent practice effect is difficult to interpret because V. P. has some spared fibers in her callosum (as we discovered after testing was finished), in her splenium (which is involved in the transfer of visual information), and in the rostral area (which may be involved in the transfer of semantic-information). J. W., in contrast, has a completely transected callosum.

According to the present view, then, the right hemisphere has difficulty in performing certain imagery tasks because it has a deficient subsystem that accesses and interprets categorical representations to arrange parts. In addition, we must assume that J. W.'s right hemisphere is deficient at devising alternative strategies. The fact that J. W. could draw the uppercase letters when a cue was given to the right hemisphere indicates that the representation was present, and that another access subsystem could retrieve it. Nevertheless, it took considerable training before J. W.'s right hemisphere learned to use drawing as a way of accessing information about a letter's shape (see Kosslyn, Holtzman, Farah, & Gazzaniga, 1985). The fact that this hemisphere

could do single-part imagery tasks shows that the problem was not simply in its ability to understand the task, or in difficulties in forming images in general.

J. W. has a very unusual right hemisphere (see Sidtis et al., 1981). It has good comprehension of language and can even read. This hemisphere appears to be unusual only in how much more it can do than most other right hemispheres, and hence it is impressive that even it cannot generate multipart images. Nevertheless, it is a special case, and we should be cautious in generalizing from it. Thus, it is important that there is converging evidence from other sources, both from brain-damaged populations and normal subjects.

Convergent Evidence in the Literature

Our interpretation of the results just described rests on the idea that separate representations of units and relations are used in image generation. There is now considerable support for this claim in the neuropsychological literature. Particularly compelling is a case study by Deleval, De Mol, and Noterman (1983). This patient experienced impaired imagery following left-hemisphere damage and claimed that (translated by Farah et al., in press),

> When I try to imagine a plant, an animal, an object, I can recall but one part, my inner vision is fleeting, fragmented; if I'm asked to imagine the head of a cow, I know that it has ears and horns, but I can't revisualize their respective places. (p. 71)

Grossi, Orsini, and Modafferi (1986) also describe a case in which there appears to be a deficit in arranging parts in an image following left-hemisphere damage (although impaired imagery per se was not definitively implicated in their studies). Farah et al. (in press) describe a similar left hemisphere-damaged patient who had a deficit in generating images, as indicated by tasks that had been previously validated to require imagery.

Similarly, there is additional evidence that the left hemisphere is critically involved in generating multipart images. In her excellent analytical review, Farah (1984) found that damage to the posterior left hemisphere was strongly correlated with loss of imagery in the case study literature (see also Farah et al., in press). In addition, Farah (1986) asked normal subjects to use imagery as a prime in a task that required discriminating among various symbols; the imaged primes were more effective in the right visual field (left hemisphere) than vice versa, which is consistent with the idea that this hemisphere is better able to generate multipart images. Cohen (1975) obtained very similar results in a task requiring normal subjects to form an image in preparation for making a normal/mirror-reversal judgment about letters.

Perhaps the most striking clinical support for the claim that shape and spatial relations are processed by separate mechanisms in imagery is provided by Levine, Warach, and Farah (1985). They found two patients with complementary imagery disorders: One could image shape but not locations, and the other could image locations and spatial relations but not shapes. Both patients had similar impairments in imagery and perception. The shape disorder followed damage to the temporo-occipital regions, whereas the spatial relations disorder followed damage to the parieto–occipital regions. Levine et al. (1985) make the point that although patients who have both imagery and perceptual deficits tend to have the same type of deficit in both kinds of processing, one can have an imagery deficit without a perceptual one or vice versa. If the present theory is correct, damage to low-level perceptual subsystems (e.g., those concerned with figure/ground segregation) should impair perception while sparing imagery, whereas damage to the categorical relations-encoding, coordinate location-encoding, and shape-encoding subsystems should affect both imagery and perception. Similarly, damage to the subsystem that accesses and interprets categorical representations to shift attention should impair both functions. In contrast, damage to the subsystem that activates visual memories to form an image should disrupt imagery but have only subtle effects on perception.

Mechanisms of Hemispheric Differentiation

The results from our studies of image generation hint that hemispheric specialization will be understood not in terms of general dichotomies among types of materials or tasks (e.g., see Bradshaw & Nettleton, 1981; Springer & Deutsch, 1981), but in terms of the underlying structure of information processing. However, our predictions rested on only a vague notion of the principles of lateralization; we hypothesized that the subsystem that accesses and interprets categorical relations to arrange parts would be lateralized on the left because it seemed similar to processes involved in language. In order to develop a theory of how visual functions are lateralized, we must have a more explicit theory of the lateralization principles. Thus, in this section I develop a computational mechanism to account for hemispheric specialization. This mechanism will lead us to make predictions about the lateralization of additional subsystems, will help us to account for much of the data in the literature, and—perhaps most important—will allow us to explain the variability in laterality so evident in the literature.

Four Macroproperties of the Brain

Why should one expect lateralization of any function? The present hypothesis follows from a theory of the mechanisms that result in an individual's experiences shaping the functional organization of the two hemispheres of the brain. This theory rests on a set of four relatively simple macroproperties of the brain. These properties are functional characterizations of the activity of populations of neurons; there are many ways in which individual neurons could act to produce these macroproperties, but we need not be concerned with these details for present purposes. These macroproperties are relatively uncontroversial; what is original here is putting them together and observing the consequences as they interact. The relevant properties are as follows:

Processing Subsystems

As a working hypothesis, I have assumed that the brain is functionally organized into a collection of separate processing subsystems. This assumption has proven to have considerable empirical utility, but can also be defended on a number of other grounds. First, detailed studies of the neuroanatomy and neurophysiology of the brain indicate that (at least some) different areas are involved in performing specialized functions (e.g., such as those discussed earlier in this article). The various input and output projections define distinct areas, some of which have been identified with specific functions (e.g., for visual processing see Cowey, 1985; Van Essen, 1985; Van Essen & Maunsell, 1983). Second, the notion of distinct processing subsystems is supported by the subtle and distinct patterns of behavioral dysfunction following brain damage (e.g., see Heilman & Valenstein, 1985; Luria, 1980). Presumably, the behavioral deficits reflect damage either to some of the subsystems proper or to their interconnections (cf. Geschwind, 1965). Third, logically, some operations must be performed before others. For example, "figure" must be parsed from "ground" before a representation of the shape of a stimulus can be formed, and a representation of the shape must be formed from the input before memory can be entered and the stimulus recognized. Because these functions are often very different, it is more efficient to have separate processing subsystems for each one; computer programmers have long since discovered that there is an enormous trade-off between the generality of a program and its complexity: all other things being equal, special-purpose programs are virtually always simpler than more general ones. Fourth, a functional componential structure makes sense if the system evolved piecemeal, with new subsystems being added, or old ones being modified, to work with those already available. A modularized system is easiest to alter, which is one reason why modularization is a hallmark of good computer programming.

Exercise

A processing subsystem is a functional description of a neural network. If such a network operates on the same pattern of input repeatedly, the subsequent internal pattern of activation and subsequent output will come to be achieved more quickly or more reliably. (Such practice effects presumably reflect actual physical changes at the cellular level, which either alter outputs from single cells or alter the number of cells that are activated; the present theory does not hinge on the precise underlying mechanism, only the emergent property.) This observation goes back at least as far as Hebb (1949) and probably to Descartes. (In Section 42 of his *Passions of the Soul,* originally published in 1649, Descartes claimed that the "pores of the brain through which the spirits previously made their way . . . have thereby become more apt than the others to be opened in the same way when the spirits again flow towards them" [pp. 343–344].) However, it is important to distinguish between simple activity in a network and actual successful computation. The present claim is that if the output from a neural net is actually used, then the weights among (i.e., strengths of) connections in the network are altered so that the network produces the output faster and with less noise (greater strength) when the input recurs in the future. This constraint ensures that neither random, resting-level activity nor "spread of activation" during access (e.g., see Anderson, 1983) will alter the network. (Note again that "connection" and "weight" are functionally defined; a functional connection may correspond to numerous neural connections and a functional weight may result from numerous properties of these connections.)

When one considers how to implement a computer simulation model of this principle, one is immediately faced with the problem of how a processing subsystem "knows" that its output was subsequently used downstream. At least in vision, a solution to this problem is suggested by the neuroanatomy. A fundamental fact about the anatomy of the visual system is that most of the pathways have both afferent and efferent tracks (Van Essen, 1985; Van Essen & Maunsell, 1983). In fact, the pathways running in each direction are typically of comparable size, which implies a rich exchange of information in both directions. This property of the system could be used in part as a way of providing reinforcement, training the subsystem that produced the output. Because training requires selectively altering weights on the connections that were used to produce the output, it requires a broad bandwidth. (For examples of computational models of this type of learning, see Hinton & Anderson, 1981, and Rumelhart & McClelland, 1986.) Such a mechanism provides a means whereby a processing subsystem can become increasingly efficient at carrying out a specific computation. This kind of modification with use plays a special role with subsystems that encode information: Feedback will train these subsystems to be sensitive to useful patterns in the environment; this process allows such subsystems to be *adaptive filters*, becoming tuned for useful information. This process will be at the heart of our theory of the mechanism of lateralization.

Transhemispheric Degradation

As discussed earlier in this article, researchers have recorded the responses of single high-level visual cells in the inferior temporal lobe (in monkeys); any given cell, obviously, is located in one cerebral hemisphere. One finding not previously mentioned is that when a stimulus is delivered directly to the hemisphere being monitored (i.e., is presented in the contralateral visual field), the cell is driven more strongly than when the stimulus is delivered to the other hemisphere and information must be passed over the major commissures (particularly the corpus callosum; e.g., see Gross et al., 1972; Schwartz, Desimone, Albright, & Gross, 1984).

This result may be due in part to the two hemispheres' sharing a common pool of activation. Holtzman and Gazzaniga (1982) found that as more stimuli (geometric shapes) were stored in one hemisphere of a split-brain patient, fewer could be stored in the other hemisphere; this finding was later replicated with words as stimuli in a larger number of subjects (M. S. Gazzaniga, personal communication, 1985). This result is particularly impressive because each hemisphere was completely ignorant of the information stored in the other. This interaction between the hemispheres suggests that a single, limited pool of activation is drawn upon by both hemispheres, and if one draws a proportionally large amount of activation, less is available for the other (cf. Kinsbourne, 1973, 1975; Kinsbourne & Hiscock, 1983). If so, then the hemisphere that receives input directly may draw more activation (rather like the way in which

using a toaster will draw more current from the power grid), leaving less for the other hemisphere.

"Central" Bilateral Control

Some activities involve coordinating rapid sequences of precise, ordered operations that extend over both halves of the body. In such cases, one does not want each hemisphere to pursue its own agenda; one needs a single set of commands for both halves of the body. These commands could simply be duplicated in each hemisphere and then initiated in tandem; however, given the physical separation of the hemispheres, it would be difficult to keep the subsystems synchronized. This problem is particularly severe in cases where open-loop commands are used, and feedback is not used to keep track of the output and to adjust the commands accordingly. These ideas imply that a relatively rapid, ordered sequence of precise operations that extend over both halves of the body will be executed in a single locus; the subsystems that actually perform the operations on a given side of the body can be thought of as slave processes, being directed by the unilateral controller. I hypothesize that the "central" bilateral control subsystems are innately lateralized, which ensures that one locus will have control over both sides (for related ideas, see Gazzaniga & LeDoux, 1978; Geschwind, 1976; Kimura, 1976, 1977; Levy, 1969; Mateer, 1978; Nottebohm, 1970, 1979; Summers & Sharp, 1979; Sussman & Westbury, 1978; Zangwill, 1976).

A Snowball Mechanism

These four properties of the brain operating together appear to be sufficient to produce functional differentiation between the two hemispheres. I assume that the infant is innately lateralized, but that lateralization of all functions is not complete; in particular, differentiation in visual hemispheric specialization progresses over age and experience, as the child has occasion to develop and use speech and to learn his or her way about the environment (cf. De Renzi, 1982, chap. 2; Witelson, 1977). The mechanism underlying this sort of differentiation depends critically on the property of bilateral control. I posit two innately lateralized unilateral control subsystems, one for each hemisphere, which will come to serve as the initial seeds (in a catalytic sense) in the differentiation process. Let us consider each hemisphere in turn.

Left Hemisphere Specialization

According to the present theory, one key to hemisphere specialization is the existence of a "central" bilateral control subsystem. Thus, it is necessary to begin with a brief review of the evidence both for such a subsystem to control speech and for an innate bias to use this system in (typically) the left hemisphere.

A unilateral speech output controller. The speech output mechanism is one example of a system that should have "central" bilateral control. When one is speaking fluently, substantial portions of an utterance are prepared in advance; one does not wait for each sound to be made before deciding on the next one. This inference is supported in part by the kinds of speech errors we make, such as scrambling the order of syllables and even words that are separated in the speech sequence; such errors should not occur if one is reading out words one at a time, with no preplanning of the entire utterance (see Dell, 1985; Garrett, 1982). In addition, this notion is supported by Sternberg, Monsell, Knoll, and Wright (1978), who found that the time to begin speaking increased linearly with the number of stressed syllables in the utterance, which suggests that the entire command is planned before production starts. Thus, one does not want to have to formulate instructions for the left and right sides of the speaking apparatus separately, synchronizing two sets of commands. Rather, it would be desirable to have a single speech output control subsystem that sends commands to the mouth, tongue, and vocal apparatus on both sides of the body to produce a string of phonemes. There is, in fact, good evidence that the area that controls speech output is on only one side of the brain (typically the left) and is situated near the motor strip (precentral gyrus; e.g., see Benson, 1967; Mazzocchi & Vignolo, 1979; Naeser, Hayward, Laughlin, & Zatz, 1981).

The idea of unilateral speech output control receives additional support using the logic of the exception that proves the rule. Consider four cases studied by Jones (1966). These patients all stuttered, and all had speech processing in both cerebral hemispheres (as indicated by sodium amytal injections, which selectively "put to sleep" one hemisphere at a time). Following surgery to remove left frontal lobe abnormalities, all patients stopped stuttering. This result is consistent with the idea that these patients stuttered because their speech was produced using two controllers, which were falling out of synchronization. Following surgery, one of the controllers presumably was removed, and hence the remaining one took over and eliminated the stuttering (see also Travis, 1931; for a brief review of relevant findings, see Corballis, 1981).

The present hypothesis is not only that a single subsystem is used to control speech movements on both halves of the body, but that the brain is innately biased to use the output controller in the (typically) left hemisphere. That is, in principle one could simply alternate between the left and right sides, controlling any single utterance from only one side. The present claim is that this does not occur; the brain favors one side. The notion that language functions are innately lateralized is supported by numerous results. For example, Molfese and Molfese (1979, 1980) found that the left hemisphere is predisposed to discriminate speech sounds even in very young infants, as indicated by selective auditory-evoked responses recorded from the scalp over the left hemisphere (see also Crowell, Jones, Kapuniai, & Nakagawa, 1973; Davis & Wada, 1977, 1978; Entus, 1977; Molfese, Freeman, & Palermo, 1975, but also see Vargha-Khadem & Corballis, 1979, for a failure to replicate Entus, 1977).[4] Additional support for an innately lateralized language mechanism on the left side comes from studies of infants who had their left hemispheres removed early in life. These people have subtle language deficits even into adulthood (see Day & Ulatowska, 1979; Dennis & Kohn, 1975; Dennis & Whitaker, 1976). Even when the left hemisphere was removed prior to 1 year of age, 10 years later there was a deficit in understanding reversible passive sentences (Dennis & Whitaker, 1976). However, there is generally remarkable recovery in most aspects of language in such

cases, especially if the left hemisphere is damaged or removed prior to 20 to 36 months of age; this observation led Lenneberg (1967) to posit that the lateralization of language occurs between 20 and 36 months. These results suggest that the left side typically is innately specialized for some aspects of language, but that, if need be, the right side can substitute at an early age but will not be quite as effective (cf. Witelson, 1977). According to the present theory, then, the infant is innately biased to use the control system in the (typically) left hemisphere; in most cases, until about 2 years of age a homologous mechanism on the other side may be recruited if necessary.[5]

The snowball effect. We begin with the claim that speech output is produced using a single control subsystem. To the extent that only the left hemisphere's control subsystem is used, lateralization will occur; the other three macroproperties of the brain will produce a snowball effect. Initially, there are subsystems in both hemispheres that produce instructions for (i.e., provide input to) the speech output controller. Even a single-word utterance is the result of such instructions to the output control subsystem. Using the speech output control subsystem will selectively draw activation (typically) to the left hemisphere. Input to this subsystem will result in feedback being sent to the sender subsystems. However, because the speech output controller is drawing activation to the left side, the feedback that must cross to the other side will be degraded. (It may be even more degraded if evoked by a degraded input, but we do not need to make this assumption to see how the mechanism works.) Hence, training the relevant links in the network is less effective, and the subsystem on the right side will receive less exercise than the corresponding one on the left side.

Thus, in the future the instruction-producing subsystems on

---

[4] These results indicate that some aspects of speech perception are innately lateralized, which at first glance seems to contradict the present claim that the output control mechanism is what is innately lateralized. However, the speech perception and production mechanisms are not independent. Logically, an infant can learn how to pronounce the phonemes of the surrounding language only after hearing them pronounced by others (cf. Teuber, 1978). Furthermore, the motor theory of speech perception posits that the same innate code used in speech perception is also used by the articulatory apparatus (see Liberman & Mattingly, 1985). This theory is supported by the finding that hearing a sound repeatedly not only adapts the perception of that sound but also alters how one pronounces it (Cooper, 1974). Particularly telling is the finding that electrical stimulation of Broca's area not only disrupts speech but also the ability to make voluntary facial movements and the ability to discriminate among phonemes (Ojemann & Mateer, 1979). In short, according to the present theory speech perception mechanisms are innately lateralized because speech perception and production share some common components, which are lateralized in order to coordinate the two sides of the articulatory apparatus during speech production.

[5] Dennis and Whitaker (1976) found that even children who had a hemispherectomy at a very young age had an apparent deficit in syntax (comprehension of reversible passives) 10 years after the left hemisphere was removed. This result may suggest that the left-hemisphere controller is favored because it is more effective. The controller presumably draws on mechanisms used in both production and perception. For example, perhaps there is a limited-capacity buffer that is used during production to hold a preprogrammed instruction set before execution and is also used for parsing the input.

the same side as the dominant speech output controller will, via the property of exercise, become more effective. They will produce better output, including that which serves as feedback upstream. And here begins the snowball: These subsystems will now fill the role of seed subsystems. That is, the subsystems that feed them, such as those that access associative memory for stored phonemic instructions (used when one wants to say a word), will in turn become better on the left side. And every time a word representation is used, its representation becomes stronger. Words name classes of entities, and hence categorical representations are ideally suited to be attached to names and used to represent word-concepts in associative memory. If so, then the result of the snowball effect should be that subsystems that produce or use categorical representations, which are usually associated with words, should in general eventually become stronger in the left hemisphere. And, subsystems that make use of subsystems that make use of such representations in turn should eventually become more efficient in the left hemisphere. This general notion is supported by evidence from studies of stroke patients and split-brain patients that the left hemisphere has a special role in arithmetic and inference (see Heilman & Valenstein, 1985; Luria, 1980).[6]

Thus, the theory rests on the ideas that (a) only one "central" control subsystem is used for an utterance, and one side is innately more likely to be used; (b) sender processing subsystems on the other side receive degraded feedback from the lateralized target control subsystem (because that hemisphere is less activated), and hence training is less effective than it is for the corresponding sender subsystems on the same side; and (c) these initially lateralized subsystems then serve as second-order seeds, providing more effective feedback to subsystems on the same side that send them input, and this effect is compounded, resulting in other subsystems becoming more effective on the same side as the second-order seed.

This mechanism, then, will cause the left hemisphere to become specialized for using categorical representations. Consider again when such representations will be usefully employed. I earlier argued that these representations are well suited for specifying pairwise relations among parts (e.g., a hand is connected to a wrist, a wrist to a forearm, etc.) and are especially useful for representing nonrigid objects because they preserve the structure as the object flexes, bends, or moves. Thus, such representations will be useful for storing prototypical descriptions of an object's parts and how they are arranged; many researchers in artificial intelligence and cognitive science have argued that such representations are stored for use during recognition (e.g., see Ballard & Brown, 1982; Latto, Mumford, & Shah, 1984; Marr, 1982; Palmer, 1977; Winston, 1975). If so, then subsystems that produce such representations will become stronger on the left side, following the logic of the snowball effect.

Thus, the snowball mechanism leads one to expect three kinds of lateralization of visual processing in the left hemisphere. First, the categorical relation-encoding subsystem will become very effective because it produces representations that will correspond to those stored in left-hemisphere associative memory. This subsystem will become reinforced for encoding information that is useful for subsystems further downstream.

Second, the shape-encoding subsystems on the left side will become more effective at producing representations of easily categorized (and named) shapes. That is, the output from this subsystem is sent to an associative memory containing word-concepts, which are more easily applied to some shapes than others (e.g., Jolicoeur, Gluck, & Kosslyn, 1984). Thus, feedback will train the left ventral system to be adept at encoding easily categorized shapes.

Third, the subsystem that accesses and interprets categorical representations to shift attention will become more effective on the left side. If this subsystem is effective in its attempt to access appropriate information in associative memory, it will receive feedback. Because the appropriate information is more likely to be stored in the left hemisphere, the subsystem will become more effective in the left hemisphere. This left-hemisphere specialization leads us to expect the findings on image generation described in the previous section.

Right Hemisphere Specialization

The snowball mechanism will also produce right-hemisphere specialization, starting with a different initial seed subsystem. We again begin by considering a likely candidate for the role of an innately lateralized seed.

A unilateral search controller. The principle of unilateral control of rapid, bilateral operations, also applies to our control of rapid shifts of attention over a scene. This sort of visual search is used in navigation, when one is systematically examining the environment as one is moving. For example, when a person is driving, he or she systematically scans the environment, not simply shifting attention to a single place but setting up a sequence of such shifts. Indeed, when the driver notices something, the scan pattern may have moved on, and he or she will do a double take, returning to the point of interest. In such cases, one does not want to have to coordinate corresponding operations in the two sides of the brain. That is, a search path can cross the midline and hence fall under the purview of the contralateral hemisphere. But one does not want each hemisphere to have its own agenda; one wants a coordinated search plan extending across the entire field. Nor does one want duplicate sets of instructions in both hemispheres, which would have to be tightly synchronized. Rather, one wants a single locus of control for rapid, coordinated programming of the slave subsystems that position attention in each hemisphere. (Note that this reasoning applies only to rapid sequences; there is no reason why a number of different subsystems cannot program single shifts of attention.)

Thus, it is not surprising that in most right-handed males, one hemisphere—typically the right—appears to have a special role in controlling such visual search (e.g., De Renzi, 1982).[7]

---

[6] After writing this, I discovered that Levine (1982, p. 659) had independently formulated a similar proposal.

[7] Unlike the speech output control mechanism, there is still debate over the special role of the right hemisphere in attention allocation (for a review, see De Renzi, 1982). Some have suggested that the locus of the search control is not innately specified but is usually located on the right side because language functions have recruited the corresponding

This controller cannot be localized with certainty to any particular structure; however, for my purposes it is enough to be able to localize this controller to the right hemisphere. This control function must be distinguished from a wide range of other attentional functions; at present there are at least four loci, presumably subserving different functions, implicated in attentional shifts: the posterior parietal lobe, the frontal lobes, the limbic system, and the reticular activating system (see Heilman, Watson, & Valenstein, 1985; Mesulam, 1981; Posner, Inhoff, Friedrich, & Cohen, 1985). Not all of these mechanisms need be lateralized, or need be lateralized in the same way.

Evidence from studies of brain-damaged children is consistent with the idea that there is an innate bias to control such rapid search paths in the right hemisphere, although the extant literature is more suggestive than compelling. Indeed, the best that can be said is that the available findings do not contradict the present hypothesis. For example, Kohn and Dennis (1974) tested children who had suffered damage to the right hemisphere prior to 1 year of age and who subsequently had that hemisphere removed. Many years later these children had difficulty with the Semmes map-reading test, which requires extrapersonal spatial orientation. Similarly, Woods and Teuber (1973) found that patients who suffered brain damage as children showed more severe deficits in performance scores on the Wechsler Intelligence Scale for Children (WISC) if they had damage to the right rather than left hemisphere (see also Rudel & Denckla, 1974; for a review of relevant findings, see De Renzi, 1982, chap. 2).

The snowball effect. The theory of right-hemisphere development is analogous to the theory of left-hemisphere development. In this case the property of "central" bilateral control underlies a unilateral locus for one component of our attentional mechanism, namely that involved in controlling rapid systematic search patterns over space. If the dominant bilateral search controller is on the right side, then subsystems on the right side that provide it with instructions will receive better training than those on the left side. The instructions to the search controller are based in part on information about the locations of objects, which helps one decide where to look next for a path. As a person moves around familiar environments such as the home, location information will be stored. This stored information will later be used to help one navigate (e.g., to set up a route when entering a room), and hence will be used to compute search patterns. Thus, this information will come to be stronger in the right-hemisphere associative memory. Thus, whereas the left-hemisphere associative memory develops a catalog of categorical representations useful for language, the right will tend to develop encodings of shape and spatial relations that are useful for navigation.

The logic of the snowball mechanism leads us to expect lateralization of three kinds of visual processing in the right hemisphere. First, the coordinate location-encoding subsystem will become more effective in this hemisphere. Coordinate representations of locations are more useful for navigation than are categorical representations; navigating between objects requires encoding the actual metric relations between them. For purposes of navigation, generalization over a class—one of the virtues of categorical representations—is a decided drawback; one needs to know about the specific case, not its general category. Thus, the output from the coordinate location-encoding subsystem will be useful for setting up instructions for the control subsystem, and hence this subsystem will be trained, and such training will be more effective on the right side. If so, the right hemisphere should become more adept at encoding subtle metric spatial relations.

Second, the shape-encoding subsystem on the right side will become trained to encode shapes as they appear at a particular time. One wants to know the shape of an object as it appears from a particular point of view in order to reach it or avoid it, as appropriate. Rather than producing a representation likely to correspond to a name, the goal here is to encode how an object or part is positioned in space. These representations are useful both for parts (as when one reaches for a handle of a drawer) and for entire objects (as when one is walking through a room).

The reason for positing separate categorical relation-encoding and coordinate location-encoding subsystems is that they perform qualitatively different computations; the first takes two locations and produces a categorical relation between them, whereas the second takes one or more locations and produces their coordinates relative to a single origin. In contrast, the left and right shape-encoding subsystems perform the same computation, producing a representation of shape for higher level processing; the only difference is that the right-sided subsystem comes to be more narrowly tuned, whereas the left-sided subsystem funnels a range of shapes into a single representation. Hence, I do not posit two distinct types of shape-encoding subsystems.

Third, again mirroring the logic of left-hemisphere development, the right hemisphere should become better at accessing stored coordinate representations and using them to position attention at a specific location. This should be true not only when rapid sequences of attentional shifts are programmed, requiring the attention search controller, but also when only a single shift is made (which does not require the controller because it does not require tight synchronization across the midline). In other words, there should be an analogue to the subsystem that accesses and interprets categorical representations to arrange parts in images; this analogous subsystem uses stored coordinate representations rather than categorical representations and should be more effective in the right hemisphere. This hypothesis was not expected in advance but rather was a consequence of the reasoning described here.

This notion leads one to expect that the right hemisphere will be better at top-down examination of previously seen pictures. In these cases, it will be better at directing attention to precise locations where specific objects or parts thereof should be found. In addition, this idea leads to an unexpected prediction: The right hemisphere should be better at constructing images

portions of the left hemisphere (see Bradshaw & Nettleton, 1981; Gazzaniga & LeDoux, 1978). Note also that the sort of process discussed here should be distinguished from processes that specifically disengage attention, which do not seem to have a "central" controller (Posner, Inhoff, Friedrich, & Cohen, 1985).

of multipart objects when coordinate representations are used to position parts. That is, if the right hemisphere becomes better at positioning the attention window to precise locations during perception, it should also be better at doing so during imagery and should be able to position imaged objects in a scene or parts on an object if coordinate locations are stored (which is likely if the spatial relations are important and subtle, as is true for faces). Finally, because the slave subsystems that actually move the attention window will be used equally often by other subsystems in both hemispheres, they should not become lateralized.

The present conception of right-hemisphere function bears on an intriguing finding in the clinical literature. Damage to the right parietal lobe can result in a patient's ignoring the left half of space. Damage to the left parietal lobe infrequently produces this deficit, and when it does the impairment is much more transient (see De Renzi, 1982). Neglect of the left side of space following damage to the right parietal lobe occurs not only in perception, but also in visual mental imagery (see Bisiach & Luzzatti, 1978; Bisiach, Luzzatti, & Perani, 1979). For example, Bisiach and Luzzatti (1978) asked such patients to imagine standing on one end of a plaza and describe what they could "see" in their images. The patients named buildings to the right side of their vantage point in the image but neglected buildings to the left. Then the patients were asked to imagine standing on the opposite end of the plaza, facing their previous position. The patients now named the buildings previously ignored (which now were to their left side) and neglected those just named (which were now to their right side).

The neglect syndrome is enormously complex and can occur following lesions to a number of different systems (see Mesulam, 1981). Thus, it is unlikely that any single account will cover all of its facets. However, Ratcliff (1982, p. 324) offers the outlines of an explanation for one form of neglect that is consonant with the present approach. Ratcliff suggests that neglect may reflect disruption of the process that sets up search patterns. His idea is that the right-hemisphere search mechanism deals with both sides of space, whereas the left hemisphere deals only with the contralateral parts of space. Thus, right-hemisphere damage disrupts searching the left part of space, but not the right because the left-hemisphere system can take over here. Left-hemisphere damage, in contrast, leaves the bilateral right-hemisphere system intact and thus does not usually produce neglect. This notion fits the present claim that the right hemisphere has a visual search control subsystem that coordinates search over both sides of space.

As will be discussed in the section on variability, these are modal expectations that may be violated in a given individual depending on a number of factors that influence the progression of the snowball lateralization process.

Neuropsychological Evidence for Specialized Representations of Spatial Relations

The analyses in the first part of this article led to the hypothesis that the brain computes two different kinds of spatial-relation representations. As discussed in the previous section, if each type of representation is computed by a separate processing subsystem, then the snowball mechanism predicts that the

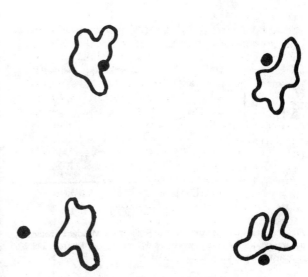

Figure 2. Examples of stimuli used in the Kosslyn, Barrett, Cave, and Tang (1986) study.

two subsystems will become lateralized. The left hemisphere should become more effective at assigning a spatial relation to a category, such as "outside of" or "attached to," whereas the right hemisphere should become more effective at representing locations using a metric coordinate scheme that specifies distances effectively. If data are found supporting this hypothesized lateralization of function, they would not only illuminate the nature of hemispheric specialization but would also provide evidence for the existence of two distinct processing subsystems.

Kosslyn, Barrett, Cave, and Tang (1986) tested the hypothesis that categorical relations are computed better in the left hemisphere whereas coordinate relations are computed better in the right hemisphere. In the first experiment, subjects (normal college students) were shown stimuli like those illustrated in Figure 2. These stimuli were line drawings of blobs, with a dot being either on the line or outside of it. The subjects were asked to fixate directly ahead, and a stimulus was presented 1.5° to the left or right of fixation in a tachistoscope. Two groups were tested, differing only in the instructions given to the subjects. One group was to respond "true" if the dot was on the line and "false" if it was off the line. The other group was to respond "true" if the dot was within 2 mm of the line (including being on the line), and "false" if it was farther than 2 mm from it (subjects were shown a sample 2-mm distance at the beginning of the experiment). Our prediction was that the left hemisphere would be more effective at categorizing the dot/line relation as on or off, whereas the right hemisphere would be more effective at representing the metric spatial information.

As is evident in Figure 3, these predictions were borne out: The on/off judgment was easier when the stimuli were presented to the left hemisphere, whereas the near/far judgment was easier when the stimuli were presented to the right hemisphere. The near/far task was also easier in general, which may simply reflect the particular stimuli we used (the discrimination was relatively easy over the distances we used).

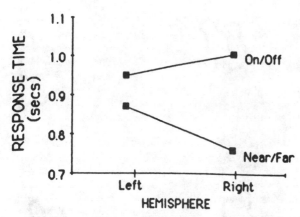

Figure 3. Results of the experiment in which subjects judged whether a dot was on or off a blob or whether a dot was near or far from a blob (Kosslyn, Barrett, Cave, & Tang, 1986).

A second experiment was conducted to provide convergent evidence for the claim. This time, subjects saw stimuli consisting of a plus and a minus sign, placed side by side. On half the trials the plus was to the right of the minus, and on half the trials it was to the left; in addition, on half of each of these types of trials the stimuli were less than 1 in. apart, whereas on the other half they were greater than 1 in. apart. Subjects again began each trial by fixating straight ahead, and a pair of stimuli was lateralized. Two groups again were tested, differing only in the instructions administered. One group was asked to decide whether the plus was to the right of the minus. We expected the left hemisphere to be better at this sort of categorical judgment. The other group was asked to decide whether the stimuli were greater or less than an inch apart. We expected the right hemisphere to be better at this sort of metric judgment. These expectations were confirmed, as is illustrated in Figure 4.

In short, we have evidence that the two hemispheres have different facility in computing categorical and coordinate representations of spatial relations. This finding is, of course, consistent with the finding that the left hemisphere is better at using categorical relations to place parts correctly in an image. In addition, our claim is consistent with the finding that the left hemisphere can encode line orientation better than the right hemisphere when only vertical, horizontal, or 45° diagonal orientations are used (all of which are easy to categorize), whereas the right hemisphere is better than the left when nonstandard (and difficult to categorize) oblique orientations are used (Umilta et al., 1974). When a categorical representation can be used, the left hemisphere is better; when a coordinate representation is more useful, the right hemisphere is better.

Similarly, the current results are consistent with findings on the ability of patients to recall dot location. Taylor and Warrington (1973), Warrington and Rabin (1970), and Hannay, Varney, and Benton (1976) all found that left-hemisphere damage disrupts dot localization more than right-hemisphere damage does. Ratcliff and Davies-Jones (1972) did not find this difference, but this null finding may have been a consequence of the task being too easy; when Hannay et al. (1976) used a more

difficult version of the task, the right hemisphere-damaged patients were again inferior. However, it is worth noting that the literature on dot localization in normal subjects is not so coherent; the right-hemisphere advantage is not consistently observed (e.g., see Bryden, 1976). We will shortly address possible bases for this sort of inconsistency in the literature.

Image Transformations

Our analysis of visual image transformations begins with the observation that different processes are useful for accomplishing different types of tasks. Some image transformations involve adding or deleting parts of an object or scene or juxtaposing two things in a novel way. For these sorts of transformations, if the parts or objects are stored in memory as separate perceptual units, the transformation can be accomplished by letting an initial image fade and then generating a new image of the object at a different position or size. Kosslyn (1980) called this a *blink transformation* because the object is altered in a discrete step. For example, this sort of transformation is useful if one wants to imagine what a person would look like riding an elephant, or if one wants to know how a lion would look with rabbit ears. If the present theory is correct, and if blink transformations require the image generation-processing subsystems, then they should be especially difficult in the right hemisphere.

In contrast, the present theory leads us to expect that other transformation tasks cannot be accomplished by letting an initial image fade and generating a new version of the object or scene. In particular, blink transformations should be difficult or impossible when the image is to be altered in a way that distorts the foundation parts, making it difficult or impossible to locate where to-be-altered parts should be added, deleted, or changed. In such cases the imaged object is apparently transformed by incrementally altering the metric spatial relations within and among parts in the image, monitoring the appearance as it changes. Kosslyn (1980) called these kinds of alterations *shift transformations*. Shift transformations are useful when one is mentally simulating movement and monitoring coordinate spa-

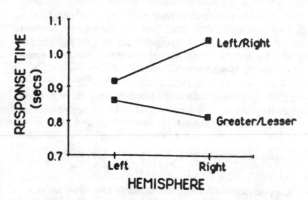

Figure 4. Results from the experiment in which subjects judged whether a minus sign was to the left or right of a plus sign or whether a minus sign was within an inch of a plus sign (Kosslyn, Barrett, Cave, & Tang, 1986).

tial relations, such as occurs when one projects oneself forward along a path in the forest, looking to "see" whether one can fit through the available spaces.

Shift Transformation Subsystems

Shift transformations involve altering an existing image, whereas blink transformations involve letting an initial image fade and then accessing stored information and generating a new image. Thus, it is not surprising that Kosslyn (1980, chap. 8) found that blink transformations generally tend to be more time-consuming than shift transformations. This finding may explain why people typically prefer to use shift transformations even when blink transformations are feasible. That is, the most basic finding about image transformations is that they typically require more time for greater alterations. For example, the time to rotate an object in an image increases (typically linearly) with each degree of additional rotation, as if the object were being spun around an axis (see Shepard & Cooper, 1982). Apparently, the representation of position is altered so that the transformed object moves through a trajectory, occupying intermediate positions as it is being transformed. However, at first glance, it is not at all clear why a series of small increments of change are used in most image transformations. Images, unlike actual objects, are not constrained by the laws of physics to pass through the intermediate points along a trajectory (real movement cannot be instantaneous). Why are images not shifted in large steps?

We can account for the incremental property of shift transformations with the following assumptions:

1. Regardless of whether an image is formed by retaining perceptual input (as is done in most of Shepard & Cooper's [1982] experiments) or by activating information stored in memory, high-resolution images of objects are composed of distinct parts. This assumption follows from the observation that forms are parsed into units during perception, and these units are later stored (see the first part of this article).

2. The representations of the locations of parts are manipulated individually when the image is transformed. This idea follows because a coordinate representation must be manipulated when one needs to alter a viewer-centered representation, such as by changing orientation or size; categorical representations do not embody the metric spatial relations among objects or parts (indeed, such representations are used to abstract out what is constant over such variations). In a coordinate representation, the location of each separate part is specified as a separate representation.

3. The behavior of the brain is subject to random perturbation. This observation is true of all physical systems; noise is pervasive.

Therefore, the locations of parts of an imaged object are not altered equally with each increment of transformation; there is noise in the movement operation, and the parts become misaligned.

4. In order to realign the locations, there must be a representation of spatial relations that does not change with different coordinate positions of the parts. I have argued earlier that just

this type of categorical relation is encoded during perception and is used to generate images of most multipart objects.

Presumably, the amount of misalignment is proportional to the size of the shift (i.e., variability is usually proportional to the mean), with larger shifts resulting in greater scrambling. If so, then there is a simple reason why images are transformed in a series of small increments: If the positions are too scrambled, it will be difficult simply to identify the corresponding parts and use stored categorical representations to realign them.

This analysis leads us to posit two additional processing subsystems: One subsystem is required to alter the representation of the positions of parts of an imaged object. These are metric spatial locations, and hence this operation would change coordinate representations in the dorsal system. A second processing subsystem is required to look up and use categorical representations of the spatial relations to direct the position-alteration subsystem to realign any misaligned parts. Finally, the inspection-processing subsystems must also be used in image transformations; the realign subsystem must make use of the categorical relations-encoding subsystem (which will allow one to compare the present relations to the proper ones), coordinate location-encoding subsystems (which provides a way to monitor the precision of the position alteration), and shape-encoding subsystems to discover the current locations of the parts, which is necessary before it can compute how to realign them. (In addition, in some tasks these subsystems are used to locate the top of the object to provide information about the shortest way to rotate; they presumably also are used to make the requisite judgment when the object has been transformed far enough; see Shepard & Cooper, 1982.)

Shift Transformations in the Two Hemispheres

The snowball mechanism leads us to make predictions about the role of the two hemispheres in shift transformations. First, the repositioning operation performed by the position-alteration subsystem depends on altering the topographic representation of the layout of individual parts. The processing subsystem that produces this coordinate representation is more effective in the right hemisphere. Thus, the snowball mechanism leads us to expect that the position-alteration subsystem should become more effective in the right hemisphere, given that this processing subsystem will receive feedback when it produces useful (e.g., recognizable) configurations of coordinate location representations. Second, if the figure is complex, categorical representations will be used to realign the parts. When the realign subsystem provides useful input to the position-alteration subsystem, it receives feedback. The origin of this feedback will be on the right side, and hence this factor will push toward a right-sided lateralization of the realign subsystem. However, the representations used by the realign subsystem should be encoded more effectively in the left hemisphere, for the reasons outlined in the previous section. Thus, we expect both hemispheres to be involved when complex forms undergo shift transformations.

Consistent with these expectations, there is some evidence suggesting the right hemisphere is better at actually transforming the representation of relative location. For example, Ratcliff

(1979) found that subjects with right parietal-lobe damage have selective difficulty performing a simple mental rotation task. Similarly, Weisenberg and McBride (1935) found that such patients have difficulty in deciding whether two shaded sides of an unfolded cube would be adjacent when the sides were folded to form the cube, and Le Doux, Wilson, and Gazzaniga (1977) found that the isolated right hemisphere of a split-brain patient was better at spatiomanipulation tasks.

Also consistent with predictions, there is some evidence that the left hemisphere is used when multipart shapes are transformed in an image (in such cases, the ability to realign parts should be critical). Kosslyn, Berndt, and Doyle (1985) tested two aphasic patients, both of whom had left-hemisphere damage; one patient corresponded quite closely to the classic syndrome of Broca's aphasia and one corresponded quite closely to the classic syndrome of Wernicke's aphasia. These patients were asked to evaluate pairs of two-dimensional shapes that were formed by selecting five cells in a 4 × 5 grid that were each connected to at least one other cell, and eliminating all but these cells (producing a set of connected boxes). The subjects were shown a pair of these forms and asked whether they were identical irrespective of orientation about the circle; the left form was always vertical and the right was at a variety of orientations. On half of the trials the two forms were identical, and on half they were mirror reversals of one another. The results were clearcut: Both patients showed large decrements in mental rotation ability. Indeed, the rate of rotation was almost 10 times slower than that of a group of normal control subjects. It is also of interest that the one subject who could understand the instructions showed no such deficit in image scanning, suggesting that the rotation deficit was selective (scanning should not require use of categorical representations). This finding suggests that the left hemisphere plays some role in the rotation of complex forms in images.

Other studies have provided mixed evidence for hemispheric specialization for image transformations, as inferred from deficits following unilateral brain damage (e.g., see Butters, Barton, & Brody, 1970; De Renzi & Faglioni, 1967; see De Renzi, 1982, chap. 6, for a review) and from studies of normal subjects receiving lateralized stimuli (e.g., see Cohen, 1975; Hatta, 1978; Simion, Bagnara, Bisiacchi, Roncato, & Umilta, 1980). Overall, the findings can most easily be interpreted as indicating bilateral involvement, which is not surprising if the present theory is correct.

Variability in Lateralization and Task Performance

I originally set out to use the theory to explain representative findings in four areas, part/whole recognition, face recognition, drawing, and dot localization. I soon discovered that the basic phenomena are highly unstable, and it simply is unclear what a "representative" finding is. For example, Martin (1979) and Sergent (1982) found that the right hemisphere was better at recognizing large shapes and the left at recognizing small shapes, but Alivisatos and Wilding (1982) and Boles (1984) were unable to replicate these findings. Similarly, the characterization of deficits in drawing ability following unilateral brain damage is inconsistent from study to study (e.g., see Gainotti &

Tiacci, 1970; Warrington, James, & Kinsbourne, 1966). White (1972) reviews evidence that this state of affairs is common in neuropsychology.

Perhaps the greatest promise of the present approach over previous ones lies in its potential for explaining variability. That is, it is important to realize that the variability is a result in its own right. Although many experiments on cerebral laterality are methodologically flawed (for critiques, see Beaumont, 1982; Kinsbourne & Hiscock, 1983; White, 1972), the experiments are no worse than those in other areas of neuropsychology that produce consistent results; the pervasiveness of this instability of results from study to study would seem to rule out ascribing all of the variability to sloppy experimentation or the like (cf. Hardyck, 1983). It seems likely that there is both between-subjects variability (especially evident in the clinical literature) and within-subjects variability (especially evident in the divided visual field literature with normals).

Between-Subjects Variation in Laterality

It is probably a mistake to think that there is only one way that the right and left hemisphere can be configured. Talk of left-hemisphere or right-hemisphere specialization per se is an idealization. Indeed, the very principles that underlie the snowball mechanism also lead us to expect great individual differences in laterality (cf. Bryden, 1975). The theory posits two potential sources of individual differences in lateralization. One is the magnitude of the bias to use the dominant seed processing subsystems. If one is biased to use the speech output-control subsystem on the right side, development of categorical representation will also be promoted on this side. Similarly, if one is biased to use the visual search control subsystem on the left side, the accompanying sorts of specialization will also be on this side. Indeed, the greater the bias to use a seed subsystem on a given side, the greater will be the accompanying lateralization. The present theory does not specify why one should be biased to use the seed subsystems on any particular side. Annett (1985) and Geschwind and Behan (1982, 1984) offer theories of why innate lateralization occurs as it does, which rest on claims about genetic differences and prenatal hormonal differences, respectively.

The second critical parameter for individual differences is the amount of transhemispheric degradation. There are probably individual differences in the degree of imbalance in activation between the hemispheres when one hemisphere is initially used. The larger the imbalance, the greater the transhemispheric degradation of feedback, and the greater the degradation of transhemispheric feedback, the more extreme the asymmetry in development.

One index of how a person is lateralized is handedness (see Annett, 1985; Bryden, 1973; Springer & Deutsch, 1981). If strongly right-handed people are strongly lateralized in general, then they should have strongly lateralized spatial-relations subsystems. And if ambidextrous or left-handed people typically are less strongly lateralized in general, then these people should not have strongly lateralized spatial-relations subsystems. This idea was explored in another experiment. In this experiment, Kosslyn, Barrett, Cave, and Tang (1986) simply replicated the

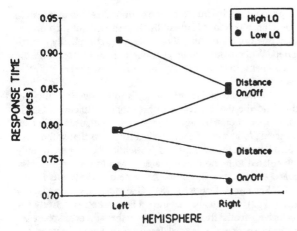

Figure 5. Results from the experiment in which subjects judged whether a dot was on or off a blob or whether a dot was near or far from a blob, broken down by handedness (score on the Edinburgh Handedness Inventory; Kosslyn, Barrett, Cave, & Tang, 1986).

procedure described previously in which subjects were asked to decide whether a dot was on or off a blob or whether a dot was near or far from a blob. In addition, we administered the Edinburgh Handedness Inventory (Oldfield, 1971) to the subjects, which assesses how strongly right-handed a person is. As before, the stimuli were lateralized, and we measured decision times and errors.

The results of this experiment are illustrated in Figure 5. As is evident, the strongly right-handed subjects showed the effect we observed before, with left-hemisphere superiority for the categorical task and right hemisphere superiority for the metric task. In contrast, the two hemispheres of ambidextrous subjects did not show any consistent differences for the two tasks, suggesting that they were not as specialized as the hemispheres of strongly right-handed people. When the handedness factor was ignored, the previously observed interaction was still statistically significant.

Thus, we not only replicated the result, but found evidence for individual differences in lateralization. Annett (1985) offers some interesting speculations about why handedness is correlated with other forms of laterality, but for present purposes we need only accept the empirical fact of a correlation.

The between-subjects inconsistencies in the clinical literature may be a result of more than individual differences in lateralization; there are at least three additional factors possibly at work here. First, in many studies patients with many different types of deficits often seem to be grouped together, often on the basis of a gross anatomical diagnosis. Small differences in localization of a lesion may have large effects (e.g., see Newcombe & Russell, 1969). Second, the tasks are often too coarse to allow one to characterize the nature of the functional breakdown. And to make matters worse, different investigators often use gratuitously different tasks when trying to assess the same functions. The tasks need to be motivated by a theory of the possible processing subsystems, and a series of tasks like those used in our work with J. W. is necessary to converge on a description

of the nature of a deficit. Third, the findings are often heavily contaminated by interpretation. For example, the lore is that drawings by patients with left-hemisphere damage are disrupted in ways different from drawings made by patients with right-hemisphere damage (e.g., see Walsh, 1978). Right-hemisphere damage purportedly results in drawings that contain correct details but have incorrect global organization; left-hemisphere damage purportedly has roughly the reverse effect. After examining illustrative examples, I personally have difficulty in seeing the characterized differences (e.g., see McFie & Zangwill, 1960). (On discussing this matter with clinicians, it seems that part of the problem here is that the process of drawing may not be the same for all patients, and the experimenter literally sees the product differently having observed the drawing process.)

Within-Subjects Contributions to Variability

It seems likely that not all of the variation in the empirical results can be ascribed to individual differences in laterality. For example, consider additional recent results from our laboratory: Normal subjects were tested in the imagery letter-classification task used with J. W. (Kosslyn and Feldman, 1986). The lowercase cues were lateralized, and separate mean response times were computed for trials in which the cue was given to each hemisphere. The first result was a failure to replicate the left-hemisphere advantage found for J. W.; this failure occurred in two separate experiments. The second result occurred when subjects were tested on two sets of trials back-to-back. This was done to discover whether there were stable within-subject differences in lateralization of the task. Two tasks were used, the straight/curved task and a task that required subjects to judge whether there was a vertical line at the extreme left of the uppercase letter; we counterbalanced which task was presented first (this was done to discourage subjects from simply memorizing the responses). Not only did we fail to find strong positive correlations between the sessions (when we examined the size of each subject's left-hemisphere advantage), but we found a large negative correlation from session to session—which hemisphere was faster actually reversed.

The letter-classification experiments with normal subjects suggest a possible solution to this puzzle. When queried after each session, some subjects claimed to have formed images of specific exemplars of the letters, which were vivid, in context (e.g., on a page), and seemed "external"; other subjects claimed to have formed images of prototypes, which were not very vivid, not in context (e.g., seemed to be floating), and seemed "internal." When the data were analyzed separately for the different types of reports, there was a significant right-hemisphere advantage when vivid, in-context, external images were reported, whereas there was a significant left-hemisphere advantage when nonvivid, out-of-context, internal images were reported. This result makes sense if categorical relations are used to generate images of prototypes, whereas coordinate relations are used to image specific exemplars. These findings must be regarded as preliminary but certainly suggest that progress can be made in understanding these phenomena.

Thus, J. W.'s right hemisphere was apparently not only deficient in using categorical relations effectively, but did not have the "executive" wherewithal to adopt an alternative strategy. This point was brought home by our ability to train the hemisphere to form images of letters by teaching it to "mentally draw" the letters (see Kosslyn, Holtzman, Farah, & Gazzaniga, 1985). The information was present to allow him to perform the task using a different strategy, but there was a problem in using it effectively.

In short, different strategies can be used to accomplish approximately the same end (see Cohen, 1982; Springer & Deutsch, 1981). A "strategy" is a way of describing the operation of a combination of processing subsystems, each operating on the output of the previous one. In our experiments the strategies were only subtly different, and had we not developed a theory we would not have known what to ask the subjects in order to discern which strategies were being used. However, we do not know why subjects change strategies; we need both a theory of possible strategies and a theory of selection principles to predict how a normal subject will perform on any given session. This is a gaping hole in the present formulation.

Conclusions

In this article I have attempted to illustrate the value of using a computational approach in conjunction with neurological and behavioral data. The present approach rests on using empirical data and computational constraints to formulate hypotheses about the nature of individual processing subsystems. In this article I have provided the motivation for a total of 12 subsystems hypothesized to be used in both visual imagery and visual perception, which of course is only a beginning. These subsystems are summarized in Table 1. In addition, I used four ideas about macroproperties of the brain to generate predictions of how these subsystems become lateralized. This mechanism is sensitive to three parameters: the magnitude of the bias to use each of the two "seed subsystems" on a given side, and the degree to which information becomes degraded when it crosses hemispheres. All else being equal, these three parameters result in the various subsystems' becoming lateralized to greater or lesser degrees. In addition, when performing a given task, the strategy used (i.e., which subsystems are recruited) will determine which hemisphere has a greater role in producing the final response.

One could ask whether the present approach is really an advance over previous approaches. Before answering that question, let us consider the alternatives. On the one hand, one could simply try to compile a list of properties of the two hemispheres. For example, we could conclude that the right hemisphere has a deficit in generating images of complex patterns and leave it at that. This approach has several drawbacks. For one, there is inter- and intrasubject variability, which precludes drawing firm generalizations. For another, even if the generalization is qualified, this enterprise will never be finished; a new phenomenon to investigate can always be discovered or an old phenomenon can be reconstrued and investigated anew. But more fundamentally, something more than a catalog of phenomena associated with the two hemispheres is needed. What is needed are general underlying principles that will cut across a wide range

of phenomena, leading to a simpler understanding than would flow from a very long (endless) list. Indeed, without such principles, one can say nothing about cases not yet explicitly investigated. Without such principles, one does not understand the phenomena; one cannot say why the hemispheres differ as they do.

The other alternative, of course, is to formulate principles that underlie the differences in hemispheric function. This is the more common traditional approach, which usually focuses on trying to identify dichotomous dimensions that will distinguish between the hemispheres. These dichotomies are usually formulated to be intuitively plausible and to rest on everyday concepts (e.g., see Bradshaw & Nettleton, 1981; De Renzi, 1982; Springer & Deutsch, 1981). One salient exception is Sergent (1982), who claims that the left hemisphere selectively encodes high-spatial frequencies, whereas the right hemisphere selectively encodes low-spatial frequencies. Unfortunately, the critical experiments have failed to replicate (see the previous section on variability in lateralization and task performance), and the idea has little ecological validity (spatial frequency shifts up as an object moves farther away, and hence higher spatial frequencies are not indicative of parts as opposed to objects). Is the natural-computation, mechanistic approach adopted here an advance over the traditional approach? I think so, for a number of reasons.

First, the traditional accounts have proven to have limited usefulness. The elegance and simplicity of a dichotomy usually disappear when the dichotomy is confronted with actual empirical results in need of explanation. For example, it is often not clear how to decide what is "analytic" or "holistic" in a given situation, and the criteria for applying the dichotomy become complicated (cf. Bertelson, 1982; Marshall, 1981; Moscovitch, 1979). The phenomena researchers are trying to understand are exceedingly complex (indeed, among the most complex in all of nature), and thus it is not surprising that theories become complex in practice. However, when dealing with a complex theory, one is faced with the problem of knowing exactly what is predicted. Even when parameter values are fixed, the sheer number of parameters can be daunting. And if the parameter values are not fixed, an explanation can be generated for virtually any effect or its converse (cf. Marshall, 1981). The present approach is useful because it is a precursor to building a computer simulation model. Such a model forces one to be explicit and consistent. Once the model is cast, it operates in a specific way and no amount of hand waving will change that; if the model does not generate successful predictions, it must be revised. The usual accounts of hemispheric differences are not very helpful as guides for building such an explicit model.

Second, the present approach is an advance over a more commonsense, intuitive approach because it leads to novel, sometimes counterintuitive, predictions that may in turn lead to important insights. To cite the present example, in some cases the left, not the right, hemisphere is superior at some aspects of mental imagery. The standard view that imagery is a right-hemisphere phenomenon is incorrect (see also Erlichman & Barrett, 1983; Farah, 1984). However, it remains possible that imagery is more important for right-hemisphere processing than left-hemisphere processing; if so, then understanding the

Table 1
The Hypothesized Subsystems

Subsystem	Input	Purpose	Output
Shape encoding	Pattern from attention window	Encode shape into associative memory	Representation of shape
Spatiotopic map construction	Location of units in low-level retinotopic maps, location of attention window, eye, head, body position	Form map of locations in actual space	Map, with location of attention window
Categorical relations encoding	Two locations	Encode categorical representation of spatial relation between the two	Categorical representation
Coordinate location encoding	One or more locations	Encode coordinates of units relative to a single origin	Coordinate representation
Visual memory activation	Part name from associative memory	Activate stored visual representation to form image or to prime during perception	Pattern of activation in the visual buffer
Categorical relations access and interpretation	Instruction to look up categorical representation of location of part	Look up part location, then direct attention window to location of part. In perception, the part is then sent to shape-encoding subsystems. In imagery, a new part is then imaged (via the visual memory activation subsystem) at that location	Instructions to the attention-shift subsystem to shift attention
Coordinate location access	Instruction to look up coordinate representation of location of part	Same as above, but using coordinate representation	Same as above
Attention shift	Specification of a new location	Shifts location of attention window	New location attended
Position alteration	Part in the visual buffer and coordinate representation of part's location	Shift representation of location of part	Repositioned parts
Part realignment	Same as above, plus categorical representation of part relation	Realign locations of parts to conform with categorical relation	Directions for position alteration subsystem on how to realign location representations
Speech output controller	Instructions for sound sequence	Program articulatory apparatus bilaterally to produce a word	Instructions to articulatory apparatus on sound to make
Search controller	Instructions for scan path	Program a systematic scan path over both sides of space	Instructions to attention-shift subsystem on scan path to take

limitations of right-hemisphere imagery may have far-reaching consequences.

The predictions made in this article are based on the insight that "imagery" is too coarse a level of analysis; the function decomposes into numerous subabilities, which in turn are carried out by numerous separate subsystems. And these subsystems appear to be differently lateralized. Thus, neither imagery as a whole nor individual imagery abilities, such as image generation or image transformation, are lateralized solely to one side or the other. Understanding the different characteristics of the hemispheres depends on first having a rather subtle analysis of processing, which would not result from the traditional approach. The predictions derived from a theory like the present one often result from the interaction of numerous processing subsystems and can be difficult to anticipate, which is one reason a computer simulation model is desirable. Indeed, actually building a simulation model may lead to new hypotheses about possible subsystems. For example, as Kosslyn, Flynn, and Amsterdam (1987) implemented a new model, we found that the subsystem that accesses and interprets categorical representations to arrange parts can be decomposed into three distinct subsystems: one that accesses stored location-part information, one that uses this information to compute where to focus attention, and one that acts as an executive, coordinating the others. We have not yet attempted to investigate these distinctions, but the predictions are clear; it may be that we can pinpoint J. W.'s deficit even more precisely than before.

Third, the present approach is an advance over previous approaches because it does not focus solely on generalizations about an idealized, typical pair of hemispheres. Rather, the same mechanisms that lead us to expect laterality also lead us to expect variability between individuals. Indeed, the present theory leads us to expect nonrandom variability in information processing both between individuals and within a given individual at different times and in different circumstances. Variability of the magnitude and frequency found in the neuropsychological literature is probably not simply a result of measurement error; rather, these are phenomena that must be explained in their own right. Although many researchers have considered variability, mechanistic accounts for the causes of variability have not been developed previously.

Fourth, another virtue of the present approach is that researchers may build on the theory. That is, one property of a theory of processing subsystems is that the theory itself can be modular. We can add to the theory by expanding the number of processing subsystems examined, without affecting the portions of the theory previously developed. Indeed, if we can simply add without having to modify the previously posited processing subsystems, this would be a sign that the earlier theory is correct, that the actual subsystems have been characterized. This modular property is fortunate, given the ultimate goals of the present theory. The theory ultimately should allow us to account for all of the major findings on visual hemisphericity (e.g., see Benton, 1982, 1985; Bradshaw & Nettleton, 1981; DeRenzi, 1982; Hardyck, 1983; Ratcliff, 1982; Springer & Deutsch, 1981; White, 1969).

A major weakness of the present theory as here presented is that the theory specifies only a few of the subsystems, and there clearly are many more (for an overview of what is known about high-level vision, see Pinker, 1985). Without knowing what the subsystems do, one cannot develop a theory of how function is lateralized. The fine-grained breakdown in function following brain damage hints at many specialized processing subsystems. For example, Newcombe and Russell (1969) found selective deficits in different spatial abilities following right-parietal damage, and the deficits depended in part on the precise location of the damage within the parietal lobe itself. The subsystems underlying this selective breakdown must be specified by the theory. A glaring weakness of the present theory is that it has almost nothing to say about the details of the mechanisms that direct attention, which is an area currently under intense study. In particular, Posner and his colleagues (e.g., see Posner,

Walker, Friedrich, & Rafal, 1984; Posner et al., 1985) have discovered much about the underlying structure of attention. These researchers have developed an approach that is in many ways similar to the present one, which ultimately should allow us to combine a theory of attention with a theory of representation. Indeed, they have shown that the slave subsystem we hypothesize that actually shifts attention can be decomposed into at least three more specialized subsystems: one that disengages attention, one that shifts attention, and one that engages attention.

One way of testing a theory like the present one is to construct a simulation model and discover differences in how it lateralizes depending on the precise parameter values. For example, we could explore the importance of magnitude of bias to use the left speech output controller with different degrees of transhemispheric degradation. In addition, we could "lesion" the model. The effects of disrupting the model in selected ways will constitute precise predictions of behavioral deficits following brain damage. It would also be interesting to do the obverse, to start with a known deficit and see what sorts of lesions are necessary to make the simulation mimic the deficit. If this procedure is successful, we may be on the road to developing a new, more precise diagnostic tool. This obviously will not be an easy endeavor, but the combination of neuroanotomical, neurophysiological, neuropsychological, and computational constraints makes it possible. If nothing else, such a project would serve to sharpen the issues and direct a program of theory-driven empirical research.

References

Alivisatos, B., & Wilding, J. (1982). Hemispheric differences in matching Stroop-type letter stimuli. *Cortex, 18,* 5–21.

Andersen, R. A., Essick, G. K., & Siegel, R. M. (1985). Encoding of spatial location by posterior parietal neurons. *Science, 230,* 456–458.

Anderson, J. R. (1983). Spreading activation. In J. R. Anderson & S. M. Kosslyn (Eds.), *Tutorials in learning and memory: Essays in honor of Gordon H. Bower* (pp. 61–90). San Francisco: Freeman.

Annett, J. (1985). *Left, right, hand and brain: The right shift theory.* Hillsdale, NJ: Erlbaum.

Ballard, D. H., & Brown, C. M. (1982). *Computer vision.* New York: Prentice-Hall.

Bauer, R. M., & Rubens, A. B. (1985). Agnosia. In K. M. Heilman & E. Valenstein (Eds.), *Clinical neuropsychology* (pp. 187–241). New York: Oxford University Press.

Beaumont, J. G. (Ed.). (1982). *Divided visual field studies of cerebral organization.* New York: Academic Press.

Benson, D. F. (1967). Fluency in aphasia: Correlation with radioactive scan localization. *Cortex, 3,* 373–394.

Benton, A. L. (1982). Spatial thinking in neurological patients: Historical aspects. In M. Potegal (Ed.), *Spatial abilities: Developmental and physiological foundations* (pp. 253–275). New York: Academic Press.

Benton, A. L. (1985). Visuoperceptual, visuospatial, and visuoconstructive disorders. In K. M. Heilman & E. Valenstein (Eds.), *Clinical neuropsychology* (pp. 151–185). New York: Oxford University Press.

Bertelson, P. (1982). Lateral differences in normal man and lateralization of brain function. *International Journal of Psychology, 17,* 173–210.

Bisiach, E., & Luzzatti, C. (1978). Unilateral neglect of representational space. *Cortex, 14,* 129–133.

Bisiach, E., Luzzatti, C., & Perani, D. (1979). Unilateral neglect, representational schema, and consciousness. *Brain, 102*, 609–618.

Boles, D. B. (1984). Global versus local processing: Is there a hemispheric dichotomy? *Neuropsychologia, 22*, 445–455.

Bower, G. H., & Glass, A. L. (1976). Structural units and the reintegrative power of picture fragments. *Journal of Experimental Psychology: Human Learning and Memory, 2*, 456–466.

Bradshaw, J. L., & Nettleton, N. C. (1981). The nature of hemispheric specialization in man. *Behavioral and Brain Sciences, 4*, 51–91.

Brooks, L. (1968). Spatial and verbal components of the act of recall. *Canadian Journal of Psychology, 19*, 289–299.

Bryden, M. P. (1973). Perceptual asymmetry in vision: Relation to handedness, eyedness, and speech lateralization. *Cortex, 9*, 418–435.

Bryden, M. P. (1975). Speech lateralization in families: A preliminary study using dichotic listening. *Brain and Language, 2*, 201–211.

Bryden, M. P. (1976). Response bias and hemispheric differences in dot localization. *Perception and Psychophysics, 19*, 23–28.

Butters, N., Barton, M., & Brody, B. A. (1970). Role of the right parietal lobe in the mediation of cross-modal associations and reversible operations in space. *Cortex, 6*, 174–190.

Cohen, G. (1975). Hemispheric differences in the utilization of advance information. In P. M. A. Rabbit & S. Dornic (Eds.), *Attention and performance* (Vol. 5, pp. 20–32). New York: Academic Press.

Cohen, G. (1982). Theoretical interpretations of lateral asymmetries. In J. G. Beaumont (Ed.), *Divided visual field studies of cerebral organization* (pp. 87–111). New York: Academic Press.

Cooper, W. E. (1974). Perceptuomotor adaptation to a speech feature. *Perception and Psychophysics, 16*, 229–234.

Corballis, M. C. (1981). Toward an evolutionary perspective on hemispheric specialization. *Behavioral and Brain Sciences, 4*, 69–70.

Cowey, A. (1985). Aspects of cortical organization related to selective attention and selective impairments of visual perception: A tutorial review. In M. S. Posner & O. S. Marin (Eds.), *Attention and performance* (Vol. 11, pp. 41–62). Hillsdale, NJ: Erlbaum.

Cowey, A., & Weiskrantz, L. (1967). A comparison of the effects of inferotemporal and striate cortex lesions on the visual behaviour of rhesus monkeys. *Quarterly Journal of Experimental Psychology, 19*, 246–253.

Crowell, D. H., Jones, R. H., Kapuniai, L. E., & Nakagawa, J. K. (1973). Unilateral cortical activity in newborn humans: An early index of cerebral dominance. *Science, 180*, 205–208.

Davis, A. E., & Wada, J. A. (1977). Hemispheric asymmetries in human infants: Spectral analysis of flash and click evoked potentials. *Brain and Language, 4*, 23–31.

Davis, A. E., & Wada, J. A. (1978). Speech dominance and handedness in the normal human. *Brain and Language, 5*, 42–55.

Day, P. S., and Ulatowska, H. K. (1979). Perceptual, cognitive and linguistic development after early hemispherectomy: Two case studies. *Brain and Language, 7*, 17–33.

Deleval, J., De Mol, J., & Noterman, J. (1983). La perte des images souvenirs. *Acta Neurologica Balgigue, 83*, 61–79.

Dell, G. S. (1985). Positive feedback in hierarchical connectionist models: Applications to language production. *Cognitive Science, 9*, 3–23.

Denis, M. (1982). Imagining while reading text: A study of individual differences. *Memory and Cognition, 10*, 540–545.

Dennis, M., & Kohn, B. (1975). Comprehension of syntax in infantile hemiplegics after cerebral hemidecortication: Left-hemisphere superiority. *Brain and Language, 2*, 472–482.

Dennis, M., & Whitaker, H. A. (1976). Language acquisition following hemidecortication: Linguistic superiority of the left over the right hemisphere. *Brain and Language, 3*, 404–433.

De Renzi, E. (1982). *Disorders of space exploration and cognition.* New York: Wiley.

De Renzi, E., & Faglioni, P. (1967). The relationship between visuospatial impairment and constructional apraxia. *Cortex, 3*, 327–342.

Desimone, R., Albright, T. D., Gross, C. G., & Bruce, C. J. (1984). Stimulus selective properties of inferior temporal neurons in the macaque. *Journal of Neuroscience, 4*, 2051–2062.

Diamond, R., & Carey, S. (1986). Why faces are and are not special: An effect of expertise. *Journal of Experimental Psychology: General, 115*, 107–117.

Entus, A. K. (1977). Hemispheric asymmetry in processing of dichotically presented speech and nonspeech stimuli by infants. In S. J. Segalowitz & F. A. Gruber (Eds.), *Language development and neurological theory* (pp. 63–74). New York: Academic Press.

Erlichman, H., & Barrett, J. (1983). Right hemisphere specialization for mental imagery: A review of the evidence. *Brain and Cognition, 2*, 55–76.

Farah, M. J. (1984). The neurological basis of mental imagery: A componential analysis. *Cognition, 18*, 245–272.

Farah, M. J. (1985). Psychophysical evidence for a shared representational medium for mental images and percepts. *Journal of Experimental Psychology: General, 114*, 91–103.

Farah, M. J. (1986). The laterality of mental image generation: A test with normal subjects. *Neuropsychologia, 24*, 541–551.

Farah, M. J., Levine, D. N., & Calvanio, R. (in press). A case study of mental imagery deficit. *Brain and Cognition.*

Finke, R. A. (1980). Levels of equivalence in imagery and perception. *Psychological Review, 86*, 113–132.

Finke, R. A., & Shepard, R. N. (1986). Visual functions of mental imagery. In K. R. Boff, L. Kaufman, & J. P. Thomas (Eds.), *Handbook of perception and human performance* (pp. 37-1–37-55). New York: Wiley.

Gainotti, G., & Tiacci, C. (1970). Patterns of drawing disability in right and left hemispheric patients. *Neuropsychologia, 8*, 379–384.

Garrett, M. J. (1982). Production of speech: Observations from normal and pathological language use. In A. W. Ellis (Ed.), *Normality and pathology in cognitive functions* (pp. 19–76). New York: Academic Press.

Gazzaniga, M. S., & Le Doux, J. E. (1978). *The integrated mind.* New York: Plenum.

Geschwind, N. (1965). Disconnexion syndromes in animals and man. *Brain, 88*, 237–294, 585–644.

Geschwind, N. (1976). The apraxias: Neural mechanisms of disorders of learned movement. *American Scientist, 63*, 188–195.

Geschwind, N., & Behan, P. (1982). Left-handedness: Association with immune disease, migraine, and developmental learning disorder. *Proceedings of the National Academy of Science USA, 79*, 5097–5100.

Geschwind, N., & Behan, P. (1984). Laterality, hormones and immunity. In N. Geschwind & A. M. Galaburda (Eds.), *Biological foundations of cerebral dominance* (pp. 211–224). Cambridge, MA: Harvard University Press.

Gross, C. G. (1973). Visual functions of inferotemporal cortex. In R. Jung (Ed.), *Handbook of sensory physiology* (Vol. 7, pp. 451–482). Berlin: Springer-Verlag.

Gross, C. G., Bruce, C. J., Desimone, R., Fleming, J., & Gattass, R. (1981). Cortical visual areas of the temporal lobe. In C. N. Woolsey (Ed.), *Cortical sensory organization II: Multiple visual areas* (pp. 187–216). Clinton, NJ: Humana Press.

Gross, C. G., Desimone, R., Albright, T. D., & Schwartz, E. L. (1984). Inferior temporal cortex as a visual integration area. In F. Reinoso-Suarez & C. Ajmone-Marsan (Eds.), *Cortical integration* (pp. 291–315). New York: Raven Press.

Gross, C. G., & Mishkin, M. (1977). The neural basis of stimulus equivalence across retinal translation. In S. Harnad, R. Doty, J. Jaynes, L. Goldstein, & G. Krauthamer (Eds.), *Lateralization in the nervous system* (pp. 109–122). New York: Academic Press.

Gross, C. G., Rocha-Miranda, C. E., & Bender, D. B. (1972). Visual properties of neurons in inferotemporal cortex of the macaque. *Journal of Neurophysiology, 35,* 96–111.

Grossi, D., Orsini, A., & Modafferi, A. (1986). Visuoimaginal constructional apraxia: On a case of selective deficit of imagery. *Brain and Cognition, 5,* 255–267.

Hannay, H. J., Varney, N. R., & Benton, A. L. (1976). Visual localization in patients with unilateral brain disease. *Journal of Neurology, Neurosurgery and Psychiatry, 39,* 307–313.

Hardyck, C. (1983). Seeing each other's points of view: Visual perceptual lateralization. In J. B. Hellige (Ed.), *Cerebral hemispheric asymmetry: Method, theory, and application* (pp. 219–254). New York: Praeger.

Hatta, T. (1978). Visual field differences in a mental transformation task. *Neuropsychologia, 16,* 637–641.

Hebb, D. O. (1949). *The organization of behavior.* New York: Wiley.

Hecaen, H., & Albert, M. L. (1978). *Human neuropsychology.* New York: Wiley.

Heilman, K. M., & Valenstein, E. (Eds.). (1985). *Clinical neuropsychology.* (2nd ed.). New York: Oxford University Press.

Heilman, K. M., Watson, R. T., & Valenstein, E. (1985). Neglect and related disorders. In K. M. Heilman & E. Valenstein (Eds.), *Clinical neuropsychology* (2nd ed., pp. 243–293). New York: Oxford University Press.

Hinton, G. E., & Anderson, J. A. (1981). *Parallel models of associative memory.* Hillsdale, NJ: Erlbaum.

Holmes, G. (1919). Disturbances of visual space perception. *British Medical Journal, 2,* 230–233.

Holtzman, J. D. (1984). Interactions between cortical and subcortical visual areas: Evidence from human commissurotomy patients. *Vision Research, 24,* 801–813.

Holtzman, J. D., & Gazzaniga, M. S. (1982). Dual task interactions due exclusively to limits in processing resources. *Science, 218,* 1325–1327.

Hubel, D. H., & Weisel, T. N. (1977). Functional architecture of macaque monkey visual cortex. *Proceedings of the Royal Society of London* (Series B), *198,* 1–59.

Ingle, D. (1967). Two visual mechanisms underlying the behavior of fish. *Psychologische Forschung, 31,* 44–51.

Jackson, J. H. (1864). Clinical remarks on defects of expression (by words, writing, signs, etc.) in diseases of the nervous system. *Lancet, 1,* 604–605.

Jackson, J. H. (1915). On the duality of the brain. *Brain, 38,* 80–103. (Originally published in 1874)

Jolicoeur, P., Gluck, M. A., & Kosslyn, S. M. (1984). Words and pictures: Making the connection. *Cognitive Psychology, 16,* 243–275.

Jolicoeur, P., & Kosslyn, S. M. (1983). Coordinate systems of visual long-term memory representations. *Cognitive Psychology, 15,* 301–345.

Jones, R. K. (1966). Observations on stammering after localized cerebral injury. *Journal of Neurology, Neurosurgery and Psychiatry, 29,* 192–195.

Jones-Gotman, M. (1979). Incidental learning of image-mediated or pronounced words after right temporal lobectomy. *Cortex, 15,* 187–197.

Jones-Gotman, M., & Milner, B. (1978). Right temporal lobe contribution to imagery-mediated verbal learning. *Neuropsychologia, 16,* 61–71.

Kimura, D. (1976). The neural basis of language qua gesture. In H.

Whitaker & H. A. Whitaker (Eds.), *Studies in neurolinguistics* (Vol. 2, pp. 145–156). New York: Academic Press.

Kimura, D. (1977). Acquisition of a motor skill after left hemisphere damage. *Brain, 100,* 527–542.

Kinsbourne, M. (1973). The control of attention by interaction between the hemispheres. In S. Kornblum (Ed.), *Attention and performance* (Vol. 4, pp. 239–256). New York: Academic Press.

Kinsbourne, M. (1975). The mechanism of hemispheric control of the lateral gradient of attention. In P. M. A. Rabbitt & S. Dornic (Eds.), *Attention and performance* (Vol. 5, pp. 81–97). New York: Academic Press.

Kinsbourne, M., & Hiscock, M. (1983). The normal and deviant development of functional lateralization of the brain. In P. Mussen, M. Haith, & J. Campos (Eds.), *Handbook of child psychology* (4th ed., Vol. 2, pp. 157–282). New York: Wiley.

Kitterle, F. L. (1986). Psychophysics of lateral tachistoscopic presentation. *Brain and Cognition, 5,* 131–162.

Kohn, B., & Dennis, M. (1974). Selective impairment of visuo-spatial abilities in infantile hemiplegics after right cerebral hemidecortication. *Neuropsychologia, 12,* 505–512.

Kosslyn, S. M. (1975). Information representation in visual images. *Cognitive Psychology, 7,* 341–370.

Kosslyn, S. M. (1980). *Image and mind.* Cambridge, MA: Harvard University Press.

Kosslyn, S. M. (1983). *Ghosts in the mind's machine.* New York: Norton.

Kosslyn, S. M., Backer, C., & Provost, D. (1985). *Sequential processes in image generation: An objective measure* (Tech. Report No. 6). Arlington, VA: Office of Naval Research.

Kosslyn, S. M., Ball, T. M., & Reiser, B. J. (1978). Visual images preserve metric spatial information: Evidence from studies of image scanning. *Journal of Experimental Psychology: Human Perception and Performance, 4,* 47–60.

Kosslyn, S. M., Barrett, A., Cave, C. B., & Tang, J. (1986). *Evidence for two types of spatial representations: Hemispheric specialization for categorical and coordinate relations.* Manuscript in preparation.

Kosslyn, S. M., Berndt, R. S., & Doyle, T. J. (1985). Imagery and language: A preliminary neuropsychological investigation. In M. S. Posner & O. S. Marin (Eds.), *Attention and performance* (Vol. 11, pp. 319–334). Hillsdale, NJ: Erlbaum.

Kosslyn, S. M., Cave, C. B., Provost, D. A., & von Gierke, S. M. (1986). *Sequential processes in image generation: Evidence from an objective measure.* Manuscript submitted for publication.

Kosslyn, S. M., & Feldman, J. (1986). *Image generation and the cerebral hemispheres: Alternative strategies.* Manuscript in preparation.

Kosslyn, S. M., Flynn, R. A., & Amsterdam, J. B. (1987). *Toward a neurologically plausible theory of high-level vision.* Manuscript in preparation.

Kosslyn, S. M., Holtzman, J. D., Farah, M. J., & Gazzaniga, M. S. (1984). *A computational analysis of mental image generation: Evidence from functional dissociations in split-brain patients* (Tech. Rep. No. 4). Arlington, VA: Office of Naval Research.

Kosslyn, S. M., Holtzman, J. D., Farah, M. J., & Gazzaniga, M. S. (1985). A computational analysis of mental image generation: Evidence from functional dissociations in split-brain patients. *Journal of Experimental Psychology: General, 114,* 311–341.

Kosslyn, S. M., & Jolicoeur, P. (1980). A theory-based approach to the study of individual differences in mental imagery. In R. E. Snow, P. A. Federico, & W. E. Montague (Eds.), *Aptitude, learning, and instruction: Cognitive processes analyses of aptitude* (Vol. 1, pp. 139–175). Hillsdale, NJ: Erlbaum.

Larsen, A., & Bundesen, C. (1978). Size scaling in visual pattern recognition. *Journal of Experimental Psychology: Human Perception and Performance, 4,* 1–20.

Latto, A., Mumford, D., & Shah, J. (1984). The representation of shape. In *Proceedings of IEEE Workshop on Computer Vision, Annapolis, MD* (pp. 183–191). Washington, DC: Institute of Electrical and Electronics Engineers.

Le Doux, J. E., Wilson, D. H., & Gazzaniga, M. S. (1977). Manipulospatial aspects of cerebral lateralization: Clues to the origin of lateralization. *Neuropsychologia, 15,* 743–750.

Lenneberg, E. H. (1967). *Biological foundations of language.* New York: Wiley.

Levine, D. N. (1982). Visual agnosia in monkey and man. In D. J. Ingle, M. A. Goodale, & R. J. W. Mansfield (Eds.), *Analysis of visual behavior* (pp. 629–670). Cambridge, MA: MIT Press.

Levine, D. N., Warach, J., & Farah, M. J. (1985). Two visual systems in mental imagery: Dissociation of "what" and "where" in imagery disorders due to bilateral posterior cerebral lesions. *Neurology, 35,* 1010–1018.

Levy, J. (1969). Possible basis for the evolution of lateral specialization of the human brain. *Nature, 224,* 614–615.

Ley, R. G. (1979). Cerebral asymmetries, emotional experience, and imagery: Implications for psychotherapy. In A. A. Sheikh & J. T. Shaffer (Eds.), *The potential of fantasy and imagination* (pp. 41–65). New York: Brandon House.

Liberman, A. M., & Mattingly, I. G. (1985). The motor theory of speech perception revised. *Cognition, 21,* 1–36.

Luria, A. R. (1980). *Higher cortical functions in man.* New York: Basic Books.

Marr, D. (1982). *Vision.* San Francisco, CA: Freeman.

Marshall, J. C. (1981). Hemispheric specialization: What, how, and why. *Behavioral and Brain Sciences, 4,* 72–73.

Martin, M. (1979). Hemispheric specialization for local and global processing. *Neuropsychologia, 17,* 33–40.

Mateer, C. (1978). Impairments of nonverbal oral movements after left hemisphere damage: A follow up of analysis of errors. *Brain and Language, 6,* 334–341.

Mazzocchi, F., & Vignolo, L. A. (1979). Localisation of lesions in aphasia: Clinical-CT scan correlations in stroke patients. *Cortex, 15,* 627–654.

McClelland, J. L., & Rumelhart, D. E. (1981). An interactive activation model of context effects in letter perception: Part 1. An account of basic findings. *Psychological Review, 88,* 375–407.

McFie, J., & Zangwill, O. (1960). Visual-constructive disabilities associated with lesions of the left cerebral hemisphere. *Brain, 83,* 243–260.

Mesulam, M.-M. (1981). A cortical network for directed attention and unilateral neglect. *Annals of Neurology, 10,* 309–325.

Milner, B. (1968). Visual recognition and recall after right temporal-lobe excision in man. *Neuropsychologia, 6,* 191–210.

Mishkin, M. (1982). A memory system in the monkey. *Philosophical Transactions of the Royal Society of London, Series B, 298,* 85–95.

Mishkin, M., & Ungerleider, L. G. (1982). Contribution of striate inputs to the visuospatial functions of parieto-preoccipital cortex in monkeys. *Behavioural Brain Research, 6,* 57–77.

Mishkin, M., Ungerleider, L. G., & Macko, K. A. (1983). Object vision and spatial vision: Two cortical pathways. *Trends in NeuroSciences, 6,* 414–417.

Molfese, D. L., Freeman, R. B., & Palermo, D. (1975). The ontogeny of brain lateralization for speech and nonspeech stimuli. *Brain and Language, 2,* 356–368.

Molfese, D. L., & Molfese, V. J. (1979). Hemisphere and stimulus differences as reflected in the cortical responses of newborn infants to speech stimuli. *Developmental Psychology, 15,* 505–511.

Molfese, D. L., & Molfese, V. J. (1980). Cortical responses of preterm infants to phonetic and nonphonetic speech stimuli. *Developmental Psychology, 16,* 574–581.

Moran, J., & Desimone, R. (1985). Selective attention gates visual processing in the extrastriate cortex. *Science, 229,* 782–784.

Moscovitch, M. (1979). Information processing and the cerebral hemispheres. In M. S. Gazzaniga (Ed.), *Handbook of behavioral neurobiology* (Vol. 2, pp. 397–446). New York: Plenum Press.

Naeser, M. A., Hayward, R. W., Laughlin, S. A., & Zatz, L. M. (1981). Quantitative CT scan studies in aphasia. I. Infarct size and CT numbers. *Brain and Language, 12,* 140–164.

Newcombe, F., & Russell, W. R. (1969). Dissociated visual perceptual and spatial deficits in focal lesions of the right hemisphere. *Journal of Neurology, Neurosurgery and Psychiatry, 32,* 73–81.

Nottebohm, F. (1970). Ontogeny of bird song. *Science, 167,* 950–956.

Nottebohm, F. (1979). Origins and mechanisms in the establishment of cerebral dominance. In M. S. Gazzaniga (Ed.), *Handbook of behavioral neurobiology* (Vol. 2, pp. 295–344). New York: Plenum Press.

Ojemann, G. A., & Mateer, C. (1979). Human language cortex: Localization of memory, syntax and sequential motor-phoneme identification systems. *Science, 205,* 1401–1403.

Oldfield, R. C. (1971). The assessment and analysis of handedness: The Edinburgh Inventory. *Neuropsychologia, 9,* 97–114.

Paivio, A. (1971). *Imagery and verbal processes.* New York: Holt, Rinehart & Winston.

Palmer, S. E. (1977). Hierarchical structure in perceptual representations. *Cognitive Psychology, 9,* 441–474.

Pinker, S. (1985). Visual cognition: An introduction. In S. Pinker (Ed.), *Visual cognition* (pp. 1–63). Cambridge, MA: MIT Press.

Pohl, W. (1973). Dissociation of spatial discrimination deficits following frontal and parietal lesions in monkeys. *Journal of Comparative and Physiological Psychology, 82,* 227–239.

Posner, M. I., Inhoff, A. W., Friedrich, F. J., & Cohen, A. (1985). *Isolating attentional systems: A cognitive-anatomical analysis.* Paper presented at the meetings of the Psychonomics Society, Boston, MA.

Posner, M. I., Walker, J. A., Friedrich, F. J., & Rafal, R. D. (1984). Effects of parietal lobe injury on covert orienting of visual attention. *Journal of Neuroscience, 4,* 1863–1974.

Ratcliff, G. (1979). Spatial thought, mental rotation and the right cerebral hemisphere. *Neuropsychologia, 17,* 49–54.

Ratcliff, G. (1982). Disturbances of spatial orientation associated with cerebral lesions. In M. Potegal (Ed.), *Spatial abilities: Developmental and physiological foundations* (pp. 301–331). New York: Academic Press.

Ratcliff, G., & Davies-Jones, G. A. G. (1972). Defective visual localisation in focal brain wounds. *Brain, 95,* 49–60.

Reed, S. K. (1974). Structural descriptions and the limitations of visual images. *Memory and Cognition, 2,* 329–336.

Reed, S. K., & Johnsen, J. A. (1975). Detection of parts in patterns and images. *Memory and Cognition, 3,* 569–575.

Rudel, R. G., & Denckla, M. B. (1974). Relation of forward and backward digit repetition to neurological impairment in children with learning disabilities. *Neuropsychologia, 12,* 109–118.

Rumelhart, D. E., & McClelland, J. L. (Eds.). (1986). *Parallel distributed processing* (Vol. 1). Cambridge, MA: MIT Press.

Sagi, D., & Julesz, B. (1985a). "Where" and "what" in vision. *Science, 228,* 1217–1219.

Schneider, G. E. (1967). Contrasting visuomotor functions of tectum and cortex in the golden hamster. *Psychologische Forschung, 31,* 52–62.

Schneider, G. E. (1969). Two visual systems. *Science, 163,* 895–902.

Schwartz, E. L., Desimone, R., Albright, T. D., & Gross, C. G. (1984). Shape recognition and inferior temporal neurons. *Proceedings of the National Academy of Science USA, 80,* 5776–5778.

Segal, S. J. (1971). Processing of the stimulus in imagery and perception. In S. J. Segal (Ed.), *Imagery: Current cognitive approaches* (pp. 69–100). New York: Academic Press.

Segal, S. J., & Fusella, V. (1970). Influence of imaged pictures and sounds on detection of visual and auditory signals. *Journal of Experimental Psychology, 83,* 458–464.

Sergent, J. (1982). The cerebral balance of power: Confrontation or co-operation? *Journal of Experimental Psychology: Human Perception and Performance, 8,* 253–272.

Shepard, R. N., & Cooper, L. A. (1982). *Mental images and their transformations.* Cambridge, MA: MIT Press.

Shepard, R. N., & Metzler, J. (1971). Mental rotation of three-dimensional objects. *Science, 171,* 701–703.

Sidtis, J. J., Volpe, B. T., Wilson, D. H., Rayport, M., & Gazzaniga, M. S. (1981). Variability in right hemisphere language function: Evidence for a continuum of generative capacity. *Journal of Neuroscience, 1,* 323–331.

Simion, F., Bagnara, S., Bisiacchi, P., Roncato, S., & Umilta, C. (1980). Laterality effects, levels of processing, and stimulus properties. *Journal of Experimental Psychology: Human Perception and Performance, 6,* 184–195.

Springer, S. P., & Deutsch, G. (1981). *Left brain, right brain.* San Francisco: Freeman.

Sternberg, S., Monsell, S., Knoll, R. L., & Wright, C. E. (1978). The latency and duration of rapid movement sequences: Comparisons of speech and typewriting. In G. E. Stelmach (Ed.), *Information processing in motor control and learning* (pp. 118–152). New York: Academic Press.

Summers, J. J., & Sharp, C. A. (1979). Bilateral effects of concurrent verbal and spatial rehearsal on complex motor sequencing. *Neuropsychologia, 17,* 331–343.

Sussman, H. M., & Westbury, J. R. (1978). A laterality effect in isometric and isotonic labial tracking. *Journal of Speech and Hearing Research, 21,* 563–579.

Taylor, A. M., & Warrington, E. K. (1973). Visual discrimination in patients with localized brain lesions. *Cortex, 9,* 82–93.

Teuber, H. L. (1978). The brain and human behavior. In R. Held, H. W. Leibowitz, & H. L. Teuber (Eds.), *Handbook of sensory physiology: Perception* (Vol. 8, pp. 879–920). Berlin: Springer-Verlag.

Travis, L. E. (1931). *Speech pathology.* New York: Appleton-Century-Crofts.

Treisman, A. M., & Gelade, G. (1980). A feature integration theory of attention. *Cognitive Psychology, 12,* 97–136.

Treisman, A. M., & Schmidt, H. (1982). Illusory conjunctions in the perception of objects. *Cognitive Psychology, 14,* 107–141.

Tyler, H. R. (1968). Abnormalities of perception with defective eye movements (Balint's syndrome). *Cortex, 4,* 154–171.

Ullman, S. (1984). Visual routines. *Cognition, 18,* 97–160.

Umilta, C., Rizzolatti, G., Marzi, C. A., Zamboni, G., Franzini, C., Camarda, R., & Berlucchi, G. (1974). Hemispheric differences in the discrimination of line orientation. *Neuropsychologia, 12,* 165–174.

Ungerleider, L. G., & Mishkin, M. (1982). Two cortical visual systems. In D. J. Ingle, M. A. Goodale, & R. J. W. Mansfield (Eds.), *Analysis of visual behavior* (pp. 549–586). Cambridge, MA: MIT Press.

Van Essen, D. (1985). Functional organization of primate visual cortex. In A. Peters & E. G. Jones (Eds.), *Cerebral cortex* (Vol. 3, pp. 259–329). New York: Plenum Press.

Van Essen, D. C., & Maunsell, J. H. R. (1983). Hierarchical organization and functional streams in visual cortex. *Trends in NeuroSciences, 6,* 370–375.

Vargha-Khadem, F., & Corballis, M. C. (1979). Cerebral asymmetry in infants. *Brain and Language, 8,* 1–9.

Walsh, K. W. (1978). *Neuropsychology: A clinical approach.* New York: Churchill Livingstone.

Warrington, E. K., James, M., & Kinsbourne, M. (1966). Drawing disability in relation to laterality of lesions. *Brain, 89,* 53–82.

Warrington, E. K., & Rabin, P. (1970). Perceptual matching in patients with cerebral lesions. *Neuropsychologia, 8,* 475–487.

Weisenberg, T., & McBride, K. E. (1935). *Aphasia: A clinical and psychological study.* New York: Commonwealth Fund.

White, M. J. (1969). Laterality differences in perception: A review. *Psychological Bulletin, 72,* 387–405.

White, M. J. (1972). Hemispheric asymmetries in tachistoscopic information-processing. *British Journal of Psychology, 63,* 497–508.

Winston, P. H., Ed. (1975). *The psychology of computer vision.* New York: McGraw-Hill.

Witelson, S. F. (1977). Early hemisphere specialization and interhemispheric plasticity: An empirical and theoretical review. In S. J. Segalowitz & F. A. Gruber (Eds.), *Language development and neurological theory* (pp. 213–288). New York: Academic Press.

Woods, B. T., & Teuber, H. L. (1973). Early onset of complementary specialization of cerebral hemispheres in man. *Transactions of the American Neurological Association, 98,* 113–115.

Zangwill, O. (1976). Thought and the brain. *British Journal of Psychology, 67,* 301–314.

Received September 11, 1985
Revision received August 28, 1986 ∎

Index